T0228877

TRANSACTION PROCESSING:

CONCEPTS AND TECHNIQUES

The Morgan Kaufmann Series in Data Management Systems

Series Editor, Jim Gray

Jim Gray
DIGITAL EQUIPMENT CORPORATION

Andreas Reuter
UNIVERSITY OF STUTTGART

TRANSACTION PROCESSING:
CONCEPTS AND TECHNIQUES

MORGAN KAUFMANN PUBLISHERS
An Imprint of Elsevier
SAN FRANCISCO, CALIFORNIA

Senior Editor: *Bruce M. Spatz*
Manufacturing Manager: *Yonie Overton*
Project Management: *Professional Book Center*
Text Designer: *Gary Head*
Cover Designer: *Wells Larson Associates*
Copyeditor: *Jeanne Thieme*
Compositor: *Impressions, a division of Edwards Brothers, Inc.*
Indexer: *Stephen Katigbak*
Proofreader: *Caryl Riedel*
Printer: *Edwards Brothers, Inc.*

Software: Compatible software for course use is available from Transarc Corporation. Information about academic site licenses for the Encina family of products and further details about Encina can be obtained by contacting Encina University Coordinator at 412-338-4400 or via the internet: encina@transarc.com

Morgan Kaufmann Publishers, Inc.
An Imprint of Elsevier
Editorial Office:
340 Pine Street, Sixth Floor
San Francisco, CA 94104

© 1993 Morgan Kaufmann Publishers, Inc.
All rights reserved

No part of this publication may be reproduced, stored in a retrieval system, or transmitted in any form or by any means electronic, mechanical, photocopying, recording, or otherwise without the prior written permission of the publisher.
Permissions may be sought directly from Elsevier's Science and Technology Rights Department in Oxford, UK. Phone: (44) 1865 843830, Fax: (44) 1865 853333, e-mail: permissions@elsevier.co.uk. You may also complete your request on-line via the Elsevier homepage: http://www.elsevier.com by selecting "Customer Support" and then "Obtaining Permissions".

Printed and bound by CPI Group (UK) Ltd, Croydon, CR0 4YY

Transferred to Digital Print 2011

ISBN-13: 978-1-55860-190-1
ISBN-10: 1-55860-190-2

Library of Congress Cataloging-in-Publication Data

Gray, Jim, 1944-
    Transaction processing : concepts and techniques / Jim Gray, Andreas Reuter.
        p. cm. — (The Morgan Kaufmann series in data management systems)
    Includes bibliographical references and index.
    ISBN-13: 978-1-55860-190-1   ISBN-10: 1-55860-190-2
    1. Transaction systems (Computer systems) I. Reuter, A. (Andreas) II. Title. III. Series.
    QA76.545.G73 1993
    004'.33—dc20
                                                                    92-25954
                                                                    CIP

Foreword

Bruce Lindsay
IBM Almaden Research Center
San Jose, California

Commercial, governmental, scientific, and cultural activities are becoming increasingly dependent on computer-based information resources. As increasing amounts and varieties of information are captured and maintained by computer systems, the techniques for exploiting, managing, and protecting this information become critical to the well-being, and indeed the very survival, of modern industrialized societies.

Transaction processing technology is the key to the coherent management and reliable exploitation of computer-based information resources.

Transaction processing encompasses techniques for managing both the stored information itself and the application programs which interpret and manipulate that information. From database recovery and concurrency control to transaction monitors that initiate and control the execution of applications, transaction processing technology provides mechanisms and facilities needed to protect and manage the critical information resources which underlie many (if not most) commercial, scientific, and cultural activities.

In order for the increasingly vast quantity of computer-based information to be useful, it must accurately reflect the real world and be available to the application programs that interpret and exploit the information. In general, exploiting stored information involves accessing and modifying related data items which *collectively* describe or model the status and evolution of real-world phenomena and activities. Because multiple data items must usually be accessed or updated together to correctly reflect the real world, great care must be taken to keep related data items mutually consistent. Any interruption of updates to related items, or the interleaving of updates and accesses, can make the data inconsistent.

The key to maintaining data consistency is to identify the sequences of accesses and updates that represent the interrogation and modification of related data items. Such sequences are called *transactions*. Transaction processing technology ensures that each transaction is either executed to completion or not at all, and that concurrently executed transactions behave as though each transaction executes in isolation. The significance of this technology is magnified by the fact that these guarantees are upheld despite failures of computer components, distribution of data across multiple computers, and overlapped or parallel execution of different transactions.

Twenty-five years of intense effort in commercial and university laboratories has led to transaction processing technologies capable of all-or-nothing execution and isolation of concurrent transactions. This book presents, for the first time, a comprehensive description of the techniques and methods used by transaction processing systems to control and protect the valuable information resources they manage. The authors describe, in detail, the state-of-the-art techniques used in the best-of-breed commercial and experimental transaction processing systems. They concentrate on proven techniques that are effective and efficient. Detailed explanations of *why* various problems must be solved and *how* they can be addressed make this book useful to both the serious student and to system developers.

The authors, Dr. James Gray and Professor Andreas Reuter, have between them five decades of direct experience with the implementations of both commercial and experimental transaction processing systems. They have both made significant contributions to the art of transaction processing and are famous for their scientific publications and their ability to explain the fruits of their research. This book is a distillation of their deep understanding of transaction processing issues and their hard-won appreciation of the most effective techniques for implementing transaction processing methods. The authors' ability to distinguish between fundamental concepts and speculative approaches gives the reader a firm and practical basis for understanding the issues and techniques of transaction processing systems.

This book covers all aspects of transaction processing technology. The introductory chapters give the reader a basic understanding of transaction concepts and the computing environment in which transactions must execute, including important assumptions about the component failures which the transaction processing system must tolerate. The explanation of the role of transaction processing monitors, which control the activation and execution of application programs and the facilities they provide, sets the stage for the presentation of concurrency control and recovery techniques. The discussion of transaction isolation covers concurrency control issues from the hardware level to the isolation semantics for records and indexes. The important and complex technology of transaction recovery in the face of failures is covered in great detail. From record management to distributed commit protocols, the recovery techniques needed to ensure all-or-nothing execution and data persistence are presented and explained. The transaction recovery and isolation techniques are then applied to the design and implementation of record-oriented storage and associative indexes. Students and developers of database systems will find much useful information in these chapters. The book concludes with a survey of transaction processing systems from both the commercial and the academic worlds.

Throughout the book, the authors provide in-depth discussions of the underlying issues, and detailed descriptions of proven techniques. The concepts are illustrated with numerous carefully designed figures. In addition, the techniques are accompanied by code fragments that increase the reader's appreciation of the implementation issues.

Transaction Processing: Concepts and Techniques is both comprehensive in its coverage of transaction processing technology and detailed in its descriptions of the issues and algorithms. In-depth presentations of the techniques are enlightening to the student and a resource for the professional. The importance of transaction processing technology to the information management needs of industrialized societies makes it essential that this technology be well understood and widely applied. This book will serve as a guide and a reference for the many individuals who will apply and extend transaction processing concepts and techniques in the years ahead.

Contents

PART TWO—The Basics of Fault Tolerance

PART THREE—Transaction-Oriented Computing

PART FOUR—Concurrency Control

PART FIVE—Recovery

PART SIX—Transactional File System:
A Sample Resource Manager

PART SEVEN—System Surveys

PART EIGHT—Addenda

Buying books would be great if we could also buy the time to read them.

ARTHUR SCHOPENHAUER: PARERGA UND PARALIPOMENA

Preface

Why We Wrote this Book

The purpose of this book is to give you an understanding of how large, distributed, heterogeneous computer systems can be made to work reliably. In contrast to the often complex methods of distributed computing, it presents a distributed system application development approach that can be used by mere mortals. Why then doesn't the title use a term like *distributed systems*, *high reliability*, *interoperability,* or *client-server*? Why use something as prosaic as *transaction processing*, a term that for many people denotes old-fashioned, batch-oriented, mainframe-minded data processing?

The point is—and that's what makes the book so long—that the design, implementation, and operation of large application systems, with thousands of terminals, employing hundreds of computers, providing service with absolutely no downtime, cannot be done from a single perspective. An integrated (and integrating) perspective and methodology is needed to approach the distributed systems problem. Our goal is to demonstrate that transactions provide this integrative conceptual framework, and that distributed transaction-oriented operating systems are the enabling technology. The client-server paradigm provides a good way of structuring the system and of developing applications, but it still needs transactions to control the client-server interactions. In a nutshell: without transactions, distributed systems cannot be made to work for typical real-life applications.

This is not an outrageous claim; rather it is a lesson many people—system implementors, system owners, and application developers—have learned the hard way. Of course, the concepts for building large systems have been evolving for a long time. In fact, some of the key ideas were developed way back when batch processing was in full swing, but they are far from being obsolete. Transaction processing concepts were conceived to master the complexity in single-processor online applications. If anything, these concepts are even more critical now for the successful implementation of massively distributed systems that work and fail in much more complex ways. This book shows how transaction concepts apply to distributed systems and how they allow us to build high-performance, high-availability applications with finite budgets and risks. We've tried to provide a sense of this development by discussing some of the "lessons from history" with which we're familiar. Many of these demonstrate the problems that transactions help to avoid, as well as where they hide the complexity of distributed systems.

There are many books on database systems, both conventional and distributed; on operating systems; on computer communications; on application development—you name it. The partitioning of interests manifest in these terms has become deeply rooted in the syllabi of computer science education all over the world. Education and expertise are organized and compartmentalized. The available books typically take their readers through the ideas in the technical literature over the past decades in an enumerative style. Such presentations offer many options and alternatives, but rarely give a sense of which are the good ideas and which are the not-so-good ones, and why. More specifically, were you ever to design or build a real system, these algorithm overviews would rarely tell you how or where to start.

Our intent is to help you solve real problems. The book is focused in that we present only one or two viable approaches to problems, together with explanations; but there are many other proposals which we do not mention, and the presentation is not encyclopedic. However, the presentation is broad in the sense that it presents transaction processing from a systems perspective. To make large systems work, one must adopt a genuine end-to-end attitude, starting at the point where a request comes in, going through all the system layers and components, and not letting go until the final result is safely delivered. This necessarily involves presentation management in the terminals, the communication subsystem, the operating system, the database, the programming language run-time systems, and the application development environment. Designing a system with that sort of integration in mind requires an altogether different set of criteria than designing an algorithm within the narrow confines of its functional specification. This holistic approach is not one that we've found in other presentations of distributed systems and databases. However, since the beginning of this project in 1986, we've been convinced that such an approach is necessary.

Topic Selection and Organization

Since the end-to-end perspective forced us to cover lots of ground, we focused on the basic ideas of transaction processing: simple TP-systems structuring issues, simple transaction models, simple locking, simple logging, simple recovery, and so on. When we looked at the texts and reference books available, we noticed that they are vague on the basics. For example, we haven't found an actual implementation of B-trees in any textbook. Given that B-trees are *the* access path structure in databases, file systems, information retrieval systems, and who knows where, that is really basic. This presentation is like a compiler course textbook or like Tanenbaum's operating system book. It is full of code fragments showing the basic algorithms and data structures.

The book is pragmatic, covering basic transaction issues in considerable detail. Writing the book has convinced us that this is a good approach, but the presentation and style may seem foreign. Our motive is to document this more pragmatic perspective. There is no theory of structuring complex systems; rather, the key decisions depend on educated judgment and adherence to good engineering principles—pragmatic criteria. We believe that these principles, derived from the basic concept of transaction-oriented processing, will be important for many years to come.

Looking at the table of contents, you will find a forbidding number of chapters (16), but they are organized into seven subject areas, which can be read more or less independently, and in different order.

The first topic is an overview of transaction processing in general (Chapter 1). It presents a global system view. It introduces the basic transaction properties: *atomicity* (all-or-nothing), *consistency* (a correct transformation of state), *isolation* (without concurrency anomalies), and *durability* (committed changes survive any system failures)—ACID, for short. The nontechnical reader can end there and still gain a broad understanding of the field.

Chapter 2 is meant for readers vaguely familiar with the basic terminology of computer science. The chapter introduces the most important terms and concepts of hardware, software, protocol standards, and so on—all the terminology needed for the technical discussions later in the book.

Chapter 3 explains why systems fail and gives design advice on how to avoid such failures. It reviews hardware and software fault-tolerance concepts and techniques (fail-fast, redundancy, modularization, and repair). If you want to learn how to build a module with a mean-time-to-failure of 10,000 years, using normal, faulty, off-the-shelf components, this is where to look. Chapter 3 explains the significance of transactions in building highly available software.

Chapters 4 through 6 present the theory and use of transactions. Chapter 4 gives a detailed discussion of what it means to structure applications as transactions. Particular attention is paid to types of computations not well-supported by current flat transactions. These applications require extension and generalization of the transaction concept. Chapter 5 explains what transaction-oriented computation means for the operating system and other low-level components by describing the role of the TP monitor. It also explains how a transaction program interacts with the system services. Chapter 6 is for programmers. It contains lots of control blocks and code fragments to explain how transactional remote procedure calls work, how request scheduling is done, and other such subtleties. Readers not interested in bit-level events should skim the first half of that chapter and start reading at Section 6.4 about transactional queues.

Chapters 7 and 8 present the theory and practice of concurrency. Transaction processing systems hide all aspects of parallel execution from the application, thereby giving the *isolation* of the ACID properties. Chapter 7 presents the theory behind these techniques, and Chapter 8 demonstrates how to implement this theory with locking.

Chapters 9 through 12 present transaction management and recovery, that is, everything related to making transactions atomic and durable. Chapter 9 explains how logging and archiving are done. Chapter 10 explains how to write a transactional resource manger like a database system or a queue manager. It explains how the resource manger joins the transaction, how it writes log records, gets locks, and participates in transaction commit or rollback. A simple resource manger (the one-bit resource manger) is used to demonstrate the techniques. Chapter 11 takes the transaction manager perspective; it must always reliably know the state of a transaction and which resource managers are working on the transaction. The implementation of a simple transaction manager is laid out in Chapter 11—again, something to be skipped by those who do not need to know all the secrets. Chapter 12 is a catalog of advanced concepts and techniques used by transaction managers.

Chapters 13 through 15 deal with yet another self-contained topic: the implementation of a very important resource manager, a transactional file system. Starting from the bare metal (disks), space management is sketched, and the role of the buffer manager in the system is explained in some detail. Next comes the abstraction of varying-length tuples from fixed-length pages, and all the file organizations that support tuple-oriented access. Finally, Chapter 15 talks about associative access, focusing primarily on B-trees and how to implement them in a highly parallel environment. All this is done in a way that provides the ACID properties: the resulting files, tuples, and access paths are transactional objects.

Chapter 16 gives an overview of many commercially available systems in the transaction processing arena. We have tried to highlight the features of each system. This is not a competitive comparison; rather it is a positive description of the strengths of each system.

At the end, there is an extended glossary of transaction processing terminology. Having such a large glossary is a bit unusual in a textbook like this. However, as the motto of Chapter 5 indicates, terminology in the field of transaction processing is all but well-established. So the glossary has to serve two purposes: First, if you are uncertain about a term, you can look it up and find our interpretation. Second, by being used this way, the glossary might actually help to promote a more homogeneous terminology in the field.

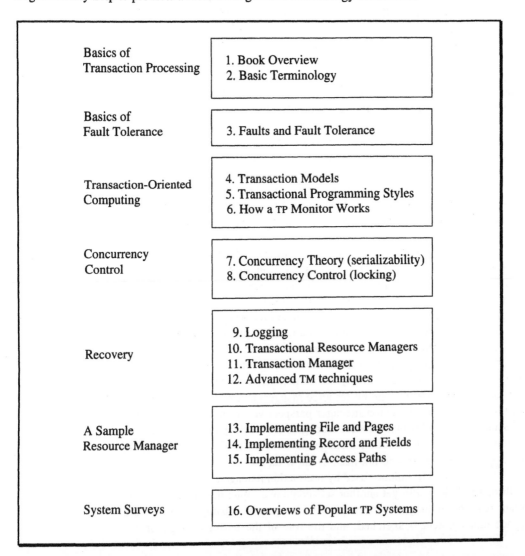

Basics of Transaction Processing	1. Book Overview 2. Basic Terminology
Basics of Fault Tolerance	3. Faults and Fault Tolerance
Transaction-Oriented Computing	4. Transaction Models 5. Transactional Programming Styles 6. How a TP Monitor Works
Concurrency Control	7. Concurrency Theory (serializability) 8. Concurrency Control (locking)
Recovery	9. Logging 10. Transactional Resource Managers 11. Transaction Manager 12. Advanced TM techniques
A Sample Resource Manager	13. Implementing File and Pages 14. Implementing Record and Fields 15. Implementing Access Paths
System Surveys	16. Overviews of Popular TP Systems

Chapters 1 through 15 contain historical notes that explain how things were developed, where certain ideas appeared first, and so on. In contrast to many other areas in computer science, transaction processing developed primarily in industrial research and development labs. Some ideas conceived and implemented in commercial products were rediscovered years later and published as scientific results. In the historical notes we try give credit to both contributions, to the best of our knowledge.

Most chapters also have exercises ranging from short refreshers to term projects. The answers to most of them are provided at the end of each chapter. Following Donald Knuth, each exercise has a qualifier of the form [section, level]. The exercise applies to the material in the section indicated. The level is an indicator of how difficult the exercise is:

[10]   One minute (just to check whether you have followed the text)

[20]   15–20 minutes for full answer

[25]   One hour for full written answer

[30]   Short (programming) project: less than one full day of work

[40]   Significant (programming) project: two weeks of elapsed time

In addition, we have used the ratings *[project]* for anything that is likely to be higher than [40], and *[discussion]* for exercises that ask readers to go out and explore a certain subject on their own.

The original plan for the book was to include SQL implementation and application design along with transactions. As the work progressed, we realized that there was not space or time for these topics. So, as it stands, this book is about how to implement transactions. Ceri and Pelagatti's excellent book [1984] covers the high-level database issues (SQL, normalization, optimization, and also some transaction management issues).

Learning with this Book

The book is intended for advanced undergraduates, graduate students, and for professional programmers who either want to understand what their transaction processing system is doing to them (e.g., a CICS/DB2 user) or who need a basic reference text. It assumes that you have a reading knowledge of SQL and C.

The content of this book has no exact counterpart among computer science classes at a university. The compartmentalization of subjects is inherent in the structure of the curriculum, and as yet there is no standard class on transaction processing. However, the book has already been used in a variety of undergraduate and graduate courses during our various stages of draft manuscript. We feel the approach we have taken is appropriate within the existing structure of computer science, but we hope that exposure to our approach will help to eliminate compartmentalized thinking. Here are some suggestions for emphasizing different aspects of the coverage:

Just getting the idea: Chapter 1, Sections 2.7, 4.1–4.2, 5.1–5.3, 5.5–5.7, and Chapter 16.

An introduction to transaction processing: Chapters 1 and 2, Sections 3.1–3.6, Chapters 4 and 5, Sections 6.4–6.5, 7.1–7.6, Chapters 9, 10, 16.

Database systems: Chapters 1, 4, 7, 10, 13, 14, 15.

Distributed systems: Chapters 1, 2, 3, 4, 7, 8, 10, 11, 12, 16.

Operating systems: Chapters 1, 2, 3, 5, 6, 7, 8, 10, 11, 13, 16.

Advanced coverage: Read everything. In advanced courses, Chapters 1 and 3 can be skipped or done away with quickly. In addition, one could use the books by Tanenbaum on operating systems and computer networks, by Ceri and Pelagatti on distributed databases, by Oszu and Valduriez on principles of distributed databases, and one of Date's books on databases in general.

Many other combinations are conceivable. Those who are already familiar with the subject can skip Chapters 1 and 2; we recommend browsing them, just to grasp the terminology used throughout the book.

Chapter 3 can be skipped, but we recommend you read it. Transactions may seem all too obvious at the first glance. However, Chapter 3 carefully explains why transactions are the right exception-handling model and are a key to building highly available systems. The techniques described therein help provide a better understanding of what fault tolerance at the system level means, and they can be put to use almost immediately for anyone building applications.

We sketched the few dependencies that exist among the chapters while introducing the subject areas. If you read the entire book, you will notice some redundancy among the chapters. This feature allows chapters to be used independently.

To enhance course use of this book, instructors might consider using software available from Transarc Corporation through the Encina University Program. The Encina products are designed to enable distributed, standards-based online transaction processing in open computing environments. Many of the topics in this book could be explored through course projects using the Encina family of modular products: for example, distributed transaction management, transactional remote procedure calls, advanced lock and recovery models, shared logging systems, a record-oriented resource manager, and a transaction monitor. Contact information about the Encina family of products and academic site licences can be found on the copyright page of this book.

If you have time enough, and if you are thoroughly interested in transaction processing, get copies of papers by Bjork and Davies [1972; 1973; 1978]. These early articles started the whole field, and it is instructive to read them from our current perspective. One appreciates that transactions evolved not so much as a natural abstraction, but as a radical attempt to cut out complexity that otherwise proved to be unmanageable. When reading these seminal papers, you will also find that the vision outlined there has not yet become reality—not by a wide margin.

Concluding Remarks

As the acknowledgments indicate, drafts of this book were reviewed and class-tested for two years (1990–1991). Not only has this improved the presentation and accuracy of the text, it also changed the overall design of the book. New chapters were added, others were dropped, and the book doubled in size. The review process and heated debates also changed the way the material is organized. One of us started top-down, whereas the other one wrote bottom-up. In the end, we both reversed our approaches.

Apart from that, errors remain errors, and they must be blamed on us with no excuse. We will be very grateful, though, if you let us know the ones you find. Please send such comments to the authors in care of the publisher, or to the electronic mailbox Gray@microsoft.com.

Acknowledgments

This book benefited from the detailed criticism and advice of many people. We gratefully acknowledge their guidance. We are *especially* grateful to Frank Bamberger, Phil Bernstein, Noel Herbst, Bruce Lindsay, Dave Lomet, Dan Siewiorek, Nandit Soparkar, Kent Treiber, and Laurel Wentworth for detailed advice on improving the emphasis or focus of the book. More than anything else, the criticism of Betty Salzberg and her classes shaped the presentation of this book. Thank you all.

Phil Bernstein at Digital
Frank Bamberger at Citibank
Edward Brajinski at Digital
Mike Carey at Wisconsin
Stefano Ceri at Milano
Edward Cheng at Digital
Joe Coffee at Northeastern
Mike Cox at Princeton
Flaviu Cristian at IBM
Gary Cuhna at Northeastern
Walker Cunningham at Morgan Kaufmann
Allyn Dimock at Northeastern
Robert Drum at Northeastern
Dan Duchamp at Columbia
Amanda Carlson at HP
Jeff Eppinger at Transarc
Georgios Evangelidis at Northeastern
Scott Fitzgerald at Northeastern
Hector Garcia-Molina at Princeton
Amal Gebrael at Northeastern
Yujia Haung at Northeastern
Ricky Ho at G.O. Graphics
Walter Hursch at Northeastern
Meichun Hsu at Digital
Pat Helland at HAL
Noel Herbst at Tandem
Pete Homan at Tandem
Olaf Kruger at Northeastern
T.J. Jafar at Northeastern
Jim Johnson at Digital

Johannes Klein at Digital
Angelica Kokkinaki at Northeastern
Jacek Kruszelnicki at Northeastern
Olaf Kruger at Northeastern
Lori Ann Lashway at Polaroid
Don Langenhorst at Northeastern
Bruce Lindsay at IBM
Dave Lomet at Digital
Randell MacBlane at USL
Dorthy Minior at GSSI
Elliot Moss at U. Massachusetts
Ron Obermarck at Digital
Jeffry Picciotto at Mitre
Franco Putzolu at Tandem
Xinyang Qian at Northeastern
Ron Regan at Northeastern
Dennis Roberson at Digital
Eleana Rosenzweig at Northeastern
Daphne Ryan at Northeastern
Betty Salzberg at Northeastern
Tom Sawyer at Tom Sawyer
Fabio Schreiber at Milan
Linda Seiter at Northeastern
Mark Sherman at Transarc
Dan Siewiorek at CMU
Eric Skov at Northeastern
Donald Slutz at Tandem
Mark Smith at U. Massachusetts
Narjit Sindupal at ATT
Nandit Soparkar at U. Texas
Christos Stamelos at Northeastern

Kent Treiber at IBM
Mike Ubell at Digital
Tom Vancor at BGS
Vic Vyssotsky at Digital
Laurel Wentworth at Digital
Gary Warner at Northeastern

Bill Wisnaskas at Northeastern
David Wong at Northeastern
Robert Wu at Digital
Hans-Jörg Zeller at Tandem
Ying Zhou at Northeastern

Walker Cunningham, our developmental writer, carefully criticized all the chapters. His efforts made an enormous difference in the clarity of the book.

Our colleagues heavily influenced certain chapters. Betty Salzberg suggested the need for Chapter 2 (terminology). Dan Siewiorek and Vic Vyssotsky contributed heavily to the chapter on fault tolerance. Bruce Lindsay and Harald Sammer influenced our presentation of transaction concepts. Phil Bernstein, Noel Herbst, Bruce Lindsay, and Ron Obermarck caused us to rethink our presentation of transaction management. Dave Lomet and Franco Putzolu contributed heavily to the chapters on record and file management. Frank Bamberger, Elliot Moss, Don Slutz, and Nandit Sopakar gave us valuable overall criticism of the book.

Charlie Davies, the visionary who launched our field 20 years ago, deserves mention here. Charlie's work on *spheres of control* is little known. His papers are obscure, but all who came in contact with him were inspired by his vision. Workers in the field are still trying to work out the details of that vision. Chapter 4 presents his ideas in more modern terms.

Transaction processing is a field in which practice has led theory. Commercial systems often implement ideas long before the ideas appear in an academic setting. One is reminded of Galileo claiming the invention of the telescope to the doges of Venice while merchants were selling mass-produced Dutch telescopes in the streets below.

Throughout the book, we are faced with a dilemma. Does one give credit to the first to publish an idea? Or, does one give priority to the earlier development and implementation of the idea in a product? Academic tradition and U.S. patent law give priority to the first to publish. We have tried to credit both. The historical notes in each chapter recount, as best we can, the parallel commercial and academic development of the ideas. Perhaps the point is moot; implementors don't want credit for ideas, they want the cash.

One implementor, Franco Putzolu, has deeply influenced our field in general, and the authors in particular. Franco has never written a paper or a patent, but his ideas and code are at the core of System R, SQL/DS, DB2, Allbase, and NonStop SQL. These designs have been widely copied by others and are repeated here. Franco Putzolu deserves much of the credit for this book.

Bruce Spatz, our publisher, gave us excellent guidance on the focus of the book. He arranged for many reviews, arranged the classroom tests, and encouraged us when we needed it most. We also are very grateful to our project manager, Jennifer Ballentine of Professional Book Center, and Jeanne Thieme, our copyeditor, for their contributions to this book.

Andreas's students contributed to the book in many ways: They read draft versions, used it for teaching, tried the exercises, worked on the references, and so on—typical student slave labor. Moreover, the absence of their supervisor when he periodically got serious about "finishing that book *now*" meant they had to work on their own much more than one would wish.

Gabriele Ziegler, Andreas's secretary, deserves special thanks for keeping him organized during the whole endeavor—not an easy assignment. She had to pacify many people who had good reason to be angry for his not responding for days or weeks when he was again "finishing that book *now*."

Christiane Reuter almost wrote a chapter on application design, but decided against it. However, she took care of the authors during the first long writing assignment in Ripa—not a simple task given the quality of the local power and the dreadful weather. She also accepted the multiyear ordeal of late nights and lost weekends.

Tandem Computers and Digital Equipment Corporation were very generous in their support of Jim Gray's efforts on this book.

Thanks to all of you who kept us going, even kept us amused, and tolerated our obsessions and varying tempers.

Jim Gray

Andreas Reuter
University of Stuttgart

Trademarks

Ada is a trademark of the U.S. Government, Ada Joint Program Office.

ACP (Airlines Control Program), AIX, AS/400 (Application System/400), CPI-C (Common Programming Interface-Communications), DL1, DB2, Expedited Message Handling (IMS Fast Path), IBM, IMS/DB(DataBase), IMS Fast Path, IMS/XRF, IMS/TM, IMS/DC, IMS, IBM-SAA (System Application Architecture), IBM PS2, IMS Extended Reliability Feature, MVS OS/2, OS/360, Presentation Manager, RS/6000, SNA, System/370, System/38, XRF (Extended Recovery Feature) are trademarks or registered trademarks of International Business Machines Corporation.

Apollo's Domain is a trademark or registered trademark of Hewlett Packard Computer Company.

Burroughs is a registered trademark of Burroughs Corporation.

CDD/Plus (Common Data Dictionary/Plus), CDD/Repository (Common Data Dictionary/ Repository), DECforms, DECdta, DECtp, DECintact, DECq, DECnet, Rdb, Rdb/VMS, RTR (Reliable Transaction Router), VAX/VMS, VAX cluster, VMS, VMS Lock Manager are trademarks or registered trademarks and VAX is a registered trademark of Digitial Equipment Corporation.

CODASYL is a trademark or registered trademark of Conference In Data Systems Language.

Com-Plete is a trademark or registered trademark of Software A.G.

Encina is a trademark or registered trademark of Transarc Corporation.

Ethernet is a trademark or registered trademark of Xerox Corporation.

FastPath is a trademark or registered trademark of Intel Corporation.

FORTRAN is a trademark or registered trademark of SofTech Microsystems, Inc.

Guardian, NonStop SQL, Pathway are trademarks or registered trademarks of Tandem Computers.

HPALLbase, HP9000, Precision Architecture are trademarks or registered trademarks of Hewlett Packard Computer Company.

Ingres, Postgres System are trademarks or registered trademarks of INGRES Corporation.

Interbase is a trademark or registered trademark of Borland International, Inc.

MS/DOS, Mach 10 are trademarks and Windows is a registered trademark of Microsoft Corp.

Multics is a trademark or registered trademark Honeywell Computer Systems.

Macintosh, Macintosh News are registered trademarks of Apple Computer Company.

New NextStep, NextStep, Next are trademarks or registered trademarks of NEXT Computer Corporation.

NCR, TOPEND are trademarks or registered trademarks of National Cash Register Corporation.

Oracle is a trademark or registered trademark of Oracle Corporation.

Open Look is a trademark or registered trademark of UNIX System Laboratories, Inc.

Sun Microsoft, Sun RPC are trademarks or registered trademark of Sun Microsystems, Inc.

Tuxedo, UNIX are registered trademarks of AT&T Bell Laboratories.

TCP/IP is a trademark or registered trademark of Defense Advanced Research Projects Administration.

x.25 is a mark of the Comite Consultiatif Internationale de Telegraphique et Telephonique.

All other brand and product names referenced in this book are trademarks or registered trademarks of their respective holders and are used here for informational purposes only.

PART ONE

The Basics of
Transaction Processing

Six thousand years ago,
the Sumerians invented writing
for transaction processing

1

Introduction

1.1 Historical Perspective

Six thousand years ago, the Sumerians invented writing for transaction processing. The earliest known writing is found on clay tablets recording the royal inventory of taxes, land, grain, cattle, slaves, and gold; scribes evidently kept records of each transaction. This early system had the key aspects of a transaction processing system (see Figure 1.1):

Database.   An abstract system state, represented as marks on clay tablets, was maintained. Today, we would call this the *database*.

Transactions.   Scribes recorded state changes with new records (clay tablets) in the database. Today, we would call these state changes *transactions*.

The Sumerians' approach allowed the scribes to easily ask questions about the current and past state, while providing a historical record of how the system got to the present state.

The technology of clay-based transaction processing systems evolved over several thousand years through papyrus, parchment, and then paper. For over a thousand years, pa-

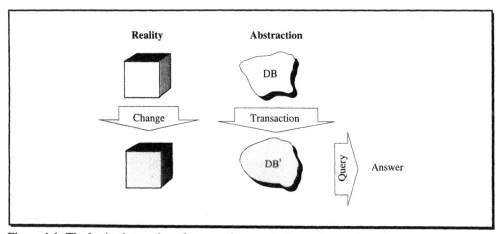

Figure 1.1: The basic abstraction of transaction processing systems.   The real state is represented by an abstraction, called the *database*, and the transformation of the real state is mirrored by the execution of a program, called a *transaction*, that transforms the database

per, ink, and ledgers were the technology for transaction processing. The most recent innovation began late in the 1800s when Herman Hollerith built a punched-card computer system to record and report the 1890 United States census. During the first half of the twentieth century, the need for transaction processing fueled the evolution and growth of punched-card equipment. These early computers were used primarily for inventory control and accounting. In effect, they replaced clay tablets with paper tablets (cards); their virtue was that the systems could search and update about one "tablet" (card) per second.

The second half of the twentieth century saw two main developments in transaction processing: *batch* transaction processing based on magnetic storage (tape and disc), followed by *online* transaction processing based on electronic storage and computer networks. These two developments were largely responsible for growth in the computer industry, and transaction processing applications accounted for the majority of computer systems revenues. Today, the primary use of general-purpose computers is still transaction processing. Typical applications and examples include the following:

Communications.   Setting up and billing for telephone calls, electronic mail, and so on.

Finance.   Banking, stock trading, point of sale, and so on.

Travel.   Reservations and billing for airlines, hotels, cars, trains, and so on.

Manufacturing.   Order entry, job and inventory planning and scheduling, accounting, and so on.

Process control.   Control of factories, warehouses, steel, paper, and chemical plants, and so on.

Consider the example of a telephone call. Each time you make a phone call, there is a call setup transaction that allocates some resources to your conversation; the call teardown is a second transaction, freeing those resources. The call setup increasingly involves complex algorithms to find the callee (800 numbers could be anywhere in the world) and to decide who is to be billed (800 and 900 numbers have complex billing). The system must deal with features like call forwarding, call waiting, and voice mail. After the call teardown, billing may involve many phone companies (e.g., direct dial from San Francisco to Madagascar involves several phone companies).

As another example, computer integrated manufacturing (CIM) is a key technique for improving industrial productivity and efficiency. Just-in-time inventory control, automated warehouses, and robotic assembly lines each require a reliable data storage system to represent the factory state. In addition, computers control and monitor the flow of goods through the factory.

As with most modern enterprises, these two applications—telephony and manufacturing—require vast quantities of software. In the past, such systems were often implemented using specialized computers and ad hoc techniques. This meant that the applications had to be reprogrammed for each new generation of computers. However, the development effort for these applications has become so huge that the investment must be preserved for several hardware generations. As a result, standard software is now used to ensure that the application will work on the next generation of computer systems. Project risks and costs are also reduced by using high-level tools to improve programmer productivity. Consequently, system control functions are being implemented using standard transaction processing systems, standard operating systems, standard database systems, and general-purpose hardware.

1.2 What Is a Transaction Processing System?

This chapter views a transaction processing system from many different perspectives: a user perspective, a programmer perspective, an administrator perspective, and a TP system implementor perspective. Because each views the system quite differently, it is difficult to give a single definition of what a transaction processing system is and what it does. If forced to do so, however, most will agree to the following statement:

> A *transaction processing system* (TP system) provides tools to ease or automate application programming, execution, and administration. Transaction processing applications typically support a network of devices that submit queries and updates to the application. Based on these inputs, the application maintains a database representing some real-world state. Application responses and outputs typically drive real-world actuators and transducers that alter or control the state. The applications, database, and network tend to evolve over several decades. Increasingly, the systems are geographically distributed, heterogeneous (they involve equipment and software from many different vendors), continuously available (there is no scheduled down-time), and have stringent response time requirements.

The term transaction processing system is generally used to mean a *complete* system. A TP system includes application generators, operations tools, one or more database systems, utilities, and, of course, networking and operating system software. Historically, TP system meant *Tele-Processing system* and denoted a program supporting a variety of terminal types and networking protocols. Some current transaction processing systems evolved from teleprocessing systems, further complicating the terminology. As used here, the term *TP system* has the connotation of transaction processing.

A TP system is a big thing; it includes application generators, networks, databases, and applications. Within the TP system, there is a core collection of services, called the *TP monitor*, that manage and coordinate the flow of transactions through the system.

All these definitions use the term *transaction*. What exactly is a transaction? It has the following various meanings:

(1) The request or input message that started the operation.   *transaction request/reply*

(2) All effects of the execution of the operation.   *transaction*

(3) The program(s) that execute(s) the operation.   *transaction program*

These ambiguities stem from the various perspectives of people involved in the transaction. The end user sees only the request and reply and, consequently, thinks in those terms. The operator and the auditor primarily see the request execution, so they take that view. The system administrator largely deals with the naming, security, and the transaction programs; he therefore often thinks of the transaction as the program source rather than the program execution.

This book adopts the second definition: *A transaction is a collection of operations on the physical and abstract application state*. The other two transaction concepts are called the *transaction request/reply* and the *transaction program*.

Transaction processing systems pioneered many concepts in distributed computing and fault-tolerant computing. They introduced distributed data for reliability, availability, and performance; they developed fault-tolerant storage and fault-tolerant processes for availability; and they developed the client-server model and remote procedure call for distributed computation. Most important, they introduced the transaction ACID properties—atomicity, consistency, isolation, and durability—that have emerged as the unifying concepts for distributed computation.

This book contains considerably more information about the ACID properties. For now, however, a transaction can be considered a collection of actions with the following properties:

Atomicity. A transaction's changes to the state are atomic: either all happen or none happen. These changes include database changes, messages, and actions on transducers.

Consistency. A transaction is a correct transformation of the state. The actions taken as a group do not violate any of the integrity constraints associated with the state. This requires that the transaction be a correct program.

Isolation. Even though transactions execute concurrently, it appears to each transaction, T, that others executed either before T or after T, but not both.

Durability. Once a transaction completes successfully (commits), its changes to the state survive failures.

As an example, a banking debit transaction is atomic if it both dispenses money and updates your account. It is consistent if the money dispensed is the same as the debit to the account. It is isolated if the transaction program can be unaware of other programs reading and writing your account concurrently (for example, your spouse making a concurrent deposit). And it is durable if, once the transaction is complete, the account balance is sure to reflect the withdrawal.[1]

It may be hard to believe that such a simple idea could be very important, but that is the point. Transactions specify simple failure semantics for a computation. It is up to the system implementors to provide these properties to the application programmer. The application programmer, in turn, provides these properties to his clients.

The application program declares the start of a new transaction by invoking Begin_Work(). Thereafter, all operations performed by the program will be part of this transaction. Also, all operations performed by other programs in service of the application program will be part of the transaction. The program declares the transaction to be a complete and correct transformation by invoking Commit_Work(). Once the transaction successfully commits, the transaction's effects are durable. If something goes wrong during the transaction, the application can undo all the operations by invoking Rollback_Work(). If there is a failure during the transaction's execution, the system can unilaterally cause the transaction to

---

[1] The term ACID was coined by Haërder and Reuter [1983]. The term *serializable* is a commonly used synonym for isolated. The terms *persistent* and *stable* are widely used synonyms for durable. None of these alternatives (e.g., PACS, SACS) gives a nice acronym like ACID.

be rolled back. Begin-Commit or Begin-Rollback, then, are used to bracket the ACID transformations.

This is a simple and modular way to build distributed applications. Each module is a transaction or sub-transaction. If all goes well, the transaction eventually commits and all the modules move to a new durable state. If anything goes wrong, all the modules of the transaction are automatically reset to their state as of the start of the transaction. Since the commit and reset logic are automatic, it is easy to build modules with very simple failure semantics.

Many of the techniques used to achieve the ACID properties have direct analogies in human systems. In retrospect, we have just abstracted them into computer terms. The notions of atomicity and durability are explicit in contract law, in which a notary or escrow officer coordinates a business transaction. Even more explicit is the Christian wedding ceremony, in which two people agree to a marriage. The marriage commit protocol goes as follows: The minister asks each partner, "Do you agree to marry this person?" If both say "yes," then the minister declares the marriage committed; if either fails to respond, or says "no," then the marriage is off (neither is married). Transaction processing systems use a protocol directly analogous to this to achieve all-or-nothing atomic agreement among several independent programs or computers. Translated into computer terms, this idea is called the *two-phase commit protocol*: it has a voting phase, in which all participants prepare to commit, followed by a second commit phase, in which they execute the commit. A distinguished process acts much as the minister, coordinating the commit. This protocol allows all participants in a distributed computation to either agree to change state or agree to stay in the old state.

The transaction concept is the computer equivalent to contract law. Imagine a society without contract law. That is what a computer system would be like without transactions. If nothing ever goes wrong, contracts are just overhead. But if something doesn't quite work, the contract specifies how to clean up the situation.

There are many examples of systems that tried and failed to implement fault-tolerant or distributed computations using ad hoc techniques rather than a transaction concept. Subsequently, some of these systems were successfully implemented using transaction techniques. After the fact, the implementors confessed that they simply hit a complexity barrier and could not debug the ad hoc system without a simple unifying concept to deal with exceptions [Borr 1986; Hagmann 1987]. Perhaps even more surprising, the subsequent transaction-oriented systems had better performance than the ad hoc incorrect systems, because transaction logging tends to convert many small messages and random disk inputs and outputs (I/Os) into a few larger messages and sequential disk I/Os.

This book focuses on the definition and implementation of the ACID properties. First, let's look at transaction processing systems from the perspectives of various people who use or operate such systems: users, system administrators, system operators, application designers, and application implementors. Each has a different view of the system. Later chapters take the system implementor's perspective—the person who has to implement all these other views.

A sample application system is needed to make the various views concrete. Funds transfer is the standard example application used for transaction processing systems because it deals with a simple, abstract, and valuable commodity. It is also one of the major application areas of transaction processing systems. For the sake of variety, let's consider a forms-oriented electronic mail application from the various perspectives.

1.2.1 The End User's View of a Transaction Processing System

The end user's view of the mail system is that there are mailboxes associated with people, and there are messages (see Figure 1.2). The user first identifies himself to the system and presents a password or some other item that authenticates him to the system. When this transaction completes, the user is presented with a list of incoming messages. The user can read a message, reply to it, delete it, send a new message, or cancel a message he has sent. Each of these operations is an ACID transaction. The read operation can see the whole message (no part of the message will be missing), while the delete operation removes the whole message. The interactions between send and cancel is the most instructive aspect of this example. If the system fails while the user is composing a message and before the user issuing a send, then the message is not sent and the user's input is lost. After the user successfully issues the send, the message is delivered. Thus, the send is an ACID transaction. Two more transactions are involved: The message is delivered to the receiver's mailbox, and the message is read by the receiver. These are also ACID units. The sender may cancel (erase) an unread message, but the cancel will have no effect if the message has already been read by the receiver. The cancel is another ACID transaction; it is called a *compensating* transaction, since it is trying to compensate for the effects of a previously committed transaction.

The operation of composing a mail message may involve updating many database records representing the message, and it may require inquiries to remote name servers to

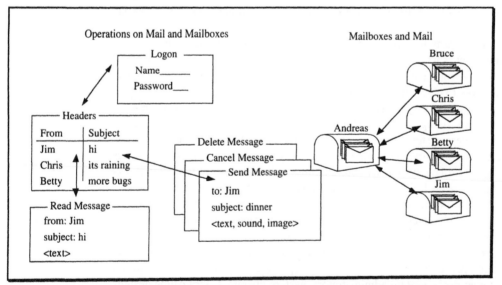

Figure 1.2: End user's view of a transaction processing system as a set of operations on abstract objects. In this case, the objects are mail messages and mailboxes. At the left, the diagram shows the menu hierarchy of operations that the user sees. The objects on the right are the transactional objects managed by the system. The user expects each operation to be atomic, consistent, isolated, and durable (ACID). The operations are presented to the user as input and output fields containing text, sounds, or images. To generalize this model, the end user views the system as a pre-programmed device with well-defined *operations on objects*. The object states are durable (persistent, stable), and the operations are atomic (all-or-nothing), consistent (transforms of high-level abstractions such as mail messages and mailboxes are complete), isolated (concurrent updates are applied sequentially), and durable (messages are not lost).

check the correctness of the mail address; all this work is packaged within the one ACID unit. If anything goes wrong during the message composition, all the operation's updates are reversed, and the message is discarded; if all goes well, all the operation's updates are made durable, and the message is accepted for delivery. Similarly, delivery of the message to the destination may encounter many problems. In such cases, the transaction is aborted, and a new delivery transaction is started. Eventually, the message is delivered to (inserted in) the destination mailbox. After that, it can be read by the recipient and replied to or deleted. Of course, to make the message durable, it is probably replicated in two or more places so that no single fault can damage it; that, again, is transparent to the end user, who thinks in terms of composing, sending, reading, and canceling messages. For each of these operations, the electronic mail application provides the end user with ACID operations on durable objects.

In this example, operations are shown to humans as a forms-oriented interface with text, voice, and button inputs. Output forms contain text, sounds, and images. In many other applications, the *user* is not a person, but rather a physical device such as a telephone switch, an airplane flap, or a warehouse robot. In these cases, the inputs are the readings of position and tactile sensors, while the outputs are commands to actuators. The sensors present the transaction processing system with input messages that invoke a transaction, and the transducers act on the transaction's output messages.

1.2.2 The Administrator/Operator's View of a TP System

The administrator of this electronic mail system has users in Asia, Australia, the Americas, Europe, and Africa (see Figure 1.3). There are administrative staff on each of these continents. In addition, the system has gateways to other mail systems, and the administrator cooperates with the managers of those systems.

The primary functions of the administrator are to add and delete users, provide them with documentation and training, and manage the system security. The security and administration interface provides forms and transaction programs that allow the administrator to

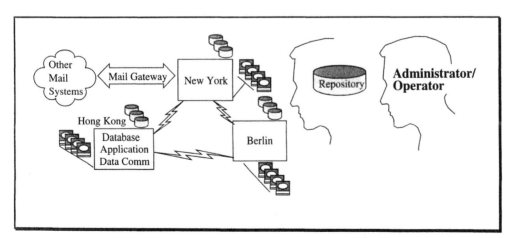

Figure 1.3: The system administrator/operator's view of the transaction processing system. This view consists of physical nodes containing hardware and interacting software modules. The application includes interfaces to facilitate administering and operating the system. The repository is a database that records the system configuration. The administrator views the system through the repository.

add users, change passwords, examine the security log to detect violations, and so on. These administrative transactions are ACID operations on the user database and the security database. They are just another aspect of the application and are programmed with the same high-level transaction processing tools used by other application designers.

Most of the software and hardware of a mail system are standard, but there are a few custom features that each organization has added. In particular, let us assume that the mail system software is a turn-key application provided by the vendor or by some third-party software house. The administrator has to plan for the installation of new software from the vendor as well as for installation of software from his own application development group. Such software upgrades and changes must be put through a careful integration, quality assurance, field testing, and then incremental installation on the various nodes of the network.

Besides these tasks, the system administrator monitors system performance and plans equipment upgrades as mail messages consume more storage and as increasing mail volume consumes disk space, processors, and network bandwidth. Once the system is installed, the administrator gets periodic reports on system utilization, indexed by component and by user. Again, these are standard applications that use the output from a performance monitor to populate a performance database; they use a report writer to generate formatted displays of the data.

The system administrator has a daunting job: He must manage thousands of users and myriad hardware and software components. He needs the help of a computer to do this. The administrative interface is an integral part of any transaction processing system and application. Like any other transaction processing application, it is programmed to provide a forms-oriented transactional interface to the system configuration. The system configuration is represented as a database, called the *repository* or *system dictionary*. The administrator can alter the configuration using standard transactions, inquire about the configuration using standard reports, or read the configuration using a non-procedural language, such as SQL, to generate specialized reports. The repository concept is developed in more detail in Subsection 1.3.2. The key point is that the system configuration should be represented as a database that can be manipulated using the high-level software tools of the transaction processing system.

While the system administrator makes policy decisions and plans system growth, the system operator performs the more tactical job of keeping the system running. He monitors system behavior, and when something breaks, he calls the repair man. Additionally, he performs operational tasks such as installing new software, connecting new hardware, producing periodic reports, moving archival media off site, and so on. There is an increasing tendency to automate operations tasks, both to reduce errors and to reduce staff costs.

Table 1.4 gives a sense of the scale of administration and operation tasks on systems with thousands or hundreds of thousands of components. If each terminal has a mean-time-to-failure of three years, then the operator of a large system will have to deal with a terminal failure about every 15 minutes. Similarly, he will have to deal with one disk failure a week and one processor failure per week. Just diagnosing and managing these events will keep an operations staff busy.

Perhaps the most important message in Table 1.4 is that a transaction processing system has thousands—up to millions—of components. Tracking these components, diagnosing failures, and managing change is a very complex task. It is structured as a transaction processing application, with a database (the repository) and a collection of well-defined operations that transform the database. Other operations produce reports on the current system configuration and how it got to that state.

Table 1.4: Representative counts of the components of small and large transaction processing systems. There are so many components in a system that a special database (called the *repository*) is needed to keep track of them and their status. Notice especially the hundreds of thousands of terminals, tapes, and source files.

Hardware	Small/Simple	Medium	Large/Complex
Terminals or users	100	10,000	100,000
Hosts	1	10	100
Disks (capacity)	10 (= 10GB)	100 (= 100GB)	1K (=1TB)
Archive tapes (capacity)	1K (= 1TB)	10K (= 10TB)	100K (= .1PB)
Software			
Transaction programs, reports, screens, database files	400	4,000	40,000
Source and old versions of programs, reports, and screens	1,000	10,000	100,000
Domains/ fields (within tables)	1,000	10,000	100,000

The system administrator, system operator, and application designer also face performance problems. The system often runs both *interactive transactions*, which are processed while the client waits for an answer, and *batch transactions*, which are submitted but may be processed later. Interactive transactions are necessarily small, since they must be processed within the few seconds that the client is willing to wait. If the system is overloaded or poorly configured, response times can increase beyond an acceptable level. In this case, the operator and the administrator are called upon to *tune* the system for better performance. As a last resort, the administrator can install more equipment. Increasingly, this tuning process is being automated. Most systems provide tools that measure performance, recommend or perform tuning actions, and recommend the type and quantity of equipment needed to process a projected load.

Estimating the performance of a TP system is difficult because the systems are so complex and because their performance on different problems can be very different. One system is good at batch jobs, another excels on interactive transactions, and yet a third is geared toward information retrieval applications (reading). Gradually, various usage patterns are being recognized, and standard benchmarks are being defined to represent the workload of each problem type.

An industry consortium, the Transaction Processing Performance Council (TPC), has defined three benchmarks. With each of these benchmarks, named A, B, and C, comes a scaleable database and workload, allowing the benchmarks to be run on computers, networks, and databases of every size, from the smallest to the largest. They can also be scaled up to the largest computers, networks, and databases. Using these benchmarks, each system gets three throughput ratings, called *transactions-per-second* (tps-A, tps-B, and tps-C). As the tps rating rises, the network size and database size scale accordingly.

These benchmarks also measure system price/performance ratio by accounting for the five-year price of hardware, software, and vendor maintenance. This five-year price is then divided by the tps rating to get a price/performance rating ($/tps).

The three benchmarks can be roughly described as follows:

TPC-A is a simple banking transaction with a 100-byte message input, four database up-dates, and a 200-byte message output to the terminal. It includes simple presentation services. The database operations are a mix of main-memory, random, and sequential accesses. The system definition and price includes ten terminals per tps.

TPC-B is TPC-A with the terminals, network, and two-thirds of the long-term storage removed. It is a database-only benchmark designed to give high tps ratings and low $/tps ratings to database systems. Its price/performance rating is typically ten times better than the more realistic TPC-A rating.

TPC-C is an order entry application with a mix of interactive and batch transactions. It includes realistic features like queued transactions, aborting transactions, and elaborate presentation services. As a group, the TPC-C transactions are about ten times more complex than TPC-A; that is, TPC-C tps ratings are ten times lower for the same hardware. TPC-C has just been approved as a standard. It will likely supplant TPC-A and TPC-B as an important performance metric.

TPC-C approximates a typical interactive transaction workload today. As computers and networks get faster, and as memories grow in size, the typical transaction is likely to grow larger and more complex than those in TPC-C. Table 1.5 gives a rough description of the cpu, I/O, and message costs of TPC-A, TPC-C, and a hypothetical large batch program. The TPC will likely define such a batch workload as TPC-D. The specifications for the TPC benchmarks and several other benchmarks are in the *Benchmark Handbook for Database and Transaction Processing Systems* [Gray 1991].

1.2.3 Application Designer's View of a TP System

Now let us look at the sample mail system from the perspective of the application designer or application implementor. In the past, the roles of application designer and application implementor were separate. With the advent of application generators, rapid prototyping, and fourth-generation programming languages, many implementation tasks have been automated so that the design *is* the implementation.

Applications are now routinely structured as *client* processes near the user, making requests to *server* processes running on other computers. In the mail system, the client is the mail program running on Andreas' workstation, and the server is running on the Berlin host

Table 1.5: Typical performance measures of interactive transactions. Interactive transactions respond within seconds. By contrast, batch transactions can run for hours or days and thus consume huge amounts of data and processing.

Performance/transaction	Interactive transactions only		
	Small/Simple	**Medium**	**Large/Complex**
Instructions/transaction	100K	1M	100M
Disk I/O/transaction	1	10	1000
Local Messages (bytes)	10 (5KB)	100 (50KB)	1,000 (1MB)
Remote Messages (bytes)	2 (300B)	2 (4KB)	100 (1MB)
Cost/transaction/second	10k$/tps	100k$/tps	1M$/tps
Peak tps/site	1,000	100	1

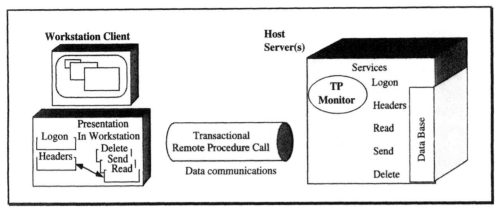

Figure 1.6: The structure of a forms-oriented application in which presentation services are performed in the client. The client program was generated by an application generator. The client actions generate remote procedure calls to the TP monitor running in the shared host computer that stores the mailboxes and messages. The TP monitor launches one or another services to perform the requested operations against the database. Of course, the host could be geographically distributed (as in Figure 1.3), and the client could store part of the database and perform some service functions locally.

(see Figure 1.3). Of course, the client could be a gas pump, a warehouse robot, or a bar code reader. In all cases, the concepts would be the same.

The client program executes as a process in the user's workstation, providing a graphical and responsive interface to the human user. This aspect of the application, called *presentation services*, gathers data and navigates among the forms. If access to other services is required, the client passes the request to a server running on a local or remote host, as shown in Figure 1.6.

The request to the server (service) arrives at the host as a message directed to the transaction processing monitor at that host. The TP monitor has a list of services registered with it. In the mail system example, these services are application-specific functions, such as logon to the mail system, read a message, delete a message, send a message, and so on. When a service request arrives, the TP monitor looks up the service in its repository and checks that the client is authorized to use that service. The TP monitor then creates a process to execute that service, passing the text of the initial request to the server process. The server process then performs its function, accessing the database and conversing with the client process. If the service is very simple, it accesses its database, replies, and terminates. If the service is more complex, it replies and waits for further requests from the client. One service may call on other services and may implicitly access remote services by accessing data stored at remote sites.

What did the application designer do to produce the client and server code? The client code was probably built with an application generator that produced a subroutine for each input/output form shown in Figure 1.2. The designer painted each form, defining input fields, output fields, and buttons that navigate to other forms. For example, the logon form gathers the client name and password, then passes them to the host, invoking the mail server logon service via a remote procedure call. The service tests the password and returns the result of the test to the client. If the logon is successful, the service will have allocated a *context* for the client on the server, so that subsequent calls can quickly refer to the client's mailbox and status on the host. The logon form then invokes the header form, which in turn calls the header service on the mail server host to enumerate the recent incoming and outgoing messages. The generated code for the logon client has a format something like this:

```
logon_client ()                                    /* automatically generated client code.          */
   {char       user_name[];                        /* user name entered in logon form.              */
    char       password[];                          /*user password entered in logon form.           */
    boolean    logged_on = FALSE;                   /* flag says user not yet authenticated (logged on)  */
    long       mailbox;                             /* Once logged on, this is the user mailbox      */
    while (! logged_on)                             /* get id and password and logon to server       */
        {   Begin_Work();                           /* start a transaction                           */
            ACCEPT user_name,password FROM logon_form; /* read user name and password               */
            CALL logon_service(user_name,password) returning(logged_on, mailbox); /* ask service    */
            if(logged_on) DISPLAY "ok";             /* to check password.                            */
            else DISPLAY "invalid name or password";    /* If bad password then display error        */
            Commit_Work();                          /* logon transaction complete, commit it         */
        }                                           /* loop until a correct name and password is entered */
    CALL headers(mailbox);                          /* invoke first user-level form (after user logon)  */
    CALL logoff_service(mailbox);                   /* logoff when menu tree returns                 */
    };                                              /* end of logon code.                            */
```

This client code is represented as the Logon box in the workstation of Figure 1.2. It is written in a programming language with standard syntax and control flow, but it also has the screen handling functions of a presentation service (the ACCEPT and DISPLAY verbs), remote procedure call functions that allow it to invoke services at any node in the network (the CALL verb), and transaction verbs that allow it to declare transaction boundaries (Begin and Commit verbs).

The client programming language is often *persistent*. This means that if the client process fails or if the transaction aborts, the process and its persistent state will be reinstantiated as of the start of the transaction. For example, if the power fails and the processor restarts, then the client process will be recreated as if the transaction had simply aborted. Persistent programming languages tie the application state together with the database state and the network state, making changes to all aspects of state atomic—all-or-nothing.

The server code may also have been produced by an application generator. For example, the logon server has to check that the user password is correct and then *open* the user's mailbox, thereby producing a *token* that will identify this client mailbox on subsequent calls. This application logic is so simple that there may be a template for it already present in the system. If not, the application designer will have to write a few lines of SQL and C code to perform these functions.

To summarize, the transaction processing system presents the application designer with a distributed computation environment and with a collection of application-generation tools to speed and simplify the design and implementation task. These application generators are used both for rapid prototyping and developing the actual application. The application designer either paints screens or writes code fragments that are attached to clients or services. All these screens, clients, and services are registered in the system repository. When an application executes, the client invokes services via a transactional remote procedure call mechanism.

1.2.3.1 Transactional Remote Procedure Calls

What is a transactional remote procedure call mechanism? It is best to develop this idea in stages. A *procedure call mechanism* is a way for one program to call another—it is the subroutine concept, a familiar part of virtually all programming languages. In general, all procedures are part of one address space and process. *Remote procedure calls* (RPCs) are a way for one process to invoke a program in another remote process as though the subroutine in the remote process were local. It appears to both the caller and the callee that they are both in the same process; the remote procedure call looks like a local procedure call.

Remote procedure calls, however, need not be remote. The client and the server can be in the same computer and still use the same interface to communicate. Local and remote procedure calls have the same interface, so that the client program can move anywhere in the network and still operate correctly. The client and the server need not know each other's location. Locating the client at a particular site is a performance and authorization decision. If the client interacts heavily with the input/output device, then the client belongs near the data source; if the client interacts more heavily with a single server, then the client probably belongs near the server.

Given these approximate definitions of procedure call and remote procedure call, we can now discuss the concept of *transactional remote procedure call*. Transactional remote procedure calls are a way to combine the work of several clients and servers into a single ACID execution unit. The application declares the transaction boundaries by calling Begin_Work(). This starts a new transaction and creates a unique transaction identifier (trid) for it. Once a transaction is started, all operations by the client are tagged by that transaction's identifier. The transaction identifier is sent with all service requests, so that the operation of that service is also within the scope of the transaction. When the transaction commits, all the participating services also commit the operations of that transaction. The commit logic is implemented by the TP monitors of each participating node. They all go through a wedding ceremony protocol (two-phase commit protocol) coordinated by a trusted process. Recall that the two-phase commit protocol is: Q: "Do you commit?" A: "I do." Q: "You are committed." A: "Great!" If anything goes wrong, everything rolls back to the start of the transaction.

In transactional systems, servers are generally called *resource managers*. A resource manager is the data, code, and processes that provide access to some shared data. Transaction processing systems make it easy to build and invoke resource managers. The mail system of our running example is a resource manager. RPC is the standard way for an application program to invoke a resource manager.

Transactional remote procedure call (TRPC) is just like remote procedure call, except that it propagates the client's transaction identifier, along with the other parameters, to the server. The TRPC mechanism at the server registers the server as part of the client's transaction. Figure 1.7 shows the flow of messages among clients and servers in a typical transaction. Each of the local and remote procedure calls in Figure 1.7 are tagged with the client's transaction identifier.

1.2.3.2 Failure

What happens if something goes wrong in the middle of this? For example, what if the user hits the cancel key, or if the server decides that the input is wrong, or if there is a power failure, or if the server fails in some way, or if something else fails? If the failure happens

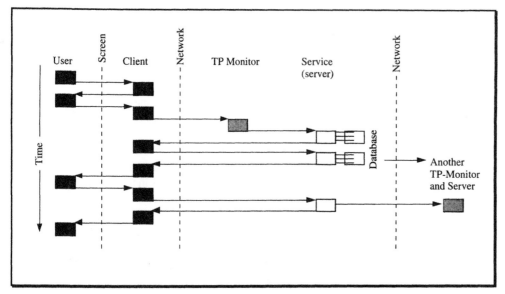

Figure 1.7: The data flow among the active components of the distributed computation shown in Figure 1.6. The user interacts with the screen interface. The client reads and writes the screen and communicates with servers via remote procedure calls (shown as bold lines). The initial invocation of the service is performed by the TP monitor that creates the server process. The server then interacts with the database and the client. The server may also make further calls to other servers and transparently access remote data via the database system. This figure shows a client calling a single server, but a client may invoke several services within one transaction. Client-server interactions can be structured as a single transaction or as a sequence of transactions.

after the entire operation completes, then the client and the server should remember the state changes, and both should return to the state at the end of the transaction—that is the durability property. On the other hand, if the failure happens *before* the operation completes, then some resource manager may not be able to commit the transaction. To be safe, the client and the server should return to their states as of the start of the transaction. All subsequent updates should be undone, the windows on the workstation should return to their original states, and the database should return to its original state—this the atomicity property.

The TP monitor automatically performs this reset, or reconstruction logic, in case of failure. The application program (client) declares the start of a computation that is to be treated as an ACID unit by issuing a Begin_Work() verb. When the computation is complete (when it is a correct transformation), the client issues a Commit_Work() verb. All actions of the transaction between the Begin_Work() and Commit_Work() verbs will be treated as a single ACID group. If the computation fails before the Commit_Work(), or if any part of the computation invokes the Rollback_Work() verb, then the state of the system will be returned to the situation as of the Begin_Work(). In particular, the client, the servers, the screen, and the database will all be reset to that state. This simplifies the exception handling for the application designer. All this undo work is automatic.

As explained later, many transaction systems allow *nested* transactions and partial rollback of a transaction. The presentation here begins with the simple model of *flat* transactions with no intermediate *savepoints*. Chapters 4 and 5 explore generalizations of this simple model.

1.2.3.3 Summary

A transaction processing system is an application development environment that includes presentation services, databases, and persistent programming languages. A TP system also provides transactional remote procedure calls, which allow the application to be distributed as clients and servers in a network of computers.

Transaction processing systems provide the application programmer with the following computational model:

Resource managers. The system comes with an array of *transactional resource managers* that provide ACID operations on the objects they implement. Database systems, persistent programming languages, queue managers (spoolers), and window systems are typical resource managers.

Durable state. The application designer represents the application state as durable data stored by the resource managers.

TRPC. Transactional remote procedure calls allow the application to invoke local and remote resource managers as though they were local. They also allow the application designer to decompose the application into client and server processes on different computers interconnected via transactional remote procedure calls.

Transaction programs. The application designer represents application inquiries and state transformations as programs written in conventional or specialized programming languages. Each such program, called a *transaction program*, has the structure:

```
Begin_Work() ;
<any sequence of calls to resource managers>
if (success)   Commit_Work();
else           Rollback_Work();
```

In other words, the programmer brackets the successful execution of the program with a Begin-Commit pair and brackets a failed execution with a Begin-Rollback pair.

Consistency. The work within a Begin-Commit pair must be a correct transformation. This is the C (consistency) of ACID.

Isolation. While the transaction is executing, the resource managers ensure that all objects the transaction reads are isolated from the updates of concurrent transactions. Conversely, all objects the transaction writes are isolated from concurrent reads and writes by other transactions. This is the I of ACID.

Durability. Once the commit has been successfully executed, all the state transformations of that transaction are made durable and public. This is the D (durability) of ACID.

Atomicity. At any point before the commit, the application or the system may abort the transaction, invoking rollback. If the transaction is aborted, all of its changes to durable objects will be undone (reversed), and it will be as though the transaction never ran. This is the A (atomicity, all-or-nothing) of ACID.

The example mail system and its administrative and operations interface were programmed in this way as an application using the tools of the transaction processing system. Sample tools included the database system, the presentation management system, and the application generator. The next subsection gives a hint of how each of these tools is built and how they fit into the transaction processing system.

1.2.4 The Resource Manager's View of a TP System

We have seen thus far that a transaction processing system includes a collection of subsystems, called *resource managers*, that together provide ACID transactions. As application generators, user interfaces, programming languages, and database systems proliferate and evolve, resource managers are continually being added to the TP system.

The transaction processing system must be extensible in the sense that it must be easy to add such resource managers. There are many database systems (e.g., DB2, Rdb, Oracle, Ingres, Informix, Sybase), many programming languages (e.g., COBOL, FORTRAN, PL/I, Ada, C, C++, persistent C), many networks (e.g., SNA, OSI, TCP/IP, DECnet, LAN Manager), many presentation managers (e.g., X-windows, News, PM, Windows), and many application generators (CSP, Cadre, Telos, Pathmaker). Each customer seems to select a random subset from this menu and build an application from that base. A transaction processing system facilitates this random selection. The TP system provides a way to interconnect applications and resource managers, while providing the ACID properties for the whole computation.

The key to this resource manager interoperability is a standard way to invoke application services and resource managers. Such a mechanism must allow invocation of both local and remote services. As explained in the previous section, the standard mechanism for doing this is a remote procedure call. The transactional remote procedure call is an extension of the simple procedure call. It allows the work of many calls and servers to be coordinated as an ACID unit.

The resulting computation structure looks like a graph, or tree, of processes that communicate with one another via these transactional remote procedure calls. The TP system provides the binding mechanisms needed to link the client to servers. The linkage could be local or remote:

Local. Client and server are in the same address space or process, in which case the server code is bound to the client code and the invocation is a simple procedure call.

Remote. Client and server are in different processes, in which case the invocation consists of the client sending a message to the server and the server sending a reply to the client. This is a remote procedure call.

The caller cannot distinguish a local procedure call from a remote procedure call; they have the same syntax. Local calls generally have better performance, but remote calls allow distributed computation and often provide better protection of the server from the client. Figure 1.8 illustrates the typical call structure of an application invoking various application services and various resource managers. Each box is optionally a process, and the connection among boxes is via a local or remote procedure call.

Aside from managing the creation and intercommunication of processes performing the transaction, each TP monitor has a set of core services that it provides to the resource managers. These services help the resource managers implement ACID operations and provide

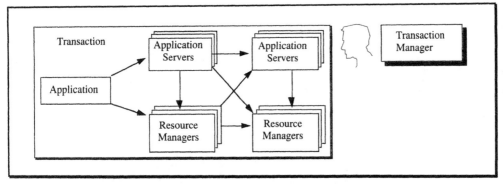

Figure 1.8: The execution of a transaction is spread among application programs (clients and servers) and resource managers. Services and resource managers can be invoked by local or remote procedure calls. Local services and servers are bound to the caller's address space, while remote ones run in separate processes, perhaps on remote computer systems. The entire computation occurs within the scope of a single transaction. The transaction manager monitors the progress of transactions, connects clients to servers, and coordinates the commit and rollback of transactions.

overall execution control of the application program that invokes the individual resource managers.

The basic control flow of an application is diagrammed in Figure 1.9. The Begin_Work() verb starts the transaction, registering it with the *transaction manager* and creating a unique transaction identifier. Once the application has started a transaction, it can begin to invoke resource managers, reading and writing the terminal as well as databases, and sending requests to local and remote services.

When a resource manager gets the first request associated with that transaction, it *joins* the transaction, telling the local transaction manager that it wants to participate in the transaction's commitment and rollback operations. It is typical for several resource managers to join the transaction. As these resource managers perform work on behalf of the transaction, they keep lists of the changes they have made to objects. As a rule, they record both the old and the new value of the object. The transaction processing system provides a logging service to record these changes. The *log manager* efficiently implements a sequential file of all the updates of transactions to objects. Of course, the other resource managers have to tell the log manager what these updates are.

To provide isolation, resource managers *lock* the objects accessed by the transaction; this prevents other transactions from seeing the uncommitted updates of this transaction and prevents them from altering the data read or written by this uncommitted transaction. The transaction processing system provides a *lock manager* that other resource managers can use.

When the transaction issues Commit_Work(), the transaction manager performs the two-phase commit protocol. First, it queries all resource managers that joined the transaction, asking if they think the transaction is a consistent and complete transformation. Any resource manager can vote no, in which case the commit fails. But if all the resource managers vote yes, then the transaction is a correct transformation, and the transaction manager records this fact in the log, informing each resource manager that the transaction is complete. At this point, the resource managers can release the locks and perform any other operations needed to complete the transaction.

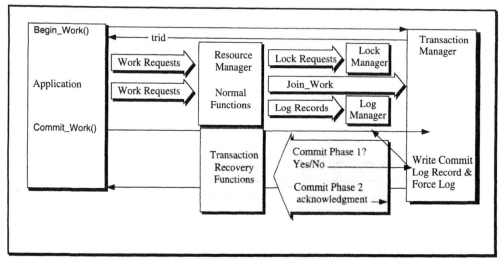

Figure 1.9: The role of the core services (transaction manager, log manager, and lock manager) in the execution of a transaction. The transaction scheduler (not shown) sets up the processes that execute the transaction.

If the transaction should fail during execution, or if a resource manager votes no during phase 1 of the two-phase commit, then the transaction manager orchestrates transaction roll-back. In this case, the transaction manager reads the transaction's log and, for each log record, invokes the resource manager that wrote the record, asking the resource manager to undo the operation. Once the undo scan is complete, the transaction manager invokes each resource manager that joined the transaction and tells it that the transaction was aborted.

The transaction manager also orchestrates transaction recovery if a node or site fails. It provides generic services for the failure of a single object, the failure of a resource manager, and the failure of an entire site. The following paragraphs sketch how the transaction manager helps in system recovery.

If a site fails, the TP system restarts all the resource managers. Several transactions may have been in progress at the time of the failure. The resource managers contact the transaction manager as part of their restart logic. At that time, the transaction manager informs them of the outcome of each transaction that was active at the time of the failure. Some may have committed, some may have aborted, and some may still be in the process of committing. The resource manager can recover its committed state independently, or it can participate in the transaction manager's undo and redo scan of the log.

If a resource manager fails but the rest of the TP system continues operating, the transaction manager aborts all uncommitted transactions involved with that resource manager. When the resource manager returns to service, the transaction manager informs the resource manager about the outcome of those transactions. The resource manager can use this information and the transaction log to reconstruct its state.

If a particular object is lost but the resource manager is otherwise operational, then the resource manager can continue to offer service on other objects while the failed object is reconstructed from an archive copy and from a log of all committed changes to that copy. The transaction manager and the log manager aid recovery from an archive copy of the object.

Each site usually has a separate transaction manager. This allows each site to operate independently of the others, providing *local autonomy*. When the transaction's execution is

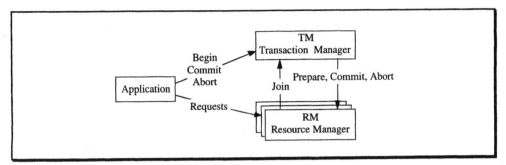

Figure 1.10: The X/Open transaction processing model. As in Figure 1.9, the application starts a transaction managed by the local transaction manager. As the application invokes resource managers, they join the transaction. When the application commits or aborts, the transaction manager broadcasts the outcome to the resource managers. In this model, the resource managers have private locks and logs, and the transaction manager does not provide an undo scan of the transaction log.

distributed among several sites, it is distributed among several transaction managers. In that case, the two-phase commit protocol for multiple processes generalizes easily to multiple transaction managers.

As explained in Subsection 2.7.4, the X/Open consortium draws Figure 1.9 differently. It assumes that each resource manager has a private log and a private lock manager, and X/Open assumes that the resource manager performs its own rollback, based on a single rollback call from the transaction manager, in case the transaction aborts. The resulting simpler picture is shown in Figure 1.10.

Figures 1.9 and 1.10 describe centralized transactions involving a single transaction manager. When multiple transaction managers are involved, the figure becomes more complicated since the transaction managers must cooperate in committing the transaction. Figure 1.11 diagrams this design. More detailed discussions of the X/Open model are found in Subsections 2.7.4 and 16.6.

1.2.5 TP System Core Services

To summarize, the following are the *core services* of the transaction processing monitor:

Transactional RPC. Authorizes, schedules, and invokes the execution of services (servers).

Transaction manager. Orchestrates the commit and rollback of transactions as well as the recovery of objects, resource managers, or sites after they fail.

Log manager. Records a log of changes made by transactions, so that a consistent version of all objects can be reconstructed in case of failure.

Lock manager. Provides a generic mechanism to regulate concurrent access to objects. This helps resource managers provide transaction isolation.

Resource managers extend the transaction processing system by using these core services. Generally, there is a separate TP system at each site or cluster of a computer network. These TP monitors cooperate to provide a distributed execution environment to the user.

The bulk of this book is dedicated to explaining the concepts of each of these core services and how they are implemented. It also explores how database system resource

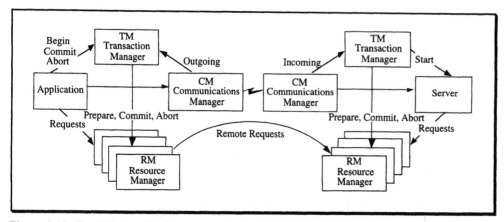

Figure 1.11: The X/Open distributed transaction processing model. As in Figures 1.9 and 1.10, the application starts a transaction managed by the local transaction manager. When the application, or some resource manager acting on behalf of the application, makes a remote request, the communications managers at each node inform their local transaction managers of the incoming or outgoing transaction. Transaction managers at each node manage the transaction's work at that node. When the transaction commits or aborts, the transaction managers cooperate to provide the atomic and durable commit.

managers use these facilities. Before diving deeper into the TP system implementor's view, let us return to the top-level view of the transaction processing system.

1.3 A Transaction Processing System Feature List

Rather than viewing the system from the perspective of a particular user, we can look at the typical features of transaction processing systems. The most obvious of these features are the application design and generation tools that, in turn, are built around the repository. Underlying the application generators and the repository are a database system used to store persistent data (often an SQL database) and a data communications system used to provide an abstract interface to terminals, workstations, and other input-output devices and remote requestors. Behind this DataBase-DataCommunications (DB-DC) layer is the TP monitor itself, with its core services. Peripheral to these mainline features are ancillary tools used to administer, tune, and operate the system. Of course, this all runs on a substrate consisting of an operating system, a network, and computer hardware. The feature list here focuses on application generation, the repository, the database, data communications, transaction management, and operations.

1.3.1 Application Development Features

The goal and promise of application generators is to automate programming by translating designs directly into executable systems. Their major success has been in the transaction processing area. Typical projects report that 90% of clients and servers are automatically generated via point-and-click graphical programming interfaces. Application generators allow rapid prototyping, reduce project risk, and improve system usability. What this really means is that application generators are able to generate most of the generic functions of the application from a standard toolbox, thereby leaving complex domain-specific issues (such as discounts, tax codes, and work scheduling) to conventional programming. This residual or core code is usually written in a standard programming language (e.g., COBOL, C, FORTRAN, SQL).

In addition, there are tools that analyze a schematic description of the database design and ultimately produce an optimized set of SQL data-definition statements to represent the database. Screen design aids allow the designer to *paint* the screens associated with each transaction. The resulting graphics are translated to programs that read and write such forms.

Once the application has been generated in this way, tools are provided to populate the database with synthetic data and to generate a synthetic load on the system. Tracing and debugging tools are used to test and certify the correctness of the programs.

Most such systems provide a *starter system*, a simple application that nevertheless includes fairly comprehensive administrative and operations functions, a security system, an accounting system, and operations procedures. These preprogrammed tools are then applicable to new applications built with the application generator. They also address the important issues of operator and administrator training.

1.3.2 Repository Features

The repository holds descriptions of the objects in the system and records the interdependencies among these objects. Repositories are also called *dictionaries* or *catalogs*. The catalogs of SQL database systems provide a concrete example of a repository: They track the database tables, indices, views, and programs. The SQL system catalog also tracks the dependencies among these objects; for example, this program uses that view, which in turn uses those indices and tables. When someone changes a table, the SQL system automatically recompiles all the affected programs. Before making the change, the administrator can run a standard report to display the programs that will be affected by the change. All this is inherent in the SQL catalogs. The shortcoming of this example is that the SQL system is only aware of the database part of the application. If the change should propagate to a client, the SQL system will not know about it.

The need for a repository is implicit in Figure 1.3 and Table 1.4. The typical system has thousands of terminals and users and hundreds of applications, screens, tables, reports, procedures, and archive copies of these objects. When old versions of applications, procedures, and other objects are considered, the number of objects grows well beyond 10,000. Remembering this information is difficult, and changing it is error-prone, because any change is likely to involve changing many system components. For example, adding a field to a screen alters the screen, probably alters the client software and the server interface, and probably adds a column to a table. All these changes must be made together (as an ACID unit). The change should be expressed once and should automatically be propagated to each consumer of the object. If the changes do not work out, then they should *all* be reversed, so that the system returns to its previous state. Implementing such a change manually is a recipe for disaster. Chapter 3 points out that such operational mistakes cause many system failures.

The operations problem is a classic inventory and bill-of-materials problem.[2] Changing a system is analogous to building a new version of a complex mechanism. The manufacturing industry learned long ago that computers can automate most of the bill-of-materials logic. The computer industry is just learning that the same techniques apply to manufacturing software systems.

Take the UNIX MAKE facility, in which a root file points to a list of subsidiary files is a bill-of-materials for the root. To make a root, one must make all the subsidiary files. These files, in turn, are MAKE files for subcomponents of that root. This is an example of bill-of-materials done in an unstructured way. The bill-of-materials is represented as ASCII text that is a free-form representation of the information. Because the information is not structured in a uniform way, it is hard to find all the components that use a particular subsystem, it is hard to find all versions of a particular subsystem, and there is no connection between the bill-of-materials and the end-product. That is, once you MAKE something, the result is not attached to its bill-of-materials; put another way, there is no version management.

Here, then, is the key idea of the repository (see Figure 1.12):

Design.   Capture all application design decisions in a database.

Dependencies.   Capture all application design and module dependencies in a database.

Change.   Express change procedures as transactions on this database.

This is not a new idea; it is just an application of the bill-of-materials idea to a new domain. Capturing all design decisions in structured form (i.e., machine-readable form) reduces errors and simplifies maintenance. Automating change reduces errors and improves productivity.

A good repository needs to be *complete*. It needs to describe all aspects of the system—not just the database, the programs, or the network. The repository stores the system bill-of-materials. To be complete, the repository must be *extensible*: It must be possible to add new objects, relationships, and procedures to it. The application designer must be able to define a new kind of object without re-implementing the repository. The true test of extensibility is whether the repository has a core that implements the repository objects, with extensions that implement the other objects (such as screens, tables, clients, and servers). For example, the SQL catalogs should just be an extension of the repository. If the vendor has extended the repository in this way, using the repository's built-in extension mechanism, then the application designer will probably be able to make comparable extensions using the same mechanism.

A repository should be *active*; that is the description of the object should be consistent with the actual state of the object. For example, if a domain is added to a file, or if a field is added to a screen, then the description of the object should reflect this change. Repositories without this property are called *passive*.

Active repositories are essential, but also very difficult to implement efficiently. The active repository concept, taken to its limit, requires that each time a record is added to a sequential file, the file's record-count be updated in the catalog. Doing this would add a ran-

---

[2] As the name suggests, the bill-of-materials for an item is a list of assemblies used in the item. These assemblies may have subassemblies, so the bill-of-materials is actually a tree of dependencies. For example, a computer has a processor, memory, network interface, and power supply. Each of these components in turn has a bill of materials.

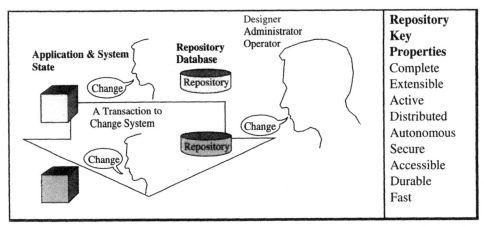

Figure 1.12: The repository describes the system state in a durable, secure, active database.
This database is changed by transactions that alter the repository, along with the system state. The
desirable properties of a repository are listed at the right.

dom update to every sequential insert—an overhead of several hundred percent. Even more
troublesome, the repository is often built on top of the operating system, file system, and
network system. With this *layered* and *portable* design, some changes to the operating system configuration, file system, or network system may not be registered with the repository
layered above them. For example, replacing the existing COBOL compiler with a new version of the compiler could be disastrous for the application: the new version may have a new
bug. If such a change is done via the repository, the old compiler will be saved for the application. If the change is done directly via the file system, without involving the repository,
the change will cause the application to fail. To be truly active, the repository must register
the dependency of the application on the old COBOL compiler and prevent its deletion from
the system until the associated applications are also deleted.

If the application is distributed among autonomous sites, then the repository must also
be distributed to provide *local autonomy:* the ability to operate on local objects, even though
the site is disconnected from the others. If the repository is truly active, then a site cannot
operate without it. For example, files cannot be created, altered, or deleted if the repository
is unavailable (down). Thus, the repository must always be available. To achieve this, the
descriptors and dependencies of all objects stored at a site must also be stored at that site. If
an object is replicated or partitioned among many sites, then its descriptors must be replicated at each site. If an object at one site depends on an object at another site, then the dependency must be registered at both sites.

The repository is one database. It is distributed, partitioned, and replicated, and it has
some interesting transactions associated with it. It is a relatively small database (less than a
million records), but it has high traffic. Bottlenecks and other performance problems have
plagued many repository implementations to date. Thus, a repository must be *fast,* so that it
does not hinder performance.

Using a database representation for the repository gives programmatic access to the data
for ad hoc reports and provides a report writer to produce standard reports on the system
structure and status. In addition, the database provides durable storage with ACID state transformations (transactions). Thus, these reporting and durability requirements are

automatically met. Since the repository holds all the information about the system, it must be *secure*, so that unauthorized users and programs cannot read or alter it.

To summarize, the repository is a database that describes the *whole* system, along with programs to manage that database. The repository should be *complete, extensible, active, secure,* and *fast*. It should provide standard reports and allow programs to access the data in ad hoc ways subject to *security* restrictions. If the repository is distributed, then it should provide *local autonomy*. Such a repository provides the basis for application development tools, system administration tools, and operations tools (see Figure 1.12).

No one has yet built a proper repository. Application generators come closest. Their repositories often meet the requirements of being active on the objects they manage, and they are extensible, accessible, secure, and fast. But they are not complete. They capture only design information of the application, not the operational information of the system, such as files, disks, networks, and information hiding in system configuration files. Since the latter objects represent reality, they can change without the design repository sensing the change. In that respect, design repositories are not active. In fact, an unhealthy split has evolved between design repositories and operational repositories.

Two of the most advanced repositories are CDD/R from Digital and Pathmaker from Tandem. CDD/R is the basis for Digital's transaction processing system (ACMS), its software development environment (Cohesion), and its database system (Rdb). Pathmaker is an application generator for Tandem's Pathway system. Figure 1.13 shows most of the database schema for the Pathmaker repository. (Not shown is the authorization database or the SQL repository; these would add another 20 tables to the 34 shown in the diagram.) Each box represents a database table. The tables describe people, projects, the system configuration, screens, clients (requesters), services, and how they are packaged into servers. The tables also describe the message formats for client-server interaction.

1.3.3 TP Monitor Features

The TP monitor provides an execution environment for resource managers and applications. When requests arrive from local or remote clients, the TP monitor launches a server to perform the request. If the request arrives with a transaction identifier, then the server becomes part of that pre-existing transaction. If the request is not already transaction protected, then the TP monitor or server starts a new transaction to cover the execution of the request. Thus, the TP monitor provides a transactional RPC mechanism.

Before creating a server for a request, the TP monitor authorizes the client to the service. The client has usually been authenticated by the TP monitor as a particular person or group of persons (e.g., all stock clerks). The TP monitor checks that the client is authorized to invoke that service. This authorization check is stated as a function of the client group, client location, and time. For example, local stock clerks may run the invoice transaction during business hours. Optionally, the TP monitor records the security check or security violation in an audit trail.

If the client is authorized to invoke the service, then starting the service becomes a scheduling decision. If the system is congested, the start may be delayed. The TP monitor may have a preallocated pool of server processes and may assign them to requests on demand. Such a process pool is called a *server class*. If all members of the server class are busy, the request must wait or a new server process must be allocated. The TP monitor may

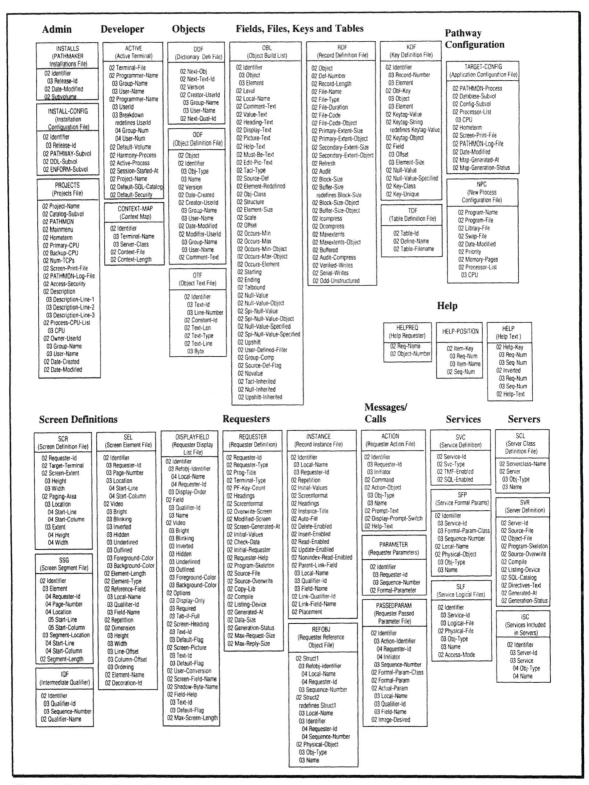

Figure 1.13: The tables of Tandem's Pathmaker repository.

create a server, put the request in a server class queue, or even put the request in a queue for later (e.g., overnight) service. This server class scheduling and load balancing is a key responsibility of the transaction processing monitor.

Once the process is scheduled and is executing the request, the service can invoke other resource managers and other services that, in turn, join the transaction. The transaction manager tracks all servers and resource managers joined to the transaction and invokes them at transaction commit or rollback. If the transaction is distributed among many sites of a computer network, the transaction manager mediates the transaction commitment with transaction managers operating at other sites.

The application view of transactions is that a transaction consists of a sequence of actions bracketed by a Begin-Commit or Begin-Rollback pair. The Begin allocates a transaction identifier (trid). Each subsequent action is an operation performed by some resource manager as either a local or a remote procedure call. These procedure calls implicitly carry the trid. All operations on recoverable data generate information (log data) that allows the transaction to be rolled back (undone) or atomically and durably committed. In addition, to isolate the transaction from concurrent updates by others, each resource manager ordinarily acquires locks on the objects accessed by the transaction. The trid is the tag used for locks and log records. It is the ACID object identifier.

Any process executing on behalf of the transaction will have the transaction's trid. If the process is running on a transaction-oriented operating system, the trid is part of the process state. If transactions have been grafted onto the operating system by the TP monitor's RPC mechanism, then the trid is a global variable of the process.

Transactions can declare *savepoints*—points within the transaction execution to which the application can later roll back. This partial rollback creates the ability for servers or subroutines to raise and process exceptions cleanly. A savepoint is established when the invocation starts. If anything goes wrong, the service can roll back to that savepoint and then return a diagnostic. The server can tell the client that the call failed and was a null operation. This

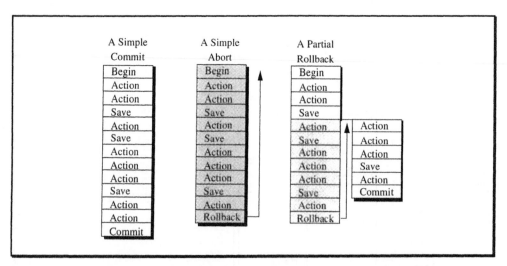

Figure 1.14: The different types of transaction executions.   In the normal case (≈97%) the transaction executes and commits. In some cases (≈3%) the transaction aborts, either it calls rollback or it is rolled back by the system. In other cases, the transaction does a partial rollback to an intermediate savepoint and then continues forward processing.

provides simple server error semantics without aborting the entire transaction. Applying this concept more broadly, the work after a savepoint looks like one transaction *nested* within another. The subtransaction can abort independently of the parent transaction, but the transaction can commit only if all its ancestor transactions commit.

In summary, a TP monitor authorizes client requests to servers, invokes servers, and provides a transactional execution environment to servers and resource managers so that they can implement ACID operations on durable objects. Besides managing individual transactions, the transaction manager also manages the resource managers. It invokes the resource managers at system startup and system checkpoint, and it coordinates the recovery of resource managers at system restart. It also orchestrates the recovery of objects from archival storage.

1.3.4 Data Communications Features

In discussing data communications, one has to consider the *classic world* of mainframes driving dumb terminals—terminals with no application logic—and the *client-server world* of clients doing all presentation management and driving servers via transactional RPCs (TRPCs). Technology is quickly making the classic approach obsolete; workstations, gas pumps, and robots are now powerful, self-contained computers. The older transaction processing systems, rooted in the classic design, are evolving to handle the new client-server approach depicted in Figure 1.6. Meanwhile, a new generation of transaction processing systems designed for the client-server model is emerging.

In both the classic and client-server designs, data communications provides an application programming interface to remote devices. The data communications software runs atop the native operating system and networking software of the host computer. There are many kinds of computer networks and networking protocols. The TP system's data communications subsystem provides a convenient and uniform application programming interface to all these different network protocols. In the OSI model, data communications is at the application or presentation layer (layer 6 or 7).

The data communications system is charged with reliable and secure communications. To prevent forgery or unauthorized disclosure, security is generally achieved via message encryption. Reliability is achieved by recording each output message in durable storage and resending it until it is acknowledged by the client. To avoid message duplication, each message is given a sequence number. The client acknowledges, but ignores, duplicate messages.

The ideal data communications system provides a uniform interface to the various communications protocols, so that higher layers do not need to be aware of the differences among the standards.[3] Applications want a single form of remote procedure call and do not want to learn about all the different ways networks name their transactions (SNA/LU6.2, OSI/TP, IMS, Tandem TMF, DECdtm, and Tuxedo all have different naming schemes.) The gateway process interfacing to that world masks these differences and translates them into the local standard interface. The data communications software provides this layer and, in doing so, provides a uniform interface to the plethora of network protocols. The resulting picture looks something like Figure 1.15.

---

[3] God must love standards: He made so many of them.

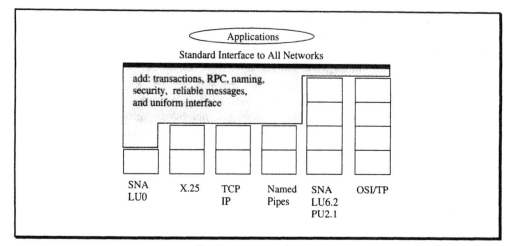

Figure 1.15: The data communications subsystem and presentation services provide a uniform interface to the data communications protocols used by clients and terminals. This protocol must add many features to simple protocols, like SNA/LU0 or TCP/IP, but needs to add less functionality to a protocol stack like SNA/LU6.2 or OSI/TP.

1.3.4.1 Classic Data Communications

In a classic data communications system, the terminal is a forms-oriented device, a gas pump, or a bar-code reader with little or no internal logic. All the presentation services logic (formatting of the display) is managed by the application running in the host. There is extreme diversity among terminal types and sub-types. The IBM 3270 terminal, for example, came with small and large screens, color, many different fonts and keyboards, a lightpen, and a printer. These options made it very hard to write generic applications; thus, *device independence* became the goal of the data communications subsystem. Over the last 30 years, transaction processing systems have evolved from cards to teletypes to character-mode displays to point-and-click multimedia user interfaces (see Table 1.16). Application designers want to preserve their programming investment; they want old programs to run on new input/output devices. Thus, teletypes emulated card readers and card punches (the source of 80-character widths). Today, many window systems emulate teletypes emulating card readers. Is this progress? No, but it is economical, since rewriting the programs would cost more than using the emulator.

In contrast to input/output devices, data storage has not changed much when compared to device interfaces. The rapid evolution and diversification of user interfaces shows every sign of continuing. The trend for data storage is for the database to move away from slow disc-based access to random-access memory. Programs written today must be insulated from such technology changes.

To insulate applications from technology changes in terminals, the classic data communications system presents an abstract, record-oriented interface to the application and presents a device-specific, formatted data stream to the device. This is a great convenience. For example, the programming language COBOL excels at moving records about. The COBOL program simply reads a record from the terminal, looks at it, and then inserts it in the

Table 1.16: The evolution of database storage devices and input/output devices used in transaction processing systems. The point is that most of the change has been in the area of input/output devices. If programs are to have a lifetime of more than a few years, they must have both database data independence and terminal device independence.

Year	Database Devices	Input/Output Devices
1960	Cards, Tape, Disc	Cards/Listings
1970	Disc	Keyboard/Teletype
1980	Disc	Keyboard/Character-mode CRT
1990	Disc	Keyboard/Mouse/Bitmap display

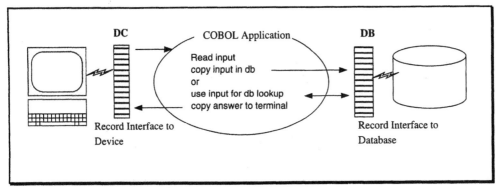

Figure 1.17: The structure of an application running on a classic transaction processing system. The DB-DC system provides a record-oriented interface to both the database (disc) and the network (terminals). The application just moves records from place to place. The details of terminal formats are left to the data communications system.

database; or perhaps it uses the record as a search condition on the database and moves the resulting records to the terminal. This logic is shown in Figure 1.17.

Presentation services provide device independence by using the technique diagrammed in Figure 1.18. First, an interactive *screen painter* produces a form description. The designer specifies how the screen will look by painting it. The screen painter translates this painting into an abstract *form description,* which can then be compiled to work for many different kinds of devices (e.g., each of the many character-mode displays and each of the many window systems). The description specifies how the form looks on the screen in abstract terms. In painting the screen, the designer says things like "this is a heading," "this is an input field," "this is an output field," "this is a decoration," and so on. Integrity checks can be placed on input fields. Ideally, all this is prespecified, since many inputs are database domains with well-defined types and integrity constraints. For example, the repository definitions of the part-number domain and customer name domain immediately imply a complete set of display attributes, help text, and integrity checks. Once the form is defined, it implies two records used to communicate with the application program: (1) an input record consisting of the input fields and their types, and (2) an output record consisting of the output fields and their types. The form may have function keys, menus, buttons, or other attributes that also appear as part of the input record.

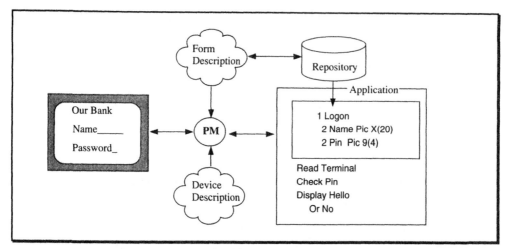

Figure 1.18: How presentation management gives device independence.   The forms painter generates an abstract description of the form. The input and output fields of the form imply an input-output
record structure for the program. The abstract form, when combined with a particular device description, can be used to read and write the device. The repository stores the forms descriptions, the record
descriptions, and the device descriptions.

When the application reads a form, the presentation manager displays the form, gathers
the input data, checks it against the form's integrity constraints, and then presents the form's
input data as a record to the application. Conversely, when the application writes a record to
the form, the presentation manager takes the form description, the device description, and
the application data fields, and builds a device-specific image. In this way, the same program
can read and write a teletype, a 24-by-80 character-mode terminal, a window of an X-Windows terminal, or a window of a PC running Microsoft Windows. That is device independence.

Along with the core service of device independence, the presentation manager also
provides the screen painter and a screen debugging facility. It manages the form, screen,
device, and record objects in the repository.

The presentation manager is the largest and most visible part of the data communications system. It often constitutes the bulk of the transaction processing system. For example,
adding support for a *single* device feature—color displays on the 3270 terminal—involved
adding 15,000 lines of code to CICS. This was more than the code needed to add distributed
transactions to CICS. In general, data communications is bigger than the database system, TP
monitor, and repository combined.

1.3.4.2 Client-Server Data Communications

Modern transaction processing systems are moving the bulk of presentation management to
the client. The client interfaces to the TP monitor by issuing transactional RPCs. In this
world, presentation services are an integral part of the client system.

When presentation services move to the client, the server has little control or even concern about how the data is gathered or displayed. The transaction processing monitor at the
server receives a remote procedure call from the client. Moving presentation services func-

tions to the workstation is a vast simplification because the workstation has only a single device type, commonly a window.

System administration still presents the problem of many different clients, each with its own environment (e.g., DOS, OS/2, UNIX, Macintosh), its own presentation services, (e.g., PresentationManager, X-Windows, Motif, OPENLOOK, NextStep, Macintosh), and its own look and feel. The administrative problem, then, is still a nightmare, because each terminal has now been replaced with a complex workstation complete with local database, operating system, and networking system. If the system is centrally administered, the administrators can simplify the number of cases by dictating a *supported* set of environments.

In this client-server computation model, servers export transactional services, and workstation clients can pick any presentation format they like. The main job of the client-server data communication system is to provide transactional RPCs to these clients and servers. For an illustration of this situation, refer to Figure 1.6.

1.3.5 Database Features[4]

Database systems store and retrieve massive amounts of structured data. They provide a mechanism to *define* data structures that represent objects, and they provide a non-procedural interface to *manipulate* (read and write) that data. The interface is non-procedural in the sense that the program or person accessing the data need not know the location of the data (local, remote, main memory, disc, archive) or the detailed access paths used to find the data. Rather, the application requests operations on the abstract records or objects, while the database is responsible for mapping such abstractions to the concrete hardware. The definition of the data includes assertions about the data values and relationships. The database system enforces these assertions when the data is updated or when the transaction commits. Each database system acts as a resource manager and thereby provides ACID operations on its data. Each database system also provides utilities to manage and *control* the use of the data.

Because databases tend to last for decades, it is important that the representation and programs be adaptable to change. For a start, this requires that the database be an international standard (e.g., CODASYL or SQL), so that it can be moved to new equipment when the current computers are replaced with different models from different vendors. The database must insulate the applications from the location of the data and from the exact representation of the data. These ideas—*location transparency* and *data independence*—are very similar to the device independence issue discussed in Subsection 1.3.4.1.

To ease programming and operations, the database system should be integrated with a repository and with one or more application generators. These application generators give a visual interface to database definition, manipulation, and control. They automate much of the design process.

---

[4] We assume that the reader already knows C and SQL. If that is not the case, then there are many good books on the topics. For SQL in particular, *An Introduction to DB2* [Date and White 1989] is a very readable tutorial. The following whirlwind tour presumably recapitulates what you already know from having read such a book. This book takes a dogmatic SQL view of databases, ignoring the "old" network proposals and the "new" object-oriented proposals. We are enthusiastic about the object-oriented ideas, but this is not the place to explore them. Sticking to SQL simplifies the presentation. Most of the transaction concepts and techniques used for relational databases will be needed in object-oriented databases as well.

The database system should allow the designer to place parts of the database at different sites. As a rule, data is placed on computers near the data source or the data consumers (or both). This creates *partitioned* data—some parts of the table are here and some parts are there. If the same data is placed at many sites, it is said to be *replicated*. The repository gave a good example of this. For the sake of local autonomy, parts of the repository are replicated at each site. Some other parts of the repository are partitioned, since only the local node needs to know about local objects. Database systems providing transparent access to replicated and partitioned data are called *distributed database systems*.

1.3.5.1 Data Definition

SQL defines a standard set of *atomic types*[5] (numbers, character strings, timestamps, users, and so on). User-defined types, called *domains,* can be defined in terms of atomic types and other domains. For example, part number or customer name can be defined as domains. Each domain has a name (e.g., partno) along with constraints on the domain values (e.g., birthyear > 1850), formatting information (e.g., display as Kanji with heading 漢), and comment information. These domain definitions are registered in the repository (the SQL catalogs describing all SQL tables are part of the repository) and can then be used to define fields in tables, screens, reports, and program variables.

SQL tables are sets of records, each record being a sequence of values. The distinguishing feature of a relational database is that all the records of a table have the same format (the same sequence of types or domains). This uniformity means that each record of the table has exactly the same form. Consequently, set-oriented operations like SORT, PROJECT, and SELECT apply to all records of a table in a natural way. Just as important, the result of each of these relational operators is again a table (relation); thus, the operators can be composed arbitrarily to form complex queries and operations on the database.

Since each operation produces a table as output, it is possible to define virtual tables, called *views*, that are computed from one or more underlying tables. Views provide data independence: If a table definition is altered, the old table format can often be defined as a view of the new table format, and old programs can operate unchanged by using the view to access the table (as in Figure 1.19).

Tables can constrain the values allowed in them. Table columns inherit the constraints of their constituent domains. The table definition can specify that some column values are *unique*; that is, no other record in the table can have this value. The next step is to specify that some set of field values must occur in some other table; for example, invoice part numbers must appear in the parts table. Such rules are called *referential integrity* constraints. Inserts, updates, and deletes will be rejected if they violate these constraints. The generalization of all these ideas is to invoke a procedure each time a record is read or written. The procedure can reject or accept the update and, in fact, may have side effects causing other records to be updated, inserted, or deleted. In their general form, such *trigger* procedures allow arbitrary views to be updated. They can translate a view update into a particular sequence of updates on the underlying tables, thereby resolving the ambiguity inherent in general view updates.

---

[5] The term *atomic type* should not be confused with transaction atomicity. Programming language type systems are built from *basic types* (atomic types) and *constructors*. The basic types are character, integer, real, pointer, and so on. Records, vectors, and lists are constructors. Transaction atomicity is a completely independent concept.

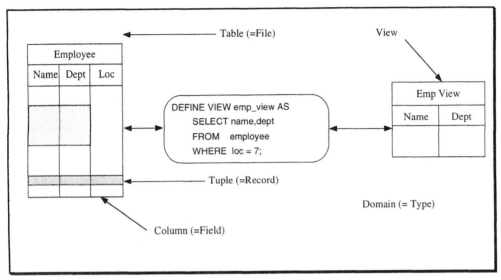

Figure 1.19: The basic concepts of logical data definition in a relational database system.

The general syntax of SQL data-definition operations is shown below:

$$
\begin{Bmatrix} \text{CREATE} \\ \text{ALTER} \\ \text{DROP} \end{Bmatrix} \begin{Bmatrix} \text{DOMAIN} \\ \text{TABLE} \\ \text{INDEX} \\ \text{CONSTRAINT} \\ \text{VIEW} \\ \text{TRIGGER} \end{Bmatrix}.
$$

Here is a simple SQL table definition showing the use of column constraints, referential integrity constraints, and uniqueness constraints:

```
CREATE TABLE accounts (   acct_id     integer PRIMARY KEY,
                          cust_id     integer FOREIGN KEY REFERENCES customer,
                          balance     decimal(9,2) CHECK balance >= 0
                );
```

The SQL standard covers the *logical data definition* issues. There are also *physical data definition* issues: where to place the data and how to organize it. The table needs to be stored somewhere. The database system has a pool of storage, and, if not instructed otherwise, it will automatically place the table in that pool and organize the records as a heap or sequential file. The database tries to pick reasonable defaults for the physical file attributes. Some of the file attributes that users often want to specify include organization (how the records are clustered—sequential, keyed, hashed), access paths (primary and secondary indices on the data to speed lookups), location (if the data is to be replicated or partitioned, the criteria must be specified), space allocation (block and extent size), and so on. These features are not standard, but vary from system to system. An extension of the previous example using Tandem's NonStop SQL syntax shows about one-fifth of these options. It partitions the table among two nodes and specifies the blocksize and extentsize:

```
CREATE TABLE \node1.$data.accounts
                    (    acct_id        integer PRIMARY KEY,
                         cust_id        integer FOREIGN KEY REFERENCES customer,
                         balance        decimal(9,2) CHECK balance >= 0
                    )
    \node2.$data    FIRST KEY   10000,   -- account id > 10000 are stored at node2
                    BLOCKSIZE 4096,      -- size of pages (minimum disk transfer)
                    EXTENT      100;     -- allocate 100 pages per extent
```

All this logical and physical information is registered by the SQL system in sets of tables, called the SQL catalogs, within the repository. If a particular table is partitioned or replicated at many sites, then, for the sake of node autonomy, the table's definition is replicated in catalogs at each of those sites.

1.3.5.2 Data Manipulation

A key principle of the relational model is the use of one language for data definition, data manipulation, and data retrieval. In addition, the same language is used for both interactive queries and for programmatic access. This vastly reduces documentation and education— you only have to learn one language, then apply it in many contexts. Using the same language for a programmatic and conversational interface also provides a useful way to test queries: You can interactively enter your program and see the answer. The key concept that makes this work is that each operator takes relations as parameters, and a read operation returns a relation as its result. Relations have a natural display format and can be fed to further operators. In particular, views can be defined in terms of queries, as in Figure 1.19. The data-definition language borrows the expression handling and procedures from the data- (see Table 1.16) language to define constraints and triggers. The SQL SELECT operator forms the core of this logic. It is composed of three common operators: PROJECT, which discards some columns, SELECT, which discards some rows based on a predicate, and JOIN, which combines records from two tables to form a third table (see Figure 1.20).

The basic theorem of relational databases says that these operators are *Gödel complete*: They are equivalent to first-order predicate calculus [Codd 1971]. But the relational calculus is not *Turing complete*: It cannot describe all computable functions. A Turing-complete computational model is needed to write general programs. There is no need to invent such a language; almost any programing language will do. Consequently, SQL is always combined with a programming language. COBOL and C are the most popular ones today and create the languages CobSQL and CSQL .

The basic style of SQL, then, can be characterized as follows:

(1) Use the SELECT statement to define sets of records.

(2) Apply set-oriented INSERTs, UPDATEs, and DELETEs where possible.

(3) Use a conventional programming language to manipulate sets when the database language is inadequate.

The connection between the host language and SQL has been called an *impedance mismatch* because SQL works on *sets of records* while the host language works on *individual records*. In addition, the SQL data types do not exactly match the host language data types.

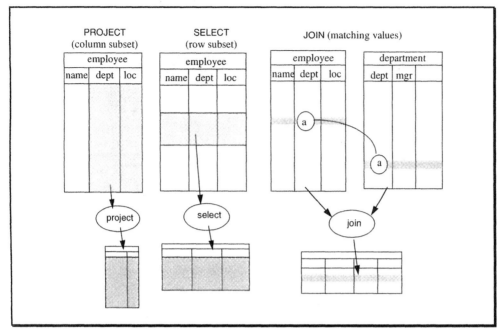

Figure 1.20: The three basic relational operators: project, select, and join. Each relational operator produces a new relation (table) based on one or more input tables.

The way around the set-of-records problem is the same technique used to deal with files: The program deals with the set one record at a time. The program defines the set by a select statement and defines a *cursor* to address the current position in the set. The program then opens the cursor to allow it to fetch the next record, moves the cursor forward or backward in the set, and updates or deletes the cursor's current record (see Figure 1.21). The datatype mismatch is handled by coercion (conversions between the SQL data types and the host language types).

1.3.5.3 Data Control

Data control is a catch-all. It includes security verbs (GRANT, REVOKE), concurrency control verbs (LOCK, SET TRANSACTION), and transaction verbs (BEGIN WORK, COMMIT WORK).

The basic security model of SQL is that tables are owned by users. Programs run as agents for users. SQL systems allow the owner to grant and revoke access to the tables he owns. By using views, the owner can grant others the authority to access a value-specific subset of the database. SQL's elaborate security model evolved from a timesharing system in which users share files. This model is inappropriate for a transaction processing system in which clients invoke servers that in turn access the data. If you think of the mail system example again, the servers at a node implement the mail database for all clients as a single set of tables. The servers typically run under the authority of the mail system and have access to all the tables. The servers authorize the clients to services on particular mailboxes. The mail system uses SQL security to completely hide the data from others; it encapsulates the data. Users can access the data only by invoking mail procedures, which in turn access the mail

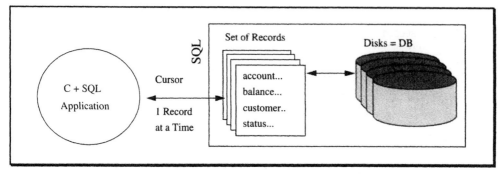

Figure 1.21: Record-at-a-time programs deal with a set-oriented system like SQL by defining cursors on the set and then operating on one record at a time. This is analogous to the way programs operate on sets of records in files.

database. Security is a systems issue, and the database security must be integrated with the rest of the system.

Similar comments apply to transaction verbs. Historically, the database was the only transactional resource manager; it therefore implemented transaction verbs. In fact, COMMIT WORK and ROLLBACK WORK are SQL verbs. As other transactional systems appear (such as persistent programming languages and transactional user interfaces), the transaction verbs become a system-wide facility, and the database system is just a part of the picture. It must operate as a resource manager within the context of the transaction processing system. The X/Open standards body is in the process of defining such system-wide transaction verbs (see Section 16.6).

In summary, security and transaction control are systems issues. The database must interoperate with the security and transaction mechanisms of the host operating system and the host transaction processing system.

1.3.5.4 Data Display

Once tables have been defined and populated with data, it is essential to have tools to browse the data and generate ad hoc reports. Such tools generally support a batch-oriented report writer that, given an SQL query and a report layout, produces a file or listing containing the answer. The report may consist of tables, charts, and graphs, or the output file may be fed to a tool like Lotus or Excel for data analysis and presentation.

With the move to online databases, these batch reports increasingly are being replaced by online reports in which an input form specifies the parameters to the query, and the output form specifies the answer. Again the output may be tables, reports, or graphs.

Virtually all systems come with a database browser that produces a form-per-record or a tabular display (see Figure 1.22). Such browsers let users query and edit databases much as one would query and edit text files. These displays can automatically be generated from the descriptive information about the table in the repository.

1.3.5.5 Database Operations Utilities

Database utilities provide the operations tools needed to manage the database. Increasingly, these utilities run automatically, performing database archiving, recovery, reorganization, and redesign. Performance is usually a major issue for utilities. For example, if loading or

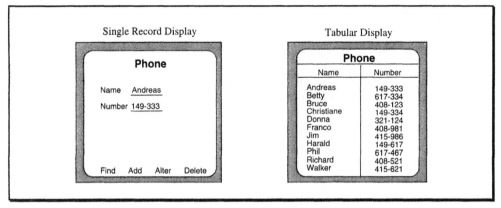

Figure 1.22: Database browser screens in two formats are automatically generated for each table from the information in the repository (SQL catalogs).

archiving runs at one megabyte/second, then loading or dumping a terabyte database will take a million seconds, or about 12 days. There are no easy answers to this problem. Historically, utilities required exclusive access to the database; all other activities were suspended. This standalone approach is not acceptable for systems that must be continuously available for online transactions. The requirements are clear: (1) all utilities should run in the background without disrupting service, and (2) no utility should take more than a day to do its job.

At present, there is considerable activity to make all database utilities *online* (operates on the data while others are reading and writing it), *incremental* (works on a few megabytes at a time), *restartable* (continues if stopped due to a fault or overload), and *parallel* (operates on multiple processors and disks in parallel to speed up the operation). Such utilities now exist for loading, dumping, recovering, and reorganizing databases (e.g., reclustering B-trees), and for collecting garbage and compacting disks. We know algorithms to build indices while the system is operating and the base table is changing, but no one has incorporated these algorithms into production systems yet. Certain operations, like dropping a table's column, invalidate the table. Such operations may force the application to be recompiled or even reprogrammed. There are no proposed solutions for such problems.

Other utilities produce either batch or interactive reports on the performance of the system. At present, the typical style is to provide a report telling which programs access which tables. These reports are usually broken down by table or by statement within program. Associated with each entry is a processor cost, a disk I/O cost, and, if the system is distributed, a message cost. This information can be used to analyze system performance.

Tools are emerging that analyze performance information and suggest better physical designs. In the future, the tools will be integrated with the utilities to make the system self-tuning.

1.3.6 Operations Features

As explained in Subsection 1.2.2, system administration and operations are a major part of the cost of owning a transaction processing system. The routine and mundane should be automated, both to reduce staff costs and to reduce errors. Humans should only be asked to deal with exceptional situations. Database archiving and reorganization are examples of such routine tasks.

There should be a forms-oriented interface to display the system status and performance at several levels of abstraction (e.g., application, process, file, or device). These displays should include mechanisms to detect problems, diagnose them, and suggest remedies. The system should also track problems (e.g., broken hardware and software) and generate reports on the status of pending problems. The repository is the key mechanism for storing all this information. It is also the basis for writing operations applications using high-level tools.

The system provides the mechanism for security, recovery, and change control, but the operations and administration staff must design the policy, specifying how these mechanisms will be used. For example, there needs to be a policy on how to change users, devices, applications, and system software.

Once the policies are in place, the administration and operations staff should conduct frequent fire drills and audits to assure that the policies work and are actually being followed.

1.3.7 Education and Testing Features

Education is an important area where we have no sage advice—only the following platitudes. It is important for the transaction processing system to use a standard interface (such as SQL, COBOL, or PresentationManager), and a standard look and feel (such as Motif, OpenLook, or Macintosh), so that users do not have to learn new skills. Programmer and user-skill portability is probably more important than program portability. This is the main theme of IBM's System Application Architecture [IBM-SAA]. Use of such standards reduces the need for education and training. That, in turn, has substantial benefits for the cost of system ownership.

Education on how to operate or use the system can be provided as *imbedded education*. This can take the form of help text for each function and a training mode in which operations against a toy version of the database are rolled back at the end of the operation.

Again, the imbedded education comes from the repository. The documentation of all functions and the meaning of all fields of each screen should be recorded in the repository. Likewise, the documentation on each entity, its possible values, referential integrity constraints, and diagnostic messages should all be recorded in the repository (in the different national languages). If this is done, help text for using and operating the system can be extracted automatically from the repository. Of course, the text will have to be manually translated to the user's native language (German, Korean, etc.).

The system must provide utilities to generate sample databases for testing. It must also generate and run multi-user input scripts to test the system for correctness (regression testing) and for performance under high load (stress testing).

1.3.8 Feature Summary

The transaction processing system includes one or more application generators built around a system repository. The repository is a database describing the entire system design and implementation. It is the mechanism whereby the administrator can assess and control change; its tools can automate—or at least guide—the administrator, operator, and designers through complex tasks.

The transaction processing system also includes a TP monitor that provides the core services of authorizing, scheduling, and executing transactions and resource managers. It provides the mechanisms to coordinate transaction commitment and isolation, along with an execution environment for resource managers. It coordinates their startup and checkpointing, as well as recovery of objects from the archive.

The transaction processing system has two key resource managers: database (DB) and data communications (DC). Thus, transaction processing systems are sometimes called DB-DC systems. The database is typically an SQL database system with data definition, data control, and data-manipulation verbs. The objects implemented by the database—tables, views, statements, and cursors—are transactional. The data communications component provides the basis for a transactional RPC mechanism. In the past, the data communications component also provided presentation services for dumb terminals, giving the application program a record-oriented, terminal-independent interface that is a major component of old transaction processing systems. As systems adopt client-server architectures, presentation services are being moved to the client and appear to be part of the workstation operating environment. This relieves the data communications system of these chores.

1.4 Summary

Transaction processing is thousands of years old; today, it is the dominant application of general-purpose computers. This chapter took a particular transaction processing application, electronic mail, and viewed it from the perspectives of those who use or operate it. A feature list describing the various components of a complete transaction processing system was presented. Underlying this chapter is the theme that transaction processing systems are in rapid evolution.

Traditional transaction processing systems are increasingly presented with many resource managers: databases, persistent programming languages, and type-specific resource managers. This diversity is forcing systems into a more open architecture than the classic DB-DC model. The movement of presentation services to clients, along with the increasing interconnection of transaction processing systems, is forcing a fully distributed design.

The main theme of this chapter is that the transaction concept is emerging as a paradigm for handling exceptions. Exceptions become increasingly important as client-server LAN-based systems evolve from simple disk and file servers to systems supporting distributed computation. When one member of the computation faults, the rest of the computation can be aborted, and a consistent system state can be reconstructed. Transactional RPC is being added both to the traditional transaction processing systems and to distributed operating systems, thus blurring the distinction between them.

A second theme of this chapter is that a transaction processing system is a large web of application generators, systems design and operations tools, and the more mundane language, database, network, and operations software. The repository and the applications that maintain it are the mechanisms needed to manage the TP system. The repository is a transaction-processing application. It represents the system configuration as a database and supplies change control by providing transactions that manipulate the configuration and the repository as a single transaction.

The transaction concept, like contract law, is intended to resolve the situation when exceptions arise. The first order of business in designing a system is, therefore, to have a clear model of system failure modes. What breaks? How often do things break? That is the topic of Chapter 3, which gives an empirical and abstract model of computer faults and computer fault tolerance. Once that is out of the way, the rest of the book develops the concepts and techniques used in transaction processing systems.

1.5 Historical Notes

National Cash Register (NCR, now part of AT&T) likes to point out that it was automating transaction processing at the turn of the century. Batch transaction processing using cards began in the 1890s, and it was in full swing by 1940. The first online transaction processing systems using teletypes, computers, and magnetic storage were built in about 1960; they were contemporary with early time-sharing systems.

By the late 1960s, database systems had been recognized as generic utilities, and the techniques to implement them for batch processing were well developed. Notably, the COBOL committee had a task group to define a standard database language (DBTG). The database community went on to evolve the relational model that was prototyped in the 1970s and standardized as SQL in 1987. Today, most database systems are SQL-like.

While this was happening, terminal monitors gradually evolved to support remote procedure calls. The most successful of these was (and still is) IBM's Customer Information and Control System (CICS). In the early 1970s, a typical CICS system was supporting 400 terminals on a processor with .5 MIPS, 256 KB of memory, and four disks of 20 MB each. Each input message would invoke a program to service it. Programs were usually short and simple, using the CICS file management system and other services. Systems routinely ran four such transactions per second. By the late 1970s, most database vendors had discovered CICS and were attaching their database products to it as resource managers. This produced a DB-DC system that could be used for transaction processing. This whole experience pointed out the need for a clean interface to resource managers.

Several other significant transaction processing systems evolved in that era. A reservation system, originally built by American Airlines, became an IBM product called SABRE. It was subsequently renamed Airlines Control Program (ACP), and then again renamed Transaction Processing Facility (TPF). TPF is designed for speed. Until quite recently, it was programmed only in assembly language, had only three record sizes ($\approx$400 bytes, $\approx$1000 bytes, and $\approx$4000 bytes), and all programs had to fit in a single record. TPF has few of the amenities mentioned in this chapter, but it is running most airlines reservations systems today and has the highest transaction throughput rates. It is fair to say that TPF trades people cost for computer cost, economizing on hardware. That was essential thirty years ago, but it is not a good trade-off today.

Both TPF and CICS were surprises. IMS was intended to be the real DB-DC system. CICS was only a TP monitor for uniprocessors, and TPF was too hard to use. By contrast, IMS had most of the niceties described here, and it had them very early (about 1973). It had ACID transactions, device independence, and data independence. IMS presented the application with the same hierarchical data model for both DB and DC, but IMS was late to exploit relational databases, TRPC, and intelligent networks. Gradually, CICS outnumbered it, and now CICS, combined with IBM's DB2 relational database, is the typical system being built. Today there are about 30,000 CICS systems and about 8,000 IMS systems. By that measure, IBM dominates the high end of the transaction marketplace. When one considers small systems each supporting tens of terminals, IBM's AS400 and CICS are the dominant products.

During the 1980s, several new transaction processing systems emerged, notably Encompass from Tandem and ACMS from Digital. These systems evolved rapidly and, due to their late start, have a more modern look. They are popular for distributed transaction processing applications.

Relational databases evolved parallel with transaction processing systems. At first they operated with one or two processes per terminal and, therefore, could not be scaled to very large terminal networks. Gradually they rediscovered the TP monitor architecture, in which a few servers perform work for many clients. Today, many database systems execute as servers in a host operating system. They provide stored procedures that, when invoked by clients, are executed by the database system as services. This is a form of transactional remote procedure call.

Fundamental changes are taking place today. One trend is the integration of transaction processing functionality with the operating system. For example, IBM's MVS system has a subsystem interface, a standard transactional local and remote procedure call (MVS/APPC), an integrated transaction manager, a log manager, and an integrated lock manager (IRLM). DEC's VMS has a transaction manager as a standard part of the operating system (DECdtm), and VMS provides a generic lock facility. The oldest such system, Tandem's Guardian system, has an integrated log and transaction manager (TMF), a transactional RPC (the message system and Pathway), and the database lock manager is a generic lock manager. Standard transaction protocols are being defined by IBM, ISO, and X/Open. Transactional RPC, then, is becoming ubiquitous.

A second major trend is the emergence of new transaction processing systems, typically on UNIX systems. Digital is introducing ACMS, IBM is introducing CICS, NCR is introducing Topend, and Transarc is introducing Encina. All these are new or reimplemented TP systems joining the Tuxedo TP system, which has long run on UNIX. Each of these systems is designed or redesigned to fit the X/Open definition of distributed transaction processing (see Section 2.7 or 16.6). This trend to open transaction processing systems, and the trend to have a standard transactional remote procedure call mechanism, will be an enabling technology for distributed applications.

Exercises

1. [1.2, 10] You have an interest-bearing checking account at some bank. The standard transaction is to write a check debiting the account or to deposit funds in the account—the so-called DebitCredit transaction. Describe four scenarios—one for each of the four ACID properties—including one that violates one property but does not violate the other three.

2. [1.2, 10] Describe eight different transaction programs on the checking account.

3. [1.3, 20] Find a *complete* manual set for some TP system (e.g., the IBM manual set for CICS and related products is a wall 2 meters high and 3 meters long, giving about 18 linear meters of manuals). Measure the linear feet of manuals in the following areas: hardware, operating system, database, networks, languages (e.g., COBOL), tools (edit, debug, bind, make), operator and administrator utilities, application generators, and applications. Draw a pie chart of the result. This pie chart approximately reflects the relative size of each component.

4. [1.3, project] Find a TP system and a person in each role (user, administrator, designer). Interview each person about how the system works and what he likes and dislikes about it. Write a ten-page description of the system from each perspective.

5. [1.3, project] Find a modern application generator that supports windows, graphics, and rapid prototyping. Implement the user interface shown in Figure 1.2. Describe the resulting database design in SQL. Produce a diagram of the application generator's repository/dictionary. Now imagine that the database is on the host. Describe the services on the host and their input and output parameters.

6. [1.2, 15] There are some interesting consequences of Figures 1.2 and 1.3. What is the information flow if a European user visits Australia and wants to read his mail while in Perth by connecting to the Hong Kong regional center?

7. [1.3.2, 15] List 20 objects that ought to be recorded in a complete repository.

Answers

1. A: The check gets lost in mail and so the bank database is not updated. C: You write a check for more than the current account balance. I: The bank pays you interest after you write a check but before the check is cashed. D: You lose your checkbook and balance.

2. CreateAccount, DebitCredit, CloseAccount, PayInterest, MonthlyStatement, YearlyStatement, Query, CancelCheck. Explain the function of each of these.

3. For the Tandem System: There are 56 linear feet of software manuals from the vendor (and 23 feet of hardware maintenance manuals). Third-party applications are about 200 additional feet. Ignoring the hardware and applications manuals the pie chart is:

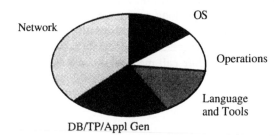

4. Hint: Break into groups of two or three to do this project. Contact a hospital, bank, retailer, manufacturer, library, or phone company. Treat all information you receive as confidential, and have the interviewee review the report before distribution. This exercise should go on in parallel with the class. It is very educational.

5. Hint: Look at Paradox on a PC or 4th Dimension on a Macintosh.

6. Presumably, the workstation client sends his request to the local host that happens to be in Hong Kong (see Figure 1.3). The Hong Kong system could either forward the request (RPC) to the home mail system of this European user (Berlin), or it could access the Berlin mailbox directly from Hong Kong, using the distributed database facilities. It is likely that for manageability and performance reasons, the logon and subsequent services will be performed for the client by a Berlin server rather than the Hong Kong server. This logic is application specific and is part of the application design.

Humpty Dumpty: "When I use a word, it means exactly what I chose it to mean; nothing more nor less."
Alice: "The question is, whether you can make words mean so many different things."
Humpty Dumpty: "The question is, which is to be master, that's all."

LEWIS CARROLL

2

Basic Computer System Terms

2.1 Introduction

Texts on computer systems introduce many more terms and concepts per page than do texts in other disciplines. This is a fundamental aspect of the field: Its goal is to recognize and define new computational structures and to refine those concepts. Besides the proliferation of terms, there is also widespread use of different terms to mean the same thing. Here are some synonyms one often encounters:

> field = column = attribute =...
> record = tuple = object = entity = ...
> block = page = frame = slot = ...
> file = data set = table = collection = relation = relationship =...
> process = task = thread = actor = ...

Of course, each author will maintain that a thread is not exactly the same as a task or a process—there are subtle differences. Yet the reader is often left to guess what these differences are.

In writing this book, we have tried to use terms consistently while mentioning synonyms along the way. In doing so, we have had to assume a basic set of terms. This chapter reviews those terms and defines them. All the terms presented here are repeated in the Glossary in a more abbreviated form.

This chapter also conveys our view that processors and communications are undergoing *unprecedented* changes in price and performance. These changes imply the transition to distributed client-server computer architectures. In our view, the transaction concept is essential to structuring such distributed computations.

The chapter assumes that the reader has encountered most of these ideas before, but may not be familiar with the terminology or taxonomy implicit in this book. Sophisticated readers may want to just browse this chapter, or come back to it as a reference for concepts used later.

2.1.1 Units

It happens that $2^{10} \approx 10^3$; thus, computer scientists use the term *kilo* ambiguously for the two numbers. When being careful, however, they use k (lowercase) for the small kilo (10^3) and K for the big kilo (2^{10}). Similar ambiguities and conventions apply to *mega* and *giga*. Table 2.1

Table 2.1: The standard units and their abbreviations.

Magnitude	Name	Abbreviation	Unit	Abbreviation
$10^{18} \approx 2^{60}$	exa	e, E	bit	b
$10^{15} \approx 2^{50}$	peta	p, P	byte (8 bits)	B
$10^{12} \approx 2^{40}$	tera	t, T	bits per second	bps
$10^{9} \approx 2^{30}$	giga, billion	g, b, G, B	bytes per second	Bps
$10^{6} \approx 2^{20}$	mega	m, M	instructions per second	ips
$10^{3} \approx 2^{10}$	kilo	k, K	transactions per second	tps
$10^{0} \approx 2^{0}$				
10^{-3}	milli	m		
10^{-6}	micro	μ		
10^{-9}	nano	n		
10^{-12}	pico	p		
10^{-15}	femto	f		

defines the standard units and their abbreviations and gives the standard names and symbols for orders of magnitude.

2.2 Basic Hardware

In Bell and Newell's classic taxonomy [1971], hardware consists of three types of modules: *processors*, *memory*, and *communications* (switches or wires). Processors execute instructions from a program, read and write memory, and send data via communications lines. Figure 2.2 shows the overall structure of a computer system.

Computers are generally classified as supercomputers, mainframes, minicomputers, workstations, and personal computers. However, these distinctions are becoming fuzzy with current shifts in technology. Today's workstation has the power of yesterday's mainframe. Similarly, today's WAN (wide area network) has the communications bandwidth of yesterday's LAN (local area network). In addition, electronic memories are growing in size to include much of the data formerly stored on magnetic disk.

These technology trends have deep implications for transaction processing. They imply the following:

Distributed processing. Processing is moving closer to the producers and consumers of the data (workstations, intelligent sensors, robots, and so on).

Client-server. These computers interact with each other via request-reply protocols. One machine, called the *client*, makes requests of another, called the *server*. Of course, the server may in turn be a client to other machines.

Clusters. Powerful servers consist of *clusters* of many processors and memories, cooperating in parallel to perform common tasks.

Why are these computer architecture trends relevant to transaction processing? We believe that to be programmable and manageable, distributed computations require the ACID

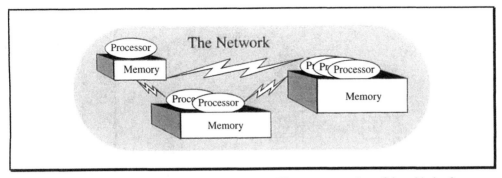

Figure 2.2: Overall structure of a computer system. The system consists of three kinds of components: processors, memory, and communications (wires), which form the network.

transaction properties. Thus, we believe that the transaction techniques described in this book are an enabling technology for distributed systems.

To argue by analogy, engineers have been building highly parallel computers since the 1960s. However, there has been little progress in parallel programming techniques. Consequently, programming parallel computers is still an art, and few parallel machines are in actual use. Engineers can build distributed systems, but few users know how to program them or have algorithms that use them. Without techniques to structure distributed and clustered computations, distributed systems will face the same fate that parallel computers do today.

Transaction processing provides some techniques for structuring distributed computations. Before getting into these techniques, let us first look at processor, memory, and communications hardware, and sketch their technology trends.

2.2.1 Memories

Memories store data at addresses and allow processors to read and write the data. Given a memory address and some data, a memory *write* copies the data to that memory address. Given a memory address, a memory *read* returns the data most recently written to that address.

At a low level of abstraction, the memory looks like an array of bytes to the processor; but at the processor instruction set level, there is already a memory-mapping mechanism that translates logical addresses (virtual memory addresses) to physical addresses. This mapping hardware is manipulated by the operating system software to give the processor a virtual address space at any instant. The processor executes instructions from virtual memory, and it reads and alters bytes from the virtual memory.

Memory performance is measured by its access time: Given an address, the memory presents the data at some later time. The delay is called the *memory access time*. Access time is a combination of *latency* (the time to deliver the first byte) and *transfer time* (the time to move the data). Transfer time, in turn, is determined by the *transfer size* and the *transfer rate*. This produces the following overall equation:

$$\text{memory access time} = \text{latency} + \frac{\text{transfer size}}{\text{transfer rate}} \qquad (2.1)$$

Memory price-performance is measured in one of two ways:

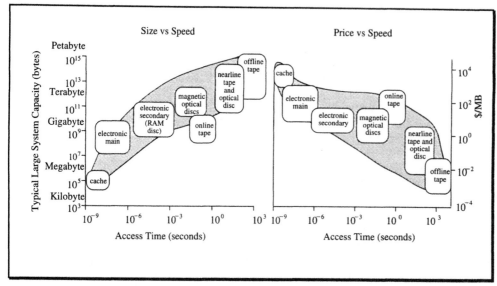

Figure 2.3: The price-performance tradeoff. Fast memory is expensive and therefore small; high-capacity memory is typically slower. Magnetic and optical disk currently offer the lowest-cost online memory, and archive robots multiplexing thousands of tapes among a few tape drives currently offer the lowest-cost nearline memory. Prices are typical of those in 1990.

Cost/byte. The cost of storing a byte of data in that media.

Cost/access. The cost of reading a block of data from that media. This is computed by dividing the device cost by the number of accesses per second that the device can perform. The actual units are cost/access/second, but the time unit is implicit in the metric's name.

These two cost measures reflect the two different views of a memory's purpose: (1) it stores data, and (2) it receives and retrieves data. These two functions are different. A device that does one cheaply probably is expensive for doing the other. Figure 2.3 shows the spectrum of devices and their price-performance as of 1990. Notice that the cost/byte and cost/access of these devices span more than ten orders of magnitude in capacities, access times, and cost/access.

Two generic forms of memory are in common use today: electronic and magnetic. *Electronic memories* represent information as charges or currents passing through integrated circuits. *Magnetic memories* represent information as polarized magnetic domains on a magnetic media.

Magnetic memories are non-volatile; they do not lose data if the power is turned off. Most electronic memory needs a power source to maintain the data. Increasingly, batteries are being added to electronic memories to make them non-volatile. The more detailed properties of these two memory technologies are discussed in the following two subsections. Discussion then turns to the way electronic and magnetic storage are combined into a memory hierarchy.

2.2.1.1 Electronic Memory

Byte-addressable electronic memory is generically called *main* memory, while block-addressable bulk electronic memory is variously called *secondary storage*, *extended memory*, or *RAM disk*. Usually, the processor cannot directly manipulate secondary memory. Rather, a secondary memory block (say, 10 KB) must be copied to main memory, where it is read and updated; the changed result is then copied back to secondary memory.

Electronic memories are getting much bigger. Gordon Moore observed that integrated circuit memory chips started out at 1 Kb/chip in 1970, and that since then their per-chip capacity has been increasing by a factor of four about every three years. This observation is now called *Moore's Law*:

$$\text{MemoryChipCapacity(year)} = 4^{\frac{(\text{year} - 1970)}{3}} \text{ Kb/chip for year in } [1970...2000] \qquad \text{Moore's Law} \qquad (2.2)$$

Moore's Law implies that the 16 Mb memory chip will appear in 1991, and that the 1 Gb (gigabit) chip will appear in the year 2000. These trends have interesting implications for disks, for databases, and for transaction processing systems, but let us stick to processors and memories for a moment longer.

Memories are getting much *bigger*, while processors are getting *faster*. Meanwhile, inexpensive electronic memories are not getting much faster. Their access times are measured in tens of nanoseconds. Thus, a fast processor (say, a 1 bips machine) might spend most of its time waiting for instructions and data from memory. To mask this problem, each processor is given a relatively small, high-speed *cache* memory. This cache memory is private to the processor (increasingly, it is on the processor chip). The processor cache holds data and programs recently accessed by the processor. If most memory accesses "hit" the cache, then the processor will rarely wait for data from main memory.

The cache concept recurs again and again. Main memory is a cache for disk memories. Disk memories, in turn, may serve as a cache for tape archives.

2.2.1.2 Magnetic Memory

Magnetic memory devices represent information as polarized magnetic domains on a magnetic (or magneto-optical) storage media (see Figure 2.4). Some form of mechanical transport, called the *drive*, moves these domains past an electronic (or magneto-optical) read-write station that can sense and change the magnetic domains. This movement trades time for capacity. Doubling the area of the storage media doubles the capacity, but it also doubles the latency. Since magnetic media is very inexpensive, this time-space trade-off provides a huge spectrum of access time versus cost/byte choices (see Figure 2.3).

Two basic topologies are used to exploit magnetic media: the line (a tape) and the circle (a disk). The line has the virtue that it goes on forever (according to Euclid). The circle has the virtue that, as it rotates, the same point returns again and again. If the circle is rotated 100 times a second, the maximum latency for a piece of data to pass by the read station is 10 milliseconds. For a tape, the maximum read time depends on the tape length (≈ 1 km) and the tape transport speed. A maximum read time of one minute is typical for a tape. In general, tapes have excellent cost/byte but poor access times, while disks have higher cost/byte but better access times. In addition, magnetic tapes and floppy disks have become the standard media for interchanging data among computers.

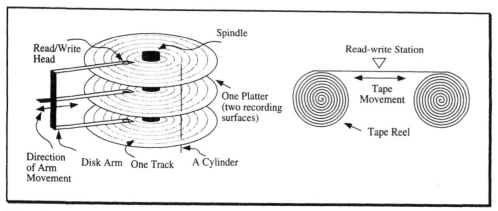

Figure 2.4: The two basic topologies of magnetic storage media: disk and tape.   Disks rotate, passing the data in the cylinder by the electronic read-write heads every few milliseconds. This gives low access latency. The disk arm can move among cylinders in tens of milliseconds. Tapes have approximately the same storage density and transfer rate, but they must move long distances if random access is desired. Consequently, tapes have large random access latencies—on the order of seconds.

Disks

Disk devices usually stack several (say, ten) *platters* together on a single *spindle* and then rotate them as a unit (see Figure 2.4). For each platter, the *disk arm* assembly has one read-write *head*, mounted on a fixed structure. The circle of data on a particular surface is called a *disk track*. As the disk platters rotate, the disk arm sees a *cylinder's* worth of data from the many read-write heads. To facilitate reading and rewriting the data, each track is formatted as fixed-size *sectors* of data (typically about 1 KB). Sectors are the smallest read/write unit of a disk. Each sector stores self-correcting error codes. If the sector fails (that is, has an uncorrectable defect), a spare sector in the cylinder is used to replace it. The arm normally can move in and out across the platters, thereby creating hundreds or thousands of cylinders. This lateral movement is called *seeking*.

Disks have a three-dimensional address space: a sector address consists of (1) the cylinder number, (2) the track number within that cylinder, and (3) the sector number on that track. Disk controllers are getting more and more intelligent; they remap defects, cache recently read or written pages, and even multiplex an array of disks into a single logical disk to provide high transfer rates or high availability.

Modern disk controllers give a geometry-independent view of the disk. Such controllers have only two parameters: (1) the sector size and (2) the number of sectors. But the underlying three-dimensional geometry and performance of the disk has not changed. Consequently, disk access times are determined by three parameters:

$$\text{Disk Access Time} = \text{Seek\_Time} + \text{Rotational\_Latency} + \frac{\text{Transfer\_Size}}{\text{Transfer\_Rate}} \qquad (2.3)$$

High disk transfer rates come from *disk striping*, which partitions the parts of a large object among *n* disks. When the object is read or written, the pieces of it are moved in parallel to or from the *n* disks, yielding an effective transfer rate of *n* times the transfer rate of individual disks.

Today, average seek and rotation times are on the order of 10 milliseconds, rotation times are on the same order, and transfer rates are between 1 MBps and 10 MBps. These times are unlikely to change dramatically in the next decade. Consequently, access patterns to disks will remain a critical performance issue. To picture this, consider two access patterns to a megabyte of data stored in 1000 sectors of a disk:

Sequential access.   Read or write sectors $[x, x + 1, ..., x + 999]$ in ascending order. This requires one seek (10 ms) and half a rotation (5 ms) before the data in the cylinder begins transfering the megabyte at 10 MBps (the transfer takes 100 ms, ignoring one-cylinder seeks). The total access time is 115 ms.

Random access.   Read the thousand sectors $[x, ..., x + 999]$ in random order. In this case, each read requires a seek (10 ms), half a rotation (5 ms), and then the 1 KB transfer (.1 ms). Since there are 1000 of these events, the total access time is 15.1 seconds.

This 100:1 time ratio between sequential and random access to the same data demonstrates the basic principle: *sequential access to magnetic media is tens or thousands of times faster than random access to the same data.* Furthermore, transfer rates are increasing faster than access rates, so the speed differential between sequential and random access to magnetic media is increasing with time. This has two implications:

Big blocks.   Transfer units for random accesses (block sizes) should be large so that transfer time compares to access time.

Data clustering.   Great care should be taken by data management systems to recognize and preserve data clusters on magnetic media, so that the big blocks will move useful data (by prefetching it or postwriting it).

Chapter 13 explains how database systems use large electronic memories to cache most of the active data. While reads to cached data do not generate disk activity, writes generate a sequence of log records describing the updates. The log records of all updates form a single sequential stream of writes to magnetic storage. Periodically, the cached data is written to secondary storage (disk or nonvolatile electronic memory) as large sequential writes that preserve the original data clustering. This logging technique is now being applied to other areas, notably directory management of file servers.

A more radical approach keeps recently used data in electronic memory and writes changed blocks to magnetic storage in a sequential stream. This strategy, called a *log-structured file system*, converts *all* writes to sequential writes. Unfortunately, for many applications a log-structured file system seems to make subsequent reads of the archived data more random. There will be many innovations in this area as the gap between sequential and random access widens.

Our ability to read and write magnetic domains per unit area has been growing by a factor of ten every decade. This observation, originally made by Al Hoagland, is expressed in the formula:

$$\text{MagneticAreaDensity(year)} = 10^{\frac{(\text{year} - 1970)}{10}} \text{ Mb/inch}^2 \text{ for year } [1970...2000] \quad \text{Hoagland's Law} \quad (2.4)$$

Hoagland's Law suggests that the capacity of individual disks and tapes will continue to increase. Of course, the exponential growth predicted by Moore's Law, Hoagland's Law, and Joy's Law (Equations 2.3, 2.4, 2.8) must come to an end someday.

Tapes

Magnetic tape memories do not have the same high densities that magnetic disks have, because the media is flexible and not matched to the read-write head.[1] Tapes, however, do have much greater area. In addition, this area can be rolled into a reel to yield spectacular volumetric memory densities (terabytes/meter^3). In 1990, a typical tape fit in the palm of your hand and stored about a gigabyte.

Mounted tapes have latencies of just a few milliseconds to read or write data at the current position, in part because they use a processor to buffer the reads and writes. But the latency for a random read or write to a tape drive is measured in tens of seconds. Once a transfer starts, tape transfer rates are comparable to disk transfer rates (say, 10 MBps). Tapes, then, are the ultimate sequential devices. Tapes are typically formatted in blocks for error control and to allow rewriting.

Because a tape drive costs about as much as a disk drive (around $10/MB), tapes mounted on a tape drive have a relatively high cost/byte (see Figure 2.3). But when the tape is offline—removed from the reader—the cost/byte is reduced by a factor of a thousand, to just the cost of the media (around $10/GB). There is an intermediate possibility: *nearline* tape robots, which move a few thousand tapes between a storage rack and a few tape readers. The robot typically has between 2 and 10 tape drives and can dismount one tape and mount another in 40 seconds.

Tape robots are another example of trading time for space. The cost of the tape readers and the tape robot is amortized across many tapes (say, 10,000). If the robot costs $500,000, the unit cost of each tape is increased by a factor of six—from, say, $10 to $60 per gigabyte. The offline figure ignores the price of the reader needed for the offline tapes, as well as the cost of the four shifts of human operators needed to feed the reader. When those considerations are added, tape robots are very attractive.

2.2.1.3 Memory Hierarchies

The simple memory boxes shown in Figure 2.2 are implemented as a memory hierarchy (see Figure 2.5). Small, fast, expensive memories at the top act as caches for the larger, slower, cheaper memories used at lower levels of the hierarchy. Processor registers are at the top of the hierarchy, and offline tapes are at the bottom. In between are various memory devices, that are progressively slower, but that also store data less expensively.

A perfect memory would always know what data the processor needed next and would have moved exactly that data into cache just before the processor asked for it. Such a memory would be as fast as the cache. Memories cannot predict future references, but they can guess future accesses by using the *principle of locality:* data that was used recently is likely to soon be used again. By using the principle of locality, memories cache as much recently used data, along with its neighboring data, as possible. The success of this strategy is measured by the cache *hit ratio*:

$$\text{hit ratio} = \frac{\text{references satisfied by cache}}{\text{all references to cache}} \qquad (2.5)$$

---

[1] Tapes are undergoing a revolution in 1991 by increasing from 100 MB linear objects to 10 GB objects. This change is the result of switching to VCR helical scan technology and other recording innovations. This section was written in anticipation of that transition.

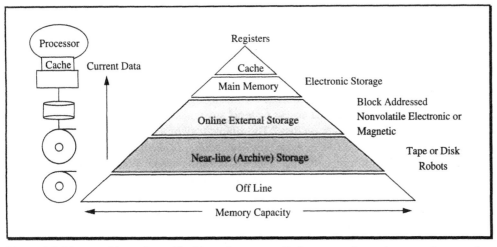

Figure 2.5: Memory hierarchy.   The hierarchy uses small, fast, expensive cache memories to cache some data present in larger, slower, cheaper memories. If hit ratios are good, the overall memory speed approximates the speed of the cache.

When a reference *misses* the cache, it must be satisfied by accessing the next level in the memory hierarchy. That memory is just a cache for the next-lower level of memory; thus it, too, can get a miss, and so on.

Unless cache hit rates are very high (say, .99), the cache memory has approximately the same access time as the secondary memory. To understand this, suppose a cache memory with access time C has hit rate H, and suppose that on a miss the secondary memory access time is S. Further, suppose that $C \approx .01 \cdot S$, as is typical in Figure 2.3. The effective access time of the cache will be as follows:

effective cache access time
$$
\begin{aligned}
&= H \cdot C + (1 - H) \cdot S \qquad\qquad (2.6)\\
&\approx H \cdot (.01 \cdot S) + (1 - H) \cdot S\\
&= (1 - .99 \cdot H) \cdot S\\
&\approx (1 - H) \cdot S
\end{aligned}
$$

Therefore, unless H is very close to unity, the effective access time is much closer to S than to C. For example, a 50% hit ratio attains an effective memory 50 times slower than cache; a 90% hit ratio attains an effective memory 11 times slower than cache. If the hit ratio is 99%, the effective memory is half as fast as cache. To achieve an effective memory speed within 10% of the cache speed, the hit rate must be 99.98%.

This simple computation shows that high hit ratios are critical to good performance. There are two approaches to improving hit ratios:

Clustering.   Cluster related data together in one storage block, and cluster data reference patterns and instruction reference patterns to improve locality.

Larger cache.   Keep more data in a larger cache, in the hopes that it will be reused.

Moore's Law (Equation 2.2) says that electronic memory chips grow in capacity by a factor of four every three years. Hence, future transaction systems and database systems will have huge electronic memories. At the same time, the memory requirements of many applications continue to grow, suggesting that the *relative* portion of data that can be kept close to the processor will stay about the same. It is therefore unlikely that everything will fit in electronic memory.

The Five-Minute Rule

How shall we manage these huge memories? The answers so far have been clustering and sequential access. However, there is one more useful technique for managing caches, called the *five-minute rule*. Given that we know what the data access patterns are, when should data be kept in main memory and when should it be kept on disk? The simple way of answering this question is, *Frequently accessed data should be in main memory, while it is cheaper to store infrequently accessed data on disk.* Unfortunately, the statement is a little vague: What does *frequently* mean? The five-minute rule says frequently means five minutes, but the rule reflects a way of reasoning that also applies to any cache-secondary memory structure. In those cases, depending on relative storage and access costs, *frequently* may turn out to be milliseconds, or it may turn out to be days (see Equation 2.7).

The logic for the five-minute rule goes as follows: Assume there are no special response time (real-time) requirements; the decision to keep something in cache is, therefore, purely economic. To make the computation simple, suppose that data blocks are 10 KB. At 1990 prices, 10 KB of main memory cost about $1. Thus, we could keep the data in main memory forever if we were willing to spend a dollar. But with 10 KB of disk costing only $.10, we presumably could save $.90 if we kept the 10 KB on disk. In reality, the savings are not so great; if the disk data is accessed, it must be moved to main memory, and that costs something. How much, then, does a disk access cost? A disk, along with all its supporting hardware, costs about $3,000 (in 1990) and delivers about 30 accesses per second; access per second cost, therefore, is about $100. At this rate, if the data is accessed once a second, it costs $100.10 to store it on disk (disk storage and disk access costs). That is considerably more than the $1 to store it in main memory. The break-even point is about one access per 100 seconds, or about every two minutes. At that rate, the main memory cost is about the same as the disk storage cost plus the disk access costs. At a more frequent access rate, disk storage is more expensive. At a less frequent rate, disk storage is cheaper. Anticipating the cheaper main memory that will result from technology changes, this observation is called the five-minute rule rather than the two-minute rule.

The five-minute rule: Keep a data item in electronic memory if its access frequency is five minutes or higher; otherwise keep it in magnetic memory.

Similar arguments apply to objects stored on tape and cached on disk. Given the object size, the cost of cache, the cost of secondary memory, and the cost of accessing the object in secondary memory once per second, *frequently* is defined as a frequency of access in units of accesses per second (a/s):

$$\text{Frequency} \approx \frac{(\text{Cache\_Cost/Byte} - \text{Secondary\_Cost/Byte}) \bullet \text{Object\_Bytes}}{\text{Object\_Access\_Per\_Second\_Cost}} \quad \text{a/s} \qquad (2.7)$$

Objects accessed with this frequency or higher should be kept in cache.

Future Memory Hierarchies

There are two contrasting views of how memory hierarchies will evolve. The one proclaims *disks forever,* while the other maintains that *disks are dead.* The disks-forever group predicts that there will never be enough electronic memory to hold all the active data; future transaction processing systems will be used in applications such as graphics, CAD, image processing, AI, and so forth, each of which requires much more memory and manipulates much larger objects than do classical database applications. Future databases will consist of images and complex objects that are thousands of times larger than the records and blocks currently moving in the hierarchy. Hence, the memory hierarchy traffic will grow with strict response time constraints and increasing transfer rate requirements. Random requests will require the fast read access times provided by disks, while the memory architecture will remain basically unchanged. Techniques such as parallel transfer (striping) will provide needed transfer rates.

The *disks-are-dead* view, on the other hand, predicts that future memory hierarchies will consist of an electronic memory cache for tape robots. This view is based on the observation that the price advantage of disks over electronic memory is eroding. If current trends continue, the cost/byte of disk and electronic memory will intersect. Moore's Law (Equation 2.2) "intersects" Hoagland's Law (Equation 2.4) sometime between the years 2000 and 2010. Electronic memory is getting 100 times denser each decade, while disks are achieving a relatively modest tenfold density improvement in the same time. When the cost of electronic memory approaches the cost of disk memory, there will be little reason for disks. To deal with this competition, disk designers will have to use more cheap media per expensive read-write head. With more media per head, disks will have slower access times—in short, they will behave like tapes.

The disks-are-dead group believes that electronic memories will be structured as a hierarchy, with block-addressed electronic memories replacing disks. These RAM disks will have battery or tape backup to make them non-volatile and will be large enough to hold all the active data. New information will only arrive via the network or through real-world interfaces such as terminals, sensors, and so forth. Magnetic memory devices will be needed only for logging and archiving. Both operations are sequential and often asynchronous. The primary requirement will be very high transfer rates. Magnetic or magneto-optical tapes would be the ideal devices; they have high capacity, high transfer rates, and low cost/byte. It is possible that these tapes will be removable optical disks, but in this environment they will be treated as fundamentally sequential devices.

The conventional model, disks forever, is used here if only because it subsumes the no-disk case. It asks for fast sequential transfers between main memory and disks and requires fast selective access to single objects on disk.

2.2.2 Processors

As stated earlier, processors execute instructions that read and write memory or send and receive bytes on communications lines. Processor speeds are measured in terms of instructions per second, or *ips*, and often in units of millions, or *mips*.

Between 1965 and 1990, processor mips ratings rose by a factor of 70, from about .6 mips to about 40 mips.[2] In the decade of the 1980s, however, the performance of microprocessors (one-chip processors) approximately doubled every 18 months, so that today's microprocessors typically have mips ratings comparable to mainframes (often in the 25 mips range). This rapid performance improvement is projected to continue for the next decade. If

---

[2] This is the approximate scalar performance of IBM 360 processors (or their descendants in the IBM System/9000) when running scalar (as opposed to scientific) programs, such as SQL requests or a COBOL compilation.

that happens, processor speeds will increase more in the next decade than they have in the last three decades. Bill Joy suggested the following "law" to predict the mips rate of Sun Microsystems processors to the year 2000.

$$\text{SunMips(year)} = 2^{\text{year} - 1984} \text{ mips for year in } [1984...2000] \qquad \text{Joy's Law (2.8)}$$

In reality, things are going a little more slowly than this; still, the growth rate is impressive. Billion-instructions-per-second (1 bips) processors are likely to be common by the end of the decade.

These one-chip processors are not only fast, but they are also mass produced and inexpensive. Consequently, future computers will generally have many processors. There is debate about how these many processors will be connected to memory and how they will be interconnected. Before discussing that architectural issue, let us first introduce communications hardware and its performance.

2.2.3 Communications Hardware

Processors and memories (see Figure 2.2) are connected by wires collectively called the *network*. Regarded in one way, computers are almost entirely wires. But the notion of wire is changing: While some wires are just impurities on a chip, others are fiber-optic cables carrying light signals. The basic property of a wire is that a signal injected at one end eventually arrives at the other end. Some wires do routing—they are switches—while others broadcast to many receivers; here, the simple model of point-to-point communications is considered.

The time to transmit a message of M bits via a wire is determined by two parameters: (1) the wire's *bandwidth*—that is, how many bits/second it can carry—and (2) the wire's length (in meters), which determines how long the first bit will take to arrive. The distance divided by the speed of light in the media ($C_m \approx 200$ million meters/s in a solid) determines the transmission *latency*. The time to transmit Message_Bits bits is approximately

$$\text{Transmit Time(Message\_Bits)} = \frac{\text{Distance}}{C_m} + \frac{\text{Message\_Bits}}{\text{Bandwidth}} \text{ seconds} \qquad (2.9)$$

Transmit times to send a kilobyte within a cluster are in the microsecond range; around a campus, they are in the millisecond range; and across the country, the transmit time for a 1 KB message is hundreds of milliseconds (see Table 2.6).

The numbers in Table 2.6 are "old"; they are based on typical technology in 1990. The proliferation of fiber-optic connections, both locally and in long-haul networks, is making 1 Gbps local links and 100 Mbps long-haul links economical. Bandwidth within a cluster can go to a terabit per second, if desired, but it is more likely that multiple links in the 1 Gbps range will be common. Similar estimates can be made for MANs and WANs. The main theme here is that bandwidth among processors should be plentiful and inexpensive in the future. Future system designs should use this bandwidth intelligently. Table 2.7 gives a prediction of typical point-to-point communication bandwidths for the network of the year 2000. These predictions are generally viewed as conservative.

Table 2.7 indicates that cluster and LAN transmit times will be dominated by transfer times (bandwidth), but that MAN and WAN transmit times will be dominated by latency (the speed of light). Parallel links and higher technology can be used to improve bandwidth, but there is little hope of improving latency. As we will see in Section 2.6, cluster, LAN, and

Table 2.6: The definition of the four kinds of networks by their diameters. These diameters imply certain latencies (based on the speed of light). In 1990, Ethernet (at 10 Mbps) was the dominant LAN.[3] Metropolitan networks typically are based on 1 Mbps public lines. Such lines are too expensive for transcontinental links at present; most long-distance lines are therefore 50 Kbps or less. As the text notes, things are changing (see Table 2.7).

Type of Network	Diameter	Latency	Bandwidth	Send 1 KB
Cluster	100 m	.5 µs	1 Gbps	10 µs
LAN (local area network)	1 km	5. µs	10 Mbps	1 ms
MAN (metro area network)	100 km	.5 ms	1 Mbps	10 ms
WAN (wide area network)	10,000 km	50. ms	50 Kbps	210 ms

Table 2.7: Point-to-point bandwidth likely to be common among computers by the year 2000.

Type of Network	Diameter	Latency	Bandwidth	Send 1 KB
Cluster	100 m	.5 µs	1 Gbps	5 µs
LAN (local area network)	1 km	5. µs	1 Gbps	10 µs
MAN (metro area network)	100 km	.5 ms	100 Mbps	.6 ms
WAN (wide area network)	10,000 km	50. ms	100 Mbps	50 ms

MAN times are actually dominated by software costs—the processing time to set up a message and the marginal cost of sending and receiving each message byte.

2.2.4 Hardware Architectures

To summarize the previous two sections, processor and communications performance are expected to improve by a factor of 100 or more in the decade of the 1990s. This is comparable to the improvement in the last three decades. In addition, the unit costs of processors and long-haul communications bandwidth is expected to drop dramatically.

2.2.4.1 Processor-Memory Architecture

How will these computers be interconnected? Where are processors in the memory hierarchy? How do processors fit into the communications network? The answers to these questions are still quite speculative, but we can make educated guesses. First, let us look at the question of how processors will attach to the memory hierarchy. Figure 2.8 shows three different strategies for this.

Shared nothing. In a *shared-nothing* design, each memory is dedicated to a single processor. All accesses to that data must pass through that processor.[4] Processors communicate by sending messages to each other via the communications network.

Shared global. In a *shared-global* design, each processor has some private memory not accessible to other processors. There is, however, a pool of *global* memory shared by

---

[3] Note here that the discussion has switched from bytes (B) to bits (Mb).

[4] An exception: In some shared nothing systems, if a processor fails, some of its memory may be accessible to another processor.

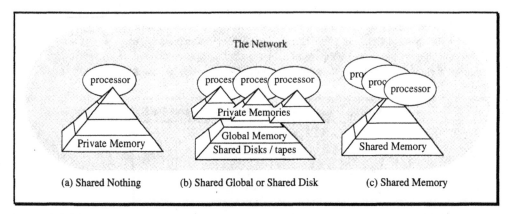

Figure 2.8: Three strategies for attaching processors to the memory hierarchy. The leftmost design (a) shows a processor with only private memory; this is called a shared-nothing design, since the processor shares only the network with other processors. The center design (b) shows each processor with an *n*-level private memory (cache) and some shared-common memory (typically disk or block-oriented tertiary electronic memory). The rightmost design (c) shows multiple processors accessing a common memory. As processors become faster (say, 1 bips), shared-memory designs are no longer economical because processors need on-chip caches (private memories). Thus, only the shared-nothing and shared-global designs will be common in the future. The text argues that even global memories will be uneconomical in the future.

the collection of processors. This global memory is usually addressed in blocks (units of a few kilobytes or more) and is RAM disk or disk.

Shared memory. In a *shared-memory* design, each processor has transparent access to all memory. If multiple processors access the data concurrently, the underlying hardware regulates the access to the shared data and provides each processor a current view of the data.

Pure shared-memory systems will probably not be feasible in the future. Each processor needs a cache, which is inherently private memory. Considerable processor delays and extra circuitry are needed to make these private caches look like a single consistent memory. If, as often happens, some frequently accessed data appears in all the processor caches, then the shared-memory hardware must present a consistent version of it in each cache by broadcasting updates to that data. The relative cost of cache maintenance increases as the processors become faster.

One can picture this by thinking of the processor *event horizon*—the round-trip distance a processor can send a message in one instruction time. This time/distance determines how much interaction the processor can have with its neighboring processors. For a 1 bips processor, the event horizon is about 10 centimeters ($\approx$4 inches). This is approximately the size of a processor chip or very small circuit board. Since wires are rarely straight, the event horizon of a 1 bips processor is on chip. This puts a real damper on shared memory.

As cache sizes grow, much of the program and data state of a process migrates to the cache where that process is running. When the process runs again, it has a real *affinity* to that processor and its cache. Because running somewhere else will cause many unneeded cache faults to global memory, processes are increasingly being bound to processors. This effectively partitions global memory, resulting in a software version of the shared-nothing design.

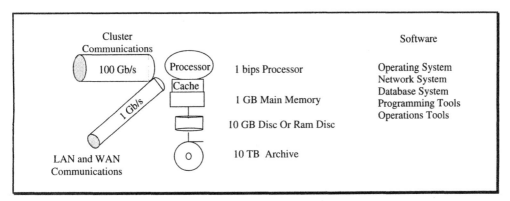

Figure 2.9: The computer of a future tape robot. The processor has substantial local storage to manage and optimize the robot and to record the catalog of tapes. Such processors will be the building blocks of system clusters.

As a related issue, each device will be managed by a free-standing, powerful computer that can execute client requests. Requests will move progressively closer to the devices. Each keyboard and display, each disk, each tape robot, and each communications line will have its own dedicated processor. Consider, for example, the controller for a tape robot. This processor will manage an expensive device. The controller's job is to optimize access to the device, deal with device failures, and integrate the device into the network. The controller will store a catalog of all the tapes and their contents and will buffer incoming data and prefetch outgoing data to optimize tape performance. Programming this software will require tools to reduce development and maintenance costs. Thus, the tape robot will probably run a standard operating system, include a standard database system, and support standard communications protocols. In other words, the tape robot controller is just a general-purpose computer and its software, along with a standard peripheral. Figure 2.9 diagrams this hardware.

Similar arguments apply to display controllers, disk controllers, and bulk electronic memory controllers (RAM-disks). Each is becoming a general-purpose processor with substantial private memory and a memory device or communications line behind it. Global memory devices are becoming processors with private memory.

2.2.4.2 Processor-Processor Architecture

Based on the previous discussion, shared-nothing and shared-global processors are likely to be grouped to form a single management entity called a *cluster*. The key properties of these clusters (see Table 2.7) are:

High communication bandwidth. Intra-cluster links can move bulk data quickly.

Low communication latency. Intra-cluster links have latency of less than 1 μs.

Clusters include software that allows a program (process) to access all the devices of the cluster as though they were locally attached. That is, subject to authorization restrictions, any program running in one processor can indirectly read or write any memory or wire in the cluster as if that device were local to the program. This is done by using a client-server mechanism. Clusters are available today from Digital (VAXcluster), IBM (Sysplex), Intel (Hypercube), Tandem (T16), and Teradata (DBC/1012).

Structuring a computation within a cluster poses an interesting trade-off question: Should the program move to the data, or should the data move to the program? The answer is yes. If the computation has a large state, it may be better to move the data than to move the process state; on the other hand, if the data is huge and the client process and the answer are small, then it is probably better to move the program to the data. Remote procedure calls are one way of moving programs so that they can execute remotely.

In summary, the processor-memory architecture is likely to move toward a cluster of shared-nothing machines communicating over a high-speed network. Clusters, in turn, communicate with other clusters and with clients via standard networks. As Table 2.7 suggests, these wires have impressive bandwidth, but they have large latencies because they span long distances. These trends imply that computations will be structured as clients making requests to servers. Remote procedure calls allow such distributed execution, while the transaction mechanism handles exceptions in the execution.

2.3 Basic Software—Address Spaces, Processes, Sessions

Having made a quick tour of hardware concepts, terms, and trends, let us look at the software analogs of the hardware components. Address spaces, processes, and messages are the software analogs of memories, processors, and wires. Following that basic client-server concepts are discussed.

2.3.1 Address Spaces

A *process address space* is an array of bytes. Each process executes instructions from its address space and can read and write bytes of the address space using processor instructions. The process address space is actually virtual memory; that is, the addresses go through at least one level of translation to compute the physical memory address.

Address spaces are usually composed of memory *segments.* Segments are units of memory sharing, protection, and allocation. As one example, program and library segments in one address space can be shared with many other address spaces. These programs are read-only in the sense that no process can modify them. As another example, two processes may want to cooperate on a task and, in doing so, may want to share some data. In that case, they may attach a common segment to each of their address spaces. Figure 2.10 shows these two forms of sharing. To simplify memory addressing, the virtual address space is divided into fixed-size segment slots, and each segment partially fills a slot. Typical slot sizes range from 2^{24} to 2^{32} bytes. This gives a two-dimensional address space, where addresses are ⟨segment_number, byte⟩. Again, segments are often partitioned into *virtual memory pages*, which are the unit of transfer between main and secondary memory. In these cases, virtual memory addresses are actually ⟨segment, page, byte⟩. If an object is bigger than a segment, it can be mapped into consecutive segments of the address space.

Paging and segmentation are not visible to the executing process. The address space looks like a sequence of bytes with invalid pages in the empty segment slots and at the end of partially filled segment slots.

Address spaces cannot usually span network nodes: that is, address spaces cannot span private memories (see Figure 2.8). Global read-only and execute-only segments can be

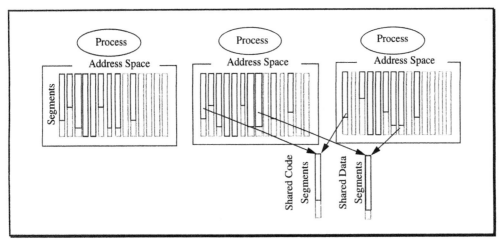

Figure 2.10: Memory segmentation and sharing. A process executes in an address space—a paged, segmented array of bytes. Some segments may be shared with other address spaces. The sharing may be execute-only, read-only, or read-write. Most of the segment slots are empty (lightly shaded boxes), and most of the occupied segments are only partially full of programs or data.

shared among address spaces in a cluster. However, since keeping multiple consistent copies of a read-write shared segments is difficult, this is not usually supported.

2.3.2 Processes, Protection Domains, and Threads

Processes are the actors in computation; they are the software analog of hardware processors. They execute programs, send messages, read and write data, and paint pictures on your display.

2.3.2.1 Processes

A *process* is a virtual processor. It has an address space that contains the program the process is executing and the memory the process reads and writes. One can imagine a process executing C programs statement by statement, with each statement reading and writing bytes in the address space or sending messages to other processes.

Why have processes? Well, processes provide an ability to execute programs in parallel; they provide a protection entity; and they provide a way of structuring computations into independent execution streams. So they provide a form of fault containment in case a program fails.

Processes are building blocks for transactions, but the two concepts are orthogonal. A process can execute many different transactions over time, and parts of a single transaction may be executed by many processes.

Each process executes on behalf of some user, or *authority*, and with some *priority*. The authority determines what the process can do: which other processes, devices, and files the process can address and communicate with. The process priority determines how quickly the process's demand for resources (processor, memory, and bandwidth) will be serviced if other processes make competing demands. Short tasks typically run with high priority, while large tasks are usually given lower priority and run in the background.

2.3.2.2 Protection Domains

As a process executes, it calls on services from other subsystems. For example, it asks the network software to read and write communications devices, it asks the database software to read and write the shared database, and it asks the user interface to read and write widgets (graphical objects). These subsystems want some protection from faults in the application program. They want to encapsulate their data so that only they can access it directly. Such an encapsulated environment is called a *protection domain*. Many of the resource managers discussed in this book (database manager, recovery manager, log manager, lock manager, buffer manager, and so on) should operate as protection domains. There are two ways to provide protection domains:

Process = protection domain. Each subsystem executes as a separate process with its own private address space. Applications execute subsystem requests by switching processes, that is, by sending a message to a process.

Address space = protection domain. A process has many address spaces: one for each protected subsystem and one for the application (see Figure 2.11). Applications execute subsystem requests by switching address spaces. The *address space protection domain* of a subsystem is just an address space that contains some of the caller's segments; in addition, it contains program and data segments belonging to the called subsystem. A process *connects* to the domain by asking the subsystem or OS kernel to add the segment to the address space. Once connected, the domain is callable from other domains in the process by using a special instruction or kernel call.

The concept of an address space as a protection domain was pioneered by the Burroughs descriptor-based machines. Today, it is well represented by IBM's AS400 machines, by the cross-memory services of the MVS/XA system, and by the four protection domains of the VAX-VMS process architecture. The concept of a process as a protection domain was pioneered by Per Brinch Hansen [1970] and is well represented by the UNIX operating systems of today.

Most systems use both process domains and address space domains. The process approach is the only solution if the subsystem's data is remote or if the underlying operating

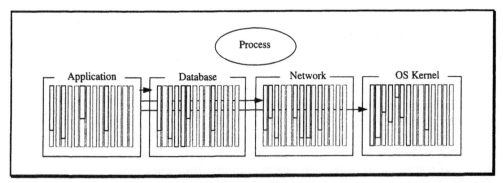

Figure 2.11: A process may have several protection domains. At the least, it has the application domain and the kernel domain. In addition, it may have other protection domains (address spaces) that allow it to execute protected subsystems without incurring a process dispatch.

system has a very simple protection model. But even that approach has at least two address spaces for each process: (1) the application domain and (2) the privileged operating system kernel domain that implements address spaces, processes, and interprocess communication. Typically, the hardware implements an instruction to switch from user mode to this privileged mode.

The process protection domain approach is the most general: it works in networks and in shared-memory systems. The drawback of using processes to implement protection domains is that a domain switch requires a process switch, and it may require copying parameters and results between the processes.

Structuring applications as multiple address space protection domains per process has real performance advantages. The multiple-address-space-per-process approach avoids most of these data copies. When the application calls the database system, the process assumes a new address space that shares the caller's memory segments and the database system's memory segments. The call begins executing at a standard location in the database system program. The database system can directly address the caller's data as well as the database code and data. When implemented in hardware, such domain switches can be very rapid (≈100 instructions for a call plus return). This is much faster than the round-trip process switch, which involves several kernel calls and process dispatches. When the additional costs of parameter passing and authority checking are added, the cost of process switching rises substantially.

2.3.2.3 Threads

Address space protection domains show the need for multiple address spaces per process. There is a dual need for multiple processes per address space. Often the simplest way to structure a computation is to have two or more processes independently access a common data structure. For example, to scan through a data stream, one process is appointed the producer, which reads the data from an external source, while the second process processes the data. Further examples of cooperating processes, such as file read-ahead, asynchronous buffer flushing, and other housekeeping chores, are given in later chapters of this book.

Processes can share the same address space simply by having all their address spaces point to the same segments. Most operating systems do not make a clean distinction between address spaces and processes. Thus a new concept, called a *thread* or a *task*, is introduced to multiplex one operating system process among many virtual processes. To confuse things, several operating systems do not use the term process at all. For example, in the Mach operating system, *thread* means process, and *task* means address space; in MVS, *task* means process, and so on.

The term *thread* often implies a second property: inexpensive to create and dispatch. Threads are commonly provided by some software that found the operating system processes to be too expensive to create or dispatch. The thread software multiplexes one big operating system process among many threads, which can be created and dispatched hundreds of times faster than a process.

The term *thread* is used in this book to connote these light-weight processes. Unless this light-weight property is intended, *process* is used. Several threads usually share a common address space. Typically, all the threads have the same authorization identifier, since they are part of the same address space domain, but they may have different scheduling priorities.

2.3.3 Messages and Sessions

Sessions are the software analog of communication wires, and messages are the software analog of signals on wires. One process can communicate with another by sending it a message and having the second process receive the message.

Shared memory can be used to communicate among processes within a processor, but messages are used to communicate among processors in a network. Even within a processor, messages can be used among subsystems if the underlying operating system kernel does not support shared-memory segments (see Subsection 2.3.2.2).

Most systems allow a process to send messages to others. The send routine looks up the recipient's process name to find its address—more on that below—and then constructs an envelope containing the sender's name, the recipient's name, and the message. The resulting envelope is given to the network to deliver, and the send routine returns to the caller. Such simple messages are called *datagrams*. The recipient process can ask the network if any datagrams have recently arrived for the recipient, and it can wait for a datagram to arrive.

More often, the communication between two processes is via a pre-established bidirectional message pipe called a *session*. The basic session operations are open_session(), send_msg(), receive_msg(), and close_session(). The naming and authentication issues of sessions are described in Section 2.4, but the basic functions deserve some comment here.

There is a curious asymmetry in starting a session. Once started, however, sessions are completely symmetric in that each side can send and receive messages via the session. The asymmetry in session setup is similar to the asymmetry in establishing a telephone conversation: one person dials a number, the other person hears the ring and picks up the phone. Once this asymmetric call setup is done and the two people have identified each other, the telephone conversation itself is completely symmetric. Similarly, in starting the session, one process, typically a server, listens for an open_session datagram from the network. Another process, call it the client, decides it wants to talk to the server; hence, the client sends an open_session datagram to the server and waits for a response. The server examines the client's open_session request and either accepts or rejects it. Once the server has accepted the open request, and the client has been so informed, the client and server have a symmetric relationship. Either side can send at any time, and either side can unilaterally close the session at any time. The client-server distinction provides a convenient naming scheme, but the session endpoints are peers. The term *peer-to-peer communication* is often used to denote this equality.

Since datagrams seem adequate for all functions, why have sessions at all? The answer is that sessions provide several benefits over datagrams:

Shared state.   A session represents shared state between the client and the server. The next datagram might go to any process with the designated name, but a session goes to a particular instance of that name. That particular process can remember the state of the client's request. When the client is done conversing with the server, it closes the session, and the server waits for a new client's open_session() request.

Authorization-encryption.   As explained in the next section, clients and servers do not always trust each other completely. The server often checks the client's credentials to see that the client is allowed (authorized) to perform the requested function. This authorization step requires that the server establish the client's identity, that is, authenticate the client. The client may also want to authenticate the server. Once they have authenticated each other, they can use encryption to protect the contents and sequence of the messages they exchange from disclosure or alteration. The authentication and encryption protocols require multi-message exchanges. Once the session encryption key is established, it becomes shared state.

Error detection and correction.   Messages flowing in each session direction are numbered sequentially. These sequence numbers can detect lost messages (a missing sequence number) and duplicate messages (a repeated sequence number). In addition, since the underlying network knows that the client and server are in session, it can inform the endpoints if the other endpoint fails or if the link between them fails. In this way, sessions provide simple failure semantics for messages. This topic is elaborated in the next chapter.

Performance and resource scheduling.   Resolving the server names to an address, authenticating the client, and authorizing the client are fairly costly operations. Each of these steps often involves several messages. By establishing a session, this information is cached. If the client and server have only one message to exchange, there is no benefit. But if they exchange many messages, the cost of the session setup functions is paid once and amortized across many messages.

2.4 Generic System Issues

With the basic software concepts of process, address space, session, and message now introduced, the generic client-server topics of communication structure, naming, authentication, authorization, and scheduling can be discussed. Then particular topics of a file system and a communications system are covered in slightly more detail.

2.4.1 Clients and Servers

As mentioned earlier, computations and systems are structured as independently executing processes, either to provide protection and fault containment, or to reflect the geographic dispersion of the data and devices, or to structure independent and parallel computations.

How should a computation consisting of multiple interacting processes be structured? This simple question has no simple answer. Many approaches have been tried in the past, and more will be tried in the future.

One of the fundamental issues has been whether two interacting processes should behave as peers or as clients and servers. These two structures are contrasted as follows:

Peer-to-peer.   The two processes are independent peers, each executing its computation and occasionally exchanging data with the other.

Client-server.   The two processes interact via request-reply exchanges in which one process, the *client*, makes a request to a second process, the *server*, which performs this request and replies to the client.

The debate over this structuring issue has been heated and confused. The controversy centers around the point that peer-to-peer is general; it subsumes client-server as a special case. Client-server, on the other hand, is easy to program and to understand; it is fine for most applications.

To understand the simplicity of the client-server model, imagine that a program wants to read a record of a file. It can issue a read subroutine call (a procedure call) to the local file system to get the record's value from the file. Virtually all our programming languages and programming styles encourage this operation-on-object approach to computing, in this case,

read(file, record_id) returns (record_value).

This programming model is at the core of object-oriented programming, which applies methods to objects. In client-server computing, the server implements the methods on the object. When the client invokes the method (procedure, subroutine), the invocation parameters are sent to the server as a message, then the server performs the operation and returns the response as a message to the client process. The invocation software copies the response message into the client's address space and returns to the client as though the method had been executed by a local procedure.

The transparent invocation of server procedures is called *remote procedure call* (RPC). To the client programmer (program), remote procedure calls look just like local procedure calls. The client program stops executing, and a message is sent to the server, which executes and replies to the client. On the server side, the invocation also looks just like a local procedure call. That is, the server thinks it was called by a local client. The mechanisms that achieve this are elaborated in Chapter 6, but the basic idea is diagrammed in Figure 2.12.

The RPC model seems wonderful. It fits our programing model, it is simple, and many standard versions of it are emerging. What, then, is the controversy about? Why do some prefer the peer-to-peer approach? The answer is complex. The client-server model postulates

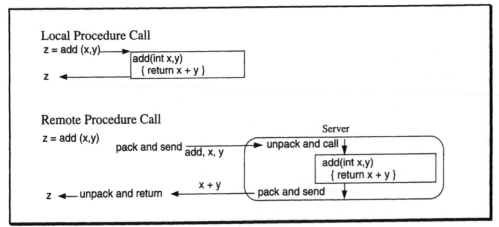

Figure 2.12: Local and remote procedure calls. Remote procedure call mechanisms give the client and the server the illusion that they are local to each other. The RPC mechanism packs the client's parameters as a message sent to the server. At the server process, the RPC invocation mechanism unpacks the parameters and invokes the server method with a local call. The results of the server method are packed by the RPC mechanism as a reply message that is returned to the client. The client RPC mechanism unpacks this reply, moves it to the client address space, and continues the client execution. In their pure forms, local procedure call and a remote procedure call look identical to the client and the server.

a one-to-one relationship between requests and replies. While this is fine for most computations, there are cases in which one request generates thousands of replies, or where thousands of requests generate one reply. Operations that have this property include transferring a file between the client and server or bulk reading and writing of databases. In other situations, a client request generates a request to a second server, which, in turn, replies to the client. Parallelism is a third area where simple RPC is inappropriate. Because the client-server model postulates synchronous remote procedure calls, the computation uses one processor at a time. However, there is growing interest in schemes that allow many processes to work on problems in parallel. The RPC model in its simplest form does not allow any parallelism. To achieve parallelism, the client does not block waiting for the server response; rather, the client issues several requests and then waits for the answers.

It appears that the debate between the remote procedure call and peer-to-peer models will be resolved by constructing the underlying mechanisms—the messages and sessions—on the peer-to-peer model, while basing most programming interfaces on the client-server model. Applications needing a non-standard model would use the underlying mechanisms directly to get the more general model.

One other generic issue concerning clients and servers deserves discussion here. Where do the servers come from? Here, there are two fundamentally different models, *push* and *pull*. In the push model, typical of transaction processing systems, the servers are created by a controlling process, the transaction processing monitor (TP monitor). As client requests arrive, the TP monitor allocates servers to clients, pushing work onto the servers. In the pull style, typical of local network file servers, an ad hoc mechanism creates the servers, which offer their services to the world via a public name server. Clients looking for a particular service call the name server. The name server returns the names of one or more servers that have advertised the desired service. The client then contacts the server directly. In this model, the servers manage themselves, and they pull work into the system. Pull results in higher server utilization since idle servers advertize for work, rather than having busy clients search for idle servers.

To summarize, the client-server structure lends itself to a request-reply programming style that dovetails with procedural programming languages. The server implements operations (methods, procedures) on objects, much in the style of object-oriented programming. The client invokes these procedures as though the objects were local, and the remote procedure call mechanism orchestrates the execution of the procedure by a remote server.

2.4.2 Naming

Every object, whether a process, a file, or a device, has a *name*, an *address*, and a *location*. The name is an abstract identifier for the object, the address is the path to the object, and the location is where the object is. As an example, the telephone named Bruce Lindsay's Office has the address 408-927-1747 and is located at some electronic address inside IBM's phone network. The name never changes, but Bruce may change locations, moving his telephone to a new office with the same phone number, or he may change addresses by going to MIT for a year.

An object can have several names. Some of these names may be synonyms, called *aliases*. Let us say that Bruce and Lindsay are two aliases for Bruce Lindsay. For this to be explicit, all names, addresses, and locations must be interpreted in some context, called a *directory*. For example, in our RPC context, Bruce means Bruce Nelson, and in our publishing context, Bruce means Bruce Spatz. Within the 408 telephone area, Bruce Lindsay's address is 927-1747, and outside the United States it is +1-408-927-1747 (where the + stands for the international access code used to get to the root of the international telephone address space in the caller's country).

Names are grouped into a hierarchy called the *name space*. An international commission has defined a universal name space standard, X.500, for computer systems. The commission administers the root of that name space. Each interior node of the hierarchy is a directory. A sequence of names delimited by a period (.) gives a *path name* from the directory to the object.

No one stores the entire name space—it is too big, and it is changing too rapidly. Certain processes, called *name servers*, store parts of the name space local to their neighborhood; in addition, they store a directory of more global name servers.

Clients use name servers to resolve server names to addresses. They then present these server addresses, along with requests, to the network. The network transports the requests to the server location, where it presents the request to the server (when the server asks for it). This is the scenario whereby sessions are established between clients and servers, and whereby remote procedure calls are implemented.

There is a startup problem: clients have to find the name and address of the local name server. To facilitate this, name servers generally have *well-known names* and addresses. A client wanting to resolve a name to an address sends a message to the well-known address or broadcasts the message to a well-known name on the local network. Once the name server responds to the client, the client knows the local name server's address. The client can then ask the local name server for the addresses of more global name servers.

2.4.3 Authentication

When a client first connects to a server, each may want to establish the identity of the other. Consider the simple case of accessing your bank from your workstation. The bank wants to be sure that the person at the workstation is you, and you want to be sure that you are talking to your bank and not some Trojan horse that will steal your passwords and financial data. In computer terms, each process wants to *authenticate* the other: to establish the *authorization identity*, or *authid,* of the other. Every process executes under some authorization identity. This identity usually can be traced back to some person and, therefore, often is called the *userid.*

How can the client authenticate itself to a server? How can it convince the server of the client's authorization identity? Conversely, how can the server convince the client? There are many answers to these questions, and there are many subtleties. Generically, however, there are two solutions: either (1) the client and the server must have a shared secret, or (2) the client and the server must trust some higher authority.

Passwords are the simplest case of shared secrets. The client has a secret password, a string of bytes known only to it and the server. The client sends this password to the server to prove the client's identity. A second secret password is then needed to authenticate the server to the client. Thus, two passwords are required.

Another shared secret approach, called *challenge-response,*[5] uses only one password or key. In this scheme, the client and the server share a secret encryption key. The server picks a random number, N, and encrypts it with the key as EN. The server sends the encrypted

---

[5] Challenge-response is the basis of IBM's SNA authentication mechanism.

number, *EN*, to the client and challenges the client to decrypt it using the secret key, that is, to compute *N* from *EN*. If the client *responds* with *N*, the server believes the client knows the secret encryption key. The client can also authenticate the server by challenging it to decrypt a second random number. This protocol is especially secure because it sends only random numbers between the client and the server, no third party can see the shared secret. It may seem to introduce extra messages, but it turns out that the challenges and responses can piggyback on session-open messages, so that no extra message flows are needed.

A third scheme uses no shared secrets at all. Each authid has a pair of keys—a *public encryption key, EK*, and a *private decryption key, DK*. The keys are chosen so that $DK(EK(X)) = X$, but knowing only *EK* and *EK(X)* it is hard to compute *X*. Thus, a process's ability to compute *X* from *EK(X)* is proof that the process knows the secret *DK*. Each authid publishes its public key to the world. Anyone wanting to authenticate the process as that authid goes through the challenge protocol: The challenger picks a random number *X*, encrypts it with the authid's public key *EK*, and challenges the process to compute *X* from *EK(X)*.

All these schemes rest on some form of key, but where do the keys come from? How do the client and the server get them securely? This issue, called *key distribution*, immediately brings some higher authority into the picture: someone or something that can make keys and securely distribute them. Such entities are called *authentication servers*. There are many different ways to structure authentication servers, but a fairly simple scheme goes as follows: The network is partitioned into *authentication domains*. Authorization identifiers become local to a domain in that an authorization identifier has a two-part name: (1) the authentication domain and (2) the authorization id within that domain. For example, if Sam is working in the government authentication domain called Gov, then Gov.Sam is Sam's authid in the government authentication domain. All requests by Sam will be authorized against this authid. Authentication servers have a trusted way of securely communicating with each other so that they can certify these authids and their public keys. This communication mechanism is itself set up by some higher (human) authority.

A process acquires its authid by connecting to a local authentication server and authenticating itself. This authentication can be done via passwords, by challenge-response, or by some other scheme. Suppose a client in one authentication domain wants to talk to a server at a remote node and, at a remote authentication domain. Consider how the server authenticates the client: The server asks its authentication server for the client's public key. The server's authentication server asks the authentication server "owning" the client for the client's public key. The authentication servers return the client's public key to the server, which can then perform the challenge-response protocol. The main issue is trust—who trusts whom about what. In the scenario described above, trust takes two forms: (1) a process trusts its local authentication server to provide correct public keys, and (2) each authentication server trusts other authentication servers to provide the public keys of authids in their domains.

2.4.4 Authorization

What happens once a process has established an authid and a server has authenticated a client as having that authid? The server now knows who the client is and what the client wants to do. The question then becomes, Is the client's authid allowed to perform that operation on that object? This decision, called *authorization*, can be expressed as the following simple predicate:

```
boolean = Authorize( object, authid, operation);
```

The Authorize() predicate can be viewed as a three-dimensional boolean array or as an SQL table. The array, called the *access control matrix*, is quite sparse and stores only the TRUE entries. Usually, a column of the array is stored with the object. That is, the authorization logic keeps a list of ⟨authid,operation⟩ pairs for an object, called the object's *access control list*. Alternatively, SQL systems routinely keep a three-column privileges table indexed by ⟨object, authid⟩. Either scheme quickly answers the authorization question.

The object owner often wants to grant access to everybody, or to all bank tellers, or to everybody in his group. Thus far, we have not encountered the concept of an *authority group*—a list of authids, or a predicate on authids. The group concept eases administration of the access control matrix and collapses its size. For example, to grant everybody in group G read authority on object O, the ⟨O, G, read⟩ element would be added to the privileges table. When a member of the group wanted to read the object, the authorization test would check the requestor's membership in group G.

Some systems, especially governmental ones, want to know each time an authentication or authorization step happens. At such points, a record or message about the step must be sent to a security *auditing* server, which collects this information for later analysis.

Once the authorization check has been passed, the requestor is given a *capability* to operate on the object. This capability is often just a control block stored in the client's context at the server. For example, if the client opens a file, the server allocates a file control block, which indicates the read-write privileges of the client. Thereafter, the client refers to the control block by a token, and the server uses the contents of the control block to avoid retesting the client's authority on each call. Occasionally, the client must be given the capability directly; an example is if the server does not maintain client state. In this case, the server generally encrypts the control block and sends it to the client as a *capability*. When the client later presents the encrypted control block, the server decrypts it, decides that it is still valid, and then acts on it.

When a client calls a server, the server may, in turn, have to call a second server to perform the client's request. For example, when your client calls a mail server and asks it to send a file, the server has to get the file either indirectly from your client or directly from the file server. When the mail system server goes to the file server, the mail system wants to use your (the client's) authority to access the file. A mechanism that allows a server to act with the authority of the client is called *amplification*. Amplification is difficult to control because of the question of how and when the server's amplified authority gets revoked. However, some form of amplification is essential to structuring client-server computations.

2.4.5 Scheduling and Performance

Once a server starts executing a request, the performance of the server becomes an issue. From the client's perspective, performance is measured by the server's *response time*: the time between the submission of the request and the receipt of the response. Response time has two components: (1) *wait time*—the time spent waiting for the server or, once the server is executing, the time spent waiting for resources, and (2) *service time*—the time needed to process the request when no waiting is involved. As the utilization of a server or resource

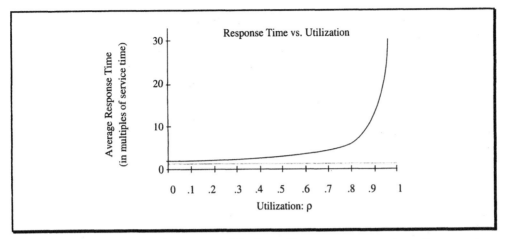

Figure 2.13: Server response time versus utilization. The average response time of a server rises dramatically as its utilization rises. This graph shows a typical situation, in which the server's response time increases due to queueing delays, following Equation 2.10. At 90% utilization, the server's response time is ten times longer; at 95% utilization it is 20 times longer. Often, performance improvement is more a matter of reducing queues than of reducing service time itself.

increases, the wait time rises dramatically. In many situations,[6] the average response time can be predicted from the server utilization, ρ, by the formula,

$$\text{Average\_Response\_Time}(\rho) = \frac{1}{1 - \rho} \bullet \text{Service\_Time} \tag{2.10}$$

Equation 2.10 is graphed in Figure 2.13. Notice that for low utilization—say, less than 50%—the response time is close to the service time, but then it quickly rises. At 75% utilization it is four times the service time, and at 90% utilization, it is ten times the service time.

There are two ways to improve response time: reduce service time or reduce wait time. This subsection deals primarily with ways to reduce wait time of critical jobs by scheduling them in preference to less-critical jobs. Each process has an integer *priority*, that determines how quickly the process's resource requests will be granted. In general, a high-priority process should be scheduled in preference to a low-priority process, and processes with the same priority should be scheduled so that they all make approximately the same rate of progress. A typical scheme is for high-priority requests to preempt low-priority requests and for requests of the same priority to be scheduled using a round-robin mechanism. Batch jobs get low priority and run in the background, while interactive jobs get high priority and are serviced as quickly as possible.

Servers generally service clients in priority order. To do this, the server must have a queue of requests that it can sort in priority order. This, in turn, suggests that many clients are waiting for the server. Such waiting is exactly what priority scheduling tries to avoid. Rather than having a single server process, then, each request should have its own server process. This concept, called a *server class*, is discussed in Chapter 6. Server classes reduce queueing for servers.

---

[6] The assumptions are m/m/1: Poisson arrivals, negative exponential service times, and a single server [Highleyman 1988].

What should the server priority be, once the server starts executing a client request? In many systems, the server has its own priority, independent of the client. Often, server priorities are high compared to any other priorities, so that services have short wait times. However, this approach—fixed server priorities—breaks down in a client-server environment. A low-priority client running on a workstation can bombard a high-priority server with long-running requests, creating a *priority inversion* problem: a server performing low-priority requests at high priority, thereby causing truly high-priority work to wait for the low-priority task to complete. The server should run requests at the client's priority, or perhaps at the client's priority plus 1, so that client requests are executed in priority order.

2.4.6 Summary

This section introduced several client-server issues. First, RPCs were defined and the general peer-to-peer versus RPC issue was reviewed. Then, the issues of naming, authentication, and authorization were sketched. Finally, the issue of scheduling clients and servers in a network was reviewed. The discussion now turns briefly to file systems in a client-server environment.

2.5 Files

Files represent external storage devices to the application program in a device-independent way. A file system abstracts physical memory devices as files, which are large arrays of bytes. Chapters 13–15 describe a transactional file system in detail. This section gives a brief background on standard file systems.

2.5.1 File Operations

Files are created and deleted by the create() and delete() operations. In reality, the create operation has a vast number of parameters, but for present purposes a file name will suffice. As discussed in the previous section, names are merely strings of characters that are resolved to an address by looking in some name server. The file system usually acts as a name server, implementing a hierarchical name space. A file server with the name "net.node.server" might implement a file named "a.b.c" with the resulting file name "net.node.server.a.b.c". The local file system and remote file servers accept file creation operations in a manner similar to this:

```
enum        STATUS = {OK, FAILED};      /* success or failure from the file routines          */
typedef     char * filename;
STATUS      create( filename );
STATUS      delete( filename );
```

Once created, a file can be accessed in one of two ways. The first approach is to *map* the file to a slot of a process address space, so that ordinary machine instructions can read and write the file's bytes. Address spaces share memory by mapping the same file. For example, processes running a certain program map the binary version of that program to their address spaces. The operations for such *memory-mapped files* are something like this:

```
STATUS      map_file( filename, address_space, slot);
STATUS      unmap_file( address_space, slot);
```

A second approach, and by far the most common, is to explicitly copy data between files and memory. This style first *opens* the file and then issues read and write file actions to copy the data between the file and memory. These are the approximate operations for such *explicit* file actions:

```
typedef     struct {} FILE;            /* the standard UNIX FILE handle definition       */
STATUS      open(filename, * FILE);
STATUS      close(* FILE);
```

The execution of the open() routine gives a good example of the concepts of the previous section. When a client invokes the open() routine, code in the client's library goes through the following logic: First, it must look up the name to find the file server owning that file. Often, the name is cached by the client library, but let us suppose it is not. In that case, the client asks the name server for the file server address. The client then sends the open request to the file server at that address. The file server authenticates the client and then looks for the file in its name space. If the file is found, the file server looks at the file descriptor, which, among other things, contains an access control list. The file server examines the file's access control list to see if the client is authorized to open the file. If so, the file server creates a capability for the file (a control block that allows quick access to the file) and returns this capability to the client.

Given one of these file capabilities, the client can read and write bytes from the file using the following routines:

```
STATUS      read (FILE, file_address, memory_address, length); /* move file bytes to memory        */
STATUS      write(FILE, file_address, memory_address, length); /* move memory bytes to file        */
```

Notice that these are not exactly the UNIX routines; the standard UNIX read routine sequentially reads or writes the next bytes of the file. UNIX file positioning is done by a separate call, lseek(). Combined addressing and data copy operations are typical of random file access.

The two approaches, mapped files and explicit file access, are equivalent. The benefit of memory-mapped files is obvious: they make file access automatic. Historically, database implementors have preferred explicit access because database systems encapsulate files. Database systems carefully control file placement in memory (for clustering) and control data copies from memory to provide transactional file semantics. For 30 years, there has been a heated debate over whether memory-mapped files or explicit file access is better. The fact that this debate has continued for so long suggests that both approaches have merit.

2.5.2 File Organizations

A file system's primary role is to store the contents of named files and to provide read and write access to them. File systems maintain other descriptive information about the file to control and direct access to it. As a rule, the file system keeps a *descriptor* for each file. The descriptor contains the file name, the authid of the file creator, and an access control list of who can do what to the file. The descriptor also keeps information on the time the file was

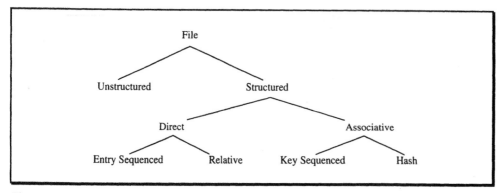

Figure 2.14: Structured and unstructured files described as a tree.   Files can be unstructured—meaning they have no obvious internal structure—or they can be structured as a collection of records. Records within a structured file can be either directly or associatively addressed. Directly addressed files either insert new records at the end of the file (entry sequenced) or insert each new record at an array address (relative). Associative files can either hash the key or store the records in key-sequenced order.

created, when it was last accessed, and when it was last archived. Of course, the file size, along with a description of how the file is mapped to storage, is part of the descriptor.

File descriptors also cover the file contents. Often a file is *unstructured*; that is, it has no simple structure. For example, the binary image of a photograph has no regular structure; a simple byte stream file is likewise unstructured. By contrast, a *structured file* is a collection of *records* with similar structure. Structured files are dichotomized by their record addressing scheme: some file organizations address records associatively (by the record contents), while others only address records directly (by the record address in the file). Chapters 13–15 describe the semantics and implementation of structured files in considerable detail. The following simple description of structured files should suffice until then (see Figure 2.14).

Entry sequence is the simplest file structure. The name comes from the way records are inserted in the file. Each new record is added to the end of the file, so that the records are stored in the sequence they entered the file. Each record address is the byte offset of the record relative to the start of the file (or some similar scheme). Entry-sequenced files can be read sequentially—first record, second record, and so on—or a record can be directly addressed by using its byte offset.

Relative files are an array of records. Initially, the array is empty. When a record is inserted into a relative file, its array index must be specified as part of the insert. Subsequently, records can be read from the file either in array order or directly by array address.

Associatively accessed files are accessed via a *record key* composed of one or more subfields of the record. All records with a given key value can be quickly retrieved. Each time a record is inserted or updated, the record's key is used to place the record in the file. There are two common record placement strategies, *hashed* and *key-sequenced*.

Hashed placement of records in a file is similar to hashing in main memory structures. The file is divided into an array of buckets. Given the key, one can quickly find the record by hashing the key to compute a bucket number and then searching that bucket for the record.

Key-sequenced placement stores the records sorted in key order. Key sequencing clusters related records together and allows sequential scanning of records in sorted order. Earlier sections of this chapter point out the benefits of this clustering and sequential access to data. When a new record arrives, its key is computed and the record is placed near records with related keys. Record insertion is a little expensive, but there are ingenious algorithms that make it competitive with hashing. Given a key value, it is easy to find the record by using binary search on the file or by using some indexing structure.

It is often desirable to associatively access a file via two different keys. For example, it is often convenient to access employees by either name or employee number. Suppose the employee records are stored in an associative file keyed by employee number (empno). Then a second associative file, keyed by employee name (empname), could store a record of the form <empname, empno> for each record in the employee file. By first looking in this second file under the empname key to find the empno, and then using this empno to associatively access the employee file, the system can fairly quickly find the desired employee record. Such index files are called *secondary indices*. It is often convenient to think of the direct address of a record as its key. If this is done, then secondary indices can be defined on direct files as well as on associative files.

Most systems allow file designers to define many secondary indices on a base file. The file system automatically maintains the records in the secondary indices as records are inserted into, updated in, and deleted from the primary file. Of course, the definition of the secondary index must be stored in the file descriptor. When a file is first opened, the descriptor is read by the server, and all subsequent record operations on the file cause the relevant secondary indices to be used and maintained.

2.5.3 Distributed Files

Parts of a file may be *distributed* among servers in a computer network. This distribution can take two forms: The files can be *partitioned* (fragments of the file are stored in different nodes), or the files can be *replicated* (the whole contents of the files are stored at several nodes).

The definitions of partitioning and replication are fairly simple. A file is broken into *fragments* by declaring the key boundaries of each fragment: All records within that key range belong to that fragment. For example, if a file is keyed by sales region and customer number, then the file might be fragmented by region, with each region having a separate fragment. These fragments might be partitioned among the computers of the various regions, with each region storing the fragment for that region. In addition, all the fragments might be replicated at central headquarters.

The descriptor of each fragment contains a complete description of the entire file. When a client opens the file, the file system looks at the descriptor and thereby knows about all the fragments. When the client issues a read-by-key, the request is dispatched to one of the servers managing that fragment. When the client issues a record insert, delete, or update operation, the request is dispatched to all servers managing the fragment that holds the record. Associated secondary index reads and writes are handled similarly.

If the file servers are transactional, then these update operations will be atomic, and the mutual consistency of the fragments, replicas, and their secondary indices will be main-

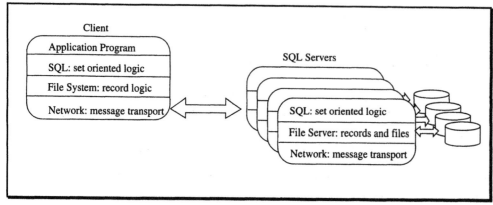

Figure 2.15: The layers of abstraction in a client-server SQL system.   The client makes calls on the local SQL libraries. These libraries may go directly to a remote SQL server via the network, or the client library may use the local file system to manage local sets of records. On the server side, the SQL system is usually built on a file server that manages the physical memory devices.

tained. If the file system is not transactional, then the fragments will quickly lose consistency as messages are lost or network nodes fail.

2.5.4 SQL

The record-oriented file system described previously is an advance over unstructured files, but it is still quite primitive. For example, the declaration of record attributes is often implicit, the logic to navigate via secondary indices is up to the client, and the client program is not insulated from changes to the file structure, such as adding or dropping indices.

There have been many attempts to raise the file-system level of abstraction. The current standard solution is the language SQL, which offers set-oriented, non-procedural data definition, manipulation, and control. (Subsection 1.3.5 gave a brief tour of SQL's features.) The main point to be made here is that SQL is a software layer executed partly in a separate protection domain of the client process and partly in a server process (see Figure 2.15). SQL calls are much like file system calls in the sense that they create and delete SQL tables (similar to files) and read and write these tables. SQL tables are usually supported by the physical file organizations outlined in Figure 2.14. Portable SQL systems often begin with unstructured files and build everything from scratch. SQL systems, integrated with their operating system, typically add SQL semantics to the record structures of the native file system.

2.6 Software Performance

Having discussed all these concepts in the abstract, let us now give them some substance. How much does all this cost? How expensive is a message? How expensive is a process? How expensive is a transaction?

The performance issues in Section 2.2 were discussed in terms of hardware. Communications performance was measured by wire bandwidths and latencies. Memory performance was in terms of latencies and transfer rates of electronic and magnetic memories. Unfortunately, both for today and for many years to come, software dominates the cost

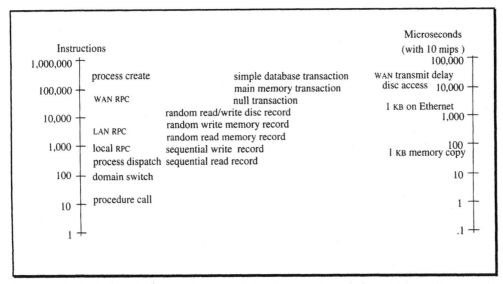

Figure 2.16: Typical performance of commercial systems. The chart at the left gives the approximate instruction cost of major operating system, transaction processing system, and database system operations. The chart at the right is in terms of microseconds. It maps the instructions on the left to a 10-mips machine and shows the latencies of disks, LANs, and WANs.

of databases and communications. It is possible, but not likely, that the newer, faster processors will make software less of a bottleneck. This section gives a sense of typical software costs for storing and fetching records from a database, typical costs for sending a message, and typical costs for doing a remote procedure call. It also discusses how these numbers compare to latencies of the underlying physical devices.

In discussions such as this, it is important to distinguish carefully between what is possible and what is common. A research prototype with the fastest database or the fastest message system slows down as it becomes a product. This slowdown comes from adding maintenance features to the code (for example defensive programming), placing the code in its own protection domain, adding diagnostics, restructuring the code so that it is easy to understand and maintain, and so on. Figure 2.16 shows typical performance numbers from commercial systems.

Figure 2.16 shows that RPCs are two or three orders of magnitude more expensive than local procedure calls. The figure also shows that with two 10-mips machines, sending a 1 KB message via Ethernet is limited by bandwidth rather than by processor speed. It shows that such machines can sequentially scan files at the rate of several thousand records per second, but that they only process a few hundred records per second in random order. Finally, it indicates that simple transactions (for example, the standard TPC-A transaction [Gray 1991]) require over 100,000 instructions to process, and that typical 10-mips systems can run about 50 such transactions per second.

When this discussion turns to future machines with 100 mips, or even with 1 bips, then all the instruction times decline by one or two orders of magnitude, bringing the software cost of a LAN RPC down to 100 or even 10 μs. As shown in Table 2.7, this is still more than the wire latencies for comparable communications in future clusters (≈5 μs), but is much less than MAN or WAN latencies (>500 μs) or disk latencies (>10,000 μs).

Perhaps the main conclusion to draw from this discussion is that the basic primitives discussed in this book—processes, sessions, messages, RPCs, transactions, files, records, SQL operations, and so on—are *large* operations. They are used for structuring a computation into a few fairly large steps.

The huge costs of these operations are not inevitable. There are lightweight analogs to most of these operations. Such lightweight systems sacrifice some of the niceties in favor of a ten-fold speedup. The resulting system is often called the *fast-path*. For example, IBM's Transaction Processing Facility (TPF) can create a process in 1,000 instructions and can run the simple DebitCredit transaction in about 40,000 instructions. But this process is really a thread (no protection domains) running on a macro package to a very simple operating system. IBM's IMS Fast Path system also runs that transaction in about 40,000 instructions by carefully optimizing the simple and common cases.

2.7 Transaction Processing Standards

Background in one more area is needed to understand distributed computing: standards for portability and for interoperation. There is a bewildering array of standards proliferating in our field. Two very important ones define a standard transactional client-server interface. They deserve to be introduced at this early stage.

2.7.1 Portability versus Interoperability Standards

This section gives a brief tour of the data communication standards relevant to transaction processing systems. Standards are defined with one or two goals in mind:

Portability. By writing programs in standard languages, the programs can be run on (ported to) many different computer systems.

Interoperability. By defining and implementing standard ways to exchange data, computers from different manufacturers can exchange data without any special conversion or interfacing code.

Programming languages such as FORTRAN, COBOL, and C are examples of portability standards. These standards require that when a program is ported to a new system, it must be recompiled for the instruction set and operating system of the new machine (as diagrammed in Figure 2.17).

2.7.2 APIs and FAPs

Most communications standards are defined for interoperability. When two software or hardware modules want to communicate (interoperate), they must agree to both a common language, or set of messages, and a protocol to exchange these messages. Standards are defined to attain interoperation among many computer vendors and to minimize the number of different languages. In discussing standards, it is important to see the distinction between the programming interface, called the *application programming interface* or API, and the communication protocol, called the *formats and protocols* or FAP. The API is syntax, while

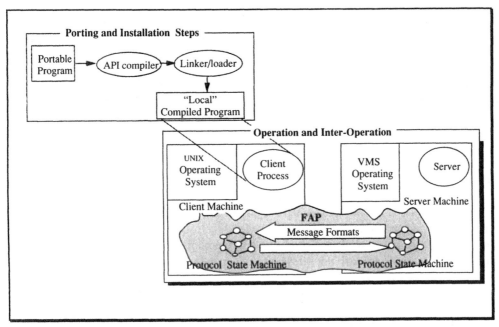

Porting and Installation Steps

Portable Program → API compiler → Linker/loader

"Local" Compiled Program

Operation and Inter-Operation

UNIX Operating System

Client Process

VMS Operating System

Server

Client Machine

Server Machine

FAP
Message Formats

Protocol State Machine   Protocol State Machine

Figure 2.17: Portability and interoperability standards. A portability standard allows a program to be run on a new machine, and an interoperability standard allows two machines to exchange data. The box at the upper left shows the steps needed to install a portable program in a process. The standard language (for example, FORTRAN, COBOL, SQL) must be compiled into instructions for the client machine and must be connected to the libraries of the client operating system. Then the program can execute. By contrast, an interoperability standard allowing two machines to interoperate consists of message formats and communications protocols in the form of a state machine, called a FAP (formats and protocols). Both computers must agree to the same FAP, but they may use completely different application programming interfaces to their local protocol machines.

the FAP is semantics. The API can be different at the two endpoints, but the FAP is a shared definition and must be the same at both endpoints. As an example from conventional programming, a Pascal program can call a C program. These programs have two different APIs (languages), but if they are to interoperate, they must agree on the way parameters are represented (for example, how arrays are mapped in storage), and they must agree on a procedure calling protocol and stack layout. In this simple case, then, the mechanics of procedure call are something like a FAP.

In communications, the FAP has two parts: (1) a detailed description of the message formats that flow on the wire or session between the endpoints, and (2) the protocol—a description of when these messages flow (see Figure 2.17). LU6.2 is further described in Subsection 16.3.5.

Message formats are the simple part of the FAP. For example, a FAP might say that a data message has the format

```
struct message {  int    address;
                   int    length;
                   char   buffer[length];
                   int    checksum;
                   };
```

where integers are twos-complement binary integers, length is the number of bytes in the buffer field, and the buffer field is an array of characters encoded with ASCII byte encoding standard number 12345. The message formats give the exact encodings of information and the exact layout of these bits in a message.

Protocols are the major part of a FAP. They define in what order messages should be sent, how the two endpoints should act on receipt of each message, and how they should act on error conditions. To take a human example, a telephone call begins with the caller dialing the callee, waiting for a ring, waiting for an answer, conversing, and then hanging up. The callee waits for a ring, answers the phone, converses, and then hangs up. Rules for handling exception conditions (for example, wrong numbers, when the callee is busy, when the callee does not answer) must be specified. Rules to handle exceptions dominate protocol definitions.

Protocol rules are often described as a state machine plus an action for each state transition. The state machine is usually expressed as a decision table, where each state transition has a semantic action. The actions are defined in a procedural programming language. Typical events driving the state machine are arriving messages, time events, and client requests.

Application programmers never see the FAP; rather, they use an API to the FAP. The API is a set of subroutines that drive the state machine, or a special language that translates to such a set of subroutines. The API tends to vary from one language to another, because the host programming syntax and data types are different. For example, the COBOL interface is slightly different from the C interface (see Figure 2.17).

APIs come in many forms. Some, like C, COBOL , and SQL, are syntactic APIs; these are programming languages. Another form of API is a set of procedure calls or subroutines. UNIX, MS/DOS, and other operating systems are defined in this way. X-Windows and many other client-server systems are also defined by a standard *call-level interface* (CLI). The ultimate in portability is the definition of a CLI for a particular computer system: such an interface is called an *application-binary interface* (ABI). An ABI allows shrink-wrapped software to be installed on a machine without any special compilation steps and with a very simple linkage operation (linking the programs to the operating system library). MS/DOS on Intel 386 machines is the most common ABI today, but each computer family defines an ABI.

The respective benefits of a standard API and a standard FAP can be recapped in this way: A standard API makes a program portable, while a FAP allows two computers to interoperate. The concepts are orthogonal.

The proliferation of computers has created a comparable proliferation of communication standards. These standards can be classified as *de jure standards*—those defined by an international standards body—and *de facto standards*—those defined by an industry leader or an ad hoc consortium. It is common for a de facto standard to become a de jure standard over time. This happened to FORTRAN, SDLC, Ethernet, C, and SQL, and it is now happening in the transaction processing area.

2.7.3 LU6.2, a de facto Standard

Transaction processing communication standards provide an interesting example of these ideas. IBM has a de facto networking standard called Systems Network Architecture (SNA). SNA has many aspects, but one part of it defines a protocol to invoke remote transactional servers. This FAP, called LU (logical unit) 6.2, defines how a client can invoke a remote transactional server and establish a session with it. Since one server may invoke others, the set of servers and sessions forms a tree. LU6.2 specifies the formats and protocols to coordinate the atomic commitment of all members of such a tree of servers.

There are many application programming interfaces to LU6.2. They are generically called APPC (*advanced program-to-program communication* or *application peer-to-peer communication*). The original APPC implementation was done by IBM's CICS and had a syntactic style API of the form

EXEC CICS SEND_DATA RESOURCE session DATA buffer LENGTH length RETURNS ERROR status;

This syntactic standard requires a preprocessor (much as SQL does) and is not convenient for non-CICS environments. IBM adopted a procedural interface (a CLI) when it added LU6.2 to its standard list of programming interfaces. The result, known as *common programming interface for communications* (CPI-C), has a format like this:

status = cpic_send_data(session, buffer, length);

The procedural standard varies only slightly from language to language, the variation being the different calling conventions and datatypes of each language. This CLI approach simplifies the API by eliminating a special compiler for the API (see Figure 2.17). CPI-C (pronounced *sip-ich*) standardizes the LU6.2 API across all computer environments.

2.7.4 OSI-TP with X/Open DTP, a de jure Standard

Subsequent to IBM's SNA de facto standard, the International Standards Organization (ISO) has been defining a network architecture called *Open Systems Interconnection* (OSI). Several aspects of OSI define function in ways roughly equivalent to LU6.2 One standard, called *Remote Operations Services* (ROSE), defines how a client can invoke a server. Another standard, called *Commit, Concurrency Control, and Recovery* (OSI-CCR), defines the commit message protocols on a single session. A third standard, *Transaction Processing* (OSI-TP), defines how transaction identifiers should be created and managed. OSI-TP also specifies how commit should propagate in the tree of sessions and how session endpoints can resolve incomplete transactions after a failure. Fortunately, OSI-TP and LU6.2 are quite similar. To some extent, OSI-TP is a redefinition of LU6.2 in OSI terms. The redefinition repaired several minor LU6.2 flaws.

All the OSI standards of the previous paragraph are FAPs; they have no API. Thus, they allow transaction processing systems to interoperate, but they do not provide a way to write portable transaction processing applications or servers. A second standards body, X/Open, recognized this problem and is defining the X/Open *Distributed Transaction Processing* standard (X/Open DTP) to solve it. This standard defines the concept of resource managers coordinated by a transaction manager. Any subsystem that implements transactional data can be a resource manager (RM). Database systems, transactional file systems, transactional queue managers, and transactional session managers are typical resource managers. The transaction manager (TM) coordinates transaction initiation and completion among these resource managers. It also communicates with other transaction managers to coordinate the completion of distributed transactions.

X/Open DTP defines a library of procedures (a CLI) to begin a transaction, to declare a transaction abort, and to commit a transaction. This application-TM CLI is called the TX-interface. X/Open also defines a subroutine library for the resource managers to register with their local transaction manager, and for the transaction manager to invoke them at system restart and at transaction begin, commit, and abort. This TM-RM call-level interface comprises the so-called XA-interface. As described, this is sufficient for a portable, one-node transaction processing application or resource manager. Two mechanisms are needed for transactions or resources to be distributed: (1) a remote invocation mechanism and (2) a distributed transaction mechanism. Remote invocation is provided by ISO's ROSE and by the many remote procedure call mechanisms. X/Open DTP specifies that the FAP for coordinating distributed transactions, the TM-TM interface, is OSI-TP.

The X/Open DTP design allows database vendors to write portable systems that act as resource managers and allow customers to write portable applications. It also allows vendors to write portable transaction managers. The standard is still evolving; this text attempts to follow its terminology and notation. A general picture of the X/Open DTP design is shown in Figure 2.18.

The work flow in X/Open DTP is approximately as follows. In the single-node case, an application invokes the TM to begin a transaction. It then invokes one or more resource managers, which may join the transaction. If the application fails, or if it asks the TM to abort the transaction, then the TM calls each resource manager and asks it to abort that

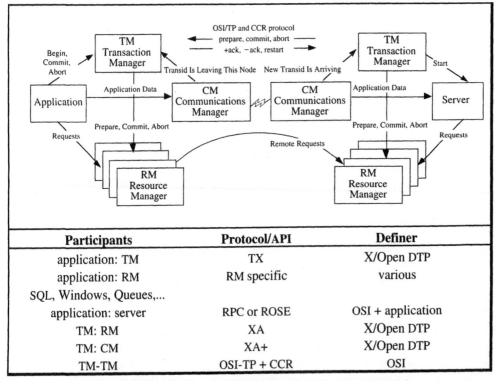

Participants	Protocol/API	Definer
application: TM	TX	X/Open DTP
application: RM	RM specific	various
SQL, Windows, Queues,...		
application: server	RPC or ROSE	OSI + application
TM: RM	XA	X/Open DTP
TM: CM	XA+	X/Open DTP
TM-TM	OSI-TP + CCR	OSI

Figure 2.18: The many standards involved in a distributed transaction. Each resource manager (RM) registers with its local transaction manager (TM). Applications start and commit transactions by calling their local TM. At commit, the TM invokes every participating RM. If the transaction is distributed, the communications manager informs the local and remote TM about the incoming or outgoing transaction, so that the two TMs can use the OSI-TP protocol to commit the transaction.

transaction. If the application calls commit, then the transaction manager calls each resource manager and asks it to commit (see Figure 2.18).

If an application is distributed, then the application or a resource manager at one TM invokes an application or resource manager controlled by a second TM. In this case, both TMs are involved in the transaction commit. In order for the transaction managers to sense the distributed transaction, the communication managers (the network software) must inform them that the transaction is being distributed. This is shown in Figure 2.18, where the transaction manager on the left hears about the outgoing transaction identifier, and the transaction manager on the right hears about the incoming transaction identifier (this is called the XA+ interface). When the application commits or aborts, the two transaction managers will use the OSI-TP protocols to coordinate the transaction commit.

In summary, the combination of OSI and all its standards (notably ROSE, CCR, and TP) results in a transaction processing FAP. X/Open DTP provides a transaction processing API. To the reader unfamiliar with this material, the acronyms may be daunting. The important concepts to remember are that one mechanism, a FAP, is needed for interoperation, and a second mechanism, an API, is needed for portability.

A FAP can have many different APIs. Within the world of APIs, there are two kinds of interfaces: syntactic APIs like SQL, and procedural APIs like the UNIX libraries. Such procedural APIs are called CLIs, which stands for *call-level interface*. A CLI can be combined with an operating system definition and a machine definition to allow a standard binary interface for applications, better known as shrink-wrapped software. You can compile a program that uses the UNIX library and port it to any binary compatible UNIX machine. A syntactic API does not provide such binary compatibility. The source program must be recompiled on the target machine.

2.8 Summary

This chapter has covered the basic hardware and software concepts from the perspective of client-server distributed computing. Section 2.2 discussed hardware trends. It argued that the declining price of hardware is encouraging decentralization of computers by moving the processing and data closer to the data sources or consumers. These hardware trends also encourage structuring server machines as clusters of processors offering server interfaces to their data. The hardware discussion also introduced memory hierarchies and the technology trends of memory devices.

The basic software notions of address space, process, message, and session were then reviewed. With these concepts in place, the issues of client-server computing were outlined. First, remote procedure call was defined and contrasted with peer-to-peer structures. Then the issues of naming, authentication, authorization, and performance were surveyed, with particular focus on a client-server architecture.

This material was followed with a brief survey of file system terminology. File operations and organizations were described by way of introducing the standard types of files: keyed, hashed, relative, and entry sequenced.

The presentation then showed how expensive all these objects are. It pointed out that processes, RPCs, records, and transactions are large objects, consisting of many thousands of instructions. A computation is structured as, at most, a few hundred such operations per second. This is programing in the large.

The chapter ended with a brief tour of TP standards: This alphabet soup described the players and the current state of play. It mentioned the industry standard LU6.2 and CPI-C from IBM, as well as the de jure standards OSI-TP and X/Open DTP. It is important to be aware of these standards. They are treated in more detail in later chapters.

The underlying theme of Section 2.4 was that distributed computing is coming; in fact, it has already arrived. Distributed computing needs principles to structure it. Client-server, naming, authentication, authorization, and scheduling are essential techniques for structuring distributed computations. The transaction mechanisms described in the remainder of this book are also key to structuring distributed computations.

Exercises

1. [2.1, 5] A Kb is 2.4% bigger than a KB. How much bigger is a GB than a Gb?

2. [2.2.1.2, 15] Using Figure 2.3, compute the cost/access/second of a tape robot storing a nearline terabyte with a single tape drive. What if the robot has ten tape drives (and the same price)?

3. [2.2.1.2, 10] If a disk spins twice as fast, what is the new transfer rate, latency, and seek time? If MAD increases by a factor of four what is the new transfer rate?

4. [2.2.1.2, 10] In the example of Subsection 2.2.1.2 comparing sequential to random access, sequential was faster by a factor of 151:1. Suppose the requests had been for a thousand 1 MB records rather than a thousand 1 KB records. What would the relative advantage of sequential be? At what transfer size is there a 10:1 advantage?

5. [2.2.1.3, 10] Given the cost/access for a tape robot, and given the costs for disks used in the discussion of the five-minute rule, and assuming that the object size is 1 MB, what is the break-even frequency for a tape robot at which it makes more sense to store the data on disk than to access it on tape each time? Assume the most optimistic cost/access for a tape robot from Problem 2.

6. [2.2.1.3, discussion] (a) Are disks dead? (b) Given Hoagland's Law and Moore's Law, and the prices from Figure 2.2, in what year will the laws intersect? (c) At that time, what will a tape look like in terms of capacity and latency?

7. [2.2.2, 10] The processor event horizon is the round-trip time/distance a signal can propagate between processor steps (clocks). This time/distance determines how much interaction the processor can have with its neighboring processors. What is the processor event horizon of a 1 bips processor given that the speed of light on a chip is about $2 \cdot 10^8$ m/s?

8. [2.2.3, 5] What fraction of the 1 KB send time is wire latency for a 1990 cluster or WAN (Table 2.6)? What about the year 2000 cluster or WAN?

9. [2.2.4, 25] Suppose a 1 bips processor has a big cache, which gives it 99% hit rates (a very good number). (a) What is the data request rate to main memory if each instruction generates two references? (b) If main memory has 20 ns access times, what is the effective cache speed? (c) Suppose a frequently accessed piece of data is stored in a *shared* RAM disk as a 4 KB block, or it is stored in a server. The RAM-disk copy proceeds at 1 GBps, and so the processor can read or write it in 4 µs. Consider the read/write rules for the RAM-disk pages. What kind of synchronization is needed with other processors so that this processor can read and update the RAM-disk page? Suppose the RAM disk is a processor itself, which accepts RPCs. What is the cost of doing a read or an update to the RAM disk via RPC versus the cost of doing it via data reservation and moving?

10. [2.4.1, 10] Suppose a client wants to transfer a 1 MB file to a server over a WAN with 50 ms one-way latency and .1 MBps transfer rate. Assume 1 KB message packets and ignore message addressing and checksumming overheads. Also ignore CPU time at the client and server. What is the best RPC time to transfer the file? What is the best peer-to-peer time to transfer the file?

11. [2.4.1, 10] Consider an RPC where the client uses four-byte one's-complement integers and the server uses eight-byte two's-complement integers. Who is responsible for the translation of the parameters? What if the translation is impossible?

12. [2.3.3, 5] Suppose my system uses passwords over Ethernet, as described in Subsection 2.4.3. (a) How would you break into my system? (b) It was mentioned that challenge-response messages can piggyback on open_session messages. How does that work?

13. [2.4.5, 10] In Subsection 2.4.5, there was considerable discussion of process priorities. Where do priorities come from? In a network, how does the server know the client priority? Does it make sense for separate threads in an address space to have separate priorities?

14. [2.4.5, 5] In Subsection 2.4.5 it was suggested that the server run at the client priority plus one? Why is that a good idea?

15. [2.5.2, 10] The end of Subsection 2.5.2 mentioned that implementors of structured files do not want to give users memory-mapped access to the files. Why?

16. [2.5.3, 10] Consider the accounts SQL table defined in Subsection 1.3.5.1. It was partitioned by primary key (account id). How would record read and insert be executed if the table were partitioned by customer number instead?

17. [2.6, 10] Suppose a transaction consists of an two LAN RPCs, four random in-memory record reads, and the null transaction overhead. Using Figure 2.16, what is the approximate instruction cost of such a transaction and what is its elapsed time on a 10 mips processor?

18. [2.6, 20] Suppose a transaction has a 5 ms service time and that there are no bottlenecks (resources that are 100% utilized and so limit the system throughput). Suppose the average transaction response time must be 100 ms or less. Using Equation 2.10, determine the maximum transaction throughput of the system that still satisfies this response time requirement. Do the same calculation for a processor that is ten times slower.

19. [2.7.1, 10] Shrink-wrapped software that you copy to a computer and then run immediately is the ultimate in portability. Suppose the program is stand-alone (no networking is involved). What standard interfaces do you need to write such a program? Hint: Such standards are called application binary interfaces (ABIs).

20. [2.7.1, 15] X/Open did not define an API for the TM-TM. It just specified a FAP, namely OSI-TP. Under what circumstances would the TM-TM interface need an API?

21. [2.7.2, 20] Try to design a FAP for a human telephone. The FAP should describe both the caller and the callee role. That is, unless the phone is "off hook," the caller is a potential callee (if the phone rings). Proceed with this exercise as follows: (a) Write the error-free FAP. (b) Pick five error cases, add them to your FAP, and notice how much larger the program/decision table has grown. (c) Enumerate ten more error cases. (d) Based on the measurement sub-problem (b), extrapolate the size of the FAP to handle these exceptions (note that the extrapolation is often combinatorial, not linear).

Answers

1. 10%.

2. Robot access time is in the [30 second, 2 minute] range and access/second is between [.008,.033]. Cost per byte is in the [.01$/MB to 1$/MB] range. So the minimum cost is 10 k$ and the maximum cost is 1M$. The best case is 10,000/.033 ≈ 300 k$/a/s. The worst case is 120 m$/a/s. If the robot includes ten tape drives, these numbers drop by a factor of ten to between 30 k$/a/s and 12 m$/a/s.

3. Transfer rate is determined by how fast the bits pass the read-write heads. So double the spin doubles the transfer rate and cuts the latency in half, but it should not affect the seek time. If the magnetic area density increases by a factor of four, then the linear density doubles. So the transfer rate doubles, and the seek and latency are unchanged.

4. Computation is the same except that the total transfer time goes from 0.1 sec to 100 sec. The cost ratios are 100 seconds for sequential and 115 seconds for the random case, and the ratio is 1.15:1. At 10:1 the following equation holds: $10(L + 1000BT) = 1000(L + BT)$, where L is the latency and BT is the time to transfer a block. A little algebra gives $BT = 1.65$ ms. At 10 MB ps, this is a 16.5 KB block.

5. Using Equation 2.7, (Disk_Cost/Byte – Tape_Cost/Byte) • Object_Bytes = 10$ – .1$ = 9.9$. From Problem 2, the best cost/access is for the ten-drive robot and is about 30 k$/a/s, so frequently = $(9.9/3 • 10^4) ≈ 1$ access per 3,000 seconds, or about 1 access per fifty minutes. So a tape robot satisfies the fifty-minute rule.

6. (a) We don't know. (b) About 2010. (c) 100 GB, same latency.

7. A 1 bips processor has a 10^{-9} clock, and the signal must travel out and back, so event horizon is 10^{-1} meters or 10 cm. This is approximately the size of a processor chip or a very small circuit board. Since wires are rarely straight, have capacitance and resistance, the event horizon of a 1 bips processor is about 1 cm. This puts a real damper on shared memory.

8. 1990: cluster: 5%; WAN: 25%; 2000: cluster: 83%; WAN: 100%.

9. (a) 20/ns, (b) 1.2 ns, (c) high!

10. A thousand RPCs are needed. They each have a 100 ms round-trip time, plus the message transmit time of 10 ms on a .1 MBps link. So each RPC needs 110 ms, and the total time is 110 seconds. In a peer-to-peer design, the client can send packets and the server can ack the last one. So the elapsed peer-to-peer time is about 10 seconds. This is the sort of example that makes peer-to-peer converts.

11. The RPC mechanism at the client or server must do the translation. If the translation is impossible (can't fit 2^{33} into a four-byte integer) then the RPC must signal an exception.

12. (a) To find passwords, tap the Ethernet, watch the passwords go by, and use them later. (b) In challenge-response, the client can send a challenge in the open message, the server can send a response and a challenge in the reply to the open message, and the client can send its response to the challenge on the first client request to the server.

13. Priority is a process-global variable. It is set by some administrative policy (e.g., person). The RPC invocation code should include the client priority in the message. The RPC receipt code should process requests in priority order and should set the server priority to the client priority plus one. Yes, different threads may be working for different clients and so should have different priorities.

14. It is desirable for servers to run at higher priority than clients so that clients do not preempt their servers or servers working for other clients with the same priority. If clients can preempt servers, server queues can get very long.

15. Access to structured files is complex, involving secondary indices, key lookups, and space allocation in a file. The file system wants to encapsulate these operations. The file system itself may run in a separate protection domain from the client, and the file system may memory map the files, but the file system does not want to give users byte-level access to the files. Incidentally, these issues are less relevant to clients with private files. They may not be willing to pay for the benefits of encapsulation.

16. The file would now be key sequenced on the account number key. Insert would send its update to the fragment based on the partitioning criterion. Sequential read of the table would be unchanged, but it would be in customer-number order. Read by customer number would send a read to the designated partition. To support read by primary key (account id) and to quickly test for primary key uniqueness, a secondary key-sequenced index would be created on the account id. This secondary index would be used to satisfy any read-by-primary-key requests. Maintenance of the secondary index would add extra work to any insert, update, and delete calls.

17. 2 LAN RPC $\approx$ 2 • 3,000 instructions; 4 random in-memory record accesses is $\approx$ 4 • 3000; null transaction is $\approx$30,000 instructions; so the total is 48,000 instructions or 4.8 ms.

18. The transaction response time must be about 100 ms, which is 20 times the basic service time. So, using Equation 2.10, 20 = 1/(1 − ρ), and so ρ = .95. Given that the machine is 95% utilized and that each transaction uses 5 ms (.5%), the system should be able to run (.95/.005) = 190 transactions per second. If the processor is 10x slower, the service time becomes 50 ms, the expansion factor is 2, ρ = . 5, and the system can run (.5/.05) = 10 transactions per second. Notice that a 10x increase in power gives a 20x rise in throughput. This phenomenon is called transaction acceleration. If the processor is 10x faster, the expansion is 200, ρ = .995, and the throughput is 1,990 transactions per second. Notice that at the high end, the tps scales almost linearly with service time. It is only for ρ < . 9 that the transaction acceleration is dramatic.

19. The program must be a binary, so the instruction set of the machine must be standardized. The format of runable binary programs must be standardized. The operating system interface to launch the program and any external libraries used by the program must be standardized. MS/DOS defines such a standard for the Intel x86 series of processors, MacOS and SunOS have comparable standards.

20. The goal of X/Open DTP was portable applications and portable resource managers. X/Open views transaction managers as integrated with the host system and not portable, so only an interoperability standard was defined. The TM interfaces to the other TM via a communications manager implementing the OSI protocols (ROSE, CCR, TP, and so on). These interfaces are extensive and complex. X/Open decided to avoid defining an API to each of them. Others are defining an RPC interface among TMs to allow portable TMs.

21. (a) The error-free case:

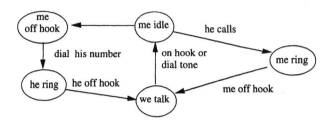

(b) Five interesting errors are: On the caller side, no dial tone, wrong number, nonexistent number, no answer after five rings, right number but wrong person. On the callee side, he hangs up just as I answer, we speak different languages (so I cannot understand him), we have a bad connection (so I cannot understand him), ... (d) These errors tend to make the state machine much bigger. Often a single error can add transitions to many states.

PART TWO

The Basics of Fault Tolerance

Nothing can go wrong.
can go wrong, . . .

3

Fault Tolerance

3.1 Introduction

This chapter presents three views of fault tolerance: the hardware view, the software view, and the global (holistic) view. It sketches the fault-tolerance problem and shows that the presence of design faults is the ultimate limit to system availability; we have techniques that mask other kinds of faults.

After a brief historical perspective, the chapter begins with standard definitions. Next, some empirical studies and measurements of current systems and typical module failure rates are presented. Then hardware approaches to fault tolerance are surveyed. This leads to the issue of software fault tolerance (tolerating software bugs). The bulk of the chapter presents the fault model and software masking techniques typical of non-transactional systems. Transaction processing systems use these more primitive techniques to implement transactional storage, execution, and messages. The chapter then mentions the meta-system design rules (KISS, Murphy's Law, and end-to-end arguments) and concludes with a discussion of system delusion that demonstrates an end-to-end issue.

The material of this chapter requires some very simple probability theory. For readers who may have forgotten this theory, the chapter begins with a crash course on probability. Readers who already know this material can skip it, but if you do not know it, don't panic! It is easy.

3.1.1 A Crash Course in Simple Probability

The *probability* of an event, A, happening in a certain period is denoted *P(A)*. Probabilities range between zero and one. Zero probability means that the event never occurs; one means that the event certainly occurs. The probability that an event, A, does not occur is $1 - P(A)$. A and B are *independent events* if the occurrence of one does not affect the probability of the occurrence of the other. Given independent events A and B, consider the following possibilities and their equations:

Both happen. The probability of both A and B happening in that period is the product of their probabilities:

$$P(A \text{ and } B) = P(A) \bullet P(B) \tag{3.1}$$

At least one happens. The probability of at least one of A and B happening is the probability that A happens plus the product of the probability that A does not happen and that B happens:

$$P(A \text{ or } B) \qquad = P(A) + (1 - P(A)) \bullet P(B)$$

$$= P(A) + P(B) - P(A) \bullet P(B) \qquad (3.2)$$

This equation has a small term $P(A) \bullet P(B)$ that can be ignored if both probabilities are very small.

$$\approx P(A) + P(B) \quad \text{if } P(A) << 1 \text{ and } P(B) << 1 \qquad (3.3)$$

For example, if the chance a system fails in a day is .01, the chance the telephone network fails is .02, and the chance the terminal fails is .03, then the chance of all three failing (using Equation 3.1) is .01 $\bullet$ .02 $\bullet$ .03, or $6 \bullet 10^{-6}$. The chance of any one of the three failing (using Equation 3.3) is .01 + .02 + .03, or .06.

Failure rates are often *memoryless*: If the system has been operating for a month, it is no more likely to fail now than it was a month ago. It is as though in each time unit the system flips the failure coin, and with probability $P(A)$ the coin comes up fail; otherwise, the system keeps working without failure. To illustrate: The chance of your dying in the next ten minutes is just about the same as the chance of your dying tomorrow at this time. In the short term, then, your death rate (hazard) is memoryless. Of course, when you are 100 years old the hazard function is likely to be higher.

Failure rates are such tiny numbers (say, 10^{-6}) that the reciprocals of the probabilities are used. If the event rate $P(A)$ is memoryless and much less than one, the *mean time* (average time) before the event is expected to occur $MT(A)$ is the reciprocal of the rate, or $1/P(A)$:

Mean time to event. If the probability $P(A)$ of event A per unit of time is much less than one and is memoryless, then the *mean time to event A* is the reciprocal of the probability of the event:

$$MT(A) \qquad = \frac{1}{P(A)} \qquad (3.4)$$

The mean time to failure of the components used in the previous example is 100 days (1/.01) for the system, 50 days (1/.02) for the network, and 33 days (1/.03) for the terminal. The mean time to any of them failing is about 17 days (1/.06), and the mean time to all of them failing is 170,000 days (1/(6 $\bullet$ 10^{-6})).

System designers are often presented with modules A, B, C, which fail independently and have mean times to failures $MT(A)$, $MT(B)$, $MT(C)$. If they are simply combined into a group G, then the failure of any one is likely to fail the whole group. What is $MT(G)$? Using Equation 3.3, the probability, $P(G)$, that any one of them fails is approximately $P(A) + P(B) + P(C)$. So, using Equation 3.4:

Mean time to any event. If events A, B, C have mean time $MT(A)$, $MT(B)$, $MT(C)$, then the mean time to the first one of the three events is:

$$MT(G) \qquad \approx \frac{1}{P(A) + P(B) + P(C)} \quad \text{using Equations 3.3 and 3.4.}$$

$$= \frac{1}{\left(\dfrac{1}{MT(A)} + \dfrac{1}{MT(B)} + \dfrac{1}{MT(C)}\right)} \tag{3.5}$$

Given N events A, all with the same mean time to occur, $MT(A)$, the mean time to the first event is:

$$MT(NG) \qquad = \frac{MT(A)}{N} \tag{3.6}$$

This is the math needed for this chapter. But, it is very important to understand three key assumptions that underlie these assumptions: (1) The event probabilities must be independent, (2) the probabilities must be small, and (3) the distributions must be memoryless. Exercises 1 and 2 explore these points.

3.1.2 An External View of Fault Tolerance

Fault tolerance is a major concern of transaction processing. Early batch transaction processing systems achieved fault tolerance by using the *old master-new master* technique, in which the batch of transactions accumulated during the day, week, or month was applied to the old master file, producing a new master file. If the batch run failed, the operation was restarted. To protect against loss or damage of the transaction file (typically a deck of cards), or the master file (typically a tape), an archive copy of each was maintained. Recovery consisted of carefully making a copy of the old master or transaction batch, then using the copy to rerun the batch (see Figure 3.1). Copies of the old masters were retained for five days, then week-

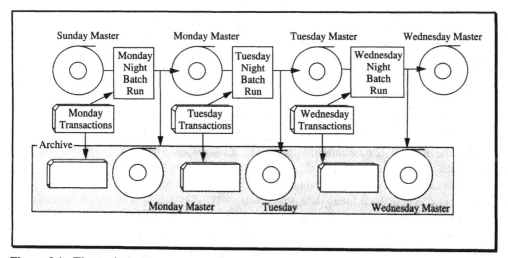

Figure 3.1: The typical old master-new master batch transaction processing scenario. Each day's transactions were represented as a deck of cards. One copy of this deck was sent to the archive for safekeeping, while the second copy was presented to the night batch run with the old master file. The program produced two identical copies of the new master file: one for the archive and one to be used in the next daily run. If a run damaged any of the data, the archive copies could be used to rerun the job.

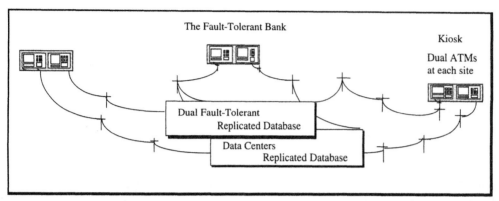

Figure 3.2: Evolution of the system in Figure 3.1 to an online transaction processing system with high availability. The batch transaction requests now arrive as messages from remote computers (automated teller machines, or ATMs) operated directly by the customer. The ATMs have been duplexed because they are the least reliable components of the system. The old master-new master files have been replaced by an online replicated database stored at two geographically remote sites. During normal operation, each site does half the work. In case of a failure, one site can perform all the work. This design tolerates any single fault and several multi-fault scenarios.

old, month-old, and year-old copies were kept. In addition, all transaction inputs were kept. With this data, any old state could be reconstructed.

Programs had internal checks to detect missing and incorrect data. When data was corrupted or missing, the redundant data in the old masters and in the transaction histories made it possible to reconstruct a correct current state.

This design tolerated any single failure and could tolerate several multi-failure scenarios. A failure might delay the batch processing, but the system could tolerate any failure short of destruction of both the archive and active copies of the files. In modern terminology, the old master-new master scheme tolerates any single fault; it is single-fault tolerant. It could be made n-fault tolerant by making $n + 1$ copies of each item, with $n + 1$ tape drives and operators, and storing them in $n + 1$ archives. But this was rarely done—single-fault tolerance was usually considered adequate, especially since the master file could probably be reconstructed from the old, old master (the Sunday Master in Figure 3.1) and the log (all the transactions since Sunday).

The more modern version of the same system is shown in Figure 3.2. In that system, the transactions are not batched but are processed while the customer waits. Using online transaction processing, or OLTP, the database is continuously updated by transactions. The new master database has been replaced by the online database, and the archive has been replaced by a second, geographically remote data center. This second center has a current replica of the data and can take over service in case the primary data center fails.

The bank with the system depicted in Figure 3.2 has gone to considerable lengths to provide its customers with a highly available service. It bought dual fault-tolerant data centers, dual telephone networks, and installed dual automated teller machines (ATMs) at each kiosk. In this example, the ATMs are the most unreliable component of the system, yielding about 99% availability. To mask the unreliability of the ATMs, the bank puts two at each customer site. If one ATM fails, the client can step to the adjacent one to perform the task. This is a good example of analyzing the overall system availability and applying redundancy where it is most appropriate.

Table 3.3: Availability of typical systems classes. In 1990, the best systems were in the high-availability range with Class 5. The best of the general-purpose systems were in the fault-tolerant range.

System Type	Unavailability (min/year)	Availability	Class
Unmanaged	52,560	90.%	1
Managed	5,256	99.%	2
Well-managed	526	99.9%	3
Fault-tolerant	53	99.99%	4
High-availability	5	99.999%	5
Very-high-availability	.5	99.9999%	6
Ultra-availability	.05	99.99999%	7

Figure 3.2 raises the issue of what it means for a *system* of many components to be available. If the bank in that figure has 10,000 ATM kiosks, some kiosks (pairs of ATMs) will be out of service at any instant. In addition, it is always possible that the database is down, or at least the part that some customer wants to access is unavailable (being recovered). The system is probably never completely "up," so the concept of *system availability* becomes:

System availability. The fraction of the offered load that is processed with acceptable response times.

System availability is usually expressed as a percentage. To apply this idea, suppose the ATMs in Figure 3.2 average one unscheduled outage every 100 days, and the problem takes on average a day to fix.[1] Such a high failure rate (1%) dominates the system availability. From the customer's perspective the system availability is 99% (=100% − 1%) without the duplexed ATMs. If the ATMs are duplexed at each site and if they have independent failure modes, then the customer is denied service only if both ATMs are broken. What is the chance of that? Using Equation 3.1, if the probability of one ATM failing in a day is 1%, then the chance of both breaking in the same day is .01% (.01 • .01). The ATM-pair availability is therefore 99.99%. Using Equation 3.4, this is a 10,000-day mean time to both failing. With 10,000 such kiosks, only one would normally be out of service at any instant.

A 99% availability was considered good in 1980, but by 1990 most systems are operating at better than 99.9% availability. After all, 99% availability is 100 minutes per week of denied service. As the nines begin to pile up in the availability measure, it becomes more convenient to think of availability in terms of denial-of-service measured in minutes per year. For example, 99.999% availability is about 5 minutes of service denial per year (see Table 3.3). Even this metric, though, is a little cumbersome so we introduce the concept of *availability class*, or simply *class*. This metric is analogous to the hardness of diamonds or the class of a clean room:

---

[1] The fact that they go out of service for 20 minutes each day to be emptied of deposits and to be refilled with cash is ignored because that can be rescheduled until the other machine is working. The failure of both ATMs due to a power outage is also not considered here.

Availability class.   The number of leading nines in the availability figure for a system or
module. More formally, if the system availability is A, the system class is

$$\lfloor \log_{10}(\frac{1}{1-A}) \rfloor.$$

Alternatively, the denial-of-service metric can be measured on a system-wide basis or
on a per-customer basis. To see the per-customer view, consider the 99% available ATM that
denies service to a customer an average of one time in 100 tries. If the customer uses an
ATM twice a week, then a single ATM will deny a customer service once a year on average
($\approx 2 \bullet 52$ weeks $= 104$ tries). A duplexed ATM will deny the customer service about once every hundred years. For most people, this is the difference between rarely down and never
down.

To give a sense of these metrics, nuclear reactor monitoring equipment is specified to be
class 5, telephone switches are specified to be class 6, and in-flight computers are specified
to be class 9. In practice, these demanding specifications are sometimes met.

3.2 Definitions

Fault tolerance discussions benefit from terminology and concepts developed by an IFIP
Working Group (IFIP WG 10.4) and by the IEEE Technical Committee on Fault-Tolerant
Computing. The following sections review the key definitions set forth by these organiza-
tions.

3.2.1 Fault, Failure, Availability, Reliability

A system can be viewed as a single module, yet most systems are composed of multiple
modules. These modules have internal structures consisting of smaller modules. Although
this presentation discusses the behavior of a single module, the terminology applies recursively to modules with internal modules.

Each module has an ideal *specified behavior* and an *observed behavior*. A *failure* occurs
when the observed behavior deviates from the specified behavior. A failure occurs because
of an *error*, or a defect in the module. The cause of the error is a *fault*. The time between the
occurrence of the error and the resulting failure is the *error latency*. When the error causes a
failure, it becomes *effective*; before that, the failure is *latent* (see Figure 3.4).

For example, a programmer's mistake is a *fault*. It creates a *latent error* in the software.
When the erroneous instructions are executed with certain data values, they cause a *failure*
and the error becomes *effective*. As a second example, a cosmic ray (*fault*) may discharge a
memory cell, causing a memory *error*. When the memory is read, it produces the wrong answer (memory *failure*), and the error becomes *effective*.

The observed module behavior alternates between *service accomplishment,* when the
module acts as specified, and *service interruption,* when the module's behavior deviates
from the specified behavior. These states are illustrated in Figure 3.4.

Module reliability measures the time from an initial instant to the next failure event.
Reliability is statistically quantified as *mean-time-to-failure* (*MTTF*); service interruption
is statistically quantified as *mean-time-to-repair* (*MTTR*).

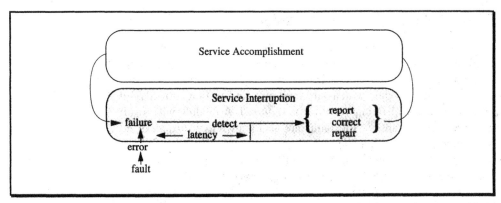

Figure 3.4: The failure-repair cycle. Usually, a module's observed behavior matches its specified behavior; it is in the *service accomplishment state*. Occasionally, a fault causes an error that eventually becomes effective, resulting in a module failure (observed behavior does not equal specified behavior). Then the module enters the *service interruption state*. The failure is detected, reported, corrected, or repaired, and then the module returns to the service accomplishment state.

Module availability measure the ratio of service-accomplishment to elapsed time. Availability is statistically quantified as

$$\frac{MTTF}{MTTF + MTTR}$$

3.2.2 Taxonomy of Fault Avoidance and Fault Tolerance

Module reliability can be improved by reducing failures, and failures can be avoided by *valid construction* and by *error correction*. The following taxonomy of validation and correction from the IFIP Working Group [Laprie 1985] may help to define the terms.

Validation can remove errors during the construction process, thus ensuring that the constructed module conforms to the specified module. Since physical components fail during operation, validation alone cannot ensure high reliability or high availability. *Error correction* reduces failures by using redundancy to tolerate faults. Error correction is of two types.

The first type of error correction, *latent error processing*, tries to detect and repair latent errors before they become effective. Preventive maintenance is an example of latent error processing. The second type, *effective error processing*, tries to correct the error after it becomes effective. Effective error processing can either *mask* the error or *recover* from the error.

Error masking uses redundant information to deliver the correct service and to construct a correct new state. Error correcting codes (ECC) used for electronic, magnetic, and optical storage are examples of masking. *Error recovery* denies the requested service and sets the module to an error-free state. Error recovery can take two forms.

The first form of error recovery, *backward error recovery*, returns to a previous correct state. Checkpoint/restart is an example of backward error recovery. The second form, *forward error recovery*, constructs a new correct state. Redundancy in time, such as resending a damaged message or rereading a disk page, is an example of forward error recovery.

3.2.3 Repair, Failfast, Modularity, Recursive Design

Section 3.7 specifies the correct behavior and some faults of the classic software modules: processes, messages, and storage. A failure that merely constitutes a delay of the correct behavior—for example, responding in one day rather than in one second—is called a *timing failure*. Faults can be *hard* or *soft*. A module with a hard fault will not function correctly—it will continue with a high probability of failing—until it is *repaired*. A module with a soft fault appears to be repaired after the failure. Soft faults are also known as *transient* or *intermittent* faults. Timing faults, for example, are often soft.

Recall that the time between the occurrence of a fault (the error) and its detection (the failure) is called the fault latency. A module is *failfast* if it stops execution when it detects a fault (stops when it fails), and if it has a small fault latency (the *fail* and the *fast*). The term *failstop* is sometimes used to mean the same thing.

As shown later, failfast behavior is important because latent errors can turn a single fault into a cascade of faults when the recovery system tries to use the latent faulty components. Failfast minimizes fault latency and so minimizes latent faults.

Modules are built recursively. That is, the system is a module composed of modules, which in turn are composed of modules, and so on down to leptons and quarks. The goal is to start with ordinary hardware, organize it into failfast hardware and software modules, and build up a system (a super module) that has no faults and, accordingly, is a highly available system (module). This goal can be approached with the controlled use of redundancy and with techniques that allow the super-module to *mask*, or hide, the failures of its component modules. Many examples of this idea appear throughout this chapter and this book.

3.3 Empirical Studies

As Figures 3.1 and 3.2 show, there has been substantial progress in fault tolerance over the last few decades. Early computers were expected to fail once a day (very early ones failed even more often). Today it is common for modules, workstations, disks, memories, processors, and so on, to have mean-time-to-failure (MTTF) ratings of ten years or more (100,000 hours or more). Whole systems composed of hundreds or thousands of such modules can offer MTTF of one month if nothing special is done, or 100 years if great care is taken. The following subsections cite some of the empirical data that support this claim.

3.3.1 Outages Are Rare Events

In former times, everyone knew why computers failed: It was the hardware. Now that hardware is very reliable, outages (service unavailability) are rare, and, since much of our experience is anecdotal, patterns are not so easy to discern. The American telephone network had two major problems in 1990. In one outage, a fire in a midwest switch disabled most of the Chicago area for several days; in another outage, a software error clogged the long-haul network for eight hours. The New York Stock Exchange had four outages in the 1980s. It closed for a day because of a snowstorm, it closed for four hours due to a fire in the machine room, it closed 45 seconds early because of a software error, and trading stopped for three hours due to a financial panic. The Internet was accidentally clogged by a student one day, and so on.

If we look at hundreds of events from many different fault-tolerant systems, the main pattern that emerges is that these events are rare—in fact, very rare. Each is the combination of special circumstances. Some patterns do emerge, however, if we look at the sources of failures.

Perhaps the first thing to notice from the anecdotes above, and this is borne out in the broader context as well, is that *few of the outages were caused by hardware faults.* Fault-tolerance masks most hardware faults. If a fault-tolerant system failed due to a hardware fault, there was probably also a software error (the software should have masked the hardware fault) or an operator error (the operator did not initiate repair) or a maintenance error (all the standby spares were broken and had not been repaired) or an environmental failure (the machine room was on fire). As explained in greater detail in Sections 3.5 and 3.6, hardware designers have developed very simple and effective ways of making arbitrarily reliable hardware, and software designers have developed ways to mask most of the residual hardware faults. As hardware prices plummet, the use of these techniques is becoming standard.

Outages (denial of service) can be traced to a few broad categories of causes:

Environment.   Facilities failures such as the machine room, cooling, external power, data communication lines, weather, earthquakes, fires, floods, acts of war, and sabotage.

Operations.   All the procedures and activities of normal system administration, system configuration, and system operation.

Maintenance.   All the procedures and activities performed to maintain and repair the hardware and facilities. This does not include software maintenance, which is lumped in with software.

Hardware.   The physical devices, exclusive of environmental support (air conditioning and utilities).

Software.   All the programs in the system.

Process.   Outages due to something else. Examples are labor disputes (strikes), shutdowns due to administrative decisions (the stock exchange shutdown at panic), and so on.

This taxonomy gives considerable latitude to interpretation. For instance, if a disgruntled operator destroys the system, is the damage due to sabotage (environment) or operations? Sabotage (environment) is probably the correct interpretation, because it was not a simple operations or maintenance mistake. If the system is located in an area of intense electrical storms, but lacks surge protection, is environment or process the cause? Process should probably be held accountable, because the problem has a solution that the customer has not installed.

3.3.2 Studies of Conventional Systems

Given this taxonomy, what emerges from measurements of "real" systems? Unfortunately, that is a secret. Almost no one wants to tell the world how reliable his system is. Since hundreds or thousands of systems must be examined to see any patterns, there is little hope of forming a clear picture of the situation.

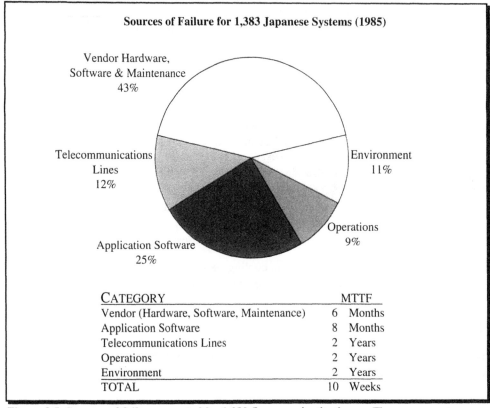

Sources of Failure for 1,383 Japanese Systems (1985)

Vendor Hardware,
Software & Maintenance
43%

Telecommunications
Lines
12%

Environment
11%

Operations
9%

Application Software
25%

CATEGORY	MTTF	
Vendor (Hardware, Software, Maintenance)	6	Months
Application Software	8	Months
Telecommunications Lines	2	Years
Operations	2	Years
Environment	2	Years
TOTAL	10	Weeks

Figure 3.5: Sources of failure reported by 1,383 Japanese institutions.   The average outage was 90 minutes [Watanabe 1986]. The ten-week figure can be computed using Equation 3.5.

The most extensive public study was done by the Japanese Information Processing Development Corporation (JIPDEC) in 1985. It surveyed the outages reported by 1,383 institutions in 1985 [Watanabe 1986]. The institutions reported 7,517 outages, with average durations of 90 minutes, resulting in a MTTF of about ten weeks and an availability of 99.91%. The study is summarized in Figure 3.5.

This study is especially interesting since these are not fault-tolerant systems. They are just ordinary computers managed by people who have a justly deserved reputation for careful planning and good quality. These statistics compare favorably with the *best* numbers reported by comparable groups in the United States, and are better by a factor of ten than typical reports (see, for example, the study by Mourad [1985]).

The categories shown in Figure 3.5 do not correspond exactly to the ones introduced earlier; they lump hardware, vendor software, and vendor maintenance together. But the study shows one thing very clearly: if the vendor provided perfect hardware, software, and maintenance, the system MTTF would be four months (this is an application of Equation 3.5). *If the goal is to build systems that do not fail for years or decades, then all aspects of availability must be addressed—simple hardware fault tolerance is not enough.*

Table 3.6: Summary of Tandem reported system outage data.

	1985	1987	1989
Customers	1,000	1,300	2,000
Outage Customers	176	205	164
Systems	2,400	6,000	9,000
Processors	7,000	15,000	25,500
Disks	16,000	46,000	74,000
Reported Outages	285	294	438
System MTTF	8 years	20 years	21 years

3.3.3 A Study of a Fault-Tolerant System

A more recent study of a fault-tolerant system provides a similar picture. Unfortunately, the study was based on outages *reported* to the vendor, and therefore it grossly underreports outages due to environment, operations, and application software. It really captures only the top wedge of the figure above. But since data is so scarce in this area, the results are presented with that caveat. The study covered the reported outages of Tandem computer systems between 1985 and 1990, encompassing approximately 7,000 customer years, 30,000 system years, 80,000 processor years, and over 200,000 disk years. The summary information for three periods is shown in Table 3.6.

Table 3.6 summarizes the statistical base, and Figures 3.7 and 3.8 display the information by category. They show the causes of outages and the historical trends: Reported system outages per 1,000 years (per millennium) improved by a factor of two by 1987 and then held steady. Most of the improvement came from improvements in hardware and maintenance, which together shrank from 50% of the outages to under 10%. By contrast, operations grew from 9% to 15% of outages. Software's share of the problem got *much* bigger during the period, growing from 33% to more than 60% of the outages.

Figure 3.7 seems to imply that operations and software got worse, but that is not the case. Figure 3.8 shows that software and operations MTTF stayed about constant, while the other fault sources improved considerably.

Two forces explain the maintenance improvements: technology and design. Disks give the best example of both forces. In 1985, each disk had to be serviced once a year. This involved powering down the disk, replacing an air filter, adjusting the power system, and sometimes adjusting head alignment. In addition, the typical 1985 disk required one unscheduled service call per year for repair. This resulted in 32,000 tasks per year in 1985 for customer engineers, and it created many opportunities for mistakes. In addition, the disk cabinets and connectors were not designed for maintenance, rendering maintenance tasks awkward and requiring special tools. If technology and design had not changed, engineers would have been performing 150,000 maintenance tasks per year in 1989—the equivalent of 175 full-time people just doing the error-prone task of disk maintenance.

Instead, 1990-vintage disks have no scheduled maintenance. Fiber-optic connectors reduce cabling and connectors by a factor of 20, and installation and repair require no tools (only thumb screws are used). All field-replaceable units have built-in self-test and light-emitting diodes that indicate correct operation. In addition, disk MTTF rose from 8,000 hours to over 100,000 hours (observed) since 1985. Disk controllers and power supplies

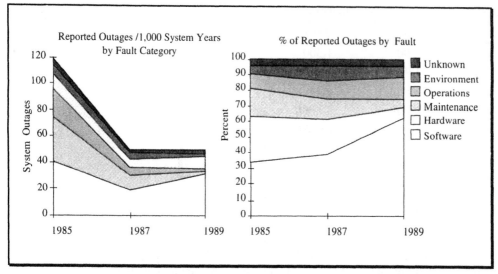

Figure 3.7: Graphs showing the declining frequency of outages by cause and the relative contribution of each fault category to system outages. The data reflect a shift from hardware and maintenance to software and, to a lesser extent, operations as the main causes of outages. Underreporting of environment and operations outages should be considered when reading these graphs.

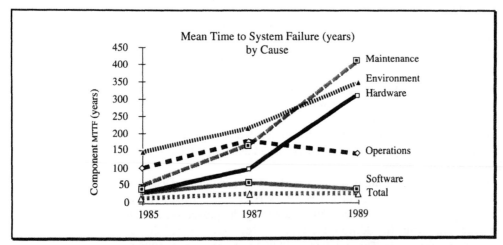

Figure 3.8: Graph showing the trend in mean time to system failure by fatal cause. Note that software and operations held about constant, while hardware, maintenance, and environment improved dramatically.

experienced similar dramatic improvements. The result was that the disk population grew by a factor of five while the absolute number of outages induced by disk maintenance shrank by a factor of four—a 2,000% improvement. Almost all the reported disk maintenance problems were with older disks or were incident to installing new disks.

This is just one example of how technology and design have improved the maintenance picture. Since 1985, the size of Tandem's customer engineering staff has held almost constant and shifted its focus from maintenance to installation, even while the installed base tripled. This is an industry trend; other vendors report similar experience. Hardware maintenance is being simplified or eliminated.

Other hardware experienced a similar improvement in MTTF. Based on Table 3.6, during 1989 there were well over 30,000 hardware faults, yet only 29 resulted in a reported system outage. The vast majority were masked by the software (the Tandem system is single-fault tolerant, requiring two hardware faults to cause an outage). The MTTF of a duplexed pair goes up as the square of the MTTF of the individual modules (see Section 3.6). Thus, minor changes in module MTTF can have a dramatic effect on system MTTF. The clear conclusion is that hardware designers did a wonderful job. Hardware faults were rare, and all but 4% of the ones that did occur were masked by software.

While hardware and maintenance show a clear trend toward improvement, operations and software did not improve. The reason for this lies in the fact that few tools were provided to the operators; thus there is no reason to expect their performance to have changed. According to Figure 3.8, every 150 system-years some operator made a mistake serious enough to crash a system. Clearly, mistakes were made more frequently than that, but most operations mistakes were masked by the system, which has some operator fault tolerance.

Operations mistakes were split evenly between two broad categories: configuration and procedures. Configuration mistakes involve such things as having a startup file that asks the transaction manager to reinitialize itself. This works fine the *first* time the system starts, but it causes loss of transactions and data integrity when the system is restarted from a crash. Mixing incompatible software versions or using an old version of software are common configuration faults. The most common procedural mistake is letting the system fill up by allowing a file to get so big that either there is no more disk space for it or no new records can be added to it.

No clearer pattern of operations faults emerges from the Tandem study. The basic problem of improving operations is that the only known technique is to eliminate or automate the operations process, replacing operators with software.

As Figure 3.7 shows, software is a major source of outages. The software base (number of lines of code) grew by a factor of three during the study period, but the software MTTF held almost constant. This reflects a substantial improvement in software quality. But if these trends continue, the software will continue to grow at the same rate that the quality improves, and software MTTF will not improve. The software in this study uses many of the software fault tolerance techniques described later in this chapter. But that is not enough; a tenfold improvement in software quality is needed to achieve Class 5 availability. At present, no technique offers such an improvement without *huge* expense. Section 3.6 surveys the most effective approaches: *N*-version programming and process-pairs combined with transactions.

Thus far, we examined the failure rates of whole systems. We now look at typical failure rates for system components such as processors, disks, networks, and software.

3.4 Typical Module Failure Rates

System designers need rules of thumb for module failure modes, rates, and repair times. There are huge variations among these. Intervals between failures seem to obey exponential, or even hyper-exponential distributions. This makes talking about averages deceptive. In addition, failure rates often vary over time, following a bathtub curve (see Figure 3.9). The rate in the beginning, often called the *burn-in* rate, is high. After that, the rate remains low and

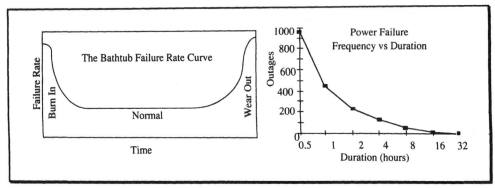

Figure 3.9: Two standard failure curves. On the left is the standard bathtub curve showing that failure rates of hardware and software modules are high at first (during burn-in) and lower in mid-life (during normal operation); failure rates then rise as the module wears out. Software modules age due to maintenance. The curve on the right shows the frequency of power outages of a certain duration. Most outages were for 30 minutes or less, but some lasted over 8 hours. This negative exponential curve is typical of failure rates and repair times [Tullis 1984].

nearly constant for many years. Then the device begins to age mechanically, or *wear out*, and the rate rises. Failure rates are usually quoted for the bottom of the bathtub curve. To mask burn-in, manufacturers often operate modules for a few hours or days to detect burn-in faults. Only modules passing this burn-in period are sent to customers.

Two kinds of failure rates are of interest: *quoted* and *observed*. Quoted failure rates are those promised by the vendor, while observed failure rates are those seen by the customer. For phone lines and for some modules, the observed numbers are much better than the quoted numbers because the quoted numbers are often guarantees, and the customer has a right to complain if the rate falls below the quoted rate. MTTF is usually quoted in hours, generally with only the first digit significant. Often only the magnitude of the MTTF is significant, so that 10,000 hours could actually be 7,000 or 12,000. With about 8,760 hours in a year, each year has about 10,000 hours. A 50,000-hour MTTF, therefore, means about a 5-year MTTF. Given these very approximate measures, here are some typical MTTFs:

Connectors and cables. Connectors and cables are commonly rated at 1,000 years MTTF. Their failure modes are corrosion of contacts, bent connector pins, and electrical erosion. Connectors and cables have high burn-in failure rates.

Logic boards. Depending on cooling, environment, and internal fault masking, logic boards are rated at between 3 and 20 years MTTF. The ratio of soft to hard faults varies from a low of 1:1 to 5:1 (typical) to greater than 10:1 for badly designed circuits.

Disks. Workstation and PC disks are notoriously unreliable (one-year MTTF observed), whereas "expensive disks" are quite reliable (rated at 5 years, with over 20 years MTTF observed). Table 3.10 gives these statistics (the term ECC refers to the extensive error correcting codes found in disk controllers to mask bad spots on the disk). Recent (June 1990) reports of IBM drives report 570 months MTTF for a population of 3,889 drives. This is approximately a 50-year MTTF. These drives will be obsolete long before they wear out or fail.

Table 3.10: MTTF **of various disk failures** [Schulze 1989].

Type of Error	MTTF	Recovery	Consequences
Soft data read error	1 hour	Retry or ECC	None
Recoverable seek error	6 hours	Retry	None
Maskable hard data read error	3 days	ECC	Remap to new sector and rewrite good data
Unrecoverable data read error	1 year	None	Remap to new sector, old data lost
Device needs repair	5 years	Repair	Data unavailable
Miscorrected data read error	10^7 years	None	Read wrong data

Workstations. Workstation reliability varies enormously. The marketplace is extremely competitive, and manufacturers often economize by having inadequate power, cooling, or connectors. A minimal good-quality terminal is usually rated at three to five years (the display is often the weak link). Workstation hardware is usually rated at one to five years, disks often being the weak link. Workstation software seems to have a two-week MTTF [Long 1990].

Software. Production software has ≈ 3 design faults per 1,000 lines of code. Most of these bugs are soft; they can be masked by retry or restart. The ratio of soft to hard faults varies, but 100:1 is usual (see Subsection 3.6.2).

Data communications lines (USA). The telephone systems of North America and northern Europe are among the most reliable systems in the world. They are spectacularly well managed and provide admirable service. (The story is not so pleasant elsewhere.) With the advent of fiber optics, line quality is getting even better. Line quality is measured in error-free seconds. Raw fiber media rates are 10^{-9} BER (bit error rate). This suggests that one message in a million is lost. When all the intermediate components are added, error rates often rise to 10^{-5}. If a message is about a kilobit, this suggests that 1:100 or 1:1000 messages are corrupted. These are soft error rates. Hard errors (outages) vary enormously and are clustered in bursts. Suppliers usually promise 95% error-free seconds, 10^{-6} BER , and 99.7% availability. There are frequent dropouts of 100 ms or less when no good data is transmitted. Duplexing the lines via independent paths should mask almost all such transient faults. Such duplexing is a service provided in most countries.

LANs. Raw cable and fiber are rated at 10^{-9} BER and 10^{-6} bad messages per hour. Most LAN problems arise from protocol violations or from overloads. One study of an Ethernet LAN over a 7-month period observed nine overload events due to broadcast storms, thrashing clients, babbling nodes, protocol mismatch, and analog noise [Maxion 1990]. This suggests a 3-week MTTF.

Power failures. Power is the most serious problem outside Japan and northern Europe. Based on Table 3.11, any system wanting MTTF measured in years should carefully condition its input power and should install a local uninterruptible power supply. In one

Table 3.11: Frequency and average duration of power outages in Europe and North America.
Power in Japan is reputed to be comparable to that in Germany. Power in the Third World is reputed to
be worse than that in Italy. Areas with severe electrical storms should expect much worse service.
These numbers do not include sags (outages of less than a second) and surges (over-voltages that can
burn out equipment). North American source is Tullis [1984].

		Out min/year	Events/year	Avg event(min)
North America		125	2.3	54
England		67	0.72	92
France	urban	33	0.8	41
	rural	390	5	78
Germany	urban	7	0.33	20
	rural	54	1.2	45
Italy	urban	120	2.5	48
	rural	300	5	60

European numbers exclude pre-arranged outages.

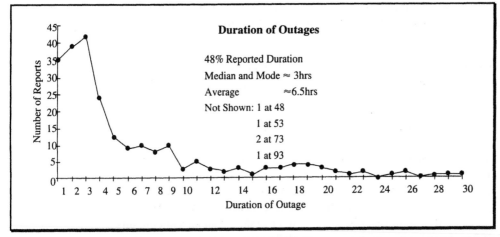

Figure 3.12: The duration of system outages. Only 48% of the reported outages reported the duration. Of those, the statistics are shown above. Three long outages (due to a tornado and flood) are not shown in the graph [Gray 1990].

study of a North American customer who did not do this, 75% of unscheduled outages were related to power failure. Table 3.11 summarizes the rates.

These statistics indicate how frequently modules fail. The other important number is how quickly they are repaired. How long does it usually take a system to be repaired? Several studies indicate that two hours is a typical module repair time if the site is near a service center and reservoir of spare parts. Once repair is complete, the system must initiate recovery. The network probably will have shut down by then (most time-outs are less than two hours). One end-to-end indication of system repair times is the Japanese study mentioned previously (see Figure 3.5), which reported an average of 90 minutes. Another study of outage durations reports a median and mean of twice that (see Figure 3.12)—essentially two hours to diagnose and repair the system and about one hour to bring the application and network back to full operation.

Based on Figure 3.12, outages roughly follow a Poisson distribution. The distribution, however, has a very long tail, since long outages are over-represented.

The statistics in this section tell us that modules fail. The question, then, is how can we build a highly reliable system out of imperfect modules? The next few sections present the various approaches to this problem. First, the hardware approach is covered, then fault-tolerant and failfast software, and finally software masking of software and hardware faults.

3.5 Hardware Approaches to Fault Tolerance

John von Neumann pioneered the idea of building fault-tolerant computer systems. Starting with unreliable components, a model of neurons, he did a design for the human mind (a giant brain) with a 60-year MTTF. His charming and seminal paper concludes that the design requires a redundancy of about 20,000: 20,000 wires in each bundle and 20,000 neurons making each decision. Such redundancy was needed in his view, because he considered any fault in the system as a failure. His system had only one level of modularity, it lacked the notion of failfast, and it lacked the notion of repair. These three ideas and their interaction are extremely important. Because they allow computer systems to get by quite well with 10^4 times lower redundancy (2 rather than 20,000), they are well worth understanding.

3.5.1 The Basic *N*-Plex Idea: How to Build Failfast Modules

Failfast modules are easily constructed from ordinary hardware. The simplest design, called *pairing* or *duplexing,* connects the inputs and outputs of two modules to a comparator that stops if the module outputs disagree; this is the failfast aspect of the design. Although a pair fails about twice as often as a single module, a failfast module gives clean failure semantics; it also reduces the number of cases fault-tolerant software needs to deal with by converting all failures to a very simple class: stopping. To provide both failfast behavior and increased module MTTF, modules are *n*-plexed, and a voter takes a majority of their outputs. If there is no majority, the voter stops the *n*-plex module. The most common case in the *n*-plex design in which *n* is greater than 2 ($n = 2$ is simply pairing) is $n = 3$. This is generally called *triple module redundancy*, or TMR. The double and triple redundancy cases are shown in Part A of Figure 3.13.

The basic *n*-plex design generalizes to a recursive one that allows failfast modules to be aggregated into bigger failfast modules, and that tolerates voter failures and connector failures. In that design, each *n*-plexed module has *n* voters and *n* outputs (see Part B of Figure 3.13).

3.5.2 Failfast versus Failvote Voters in an *N*-Plex

As the voting scheme is described in the previous section, the voter requires that a majority of the modules be available. If there is no majority, the voter stops. This is called *failvote.* An alternative scheme, called either *failfast voting* or *failfast* represents a fundamental refinement. This scheme has the voter first sense which modules are available and then use the majority of the available modules. Thus, a failfast voter can operate with less than a majority of the modules.

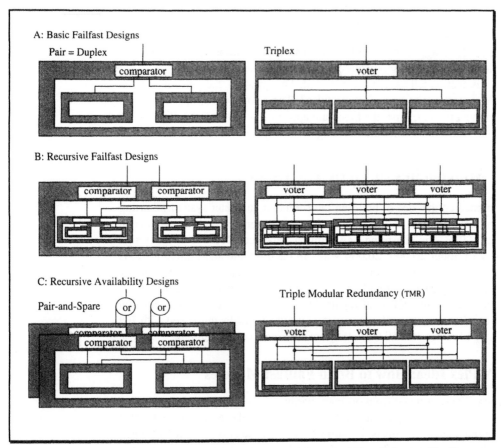

Figure 3.13: The two evolutions of hardware modules to high-availability designs. The first step is to use a voter to get failfast behavior. The second step is to make the design recursive and to tolerate voter failures by n-plexing the voters. The third step is to add redundancy, so that failfast failures are masked by the redundant modules. Note that the second and third steps are the same for TMR. These ideas, of course, generalize to n-plexed modules.

If each of the component modules is failfast, then a failfast voter can operate by observing the outputs of the *non-faulty* modules. In theory, a voter combining the outputs of failfast sub-modules never detects a mismatch; it just detects missing votes from failed modules. For example, disk modules are usually assumed to be failfast. A failfast voter managing a pair of disks can detect disk failures and can still operate if only one of the two disks is functional. This permits the supermodule (disk pair) to function with only one module.

Even if the component modules are not failfast, the voter can still operate with failfast voting. To do so, a module is marked as failed each time it miscompares, and the voter ignores its inputs until it is repaired. Thus the voter forms a majority from the non-faulty modules. Take as an example a 10-plexed module composed of ordinary (not necessarily failfast) modules. A failvote voter operating the 10-plex will fail when five modules have failed. A failfast voter will continue operating until the ninth module fail, because a failfast voter on non-failfast modules requires only two available modules to operate. This indicates that failfast voting has better reliability than failvote voting.

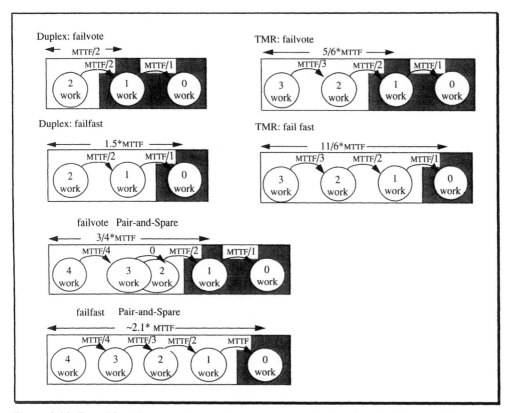

Figure 3.14: Transition diagrams to estimate the MTTF of a duplexed or triplexed module. The diagrams are based on the MTTF of the component modules and assume no voter failures and no repair. Shaded areas represent the failed regions. In unshaded areas, the assembly is delivering service. Modules can be constructed as failfast or failvote. In the failfast case, the voter ignores modules with no output and modules that have failed in the past. This enables it to operate with a single module. In the failvote case, the voter must have a majority of correct inputs. Because failures are independent with exponential distributions, the means are additive.

Consider a failvote *n*-plex and ignore failures of the voters (comparators) and connectors. (For the scenario that follows, refer to Figure 3.14.) Given modules, each of which is failfast, with an MTTF of 10 years, the MTTF of the paired supermodule is about five years (10/2 years, using Equation 3.6).[2] The MTTF for the triplex system is about 8.3 years (using Equation 3.6, it is 10/3, or about 3.3 years to the first failure and 10/2, or 5 years to the second and fatal failure). The analysis of pair-and-spare is a little more tricky, since the first pair will fail the first time one of the four processors fails. Equation 3.6 says that is expected to happen in 10/4, or 2.5 years. After one pair fails, the remaining pair is expected to operate for five years, as computed here. Thus, pair and spare has a 7.5-year MTTF. This logic (simply adding the times), incidentally, shows how the memoryless property simplifies analysis.

So far, all this redundancy does not look like a good idea. *All three schemes cut the MTTF, making failure more likely.* However, there are two extenuating circumstances. First,

---

[2] Faults are assumed to be independent and memoryless, as explained at the start of the chapter. The trivial analysis presented here derives from the presentation in [Siewiorek and Swartz 1982].

and most important, *n*-plexing yields failfast modules. Failfast modules have vastly simplified failure characteristics; they either work correctly or they stop. This simplicity makes it possible to reason about their behavior. If modules can have arbitrary failure behavior, there is little hope of building fault-tolerant systems.

The second benefit of triplexing and pair-and-spare is that if soft (transient) faults dominate, then pair-and-spare or TMR can be a big improvement (recall that modules continue to function after soft errors). Both schemes mask virtually all soft faults, and two of the three would have to have exactly the same fault for the voter to pass on the faulty result. Thus if the ratio of hard faults to total faults is 1:100, and if TMR masks all transient faults, the module MTTF rises by a factor of 100 to become 1,000 years MTTF; in addition, TMR failvote improves the MTTF from about 8.3 years to about 8,333 ($\approx 10,000 \cdot (1/3 + 1/2)$) using Figure 3.14).

3.5.3 *N*-Plex plus Repair Results in High Availability

The key to getting this hundred-fold MTTF improvement is repairing the faulted module immediately after the fault. If the module has no internal state, recovery from a soft fault is easy; the module goes on to compute the next state from its next inputs. But typically, the faulted module is a processor or memory with an incorrect internal state. To repair it, the design must somehow resynchronize the faulted module with the other two modules. The easy way to do this is to reset all the modules to their initial states, but this will probably reflect the fault outside the module. Mechanisms to resynchronize the faulted module without disrupting the service of the other two modules are usually complex and ad hoc. For storage modules, such mechanisms consist of rewriting the state of the faulted storage cell. For processing modules, they generally set the state (registers) of the faulted processor to the state of one of the good processors.

The huge benefit of tolerating soft faults is just one aspect of the key to availability: *repair*. Soft errors postulate instant mean time to module repair; when the module faults, it is instantly repaired. Failvote duplex and failfast TMR both provide excellent reliability and availability if repair is added to the model.

The failure analysis of a failvote *n*-plex is easy to follow. Each module goes through the cycle of operation, fault, repair, and then operation again. The supermodule (the *n*-plex module) will fail if all the component modules fail at once. More formally, the *n*-plex will fail if all but one module are unavailable, and then the available module fails. The analysis first determines the probability that a particular module, *N*, will be the last to fail (all others have already failed and are still down). The probability that a particular module is unavailable is

$$P_1 \approx MTTR/(MTTF + MTTR)) \approx (MTTR/MTTF) \text{ since } MTTR \ll MTTF . \tag{3.7}$$

Using Equation 3.1 with Equation 3.7, the probability that the other $n - 1$ modules are unavailable is then

$$P_{n-1} \approx P_1^{n-1} = (MTTR/MTTF)^{n-1}. \tag{3.8}$$

Using Equation 3.4, the probability that a module, *N*, fails is

$$P_f \approx 1/MTTF. \tag{3.9}$$

Table 3.15: MTTF estimates for various architectures using 1-year MTTF modules with 4-hour MTTR. Note: in the cost column, the letter ε represents a small additional cost.

	MTTF	Equation	Cost
Simplex	1 year	MTTF	1
Duplex: failvote	≈0.5 years	≈MTTF/2	2+ε
Duplex: failfast	≈1.5 years	≈MTTF(3/2)	2+ε
Triplex: failvote	≈.8 year	≈MTTF(5/6)	3+ε
Triplex: failfast	≈1.8 year	≈ MTTF(11/6)	3+ε
Pair and Spare: failvote	≈.7 year	≈MTTF(3/4)	4+ε
Triplex: failfast with repair	>10^6 years	≈$MTTF^3/3MTTR^2$	3+ε
Duplex failfast + repair	>10^3 years	≈$MTTF^2/2MTTR$	2+ε

Equation 3.1 can combine Equations 3.8, and 3.9 to compute the probability that the last module N fails, and that all the other modules are unavailable:

$$P_f \cdot P_{n-1} \approx (1/MTTF) \cdot (MTTR/MTTF)^{n-1} \tag{3.10}$$

This is the probability that module N causes the n-plex failure. There are n such identical modules. To compute the probability that any one of these n modules causes an n-plex failure, Equation 3.10 is combined n times using Equation 3.3:

$$P_{n\text{-plex}} \approx \left(\frac{n}{MTTF}\right) \cdot \left(\frac{MTTR}{MTTF}\right)^{n-1} \tag{3.11}$$

Equation 3.11 is therefore the probability that a failvote n-plex will completely fail. Using Equation 3.4 with Equation 3.11 gives the mean time to total failure for a failfast n-plex:

$$MTTF_n \approx \left(\frac{MTTF}{n}\right) \cdot \left(\frac{MTTF}{MTTR}\right)^{n-1} \tag{3.12}$$

Applying Equation 3.12 and using the 1-year MTTF with a 4-hour MTTR,

$$MTTF_{pair} \approx \frac{MTTF^2}{2\,MTTR} = 1095 \text{ years.} \tag{3.13}$$

The corresponding result for a TMR group is

$$MTTF_{TMR} \approx \frac{MTTF^3}{3\,MTTR^2} = 1,600,000 \text{ years.} \tag{3.14}$$

Starting with two modest one-year MTTF modules, we have now built a one-millennium module! Thousands of these could be used to build a supermodule with a one-year MTTF. The construction can be repeated to obtain a system with a one-millennium MTTF—a powerful idea (see Table 3.15).

3.5.4 The Voter's Problem

There is a nasty flaw in the previous reasoning: Namely, the assumption that *the voters and connectors are faultless.* The recursive construction was careful to replicate the voters and connectors for this very reason, so that the construction actually tolerates failures in

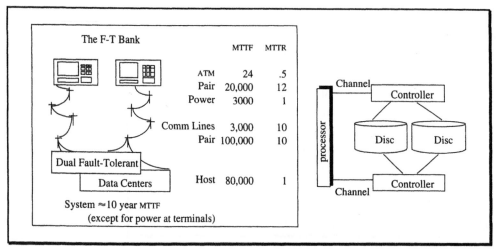

The F-T Bank

	MTTF	MTTR
ATM	24	.5
Pair	20,000	12
Power	3000	1
Comm Lines	3,000	10
Pair	100,000	10
Host	80,000	1

Dual Fault-Tolerant Data Centers

System ≈10 year MTTF (except for power at terminals)

Figure 3.16: Two real examples of moving the voter into the client. In one case the client is the bank customer who uses a second (adjacent) ATM if the first one fails. Every ATM kiosk has at least two ATMs, since they are the least reliable component. To make this work, the ATMs must be failfast. Analogously, the processor must access the duplexed pair of disks via an alternate channel if one channel or controller of a disk pair fails. Likewise, for this to work, the channels, controllers, and disks must be failfast.

connectors and voters. Fundamentally, however, system reliability and availability are limited by the reliability of the top-level voters.

In some situations, voting can be carried all the way to the physical system. For example, by putting three motors on the airplane flaps or reactor rods and having them "vote" at the physical level, two can overcome the force of the third. Often the voter cannot be moved to the transducer. In those situations, the message itself must be failfast—it must have a checksum or some other consistency check—and the client must become the voter. Two examples of moving the voter to the client appear in Figure 3.16.

The first example in Figure 3.16 is a repetition of the banking system depicted in Figure 3.2. It shows the failure rates for the various system components and indicates that the ATM is the least reliable component. But using the pair-and-spare scheme produces instant repair times (repair in the sense of providing service): If one ATM fails, the client can step to the adjacent ATM. That moves the voter into the customer. If each ATM is failfast, the customer can operate with a correct one.

The second example in Figure 3.16 shows a disk pair. Data is read from either disk and written to both. Each disk and each controller is a failfast module. In addition, the wires are failfast, because the messages they carry are checksum protected. If the message checksum is wrong, the message is discarded. But the client (the processor in this case) must try the second channel (the second path) to the device if the first fails, much as the bank client must try the second ATM if the first fails. These are both examples of moving the voter into the client.

3.5.5 Summary

The foregoing presentation is from the traditional perspective of hardware fault tolerance. The next two sections develop similar ideas from a software perspective. To bridge these two perspectives, it is important to see the following connections:

Failfast is atomic. Failfast means that a hardware (or software) module either works correctly or does nothing. This is the atomic, all-or-nothing aspect of the ACID property (the A in ACID). Atomicity vastly simplifies reasoning about the way a system will fail.

Failfast is possible. There may be skepticism that it is possible to build failfast modules, but Figure 3.13 shows how to build arbitrarily complex hardware systems with the failfast property through suitable use of redundancy.

Reliable plus repair is consistent and durable. If modules fail and are repaired, then a module will always make correct state transitions (eventually), and the module state will be durable. The module will eventually be repaired and continue service. Consistent and durable are represented by the C and D of ACID.

To summarize, reliability plus repair means doing the right thing *eventually*; the module may stop, but eventually it is repaired and continues to function. Failfast is the A of ACID, and reliability plus repair are the A, C, and D of ACID. High availability modules can be built by *n*-plexing failfast modules and by using a failfast voting scheme.

Historically, transaction processing systems have been geared toward reliability—never losing the database. But for many reasons, they often delivered poor availability. Many TP systems were designed in an era when one failure per day was considered typical and when 98% availability was considered high. Technology advances and declining hardware prices have shifted the emphasis from reliability to availability, which means doing the right thing and doing it *on time*. *Repair* is the key to reliability, since with enough repair the job eventually gets done. *Instant repair* is the key to high availability: It almost always masks the failure such that module failures do not cause a denial of service. Combined with failfast, instant repair makes all single faults appear to be soft faults. Both TMR and pair-and-spare provide instant MTTR for hardware faults. These techniques make it possible to buy conventional components off the shelf and combine them to build super-reliable and super-available modules. The next sections show how to achieve instant software MTTR, implying highly available software systems.

3.6 Software Is the Problem

Both the Japanese study and the Tandem study of the causes of system failures point to software as a major source of problems (Subsection 3.3.2). There is a clear trend toward using software to mask hardware, environmental, operations, and maintenance faults. Thus, as all the other faults are masked, the software residue remains. In addition, software is being used to automate operations and simplify maintenance. All this implies millions of new lines of code. In general, production programs engineered using the best techniques (structured programming, walk-throughs, careful code inspections, extensive quality assurance, alpha and beta testing) have two or three bugs per thousand lines of code. Using this rule of thumb, a few million lines of code will have a few thousand bugs—megalines have kilobugs.

It is important to realize that *perfect software is possible—it's just a matter of time and money*. The following program, for example, is perfect at adding unsigned integers modulo the machine word size:

```
/* a perfect program to add two unsigned integers (modulo the machine word size)          */
Ulong add(Ulong a, Ulong b)
          { return a + b; }
```

As an amusing side note, our first version of this program had two bugs! It advertised *add* rather than *modulo word size add*, and it used signed integers, which meant it would get overflow and underflow traps on some machines. Now that it has been through QA, it is a perfect program: It does what it says it does.

Writing perfect software takes time for careful design, and money to pay for it. The U.S. space shuttle software is a case in point. At present, it costs $5,000 per line of code. This price[3] includes careful design, code reviews, testing, and then more testing. Yet each time a shuttle flies, the pilots are given a known bug list. One such bug was that if two people typed on two keyboards at the same time, the input buffer would get the OR of the two keyboard inputs (the workaround was to only use one keyboard at a time). How could such a gross error get past such an expensive test process? Obviously, the U.S. government did not have enough time and money. No one, though, has more time and money than the U.S. government, which means that for practical purposes, perfect software of substantial complexity is impossible until someone breeds a species of super-programmers.

Few people believe design bugs can be eliminated. Good specifications, good design methodology, good tools, good management, and good designers are all essential to quality software. These are the fault-prevention approaches, and they do have a big payoff. However, after implementing all these improvements, there will still be a residue of problems.

3.6.1 *N*-Version Programming and Software Fault Tolerance

The main hope of dealing with design faults is for designers to develop techniques to tolerate design faults, much as hardware designers are able to tolerate hardware faults. Of course, hardware design *is* software, so hardware designers have the same problem: Their techniques to tolerate physical hardware faults do not mask *design* faults. There are two major software fault tolerance techniques:

N-version programming.   Write the program *n* times, test each program carefully, and then operate all *n* programs in parallel, taking a majority vote for each answer. The resulting design diversity should mask many failures.

---

[3] A rule of thumb is that business software costs $10 to $100 per line of code, and system software costs $100 to $1,000 per line of code. At $5,000 per line of code, the cost for the shuttle and other military projects is about an order of magnitude higher than the industrial norm. The price differential comes from much more careful design and testing.

Transactions. Write each program as an ACID state transformation with consistency checks. At the end of the transaction, if the consistency checks are not met, abort the transaction and restart. Rerunning the transaction the second time should work.[4]

Both these approaches are statistical and both have merit, but both can fail if there is a fault in the original specification.

The *n*-version programming approach is expensive to implement and to maintain. That is because to get a majority, *n* must be at least 3. In addition, the *n*-version programming approach suffers from the "average IQ" problem. If *n* students are given a quiz, all of them will get the easy problems right, some will get the hard problems right, and almost none will get the hardest problem right (if it is a good quiz). Also, several will make the same mistakes. An *n*-version program taking this quiz would score in the 60th percentile. It would solve all the easy problems and might even solve a few of the harder problems. However, there would be no consensus, or consensus would be wrong, on the hardest problems.

A final problem with *n*-version programming is that module repair is not trivial. Since each module has a completely different internal state, one cannot simply copy the state of a good module to the state of a failing module. Without repair, *n*-plexing has a worse MTTF than simplexing (see Table 3.15).

N-version programming is often used in high-budget projects employing many low-budget programmers. You can imagine the controversy surrounding this idea. Better results might be obtained by spending three times more on better-quality programmers and on better infrastructure, or on more careful testing of one program.

3.6.2 Transactions and Software Fault Tolerance

Transactions are even more of a gamble. When a production computer system crashes due to software, computer users do not wait for the software to be fixed. They don't wait for the next release, but instead restart the system and expect it to work the next time; after all, they reason, it worked yesterday. By using transactions, a recent *consistent* system state is restored so that service can continue. The theory is that it was a *Heisenbug* that crashed the system. A Heisenbug is a transient software error (a soft software error) that only appears occasionally and is related to timing or overload. Heisenbugs are contrasted to *Bohrbugs* which, like the Bohr atom, are good, solid things with deterministic behavior.

Although this is preposterous, the test of a theory is whether it explains the facts—and the Heisenbug theory does explain many observations. For example, a careful study by Adams [1984] of all software faults of large IBM systems over a five-year period showed that most bugs were Heisenbugs. The Adams study dichotomized bugs into *benign* bugs—ones that had bitten only one customer once—and *virulent* bugs—ones that had bitten many customers or had bitten one customer many times. The study showed that the vast majority (well over 99%) of the bugs were benign (Heisenbugs). Adams also concluded from this study that customers should not rush to install bug fixes for benign bugs, as the expense and risk are unjustified.

There are several other instances of the Heisenbug idea. Most large software systems have data structure repair programs that traverse data structures, looking for inconsistencies.

---

[4] The fault-tolerance community often uses the term *recovery blocks* to mean transactions. But the recovery block concept is more like a checkpoint-restart mechanism than an ACID unit. It lacks the notions of isolation and durability.

Called *auditors* by AT&T and *salvagers* by others, these programs heuristically repair any inconsistencies they find. The code repairs the state by forming a hypothesis about what data is good and what data is damaged beyond repair. In effect, these programs try to mask latent faults left behind by some Heisenbug. Yet, their techniques are reported to improve system mean times to failure by an order of magnitude (for example, see the discussion of functional recovery routines in Mourad [1985] or in Chapter 8 of this book).

Heisenbug proponents suggest crashing the system and restarting at the first sign of trouble; this is the failfast approach. It appears to make things worse, since the system will be crashing all the time, and the database and network will be corrupted when the system is restarted. This is where transactions come in. Transactions, and their ACID properties, have four nice features:

Isolation. Each program is isolated from the concurrent activity of others and, consequently, from the failure of others.

Granularity. The effects of individual transactions can be discarded by rolling back a transaction, providing a fine granularity of failure.

Consistency. Rollback restores all state invariants, cleaning up any inconsistent data structures.

Durability. No committed work is lost.

These features mean that transactions allow the system to crash and restart gracefully; the only thing lost is the time required to crash and restart. Transactions also limit the scope of failure by perhaps only undoing one transaction rather than restarting the whole system. But the core issue for distributed computing is that the whole system cannot be restarted; only pieces of it can be restarted, since a single part generally doesn't control all the other parts of the network. A restart in a distributed system, then, needs an incremental technique (like transaction undo) to clean up any distributed state. Even if a transaction contains a Bohrbug, the correct distributed system state will be reconstructed by the transaction undo, and only that transaction will fail.

The programming style of failfast software designs is called *defensive programming* by analogy with the defensive automobile driving style advocated by traffic-safety experts. Defensive programming advocates that every software module check all its inputs and raise an exception if the inputs are incorrect. This essentially makes the software module failfast. The module checks all its parameters, and as it traverses internal data structures it checks their integrity. To give a specific example, a program traversing a doubly linked list checks the back-pointer in the next block to be sure that it points to the previous block, and the program checks other redundant fields in the block for sanity. If a list element does not satisfy these tests, then an error has been detected, and it is repaired by discarding the block or by repairing it. Whenever a module calls a subroutine, the callee checks the parameters for sanity, and the caller checks the routine's results. In case an error is found, an exception handler is invoked. Exception handlers are much like the repair programs mentioned earlier in this section. The exception handler either masks the exception (if it is an internal inconsistency that can be repaired), or the module reflects the exception back to the caller (if it is the caller's error). In extreme cases, the exception handler cannot mask the fault and, consequently, reflects it as a transaction abort, a subsystem restart, or another coarse form of recovery.

Failfast creates a need for instant crash and restart. This again may seem a preposterous approach, but computer system architectures are increasingly adopting this approach. The concept of *process pair* (covered in Subsection 3.7.3) specifies that one process should instantly (in milliseconds) take over for the other in case the primary process fails. In the current discussion, we take the more Olympian view of *system pairs,* that is two identical systems in two different places. The second system has all the data of the first and is receiving all the updates from the first. Figure 3.2 has an example of such a system pair. If one system fails, the other can take over almost instantly (within a second). If the primary crashes, a client who sent a request to the primary will get a response from the backup a second later. Customers who own such system pairs crash a node once a month just as a test to make sure that everything is working—and it usually is.

If Heisenbugs are the dominant form of software faults, then failfast plus transactions plus system pairs result in software fault tolerance. Geographically remote system pairs tolerate not just Heisenbugs, but many other problems as well. They tolerate environmental faults, operator faults, maintenance faults, and hardware faults. Two systems in two different places are not likely to have the same environmental problems: They are on different power grids, different phone grids, and different earthquake faults, and they have different weather systems overhead. They have independent operations staffs, different maintenance personnel, and different hardware. All this means that the two systems have largely independent failure modes. Section 12.6 develops the concept of system pairs in more detail.

3.6.3 Summary

Software faults are the dominant source of system failures. All other faults can be masked with a combination of redundancy, geographic diversity, and software to automate tasks. Software can automate system operations and mask operations and maintenance failures. Software faults, however, remain an unsolved problem.

There are two approaches to software fault tolerance: *n*-version programming and transactions. The two approaches could be combined. Advocates of *n*-version programming aim to combine several incorrect programs into a better, more reliable one. *N*-version programming may also be a good way to write failfast programs. Transaction advocates aim to detect incorrect programs and minimize their effects by undoing them. Transactions encourage a failfast design by allowing the system to quickly crash and restart in the most recent consistent state. By having a standby system, restart can begin within milliseconds.

3.7 Fault Model and Software Fault Masking

The application of the pair-and-spare or *n*-plex techniques to software modules is not obvious. How do you pair-and-spare a software module? How do you *n*-plex messages, remote procedure calls, and the like? The answer to these questions—process pairs—is neither trivial nor a direct application of the hardware *n*-plex and pair-and-spare approaches described in the previous section. To the authors' knowledge, the best approach to process pairs was worked out in an unpublished classic written by Butler Lampson and Howard Sturgis in 1976 at Xerox. At about the same time Joel Bartlett designed and implemented similar ideas for Tandem's Guardian operating system. The Lampson-Sturgis model has widely influenced subsequent work in the field; but, unfortunately it is not widely available.

Bartlett's work is even more inaccessible. The presentation here borrows heavily from those original works. The process pair discussion comes from experience with Bartlett's design.

Designing fault-tolerant programs requires a model. The model must define correct behavior, and if the programs are to deal with faults, the model must describe the kinds of faults and their relative frequencies. Given such a model, programs can be written, system reliability can be estimated using probabilistic methods, and proofs that the programs are correct can be made with any desired degree of formality. The validity of the model cannot be established by proof, since there is no formal model of reality. The strongest possible claim is that the physical system behaves like the model with probability p, and that p is very close to 1. This claim can only be established empirically, by estimating p from measurements of real systems.

The model here involves three entity types: *processes, messages, and storage.*[5] Each has a set of desired behaviors and a set of failure behaviors. This section shows how to transform each of the three entities from failfast entities into highly reliable and even highly available entities.

Faulty behavior is dichotomized into *expected* faults (those tolerated by the design), and *unexpected* faults (those that are not tolerated). Unexpected faults can be characterized as dense faults or Byzantine faults:

Dense faults.   The algorithms will be *n*-fault tolerant. If there are more than *n* faults within a repair period, the service may be interrupted.

Byzantine faults.   The fault model postulates certain behavior—for example it may postulate that programs are failfast. Faults in which the system does not conform to the model behavior are called Byzantine.

It is highly desirable that the system be failfast in the dense fault cases. That is, if there are more than n-faults in the repair window, the system should stop rather than continue the computation in some unspecified way. It is possible to measure the rate of unexpected faults in real systems and observe that the rate is small. Some representative measurements appeared in Sections 3.3 and 3.4.

Picking the model is a very painful and delicate process. One is constantly torn between simplicity and completeness. For example, when a storage module breaks and is repaired, in our model it returns to service in the empty state. A more complete model would have two kinds of repair. But a more complete model would be much bigger and would not make the ideas much clearer. The goal here is to provide a basis for understanding the fundamental issues and algorithms.

3.7.1 An Overview of the Model

The model describes each aspect of the system—storage, processors, and communications—by presenting a program that simulates the behavior of such entities, complete with their failure characteristics. For example, a storage module reads and writes data at storage addresses, but it also occasionally writes the data to the wrong place, invalidates a page, or

---

[5] It would be possible to dispense with storage, since storage modules are just processes. This is the view of the actor's model [Agha 1986]. No one has been able to unify the concepts of process and messages. Perhaps, by analogy with energy and matter, the two concepts are interchangeable, but both are needed because their functions are so different.

damages the whole store (the latter two events require the store to be repaired). Given these errant storage modules, the presentation then shows programs to mask the failures through failvote duplexing and writes a program to repair the failures in the background.

The presentation then models processes and messages. Messages can be lost, duplicated, delayed, corrupted, and permuted. By implementing sessions, timeouts, and message sequence numbers, all message failures are converted to lost messages. By combining this simple failure model with message acknowledgment and sender timeout plus message retransmission, the message system becomes highly available.

These techniques for building reliable stores and reliable messages demonstrate how software masks hardware faults, but they have little to do with masking software faults. Still, the presentation is instructive in that it sets the stage for the software fault tolerance discussion that follows.

Processes fail by occasionally being delayed for some repair period, having all their data reset to the null state, and then having all their input and output messages discarded. The presentation then uses this model to show how to build process-pairs. One process, called the primary, does all the work until it fails; then the second process, called the backup, takes over for the primary and continues the computation. During normal processing, the primary periodically sends *I'm Alive* messages to the backup. If the backup does not receive an *I'm Alive* message from the primary for a couple of messages periods, it assumes the primary has failed and takes over for the primary. Three kinds of takeover are described:

Checkpoint-restart.   The primary records its state on a duplexed storage module. At takeover, the backup starts by reading these duplexed storage pages.

Checkpoint message.   The primary sends its state changes as messages to the backup. At takeover, the backup gets its current state from the most recent message.

Persistent.   The backup restarts in the null state and lets the transaction mechanism clean up (undo) any recent uncommitted state changes.

The benefits and programming styles of these three forms of process pairing are contrasted. To preview that discussion:

Quick repair.   Process pairs obtain high availability processes by providing quick process repair.

Basic Pairs must Checkpoint.   Certain programs are below the transaction level of abstraction and must therefore use some form of checkpointing to get highly available program execution. Examples of such primitive programs are the transaction mechanism itself, the operating system kernel, and the programs that control physical devices (disks and communications lines).

Persistent is Simple.   Checkpointing of any sort is difficult to understand. Most people will want to use transactional persistent processes instead.

Process pairs mask hardware failures (processor failures) as well as transient software failures (Heisenbugs). As such, they are the key to software fault tolerance.

This concludes the overview. The following discussion turns to describing the behavior of storage, processes, and messages by the behavior of programs that simulate their behavior. The Lampson-Sturgis model is very instructive and provides a clear way of contrasting some subtle issues. However, the material is very challenging. Readers who do not care to delve in depth into this subject may wish to skim the rest of this section.

3.7.2 Building Highly Available Storage

Reliable storage is built as follows: First, the basic storage operations and failure behavior are defined. Then higher-level operations are defined; with high probability, these mask the failure behavior by n-plexing the devices. This is the analog of the hardware discussion of Section 3.6, but it is less abstract, since specific modules and specific failure modes are involved.

3.7.2.1 The Structure of Storage Modules

A storage module contains an array of *pages* and a *status* flag. If the module status is FALSE, then it has failed, and all operations on it return FALSE. Each page of a store has an *address,* a *value*, and a *status*. Addresses are positive integers up to some limit. The status is either TRUE or FALSE. If the page status is FALSE, the page value is invalid; otherwise, the page value stores the data most recently written to it. Two operations are defined on storage modules—one to write page values, and another to read them. Rewriting a page makes it valid (makes its status TRUE). Intuitively, these definitions are designed to model disks or RAM disks.

3.7.2.2 Definition of Store and of Store Read and Write

The definitions of the data structures for the programs are given in the following listing and are illustrated in Figure 3.17.

```
#define  MANY         100000          /*a big number (system will have many entities)  */
#define  MAXSTORES    MANY            /*with many stores                               */
#define  MAXSTORE     MANY            /* each holding many pages.                       */
#define  VSIZE        8192            /* size of a page value (also used for messages)  */
typedef  char *       avalue;         /* each value will be 8kB                          */
typedef  Ulong        address;        /* address is integer 0≤x<MAXSTORE                */
typedef  struct {                     /* template for a page                            */
         Boolean   status;            /* status is true if page is ok                   */
         char      value[VSIZE];      /* value of the page                              */
         } apage;                     /*                                                */
typedef  struct{                      /* define the template for a storage module       */
         Boolean   status;            /* flag indicates that module is functioning      */
         apage     page[MAXSTORE];    /* storage module has many pages                  */
         } astore;                    /*                                                */
astore   stores[MAXSTORES];           /* allocates the array of many stores             */
```

Storage objects support two operations: read and write. They are defined by the simple code fragments that follow. Notice in particular that writes may occasionally fail (with probability pwf) by having no effect.

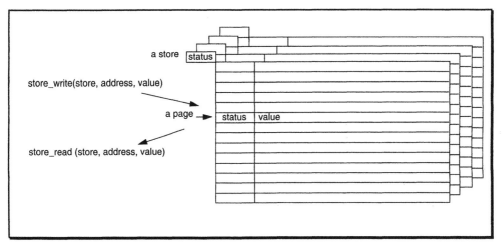

Figure 3.17: The data structures and verbs used by the model of storage. There are many stores, each of which carries a status flag indicating it is valid. Each store consists of many pages; each page has a status flag and a value. Such stores model disks and RAM disks.

```
#define        pwf      1E-6              /*probability write has no effect (1 in a million)      */
float          randf();                   /* returns a random float 0<x<1 (never 0 or 1)         */
/* write a value to a particular page of a particular store.                                     */
Boolean store_write(astore store, address addr, avalue value) /*                                 */
    { if (addr >= MAXSTORE) return FALSE;     /* return false if bad address                     */
    if (!store.status) return FALSE;          /* return false if store has faulted               */
    if (pwf > randf()) return TRUE;           /* sometimes write faults by doing nothing         */
    store.page[addr].status = TRUE;           /* set page status to valid                        */
    copy(store.page[addr].value,value, VSIZE); /* else store.page[addr].value=value              */
    return TRUE;                              /*                                                 */
    };                                        /*                                                 */
Boolean store_read(astore store, address addr, avalue value)  /*                                 */
    { if (addr >= MAXSTORE) return FALSE;     /* return false if bad address                     */
    if (!store.status) return FALSE;          /* return false if store has faulted               */
    if (!store.page[addr].status) return FALSE; /* or bad page value                             */
    copy(value,store.page[addr].value, VSIZE); /* else value=store.page[addr].value              */
    return TRUE;                              /*                                                 */
    };                                        /*                                                 */
```

These programs model, or simulate, durable storage devices such as disks, tapes, and battery-protected electronic RAM. For simplicity, the code does not model soft read faults (a read that fails but will be successful on retry). It does model the simple case of a write occasionally having no effect at all (null writes in the third statement of store_write()). This happens rarely, with a probability pwf (probability of write failure). As explained in the next paragraph, address faults (a write of a page other than the intended page) are modeled by page decay (spontaneous page failure) and by null writes (writes that have no effect).

The model assumes that reads and writes of incorrect locations produce a FALSE status flag and consequently are detectable errors. Both appear to be a spontaneous decay of the page (see below). Incorrect reads and writes are typically detected by storing the page address as part of the page value, so that a read of a wrong page produces a FALSE status flag. This mechanism also detects a write of a correct value to an incorrect address when the overwritten data is subsequently read, because the page address stored in the value will not match the page's store address. In addition, each page is covered by a checksum that is used as follows:

Write.   When a page is written, the writer computes the page checksum and stores it in the page, and

Read.   When the page is read, the checksum is recomputed from the value and compared to the original checksum stored in the page.

If the checksums do not match, the page is invalid. All this validity checking is implicit in the status flag.

3.7.2.3 Storage Decay

Each store and each page may fail spontaneously, or a page may fail due to an incorrect store_write(). The spontaneous failure is modeled by a *decay process* for each store. Operating in the background, this decay process occasionally causes a page to become invalid (status = FALSE) or even invalidates the entire store. The model postulates that store and page errors are independent and that the frequency of such faults obeys a negative exponential distribution with means MTTVF and MTTSF, respectively. Table 3.10 suggests values for such means. The storage decay process is given in the code segment that follows.

```
/* There is one store_decay process for each store in the system              */
#define  mttvf    7E5             /* mean time (sec) to a page fail, a few days  */
#define  mttsf    1E8             /* mean time(sec) to disk fail is a few years  */
void store_decay(astore store)                       /*                          */
    { Ulong  addr;                          /* the random places that will decay   */
    Ulong page_fail = time() - log (mttvf*randf());  /* time in seconds to next page decay  */
    Ulong store_fail = time() - log (mttsf*randf()); /* time in seconds to next store decay */
    while (TRUE)                             /* repeat this loop forever             */
        { wait(min(page_fail,store_fail) - time());  /* wait for next event          */
        if (time() >= page_fail)             /* if the event is a page decay        */
            { addr = randf()*MAXSTORE;       /* pick a random address               */
            store.page[addr].status = FALSE; /* set it invalid                      */
            page_fail = time() - log(randf())*mttvf; /* pick a wait time for next fault */
            };                               /* negative exp distributed, mean mttvf */
        if (time() >= store_fail)            /* if the event is a storage fault     */
            { store.status = FALSE;          /* mark the store as broken            */
            for (addr = 0; addr < MAXSTORE; addr++)  /*invalidate all page values   */
                store.page[addr].status = FALSE; /*                                 */
            store_fail = time() - log(randf())*mttsf; /* pick a time for next fault  */
            };                               /* negative exp distributed, mean mttsf */
        };                                   /* end of endless while loop           */
    };                                       /*                                     */
```

As defined, storage gradually decays completely. According to the parameters described earlier, half the stores will have decayed after three years. Such stores are not reliable—reliable devices continue service from their pre-fault state when the fault is repaired. The model assumes that each store and each store page are failfast and are repaired and returned to service in an empty state; that is, all pages have status = FALSE. Algorithms presented next will make them reliable.

3.7.2.4 Reliable Storage via *N*-Plexing and Repair

In Section 3.6, we saw that repair is critical to availability. The goal is to build reliable stores from off-the-shelf, unreliable components. A reliable store can be constructed by *n*-plexing the stores, by reading and writing all members of an *n*-plex group, and by adding a *page repair process* for each group of stores. Storage is assumed to have exponentially distributed repair times with a mean of a few hours (MTSR $\approx 10^4$ seconds). This includes the latency to detect storage faults.

The idea here is to divide the stores into groups of *n* members and then to pretend that there are only

$$\frac{MAXSTORES}{n}$$

logical stores. Each reliable_write() attempts to write all members of the group, and each reliable_read() attempts to read all members of the group.[6] The write case is easy and is represented by the following code:

```
#define nplex    2                                 /* code works for n>2, but do duplex    */
Boolean reliable_write(Ulong group, address addr, avalue value) /*                          */
    { Ulong      i;                                 /* index on elements of store group      */
    Boolean status = FALSE;                         /* status is true if any write worked    */
    if (group >= MAXSTORES/nplex) return FALSE;     /* groups = 1/nth of stores              */
    for (i = 0; i < nplex; i++ )                    /* write each of the n stores in the group. */
        status = status ||                          /* status indicates if any write worked  */
            store_write(stores[group*nplex+i],addr,value);  /*                               */
    return status;                                  /* and return status                     */
    };                                              /*                                       */
```

Note that a really careful design might read the value after writing to make sure that at least one of the pages now has the correct value.

The reliable_read() faces two problems:

All fail.   If none of *n* members can be read, then reliable_read() fails. This should be rare. If its frequency is unacceptably high, then *n* can be increased.

Ambiguity.   If *some* of the *n* members are readable (all have good status) but give different values, there is a dilemma: which value should the reliable_read() return? The problem can easily arise if some earlier writes fail (had no effect or had an address fault). This problem can't be solved by increasing *n*; in fact the frequency of the problem increases with *n*. Setting *n* to 1 "solves" the problem but does not give a reliable store.

---

[6] Concurrently writing *n* replicas creates synchronization problems if multiple writers race multiple readers and writers. For the moment, assume that each operation is serialized as a unit. Serializing the operations is covered later.

One solution to resolving ambiguous reads is to take the majority view, the most popular value. But that only works if there is a majority value. If there are two stores and two values (the most common case), there is no majority.

The premise is that there is a correct value—the most recently written one.[7] Thus it is postulated that each page has a *version* generated at the time of the write as part of the value.[8] The key property is that version numbers increase monotonically. Page value versions are assumed to have the property

(version(value1) > version(value2)) *if and only if*

(value1 was written more recently than value2).

If the *n*-plex reliable_read() discovers a version mismatch, it takes the most recent value and writes that to all other members of the group. In addition, if it finds a member with bad status, it rewrites that member with the most recent version. This could be left to the repair process, but it is repeated here to minimize the latency between fault detection and repair. The reliable read code for *n*-plex stores follows.

```
Ulong version(avalue);                              /* returns version of a value              */
/* read an n-plex group to find the most recent version of a page                             */
Boolean reliable_read(Ulong group, address addr, avalue value) /*                             */
    { Ulong       i       = 0;                      /* index on store group                    */
    Boolean       gotone  = FALSE;                  /* flag says had a good read               */
    Boolean       bad     = FALSE;                  /* bad says group needs repair             */
    avalue        next;                             /* next value that is read                 */
    Boolean       status;                           /* read ok                                 */
    if (group >= MAXSTORES/nplex) return FALSE;     /* groups = 1/nth of stores                */
    if (addr >= MAXSTORE) return FALSE;             /* return false if bad address             */
    for (i = 0; i < nplex; i++ )                    /* for each page in the nplex set          */
        { status = store_read(stores[group*nplex+i],addr,next); /* read its value              */
        if (! status ) bad = TRUE;                  /* if status bad, ignore value             */
        else                                        /* have a good read                        */
            if (! gotone)                           /* if it is first good value               */
                {copy(value,next,VSIZE); gotone = TRUE;}/* make it best value                  */
            else if ( version(next) != version(value))  /* if a second value, compare          */
                { bad = TRUE;                       /* if different, repair needed             */
                if (version(next) > version(value)) /* if new value is best version            */
                copy(value, next, VSIZE);           /* copy it to best value                   */
        };          };                              /* end of read all copies                  */
    if (! gotone) return FALSE;                     /* disaster, no good pages                 */
    if (bad) reliable_write(group,addr,value);      /* repair if saw any bad pages             */
    return TRUE;                                    /* success                                 */
    };                                              /*                                         */
```

---

[7] This is a major difference between the software view of redundancy and the hardware view. The hardware view must insist on a majority, because it has no understanding of the data being stored. The software often has very clear ideas about the meaning of the data.

[8] In Subsection 10.3.7 this version is the log sequence number (called the page LSN), but it could just as well be a timestamp reliably generated by the hardware.

If an *n*-plexed page is not read for many years, all *n* copies of it will likely decay. To prevent this scenario, a store repair process runs in the background for each *n*-plex group. This process merely reads each page of the group once a day (or at some other frequency). The reliable_read() routine performs any needed repair. As part of its normal operation, it reads all copies and updates them if any disagree or are bad. The store repair process repairs any broken pages in a store within a day of its failure, since it visits each page about that often.

```
/* repair the broken pages in an n-plex group. Group is in 0,...,(MAXSTORE/nplex)-1        */
void store_repair(Ulong group)                    /*                                       */
    { int    i;                                   /* next address to be repaired           */
     avalue  value;                               /* buffer to hold value to be read       */
    while (TRUE)                                   /* do forever                            */
        for (i = 0; i <MAXSTORE; i++)             /* for each page in the store            */
            { wait(1);                             /* wait a second                         */
             reliable_read(group,i,value);         /* do a reliable read (that will repair pages */
    };       };                                    /*                      if they do not match)  */
```

3.7.2.5 Optimistic Reads of the *N*-Plex Group

N-plexing of disks and other storage is common and is implemented as described previously. Writes are done to both disks. But often, especially in the duplexed disk case, the read operation is *optimistic*: it is directed to only one disk. If that fails, then the other disk is consulted. The logic is something like this:

```
Boolean optimistic_read(Ulong group,address addr,avalue value) /*                          */
    {if (group >= MAXSTORES/nplex) return FALSE;   /* return false if bad disk address      */
    if (addr >= MAXSTORE) return FALSE;            /* return false if bad page address      */
    if (store_read(stores[nplex*group],addr,value)) /* read one value and if that is ok     */
        return TRUE;                               /* return it as the true value           */
    else                                           /* if reading one value returned bad     */
        return (reliable_read(group,addr,value));  /* then do n-plex read and repair.       */
    };                                             /*                                       */
```

Optimistic reading is dangerous. Suppose one of the *n* store_write() operations within a reliable_store_write() fails; that is, suppose it is a null operation. Then, that storage group of pages will have different page values and different page versions. If only one member of the *n*-plex is read, it may have the old version rather than the new version, a *stale read*. Stale reads occur half the time for a duplexed disk page damaged by a failed write. Believers in optimistic reads assume each disk is failfast. If so, the writer can sense the write failure and immediately initiate recovery. Recovery from the write failure includes retrying the write, sparing the page to a new location (remapping the address to a new storage page), or ultimately invalidating the whole storage module containing the bad page. The stale write problem often is not carefully thought through, and it is a typical flaw in optimistic *n*-plex schemes. To summarize, optimistic reads get the performance benefits of reduced read traffic but risk reading stale data.

The implementation of storage operations assumes that each *n*-plexed read and write is atomic. That is, if I do a read while you are doing a write, then I will see the store as it was

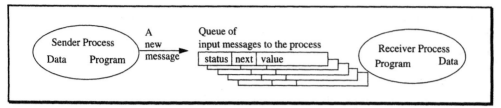

Figure 3.18: The flow of a message sent by a process to the input queue of another process.
Message_send() operation copies data from the sender's address space to a message that is transported to the receiver. When the receiver process executes message_get(), the data is copied to the receiver's address space. A status flag indicates whether the message has been corrupted in transit. When a process fails, its data and input message queue are reset to their initial (null) state.

before or after your write, but not the state during your write. A similar assumption applies to two concurrent write operations. The usual way to ensure this one-at-a-time serialization is to have some (reliable and available) process perform the storage reads and writes for everyone else. Such a server, which serializes the requests, could be appointed for each n-plex page or for any larger group. Alternatively, a locking scheme can be used. A highly available and reliable server manages the lock requests for individual pages and serializes access to the pages, but it actually does none of the work. Each of these designs suggests the need for reliable processes, which is the next topic.

The preceding discussion covered n-plexing of storage. A different approach is to use one or more stores to hold an error-correcting code for a set of stores [Patterson et al. 1988]. This approach could also be described and analyzed using the model presented here. That is left as a term-project exercise.

3.7.2.6 Summary

A simple model of storage and storage failures captures much of the logic used in I/O subsystems. It allows careful definition of n-plexed storage modules and illustrates the version mismatch problem for n-plex stores as well as the stale-version problem for optimistic reads. In addition, it points out the need for the store_repair() process and the simplicity of that process. Given the statistics used by this model (see Sections 3.3 and 3.4), a computation of the probability of various failure modes shows that duplexing modern disks and other nonvolatile storage devices provides highly reliable and highly available storage.

3.7.3 Highly Available Processes

Highly reliable and available processes can be constructed from failfast processes and messages. Processes and their interactions cannot be discussed without talking about messages; unfortunately, the opposite is also true. Because we have to begin somewhere, we start by defining messages. The treatment of messages beyond their definition is reserved for the next subsection. Indeed, it will turn out that reliable messages require reliable processes to implement them.

3.7.3.1 Messages Defined

Processes interact by sending messages to one another or by writing to shared storage that is later read by others. A *message* is a value sent from one process to another. Figure 3.18 diagrams the flow of a message from a sending process to a receiving process.

Message delivery is not reliable. Some messages are lost (they are never delivered). Some may be delayed, arbitrarily permuting the message delivery order to a process's input queue. Even if a message is delivered, there is some small chance it will be *corrupted,* so that the message data is unreadable. The loss and corruption of messages is quantified as the probability of message failure, pmf. There is a comparable chance that the message will be *duplicated*, so that the message appears twice in the process's input queue. The following example code demonstrates the external definition of message gets and sends.

```
/* definitions of constants and data structures used by the message simulation    */
#define  pmf      1E-5              /* probability of message failure (loss or corrupt)  */
#define  pmd      1E-5              /* probability of message duplication     */
typedef struct Message * amessagep;  /* pointer to a message structure        */
typedef  struct Message{            /* struct defining message formats       */
        Boolean     status;         /* status is true if message data (value) is ok  */
        amessagep  next;           /* pointer to next input message of this process  */
        avalue     value;          /* data in the message                   */
        } amessage;                 /*                                       */
```

```
/* Send a message to a process, returns true if process exists              */
Boolean message_send(processid him, avalue value); /*                       */
/* Get the next input message of this process: Returns true if there is a message else false.  */
/*                     In true case, valuep addresses message, status is msg status    */
Boolean message_get(avalue * valuep, Boolean * msg_status);     /*          */
```

The next piece of code gives a sense of how these routines are used, and it defines a useful routine. This get_msg() routine discards corrupt input messages and returns false if there are no good new messages in the process input queue, or returns true and the data of the next input message.

```
/* return pointer to next valid input message in valuep and return TRUE or return FALSE  */
Boolean get_msg(avalue * valuep)               /*                           */
   { Boolean     msg_status = FALSE;           /* flag says msg value is not corrupt  */
     Boolean     msg_exists = FALSE;           /* flag says next input msg exists    */
     while (msg_status = FALSE)                /* read until have good msg or queue empty  */
        {   msg_exists = message_get(&valuep, &msg_status); /* get next msg if it exists  */
            if (!msg_exists) break;}           /* if input queue is empty, quit read loop  */
     return msg_exists;                        /* return msg to caller            */
   };                                          /*                             */
```

This completes our brief overview of messages. Messages are explored further in Subsection 3.7.4, following the introduction of reliable processes.

3.7.3.2 Process Fault Model

A process executes a program, transforms the process state, and displays an execution behavior. The process's *external behavior* is a sequence of store_read(), store_write(), message_send(), and message_get() operations. This external behavior is created by the process executing its program logic on the process state. Each process state is a bundle of bytes containing its program and data. Each process has two states, an *initial state* that never changes and a *current state* that changes at each program step. In addition, each process has an *input queue,* an unordered set of messages sent to it by other processes.

```
#define  MAXPROCESS  MANY               /* the system will have many processes        */
typedef Ulong processid;                /* process id is an integer index into array  */
typedef struct {char program[MANY/2];char data[MANY/2]} state; /* state is program + data */
struct { state        initial;          /* process initial state                      */
         state        current;          /* value of the process state                 */
         amessagep    messages;         /* queue of messages waiting for process      */
         } process [MAXPROCESS];        /*                                            */
```

A process fails by stopping for a while (say, an hour) to be repaired, then being reset to its initial state, and having all its unprocessed input messages discarded. That is analogous to a restart of processors in many operating systems. At any instant, each process runs the risk of faulting. After a reset, the process executes its restart logic and continues processing. Of course, it runs the risk of experiencing another reset during the restart.

Here is a way to think of process faults: Imagine that each process is implemented by a lower-level automaton that usually executes the next step of the process, but sometimes stops the process execution for a repair period, discards all the process' messages, resets the process to the initial state, and then continues the process execution from the initial state (this state includes the process' program). In addition, the process may have defensive programming tests that cause it to failfast by calling panic() if the test is false. These calls to panic are modeled as just another aspect of the execution automaton occasionally failing the process. Such an automaton is defined as follows:

```
/* Process Decay : execute a process and occasionally inject faults into it            */
#define  mttpf    1E7                    /* mean time to process failure ≈4 months     */
#define  mttpr    1E4                    /* mean time to repair is 3 hours             */
void process_execution(processid pid)    /*                                            */
    { Ulong      proc_fail;              /* time of next process fault                 */
      Ulong      proc_repair;            /* time to repair process                     */
      amessagep  msg, next;              /* pointers to process messages               */
      while (TRUE)                       /* global execution loop                      */
          { proc_fail = time() - log(randf())*mttpf;  /* the time of next fail          */
            proc_repair = -log(randf())*mttpr;        /* delay in next process repair   */
            while (time() < proc_fail)   /*                                            */
                { execute(process[pid].current);};   /* execute for about 4 months  (work)  */
            (void) wait(proc_repair);    /* wait about 3 hrs for repair        (break) */
            copy(process[pid].current,process[pid].initial,MANY); /* reset to initial state (fix). */
            while (message_get(msg,status) {};   /* read and discard all msgs in queue  */
    };  };                               /* bottom of work, break, fix loop            */
```

3.7.3.3 Reliable Processes via Checkpoint-Restart

So far, the processes described are failfast: they either execute the next step, or they fail and reset to the null state. They are not reliable because they do not repair their state upon failure. This failure behavior is similar to the storage failure model in which stores return to service in the null state. Some mechanism is needed to repair the process state, that is, to bring it up to its most recent value.

There are many ways to build such reliable processes from failfast processes. For simplicity, assume that every process' state fits within a single page. It is then easy to generalize to larger processes.

The following discussion proceeds by example, showing three different ways to implement the same server process. The server's job is to return a unique sequence number, called here a *ticket*, to each client upon request. It must never return the same ticket number to two different client requests. Clearly, to achieve this the server must reliably remember the most recently granted ticket number.

The simplest design is the *checkpoint-restart* approach. The process keeps two copies of its state in reliable storage. At each state change, it overwrites the oldest state value (ticket number) in reliable storage. At restart, it reads both state values and resumes execution from the most recent one (see Figure 3.19). The following code gives a simple example of a reliable checkpoint-restart process.

```
/* A checkpoint-restart process server generating unique sequence numbers for clients.    */
checkpoint_restart_process()                          /*                                   */
    { Ulong  disk = 0;                                /* a reliable storage group with state */
    Ulong    address[2] = {0,1};                      /* page address of two states on disk  */
    Ulong    old;                                     /* index of the disk with the old state */
    struct   { Ulong  ticketno;                       /* process reads its state from disk.  */
               char          filler[VSIZE];           /* newest state has max ticket number  */
               } value [2];                           /* current state kept in value[0]      */
    struct   msg{                                     /* buffer to hold input message        */
               processid   him;                       /* contains requesting process id      */
               char          filler[VSIZE];  } msg;   /* reply (ticket num) sent to that address */
/* Restart logic: recover ticket number from persistent storage                             */
    for (old = 0; old<=1, old++)                       /* read the two states from disk       */
        { if (!reliable_read(disk,address[old],value[old] ))  /* if reliable read fails      */
            panic(); };                               /* then failfast                       */
    if (value[1].ticketno < value[0].ticketno) old = 1;  /* pick max seq no and determine    */
        else { old = 0; copy(value[0], value[1],VSIZE);};  /* which value is old.            */
/* Processing logic: generate next number, checkpoint, and reply                            */
    while (TRUE)                                       /* do forever                          */
        { while (! get_msg(&msg)) {};                  /* get next request for a ticket number */
        value[0].ticketno = value[0].ticketno + 1;     /* increment ticket number             */
        if ( ! reliable_write(disk,address[old],value[0])) panic(); /* checkpoint             */
        old = (old + 1) % 2;                           /* use other disk for state next time  */
        message_send(msg.him, value[0]);               /* send the ticket number to client    */
    };   };                                            /* endless loop to get messages.       */
```

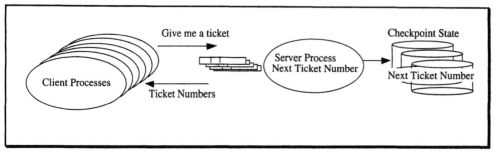

Figure 3.19: The checkpoint-restart model of reliable process execution. The process records all state transitions in the checkpoint state. When the process fails and is restarted, it refreshes its most recent state from the checkpoint-restart state. Such repair and restart yield reliable but not highly available processes, since repair times can last for hours.

Checkpoint-restart is a classic technique that has been widely used for decades (see Figure 3.1). Its major problem is that the repair time for the process can be quite long, since the process does not resume service until it is started and refreshes its state from persistent storage. The total repair time is therefore the process repair time plus the restart time, which, according to the model, is several hours altogether.

Because of the long repair times, checkpoint-restart yields highly reliable process execution, but not highly available process execution. The goal is to continue the process execution immediately after the process faults, meaning instant (almost zero) MTTR of process faults. If the fault is caused by hardware, it is likely that pair-and-spare hardware or triplexed hardware can mask it. If the fault is caused by software, by operations, or by environment (as most faults are), then the process and processors will fault, and the process will stop. Why not have a second process in a second processor take over from the first if the first process fails? That idea, called process pairs, is the next technique.

3.7.3.4 Reliable and Available Processes via Process Pairs

The *process pair* technique is somewhat analogous to *n*-plexed storage; it is a collection of *n* processes dedicated to providing a service. One of the processes is *primary* at any time. The primary process delivers the service. If the primary fails, the backup process continues the service. Clients send their requests to the primary, and if the primary fails, the new primary informs the clients of its new role.[9]

The two-process case, *process pairs*, is subtle enough. It allows a second process to *take over* from the primary. There are two delicate aspects of takeover:

Detection. Knowing that the primary is dead (being repaired).

Continuation. Knowing the most recent state of the primary.

As with all aspects of fault tolerance, detecting the primary failure is purely statistical. Because the primary can send messages only when it *is* operating, a failed primary cannot

---

[9] There is a generalization of process pairs to groups of *n* processes. But, as we will see, process pairs are close to or beyond the complexity barrier. In addition, the MTTF equations suggest that process pairs offer very long MTTF (≈30,000 years). For this reason the *n*-plex generalization is not considered here.

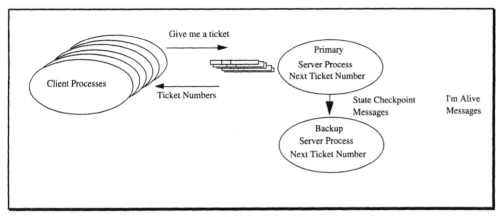

Figure 3.20: The process-pair model of reliable process execution. The primary server process sends all its state transitions to the backup process. When the primary process fails, the backup takes over, executing in the most recent state. This can yield takeover times measured in microseconds or milliseconds, providing high availability. The backup detects primary failure by noticing that no *I'm Alive* messages have arrived from the primary in a long time.

inform the backup that the primary is broken. For this reason, the primary sends *I'm Alive* messages to the backup on a regular basis. If one *I'm Alive* message fails to arrive on time, it is assumed to be delayed or damaged. But if several *I'm Alive* messages fail to arrive within a reasonable time, the backup assumes that the primary did not send them and is being repaired.

Suppose the backup has decided that the primary is dead. What should it do? How can it continue the computation from the most recent primary state? First, it needs to know the most recent primary state. The usual technique is for the primary to combine state-change messages to the backup with the *I'm Alive* messages, so-called *checkpoint messages*. For example, in Figure 3.20 the *I'm Alive* messages are being sent frequently to the backup. Clearly, the state-change messages can piggyback on the *I'm Alive* messages, or they can act as surrogates for them. The basic logic of a process-pair program is shown in Figure 3.21.

The idea presented in Figure 3.21 is that both processes start out in the restart state. One process (say, the even-numbered one) is the default primary and takes priority by waiting only one second to see if the other is alive. After two seconds, either the default primary process will have generated an *I'm Alive* message to the default backup, or the backup decides the primary is dead. In that case, the backup becomes the primary. In any case, whichever becomes the primary broadcasts its identity to all concerned and then goes into a loop of looking for input and processing it. This loop continuously sends *I'm Alive* messages to the backup, whether there is any input or not. For its part, the backup sleeps for a second, looks to see what the new state is, and then goes back to sleep. The "newer state" test is designed to avoid the possible permutation of messages in the input queue by ignoring states older than the current backup's state. This test also discards duplicate messages. If the backup does not get a new state within a second, then the primary must be dead, since the primary ought to be able to send hundreds of *I'm Alive* messages in that time. If the primary is dead, the backup broadcasts that it is the new primary and waits for requests.

There is one more delicate takeover issue. At takeover, the backup is in the same state the primary was in when it sent the checkpoint message to the backup. But the primary may have failed before sending the reply that the last state transition generated (the bottom box of

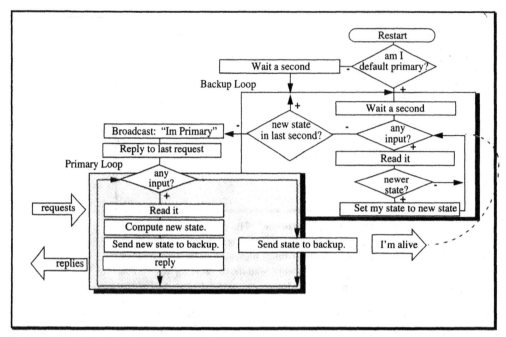

Figure 3.21: The logic for a process pair. The primary process spends most of its time in the shaded box (primary state), where it reads requests, computes the new state, sends the new state to backup, and then replies. If it has nothing else to do, the primary simply sends out an *I'm Alive* message, presumably generating thousands per second. The backup, executing exactly the same program, consumes these *I'm Alive* and state checkpoint messages. If no messages from the primary arrive at the backup for one second, the backup assumes the primary is dead and takes over the responsibilities of the primary.

Figure 3.21). So, if a reply was owed to a client, the reply is resent. This may generate a duplicate message to the client, but that was a possibility of the message system anyway.

To continue the discussion of Figure 3.21: If the maximum propagation time for messages is one millisecond, and the maximum service time for a request is a millisecond, then waiting ten milliseconds (five message cycles) is long enough to detect process failure. This period is long enough for five consecutive lost *I'm Alive* messages if processors are dedicated to processes. Thus, process takeover times of ten milliseconds can easily be achieved. Typically, though, the primary shares the processor with other processes and, for resource consumption reasons, does not continuously send *I'm Alive* messages. Consequently, a longer latency is more typical.

In fault-tolerant operating systems, process pairs are a basic notion provided by the system. Such operating systems inform the backup process when the primary process fails and automatically redirect all new client requests to the backup process. This means that the primary can dispense with the idle state checkpoint messages and the *I'm Alive* messages. It also means that the backup can dispense with the one-second waits, because all the messages are important. The backup can also dispense with the broadcast to clients at startup and takeover. These are just performance optimizations; the programming style of checkpointing state changes is the same for this simple model and for the "real" fault-tolerant systems.

Adapting the checkpoint_restart_process() example to process_pair_process() using the logic of Figure 3.21 is straightforward (about one page of C code). The complexity of process pairs apparent in the above explains why the discussion here is restricted to process pairs, rather than including *n*-plexed processes.

3.7.3.5 The Finer Points of Process-Pair Takeover

No known technique continues process execution immediately after a fault.[10] The known techniques offer takeover times on the order of a few message propagation delays. In a cluster or local network, this takeover can happen in milliseconds when software overheads are considered; in long-haul nets, the message propagation delays imply that takeover times will be on the order of tens or hundreds of milliseconds (see Section 2.9 for a discussion of message propagation times). To clients operating on a time scale of seconds, this takeover may appear immediate. Certainly, it is a big improvement over the availability offered by the checkpoint-restart approach, which has outages measured in minutes or hours.

There are a few additional details. If state-change checkpoint messages were permuted in the backup process' input queue, then an old state might replace a newer one. The permuted messages problem is easily solved by having the primary process sequence number the state-change messages, and by having the backup ignore old ones—ones with sequence numbers less than the current sequence number. The next problem is much more serious. If the checkpoint messages are lost *and* the primary fails, then the backup will not be in the correct state. At this point, one must appeal to the single-fault tolerance assumption. These are process pairs; they tolerate single faults. If both a process and the message fail, then there is a double failure, which is not protected. Assuming independence of failures, the mean time to such failures is approximately MTTPF/pmf, the time to a process failure over the chance that the most recent message was lost. For the numbers chosen in the process and message model above, that is ($\approx (10^7/10^{-5}) = 10^{12}$) seconds, or about thirty-thousand years. If that answer is not acceptable, then a safer approach is to have the backup acknowledge receipt of the state change before the primary responds to the client. But now the primary has to sense backup failures (it has to know when to stop waiting for the backup to acknowledge). This acknowledged-checkpoint strategy is the one used in the Tandem Computer's process pairs; for the sake of simplicity, however, it is not the one described here.

The ticket-number generator program was used to demonstrate checkpoint-restart logic. This three-line program is not very demanding, either as a checkpoint-restart process or as a process pair. Its only requirement is that it never generate the same ticket number twice. As such, it fails to expose one of the most delicate issues in takeover. Suppose the primary is performing some real operation, such as advancing the rods in a nuclear reactor by one inch, and then it fails. The backup may be in a quandary: did the primary perform the operation or not? The backup cannot tell unless it "looks" at the rods. Sometimes, though, it is not possible to "look."

A whole vocabulary has been built up around this problem. First, an operation is *testable* if the program can reliably establish whether the operation has been performed and

---

[10] One scheme, called atomic broadcast, sometimes works. In atomic broadcast, the client sends requests to N different servers and accepts the first response. This works well if all requests to the servers commute (if ordering is not important). Read-only servers have this property. In general, however, requests do not commute. Thus, if two clients broadcast their requests to *n* servers, the servers may process the requests in different order. This can produce different final states and different answers. For this reason the *n*-server design forces the servers to agree to an ordering of the requests in the general case. Such an ordering mechanism is called *atomic broadcast*. It synchronizes the servers and so introduces delays in transaction (request) processing.

the desired effect achieved. Writing pages to disk is testable (they can be read to see if they have changed). Moving reactor arms to a particular position is testable, but movement to a relative position is not: "move to position X is testable," while "move 1 inch" is not testable. Writing to a display or printing on paper is not testable. In general, many physical operations are not testable. The safe thing, then, is to redo the operation: move the reactor arm to position X again, write to the display again, print the message again, and write to the disk again. But not all operations can safely be redone. An operation is *restartable* or *idempotent* if redoing it is safe; that is, if redoing it an arbitrary number of times is equivalent to doing it once. Moving the reactor rods one inch is not restartable, printing a check is not restartable (n operations are likely to print n checks), and inserting a record at the end of a file is not restartable (it may insert the record n times); but moving the rods to position X, writing a disk page, and writing a display are probably idempotent operations.

In Figure 3.21, resending the reply message at takeover is trying to deal with the idempotence issue. The takeover process cannot tell whether the client received the reply to his request, so the server resends the reply on the premise that the message will be discarded by the client if it is a duplicate. The operation is not testable, but it is assumed to be idempotent.

3.7.3.6 Persistent Processes—The Taming of Process Pairs

As can be seen from the previous discussion, writing process pairs is very demanding. Indeed, it is the authors' experience that everyone who has written one thinks it is the most complex and subtle program they have ever written. However, reliable systems use these techniques, and those systems do mask many failures.

There is a particularly simple form of process pair called a *persistent process pair*. Persistent process pairs have a property that is variously called *context free, stateless,* or *connectionless*. Persistent processes are almost always in their initial state. They perform server functions, then reply to the client and return to their initial state. The primary of the persistent process pair does not checkpoint or send *I'm Alive* messages, but just acts like an ordinary server process. If the primary process fails in any way, the backup takes over in the initial state.

Persistent process pair takeover works as follows. The underlying fault-tolerant operating system knows that the primary and backup are a process pair. If the primary fails, or if the processor on which the primary is executing fails, the operating system of the backup process senses the failure and informs the backup process of the failure. The operating system also redirects all client messages to the backup. In this situation, the backup takes over in its initial state and begins offering service.

As described, persistent processes are easy to program and make high-availability servers, but these servers seem to provide little more than encapsulation of the server logic to the client. The servers do not maintain network state or database state. To make persistent processes useful, someone else must maintain such states.

For example, imagine that such a persistent process acted as your mailbox. It would receive messages for you, but would always return to the null state (no messages for you)—not a very useful program. Similarly, if the server actually kept your state in a file, the updates to receive or discard a mail message might be partially incomplete at the time the server failed. In this case, your mailbox file would be left in that state by the backup persistent process when it took over in the null state.

These examples hint at the solution. A persistent process server should maintain its state in some form of transactional storage: a transaction-protected database. When the primary process fails, the transaction mechanism should abort the primary's transaction, and the backup should start with a consistent state. On the other hand, if the server calls commit_ work() after making the changes, the transaction mechanism should reliably deliver the server's message to the client as part of the atomicity guarantee of ACID transactions.

Given that, the transaction mechanism returns the database and the network to their state as of the start of the server function. Persistent processes need not send application check-point messages to indicate state changes, since the initial state is the takeover state. When running on a fault-tolerant system that provides persistent process pairs as a primitive, the program need not concern itself with takeover or message retransmission. That logic is handled for the program by the underlying system. All this makes persistent process pairs very easy to program. They have the following form:

```
persistent_process()                        /* prototypical persistent process              */
    { wait_to_be_primary();                  /* wait to be told you are primary              */
    while (TRUE)                              /* when primary, do forever                     */
        { begin_work();                       /* start transaction or subtransaction          */
        read request();                       /* read a request                               */
        doit();                               /* perform the desired function                 */
        commit_work();                        /* finish transaction or subtransaction         */
        reply();                              /* reply                                        */
        };                                    /* did a step, now get next request             */
    };                                        /*                                              */
```

The following code illustrates the checkpoint-restart ticket server of Subsection 3.7.3.3 reprogrammed as a transactional server.

```
/* A transactional persistent process that acts as a server generating unique tickets for clients  */
persistent_ticket_server()                   /* current state kept in sql database           */
    { int     ticketno;                       /* next ticket number (local variable from DB)  */
    struct    msg{                            /* buffer to hold input message                 */
              processid    him;               /* contains requesting process id               */
              char         filler[VSIZE];     /* reply (ticket number) sent to that addr       */
              } msg;                          /*                                              */
    /* Restart logic: recover ticket number from persistent storage                          */
    wait_to_be_primary();                     /* wait to be told you are primary              */
    /* Processing logic: generate next number, checkpoint, and reply                         */
    while (TRUE)                              /* do forever                                   */
        { begin_work();                       /* begin a transaction                          */
        while (! get_msg(&msg));              /* get next request for a ticket number         */
        exec sql update ticket set ticketno = ticketno + 1; /* increment the next ticket number */
        exec sql select max(ticketno)         /* fetch current ticket number                  */
              into :ticketno                  /*    into program local variable               */
              from ticket;                    /*    from SQL database                         */
        commit_work();                        /* commit transaction                           */
        message_send(msg.him, value);         /* send the ticket number to client             */
    };  };                                    /* endless loop to get messages.                */
```

Notice that to become a process pair, the ticket server application did nothing more than represent its state in transactional storage and call the operating system routine wait_to_be_primary(). There are no checkpoint messages, no *I'm Alive* messages, and no takeover logic. Yet this process has much higher availability than the checkpoint-restart process. In addition, if the transaction did complex updates to its database, each group of updates (transactions) would have all the ACID properties.

3.7.3.7 Reliable Processes plus Transactions Make Available Processes

Transactions provide highly reliable execution, but ACID says nothing about availability. All the ACID properties are reliability properties. Process pairs provide highly available execution (processes), but they are hard to program because takeover is so delicate. The transaction ACID properties provide clean takeover states: transactions combined with persistent process pairs give both high reliability and high availability by allowing simple programs to use process pairs.

Virtually all fault-tolerant application-level process pairs are now programmed as persistent processes. Only low-level processes (device drivers, disk servers, TP monitors, and the transaction mechanism itself) are programmed as raw process pairs. These more basic processes cannot use the persistent process approach, primarily because they are below the level of abstraction that provides the high-level process-pair and transaction mechanisms.

Highly available systems contain many process pairs. The storage repair processes mentioned previously need to be process pairs. If the storage is shared and access to it must be serialized, then the storage servers should be process pairs. If reliable storage is to be implemented, then the reliable writes should indeed be reliable (write *all n* of the *n*-plex). To protect against faults within the reliable write code, it should be run as a process pair, and so on.

Process pairs depend critically on the premise of single failure (only one processor fails) during the repair period. If the pair of processes has a shared power supply (or shared memory or any other single point of failure that can disable them both), then this assumption is violated. The processes must therefore be connected to each other, to their storage, and to their clients via dual networks. They must have independent power supplies and, of course, they must have different processors and memories. In addition, each component should have independent failure modes and be failfast. It is fair to say that today most hardware systems are not constructed to meet these demands. Several attempts to build process-pair systems have failed. Yet there are two successful examples, Tandem's Guardian system and IBM's XRF system. The XRF design demonstrates that it is possible to retrofit these ideas to a pre-existing general-purpose transaction processing system (IMS in this case).

In summary, given failfast processes that fail independently, there are two ways to get highly reliable processes (checkpoint to storage or checkpoint to a backup process) and one way to get available processes (process pairs). The model allows us to talk about and analyze both.

3.7.4 Reliable Messages via Sessions and Process Pairs

Having shown how to convert faulty processes and faulty storage to highly available processes and storage, the discussion turns to converting faulty messages to highly reliable messages. This section first defines the behavior and fault model for messages. It then shows how sessions, session sequence numbers, acknowledgment, timeout, and retransmission can all be combined to provide reliable message delivery. Since either the message source process or the destination process can fail, process pairs are part of the mechanism needed to convert faulty messages into reliable messages.

3.7.4.1 Basic Message Model

A process can send a message to another process by invoking message_send(), which specifies the process identifier and the message data. This copies the message data from the sender's address space to the receiver's input queue. The receiver can then call message_get() to copy the message from its input queue to its address space.

The message and process queue definitions were already given. Here is the code to implement message_send and message_get:

```
/*send a message to a process:        returns true if the process exists              */
Boolean message_send(processid him, avalue value)  /*                                 */
        { amessagep    it;                          /* pointer to message created by this call   */
        amessagep  queue;                           /* pointer to process message queue   */
        if (him > MAXPROCESS) return FALSE;          /* test for valid process            */
loop:   it = malloc(sizeof(amessage));              /* allocate space to hold message and fill   */
        it->status = TRUE; it->next = NULL;          /* in the fields                     */
        copy(it->value,value,VSIZE);                 /* copy message data to message body  */
        queue = process[him].messages;               /* look at process message queue      */
        if (queue == NULL) process[him].messages = it;  /* if the queue is empty then     */
        else                                         /* place this message at head of queue  */
            {while (queue->next != NULL) queue = queue->next; /* else find end of queue    */
             queue->next = it;}                       /* and place the message at queue end .   */
        if (randf() < pmf) it->status = FALSE;        /* sometimes message is corrupted.   */
        if (randf() < pmd) goto loop;                 /* sometimes the message is duplicated  */
        return TRUE;                                  /*                                   */
        };                                            /*                                   */

/* get the next input message of this process:     returns true if there is a message   */
Boolean message_get(avalue * valuep, Boolean * msg_status)/*                            */
        { processid   me = MyPID();                   /* caller's process number           */
        amessagep  it;                                /* pointer to input message          */
        it = process[me].messages;                    /* find caller's process message queue  */
        if (it == NULL) return FALSE;                 /* return false if queue is empty     */
        process[me].messages = it->next;              /* take first message off the queue   */
        *msg_status = it->status;                     /* record its status                 */
        copy(valuep,it->value,VSIZE);                 /* value = it->value                 */
        free(it);                                     /* deallocate its space              */
        return TRUE;                                  /* return status to caller           */
        };                                            /*                                   */
```

Messages have simple failure modes; some fraction of them spontaneously decay (status = FALSE) and some fraction of them are duplicated. This models failure of communication lines, buffer overflows, and the like. It also models the retransmission logic underlying message systems that occasionally duplicate a message. In addition, the messages in a process's input queue may be arbitrarily permuted. This models the possibility that messages can be arbitrarily delayed in the network.

3.7.4.2 Sessions Make Messages Failfast

As defined, messages are not failfast; corrupt and duplicate messages are delivered, and messages are delivered out of order. The first step in making messages reliable is to give them simple failure semantics—failfast semantics. To make all messages failfast, faulty messages are converted to lost messages. Message semantics, then, are as follows: (1) messages are delivered in order, and (2) some messages are lost. In the simplified model, the only form of message failure is a lost message.

First, let's convert corrupt messages to lost messages. The message status flag models the idea that the message contents are self-checking, so that corrupt messages can be detected and discarded. It is standard to compute a message checksum at the source and to send the checksum as part of the message. The receiver recomputes the checksum and compares it to the sender's checksum. If the two checksums are different, the message has been corrupted and is discarded. This converts a corrupt message to a lost message. The get_msg() procedure defined in Subsection 3.7.3.1 discards all such corrupt messages.

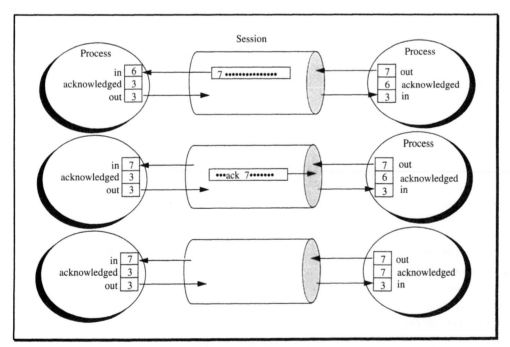

Figure 3.22: The three steps of sending a message via a session between two processes. Each session endpoint maintains three sequence numbers. A new message is tagged with the sender's next *out* sequence number. The receiver increments its *in* sequence number when the next sequential message is received. The receiver sends an acknowledgment message for that sequence number. When the sender gets the acknowledgment, it increments its *acknowledged* sequence number. This mechanism detects duplicate and delayed messages.

The simplest approach to detecting and discarding duplicate and permuted messages is to use sessions and message-sequence numbers. A *session* is a bidirectional message pipe between two processes. Sessions have the following semantics: (1) messages are delivered to the destination in the order they were sent, and (2) no messages are duplicated or lost, but messages can be delayed. Sessions are variously called connections, sockets, pipes, dialogs, opens, ports, and myriad other names. In this text, sessions are represented by pipe icons, as shown in Figure 3.22.

Sessions implement these semantics by having the two session endpoints each maintain three sequence numbers: (1) the *out* sequence number, which is the sequence number of the most recently sent message on that session, (2) the *in* sequence number, which is the sequence number of the most recently received message on that session, and (3) the *acknowledged* sequence number, which is the sequence number of the most recently acknowledged message.

Each message from one process to another carries a sequence number. When a new message is sent to that receiver, the sender's *out* sequence number is incremented and used to tag the sender's message. When the receiver gets the message, if the sequence number is one greater than the most recent message, the recipient knows it is the next message and accepts it. The recipient increments the *in* sequence number and sends an (unsequenced) *acknowledgment message* to the sender, saying that the new message arrived.

Sequence numbers detect duplicate and delayed messages as follows: If a message is duplicated, the message sequence number is also duplicated; thus the recipient can detect a duplicate message by noticing that the message sequence number is equal to the most recently acknowledged sequence number. In this case, the recipient discards the message and does not change its *in* sequence number. In either case, the recipient acknowledges the message to the sender.

If a message is delayed and hence arrives out of order, the recipient can see that the message sequence number is less than the most recently acknowledged message and consequently can discard the message. It need not acknowledge such messages.

As described so far, sessions create the simple failure semantics of sending messages in order, thereby making messages failfast. If there were no failures, such sessions would work perfectly. But, as soon as there is a message failure, the session starts discarding all future messages in that direction. So far, then, the design has made messages failfast. The next step is to make messages reliable by repairing lost messages.

3.7.4.3 Sessions plus Retransmission Make Messages Reliable

To restate the session message-sending protocol: When one process sends a message to another, the sender increments the session *out* sequence number and tags the message with the session name (the names of the two processes) and the sender's current *out* session sequence number. The sending process then waits for an acknowledgment message, called an *ack*, from the recipient. The ack message carries the session name and the original message sequence number. Because message failures cause messages to be lost, the acknowledgment may never arrive. In such cases, the sender must resend the message.

To repair lost messages, the sender has a *timeout* period. If the sender does not receive an ack within a timeout period, it *retransmits* the message and continues to do so until an ack is received. If the sender and receiver are functioning, the message eventually is delivered, and the ack is delivered. When that happens, the sender declares the message delivered and increments its acknowledged sequence number.

3.7.4.4 Sessions plus Process Pairs Make Messages Available

The discussion so far has focused on message failures and ignored process failures. What if the sending or receiving process fails? In that case, the message has nowhere to go or no sender to retransmit it. A session is only as reliable as its two endpoints.

The obvious solution to making reliable session endpoints is to make each endpoint a process pair. In this design, sessions connect process pairs so that delivery of new messages to the backup is automatic if the primary fails. Messages that have already been sent to the primary are probably lost and will not arrive at the backup. The sequence numbers of the primary are also maintained as part of the backup process state. If a process fails, that endpoint of the session switches to the backup of that process pair. The backup will have the current sequence numbers, and if it is sending, it will have a copy of the current message.

The logic for this is simple: The sender first checkpoints the message to the backup and then sends the message. If the backup takes over, it resends the message and continues the session. The receiver checkpoints received messages to its backup before acknowledging them. This logic is diagramed in Figure 3.23.

At process-pair takeover, the backup process broadcasts its new identity and resends any unacknowledged messages that the primary process was trying to send. The other session endpoint may get a takeover broadcast from the backup process of the process pair. In that case, the other endpoint begins sending the message to the former backup process,

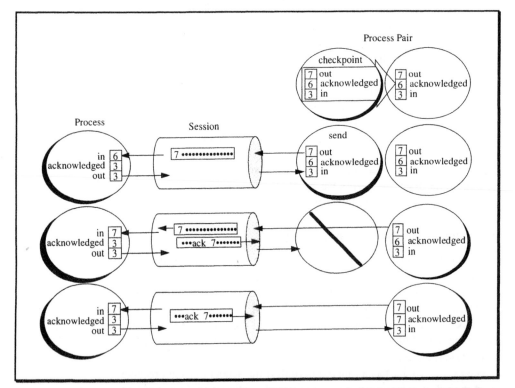

Figure 3.23: The process pair logic for sessions. Each session endpoint is a process pair. Before sending a message or an acknowledgment, the process checkpoints the state change to its backup. When a process fails, the session endpoint switches to the backup process that takes over the session. Now all messages flow to the backup.

which is now the new primary process of the process pair. When the message is finally delivered and acknowledged, the next message can be sent via the session.

To restate this development: Session sequence numbers convert permuted messages and duplicate messages into lost messages, making all messages failfast and making sessions failfast-communications services. Acknowledgment, timeout, and retransmission make messages reliable by resending them. Messages eventually get through. Process pairs make the endpoints available; they are persistent in sending the messages until they are acknowledged. Messages are as available as the processes that send them and the wires that carry them. If the processes are duplexed, and the wires are n-plexed, the messages can be made highly available. The various time constants (acknowledge times and takeover times) are limited by message delay and processor speed. It is possible to give reliable delivery within seconds for wide-area systems ($\approx$10,000 km) and within tens of milliseconds for local area systems (1 km). These time constants are discussed in Section 2.6.

3.7.4.5 The Code for Sessions and Messages

The code to implement sessions, acknowledgment and retransmission, and process-pair checkpoint and takeover is instructive. First, sessions and message formats are defined, and an array of sessions is added to the state of each process. These sessions hold the endpoint names and the sequence numbers.

```
/* definition of a session address, the source and destination processes (or process pairs)   */
typedef struct    Session * asessionp;             /* typedef for session pointer               */
typedef struct    Session{                         /* typedef for sessions                      */
                  processid    source;             /* source process (or pair) of session (sender) */
                  processid    target;             /* destination process of session (receiver) */
                  Ulong        in;                 /* sequence number of most recently acked msg */
                  Ulong        out;                /* sequence number of most recently sent msg */
                  Ulong        ack;  } asession;    /* sequence number of most recent ack        */
enum MSG_TYPE { MSG_NEW,MSG_ACK,MSG_TAKEOVER};  /*                                              */
typedef struct Session_message * a_session_messagep;  /* typedef for session pointer            */
typedef struct Session_message{                    /* typedef for messages flowing on sessions  */
                  asession      session;           /* a msg has session name plus sequence nums */
                  MSG_TYPE      type;              /* message type: data, ack, takeover.        */
                  avalue        value;             /* data if this is a data message            */
                  } a_session_message;             /*                                           */
/* each process has an array of sessions and for each session a list of input messages          */
asession      my_session[MAXPROCESS];              /* sessions belonging to this process        */
amessagep   in_msg_queue[MAXPROCESS];              /* process queue of acked input messages     */
void initialize_sessions(void)                     /*                                           */
    { int him;                                     /*                                           */
    for (him = 0; him<MAXPROCESS; him++)           /* initialize global structures              */
       {my_session[him].source = MyPID();          /* session is from my process id             */
       my_session[him].target = him;               /* to his process id                         */
       my_session[him].in = my_session[him].ack = my_session[him].out = 0;  /* seq numbers start at zero */
       in_msg_queue[him] = NULL;                    /* process input queue is null initially     */
    };   };                                        /* end of initialization of process session arrays */
```

In addition, assume that the message_send() and message_get() routines have been abstracted to session_send() and session_get() routines. These routines send and get messages that carry a session descriptor and a message type (that is, they manipulate the a_session_message type rather than just a_message type). These routines pack and unpack the session descriptor and message type descriptor as added framing information on messages. Session_send() fills in the session descriptor and value for each message. Session_get() extracts these two fields from the next process input message and returns them. Session_get() must read the message to find the session name and the sequence number. If the message is corrupt (status = FALSE), session_get() cannot read these fields and discards such messages. Consequently, it has no status parameter; any message it returns is not corrupt. These are the interfaces:

Boolean **session_get(asession *session, MSG_TYPE *type, avalue * value);**
Boolean **session_send(asession session, MSG_TYPE type, avalue value);**

The reliable_send_message() routine sends the message, waits for the timeout period, and if no acknowledgment message has arrived, it sends the message again. It continues this until the message has been acknowledged (the acknowledgment mechanism is explained momentarily):

```
const Ulong   timeout = 1;                              /* sender's timeout for ack wait               */
void reliable_send_message(processid pid, avalue value)  /* send a message reliably                    */
    { asessionp sessionp= &my_session[pid];              /* point at the session to that process        */
    sessionp->out = sessionp->out + 1;                   /* increment session out sequence number       */
    checkpoint(*sessionp,value);                         /* checkpoint session and msg to backup        */
    do                                                   /* keep sending until msg is acknowledged      */
        {session_send(*sessionp, MSG_NEW, value);        /* send                                        */
        wait(timeout);}                                  /* wait a second                               */
    while (sessionp->out != sessionp->ack);              /* repeat until message is acknowledged        */
    };                                                   /*                                             */
```

In this design, the sender continues sending until the receiver acknowledges the message. The receiver may be doing something else at the moment—computing, writing storage, or even sending a message to some third process. The receiver, therefore, may not be interested in acknowledging the sender's message right away. Waiting for the receiver's acknowledgment might cause message deadlock, with each process waiting for an acknowledgment from the next. To avoid such deadlocks, and to speed message flows, acknowledgments should be generated quickly and asynchronously from the receiver's application program logic. This means that each process should regularly poll its input sessions for messages. Such a requirement, however, would make programs both unreadable and error-prone.

Even more fundamental, perhaps, is the fact that the sender in the code above assumes someone else is going to update the acknowledgment sequence number. The reliable_ send_message() code could perform this logic, but it would vastly complicate the code. In general, this is the kind of logic that another process should manage as a service for all processes in the address space.

To preserve the program structure, almost all systems use the concept of multiple processes sharing one address space to perform such asynchronous tasks (see Chapter 2). Such lightweight processes are often called *threads,* but the generic term *process* is used here. These processes execute continuously and autonomously from the main application, communicating with it primarily via shared memory. The main application function is implemented as one or more processes (threads), and service functions such as message acknowledgment are implemented as other processes.

Each address space has a *listener* process that performs message acknowledgment and increments message sequence numbers for the application process executing in that address space. The listener is constantly polling the application process's sessions. When a message arrives, the listener executes the sequence number logic. If the message is a data input message, the listener acknowledges the message and places it in the session's message queue for the application program process. If the message is an acknowledgment, the listener implements the ack sequence number logic. Figure 3.24 illustrates the role of the listener .

The listener process executes continuously, running at high priority. When there are no input messages, it waits for the next event (in the sample code it waits for a second rather than for an event). In most designs, the listener places a limit on how many messages it will accept from a sender. This is called *flow-control.* Otherwise, senders could flood the receiver with messages, consuming all the listener's storage. For simplicity, such refinements are not included in the example. Also for simplicity, the code does not deal with takeover (process pairs). The listener maintains the process sequence numbers and the FIFO session message queues.

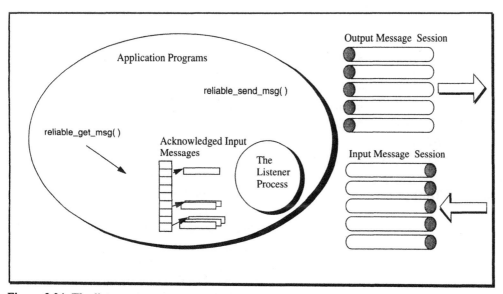

Figure 3.24: The listener process manages message acknowledgment for the processes executing in the address space. It executes asynchronously within the address space of the application process. Its job is to quickly acknowledge input messages arriving via the input sessions, adding them to the process input queue. It also manages the session sequence numbers and checkpoints changes to the backup process of the process pair.

```
/* The listener process runs in the background of each address space. It acknowledges input        */
/* messages and records the acknowledgement of sent messages                                       */
void listen(void)                                      /*                                           */
    {asession      session;                            /* the session the message arrived on        */
    processid      him;                                /* identity of message sender                */
    MSG_TYPE       type;                               /* type of message (data, ack, other)        */
    Ulong          seqno;                              /* sequence number of message                */
    avalue         value;                              /* contents of message                       */
    amessagep      it;                                 /* pointer to new msg added to queue          */
    amessagep      queue;                              /* pointer to session message queue           */
    initialize_sessions();                             /* initialize global structures              */
    while (TRUE)                                       /* do forever: read msgs and ack them         */
        { while (session_get(&session,&type,&value))   /* get message, if none wait a second         */
            { him = session.source;                    /* who sent the message                       */
            seqno = session.out;                       /* extract message sequence number            */
            switch (type)                              /* what kind of message                       */
                {case MSG_NEW:                          /* a new data message                        */
                    { if (my_session[him].in == (seqno - 1)) /* if it is the next message            */
                        {it = malloc(sizeof(amessage))  /* get and format the message block          */
                        copy(it->value,value,VSIZE);    /* copy message to queue element             */
                        it->next =NULL;                 /* it is at the end of the enqueue            */
                        if (in_msg_queue[him] == NULL)  /* if queue is empty add                      */
                            in_msg_queue[him] = it;     /* element to queue head                      */
                        else { for(queue = in_msg_queue[him] ; queue->next != NULL ; ); /*           */
                                queue = queue->next;    /* else go to end of the queue                */
                                queue->next = it;};     /* and insert new message                     */
                        my_session[him].in ++;          /* increment sequence number                  */
                        checkpoint(my_session[him],value);} /* ckpt session and message to backup     */
                    session_send(session,MSG_ACK,value);} /* ack message in any case                 */
                case MSG_ACK:                           /* got an ack for a message                  */
                    {if (session.out == my_session[him].out) /* if it ack's most recent send          */
                    my_session[him].ack ++;}            /* increment acknowledged seqno               */
                case MSG_TAKEOVER:                      /* process pair takeover message             */
                    {};                                 /* logic not handled in this example          */
                default: {};                            /* ignore message by default                  */
                };                                      /* end of case switch on message type         */
            };                                          /* end of get message loop                    */
        wait(1);                                        /* nothing in input queue, wait a second      */
    };    };                                            /* end of listener infinite loop.             */
```

The picture thus far is that the listener acknowledges receipt of messages promptly and
saves these messages as part of the process (pair) state. The acknowledged input messages of
each session are chained from the in_msg_queue[] of that session in most-recent-last order. It
should now be clear that reliable_send_message() does reliably send messages. It retrans-

mits every second until the message is acknowledged and the listener records that acknowledgment by incrementing the session.ack sequence number.[11]

Reliable_get_message() gets the next message value from a particular session by accessing the message queue maintained by the listener. The code to reliably get a message follows:

```
Boolean reliable_get_message(processid him, avalue value)   /* get a message                          */
   { amessagep msg = in_msg_queue[him];                      /* points a first msg in queue            */
   if (msg == NULL) return FALSE;                            /* return false if queue empty            */
   in_msg_queue[him] = msg->next;                            /* remove msg from queue                  */
   copy(value,msg->value,VSIZE);                             /* copy msg value (value = msg->value)    */
   free(msg);                                                /* deallocate message storage block       */
   return TRUE;                                              /*                                        */
   };                                                        /*                                        */
```

3.7.4.6 Summary of Messages

Reliable_get_message() and reliable_send_message(), combined with the listener process, convert ordinary messages into failfast messages. They discard corrupt messages, duplicates, and permutations. Sender timeout and retransmission until acknowledgment transform failfast messages into reliable messages. Process pairs make the session endpoints available, thereby transforming reliable messages into highly available messages. This sequence of steps shows how ordinary unreliable messages can be transformed into a reliable and available message service.

Fault-tolerant operating systems provide the reliable message get and send logic, the listener logic, and the logic to redirect messages to the backup of a process pair at takeover. For this reason, most application programmers are unaware of the acknowledgment-timeout-retransmission issues; they are even unaware of the checkpointing of the message sends and acknowledgments to the backup. But it is useful to have this simple model of how the underlying message system works.

One nice way to talk about messages is to say that raw messages may be delivered zero or more times. By adding sequence numbers and discarding duplicates, messages are delivered *at most once*. Such messages, however, may be delivered once or not at all. By adding retransmission, messages are delivered to a process *exactly once*. But this just means the message was delivered to the listener. Perhaps the message was never delivered to the application, or was never acted upon by the receiver. By adding process pairs, the message is *processed exactly once*. Consequently, these techniques give a simple form of message atomicity and durability (the A and D of ACID).

3.7.5 Summary of the Process-Message-Storage Model

The preceding gives a simple simulation model of the three components of a computer system. The message and storage models show how software can mask hardware faults by

---

[11] Both reliable_get_message() and reliable_send_message() share the session and message queue data structure with the listener process. Updates to this shared data structure must be synchronized by a semaphore or by the use of atomic machine instructions as described in Chapter 12. That issue is ignored here.

using redundancy in hardware, duplexing storage, wires, and processors. It also shows how software can use redundancy in time by retransmitting a message if the first one fails.

This material gives a sense of three styles of software fault tolerance: checkpoint-restart, process pairs, and persistent processes. It also gives a sense of the relative difficulty and benefits of the three styles, with the goal of convincing the reader that, if possible, persistent processes plus transactions should be used to obtain highly available program execution.

In addition, this simplified model (leave aside the actual implementation) is fairly complex. No formal or theoretical development of these ideas is available—it would be too difficult and complex to handle. In contrast, the model might work well for simulation studies to help quantify the relative benefits of design alternatives.

3.8 General Principles

We have all learned the following two rules, and done so by bitter experience:

KISS.   Keep It Simple, Stupid!

Murphy.   Whatever can go wrong will go wrong at the worst possible time and in the worst possible way.

Modularity, failfast, n-plexing, and ACID are all attempts to deal with these rules. Imagine programming a module that either works or misbehaves arbitrarily, and trying to tolerate the arbitrary misbehavior. That is the behavior predicted by Murphy's law. Failfast, also called all-or-nothing (atomicity), simplifies failure modes. Simplicity is what KISS is about. Don't be fooled by the many books on complexity or by the many complex and arcane algorithms you find in this book and elsewhere. Although there are no textbooks on simplicity, simple systems work and complex ones don't. Modularity, failfast, n-plexing, and ACID are mechanisms that simplify design, and make it easier to build systems with high functionality yet simple structure.

Given that things fail, and given that they fail fast, then repair is important to both reliability and availability. Process pairs, disk pairs, system pairs, and quick message retransmission all yield repair times measured in milliseconds—in effect, instant repair for people and physical processes that operate on time scales of seconds.

If faults are independent, then single-fault tolerance, combined with repair, yields MTTFs measured in decades or millennia. At these rates, other factors become significant (labor disputes, fires, floods, business panics, or whatever). The next improvement is several orders of magnitude away and is justified only rarely, generally only when human life is at stake.

Designing a fault-tolerant system needs a model of fault modes and their frequencies. The hardware and software design should minimize module interdependencies to get good fault containment. If faults are to be independent, the modules should have independent failure modes—suspenders and a belt, rather than two pairs of suspenders or two belts. This is sometimes called *design diversity*.

A model of fault tolerance needs to be *end-to-end*. It needs to look at the whole system, including operations and environment, to make estimates of system reliability and availability and to tolerate faults at the highest level of abstraction. The next section has an extended example of end-to-end problems.

The models used in the previous three sections are not end-to-end: They focus on the narrow topics of hardware or software fault tolerance. But they do allow careful discussion of the key fault-tolerance architectural issues. The message model and storage model of the previous section are relatively easy to understand and use. In contrast, the process pair model is intellectually challenging for the brightest people. As such, process pairs are a dangerous tool. Transactions combined with persistent process pairs are a solution. They provide simple process pairs (persistent execution) and a simple fault model.

In the limit, all faults are software faults—software is responsible for masking all the other faults. The best idea is to write perfect programs, but that seems infeasible. The next-best idea is to tolerate imperfect programs. The combination of failfast, transactions, and system pairs or process pairs seems to tolerate many transient software faults.

3.9 A Cautionary Tale—System Delusion

The focus here on system failures ignores the common end-to-end problem of *system delusion*: The computer system and its communications and terminals are up, but the output is untrustworthy or useless because the database is inconsistent with reality. System delusion generally results from *incorrect transactions* and from *unrecorded real-world activities*.

A specific example of system delusion may help in understanding the problem. Company X built an elaborate system to optimize and control the inventory of spare parts used for repairs. The application tracks many field locations, each with various types of in-use parts and spare parts. It also tracks a few central stock locations where parts ordered from manufacturers are stored until they are needed in the field. The stock locations also receive from field sites any unneeded spares and any defective parts that require repair. In principle, each field location does a transaction any time it uses a part or removes it from use, and a transaction each time it needs parts from central stock or returns parts to central stock. A central administrator runs transactions to release parts from central stock to the field, to order more parts from vendors, to record their receipt, and so on. As stated, this is a classic inventory-control problem.

As it turns out, the big problem with this system is not system failures. These do occur, but they are minor compared to the difficulties caused by unrecorded activities and by incorrect transactions.

Unrecorded real-world activities were a problem for various reasons. For example, optimal spare stocking levels are not intuitively obvious to people in the field. Most field managers gradually acquired extra spares, beyond what a reasonable inventory manager would agree was needed. Exactly how the field managers did this wasn't entirely clear, but they did it. Then, every once in a while they would get tired of seeing spares sitting around gathering dust and would dump the excess into cartons and send it back to central stock, but without any indication of where it was sent from (this to avoid admitting they had the stuff in the first place). Such activities guaranteed that the transaction system was constantly out of touch with reality, which made inventory management remarkably difficult. In particular, the spare reorder process tended to be seriously unstable.

This problem was eventually solved by adding heuristics to detect locations reporting activities inconsistent with recorded stocks. These tests triggered a physical reinventory of those sites. Even that was an art. For example, the field managers routinely hid excess inventory in the women's rest rooms.

Another example demonstrates the difficulties caused by incorrect transactions. An improperly trained clerk, told to change the accounting classification of a very large number of parts, spent two weeks deleting these parts from the database. When this was discovered, it was impossible to just roll forward from two weeks ago because, although database backups and log tapes were available, the incorrect deletions had caused various other things to happen that had real-world consequences. Complicating the situation, the deletions had caused the deleted part descriptions to disappear entirely from the on-line database (in hindsight, a serious flaw in application design). So, several people spent a month going back through the journal tapes looking for and recreating the deleted modules. Meanwhile, nobody really trusted the output of the transaction system; as a result, a lot more people spent time manually reviewing transactions.

The point of these two stories is that a transaction system is part of a larger closed-loop system that includes people, procedures, training, organization, and physical inventory, as well as the computing system. Transaction processing systems have a stable region; so long as the discrepancy between the real world and the system is smaller than some threshold, discrepancies get corrected quickly enough to compensate for the occurrence of new errors. However, if anything happens (as in the case of the improperly trained clerk) to push the system out of its stable zone, the system does not restore itself to a stable state; instead, its delusion is further amplified, because no one trusts the system and, consequently, no one has an incentive to fix it. If this delusion process proceeds unchecked, the system will fail, even though the computerized part of it is up and operating.

More generally, this is an end-to-end argument. Most transaction processing systems are vulnerable to failure by getting out of touch with reality. System delusion doesn't happen often, but when it does there is no easy or automatic restart. Thus, to the customer, fault tolerance in the transaction system is part of a larger fault-tolerance issue: How can one design the entire system, including the parts outside the computer, so that the whole system is fault tolerant? This may involve such exotic things as finding heuristics that detect transactions and data patterns that are seriously out of touch with reality. System designers must consider such organizational and operational issues as part of the overall system design.

3.10 Summary

The first section of this chapter reviewed empirical studies of computer systems and showed that the major sources of failure are environment, software, and operations. Hardware, maintenance, and process are relatively minor failure sources today, and the trend is for them to become even more reliable.

The next section described how hardware designers do it: they use either pair-and-spare or TMR to get failfast modules with instant mean time to repair of a single fault. Repair was shown to be a critical part of the design.

The discussion then turned to software, exploring two approaches: n-version programming and transactions. Both schemes try to mask transient software failures. It was shown that n-version programming without repair is of questionable value.

Next, a more detailed software fault masking view was explored. Simple fault models for processes, storage, and messages were defined. These unreliable entities are first transformed into failfast stores, processes, and messages. Then they are transformed into reliable and available entities. N-plexing of storage with a version number for each logical page provides highly available storage. Sequence numbers, acknowledgment, timeout, and retransmission provide reliable messages, and process pairs provide highly available execution. Process pairs are needed to ensure that messages are delivered reliably and that replicated storage groups are updated reliably. These concepts are the basis for understanding the algorithms used in "real" fault-tolerant systems.

At a low level, hardware designers must deal with pair-and-spare or TMR, and software gurus must deal with process pairs. Fortunately, most of us are handed this substructure and even a transaction processing system built on top of it. Given these, we can build applications and subsystems using ACID transactions, persistent processes, system pairs, reliable messages, and reliable storage. Mid-level software—such as database systems, compilers, repositories, operator interfaces, performance monitors, and so on—can all be written atop this base as "ordinary" applications. The transaction mechanism with failfast hardware and instant repair can then mask most systems programming faults, most application programming faults, most environmental faults, and most operations faults.

The chapter concluded with some free design advice: keep it simple and worry about end-to-end issues. To drive home the end-to-end point, an extended example of system delusion was described—a system that was "up" but was completely out of touch with reality because it did not tolerate faults in the organization it served.

3.11 Historical Notes

Fault tolerance has been important since the inception of computers, and there have been an enormous number of contributors to the field. Von Neumann's early work is generally cited as the beginning, but Charles Babbage mentioned the need for redundancy. Of course, auditors have been performing duplicate calculations and keeping multiple copies of things for millennia. Error detection and correction has been a key part of data transmission for many decades.

The empirical measurements are based on Eiichi Watanabe's translation of a study done by the Japanese. In addition, we benefited from the work of Ed McClusky's students at Stanford in the mid 1980s [Mourad 1985], and from Ed Adams's study of IBM software faults [Adams 1984]. Many people, who wish to remain anonymous, gave us statistics on the availability of their (or their competitors') systems. Those statistics are encrypted within this chapter.

Disk duplexing was widespread soon after disks were invented; disks were very unreliable at first, making duplexing essential. As disks became more reliable, duplexing became more exotic, but it had a rebirth as disks got cheaper.

The ideas for failfast, pair-and-spare, and TMR were worked out by the telephone companies, the military, and the deep-space missions. The book by Avizienis [1987] gives a good survey of those developments. Avizienis' later study [1989] and Abbot [1990] do a good job of reviewing work on *n*-version programming. The seminal text on fault-tolerant computing by Dan Siewiorek and Robert Swarz [1982] contains a wealth of information. Section 3.5 borrows heavily from their analysis of availability and reliability. The tutorial by Flaviu Cristian [1991] gives a good summary of current work in fault-tolerant systems from a software perspective. Bruce Lindsay is credited with coining the term Heisenbug.

The ideas for process pairs have deep roots as well. The presentation in this chapter draws heavily from the process-pair design of Joel Bartlett in Tandem's Guardian operating system done in 1974, and from the Lampson and Sturgis paper [1976]. Alsberg and Day

[1976] had similar ideas in that era, but seem not to have developed them. The model of storage and messages is based on the Lampson-Sturgis model [Lampson 1979 and Lampson 1981].

The ideas for system pairs also go back a long way. Many such systems have been built since 1960. General-purpose systems are just beginning to emerge. The first organized approach to this problem was SDD-1. Typical reports describing that system are Bernstein and Goodman [1984] or Hammer [1980]. Notable commercial systems are IBM's XRF [IBM-IMS-XRF] and Tandem's RDF [Tandem-XRF]. Intensive research on this topic is proceeding at Princeton [Garcia-Molina 1990], IBM Research [Burkes 1990], and Tandem [Lyon 1990].

The taxonomy of *at least once*, *at most once*, and *exactly once* message semantics is due to Alfred Spector. The concept of the *testability* of an operation is due to Randy Pausch [1987].

Exercises

1. [3.1, 10]. This exercise is designed to get you thinking about failure rates. Suppose you are 20 years old and you learn that one 20-year old in a thousand will die this year. (a) What is your mean time to failure? (b) What is your failure rate per hour? (c) If there are 100 people in your class, all the same age, what is the chance one of them will die this year? (d) Why is the answer to question (a) so much higher than your life expectancy? (e) Is this failure rate memoryless on the time scale of weeks and on the time scale of decades?

2. [3.1, 20]. Even though the mean time to failure of a module is one year, a module may operate for many years without any failure. The probability of a failure within a certain time may be estimated as follows: The arrival rate of failures is $\lambda = 1/\text{MTTF}$. Suppose, as is often done, that failure rates obey the standard negative exponential distribution that has the formula $f(t) = \lambda \cdot e^{-\lambda t}$. Then the chance of not failing between now and time T is the integral of this function

$$F(T) = \int_0^T \lambda e^{-\lambda t} = 1 - e^{-\lambda T} \qquad (3.15)$$

Returning to the original example, what is the chance of failing within .5 year, within 1 year, within 2 years, and within 10 years?

3. [3.1, 10]. Suppose your car has four failure modes with the following mean times to failure: wreck: 20 years, mechanical: 1 year, electrical: 3 years, flat tire: 3 years, and out-of-gas: 3 years. (a) What is the mean time to failure of the car? (b) How much better would it be if you never ran out of gas?

4. [3.1, 10]. Suppose a module has MTTF of one year and that its failure rate is memoryless. Suppose the module has operated for five years without failure. Use Equation 3.15 to estimate the chance it will not fail in the next year.

5. [3.2, 10]. Compute the availability and reliability of the New York Stock Exchange. Suppose it is open 250 days per year, eight hours each day. The text asserts that during the decade of the 1980s it had four outages: (1) a day because of a snowstorm, (2) four hours due to a fire in the machine room, (3) 45 seconds because of a software error, and (4) trading stopped for three hours due to a financial panic. What was its quantitative (a) reliability, (b) availability, (c) availability class?

6. [3.2, 15]. (a) Give examples of your car's (or other complex appliance) latent faults, soft faults, hard faults, environmental faults, operations faults, maintenance faults, and hardware faults. (b) Categorize them by class and frequency. (c) Suggest some design changes that would improve availability.

7. [3.3, 10]. (a) Derive the total MTTF of Figure 3.5 from the component MTTFs. (b) Assuming the systems operate continuously, what is the average system reliability and availability? (c) If the vendor caused no faults, what would be the reliability, availability, and availability class?

8. [3.4, project]. Get and read the fault specifications for (a) your computer, (b) a module (e.g., a disk), (c) a communications line, (d) a LAN, including the adaptors and drivers, (e) the power of your local power company, and (f) an uninterruptable power supply.

9. [3.4, 10]. A factory with a 10^8\$/year budget is continuously operated by a computer system that is 99% available. (a) How many hours a year is the system out of service? (b) What is the direct cost of these outages? (c) If four hours of the outage are due to power failures, and if those problems can be solved by installing a 50k\$/year uninterruptable power supply, is it a good investment? (d) What if the power failure affects the entire factory?

10. [3.4, 10]. Based on Table 3.11, what is the reliability, availability, and availability class of power in (a) urban Germany, (b) rural France, (c) North America? Remember, the statistics for Europe are unscheduled outages measured by the power company, while the North American statistics are measured by a customer (a phone company).

11. [3.5, 5]. (a) What percentage worse is the MTTF of failvote duplex than the MTTF of the simplexed module? What is the percentage for failfast duplex?

12. [3.6, 15]. Suppose a set of n-version programs is to be run failvote without repair. (a) How many versions of the programs must be written to double the MTTF of the typical program? (b) If 50 copies are written and run with a failfast voter, what will be the increase in the MTTF?

13. [3.6, 10]. Suppose that a software system has mean time to failure of one year, and on average it takes an hour to repair the software fault. If, as several studies indicate, more than 99% of software faults are Heisenbugs, and if transactions plus persistent process pairs mask all such bugs with mean repair times of one minute, what is the mean time to reliability, availability, and availability class of the system implemented (a) without process pairs and transactions and (b) with process pairs and transactions?

14. [3.7.1, 10]. In the discussion of storage pages, three values were stored in each page to compute the page validity: a checksum, an address, and a version number. Give examples of failures that would be detected by each of these redundant values.

15. [3.7.1, 15]. In the discussion just after the definition of store_write(), several failure modes were considered and mechanisms to detect them were explained. (a) There is one case that is not detected; what is it? (b) How is it detected by mechanisms introduced later in the chapter?

16. [3.7.1, 10]. On average, the store decay process fails one of the 10^5 pages of a store every $7 \cdot 10^5$ seconds. There are about $3 \cdot 10^7$ seconds in a year. Ignoring faults of the entire store, how many pages will have decayed after one year? Hint: use Equation 3.15 of Problem 2.

17. [3.7.1, 5]. Suppose a n-plexed storage system implements optimistic reads by choosing a storage module at random. Suppose the storage group of that page just experienced a null write. What is the probability the optimistic read will get a stale value?

18. [3.7.1, 10]. What is the MTTF of a 3-plexed failfast voter storage group with the repair process operating in the background? Use the statistics in the model, consider only page failures (ignore whole-store failures), and assume n-plexed reliable reads take $n \cdot 30$ ms.

19. [3.7.1, 15]. In the code for reliable_write(), add the logic for read-after-write to check that the write was successful. If the write had a fault, include the logic to repair the page.

20. [3.7.1, project]. Describe and analyze a RAID5 approach [Patterson 1988] in the style of the n-plex store approach. Be particularly careful about the atomicity of data plus parity writes (somewhat analogous to the version problem, but more serious).

21. [3.7.2, 15]. (a) What is the reliability and availability of the basic processes of Subsection 3.7.2? (b) Ignoring message failures, what is the availability and class of the checkpoint_restart() process? (c) What is the availability and class of the corresponding process_pair() process?

22. [3.7.2, 15]. Suppose the disks used by the checkpoint_restart() process are all duplexed. How many different places store a version of the process state?

23. [3.7.4, 15] Program the listener logic as a checkpoint-restart process.

24. [3.7.3, 10]. Figure 3.21 describes process pairs. Suppose both the primary and backup processes start at approximately the same time. What causes the backup to sense that it is the backup?

25. [3.7.3, 20]. Program the checkpoint_restart_process() as a process_pair() process using the flowchart of Figure 3.21.

26. [3.7.2, 15]. Make the storage repair process of Subsection 3.7.2.4 a process pair. Hint: It could restart at zero on takeover, giving it no state aside from the group number; or it could restart at the current page, making the address of the current page being scanned ("i" in the program) the only changeable (checkpointable) state.

27. [3.7.4, 15]. When the sessions connect process pairs, the sender checkpoints outgoing messages and the receiver checkpoints its acknowledgment messages. Two questions: (a) Why must these checkpoints precede the message transmission? (b) Why does the sender not need to checkpoint the receipt of the acknowledgment message?

28. [3.7.4, 10]. For simplicity, reliable messages (a_session_message) carry the entire session descriptor. But MSG_NEW messages and MSG_ACK messages need only a subset of the fields. What fields are actually needed?

29. [3.7.4, 20]. Write the declares for the checkpoint messages sent by the listener to its process pair during normal operation, and when a process is repaired. Describe when these messages are sent, and describe the backup's logic. Assume no messages are lost or permuted (the underlying system is doing the ack protocol for you).

30. [3.7.4, 20]. Generalize reliable_send_message() to be asynchronous by expanding the listener to include retransmission and by adding a queue of unacknowledged outgoing messages for each session. The maximum gap allowed between session.out and session.ack is called the *window* in data communications and the *syncdepth* in Guardian.

Answers

1. (a) 1000 years. (b) ≈10⁻⁷. (c) 0.1. (d) Because it is measured at the bottom of the bathtub. As people age, the failure rate rises. (e) The rate is approximately memoryless on the time scale of weeks, but it is not memoryless when measured on the scale of decades; infants and very old people have high mortality rates.

2. 39, .63, .86, .99995.

3. Using Equation 3.5, (a) ≈.5 years, (b) ≈.58 years.

4. Since the failure rate is memoryless, the MTTF is the same five years later. The fact that it has operated for five years without a problem is irrelevant. The chance it will fail in the next year is $1 - e^{-1}$, which is about .63.

5. The period involved 10•8•250 hours or 20,000 hours. The MTTF was 5,000 hours. The MTTR was (8+4+3+.01)/4 = 3.75 hours. So the availability was 99.93%. So (a) 5,000 hours, (b) 99.98%, (c) Class 3 (≈ 3.9).

6. (c) Cars often fail due to a dead battery or running out of gas. Add a reserve battery and reserve gas tank. According to one study, in the United States about 30% of car maintenance breaks something else. So, redesign the car to have less-frequent maintenance.

7. (a) Use Equation 3.5. (b): reliability is MTTF of 10 weeks, availability is MTTF/(MTTF+MTTR)= 99.91%. (c) Class 3.

9. (a) 88. (b) 10⁶$. (c) 11k$/hr => 44k$, so maybe. (d) If restart time after failure is long (≈30 minutes), then the UPS may be a good investment.

10. MTBF = reliability: (a) 36 months, (b) 2.4 months, (c) 5.2 months. Availability = MTTF/(MTTF+MTTR) (a) 99.9986%, (b) 99.9259%, (c) 99.9762%. Germany is class 4; France and North America are class 3.

11. Using Figure 3.14, duplex failvote MTTF is 50% of simplex MTTF, and duplex failfast MTTF is 150% of simplex MTTF.

12. (a) 19. Running the programs with a failvote voter will always result in a shorter MTTF than the MTTF of a simplex module. If a failfast voter is used, then using analysis similar to the diagrams in Figure 3.14: the first failure in the *n*-plex comes in time MTTF/*n*, the next in time MTTF/(*n* − 1), and so on. The voter needs at least 3 modules to form a majority. So we need to find an *n* such that 1/*n* + 1/(*n* − 1) +...+ 1/3 > 2. 19 is the smallest such number. (b) Using the same logic, 50 copies with a failfast voter will improve the MTTF by a little less than a factor of 3.

13. (a) Reliability is 1 year MTTF and availability is 99.98858%. (b) MTTF would rise to more than 100 years, and availability would be more than 60 times higher at 99.99981%. They are class 3 and class 5 respectively.

14. The checksum will detect page value corruption if some bits decayed. The address will detect a store-write address fault that wrote to this page by mistake. Version number detects stale data.

15. (a) Stale writes (that is, writes that have no effect on the page to be changed) are not detected by the mechanisms described. (b) Later, storage modules are n-plexed and the latest version of each page is used on each read. This mechanism detects, masks, and repairs stale writes.

16. [MTTF = $7 \cdot 10^{10}$ seconds $\approx 2.2 \cdot 10^3$ years and the fault arrival rate is $\lambda = 1/(2.2 \cdot 10^3) = 4.5 \cdot 10^{-2}$ faults/year. So the simple answer is 10^5 pages times 1 year times λ. This translates to 4500 failed pages per year. The more careful analysis uses Equation 3.15 (page 152) to get the same answer: The probability of a particular page failing in a year is $(e^{-2.2 \ 10^{-3}}) \approx 1/2 \cdot 10^{-3}$. Now the population times the probability of failure gives $10^5 \cdot 4.5 \cdot 10^{-2} = 450$.

17. $1/n$.

18. The page repair process checks and repairs a page every $1 + .03n$ seconds, which is about 1 second. So the mean time to page repair is MANY/2 seconds. Using Equation 3.12, the answer is MTTF^3/3MTTR^2 = $(10^8)^3/3(10^3)^2 = 10^{24}/3 \ 10^6$ = 3E17 seconds = 10^{10} years. This is approximately the age of the universe, so there is little incentive to build 4-plexed modules.

21. (a) The reliability (MTTF) is about 11 weeks, which is about 2.6 months. The availability is MTTF/(MTTF+MTTR) which is 99.90%. (b) Fails every 10^7 seconds for 10^4 seconds, so 99.9% = class 3. (c) Process pair takeover takes ≈ 2 seconds, happens every $10^7/2$ seconds, so 99.99996% = class 6. Interestingly, they have the same MTTF.

22. Six: two pair on disk and one pair in volatile storage.

24. The backup waits for a second and then looks to see if it has received a message. The primary skips the wait statement and will have sent an *I'm Alive* message by then.

27. (a) If the process fails after the message transmission, the backup must retransmit the message or acknowledgment. (b) If the backup does not know about the acknowledgment, it will resend the message at takeover and the receiver will treat it as a duplicate and re-acknowledge it.

28. By looking at the listener process, MSG_NEW needs session.target, session.source and session.out, and MSG_ACK needs session.target and session.out.

29. Add some new message types: (1) MSG_CHECKPOINT, which looks just like a data message and is used to record received messages and sequence number updates, (2) MSG_DELIVERY, which is used to record the delivery of a message from the input queue to the application (generated by reliable_get_message()), (3) MSG_IM_BACK, which the backup sends to the primary after repair, requesting a new copy of the state, and finally (4) MSG_STATE, which is a copy of the current state (sequence numbers and input queue) sent by the primary in reply to an *I'm Back* message.

PART THREE

Transaction-Oriented Computing

How long halt ye between two opinions?

1 KINGS 18:21

4

Transaction Models

4.1 Introduction

Transactions are a way of making ACID operations a general commodity. In computer systems, atomic actions are commonplace up to a certain level, and everybody takes them for granted. Consider, for example, an SQRT function invoked from a Pascal program. The invocation is synchronous from the program's point of view; that is, it waits until the result has been computed. The function will either return the right value of the square root, or it will return an error code, but it will not change any data structures or parameters in an unpredictable way. Whether it does the computation using an iterative algorithm, a table lookup, or by asking a number-crunching friend is irrelevant to the caller; under no circumstances will it produce "partial" square roots or otherwise incorrect results. It also will not return somebody else's square root if the function is invoked by many programs at the same time.

The square root procedure, in turn, relies for its implementation on some lower level operations, such as machine instructions, which it assumes to be executed atomically. And, on the other hand, the procedure can be part of an even higher level atomic operation (e.g., solving quadratic equations). Atomicity, then, definitely does not mean that something is executed as one instruction at the hardware level with some magic in the circuitry preventing it from being interrupted. Atomicity merely conveys the impression that this is the case, for it has only two outcomes: the specified result or nothing at all, which means in particular that it is free of side effects.

Note that atomicity is defined only from the perspective of the caller of the operation, because almost no atomic action—including machine instructions—is truly atomic at all levels of implementation. Making operations appear atomic actually requires a considerable amount of design and implementation effort—which most of this book is about—and, of course, atomicity does not come for free.

Achieving atomicity is fairly simple as long as the operations are read-only. If anything goes wrong, the operation can either be retried or return an error code (which conforms to the specification); no damage will be done to any part of the system.[1] But whenever a state

---

[1] This is not to say that all read-only computations should be made atomic under all circumstances. Think, for example, of a technical simulation running some 10 hours. Atomicity would mean starting all over again if something goes wrong along the way. Major portions of this chapter deal with the question of how to reconcile the ACID paradigm with long-running applications.

that is not internal to the operation (like a field in the database) has to be changed, or a message has to be sent, or a real action (such as opening a valve) has to be performed, no action can take effect before the entire operation has completed. Thus, it must be possible to revoke the changes in case the operation fails, and concurrent users of the system must be protected from accessing preliminary data. All these issues are covered in other chapters of this book. In this chapter, we look specifically at how to organize *complex* applications—those supporting concurrent users on shared databases and in distributed systems—into units of work that can be viewed as atomic actions. As it turns out, exercising adequate control requires more than just simple atomic operations. The variety of transaction models reflects the trade-off between the simplification in system design through atomicity and isolation, and the price one has to pay for it.

4.1.1 About this Chapter

The first section of this chapter contains a detailed discussion of atomic actions and how they are different from other types of actions. On that basis, the classical "flat" transaction is defined precisely. The standard debit/credit transaction is used to illustrate the programming style induced by ACID transactions, and their influence on structuring applications. By discussing some simple extensions of the example, it is demonstrated that many situations exist in which more flexible means of control would be required than flat transactions provide. A short review of the literature in the field of transaction processing shows that transaction models abound (extended, generalized, advanced, etc.). The major part of the chapter attempts to present a systematic view of how computations can be organized into related or unrelated pieces of work, each of which has some or all of the ACID properties.

The discussion begins with a brief account of the concept of *spheres of control* that was developed by Larry Bjork and Charles Davies in the early 1970s. It was the first attempt to investigate the interrelated issues of control, recovery, and concurrency in integrated systems in a coherent fashion. Although these ideas were never fully realized, they gave rise to the development of the transaction paradigm. By slightly extending their notion of control dependencies, a simple formalism is introduced that allows us to describe and control transactions, and structures built from transactions, in a coherent way. The last section discusses the role of different transaction models in an integrated transaction system.

4.2 Atomic Actions and Flat Transactions

Atomic actions are the basic building blocks not only for structuring the application, but also for most of the system architecture to be described in this book. Atomicity is more than a mere definition; it requires precise specifications for two fundamental aspects of each operation. One is the question of when and how the results of the operation are made accessible to other operations in the system; this has to do with completing an operation successfully. The other aspect is the "nothing" case of all-or-nothing: How can the (partial) results of an operation that do not complete successfully be rolled back such that no side effects (or only well-controlled side effects) occur? Note that these two questions are not equivalent: Controlling the propagation of results prevents other actions from being affected in case the operation has to be backed out. This does not automatically imply, though, that the action *can* really be reset to its original state. There is no problem with read actions—they do not change the state—but all update operations must ensure that the original state of the system they affect can be reestablished, provided that the propagation of results is performed properly.

We also have to be specific about the circumstances under which an action is to be atomic. Achieving this property under the assumption that the system is functioning normally is fairly simple, as is demonstrated in Chapter 10. Making the same action atomic in the presence of system crashes (without any hardware components being damaged) requires more effort, and this continues as more types and degrees of failures (loss of disks, loss of machine rooms, etc.) are considered. In most of the following discussion, atomicity of actions is supported by recovery mechanisms that tolerate crashes of processes, system crashes, and loss of one hardware component required for executing the operation. All higher levels of atomicity, and thus fault tolerance, are given special treatment.

4.2.1 Disk Writes as Atomic Actions

To give an idea of what atomicity implies in terms of implementing an operation and controlling its effects, this subsection analyzes a very common operation: writing a block to disk. In Chapter 3, this operation was investigated with respect to its level of fault tolerance. Here, we will reconsider some of the arguments to illustrate what is required to make an action atomic. Since it works most of the time, application programmers rarely think about the exact (failure) properties of such an operation. As long as the system stays up, it is assumed to work correctly, and if there is a crash while writing a file, much greater damage than just one block must sometimes be repaired. The standard UNIX file system has the reputation of losing and misplacing files as a consequence of system crashes that affect writes to the file directory. Many UNIX programmers have come to accept as a fact of life the necessity of running FSCHK after restart and inquiring about their files at the lost-and-found. Yet it need not be a fact of life; it is just a result of not making things atomic that had better not be interrupted by, for example, a crash.

If there were an atomic operation to write blocks to disk, then it would provide a good basis for making more complex file operations atomic, too. This discussion is deferred to Chapter 13; for the moment, let us just define precisely which properties the disk write operation has and what is required to achieve certain levels of atomicity. Essentially, the disk write operation comes in four quality levels:

Single disk write. Atomicity of a disk write operation would mean that either the entire block is correctly transferred to the specified slot, or the slot remains unchanged. Actual disks do not behave this way. Rather, they have the flavor of the storage model described in Chapter 3. The block on disk can be left half-changed, and the controller returns an error code indicating that this happened. It might even produce a normal return code in spite of the fact that, due to some transient error in the controller's circuitry or a fault in the disk media, the block was not written correctly. And if there is a power loss in the middle of the operation, it might happen that the first part of the block is written, but the rest is not. In all these cases the outcome of the action is neither all nor nothing, but something in between.

Read-after-write. This implementation of the disk write first issues a single disk write, then rereads the block from disk and compares the result with the original block. If the two are not identical, the sequence of writing and rereading is repeated until the block is successfully written. Although this is better than a single write, it still does not achieve atomicity. There are three reasons why this is so: (1) There are no provisions to return to the initial state; that is, the old contents of the block are not kept by the component implementing the write operation. (2) The block on disk can be bad, so that the write will still be unsuccessful after a specified maximum number of attempts. (3) If the system crashes while executing this operation, the block can be in an undefined state.

Duplexed write. In this implementation each block has a version number, which is increased upon each invocation of the operation. Each block is written to two places, A and B, on disk. First, a single disk write is done to A; after this operation is successfully completed, a single disk write is done to B. Of course, when using this scheme, one also has to modify the disk read. The block is first read from position A; if this operation is successful, it is assumed to be the most recent, valid version of the block. If reading from A fails, then B is read. For this scheme to protect against single disk failures, A and B must be on different physical disks, with separate controllers, and must go through separate I/O paths. It also must not happen that a write operation pretends to be successsful but actually changes the wrong slot; this can be detected by read-after-write. The basic technique used here is the same as the one introduced in Chapter 3 to make storage, messages, and processes failfast, assuming single component failures. Given the behavior of real disks, there are many refinements of the duplexed write scheme. Consider the case that the write to position A fails in such a way that the block on disk remains unchanged; then it is necessary to access *both* blocks when reading and pick the one with the higher version number, if both are readable. Another problem is how to assign a new writing position to a block if one goes permanently bad.

Logged write. The basic strategy of the logged write is as follows: The old contents of the block are first read and then written to a different place (on a different storage device), using the single disk write operation. Then the block is modified, and eventually a single disk write is performed to the old location. To protect against unreported transient errors, the read-after-write technique could be used. If writing the modified block was successful, the copy of the old value can be discarded. With this method, it is possible to recover from a system crash by rewriting the copy of the old contents of the block to its original position. Atomicity is lost if the block on disk goes bad, or if all blocks go bad (i.e., if the disk as a whole is damaged).

This last technique may seem strange at first, but this is only because it is presented in the context of a single block write operation. In fact, a number of database systems achieve their atomicity at the disk level in exactly this way, but they group a larger number of operations together for that purpose. Later in this text, writing the old contents of the block to be modified is called "before image logging."

Some aspects relevant for a real system design are ignored in the preceding discussion. In particular, there is no clear failure model for the components on which the operation is implemented. For example, should the design tolerate the case that the block is written completely, but to the wrong slot? Can it happen that the single write operation returns normally, but the block got modified somehow during the write operation without a parity check indicating what happened? Can two different processes write to the same place on disk concurrently?

The principles of fault tolerance outlined in Chapter 3 make it very clear that any statement about reliability, availability, and thereby atomicity must be founded on a complete model of the system, including everything that can go wrong. This necessarily implies explicit statements about what is assumed not to go wrong, that is, the residual risk in the system design. But that is not the subject of this chapter. It only illustrates what has to be considered and specified in order to define exactly what kind of atomicity, if any, an operation as simple as a disk write has.

It is also worth noting that all implementations of the disk write except for the duplex write can easily get into the situation where the block simply cannot be written because the target slot has gone bad. One of the exercises at the end of this chapter considers what atomicity means under these circumstances and how it can be achieved.

From the preceding discussion, we can conclude that even simple operations cannot simply be declared atomic; rather, atomicity is a property for which the operations have to be designed and implemented. It is also clear that because of the overhead incurred by fault tolerance in general, the decision concerning which types of operations to make atomic in which situations is extremely critical. It is a decision that must be made by the implementor of a transaction processing system as well as by the designer of transaction-oriented applications.

4.2.2 A Classification of Action Types

The discussion in the previous subsection must not be taken to mean that transaction systems have to be built with atomic operations at all levels. On the contrary, the crucial architectural issue is to provide the system with the means for achieving the ACID properties wherever they are required, based on lower-level operations that do not have these properties. As explained later in this chapter, even at the top (application) layer, there are situations where the ACID properties cannot be applied; yet transactions can help to control such environments.

It is useful to distinguish between three types of actions as the basic building blocks for every type of service the system can provide:

Unprotected actions. These actions lack all of the ACID properties except for consistency. Note that the following discussion is based on the assumption that the system only contains correct software components. Unprotected actions are not atomic, and their effects cannot be depended upon. Almost anything can fail. A single disk write is an example of an unprotected action.

Protected actions. These are actions that do not externalize their results before they are completely done. Their updates are commitment controlled, they can roll back if anything goes wrong before the normal end, and once they have reached their normal end, there will be no unilateral rollback—what has happened remains. Protected actions have the ACID properties.

Real actions. These actions affect the real, physical world in a way that is hard or impossible to reverse. Drilling a hole is one example; firing a missile is another. Real actions can be consistent and isolated; once executed, they are definitely durable. But in the majority of cases, they are irreversible, which means it is much more difficult to make them appear atomic, because the option of going back in case the proper result cannot be achieved does not exist. In some cases, pretending atomicity for a real action is not possible at all.

Protected actions are easy to distinguish from the rest, but the difference between unprotected and real actions may appear artificial. One might argue, for example, that writing a disk block is a real action: it affects physical reality, and if it is interrupted in the middle, the slot will not be readable.

The distinction really is determined by the question of whether or not it is *possible* to reverse the effects of the original operation by executing something that is similar to the original operation. For the disk write this is easy. If the original contents of the corrupted slot are still available (where to get the original from is not an issue here), then it just takes another write to make the slot readable again. On the other hand, there is no "undrill" operation, and missiles, once on their way, are hard to get back to the launching site.[2] This difference is much more than just an interesting observation. Since unprotected actions can be reversed (or *undone*, as this is called later in the book), they can be included in a higher-level operation, which as a whole has the ACID properties. The implementation of that higher operation must know about the reversal mechanisms and apply them in case a rollback is necessary. This is exactly what happens in a database system: at the user level, all interactions are enclosed by transactions; while some layers down the hierarchy, unprotected read/write operations are used to access the database. For real actions, there may be repair procedures to contain the damage done by a real action that should not have happened, but repairing something is fundamentally different from reversing a state. What happens, then, if a real action is to be part of a higher-level protected action?

Figure 4.1 illustrates the essential aspects of the problem. Whereas the SQL operations can be undone, the real action cannot. To be part of a higher-level protected action, it must receive special treatment. Among the possibilities, the scenario in Figure 4.1 is one that employs conventional wisdom: when doing something that is very hard or impossible to revoke, try to make sure that all the prerequisites of the critical action are fulfilled. A paratrooper first puts on the parachute, checks that all the straps are in the right positions, and so on, before he commits to execute the real action—exiting from the airplane. If there were a mechanism for effectively undoing the real action, the steps could as well be executed in different order, such as putting on the chute in midair and hoping for the best.

Thus, for a general system and application design, we can state the following rules of thumb:

Unprotected actions must either be controlled by the application environment, or they must be embedded in some higher-level protected action. If this cannot be done, no part of the application, including the users, must depend on their outcome. Operations on temporary files used for storing intermediate results can be treated as unprotected actions.

Protected actions are the building blocks for reliable, distributed applications. Most of this text deals with them.

Real actions need special treatment. The system must be able to recognize them as such, and it must make sure that they are executed only if all enclosing protected actions have reached a state in which they will not decide to roll back.

---

[2] There are means for destroying them if they are seriously off track, but this obviously does not reconstitute the status quo ante.

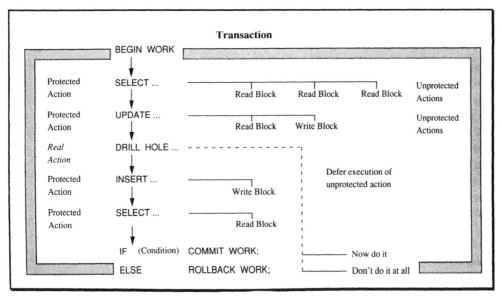

Figure 4.1: Protected versus real actions in a transaction-oriented environment. A real action can be made part of a higher-level protected action or transaction. To do so, it must be implicitly rearranged to take effect no sooner than when the final success of the encompassing transaction can be guaranteed.

Real actions also turn out to be special when considering recovery from a failure. Assume the system comes back after a crash and finds that a certain transaction (for example, the one in Figure 4.1) had completed successfully before the crash and wants to ensure that all consequent actions have been executed. Protected actions are easy in that respect. They can always be implemented in such a way that repeated execution (during recovery) yields the same result; they can be made *idempotent*. Real actions may be idempotent (drilling a hole, for example, provided one gets the metal back into exactly the same position), but many are not. Dispensing money through an automated teller machine is not idempotent; neither is applying a specific X-ray dose to a patient. The question here is whether the real action is testable; that is, whether the environment in which the action is executed allows for some kind of subsequent read operation that can tell if the real action has happened or not. Testable real actions are easy to manage in a recovery situation; for nontestable real actions there is no good solution in a transactional environment.[3]

4.2.3 Flat Transactions

Flat transactions are the simplest kind of all. The term and concept has been used from the beginning of this book, but in this subsection it is defined more carefully. This definition includes an investigation of the properties of flat transactions, both from the progammer's perspective and from a control point of view. The result of this investigation is the motivation to explore extensions of the flat transaction model.

---

[3] There is probably no good solution for them in any kind of environment.

Let us start by reviewing the ACID properties, which make a transaction different from a normal, unprotected type of program execution:

Atomicity.   A state transition is said to be atomic if it appears to jump from the initial state to the result state without any observable intermediate states—or if it appears as though it had never left the initial state. Again, this is a description from the perspective of the instance invoking the atomic action. The atomicity of a state transition effected by a transaction is a general, unconditional property. It holds whether the transaction, the entire application, the operating system, or other components function normally, function abnormally, or crash. Note also that this is more than a mere definition. For a transaction to be atomic, it must behave atomically to any outside "observer." That is, under no circumstances may a transaction produce a result or a message that later disappears if the transaction rolls back. (The technical implications of this requirement are discussed in more detail in Chapter 11.) A simple consequence, which is discussed later in this chapter, is the following: if a transaction encounters an error condition that causes it to roll back, there is no way compliant with the ACID paradigm to allow it to send an error message to the application program. Being atomic, a failed transaction by definition has done nothing; in particular, it has sent no messages.

Consistency.   A transaction produces consistent results only; otherwise it aborts. A result is consistent if the new state of the database fulfills all the consistency constraints of the application; that is, if the program has functioned according to specification.[4] Simple as that may seem, it has a number of subtle ramifications. First, the transaction must see a consistent database to start with. Further, not only must the input state of the transaction be consistent, it must remain consistent for the duration of the transaction. This leads to the second point: a piece of data is consistent if it complies with all the consistency constraints. Certainly, it is impossible to check them all each time a new transaction starts; the database is large, and there are many integrity rules. Here, then, is the other way to put it: data is consistent if it has been produced by a committed transaction. This is where (in today's systems at least) the definition becomes somewhat circular. When a transaction calls COMMIT WORK, the system underneath has no means for checking all the consistency constraints there are. Most of them are them are not formalized in the first place, and if they were, it would be very expensive to go through all of them. So, rather than guaranteeing that a transaction will end successfully only if it has produced a consistent result, the commit itself is taken as the guarantee that the result is consistent. If later it is found that the update done by some transaction was, in fact, inconsistent, there is nothing a flat transaction system can do about it. Control does not extend beyond transaction boundaries. Loosely speaking, one might say that a committed transaction has turned into a real action, with all its consequences. It is important to keep in mind that the consistency definition that comes with the transaction paradigm is largely a syntactic one.

Isolation.   Isolation simply means that a program running under transaction protection must behave exactly as it would in single-user mode. That does not mean transactions cannot

---

[4] This assumes the specification is correct and complete.

share data objects. Like the other definitions, the definition of isolation is based on observable behavior from the outside, rather than on what is going on inside. Isolation is not an entirely independent requirement; rather, it must be achieved to guarantee consistent input data, which is a prerequisite for consistent output. (And, of course, isolation is also required to make the acronym pronounceable.)

Durability.   Durability requires that results of transactions having completed successfully must not be forgotten by the system; from its perspective, they have become a part of reality. Put the other way around, this means that once the system has acknowledged the execution of a transaction, it must be able to reestablish its results after any type of subsequent failure, whether caused by the user, the environment, or the hardware components. It also implies that there is no automatic function for revoking a completed transaction. The only way to get rid of what a completed transaction has done is to execute another transaction with a counter-algorithm. This concept is treated more precisely when discussing open nested transactions and other generalizations of the basic model, later in this chapter.

Flat transactions represent the simplest type of transaction, and for almost all existing systems it is the only one that is supported *at the application programming level*. The emphasis is important because, as we will later see, many systems exhibit some properties of more general transaction models without allowing those more flexible transaction models to be used as a general programming model.

A flat transaction is the basic building block for organizing an application into atomic actions. It can contain an arbitrary number of simple actions; these actions may, in turn, be either protected, real, or even unprotected, if necessary. Putting a flat transaction as an execution unit around a sequence of either protected or real actions makes the whole appear indivisible as far as the application is concerned. Note that the question of whether the actions inside are executed sequentially or in any kind of parallel or semi-parallel fashion is irrelevant, because we can speak only about the entire transaction; there is no way of making reference to an intermediate state of execution. Consequently, the structure of this execution has no significance at all.

These transactions are called *flat* because there is only one layer of control by the application. Everything inside the BEGIN WORK and COMMIT WORK brackets is at the same level; that is, the transaction will either survive together with everything else (commit), or it will be rolled back with everything else (abort). Figure 4.2 shows the three different outcomes a flat transaction can have; there are no other possibilities. The percentages quoted in the figure pertain to classic TP applications such as order entry, accounting, inventory control, and so forth. Structurally different applications, when using transactions, will probably be characterized by different numbers.

The major restriction of flat transactions is that there is no way of either committing or aborting parts of such transactions, or committing results in several steps, and so forth. All the suggestions described later in this chapter for extending the simple transaction model are aimed at introducing more dimensions of control to this boring flatland. But before dwelling on such landscaping efforts, let's look at a typical example for a flat transaction to understand why we need more means for control in the first place.

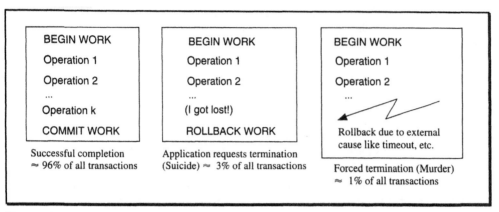

Figure 4.2: The three outcomes of a flat transaction. Atomicity of a transaction manifests itself in three different situations. The first one is the commit case (the "all" of all-or-nothing). The other two are the "nothing" case, either because the transaction program gives up, or because the transaction is prevented from completing due to some outside event, such as a timeout or a crash.

4.2.3.1 The Debit/Credit Transaction

The debit/credit transaction can be considered the literature's most popular flat transaction example. It is prototypical in two respects. Historically, transaction systems were first developed for banking applications, and the debit/credit transaction is a very simplified version from that domain; and technically, this transaction is the basis of the only industry-standard benchmarks for transaction systems, the TPC-A and TCB-B benchmarks [Gray 1991].

Without going into any detail, this is what the debit/credit transaction does: Given a database with a well-defined size that must be related to the throughput the system is to achieve, a transaction receives a message from the terminal[5] that requests it to debit or credit a certain amount to an account. The transaction modifies the account as requested, modifies the record of the teller where the transaction originates (to maintain a running balance), does the same thing for the branch record, and finally inserts into the history relation a tuple that contains all the parameters of the transaction, including a timestamp. The new account balance is given back to the application program, which can then respond to the user with a response message.

The following code is quoted from the benchmark definition with only minor modifications. As an aid to understanding this (very simple) transaction, the declaration of the accounts relation is included; the other relations are declared accordingly.

```
exec sql CREATE TABLE accounts (
         Aid            NUMERIC(9),
         Bid            NUMERIC(9) FOREIGN KEY REFERENCES branches,
         Abalance       NUMERIC(10),
         filler         CHAR(48),
         PRIMARY KEY(Aid) );
```

The code of the transaction program itself looks as follows:

---

[5] To be precise, the TPC-A benchmark requires messages from and to (simulated) terminals; that is, the system to be measured must include a network. The TPC-B version allows batch transactions, so the input can simply be read from a file. This distinction is not relevant at the moment.

```
/***                  main program with the invocation environment                    ***/
/* global declarations                                                                  */
exec sql BEGIN DECLARE SECTION;              /*declare working storage                  */
long Aid, Bid, Tid, delta, Abalance;         /* account id, branch id, teller id, debit or */
                                             /* credit amount, account balance          */
exec sql END DECLARE SECTION;                /* front end for the transaction program   */
DCApplication()                              /*                                         */
{read input msg;                             /* deal with request messages              */
    exec sql BEGIN WORK;                     /* start the flat transaction              */
    Abalance = DoDebitCredit(Bid, Tid, Aid, delta);  /* invoke transaction program       */
    send output msg;                         /* send response to terminal               */
    exec sql COMMIT WORK;                    /* successful end of transaction           */
}                                            /*                                         */
/* subroutine for doing the database accesses defined for TPC debit/credit transaction  */
long     DoDebitCredit(long Bid, long Tid, long Aid, long delta)/*                      */
{
    exec sql UPDATE accounts                 /* apply delta to the account balance      */
        SET    Abalance = Abalance + :delta  /*                                         */
        WHERE    Aid = :Aid;                 /*                                         */
    exec sql SELECT Abalance INTO :Abalance  /* read new value of balance               */
        FROM accounts                        /*                                         */
        WHERE    Aid = :Aid;                 /*                                         */
    exec sql UPDATE tellers                  /* apply delta to teller balance           */
        SET    Tbalance = Tbalance + :delta  /*                                         */
        WHERE Tid = :Tid;                    /*                                         */
    exec sql UPDATE branches                 /* apply delta to branch balance           */
        SET    Bbalance = Bbalance + :delta  /*                                         */
        WHERE Bid = :Bid;                    /*                                         */
    exec sql INSERT INTO history(Tid, Bid, Aid, delta, time)  /*  insert parameters of transaction */
        VALUES (:Tid, :Bid, :Aid, :delta, CURRENT);   /*  into application history       */
    return(Abalance);                        /* return modif. account balance to caller */
}                                            /* end of DebitCredit - subroutine         */
```

When looking at this bare-bones transaction, remember that all it has to do is create "typical" requests to the SQL database such that the resulting measurement data allow for conclusions about the system's performance in a real-life environment. It is not intended to reflect the flow of logic in an application program that deals with real tellers or automated teller machines (ATMs).

The example, however, does contain the minimal structure every transaction program must have. The BEGIN WORK statement declares the start of a (flat) transaction. All protected actions executed from now on are part of the same ACID unit of work. The protected actions in this example are updates to an SQL database. The consistency constraints in this assumed application are such that each debit and each credit requires the four steps shown: modification of the account, update of the teller balance, update of the branch balance, and insertion of a history record describing the transaction. Any execution performing only parts of these updates is considered inconsistent and must not happen. The COMMIT WORK statement is invoked to indicate that the new consistent state of the system has been reached. If control returns to the application from the COMMIT call, it can rest assured that the previous piece of work has been endowed with all ACID properties. Durability in particular guarantees that nothing[6] can cause the updates to be lost from now on.

The benchmark transaction does not contain a ROLLBACK verb, a situation that is not typical of a real transaction. So let us bring that simple transaction a bit closer to real life by including a check on the account balance and refusing any debit that overdraws the account. The subroutine DoDebitCredit can remain unchanged; the consistency check can be done entirely within the DCApplication. The transaction then looks as follows:

```
DCApplication()                            /*                                                */
{    receive input message;                /* deal with request messages                     */
     exec sql BEGIN WORK;                   /* start the flat transaction                     */
     Abalance = DoDebitCredit(Bid, Tid, Aid, delta);   /* invoke transaction program         */
     if ((Abalance < 0) && (delta < 0))     /* check if it a debit and account overdrawn      */
        {   exec sql ROLLBACK WORK;      }  /* if so: don't do it                             */
     else                                   /* this the good case: either credit or            */
     {                                      /* enough money in account                        */
     send output message;                   /* send response to terminal                      */
        exec sql COMMIT WORK;               /* successful end of transaction                  */
}    }
```

Following the flow of logic, we can see that even in the case where a debit is eventually refused, all the updates are done before the checking is performed. But since all of this happens within an ACID transaction, no harm is done, and the ROLLBACK makes sure that all the records are returned to their previous states. The program can therefore do whatever needs to be done in a fairly straightforward way, without having to twist its logic into what is called a "defensive" programming style. Without transaction protection, what usually has to be done is to: first go through all the data to see if all the update-dependent conditions hold, and then go through the data a second time to actually do the updates. With ACID protection, there is no need to do that defensive programming. One can just go ahead and do the updates, meanwhile gathering the data needed for consistency checks, and finally see if it all makes sense. If not, then ROLLBACK.

One might wonder why the code does not send an error message in the clause with the ROLLBACK WORK. Recall, however, that atomicity means a transaction either does everything or does nothing at all. Rollback establishes the "nothing" case, which implies that no messages will be delivered. Strange as it may seem, there is no way of sending an error (output) message directly from a transaction that aborts, provided we view all operations as protected. The problem of how to send such error messages is picked up again in the exercises.

---

[6] That is, nothing within the specifications of the system. If more errors than the system was designed for occur at the same time, then this guarantee does not hold (see Chapter 3).

We must appreciate that transactions cover not only database operations: the ACID properties hold for everything executed between BEGIN WORK and COMMIT WORK.[7] This is particularly important for outgoing messages if we imagine the message going to an automated teller machine (ATM). The ACID paradigm makes sure that either the message will be sent (the cash will be dispensed), which means that the entire transaction will be successfully completed, or the transaction will fail, in which case no money will be released. Other constellations cannot occur under transaction protection.

4.2.4 Limitations of Flat Transactions

For a simple state transformation, such as debiting or crediting an account, an atomic unit of work is certainly appropriate, and it is this type of application for which transactions were originally designed. But like every simple, rigorous, and successful concept, the flat transaction model was soon subject to numerous attempts at extending its scope, generalizing its semantics, and, in short, making it more powerful in a broad sense. There are two driving forces behind this. The first is that a simple control structure will not be able to model application structures that are significantly more complex; to support such applications by basic system services, it could be desirable to provide the transaction model with more expressive power. The second motivation is the general tendency to take an idea to its conceptual limit.

In either case, there is the imminent risk of sacrificing one of the major virtues of flat transactions—simplicity—which makes ACID transactions so successful in isolating the application from faults. During the following discussion, therefore, it must be kept in mind that extending the transaction concept is not a case of "the more the better"; rather, a delicate balance must be maintained between expressive power on one hand and usability (simplicity) on the other. The location of the point that separates useful transaction concepts (in the sense that they help simplify and better control applications) from those concepts that are too baroque (and thus create more problems than they solve) cannot be determined by rigorous measurement. It can, though, be determined to a certain degree by preferences of style, experience, and other such criteria.

Let us now turn and look at two examples demonstrating fairly simple application structures that are not adequately supported by flat transactions: trip planning and bulk updates.

Trip planning. This is a typical travel agency application. Let's assume you want to go from Bolinas, California, to Ripa, Italy. Since there are no direct flights between the two places, you must book a number of connecting flights, perhaps some trains, and so on. You also have certain ideas about how often you are willing to change planes, where you might want to stay overnight, and other such requirements. The travel agent, using a transaction system that gives him access to all the required databases of airlines, train companies, and car rental agencies, tries to come up with an itinerary for you.

---

[7] A popular misunderstanding has it that transactions are bound to databases. Although it is true that historically, transactions have evolved from the database domain, it must be understood clearly that they establish a general execution paradigm that ideally covers all the subsystems invoked in their course. The problem, as is shown later, is that not all system components are able to support the protocols required for transaction processing.

Assuming you actually start out at the San Francisco airport, then the first round of interactions might look like the example below. (What follows is not meant to be code; it only casually alludes to the transactional verbs.)

BEGIN WORK
S1:   book flight from San Francisco to Frankfurt
S2:   book flight from Frankfurt to Milan, same day
S3:   book flight from Milan to Pisa, same day
                    Problem: There is no way to get to Ripa from Pisa
                            the same day, except in a rental car. But
                            you do not want to drive at night.

What can the travel agent do in that situation? One solution might be to have you go from Milan to Florence rather than Pisa, and then go by train from there. Or the situation might require your going from Frankfurt to Genoa, or perhaps somewhere else. The point is, given a flat transaction model, the travel agent has only two choices: (1) Issue ROLLBACK. This gives up much more of the previous work than is necessary; in particular, there is no need to give back the reservation on the flight to Frankfurt. (2) Explicitly cancel all the reservations that are no longer useful. This might be very cumbersome if the amount of work is a little larger than that in the example shown above. Furthermore, explicit cancelation might not be so easy, because some of the very cheap special fares come with a high cancelation fee.

What would be needed to support such an application is a *selective* rollback. Rather than aborting the whole transaction, it should be possible to, say, roll back to position S2. That would require the system to undo everything that was done after S2, but keep the work done up to that point and allow processing to continue from there. If such a feature is not available, the application design is actually forced to use a pre-transactional programming style, where updates no longer needed have to be explicitly reversed by the application.

Bulk updates. This problem is much simpler to illustrate than the previous one. Assume that at the end of a month a bank has to modify all of its one million accounts by crediting or debiting (depending on the sign of account_balance) the accumulated interest. Conceptually, this is trivial. Why not write the following piece of code and be done with it?

```
ComputeInterest()
{     real    interest_rate;      /* monthly interest rate                          */
      receive (interest_rate);    /* receive request to compute the accumulated     */
                                  /* interest and to modify all accounts            */
                                  /* accordingly                                    */
      exec sql   BEGIN WORK;   /* start the transaction                             */
      exec sql   UPDATE checking_accounts       /*                                  */
                 set account_balance =          /*                                  */
                       account_balance * (1+interest_rate);/* modify all accounts   */
      send ("done");                 /*                                             */
      exec sql   COMMIT WORK; /*                                                    */
      return;                     /*                                                */
};                                /*                                                */
```

Note that the UPDATE applies to all tuples in the relation, because there is no WHERE clause to restrict it.

Just considering the logic, there is nothing wrong with the solution just given. But what about a failure of the system or of some of its components? If 934,767 accounts have been modified—which will have taken quite some time—and the database process crashes after that, the transaction paradigm says exactly what has to happen: all modifications being one atomic state transition, they all have to be rolled back. Of course, this is undesirable for at least two reasons. First, the account updates that have been performed so far are not invalid in any sense, and second, rolling back 934,767 updates takes about as long as it took to do them in the first place.

On the other hand, it has to be guaranteed that each account tuple is updated *exactly once* . With flat transactions, the only way of getting this guarantee from the system is the "bulk" transaction shown in our example. Making each tuple update a stand-alone transaction in order to minimize the loss in case of a crash is no solution, because then the system will have no information about which account was updated last before the crash; that is, where it has to pick up work again after recovery. (An aside: In terms of concepts that are rigorously defined later in this book, the system does have information, strictly speaking, about which was the last successful update because it writes that update to the log. If the application understands how the log works, what its record structure is like, and so on, it can look over the system's shoulder by reading the log for its own purposes. For the moment, it is sufficient to understand clearly that this is a "dirty" solution because the log is not part of a data model such as SQL; and using the dirty solution means exceeding the capabilities of a simple flat transaction environment with its standard database resource managers. But this is exactly what new and extended transaction models are all about. We return to this subject a number of times throughout this text.)

For each of the problems of the standard flat transaction, extensions to the transaction model have been proposed. Complex updates are supported by savepoints or by nested transactions, bulk updates are supported by chained transactions or sagas, and so on. This could go on forever. A new type of application results in a new, specialized transaction model. Each model is at least partially incompatible with the other models—certainly not a desirable way of proceeding.

For the rest of this chapter, extensions to the flat transaction model are presented in a systematic way. Most of these extensions are mere proposals in scientific papers, though some have been implemented in one system or another. We should be very careful, however, not to let the general perspective of this book be distorted by what follows: The discussion of limitations of ACID transactions and the description of suggested remedies must not create the impression that ACID transactions are a temporary solution that must be dispensed with—and the sooner the better. To the contrary, flat transactions and the techniques to make them work account for more than 90% of this book. No matter which extensions prove to be most important and useful in the future, flat transactions will be at the core of all the mechanisms required to make these more powerful models work. The discussion in this chapter therefore serves a twofold purpose: to aid in understanding flat transactions and their ramifications through explanation of extended transaction models, and to clarify why any generalized transaction model has to be built from primitives that are low-level, flat, system transactions.

To get a more systematic perspective on transaction oriented processing, let us step back for a moment and consider in detail how state transitions can interact and what that means in terms of isolation and recoverability. The key concept for this was proposed in the early 1970s and actually triggered the subsequent development of the transaction paradigm: the notion of spheres of control.

4.3 Spheres of Control

At the core of the notion of spheres of control is the observation that controlling computations in a distributed multiuser environment primarily means

(1) Containing the effects of arbitrary operations as long as there might be a necessity to revoke them, and

(2) Monitoring the dependencies of operations on each other in order to be able to trace the execution history in case faulty data are found at some point.

Any system that wants to employ the idea of spheres of control must be structured into a hierarchy of abstract data types. Whatever happens inside an abstract data type is not externalized as long as there is a chance that the result might have to be revoked for internal reasons. Thus, passing a result across the interface of an abstract data type is a commitment on the ADT's part, confirming that the result is correct (from its local perspective). Take as an example an ADT implementing disk read and write operations. If it internally uses read-after-write plus duplexed write, then it cannot expose any block contents the validity of which has not yet been confirmed according to the protocol. For such small ADTs it is reasonable to assume that data are not externalized as long as their validity has not been determined. However, in a hierarchy of ADTs, where the low-level ones are used to implement the more complex objects, the question of when to externalize a result becomes more difficult. This leads to the notion of dynamic dependencies among spheres of control.

Think of SQL as an abstract data type. There are interface operations for selecting tuples, for updating them, and so on. Now look at the debit/credit transaction. Each update operation is a complete, self-contained ADT invocation. Yet the first one executing correctly would not be sufficient reason to commit its result (the new contents of the tuple) to the outside world, unless the other three update operations are also successful. Therefore, beyond the static structuring into a hierarchy of abstract data types, it must be possible to dynamically create new spheres of control to contain the commitment of data. These dynamic spheres are determined by consistency constraints and dependencies on shared data, messages, or other objects.

To keep the discussion focused on the important issue of dynamically expanding spheres of control, we assume that each invocation of an abstract data type is an atomic action from the perspective of the caller. The callee assumes the same attitude, again using atomic operations from its supporting layer, and so forth, down to the hardware level.

4.3.1 Definition of Spheres of Control

Based on the structural framework just sketched, Davies [1978] established the notion of *spheres of control* (SoC); the following definitions are largely quoted from his paper:

Process[8] control.   Process control ensures that the information required by an atomic process is not modified by others, and it constrains the dependencies that another process may place on the updates made by this process.

Process atomicity.   Process atomicity is the amount of processing one wishes to consider as having identity. It is the control over processing that permits an operator to be atomic at one level of control, while the implementation of that operator may consist of many parallel and/or serial atomic operators at the next lower level of control.

Process commitment.   While a function is in process, changes of state are being made only by that function or they are expressly known to that function. This allows the establishment of a single point to which one can return for rerun purposes independently of the error detected or the number of functions since that point. Preventing process commitment by holding (controlling) the use of its results permits the system to perform a unilateral backout (process undo) over much larger units of process. *Unilateral* here means without having to request permission from each participant in a process. In summary, process commitment control is the containment of the effects of a process, even beyond the end of the process.

For readers already familiar with the transaction paradigm, it is important to realize that in the concept of spheres of control, the commitment of data produced by an atomic process is not strictly bound to the completion of that process. It is quite possible at the end of a process to create dynamically a new (enclosing) process that will control the commitment of the results of the first process. As an example, consider Figure 4.3.

The spheres with the solid lines in Figure 4.3 represent a predefined hierarchy of functions, each executing in its own sphere of control as an atomic process; that is, they are instantiations of some abstract data types. The highest-level processes, A1 and A2, are invoked sequentially. If, however, A1 decides that some of its results are not yet ready to be committed to the outside world, A2 can nevertheless start working on these data—but only after a new, higher-level sphere of control, S, has been created. S now contains the joint activities of both A1, A2, and whatever might follow after that. S can be terminated as soon as all processes depending on A1's results have terminated, and it has been decided to commit these results.

In other words, the dynamically created spheres for commitment control allow processing data that are dubious and would otherwise require the consuming application to stop or undergo some checking procedure. Similar control mechanisms can be found in many real-life situations, as the following example illustrates.

Assume Andreas and Jim are two SoCs, and Andreas SoC wants to sell his house to Jim SoC. Now each SoC has to commit some data. The SoC named Andreas has to hand over the house title to the SoC named Jim. He is reluctant to do this, though, because he does not trust Jim and would rather get the money first. Jim, on the other hand, has to give the money to Andreas. He, too, is reluctant to do his part, because he does not trust Andreas and would rather get the title first. In this situation, it is the usual procedure to create a dynamic sphere of control (the escrow officer, in this case) encompassing both Andreas SoC Jim SoC. This

---

[8] The term *process* is used throughout Bjork's and Davies' papers. Its meaning is not confined to processes in the operating system's sense of the word. For the purposes of the presentation, one could as easily read *action*, *operation*, or—as will become obvious later—*transaction*.

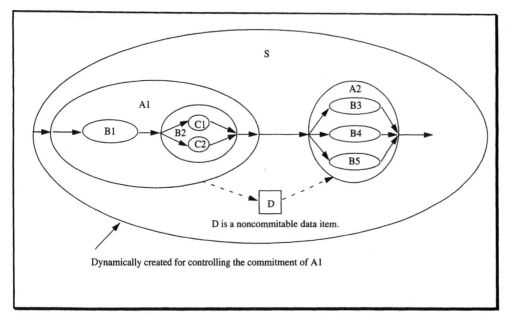

Figure 4.3: Spheres of control: the basic idea. Spheres of control come in two varieties. One is statically established by structuring the system into a hierarchy of abstract data types. The other results from dynamic interactions among spheres of control on shared data, which cannot be committed yet. Each sphere of control is viewed as an atomic action from the perspective of all processes executing at the same or a higher layer.

higher SoC controls both commitments and can also decide to do a unilateral backout if anything goes wrong (such as Andreas's house falling down because of old age).

4.3.2 Dynamic Behavior of Spheres of Control

This house-buying example illustrates the use of spheres of control to contain undesired dependencies *before* they occur. However, the concept also allows the description of process dependencies on data that are found to be erroneous long after they have been created (and committed). This is demonstrated by the scenario in Figure 4.4a, which is an abridged version of a more detailed discussion [Bjork 1974].

In Figure 4.4a, time is assumed to be passing from left to right; there are three completed spheres of control, A, C, and E, with no higher-level sphere around them. If the indicated problem in B is found, there is no way to unilaterally backout the work done so far, because other processes that may or may not depend on faulty data can already have committed their results; in the example, this is the process having executed in sphere E. The first thing to do, then, is to trace back and find out which process created the wrong data item (it was A in the example) and enclose the already-completed SoC into a dynamically created new SoC to serve as the recovery environment. This effectively means reestablishing a system state that was in effect at an earlier point in time. The result is shown in Figure 4.4b.

A next step, which is not shown here, would consist of looking inside A, which of course might encompass a number of lower-level SoCs, to determine exactly where the faulty data came from. After this has been established, the final step consists of again going

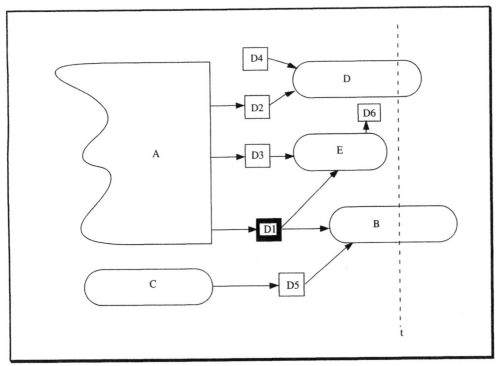

Figure 4.4a: Beginning of scenario: containment of faulty data after the fact. Sphere of control A has been going on for some time; at the indicated point in time *t*, a problem is discovered in the process protected by B. Data item D1 is determined to be the cause of the problem.

forward in time to do recovery for all processes that have become dependent on any data produced by the process that created D1. This leads to an extension of SoC F, as shown in Figure 4.4c.

Atomicity, therefore, is only one aspect of the concept of sphere of control. The complementary notion of commitment control is equally important, because, as observed above, as soon as an update is exported by a process, it makes its way through the system. Other spheres of control, using the updated data as input, become dependent on it. There is no realistic way to avoid this. Preventing SoCs from becoming dependent on intermediate results would mean that no data can be externalized until the data has become globally consistent (from the perspective of the highest-level sphere of control). For all nontrivial operations on shared data, this is infeasible. Apart from the performance problems incurred, one consequence would be to give up any hierarchical control structure in favor of a single-level, monolithic design. In order, then, for any useful work to be done, data must be externalized to other processes on a regular basis,[9] even before it can be trusted to be "ultimately" correct. As a consequence, the system must keep track of who created, updated, and deleted which data, who became dependent on it by reading or displaying it, and so on. This execution history must kept for as long as control might still need to be exercised.

---

[9] [Davies 1972] observes that displaying data on the screen means some kind of commitment. If, however, the action supplying this data is atomic, then special precautions are required for decommitting (revoking) the data from the user.

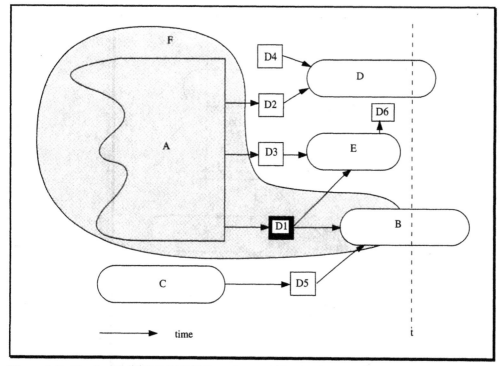

Figure 4.4b: Tracing dependencies backward in time.   A dynamic sphere of control, F, is extended backward in time to contain the SoC that created the invalid data item D1.

Note that this is not necessarily an unrealistic requirement. In many human organizations, such rules have been in effect for a long time, and the way they are implemented is by keeping written accounts, receipts, and other physical history. The type and duration of such record keeping is regulated by law in most cases. The idea is to keep the application accountable, whether for controlling purposes, for legal purposes, or for whatever. Automated systems have largely followed these rules by writing the specified information to archival storage and then forgetting about the rules, as far as the system structure is concerned.

Keeping the actual execution history with data dependencies and the values associated, as is suggested by the SoC concept, is definitely not the state of the art in current application systems. It would, among other things, require that objects not be updated, but rather that a new version be created every time a data object is assigned a new value. To appreciate this, we have to understand that there is no fundamental need to keep a database at all; the log contains all the information there is. The only reason for storing the database (i.e., the current end-of-the-log) is performance of retrieval operations. Larry Bjork described such a design in technical reports; David Reed [1978] elaborated very similar ideas in his thesis on time domain addressing.

Apart from the problems of implementing a system that keeps a complete history of all its objects—including information about which version of some object was dependent on which versions of other objects at any point in time—there is another fundamental difficulty: looking back at Figures 4.4b and 4.4c, there is nothing said about what is actually done in the recovery sphere F. This is not an omission, but rather reflects the fact that once there is a

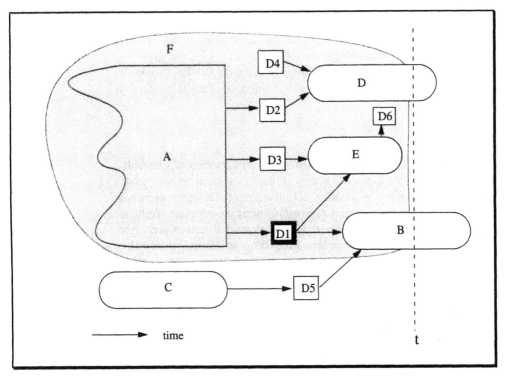

Figure 4.4c: Creating dynamic dependencies to encompass all processes affected by the correction of an error. After the cause of the faulty data has been determined, the recovery sphere of control, F, is expanded forward in time. It must encompass all processes that potentially have to be recovered because they have used the invalid data item D1.

necessity to establish a sphere of control that has to contain errors by going backwards in time, all the actual recovery steps are completely application dependent.

Consider the following example: Somebody walks up to an ATM and gets money out of it. The system has committed physical data (greenbacks) based on the account balance, which was sufficiently high because some hours before a check was credited to that account. The process clearing the checks had done its job and committed its data to the process keeping the accounts. If two days later it is determined that the check was forged, the data committed by the check clearing process turns invalid. Now, the business of extending a recovery sphere of control back in time begins to determine the point where the check entered the system. From then on, history is replayed in a forward direction to recover all processes that have become dependent on the falsification. One of these processes is the person with the money.[10]

To avoid any misconceptions, we should point out that none of the current models used for building applications (including flat transactions) could automatically cope with such a situation. If something of that type occurs, it would be an exception that must be taken care of "manually" by the application. The same is true for the concept of spheres of control; it makes no prescriptions on *how* the effects of the forged check can be contained and compensated for. But the big difference from simpler schemes is that spheres of control allow

---

[10] Is it fair to say that detective stories by and large deal with little more than expanding spheres of control backward in time and running a forward recovery from there?

description of (and thereby control of) dependencies that are relevant for the application. With models like flat transactions, these dependencies are not understood by the system; they are documented in procedural regulations of the operation, at best.

The notion of recovery spheres of control, then, is purely conceptual. All the system can do is keep the history of versions and data dependencies. Everything else has to be done by the application.

4.3.3 Summary

Spheres of control are based on a hierarchy of abstract data types, which execute atomically. If a computation involves many such spheres of control, it may become necessary to use data the final correctness of which cannot be decided at a given point. To make the whole computation appear atomic to the outside, commitment control must be exercised for these data. This requires the dynamic creation of a sphere of control around all actions accessing the data. Which computation depends on which version of the data must be recorded so that the execution history can be traced in case of a subsequent problem. Based on the recorded dependencies, all affected computations can be redone or invalidated. A consequence of this is that all versions of all data elements must be kept around forever. It is important to understand that the data on which processes can become dependent comprise everything that can possibly be shared among different activities: data in a database, messages, timer values, and sensor inputs. Though the issue is beyond the scope of this discussion, it is important to note that reversing history becomes particularly tricky when some of the data involved are intrinsically irreversible (a timer, for example).

The notion of spheres of control is both general and powerful, but it has never gotten fully formalized. Due to its generality, it is likely to be difficult (and expensive) to build a system exploiting it in full. Flat transactions, on the other hand, are simple and easy to implement, but they only describe what is the bottom level of atomic actions in the SoC model. What is needed is something more implementable than spheres of control, and something more powerful than flat transactions.

4.4 A Notation for Explaining Transaction Models

In the literature, suggested transaction models abound. Flat transactions have finally made their way into all commercially available database systems, and they are about to be used in operating systems and communication systems. The implementation techniques are well-understood, and so are the limitations.

Consequently, many attempts have been made to extend the flat transaction model so that it can adequately model more complex situations. Such proposals often start from a specific application, analyze its dynamic behavior, specify a fault model, and then add as many features to the classical ACID transaction model as are needed to support that application. The point is that these application-specific extensions result in a new, closed transaction model that may not support some other applications. Furthermore, it is sometimes hard to determine if and how these various transaction models can coexist, in the sense that different applications use different models while sharing some of the data they work on.

Because this is an area of active research, this chapter can do little more than give an overview of the current state of discussion: no Grand Unified Theory of Transactions has yet been developed. To give a better impression of what differences there are between transac-

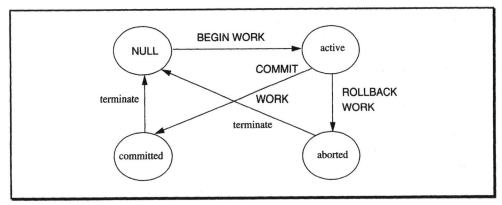

Figure 4.5: State-transition diagram for a flat transaction as seen by the application. By issuing BEGIN WORK, the transaction is pulled out of the NULL state into the active state. From this state, it can either move on to the committed state (COMMIT WORK) or to the aborted state (ROLLBACK WORK). From there the transaction is brought back to the NULL state by the system; this is shown as the "terminate" transition.

tion models—beyond the fact that they are meant to support different types of applications— the various transaction models are presented here not only by example, but by also with a notation that focuses on the structural aspects of how spheres of control are created and destroyed.

4.4.1 What Is Required to Describe Transaction Models?

It sometimes is useful to describe transactions as state machines. For example, when specifying the interactions of a certain transaction type with its operational environment, a finite automaton says unambiguously which state a transaction can be in, depending on which events can occur. The basic flat transaction is described by the simple state machine shown in Figure 4.5.

For single transactions, such a representation is very clear and comprehensive. It is easy to elaborate on finite state machines, especially when considering implementation details. The active state can then be divided into more intermediate states; so can the committed state, the aborted state, and so forth. A good example for this is presented in the discussion of the two-phase commit protocol in Chapter 10.

However, when describing phenomena for which it is not possible to define a priori a fixed number of states, finite state machines are not appropriate (this is the case with dynamically created spheres of control to reflect data dependencies).[11] Therefore, we will use a slightly different notation, which is not as amenable to formal analysis as state machines are, but which may help in understanding the dynamic behavior of different transaction models.

To keep things simple, the approach adopted here takes the SoC model's attitude of using atomic state transitions as the basic building blocks. In this model, therefore, a flat transaction that does not interact with other transactions and encounters no dependencies on data

---

[11] For readers who are familiar with that kind of problem, we might add that one could still try to use state machines and model their interactions by using the Cartesian product of the transactions involved. But if these transactions are not simple, or if more than two transactions are involved, such product representations get quickly out of hand.

objects is an *elementary particle*. The observable behavior is completely described by Figure 4.5. Note, though, that the state machine in the figure describes the flat transaction *type*. Each instance of a flat transaction, after it has appeared on the scene, stays active for a while, and then commits or aborts. Once it has reached one of these two completion states, it remains in that state forever, and because SoC scenarios always describe histories of execution, they contain information only about instances, not about types. The same approach is taken here, and the various transaction models are introduced by explaining the evolution of the instances involved over time. Each instance has a name that identifies it eternally.

The next aspect adopted without modification from the SoC model is the distinction into two categories of dependencies among atomic actions:

Structural dependencies. These reflect the hierarchical organization of the system into abstract data types of increasing complexity. Consider as an example Figure 4.3. The atomic action surrounded by SoC B4 is structurally dependent on A2, because the implementation of A2 uses B3 (as well as B4 and 5). The consequence of this—forgetting about sphere S for the moment—is that none of the results produced by B3 can finally be committed (even though they appear perfectly good from B3's perspective) until A2 decides to commit. The reason is simple: A2 appears as an atomic action to the outside. So, as long as it has not decided which way to go (all or nothing), everything it has done—either by itself or by invoking lower-level atomic actions—must remain contained inside A2's sphere of control. In that sense, the commit of B3 depends on the commit of A2. Structural dependencies are fixed in that the invocation hierarchy is hard-wired in the code; even if it is not, each instance to which A2 belongs invokes an instance of abstract data type B. As soon as the instance of B gets invoked, its fate depends on the invoking instance of A.

Dynamic dependencies. As explained previously, this type of dependency arises from the use of shared data. Let us briefly recapitulate the idea illustrated in Figure 4.3. Up to a certain point, A1 and A2 are disjoint atomic actions. Some action within A1 has produced data object D, but A1 is still active. If someone inside A2 uses D, then it is quite obvious that any results based on that become wrong at the moment A1 decides to roll back, because that makes D return to its previous value. As a consequence, A2 has become dependent upon A1 in the sense that A2 can commit only if A1 does. This sounds like the description of structural dependencies, but there is a major difference: structural dependencies reflect the *invocation hierarchy* of the system, whereas dynamic dependencies can envelop any number of otherwise unrelated atomic actions.

The SoC model describes dependencies by drawing circles around other circles. This is convenient as long as dependencies are strictly hierarchical, which is true for structural dependencies. Data dependencies, however, are not at all hierarchical. Any atomic action (at any level) can be involved in dynamic dependencies with many other atomic actions at different levels of the invocation hierarchy. Thus, while adopting the notion of dependencies from the SoC model, we use a different graphical metaphor (introduced in the next subsection). We also reduce data dependencies to the description of the fact that such a dependency exists; the data elements that caused the dependency do not show up in our formalism. While this may seem for now to be a drastic loss in descriptive power, we will later see that it is not.

There is but one major difference between the SoC model and the approach to describing transaction models taken here. Spheres of control are supposed to be around forever; no modifying or purging of history is allowed; and, as is shown in the scenario of Figures 4.4a–4.4c, the model allows enfolding spheres of control into new ones long after the original SoCs have completed. In other words, as long as an atomic action has at least one sphere of control around itself, it is neither committed nor aborted. Once committed or aborted, it has no sphere of control between itself and the universe, and it remains forever in the state it has assumed. The name of the atomic action and its final outcome are remembered forever. Considering the tremendous hurdles of implementing such a scheme, this feature is not included in our considerations.

4.4.2 Elements of the Notation

The fundamental observation to be made about transaction models is that they impose different rules about structural and dynamic dependencies among atomic actions and the effects they have on related actions. These rules can come in great variety, but they all have a very simple structure, once the restrictions outlined in Subsection 4.4.1 have been accepted. There are two parts to a rule: an active part and a passive part. Here is what they are about:

Active part. As can be seen from Figure 4.5, there are three events causing an atomic action to change its state: the BEGIN WORK, the ROLLBACK WORK, and the COMMIT WORK. Transaction models can define conditions that trigger these events. Consider the example in Figure 4.3 again: the event ROLLBACK WORK for atomic action B3 can be triggered by the program running inside B3 (this is true for all atomic actions); but, because of the structural dependency, there is an additional condition saying that the abort of A2 triggers the rollback of B3.

Passive part. Atomic actions that depend on other transactions might not be able to make certain state transitions all by themselves. For example, the signal COMMIT WORK for B3 is not sufficient to actually commit B3; that can only happen if A2 is ready to commit, too, since A2 is the higher-level sphere of control. Accordingly, there must be rules specifying the conditions for performing a state transition that has been signalled.

That is all there is. Transaction models are simply distinguished by different sets of rules for creating the events that drive atomic actions and for the conditions under which the rules can take effect. Before setting up the syntax for these rules, which are used in the rest of this chapter, let us look at a graphical notation that illustrates the key parts of the rules. The building block of the graphical representation is shown in Figure 4.6.

As explained, each instance of an atomic action can receive three types of signals;[12] they are shown as three "ports" at the top of the rectangle representing the atomic action. After a finite time, the action will inevitably end up in one of two states, aborted or committed, with no sphere of control around it. These are shown at the bottom of the rectangle. By having one box for each possible outcome, it is possible to attach conditions to the outcomes according to the passive rules. (This will become clear during the following discussion.) Let

---

[12] Note that these signals do not necessarily have to come from the outside; under normal conditions, abort and commit are signalled by the code executing under the protection of the sphere of control.

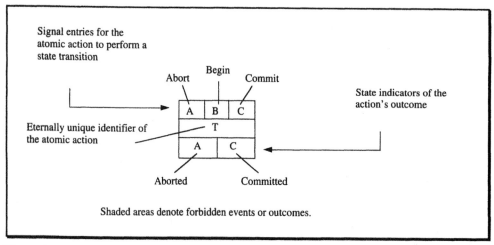

Figure 4.6: A graphical notation for general transaction models. For the graphical representation of a transaction model, each instance of an atomic action is depicted as a box with three entries at the top representing the signals for state transitions the action can receive, and two entries at the bottom representing the two (mutually exclusive) final outcomes of the action.

us start using the graphical notation by applying it to the simplest transaction model of all, flat transactions. The result is shown in Figure 4.7.

Let us first explain the system transaction. It is a "permanent" transaction in that as long as the system is up, it is always active. There is no way to commit the system transaction. A system crash aborts the system transaction, and the operational model one can apply to this notation is that restart begins when the abort of the system transaction takes effect. As Figure 4.7 shows, its abort triggers a ROLLBACK WORK signal to the flat transaction T, which consequently aborts as well. This models the fact that classic flat transactions are rolled back if affected by a crash. Why does this need a "system" transaction? Would it not be simpler to use the same restart interpretation that is applied to the system transaction and apply it to each atomic action that is not yet committed, thus avoiding the system transaction altogether? For flat transactions, it would. More sophisticated transactions, for which this artifact of a system transaction is really helpful, are discussed in Sections 4.6 and 4.11.

Beyond this, there is little to say about Figure 4.7. Forbidden states and events are shaded. A transaction that is running cannot be started again; a terminated transaction cannot react to any events, and it cannot change its final state. It is simply an inert part of execution history. Figure 4.7 makes it quite clear why flat transactions are so ill-suited to model complex computations: apart from the dependency on the system transaction's abort, they are completely self-contained and independent of their environment, and they can roll back or commit at their leisure.

4.4.3 Defining Transaction Models by a Set of Simple Rules

Before proceeding to more expressive transaction models, let us establish the syntax for the rules illustrated by the graphical metaphors we have shown. Each transaction model talks about the relationship between a number of atomic actions (the flat transaction model has just one, but we are about to leave this boring flatland). For each atomic action that is part of

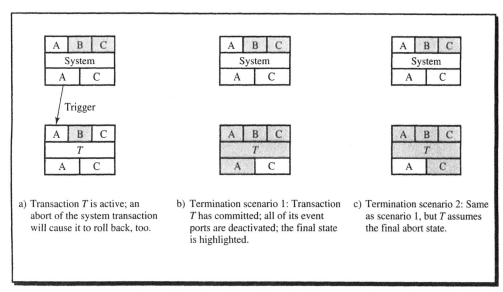

a) Transaction *T* is active; an abort of the system transaction will cause it to roll back, too.

b) Termination scenario 1: Transaction *T* has committed; all of its event ports are deactivated; the final state is highlighted.

c) Termination scenario 2: Same as scenario 1, but *T* assumes the final abort state.

Figure 4.7: Describing flat transactions by means of the graphical notation. A flat transaction is nothing but an atomic action with only one structural dependency. This dependency says that if the system transaction aborts, the flat transaction is forced to abort, too. The system transaction is always in the active state, never commits, and aborts only as a result of a system crash. Once a flat transaction has committed, it stays around without any dependencies, only documenting which final result is related to its name. All incoming ports that cannot receive events and all final states that cannot be assumed are shaded.

the model definition, we write down a set of rules—one for each state transition an atomic action can perform. So far (for the flat transaction model), there are three, corresponding to the verbs BEGIN WORK, ROLLBACK WORK, and COMMIT WORK. These rules are identified by $S_B(T)$, $S_A(T)$, and $S_C(T)$, respectively. T is the identifier of the atomic action, and S can be thought of as the initial of "signal." As explained next, the rule associated with a signal is activated whenever the respective event occurs. More sophisticated transaction models allow for more operations and therefore have more rules.

The structure of an arbitrary rule is as follows:

⟨rule identifier⟩:⟨preconditions ⟩ → ⟨rule modifier list⟩, ⟨signal list⟩, ⟨state transition⟩

Of course, the state transition in a rule with identifier $S_B(T)$ must be BEGIN WORK, the $S_A(T)$ rule must do a rollback, and so on. The idea behind these rules is quite simple: whenever a signal for a state transition arrives, it is not executed until the preconditions are fulfilled. The preconditions are simple predicate expressions. The most important predicates used in them are predicates about the completed state of other atomic actions: $A(T)$, saying that atomic action T is in the aborted state, and $C(T)$, saying that the atomic action T is in the committed state. For some transaction models, additional predicates are required; they are explained as needed.

The left side of the rule corresponds to the arrow in the graphical notation shown in Figure 4.7: the rule identifier specifies which signal port the arrow points to, and the precondition says where it comes from. The right side of the rule has three parts; the last one is essentially redundant, as was mentioned previously, but it is kept for clarity. The middle part describes which signals are generated as part of the state transition the rule specifies; in terms of the graphical notation, it says that an event such as ''action X has committed'' travels along an arrow that originates from that port. The signals are simply the names of rules that are to be activated by the signal; that is, they name the endpoint of the arrow.

The first clause of the rule's right-hand side is used to introduce additional arrows as they are needed, or to delete arrows that have become obsolete. These arrows, as explained, correspond to signals, that is, to the middle part of a rule. Consequently, a rule modifier looks like this:

⟨rule modifier ⟩::= +(⟨rule identifier⟩|⟨signal⟩).[13]

A minus sign in front of the clause on the right-hand side, instead of the plus sign shown, says that an existing arrow is to be removed. Another form of the rule modifier reads like this:

⟨rule modifier⟩ ::= delete(X),

where X stands for the identifier of an atomic action. This expression says that all rules pertaining to X and all references to it are to be deleted.

To understand how these rules can be used to decide what to do in a specific situation (that is, to implement a certain transaction model), the following intuitive interpretation is offered. Whenever an event—one of the three possible types—occurs, the rule that it identifies is checked. If the preconditions do not hold, the rule is simply marked to indicate that the event has occurred, and nothing else happens. If the precondition holds, the right-hand side is executed, which results in more signals, and so on. So far, this sounds very much like rule processing with forward chaining, and to a certain degree it is. But the point is that all actions triggered by one event are executed atomically; that is, the whole chain of dependent events is completed before any nonrelated event is considered. Once an atomic action has reached a final state, all its rules are deleted, and all signal entries pointing to one of them are removed. Only the predicate saying which state it has reached is remembered. Furthermore, all rules that are not referred to in any signal clause are deleted. The absence of signals pointing to a rule indicate stale actions that need not be further considered.

If this sounds a bit vague at the moment, keep the intuitive example in mind. The principle of executing a whole series of dependent events atomically before doing anything else comes up repeatedly throughout this text. In fact, we have already seen a very prominent example of this in the introduction to the book: the two-phase commit protocol.

The rules for the flat transaction model are extremely simple; there are no preconditions and no new events that need to be signalled:

$S_B(T)$: → +(S_A(system)|$S_A(T)$),,BEGIN WORK
$S_A(T)$: → (delete($S_B(T)$), delete($S_C(T)$)),,ROLLBACK WORK
$S_C(T)$: → (delete($S_B(T)$), delete($S_A(T)$)),,COMMIT WORK

---

[13] The clause ⟨rule modifier list⟩ is a sequence of ⟨rule modifier⟩s.

The first rule establishes the structural dependency from the system transaction and then starts the flat transaction itself. The other rules specify the effects of the abort and commit events. In flat transactions, these effects are straightforward: the appropriate state transition must be executed, and since both resulting states are final states, the rules pertaining to the terminated transaction must be removed. If we only had to cope with flat transactions, all this machinery of rules and graphical notations would not be needed; but it turns out to be very convenient once we consider more complex execution schemes.

4.5 Flat Transaction with Savepoints

The "all-or-nothing" characteristic of flat transactions is both a virtue and a vice. It gives the simplest of all possible failure semantics, but if anything goes wrong along the way, the application programmer has only two options: he can thread his way back through the application logic by repairing this and reestablishing that (the conventional method), or he can invoke ROLLBACK WORK, thereby giving up everything that has been done so far.

The latter approach is much simpler, and for very short applications, such as debit/credit, it is quite appropriate.[14] But as we saw in the trip planning scenario, there are situations in which a little more context is accumulated, not all of which is invalidated by a single error in processing along the way. If that is true, then giving up the entire context is both undesirable and too expensive. Having the option of stepping back to an earlier state *inside the same transaction* would be a better support for such applications. That is, if one does not want to allow transactions inside transactions, there must be some other way of informing the system about a state of the application program that should be remembered so that the application can return to it later on if something goes wrong. This is what savepoints are all about.

4.5.1 About Savepoints

A savepoint is established by invoking the SAVE WORK function, which causes the system to record the current state of processing (this is explained in detail in Chapters 10 and 11). This returns to the application program a handle that can subsequently be used to refer to that savepoint. Typically, the handle is a monotonically increasing number. The only reason why an application program needs an identifier for a savepoint is that it may later want to reestablish (return to) that savepoint. To do that, the application invokes the ROLLBACK WORK function, but rather than requesting the entire transaction to be aborted, it passes the number of the savepoint it wants to be restored. As a result, it finds itself reinstantiated at that very savepoint. This idea is illustrated in Figure 4.8.

If savepoints are established at partially consistent states of the application program, they can be used as internal restart points when problems are subsequently found. Depending on the application logic, one can decide to return to the most recent savepoint, or to any other earlier savepoint.

Looking more closely at Figure 4.8, we can make some interesting observations about the way savepoints are used. First, the successful execution of the BEGIN WORK statement establishes the transaction's first savepoint; it is guaranteed to have number 1. It is worthwhile considering the subtle difference between rolling a transaction back completely

---

[14] This is not always true. If the input message is part of the transaction, then invoking ROLLBACK will dispose of the input message, which is considered bad form. However, let us ignore such detail for the moment.

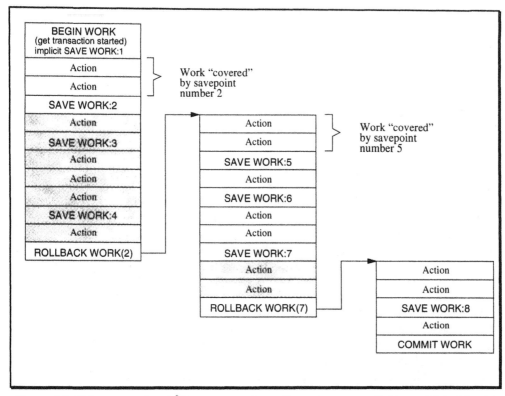

Figure 4.8: Using savepoints inside a transaction. Savepoints are explicitly established by the application program and can be reestablished by invoking a modified ROLLBACK function, which is aimed at an internal savepoint rather than at the beginning of the transaction. For reference, savepoints are numbered. The BEGIN WORK of a transaction implicitly establishes savepoint number 1.

(aborting it) and rolling back to savepoint 1. In the first case, the transaction disappears from the scene, gets detached from the program that was running it, and loses all its resources. When rolling back to savepoint 1, the transaction stays alive, keeps its resources, and simply returns to a state where it has not yet done anything. The usefulness of that feature is further elaborated in Exercise 4.13.

The other thing to note is that savepoint numbers increase monotonically within a transaction. Consider the example in Figure 4.8. Having returned to savepoint 2, one would expect the next savepoint number to be 3, since all the previous work has been given up. However, the savepoint number is 5; that is, the ROLLBACK does not affect the savepoint counter. At first sight it might seem arbitrary whether numbering should work this way or that way. This is not the case, though, since increasing numbers monotonically allows the complete execution history of the transaction to be maintained in the savepoints it has taken—including all the changes of mind along the way. On the one hand, this gives the application programmer a high degree of flexibility; on the other hand, it may lead to very unstructured programs. Look at Figure 4.8 one more time: there is nothing that prevents the application program, after having generated savepoint number 8, from requesting a rollback to savepoint 4. The system will perform as it is told, but the application had better know what it is doing.

4.5.2 Developing the Rules for the Savepoint Model

Let us now apply the notation to the savepoint model. The graphic representation is easy. The basic idea is to regard the execution between two subsequent savepoints as an atomic action in the sense of spheres of control. The transaction as such is rooted at the savepoint 1 action, which corresponds to the **BEGIN WORK**. Like a flat transaction, this transaction will receive an abort signal from the system transaction in case of a crash. The completion of a savepoint creates a new atomic action that is structurally dependent on its predecessor, and so forth. It is important to note that since execution can only take place in the atomic action that was created last, only this one can initiate commit. Consequently, the commit signal percolates up through all the intermediate atomic actions until the whole transaction is committed. This is illustrated in Figure 4.9.

In the same vein, it is only the most recently created atomic action that can invoke **ROLLBACK**. However, the question of how far back rollback extends depends on what the

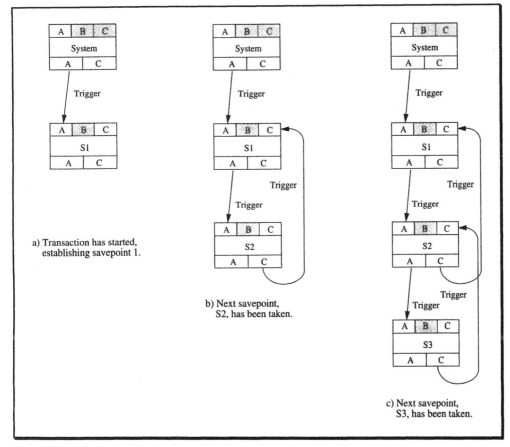

a) Transaction has started, establishing savepoint 1.

b) Next savepoint, S2, has been taken.

c) Next savepoint, S3, has been taken.

Figure 4.9: The graphical representation of flat transactions with savepoints. The model of flat transactions with savepoints consists of a sequence of atomic actions that are threaded together by triggered commits (from the current position back to the beginning of transaction) and by triggered aborts originating at the system transaction as a consequence of a crash. A rollback from the current position back to a savepoint or an abort of the entire transaction requires explicit abort signals to each of the atomic actions in the inverse order of their invocation.

target of the rollback is. It can be a savepoint along the way, or the whole transaction can be aborted. The graphical notation is not quite capable of depicting this kind of value-dependent rollback, so let us now turn to the rules.

As before, there is a rule for each state transition a transaction can make; but for this model, rollback needs to be parameterized by the identifier of the savepoint the transaction is to be rolled back to. Since we are modeling the sequence of savepoints by a sequence of atomic actions, the target of the rollback is assumed to be specified as the identifier of the oldest atomic action to be rolled back; if this is the identifier of the starting action, then the rollback aborts the transaction. Let the identifier of the rollback target be R. The transaction itself has the identifier S_1, which, according to the modeling convention, is the identifier of the first atomic action in the sequence. To keep the focus on the important parts of the rules, the delete clauses in the abort and commit rules are omitted. They look exactly like in the case of flat transactions.

$$
\begin{aligned}
&S_B(S_1): &&\rightarrow +(S_A(\text{system})|S_A(S_1)),, \text{BEGIN WORK} \\
&S_A(R) \ :(R<S_1) &&\rightarrow \ ,,\text{ROLLBACK WORK} \\
&S_C(S_1): &&\rightarrow \ ,,\text{COMMIT WORK} \\
&S_S(S_1): &&\rightarrow +(S_A(S_1)|S_A(S_2)), S_B(S_2),
\end{aligned}
$$

The last rule is a new type and describes what to do on behalf of action S_1 when the savepoint signal arrives (subscript S). The rules for taking an arbitrary savepoint after the first one look very similar. The only difference is that subsequent atomic actions are not rooted at the system transaction, and both commit and rollback signals are passed backwards to the predecessor. Here is the rule set for an atomic action S_n representing some intermediate savepoint that was generated by S_{n+1}:

$$
\begin{aligned}
&S_B(S_n): &&\rightarrow \ ,,\text{BEGIN WORK} \\
&S_A(R) \ :(R<S_n) &&\rightarrow \ ,S_A(S_{n-1}), \text{ROLLBACK WORK} \\
&S_C(S_n): &&\rightarrow \ ,S_C(S_{n-1}), \text{COMMIT WORK} \\
&S_S(S_n): &&\rightarrow +(S_A(S_n)|S_A(S_{n+1})), S_B(S_{n+1}),
\end{aligned}
$$

An analysis of this description shows that it does not allow something previously described as being possible in principle: In this model, if the transaction rolls back from, say, savepoint 5 to savepoint 2, all the atomic actions on the way back are aborted; that is, they go into a final, immutable state. As a consequence, there is no way to later roll back to savepoint 3 or 4. After having returned to savepoint 2, the transaction can either roll back further or roll back to a savepoint that was established after the rollback. This restriction, which enforces structured programming very nicely, is a consequence of modeling each savepoint interval as an atomic action.

4.5.3 Persistent Savepoints

There is an idea that has been discussed in the field of transaction processing for quite some time, and no commonly accepted conclusion seems to be within reach. It is the idea of persistent savepoints. As can be seen from the rule set in Subsection 4.5.2, an abort signal resulting from a system crash is passed down the chain of atomic actions, which is to say that all savepoints perish in case of a system failure.

Making savepoints persistent implies that whenever a savepoint is taken, the state of the transaction is not just recorded in some control blocks in volatile memory, but rather is kept in persistent storage (or durable storage, as it is usually called in this book). That allows restart to proceed as follows: the last unfinished savepoint interval is rolled back, just as in any incomplete transaction, but the state as of the previous successful persistent savepoint is reestablished. The benefit is a (possibly drastic) reduction of work lost. We suggest transactions using persistent savepoints be called *Phoenix transactions*, because they are reborn from the ashes.

Put this way, the idea sounds like a good one. In fact, we could convince ourselves that the model description and the rules could easily be modified to accommodate that idea. All that is needed is to sever the ties to the system transaction that causes the abort upon restart. While this is an easy solution at the level of modeling the behavior, actually implementing persistent savepoints is far from simple: It is not sufficient to just recover the data that the transaction has worked on; since a savepoint can be generated anywhere in a transaction program, the processing state of that program must be reestablished as well to make sure execution continues along the right path when the work is picked up again after restart.

The point, then, is that the idea of persistent savepoints is not primarily linked to the underlying transaction model. The difficulty is caused by the fact that conventional programming languages, such as COBOL, C++, Pascal, and so on, do not understand transactions, and there is no easy way to fix that. When using transactions with savepoints it is important to understand that savepoints, like transactions themselves, provide the control and therefore the means for state restoration for only those components that understand transactions (including savepoints). For example, this implies that if an application invokes the ROLL-BACK WORK function, its state will only partially be reestablished. Some components, such as the database manager, cooperate and fully support the protocol. But the memory manager and the run-time system of a conventional programming language ignore both transactions and savepoints completely. In other words, the database contents will return to the state as of the specified savepoint, but the local programming language variables will not.

The reason for this situation is simply that conventional programming languages lack durability and persistence. When a program is loaded, the variables either come with a predefined initial value or have to be initialized explicitly by the program. When the program terminates, normally or abnormally, the variables cease to exist. Since there is no concept of value stability or assignment history, there is no means of reestablishing some previous state. Put the other way around, if we have persistent savepoints, then after restart the transactional environment comes back at the most recent savepoint. The application's programming environment, on the other hand, resurfaces in its initial state: there is a clear mismatch of concepts.

Why was all this not discussed in the explanation of the ROLLBACK operation for flat transactions? Since aborting a transaction does not affect the program state either, the same set of arguments obviously holds for both transaction aborts and for savepoints. Usually, however, the implicit assumption is made that at the beginning of a transaction, the program does not rely on any state it keeps in local variables; rather, it initializes everything and then starts, using the parameters from the message it receives. The programming discipline imposed by the use of savepoints is demonstrated in detail in Chapter 5.

Without support from a persistent programming language, the only type of persistent savepoint that can likely be handled as easily as a rollback is persistent savepoint 1, the state of the transaction right after it has executed BEGIN WORK. At that point, the invocation context of the transactional environment is already set up, the input message is there, and so on. But, on the other hand, the application should not yet have built up any context in its local program variables. Thus, reestablishing a transaction in that state after a crash enables the application to simply continue processing without having to worry about lost messages; at the same time, there is no risk of a discrepancy between the transactional and the non-transactional view of things.

4.6 Chained Transactions

Chained transactions are a variation on the theme of savepoints. Given the deficiencies of a normal programming environment, they try to achieve a compromise between the flexibility of rollback and the amount of work lost after a crash. The concept, though, requires some cooperation on the programmer's part.

The idea of chained transactions is that rather than taking (volatile) savepoints, the application program commits what it has done so far, thereby waiving its rights to do a rollback; at the same time, however, it is required to stay inside a transaction. In particular, it does not want to lose the database objects it has acquired during the previous processing; if it has SQL cursors open, it wants to keep the cursors and their positions. Standard SQL closes all cursors upon commit. This request, which expresses a commit plus the intent to keep going, is called CHAIN WORK. It is a combination of COMMIT WORK and BEGIN WORK in one command. Note that this is not the same as calling COMMIT WORK and then starting a new transaction. The combination of both statements keeps the database context bound to the application, whereas a normal commit gives up all the context. One might object that even with a normal COMMIT/BEGIN sequence the next transaction could simply reestablish the previous context and keep going. However, between the COMMIT and the BEGIN, since they are separate statements, some other transaction could have arbitrarily changed the database, so that the next transaction in the sequence finds the world to be different from what it expects.

With transaction chaining, one can commit one transaction, release all the objects that are no longer needed, and pass on the processing context that is still required to the next transaction that is implicitly started. Note that the commitment of the first transaction and the beginning of the next are wrapped together into one atomic operation. This, in turn, means that no other transaction can have seen (or altered) any of the context data that is passed from one transaction to the other. Figure 4.10 shows the graphical representation of that transaction model.

As Figure 4.10 shows, the structural dependencies are not strong; the only guarantee is that the commitment of a transaction in the chain causes the next transaction to be started— if there is a next transaction. Apart from that, each transaction behaves like a flat transaction. The rules are accordingly simple. The list describes an arbitrary transaction in the chain (neither the first nor the last one); again, the delete clauses in the abort rule are omitted:

$S_B(C_n)$: $\rightarrow$ +(S_A(system)|$S_A(C_n)$), ,BEGIN WORK
$S_A(C_n)$: $\rightarrow$,,ROLLBACK WORK
$S_C(S_n)$: $\rightarrow$,$S_B(C_{n+1})$, COMMIT WORK

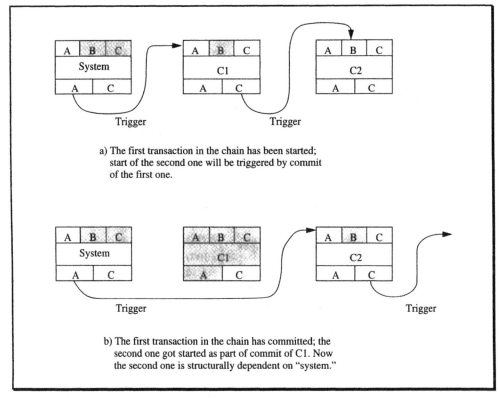

a) The first transaction in the chain has been started; start of the second one will be triggered by commit of the first one.

b) The first transaction in the chain has committed; the second one got started as part of commit of C1. Now the second one is structurally dependent on "system."

Figure 4.10: The graphical representation of chained transactions.   Chained transactions are modeled by a sequence of atomic actions, executed one at a time. As part of commit processing, a signal is generated that causes the next atomic action to do BEGIN WORK. The important thing is that this transition is atomic. Either C1 commits, then C2 begins, or C2 fails to begin, but then C1 does not commit either.

When comparing chained transactions to the savepoint model, we can make the following observations (one transaction in the chain is compared to one savepoint interval):

Workflow structure.   Chained transactions allow a substructure to be imposed on a long-running application program, just as savepoints do. The database context is preserved in both cases; in particular, cursors are kept open.

Commit versus savepoint.   Since the chaining step irrevocably completes a transaction, rollback is limited to the currently active transaction. This corresponds to restoring the *previous savepoint only*, rather than selecting an *arbitrary* savepoint. Again, this considers the effects of a chained transaction assuming they were to *replace* savepoints. It is a different story if savepoints are used within chained transactions.

Lock handling.   The COMMIT allows the application to free locks (explained in Chapter 7) that it does not later need. This can be very important for performance reasons; a savepoint does not affect any locks acquired so far.

Work lost. Savepoints allow for a more flexible state restoration than do flat transactions only as long as the system functions normally. After a crash, the entire transaction is rolled back irrespective of any savepoints taken so far, the idea of persistent savepoints notwithstanding.

Restart handling. The chained transaction scheme, on the other hand, reestablishes the state of the most recent commit; that is, less work is lost in that situation. But if chained transactions are used as a "most recent savepoint" scheme, the whole problem of reestablishing the program state, as discussed for persistent savepoints, comes up again. Unless the application programmer makes sure that at the moment CHAIN WORK is invoked there is no relevant processing context hidden in local program variables, restarting a chain might face the same problems as persistent savepoints do.

Observant readers (that is, everybody) will notice that the description of the chained transaction model in Figure 4.10, as well as in the rules, has nothing special to say about the case of transaction rollback. The last transaction in the chain is aborted, and that is that. This is what existing implementations of the chained transaction model have to offer.

However, the idea behind chaining could be extended in such a way as to get a whole sequence of transactions executed as one larger thing. From the application's point of view, the whole chain is likely to be the sphere of control; the individual transactions are merely technical tricks to get higher reliability. What should actually happen in case one of the transactions in the chain aborts? The reader can ponder this for a while but will almost certainly find that there is no generally good answer.

To settle this problem for the moment, we adopt the following view. If a transaction in the chain aborts during normal processing, then the chain is broken, and the application has to determine how to fix that. However, if a chain breaks because of a system crash, the last

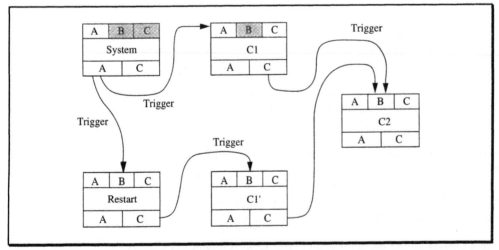

Figure 4.11: Restart processing in a chained transaction.   To continue processing a chain of transactions after a crash, a restart action is introduced. The "restart" gets activated as a consequence of "system" aborting. It does whatever the transaction system needs for restart (see Chapter 6), and upon commit triggers the new instance of C1 to start over again. C1' has the same dependencies C1 had.

transaction, after having been rolled back, should be restarted. This interpretation is shown graphically in Figure 4.11.

The scenario shows the use of the "system" action for something else than aborting other transactions. Rather, the abort of "system" triggers another generic action called "restart," which, as part of its commit, starts a new instance of the last transaction in the chain that got rolled back through its dependency from "system." Writing the rules for that is the subject of Exercise 4.15. Of course, the problem then is where to find the input for C1' once it has been restarted after a crash; that is discussed in Section 4.10.

4.7 Nested Transactions

Nested transactions are a generalization of savepoints. Whereas savepoints allow organizing a transaction into a *sequence* of actions that can be rolled back individually, nested transactions form a *hierarchy* of pieces of work. Their basic structure can be illustrated using the trip planning example discussed in Subsection 4.2.4. There is a top-level transaction controlling the whole trip planning activity, and nested within it are lower-level transactions, called subtransactions, controlling each of the partial transfers. Rather than taking a savepoint after each partial transfer, each of these subtransactions becomes a self-contained but dependent action (with the *A*, *C*, and *I* properties of ACID), which can be completed or rolled back individually. Of course, nesting can be continued over as many levels as there are abstraction layers in the application; it is a quite natural example of the nesting of spheres of control. The basic idea is illustrated in Figure 4.12.

4.7.1 Definition of the Nesting Structure

The formal definition of a nested transaction is very straightforward, although we will later see that the simple concept can be extended in many ways. For the moment we use the definition of nested transactions developed in Moss [1981], which can be paraphrased as follows:

(1) A nested transaction is a tree of transactions, the sub-trees of which are either nested or flat transactions.

(2) Transactions at the leaf level are flat transactions. The distance from the root to the leaves can be different for different parts of the tree.

(3) The transaction at the root of the tree is called the *top-level transaction*; the others are called *subtransactions*. A transaction's predecessor in the tree is called a *parent*; a subtransaction at the next lower level is also called a *child*.

(4) A subtransaction can either commit or roll back; its commit will not take effect, though, unless the parent transaction commits. By induction, therefore, any subtransaction can finally commit only if the root transaction commits.

(5) The rollback of a transaction anywhere in the tree causes all its subtransactions to roll back. This, taken with the previous point, is the reason why sub-transactions have only *A*, *C*, and *I*, but not *D*.

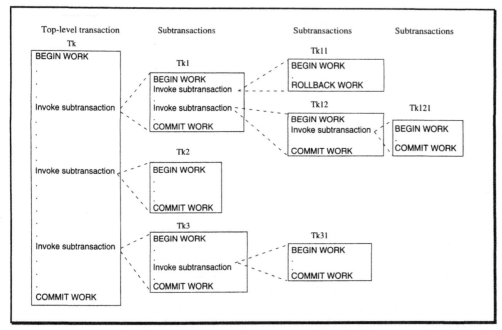

Figure 4.12: Nested transactions: the basic idea. A nested transaction is a tree of transactions. Starting at the root, each transaction can create lower-level transactions (subtransactions), which are embedded in the sphere of control of the parent. Transactions at the leaf level are flat transactions, except that they lack the durability of non-nested flat transactions.

In Moss's model of nested transactions, actual work can only be done by the leaf-level transactions. Only they can access the database, send messages, and acquire other types of resources. The higher-level transactions only organize the control flow and determine when to invoke which subtransaction.

In the following discussion, these restrictions are not observed. On the contrary, it is argued that by applying transaction nesting to a layered abstraction of objects, it is possible to increase the level of parallelism on shared objects, compared to a flat environment. However, this requires transactions at all levels to actively maintain their own objects. The behavior of nested transactions is summarized in the following three rules:

Commit rule. The commit of a subtransaction makes its results accessible only to the parent transaction. The subtransaction will *finally* commit (i.e., release its results to the outside world) only if it has committed itself locally and all its ancestors up to the root have finally committed. Consequently, any subtransaction can finally commit only if the root transaction commits.

Rollback rule. If a (sub-) transaction at any level of nesting is rolled back, all its subtransactions are also rolled back, independent of their local commit status. This is applied recursively down the nesting hierarchy. The immediate consequence is that if the root transaction is rolled back (e.g., because of a system crash), all its subtransactions are also rolled back, whether or not they have already done their local commit.

Visibility rule. All changes done by a subtransaction become visible to the parent transaction upon the subtransaction's commit. All objects held by a parent transaction can be made accessible to its subtransactions. Changes made by a subtransaction are not visible to its siblings, in case they execute concurrently.

It is important to note that subtransactions are not fully equivalent to classical flat transactions. The key point is that they are valid only within the confines of the surrounding higher-level transaction. They are *atomic* from the perspective of that parent transaction; they are *consistency preserving* with respect to the local function they implement; they are *isolated* from all other activities inside and outside the parent transaction; but they are not durable because of the commit rule. Except for the aspect of durability, then, nested transactions closely resemble the nesting of spheres of control described in Section 4.3.

The graphical representation of this transaction model is shown in Figure 4.13. The box for the system transaction is not shown, because its relation to the root transaction is the same as in the case of a simple flat transaction. What is new in this figure is the arrow pointing back from a committed state of a subtransaction to the committed state of the parent transaction. This is to depict the conditional state transition in the subtransaction. For example, T1 will enter the committed state only if the predicate C(T) is true. These backward

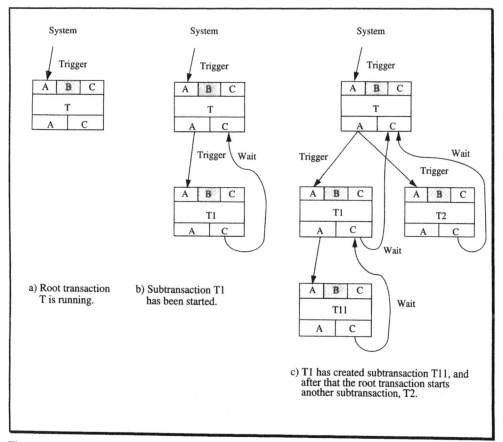

a) Root transaction T is running.

b) Subtransaction T1 has been started.

c) T1 has created subtransaction T11, and after that the root transaction starts another subtransaction, T2.

Figure 4.13: Graphical representation of nested transactions. The dependencies between the atomic actions establishing a nested transaction are purely structural. Abort signals are passed top down from the root to the leaves. The transition into the committed state in each atomic action depends on whether the parent action has made that transition.

arrows labeled "wait" correspond to the precondition clauses on the left-hand side of the rules.

Given the considerations explained for the savepoint model and for chained transactions, describing the rules for nested transactions is straightforward. Consider an arbitrary subtransaction T_{kn}, which has parent T_k. Its behavior is determined by the following rules:

$$S_B(T_{kn}): \qquad \rightarrow +(S_A(T_k)|S_A(T_{kn})), \text{,BEGIN WORK}$$
$$S_A(T_{kn}): \qquad \rightarrow \text{,,ROLLBACK WORK}$$
$$S_C(T_{kn}): \quad C(T_k) \quad \rightarrow \text{,,COMMIT WORK}$$

It is surprising that the rule set for nested transactions is simpler than the one for savepoints, although nested transactions seem to be the more powerful concept. The reason is that the building blocks of our description method are single atomic actions—much closer to the spirit of nested transactions than to sequential savepoints. Therefore, the fewer restrictions placed on the flexibility of atomic actions, the simpler the rules. Once the model requires curtailing the autonomy of the atomic actions, the rules get accordingly more complicated.

4.7.2 Using Nested Transactions

Nested transactions provide a powerful mechanism for fine-tuning the scope of rollback in applications with a complex structure. It is worth noting that there is a strong relationship between the concept of modularization in software engineering and the nested transaction mechanism. So far, there have been few attempts to capitalize on this relationship. Barbara Liskov's Argus project is a notable exception [Liskov 1988]; another more recent attempt to make nested transactions generally available is the Camelot prototype [Eppinger 1991]. The commercial "successor" of this prototype is the Encina TP monitor, with the programming language Transactional C; the run-time system of that language supports the notion of nested transactions [Transarc-Encina 1991].

The effect of combining nested transactions with a modularization hierarchy is easy to understand; see Figure 4.14 for an example. A well-designed module produces effects only via its interface. If no global variables are used, there can be no side effects, which means that even if a module fails, it will not corrupt any data structures used by the outside world; that is, by other modules. Although this is standard gospel, it is simply not true for database applications, because the database itself constitutes a very large global variable. Even if the software implementing the database application has a clean module structure, none of its modules will be free of side effects if it modifies the database—unless it is protected by a transaction.

The structure of Figure 4.14 closely resembles Figure 4.12, but whereas a transaction control structure is depicted in the earlier figure, Figure 4.14 shows a sample module hierarchy. The point is that the structural similarity can be exploited to build more reliable software. In other words, modularization and nested transactions complement each other. Modular design takes care of the application structure and encapsulates local (dynamic) data structures; the transactions make sure that the *global* data used by these modules are isolated and recovered with the same granularity.

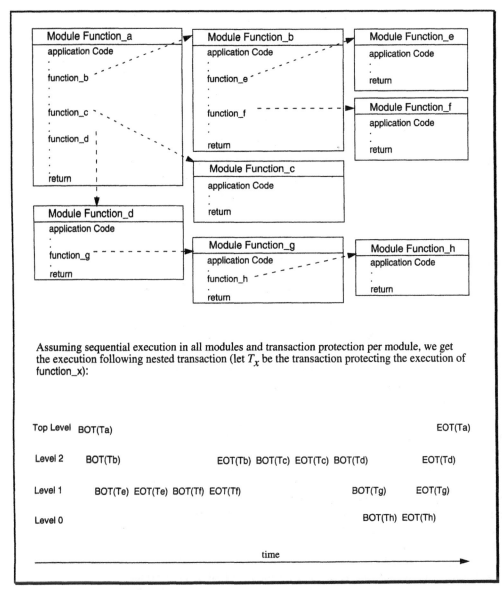

Figure 4.14: Combining the module concept with nested transactions. Each module execution is protected by a (sub-) transaction. The role of the top-level transaction is determined by the application requirements; the nesting structure follows the invocation order.

The first idea along this line (based on spheres of control) was introduced by Randell [Randell, Lee, and Treleaven 1978] under the name of *recovery blocks*, but it never gained much attention. The problem was that—viewed as units of execution—recovery blocks only had the C property of ACID. Argus was the first transaction-oriented approach in that direction, but it lacked a database and the proper operating system basis. The surprising fact therefore remains that although these techniques would obviously facilitate the design, implementation, and maintenance of large systems, they are not used in reality, because there is almost no system support for them—again with the exception of very recent developments such as Transactional *C*.

Even current database systems, except for the limited case described in Section 4.8, do not rely on nested transactions for their own implementation. This is quite surprising, because nesting the scope of commitment and backout is commonplace even in today's SQL systems (although the user cannot influence it). This is particularly true for SQL statements that are executed as part of a transaction. Think of this transaction as the root transaction and the SQL statements as the subtransactions. Obviously, an SQL update statement commits its modifications to the top-level transaction. If it fails (assume an INSERT being rejected because a unique value condition is violated), it is implicitly undone and so appears to be atomic even in case of a failure. In other words, update SQL statements have all the properties of subtransactions, but since the implementation techniques are typically ad hoc rather than guided by the idea of transaction nesting, the general mechanism is not available for the application programmer.

4.7.3 Emulating Nested Transactions by Savepoints

It is interesting to note that even if a system does not support nested transactions, their effect with respect to hierarchical domains of recovery (as explained earlier) can nevertheless be obtained by using savepoints. The idea is simply that whenever a new subtransaction T_{ki} is started—no matter at which level—this is the very point to which control must return in the event that subtransaction is rolled back. Since the purpose of a savepoint is to establish a point to fall back to, it is invoked immediately before starting T_{ki}, and its name is associated with T_{ki} in the sense that it defines the target of the transaction's rollback. This principle is illustrated in Figure 4.15. For simplicity, the savepoints have been given the same indices as their associated transactions.

The figure also shows that the savepoint scheme gives even more flexibility in terms of transaction-internal recovery than does the concept of nested transactions. For example, with savepoints it is possible (say, after the completion of T_{k3}) to restore the state as of s_2; this is not possible in a hierarchy of transactions. This is but another aspect of the general question of how much structure, and how many restrictions, a control mechanism should impose.

Since an arbitrary subtransaction T_{ki} has to be associated with a savepoint S_{ki} that stabilizes the system state *at its beginning*, it is obvious that a rollback will remove all savepoints created after that. If all subtransactions are executed in a synchronous, sequential fashion, these later savepoints can only be related to T_{ki}'s subtransactions T_{kij}, which are implicitly rolled back if T_{ki} is rolled back. Of course, the associated savepoints of all of T_{ki}'s younger siblings are also created after S_{ki}, but since a commit (T_{ki}) must have happened before that, they cannot be affected by a rollback of T_{ki}.

However, if subtransactions are allowed to execute in parallel, the nesting order will no longer be monotonically mapped onto the sequence of savepoints. Therefore, reestablishing the state of the savepoint associated with a transaction will affect arbitrary transactions, rather than only the sub-tree of the aborting transaction. In other words, the emulation of nested transactions by savepoints is limited to systems where everything within a top-level transaction is executed sequentially. Intratransaction parallelism requires genuine support for nested transactions.

There is yet another subtle point that may not become completely clear until the concepts for isolation have been introduced in Chapter 7, but let us briefly mention it anyway.

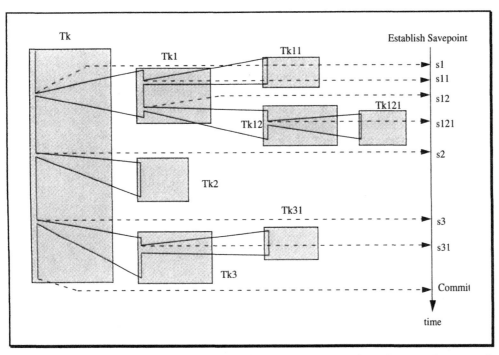

Figure 4.15: Nested transactions versus savepoints. The correspondence between the scope of recovery of nested transactions and those established by savepoints can easily be derived from this figure: if at the beginning of a subtransaction a savepoint is generated, then rolling back to that savepoint has the same effect as an abort of the corresponding subtransaction.

In a nested transaction, all the locks acquired by a subtransaction are *counter-inherited* by (transferred to) the parent transaction when the subtransaction commits. In other words, the objects that have been locked by the subtransaction are kept locked after its commit,[15] but now the parent transaction is the "owner" of the locks. Conversely, a parent transaction can give locks on objects to a subtransaction (locks are *inherited* by the subtransaction) at the moment it starts; this can be done selectively, or all of the parent's locks can be given to the subtransaction while it runs.

This is where the difference between nested transactions and the emulation of nesting by savepoints within a flat transaction comes in. Nested transactions imply different names for the (sub-)transactions, and therefore different holders of locks on the database objects. So, for example, a parent transaction P can hold exclusive locks on objects X and Y. If it invokes a subtransaction S_1, it can either pass none of its locks or all of them, or it can decide to just pass the lock on X to its child transaction S_1. In the latter case, S_1 can now can access X, but not Y. Assume S_1 acquires an exclusive lock on Z and then commits. Now P has (exclusive) locks on all three objects, X, Y, and Z (via counter-inheritance). It may then start another subtransaction S_2, which is given the lock on Y and therefore can access neither X nor Z.

---

[15] If the subtransaction aborts, all the locks that were newly acquired by that subtransaction are dropped, but those that were given to it by the parent in the beginning are returned to the parent.

When emulating nested transactions by savepoints, there is no choice as to which locks should be inherited by a subtransaction and which should be kept by the parent transaction. There is only one flat transaction, which owns *all the locks* that have been acquired since begin-of-transaction, and within which the savepoints are generated. In other words, at any point of such a transaction, all locked objects that have been touched so far are available and accessible, independent of the number of savepoints taken. In the scenario just mentioned, the operations pertaining to S_1 are effectively part of the surrounding transaction; thus, both X and Y are accessible. Likewise, the operations equivalent to S_2 are executed in the same environment and therefore have access to X, Y, and Z. The effect of emulating nested transactions by savepoints, then, is indistinguishable only with respect to recovery; that is, the possibility of selectively aborting subtransactions. The locking behavior achieved by the savepoint method is not as flexible as the general nested transaction model; it corresponds to the case in which each parent transaction gives all its locks to each subtransaction. This, in fact, is exactly what Moss [1981] proposed on nested transactions.

4.8 Distributed Transactions

A distributed transaction is typically a flat transaction that runs in a distributed environment and therefore has to visit several nodes in the network, depending on where the data is. The conceptual difference between a distributed transaction and a nested transaction can be put as follows:

The structure of nested transactions is determined by the functional decomposition of the application, that is, by what the application views as spheres of control. The structure of a distributed transaction depends on the distribution of data in a network. In other words, even for a flat transaction, from the application's point of view a distributed transaction may have to be executed if the data involved are scattered across a number of nodes.[16]

Assume that transaction T runs at node A, which requires two tables, X and Y, to be joined. Since only X is locally available, Y must be accessed through the network. This causes subtransactions T_1 and T_2 of T to be spawned at two other nodes, B and C, each of which holds a partition of Y. The invocation structure of such a distributed transaction is exactly like the one of a nested transaction. The dependencies, though, are different, as can be seen in Figure 4.16.

As mentioned, the decomposition into subtransactions does not reflect a hierarchical structure in the programs to be executed, but is induced by the placement of the data in the network. Consequently, the subtransactions are not really executing at a lower level of control, as is the case in nested transactions. Rather they are "slices" of the same top-level transaction. In other words: simple flat transactions (from the application's perspective) may be executed as distributed transactions if they run in a distributed database system and the data they access are scattered across multiple nodes. If a subtransaction issues COMMIT WORK, this signals the commit of the entire transaction, which forces all other subtransactions to commit. By comparison, in a nested transaction this is simply a local commit of that

---

[16] Note that this distinction is biased towards the application perspective. When viewed from the data manager's perspective, it is quite obvious that accessing data from a remote site requires different modules to be invoked than does accessing local data, resulting in a transaction structure that quite naturally reflects its task structure. Again, then, the terminology in some parts depends on what abstraction level we are actually looking at.

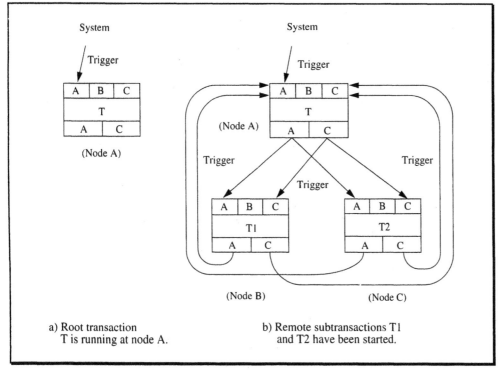

System
Trigger

A	B	C
T		
A		C

(Node A)

System
Trigger

(Node A)

A	B	C
T		
A		C

Trigger

Trigger

Trigger

A	B	C
T1		
A		C

Trigger

A	B	C
T2		
A		C

(Node B)   (Node C)

a) Root transaction
   T is running at node A.

b) Remote subtransactions T1
   and T2 have been started.

Figure 4.16: Graphical representation of distributed transactions. Distributed transactions are a restricted type of nested transactions that are used, for example, in distributed databases. Two subtransactions are shown. Other subtransactions at any level are appended in exactly the same way.

subtransaction, the final success of which depends on the commit of its ancestors in the tree. Distributed subtransactions normally cannot roll back independently, either; their decision to abort also affects the entire transaction. This all means that the coupling between subtransactions and their parents is much stronger in our model. The description of the distributed transaction model by the state transition rules is left as Exercise 4.17.

4.9 Multi-Level Transactions

Multi-level transactions are a generalized and more liberal version of nested transactions. They allow for the early commit of a subtransaction (also called pre-commit), and thereby give up the possibility of a unilateral backout of the updates. But rather than just letting the subtransaction go away, they assume the existence of a compensating transaction, which can semantically reverse what the original subtransaction has done in case the parent transaction decides (or is forced) to roll back. This compensating transaction can, of course, be another nested or multi-level transaction. Since these commit-compensation dependencies are enforced at all levels of nesting, it is guaranteed that all updates can be revoked, even if the root transaction fails and a whole number of subtransactions have committed before.

Note again the important differences in techniques used to achieve atomicity: as long as strict commitment control can be exercised over the modified data (that is, as long as they are not externalized to any instance outside the modifying transaction), it is possible at any point in time to decide to roll back, which then can be done by just reestablishing the old value. Clearly, if nobody has witnessed the attempt to create a new value, nobody can be affected by the decision not to do the updates. Chapter 7, on isolation concepts, discusses when to externalize data such that the I property of ACID is maintained.

4.9.1 The Role of a Compensating Transaction

If commitment control is relinquished before the application can be sure that the updates will really survive, then there is the risk of having to go through the time traveller's recovery scenario shown in Figures 4.4b and 4.4c. Given the fact that going back to the past is not a realistic option in an online system, the only possibility is to install a compensating transaction for what is about to be committed at that moment and keep the compensating transaction around in case the pre-committed results turn out to be invalid. If this does not happen, the compensating transactions can be thrown away unused when the root transaction commits.

This is shown in the graphical representation in Figure 4.17. N is the subtransaction nested below T, and CN is the corresponding compensating transaction. As long as N is running, there is no need for CN. But note that the relationship of N to T is not exactly the same as for a nested transaction; the point is that N can commit independently of T. When it does so, however, CN enters the scene. CN does not start, though, because it does not have to do anything if T commits. If T rolls back, though, CN is started, and then it must by definition commit. It is easy to see why that is so. T is the root transaction that determines the outcome of the entire top-level atomic action. If it is an abort, then none of its effects must remain in the system. But, according to the assumptions, N has already committed and externalized its results. This is the point where the spheres-of-control model embarks on its time travel back into the distant past. Lacking the means to implement that, multi-level transactions do the next best thing: they run a transaction in the present that makes the system look as though the precocious atomic action N had never been executed. This, in turn, creates the effect of T never having run.

Remember that an abort is a transaction's last resort; if an abort fails, the system is inconsistent. In the multi-level transaction model, however, the abort of one atomic action (T) is unconditionally linked to the commit of another one (CN), which means CN must not fail, no matter what. This is indicated in Figure 4.17, in which both the abort signal port and the aborted state of CN are shaded. Of course, this is just another way of saying "this must not happen"; it gives no indication of how that is done. The following rules are a little more specific.

The rules for the root transaction are again identical with those for a flat transaction. So let us first specify the rules for subtransaction N.

$$S_B(N): \qquad \rightarrow \text{,,BEGIN WORK}$$
$$S_A(N): \qquad \rightarrow \text{,,ROLLBACK WORK}$$
$$S_C(N): \qquad \rightarrow +(S_A(T)|S_B(CN)), \text{,COMMIT WORK}$$

When CN actually gets started, it must make sure that it will survive a crash or will be restarted after an abort caused by some internal malfunction. This calls for a trick similar to

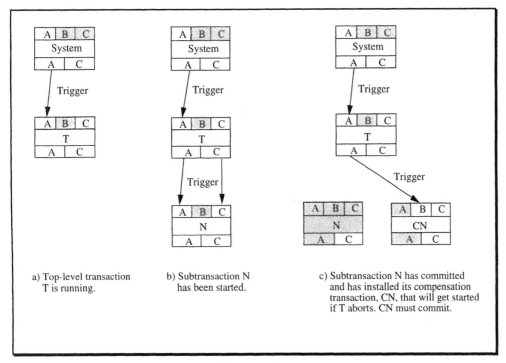

a) Top-level transaction
  T is running.

b) Subtransaction N
  has been started.

c) Subtransaction N has committed
  and has installed its compensation
  transaction, CN, that will get started
  if T aborts. CN must commit.

Figure 4.17: Graphical representation of a multi-level transaction T with one subtransaction N.
The subtransaction can commit before T does. In that case, a compensating transaction, CN, started by
an abort of T, is installed. Since by definition an abort must not fail, the compensating transaction CN
must commit; it has no abort option.

the one used for chained transactions: we introduce another instance of CN, called CN',
which runs the same code, gets the same data, but has a different name.[17] These are the rules
for CN:

$$S_B(CN): \qquad \rightarrow \ +(S_C(restart)|S_B(CN')),,BEGIN\ WORK$$
$$S_A(CN): \qquad \rightarrow \ ,S_B(CN'),\ ROLLBACK\ WORK$$
$$S_C(CN): \qquad \rightarrow \ delete(CN'),,COMMIT\ WORK$$

The problem with CN not being allowed to abort for whatever reason, indicated in Figure
4.17 by merely shading two boxes, is spelled out here in two places. When starting CN, its
alter ego, CN', is installed by linking its begin port to the committed state of the restart
transaction. This ensures that the compensation continues after restart. Furthermore, an internal abort, which of course we cannot prevent (some SQL error might cause it), is linked to
the start of CN', so it will also take over in that case.

On the other hand, if T eventually commits, all the compensating transactions that have
been introduced must be disposed of, because it is clear that they will never receive their
"begin" signal. These delete clauses in the rule system have been omitted for simplicity.

---

[17] Remember that in our SoC-inspired model, an atomic action can only run once; this means,
among other things, that it cannot be restarted.

4.9.2 The Use of Multi-Level Transactions

At first glance, multi-level transactions may appear fairly contrived. One could argue in particular that the notion of a repair transaction for compensating updates that have been committed before the actual end of the top-level transaction is just a trick that brings the system back into a (formally) safe state again. But is it reasonable to assume the existence (let alone safeness) of such compensations?

The expression "real life" is often used when justifying something that escapes nice, simple, formal treatment. In this case, however, it is sufficient to stay within the confines of computer systems and, more specifically, databases. A very simple scenario is shown in Figure 4.18.

The application transaction T consists of a number of SQL statements, which can be viewed as subtransactions, as pointed out in Section 4.7. But apart from just appearing to be atomic from the application programmer's perspective, each SQL statement in turn is implemented by a sequence of operations on the internal storage structures, which also can be viewed as subtransactions, and so forth. Consider the "insert tuple" part of the INSERT statement. It is easy to make this a subtransaction, consisting of two leaf-level actions: one action puts the new tuple into a page, which involves finding a page with enough free space and doing some other bookkeeping; the other action makes the new tuple addressable by putting its page number into the entry of some system-internal address translation table that corresponds to its unique identifier.

To explain the potential advantage of multi-level transactions, we must consider this in a little more detail. Let us first assume T was executed as a nested transaction according to the rules laid out in Section 4.7. All objects that have been modified along the way through

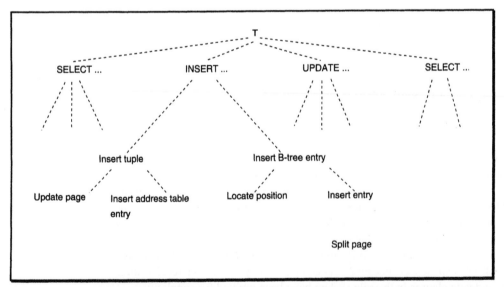

Figure 4.18: Viewing SQL statements as multi-level transactions. The statements are nested within the top-level application transaction. The effects of each statement can be committed at their level of implementation before the surrounding top-level transaction commits, provided the objects they implement are commitment-controlled at a higher level, and provided there is a counter-action that can compensate the original action.

the hierarchy of operations—such as the address table, the page where the tuple is inserted and so on—are commitment controlled. This is to say that upon the termination of a subtransaction, its new state is made accessible to the respective parent transaction, but not to anybody else; the option for unilateral rollback "just in case" is kept open. Consequently, all these objects remain protected until T finally commits, which means that nobody else can access the page where the tuple was inserted, nobody else can read through the modified portion of the B-tree, and so on. It is easy to imagine that this last restriction, in particular, can turn out to be detrimental for system performance in an environment where many transactions are to be executed in parallel using the same B-tree access path.

Now let us assume the same hierarchy of actions, executed as a multi-level transaction. According to the assumptions of this model, a subtransaction will commit its updates as soon as it is done. This means, for example, that both the page holding the new tuple and the page holding the address table entry are accessible to other (sub-) transactions, whether or not they are related to T. But, of course, T can still decide to roll back later on, in which case the tuple must be removed from its page, the corresponding entry must be deleted from the address table, and so on. Since the right of doing a unilateral backout has been waived by committing the updates early, removing the invalid modifications requires an explicit compensation action. Figure 4.19 illustrates the interplay between the original sequence of actions and their compensating counterparts, using the "insert tuple" example. It shows that for each step in the original transaction, there is an inverse step in the compensating transaction. (By the way, the compensating transaction is a DELETE statement.)

To appreciate that this might be a big advantage over a system that does not allow subtransactions to pre-commit, assume a page into which many transactions want to insert at about the same time. This could be the end-of-file of a relation with a heavy insert load. If no pre-commit is allowed, the page is isolated from other transactions as long as the one transaction currently doing an insert has not committed. Assume this takes about 300 ms. All other insert transactions have to wait during that time, which effectively allows for three insert transactions per second. If the subtransaction handling the page insert is allowed to precommit, however, then the other transactions are held up for its duration only. If a page insert takes 10 ms, then the same set of transactions suddenly can run at a throughput of 100 inserts per second.

Assume for the moment that a compensating action can always be defined for any given action.[18] Then, by running all compensations in the inverse order of the original actions, the initial state of the entire transaction can be reestablished. But how can the transaction be kept isolated if parts of its results are committed early? Specifically, how can some other transaction be prevented from deleting the new tuple from its page before T is committed? To understand the problem of atomicity in multi-level transactions, let us consider the sequence of updates in bottom-up order.

At the page level, there is no problem. All the page headers and table entries are updated according to their local consistency constraints by the "insert tuple" subtransaction. This means that no concurrent activity can inadvertently overwrite the space occupied by the new tuple or reuse the unique identifier assigned to it. Even if other transactions add tuples to or delete tuples from the same page, the compensating transaction will still be able to execute correctly, because it makes no reference to the specific offset in the page where the tuple

---

[18] This assumption does not hold in all environments. Think of real actions; it is easy to come up with examples of that category which defy both rollback and compensation.

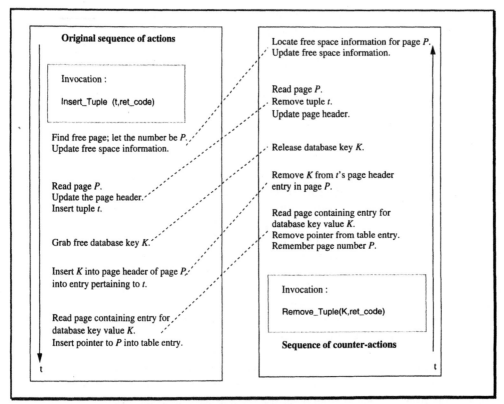

Figure 4.19: Maintaining tuples in a page by nested subtransactions.   If inserting a tuple into a page is implemented as a nested transaction that commits before the root transaction does, there must be a corresponding compensating transaction that guarantees to remove the tuple from the page if this is necessary—even if the page has subsequently been modified by other (unrelated) transactions.

was stored. The only parameter it gets is the identifier of the tuple, which is by definition stable as long as the tuple exists.

What must be guaranteed, though, in order to maintain the atomicity of T, is the *existence of the tuple t* as such. According to the multi-level transaction model, the "insert tuple" subtransaction controls nothing, because it commits as soon as it has done its job. The same holds for the INSERT subtransaction at the next higher layer; after all partial actions related to the INSERT have been completed, the subtransaction commits and therefore releases control over the tuple.

This leads us to the crucial point of multi-level transactions, as opposed to simple, nested transactions. Nested transactions are simply an execution model that places no restrictions on what the subtransactions do and which objects they manipulate. Multi-level transactions, however, require a hierarchy of abstract data types, as was already mentioned for the concept of spheres of control. The principle can be stated as follows:

Abstraction hierarchy.   The entire system consists of a strict *hierarchy* of objects with their associated operations.

Layered abstraction.   The objects of layer *n* are completely implemented by using operations of layer *n*−1.

Discipline.   There are no shortcuts that allow layer n to access objects on a layer other than $n-1$.

In the example of Figure 4.19, this principle means that an application (which is always represented by a top-level transaction, T) is implemented by using relations, views, and tuples together with the SQL operators. Each SQL operator in turn is implemented by a set of functions on internal storage structures (which we have not yet defined precisely), each of which relies on a set of single-page operations.

The upshot of this is that each layer exercises commitment control over the updates of objects needed for its implementation. Since there is an object hierarchy, protecting an object at a higher level *implicitly* protects all the objects needed for its implementation at the lower levels, even if these objects have no direct protection at all. Put in terms of the example, having executed the "insert tuple" subtransaction, the updates on the data page as well as on the page holding the address table are committed. Now everybody else can access these pages, yet nobody can access the tuple t, because such an access would have to go through the SQL layer (according to the layering assumption), and at that layer transaction T is still controlling the commitment of tuple t. In other words, another transaction can get to page P, but it will not be possible to do so by trying to access tuple t, as long as T has not finally committed.

It is also worth noting that the principle of multi-level transactions relies on an *object mapping* hierarchy, not on a containment hierarchy. This difference is illustrated in Figure 4.20 (again using the same example).

Given the preceding discussion, it should be clear that multi-level transactions are a means for fine-tuning the granule of commitment control. Just considering the atomicity requirements of transaction T, it would be perfectly legitimate to simply use the nested transaction model and thereby keep all objects at all levels of implementation under commitment control. But since the objects that really need to be controlled (e.g., tuple t) are often much smaller than the objects they are mapped into at lower layers of the implementation

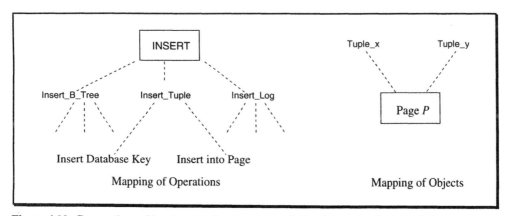

Figure 4.20: Comparison of implementation layers and (object) mapping layers.   Whereas operations at one layer, n, are mapped hierarchically on operations at layer $n-1$, the objects layer $n-1$ is responsible for can be part of the implementation of many layer-n objects. The latter effect is the reason why early commit of a layer-n transaction is desirable in many cases; the first property assures that atomicity and isolation for higher levels can be maintained.

hierarchy (e.g., files), this might create unnecessary obstacles for other transactions running concurrently. There is no good reason for making a file unavailable just because a 100-byte tuple that needs to be commitment controlled has been stored in it. Executing a compensating action in case of a rollback is more expensive than merely restoring the old value, but if rollback is not a frequent operation, the advantages of having smaller units of commitment control will outweigh the cost of compensation by a wide margin.

To summarize, then, multi-level transactions are nested transactions with the ability to pre-commit the results of subtransactions. Of course, there are other examples of committing results early: unprotected actions commit whenever they are executed. Transaction models such as open nested transactions, sagas, and engineering transactions (all of which are described in subsequent sections) also make use of the early commitment of certain updates. But the main difference between all these models and multi-level transactions must be clearly understood: only multi-level transactions have all the ACID properties, because their scheme of layering object implementation makes it possible to protect updates at lower layers by isolating higher-layer objects. This achieves isolation for the root transaction, and thereby the possibility of executing the root transaction atomically. This guarantee does not hold for the other transaction models mentioned.

4.10 Open Nested Transactions

Open nested transactions are the "anarchic" version of multi-level transactions. Subtransactions can abort or commit independently of what the status or the final outcome of the parent transaction is. There are no restrictions with respect to the semantic relationships of parent and child transactions. In particular, no object hierarchy, or anything like it, is assumed. There is obviously no sphere of control except, perhaps, for the leaf-level transactions—thus, open nested transactions are unprotected actions, according to the terminology established previously.

Another way of putting this is to say that open nested transactions are just a means for firing off other top-level transactions without exercising any further control over them. Since there is little to say about open nested transactions from the perspective of consistency, atomicity, and so on, they are not considered in detail here. Chapter 5 contains an example of how to use open nested transactions for some special purposes in client-server environments. If open nested transactions are used in such a deliberate, well-controlled fashion, they are often referred to as *nested top-level transactions*.

Incidentally, the adjective *open* in the name open nested transaction has a different connotation than it does, for example, in *open systems*. In the latter case the term refers to extensibility, standard interfaces, and so on, whereas open nested transactions are (presumably) so called because they do not maintain a closed sphere of control.

4.11 Long-Lived Transactions

With all the transaction models introduced so far there is one problem (already mentioned in Subsection 4.2.4), which concerns how to proceed when the unit of consistent state transition requires updating all of the bank's one million account records at the same time. By making the whole update operation a flat transaction, the "exactly once" semantics are obtained, but the price of restart is unacceptably high. Neither making a nested transaction nor taking savepoints will help, because in either case the ACID property is still maintained for the entire transaction. Such additional structuring may help to organize normal processing, but it does not contain the amount of work lost[19] in case of a crash.

Now assume the bulk of the one million updates is decomposed into a sequence of a million single (chained) transactions. This improves the situation considerably, because whenever a failure occurs, it is only the last (i.e., the ongoing) transaction that gets rolled back. This would not make much sense for performance reasons, but let us ignore that for the moment. The interesting question here is whether or not a certain transaction model is adequate for the processing requirements of long-lived computations such as updating one million accounts.

Although chained transactions can contain the amount of work lost in case of a system crash, they no longer guarantee atomicity for the overall computation. The reason is simply that when the chain of transactions is being processed and something goes wrong, the responsibility of the transaction system at restart is to make sure that the updates of all complete transactions in the chain are not lost, and that the ongoing transaction that was interrupted by the crash is rolled back. However, the definition of the chained transaction model does not include any state information about the chain as a whole. In particular, at restart the system knows that the transaction that got rolled back must be started again, but there is no built-in mechanism to determine in which state the restart should begin. As treated in Section 4.5, the matter of chained transactions is concerned with control flow only. The question of where (and how) the state information about the chain as a whole is kept has not yet been considered.

There is another important difference between a sequence of individual transactions and a huge batch transaction: a batch transaction that updates all account records as one ACID unit of work makes all effects visible at the same point in time, namely at its commit. A chain of transactions releases the updated values gradually; there are as many commit points as the chain has elements. Updating all accounts in one ACID unit ensures that no intermediate update occurs, such as inserting a new account record while the ComputeInterest application is still running. If the computation is broken up into a sequence of separate transactions, this guarantee cannot easily be maintained.

Given that a single flat transaction is not the appropriate model, there needs to be a way of structuring the update work such that the loss due to a crash is minimized, but that the information about where to continue after a crash is automatically maintained. The question is how to do that.

Looking at the account tuples certainly does not help, unless one assumes some special timestamp attributes saying when the last interest accumulation for the account has been done. Basically, all data needed to restart the transaction chain at the right point are contained in the log—something that is maintained by lower-level components of the system to support recovery (see Chapter 9). But a typical application program, which is speaking SQL and some standard programming language, does not know anything about a log and should not need to deal with it. Rather, there should be an easier way for an application to make sure that a piece of work it has begun before a crash is picked up afterwards at the right position.

---

[19]Note the change in perspective: what has always been the virtue of atomicity suddenly turns into the vice of "work lost." Real applications are like that.

Before describing a solution to the ComputeInterest problem, we must first understand the notion of *transaction processing context*. Since this term appears repeatedly throughout this text, it is important to have a clear idea of what it consists of and what it is used for.

4.11.1 Transaction Processing Context

Consider a very simple transaction program with the following structure:

```
SimpleProgram()
    {    BEGIN WORK;
         read (input_message);
         /* perform computation on input message */;
         send (output_message);
         COMMIT WORK;
    };
```

The program receives a work request through an input message, does what it has been asked, and returns the result in an output message. The execution is covered by a flat transaction. At first glance, this will strike no one as particularly worth considering. Reduced to their bare bones, though, isn't that what all transaction programs look like?

We can easily convince ourselves that this is not the case. Strictly speaking, what the above program says is that

$$output\_message = f(input\_message).$$

The result is completely and unambiguously determined by the parameters in the input message and by the function definition f. In that sense, SimpleProgram is an implementation of f.

There are many examples of programs working in this manner: the square root function, the maximum function, and all the other mathematical subroutines. But now consider the following sequence of SQL statements:

```
exec sql    DECLARE CURSOR c AS
            SELECT      a,b,c
            FROM        rel_a
            WHERE       d = 10
            ORDER BY    a ASCENDING;
exec sql    OPEN CURSOR c;
do { exec sql FETCH NEXT c INTO :a, :b, :c;
            /* perform computation */
    } while (SQLCODE == 0);
exec sql CLOSE CURSOR c;
```

This portion of an application program declares a cursor and then processes all qualified tuples in a loop. The SQL server has the basic structure of waiting for an input message, working on it, and sending the result back to the client. But what does the input message actually contain in case of the fetch command? It names the cursor and points to locations where the attribute values of the "next" tuple should be stored. However, the information about what the next tuples are and how the cursor is defined in the first place is not passed with the input message to the SQL server. That means the result produced depends on more than just the values in the request message; there must be contextual information to augment the input parameters. This information is referred to as *context*, for short. Servers usually are not simple functions; rather, they are transformations of the type

$$f(\text{input\_message}, \text{context}) \rightarrow \{\text{output\_message}, \text{context}\}.$$

Programs where context is the empty set are called *context-free*, the others are called *context-sensitive*.

But whereas the context-free view embodied by the SimpleProgram is too simple to describe the structure of real transaction programs, introducing a "context" without further specification is just too general to be useful. If we allow the context to comprise everything that influences the outcome of the computation, except for the input message and the algorithm, then we have to include the entire database, the states of all other concurrent computations, the state of the application using the TP system, and so forth. This ultimately leads to the notion of the universal interconnectedness of everything—which is notoriously hard to disentangle.

To appreciate this rapid expansion of context, consider the read loop using the cursor c. What determines the result delivered by the invocation of a statement "fetch next c into. . . ."? First, the current position of the cursor determines which tuple qualifies as the next one. The cursor position is a context that is *private* to the program containing the read loop. Second, the contents of the database itself determines which "next" tuple can be retrieved. If the same program is executed twice, and we compare the results of both runs, then starting from identical cursor positions the fetch operation can return different tuples because the global context—that is, the database—has changed.

Now, what influences the contents of the database? Of course, it is the set of all other transactions updating the database, and they in turn—you get the idea.

The only type of context that really matters for structuring long-lived transactions is the first one, private context. Restricting discussion to private context strictly delimits the scope of what qualifies as context, because all the entities that can own private context do exist only temporarily, or they can keep only certain amounts of context data at any given point in time. For our present purposes, a context owner can be a:

Transaction. Cursor c introduced earlier falls into this category. Since SQL cursors cannot be passed across transaction boundaries, a cursor position is a typical example of transaction context.

Program. If a program executes a series of transactions, then program context contains the information about which transaction was committed last. This is explained in detail in Subsection 4.11.2.

Terminal. Terminal context may contain a list of users who are allowed to use this terminal, a list of functions that can be invoked from that terminal, the last window that was displayed on that terminal, and so on.

User. User context may contain the next password the user must produce in order to be admitted, or the last order number the user has worked on, and so forth.

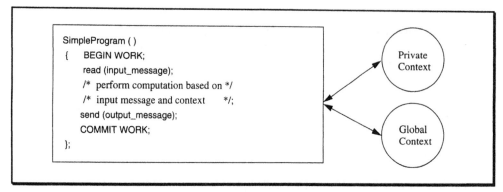

Figure 4.21: Relationship of servers and their processing context. A context-sensitive transaction program performs its computations based on the parameters in the input message and on some state information called context. The context contains execution history; that is, results of previously executed steps that have some bearing on the current request. The result is an output message back to the client, and a modified context.

The interaction of a transaction program and its context is illustrated in Figure 4.21. If processing structures are considered from the perspective illustrated in Figure 4.21, the notion of context becomes ubiquitous, though mostly unnoticed. Opening a file establishes context on both sides, the application program and the file system. This context contains the authorization status of the user of the file, the position of the end-of-file pointer, and other things. All higher-level communication protocols need context; Chapter 6 explores the concept of sessions as a means for maintaining processing context. Even simple pseudo–random number generators need context (the random number they produced upon the previous invocation).

Now, what does the ComputeInterest example have to do with context? If all accounts are updated within one transaction, there is no need for maintaining context. The input message contains the interest rate and otherwise just says ''Do it.'' If it fails, the same thing can be done over again; it is context-free.

Splitting the job up into a sequence of transactions results in the following structure:

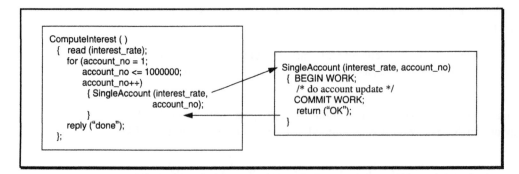

The transaction program to update a single account is still context-free, because the next account number to be processed is passed in the input message. However, the surrounding program that keeps the context is not, because if something happens along the way, and the program is invoked again with the same input message, the result with respect to the database will be different. The point is that SingleAccount changes durable memory (the accounts database). The database therefore ''remembers'' how far the account update has proceeded, thereby establishing processing context that must be maintained properly if the results are to be right. This kind of context management (keeping it in a local program variable) is sufficient only as long as nothing happens. After a crash, however, the program (its reinstantiated version, that is) and the database are out of synch. To avoid this, the program's context must be kept in durable memory, too; this, in turn, has some impact on SingleAccount.

Let us summarize what has been said so far. Programs frequently use information in addition to the input parameters; this information is called *context* and is (potentially) modified every time the program is invoked. Context can consist of simple counters (how often the program was called), user-related data (last screen sent), information about durable storage (last record read, most recently modified tuple), and much more. All programs that read durable storage (a database, for instance) and modify it based on what they see become dependent on that context, whether they like it or not.

Furthermore, context can be volatile or durable. An end-of-file pointer is usually volatile context, because it need not be recovered. After a crash the file must be opened again, which implicitly sets the end-of-file pointer. However, the context that says how far the sequence of ComputeInterest transactions has gotten must be durable for the reasons explained.

Throughout this text there are frequent references to context of all kinds, both volatile and durable. All of these are varieties of the principle just sketched.

4.11.2 The Mini-Batch

What is obviously missing in the transaction models introduced so far is the capability of keeping the transaction processing context beyond the boundaries of top-level transactions, so that it can be used to control the state at which the system should be recovered after a crash. One way to cope with this (the *only* way for most existing transaction processing systems) is for the application to maintain the context as a database record. Each time a transaction commits, the context in the database is advanced.

A solution to the example problem, then, could consist of executing a sequence of transactions, each of them updating only a small number of accounts (called mini-batches) while the atomicity of the whole task is maintained by the application through the use of context data stored in the database. The code given next illustrates this approach. It can be considered an example of the chained transaction model (in the crash-resistant variety), with the maintenance of the state of the chain made explicit.

This program is worth contemplating for a while. It actually contains a sequence of transactions, not all of which are doing account updates. There is no higher-level transaction to encompass them, and yet the overall effect of incrementing each account exactly once is achieved. The way this is done is by maintaining the program's state (the relevant part of it) in the batchcontext relation—something that could just as well be done in the transaction management system.

```
ComputeInterest (interest_rate)
      {       long account_no,last_account_done, batch_date;
              double account_total, interest_rate;
              int logsize;
           #define stepsize 1000;
           #include <string.h>;
           #define max_account_no 999999;
```
/* For simplicity we will assume that the accounts are numbered from 1 to 1000000.   */
/* batchcontext is the relation containing the identifier of the last mini-batch   */
/* processed completely. See if it contains an entry.   */
```
              logsize = 0;
              exec sql SELECT COUNT(*) INTO :logsize FROM batchcontext;
              if (SQLCODE != 0 || logsize == 0)
```
/* Either there is no relation batchcontext, or it is empty. This will be the case   */
/* if a chain of transactions is started from the beginning. If there is a   */
/* restart after a crash, batchcontext will contain a tuple.   */
```
                { exec sql BEGIN WORK;
                      exec sql DROP TABLE batchcontext;
                      exec sql CREATE TABLE batchcontext (last_account_done INTEGER);
```
/* initialize batchcontext by storing a tuple into it which in the beginning says   */
/* that no mini-batch has been completed yet (last_account_done = 0).   */
```
                      last_account_done = 0;
                      exec sql INSERT INTO batchcontext VALUES(:last_account_done);
                      exec sql COMMIT WORK;
                }
            else
```
/* The restart case. Processing must resume after the mini-batch named by the batchlog tuple   */
```
                  { exec sql SELECT last_account_done   /* There will be exactly one qualified tuple   */
                              INTO:last_account_done
                              FROM batchcontext;
                  }
```
/* Now processing of the chain of transactions can be resumed at the right point   */
```
              while (last_account_done < max_account_no)        /* loop over all accounts             */
                  { exec sql BEGIN WORK;                         /* initiate the next mini-batch       */
                      exec sql UPDATE accounts
                              SET account_total = account_total * (1+ :interest_rate)
                              WHERE account_no BETWEEN
                                      :last_account_done+1 AND :last_account_done + :stepsize;
```
/* update the batchcontext tuple by setting last_account_done to highest account number of this   */
```
                      exec sql UPDATE batchcontext                /* mini-batch                        */
                              SET last_account_done = last_account_done+ :stepsize;
                      exec sql COMMIT WORK;                       /* commit this transaction.          */
                      last_account_done = last_account_done + stepsize;   /* next mini-batch           */
                }
```

```
/* now the last mini-batch has been completed; discard batchcontext.                    */
      exec sql BEGIN WORK;
      exec sql DROP TABLE batchcontext;
      exec sql COMMIT WORK;
      return;
}
```

Note also that the program does not achieve strict atomicity for the entire computation. Each of the transactions in the chain is atomic, but if something goes wrong, the program will continue only in the forward direction. For the example at hand, this makes sense, because it is reasonable to assume that the interest for an account will eventually be computed, if only one tries patiently enough. There are, however, other types of long-lived activities that may take much longer than the ComputeInterest program, and for which a successful termination cannot always be guaranteed.

Examples can be found in the areas of engineering design, office automation, and elsewhere. Providing adequate transaction support for such applications is an area of active research. The mini-batch solution is also susceptible to disturbances by other transactions of the set of accounts it works on. At any moment, isolation is guaranteed only for the account tuples a step transaction is accessing; but it is quite possible for new accounts to be inserted in front of and behind the segment of **stepsize** accounts that are updated as an atomic unit of work.

For the moment, the requirements for long-lived transactions can be summarized as follows:

Minimize lost work. It must be possible to split up bulk transactions in order to control the amount of lost work in case of a program or system crash.

Recoverable computation. Activities that inherently take days, weeks, or even longer—but still represent one unit of work from an application perspective—must be organized into smaller pieces such that the system can be shut down as often as needed while they are still in progress. In other words, there must be ways to temporarily stop the computation without having to commit the results *and* without causing rollback because of shutdown. Note that the normal ACID transaction model has no notion of "suspending" a transaction such that it can survive system shutdown/restart.

Explicit control flow. The system must be able to control the sequence of transactions belonging to one long-lived transaction. At any point in time, and under all failure conditions, it must be possible to either proceed along the prespecified path or remove from the system what has been done so far.

Long-lived activities, therefore, should ideally not only have the "exactly once" semantics we have demonstrated; they should also be atomic, like any other transaction. Note that this sounds very much like a paraphrase of the definition of spheres of control—and it is.

4.11.3 Sagas

A first attempt towards the goal of providing system support for the execution of mini-batch-like sequences of transactions is the *saga*, as described in Garcia-Molina and Salem [1987]. The concept is in two respects an extension of the notion of chained transactions:

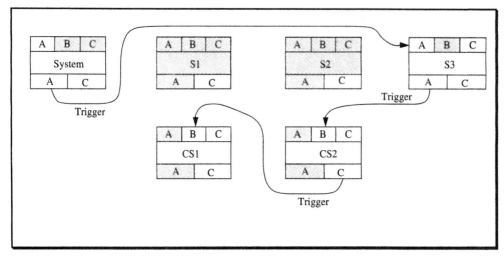

Figure 4.22: Graphical representation of a saga.   Sagas are simply chained transactions for which a backward chain of compensating transactions is established as the original chain proceeds in a forward direction.

(1) It defines a chain of transactions as a unit of control; this is what the term *saga* refers to.

(2) It uses the compensation idea from multi-level transactions to make the entire chain atomic.

Informally, a saga has the following properties:

It is a set of flat transactions $s_1, s_2, \ldots, s_n$. In the simplest case, these are executed sequentially.[20] For each of the transactions s_i ($1 \leq i < n$) there is a compensating transaction cs_i, which will semantically undo the effects of s_i. The final outcome of a saga will be either the execution sequence

(1) $s_1, s_2, \ldots s_i, \ldots, s_n - 1, s_n$

or, in case something goes wrong along the way in step j, the sequence

(2) $s_1, s_2, \ldots s_j$(abort), $cs_j - 1, \ldots, cs_2, cs_1$.

Sequence (1) is the saga's commit case; sequence (2) is the rollback scenario. As with chained transactions, only the transaction interrupted by a failure can be rolled back unilaterally. For all the transactions executed before, there must be a semantic compensation, because the updates have already been committed. The graphical representation of a saga is shown in Figure 4.22.

As the figure shows, atomicity is achieved by starting the compensation sequence whenever the transaction that is currently executing rolls back. In particular, the model makes no attempt to pick up the pieces after a crash and continue executing the saga. It does,

---

[20] Allowing for parallel execution within a saga is a straightforward matter, but this issue is omitted for the moment.

however, run the chain of compensating transactions backwards. Exercise 4.20 asks the reader to come up with a modified graphical representation describing recoverable sagas. Putting the graphical scenario of Figure 4.22 in the rule notation is the topic of Exercise 4.21.

4.12 Exotics

Considering the current state of the art, almost every transaction model, except flat transactions and distributed transactions, can be considered exotic. Of course, there are some systems that support savepoints, while others have something like transaction chaining, but in general there is no agreement on what should constitute a basic set of transaction services or who should provide them. The discussion in the previous sections suggests that there is a certain class of transaction models (i.e., those that can be formalized using the rule notion) that follows naturally from the simple ACID transaction model. The common trait of all these models is that they are founded on the notions of structural and dynamic dependencies. In other words, all the additional structure that distinguishes the different transaction models simply denotes different protocols for deciding if and when state transitions can be externalized (committed). For the purpose of this chapter, therefore, all transaction types that can be constructed using dependencies, as demonstrated in previous sections, are considered "natural" extensions of ACID transactions and are therefore *not* exotic.

In the literature, there are suggestions for other transaction models that are much more complex. In particular, their structure is defined by more criteria than just controlling the commit of updates. As an example, we briefly introduce the idea of cooperating transactions, which are suggested primarily for applications like computer-aided design (CAD). The basic scenario is shown in Figure 4.23.

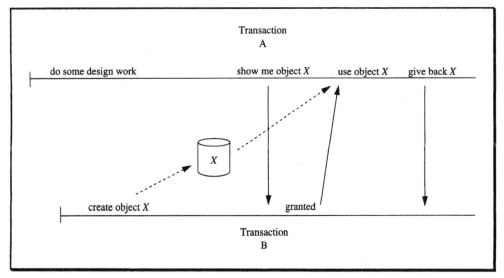

Figure 4.23: One aspect of cooperative transactions. Cooperative transactions allow for explicit interactions among collaborating users on shared (design) objects. At that level of cooperation, though, notions such as atomicity are not powerful enough to model the complex rules of state transitions the application wants to support.

There are two transactions encompassing some design activities, which are at least partially shared among several designers. At some point in time, designer Andreas, running transaction A, explicitly requests access to a design object X, which he knows designer Jim is working on right now.[21] Jim is modifying object X under the protection of transaction B. The cooperating transaction model now provides methods by which transaction B can decide to suspend its own activities on X and give it to A, with two strings attached: first, A must understand that object X is preliminary and must not try to change it; and second, A must eventually return object X to transaction B so B can resume its work on X.

This method of handing out objects that are not yet in a committed state and requesting them back later is substantially different from the dynamic data-induced dependencies discussed earlier in this chapter. The notion of spheres of control and all transaction models derived from it implicitly assume that dependencies incurred by accessing shared data are undesired effects, due to the parallel execution of transactions. Consequently, data dependencies are monitored and handled inside the system; the transaction models are designed such that any aspects of these dependencies are transparent to the application.

In our scenario, however, it is assumed that knowing and handling such dependencies is inherent to the application. Designer Andreas knows that X is not a final version; Jim knows that Andreas uses the current state of X—he may even know what Andreas uses it for, although he also may not approve of it. Of course, there is still a possibility of "normal" data dependencies on X, if some other transaction that is not part of the design process tries to access X while Jim is still polishing it. Thus, this method of explicit, application-driven sharing of objects introduces two additional concepts to the way transactions control their objects:

Prerelease upon request.   Object X is isolated until the surrounding sphere of control has decided to commit. However, there may be special transactions that are allowed to access it anyway, without creating a commit dependency on it. Such transactions must be run by users who are members of the same design team as the owner of X, or some other distinguished group.

Explicit return.   The transaction that selectively releases commitment control knows who has access to the object and what kind of access is requested to the object, and it gets informed as soon as the object is returned to its original sphere of control.

As shown, there is much more information about the interaction among these two (or generally more) transactions that can be used to decide what should happen if, say, transaction B wants to commit its updates before A is finished, or if transaction B rolls back after A has been granted access to object X, and so forth. All this becomes very much dependent on the application semantics that are to be supported by the model of cooperating transactions. It is not clear whether a simple formal model, such as the graphical or the rule notation, will be sufficient to capture all the application-oriented aspects, or whether simply another execution model is required for such environments, which—for the sake of clarity—should not be called transaction.

---

[21] For the identity of the objects under discussion, the reader is referred to the control blocks and interface definitions in Chapters 6–12.

4.13 Summary

Transaction models try to provide an adequate formal template for processing patterns in an application, much as data models try to reflect the object structure in an application. The term *processing pattern* is deliberately vague, because it can have a large number of facets, and the different transaction models are mostly distinguished by which aspect they are intended to support particularly well.

The current state of the art is characterized by flat transactions, which focus on four aspects; namely, atomicity in the presence of crashes, controlled state transitions with regard to consistency constraints, isolated execution in a concurrent environment, and durability of results in the presence of losses of external storage media. These properties are captured by the ACID acronym, and flat transactions provide a single execution framework to take care of all four aspects.

This has the great advantage of conceptual and formal simplicity, and it has proved to be a very powerful concept over that last 25 years or so. However, with applications getting bigger, more integrated, and thus more complex, there are numerous types of processing that are not well-served by the simplicity of flat transactions.

As a starting point into the fertile field of advanced transaction models, the notion of spheres of control is briefly reviewed. There are two reasons for beginning here: first, this is where transaction processing started; and second, it is still more general than all the other models discussed in the literature. The basic idea behind spheres of control is to keep the entire history of processing around forever. This requires a temporal data model, and it makes it possible to keep complete track of which data value depends on which other values. Thus, if any value is changed (lost, corrected, or whatever), one can determine all the resulting changes that become necessary. How this is implemented, especially if some of the resulting actions are real actions, is not part of the formal model; that, of course, is the key difficulty in applying the notion of spheres of control in general.

The main part of this chapter described different extensions of the flat transaction model, all of which are much less powerful than the spheres of control but, on the other hand, are more amenable to implementation. Savepoints and nested transactions try to give more control over dynamically backing out from incorrect parts of a computation without having to give up the entire transaction. These models blend very well with the notion of modularization.

Chained transactions allow for committing certain stable, intermediate results (so they will not be lost in case of a crash) while still keeping control over resources that should not be allocated to other users (transactions).

Multi-level transactions are a variant of nested transactions that allows for an early commit of intermediate results inside a transaction—at a certain level of abstraction. If there is a well-defined implementation hierarchy of the objects manipulated by the transaction, then modifications at lower levels can be committed early, provided isolation is still controlled at higher levels, and provided there are counter-actions at the lower-level objects that can be executed in case of a rollback. Open nested transactions are a very weak type of cooperation among flat transactions, which can be useful in some special situations.

The chapter's last section described the problem of long-lived computations, which is characterized by the trade-off between the amount of work lost if the transaction covers the whole computation and the difficulty of determining the correct processing state after a crash in case the computation is divided into a series of transactions. This discussion introduced the notion of transaction context, which will prove important in many of the following chapters. One of the key observations about models for long-lived computations is that they either assume that only forward recovery is needed after a crash (for the long computation as a whole), or they assume that there are compensating transactions that permit semantically undoing what previous transactions have done. Of course, both assumptions are justified only in certain types of applications.

4.14 Historical Notes

Where wast thou when I laid the foundations of the earth?
Declare, if thou hast understanding.

Job 38:4

Transactions, as pointed out in Chapter 1, are a very old idea. That is, the idea itself is old, but the term has undergone a number of changes in meaning. The traditional semantics can be derived from the literal interpretation: a transaction is an action (usually involving two parties) that transforms the state of the system. In that sense, the Sumerians used transactions: a farmer came to the Royal Storage to deliver his duty,[22] and a clerk chiseled the fact onto a clay tablet. Maybe the farmer even got a receipt; one would have to dig for it.

Use of the term came into full swing with the invention of bookkeeping, a technique that abstracts everything—people, goods, services—into numbers in columns. Whatever caused numbers to be added to columns (remember that there is nothing resembling modification in bookkeeping) was a transaction. That was also the first time the business-oriented interpretation of transaction met with another, quite different type of abstraction: atomicity. Bookkeeping requires certain sums to balance. If an amount is entered into a debit column, then the same amount must be entered into a corresponding credit column; otherwise the system is not in a legal state. Entering just one number and then going to lunch leaves the system in an inconsistent state; the sums do not match.

Atomicity has been on the agenda of computer systems design right from the beginning, mostly without being stated explicitly. More than anything else, the concept of modularization helped to provide the structure needed for implementing atomic state transitions. Modules embody the idea of encapsulation, which is a special variant of isolation—a necessary prerequisite for atomicity. The early discussion about abstract data types, however, focused almost exclusively on implementation abstractions. Issues such as failure abstraction and controlling concurrency were rarely considered.

The first attempt to put these ideas into a systematic framework, so that they could be formalized and serve as a basis for system specification, was the spheres of control developed by Larry Bjork and Charles Davies in the early 1970s. Interestingly, Bjork and Davies started their work by looking at how large human organizations structure their work, how they contain errors, how they recover, and what the basic mechanisms are. As shown in Section 4.2, Bjork and Davies arrived at something considerably more complex than ACID transactions. It was so general that it required time domain addressing to keep versions of

---

[22] They did not want to call it "theft," so they decided to call it "taxes," a custom, which (besides transactions) has come upon our times. (This piece of information on transaction processing history was contributed by Charles Davies.)

everything for arbitrarily long periods (again, no changes in bookkeeping). Furthermore, it was so complex that few people read the papers, and even fewer understood the implications of the ideas (the authors of this book included).

One of the very first incarnations of the principles of flat transactions was the program isolation feature in the IMS database system, which is largely due to a group of people consisting of Sid Cornelis, Larry Morgan, Ron Obermarck, Tom Sawyer, and Vern Watts. Considered in retrospect, this feature seems to have exploited the idea that the same measures that isolate modified data so that it can be rolled back if necessary (atomicity) also effectively allow concurrency control. A formal development of these ideas, along with the theoretical foundation of the theory of transaction-oriented (database) processing, was published in Eswaran et al. [1976] and in Gray et al. [1976], works that can be said to be *the* classics on flat transactions.

At about the same time, Brian Randell's group, working on a fault tolerance project, proposed the notion of recovery blocks as units of software fault tolerance. Fundamentally, these are modules designed to check the correctness of their results and, in case of inconsistency, to try another implementation of the same specification. However, this approach lacked atomicity, isolation, and durability, attributes that make transactions such a powerful concept.

In the early 1980s, attention was focused on the technical issues of concurrency control and recovery, rather than on modeling. The first discussion of transactions as a means of modeling the structure and flow of real applications was presented in Gray [1981]. It pointed out most of the deficiencies of the flat transaction model discussed in this chapter, but it suffered the fate of being frequently cited and infrequently read.

In the 1980s, the transaction concept began to blossom and to grow, developing branches and twigs and becoming more diverse. Not surprisingly, computer scientists applied to it their key passion—recursion—thus creating nested transactions. Elliot Moss, working on the Argus project, described a design of hierarchically structured transactions [Moss 1981]. It contained all the basic rules for nesting the scope of recovery and commitment control, basically rendering some of the more general ideas from spheres of control in transactional terms. It was quite obvious how to carry the ideas for achieving isolation over to nested transactions, but a formal theory of what isolation really means in that context proved to be nontrivial. The major contributions in this area came from Catriel Beeri and others [Beeri et al. 1983], Nancy Lynch [Lynch 1983], and Gerhard Weikum [1987].

The use of nested transactions has been limited so far. Apart from tricks resembling a two-level nesting for achieving atomicity of data manipulation language (DML) statements, there are only two implementations to note. One is a database system supporting unnormalized relations, where nested transactions are used as a means for implementing the system; they are not, however, made available at the user interface. This project (DASBDS) was run in Hans Schek's group [Schek and Scholl 1986]. The other example is the Camelot system (with its precursor, TABS) that was designed by Al Spector and others [Eppinger, Mummert, and Spector 1991]. Based on the Avalon persistent programming language, it is a full-blown transaction processing system with nested transactions according to Moss's proposal. Camelot can be taken to be the first proven implementation of nested transactions as a general facility. By the time this book goes to the printer, the Encina TP monitor with Transactional C will be commercially available [Transarc-Encina 1991].

Other generalizations of the classical transaction model were applied in a more ad hoc fashion. People realized that giving up an entire transaction in case the program had gotten just slightly off the track was a nuisance, so they introduced savepoints. System R [Astrahan et al. 1979] was the first system with an implementation of that idea; see also Gray [1982]. Many others have followed since then. Chained transactions, which in a sense are complementary to savepoints, go back to IMS, where they are a by-product of *queued transaction processing* (this term is explained in Chapters 5 and 6). Another interesting implementation is HP's Allbase database products, where transaction chaining allows cursors to be passed from one transaction to the next.

Activities of long duration have been a worry to users of transaction-oriented systems from the beginning, because flat or nested transactions as they are implemented now simply do not go well with such computations. This is ironic, considering that the transaction model was inspired by the idea of spheres of control, which in turn were intended to model very complex, long-lived activities in the real world (the best laid plans . . .).

The problem has been approached from various sides, some application specific, others not. An example of the application-specific category is engineering databases. Developers in this area find virtually nothing useful in databases as they are now. The data models are insufficient, the access paths are not right, and the processing model (transactions) is utterly inadequate. There have been numerous suggestions for putting control structures around transactions, so that the dynamics of design processes can be more properly administered by the system. An overview of the issues that have to be addressed is given in Bancilhon, Kim, and Korth [1985]. A more recent account of what has been suggested and what is available can be found in Barghouti [1991]. From what we see right now, however, no clear structure has yet emerged that could lead to something like an "engineering transaction model." Perhaps there is no such thing. Many of the requirements discussed in that context sound like variations on the theme of "anything goes."

The second approach to long-lived transactions is determined by purely structural considerations, without a specific application in the background. A good example for that is the concept of sagas, which is proposed by Garcia-Molina and Salem [1987]. The idea itself had, in fact, been around for some time, and the term *saga* itself was suggested by Bruce Lindsay, but the 1987 paper describes a complete design. The key point of the saga concept is the need for compensating transactions, which are a way of extending spheres of control back in time when something goes wrong involving already committed data.

In their original version, sagas are simply linear sequences of transactions: something that can be used for structuring and controlling long batch activities in a mini-batch-like fashion. It was an obvious step to pick up the idea of compensatable transactions and put a more powerful set of control flow descriptions on top of it, to get a model that really permits describing activities that evolve in time. Some more recent proposals include *migrating transactions* [Klein 1987], *flexible transactions* [Leu 1989], and *ConTracts* [Reuter 1989]. Some very similar concepts are currently being implemented under names such as *business transactions* and *shopping cart transactions,* but none of them is yet mature enough to allow for an assessment of how adequate any is in modeling real-life applications.

Another area of active research related to extending classical transactions has to do with describing the dependencies that arise on shared data during concurrent execution. Remember that isolation requires transactions to be free of "influences" from other transactions, and vice versa. That is a very vague requirement. Obviously, everybody is welcome to change any data I do not need. And even data I need may be changed while I run, provided the change is not such that my computation becomes useless or false. For example, if I reserve a seat on a flight, other transactions at the same time can take other seats, but not mine.

Since this gets very complicated, the usual attitude towards isolation is to say: "Nobody touches my data."

This is easy to implement, but overly restrictive in some cases and unacceptable for long-lived activities. There is probably no general "good" solution. The product of the precision with which the value of a data element can be determined and the degree to which other transactions are allowed to access it seems to be limited by some kind of conservation law (which has not yet been formalized). One proposal [Peinl, Reuter, and Sammer 1988] suggests a predicate-oriented check/revalidate mechanism that tries to preserve invariants (which the application has to declare) over the database. A similar proposal that is slightly more restrictive is described under the name of *promises* [O'Neil 1992]. All of this is still very preliminary.

The most recent development in this area is the attempt to formalize the intuitive notation used by Bjork and Davies for describing spheres of control, and thus provide a formal framework for reasoning about transactional execution schemes without being restricted to a specific type of transaction. These approaches start by merging two notions: one is the description of an individual transaction as a state machine, which has long been used for driving commit protocols. The other is the notion of transaction dependencies resulting from the requirement of isolation when accessing shared data. Such dependencies can easily be given additional semantics, resulting in something like the structure graphs used in this chapter for illustrating the various transaction models. Two contributions are notable here. One is the ACTA model described in Chrysanthis and Ramamritham [1990], and the other is a theory of transaction interdependencies based on finite automata and a behavioral description using temporal logic [Klein 1991]. The description of transaction models in this chapter benefited much from discussions with Johannes Klein; the graphical notation is a simplified version of his formal model. The rule notation follows the ideas that are elaborated in Dayal, Hsu, and Ladin [1990].

Exercises

1. [4.2, 10] When writing to disk or reading from disk, there is a marginal probability of either the block being written to the wrong address, or of a block being read from the wrong address. You cannot avoid this, but what can you do to detect it?

2. [4.2, 25] Assume you have a disk all to yourself. It contains blocks numbered from 1 to N, which you can read and write with the type of operations considered in the chapter. Each block has a data portion and a forward and a backward pointer to other blocks; the forward pointer can be NULL. Block number 1 is special: It contains two pointers; the rest of its capacity in unused. The first pointer, F, points to the first free block; this free block points forward to the next free block, and backward to block 1. The next free block points forward to the third free block and backward to the first one, and so on. The other pointer, A, points to the first assigned block. This first assigned block points forward to the next assigned block and backward to block 1, and so on, just like the "free" chain. Except for block number 1, each block is either in the "free" chain or in the "assigned" chain. Consider two operations: First, *assign a new block;* which means: find a free block in the free chain, remove it from there, and link it into the assigned chain. Second, read along the assigned chain, that, starting from the block A points to, read each assigned block.

    Analyze the failure characteristics of these operations based on the block operations discussed here and in Chapter 3. What does it take to make the operation *assign a new block* atomic (under which failure assumptions)?

3. [4.2, 10] Consider the real action of drilling a hole into a piece of metal. From the application's perspective, is there an effective undo operation for that action?

4. [4.2, 20] Transactions are defined as consistency-preserving, among other things. Now look at the following scenario: An electronic fund-transfer application needs a program that manages the transfer of some amount X of money from account A to account B. X, A, and B are parameters. The obvious consistency constraint requires that X is debited to account A if and only if X is credited to account B. If this were not the case, money would either be created or destroyed. If both account updates are done in one transaction, atomicity is guaranteed for the whole operation. But somebody could come up with a design where a first transaction updates account record A, and then comes a second transaction updating account record B. Determine whether the second design is feasible at all; if so, determine under which circumstances, and what the problems are with it.

5. [4.2, discussion] Find a number of real-life situations where there is something like a commit point before which things are fairly easy to reverse, but after which an undo is expensive or even impossible. Discuss whether the situations you find are adequately modeled by the transaction paradigm.

6. [4.2, 20] Consider the code for the debit/credit transaction. The BEGIN WORK statement comes after the message from the terminal (or ATM) has been received. What would be different—if anything—if this sequence were reversed?

7. [4.2, 25] Modify the code for the debit/credit transaction, such that it will ask for the personal identification number before doing anything and block access to the account for the rest of the day after three invalid PIN inputs. Beware of the problem that in a strictly transactional world, no message can leave the system before commit. *Hint: The interaction does not necessarily have to be just one transaction. You can have a sequence of* BEGIN WORK/COMMIT WORK *pairs, if that helps.* Assume you can make messages unprotected actions. Which ones would you make unprotected, and which ones not? Consider the consequences of your design under different failure scenarios.

8. [4.2, 25] Consider a modified debit/credit transaction driving an automated teller machine (ATM). The ATM is acting as a terminal; that is, the input the customer makes at the ATM is a message to the (extended) debit/credit program, and the final message from the program makes the ATM dispense the cash. How do you guarantee the ACID properties of the whole interaction (from the request to the greenback rolling out) under the following types of failures: (a) Crash of the system running the transaction program? (b) Crash of the teller machine? (c) Crash of the communication link between the system and the teller machine? Specify exactly which features you must assume for the ATM in order to get atomicity. Are there cases in which the ACID rules can be violated? How would you suggest coping with these?

9. [4.2, 40] Make a design for running the debit/credit transaction on a normal file system, that is, without transaction support from the system. Assume sequential files and indexed files providing direct access via primary keys (e.g., account number). Write operations to both file types will always go to stable storage; buffering need not be considered. Read Chapter 10 on logging and design your own log file and the recovery routine to deal with system crashes. To simplify things, ignore the impacts of update operations in the file directory, which in real systems might cause substantial problems. Assume single user mode. *Hint: Proceed as follows: Define which files you need and what types of operations you want to execute on them. Choose the most appropriate file organization for that. Then design the modules implementing the access functions you need. Analyze the failure modes that could occur, and depending on that, decide what amount of redundancy is needed to protect the operations. Then make a consolidated design of the update*

operations with the necessary bookkeeping of log data. Finally, design the recovery routines. Make a number of walk-throughs (have other people participate) to see how the whole thing might work.

10. [4.3, 20] Assume an extended debit/credit transaction where the user operates from an ATM. He has to authenticate himself by entering the PIN first; then he can ask for his account balance, and finally he can decide to withdraw money from the account. Or he can withdraw right away without checking the balance first, or he can deposit money on the account, or. . . . So just imagine yourself using an ATM. Draw the spheres of control diagrams for some typical interactions, and describe precisely what each sphere of control is there for and which interactions on data occur.

11. [4.4, 15] Use the graphical notation introduced for the description of transaction models to specify a transaction that can send an error message and then roll back, without the message being an unprotected action. Remember, for an unprotected action there are no guarantees. It can be delivered or not, or multiple times. Our requirement here: If the transaction aborts, the error message has to be delivered at least once. If the transaction commits, then there is no error message.

12. [4.4, 15] Write down the rules for the solution to the previous exercise.

13. [4.5, 20] This is the same problem of a transaction trying to send an error message and not having done anything else in case of an error. Now assume the mechanisms you have described in the previous two exercises were not available. Could the same effect be achieved by using savepoints?

14. [4.5, 10] Assume you were writing a program for a system with persistent savepoints. There are statements to install the savepoints (SAVE WORK), and there are statements to return to a savepoint during normal operation (ROLLBACK). Where do you expect the program to wake up again after restart from a crash, and what kind of logic do you have to provide to handle that case?

15. [4.6, 20] How would you modify the rules for the chained transaction model to make the chain automatically recoverable after a crash?

16. [4.1, 4.5, 4.7, 25] Design a program structure for the trip planning example in Section 4.2, using savepoints. The savepoints are to emulate transaction nesting as explained in Section 4.7.

17. [4.8, 15] Write down the state transition rules for a distributed transaction.

18. [4.9, 30] This is an extension of Exercise 2. Consider a data structure as sketched in the following figure. A sorted list of records is maintained in blocks that are stored on disk. A fixed sorted_list_anchor points to the block with the lowest key record. Each block has a local anchor pointing to the first record in the block; this is the record with the lowest value in the sort attribute. Each record points to its successor in the block. If this forward pointer is NULL, the next-higher record is to be found in the next block. Blocks are linked together with forward and backward pointers according to the sort order of the records. Furthermore, there is a doubly linked list of free blocks, anchored at free_list_anchor. Design the algorithms for two operations: The *insert record* operation stores a record at its proper position according to the sort order. So the list must be scanned from sorted_list_anchor to find the block where the record has to go. Then the right position in the block needs to be found. If the block where the record has to go is full, get a free block and chain it between the block you are currently looking at and its successor—if there is a successor.

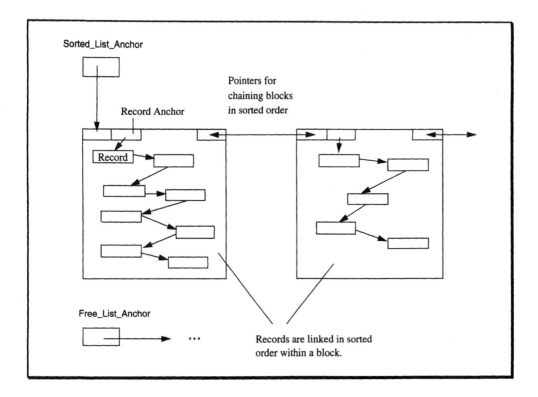

Sorted_List_Anchor

Pointers for
chaining blocks
in sorted order

Record Anchor

Record

Free_List_Anchor

· · ·

Records are linked in sorted
order within a block.

The second operation, *delete record*, also has to locate the record, remove it from its block, and return blocks that have become empty to the free list. So far, this has little to do with transaction models. The point is that you should try to design the operations using a hierarchy of abstract data types, so the multi-level transaction model can be applied. This means, in particular, that for each operation you have to specify a compensating operation. Make a careful analysis of which objects like records, blocks, pointers and so on need to be isolated, and what happens during rollback and restart, respectively.

19. [4.11 25] Write a modified version of the ComputeInterest mini-batch program that allows you to process 1,000,000 accounts with *arbitrary* (unique) account numbers. In other words, you can no longer rely on the account numbers ranging from 1 to 1,000,000; they might well range over a much larger domain. You can put the logic to control the mini-batch into your application program, or you can use any of the transaction models introduced.

20. [4.11, 10] Modify the graphical representation of a saga such that it becomes crash-resistant; that is, it will automatically be restarted after a crash.

21. 4.11, 20] Specify the state transition rules for a saga.

22. 4.2–4.11, 40] Consider the trip planning example from Subsection 4.2.4, but in a slightly extended version. You have to develop an application which assists the travel agent in customizing travel packages. For obvious consistency reasons, one wants to treat everything that pertains to one trip of the same customer as 1 unit of work. The execution model must be able to cope with requirements of the following type:

(1) I want to go from London to New York on August 24, 1992, and stay there for 5 days.

(2) Then I want to go to Los Angeles for 3 days; want to visit the Universal Studios.

(3) Next stop, Tahiti for 6 days. Want to do a boat excursion to Mooréa for 1 or 2 days.

(4) Etc.

For each stop along the way, the application has to do a couple of things: make the appropriate flight reservation, book a hotel, make arrangements for the excursions, and so forth. For each portion, it must be possible to find all relevant offers and select the cheapest (most convenient, most elegant, etc.) one. At any intermediate point, one may end up in the following situation: There is a flight to the destination, the hotel reservation is okay, the cabin on the boat has been booked (all of which required some databases to be updated), but then there is no flight to the next stop for the rest of the week. Rolling back the transaction is not a good idea, because this invalidates all the previous work. Explicitly programming the cancelation logic is cumbersome. Design an execution model for that application, choosing freely among the transaction models described in this chapter. Carefully consider the trade-offs with respect to the following criteria: amount of work lost in case of an internal or external failure; flexibility in selecting among options, revising decisions, etc.; amount of control logic that must be understood and maintained by the application; impact of commitment control on other transactions (i.e., other travel agents).

Answers

1. Assume the block with address i is written to the slot holding block k. There are two possibilities to detect this, with different efficiency. To detect it right away, read-after-write must be used. If that delivers the wrong result, recovery for block k must be initiated, and then the write of block i must be repeated. If read-after-write fails in such a way that reading block i erroneously returns the contents of block address k, an error will not be detected. However, this assumes a double failure, which the design does not generally tolerate. If no read-after-write is used, the blocks must at least be self-identifying; that is, the block address must be recorded as part of the block contents. This will detect the error the next time block k is to be read, and it can initiate recovery for that block. However, read accesses to block i after the original write error will not detect any problems with that block and therefore produce the wrong results.

2. Since you have the disk all to yourself, there is only one program at a time using it, that is, all problems related to concurrency can be ignored. The trivial answer to the problem is to include all the the necessary disk read and write operations into a transaction. This would certainly make the manipulations of the "free" chain and the "assigned" chain atomic, but the problem is that the disk subsystem typically does not support transactions. Therefore, atomicity must be achieved by judiciously using the simple block operations.

   Consider the assignment of a new block. The free block that is pointed to by F (let us call it b_n) is taken and linked immediately behind A. Both A and F must be modified in block 1; b_n itself must be modified (its forward and backward pointers); and the backward pointers of the new first block in the "free" chain (b_f) and of the old first block in the "assigned" chain (b_a) must be modified. Crashes can occur anywhere along the way.

   First, read all the blocks required: 1, b_n, b_f, and b_a. Now assume there are two auxiliary fields in block 1, named A^* and F^*, which contain the new values of A and F as long as the update process has not completed. Set $A^* = b_n$ and $F^* = b_f$. Write block 1; assume that this write is made fault tolerant by using read-after-write. Set the backward pointer in b_a to b_n and write b_a. Set the backward pointer in b_f to 1 and write b_f. Set the forward pointer in b_n to b_a, and the backward pointer in b_n to 1; write b_n. Set $A* = 0$ and $F* = 0$, and write block 1. The trick to making this update atomic lies in the use of $A*$ and $F*$. Every time the system is (re-) started, it must check if these two auxiliary fields are 0. If so, the data structures for maintaining the disk blocks are consistent. Otherwise, the update operation was interrupted; it is easy to see that $A*$ and $F*$ contain enough information to completely redo it upon restart.

With these conventions, the operation scanning the "assigned" chain can trust it to be consistent under all circumstances (except for multiple failures). It may, of course, perform a sanity check by comparing the forward and backward pointers in adjacent blocks.

3. Unless the metal is extremely precious, an effective undo to a drilling operation as part of transaction rollback is to throw away the piece with the hole and replace it with a new piece of metal.

4. If only two independent transactions are used, there is no way to preserve the atomicity of the fund transfer operation in case of a failure. It is clear that once the first transaction has committed, commitment of the second one must be guaranteed. This is similar to the situation described in the mini-batch example. A solution can therefore be based on the principle of persistent context. Here is a simple way to proceed. First, introduce a relation with the following schema:

Money_In_Transit(Deb_Account, Cred_Account, Amount, Time)

It contains a tuple for each transfer that has not yet been completed; to avoid duplicate tuples, a timestamp has been added to the schema, but it does not play any role in the following discussion.

The first transaction is always the one debiting the source account. It consists of an update to the Accounts relation, which means modifying the account balance; it then inserts a tuple into Money_In_Transit, which contains the account numbers of the source and the destination accounts, the amount to be transferred, and the timestamp. The second transaction then credits the amount to the destination account and—having done this—deletes the corresponding tuple from Money_In_Transit. It is clear that this guarantees that the transfer gets completed even if the system crashes after the first transaction has committed and before the second one has.

There are still some problems with this approach. For example, if upon execution of the second transaction the target account no longer exists, there must be some kind of compensation for the first transaction, probably including an extra credit for the interest lost while the amount was in transit. This compensation, however, may also fail because the source account has been canceled, too. What to do in such exceptional cases is completely application dependent.

All in all, splitting the transfer into two transactions does not sound like a good idea at all. However, many interbank transfers are actually handled this way. The reason is this: If it were done as one transaction, it would be a distributed transaction. In many cases, this does not work in the first place because the two banks involved use different database systems, which are not able to act as resource managers in an open distributed transaction system (see also Chapter 5). Even if this is not the case, processing the transfer as one distributed transaction is often considered too expensive. So all the interbank transfers of a day are accumulated in an equivalent to the Money_In_Transit relation (one per target bank), which is sent to the other bank at the end of the day and processed there.

5. Real-life commit points include saying yes in a marriage ceremony (or no, for that matter); signing a legal contract; letting go of a balloon; throwing a letter into the fire; emptying the Macintosh desktop trash can; converting your old jeans into short pants; cutting down a tree; telling your boss you quit; starting to work on an exam; making a bid in an auction. The last example is not adequately modeled by a transaction. If you make the bid you are committed to pay the money

unless somebody else makes a higher bid, in which case you are off the hook. In transactional terms, this is an asymmetric situation in which some participants in the transaction have to make a decision—which may or may not lead to the final commit, depending on whether other participants override this decision—without rolling back the transaction. More technically, this means that even after phase 1 of commit is completed, the transaction can return to its previous processing state. This is not supported by the classical transaction model.

It is interesting to note that many countries have introduced something like an extended phase 1 of commit in their contract laws. For example, if you order something from a mail order warehouse, you establish a contract that, unless the order is explicitly refused, binds the warehouse. It also binds you, unless you revoke the order within, say, 10 days—even if the goods have been delivered in the meantime. It is only after the expiration of that period that you are finally committed.

6. The way the code is now, the receive operation for the input message is not part of a transaction and thus is an unprotected action. In other words, the operation of removing it from the input queue is definitive and not recoverable by the system. If the transaction aborts for some reason, its rollback does not make the message reappear on the input queue, which means the message is lost and the user has to enter his request again. If the receive operation is part of the transaction, though, it has all the ACID properties (assuming the message system understands transactions). Therefore, if the transaction aborts due to, say, a system crash, recovery will make sure the message is put back onto the message queue. After system restart, the message sits there as though it had never been received by a transaction program and as though it can be delivered to the next program that wants to receive a message of that type.

7. We will not spell out the code but rather explain the rationale behind two possible approaches. The first one is simple and efficient. First, the message is received; whether this is a protected or an unprotected action does not matter for the present problem. Assume this message already contains the PIN entered the first time. If the PIN is correct, the transaction is executed normally. If not, an *unprotected* error message is sent, asking for the correct PIN. The answer is also received as an unprotected message. If it's wrong again, the interaction is repeated. While this is going on, the transaction stays open. The only minute problem with this approach is that if the transaction aborts while the user tries to enter the correct PIN, the user gets three more attempts after restart. That should be acceptable, though, in many cases.

To ensure that the client gets only three attempts no matter what, each unsuccessful attempt must be recorded in a durable way; that is, the transaction must be committed. To make sure this also works in case of transaction or system failures, durable context must be used (see the answer to Exercise 4). Here, the context relation must be declared as follows:

PIN_Context(Terminal_Id, Request_Message, Time, Attempt_Count)

The context must be related to the terminal (the ATM), and the number of invalid attempts must be counted, too. The original request message is part of the context, because the transaction does not start working on it until the correct PIN has been entered. In this solution, all messages (including the error messages) must be transaction protected. When you consider the details of this solution, you may want to think about the restart logic that processes the contents of the PIN_Context after a crash.

Now what happens after the wrong PIN is entered three times in a row? As described so far, the first solution simply aborts the transaction and forgets about the whole affair. The second solution deletes the context tuple from PIN_Context and consequently forgets the incident as well. But then, of course, the client could reinsert the card and try another round. To prevent this from happening, both solutions need a way of remembering the anomaly beyond the end of transaction; that is, the fact that there was a problem with the PIN must be made durable. One possibility is to store that information in the database, as a flag in the Accounts relation that will prevent all further access to the account through an ATM as long as the flag is set. Clearly, PIN_Context is not the right relation to keep that information. Considering the related problems, you may now appreciate the simplicity of the approach taken by many such applications, which make the information about the PIN problem durable by keeping the card in the ATM after the third false attempt.

8. The key to the solution is the (distributed) two-phase commit protocol. The ATM must be able to participate in this protocol, the purpose of which is to make sure that things are externalized (and/or made durable) if and only if the request has been processed correctly, and that there is some assurance the results can be reapplied or redelivered if something goes wrong during the process of completing the interaction. So the ATM needs a (small) durable storage that enables it to record the phase-1 decision and the outcome of phase 2, which is the fact of money having been dispensed. In case (a), if the system crashes before phase 1 the ATM will time out after a while, display an error message, and return the card. If the system crashes after the end of phase 1, the ATM is able to complete its part of the transaction (which is now sure to be successful) and report its outcome to the system as soon as it comes back. In case (b), the system will abort the transaction if the ATM crashes before the completion of phase 1, so nothing will have happened. If the ATM crashes after phase 1, the crash most likely will have affected the process of dispensing the money. With simple messages going to the screen, the normal technique for coping with such display failures is to redisplay the message; but given the nature of the messages an ATM produces, banks are reluctant to use this technique. So the additional requirement is that the dispense operation be testable. This is achieved by electromechanical counters that keep track of how often a bill has been released from which stack. This information can be sensed and compared to the most recent phase-2 record found in the ATM's durable memory. After restart, the comparison of the numbers indicates whether or not the last output message (batch of bills) was sent completely. There are some special situations in which atomicity cannot be guaranteed automatically. If, for example, a bill gets stuck in the dispenser and the client rips it off, then an inconsistency that requires human intervention may arise. Case (c) poses no new problems beyond those just covered.

9. Rather than present a complete solution, we just describe some decisions that lead toward a feasible design. First, assume four files: one for the account records, one for the branch records, one for the teller records, and one for the history records. The first three files are indexed files that use the primary key of the respective record type as the index; the history file is a sequential file. In addition, there is a log file, which is also sequential. We rule out all administration operations on these files: that is, the files already exist; they need not be expanded, reorganized, or whatever. Thus, we have to consider only the file operations read, insert, update, and delete. In case of an indexed file, a key value points to the record; in case of a sequential file, it is the next record the operations apply to. We also assume that each file operation is executed as an atomic action by the file system—a fairly optimistic assumption in the case of the indexed files.

   Given these assumptions and the fact that we consider single-user mode only, all files are, by definition, always in a state that allows the execution of file access operations, even after a crash. Hence, transaction recovery can be supported by the following convention: Before a modification is applied to any of the files (except for the log file), the current state of the record is read; in case of an insert, no read is necessary because here the current state is the null record. Then the current state of the record and the new state of the record are written to the log (which is an atomic operation). Next, the modification of the file is done. Should this modification need to be undone, then the old value of the record is found on the log. Should the file need to be reconstructed because of a loss of storage media, the new value of all modified records is on the log, too. Each end of transaction, be it via commit or abort, is documented on the log by an appropriate record. This is a simple version of the WAL protocol that is explained in detail in Chapter 10.

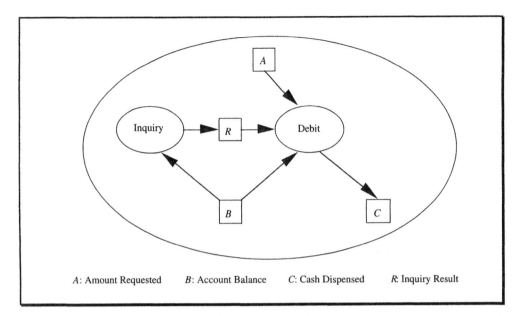

A: Amount Requested   B: Account Balance   C: Cash Dispensed   R: Inquiry Result

Considering things carefully, you will find that this design works. However, relaxing just one of the assumptions it is based on makes things much more complicated. Understanding the reasons makes it easier to appreciate that it is unfeasible to achieve the ACID properties at the application level using a conventional file system.

10. One scenario is shown in the figure above. There is an inquiry, the result of which depends on the current amount balance. This result is displayed to the client. Based on this information, the client tries to do a debit.

The result of the debit depends on three data items, namely the amount requested, the inquiry result, and the account balance via one obvious and one not-so-obvious consistency constraint. The system constraint is $A \le B$, and the client expects that $B = R$. If things work out correctly, then the debit process creates the data item called *cash*. If the debit cannot be done, the outermost sphere of control must be invoked to undo the effects of both the debit and the inquiry, because in principle the failure of the debit process indicates that the inquiry result has been invalidated, so the display most also be revoked—whatever that means.

11. Delivery of the message is made a separate transaction. It is started by the abort event of the transaction that sends the error message. In case the message transaction aborts, it is started again—which just says that the message will ultimately be delivered. The same holds in case of a system crash; here, the restart transaction will make sure that the message transaction will complete, provided it started in the first place.

12. Here is one feasible set of rules; other solutions are possible.

$$
\begin{aligned}
S_B(T): &\quad \rightarrow\ +(S_A(system)|S_A(T)),\ ,BEGIN\ WORK \\
S_A(T): &\quad \rightarrow\ delete(S_C(T)),\ S_B(message),\ ROLLBACK\ WORK \\
S_C(T): &\quad \rightarrow\ (delete(S_A(T)), \\
&\qquad\qquad delete(S_B(message))),,\ COMMIT\ WORK \\
S_B(message): &\quad \rightarrow\ +(S_C(restart)|S_B(message)),,BEGIN\ WORK \\
S_A(message): &\quad \rightarrow\ ,S_B(message),\ ROLLBACK\ WORK \\
S_C(message): &\quad \rightarrow\ (delete(S_A(message),- (S_C(restart)|S_B(message)))),,COMMIT\ WORK
\end{aligned}
$$

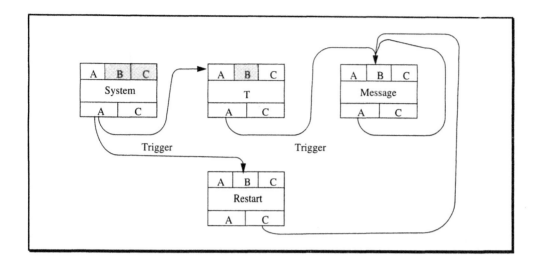

13. Since BEGIN WORK establishes a savepoint (savepoint 1), this represents a state in which nothing has been done yet, but the transaction as such exists. Now, in case of an error one can roll back to savepoint 1, thereby undoing all updates that have been applied so far; issue the (protected) error message; and then commit rather than abort. The commit is not to stabilize a new consistent state, though; it rather assists in giving the error message the ACID properties. Otherwise, there is nothing to commit.

14. The program comes back up at the statement following the most recently completed SAVE_WORK. The program's local variables have been reinstantiated, the call stack and the open control blocks have been recovered, and so on. The program basically cannot tell that a crash has occurred at all. It simply continues processing after the SAVE_WORK function, exactly as it did the first time around—but it does not know that there was a first time. A code example is presented in Subsection 5.5.4.

15. The solution is obtained by looking at Figure 4.11 and by using the type of rule that made the message transaction restartable in Exercise 12.

17. The solution is shown for the simple case of one subtransaction. The delete entries have been omitted.

$$
\begin{aligned}
S_B(T): &\quad \rightarrow \quad +(S_A(\text{system})|S_A(T)), \,,\text{BEGIN WORK} \\
S_A(T): &\quad \rightarrow \quad ,, \text{ROLLBACK WORK} \\
S_C(T): &\quad \rightarrow \quad ,, \text{COMMIT WORK} \\
S_B(T1): &\quad \rightarrow \quad (+(S_A(T)|S_A(T1)), \\
&\qquad\qquad +(S_C(T)|S_C(T1))),,\text{BEGIN WORK} \\
S_A(T1): &\quad \rightarrow \quad , S_A(T), \text{ROLLBACK WORK} \\
S_C(T1): &\quad \rightarrow \quad , S_C(T), \text{COMMIT WORK}
\end{aligned}
$$

19. A simple solution can be obtained as follows: Take the basic structure of the mini-batch solution presented in Section 4.11. Rather than using the set-oriented update statement that qualifies **stepsize** tuples, declare a cursor that ranges over all tuples that have not yet been updated.

Modify the tuples addressed by the cursor, using a loop that terminates after stepsize updates. As part of the commit process of the mini-batch, close the cursor; reopen it when starting the next mini-batch with the remaining tuples.

20. This modification requires the same tricks used to make a chained transaction recoverable. As a matter of fact, a chained transaction is a saga without the notion of compensation.

21. See Exercise 15.

Confucius, when asked what he would undertake first if he were
the ruler of the country, replied: "The rectification of names."

5

Transaction Processing Monitors: An Overview

5.1 Introduction

The many transaction processing monitors, or *TP monitors*, differ widely in functionality and scope. Each evolved to provide either essential services absent from the host system, or services the host performed so poorly that a new implementation was required. Consequently, each TP monitor is a Swiss Army knife of tools reflecting the particular holes in the surrounding system: in a contest for the least well-defined software term, TP monitor would be a tough contender.

There is no commonly accepted definition of precisely what a TP monitor is, how it interfaces to other system components, and whether it is really needed in the first place. Given that, the intent of Chapters 5 and 6 is to establish the terminology, present a reference architecture of transaction-oriented systems, define the role of a TP monitor within that framework, and demonstrate by example the transaction-oriented style of application programming. The current chapter, in particular, explains the services provided by a TP monitor; the structure of that system component is introduced in a stepwise fashion by identifying the problems of conventional approaches with respect to transaction processing. A major result of this analysis is the introduction of a mechanism called *transactional remote procedure call* (TRPC), which facilitates the cooperation of all components in a transaction processing system, and which the TP monitor implements. Chapter 6 then defines the TP monitor functions from a broader perspective. It sketches the architecture of a transaction processing operating system (TPOS) and describes some of its key implementation issues.

5.2 The Role of TP Monitors in Transaction Systems

TP monitors can be presented from three different perspectives:

The evolutionary perspective. By going back in history, we can discover which requirements determined the development of TP monitors and how these requirements, in turn,

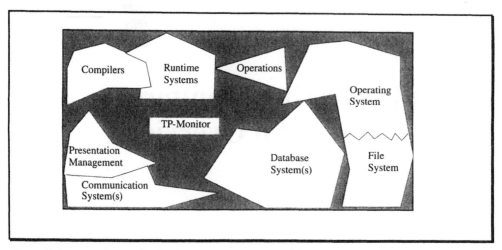

Figure 5.1: TP monitor and related system components. The TP monitor integrates different system components to provide a uniform applications and operations interface with the same failure semantics (ACID properties).

influenced the development of operating systems, database systems, and communication systems. A brief historical account is given in the historical notes (Section 5.7).

Case studies. Another approach is to analyze some real systems and define the concept of TP monitor as the class name for all possible instances—quite like an enumerated data type. There are references to TP monitor products in this book, and, to put the material into a product-oriented perspective, Chapter 16 provides actual case studies of real transaction processing systems.

An abstract model. Finally, there is the architectural perspective, which focuses on the functions an "ideal" TP monitor should provide in a transaction processing system.

This chapter takes the architectural perspective, sketching a hypothetical TP monitor. No real TP monitor is structured exactly like the model described here, but using a simple model allows the concepts to be presented in a more coherent way. Existing systems are often compromised by their system environment and history. This chapter therefore describes the essential features of a TP monitor as if one had to build from scratch, without the unavoidable system and cultural constraints. This still requires extending and unifying existing system components, particularly the operating system, communication system, and so on. These components usually have not been developed for the needs of a transaction-oriented environment.

The main function of a TP monitor is to *integrate* other system components and manage resources. As Figure 5.1 suggests, it interfaces to many different pieces of software,[1] and its main purpose is to make them work together in a special way, a way that has come to be known as *transaction-oriented processing*. Consequently, the model of a TP monitor out-

---

[1] Some people describe TP monitors as glue that ties together system components—a metaphor that implies smoothly fitting interfaces between the pieces. Looking at real systems, the analogy of mortar around and between rocks in a wall is probably more appropriate.

lined in this chapter is not a monolithic piece of software; the integration functions are spread across a number of separate system components that generally run in different processes and, depending on the environment, in different nodes. But before getting into the technical details, let us first define the term *transaction-oriented processing*. This is most easily done by contrasting it with four other styles of computing that are typically supported by operating systems.

5.2.1 The Transaction-Oriented Computing Style

Computing systems are used in a variety of ways, which are largely determined by the type of applications these systems were developed for and by the processing characteristics inherent in these applications. The size of what is perceived as a unit of work, for example, has a big influence on how resources should be allocated to such a unit and on the duration of allocation, how flexible this allocation decision must be, how much parallelism will go on in the system, how the system should behave in case of a crash, and so on. But before delving into the abstract, let us characterize all the processing styles typical of today's computer systems. Although the claim here is that most of them will disappear soon, the type of processing they were designed for still has to be supported by one of the surviving processing styles (one of which is, of course, transaction-oriented processing). Thus, it is helpful to analyze the existing style very carefully to understand what system facilities are fundamental to support each style. This section therefore introduces each of the current computing styles, in more or less the historical sequence of their evolution.

5.2.1.1 Batch Processing

Batch processing is what many older operating systems have been built for and what they are good at doing. Batch processing is characterized by the following properties:

Large units of work. Work comes in large portions at prescheduled times and with well-defined resource requirements.

Coarse-grained resource allocation. Resources are assigned to the batch job in large granules, such as files and volumes; this effectively means that the programs operate on their own private data.

Sequential access patterns. Batch jobs typically go sequentially through a (large) number of processing steps, access files in a sequential scan, and so on. Even if "random" requests are processed (think, for example, of order entry), these requests first are sorted by part numbers or customer numbers or whatever, and then the sorted batch of requests is processed sequentially against the database.

Application does recovery. Batch applications have to make their own provisions against system crashes. For that, they can use some basic operating system services, such as program checkpoints, but often applications do recovery "bare handedly." This may require the operator to rerun a batch job, based on the instructions in a runbook and some circumstantial evidence about the state of the computation at the time of the crash, such as key value in the last line printed.

Few (tens of) concurrent jobs. Since each batch job consumes resources in large quantities, there are not many batch jobs running concurrently on any given system. The basic performance criterion is minimal completion time, that is, high throughput.

Isolated execution. Each batch job executes in its own process; this process has exclusive control of the files, data streams, and other resources it uses.

5.2.1.2 Time-Sharing

Time-sharing is the terminal-oriented version of batch. While batch processing is driven through a predefined job control program, a time-sharing session is controlled by the terminal user. It has the following characteristics:

Process per terminal. Like a batch program, a terminal session is attached to a private process, giving the terminal user a complete abstract machine with memory, devices, and the like. From this environment, all the operating system services can be invoked (authorization permitting), communication with other processes can be established, and so on.

Coarse-grained resource allocation. Terminal sessions are typically long, and resources are assigned to these sessions in large granules; as in batch processing, the application works on private data.

Unpredictable demands. Since the work is controlled by the user, the actual resource demands are not as predictable for the system as they are with batch processing.

Sequential access patterns. The computations invoked during a terminal session are usually sequential in the process assigned to the terminal.

Application does recovery. The system makes no consistency guarantees after a crash. It is up to the user to reestablish the session and to figure out how far he had gotten before the crash—or when he did the last save in the editor. Achieving atomicity under such circumstances may require the user to send a message to the system operator to the effect "Please restore MYFILE, which I've just inadvertently deleted."

Hundreds of concurrent users. The number of concurrent terminal sessions can be as many as several hundred; response time is the key performance criterion.

The major observation to be made about time-sharing is that it is a way of giving interactive access to computing resources via low-bandwidth (dumb) terminals. Nowadays, terminals are being replaced by workstations and intelligent clients,[2] giving way to the client-server–oriented processing style. This means that time-sharing will soon be dead. Of course, these workstations will still run time-sharing operating systems to manage their processes, windows, and sessions, but the overall processing style will be different.

---

[2]A gas pump is an intelligent client compared to a dumb terminal.

5.2.1.3 Real-Time Processing

Real-time processing denotes a special style of computing that has been shaped by the requirements of process control and similar applications. Except for the operators at the control panels, the system is attached primarily to sensors that monitor the state of some real-world process, and to controllers that manipulate valves, magnets, wing flaps, and so on—things that operate in real time. The operational characteristics of real-time processing can be summarized as follows:

Event-driven operation.   Activities in the system are driven largely by interrupts coming from the sensor devices. The workload pattern is not preplanned.

Repetitive workload.   Events do not trigger arbitrary programs, and there are no users editing, compiling, and running new programs all the time. Rather, the set of programs that can be activated by outside events is statically defined, and the only random aspect is the sequence and the frequency in which programs are invoked. However, a program cannot suddenly be invoked needing 100 times more resources than any other previous program invocation.

Dynamic binding of devices to tasks.   The sensors and the control devices are not attached to processes in the sense of abstract machines; rather, they are bound to specific *functions* that transform the sensor signal into a series of signals to the control devices. Each of these request/response loops is very short.

Isolated execution.   Most of these functions operate on private data; there may be a small amount of shared data describing the global system state.

High availability.   The system must be highly available, because it controls a real-world process. On the other hand, there are usually no formal consistency guarantees maintained by the system. A common attitude is this: if in doubt, read the sensors again to find out what the system state is, because this is the primary object.

High performance.   The paramount performance requirement is guaranteed maximum response time under peak load, at least for the functions with the highest priority; otherwise, something might crash, melt down, or explode. Sometimes, a system is characterized as real-time if it is supposed to react real fast. The distinctive requirement, however, is that it is able to do deadline scheduling.

The distinction between real-time systems and transaction processing systems may have become historical by the time this book is published. As we will see later on, both processing styles have much in common, and processors are now fast enough to use transactions in real-time applications. Classical real-time systems used to ignore faults and were concerned with performance only in the no-fault case. They also had inadequate programming tools and, without a fault model, complex start-up logic.

5.2.1.4 Client-Server Processing

Client-server processing is the modern version of time-sharing. Rather than running everything a user requests in one process per user, services are invoked by passing requests to dedicated servers, which can reside in other processes on the same machine or in different machines of a distributed system. For the user at the terminal, there is no difference between these two styles, and the load characteristics are the same. But there are clear distinctions with respect to the system structure and the component requirements in a client-server–oriented system. First, each server provides a well-defined, special service; there is no such thing as a server providing a general abstract machine. Thus, the repertoire of a client-server environment is limited by comparison to a process in a time-sharing environment. Second, all persistent data are now encapsulated in database servers, so the data are shared among many users through that server. This means that such servers have to be highly available in order not to interrupt service to a large community of users.

5.2.1.5 Transaction-Oriented Processing

Transaction-oriented processing can be characterized by comparison to the other styles:

Sharing. Computations in a transaction-oriented system read and update databases shared among all users.

Variable requests. User requests are random; they may exhibit some statistical regularities, but the individual requests cannot be preplanned.

Repetitive workload. Users do not run arbitrary programs, but rather request the system to execute certain functions out of a predefined set. Each function is an instance of a transaction type; that is, it invokes a transaction program that implements the requested function. Typical transaction processing systems provide in the range of 100 to 1,000 different functions. Note that in this environment, all administration and operation steps are (flat) transactions in the sense defined in Chapter 4.

Mostly simple functions. Most of the functions are of moderate size; they consume 10^5–10^7 instructions and do some 10 disk I/Os. This property holds for the online transaction processing (OLTP) variety of transaction-oriented processing.

Some batch transactions. There are functions that have the size and duration of typical batch jobs. They are much like classical batch computations, except that they have the ACID properties, recoverable outputs, and some degree of data sharing with other transactions.

Many terminals. In large OLTP systems, there are from 10^3 up to 10^5 terminals (clients).

Intelligent clients. Terminals in OLTP systems are increasingly intelligent clients (workstations) that can do their own processing, keep some of their own data, run window systems, and so on.

High availability. Because of the large number of users, the system must be highly reliable and available.

System does recovery. Because of the use of shared data, there must be formal guarantees of consistency that are automatically maintained. After a crash, all users must be informed about the current state of their environment, which functions were executed, which were not, and so on. The guiding principle here is determined by the ACID properties of transactions.

Automatic load balancing.   The system should deliver high throughput with guaranteed low response times for the majority of requests.

Table 5.2 summarizes the characteristics of these computing styles.

5.2.1.6 Summary of Transaction-Oriented Computing Style

Transaction-oriented processing, especially online transaction processing (OLTP), is different from the other computing styles in both quantitative and qualitative respects. First, the number of clients to be supported is (potentially) about two orders of magnitude higher than in other configurations. Second, the users operate on a common, shared database. This implies strict control and recovery mechanisms by the system in order to prevent any inconsistencies due to parallelism and/or program failures. For small units of requested work, the overhead for allocating resources and performing the computation must be small; but it must also be possible to schedule long-running activities using the same set of basic mechanisms. In addition, TP systems have a well-defined unit of work, the transaction, which none of the other computing styles has. The transaction paradigm enables consistency in the presence of

Table 5.2: Comparison of the five basic styles of computation.   The comparison is by granularity of resource allocation, size of the unit of work, type of data usage, performance and availability requirements, and security classes.

	Batch Processing	Time-Sharing	Real-Time Processing	Client-Server	Transaction-Oriented Processing
Data	Private	Private	Private	Shared	Shared
Duration	Long	Long	Very Short	Long	Short
Guarantees of Reliability	Normal	Normal	Very High	Normal	Very High
Guarantees of Consistency	None	None	None	None(?)	ACID
Work Pattern	Regular	Regular	Random	Random	Random
Number of Work Sources/ Destination	10^1	10^2	10^3	10^2	10^5
Services Provided	Virtual Processor	Virtual Processor	Simple Function	Simple Request	Simple or Complex Function
Performance Criteria	Throughput	Response Time	Response Time	Throughput and Response Time	Throughput and Response Time
Availability	Normal	Normal	High	High	High
Unit of Authorization	Job	User	None(?)	Request	Request

failures and controlled sharing of data, properties that are indispensable for large distributed online systems.

Despite these additional responsibilities, the performance requirements of TP systems are similar to those of real-time systems. Even though no maximum response time for all requests of a certain type must be guaranteed, the usual requirement is that around 90% of all requests have a response time less than x seconds. This qualifies transaction processing systems as *soft real-time systems*.

As mentioned, transactional requests can come in different sizes, from simple one-message-in-one-message-out queries that require only a few database accesses, to long-duration, batch-like computations. Within the transaction-oriented processing style, then, we have to distinguish a number of transaction types, which are characterized by different processing patterns. Each pattern requires its own programming style, and, as we will later learn, the TP system needs to understand these patterns, because they have to be handled differently with respect to scheduling and resource allocation.

5.2.1.7 A Taxonomy of Transaction Execution

Figure 5.3 gives an overview of the criteria that influence the way transactions are scheduled and executed in a transaction processing system. Each level of the tree in Figure 5.3 corresponds to one of the categories: scheduling, input/output, and resource manager allocation. Since the categories are orthogonal, their instances can be combined freely, resulting in eight different transaction classes. Each of the three categories is briefly characterized in the following discussion.

Each level of the tree in Figure 5.3 corresponds to a different dimension that characterizes the different transaction types. Let us consider each of them briefly.

Direct versus Queued Transactions

Direct transactions have one important property: the terminal (user, client) interacts *directly* with the server program handling the request; that is, the terminal and the process running

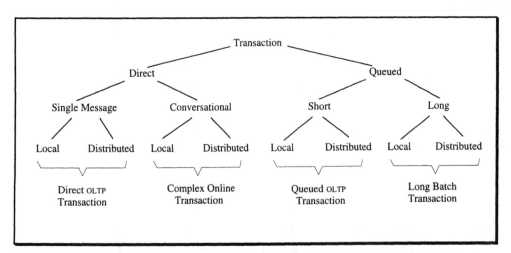

Figure 5.3: A taxonomy of transaction execution.   Transaction types are distinguished by three categories: direct versus queued, simple versus complex, and local versus distributed.

that program are associated with each other, much as two partners in a phone conversation are associated with each other.

In queued transactions, as the name suggests, requests are not dispatched for processing immediately. Rather, they are put in a queue in front of the appropriate server and scheduled for processing according to the queueing discipline (or at a specified time, or when an event occurs, or according to some other scheduling rule). The same applies to the result message(s). Note that the operations on the queue itself must have the ACID properties, just as the other operations do. As explained in Chapter 6, even direct transactions can experience some amount of queueing in situations of high load. But this sort of queueing is handled completely inside the transaction system by the TP monitor, so that the application program and the server still have the impression of a direct association.[3] Therefore, we classify a transaction as queued only if the application program has to be aware of the interface to the request queue. If no queue resource manager is visible or needs to be used, the transaction is classified as a direct transaction.

One should clearly understand that a *direct* OLTP transaction and a *queued* OLTP transaction can perform exactly the same functions; it is just that one talks to a server directly, while the other one submits the request, which does not get serviced until a server picks it up from its request queue. The direct case most accurately represents the TPC-A benchmark transaction. Queued transactions cannot interact with the client in case of an exception. Also, the transaction will be restarted from the queue after a crash or a transaction abort; such a "blind" restart with the unmodified input message makes sense only for simple computations.

Simple versus Complex Transactions

Simple transactions are short and touch only a few objects, whereas complex transactions have a rich internal structure (control flow) and/or touch many objects in the database. As a consequence, complex transactions typically stay in the system for a much longer time than simple transactions do, and they require more processing and other resources.

In the case of direct transactions, *simple* means there is a single input message from the terminal, and upon commit a single output message is delivered. Whenever the user wants to react to that output, there is no program on the other side ready to receive such a reply; another transaction must be initiated, which, in principle, runs without any knowledge of the first transaction. A *complex* direct transaction allows for repeated exchange of messages between the user and the application. Assume the program does flight reservations. A simple direct transaction would be able to receive in one message the request, complete with flight number, date, type of seat, and other details.[4] Its output would be either the confirmation of the reservation or the message that there are no seats left. A conversational transaction, on the other hand, would allow the user to first ask which flights are available; try to book on one of them; then, if that does not work, try another one; and so forth. For the whole

---

[3] To keep the telephone metaphor: The internal queueing that goes unnoticed by the transaction program is similar to what happens with transatlantic phone calls. Although both ends have the impression of a wire being switched from one end to the other, the satellite (or the submarine cable) is actually allocated to that conversation only if there are any sounds to carry. Contemplative silence is not transmitted; rather, the wire is given to another conversation.

[4] This is no simplification made up for the purpose of presentation. Watch the person working at the terminal next time you make a flight reservation. The amazingly cryptic string of characters the agent has to key in is this one input message; and, yes, the request is processed as a simple (direct or queued) transaction.

duration of this exchange, there would be a server associated with the terminal to remember what has been done so far.

Because queued transaction messages do not originate from a terminal (at least not directly), there is no possibility of exchanging messages with a terminal during execution. Queued transactions are requests put in a queue in front of a server by some program, and they are started whenever the scheduler decides to do so. Thus, there is nobody the transaction program could talk to at the other end; rather, the transaction program runs all by itself, invoking other servers along the way and finally producing some output, which goes to another queue to be picked up by someone else.

At the risk of provoking confusion, there are systems that do online transaction processing using only queued transactions. This is explained in some detail later in the chapter, but the basic idea is the following: The TP system has some components that talk to the terminals and, in particular, take their request messages and put them onto a request queue. The server processes whatever is on the queue and puts the result onto a response queue. Another component of the TP system then feeds off the result queue and sends the formatted response back to the terminal. If the queueing times involved are not too long, then the user working at the terminal still has the illusion of interacting with the application program directly.[5]

The measure of complexity in the "queued" case is the duration of the transaction and the amount of work it does. If the number of objects (tuples, blocks) it touches is in the tens, it is a short transaction; if it is in the tens of thousands, it is a long, batch-like transaction.

Local versus Distributed Transactions

Transactions may run entirely on the network node where the request originated; this is the local case. They might also invoke services from other nodes, in which case they run as distributed transactions. The point made in Figure 5.3 is that this distinction should not influence the programming style and the behavior of the transaction in any way. The distinction between nested transactions and distributed transactions, as discussed in Chapter 4, is a system-internal aspect rather than something the application has to be aware of.

The discussion so far has focused on preplanned transactions, that is, transactions that are anticipated as part of some data processing application. They are indicated by an action like pressing a function key, or by inserting a card into a reader. However, in applications such as decision support there is the need for handling ad hoc queries; such applications also have to run under transaction protection. Ad hoc queries are entered via an interactive SQL interface to the database system and are interpreted, optimized, and executed at run time. The number of result tuples they produce can be anything between none and the entire database. As a result, these queries, though they are not queued, have to be treated more like batch transactions than online transactions. Note that without proper control, ad hoc queries can block large portions of the system resources, for example, by accessing entire relations and keeping them locked for the duration of their activities.

Careful consideration reveals that all the other processing styles described previously are reflected in one of the types of transaction processing—at least with respect to duration, frequency, and performance criteria. This is no coincidence. On the contrary, one of the ba-

---

[5] To use the telephone metaphor one last time: Queued processing can be compared to a clerk who is handling requests that come in on his answering machine. He acts on them and then leaves an output message on the requestor's answering machine.

sic premises of this text is that in future systems, the distinction between different processing styles will become obsolete, because each interaction with the system and among systems will be imbedded in a transaction that adequately models the consistency requirements of the particular application. Transaction processing systems, having done online and batch processing in the past, will therefore support both client-server and real-time processing in the future; time-sharing will become obsolete.

This is not to say that the TP monitor will replace the operating system completely. Though that might be possible, the architectural model used in this book implies that the operating system is not dominated by the TP monitor. Consequently, the operating system assumed here (called a *basic operating system* in Chapter 6) can handle batch, time-sharing, and communication in more or less the conventional fashion, whereas the TP monitor takes care of OLTP style and distributed transactions. The unifying concept on which this presentation is based is a number of *basic transaction services* that can be used in all computing styles to support the transaction abstraction under all kinds of service request patterns. The basic outline of this architecture is presented in Section 5.3.

Before describing the structure of a TP monitor, let us briefly explore the informal rationale motivating the layout of the basic transaction services. The tasks identified in the next two subsections will serve as a road map for the rest of this chapter, as well as for the following chapter on transaction processing operating systems. For each problem area, there is a section explaining the concepts and implementation issues in detail. By reading only these two subsections, the reader will not know how the transaction services or a TP monitor work, but will be able to understand why they are needed.

5.2.2 The Transaction Processing Services

Transaction services must provide the application programmer with a programming environment that integrates transaction control in a seamless manner. As far as data sharing is concerned, applications can use the services provided by a database manager.[6] Database systems come with most of the mechanisms required for synchronizing access to shared data by concurrent activities, and for recovering these data to a consistent state after a program failure or a crash—that is, for executing transactions *on the objects the database knows about*. But these database programming environments are not geared toward the function request/response style that is characteristic of online transaction processing. Rather, they are designed to process pre-compiled or dynamic SQL statements—sufficient to support batch transactions and ad hoc queries that are processed in one process per user (terminal). It will become obvious in the following discussion that this is inadequate for the general case of transaction-oriented processing, where requests come in a more general client-server style, asking for some predefined service, and where one transaction can encompass multiple interactions among different clients and servers.

Apart from the technical issue of access to shared data, more system services are required to support transaction-oriented processing. This is what the transaction services have to do in addition to, but in cooperation with, a database system:

---

[6] In fact, many textbooks create the impression that database transaction control is all there is to transaction processing. But the need to support other resources with ACID properties (such as persistent queues, message integrity, and new object managers such as persistent programming languages) forces a more generic view of transaction management.

Manage heterogeneity.   If the application-level function to be implemented requires access to different (heterogeneous) databases or different resource managers (such as subsystems from different vendors), the local transaction mechanisms in each subsystem will not be sufficient to ensure the ACID properties for the whole function. Transaction services must combine all operations on autonomous objects into one transaction. The system components that provide transaction protection for their resources in such a way that the resources can be integrated into global transaction services by a TP monitor are called *resource managers* (RMs) throughout this text.

Control communication.   If the application function (or some resource manager invoked by the application) establishes communication with a remote process, the status of this communication must also be subject to transaction control by the transaction services. Of course, this requires adequate support from the communication mechanism. This is referred to as *transactional remote procedure call* (TRPC) later in the text. With respect to the messages it handles and the sessions it maintains between processes, the communication manager is a resource manager in the sense just defined.

Terminal management.   The functions are invoked by the users through terminals of different types (workstations, conventional terminals, automated teller machines, bar code readers, gas pumps, and—maybe in the near future—TV sets). The programs implementing functions must therefore communicate with these terminals through messages. Since the ACID properties of a transaction must be perceived by the user and not just by the program, sending and receiving the messages must be part of the transaction. This control must be exercised by the TP monitor. In particular, it is the TP monitor that has to deal with the problem of whether a response message was actually delivered to the user in case a failure happened at about the time of delivery. (Remember that messages leaving the system are unprotected from then on.)

Presentation services.   There is a corollary to the previous point: if the terminal uses sophisticated presentation services (an X-Windows system, for example), then reestablishing the window environment, cursor positions, and so forth after a crash of the workstation is also part of the transaction guarantee. This says that in a transactional environment an X client must act as a resource manager, implementing the ACID properties for its objects (windows) in cooperation with the other resource managers in the system.

Context management.   After a transaction has been executed on behalf of a user, the next function invocation (user input) often needs to find the context of the previous transaction run for that user, terminal, or application. (See the discussion of that problem in Section 4.10.) Storing and recovering context is bound to the sphere of control of the transaction that created or last modified the context. Other types of context are only bound to the terminal or to the user, irrespective of any previous transaction execution. Examples are: "Current authenticated userid at that terminal," "Default terminal for that user," "Account number for that user," "Current user role." Maintaining context of the different varieties is one of the TP monitor's duties. Of course, if the context definition refers to the outcome of a transaction, the context must be given ACID properties. Other types of context need not be recoverable automatically.

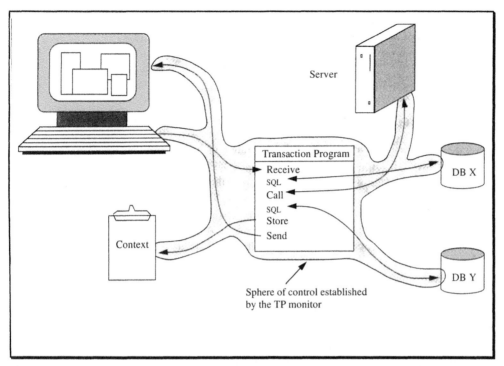

Figure 5.4: Integrated control exercised by the transaction services. A transaction program is shown, involving a workstation with a window environment, two databases, a remote server, and some application-dependent context maintenance. The whole computation is one ACID transaction.

Start/restart. Since the transaction services are responsible for virtually all the components the application needs to run, the TP monitor must also handle the restart after any failure. By doing so, all the subsystems are brought up in a state that is consistent with respect to the ACID rules.

This is not a complete list of the transaction services; it is restricted to those that have a more or less immediate impact on the way programs are written in a transactional environment. The other components of transaction services—program management, configuration management, load balancing, authorization, and administration interfaces—are described in Chapter 6.

In essence, then, the application programmer is provided with an environment that comes with the following guarantees: All local processing will be done under the protection of a transaction. The program need not worry about concurrency, failures, clean-up, and so forth. All this is managed by the underlying transaction services. All external services of the types mentioned will automatically participate in the client's transaction. Thus, the program does not have to worry about things such as reestablishing broken connections and rebuilding the context. Whatever services are made available to the application become part of the atomic state transition that the application programs see. Figure 5.4 shows a sample scenario of the integrated control exercised by the transaction services.

It is important to understand that one does not get a transaction processing system by simply taking an arbitrary set of databases, servers, file systems, and so forth, and putting some TP monitor on top. All the components that are to be integrated by the transaction services must implement a basic set of protocols that enable them to cooperate in transaction processing. This topic is discussed in detail in Section 5.3 and in Chapter 6.

5.2.3 TP System Process Structure

This section explains that many of the things a TP monitor must do are concerned with managing system resources; that is, they are similar to the duties of an operating system. In fact, some believe it would be best if the operating systems just swallowed the TP monitor, thus making transactions a basic system service. This issue is reconsidered in Chapter 6, after the similarities between operating systems and TP systems have become clear. To illustrate the issue, consider the situation as perceived by the application (Figure 5.5). A terminal (client) wants some function to be executed by an application server, which in turn needs some data from the database.

Something has to tie all these components together: the terminals (there may be many), the application programs, and the databases (consisting of many files, partitions, and so on). For each terminal, there must be a process that eventually gets the input, understands the function request, and makes sure that the function gets executed (or executes the function itself). To appreciate the problems involved in getting some program to execute on behalf of a request, one needs to understand the various aspects of mapping requests onto processes with the right program in them.

The key terms needed to describe the problem are introduced in Figure 5.6, in terms of a simple data model that represents the various components as entity types and shows what types of relationships exist among them in the general case. Let us begin the explanation with the dynamic part. A request comes in saying what service it wants. The desired service is identified by a *transaction program name* (TPN) or a *transaction code* (TAC)—these are different names for the same concept. A TPN identifies a certain piece of code that implements the service; for example, the DebitCredit program, or the ComputeInterest program.

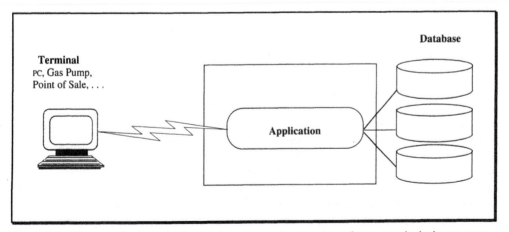

Figure 5.5: Client-application-database interaction. A user request from a terminal triggers some database application to run and to return an output message. The application accesses one or more databases. The whole computation is an ACID unit of work.

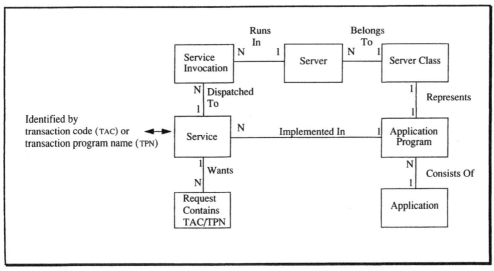

Figure 5.6: Concepts involved in transaction-oriented processing. The data model describing all the entities involved in mapping a request to a real process has six entity types. From a terminal comes a request that identifies a service the user wants to execute (account inquiry, for example). A service is implemented by some program. Typically, a number of services are bunched together into one application program. For each application program, the system entertains a server class, which is a group of processes. Each process in that group is characterized by the fact that it can execute code of the corresponding application program. An actual execution of a service request requires the request to be sent to a process of the right server class. The execution of the server on behalf of that request establishes a service invocation.

The service is implemented in an application program that usually contains code for more than one service.

The dynamic aspects are captured in the upper part of Figure 5.6. At run time, there is a server class maintained by the TP monitor for each application program. A server class is nothing but a group of processes that are able to run the code of the corresponding application program. A process that is a member of such a server class is called a server. Each request for a service must be dispatched to a server of the right server class; that is, to a process with the requested piece of code in it. This activation of a server on behalf of a service request is called *service invocation*. Throughout this book, we assume that at any point in time each server can work on only one service request.[7]

As commonly used, the word *application* denotes a set of application programs; this is also shown in Figure 5.6. For brevity, the term is used generally in what follows, even when referring to a single application *program* that processes a particular request.

Let us now return to the overview of the techniques available to map a request to a proper process. This can be done in a variety of ways, the basic versions of which are depicted in Figures 5.7a–5.7d. For each variant, the pros and cons are briefly discussed in the following subsections.

---

[7] For readers who wonder if by this assumption we rule out process-internal multi-threading in the manner of CICS, the answer is no. Rather, we adopt the habit of calling the smallest unit that can be scheduled a process; whether the respective operating system calls it a process, a task, or a thread does not matter. The point is not to burden the discussion with the problem of heavyweight processes versus lightweight processes.

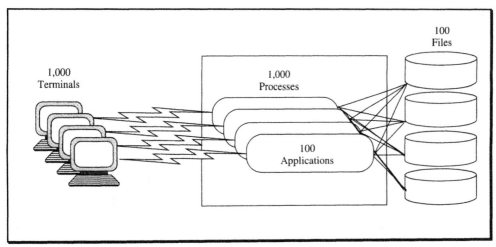

Figure 5.7a: The standard operating system solution: one process per terminal. Each process can run all applications. Each process may have to access any one of the databases. This design is typical of time-sharing systems. It has many processes and many control blocks.

5.2.3.1 One Process per Terminal

Time-sharing systems assign one server process per terminal client. At logon, each terminal is given its own process, which it holds on to for the rest of the session. All applications are linked together to form one application program; thus, a process loading this application program can provide any service for all applications. Figure 5.7a shows this implementation.

For the following reasons, the one process per terminal approach generally does not work well for transaction-oriented systems:

Too many processes. Large TP applications can have 10^4–10^5 terminals. If each terminal creates its own process, the maximum number of processes most current operating systems can handle will be greatly exceeded. (Note that these processes, in turn, call other processes; for simplicity, that is not shown in the figure, but it is explained in detail in the following chapter.) The design may also eventually violate restrictions that apply to both the addressing capabilities and the management of resources bound to processes such as virtual address spaces.

Too many control blocks. For each terminal to potentially invoke each application, all processes must open all databases that might be required. This results in a very large number of file control blocks with low utilization. In general, there are T terminals (i.e., T processes), each accessing F files, each of which has an average of P partitions. Therefore, the number of open control blocks will be $T \cdot F \cdot P$. For large systems with $T = 20,000$, $F = 1,000$, $P = 50$, this yields 10^9 control blocks, which simply spells death to the operating system. This phenomenon is often referred to as *polynomial explosion*.

Too many process switches. If there are many processes, each of them will be rarely used; the same holds for the potentially enormous number of control blocks. This has two consequences: first, the control blocks will most likely not be in main memory when they are referenced next time; and second, there will be many process switches.

Process switches are very expensive operations in most operating systems (typically 2,000–5,000 instructions). To support short interactive function requests at a high frequency, the system must be able to perform much cheaper and faster process switches.

Inflexible load balancing. The process-per-terminal scheme makes load balancing difficult. If, for example, different priorities are to be assigned to different application classes, then processes have to change priorities every time "their" terminal invokes another type of function. This is because it is the operating system that schedules processes, and the fundamental assumption here is that the TP monitor is but an application to the operating system.

Too many capabilities per process. A process comes with more capabilities than a terminal in a transaction-oriented application needs. The bank teller does not need to invoke a compiler, nor does he have to create files or send messages. In fact, he does not have to (or even want to) know about the existence of something as frightening as an operating system (or a TP monitor, for that matter). Processes are simply too mighty a resource to be allocated to a terminal.

In summary, the one-process-per-terminal approach is doomed, mainly because of the duty cycle problem with processes and control blocks. It is acceptable only for small- to medium-sized systems of less than 100 clients. For large systems, there must be a way of multiplexing processes among many requests.

5.2.3.2 Only One Terminal Process

All terminals talk to one process, which can be either the TP monitor process itself or a process running communication protocols and presentation services, such as an X-windows client. It receives the function requests and routes them to the programs that can service them. This configuration is shown in Figure 5.7b.

From a control point of view, a single process makes things easy. The TP monitor can check the function requests, schedule them according to its own policies, and so on. It is also in the ideal position to coordinate distributed transaction processing, to make output messages to the terminals recoverable, and so forth. Of course, the TP monitor process should be run as a *process pair* to achieve fault tolerant execution (see Chapter 3).

The problems of this configuration are just as obvious as the advantages. Assume the process the terminals are attached to is the TP monitor process—this is the way CICS, Complete, and many other transaction processing systems work. Then, of course, the TP monitor has to support all the communication protocols that might be used by any of the terminals out there. Second, the TP monitor is confined within one address space and one operating system process, which can be a serious limitation for large applications and for multiprocessor systems. Each page fault or other exception in the TP monitor's process will stop the whole transaction processing environment. If there is only one monitor process, it might become a bottleneck. This is aggravated by the fact that such a TP system can use only one CPU, because a single process can employ only one CPU at a time. Systems based on this approach require the application to be partitioned into different domains, with one TP monitor process serving each domain. But then each terminal can operate in only one domain, and

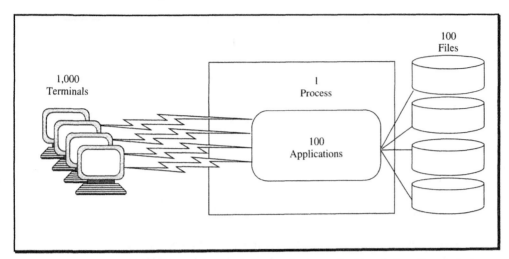

Figure 5.7b: The early TP monitor solution: only one process. In this solution, there is just one process in the entire system. It talks to all terminals, does presentation handling, receives the requests, contains the code for all services of all applications, can access any database, and creates dynamic threads to multiplex itself among the incoming requests.

if there is simply too much work flowing toward the TP monitor, there is no easy way of balancing it.

Finally, having only one process means that all applications are linked together in one address space. This makes the whole application a monolith, which is hard to organize and has no fault containment or isolation. Any application can cause all others to fail.

5.2.3.3 Many Servers, One Scheduler

In the design shown in Figure 5.7c, there is still only one process owning all the terminals and thus handling all the request and response messages, including presentation services. In contrast to the previous design, however, there are multiple processes running the applications that are made accessible to the users at the terminals. So the issue of presentation management is separated (at the level of the operating system) from the issue of request handling.

Figure 5.7c shows the basic IMS/DC configuration. It reflects the structuring into applications, server classes, and servers that was introduced in Figure 5.6 in its process structure. We now have a group of processes (that is, a server class) for each application program. For that reason, each group of processes needs to access only a small subset of the total number of files (databases). An important consequence is that different applications are fenced off against each other; in addition, there can be multiple processes running the same applications to accommodate varying load requirements. Requests for services are issued from one process running the presentation services. This process gets the messages from the clients (terminals), does authentication, identifies the service, and routes the service request to the appropriate server. The advantage is (as in the previous scenario) that there is one place for scheduling and load control. The disadvantage is also the same: under high load, the presentation services process will become a bottleneck.

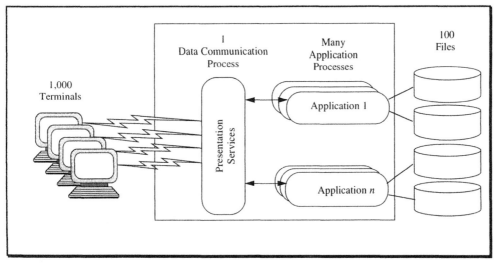

Figure 5.7c: The coexistence approach between operating system and TP monitor: many servers, one requester.   Multiple processes have one requester, which is the process handling the communication with the clients.

5.2.3.4 Many Servers, Many Schedulers

The generalization from the previous approach to this one is obvious:[8] a number of (functionally identical) presentation service processes do the terminal handling. In other words, there is in this case a server class for presentation services, just as there are server classes for the other applications. The application server classes are set up as in the previous scenario. The presentation service processes (i.e., the TP monitor running therein) serve as routers that take in the function request from the terminal, understand the function code that specifies the application to be invoked, and pass the request on to the proper member of that server class. Figure 5.7d shows the resulting configuration.

   This multiple-server approach, which, for example, is used in Tandem's Pathway and DEC's ACMS, requires an additional monitor process to supervise the functions of the other processes, to start them up, to configure them, and so on. However, as will be explained in the next chapter, this separate monitor process comprises only parts of the functionality typically ascribed to a TP monitor.

   In both approaches utilizing multiple servers, the presentation service actively multiplexes the application servers among the requests. Thus, the application servers can be simple, single-threaded processes. The presentation service process, however, must multiplex itself among the terminals it is attached to, and therefore must be multi-threaded. Whether this is supported by some kind of lightweight process mechanism in the operating system, or whether the TP monitor does its own multi-threading is not important at the moment. The net effect, though, is that expensive process switches can generally be replaced by much cheaper process-internal thread changes.

---

   [8] There is another generalization, which basically multiplies the one process of the design shown in Fig. 5.7b; it is different from the many servers, many schedulers design in that each process still contains all the applications and the TP monitor code. But because of the many processes, multiprocessors can be exploited. An example of this design is the UTM system.

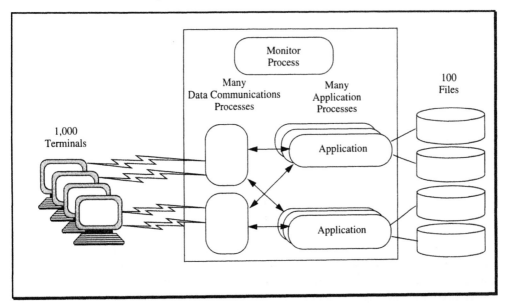

Figure 5.7d: Generalization of the coexistence approach: multiple application servers invoked by multiple requesters. The association between these groups of functionally distinct processes, load control, activation/deactivation of processes, and so on, must now be coordinated by a separate instance, the monitor process.

5.2.4 Summary

TP monitors have to fulfill a number of tasks, some of which are very close to what a basic operating system does. Depending on the actual process configuration, the influence and responsibility of a TP monitor can be more or less prominent, but its to-do list will always contain the following items:

Scheduling. The requests coming from the clients (terminals) must be mapped to the server programs implementing the application services. The techniques used for this request mapping must be more powerful than simple subroutine calls and more flexible (and cheaper) than process switches in conventional operating systems. Section 5.4 introduces the basis for this: an efficient transactional remote procedure call mechanism for the various clients and servers involved in the application.

Server class management. In configurations that are not of the one-process variety (per terminal or per system), the TP monitor is responsible for setting up the server classes, for load balancing, and for all related issues.

Authentication and authorization. Service requests must be cleared by the TP monitor before they are executed. Remember that rather than logging into the operating system, users check in with the TP monitor. But, while operating systems do authorization very infrequently (at file open, when loading a program), the TP monitor has to authorize each individual request, based on a large number of parameters such as transaction program name, terminal identifier, user name, time of day, and many more. All this has to be checked against a user profile at the time of invocation.

Resource administration.   The TP monitor is responsible for the terminals, databases, application programs, users, and all other components of the transaction processing system. Information about these components is kept in the system repository, but the only way for the application to access the repository is through the administration interface of the TP monitor.

System operation.   The TP monitor must provide the operators with sufficient information to tune the system, and inform them about any problems that occur during normal operations (broken terminals, problems in a server class, unexpected load peaks, attempts to execute unauthorized service requests, and much more). Since the TP monitor manages the whole transaction system at a very fine granularity (single-service requests), it has detailed information about what is going on in the system. In undigested form, this flood of data is useless for any operator or system administrator. One of the key problems, therefore, is to aggregate the data about the system behavior such that they become meaningful, but not to lose information in doing so.

Recovery.   After a crash, the TP monitor is responsible for bringing up the transaction processing environment. It starts all the system processes, brings up the server classes (based on the system description in the repository), and then passes control to other components of the transaction processing system (in particular, to the transaction manager; see Chapter 10). This ensures that all resource managers are recovered to their correct states according to the ACID principle. In case of problems during normal operation, such as server crashes, the TP monitor is responsible for reestablishing the process configuration. The remaining recovery activities are again coordinated by the transaction manager.

5.3 The Structure of a TP Monitor

Before exploring the technical details of a TP monitor, it is necessary to define precisely which system components make up the basic transaction services and what the interfaces look like. The following presentation, therefore, focuses on structure rather than on the implementation aspects of single components. Remember that the TP monitor *allocates* resources for other system components to do the work, rather than doing the work itself. It may help in understanding the message of this section to view the TP monitor as a very sophisticated remote procedure call (RPC) mechanism, but with a difference.

A standard RPC mechanism just forwards a call to another node—assuming that the program called is in place, and without guaranteeing that the call returns (or has a point to return to) in case of a failure while handling the call. The invocation mechanism provided by a TP monitor, however, does much more: it gets requests for some functions to be executed and is responsible for providing and scheduling all the resources needed to start and control this execution. Of course, all the other services such as scheduling, security checking, and so on, go on top of this, but the basic functionality is to attach service requests to the right piece of code and make sure that an answer is returned. This very simplistic view is illustrated in Figure 5.8, which shows what the TP monitor does to a request and which components are involved.

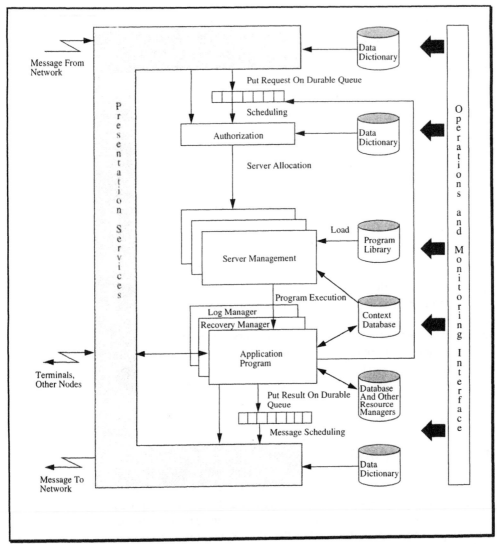

Figure 5.8: Flow of control through a TP monitor.   The diagram represents the basic functions that are needed for transaction program management. Depending on the specific system, some of these functions may be provided by components that are not part of the software package called "TP monitor."

5.3.1 The TP Monitor Components

This subsection begins with a brief overview of the components of Figure 5.8, whose structure will serve as a guideline for the rest of this chapter and the next.

Presentation services define the interfaces between the application program and the devices it talks to. They relieve the application programmer from technical details such as terminal types, format control, and scrolling. They provide device independence with respect to the terminals much in the same way that SQL provides device independence from disks, tapes, and so on. In case of an RPC they also translate data from the client format to the server format, and vice versa. In all of the older TP monitors, presentation services were an integral part (supporting the so-called virtual terminal interface). Now that there are many different presentation services, including window protocols, ASN.1, and graphics standards, it makes no sense for the TP monitor to contain all that code. Rather, there is a group of resource managers implementing a variety of presentation objects, interfacing to the TP monitor through transactional remote procedure calls.

Queue management is the component of the TP monitor that supports queued transaction processing. The main functions of a queue are to receive requests and deliver them to the appropriate servers, and to receive responses and deliver them to the proper clients. Queue services must be transactional. That means a request is on a queue if and only if the client transaction having generated the request commits. Once a request is on a request queue, it gets executed exactly once. Only if the server transaction commits is the result stored on the response queue. Each response on a queue will be delivered to the client by the TP monitor. Depending on the application and the contents of the message, delivery can be requested with different guarantees: at least once, at most once, or exactly once (which is in accordance with the ACID principle). Typically, the queue manager is implemented as a resource manager owned by the TP monitor.

Server class management ensures that for each application program, a server class is set up and active. Servers in the class are activated either by default at system startup, or on demand. Server class management includes creating processes and queues, loading the code into the appropriate address spaces, setting up the process privileges so they can access the appropriate queues, doing the required domain switches, and determining the priorities of the servers in that server class. This service interacts heavily with the load-balancing component to adapt the server class configuration to changing load patterns. We assume here that program management and loading, as well as process creation, are provided by the basic operating system.

Request scheduling is the TP monitor's most frequently executed service. It first locates the service requested. If the service is remote (at a different node in the network), the request is sent there via transactional RPC. If the service is locally available, check if a server class is set up for it. If not, invoke the load-balancing component to decide whether a new server should be created in that class, or whether the request should wait for the next server to become available. Ultimately, the scheduler passes the request to the server. Passing a request can mean a branch in the same address space, a domain switch to a different address space while holding on to the process, or a process switch.

Request authorization is part of the system-wide security provisions. The TP monitor has to check whether the incoming request is valid according to the specifications of the application. The range of possible strategies goes from simple, static authorization up to value-dependent dynamic authorization; given the specific operational characteristics of transaction systems, dynamic authorization upon each individual request is very important.

Context management denotes a TP monitor service that can be used by all transaction programs. It comprises two functions. Its first function is to store processing context that spans transaction boundaries and to retrieve it in subsequent transactions. (An example of how that might be used is given in Section 4.11.) This context database has all the ACID properties; in fact, the TP monitor might implement it using an SQL database system. The second function has to do with context inside an ongoing transaction. If a transaction invokes many different resource managers and therefore employs many different servers, intermediate results (processing state) may have to be passed from one server to the next, as the transaction invokes them. For a number of reasons (see Chapter 6) it makes sense not to pass them entirely via the invocation messages. In such situations, the TP monitor offers a service that allows one server executing for the transaction to give a certain piece of data to the TP monitor to keep, such that another server executing later within the same transaction can access it. Since this happens within one transaction, that context need not be durable, persistent savepoints notwithstanding.

Figure 5.8 shows that the TP monitor relies heavily on a data dictionary (repository) and on some additional databases. Among other things, they contain a complete description of the transaction processing environment. In existing transaction systems, there are usually several disjointed "configuration databases" separately describing the environment for each of the participating software components. To simplify the discussion, we assume here exactly one global repository, which is implemented as a distributed SQL database. All the meta-data required are kept in this dictionary; for the TP monitor, these are as follows:

(1) The nodes involved in the distributed transaction system; their names, addresses, and so on.

(2) The local components of the transaction services, such as the log manager, the transaction manager, and the communication manager.

(3) The hardware components the TP monitor has to know about, such as terminals, controllers, and physical links to other nodes used by the communication manager.

(4) The transaction programs and resource managers that are installed at this node.

(5) Access control lists associated with the application programs and resource managers.

(6) Screen format definitions associated with the application programs. This means a description of how to translate input/output messages into menus, graphics, icons, beeps, or whatever on the terminal (workstation).

(7) Server class configuration data (how many processes, how many threads, which priorities).

(8) Users known to the system, authorization codes, security profiles, and other security-related data.

(9) Operator interface configuration.

(10) Restart configurations and procedures (which resource managers to bring up in which order).

Some of these repository data structures are detailed in Chapter 6. For the moment, it is important to note that the TP monitor controls these catalogs and manages the entire transaction processing environment based on the configuration data they contain. In particular, each system restart refers to the data dictionary and tries to bring up the operational configuration described therein. The contents of these catalogs are manipulated through system transactions.

5.3.2 Components of the Transaction Services

In the previous subsection, the services of a TP monitor were presented in a cookbook style: we need this, we need that, and so on. This subsection defines the role of the TP monitor in the ensemble of components that together establish the transaction services. The whole concept of transaction-oriented processing by means of cooperating components is based on the notion of a *resource manager*. A resource manager is a subsystem that ties into the TP monitor to provide *protected actions* on its state.

Conceptually, there are three types of resource managers. The first category comprises system components that are needed for just administering the system itself—two examples are the catalog and the presentation services. In the second category are the basic components for implementing transactions; that is, those components that help maintain the ACID properties of a transaction. Examples of this category are the transaction manager, the log manager, and the communication manager. The third category is open. In it are all kinds of subsystems implementing objects that can be used by the application and that support the transaction paradigm. Examples of this third category of resource manager include a file system, an SQL database system, a queueing system, an X client, a mail system, and a manager for handling complex transactions (such as sagas, nested transactions, and so on, as described in Chapter 4).

The view taken in this book is that practically any piece of software implementing some services can be a resource manager. To qualify as a resource manager, it must be able to participate in transaction-oriented recovery. But apart from that, it might feature a very special view of the world. For example, when operating on shared data, it could use some synchronization criteria other than locking, or even some correctness criteria other than serializability. It must, however, be able to commit or roll back its part of a transaction when it is told to do so by the transaction manager.

The interplay between the components of the transaction services can best be illustrated by looking at a simple example. Consider a simple transaction with the following program structure:

```
BEGIN WORK
receive (input message);
< some SQL >
send (statistics menu) to (window w1);
COMMIT WORK;
```

Here window w1 might refer to the default window that is obtained from the "context." The resulting control flow through the components for running this transaction program is shown in Figure 5.9.

The request comes in through the network and is received by the TP monitor in a request queue. It then schedules the appropriate transaction program and provides it with a server process to run in. The first thing the application does is to register with the transaction manager by issuing a BEGIN WORK command; it gets back a transaction identifier (TRID), which from now on is used to tag all messages and requests issued on behalf of that transaction.

The UPDATE command results in a call to the resource manager named DB2. This component uses either a local favorite log or the global log manager (the latter is assumed

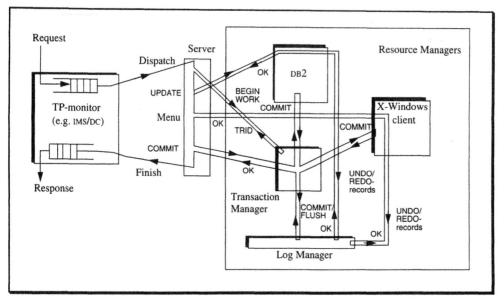

Figure 5.9: Flow of control among different resource managers during the execution of a simple transaction (no rollback). The diagram shows that the request is first acted upon by the TP monitor, which dispatches a server for it. The program executing in the server (apart from its internal processing) invokes other resource managers, such as the transaction manager, an SQL database system, and an X client. These resource managers, in turn, invoke further resource managers they depend on for the implementation of their objects. The response is finally delivered to the client through the TP monitor (not counting the statistics display via the X client). The whole thread of execution is tied together into one ACID transaction by the TP system. It is assumed that requests come in through an input queue, and responses are put on an output queue.

here); it will write all necessary UNDO and REDO records to this log via the public log interface (see Chapter 9), passing on the TRID of its client. Once control has returned to the application program, it continues execution, and the next "outside" reference goes to a resource manager that is an X client talking to PCs, workstations, and so forth. Being a participant in a transaction, the X client has to make its window contents recoverable, which requires writing UNDO and REDO information to the log. After that, the application is ready to commit.

The COMMIT WORK call goes to the transaction manager, which by now knows which resource managers (apart from itself) have something to do with this transaction. It therefore tells DB2 about the COMMIT, and this resource manager can now do whatever it needs to do for commit processing. The X client gets the same information and can now get ready to display the new window contents. After each resource manager has agreed to commit this transaction, the transaction manager writes the final log records and tells the log manager to put them on durable storage. Now, the screen can actually be written, the locks can be released, and so on. As part of this, the response message is put onto an output queue. (It is not necessary to understand precisely the necessity of some of these interactions, especially *what* is written to the log. For the moment, it is important only to understand that logging, commit coordination, and similar things need to be done. The rationale and details are explained beginning in Chapter 9.)

Finally, the TP monitor learns about the completion of the request. It can now reassign the server to another request. Note, however, that the completion of a request does not always free the server so that it can be reassigned. There are cases, for example, in which a server is reserved for a special user and thus can only be given requests from that environment. Think of the chained transaction model described in Chapter 4. If the request under one transaction has been completed (and the next transaction has already been created), it is likely that the server must be reserved for requests from that "next" transaction, because it may refer to local context variables set by the previous transaction. Of course, those variables are available only in the server process the previous transaction ran in, and not in any other server of the same class. This leads to the notion of sessions and context-sensitive scheduling, which are discussed in detail in Chapter 6.

This example is simplified (there is no scheduling, authorization, and so on) to give an idea of how transaction processing is organized by the TP monitor and how the basic transaction services work in cooperation with transaction-oriented servers. Figure 5.10 is not

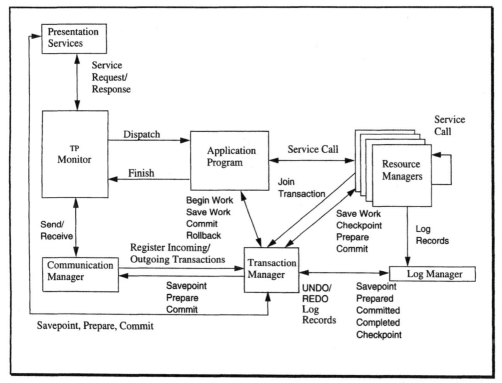

Figure 5.10: Transaction processing components and interfaces during normal processing. The figure illustrates that the TP monitor's main task is to handle the incoming requests, provide the resources for their processing, and hand back the results. Orchestrating the cooperation among the various resource managers (those that are system components and those that are provided by the application) is the task of the transaction manager. It informs all components involved in a transaction about the critical state transitions, such as prepare and commit. It also coordinates savepoints and checkpoints and, in general, makes sure that the ACID rules are maintained as far as the interaction among the resource managers is concerned. Communication with remote parts of the transaction is handled through the communication manager, which in turn talks to the transaction manager. The figure does not show any calls related to transaction rollback.

limited to showing the flow of control resulting from one invocation. Rather, to tie the components together in a transaction-oriented way, it sketches the interfaces among the components by indicating which types of calls can be issued in which direction.

The figure illustrates that once the transaction program has started, the TP monitor has little to do with transaction management. The coordination of the resource managers is done by the transaction manager, whose main purpose is to ensure that all resource managers participating in a transaction are able to recover in the correct way if that should ever be necessary. It may seem surprising at first to distinguish so strictly between the TP monitor and the transaction manager, rather than viewing them as one component. Remember, however, that the whole system is to support the transaction paradigm, not just the part that runs OLTP applications. Consequently, there will be transactions that do not come in through the TP monitor:[9] the ad hoc query interface of SQL systems gives users direct access to database transactions. These users can begin and commit transactions while running in a time-sharing process. Batch programs run sequences of transactions by talking directly to the resource managers required. Special application systems (such as those for CAD) run their own terminal environment without using the TP monitor or its terminal managers. All these activities, however, require transaction support. The logical consequence of this is to separate the components exercising *transaction control* (the transaction manager) from those that do *transaction-oriented resource scheduling* (the TP monitor). Most of the interfaces are provided or are used by the transaction manager. Because of the central role this component plays in a TP system, it is described separately (Chapters 10 through 12). This section only explains the TP monitor's interfaces.

There are, in fact, two interfaces in Figure 5.10 that belong to neither the transaction manager nor the TP monitor. One is the service calls from the application program to the various resource managers of the type described above (SQL, X-Windows, etc.). These are completely application specific and require little comment. Like all the other requests, each service call must be tagged with the TRID of the transaction to which this call belongs. The other kind of interface is the public interface to the log used by the resource managers; this is precisely defined in Chapter 9. The point is, however, that all the calls among resource managers, no matter where they originate, are so-called transactional remote procedure calls. The mechanisms to handle them are provided by the TP monitor.

5.3.3 TP Monitor Support for the Resource Manager Interfaces

Thus far we have looked at which interfaces the TP monitor uses and which interfaces it exports. But there is more; the TP monitor actually has to provide all the mechanisms required for the other components and resource managers to use these interfaces. In other words, the TP monitor must maintain the infrastructure that allows resource managers to invoke other resource managers via a transactional RPC mechanism. This means the TP monitor has primary responsibility for bringing up the resource managers, helping them recover to a consistent state, making them addressable by others, and dispatching service requests to servers of the appropriate server class. Thus, the major responsibilities of the TP monitor, with respect to the resource managers in its local configuration, are as follows:

---

[9] Of course, such requests need to be authenticated and authorized, too. This is typically done by the operating system upon logon, and by the resource managers invoked. Remember that SQL has its own security mechanism that can be used independently of a TP monitor that handles the requests.

Restart and system startup. All resource managers installed in the current configuration first have to be started. The actual recovery protocol after a crash is completely handled among the resource managers and the transaction manager, so that in this respect the TP monitor only has to make sure they are brought up.

Definition of a new resource manager. A new resource manager must be installed explicitly at its node. That means the TP monitor must enter the resource manager's description into the repository and update the configuration data so that from now on the new resource manager will automatically be brought up upon startup.

Changing the process configuration. If, for load balancing reasons, a server class must be extended, the TP monitor has to create a new process, load the code into it, or attach the process to the right address space so that it can execute the server code that is already available elsewhere.

Handling transactional remote procedure calls (TRPCs). This is the TP monitor's fundamental chore. As described previously, the components in the TP system interact through service requests. BEGIN WORK, COMMIT WORK, and the other transaction-specific calls are also service requests—directed toward a component called *transaction manager*, which knows how to act on them. Technically, however, a BEGIN WORK is simply a TRPC that is handled by the TP monitor just as any other service request would be. It is important to understand that at the level of the TP monitor and the system components it manages, we are not talking about messages, or interprocess communication, or memory sharing; whatever is required in terms of interaction is a TRPC. Since that is a very important aspect of the TP system architecture described in this book, the basic idea is illustrated in the next section. The technical aspects of how such an invocation mechanism works are presented in Chapter 6.

5.4 Transactional Remote Procedure Calls: The Basic Idea

This section is essentially a whirlwind tour of standard remote procedure calls: what they are, what happens along their way, and so on. At the end of the section, the concepts introduced are highlighted from the perspective of the specific requirements in transaction processing systems. This is the transition to the detailed description of TRPCs in Chapter 6. The explanation is based on the terms used throughout this book but should not obscure the fact that standard RPC is a mechanism that can be used (and is being used) independently of any TP system. Books on computer networks and operating systems cover that topic with much more detail. Readers who are familiar with RPCs may just browse through the following text and proceed to Section 5.5. For those who are not sure they know enough about RPCs, understand that this is not meant to be the whole story about RPCs but is intended to serve as a foundation for the material that follows.

5.4.1 Who Participates in Remote Procedure Calls?

As explained in the previous section, processing in a transaction-oriented system is based on service requests issued by clients to resource managers (servers). An application calls a server to do something; that server, in turn, invokes another server, and so forth. So far, this suggests a clear distinction between application programs requesting services (clients) and servers delivering them. Figure 1.8, however, shows that this is not so. Servers are clients to other servers, and applications can be servers to both applications and servers. The distinction, then, between applications and servers is not a technical one. Rather, it has to do with the role a component plays in the system and with the level of sophistication that is needed for its design and implementation. Applications are thought to be simpler than general servers. Structurally, both look the same; they are resource managers calling each other and the underlying transaction processing services through well-defined interfaces. Given that this chapter is on structural (implementation) issues, the term *resource manager* will be used for both applications and "real" servers throughout. Resource managers issue (transactional) remote procedure calls to other resource managers. Only in a few cases do we explicitly need to talk about applications.

The programs to be called via RPCs—the resource managers—are referred to in two ways. First, they have a resource manager name, which is a globally unique character string; this will be called RMNAME. The RMNAME is used in all external (human) interactions with the system: for reporting, invocation, and other references to the services from the outside. Second, there is a resource manager ID, called RMID, which is a 4-byte integer and is used for all practical (system-internal) purposes. The RMID identifies the resource manager at one node in the network, that is, within the name space of one instance of the transaction processing operating system (TPOS). It is handed out by the TP monitor when the resource manager is installed at the node, and it remains valid until the resource manager is removed. The definition of these data types is as follows:

```
typedef  char[BIG]    RMNAME;     /* globally unique name for the resource manager    */
typedef  Uint         RMID;       /* locally unique identifier for the resource manager */
```

Note that this is one example of the distinction between the name and the address of an object, as discussed in Chapter 2.

5.4.2 Address Space Structure Required for RPC Handling

In contrast to what their name suggests, remote procedure calls are not necessarily remote. They were invented for distributed systems to make the invocation of services at remote nodes look like local subroutine calls. The main advantage of an RPC is that subroutine calls are simple, synchronous, and thus easy to test. All more network-like alternatives, such as message passing or interrupt programming, put much higher demands on the user of such interfaces.

If the system is to be transparent with respect to the location of services in the network, then the program invoking a service does not even know whether the resource manager it needs is locally available. Hence, it cannot be required to use the syntax for a local procedure call in one case and the syntax for a remote procedure call in the other; all have to look the same. The consequence of this is that any kind of service invocation results in a local procedure call—local to the address space of the process in which the program runs. This call, of course, does not go directly to the resource manager named, but instead goes to a piece of code called the *RPC stub*, which is linked to the application program (or resource manager). The stub, among other things, finds out where the callee is located and, if it is

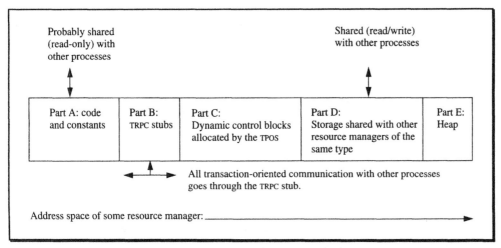

Figure 5.11: Overview of the address space structure of a resource manager process. Each process running a resource manager or an application program under a transaction processing operating system must contain a piece of code called TRPC stub, which represents the agent of the TP monitor. This stub handles all dynamic aspects of the respective resource manager/application: initialization, invocation, communication, multi-threading, and scheduling. It acts on behalf of the TP monitor and in cooperation with its peers in the other processes. It is an extension of the RPC stub that is implicit in this and that handles incoming and outgoing remote procedure calls in cooperation with the communications manager.

another node in the network, makes all the preparations to send the call across the wire as a message. This is demonstrated in the next subsection.

The point to be made here is that part of each resource manager's address space is this stub that handles all calls to other resource managers, including the local ones. Instead of *RPC stub*, the usual term in general networks, we will call it *TRPC stub* because some of the work that makes remote procedure calls transactional is also located here. The term *stub* alludes to the fact that in standard RPC mechanisms it is a very short piece of code that adapts the local call to the formats and requirements of the remote invocation mechanism via messages; conversely, this code also turns messages into local calls. The part that handles the messages and the local address tables is not short at all, but it is used for all calls. What is specific to each individual call is the piece that picks up the name and the description of the parameter list; that is the stub. For a *transactional* remote procedure call, the stub has to do more than just parameter matching.[10] This is the topic of Section 6.3. The stub must be shared among all address spaces participating in transaction processing on that node. The reasons may not be obvious now, but the discussion in Section 6.3 will provide an explanation. The TRPC stub acts as the TP monitor's agent in each address space.

Figure 5.11 gives an overview of the address space structure of a resource manager process. Part A is its code, which can be shared (read-only) with other processes running the same resource manager. Part B is the TRPC stub. As the figure shows, there are generally additional parts of the address space, some of which are determined by the style of transaction processing. In particular, the TPOS, through its agent, might keep some dynamic data

_____

[10] In that case, the stub might more properly be called a log; however, since that name is already used for something very important in the context of transaction systems, we leave it at *stub*.

structures (Part C), and the resource manager may share data structures with address spaces of other processes running the same code (Part D). None of the parts beyond B are needed immediately; rather, they are shown for completeness.

In discussing address spaces and processes, the terminology introduced in Chapter 2 is used. Not all existing transaction processing systems make the process/address space distinction. As explained in Section 5.1, there are transaction processing systems in which the TP monitor employs just one process, which uses one address space (except for the operating system domain). From the perspective of the RPC mechanism, this does not matter because the RPC stub still has to be shared—regardless of how many address spaces (and processes) there are.

5.4.3 The Dynamics of Remote Procedure Calls

Let us describe the handling of RPCs by considering the invocation of an SQL resource manager. Although this makes the discussion a little more involved, SQL databases are used throughout this text as *the* prototypical resource managers. It is therefore worth the effort to study the invocation of SQL services via remote procedure calls. To simplify things, we assume that there is only one service entry point to the SQL server. (This, of course, is not true; each resource manager can have more than one service entry point.[11])

The problem in mapping arbitrary servers onto the the RPC interface, which tries to mimic a subroutine call, is that the server's application programming interface (API) can be structurally very different from such a call. As an example, consider the API that is defined by (imbedded) SQL. It is a nonprocedural interface and has a notational convention for referring to the database name space, as well as to local program variables in the same statement, and so on. The operations described in SQL are eventually executed by some remote or local database resource manager, but the complexity required for actually invoking the SQL server is hidden beneath the SQL surface. Figure 5.12 illustrates the sequence of mappings.

First, a pre-compiler parses and translates the SQL statement, creating an internal representation of the query tree that can be interpreted directly by an SQL executor. This results in a series of assignments to data structures according to the syntax of the host language. With all that in place, the resource manager call can be generated. Since the pre-compiler generates code for the host language, this is either a normal subroutine call or a special statement that is tagged for yet another pre-compiler to look at. For clarity, let us assume the latter case. In Figure 5.12, this is the statement line:

```
!sqlselect('fastsql', format_CB, expression_CB, &variable_CB);
```

The exclamation character (!) is arbitrarily chosen to mark this function call as a resource manager invocation. In other words, it says, "This is a remote procedure call to the entry point sqlselect of a server with RMNAME 'fastsql' and with parameters. . . ." Statements tagged in this manner are recognized by a *stub compiler*.

As the name suggests, the stub compiler generates code for passing parameters of an arbitrary remote procedure call to the local stub, and vice versa. Specifically, it does two things: It first translates the statement into code that prepares parameters for the TRPC stub, and into calls to the right entries. The second task results from the observation that in a real,

---

[11] In terms of object-oriented programming, the resource manager implements an object class, and the service entry points represent its methods.

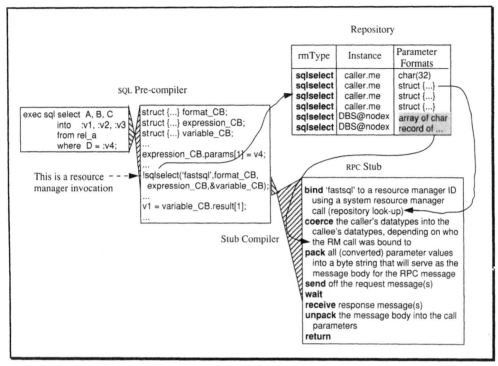

Figure 5.12: Passing the invocation of an SQL service via a remote procedure call (RPC). If the application programming interface (API) is SQL, the invocation of the database resource manager involves two steps. First, the SQL pre-compiler translates SQL into a number of control block declares, value assignments, and procedure calls, according to syntax of the host language. Some of these calls are resource manager calls, that is, TRPCs. These are translated in the second step by the stub compiler, such that the data types in the parameter list of the caller get coerced into those of the (remote) callee, and vice versa. After that, normal RPC handling takes place, all of which is done in the RPC stub. Note that each resource manager interface has to be documented in the repository.

open, distributed system the client might present the parameters of the invocation in a different manner than the server expects them—the parameters could use different data types, for example.[12] Conversely, the server hands the results back in a format the client cannot understand. The stub compiler's second task is therefore to coerce the parameter formats back and forth.

To coerce the parameters, the stub compiler looks up the prototype description of the callee in the repository. According to this description, it generates code that translates data structures and data types into one another (as long as they are compatible). This problem is of no further interest to us, but the example shown in Figure 5.12 should give an idea of what has to be done.[13]

---

[12] Even if all that were the same, one machine could be a Big Endian, and the other one a Little Endian, in which case one could not simply copy bytes from this node to that node.

[13] In OSI-compliant systems, the prototype description is based on the abstract syntax notation ASN.1, which is not elaborated here. To be precise, ASN.1 is the formats and protocol (FAP) definition, to which there are a number of application programming interfaces (APIs), generically denoted as NIDL (network interface description language).

Once the TRPC stub is called, it finds out where the service called 'fastsql' is available. The simplest way to do that is to look up a name server. The name server is an SQL database that relates RMNAMEs to NODEIDs in the network and to the local RMIDs. According to the descriptions in Chapter 1, we assume the name server to be part of the repository.

If the name binding is performed at run time rather than at compile time, then the decision of which type of parameter coercion needs to be done also happens at run time. As long as the server is not known, there is no interface description to look up. The logic the TRPC stub executes therefore comprises the following steps:

Bind the RMNAME in the invocation to a NODEID and an RMID; information is stored in the name server (repository).

Look up the callee's interface prototype description; this is also part of the repository.

Coerce the local parameter representation into the one expected by the invoked resource manager.

Pack all the transformed parameter values into a byte string; this step is called *parameter marshalling*.

Send the message (as one packet or a sequence of packets) to the peer TRPC stub, if the server executes at a remote node. If the server is local, put the message in the input queue of the respective process. This step is explained in detail in Section 6.3.

The process executing the resource manager call is now suspended until the response from the server arrives.[14] The response message itself contains a byte string that needs to be remapped into the control blocks of the invocation statement. This is done by a second portion of code, which mirrors the first one:

Unpack the byte string (reverse marshalling).

Coerce the parameter values received into the representation used by the caller.

Right after the invocation point, control returns to the application. The style of invocation described here assumes that coercing the parameter values is done at the caller's site; this is generally called the "client makes it right" method. The alternative method is "server makes it right," but it is not fundamentally different.[15]

---

[14] Of course, the process is also reactivated by a timeout event if the response is not received, but that will not be considered here.

[15] Note that this description of how a remote SQL server is invoked basically assumes dynamic SQL, which is interpreted at run time. Embedded SQL is compiled once, and from then on the generated query plan is executed. This requires a much more complicated protocol than the one we have sketched. At compile time, the client has to issue rmCalls to the SQL server for it to compile the statement, generate the access plan, and hand back an identifier for that plan (together with format control blocks and all). At run time, the rmCalls from the client refer to the access plan identifier and thereby ask the server to run that pre-compiled query. The access plan identifier serves a similar purpose as a file handle, but it is persistent. It is unique within the name space of a resource manager; that is, the concatenation of resource manager name and access plan identifier is globally unique. These problems, however, are specific to SQL rather than to resource manager invocation.

The principle underlying this method of invoking resource managers is the description of the prototype of the service interface in the repository. Note that the name of the service interface does not denote a specific process or program instantiation; rather, it refers to a generic class of services (e.g. mail, SQLDB), which generally can be provided by multiple servers. The trick is to have the code generated by the stub compiler coerce the parameter values, depending on which server the client is actually bound to. Stub compilers, on the other hand, are language dependent, and in many cases no such thing might be available. There are a couple of ways to cope with this, two of which are discussed briefly:

Local system resource managers. Transaction processing requires the invocation of a number of resource managers, which either run on the same node or on a statically assigned server node (if the client runs on a workstation). The log manager, the transaction manager, and the communications manager are examples of local system resource managers. Their interfaces constitute no surprise at run time, because they are they are part of the local operating system. Therefore, the code needed to prepare their invocation for the RPC stub is fixed and linked to each process that invokes resource managers. Note that these still are not direct subroutine calls, because even on the local node, these system resource managers may reside in a different domain or process.

Do it yourself. To include resource managers written by the application without suitable support from a stub compiler, one can either provide the parameter marshalling routines as the local resource managers do, or one can leave this completely to the client and the server. What that means is simply that the client has to deliver the parameters exactly as the RPC stub expects them—as a byte string—and the server has to know how to plough through that byte string to find its parameter values. This is close to what the RPC mechanisms in most workstation environments provide.

For the rest of this book both versions are used. All the system resource managers (components of the transaction processing system) are referred to according to their function prototype definitions, which are introduced in the chapters describing the respective types of resource manager. Marshalling is assumed to be done in the TRPC stub. For all other application-specific resource managers, there is one interface definition, rmCall, which contains as its parameters the RMNAME of the service requested, a byte string with the input parameters, and a byte string with the results. This is explained in Chapter 6.

5.4.4 Summary

This section has been a digest of how the standard remote procedure call mechanism works. The key idea is to provide a conventional call interface that allows services to be invoked from subroutines bound to the caller's address space, as well as from servers running in different address spaces at the same node, or from servers at different nodes. Since the actual transfer of control is different in each case, it must be hidden from the caller by some RPC service routine. This routine is called "transactional remote procedure call (TRPC) stub" throughout this text. The caller branches to this stub, telling it what kind of call he wants to make (name of the server and parameters), and the stub code finally does the call, puts the request into another process's input queue, or sends the request across the wire in a message. The RPC mechanism also is responsible for parameter coercion, which accounts for different data types on the caller's and the callee's side. Upon completion, the server first returns to the stub, which hands the result parameters back to the caller. At the server's side, there is the same kind of stub. That stub receives the request and transforms it into a subroutine call to the local server routine, acting fully complementary to the stub at the caller's side.

TP monitors provide all this, plus something very important: each RPC is turned into a transactional remote procedure call, which, among other things, means the following:

Bind RPCs to transactions.   The TP monitor makes sure that each invocation, before it goes out, is tagged with a TRID.

Inform the transaction manager.   When the TP monitor forwards a call to a resource manager, it informs the transaction manager about this invocation. That way, the transaction manager always knows who is participating in a transaction.

Binding processes to transactions.   When dispatching a server, the TP monitor remembers the transaction for which the server process is running and thus can inform the transaction manager if that process crashes.

The sum of the TP monitor's functioning is twofold: it extends standard RPC mechanisms to include server class management, and it provides the transaction manager with enough information to keep the dynamically expanding web of resource managers participating in a transaction within a sphere of control.

5.5 Examples of the Transaction-Oriented Programming Style

This section gives an overview of the programming style induced by the use of transaction-oriented systems. The focus here is on direct transactions—transaction programs that are directly invoked by their clients, whether users at the terminal or other resource managers in the system. The main purpose of these examples is to demonstrate the use of the transactional verbs, such as BEGIN WORK and COMMIT WORK, which are introduced as we go along. For each verb, the implications with respect to transaction management and the effects on other resource managers are explained. To achieve the desired program behavior, the effects of transactional verbs on the global state involved, and on the other resource managers that are part of a transaction, must be clearly understood. Transactions are a very powerful programming paradigm, but, just as any other power tool, they should be used with discretion to avoid surprises.

Since this chapter is entirely at an overview level, the complete range of transaction programming styles is not covered. In particular, the requirements for a transactional resource manager that keeps its own durable state are not mentioned. Such advanced topics are deferred to later chapters of the book. Queued transactions are also not talked about at this point, since the question of whether a transaction feeds off a queue or gets its requests directly makes no great difference in the way the transaction program is structured. A queued program cannot interact with the user, but it can invoke other resource managers in the same way a direct transaction can. Queued transactions are more interesting from the perspective of how they fit into the overall architecture of a TP monitor, and they are consequently presented in that context in Chapter 6. The focus here is on transaction-oriented application programs.

5.5.1 The Basic Processing Loop

The typical transactional application program has a simple sequential structure consisting of the steps shown in Figure 5.13. First, it waits for a request to arrive. This is a metaphorical description; in reality, there is no program instance sitting there and waiting for a message. It is the TP monitor that gets the message, looks at the service identifier (TPN), finds a server for it, and issues a transactional remote procedure call to the transaction program.

The difference is important for readers familiar with a real TP monitor, because in many such systems the application programs actually wait at an input message buffer for the request message to arrive. In our design, however, the application is called as if it were a subroutine, and it gets its request parameters via the parameter list. In all the following examples, we assume rmParams to denote a byte string that contains the parameters that are being passed to a server or that the server hands back to the client. Client and server, respectively, understand the contents of that string of parameters. The only intent behind this convention is to keep things simple.

One could argue that it is merely a matter of stylistic finesse whether the request parameters are passed via a message buffer or via the procedure's parameter list. Yet it is more than that: In the message-oriented style, the application program responds by sending a

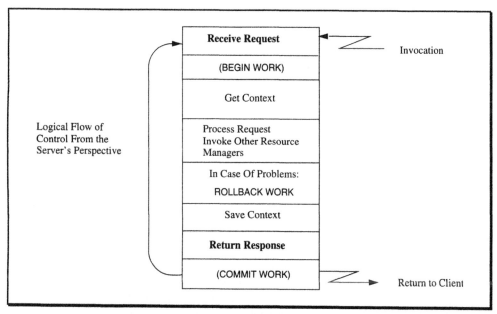

Figure 5.13: The basic structure of a transactional application or a simple resource manager. It waits for an incoming request and begins a transaction if the request does not already come with a TRID; it probably looks for processing context, then starts doing its computations, which may involve calls to other resource managers, such as an SQL database. If it runs into problems, it can invoke ROLLBACK, which will affect all clients and servers that have participated in that transaction. If everything works out correctly, it prepares a response and calls COMMIT WORK, provided the server program represents the outermost sphere of control for that activity. Control then returns to the client that has invoked the server. The server program itself, however, returns to its initial state, where it is able to receive the next request.

response message, but control (potentially) remains inside the transaction program. The program could, then, return to the beginning and start acting on the next input message, if there were one.

In the model used here, which is based on procedure calls, the program responds by returning to the caller. Thus, control is passed to the point from which the program was called—the TRPC stub in its address space.

The pros and cons of the two styles are not discussed here. The TRPC style has a number of advantages, not the least of which is simplicity. In all the following examples, therefore, the application programs look like subroutines, and they invoke other resource managers by using the generic TRPC interface rmCall. Remember that rmCall denotes the invocation of another arbitrary resource manager via transactional remote procedure call. The function prototype definition for the rmCall interface is explained in Chapter 6. For further discussions of programming styles, see Section 2.6.

5.5.2 Attaching Resource Managers to Transactions: The Simple Cases

The simplest variety of resource managers does not talk to the transactional environment at all. It exports its service interface and probably invokes other application-specific resource managers (SQL or a mail server), but otherwise ignores transactions completely. It has the following structure:

```
Boolean      IgnorantServer(rmParams *InParams, rmParams *OutResults)
   {    /* declares */
        work on input parameters          /* example of the simplest version        */
        CompCode = rmCall('HelpMe',......);  /* of a transactional resource manager   */
                                          /* checking of return code omitted         */

        prepare output parameters
        return(TRUE);
   }
```

It is interesting to note that, although there is no reference to a transaction at all in the code, this computation will automatically be made part of an ACID unit, if it is called from *inside* a transaction. If the program only does a few local computations on the input parameters, there may be nothing to isolate or to recover, as far as IgnorantServer is concerned. However, the program invokes another server, HelpMe, which might act on durable data and would therefore need a transaction around its operations. If for no other reason than this, IgnorantServer must be part of a transaction to be able to pass the TRID on to its callees. As the example demonstrates, the program can be completely unaware of this operational environment; the transaction attachment is the responsibility of the TRPC mechanism. Because it is ignorant, the server cannot be asked to vote on commit—remember that it is quite unaware of any transaction in which it is running. The transaction manager knows from the TP monitor (which, in turn, knows it from the repository) that IgnorantServer is exactly what the name suggests, and simply assumes that all such servers always vote Yes during commit. Only a crash of its process between the invocation and the return could cause the transaction to abort because of that server.

The next type of server embodies the simple ACID transaction. It explicitly begins a transaction, does its job, and then either commits or aborts. The debit/credit transaction is one example of this type; quite a few others are also mentioned in earlier chapters.

For completeness, let us declare the function prototypes for the calls to the transaction processing environment used for the SimpleServer:

```
/* basic interface prototypes provided by the TP monitor to support transaction    */
/* oriented processing. these functions are needed by both, simple applications     */
/* and by sophisticated resource managers.                                          */
typedef struct {    Ulong length;              /*                                   */
                    char data[length];         /*                                   */
                } context, *contextp;          /* byte string for storing savepoint data. */
                                               /* see chapter 4 for programming example.  */
TRID        Begin_Work(attributes, context);   /* declares begin of transaction to transaction */
                                               /* manager. since the begin is savepoint 1,      */
                                               /* context can be specified.                     */
Boolean     Commit_Work(Boolean lazy, context); /* commit transaction, write context to the    */
                                               /* log. specify if eager or lazy commit.        */
(void)      Abort_Work();                      /* roll back entire transaction; savepoint 0    */
```

Note that, in contrast to the examples in Chapter 4, we now have Begin_Work instead of BEGIN WORK, and so on. That is because the examples in Chapter 4 were pure SQL; that is, the start of a new transaction required the statement

```
exec sql BEGIN WORK;
```

Thus far, then, we have been using the SQL application programming interface (API). In this chapter, however, SQL is not always used. The examples that follow assume general transactional application programs, which therefore have to use a call-API to the transaction services. The function prototypes of this call-API are shown in the declares just given. Remembering the description of the way RPCs are handled, note that SQL's BEGIN WORK is translated by the pre-compiler into a Begin_Work() TRPC.

The basic structure of the simple flat-transaction server resembles the following:

```
Boolean     SimpleServer(rmParams *InParams, rmParams *OutResults)
    {   TRID             NewTRID;          /* TRID of the transaction started here */
        RETCODE          CompCode;         /* rmCall completion code               */
        NewTRID = Begin_Work(...);         /* start transaction                    */
        do work;                           /*                                      */
        CompCode = rmCall('HelpMe',......); /* server invocation                   */
        if   (CompCode == BAD)             /* response OK ?                        */
            {   Abort_Work();              /* abort transaction                    */
                return(FALSE);}            /* deny service                         */
        do more work;                      /*                                      */
        if    (result_ok)                  /*                                      */
            {   prepare output parameters; /* example of a resource manager that   */
                Commit_Work(...);          /* starts a transaction and completes it */
                                           /* test for success of commit           */
                return(TRUE);}             /* within the same invocation           */
        else {   Abort_Work();             /*                                      */
                 return(FALSE); }          /*                                      */
    }                                      /*                                      */
```

Such a resource manager runs under transaction protection. To do that, it invokes system resource managers (the transaction manager, in this example), using the same TRPC mechanism that invoked SimpleServer in the first place. Thus the invocation of Simple-Server does not yet have transaction protection; nor does Begin_Work. But after that, everything, including the invocation of HelpMe, runs under NewTRID.

Note that, while the IgnorantServer can be invoked from anywhere, the SimpleServer cannot. It calls Begin_Work unconditionally; if the transaction manager finds that the TRPC invoking SimpleServer already came with a TRID, it fails the call to Begin_Work[16] and, along with it, the whole server invocation. For this reason, resource managers like this one typically service dumb terminals or other nontransactional end points of the system.

The application program, however, could try to do a little better. Since each TRPC takes the identifier of the transaction that issued the call to the callee (which then also executes "under" that transaction), the transaction program can simply ask the transaction manager if it was invoked within a transaction. If so, it keeps going; if not, it begins a transaction.

Here is the prototype declaration of the function that tells a program under which TRID it is executing:

TRID	**My_TRID();**	/* returns the transaction ID on behalf of	*/
		/* which the process is running right now.	*/

For this data type there is a NULL value, called NULLTRID. Hence, the simple logic that allows the more flexible SimpleServer to be invoked from within or without a transaction:

```
if (MyTRID ()== NULLTRID)
      Begin_Work(...);
```

Context data, as introduced in Chapter 4, is an arbitrary string of data the transaction program can pass on with the savepoint request; the data will be returned by the TP monitor should the program later decide to return to the state as of the savepoint. Since both Begin_Work and Commit_Work represent special savepoints within a transaction (the first one and the last one), context can be attached to them as well.

The next type of resource manager represents a wide class of what we call *cautious resource managers*. These resource managers make use of the savepoint facility and thereby also make use of context. (Note that there are many other ways of using context, some of which are discussed later in this book.) The following code shows the basic structure of a program that makes itself recoverable in a stepwise fashion by using savepoints.

```
Boolean    CautiousServer(rmParams *InParams, rmParams *OutResults)
    {   TRID      NewTRID;                    /* TRID of the transaction started here      */
        savepoint   last_ok_state;            /* variable for remembering last savepoint   */
        context    trusted_data;              /* storage area to be kept with savepoint    */
        int        steps_p_savepoint;         /* how much work between savepoints           */
        RETCODE   CompCode;                    /* rmCall completion code                     */
        initialize trusted_data                /*                                            */
        NewTRID = Begin_Work(...,trusted_data,FALSE); /*                                      */
        last_ok_state = 1;                     /* begin is save_point no 1                   */
```

---

[16] We assume a flat transaction system; if nested transactions were supported, the Begin_Work could be interpreted as the beginning of a subtransaction. However, we do not elaborate on this aspect.

```
        while (more_work)                    /* transaction goes on for a while          */
        {    for (i=1;i<=steps_p_savepoint;i++)  /* every steps_p_savepoint call savepoint  */
            {    do work;                    /*                                          */
                 CompCode = rmCall('HelpMe',......);     /* server invocation             */
                 /* watch this space !!!                                                  */
                 do more work;               /*                                          */
                 if (error occurs)           /* when trouble: return to earlier savept.  */
                    {    last_ok_state = Rollback_Work(last_ok_state);   /* might be abort  */
                         trusted_data = Read_Context(last_ok_state);    /* read savepoint data */
                         reset local variables from
                         what has been stored in trusted_data
                         i=0;                 /* start new savept cycle                   */
            };         };                     /* take a new savepoint                     */
            save all relevant local          /*                                          */
            variables in trusted_data        /*                                          */
            last_ok_state = Save_Work(FALSE, trusted_data);    /*                          */
        };                                    /*                                          */
    if    (result_ok)                         /*                                          */
        {    prepare output parameters;       /* example of a resource manager that       */
             Commit_Work(...);                /* uses savepoints to structure its work    */
                                              /* test for success of commit               */
             return(TRUE);                    /* it still begins a transaction and        */
        }                                     /* completes it within one invocation       */
    else                                      /*                                          */
        {    Abort_Work();                    /*                                          */
             return(FALSE);                   /*                                          */
        }                                     /*                                          */
}                                             /*                                          */
```

Viewed from the outside, the CautiousServer looks very much like the SimpleServer. It unconditionally starts a transaction and finishes it within the same invocation. It invokes another server, which becomes part of the same transaction. The new aspect lies in the use of the Save_Work call. This call goes to the transaction manager but could just as well be interpreted as an invocation of a special server that maintains savepoints. Since the call is issued in a TRPC environment, it automatically extends to all resource managers that are part of the transaction. Thus, when CautiousServer calls Save_Work, not only is the savepoint logic invoked for this server, but the transaction manager also contacts HelpMe (described in Chapter 6) to participate in the savepoint. There is a corollary: the invocation of Rollback_Work to a previous savepoint by CautiousServer results in HelpMe being urged to roll back to that savepoint, too.[17] Again, this happens automatically as part of the TRPC mechanism. The function prototypes used in the previous example are declared as follows:

---

[17] Note that HelpMe can neither be forced to take a savepoint nor to roll back to one. However, if its invocation by CautiousServer is to make sense, then it is reasonable to assume that either it has nothing to save (maybe it is read-only), or it does support savepoints properly.

```
savepoint    Save_Work(Boolean persistent, context); /* take a savepoint with specified context.      */
                                                      /* indicate if it has to be persistent.           */
savepoint    Rollback_Work(savepoint);               /* return to the specified savepoint               */
                                                      /* returns the savepoint number actually reached   */
                                                      /* might be prior to the one requested             */
context      Read_Context(savepoint);                /* context from savepoint                          */
TRID         Chain_Work(Boolean persistent, context); /* commit the ongoing transaction and pass        */
                                                      /* its context to a new transaction. this          */
                                                      /* is only applicable to top-level transactions    */
```

There is a line in the code of the CautiousServer urging you to watch the space after the invocation of server HelpMe. What could be so interesting about this TRPC to warrant three exclamation marks? It is a potential complication that illustrates the surprising side effects that result when global state transitions in a transaction are applied to resource managers that are part of an invocation hierarchy. To explain this, we must investigate a little more how Save_Work calls are handled inside a transaction.

Consider such a Save_Work call, issued by some resource manager working on behalf of a transaction. As explained, the transaction manager makes sure that *all* resource managers currently associated with that transaction get notified about the savepoint request. If they want to save any state information for their resource, they can do so.

The notification mechanism is explained in detail in Section 6.3; for the moment, a simple sketch will do. Each module implementing a resource manager, such as the CautiousServer or HelpMe, has a number of extra entry points (named *callback entry points*) in addition to the designated service entry point—the only one we have considered so far. One of these entry points is called rm_Savepoint, and the convention says that the resource manager has to be called whenever a savepoint is generated for a transaction it participates in. Likewise, there is another entry point by the name of rm_Rollback_Savepoint, at which the resource manager has to be called back to perform the requested rollback operation as far as its own resources are concerned. Resource managers that do not maintain any state for the transaction obviously need not be called in either case, because there is nothing to be saved or rolled back to.

The point is the following: If we assume that any resource manager can call Save_Work and Rollback_Work, then *all* other resource managers participating in the transaction—up to the application—will get notified, provided they have the appropriate entry points. If resource manager R requests a savepoint, then both the resource manager that invoked R and those that got invoked by R will transparently be invoked at their rm_Savepoint entry points by the transaction manager.

To appreciate the consequences, return to the example of the CautiousServer and assume that HelpMe also invokes the savepoint mechanism. This means that at some point, while being invoked by CautiousServer, it can decide to call Rollback_Work. Now, what happens at the point that you were asked to watch?

While HelpMe was running, the CautiousServer—upon its invocation of Rollback_Work—was implicitly "called back" to do its part of the rollback activity. That piece of code looks like this:

```
Boolean      rm_Rollback_Savepoint(savepoint BackTo);
      trusted_data = Read_Context(BackTo);      /* read savepoint data           */
      reset local variables from                /* assume there is no problem     */
      what has been stored in trusted_data;     /* resetting the local state      */

      return(TRUE);                             /* have reset my resources        */
```

The net effect of all this is that HelpMe returns to a different state of CautiousServer from what it was called from. Although HelpMe returns "normally," it has caused side effects that are not part of its service interface. So the caller must be informed that yes, HelpMe has done its thing, but, no, it did not do so without complications along the way. Thus, if CompCode informs the caller about that, it can decide what to do, knowing that its own local variables have changed since it issued the call.

It is impossible to come up with any general prescriptions for that case, because the effects and their interaction totally depend on what the caller does during rollback and how that affects the validity of the outstanding service call. The situation is particularly delicate for callers who themselves neither do call savepoints nor have the capability to roll back, but must anticipate some of their resource managers to roll back to them. To avoid all these complications, we make the following convention: Only application programs, that is, programs running at the root of the invocation hierarchy, are allowed to invoke savepoints and roll back to a savepoint. Of course, all resource managers maintaining state must be able to act on both types of requests. Abort can still be invoked by any resource manager.

The Chain_Work call supports chained transactions, as described in Chapter 4. Given the logic of transactional remote procedure calls, it affects all resource managers that are involved in the same transaction as the one calling Chain_Work. All of them are asked to commit the current transaction and then find themselves in a new one (the new TRID is returned by the call). Of course, control returns to the resource manager that issued the call.

We can learn much about the way transactional RPC works by considering carefully the effects of Chain_Work. Assume a resource manager that looks similar to the CautiousServer but uses chained transactions instead of savepoints; call it ChainedServer (writing the code skeleton for it is left as Exercise 5.6). Not counting the system resource managers, Chained-Server employs one other resource manager, HelpMe. At some point, ChainedServer calls Chain_Work. The transaction manager goes through the two-phase commit protocol, which involves asking HelpMe for a vote on that transaction. Except for that, HelpMe does no work at this time for ChainedServer. After commit is complete, the transaction manager creates a new TRID to replace the old one and registers all resource managers that participated in the previous transaction to be part of the new one. It then returns to the caller, and Chained-Server continues processing right after the Chain_Work call. And what does all that mean for HelpMe? Unless it gets invoked again by ChainedServer, HelpMe will not do anything with respect to the new transaction. If it gets invoked, it will do its work, essentially unaware of the change of TRIDs; that is, it does what it would have done, even without an intermediate change of transactions. Note, however, that even if ChainedServer does not invoke HelpMe at all during the new transaction, HelpMe is still part of ChainedServer in the sense that it will be asked to vote again when it is time to commit the new transaction.

5.5.3 Attaching Resource Managers to Transactions:
The Sophisticated Case

The invocation scenarios in Subsection 5.5.2 are all simple in the sense that the resource managers did not actually care which transaction they were running in. They either assumed they were invoked from within an ongoing transaction, or they asked the transaction manager to create one. Once there was a transaction around them, however, they stuck to it until commit or abort. Transaction-oriented applications (as opposed to general resource managers) are characterized by that style of transaction usage.

For sophisticated resource managers, these interfaces are not sufficient. They need to know that they work for many transactions concurrently and, therefore, upon each invocation may have to check which of the ongoing transactions has issued the call in order to pick up the right context. Moreover, a sophisticated resource manager SRM, when working on a transaction $T1$, might have a reason to suspend that activity temporarily and pick up another transaction, $T2$, instead. This has to be understood by the TP monitor, because from then on the resource managers involved in $T2$ are affected by what SRM does, not by the ones participating in $T1$. If SRM returns control to a caller, it has to be to the caller that invoked SRM from within $T2$, and not the one that called from $T1$. The TRPC mechanism must therefore be able to handle dynamic reassignments of processes and transactions.

The following chapters present a number of examples for sophisticated resource managers; here, a very simple version of this species is described. It is an example of motivating the interfaces to the TP monitor required to support that type of work. The application invokes another server, which has good reasons not to run under the client's TRID, but under its own. The basic scenario is shown in Figure 5.14.

A transaction program invokes a public quotation server, which tries to find the complete reference for a quotation or all quotations on a certain subject—an electronic version of J. Bartlett's invaluable book.[18] This server has a certain attitude about its business: once it has done its lookup, it wants to charge the client for the service, regardless of the outcome of the client's transaction. However, according to the conventions of the resource manager interface, the server runs from the moment of its inception under the client's transaction identifier. Firing off a nested subtransaction does not solve the problem, because the subtransaction does not reach final commit if the client's transaction does not. Chaining, which would commit the client's preliminary (and presumably inconsistent) state, is also not an option. The server therefore has to create an independent top-level transaction, which cannot be done while running under another TRID. The transaction manager interfaces for that are declared as follows:

```
TRID     Leave_Transaction(void);              /* tell the transaction manager that process      */
                                               /* is not working on current transaction (for     */
                                               /* the moment). returns current TRID               */
Boolean  Resume_Transaction(TRID desired);     /* tells transaction manager that the process     */
                                               /* wants to resume working on a transaction        */
                                               /* that it left earlier.                           */
```

---

[18] To prevent misunderstandings with our technical audience, the reference here is to John Bartlett's *Familiar Quotations*. Readers who were thinking of Joel Bartlett were not completely off; refer back to Chapter 3 to see what he has to do with this topic.

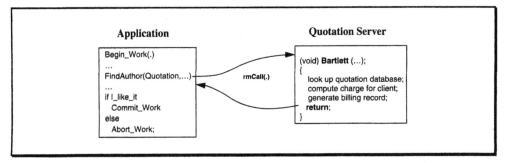

Figure 5.14: Using the interfaces for sophisticated resource managers. The figure shows an example of a server that is invoked as part of a transaction but decides to do something independent of the outcome of that transaction.

The use of these primitives is straightforward, as is shown by the following code skeleton. Note that although Bartlett works on behalf of the application that issued the call under ClientTRID, the intermediate change of TRIDs goes unnoticed by the application.[19] From its perspective, the server behaves exactly as though it had run entirely under the client's TRID. At no point will the application be associated with the new TRID; the pair (LeaveTRID, Begin_Work) has a completely different effect on the TRPC environment from that of the Chain_Work of the previous subsection.

```
Boolean     Bartlett(rmParams *InParams, rmParams *OutResults)
/* example program demonstrating the dynamic creation of a "nested" top-level transaction    */
{    .....                                      /*                                            */
    TRID    ClientTRID;                         /* declare the interface parameters           */
    TRID    MyownTRID;                          /*                                            */
    .....                                       /*                                            */

    Client_TRID = Leave_Transaction();          /* leave transaction the client runs in       */
    MyownTRID = Begin_Work(...);                /* begin independent top-level trans.         */
                                                /* provide the service requested              */

    do database lookup                          /*                                            */
    prepare reference list                      /*                                            */
    write billing record to database            /* make sure the client will be charged       */
    Commit_Work(FALSE,NULL);                    /* commit billing transaction                 */
    Resume_Transaction(ClientTRID);             /* error handling is omitted; the point       */
                                                /* is that server always commits              */
    return;                                     /* return from server                         */
}                                               /*                                            */
```

This is a very simple version of switching TRIDs. The simplicity stems from the fact that the server just wants to get its own (billing) transaction committed, no matter what. Its call to Resume_Transaction is required only to tell the TP monitor where to return. If the resume fails (which might happen because the application has meanwhile aborted), there is no

---

[19] The client's controlling department may someday find out that the server is more independent-minded about the whole ACID business than the application had thought it would be: If bills for service that do not correspond to any committed local transactions keep coming in, this is an indication of something strange going on.

effect on the server; it will return to the TRPC stub without a TRID, which means the TRPC will not return to anywhere. From the server's perspective, this is fine.

If the client's transaction is still there, the return succeeds. When it comes to commit, the server behaves exactly like the IgnorantServer[20] of the previous subsection. It does not vote on the transaction, but the transaction manager takes its return as a "no objection" with respect to the commit of the client's transaction.

Exercise 7 considers other ways to achieve the effect required by the Bartlett server with a mechanism less powerful than Leave/Resume.

5.5.4 Using Persistent Savepoints

This subsection is a short treatment of the use of *durable context,* that is, context that is reestablished after a crash. As mentioned in Chapter 4, the simplest way to achieve this effect is for the application to write whatever context it needs into the database and, at restart or on any subsequent invocation, read that tuple from the database and continue accordingly. However, since that solution uses no support from the transaction system, it is of little pedagogical value. Instead, the use of the persistent savepoint is illustrated. Although this concept is not yet available in any commercial TP monitor, it is quite easy to realize, based on the machinery that has to be in place for a distributed transaction system. Let us for the moment ignore the question of how the programming language would cooperate and just look at the effect it has on the implementation of the ComputeInterest example from Chapter 4. Here is the code:

```
#define stepsize 1000;                         /*                                        */
#include <string.h>;                           /*                                        */
#define max_account_no 999999;                 /*                                        */
ComputeInterest (interest_rate)                /*                                        */
    {   long account_no,last_account_done, batch_date; /*                                */
        double account_total, interest_rate;   /*                                        */
        int logsize;                           /* same declares as in Section 4.11.2     */
        savepoint    HereWeAre;                /* number of savepoint taken              */
        context  FinishedAccount;              /* stored with the savepoint              */
        last_account_done = 0;                 /* initialize the indicator of what       */
                                               /* has been completed so far              */
        store last_account_done in FinishedAccount    /* prepare savepoint context       */
        Begin_Work(FinishedAccount, TRUE);     /* begin work with pers. savepoint        */
        while (last_account_done < max_account_no)  /* loop over all accounts            */
            { EXEC SQL UPDATE accounts         /*                                        */
                    SET account_total = account_total * (1+ :interest_rate) /* */
                    WHERE account_no BETWEEN    /*                                        */
                        :last_account_done + 1 AND :last_account_done + :stepsize; /*     */
                last_account_done = last_account_done + stepsize;   /* next interval      */
                store last_account_done in FinishedAccount          /* prep. savept. context */
                HereWeAre = Save_Work(FinishedAccount, TRUE); /* take pers. savepoint      */
            };                                 /* end of last savepoint interval         */
        Commit_Work( );                        /* commit whole transaction               */
    };                                         /*                                        */
```

---

[20] One could devise a scheme that allows the client transaction to commit even if the server node is down at that moment; see Chapters 7 and 8 for details.

The problem description from Chapter 4 need not be repeated; let us just discuss the merits of persistent savepoints in writing the ComputeInterest application. The immediate impression is that the code is not only shorter than the solution presented in Chapter 4, but simpler. This is due to the fact that everything related to the maintenance of persistent context is now taken care of by the Save_Work function, whereas the mini-batch solution had to do the maintenance all by itself, using the batchcontext relation.

If something seems to be missing in the program—for instance, the part related to restart after a crash—consider carefully what it means to invoke a persistent savepoint and to be rolled back to it. A normal, volatile savepoint is more familiar, because it is clear how to return to a savepoint and where control in the program is after such a rollback. During normal operation, a savepoint is reestablished by calling Rollback_Work, and the instruction to be executed is the one after that call.

Persistent savepoints can be used in the same way, but, in contrast to volatile savepoints, they are also effective at restart. Each resource manager participating in the transaction with the persistent savepoint is brought up in the state as of the most recent persistent savepoint. For that to work, the run-time system of the programming language has to be a resource manager, too; consequently, it also recovers its state to the most recent persistent savepoint. Its state includes the local variables, the call stack, and the program counter, the heap, the I/O streams, and so forth. The program affected will then be restarted at the instruction following the most recent Save_Work.

From there, the program continues execution as though nothing had happened. It has no way to tell that there was crash and a restart, unless it keeps the timer in the savepoint context and finds out that the last savepoint interval took surprisingly long to complete.

Also note that we are now using the call interface to the transaction manager for Begin_Work, and so on, rather than the SQL API used in the mini-batch program. The reason is that now the ComputeInterest routine is something like a "real" resource manager. It maintains its own persistent state, even though it is just the small portion of processing context. Therefore, the transactional verbs have to apply to all components along the way, and not just to the SQL database system, as would be the case with the SQL API.

5.6 Terminological Wrap-Up

This chapter introduced the concepts behind TP monitors and the terminology that goes with them. The following recapitulates the most important terms along a complete thread of control through the TP monitor for one user-system interaction.

A user issues a *service request* at a terminal. This can be done in many different ways; examples include entering a command, pressing a function key, inserting the bank card, lifting the nozzle of a gas pump, and so on. The service request asks the system to deliver a certain predefined service on behalf of that user. The *presentation services* translate the terminal inputs into a message with a standard format according to a *forms definition* stored in the *repository*. This message is given to the TP monitor. The header of the message contains an identifier of the service requested, which is called *transaction program name* (TPN) or *transaction code*. Each TPN is associated with an *application program*. The TP monitor maintains a *server class* for that application program and dispatches the request to a *server process* of that server class. Unless the service request is part of an ongoing transaction, the program implementing the service calls BEGIN_WORK, which is a *transactional remote procedure call* (TRPC) to the *transaction manager*. The transaction manager assigns a globally unique *transaction identifier* (TRID), which tags all TRPCs on behalf of that transaction. The transaction program can contain an arbitrary number of calls to *resource managers* in the TP system; each call is handled as a transactional remote procedure call.

The transaction invoked can be *direct*, in which case the request goes from the terminal to the server without any perceptible stops in between. If further messages are exchanged with the user at the terminal during that transaction, it is called *conversational*. The other style of processing uses *queued transactions*. An incoming request is not dispatched immediately, but is stored on a *durable queue* in front of the corresponding server class. The TP monitor takes service requests off this queue according to a *scheduling* policy that is determined by the user's optimization criteria. When a request has been scheduled for execution, the TP monitor checks the *access control list* of the server class against the user's *security profile* in the repository to decide whether the request can be serviced. If so, it transfers control to the server that has been selected to handle the request. This instantiation of the transaction program with all the service calls it issues is then executed as one *transaction*.

It is important to understand that servers are not normally created and allocated upon an incoming request. Rather, they are preallocated, and the TP monitor multiplexes the client requests among the set of available servers. Deciding to shut down an existing server or to fire up a new one is a matter of *load balancing* and is therefore a rare event.

5.7 Historical Notes

As mentioned in the introduction to this chapter, the scientific community has so far shown little interest in the topic of TP monitors. Consequently, there is little literature to draw upon beyond reference manuals of existing systems. The evolution of TP monitors can be understood only by reading systems manuals and talking to people who have used or implemented such systems.

TP monitors started out as terminal drivers and were used to handle card readers, key punches, and everything that came after that. As a result, the acronym originally stood for *tele-processing* monitors. But shortly thereafter, TP monitors were developed into specialized operating systems, and this is what they still are. Because general-purpose operating systems had been designed for batch applications and for long, interactive time-sharing sessions, their unit of resource allocation was (and in most cases still is) a huge and expensive, but flexible, process. This was no appropriate platform for building systems that had to service a large[21] number of terminals. One alternative was to build a different operating system that was tailored toward the requirements of online applications. This is how ACP (the airline control program) came about. ACP has its own scheduling, message handling, file system, and so forth, and very low pathlength for the types of messages it has been designed for. Although it is more than 25 years old, the system is still around and is being used under the name of TPF (transaction processing facility).

The other option, taken by almost everybody else, was to build some kind of counter-operating system that runs on top of the (inadequate) basic operating system and pretends to be a normal application process. Within that, however, it does everything to bypass the underlying operating system; it does its own message handling and scheduling, and sometimes has its own file system. IBM's CICS (customer information control system) is one of the ear-

---

[21] In the 1960s, "large" meant something between 10^2 and 10^3; currently, a large system has some 10^5 terminals.

liest and most successful examples of this type of TP monitor. By the time CICS came along, the acronym TP meant *transaction processing* monitor, as it does today. Some vendors prefer to call these programs DC (data communication) systems.

A large number of such TP monitors have been built since the late 1960s by different vendors, for different operating system platforms, and for different purposes. Some have been built to complement a specific database system (Com-Plete, IMS/DC, UTM), while others were designed primarily to integrate different database systems (CICS, Shadow). Meanwhile, some of these systems do also support the execution of distributed transactions. The basic approach, however, is the same for all of them: use the operating system as an execution environment, and "do your own thing."

There are, however, two exceptions: DEC ACMS and Tandem Pathway. They differ from other TP monitors in two major aspects. One is a process structure that reflects the client-server paradigm of distributed processing (see Figure 5.7d). Rather than having an asymmetric configuration, where a master (TP) process invokes slave (application) tasks, there is a symmetric relation of client-server invocations that are transaction protected. The other difference is the role of the operating system, which is not bypassed to the degree it is in "classical" TP monitors. Here, the operating system provides the required RPC mechanisms, provides server classes (rather than individual processes), and even understands what a transaction is. TMF in Guardian and DECdtm in VMS are the two commercially available transaction managers at the operating system level.

Still, during the past 25 years little has happened in the area of operating systems to bridge the gap between the operating system view of things and the transactional perspective. When VMS was announced, some people claimed its processes were cheap enough to make TP monitors obsolete. Apart from its factual incorrectness, that statement reflects a misconception of what a TP monitor has to do. Most of the functions introduced in this chapter are not part of standard operating systems such as VMS.

Currently, there are only a few operating systems that have been explicitly designed for transaction processing. The standard example is Tandem's Guardian, which provides transaction support at the OS level. DEC has recently (1990) modified VMS with a component called DECdtm, which provides transaction commitment and recovery functions and is an attempt to make the operating system more transaction oriented. IBM is augmenting its MVS operating system with transactional subsystem calls. Given the fact that different implementations of UNIX[22] are being extended to support transaction processing [Transarc-Encina 1991; USL-Tuxedo 1991], there seems to be a clear trend toward integrating transaction services into general-purpose operating systems. Whether this is done by adding components on top of the OS or by actually modifying the OS itself is a pragmatic rather than a strategic issue.

Remote procedure calls have been drawing increasing attention since the early 1980s. Currently, they are mostly used in workstation environments. Birrell and Nelson's seminal paper [1984] on this topic describes all the basic implementation issues. Transactional RPCs of the type described in this book are not yet state-of-the-art, but there are clear indications that transaction systems will go as we have described them. Current product developments and standard proposals support this view. There is, however, heated debate in many groups and circles over the question of whether transactional RPC is sufficient to do what

---

[22] DECdtm, which currently is a component of VMS only, is expected to be available for Ultrix in the near future.

transaction systems have to do. Many people believe that in addition to it (or instead of it), context-sensitive peer-to-peer communication is needed, especially in cases where large amounts of data have to be exchanged. The next chapter picks up this issue and puts it into a more technical perspective. But again, judging from new implementations of transaction processing systems, the transactional remote procedure call is one of the key features for structuring such systems. A good example can be found in Spector [1991].

Exercises

1. [5.2, 20] Explain how the debit/credit transaction would be executed in each of the different types of transaction systems introduced in this chapter: process per terminal, one process, multiple processes for all terminals, client-server.

2. [5.2, 20] Consider a transaction processing system with 2,000 terminals. Each terminal can choose freely among 150 services. Each service accesses 5 databases (no 2 services access any common databases); each database on the average is partitioned across 10 files. The TP system uses the one-process-per-terminal approach. It runs on a machine with 20 mips. When the system comes up (during restart after a crash, for example), all processes must be started, each process must open its connection to "its" terminal, and all the applications running in the process must open all the files for all databases. Use the following cost measures for estimating the time required for startup: Creating a process costs 20,000 instructions; the time get a terminal reattached is 300 ms; establishing one open control block costs 2,000 instructions (ignoring the reads from the catalog). Assume everything happens sequentially.

3. [5.3, 25] A user gets a menu on its terminal with entries like "Arrivals," "Departures," "Fare Quotation," and so on—this is an airport application. Assume the user presses the function key assigned to "Arrivals," which requests all arrivals during the last hour to be displayed on the screen. Describe the flow of the service request message through the TP monitor, to the application program, and back to the terminal. Take into account that at a busy airport, more planes arrive during one hour than lines fit on a screen. So the user might want to scroll forward and backward through the information. How would you handle this? Consider the various transaction types.

4. [5.2, 5.3, 10] Consider a resource manager like an SQL database that can be called by other resource managers during their execution. Which transaction types are appropriate for such a resource manager that must accept dynamic calls?

5. [5.4, 25] Assume an application program that calls Begin_Work and then calls other resource managers via rmCall, some of which might in turn call other resource managers still, and so on. One of the resource managers downstream calls Rollback_Work. Describe exactly what happens with respect to the sequence of resource manager invocations, and which call returns where with which parameters. What can and what must the resource managers do along the way? *Hint: Draw a simple call tree, show which application (resource manager) called who. Let the tree have three levels. Then look at the resource manager that was invoked last. Note that only this one can be working on behalf of the transaction, because we are assuming sequential execution inside a transaction. Now consider what happens if this resource manager calls* Rollback_Work. *Try to figure out how control threads its way back through the call stack.*

6. [5.5, 20] Rewrite the the program skeleton of the CautiousServer by using chained transactions instead of savepoints.

7. [5.5, 10] Explain what the potential danger of the Leave/Resume pair of transaction manager calls is. How could the effect required by the Bartlett server be achieved in a more secure manner?

Answers

1. The following answer only sketches the aspects to be considered in a "process per terminal" scenario. According to the definition of this scenario, each process contains the entire code for the application and all services it requires—in this case, the code of the SQL database system runs in each process, among others.

   Consider an arbitrary terminal. Its process waits synchronously for an input from the terminal—it has nobody else to service. Once the read from the terminal has completed, the process may or may not make the request recoverable by storing it in the database or in some kind of durable context facility provided by the system. The process then starts executing the debit/credit code that it shares with all other processes. The invocations of the SQL server are process-internal calls, that is, branches within the same address space, or controlled branches to the SQL address space, depending on the architecture of the operating system. Again, execution is synchronous with respect to the process servicing the terminal. Whenever I/O has to be done in a code portion running under that process, it is deactivated and waits for completion. The same holds for page faults. After the debit/credit processing has been completed, the result is returned by the process, which issues a synchronous write to the terminal.

   This does not sound special at all. In fact, it could be the description of the simple single-user case. But that is the point. Because data and control information need to be shared, all the processes that service the terminals in a conventional synchronous fashion as far as the code is concerned need to share their global data structures: among others, the database buffer, the log buffer, the lock tables, and so on. For consistency, they have to synchronize themselves on these data structures to prevent illegal updates. Starting in Chapter 6, it will be demonstrated that a synchronization like that among thousands of processes becomes intolerably expensive.

2. Creating a process is 1 ms, so there are 2,000 ms for that. Getting all the terminals back costs 2,000 · 300 ms = 600,000 ms. Opening the files costs 2,000 · 150 · 5 · 10 · 0.1 ms = 1,500,000 ms. Ignoring the 1 ms for the process creation, this adds up to 2,100 seconds = 35 minutes.

3. The screen is handled by the presentation server. This server interprets the function key with its associated parameters and produces the proper TRPC to the "Arrival" server; it probably produces an implicit BEGIN_WORK. The TRPC is handled by the TP monitor; it checks authorization and then routes the call to a server process that runs the "Arrival" code. The server code determines the necessary database call(s)—let us assume only one is required. The call to the database server is yet another TRPC that goes through the TP monitor. If it was a set-oriented SQL Select, it returns all the arrival tuples that qualify for the query issued by the application. The application may now format the response in the style that the presentation server expects and pass it as a result when returning from the TRPC—again, via the TP monitor. The presentation server then will put the result—all arrivals asked for, maybe more than a screen—into a local context store (volatile) and call COMMIT_WORK in order not to hold on to the data for too long. Then it presents the user with the first page of result tuples; all the scrolling required is implemented in the presentation server.

4. Distributed transactions, nested transactions, open nested transactions, multi-level transactions.

5. Here we are discussing one of the key differences between a normal (remote) procedure call and a transactional remote procedure call. First assume a conventional call. In this case, the resource manager that decides request processing cannot be completed returns to its caller with a bad return

code identifying the problem. The caller resumes execution at the instruction after the call, checks the return code, and then takes appropriate action. This action most likely will consist of returning to its caller in turn, informing it about the problem caused by one of the lower-level functions. In that manner, control will return in inverse order of the call sequence by popping one entry after the other off the call stack. When control has arrived at the top level, this routine (let us assume it is the application program) will produce an error message to the user and then terminate.

In a transactional environment, things are more complicated (internally). The resource manager that runs into problems does two things: First, it calls the transaction manager at its Rollback_Work entry. After control returns from there, it returns to its caller with the bad return code just described. Now the point is that the transaction manager, when asked to roll back the transaction, invokes all participating resource managers at their rollback entries, asking them to undo the work they have done on behalf of the failing transaction. Note that all resource managers are called via TRPC by the transaction manager (provided they have specified a rollback entry), independent of their position in the call stack. So from the perspective of the resource manager that called Rollback_Work, the transaction manager at one fell swoop calls its (the resource manager's) caller, its caller's caller, and so forth, up to the top level—before control returns to the resource manager at the instruction after the Rollback_Work statement. As a matter of fact, even the resource manager itself is called by the transaction manager as a consequence of its Rollback_Work call, but at a different entry. So when control finally returns via the call stack, it will lead into resource managers that already know about the abort and have acted upon it. The call return path in that case serves for little more than passing return codes and deallocating control blocks.

A full discussion of this issue can be found in Sections 6.2 and 6.3 of Chapter 6.

7. The danger is that a program calls Leave for a transaction without ever resuming the transaction. This could be prevented by combining the functions of Leave and Begin, such that leaving a transaction implicitly starts a new one. In the same vein, one can combine the functions of Commit/Abort with Resume, which means that terminating the intermediate transaction with whatever result automatically reinstantiates the old transaction.

6

Transaction Processing Monitors

6.1 Introduction

Beginning with this chapter, and continuing up to Chapter 12, we look at the topics presented in Chapter 5, but through a magnifying lens. This close-up will reveal which concepts, algorithms, and techniques are used to provide the application with a transaction-oriented execution environment. The component structure and the sample implementations are based on the functions of the basic operating system introduced in Chapter 2; that is, on processes, address spaces, messages, and sessions. The description of how it works is focused on the core mechanisms for implementing simple ACID transactions and phoenix transactions. Due to the limited space, the implementation of the large number of other transaction types (see Chapter 4) cannot be covered.

Chapter 5 has already mentioned the variety of meanings attributed to the term TP monitor. Having defined the role of a TP monitor in a transaction-oriented system by enumerating the services it provides, we will be equally careful in specifying the interfaces used for implementing a TP monitor. A good way to structure interfaces is by layers of abstraction. Let us therefore start by considering those layers in a transaction processing system.

Table 6.1 organizes the terms in the way they are used throughout this book. It contains three central layers. First, there is the *basic operating system* (BOS), which is assumed to know little or nothing about transactions. Next comes the *transaction processing operating system* (TPOS), the main task of which is to render the objects and services of the BOS in a transactional style. For example, the basic OS provides processes; in order to exercise transaction-oriented (commitment) control, each process executing code on behalf of an application must be bound to the transaction that surrounds this execution. The basic OS also provides messages: when transaction programs send protected output messages, they must not be delivered until the transaction has committed. Therefore, messages must be bound to transactions, too. The same argument applies to interprocess communication, units of durable storage, and—in some cases—physical devices.

Finally, there are transaction oriented services, which make the TPOS manageable and usable for developing transaction-oriented applications. Table 6.1 also relates the services to the types of objects and functions they provide. For completeness, the table includes the hardware underneath and the application on top of the transaction processing services.

Table 6.1: Layering of services in a transaction processing system.   The description of functions and services throughout this book assumes five interface layers. The basic operating system uses the hardware directly. Its interfaces are used by the transaction processing operating system to provide a transactional programming environment. Sophisticated servers like databases, configuration management, window management, and so forth, use both the basic operating system and the transaction processing operating system to create a transaction-oriented programming environment. The application typically uses the transaction processing services and the interfaces to the transaction processing operating system, depending on the application's sophistication.

This is what a typical TP monitor will put atop a conventional operating system.

	Application		
Transaction Processing Services (TRAPS)	Operator Interface Configuration Load Control Programming Environment	Databases (SQL) Disaster Recovery Resource Managers Flow Control	Distributed Name Binding Server Invocation Protected User Interface
Transaction Processing Operating System (TPOS)	TRIDS Server Class Request Scheduling Resource Manager i/f. Authentication	Transaction Manager Log, Context Durable Queue Transactional File Archive	Transactional RPC Transactional Session RPC
Basic Operating System (BOS)	Process / Thread Address Space Scheduling IPC Local Naming Protection	Repository File System Directory Extents Blocks File Security	IPC Simple Sessions (Open/Close, Write/Read) Naming Authentication
Hardware	Processors	Memory	Wires, Fibers, Switches

A Transaction Processing System

The following chapters are largely concerned with the middle layer of Table 6.1, the transaction processing operating system (TPOS), and with showing how its main functions are implemented. Discussion of functions that are attributed to other layers is restricted to the degree that the functions contribute to the main purpose of the TPOS. Chapters 13–15 then use the mechanisms of the TPOS to outline the implementation of a transaction-oriented file system. The file system has the features needed as a platform for SQL. It serves as an example for a resource manager in the sense described in Chapter 5. A precise definition of the term *resource manager* is given in Section 6.2.

Bear in mind that the layering in Table 6.1 does *not* reflect a strict implementation hierarchy. Rather, it describes a separation of concerns among different system components. It is therefore perfectly reasonable to assume that the TPOS implements some of its data structures (repositories, queues) using SQL, although SQL is shown to sit on top of the TPOS. This situation is analogous to the assumption made in Chapter 3, Section 3.7, where the operating system uses SQL to keep track of its ticket numbers.

Table 6.1 tries to relate the strongly used and weakly defined term TP monitor to the service categories used in this book, by way of the services a typical TP monitor provides (according to Chapter 5). Given the overview of terms in Table 6.1, we use TPOS and TP monitor interchangeably, whenever there is no risk of confusion.

To describe the implementation of a complete TP monitor in full detail is far beyond the scope of this book. Rather, we focus on the key services provided by a TP monitor, which encircle the transactional remote procedure call (TRPC), as was sketched in Chapter 5. TRPCs are used to invoke services from resource managers under transaction protection.

The organization of this chapter follows generally the flow of a TRPC. Section 6.2 gives a detailed description of what a transactional RPC looks like and the consequences of its use on the structure of resource managers. In particular, it discusses the interfaces of a resource manager, both in its role as a server to applications and other resource managers, and as a client invoking services via TRPC. The implementation of transactional RPCs is then described in Section 6.3. It is the longest section in this chapter and covers all related aspects, such as server classes, name binding, and transaction management.

Queue management is the topic of Section 6.4. All the miscellaneous topics that have not been given their own sections, such as load balancing, authentication and authorization, and restart processing, are briefly discussed in Section 6.5.

The discussion makes use of a number of concepts in operating systems and programming languages; we will not explain these. To avoid any confusion, here are the topics that the reader is assumed to be familiar with (for the reader unfamiliar with these topics, textbooks on operating systems are a particularly good source of information):

Linking and loading.   The TP monitor is responsible for creating processes and making sure the code for the resource manager requested can be executed in them. For this, it needs to link and load the resource manager's object modules together with the stub modules of the TPOS. There is no explanation in this chapter about how exactly this is done.

Library management.   The object modules of the resource managers and application programs are stored in libraries. These can be libraries maintained by the operating system, or the TP monitor can keep it all in its own repository. There are no specific assumptions made here.

In addition to these basic techniques, we will also gloss over some TP-specific items, most notably the administrative interface. These important issues are not addressed in this book.

6.2 Transactional Remote Procedure Calls

Having introduced the notion of remote procedure call (RPC) in Chapter 5, we now proceed to explain what exactly a *transactional* remote procedure call (TRPC) is. It is much more than just an RPC used within a transaction. To get into the right mind set, think of a TRPC being as different from a standard RPC as a subroutine call is from an ACID transaction. For an illustration, go back to Figure 5.9. There, the request coming in at the upper left-hand corner is a TRPC from some other node, aimed at the application represented in the center of the figure. The application begins to work and calls various system resource managers, the database, and so on. Each of these invocations is a TRPC of its own, handled in the way just described. The database, in turn, calls system resource managers, some of which have also been called by the application, again using TRPCs.

The distinguishing feature is that all resource managers, by having been called through a transactional remote procedure call, become part of the surrounding transaction. Remember that in a standard RPC environment, the RPC and the operating system have only to make sure that once a call has arrived at the local node, there is a process running the server's code. When the call returns, the server is free again, and that is all there is to it.

A TP monitor must manage a pool of server processes, and in addition, each TRPC has to be tagged with the identifier of the transaction within which the call was issued. In particular, TRPC messages going across the network have to carry the transaction identifier with them. When scheduling a process for a request, the TPOS must note that this process now works "for" that transaction. After the call returns, the process is detached from the transaction, but the response message has to be tagged with the transaction identifier.

If that were all that distinguished a TRPC from an RPC, it would not require a section to describe it; but the point is that TRPC is not just transaction control over one resource manager invocation. Rather, transaction control must be exercised over all resource manager interactions within one transaction. Keeping all resource managers together as part of the same transaction requires more than just appending a transaction identifier to each request. The TP monitor also needs to enforce certain conventions with respect to the behavior of the resource managers issuing and receiving TRPCs, and with respect to the way transactions are administered by the nodes constituting the transaction system. The following are required for the "web" of a transaction's calls to hang together:

Control of participants.   Someone must track which resource managers have been called during the execution of one transaction in order to manage commit and rollback. As part of the two-phase commit protocol, all resource managers participating in the transaction must, in the end, agree to successfully terminate that transaction; otherwise, it will be rolled back. That means somebody must go out and ask each resource manager involved whether it is okay to commit the work of the transaction. The component responsible is called the *transaction manager* (TM), which is explained in detail in Chapter 11. It is instructive to contemplate for a moment that a resource manager does not necessarily remember that it has been called at all. Assume a simple COBOL server that gets invoked as part of transaction *T*1, reads some tuple from a database, performs some computations, inserts a tuple, and returns. Each time the server is called, it starts in its initial state; that is, all the data for doing its work must be in the parameters passed. After the server is done, it forgets everything (frees its dynamic storage); thus, there is no point in asking the server later on whether transaction *T*1 should commit; it has no information about the transaction.

Preserving transaction-related information.   As Figure 5.9 shows, the same resource manager can be invoked more than once during the same transaction—by the same or by different clients. In the process environment that we assume, each invocation can, in principle, be handled by a different process (remember the concept of server classes outlined in Chapter 5). Since each RPC finally ends up in a process, at commit each process running the same resource manager code is asked individually about its commit decision. For some types of resource managers, this may be sufficient. Assume that, upon each invocation, 10 tuples were inserted into a database; the transaction will commit if each of the 10-tuple-insert requests was successful. In other situations, however, the resource manager can only vote on commit when all the information pertaining to that transaction is available in one place. If the different invocations left their traces in different servers, this will be hard to do. The TRPC mechanism, then, must provide a means to relate multiple invocations of the same resource manager to each other.[1]

Support of the transaction protocol.   The resource managers must stick to the rules imposed by the ACID paradigm. This must be supervised by the TRPC mechanism; in case of a violation, the transaction must abort.

The long and short of all this is that the concept of transactional remote procedure calls has two complementary aspects. One is the association of requests, messages, and processes with a transaction identifier. The other aspect is the coordination of resource managers in order to implement the transaction protection around RPCs. If this sounds recursive again, bear with us until Section 6.3, where the dynamic interaction among the TPOS components is explained in some detail.

All TRPC-related issues are handled by the TPOS, though not by the TP monitor alone. As the description progresses, it will turn out that the TP monitor acts as a kind of switchboard that receives requests and passes them on, without actually acting on most of them. However, the TP monitor makes sure that these are valid transactional RPCs and that they get routed to the proper components of the TPOS or the application. The explanation of the way TRPCs are handled is divided into two parts. First, we explain the interfaces through which transactional resource managers interact with their environment—the TPOS in particular. Second, the problem of preserving transaction-related information is discussed.

6.2.1 The Resource Manager Interface

A resource manager qualifies as such by exhibiting a special type of behavior. More specifically, a resource manager uses and provides a set of interfaces that, in turn, are used according to the protocols of transaction-oriented processing. Depending on how many of the interfaces a resource manager uses (and provides), it has more or less influence on the way a transaction gets executed in the system. This is discussed extensively in this chapter, as well as in Chapter 10. Figure 6.2 gives an overview of the types of interfaces a resource manager has to deal with.

On top of Figure 6.2, there is the rmCall interface, used for invoking the resource manager's services; the results are returned as parameters to this call.[2] The function prototype declare follows. One entry in the parameter list that has not been mentioned so far, BindId, is explained in detail in Section 6.2.4, but here is the idea: since there can be many processes executing the same resource manager code, it may be necessary in some cases to know exactly which one has serviced a request within a transaction. The parameter BindId is a

---

[1] This still may sound like a subroutine using static variables to keep data across subsequent activations. Remember, though, that the TRPC's "subroutines" can have multiple instantiations in different processes at different nodes.

[2] Of course, there are other ways of returning results, such as writing to the database tuples that the client can read. But again, this has nothing to do with the resource manager interface.

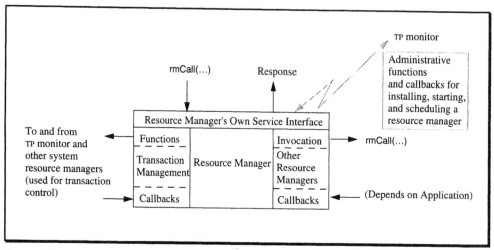

Figure 6.2: Overview of a resource manager's interfaces. The resource manager both uses interfaces from other system components and provides interfaces to other system components. There are three groups to be distinguished: the interface the resource manager exports, the interfaces it uses from other general resource managers and the system resource manager interfaces it has to call to support the transaction protocol.

handle for such an interaction between a client and a specific server that has to be used repeatedly.

```
typedef  char *          RMNAME;            /* long external name of resource manager            */
                                            /* can have structure like A.B.C if so desired       */
typedef  struct                             /* handle for identifying the specific instantiation */
    {                                       /* of a resource manager                             */
        NODEID          nodeid;             /* node where process is allocated                    */
        PID             pid;                /* process request is bound to                        */
        TIMESTAMP       birthdate;          /* time of server creation                            */
    } rmInstance;                           /* identifies a specific server                       */
typedef  struct                             /* resource manager parameters                        */
    {  Ulong      CB_length;                /* number of bytes in this control block              */
       char       CB_bytes [CB_length];     /* control block as byte string                       */
    }    rmParams;                          /*                                                    */
Boolean rmCall(RMNAME,                      /* invocation of resource mgr. named RMNAME           */
               BindId* BoundTo,             /* explained with the bind mechanism                  */
               rmParams * InParams,         /* params passed to the server                        */
               rmParams * OutResults);      /* results returned from the server                   */
```

This is about all there is to say about the service interface of a transactional resource manager. Whenever such an rmCall is issued from somewhere, it gets the TRPC treatment we have outlined. In particular, the TP monitor assures that the execution of the resource manager becomes part of the transaction in which the caller is running—provided there is an ongoing transaction. If there is none, then whatever has happened so far has no ACID properties.

Some of the interactions of a resource manager or an application program with the transaction manager, which are alluded to on the left-hand side of Figure 6.2, have already been discussed with the programming examples in Chapter 5. But as the figure indicates, a resource manager generally can not only *call* the transaction manager, it can also *be called upon* by the transaction manager. This feature, which is required for the implementation of general resource managers that keep their own durable state, is discussed in the next subsection.

6.2.2 What the Resource Manager Has to Do in Support of Transactions

The transactional remote procedure calls described up to this point cover the normal business of invoking the services of resource managers from application programs or other resource managers. It has also been pointed out that the verbs for structuring programs in a transactional fashion result in calls to system resource managers, most notably to the transaction manager. But sophisticated resource managers, especially those maintaining durable data, must also be able to respond to requests from the TPOS. For example, they must vote during two-phase commit, they must be able to recover their part of a transaction (either roll it back or redo it after a crash), they must be able to take a savepoint, and so forth. There are two ways to invoke the resource managers at these special service entries:

Single entry. The server has only one service entry point (message buffer) through which it receives all its service requests. So before acting on a request, it must determine what kind of request it is and then branch to the appropriate subroutine.

Service entry plus callback entries. Interfacing the resource managers to the transaction manager via a set of entry points is the approach taken in this book (and by X/Open DTP). As Figure 6.2 indicates, each resource manager has a service interface that defines what the resource manager does for a living. Furthermore, it declares a number of callback entries. In the resource manager's code portion these are entry points, which can be called when certain events happen. The principle is illustrated in Figure 6.3.

The function prototype declares are shown below. Note that the invocation of a resource manager by the transaction manager at such a callback entry is just another transactional remote procedure call.

```
Boolean rm_Prepare();                    /* invoked at phase 1 of commit. Returns vote.      */
Boolean rm_Rollback_Savepoint(Savepoint);  /* rollback to requested savepoint. number        */
                                         /* TRUE if ok, FALSE if needs further rollback       */
Boolean rm_Commit(Boolean);              /* invoked at phase 2 commit: param is decision      */
Boolean rm_Savepoint();                  /* invoked when the transaction takes a savepoint    */
                                         /* TRUE if ok, FALSE if this resource manager        */
                                         /* cannot establish the savepoint and must           */
                                         /* continue rollback                                 */
(void) rm_UNDO(&buffer);                 /* asks the resource mgr. to undo the effects        */
                                         /* described in the log record passed as a parameter */
(void) rm_Abort();                       /* invoked at end of abort phase,                    */
                                         /* after all undo steps have been performed          */
```

(void) **rm_REDO**(&buffer);	/* asks the resource mgr. to redo the effects */
	/* described in the log rec. passed as a param */
(void) **rm_Checkpoint**();	/* invoked by TM for taking a checkpoint. */
(void) **rm_restart**(LSN);	/* first callback from the transaction manager at */
	/* restart; passes the address of the resource */
	/* manager's recent checkpoint record. */

For example, the rm_Commit entry of a resource manager is called by the transaction manager when a transaction is in the prepared state and the two-phase commit protocol has made the decision to commit. The resource manager can then do whatever is required to commit its portion of the transaction, such as releasing locks or sending output messages. Details of what resource managers are expected to do at each of these entry points are explained in Chapters 10 and 11.

As mentioned, the number of callback entries provided by a resource manager depends on its level of sophistication. The types of servers discussed in the previous subsection need not provide any callback entries. They do not write log data, so they have nothing to undo or to redo. They also do not keep other context data in their own domain, which means their vote on commit is implicitly Yes when they return to the caller. This can be put in a simple rule of thumb: if the resource manager maintains any durable objects, it must be able to accept rollback and prepare/commit callbacks from the transaction manager. It must write log

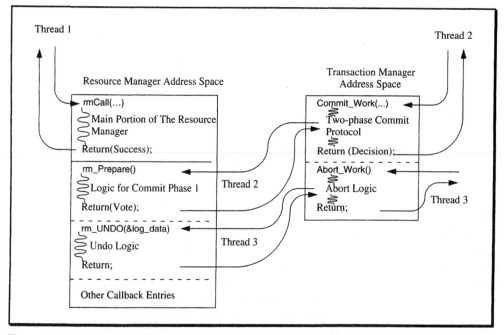

Figure 6.3: **The use of different entries into a resource manager by different threads of control.** A sophisticated resource manager, in addition to its service entries, provides callback entries to the transaction manager that allow the resource manager to participate in all phases of transaction handling, if required. This can result in multiple threads executing the resource manager's code at different entry points. The resource manager exports the callback entries to the transaction manager when it first checks in with the TP monitor.

records and, consequently, must be able to act on undo/redo callbacks. If it has all of its state maintained by other resource managers (e.g., SQL servers), then it becomes *their* problem to maintain the ACID properties of the state. There is a slight deviation from this rule in case of resource managers that do not maintain durable objects but do have to remember all invocations by the client within one transaction; for example, to check deferred integrity constraints. This is discussed in Subsection 6.2.4. The rm_Checkpoint callback is listed for completeness only; its meaning is described in Chapter 11.

The resource managers, on one hand, and the transaction manager, on the other, usually run in different address spaces, all of which may be different from the address space the TP monitor uses. All addressability issues with respect to resource managers are handled by the TP monitor. Most of the callbacks, however, are needed by the transaction manager; thus, there must be a way for the transaction manager to point to the right entry points without actually knowing the addresses. This issue is discussed in the next subsection.

There is one last call from the resource manager to the transaction manager that is needed for start-up, and especially for restart after a failure. This call, Identify, informs the transaction manager that the resource manager is in the process of opening for business and wants to do any recovery that might be necessary. The transaction manager responds by providing the resource manager with all the recovery data that might be relevant; to do that, it uses the rm_restart, rm_UNDO, and rm_REDO callbacks. Details are presented in Section 6.5. The point is that after the Identify call returns, the resource manager has caught up with the most recent transaction-consistent state and from now on can accept service requests. The function prototype declaration looks as follows:

```
/* Introduces the resource manager to the transaction manager. Asks the transaction manager    */
/* to initiate restart recovery for the resource manager if necessary.                         */
Boolean Identify(RMID);
```

The resource manager just passes its RMID and gets a boolean back; it is TRUE if the transaction manager has gone successfully through the restart logic for that resource manager. If FALSE is returned, something serious went wrong, and the resource manager cannot be declared up.

Since Identify is needed only to start up those resource managers that have to recover durable state (sophisticated resource managers), simple resource managers and application programs do not have to call Identify at all.

The right-hand side of Figure 6.2 shows the interaction between the resource manager and servers other than the system resource managers. These could be other low-level resource managers, such as the log manager or the context manager, or any other server in the system. With each of them, the resource manager could agree on additional callback entries. The invocations of these "other" resource managers need no further explanation; they are simply TRPCs.

6.2.3 Interfaces between Resource Managers and the TP Monitor

At this point, it is necessary to remember that TRPCs never go directly from the client to the server; rather, they are forwarded by the TRPC stub, which is linked to each resource manager's address space (see Figure 5.11). From a logical perspective, then, clients, servers, and system components are invoking their respective interfaces, but the TRPC stub intercepts the requests and thus enables the TP monitor to act upon them as necessary. This is to say, the

TP monitor plays a crucial role in resource manager *invocation*. The TP monitor does, how-ever, have some other roles: it is the component responsible for starting up the transaction system (bringing up the TPOS), for closing it down again, and for administering all the trans-action-related resources. Startup and shutdown are described in some detail in Section 6.5; here we only introduce the TRPCs needed after startup. The administrative functions are not explained in this book; they only require updating the repository database and, as such, are part of the general operations interface, which is not described here.

The procedure calls required for system startup and shutdown are exchanged directly among the resource managers and the TP monitor. The administrative TRPCs are exchanged among the TP monitor and the repository resource manager. All this is depicted by the "lightning" in Figure 6.2. Let us start with the function calls used to install a new resource manager or to remove an existing one:

```
/* the rmInstall function introduces a new server or application to the local TP monitor. It     */
/* provides all the information required to install, load and run this resource manager.         */
RMID rmInstall(RMNAME,                   /* globally unique name of service                      */
               &rm_callbacks[],          /* callback entries in the resource manager             */
                                         /* that are used by the TP monitor                      */
                                         /* and the transaction manager                          */
               AccessControlList,        /* used to authorize requests                           */
               stuff);                   /* more administrative info for the TP monitor          */
Boolean rmRemove(RMID);                  /* removes an installed RM from the system;             */
                                         /* checks for references from other resource mgrs.      */
Boolean rmDeactivate(RMID);              /* the resource manager is shut down (if running)       */
                                         /* and marked as inactive. This means it will not be    */
                                         /* brought up at system restart.                        */
Boolean rmActivate(RMID);                /* an inactive resource manager is marked active        */
                                         /* again and its start-up is initiated.                 */
```

The parameter list of rmInstall is very rudimentary. The first three parameters are spelled out. RMNAME is the user-supplied global external identifier for the new service; its actual uniqueness will be checked against the repository when the resource manager is installed.

The next parameter is an array of pointers to the callback entries in the resource man-ager. These callback entries are specified as relative addresses in the load module for that re-source manager; as a result, invoking that callback entry means that the TRPC stub branches to the respective address. There is a convention saying that, for example, the first element of the array is the address of the rm_Startup entry, the next element is the address of the rm_Prepare entry, and so on. The TP monitor keeps this array in the TRPC stub of the re-spective resource manager's address space. If the transaction manager issues a TRPC to such a callback entry, it has to specify three things: first, the name of the entry to be called; sec-ond, the RMID of the resource manager the call is directed to; and third, the parameters that go with the call. The TRPC stub then takes the entry name and associates it with the index in the rm_callbacks array. The copy of that array for the resource manager identified by RMID then contains the actual address to branch to.

As with the callbacks for the transaction manager, these entries need not be provided by simple resource managers; such resource managers can just be loaded or canceled.

Sophisticated resource managers, however, may have files to open (close) or other initial (terminal) work to do. Note that in a real system there is more to say about callbacks than just an address in the event the resource manager needs to be called back for the respective event. Especially in cases where *no address* is provided, additional information is required by the transaction manager. For example, if a resource manager specifies no rm_Prepare entry, this indicates that under all circumstances its vote on commit is Yes. But this convention of "no entry = blind agreement" is not generally applicable. For example, specifying no rm_Rollback_Savepoint entry might indicate that the resource manager has no durable state and therefore does not object to a rollback request. It might, on the other hand, say that the resource manager is able to abort the transaction but cannot return to any local savepoint. Thus, for each missing callback address, the transaction manager must be told the default result of that function for the respective resource manager.

The remaining parameters are left vague. They merely indicate that more information is needed when installing a new resource manager. There must, for example, be an access control list that allows the TP monitor to check whether an incoming request for that resource manager is acceptable from a security point of view. Other necessary declarations include the location from which the code for the resource manager can be loaded, which other resource managers need to be available before this one can start, what its priority should be, and what the resource consumption is likely to be (processor load and I/O per invocation). Some of these issues are discussed in Section 6.5.

The second group of functions is very straightforward; they were mentioned in the description of Identify. The transaction manager invokes the callbacks for driving the transaction protocols, and the TP monitor brings a resource manager to life by calling rm_Startup. When this TRPC returns, the TP monitor knows that this resource manager is open for service (see Section 6.5). Conversely, when rmDeactivate has been called from the administrator, the TP monitor invokes rm_Shutdown and from now on rejects all further calls to that server class.

```
(void)   rm_Startup();        /* invoked at system start-up.          */
(void)   rm_Shutdown();       /* invoked at system shutdown.          */
```

No program can participate as a resource manager in a transaction unless it has properly registered with the TP monitor. The TP monitor enters the new service to the name server, which is part of the repository, then checks its resource requirements and its dependencies on other resource managers. Note that this attitude is different from the somewhat anarchic way distributed computing is done in PC or workstation networks. There a server can come up and announce itself to the network by entering its name and address into the name server, and from then on everybody who is interested can send requests to that server directly via RPC. The scheme used by TP monitors is more controlled in the sense that there is always a TPOS, especially a TP monitor, in the invocation path. The major advantage of this approach over the anarchic one is obvious: Going through the TPOS layer allows system-wide end-to-end control, authentication, and load balancing. One can argue that the same control would be possible in the anarchic scheme by proper cooperation among the RPC mechanism and the name server. While this is true, it means that that scheme would effectively evolve into a TPOS.

6.2.4 Resource Manager Calls versus Resource Manager Sessions

Thus far, we have seen the problems of invoking different types of resource managers via transactional remote procedure calls. As mentioned at the outset, however, there is a second aspect to TRPCs that goes beyond the scope of one invocation: context. This is a loaded topic—and an important one—so we will try to give it careful treatment.

The fundamental question can be put like this: If, in the course of one transaction, a client C repeatedly invokes server class S, how should that be handled? To appreciate that there is a problem at all, note that S denotes a server *class*, and each invocation can go to a different process belonging to that class. Since these processes have separate address spaces, process S_i has no information about what process S_k has done on behalf of C. With these constraints in mind, consider the following scenarios, which are illustrated in Figure 6.4:

Independent invocations.   A server of class S can be called arbitrarily often, and the outcome of each call is independent of whether or not the server has been called before. Moreover, each server instance can forget about the transaction by the time it returns the result. Since the server keeps no state about the call, there is nothing in the future fate of the transaction that could influence the server's commit decision. Upon return, the server declares its consent to the transaction's commit, should that point ever be reached. An example for this is a server that reads records from a database, performs some statistical computations on them, and returns the result.

Invocation sequence.   The client wants to issue service requests that explicitly refer to earlier service requests; for example, "Give me the *next* 10 records." The requirement for such service requests arises with SQL cursors. First, there is the OPEN CURSOR call, which causes the SELECT statement to be executed and all the context information in the database system to be built up. As was shown, this results in an rmCall to the SQL server. After that, the FETCH CURSOR statement can be called arbitrarily often, until the result set is exhausted. If it was an update cursor, then the server cannot vote on commit before the last operation in the sequence has been executed; that is, the server must be called at its rm_Prepare() callback entry, and the outcome of this depends on the result of the previous service call.

Complex interaction.   This is the general case, of which only a simple version is shown in Figure 6.4 (Case C). The server class must remember the results of all invocations by client C until commit, because only then can it be decided whether certain deferred consistency constraints are fulfilled. Think of a mail server with which the client can interact. The server creates the mail header during the first interaction, the mail body during the next interaction, and so on. The mail server stores the various parts of a message in a database. In principle, then, all these interactions are independent; the client might as well create the body first, and the header next. However, the mail server maintains a consistency constraint that says that no mail must be accepted without at least a header, a body, and a trailer. Since this constraint cannot be determined until commit, there must be some way of relating all the updates done on behalf of the client when the server is called (back) at rm_Prepare—even if this call goes to a process that has not been called upon before. Note that all sophisticated resource managers, such as SQL database systems, entertain such complex interactions with their clients.

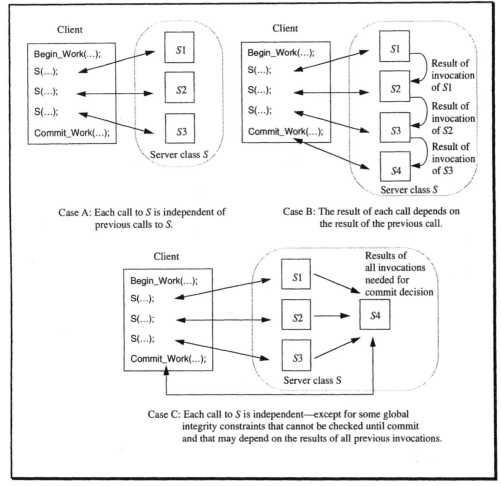

Figure 6.4: Three scenarios for dependencies among subsequent invocations of the same server class. The three cases are defined by the type of invocation and the way the server provides its service. In Case A there can be no dependency at all. In Case B, each invocation depends on the outcome of the previous call, so that the final commit decision of the server class may depend on the outcome of the last invocation. In Case C, there are no immediate dependencies during execution, but the commit decision may depend on the results of all invocations.

This whole issue of relating multiple calls of one client to the same server class is one facet of an almost religious debate that has been going on in the field of distributed computing for many years. It has to do with the question of whether computations should be *session oriented* or *service-call oriented*. This is not the place to resolve this question, but let us use the previous example to consider the fundamental issue.

This whole debate has some of the flavor of the data modeling discussions circling around the question of whether all information must be expressed by values (the relational camp), or whether positional information should be allowed, too (the hierarchical, network- and object-oriented camp). Common terms for this controversy are *connection-less* versus *connection-oriented*, *context-free* versus *context-sensitive*, *stateless* versus *stateful*, *datagram* versus *session*.

A client and a server are said to be *in session* if they have agreed to cooperate for some time, and if both are keeping state information about that cooperation. Thus, the server knows that it is currently servicing that client, what that client is allowed to do, which results have been produced for it so far, and so forth. If the session covers an invocation sequence, the server knows which records the client refers to and has context information pointing to the last record delivered to the client. Consider the request for "the *next* 10 records" issued by the client to a server it contacts for the first time—this obviously would not make any sense.

The advocates of statelessness hold that nonsensical service requests like these should not be issued in the first place. Put the other way around: each remote procedure call must contain enough information to describe completely what the service request is about, without alluding to some previous request, earlier agreement, or anything of that sort.

There are, however, many situations in which it is just very convenient to have some agreed-upon state, if only for the sake of performance. Consider the example of the cursor from which the next n tuples are read. One could think of an implementation that passes with each new request the identifier of the last record read with the previous request; that way, the server knows where to continue. But that would solve only part of the problem. Without context, each new request would have to be authenticated and authorized; that is, the server would have to decide over and again whether the client is allowed to read these records. If there is state, then the result of the security check done upon the first request is kept in the context on the server's side.

As will become obvious in the following chapters, there is even more context that needs to be preserved in order to achieve the ACID properties. For example, guaranteeing atomicity and isolation requires the server to remember all the records a transaction has touched so far—and not just the most recent one, which would be enough to support the "fetch next" semantics. Furthermore, a transaction in itself establishes a frame of reference that can (and must) be referred to by all instances that have participated in it. Just to make the decision whether "this transaction" should be committed or aborted requires some context from which to derive which state the transaction is in (from each client's or server's perspective). Of course, since a transaction can involve an arbitrary number of agents, it is by nature more general than a session, which is always peer-to-peer. But the important similarity at this point is the necessity of context that can be referred to by all instances involved. The following discussion is focused on the issue of how to achieve shared context.

The problem of "sessions" versus independent rmCalls will come up over and again during this chapter. The position taken here is that the difference between the two at the level of the resource manager interface is not that dramatic and, therefore, the issue should not be overrated (and overheated). There are situations where maintaining context on both sides lends itself naturally toward supporting certain types of (important) resource manager request patterns. In other cases, keeping the context on one side is the more economical solution. Let us briefly sketch the different methods for keeping client-server context; it turns out that client-server association via context is a fairly general phenomenon and allows for many different implementations. Four structurally different approaches are sketched in Figure 6.5.

It is easy to see that each of these techniques can, in principle, be used to maintain the relationships among server invocations as they are illustrated in Figure 6.4. This is not to say, though, that the techniques are arbitrarily interchangeable; they are quite different with

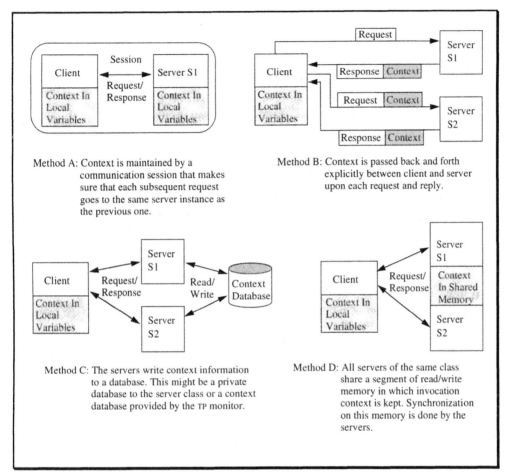

Figure 6.5: Implementing state associated with a client-server interaction.   Context information about multiple invocations of the same server class can be maintained in four different ways: (a) make sure that each invocation goes to the same process and that this process does not handle other invocations in the meantime; (b) pass the context explicitly back and forth with each request; (c) keep the context in a database; (d) have a segment of shared memory where the context is stored for all server processes.

respect to the burden they put on both the client's and the server's implementation in terms of cost for maintaining the processing context.

Having the communication system manage the context is the simplest approach for both sides. There is some magic around them, called *session*, that makes sure all invocations from the same client go to the same instance of the server. Thus, the server behaves like a statically linked subroutine, which means it can keep its context in local program variables. This applies not only to the normal service invocations, but also to any callbacks the server may get from the transaction manager. Such a session has to be managed by the TPOS; all the client or the server has to do is declare that it needs one. The price for this is considerable overhead in the TPOS for maintaining and recovering sessions; see Chapter 10, Section 10.3. Note that only this method is a session according to the established terminology. The other three techniques implement a stateful relationship between a client and a server class, but most people familiar with communication protocol stacks would not call them sessions. This text takes a somewhat less rigid perspective: whenever there is relationship between a client and server for which context is kept somewhere, it is referred to it as a *session*, provided there is no risk of confusion.

Context passing relieves the TPOS of the problem of context management. Both the client and the server side cooperate in order not to get out of sync. The server decides what context it needs to carry on in case of a subsequent call. The client stores the context in between server calls and passes it along with the next invocation. There is a subtle problem when using Method B (shown in Figure 6.5) in a scenario of the type depicted in Case C of Figure 6.4. The server instance that gets invoked via rm_Prepare needs the context for making its decision. But, because this call comes from the transaction manager, there will be no context in the parameter list. The only solution is for the client to issue some "final" service call (with context), which tells the server that the client is about to call commit. If the server does not like the situation, it calls Abort_Work. If, on the other hand, the server returns normally, the client can call Commit_Work, and the server will not be called back by the transaction manager.

Keeping the context in the database gives the responsibility of maintaining context to the server. It has to write the state that might be required to act on future invocations into a file, database, or whatever. The state information must be supplied with the necessary key attributes to uniquely identify which thread of control it belongs to. The key attributes include the TRID, client RMID, and the sequence number of the invocation. Some of the work involved in maintaining the context can be offloaded to either an SQL database system or to the context management service of the TP monitor (see Section 6.5).

The important point is that with this method, an arbitrary instance of the server can be invoked to vote on commit. Using the MyTrid call, it can find out what the current transaction is; through the TRPC mechanism, it also knows which RMID it is working for, so that it can pick up the right context from the database.

The shared memory approach is similar to the solution using a context database, except that now the whole responsibility is with the server (class). Context has to be kept in shared memory, access to which must be carefully synchronized. This solution is used by very sophisticated resource managers, such as SQL database systems, and is only applicable when all instances of the server class are guaranteed to run at the same node. Chapters 13–15 discuss some of the problems related to that type of context management.

So far, we have ignored a very important distinction with respect to the type of context that needs to be maintained from a server's perspective. Considering our various examples, one can easily see that there are two types:

Client-oriented context. This reflects the state of an interaction between a client and a server. The solutions presented in Figure 6.5 implicitly assume that this is the type of context to be managed. Typical examples are cursor positions, authenticated userids, and so on.

Transaction-oriented context. This type of context is bound to the sphere of control established by a transaction rather than to an isolated client-server interaction. Consider the following example: Client *C* invokes server *S*1, which in turn invokes server *S*3—all within *T*. After return from the service call, *C* invokes *S*2 (a different server class), which also invokes *S*3, but needs the context established by the earlier call to *S*3 from

*S*1. Case C) in Figure 6.4 describes a similar situation. The point here is that the context needed by *S*3 is not bound to any of the previous client-server interactions, but it is bound to the transaction as such.[3] This leads back to the argument about the similarities between sessions and transactions in terms of context management. Examples of transaction-oriented context are *deferred consistency constraints* and *locks* (see Chapter 7).

A general context management scheme must be able to cope with both types of state information; that is, it must distinguish whether a piece of context is identified by the client-server interaction or by the TRID. Note that communication sessions can only be used to support client-oriented context. Exercises 4 and 5 are concerned with ways to maintain both types of context based on the mechanisms introduced in Figure 6.5.

Now let us return to the example of the SQL cursor; the only way to avoid any kind of session-like notion at the TRPC level is to use Method B. In this case, all the cursor management is done by some piece of code in the client's process. The server delivers all the result tuples to that local cursor manager and can then forget about the query. Assuming that the cursor navigates over a large relation, this is an expensive solution.

To get reasonable performance, then, the server must be involved somehow. It has to maintain the result produced by the SELECT of the cursor definition and must record the current cursor position in that result set. In other words, it must be in a position to make sense of a FETCH NEXT service request. The client and server share responsibilities for maintaining context. They must decide what context information about their interaction is to be kept from now on. Having both maintain the same context would be overkill. For example, if the client issues a SELECT, which he knows returns at most one tuple, then no client context is needed; only if he wants to process a cursor must context be maintained for the client.

Transaction-oriented context must be maintained by each server that manages persistent state, no matter what the invocation patterns with its clients look like. This aspect is elaborated over the course of the next five chapters.

The ground rule is this: Each server that manages persistent objects must be implemented such that it can keep transaction-oriented context. The TRPC mechanism must provide means for servers of any type to establish a stateful interaction with a client in case this should be needed (client-oriented context). Of course, both types of context must be relinquished after they have become obsolete, either after commit/abort or after an explicit request to terminate a particular client-server interaction. The TPOS provides two mechanisms to implement client-oriented context:

Session management. If context maintenance is handled through communication sessions, then the TP monitor is responsible for binding a server process to one client for the duration of a stateful invocation.

Process management. Even if the TP monitor has no active responsibility for context management, it may use information about the number of existing sessions per server for load balancing. The rationale is that an established session is an indicator for more work in the future.

---

[3] One could argue that this type of context can be thought as being bound to the client, but that essentially creates a confusion among concepts. Note that it is the server that needs the context; the client is unlikely even to know that the context exists. Hence, it is not a good idea to bind context to a class of resource managers that have no interest in (and probably no authority on) the data involved.

For the purpose of our presentation, we use two TRPC calls to establish and relinquish a session among a client and a server; they assume that the request for a session is always issued by the server. Here are the function prototype declares:

```
typedef struct               /*                                                    */
        {rmInstance  EndA;   /* one end of stateful interaction                     */
        rmInstance  EndB;    /* other end of stateful interaction                   */
        Uint        SeqNo;   /* sequence no. to distinguish                         */
                             /* between multiple stateful interactions              */
                             /* among the same servers.                             */
        }BindId;             /* handle for a stateful interaction                   */
BindId  rmBind(rmInstance);  /* function passes the ID of the client to which a     */
                             /* a session with the server has to be established.    */
                             /* gets back a handle which identifies the interaction */
                             /* among this server and this client.                  */
                             /* returns the NULL instance if binding fails.         */
Boolean rmUnbind(BindId);    /* inverse to rmBind. waives the future use of the     */
                             /* specified binding. returns FALSE if no binding      */
                             /* with that identifier was in effect.                 */
```

It is important to understand that a BindId uniquely identifies an association between a client instance and a server instance. Therefore, each BindId points to one rmInstance on the client's side and one rmInstance on the server's side. Consider the use of these functions for handling SQL cursors. The sequence of SQL statements reads like this:

```
OPEN CURSOR
        FETCH CURSOR
        FETCH CURSOR
        ........
        FETCH CURSOR
CLOSE CURSOR
```

Using the ideas just introduced, this would be mapped onto the following sequence of TRPCs:[4]

```
rmCall (SQL,NULL,...), bindid = rmBind (ClientRMID), rmCall (SQL,&bindid,...),
rmCall (SQL, & bindid,...),...,rmUnbind (bindid).
```

The imbedded SQL calls on the client's side are turned into rmCalls to the SQL server; the first one requests the open function, the next one the fetch operations, and so forth. Upon the first request, the server issues an rmBind request to the TP monitor, because the open establishes context to which the client subsequently is likely to refer. The server instance therefore asks to be bound to that client instance to make sure future client requests are mapped correctly. After this, the server acts on the function requests. The CLOSE CURSOR request is essentially a signal to the server to destroy the context; therefore—after its local clean-up work—it invokes rmUnbind. Of course, the SQL connection module on the client's side must

---

[4] The SQL standard has the verbs CONNECT and DISCONNECT for that purpose, but since the presentation in this chapter talks about arbitrary resource managers, fictional function names are used.

be able to associate cursor names with the BindIds that are returned with the rmBind requesting to open the cursor. Since this has nothing to do with TP monitors in particular, it is not discussed here.

If rmCalls are to be issued without a preference for a particular instance of the server, rmInstance is set to NULL; otherwise, the value for it must be determined by a preceding rmBind. Note that a client can entertain an arbitrary number of simultaneous bindings with the same server class, though of course, not with the same instance. The pair of rmBind/rmUnbind operations establishes a session between the client and the server.

There is one more interesting thing to note about the binding between client and server, especially in case of an SQL server. The example makes it look as though binding was meant only to protect cursors or the work within one transaction. However, sessions are generally used in a much wider scope. Imagine that an application program starts up, and the first thing it has to do is to find its proper database. For example, it could have to run with a test database or with the production database; it could have to use the order entry database of region *A* or of region *B*, and so on. In short, all its schema names need to be bound to the right schema description. This requires control blocks to be set up on both sides—again, a session between the client and the server. Once this is established during the startup of the application, it can be used for all subsequent interactions that refer to this schema. Cursors will, of course, work correctly, because the initial SELECT, as well as the corresponding FETCH NEXT, will all be sent to the same rmInstance. Thus, the duration of an rmBind can be longer than one transaction; a client and a server "in session" can execute an arbitrary number of transactions across that session. But assuming that there is no parallelism within a transaction, each such session will, at any point in time, be used by at most one transaction. If this transaction aborts, the state on both sides will be rolled back, as atomicity demands. Since the session is essentially defined by the state kept on both ends, this implies that the session is also recovered to the beginning of the transaction. This is explained in more detail in Chapter 10.

It is interesting to consider who (i.e., at which level of programming) actually uses the rmBind/rmUnbind mechanism. A full-blown resource manager, designed to service many clients simultaneously, must be able to bind many server instances of itself—for load distribution, for throughput, or for other reasons. In that case the the resource manager's program has to use the binding mechanism explicitly.

If, on the other hand, the resource manager is just a COBOL application, then no one can expect its programmer to use such tricks. It is therefore up to, say, the SQL pre-compiler or the TP monitor to handle properly the sessions established on behalf of the SQL server in order to let the COBOL program run correctly. You can consider some of the consequences of this as an exercise.

The foregoing explicitly assumes that sessions are established by servers only. This is a simplification for the purpose of keeping the presentation free of too many extras. Depending on the type of services provided and on the level of sophistication in the implementation of the clients and servers, it might well be the client asking to be bound to a particular server. Think, for example, of a piece of software that acts as a server to one side, but is a client to other servers. If it receives a request that requires binding, then it will have to go into session with its servers to be able to service the request. The discussion of which way to set up a session under which circumstances is beyond the scope of this book. In many of today's systems, however, there is a clear distinction between clients (application programs) and servers (TP services) in terms of sophistication and complexity: applications do not want to be bothered with any aspects of concurrency, error handling, context maintenance, and so on, leaving the servers to take care of the context.

6.2.5 Summary

The TP monitor's main task at run time is to implement transactional remote procedure calls (TRPCs). TRPCs look very much like standard RPCs in that a service can be invoked via its external name (RMNAME), irrespective of which node in the network actually runs the code for it. However, TRPCs come with a much more sophisticated infrastructure, which is embodied by the TPOS.

Apart from the automatic process scheduling and load balancing that is discussed in the following sections, the TP monitor makes sure that all resource manager invocations within a transaction are part of that transaction. Thus, even a simple program that uses none of the transactional verbs becomes attached to a transaction when invoked through a TRPC. That does not mean that updates it makes to an arbitrary resource become magically recoverable, but if that simple program in turn invokes recoverable resource managers, such as SQL databases, the TP monitor tags the invocation with the transaction ID of the simple program and thus keeps the whole execution within one sphere of control.

The actual management of the transactional protocols is done by the transaction manager. The TP monitor forwards TRPCs and guarantees that they carry the right TRID and go to the right process, depending on the TRID.

Sophisticated resource managers maintain durable objects, or at least state information, about the interaction with a client for the duration of a transaction, or longer. It has been demonstrated that the TP monitor needs to support these associations among clients and servers spanning multiple TRPCs by providing session-like concepts. In some implementations, the TP monitor is responsible for keeping state that belongs to such a client-server session.

This section has taken the perspective that resource managers and applications are structurally indistinguishable. In general, an application is simpler than a full-blown resource manager—say, an SQL database system—in that it does not actively participate in most of the transaction protocols, does not have any changes to durable storage that need to be undone, and so on; in principle, however, it could do all that if the application required that level of sophistication. The TP monitor treats resource managers and applications as the same type of objects.

6.3 Functional Principles of the TP Monitor

The crucial thing about resource managers and transactional applications is that all invocations of services other than calls to linked-in subroutines have to use the TRPC mechanism. In current operating systems, there is no way to effectively enforce these conditions; yet, we must appreciate that all bypasses and shortcuts will cause part of the work to be unprotected, resulting in dire consequences for the global state of the system. Ignoring the issue of side doors, we will assume a well-designed system according to Table 6.1, where the TPOS is in full control of all its resource managers.

As is apparent in the previous section, the TP monitor's premier function is to handle TRPCs and all the resources pertaining to them. This section, therefore, focuses exclusively on this aspect. Some other services provided by the TP monitor—managing queues, authenticating users, and bringing up the system—are covered in the later sections of this chapter.

This section contains a large amount of technical detail. It begins by sketching the address space and process structure the TP monitor requires for managing its applications and resource managers. Based on that, the core data structures of the TP monitor and the transaction manager are declared. Then the logic for handling a TRPC is presented in some detail—first for a local invocation, and then for a remote invocation. This analysis shows that there are (at least) two topics that need further exploration: the binding of names of resource managers, and the dynamic interaction between the TP monitor and the transaction manager. These topics are covered in the next subsections. Finally, some subtleties omitted during the main discussion are explained. They illustrate a phenomenon that occurs with increasing frequency the closer one gets to the implementation details of a TP system: whenever things look nicely controlled and strictly synchronous, parallelism rears its head and calls for another round of complication. This is but one example of the complexities a TP system hides from the application.

6.3.1 The Central Data Structures of the TPOS

The TP monitor manages resources in terms of *server classes* (or *resource manager types*). The definition of these terms in Chapters 2 and 5 are briefly repeated here. The idea is illustrated in Figure 6.6, which is a refined version of Figure 5.11.

Remember that an RMNAME is a globally unique identifier for a service that is available in the system. At the moment the resource manager is installed at a node (function rmInstall), it gets a locally unique RMID. At run time the TP monitor maintains a server class for each active RMID. The server class consists of a group of processes with identical address space *structures*; this is to say that each member of a server class runs exactly the same code. Processes in a server class are functionally indistinguishable.

For each TRPC, the TP monitor has to find the RMID for the requested RMNAME and then the server class for that RMID. If there is no unused process in that server class, the TP monitor has to create one. Otherwise, it has to select from the server class a process to receive the request. A third option is to defer execution of the TRPC for load balancing reasons; this, however, may cause deadlocks (can you see why?). All this happens within the TRPC stub.

The reason for having multiple processes running on behalf of the same resource manager is load balancing. As the load for a certain resource manager increases, the TP monitor creates more processes for it. The considerations determining how many processes should be in a given server class are outlined in Section 6.5. For the moment, let us concentrate on the address space structure required for making server class management efficient—which means low pathlength for a TRPC.

As described in Chapter 5, for all processes using TRPCs, there is one piece of shared memory, which holds the TRPC stub. This portion is displayed in the center of Figure 6.6. Each resource manager invocation via TRPC results in a branch to that stub (within the process issuing the call), and then the processing we have already sketched begins. Of course, the TRPC-stub code is re-entrant; that is, it can be executed by many processes simultaneously, as is the case for compilers, sort routines, and editors.

The remarks about what happens when a TRPC is mapped to a process do indicate that the TRPC stub needs information about the local server class configuration, as well as about

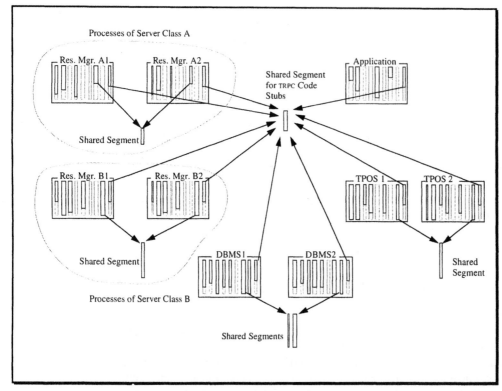

Figure 6.6: Address spaces involved in TRPC handling, and their interrelationships in a shared memory environment. To implement TRPCs, the address spaces of the processes running at a node must have a number of shared segments. Most important is the portion with the TRPC stub, which must be shared among all address spaces. The address spaces of the processes running the TPOS need to share (at least) one segment with all the global data structures of the resource managers. Except for that, members of a server class may share memory segments, but the access synchronization on these shared segments is in the responsibility of the respective resource managers.

remote resource managers that might be targets of TRPCs issued by local clients. For fast access, this information is kept in shared global data structures, for which the TP monitor is responsible. The segment(s) for these shared data structures is shown as the common segment for the two TPOS address spaces in Figure 6.6.

To give an idea of how the TP monitor and the other components of the TPOS cooperate, we now describe a global view of what the core data structures maintained by the TPOS are, how they hang together, and what access functions are available for them. Note that this section only presents the "grand design" plus a more detailed discussion of the TP monitor's data structures.

6.3.1.1 Defining the System Control Blocks

To keep things manageable, it helps to have one starting point from which all data structures can be tracked down, rather than a bundle of unrelated structures that can be located only via their names in a program. Thus, above all there is an anchor data structure providing access to the other global data structures. Its declare looks like this:

```
typedef  char *          timestamp;          /* type for referring to dates                          */
typedef  struct anchor * TPOS_AnchorP;       /*                                                      */
typedef  struct anchor                       /* TPOS anchor for the global control blocks            */
{        char            *SysName;           /* name of the local system                             */
         timestamp       DateGenerated;      /* date of last sysgen                                  */
         timestamp       DateLastStartUp;    /* date of recent system startup                        */
         char            morelikethis;       /* more administrative stuff                            */
         TPAnchorP       TPMonCBs;           /* pointer to the anchor of the TP monitor              */
         TMAnchorP       TM_CBs;             /* pointer to the anchor of transaction mgr.            */
         CMAnchorP       SM_CBs;             /* pointer to the anchor of session manager             */
         LMAnchorP       LM_CBs;             /* pointer to the anchor of log manager                 */
         IMAnchorP       IM_CBs;             /* ptr. to the anchor of lock (isolation) manager       */
} TPOS_Anchor;                               /*                                                      */
```

Of course, a real system anchor contains more than what is shown in the example. The TPOS_Anchor is one well-defined point in the TPOS, from which all the system data structures can be reached (provided the requestor has the required access privileges). Each resource manager is assumed to have its own local anchor, where this resource manager's data structures are rooted. Keeping the pointers to these anchors in the TPOS_Anchor ensures that addressability can be established in an orderly manner upon system startup; this is necessary, because the TPOS comes up before any of the resource managers is activated. Note that although all the data structures to be introduced are global TPOS data structures (in that they are required for all activities of the TPOS), each one is "owned" by one of the system resource managers, which tries to hide them (that is, their physical organization) from the other components of the TPOS. The degree to which this can be done depends on the flexibility of domain protection offered by the underlying operating system.

The declaration in our example assumes five system resource managers: the TP monitor, the transaction manager, the log manager, the lock manager, and the communication manager. This is a basic set; real systems might have more.

The anchor of a system resource manager has no fixed layout; it is declared by each resource manager for itself. The TP monitor's anchor might have the following structure:

```
typedef   struct tpa *   TPAnchorP;          /*                                                      */
typedef   struct tpa                         /* TP monitor anchor for its control blocks             */
{         char           *MyVersion;         /* version of the TP monitor running                    */
          char           Repository[64];     /* name of the repository I work with                   */
          handle         Repos_Handle;       /* handle for calls to repository                       */
          char           ContextDB;          /* name of database for keeping context                 */
          handle         CtxDB_Handle;       /* handle for calls to context database                 */
          RMID           NextRMID;           /* next RMID to be handed out                            */
          RMCB *         FirstRMCB;          /* pointer to 1st res. mgr. control block                */
          PCB *          FirstPRCB;          /* pointer to 1st process control block                  */
          SECB *         FirstSECB;          /* pointer to 1st session control block                  */
          char           *stuff;             /* more administrative data                             */
} TPAnchor;                                  /*                                                      */
```

The resource manager control blocks and the others rooted at TPAnchor need more than just declarative treatment; accordingly, they are introduced immediately following the

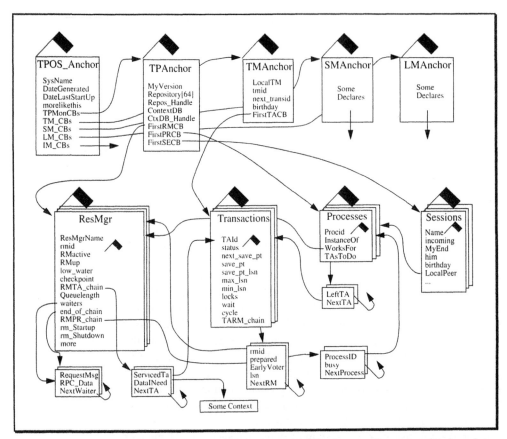

Figure 6.7: Overview of the central data structures required for transaction processing based on TRPCs. The global control blocks used by the TPOS to describe its resources are threaded together by a number of reference lists, which provide access to all elements of one control block belonging to an element of another control block. The references are keyed by the element's logical name. To resolve a reference, the control block access primitives provided by the system resource managers must be used. The flags denote the so-called semaphore data types (see Chapter 8).

description of the global data structures. Figure 6.7 gives an overview of which data structures the TPOS keeps in its different components and how they are related. To be precise: only the global data structures entertained by the TP monitor and the transaction manager are fully shown, because these are the ones needed for handling TRPCs. For the remaining system resource managers, Figure 6.7 shows the anchor structure but none of the global data structures managed by these components.

The flags attached to the control blocks in Figure 6.7 serve as metaphors for a special data type that has not yet been introduced: the *semaphore*. As explained in Chapter 8, semaphores are used to control the access of concurrent processes to data structures in shared memory. It is important to understand that the control blocks shown in Figure 6.7 will be heavily accessed, because the TPOS executes on behalf of virtually every process in the system. Since the control blocks are threaded together through different types of linked lists, it is important that update operations on these link structures be consistent. Consistency can be lost if different processes access the same control block simultaneously, applying contradictory updates to it. Again, exactly how this can happen is a subject of Chapter 8; for the

the moment, just accept that the little flags called semaphores help to make sure that a process can operate on these central data structures without being disturbed by other processes.

The small control blocks in the lower part of Figure 6.7 are used to establish fast cross-references from one type of control block to the other; they are explained in Subsection 6.3.2. Before we come to that, let us introduce the access functions to the TPOS's major control blocks.

6.3.1.2 Accessing the Central Data Structures of the TPOS

There is one system resource manager that is responsible for and encapsulates each type of control block in the central data structures. For example, the TP monitor is responsible for the resource manager control blocks, the process control blocks, and the session control blocks. The transaction manager is responsible for the transaction control blocks, and so on. The cross-reference control blocks are maintained by the resource manager at whose control block they are rooted.

Whenever a component of the TPOS executes one of its functions, the characteristics of transactional remote procedure calls require the TPOS to know:

(1) Which **process** it is executing in,

(2) Which **transaction** this execution is part of, and

(3) Which **resource manager** has issued the call.

In many cases, it also important to get the resource manager ID of the client that called upon the system resource manager. Based on such an identifier, the routine might request detailed information about the process, transaction, or resource manager. Of course, such data could be passed along with each TRPC, as is the case with remote invocations. But for local invocations, it is much more efficient to use the central control blocks where all this environmental information is kept.

For the purposes of this and the following chapters, we define a set of functions that allow controlled access of the TPOS's data structures. Here is the list of function prototype definitions:

```
PID        MyProcid();      /* returns the identifier of the process the caller is running in    */
                            /* this is actually a call to the basic OS                          */
TRID       MyTrid();        /* returns the transaction identifier the caller is executing within */
RMID       MYRMID();        /* returns the RMID of the resource manager that has issued the call */
RMID       ClientRMID();    /* returns the RMID of the caller's client                          */
```

These functions can be called from any process running in the transaction system. The three types of identifiers returned are accessible to anybody involved in the processing and thus need no additional privilege for reading them. The next group of functions is not as public; their use is restricted to system resource managers that form core parts of the TPOS. The ways of enforcing these access restrictions are not discussed here; just keep in mind that an arbitrary application is not allowed to call the functions declared in the following example code.

PCB	**MyProc();**	/* returns a copy of the central process control block	*/
		/* describing the process the caller is running in	*/
TransCB	**MyTrans();**	/* returns copy of the central transaction control block.	*/
		/* describing the transaction the caller is working for	*/
RMCB	**MyRM();**	/* returns copy of the central resource manager control	*/
		/* block describing the res. mgr. that issued the call	*/
RMCB	**ClientRM();**	/* like MyRM, but for the caller's client	*/
PCB *	**MyProcP();**	/* returns pointer to the central process control block	*/
		/* describing the process the caller is running in	*/
TransCB *	**MyTransP();**	/* returns a pointer to the central TA control block	*/
		/* describing the transaction the caller is working for	*/
RMCB *	**MyRMP();**	/* returns pointer to the central resource mgr. control	*/
		/* block describing the res. mgr. that issued the call	*/
RMCB *	**ClientRMP();**	/* like MyRMP, but for the caller's client	*/

The data structures that are returned by these functions will be explained as we go along. Processes that are entitled to call, say, MyTrans will get a copy of all descriptive data for their current transaction, but no linkage information from there to other control blocks. Access to that kind of data is reserved to those who are allowed to invoke MyTransP.

6.3.2 Data Structures Owned by the TP Monitor

If Figure 6.7 left the reader a bit puzzled, that is because it focuses on the organizational aspects of the central data structures; that is, the addressing hierarchy and the cross-referencing among the control blocks. Let us leave this to the side for a moment and consider what has to be described in the control blocks in order to handle TRPCs as laid out in the previous section. Figure 6.8 shows an entity relationship diagram with the key entities the TP monitor has to deal with, and their relationships. Don't worry about the fact that the data structures of some of these entities are not owned by the TP monitor; for the moment, we view them as logical data objects and try to come up with a data model reflecting the TP monitor's perspective of the world. Mapping this view to some kind of data structure is the next step. Now consider each of the entity types and their relationships.

First, there are resource managers, the descriptions of which are stored in the repository. For each resource manager, there is a server class (and vice versa), which is the run-time environment for that resource manager. For mapping TRPCs, these two categories can be joined into one data structure that holds the static information from the repository as well as the dynamic data, such as request rates and queue lengths. This structure, called RMCB, is introduced later in this subsection.

Server classes are associated with processes in two ways. First, there is a 1:*n* relationship that describes which processes have been allocated *for that server class*. If a process is allocated for a server class, then its own, private address space contains the code of the resource manager corresponding to the server class. In other words, the process always starts processing in the code of the server class to which it has been assigned. Assigning processes to server classes is done by the TP monitor. Once such an assignment has been established, it can only be changed by killing the process.

Despite the fixed assignment of processes to server classes, processes can switch address spaces during execution; that is, they can execute code of other resource managers.

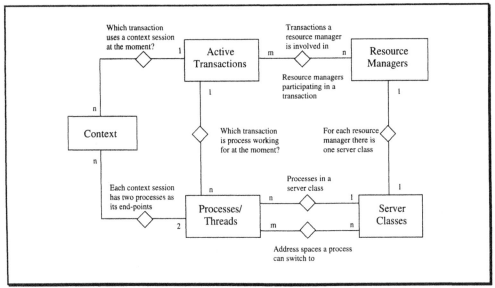

Figure 6.8: Overview of the entities and their relationships described by the TPOS's central data structures. This figure depicts a static view, but since relationships between entities may change over time, the temporal cardinality of the relationships differs from those shown. The figure does not include the anchor data structures, because there is only one instance of each per node.

This is an immediate consequence of the orthogonal process/address space design laid out in Chapter 2. Of course, any process cannot switch to any address space; that has to be restricted for both scheduling and protection reasons. Thus, we need a second relationship among processes and server classes describing which processes can "domain-switch" to which address spaces. It is this ability of a process to execute in different spaces that requires the system calls MyRMID and ClientRMID. Consider the scenario shown in Figure 6.9.

Of course, there is the static association of a process to its own resource manager, that is, to the server class running for that resource manager. Because the association is static, we have not defined a separate system call for it. Rather, it is stored at a fixed entry in the process control block.

Except for a few special situations, all execution in the system is protected by a transaction. Thus, at any point in time, a process is running code on behalf of a transaction. Over time, each process will service many transactions, but if we take a snapshot of the system each process is either idle, or it works for one transaction. Conversely, each transaction can, at one instance, have many processes working for it.

The complex m:n relationship between transactions and resource managers follows immediately from that. A transaction can invoke the services of many resource managers, and each resource manager, having many processes in its server class, can at any instant be involved in many transactions.

The last aspect is context sessions in the sense of application-level stateful interactions among clients and servers. For the implementation discussion in this chapter, we assume the session technique depicted in Figure 6.5, Method A; this means reserving a server process for a client process for the duration of the stateful interaction. Therefore, each context session is associated with exactly two processes, one for the client and one for the server. Each process, on the other hand, can entertain multiple sessions at the same time. Similar

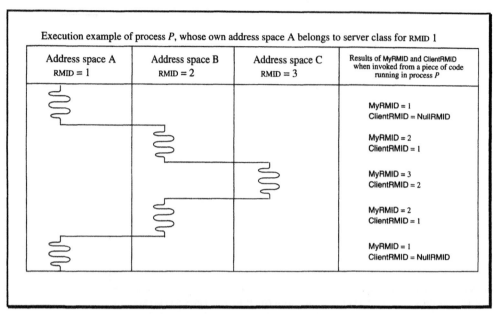

Execution example of process *P*, whose own address space A belongs to server class for RMID 1

Address space A RMID = 1	Address space B RMID = 2	Address space C RMID = 3	Results of MyRMID and ClientRMID when invoked from a piece of code running in process *P*
			MyRMID = 1 ClientRMID = NullRMID
			MyRMID = 2 ClientRMID = 1
			MyRMID = 3 ClientRMID = 2
			MyRMID = 2 ClientRMID = 1
			MyRMID = 1 ClientRMID = NullRMID

Figure 6.9: The association of processes with resource managers. Each process belongs to a fixed server class and therefore has a natural RMID associated with it. At run time, however, a process, can switch to other address spaces, by issuing TRPCs, which run for other RMIDs. Therefore, the result of the invocation of MyRMID and ClientRMID by some routine executing in process *P* has different results, depending on the address space the process is in right now.

arguments hold with respect to the relationship between sessions and transactions. A transaction can have many sessions, but a session, although it may be open for a long time, is associated with only one transaction at any instant.

The perspective taken for designing the central data structures of the TPOS, therefore, is to look at the relationships that can exist at any point in time between the various entity types. Some of the relationships are static, while others can vary at a high frequency. Maintaining these is largely the job of the TP monitor.

6.3.2.1 Declaring the Control Blocks

To start with, there must be a data structure for each of the entity types shown in Figure 6.8, and there must be an efficient way of maintaining the relationships among them. The following declarations are not meant to represent an actual implementation; rather, they contain a number of simplifications that keep the descriptions of the algorithms simple.

The first simplification is to assume a linked list of control blocks for the instances of each entity type, as is shown in the declares that follow. We could have as easily declared them as relations and used SQL to get to the required entries—this would have gone well with the explanations of the principles underlying the implementation of a TP monitor.

The first group of declares contains everything the TP monitor needs to know at run time about the resource managers installed at that node. The declares for the semaphores in Figure 6.7 have been left out to avoid confusion; but, of course, in a real system they have to be there. Note there is no control block for server classes. But, as Figure 6.8 indicates, at each node there is a 1:1 relationship between resource managers and server classes, so both entity types are represented by just one type of control block.

```
/*** control block structure for all resource managers (server classes) at the node       ***/
typedef struct    ResMgr *    RMCBP;           /*                                            */
typedef struct    ResMgr                       /* control block for describing the known resource  */
    {                                          /* managers at that node                      */
    RMNAME        rmname;                      /* global name of the resource manager        */
    RMID          rmid;                        /* the resource manager short name (identifier)  */
    Boolean       RMLocal;                     /* indicates if the RM available at the local node  */
    pointer       acl;                         /* pointer to access control list to authorize requests  */
                                               /* see explanation in Section 6.4             */
    Uint          priority;                    /* priority of this RM for local process scheduling  */
    Boolean       RMactive;                    /* indicates if the RM is activated or deactivated  */
    Boolean       RMup;                        /* status flag says resource manager is up or down  */
    Boolean       UpAfterREDO;                 /* says if the resource manager can operate normally  */
                                               /* after REDO recovery has completed          */
    Uint          QueueLength;                 /* number of requests waiting for that server class  */
    RMQUEP        waiters;                     /* pointer to the request queue for that resource mgr  */
    RMQUEP        end_of_chain;                /* points to last waiting request; append happens here  */
                                               /* queue information refers to local server class only  */
    RMTA_CBP      RMTA_chain;                  /* points to the 1st control block describing a trans-  */
                                               /* action the RM is currently working for     */
    RMPR_CBP      RMPR_chain;                  /* points to chain of control blocks for the processes  */
                                               /* allocated to this resource manager         */
    RMNO_CBP      RMNO_chain;                  /* points to chain of control blocks for the nodes in the  */
                                               /* network where this resource manager is available.  */
    procedure     rm_Startup;                  /* invoked at restart.                         */
    procedure     rm_Shutdown;                 /*invoked at system shutdown.                 */
    /* more stuff needed by the transaction manager, the log manager, and others             */
    RMCBP         next_RMCB;                    /* next in list of RM control blocks          */
    } RMCB;                                    /*                                            */
```

This is but the skeleton of a resource manager control block; for a complete system, more entries would be needed. However, the ones shown here are sufficient for the explanations of the TP monitor algorithms in the next sections. Note also that in a system that makes use of the address space/protection domain facility described in Chapter 2, there would not be just one central resource manager control block. Rather, the TP monitor would have one control block with the entries it needs, the transaction manager would have another one, the log manager would keep resource manager control blocks, and so on. (This aspect is ignored during the following presentations.)

The process control block is simple in comparison to the resource manager control block:

```
/***          control block structure for all processes in server classes              ***/
typdedef struct    Processes *PCBP;      /*                                                 */
typdedef struct    Processes             /* control block describing a process in a server class   */
    {                                    /* and its dynamic associations                     */
    PID            pid;                  /* process no. provided by the basic OS             */
    RMID           InstanceOf;           /* this is the process's own server class           */
    RMID           RunsIn;               /* server class of resource manager process runs in now   */
    RMID           ClientID              /* RMID of client having invoked RunsIn              */
    TRID           WorksFor;             /* Trid of transaction under which process currently runs  */
    Boolean        busy;                 /* does the process currently service a request ?   */
    Uint           priority;             /* priority the process has currently been assigned */
    PRTA_CBP       TAsToDo;              /* pointer to list of suspended transactions         */
    PRRM_CBP       IMayUse;              /* list of res. mgrs. to whose address spaces I may switch */
    } PCB;                               /*                                                  */
```

The third group of objects for which the TP monitor is responsible is the sessions among clients and servers. There is not very much to remember about them from the TP monitor's point of view. Note, however, that in case one end of the session is at a remote site, communication will travel along a communication session, for which the communication manager is responsible. These sessions typically are not established and released on a per-transaction basis; the cost for that would be prohibitively high. Rather, sessions are maintained between processes in different nodes over longer periods of time (in much the same spirit as the Bind/Unbind mechanism); but since they can at any point in time be used by only one transaction, it is possible to recover the state of each session in accord with the ACID paradigm. The communications manager must, of course, behave like a transactional resource manager and keep enough information about the activities of each session to able to roll back in case of a transaction failure. This is described in some detail in Chapter 12. The communications manager must also keep track of which transactions are associated with which sessions (via their processes), since it might receive messages from the network saying that a certain session is broken because of a link failure, or because the other node crashed. Those messages must then be translated into an abort message for the affected local transaction.

```
/***   control block for all sessions an RM in that node participates in                 ***/
typedef struct    Sessions     *SECBP;      /*                                               */
struct   Sessions                           /* control block describing one high-level (TP monitor) session  */
    char          name[BIG];                /* the session name                              */
    Boolean       incoming;                 /* session polarity (incoming or outgoing)       */
    PID           Initiator;                /* ID of process that initiated the binding      */
    NODEID        InitNode;                 /* node where the initiator resides              */
    PID           OtherEnd;                 /* ID of the bound side of the session           */
    NODEID        BoundNode;                /* node where the bound process runs             */
    HANDLE        handle;                   /* session handle given out by the communications manager  */
    TRID          UsedBy;                   /* transaction that is currently riding on this session  */
    char          *stuff;                   /* many other things                             */
    } SECB;                                 /*                                              */
```

Now that the data structures for the entity types have been established, we need the control blocks for the cross-references among the entity types. Let us start with the control block for the m:n relationship between resource managers and transactions. Since this chapter is on the TP monitor, these control blocks are rooted in the RMCB; they might as well be rooted in the TACB, or in both.

```
/*** template for a control block containing information about a transaction's association with   ***/
/*** a resource manager; anchored at RMTA_chain.                                                   ***/
typedef struct      rmta * RMTA_CBP;         /*                                                     */
typedef struct      rmta                     /* control block describing the association between one */
                    {                         /* resource manager and one transaction               */
    TRID            ServicedTA;              /* ID of the transaction involved                       */
    pointer         DataINeed;               /* points to a data structure the RM may want to maintain */
                                             /* for keeping state pertaining to its work on that TA  */
    RMTA_CBP        NextTA;                  /* points to control block for next transaction of RM   */
    } RMTA_CB;                               /*                                                     */
```

The interesting thing about this data structure is the variable DataINeed. It allows a resource manager (not a particular process from its server class) to maintain context for a transaction. This is a simple version of the context management techniques depicted in Figure 6.5. The way it is declared here is a mixture of keeping context data in the database and of putting it into shared memory.

Another type of control block rooted at RMCB is needed to implement volatile queues. These queues have to be kept in cases where there are more TRPCs for a resource manager than the server class has processes—and where the TP monitor for some reason decides not to create new processes. (See Section 6.4 for details.)

```
/***           template for an entry in the resource manager's request queue                      ***/
typedef struct      rmq *RMQUEP;             /*                                                     */
typedef struct      rmq                      /* control block describing one TRPC to that res. manager */
                    {                         /* that could not be scheduled immediately for lack of processes */
    pointer         RequestMsg;              /* pointer to the message contents; depends on the      */
                                             /* interface that the request is directed to            */
    pointer         RPC_Data;                /* points to a control block describing the RPC context */
    long            timeout;                 /* defines a timeout interval after which the waiting request */
                                             /* is cancelled.                                        */
    RMID            ClientType;              /* which resource manager issued the request            */
    rmInstance      ClientInst;              /* which instance of the RM issued the request          */
    RMQUEP          NextWaiter;              /* pointer to next entry in request queue                */
    } RMQUE;                                 /*                                                     */
```

The entries ClientType and ClientInst are provided to support detection of deadlocks that are caused by suspended TRPCs.

Two lists relate processes to server classes, as shown in Figure 6.8. The first one lists all the processes that may switch to a server class (i.e., to its address space), and it holds a flag saying if this is one of the processes that has been allocated for that server class. Note that the same information is also kept in the PCB entry InstanceOf.

The second list starting at PCB contains the RMIDs whose code a process is allowed to execute. That is, it can switch to the address space of the corresponding server class.

```
/***          template for an entry in the resource manager's process queue          ***/
typedef struct    rmpr * RMPR_CBP;       /*                                             */
typedef struct    rmpr                   /* control block describing a process associated with the  */
              {                          /* resource manager                          */
    PID           pid                    /* process identifier of the associated process */
    Boolean       PrimaryProc;           /* is this a process that was allocated for the resource */
                                         /* manager's server class ?                  */
    RMPR_CBP      NextProcess;           /* pointer to next entry in process list     */
              } RMPR_CB;                 /*                                            */
/***          template for an entry in the process' resource manager list             ***/
typedef struct    prrm * RMPR_CBP;       /*                                            */
typedef struct    prrm                   /* control block describing a resource manager the process */
              {                          /* can switch to                             */
    RMID          rmid                   /* ID of resource manager implemented by the server class */
    char          *stuff;                /* addressing information, depends on the OS  */
    PRRM_CBP      NextResMgr;            /* pointer to next entry in resource manager list */
              } PRRM_CB;                 /*                                            */
```

The other reference data structures mentioned in Figure 6.7 are organized in exactly the same way and therefore need not be spelled out explicitly. The transaction control block and the data structures that go with it are introduced in Chapter 11, Section 11.2.

When describing the algorithms for handling TRPCs, it will be convenient to have routines that access the control blocks declared above (such as RMCB, PCB) via their primary keys. Of course, these routines can be used only inside the components owning the respective control block. From the outside, the more restricted retrieval operations introduced at the beginning of this subsection are available.

The ancillary routines perform the following function: given the identifier of the object type, they return the pointer to the corresponding control block upon lookup, or they return the pointer to a newly allocated control block upon insert. The following prototype declaration illustrates this for the RMCB:

```
enum          operation { LOOKUP, INSERT };
RMCB *        RMCBAccess(RMID, operation);
```

The operation is INSERT if a new control block is required for the given RMID, in which case there must be no existing entry with that RMID. The function returns the pointer to the control block that has been allocated for the new resource manager. If the operation is LOOKUP, the function returns the pointer to the control block belonging to the given RMID. In either case, the function returns NULL if something goes wrong. Note that access is defined via the RMID; one can easily imagine an equivalent function for accessing RMCB via RMNAME. Similar functions are assumed for the process and the session control block.

6.3.3 A Guided Tour Along the TRPC Path

This subsection takes you through a complete TRPC thread. We start at the moment the TRPC is issued by some resource manager, follow it through the TRPC stub, see how control is transferred to the callee, and then, upon return, trace the way back to the caller. To avoid unnecessary repetition, we will divide the path into a number of steps:

Local call processing. This is what happens in the caller's TRPC stub to find out what kind of call is being made, where it is directed, and so on.

Preparing outgoing calls. In case the call is not local—that is, the server invoked runs in a different node—the communication manager has to get involved to send the message off to the other side.

Incoming call processing. When a TRPC from another node has arrived, it must be prepared so that it can be passed on to a local process.

Call delivery. After the recipient of a TRPC (be it local or remote) has been determined, it must be invoked at the proper address.

Call return. This can be described as one step, because the return path is completely set up during the call phase, no matter if it is a local or a remote call.

Let us now describe each of these steps in some detail. To do so, we rely on a mixture of explanations in plain English and portions of C code, in a style similar to that used in Chapter 3. Note, though, that what looks like C code is often just pseudo-code in C syntax. Spelling out the complete code for transactional remote procedure calls, including process scheduling and the other services of a TP monitor, would require a separate, quite sizeable book. The reader is therefore cautioned not to take the code examples as something one would want to compile and run; rather, they are a slightly stricter way of writing explanations.

6.3.3.1 Local Call Processing

A TRPC comes from an application or resource manager running in some process. Whether it is the process's own resource manager calling or not makes no difference at all. We assume the do-it-yourself format of the call introduced in Subsection 6.2.1, and now look at the corresponding entry in the TRPC stub. As pointed out repeatedly, this is part of each address space, so it is just a subroutine call to rmCall. This routine starts out checking what kind of request has been issued. It should be easy to get this information by following the (pseudo-) code for the first part of rmCall.

```
Boolean    rmCall(  RMNAME                     /* entry point to server routine                         */
                    BindId * rmname, BoundTo,  /*                                                       */
                    rmParams * InParams,       /*                                                       */
                    rmParams * OutResults);    /*                                                       */
           {                                   /*                                                       */
                 RMCBP     rmcbp;              /* pointer to control block of requested resource mgr.   */
                 PID       pid=MyProcid();     /* PID of my current process                             */
                 PCBP      pcbp=MyProcP();     /* PCB of my current process                             */
                 PID       pid_new;            /* PID and PCBP for new process to                        */
                 PCBP      pcbp_new;           /* send request to                                       */
                 PRRM_CBP  prrm_cbp;           /*                                                       */
                 Boolean   CanSwitch;          /*                                                       */
                 RMID      DestRMID;           /* RMID of callee                                        */
                 RMID      CallerClient;       /* RMID of caller's client                               */
```

```
Boolean    success;                                  /*                                                    */
CallerClient = pcbp->ClientID;                       /* remember which RMID the caller's client has        */
if (BoundTo == NULL)                                 /* no context sensitive call                          */
    { rmcbp = NameServer(rmname,                     /* look up name server for rmname                     */
                    'LOOKUP');                        /* returns pointer to RMCB                            */
    if (rmcbp == NULL)                               /* rmname is wrong or RM not active                   */
        handle_error;                                /* not covered here                                   */
    if ( !rmcbp->RMLocal )                           /* RM is not locally available                        */
        return(RemoteRMC(....));                     /* invoke procedure for remote calls                  */
                                                     /* see if I can domain-switch to desired RM           */
    DestRMID = rmcbp -> rmid;                         /* get RMID of callee                                 */
/* authorize request; see description in Section 6.4; code omitted                                         */
    CanSwitch = FALSE;                               /*                                                    */
    prrm_cbp = pcbp->IMayUse;                        /* scan list to see if my process can                 */
    while ((prrm_cbp != NULL) && !CanSwitch)   /* switch to callee's address space                         */
            { CanSwitch = ( prrm_cbp->rmid == DestRMID);   /*                                              */
            prrm_cbp = prrm_cbp->NextResMgr;           /*                                                  */
            };                                       /*                                                    */
    if ( CanSwitch )                                 /* don't need new process                             */
        { pcbp->ClientID = pcbp->RunsIn;   /* set process' assignment to RMs                               */
        pdbp->RunsIn = DestRMID;           /*                                                              */
        success = DomainSwitch(DestRMID,...); /* transfer control to destination                          */
        }                                            /* the ... denote more params                         */
    else                                             /* need new process                                   */
        {   /* Here the TP monitor's scheduling component must be invoked. It has                          */
            /* 3 options: invoke remote process (handled separately), wait in                              */
            /* queue for resource manager (see 6.3), switch to local process.                              */
            /* Only the last case is spelled out in the following.                                         */
            /* Let pid_new and pcbp_new point to process selected by scheduler.                            */
            pcbp_new->busy = TRUE;    /* set up process CB                                                 */
            pcbp_new->ClientID = pcbp->RunsIn;   /*                                                        */
            pcbp_new->RunsIn = DestRMID;         /*                                                        */
            pcbp_new->WorksFor = pcbp->WorksFor; /*                                                        */
/* prepare request message                                                                                 */
            SendIPC(pid_new,RequestMessage);         /* send request to new                                */
                                                     /* process; wakes it up                               */
            Receive(ResponseMessage);                /* wait for response                                  */
/* restore RunsIn and ClientId, etc.                                                                       */
            };                                       /*                                                    */
        return(success);                             /* return to client                                   */
        }                                            /*                                                    */
    else                                             /* TRCP flows along a session                         */
    { if (BoundTo.EndB.nodeid != NULL)               /* session to remote node                             */
        return(RemoteRMC(...));                      /* invoke procedure for session call                  */
    if (BoundTo.EndB.pid = pid)                      /* session in same process                            */
        { /* do domain switch */}                    /*                                                    */
    else                                             /* session to other local process                    */
        { SendIPC(...);   };                         /* see above                                          */
                                                     /*                                                    */
};
```

As can be seen, the stub code is mostly concerned with figuring out where to send the request. If the request is local, the stub code authorizes the client; the methods for that are presented in Section 6.5. It then decides whether it can hold on to the client's process and just do a domain switch, or if it has to find another process that is authorized to execute the callee's code. For the first case, we assume a procedure DomainSwitch that hides all the operating system–specific aspects involved. Finding a process is the task of the TP monitor's scheduler. The considerations going into that decision are also described in Section 6.5. The scheduler comes up with one out of three possible decisions: first, if too much is going on locally, then send the request to another node, even though the service is locally available. Thus, we have to continue at the point where outgoing requests are handled, represented by the routine RemoteRMC. The second possible decision is to put the requesting process on a waiting queue in front of the resource manager to which the TRPC is going. This problem is discussed in Section 6.4. The third possibility is to pick an idle process and send the request to it; this is done using the routine SendIPC.

In the event the TRPC flows along a preestablished session, the TP monitor has only to forward the request to the other end point of the session, which is completely identified in the rmInstance that serves as a handle for that session.

The problem of binding the resource manager name to a server class is slightly simplified in the program just given. Strictly speaking, a TRPC name consists of a tuple ⟨resource manager name, entry name⟩. Thus, name binding of a resource manager at one of its entry points requires the name resolution and address binding of both components of the tuple.

Binding an RMNAME to an RMID is done through the repository, which holds the information about each RMNAME in the (distributed) system as to where the service is available, and under which RMID. The TP monitor caches these binding data as far as possible; we will not discuss that in detail. If you look closely at the declarations of the RMCB and its related data structures, you will find that they are designed to cache binding information.

Binding the entry name is straightforward. It is assumed that a resource manager, at the moment it is installed by the TP monitor, declares all its service and callback entries. Since the TP monitor loads the code for the resource managers into the address spaces it has allocated for them, and since all processes in one server class have identical structures, the addresses of all the entries are known to the TP monitor. In some implementations of TP systems, the code of resource managers may have to be relocated in their address spaces at run time, but this complication is ignored here.

Figure 6.10 summarizes the name binding to be done by the TP monitor.

6.3.3.2 Preparing Outgoing Calls

If a request has to be sent to a distant node, the major work is done by the communication manager, which is responsible for setting up and maintaining the communication sessions among processes. First, the TRPC stub in the TP monitor formats the message to be sent; this is almost identical to what a standard RPC stub does, except for the TRID that is appended to the message. If the request goes along a predefined session, the handle provided by the communication manager is put in the message header as an indication for the communication manager to use that session. The handle is kept by the TP monitor in the SECB.

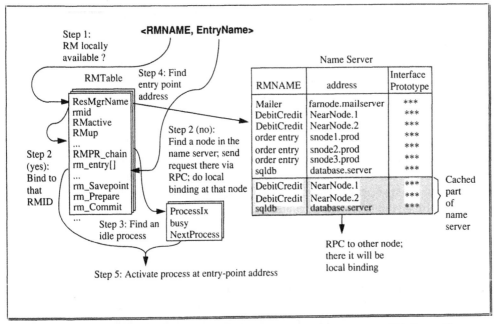

Figure 6.10: Binding RMNAME to RMID in a distributed transaction system. This figure illustrates the main steps required for binding a resource manager invocation to a node, to an RMID in that node, to a process servicing that server class, and to an entry-point address in that process.

```
typedef struct    FRMsg *msg_ptr;           /*                                                            */
typedef struct    FRMsg                     /*                                                            */
    {   RMID          addressee;            /* which server is to receive the request                    */
        TRID          req_trid;             /* trid of requestor                                         */
        NODEID        orig_node;            /* callee's node identifier                                  */
        RMID          rmid;                 /* caller's RMID                                             */
        HANDLE        handle;               /* does it go on an established RM session                   */
        TERMID        terminal_id;          /* which terminal does it come from                          */
        AUTHID        user_id;              /* authorization code of the user who started transaction    */
        AUTHID        rm_authid       .     /* authorization code of the requestor                       */
        Ulong         source_authent;       /* indicates requestor has been authenticated by             */
                                            /* his local TP monitor                                      */
        char          *stuff;               /* more header data, not needed here                         */
                                            /* some more administrative information                      */
        Ulong         data_length;          /* how many data bytes do follow that                        */
        char          payload[data_length]; /* message body                                              */
    } RequestMessage;                       /*                                                            */
```

The communication manager takes the message and checks if it has seen this transaction going out on that session before. It does so by checking the entry UsedBy in the SECB. If this is the first time, it stores req_trid in UsedBy and calls the transaction manager to inform it that this transaction is leaving the node on an outgoing session. As will be seen in Chapter

11, the transaction manager needs to know this for two reasons: first, it must include the remote resource managers in the commit decision, and because it cannot invoke them directly, it must go through the communication manager. Second, the session itself needs to be transaction protected, so that the communication manager becomes another local participant in this transaction. (This is also discussed in Chapter 10.)

6.3.3.3 Incoming Call Processing

This description can be kept short. As a request arrives from the network, it is delivered to the communication manager first. The communication manager goes through a logic similar to that of the rmCall in the case of local call processing:

If the incoming request travels along a preestablished session, then there is already a process allocated to it. Actually, this process has been suspended in its TRPC stub while waiting for the next request via this session. Thus, all the communication manager has to do is unpack the message (the inverse of what has been described for the preparation of outgoing calls) and then wake up the other end of the session; this means routing the call to the "right" resource manager process.

If there is no preestablished session, a process must be scheduled to handle the request. The option of just switching address spaces must be ruled out in this case, because the communication manager wants to hold on to its process in order to be able to handle other incoming and outgoing messages. Therefore, the scheduler of the TP monitor has to find a process that can execute in the address space of the requested server class. The process control block is then set up just as for local call processing.

There is one situation that has not yet been considered: assume the request comes in and there is no session on the receiving side for it, but the requestor's side sends a handle along, thus indicating that a session should be established (see the description of the rmBind function in Section 6.2). In this case, the communication manager has to go through its logic for establishing a session (authenticate the requestor, for example). After that is done, it has to create a new SECB for that session and have the TP monitor allocate a process for it, which is from then on bound to that session. Of course, the BindId, which is the application-level identifier of the session, is passed on to the server so that it knows it is in session with the client.

In accord with the logic of outgoing calls, the communication manager calls the transaction manager to inform it about the arrival of a new transaction on a session from the network. This also has to do with commit processing, although the role of the local transaction manager is different than in the previous case.

6.3.3.4 Call Delivery

Assume that a domain switch has been performed. The process executing the TRPC now continues in the TRPC stub of the callee's address space at the location where incoming calls from local processes are received. There is not much left to do before the resource manager can start working on the request. The first step is optional: the resource manager might want to do some additional authorization of the client's request, which for security reasons has to be performed in its own protection domain rather than outside.

The second step is strictly related to the logic of transactional RPC. The TP monitor has to check if the resource manager has already checked in with the transaction manager for the current transaction. Sophisticated resource managers could do that themselves, but simple resource managers cannot, and so it is good idea to have the TP monitor do it for them. This is the logic (we assume the same variable names and declarations as in the discussion of local call processing):

```
RMCBP          rmcbp;                    /* pointer to CB of this resource manager    */
RMTA_CBP       rmta_cbp;                 /* pointer for the list of TAs associated     */
Boolean        HaveToJoin;               /* with this resource manager                 */
TRID           trid = MyTrid();          /* current transaction                        */
if (trid != NULLTRID)                    /* check if incoming request had a trid       */
    { rmcbp = MyRMP();                   /* locate CB of this resource manager         */
      rmta_cbp = rmcbp->RMTA_chain;      /* start searching the list of assoc. TRIDs   */
      HaveToJoin = TRUE;                 /*                                            */
      while ((rmta_cbp != NULL) && HaveToJoin)    /*                                   */

            { HaveToJoin = (rmta_cbp->ServicedTA != trid);  /* look for entry with TRID */
              rmta_cbp = rmta_cbp->NextTA;               /*                            */
            };                           /*                                            */
      if (HaveToJoin)                    /* resource manager sees trid 1st time        */
          Join_Work();                   /* call transaction manager                   */
    };                                   /*                                            */
```

The effects of Join_Work are described in Chapter 10. Note that in case the incoming request has no TRID—which is quite possible if it is a message from a dumb terminal—the TP monitor cannot check in the resource manager with the transaction manager. What will happen (most likely) is that the resource manager will call Begin_Work, and as a consequence of that, the transaction manager will automatically register the resource manager as a participant of that new transaction. Once all this is done, the resource manager can start unpacking the message and act on it.

6.3.3.5 Call Return

The logic of call return handling is essentially the same, no matter which way the TRPC went. There are slight variations, though, with respect to the clean-up work in the global data structures. A TRPC returning within the same process (coming back from a domain switch) is like a return from a subroutine call. The only thing the TP monitor has to do is restore the entries RunsIn and ClientID in the process control block. A return from an outgoing call looks just like a return from a local call with a process switch involved, because the response message is first received by the communication manager, who sends it (via IPC) to the caller's process. In either case, the caller's process is suspended in the TRPC stub, waiting to be woken up again with a response message.

We can restrict the description to the case of a local return from a TRPC handled by another process. The administrative work on the TP monitor's part consists of two things: first, the process control block of the returning process must be reset; second, requests must be checked to see if there are any waiting in front of the resource manager that just completed, so that the process can immediately be scheduled for one of them. This is the logic:

```
RMQUEP          rmquep;                         /* pointer to queue of requests              */
if (  BoundTo == NULL    )                      /* if process is not bound                   */
     {   pcbp_new->busy = FALSE;                /* reset process control block               */
         pcbp_new->ClientID = NULLRMID;         /*                                           */
         pcbp_new->RunsIn = NULLRMID;           /*                                           */
         pcbp_new->WorksFor = NULLTRID;         /*                                           */
         if  (rmcbp->QueueLength ! = 0)         /* if a request is waiting:                  */
              {   rmquep = rmcbp->waiters;      /* get 1st queue element (FIFO)              */
                  rmcbp->waiters = rmquep->NextWaiter; /*                                    */
                  rmbcp->Queuelength--;         /*                                           */
                  /* enter local call processing with dequeued element                       */
              };                                /*                                           */
     };                                         /*                                           */
```

If no unserviced requests are waiting, the process enters the wait state by invoking an operating system service called "wait," which is described in Chapter 8. For convenience, our code here is written as though it were executed in the process of the original caller, which it is not. Given all the previous arguments, the reader should be able to figure out which process actually activates the process waiting in the resource manager's request queue.

6.3.4 Aborts Racing TRPCs

The discussion in Section 6.2 was simplified in a number of respects; two aspects omitted from the earlier discussion are at least mentioned here. First, the code examples were written like simple sequential programs, which they absolutely are not. Remember that TRPC processing takes place in the TRPC stub, which is in everybody's address space and thus gets executed in parallel by many processes—potentially on a number of processors. To allow for that, all the central control blocks must be protected by special functions called *semaphores*, depicted by flags in Figure 6.7. The details are described later in this book; for the moment, it should be sufficient to assume that there is a mechanism providing the required level of coordination among the processes.

The next problem is more subtle. When describing the flow of control, we have assumed that at any point in time only one process could be working on any given transaction. Because we have ruled out intratransaction parallelism, this seems to be a reasonable assumption. However, it is not quite that simple. In a distributed transaction, no matter which node is currently handling a request for that transaction, an unsolicited abort message from another node can arrive at any instant. Without control, this could cause two processes at the same node to start working concurrently on behalf of the same transaction, resulting in major inconsistencies.

Without referring to technical detail that has not yet been established, let us sketch the problem in very simple terms. Assume a process A is working for transaction T, updating some objects, generating log records, and so on. An abort message arrives because a remote site, which was also involved in T, has crashed and restarted again, and it tells all affected nodes to abort T. If a process B were allowed to run in parallel to process A (on the same node), trying to do the rollback work for T, then the following situation could occur.

Process B works its way back through the log to undo what was done on behalf of T, while process A keeps adding records to the log, which process B will never see. At some point *B* declares victory—rollback complete—while in fact the object is now in a thoroughly inconsistent state. Therefore, the TP monitor enforces a simple protocol:

(1) Whenever a process runs under a TRID, that process protects the control blocks it uses, preventing all other processes from using and, in particular, from updating them. Of course, the transaction manager protects its control blocks, too.

(2) Whenever the TP monitor tries to handle a resource manager invocation for a transaction and finds the transaction busy, it immediately rejects the call, unless it is an abort call.

(3) An abort call checks if the abort is already under way; if so, the call can be rejected without consequences.

(4) If no abort is under way, it might still be the case that a process is doing normal (forward) work for the transaction. The TP monitor checks this with its central control blocks. If a process is working for that transaction, the TP monitor waits for the call to return. Then the TP monitor blocks all the control blocks pertaining to that transaction and thus makes sure that the rollback of *T* will be executed without interruptions at this node.

This protocol is transparent to both clients and servers.[5] It is the TP monitor that reserves the control blocks before invoking the requested resource manager entry. The TP monitor frees them when the transaction is completed and the resource manager is no longer involved. In the case of abort handling, this requires some cooperation between the TP monitor and the transaction manager.

If the description of the abort racing problem sounded a bit difficult, it is. A detailed analysis of all the options there are would take up too much space. Thus, this complication is only mentioned; it is typical of a transactional remote procedure call, as opposed to standard RPC.

6.3.5 Summary

This section started out with a digest description of standard RPC mechanisms. It then proceeded to transactional remote procedure calls, focusing on what makes them different from the standard ones. The key difference is that TRPCs are not just one-time interactions between clients and servers, but that each invocation is automatically bound into the control sphere of an ongoing transaction. Some examples have pointed out that even simple programs that do not know anything about transactions are given the ACID treatment when invoked in a TRPC environment. Programs actively using the features provided by transactional remote procedure calls are called resource managers. They have to interact with their environment in a well-defined manner, which is specified as the resource manager interface. The major components of this interface have been introduced via examples.

We then proceeded to describe how the TP monitor implements TRPCs. First, the required global process and address space structure were laid out, and then the central data

---

[5] It is transparent as far as it goes. What the programmer of a resource manager must be prepared to see is a bad return code from a server call, indicating that in the meantime the abort of the transaction has been initiated. The resource manager can then just call Rollback_Work itself, and quit. The transaction manager makes sure the resource manager gets invoked at its proper callback entries in order to undo its work.

structures needed by the TP monitor were explained in detail. Finally, we took a tour along a TRPC through the TP monitor stub and the communications manager, to investigate what exactly needs to be done for mapping TRPCs onto processes. To recap the major steps: bind the name of the requested service to a server class, local or remote. If it is remote, prepare a message to be sent and hand it to the communication manager. The communication manager will check with the transaction manager to register the fact that a transaction leaves the node to continue execution elsewhere. If the call is local, a process must be allocated for handling the request. Upon return, the basic work consists in freeing resources that had been allocated to the TRPC. Some of the tasks along the way, like scheduling and authorization, have only been mentioned for the moment; they are discussed in the upcoming sections.

6.4 Managing Request and Response Queues

A look back at Figure 5.3 shows that there are two ways transactional requests can get into (and out of) the TP system. One is the "fast lane": requests are immediately authorized, dispatched, and executed, and responses are returned to the client without delay. This mode of operation is called *direct transactions* and is typically used for interactive processing. The other mode is asynchronous and involves the system queueing requests over potentially longer periods of time. So far, we have considered only direct transactions.

As mentioned in Chapter 5, queueing is used in transaction processing systems for a variety of reasons. Let us briefly recapitulate them to see which properties an implementation of transactional queueing services must have in order to meet these requirements. These are the main applications of queues:

Load control.   If there is a temporary peak in the request rate for a resource manager, it might not be a good idea to react by creating additional processes. If the load can be expected to return to normal quickly, it might be more economical to put the requests into a temporary queue in front of the server class rather than flood the system with new processes, which will rarely be used later on. Note that this type of queue is used during direct transaction processing (it was actually mentioned in the pseudo-code example) and is kept entirely in volatile storage.

End-user control.   Responses from transaction programs usually involve messages to be displayed to the user, either as text or pictures on the screen, as a ticket that gets printed, as money from a teller machine, or for whatever purpose you can name. Since this always is a real action of some sort, it is critical for the end points of the system to be in accord with the central resource managers with respect to which steps were completed and which were not. At first glance, there does not seem to be a problem, because the two-phase commit protocol is designed to take care of that, and one of our key prognoses was that in real transaction processing systems all terminals will be intelligent enough to run that protocol. With asynchronous processing, however, the system transaction updating the database may have completed successfully, whereas the subsequent output transaction presenting the result to the user was rolled back because of a system crash or simply because the user had switched off his workstation. Thus, there is a need for maintaining the output of asynchronous transactions for redelivery as long as the user has not explicitly acknowledged its receipt.

Recoverable data entry.   There are applications that are essentially driven by data entry. Data are fed into the system at a high rate, and each record is the input to a transaction that does consistency checking and takes further actions. However, there is no feedback to the data source. Such systems can be configured for high throughput rather than short response times. This is to say, the input data are put on a queue from which the server running the application takes them as fast as it can. The key point here is not to lose any input data, even if the system crashes before they get processed.

Multi-transaction requests.   The discussion in Chapter 4 made the point that under the flat transaction ACID paradigm, typical TP systems offer no control beyond transaction boundaries. Because this is insufficient for many applications, the TP monitor generally provides some additional support. Consider the example mentioned in the previous paragraph. The idea is to collect the input data at some point and make them recoverable. Then they are processed by some server $S1$, which passes results on to another server $S2$ for further processing. This can go on for an arbitrary number of steps. As long as none of the steps interacts with a user, they can all be executed asynchronously; that is, scheduled for high throughput. Some final step is then likely to present something to the outside world. Explicitly programming all this chaining of processing steps in the application would be unacceptably complicated. Lacking more general transaction models, there is a way of achieving the desired effect, at least with respect to the control flow: by employing queues. The idea is illustrated in Figure 6.11.

It is obvious from this list of requirements that two types of queues are needed: first, *volatile* queues must be provided to support the management of server classes for direct transactions. Second, *durable* (recoverable) queues must be supported for handling asynchronous transaction processing. Let us first briefly consider the implementation of volatile

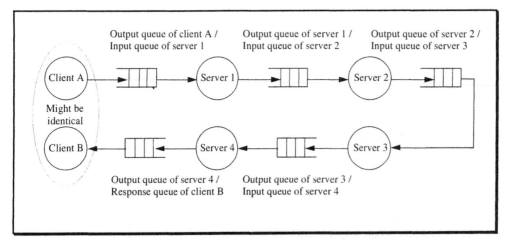

Figure 6.11: Control flow among multiple transactions managed by employing intermediate queues.   Starting with the client, where the activities originate, each transaction produces as its output a request for processing, which goes into a queue in front of the appropriate server class. The server class feeds off this queue, acting upon each request by executing a transaction, which in turn produces a request into another queue, and so on. Whether the final outcome of this transaction chain goes to the original client or to a different one depends completely on the application.

queues as part of the server class scheduler; there is really not much to say about this. After that, the techniques for providing durable queues are described in some detail.

6.4.1 Short-Term Queues for Mapping Resource Manager Invocations

The need for a short-term queueing mechanism was illustrated by the pseudo-code example in Section 6.3, which describes the handling of generic resource manager calls. There is one situation in which these queues are needed: a server class has been installed with P processes, and at some point the number of concurrent requests for that server class exceeds P. If the TP monitor decides not to initiate more processes (and if the service is not available at remote nodes), then there are two possibilities:

(1) Let the client decide what to do. That means the TP monitor rejects the call with a return code indicating overload. The client process might decide to wait for some time and then reissue the call. This method offloads the problem of how to handle wait situations to the client, who is probably not prepared to cope with it and simply calls Rollback_Work. Even if the client were able to wait in its own process, this would not be a good solution because with the reject the request disappears from the TP monitor's domain; that is, the TP monitor has no control of how much unfinished work is in the system. As a consequence, the TP monitor cannot use that information for making its scheduling decisions.

(2) The TP monitor keeps a dynamic request queue anchored at the control block for the server class. In that queue, the excessive requests are stored for dispatch at the next occasion. The next occasion arises whenever one of the processes in that server class completes its current request; that is why, upon return from a request, the temporary queue must be checked for any entries. Note that with this scheme, a resource manager invocation, which is a synchronous call from the client's perspective, turns into queued processing that is typical of asynchronous request handling. But then, the same is true for the basic operating system, where processes are queued in front of processors and other physical resources. The underlying assumption is that waits are short enough to be tolerable, even in an interactive environment.

The basic implementation problem associated with this type of queue is illustrated in Figure 6.12.

As can be seen from the declarations in Section 6.3, there is one anchor for a volatile request queue in each resource manager control block, that is, for each server class at each node. The queue itself is assumed to be maintained as a linked list of request control blocks. This is sufficient for strict FIFO processing (which we assume here); for other policies, including priorities, more sophisticated data structures would be required. The queueing aspects themselves are not particularly exciting: it is a single queue with multiple servers (processes of the server class), and each queue entry can be serviced by any of the processes. What makes things interesting, though, is the process configuration shown in Figure 6.6. Because there may be many processes in the server class, more than one of them might try to remove the same first element from the queue at the same time. An equivalent observation holds for the tail of the queue: more than one process may want to append a request to the queue at the same time. And, of course, in a queue with just one element, the first entry is also the last one, causing these processes to compete for access to the same control block. However, the following must be guaranteed:

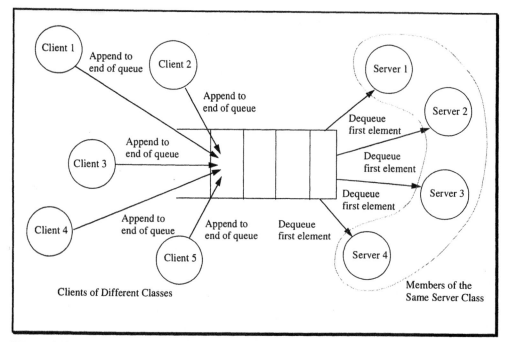

Figure 6.12: Volatile queues used to fend off peaks in the request rate for a specific server class. For each server class, a dynamic volatile waiting queue can be maintained by the TP monitor. The processes allocated to the server class feed off this queue whenever they become free by taking out the first request. New requests are appended to the end of the queue by processes issuing resource manager invocations.

(1) Each request must be taken from the queue and executed by a server exactly once.

(2) The structure of the queue must always be maintained correctly.

Chapter 8 presents methods to achieve the protection required for the moment, we will leave it at that.

It is important to understand the following point: although these server class–specific request queues contain transactional requests, there is no need to bind request queues strictly to the ACID paradigm. In other words, it is not necessary to keep the first element of such a queue reserved until it is clear whether the transaction having issued the request has committed or aborted. These queues can be accessed and modified by many transactions at the same time, the requirements just discussed notwithstanding. Given a system that supports multi-level transactions, each operation on a request queue would be a subtransaction.

6.4.2 Durable Request Queues for Asynchronous Transaction Processing

Durable queues are needed for a style of processing that, at first glance, seems to be quite different from online transaction processing. To make this point very clear, let us repeat the basic idea of queue-oriented processing: there is a transaction handling the client request; presentation services, some authentication, consistency checking, and so on, are part of that transaction. It eventually produces a request to a server, but this request is not passed to the server along a TRPC; rather, it is put onto a request queue in front of that server, and then *the client transaction commits*. The client process can then begin a new transaction that creates another request to the server, and so forth. Finally (in this example), the client will enter a wait state until the response from the server to the first of the client's requests has arrived. Before considering that in more detail, let us switch to the server's side.

In essence, the server sits there watching its work-to-do queue. Whenever there is an entry, it starts a transaction, picks an entry from the queue—according to FIFO, based on priorities, or whatever—processes the request, puts the response on a queue the client is watching, and then commits the server transaction. If there is more work in its input queue, the server does the same thing over again.

The client, as noted, enters a wait state if it is interested in the responses, and actually waits for an entry to appear in its response queue. As soon as that happens, it starts a transaction, takes the response from the queue, does whatever the response requires, and commits the transaction.

Note that for each request there are three transactions:

(1) The first transaction creates the request and enters it into the server's input queue.

(2) The second transaction processes the request in the server and enters the result into the client's response queue.

(3) The third transaction takes the response out of the client's response queue and presents it to the user (or does whatever is required).

This style of processing called queued transaction processing (QTP), which is essentially the way IMS/DC structures its work, is illustrated in Figure 6.13. Given the fact that each resource manager can act as a server to the resource managers that invoke it, and as a client to those whose services it needs, the QTP model implies *durable relationships* between a resource manager and a number of queues. A resource manager can designate some queues as input queues—queues through which it is willing to accept requests. The minimum is one

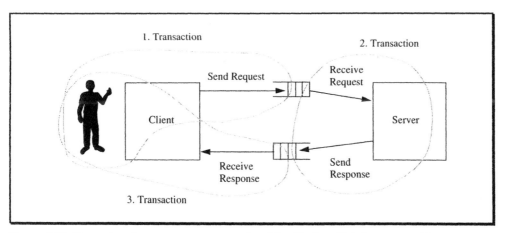

Figure 6.13: Request and response queues are durable objects. Entering a request into a request queue in front of a server is a transaction; so is the removal of the request, its processing, and the entering of the response into the client's response queue. Receiving the response via the response queue is yet another transaction.

such queue, but the resource manager may decide to have different queues for different types of clients or for different types of services it provides. Accordingly, each resource manager has to relate to different output queues that receive its results. Again, there can be a standard output queue per server class, or the server can place its results into a queue that has been designated by the client. Note that the output queue from the perspective of one resource manager is the input queue from the viewpoint of the other.

Queues, then, are distinguishable, stable objects that are manipulated through ACID transactions. They are, in fact, much like database relations. We will see later on that durable queues can be implemented as SQL relations, but we will also observe that there are good reasons for not making them part of the global database.

To understand what it means for a resource manager to have durable relationships to a queue, imagine the way direct transactions (those we have implicitly assumed so far) get executed. An activity starts at a terminal when a user hits a function key, selects a menu item, or enters his credit card. From then on, all requests flow through the system on TRPCs or sessions until the transaction commits and the final message is delivered to the user—provided the transaction commits. If it does not commit there is no final message, of course, thanks to the ACID properties. Now assume the transaction fails because of a system crash. If recovery takes a while, the user probably decides to come back later, when the system has recovered. He then wants to know what the last successful interaction with the system (the last committed transaction) was, because he has to pick up his work at that point. Using only transactions, this is a problem. The last successful transaction had gone through the two-phase commit protocol: the resource manager at the user's workstation had voted Yes, because the user had seen the result, and then all participating resource managers had forgotten about the transaction. Subsequent aborted transactions have left no traces anyway. Asking for the last successful transaction, then, is asking for something that no longer exists; one would have to read the log to find the requested information. Yet fundamentally—in the transaction paradigm—the outcome of a transaction is a durable event, though no standard interface to the system exists to allow inquiries about that type of durable event.

6.4.2.1 The Client's View of Queued Processing

Queues in the sense described here allow such questions to be asked. They maintain durable information about the association between different resource managers. Remember that in our "favorite" model of transaction systems, each end point (workstation) will be represented in the system by at least one resource manager that manages the local context and presentation services. Since each request, as well as each response, is recorded durably in a queue, there is a history of resource manager interactions that makes it possible to determine specifically what happened last between a certain client and its server. Put another way, if the client has crashed and later restarts, the client can go back to its response queue and check which response was last delivered to it before the crash. The behavior of such queue-oriented client-server interactions can be characterized by three properties.

Request-reply matching. The system guarantees that for each request there is a reply—even if all it says is that the request could not be processed.

ACID request handling. Each request is executed exactly once. Storing the response is part of the ACID transaction.

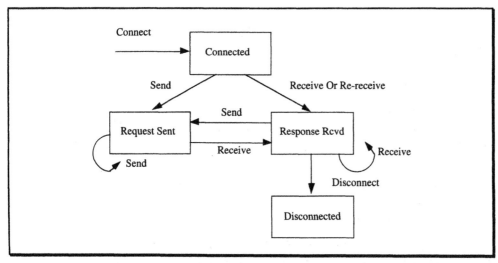

Figure 6.14: State diagram of a durable queue. A resource manager can interact with the queue only if the two are connected. Connections to a queue are also durable. From the perspective of a single service request, the behavior of a resource manager with respect to its queues is described by this state diagram. A request is entered into a durable queue, and there must be a corresponding response later on. A resource manager can disconnect from a queue only if there are no outstanding responses.

At-least-once response handling. The client is guaranteed to receive each response at least once. As explained previously, there are situations where it might be necessary to present a response repeatedly to the client. We will discuss shortly how the client must prepare itself for properly dealing with duplicate responses. The important thing about the at-least-once guarantee, though, is the fact that no responses will be lost.

Figure 6.14 shows the corresponding state diagram for the behavior of the client with respect to one request. The client has to be connected to the queueing system in order to issue requests. It then can switch back and forth between sending requests to servers and receiving responses from them. Finally, it can disconnect from the queueing system, but only after having received all responses it has asked for.

To achieve the guarantees just listed, a mechanism for relating requests to responses must be in place. The obvious way to determine which request corresponds to which response is to have a unique identifier for each request (RQID), supplied by the client, which is returned with the response. There is no need for these identifiers to be contiguous. The requests they are attached to are manipulated inside ACID transactions; consequently, there can be no holes due to lost messages or anything like that. For convenience, let us assume the TRID of the transaction issuing the request is used as the RQID.

6.4.2.2 The Client Interface to the Queueing System

With these preparations, we can now define the client's interface to the queueing system of the TPOS. Each queue is identified in much the same way resource managers are identified; in fact, the queueing system can best be thought of as a special resource manager that handles request and response queues. Thus, each queue has a globally unique name and a locally unique queue identifier, which is reflected in the following declares:

```
typedef  char[BIG]    QUNAME;       /* globally unique name for the queue              */
typedef  Uint         QUID;         /* locally unique identifier for the queue         */
typedef  TRID         RQID;         /* request identifier, based on transaction identifier  */
typedef  char         REQUEST[ ];   /* requests are passed as character strings        */
typedef  char         RESPONSE[ ];  /* responses are also passed as character strings  */
```

Before describing the functions for connecting to the queueing system, let us consider the operations that can be invoked once connection has been established. For our simple processing model, three operations are sufficient:

```
/* send passes the request to the queue identified in ToQueue and expects the response in the queue  */
/* specified in RespQueue. The request is identified by rqid.  Returns TRUE if the request was  */
/*successfully entered into the queue, FALSE otherwise.     */
Boolean      send(REQUEST DoThis, RQID rqid, QUID ToQueue, QUID RespQueue);
```

```
/* receives the next response from the queue specified in RespQueue. Some client-specific data  */
/* passed in KeepThat are stored by the queueing system if the response has been taken from the  */
/* queue successfully (as part of the "receive"-transaction). The use of this mechanism is explained  */
/* below.     */
RESPONSE receive(QUID RespQueue, char * KeepThat[1000]);
```

```
/* Presents the response of the last receive successfully executed by that client. It is used after restart of  */
/* the client to find out which was the last piece of work it has successfully executed.     */
RESPONSE  reReceive(QUID RespQueue);
```

Registering a client with a queue establishes a recoverable session between the client and the queue resource manager. This is another example of a stateful interaction between a client and a server. The queue resource manager remembers the RQIDs it has processed, and the client knows whether it can send a request to the server queue, or whether it has to wait for a response from its input queue. The session is recoverable in that after a crash of either side, it can be resumed with all state information reestablished as of the last successful transaction that updated the queue. The function prototypes for opening and closing a session with a queue are as follows:

```
typedef   struct SessionParms    *QStatePtr; /*                                                    */
struct    SessionParms                    /* parameters describing the state of the session         */
                                          /* between a client and the queueing system               */
   {      QUID     quid;                  /* identifier of the queue involved                        */
          RQID     LastSent;              /* ID of the last request sent by the client               */
          RQID     LastRcvd;              /* ID of the request the last response delivered           */
                                          /* to the client belongs to                                */
          RESPONSE  response;             /* information passed by the client with the last          */
                                          /* successful receive operation                            */
   } QState;                              /*                                                         */
```

```
/* Client identifies itself and requests to be connected to the specified queue. If the session between  */
/* the two entities had not been closed down explicitly before, the system returns the state of the  */
/* session as shown in the declare. If the session is newly established, QState contains NULL entries.  */
QState       connect(RMID MyRMID, QUID ToQueue);
```

```
/* Client closes the session with the specified queue. For this operation to complete    */
/* successfully, no responses must be left in the queue for that client.                 */
Boolean      disconnect(RMID MyRMID, QUID FromQueue);
```

The key point is that a session between a client and a queue can only be closed if there are no responses that have not yet been received by the client. By calling disconnect, the client explicitly states that it has properly processed all replies and waives all rights of future inquiries into the state of that session. In case of a failure, however, the session is kept up by the system (or is recovered if the entire node fails), and the client has to call connect after restart. The client then gets back the state of the session as declared above. This state is characterized by the RQID of the last request entered in the queue and by the RQID of the last response received by the client (more precisely, the RQID of the request that triggered this response). Excluding special error conditions, there are two cases to consider:

LastSent = LastRcvd.   The client has received the response to the last request it made. It now has to decide whether the response was processed completely—remember that part of the response handling might be a real action. If the response to the outside world is idempotent (such as a message displayed on a screen), then it can simply be repeated. If it is not idempotent, then the question is if the device the client talks to is *testable*, that is, if it can be queried about its current state. A ticket printer, for example, advances a counter that can be read from the client process each time a ticket is printed. If the client is about to respond to such a device, it reads the counter value, receives the response from the queue (passing the counter value in the parameter KeepThat), commits, and then prints the ticket. Upon restart, it gets the last value passed in KeepThat; if it is equal to the counter in the device, the response had not been processed before the crash, so printing must be done. Otherwise, the ticket has already been printed. If the response processing is not testable either, it is up to the application to put all the information required for a correct restart decision into KeepThat.

LastSent != LastRcvd.   Response processing had been completed before the crash, and a subsequent request had been entered. The response to that request has not yet arrived, so all the client has to do is to enter the request sent state.

6.4.2.3 Implementation of the Queue Resource Manager

Queues have to maintain durable, transaction-protected state. As later chapters will show, it is hard to implement something like this with only a simple (non-transactional) file system underneath. A much simpler approach—and the one taken here—is to offload all the problems related to durable state to somebody else and just focus on the queue-specific aspects. In addition to greatly simplifying the discussion, that approach has the advantage of demonstrating the power of the resource manager architecture that is the leitmotif of this book. In order to turn a simple queue manager into a regular resource manager, we only have to support the resource manager interfaces described earlier and provide the callback entries for the various transaction-specific events. The SQL resource manager takes care of the durable storage, and the TPOS, with all its transaction-oriented services, makes sure that the interaction among all components involved comes out as an ACID transaction.

To keep things simple, assume that all queues are maintained in a single relation that has been created by the following statement:

```
exec sql  CREATE TABLE sys_queues ( quid              integer   not null,
                                     q_type            char(2)   not null,
                                     from_rmid         integer   not null,
                                     to_rmid           integer   not null,
                                     timestamp         time,
                                     rqid              TRID      not null,
                                     keepthat          char(1000),
                                     request_response char(40000),
                                     no_dequeues       integer,
                                     delete_flag       char(1),
                                     primary key (quid,rqid,time)
                                   );
```

It is assumed that the binding of quid to the corresponding quname is done in the repository. All the attributes have been discussed before, with three exceptions:

q_type. Describes the usage of this queue. 'CS' denotes a queue in which a client places requests to a server; 'SC' denotes a queue with responses from a server to a client; 'SS' denotes queues for work-in-progress in multi-transaction executions (see Figure 6.11).

no_dequeues. Counter for keeping track of how often a server has tried to process that request (explained later on).

delete_flag. Tags deleted queue elements. If it is NULL, this is an active entry; if it is 'D,' the element has already been used but is kept in the relation for restart purposes.

The sessions between "other" resource managers and the queue resource manager are stored in a separate relation that has the following schema:

```
exec sql  CREATE TABLE qu_sessions (   quid               integer      not null,
                                       rmid               integer      not null,
                                       role               char(1),
                                       primary key (quid,rmid)
                                   );
```

The attribute role denotes whether the rmid participates in the session as a client or as a server.

The functions provided by the queue resource manager either establish sessions between a queue and a resource manager, or they act on entries of a single queue object; that is, on entries pertaining to one quid. This is important to note, because the client interface to the queue resource manager we have described permits referencing more than one queue object per call; see the description of the send function earlier in this section.

The first function is the send which appends an entry to a specified queue. Here is the implementation:

```
typedef    struct queue_rel    *QAttrPtr;       /* make the queue data structure addressable        */
struct     queue_rel                            /* structure matching the sys_queues relation        */
     {     QUID          quid;                   /* queue identifier                                  */
           char          q_type[2];              /* describes queue type as explained above           */
           RMID          from_rmid;              /* where do the sends come from                      */
           RMID          to_rmid;                /* where do the responses go to                      */
           char          time[8];                /* timestamp of request                              */
           RQID          rqid;                   /* request identifier                                */
           char          keepthat[1000] ;        /* application context for response matching         */
           char          request_response[40000]; /* request-response message                         */
           Uint          no_dequeues;            /* number of attempts to service the request         */
           char          delete_flag;            /* attribute to mark the request deleted             */
     } QAttr;                                    /*                                                   */
Boolean    send(QAttrPtr);                       /* resource mgr. interface for enqueueing a request  */
     {                                           /* for simplicity there is no checking if the requesting */
                                                 /* rm is in session with the designated queue        */
                                                 /* insert the parameters passed into the relation    */
           exec      sql  INSERT INTO sys_queues                                      /*              */
                          VALUES    (:(QAttrPtr->quid), :(QAttrPtr->q_type),          /*              */
                                    :(QAttrPtr->from_rmid), :(QAttrPtr->to_rmid),     /*              */
                                    CURRENT, :(QAttrPtr->rqid), :(QAttrPtr->keepthat), /*             */
                                    :(QAttrPtr->request_response), 0, NULL);/*                        */
           return(sqlcode == 0);                 /*                                                   */
     };                                          /*                                                   */
```

At first glance, one might wonder why the insert pays no attention to any queueing dis-cipline; in particular, there are no provisions for making sure that the new entry is appended at the end of the queue. That is because of the decision to use relations as the implementation vehicle for the queues. Tuples in relations have no system-maintained order whatsoever. If the user wants them ordered, he has to specify a sort order based on the attributes in the relation *when retrieving them*. In other words, the effective queueing discipline depends on how the tuples are selected when deciding which one to remove from the queue. This is part of the second operation provided by the queue resource manager, the receive function.

```
RESPONSE    receive(QUID from_there, char KeepThat [1000]);
     {                                    /* for simplicity consistency checks are omitted     */
           exec  sql  DECLARE CURSOR dequ ON        /* define a scan over all               */
                      SELECT     *    FROM sys_queues /* tuples belonging to queue           */
                      WHERE      quid = :from_there  AND /* ordered by rqid, i.e. in FIFO    */
                                 delete_flag = NULL  /* order; allow updates                 */
                      ORDER BY rqid ASCENDING        /*                                      */
                      FOR UPDATE                     /*                                      */
                      <some isolation clauses>;      /* see text for explanation             */
```

```
        while (TRUE)                                    /* try until an entry is found                */
            {   exec sql OPEN dequ;                     /* execute the select statement               */
                exec sql FETCH dequ INTO :(QAttrPtr->QAttr);/* get values from first entry that is     */
                                                        /* not worked on by another server            */
            if    ( sqlcode == 0 )                      /* found an entry                             */
                { exec sql    UPDATE WHERE CURRENT OF CURSOR dequ /*                                    */
                            SET delete_flag = 'D',      /* mark entry as deleted                       */
                QAttrPtr->KeepThat = :KeepThat;         /* store context for response matching         */
                exec sql CLOSE dequ;                    /* terminate select statement                 */
                return(TRUE);                           /* signal success                             */
                };                                      /*                                            */
                                                        /* In this case, there is no qualifying       */
                                                        /* queue entry.                               */
            exec sql OPEN dequ;                         /* close the (empty) result set               */
            wait(1);                                    /* sleep for some time; try again             */
    };      };                                          /*                                            */
```

These are the two service interfaces of the queue resource manager. It calls the database manager using embedded SQL but so far makes no references to other (system) resource managers. What about its callback entries for transaction handling? Some careful thought to this matter shows that there is actually nothing to do. For example, at startup the queue manager has neither control blocks to initialize nor anything else like that. Its callback entry therefore looks like this:

```
(void)        rm_Startup()
                    {    return; }
```

The queue resource manager's logic during commit processing is not sophisticated, either; whenever it is asked about the outcome of a transaction, it votes Yes:

```
Boolean        rm_Prepare()
                    { return(TRUE); }
```

The other callback entries look exactly the same. Neither has the queue manager any updates to undo (SQL does that), nor is there any savepoint state to write to the log, and so on. Joining the queue manager to a transaction is done automatically by the TP monitor, as described previously.

The result of these considerations, then, is that the code for the transactional queue resource manager is strikingly simple. There is really nothing else to do. And although it looks like a straightforward sequential program, the queue resource manager runs in a multiuser environment and maintains its objects under the protection of ACID transactions. This little example shows that writing resource managers in a transaction processing system is simple—provided they do not keep their own state. Keep this in mind as a general rule for dealing with such systems: whenever possible, have a transactional database system that is able to act as a resource manager to take care of your data; don't mess around with files.

Of course, this is not a comprehensive implementation of a queue resource manager. The coding is not defensive at all, and except for the functions to establish a session between a resource manager and a queue, further administrative functions are required for a complete queueing system. For example, there must be a way for the client to retract requests it no longer wants to be executed, or requests that have turned out to be invalid for other reasons (see Subsection 6.4.2.4). However, adding all this would not change the basic simplicity of the queue resource manager; it would only be more of the same.

6.4.2.4 Some Details of Implementing Transactional Queues

Two interesting details about transactional queues can be observed in the code for the dequeue function. The cryptic remark in our program about "some isolation clauses" refers to the same problem that has already been discussed for the volatile queues: since many server processes can operate on the same queue concurrently, they must protect themselves against each other. For the in-memory queues maintained by the TP monitor, critical sections are the appropriate solution. Durable queues implemented as SQL relations require a slightly different approach.

As we will see in the next two chapters, SQL database systems have a whole set of mechanisms for coordinating the operations of concurrent transactions on shared data. Without using concepts that have not yet been introduced, let us briefly consider the queue-specific problems. Dequeueing an element from a queue is part of a transaction; that is, if the transaction fails, the element must remain in the queue. Now if some transaction T_a has dequeued the first element E_1 no other transaction can take it (exactly-once semantics). On the other hand, E_1 is still the "first element"—the one with the lowest RQID. Thus, each concurrent access asking for the first element will be directed to E_1. And, of course, one cannot say it is no longer there; if T_a aborts, E_1 will remain in the queue as the first element. The only solution preserving FIFO processing in a strict sense would require all other transactions to wait until the fate of T_a is known. If T_a commits, then there is a new "first element"; if it aborts, another transaction will pick up E_1. This, however, is not acceptable from a performance perspective. The following, then, is what the SQL clause not spelled out in the code example says: scan the tuples in the selected queue in their RQID order, but if you find one that is currently being worked on by another transaction, skip it and try the next tuple.

The second remark has to do with a fairly subtle detail of queued transaction processing. If something goes wrong in a direct transaction, the transaction is rolled back, and the user can decide how to react to that. With queued transactions, the first step consists of putting the request into a server queue. Now assume the request is invalid in some way, causing the server transaction to abort. What will happen?

A server process receives the faulty request as part of its processing transaction and sooner or later has to invoke Rollback_Work. As a result, the request reappears in the queue, only to be picked up by the next server process, which also aborts its transaction, and so forth. Given a thoroughly corrupted request, this could go on forever. It is therefore a good idea to have a counter that contains the number of rollbacks caused by the request associated with each queue entry—this is what the attribute no_dequeues is there for. It is set to zero when the tuple is stored, and the plan is to increase it by one each time a transaction having received this entry aborts. The question, though, is how to do that. It basically requires that an aborting transaction produce a durable update—which, by definition, it can't. There are three obvious approaches to solving this problem:

No aborts. One could rule out the use of transaction abort for the server, forcing it to masquerade all failed transactions as successful ones. In this scenario, if something goes wrong, the server calls rollback to savepoint 1, which is the state of the transaction right after executing Begin_Work. It then updates the tuple in the sys_queues relation, setting the delete_flag back to NULL and increasing no_dequeues. After that, it calls Commit_Work.

Unprotected updates. If the update of the queue entry increasing the attribute no_ dequeues is made an unprotected action, then it is not affected by the server trans- action's rollback. If the queue resource manager were implemented on top of the basic file system, this would be an option. However, because we have chosen SQL as the im- plementation vehicle for queues, there is no such thing as an unprotected SQL operation.

Nested top-level transaction. One can try to employ the idea that was used for the Bartlett server in Chapter 5; that is, the updates that have to be detached from the scope of a rollback operation are wrapped into a separate top-level transaction. In contrast to the quotation server, this must happen only in case the server transaction aborts; thus, the logic goes into the routine associated with the rm_Abort callback entry. This is illus- trated in the following piece of code:

```
(void)   rm_Abort(QAttrPtr request);            /* updates queue entry to reflect the server abort   */
         {   TRID    NewTrid;                    /* ID of new top-level transaction                   */
             TRID    OldTrid;                    /* ID of aborting transaction                        */
             Boolean     success;                /* indicator for outcome of TA manager calls         */
             OldTrid = Leave_Transaction(); /* depart from aborting transaction                       */
             NewTrid = Begin_Work(...);              /* start the update transaction                  */
             exec sql    UPDATE sys_queues         /* update queue entry in question                  */
                         SET     delete_flag = NULL               /*                                  */
                                 no_dequeues = no_dequeues + 1   /*                                   */
                         WHERE quid = :(request->quid) and        /*                                  */
                             rqid = :(request->rqid) and          /*                                  */
                             time = :(request->time);     /* no error checking                        */
             success = Commit_Work(NULL, FALSE);          /* commit update                            */
             success = Resume_Transaction(OldTrid);/* reattach to aborting transaction                */
             return;                                  /*                                              */
         }                                        /*                                                  */
```

Readers familiar with the problems of executing concurrent transactions on shared data may point out that the above solution does not work for the following reason: the new trans- action tries to modify a tuple that has also been modified by the old transaction. When that happens, the old transaction is not completely over—the transactions manager is just going through the abort sequence—meaning that the old transaction still protects this tuple from other transactions. The queue manager, on the other hand, starts a new transaction to update the tuple. If the old transaction still holds on to it, the new transaction will wait for that transaction to finish. Given the logic, though, the old transaction will not finish before the new one has updated the tuple; in other words, nothing moves.

Those who came to that assessment are fundamentally right, but not entirely. Note that the piece of code for the nested top-level transaction is not part of the "mainline" implemen- tation of the queue manager's services; rather, it is part of a callback that gets invoked by the transaction manager at a well-defined point in time, namely at the end of the abort phase, after all undo work has been done. Chapters 10 and 11 explain that the order in which the re- source managers participating in a transaction are invoked during commit (or during abort, for that matter) can be specified according to their particular needs. If in our example the queue resource manager is invoked at its rm_Abort entry after the database system, then the logic described works correctly.

6.4.3 Summary

Queues are needed for scheduling transactional processing requests in an asynchronous fashion. The reasons for that are twofold: in direct online transaction processing, temporary system overload can cause requests for certain resource managers to wait in front of the corresponding server class. These queues are volatile. The TP monitor maintains them as temporary control blocks in its pool of shared data structures. The second type of queues is used for queued transaction processing, which by its very nature is asynchronous. Requests, rather than being expedited directly from the requestor to the server via TRPC, are forwarded through durable request queues. Adding entries to such a queue is part of one transaction; taking an entry out is part of another one. Request and response queueing helps in a number of situations, such as coupling a non-transactional end-user environment to the transaction system and implementing multi-transactional activities.

In this section, only one type of queue was implicitly assumed, the so-called ASAP queues. As the name suggests, the entries in such a queue are supposed to be processed as soon as possible. TP monitors support other types of queued processing policies as well. Batch applications are known to run for a long time, consuming many resources; thus, they should be scheduled at times with low system utilization, such as during the night. Requests for such applications are put into *timed* queues, which will not be activated before a pre-specified time. A third type of queue is called *threshold* queue; such queues are not activated unless a prespecified number of requests is in them. This is useful for applications that require resources that are not normally kept available and are expensive to set up, such as parts of tertiary storage or a communication session to a remote node. If a number of requests all requiring these resources are batched together via a threshold queue, the expensive set-up can be amortized over all of them.

6.5 Other Tasks of the TP Monitor

The previous sections explained three major aspects of the transaction processing operating system, down to the level of coding examples: the resource manager interface, including the rules for constructing transactional resource managers; the notion of server classes, including the means for implementing transactional remote procedure calls; and the implementation of queues for queued transaction processing. Some other tasks of the TP monitor in particular have only been mentioned in passing, and there is not enough space to give them an equally detailed treatment. The purpose of this section is to give an overview of the techniques typically used by TP monitors to do load balancing, authentication and authorization, and restart processing.

6.5.1 Load Balancing

The load balancing problem is easy to describe and hard to solve. Given a set of requests (in case of direct transactions) or a request queue (in case of queued processing), how many processes should be given to that server class? When a request arrives at a server class, and all processes are busy handling requests, should a new process be created for the server class, or should the request wait for a process to become available? In the same situation, if the server class is distributed among several nodes, should the request be sent there rather than kept waiting locally? All this boils down to the question of how many virtual machines of which type should be maintained, and where.

Allocating processes to a server class has many problems in common with operating systems, with one big difference: from the perspective of the basic OS, processes are created by application programs or by scripts specified by the system administrator, and these processes are meant to exist for a long time. The operating system, then, only has to select among processes that are ready to execute. The TP monitor, in contrast, has to do scheduling on a *per-request* basis, and requests are very short compared to the lifetime of an OS process. Depending on the load, the TPOS has to either create processes, which will then request CPU time from the operating system, or kill other processes that are no longer needed.

6.5.1.1 Local Process Scheduling

The operating system bases its scheduling decisions on a small set of parameters, both static and dynamic, that describe the resource requirements of a process. These are the most important ones:

Priority of the process.   The execution priority is set at process creation time and can later be modified through special system calls.

Working set size.   This says how much real memory should be available at any given point in time for the process to run properly. That means a process never needs at one time *all* the code and *all* the data structures that have been loaded into it in memory. But the system should be able to keep the process's working set[6] in real memory when the process is using the (real) processors. The size of the working set depends on what type of processes run in the system and what their response time characteristic should be—assuming that the processes run interactive programs. The working sets must be chosen such that the portion of memory used is not likely to change completely from one request to the next. Different portions of the same program can create different working set sizes for the process.

Completion time constraints.   This says that the request must be processed by a certain time.

The TP monitor, operating at a higher level of abstraction, has more information than the BOS about the requestors and the resource requirements that come with a request. Whereas the operating system often treats processes as black boxes—that is, rather than looking at the program running in a process, it observes its behavior from the outside—the TP monitor knows which server classes it creates a process for. It also keeps statistics about that server class utilization. However, this wealth of additional information may as well lead to "paralysis by analysis." Exploiting the performance characteristics for each single resource request is particularly infeasible, because it violates the requirement that each load balancing measure should save more resources than it consumes. As a consequence, there must be a mix of static decisions implemented at startup time and dynamic decisions that

---

[6] We assume the normal definition of a working set: the portion of the process's address space it references within a predefined time window.

must be very fast, based on just a few parameters, mostly heuristic ones. Static decisions can be modified when system monitoring suggests that the overall behavior of the system is outside the specification. In most systems, dynamic scheduling relies on table lookups (and therefore is essentially predetermined by the static decision), along with a few rules of thumb. To get an impression of what those rules look like, consider the following list:

(1) If the service is available in the same address space where the request originates, just keep the process and the address space. This is the case of different resource managers being linked together; a resource manager invocation is little other than a branch in the address space, with some moderation by the TRPC facility along the way. The TP monitor might, for example, change the process priority before actually branching to the destination resource manager (see the discussion of priority inversion in Chapter 2, Section 2.4).

(2) If the service is available in a different address space, the current process can bind to, or keep, the process. Otherwise, the aspects are the same as in the first case.

(3) If the service is not locally available, pick a node where it is (access to the name server) and send out the request via the communication manager. Now the request is that node's problem.

(4) If the service is locally available (not cases 1 and 2), and there is an idle process providing that service, send the request to that process.

(5) If none of the cases holds, and the service is only locally available, decide on the basis of CPU and server class utilization whether or not to create a new process. If the service is also available at other nodes, see if there is a lightly loaded one, which can (presumably) provide fast response; else queue it.

6.5.1.2 Interdependencies of Local Server Loads

Entry 5 in the rules-of-thumb list is the nontrivial one; the others rely on the static load distribution being correct. If that should not be the case, a reconfiguration of the TP system's process structure may be required. Let us forget about the remote nodes for a moment and just focus on the decision whether or not to expand the local part of a busy server class by one process.

This decision in essence determines where on the curve shown in Figure 2.13 the system will be for the next time interval. If there are more requests than processes, this indicates that higher throughput is required. Higher throughput, though, means higher response times—a situation that is tolerable only up to a certain level. Note that all performance requirements at the core read like this: provide maximum throughput, while keeping response times below t seconds in 90% of all transactions. This is, for example, the basis of the TPC benchmark definition.

Creating a new process moves the system to the right on the response-time curve; more processes mean more load on the CPU. No new process means the system stays on its curve, but the request waits in front of the server class. An intuitive reaction might suggest that it makes no difference whether the request waits in front of the CPU (having a new process) or in front of the server class. This, however, is a misleading intuition.

Consider a server class "database system" to which a sequence of requests of the same type are submitted. Each request is an instantiation of the same program, just with different parameters, and they all operate on shared data. By massive simplification, we reduce the whole system to one server with one queue. Let the arrival rate of requests[7] be R and the service time T_1. Then, assuming a simple M/M/1 queue with an infinite number of requests coming in, the average service time per request is $S_1 = T_1/(1 - T \times R)$. Implicit in this formula is that only one database request is processed at a time. If we admit more than one process per server class (say, n), we would expect the system to behave like a single queue with n identical servers. However, two assumptions are required for this to hold true: (1) there is enough CPU for everybody, and (2) there is no interference on the data. Let us grant the unlimited CPU capacity for the moment; we still have to take into account the fact that transactions will get into conflict on the shared data. A model of this is sketched in Chapter 7, Section 7.11; for the present discussion, the following argument is sufficient. If there are n processes (n transactions accessing the database concurrently), the chances for an arbitrary transaction to be delayed by another transaction are proportional to n. The degree to which data sharing among transactions may cause conflicts, and thereby transaction wait situations, is measured by c. If the duration of the delay is assumed to be fixed,[8] the original service time is increased by an amount that is proportional to n. Of course, each server now only gets $1/n$ of the total load.

This very simple model then yields the following estimate of the service time:

$$S_n = (T(1 + c\,(n - 1)))\,/\,(1 - T(R/n)(1 + c\,(n - 1)))$$

To give an idea of what that amounts to, Figure 6.15 shows a plot of Sn over n; T is set to 0.8 second, R is set to 0.9 requests per second, and c is 0.02. Note that this is not another version of Figure 2.13; here the abscissa is the number of server processes at a fixed arrival rate, whereas Figure 2.13 plots the response time over the arrival rate. The important aspect of this simple model is that CPU utilization has not been taken into account, and still there is a fairly narrow margin (given a response time threshold) within which the server class behaves properly.

Of course, a complete analysis cannot ignore CPU load as we have done here. When all processes allocated to a server class are busy and more are needed, then this not only shifts the system to the right on Figure 6.15, but it is also an indicator for a higher arrival rate, which increases R as well. A higher R affects the abstract server class as well as the physical resources (the CPU), so these effects are cumulative.

The point of this example is that request-based load balancing performed by the TP monitor must look at both the utilization of each server class and the utilization of the underlying physical resources. Just monitoring the physical resources, and basing all scheduling decisions on that, would not be sufficient. Consider the same scenario with the database server class, and assume that CPU utilization was the only criterion for the decision whether or not new processes should be admitted. Let the CPU utilization with 40 transactions running in parallel be 60%—not a very high value. As long as the utilization is below 85%, the system will allow new server processes to be created. With parallelism increasing, the service time per transaction goes up. More and more transactions actually wait for other transactions to finish, which reduces the load on the CPU. This allows more processes to be created, which further increases the service time—this is a version of thrashing, a phenomenon

---

[7] Throughout this section, only mean values are used.

[8] This is not quite right, because the duration of the actual delay also depends on the number of concurrent transactions, but for the present argument the simple (more optimistic) model will do.

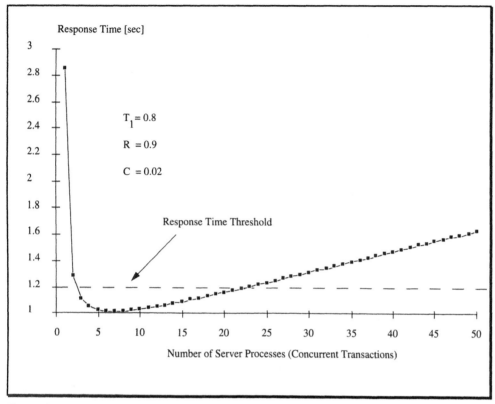

Figure 6.15: The response time of a simple database server as a function of the number of processes in its server class. Response time is shown as a function of the number of server processes in cases where increasing concurrency leads to increasing probability of access conflicts on shared data. The underlying model assumes a linear dependency of the probability of one transaction waiting for another on the number of concurrent transactions in the system.

better known from virtual memory management.[9] The transition from normal system behavior to thrashing, which is always caused by making scheduling decisions with insufficient information, is shown in Figure 6.16.

The consequence of all this can be put as follows: the TP monitor has to monitor the utilization of all server classes, as well as the utilization of the CPU(s) and perhaps other physical resources, such as communication busses and disks. For its dynamic scheduling, it then needs heuristics, which specify the minimum and maximum number of processes per class, depending on the utilization. That requires careful a priori analysis of the system load. For example, the degree of interference of transactions on data must be determined (parameter c in our model); this task is performed by the system administrator. Fully adaptive systems that, without prior knowledge, automatically achieve optimal balance with respect to a specified set of performance criteria, do not currently exist, and they probably will not for a long time.

---

[9] There is an equivalent to memory thrashing in operating systems in the buffer pool of database systems. For this discussion, however, the position is taken that memory will be unlimited in the near future, and thus should no longer create any such problems.

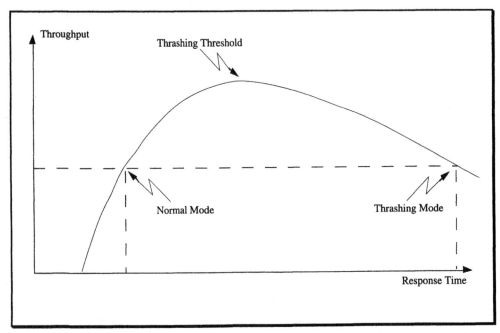

Figure 6.16: The basic shape of the threshold curve.   If request processing requires multiple re-sources, and at least one of them is overloaded—whereas request scheduling is done based on the fig-ures of a non-overloaded resource—thrashing will occur as shown by the curve. This graph is quoted from Highleyman [1989].

6.5.1.3 Scheduling Across Node Boundaries

In distributed systems, where nodes do not share memory but are connected via a high-band-width, low-latency communication channel (a fast bus or a switch), scheduling a request at a remote node is not significantly slower than scheduling it locally—especially, if the local CPU is highly loaded. Let T_c be the communication overhead for sending the request to a remote node and for sending the response back. The scheduling decision then has to be based on the following considerations:

(1) What is the expected local response time S_l, based on CPU utilization and server class utilization?

(2) What is the expected response time S_r at the remote server, given the utilization of its resources?

(3) What is the expected T_c, based on the utilization of the communication medium?

If any remote node can be found such that $S_r + T_c < S_l$, then the request should be exe-cuted at that node, rather than locally. To make these estimates, the TP monitor has to keep track of the performance figures of remote servers as well as local ones. These figures do not have to be kept current to the millisecond; the principle of locality is applicable to load bal-ancing, too, and thus states that load patterns change gradually. TP monitors supervising parts of the same server classes need to be in session with each other anyway, and one type of message that is exchanged via such sessions is a periodic sample of the utilizations, response time, and so on, of the local resources at the participating nodes. Note that the scheduling decision need not actually be made according to the response time estimates we have given. As long as the utilization samples show that all nodes are running within the prespecified load limits, each node can schedule requests to all nodes that provide that service using a round-robin scheme. Given stability of load conditions, this is cheap to implement and is a good heuristic for keeping the load evenly distributed.

Simple as that seems, this approach to global scheduling has two problems that may go unnoticed and result in high overhead as well as (potentially) poor overall performance. One is frequently referred to as *control block death*, and the other has to do with data affinity.

Control block death becomes a problem as the number of nodes and the number of processes per node increase. This is likely to happen in large systems. Assume two server classes, A and B. If there are N nodes in the system and each node has I_a processes for A and I_b processes for B, then—according to our current scheduling model—each instance of A could send its request to any instance of B. If these requests are not context-free, the instances must bind to each other: a session has to be established. Now each session requires a control block describing its end points, the context that is associated with it, and other administrative details. If the assumed configuration operates in that mode for a while, each instance of A eventually will be in session with each instance of B, yielding $c = (NI_a)(NI_b) = N^2 I_a I_b$ control blocks. As N gets large, there will be a point where the number of control blocks growing quadratically will get *too* large—this is control block death.

The problem of data affinity can best be described by referring to Figure 6.17. There is a database, which is partitioned across two nodes, 1 and 2. Node 1 is currently heavily loaded; node 2 has little to do. A request from a terminal attached to node 1 is routed to node 2, using the global balancing strategy already described.

The service effectively invoked at node 2 needs access to the database, and the TP monitor makes sure that this resource manager invocation is kept local. It turns out, though, that the data to be accessed are in partition A, so the actual data manipulation has to be requested from node 1 via RPC, adding further to its high load. The problem is that the TP monitor at node 1 could not foresee the service requests done by server class 2. And even if it had that information, the need to access data partition A may depend on parameter values in the request. But let us go even further and assume the TP monitor understood these data fields. The best thing it could do would be to keep the request for server class 2 local to node 1; this would improve things just marginally, because node 1 had too high a load to start with.

If the high load results from frequent requests to data partition A (which is frequently observed), the dynamic load balancing cannot help. A static balancing measure has to redistribute the data across the nodes such that each one gets about the same number of accesses. In current systems, such a load-sensitive data partitioning is often combined with application-specific routing; after all, the TP monitor does not understand the parameter fields. The application router knows the partitions and their value ranges and makes sure requests are routed to the node where the data are. Given the way the TP monitor works, this requires hiding the fact that the server classes are the same at each node; they only pretend to be different. Specifically, server class 2 at node 1 is announced as "server class 2 needing data from partition A," while server class 2 at node 2 is "server class 2 needing data from partition B."

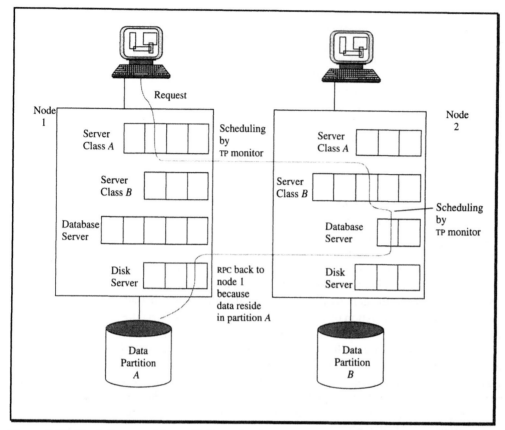

Figure 6.17: The influence of data affinity on load balancing. A request originating at node 1 is routed to node 2 by the local TP monitor, because node 2 is currently running under light load. The server at node 2, in turn, invokes the database server; this call is kept local to node 2 because of the load situation. The database server, however, finds out it needs data from partition *A*, which is managed by node 1.

6.5.2 Authentication and Authorization

The issue of authentication and authorization was touched upon in Chapter 2, in the discussion of the role of operating systems. The OS supports system security in the following areas:

User authentication. When a user is admitted to the system (given a userid), he is granted certain privileges on files, libraries, and system functions. These are specified by the system administrator, who is a trusted user with higher authority than other users. Upon admission, the user is given a secret (usually a password) by which he proves his identity to the system. From then on, the user can modify this secret in direct contact with the system, without administrative assistance. Whenever the user wants to establish a session with the system (logon), the operating system *authenticates* him by checking if he knows the secret. A userid that has been successfully authenticated is called an authorization ID (authid, for short). The two terms are used interchangeably here.

Session authentication.   This is similar to user authentication, except that the "user" is mainly a process running on a different node. The process pretends to run under a certain authid; that is, it claims to have been authenticated by its local system, but the other end typically does not believe it. One could use the simple password mechanism, but having passwords flow across the network is not a good idea. The next possibility is challenge response, as described in Chapter 2, Section 2.4. It requires two rounds of messages (which may be piggybacked).

File access control.   File security is normally protected by a two-dimensional access matrix that specifies which *subject* is allowed to do *what* on which *object*. A subject in the access matrix is either a userid, a group name (denoting a group of users), or a program in a library. An object is either a file, a group of files (a sub-tree in a hierarchical directory), or a program. The operations are the usual operations on files and programs: create, delete, read, write, link, load, and execute. In a typical situation, a user *A* is not allowed any access to file *X* but is allowed to run program *P*, which in turn reads and writes file *X*. This ensures that the user can get to the file only through controlled channels—in that case, via the program that manipulates it.

Memory access control.   In systems supporting protection rings, the operating system, with support from the hardware, ensures that boundaries between protection domains are crossed properly. That is, one can get from a lower authority domain to a higher authority domain only through special instructions or operating system calls. Higher authority domains may address or branch directly into lower authority domains. The same holds for switching address spaces while holding on to the same process.

The first of the two entries on our list describe *authentication* services (checking the identity of a subject); the last two entries are concerned with *authorization* (checking if an authenticated subject is allowed to do what it wants to do). A TP monitor has to perform all this checking for the TP system environment, and the question is whether it can just use the operating system services and leave it at that.

Judging from the current situation in that area, the answer has to be no. The reason is simple: the units for which the operating system has access control are large and long-lived: processes, sessions, and files. The TP monitor, on the other hand, handles small transactional requests, which hold on to a process only for a short time and access tuples or attribute values rather than files; they may, on the other hand, invoke services on many nodes. In other words, the TP monitor has to do authorization on a *per-request basis*, not on a session basis. Its authorization scheme can also be described by an access matrix, but one with more dimensions than the file protection matrix used by the operating system. In its general form, the problem can be stated thus: the TP monitor, upon each request for service *S* issued by a user with authid *A*, has to check whether

this user is allowed to invoke
this service (application) from
this terminal (this application) at
this day in the week (time of the day) on
this object with
these parameters.

6.5.2.1 The Role of Authids in Transaction-Oriented Authorization

In a classical time-sharing environment, for which the operating system's security mechanisms have been designed, the question of which userid an application runs under is trivial to answer. As the user logs on, he gets a process (or a number of them), which runs under his authid. Programs that are loaded into this process's address space execute under the same authid, making it easy to decide on whose behalf a request (say, for accessing a file) is issued: it is the authid of the process the program runs in. This is also what makes such systems penetrable by Trojan horses. In a transaction processing system (or, more precisely, in each client-server system), the situation is a little more involved. To appreciate this, consider Figure 6.18.

Figure 6.18 is an elaboration of the mail system application depicted in Figure 1.2. A mail system user at his workstation is logged in under userid myself. At some point, he decides to run the mail application, which executes within transaction system at his node. The application runs under the authid localadm. The local TPOS does exactly what is described in this chapter, namely, handling transactional RPCs, commit processing, and all the other services of the TPOS. On behalf of the user, it issues a call to the mail server node, where the mail system runs in a process under userid mailguy. The call arrives; from the mail server's perspective, it is user localadm that is requesting service. As this continues, the mail server uses an SQL database system to implement its services. As far as the database is concerned, the arriving SQL select has been issued by user mailguy (the database is running under DBadmin). But as the figure points out, mailguy is, in fact, working on behalf of localadm, which in turn is working on behalf of myself. What should be the criteria for access control under these circumstances?

The simple solution of having each process along the way take on the user's authid does not work. There are two reasons: first, in a distributed system, the userids cannot be expected to be known at all nodes. Second, the end user (myself, in this example) usually has fewer rights on shared resources like databases than the administrator of these services. Referring to Figure 6.18, authid DBadmin is well authorized to access the SQL database catalog, for example, whereas userid myself is not authorized to do so at all. In other words, running process *C* under myself (even if it were registered at the database node) would merely result in denial of access.

The other extreme is to collect all the authids along the way and specify access rights for these concatenations. This does not make sense either, because it is neither manageable nor even required. Request-based access control exercised by the TP monitor is usually based on a two-level scheme: it authorizes clients' requests for the servers it invokes directly (for example, is the mail server running under mailguy allowed to issue requests to the SQL database server?), and it passes the transaction's authid along with each request. This is the authid of the user who started the transaction and who eventually will receive the result. Thus, the basic idea is to authorize each invocation step individually and tell the server what the transaction's authid is; that way, the server can decide, even if it accepts *in principle* the request from the client, whether it can provide the service to the client, given that it works on behalf of that user. This attitude is reflected in the message format declared in Subsection 6.3.3.

Note that this scheme with two authids has two effects; one is restrictive, the other one permissive. The restrictive effect is easy to see: from the perspective of the SQL database,

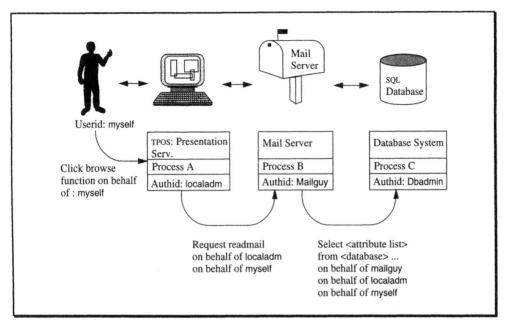

Userid: myself

Click browse
function on behalf
of : myself

Request readmail
on behalf of localadm
on behalf of myself

Select <attribute list>
from <database> ...
on behalf of mailguy
on behalf of localadm
on behalf of myself

Figure 6.18: The problem of transferring access rights in a client-server environment in a controlled manner. For handling a request of user myself to his mail application, a sequence of servers is invoked, each running under its own authid but acting on behalf of the client's authid when handling a request. This stack of authorization codes grows with the number of servers invoked.

the mail server can access all the tuples in the mail database, because that is how it implements its services. But it must be prevented, of course, from giving a user (like myself) tuples that do not belong to his mailbox. If the database knows the transaction's userid, it can properly restrict mailguys access rights where necessary. As an example of the permissive effect, take the following: assume I want to use the mail system to send a file out of my private database to Jim. As usual, the mail system calls upon the database, and, yes, it can access its files, but mailguy has no access rights on my file. Knowing, though, that its actually myself calling, these rights can be granted temporarily.

Note that the TP monitor checks only the client's authority to call the server; the second part, which uses the transaction authid, is left to the resource managers. All the TPOS does to help in that is to pass on the original authid. This reflects a simple separation of concerns: the TP monitor does not "own" the database, or the log, or the user files; the only resources it manages is the set of resource managers that run the database, maintain the log, and so on. Consequently, the TP monitor only controls access to the resource managers. Each server is left to protect its own resources, in turn.

As mentioned, authorization in TP systems is a multidimensional problem. In addition to controlling who is going to access what, restrictions can be applied on when a request can be made (certain services are made available only between, say, 9 and 5, or only on Fridays, or whatever), and on where requests are allowed to originate. For example, a user may have the right to execute a fund transfer application involving large amounts of money, but only from a special terminal in a particularly protected area. There are many more restrictions and regulations one could think of, but these are the criteria applied by normal TP monitors.

Some of them allow an invocation-specific password to be checked. The access matrix is stored in a relation that is part of the local repository and, thus, is owned by the TPOS. Accesses to it require the invocation of TPOS functions—and, of course, these accesses have to be authorized in the access matrix. There is a simple recursion problem here, which is left to the reader to figure out. A sample declaration of the TP monitor access matrix looks like this:

```
exec sql     CREATE TABLE TP_access_matrix (
                        authid          char(8)    not null,
                        nodeid          integer    not null,
                        rmid            integer    not null,
                        entry_name      char(100)       not null,
                        day_mask        char(7),
                        from_time       time,
                        to_time         time,
                        rest_node       integer,
                        rest_term       char(100),
                        inv_pswd        char(32),
                        PRIMARY KEY(authid,nodeid,rmid,entry_name)
                        );
```

6.5.2.2 When to Do Authentication and Authorization

The previous subsection dealt with authorization, and only from the perspective of which criteria go into the decision. Let us now put everything together and describe how the TP monitor controls access to its services from the moment the user logs on to the system until the last resource manager in the line is invoked. Refer back to Figure 6.17 as an illustration of the different steps.

We assume that the user at the workstation is interested only in transaction processing, so switching back and forth between a transactional and a non-transactional environment need not be considered. First, the user logs on to the TPOS; that is, a session is established between the TPOS and the user. The user can be either a human or a machine, such as an automated teller machine (ATM). Establishing the session requires authentication. Once this has happened, the TPOS considers the user working on that terminal as authenticated; that is, upon future function requests from the terminal, the TPOS performs no authentication. Thus, the possibility of the user physically changing in midsession is ruled out. As part of the logon handling, the TPOS loads the user's security profile from the repository. The profile describes general capabilities of the user, which are independent of a specific resource manager invocation. The user's password (or his public encryption key) is kept here, along with the expiration date of the password, which days of the week he is not allowed to use the system, and more things of this kind.

With this, the user has been accepted as a legal citizen; as before, his authid is myself. The TP monitor typically provides a selection menu that contains the names of applications (resource managers) the user is allowed to use. These can be all the services he is granted in the TP_access_matrix, or a restricted set of those services. The name of the entry menu is specified as part of the user profile. In case the user can run only one application (think of the ATM), the input menu of that application is displayed.

Returning to Figure 6.17, the user invokes the application running in server class *A*. This requires the TP monitor to do a lookup in the privileges relation:

```
exec sql    SELECT *
            FROM TP_access_matrix
            WHERE    authid       = 'myself'    and
                     nodeid       = 'here'      and
                     rmid         = :rmid       and
                     entry_name = 'ServiceEntry';
```

If there is no tuple, the user has no right to call the service. If there is one, the TP monitor must further check if there are date and time restrictions and if the user works on the right terminal.

It is too expensive to query an authorization database every time some client issues a resource manager call. This leads to the distinction of run-time authorization versus bind-time authorization. Assume a transactional application that needs to invoke a number of servers— for example, the mail server mentioned before. At some point, the TP monitor has to load the code for that application into a process's address space. In doing so, it has to resolve all the external references, like any linker or loader does. Some of these external references go to the stubs provided by the TPOS to handle the TRPCs. If the application supplies *constants* for the names of the services, the TP monitor can check right away if the application program makes any nonauthorized calls. If no such calls are detected, then at run time there is no need to reauthorize all the resource manager calls coming out of that process.[10] Strictly speaking, this is true only if the access condition does not contain time constraints or restrictions with respect to the terminal, because those can only be checked at run time. This leads us directly to the methods for run-time authorization.

There is nothing really new here. The process circles around, caching, as in the case of name binding. The TP monitor keeps an in-memory copy of authorized requests in a data structure that provides fast access via authid; see Section 6.3 for a discussion of how to access the TP monitor's system control blocks. If the number of users per node is not too large, the whole TP_access_matrix might fit into main memory. To further speed things up, each process control block could have a tag saying whether any authentication is necessary for resource manager calls issued by that process—except for the value-dependent parts.

So far, this all takes place in one node. In the example of Figure 6.17, the next TRPC goes to an instance of server class *B* at node 2. What does that mean in terms of authentication and authorization?

From the perspective of the process running server class *B*, neither the process at node 1 issuing the call nor the user has been heard about. That would suggest authenticating them both before accepting the request. And, indeed, a truly paranoid system might do just that. However, in normal systems, one tries to exploit the knowledge about the way requests are sent and about the components involved.

According to the architecture outlined in this chapter, remote requests are sent via the session managers of the participating nodes. Because these session managers keep at least

---

[10] There is a small problem when the access matrix is modified at run time, to the effect that access rights are revoked from a user. Then there must be means for finding out if there are any processes with bind-time authorization running under his authid.

one session between the TPOSs on either side, they have authenticated each other and have no reason to question the identity of their peers. Each TPOS administers its local resource managers by creating processes and loading the code; this is something like a session, too. If a TPOS sends out a request saying it comes from resource manager *A*, its peer in the other node can accept this as enough support for *A*'s claimed identity. If the client TPOS has also authenticated the user, it can indicate this in the request message, suggesting that the server need not do so again. Both types of confirmation can be ignored by the server in favor of doing its own authentication.

Figures 6.17 and 6.18 illustrate that as soon as there is a chain of requestors/servers working on behalf of one user, the TP monitor provides step-by-step authentication rather than end-to-end authentication. The problem of achieving higher security without losing too much flexibility and performance is an area of active research.

6.5.3 Restart Processing

Restart processing by the TP monitor has been mentioned so often that there is not much left to say. After a crash, the basic operating system first bootstraps itself back into existence. For simplicity, we assume that the log comes up very early with the operating system. This is not as bold an assumption as may appear. First, the log cannot rely on any transactional services for its recovery (see Chapter 9), because it is instrumental in giving ACID properties to other components; this is where the recursion halts. Moreover, the operating system might want to protect its file system and catalogs by something like system transactions,[11] which also require the log to come up early. By *the log* we mean the one special log that is dear to the heart of the transaction manager; it stores the commit/abort outcome of the active transactions. There may be many other logs entertained by various resource managers, but they can wait to be brought up later.

As usual, the operating system performs its restart according to a startup script that specifies which processes must be created, which programs loaded, which lines opened. As part of this script, the TPOS is brought up. That means a process is fired up with the code of the complete TPOS in it. This process is given control at the rm_Startup entry point. It then performs the following steps:

(1) Format all the system control blocks needed for managing the resource managers (See Section 6.3).

(2) Load the descriptions of all resource managers registered at that node into RMTable. Mark the log as up, and enter its processes into PRTable. From now on, all steps taken by the TP monitor to restart the TP system are guided by a TPOS startup script that is similar in function to the one used by the basic operating system for its restart.

(3) For each active resource manager, start the prespecified number of processes for that server class and load the code. If the resource manager provides an explicit rm_Startup entry, mark it as down in RMTable; the others are marked as up right away. Update the PRTable according to the processes created.

---

[11]This is not state-of-the-art in commercial operating systems. Judging from some recent developments, however, it is reasonable to assume that the log will become an integral part of the basic OS. This assumption implies that the system is in deep trouble should the log fail to come up. See Chapters 10–12 for a detailed discussion of component recovery.

(4) Call the the transaction manager at its rm_Startup entry. It opens the log, tries to find its own most recent log entries, and reestablishes its TM_Anchor. It reads the log to determine the transactions that were active at the time of the crash, as well as the resource managers involved, and formats the TATable accordingly. After this, it is ready for business again. If the transaction manager does not respond to the TP monitor, it will crash the TPOS and try restart all over again. If that fails repeatedly, panic.

(5) Call the communications manager at its rm_Startup entry. The communications manager opens its connections to the other nodes. It then calls Identify (see Section 6.2) to tell the transaction manager it is back. In response to that, the transaction manager starts feeding all relevant log records to the communications manager in order for it to recover its sessions. Once all transactional sessions have been reestablished,[12] the communications manager is also ready for business again.

With this last step, all major components of the TPOS are back. The rest of restart handling consists of bringing up all the resource managers at that node and orchestrating their recovery. Let us illustrate this procedure by looking at one arbitrary resource manager, *R*; the next steps are illustrated in Figure 6.19.

(6) Resource managers are brought up according to the sequence prescribed in the startup script. This is necessary to make sure that services required for the restart of other resource managers are in place before they are brought up. Thus, if *R* needs the database for its own restart, the database must be operational before *R* can be restarted. Remember that these dependencies can be declared as part of the registration with the TP monitor.

(7) Assume R can be brought up. The TP monitor picks a process for that server class and activates it at the rm_Startup entry point. The resource manager then does whatever is needed for its own initialization and eventually calls the Identify function of the transaction manager. The transaction manager takes this as the signal to start recovery for *R*. It starts by feeding the log records for REDO purposes (checkpoint and REDO records) to the resource manager through its rm_REDO callback entry. Note that this phase is executed single-threaded; that is, the TP monitor needs to allocate only one process for it.

(8) After the REDO phase is completed, the UNDO phase starts. When the TP monitor gets to see the first TRPC to the rm_UNDO entry of *R*, it checks its entry in the RMTable to see if the resource manager can be declared up; that is, if the remaining recovery can proceed in parallel to normal system operation. The TP monitor also has to make provisions for doing the UNDO recovery in parallel. It has been established by now which transactions R was involved in; the corresponding control blocks have been established. All the TP monitor needs to do is assign one process for each transaction *R* needs to UNDO; from then on, UNDO can run in parallel. It works the same way REDO recovery does: the transaction manager feeds the UNDO records to the resource manager through the rm_UNDO callback interface. After that is done, it returns from the Identify call, which in turn makes the resource manager return from the rm_Startup call to the TP monitor. Then, at last, *R* can be declared up again. There is an interesting aside: If UNDO is done in parallel, then the TP monitor has called rm_Startup for *R* out of one process, and *R* returns from it in many processes. The reader should be satisfied that this does not create any difficulties.

---

[12] At least on this end; a peer might have crashed meanwhile, leaving its end of the session down.

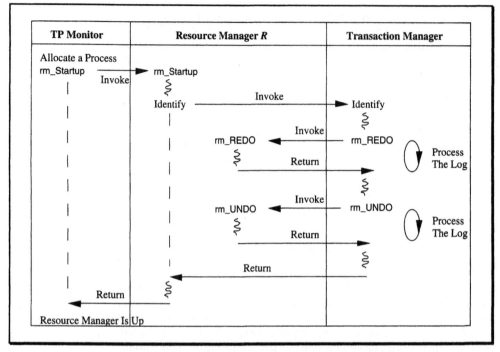

Figure 6.19: Restart processing for a resource manager maintaining durable state. This scenario shows the interaction between the TP monitor, the transaction manager, and the resource manager during resource manager restart. The TP monitor allocates a process for the RM, loads the code, and invokes it at its rm_Startup callback entry. The resource manager, after going through its local initialization, identifies itself to the transaction manager. The transaction manager scans the log to see if there is any recovery work to do for that resource manager. If so, it feeds the REDO records to the RM through the rm_REDO callback. After that, the same is done for the UNDO records. then the transaction manager returns from the Identify call, and the resource manager eventually returns from the Startup call. Once the TP monitor gets this return, it knows that the resource manager is up again.

(9) When the last resource manager has gone through UNDO for a transaction, the transaction can be removed from the TATable. This also holds in the case where a resource manager that has participated in some of the transactions fails to come up. It will be informed later on that the transactions have long been rolled back.

There is some additional work for the transaction manager in case of resource managers failing to restart; this is discussed in Chapter 11, Section 11.4.

6.6 Summary

This chapter has described the TP monitor from an implementation-oriented perspective. It becomes clear that the TP monitor is a resource manager that manages other resource managers and processor resources such as processes, threads, access rights, programs, and context. In that respect, the TP monitor is very much like an operating system, but there are important differences. For one thing, a conventional operating system allocates resources to requests on a long-term basis (a logon creates a session that can be expected to go on for minutes or hours), while a TP monitor has to allocate resources on a per-request basis. This leads to the second difference: all the administrative tasks an operating system carries each time a session is created (or opened) must be performed by the TP monitor upon each request. This applies to authentication, authorization, process allocation, and storage allocation. Not only is the rate of these tasks much higher in a transaction system, but doing these things on a per-request basis also introduces more dimensions to the decision space. This is illustrated in the complex authorization criteria a TP monitor has to apply. A third difference between operating systems and TP monitors has to do with consistency: a TP monitor must support all applications and resource managers upon restart after a crash; an operating system, on the other hand, typically takes care of its own system files (catalog, and so on) and lets everybody else do what they please.

The explanation of the implementation principles was organized into four major sections. First, the notion of transactional remote procedure call was specified. The key issue here is that all interactions in a transaction system are kept under transaction control, which applies both to the normal commit case and to an abnormal transaction termination (abort). To exercise this type of control, a well-defined resource manager interface is required, one that allows the transaction manager to communicate all transaction-related events to the applications and resource managers. Another special aspect of TRPCs is the notion of context. It allows stateful (context-sensitive) interactions among applications and resource managers (or clients and servers in general), with the guarantee of the context information being transaction protected as well.

The second part of the description dealt with the TP monitor's control blocks and their relationships to the other system resource managers' control blocks. Their use was illustrated in a detailed tour along a complete TRPC path, which included a discussion of remote invocation and the way sessions are included into the transaction web.

The third section dealt with queues, both volatile and durable. Volatile queues are a means to control the workload and to fend off peaks in the request rates for certain services. Without such queues, the TP monitor would have to reject requests, or a large number of processes would have to be created (in case of momentary request peaks). Durable queues support queued transaction processing and chained transactions. They are also a means for delivering response messages in a transaction-controlled manner; that is, these message can be given the "exactly-once" semantics, provided the application adheres to a certain protocol on these durable queues. The section also illustrated that implementing durable queues on an SQL database system is almost straightforward.

The fourth section briefly sketched the approaches to implementing further services of the TP monitor. One is load balancing. In a distributed system, the fundamental problem of dynamic load balancing is what to do with an incoming request for which there is no idle local process at the moment. One possibility is to put the request on a volatile queue. Another option is to create a new (local) process. The third possibility it to send the request to another node. It was shown that the TP monitor needs a rudimentary model of the resource manager's behavior in order to make proper decisions. It is also necessary to monitor the load of all relevant system components.

Authentication and authorization were mostly described with respect to their requirements; implementation issues were not considered. It was demonstrated by means of a simple example that authorization in a distributed system with chains of resource manager calls can lead to fairly complicated problems in determining whether a certain resource manager

A, acting on behalf of resource manager *B*, which is acting on behalf of resource manager *C*, and so on, is authorized to execute function *f* on resource *X*.

Finally, restart processing was explained in detail. We have seen which components of the system are brought up in which order, when the TP monitor takes over, in which way the resource managers are informed about the necessity of restart, and which protocol they have to adhere to in the event of restart.

6.7 Historical Notes

The "history" related to this chapter is almost exclusively product history. Because the term TP monitor is itself anything but well-defined, there is no established topic in computer science that would cover "TP monitor concepts and their implementation." It is necessary to go and look at existing TP monitors, find out what they do and how they do it, and then try to conceptualize backwards from the specific to the general. Only in this way can we determine what makes a TP monitor different from an operating system, or a communications manager, or a forms manager.

Given this situation, it is difficult to say that concept *X* was first implemented in system *S*, because it is often the case that at the time system *S* was developed, the concepts had not been sorted out completely. And even if it is possible to trace in retrospect the origin of *X* back to *S*, it is usually mixed up with many other features and optimizations that reflect the particular constraints the implementors had to face. Remember that, until just recently, no TP system has been designed and implemented *as such*. Rather, such systems resulted from tying together other components that were already there. With these caveats in mind, let us look at the origins of the concepts that we have used for structuring this chapter, namely server class management (including process scheduling), queue management, and resource manager interfaces.

Process management is what all TP monitors started out doing. Batch-oriented operating systems on .5 mips machines would just crumble under the load of 100 terminals; thus the tele-processing monitors of the early days provided cheap processes (threads) inside an (expensive) OS process, handled screen forms, loaded the programs run in the threads, and so forth. CICS was designed to do that, as were Com-Plete, INTERCOMM, Shadow, and many others.

IMS/DC took a different approach by employing multiple OS processes and dispatching the requests among them. This results in a large number of (expensive) process switches— more than an acceptable number for transaction-oriented processing. As a consequence, the underlying operating system (MVS) was extended in order to allow for fast switches from one address space to another, while holding on to the same process. To do this efficiently, the S/370 architecture was augmented by several instructions for exchanging the process's register sets, for branching into another address space, for moving data across address space boundaries, and the like—in a controlled fashion, one should add.

IMS also pioneered the use of transaction-protected queues for handling requests in a reliable fashion. IMS/DC still supports the scheme illustrated in Figure 6.13 as its only model of execution. There is another IMS, called IMS FastPath, which pioneered many ideas for high-performance transaction processing; many of them will be mentioned in chapters to come. One of them, called *expedited message handling* was a way of reliably processing requests without first having to explicitly queue them.

The description of queue management borrows heavily from Bernstein, Hsu, and Mann [1990], whose paper does a nice job of extracting the concepts from the many implementations of volatile and persistent queues in existing TP monitors. The earliest implementation of recoverable queues was in IMS/DC, which had queued transactions as the only type of processing it supported. Each request was put in a queue; a server would get a request from a queue and put its response into another queue, from whence it was finally delivered to its destination (terminal, printer, or whatever). Yet the extent to which queues should be exposed to the application in modern TP systems is still an open issue. Some people claim that queues are fine for scheduling and for recovering output messages, but that using them for implementing multi-transaction activities is awkward; it is said that such things should be handled by the transaction manager. Let us just say that this is still an area of active research.

The history of program management done by TP monitors is even fuzzier. Given their general "bypass the operating system" attitude (with the exception of ACMS, IMS/DC, Pathway and a few others), they did not use any of the standard linker/loader facilities. Rather, they maintained their own libraries for executables and did their own management of the portion of their address space that was to contain transaction program code. Without going into any detail, let us briefly summarize the reasons for implementing TP-specific program management (these issues are discussed at great length in Meyer-Wegener [1988]):

Memory.   At the time these systems were developed, main memories tended to be small (less than 1 MB), yet the number of different transaction programs to be kept available was increasing. As a result, the size of all transaction programs linked together (including their temporary storage requirements) was much larger than the memory available. In principle, one could leave the mapping problem to virtual memory management. But remember that transaction processing is driven by high rates of short requests, with response time being *the* performance measure. On the other hand, virtual memory works with acceptable performance only if paging is rare—that is, if locality is high. This, however, cannot be guaranteed if all applications of a TP environment are simply linked together and then loaded into the virtual address space of the TP monitor process(es). Therefore, many TP monitors provide means to group transaction programs, depending on which are executed together and which are not. Based on this, whole groups of programs can be replaced in memory in one (sequential) I/O operation, rather than be replaced one block after the other by demand paging.

Addresses.   Of course, the argument extends to situations where the total length of the application exceeds the maximum address space provided by the operating system. Remember that many of the systems discussed here were built at a time when addresses had, at most, 24 bits.

Process structure.   TP monitors started out doing process management for performance reasons. This often meant implementing threads on top of normal OS processes. To control these threads, of course, the TP monitors had to be able to allocate the pieces of code pertaining to the different transaction programs according to their storage management policies. Some systems apply different techniques depending on whether the transaction program code is re-entrant, partially reusable, or of unknown properties.

Code protection.   There is one last reason for doing program management inside the TP monitor: these systems typically come with a database system as the "preferred" resource manager, and with a number of tools such as 4GL systems on top. To prevent users from running programs developed on such a platform outside the proprietary environment, the executable code is stored in the database rather than in an OS library.

Remote procedure calls and, along with them, the notion of client-server computing have been implemented and used long before the name was coined and the papers were published—nothing new in the domain of transaction systems. The first commercially available versions of RPCs are probably those in Tandem's Guardian operating system and in the ICS (inter-systems communication) feature of CICS. Both came out in the mid 1970s. At about the same time, much of the research into RPC mechanisms to support computing in large workstation networks, including network file systems, was done at Xerox PARC and at MIT . It was this work, rather than the commercial systems, that influenced the subsequent development of RPCs as a general distributed operating system facility. There are two publications to mention in that respect. The first one [Birrell et al. 1982], describes a research prototype of a distributed mail server named Grapevine. It is a fairly complex exercise in distributed computing, based on the client-server paradigm. A general RPC mechanism is used to invoke remote services, a database system acts as a name server, there are provisions for load balancing and fault tolerance, and so on. That system is also worth mentioning in another respect: it used local transactions on the database, but it did not use distributed transactions for the RPC mechanism. This caused substantial problems in controlling the complexity of error situations that could occur and eventually it limited the size to which the system could be extended.

The other paper [Birrell and Nelson 1984] explains the implementation issues related to RPC, parameter marshalling, name binding, program management, piggybacking of acknowledgments, and so on. In that area, it is a classic.

This work influenced most of the RPC facilities found in today's UNIX systems, such as the de facto standard Sun RPC, or the RPC mechanism that is used in Apollo's Domain operating system; the latter one is also the basis of the RPC used for the distributed computing environment (DCE) defined by the OSF [OSF-DCE 1990]. DCE incorporates many features described for TP monitors, such as threads, distributed authentication, synchronization, remote procedure calls, but so far, it does not have transactions. It is quite likely, though, that sooner or later DCE will evolve into something that subsumes most of the functions of a conventional TP monitor.

Exercises

1. [6.2, 10] Name three properties a TRPC has that a standard RPC has not.

2. [6.2, 25] Consider an application program with the following structure:

```
Begin_Work
exec sql  UPDATE MyRelation ...
Commit_Work
```

The SQL database is one other resource manager. Draw the complete thread of TRPC invocations, starting with the Begin_Work statement.

3. [6.2, 30] Read about the RPC mechanism available in your local workstation environment. Find out whether the invocations are context-sensitive or context-free. If they can be context-sensitive, find out how context is kept and how fault tolerant it is.

4. [6.2, 30] Go back to the trip planning example discussed in Chapter 4. The application consists of a sequence of processing steps, each of which makes a reservation or cancels one. Assume that flat transactions are all the TP system gives you. Assume further that it has no sessions at the TP monitor level; that is, there is no way to reserve a process for an ongoing activity. For performance reasons, you have the requirement of making each reservation (or cancelation) a separate transaction. How do you keep the processing context?

5. [6.2, 30] Consider the mail server example discussed in Section 6.5 Assume the same system as in the previous exercise (flat transactions, no context-sensitive servers). Sending a mail message is a conversational transaction that may require multiple interactions with the user. How would you maintain the context so that at commit time (which corresponds to the request to now send the message) the global integrity constraints can be checked?

6. [6.3, 10] Explain why the TRPC stub must be shared among all the address spaces in the system.

7. [6.3, 20] As was explained in Chapter 5, there are TP monitors using only one operating system process. They do their own multi-threading inside that process. The threads are what is called *process* throughout this book. How does the addressing structure shown in Figure 6.6 look for such a single OS-process, multi-threaded TP monitor?

8. [6.3, 20] Go back to the second exercise (the simple program invoking SQL). For each piece of code involved, make the following analysis: when that piece of code is executing within that sample transaction, which process is it running in, which resource managers is it associated with, what is the current value of MyTrid?

9. [6.3, 20] Consider the methods for name binding described in Section. 6.3. Which steps have to be taken as a consequence of removing a resource manager from the system? Where do they have to be taken, and when ? *Hint: There are a number of possible solutions. You might compare the pros and cons of at least two of them.*

10. [6.3, 20] Why are special provisions needed against aborts racing normal processing? Sketch a simple scenario that shows what could go wrong if the system would not detect it.

11. [6.4, 20] Rewrite the ComputeInterest program based on the mini-batch approach, but this time use recoverable queues to keep the processing context.

12. [6.4, 40] Assume you have to write a version of the debit/credit transaction that dispenses money through an ATM. The interesting question at restart after a crash is: if a transaction was going on at an ATM when the crash occurred, was the transaction committed, and if so, was the money really dispensed? Obviously, you want to have the "exactly once" semantics for the action "dispense money"; the "at least once" semantics is not popular with the bank. Assuming the ATM is an intelligent terminal (that is, you can program it to behave as a resource manager; it has persistent memory), how would you implement the debit-service? Specify exactly which failure cases your design handles correctly, and which ones it does not.

13. [6.5, 30] Assume a bank wants to implement an extremely sensitive transaction (much money is involved one way or the other). In order to keep the risk of misuse as low as possible, it decides to use end-to-end authentication and authorization for each individual invocation of that transaction. Design a viable scheme for doing that, and specify precisely which part of the work is done by the TP monitor, and what is left to the application. *Hint: An approach to be found in some applications is to use one-time passwords. Each password is good for one transaction only; and, of course, a whole list of passwords has to be set up at the beginning of, say, each week. Take this as a staring point for your design, and see how that can be made to work.*

Answers

1. (1) Resource Manager called automatically becomes part of the ongoing transaction. (2) TP monitor does server class management, that is, it determines to which server the call is directed and creates a new server if necessary. (3) If any of the resource managers calls Rollback_Work, all the resource managers invoked during the transaction are called back by the transaction manager, independent of their position in the call stack.

2. Application to transaction manager (TM): Begin_Work.
   Application to SQL server: UPDATE ....; en route: TP monitor to TM: Join_Work for the SQL server. SQL server to log manager: log_insert. Depending on the implementation of the SQL server, there may be more TRPCs to the file manager, to the lock manager, and so on.
   Application to TM: Commit_Work. As a consequence of this, the TMissues TRPCs to the SQL server (Prepare), to the log manager (log_insert), to the SQL server (Commit), and to the log manager again (log_flush).
   The explanation for the sequence of TRPCs triggered by the Commit_Work call is given in Chapter 10.

4. The key observation is that the context has to be kept in the database, just like the restart information was stored in the database in the mini-batch example of Section 4.11. For each new trip (which may consist of many steps), a new order is prepared, and the system hands out a unique order number that from now on serves as an identifier for the context of that order, that is, for all reservations made on behalf of the customer. At the end of each reservation, the transaction commits, thereby externalizing all the updates pertaining to the reservation. As part of the same transaction a context record is written to the database, saying that the order with the given order number is currently being processed from terminal X by travel agent Y on behalf of customer Z. Thereby, the context is durably linked to all relevant entities, which means in case of a restart or when the customer comes back some days later after having reconsidered her plans, order processing can be picked up at the most recently committed state. Of course, all this context saving and restart processing has to be part of the travel agency application.

5. The solution is very similar to the answer to the previous exercise. Each new mail is identified by a system-generated MailId. All the records generated during the process of preparing a mail are tagged by the current value of MailId. As each partial transaction commits, these records are committed to the mail database. When a mail with a given MailId is to be sent, the transaction that implements the Send function reads the database to see if there is at least one tuple qualified by <MailId,"header">, because the integrity rule says there has to be a valid mail header. The Send transaction then goes on to check if there is at least one tuple qualified by <Mailid, "body">,

because there must be a mail body, and finally it is checked if there is a tuple qualified by <Mailid, "trailer">. If all checks succeed, the mail is sent, otherwise the Send function fails, and the user is asked to complete or correct the missing parts of the mail.

6. All servers of all server classes are—potentially—shared among all transactions in the system, and the dynamic mapping of function requests issued on behalf of transactions to servers is done by the TRPC stub. This requires the use of a number of shared control blocks, access to which must be strictly synchronized among all activations of the stub code.

7. The resulting address space configuration is shown in the following figure.

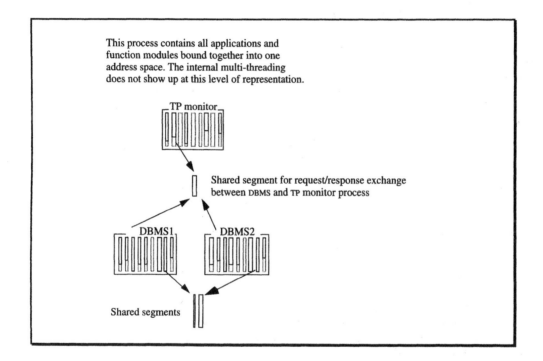

This process contains all applications and function modules bound together into one address space. The internal multi-threading does not show up at this level of representation.

TP monitor

Shared segment for request/response exchange between DBMS and TP monitor process

DBMS1   DBMS2

Shared segments

Note that the component denoted as TPOS in Figure 6.6 completely hides in the TP monitor process in the scenario assumed here.

9. First, the server class corresponding to the resource manager must be shut down. This requires all transactions using that use the resource manager to terminate. Then the control blocks pertaining to the resource manager can be deallocated. After that, the TP monitor can remove the code for the server class from its library and delete the addressing information about the resource manager from the local repository.

The first variant stops here. Of course, there may be binding information for the removed resource manager cached in other nodes, but they will learn about the deactivation of the RM upon the next TRPC . That way, news about the deactivation travels slowly, and remote clients learn it "the hard way" by getting their calls rejected. On the other hand, this method requires local activities only when removing a resource manager.

A second variant might try to inform all nodes in the system about the deactivation of the resource manager. Such a broadcast operation, however, is not trivial in a large distributed system if the messages are to be delivered reliably. One reason is that one cannot expect all nodes to be up at any point in time. So the typical method will be to first deactivate the RM locally and then spread the news by either invalidating pre-bound calls (based on cached naming information), or by piggy backing the deactivation-message on other message exchanges among the local TP monitors.

Of course, the RMNAME of the deactivated RM must not be issued again—at least not until it is guaranteed that no references to the old resource manager can come from anywhere in the network.

10. Assume a transaction T1 started at node A, and then invoked a distributed sub-transaction at node B. The TRPC returns from B, and processing continues at node A (T1 is still active). Meanwhile, node B has crashed and restarted, and as a part of the restart activities the TPOS of node B informs node A's TPOS that it has aborted T1. As a consequence, the transaction manager at node A invokes the local resource managers at their rollback entries. Consider one of these resource managers. The program might be executing along the normal path of the code in its own process, issuing calls to other RMs and so on. At the same time, the same resource manager is activiated at the rollback entry under the TP monitor's process and starts accessing and updating the same shared control blocks. Since this may lead to arbitrary consistency anomalies, abort racing must be protected against.

11. This is simple. Replace the update operation on the batchcontext relation at the end of each step by a (durable) enqueue operation. Correspondingly, retrieval of the restart information from batchcontext is replaced by a dequeue operation. Creating and dropping the batchcontext relation corresponds to the creation and deletion of a named queue used for the mini-batch application.

12. All the necessary information for a solution is given in the answer to Exercise 8 in Chapter 4. If you are still uncertain how to proceed, you might want to read the detailed explanation of the two-phase-commit protocol in Chapter 10. The key point here is to reconsider the issue that makes ATMs different from normal resource managers: at a certain point they have to perform a critical physical action that takes some seconds and cannot be undone by the system, namely dispensing the cash. The solution to the problem is based on two ideas:

—Move the dispense action to the very end of the debit transaction and make sure there can be no reason whatsoever to undo it.

—Before that, write information to durable storage that allows to check after a crash that interrupts the dispense action whether or not that action was executed successfully. Of course, such a test may require human intervention.

13. Assume there is a special resource manager $$$T handling these sensitive, high-value transactions. The TP monitor controls access to its environment by authenticating the users based on a simple password scheme. The authorization to invoke $$$T is restricted to certain users and certain terminals, that is, even a user who can use $$$T may do so from a special terminal only.

A user who has passed authentication and authorization so far is then authenticated again by $$$T, this time using a challenge-response scheme. After that is completed, $$$T is willing to accept requests from that user (at that terminal). Let us assume $$$T provides a single service, namely electronic fund transfer from account A to account B. So the only parameters the user has to provide are the account numbers (source and destination) and the amount to be transferred. Each transfer is executed as one transaction. Given that the amounts are typically in the multi-million dollar range, each individual transaction is to be further protected. One way to achieve this is that for each legal user the resource manager allows n transactions to be executed without invoking a higher authority. It does that by generating n passwords p_i ($1 \leq i \leq n$) and storing them in the database as tuples of the form <UserId,i,p_i>. For security, this relation should be stored in some encrypted form that only $$$T understands. In the beginning, the list of p_i is given to the user via some other protected channel (e.g. printing them on those special carbon copy envelopes that must be torn open to read the information). In addition, $$$T keeps context information for each legal user. The context basically contains the number of transactions executed so far. For an arbitrary user, let this value be h. Then for the next transaction this user wants to run (after having been authenticated by $$$T), the resource manager retrieves p_{h+1} from the password relation, and expects the user to provide exactly this password. Independent of whether or not the transaction is successful, the tuple with p_{h+1} is deleted from the relation. So even if the transaction fails, the transaction program goes back to savepoint 1, then does the delete and calls Commit_Work to make sure the password cannot be used again. After n such transactions, another list of passwords must be given to the user, which typically involves a higher authority.

PART FOUR

Concurrency Control

A foolish consistency is the hobgoblin of little minds,
adored by little statesmen and philosophers and divines.
With consistency a great soul has simply nothing to do. . . .
Speak what you think today in hard words
and tomorrow speak what tomorrow thinks in hard words again,
though it contradict everything you said today.

RALPH WALDO EMERSON

7

Isolation Concepts

7.1 Overview

This chapter and the next cover the concepts and techniques associated with transaction isolation. This topic is variously called *consistency* (the static property), *concurrency control* (the problem), *serializability* (the theory), or *locking* (the technique). The generic term, *isolation*, is used here, both because it fits with the ACID theme of this book (the I of ACID) and because isolation is the term used by the SQL standard.

This chapter presents the isolation definitions and theorems. These theorems state that transactions can execute in parallel with complete isolation if the objects each transaction reads and writes are disjoint from those written by others. The theorems indicate how locking can achieve this: lock everything you access and hold all locks until commit.

Refinements of these results can increase concurrency among transactions. One strategy—called *granular locks*, or *predicate locks*—allows transactions to lock subsets of an object. Another strategy allows transactions to declare the degree of sharing they will tolerate. Both these approaches preserve isolation. A third approach allows transactions to accept reduced degrees of isolation, thereby allowing greater concurrency.

After a theoretical treatment, the chapter turns to the more pragmatic issues of scheduling lock requests that are waiting. Processes waiting for one another may form a cycle called a *deadlock*. Techniques to detect and resolve deadlocks are briefly described. A simple analysis shows that deadlocks should be very rare.

The chapter concludes with some exotic ways to get even higher concurrency by exploiting operation semantics. If operations commute with one another, they may be performed in any order. This simple observation gives rise to an interesting array of techniques.

7.2 Introduction to Isolation

The system state consists of objects related in certain ways. These relationships are best thought of as *invariants* about the objects. Here are some typical invariants at different levels of abstraction:

"The checksum field of each page, P, must be CHECKSUM(P)."
"For each element, x, in a doubly linked ring, prev(next(x)) = x."
"Account balances must be positive."

"ZIP is an INDEX for the EMP table listing employees by postal code."
"EMP1 is a replica of the EMP table."
"All department managers must be employees and so must appear in the EMP table."

In addition, there are invariants about how the system may change state, for example:

"If a record is inserted into EMP, a corresponding record must be inserted into ZIP."
"If either replica of EMP is updated, the other must also be updated in the same way."
"If a program changes the account balance, it must record the change in the ledger."
"The reactor rods cannot move faster than one meter per second."

The system state is said to be *consistent* if it satisfies all these invariants. Often, the state must be made temporarily inconsistent while it is being transformed to a new, consistent state. The cases just listed give several examples of this temporary inconsistency. Changing a page invalidates its checksum until the checksum is recomputed and stored. Adding an element to a doubly-linked ring necessarily causes a temporary inconsistency when one pointer has been updated, but the second has not. Inserting a record into the EMP table cannot be exactly simultaneous with inserting records into the EMP1 table and the ZIP index. Almost any transformation involving updates to several objects temporarily invalidates their mutual consistency.

To cope with these temporary inconsistencies, sequences of actions are grouped to form transactions that preserve the consistency constraints. A transaction that is started with a consistent system state may make the state temporarily inconsistent, but it will terminate by producing a new consistent state. Transactions, then, are units of consistency. This is the C (consistency) of the transaction ACID property. If some action of the transaction fails, the system can automatically undo the actions of the transaction to return to the original consistent state. Defining transaction boundaries within application programs is a major part of application design.

If transactions are run one at a time in isolation, each transaction sees the consistent state left behind by its predecessor. However, if several transactions execute concurrently, the inputs and consequent behavior of some may be inconsistent, even though each transaction executed in isolation is correct. Concurrent transaction execution must be controlled so that correct programs do not malfunction. It is hard enough to design applications even without having to worry about inconsistent inputs caused by concurrent execution. Thus, we have the first law of concurrency, as discussed in the following section.

First Law of Concurrency Control:
Concurrent execution should not cause application programs to malfunction.

This is the I (isolation) of the transaction ACID property. The system gives the illusion that each transaction runs in isolation. The simplest way to implement isolation is to run only one program at a time. If all the programs are short, if all the data are centralized in a main memory, and if all data are accessed by a single processor, then there is no need for concurrency—the programs simply can be run in sequence. But there are a great many *ifs* in this scenario. It is more typical to have many programs with varying response times distributed among many processors with many disjoint memories. In addition, the data may be distributed among fast and slow memories, such that computation and I/O overlap. In such situations, concurrency is inherent and essential. Rather than outlaw it, therefore, systems try to control concurrency in a way that satisfies the first law of concurrency by providing the appearance of isolation. In some situations, notably the operating systems domain, the user is assumed to be a superprogrammer who delights in writing programs that explicitly deal with concurrency. In the transaction processing domain, the assumption is that programmers are mere mortals. In this domain, every attempt is made to make concurrency control automatic.

Many approaches to providing automatic isolation have been tried. There is consensus on one feasible solution—*locking*. (Though there are many other solutions, understanding one is hard enough. Thus, the other solutions are briefly treated at the end of this chapter.) Yet even within the locking approach, there is a bewildering array of variants. Most of these variants are relegated to Section 7.12, on exotics. One reason is the second law of concurrency.

Second Law of Concurrency Control:
Concurrent execution should not have lower throughput or much higher response times than serial execution.

If the concurrency control mechanism has high overhead, it may well cost more than it saves. Complex algorithms are often complex to implement and to execute. The second law favors simple algorithms.

The simplest lock protocol associates a lock with each object. Whenever a transaction accesses an object, the underlying resource manager automatically requests and holds the object's lock for that transaction until the transaction completes. If the lock is granted to another transaction at the moment, the transaction waits for the lock to become free. Locks are a serialization mechanism that assure that only one transaction accesses an object at any given time.

By refining the granularity of the lock (how much data the lock covers), increasing amounts of concurrency are allowed. A lock on the "system" allows only a single transaction to run in the system. A lock at the granularity of a record allows other transactions to access other records in the file as well as records in other files.

The concept of locking goes back thousands of years, to just after the invention of doors. The idea is familiar in the operating system domain, where locks are called *semaphores*, *monitors*, *critical sections*, or *serially reusable resources*. In addition, the concurrent programming community has long been interested in reasoning about concurrent execution that preserves invariants. Transaction isolation (locking) ideas owe a considerable debt to these earlier contributions.

The main contribution of transaction systems to concurrency control has been to refine these ideas to include automatic locking and to combine the locking algorithms with the transaction undo/redo algorithms. This approach gives application programmers a simple model of concurrency and exception conditions. Transaction processing systems automatically acquire locks and keep logs to preserve the ACID properties, thus isolating the application program(mer) from inconsistency caused by concurrency and automating the setting and releasing of locks. The application designer can ignore concurrency issues unless there are performance problems (so-called *hotspots*) in which many transactions want to access the same object. Hotspots either are eliminated by changing the application design, or they are tolerated by using an exotic concurrency control technique.

The isolation theorems are the key results that allow automatic locking. Before covering those theorems, it is instructive to look at some characteristic examples that show the three kinds of anomalies that locking prevents. These provide some intuition about the issues (and considering them puts off rather tedious proofs just a little bit longer).

7.3 The Dependency Model of Isolation

The simplest way to understand isolation results is to think in terms of transaction inputs and outputs. Think of the transaction as a set of read and write actions on the system objects. System objects include terminals, queues, database records, and even other processes. The transaction can either read an object by looking at some aspect of its state, or it can write the object by changing the object's state. Imagine that creating and destroying objects is just a matter of writing their states. Viewed in this coarse way, a transaction is a sequence of read and write actions on objects.

Two read actions by two different transactions to the same object cannot violate consistency because reads do not change the object state (the state is assumed to be initially consistent). Thus, it is only write actions that may create a problem. Two write actions to an object by the same transaction do not violate consistency because the ACID property assumes that the transaction knows what it is doing to its data; the ACID property assumes that if the transaction runs in isolation, it will correctly transform the system state. Consequently, only write-related interactions between two concurrent transactions can create inconsistency or violate isolation.

This fact can be expressed by letting I_i be the set of objects read by transaction T_i (its inputs), and O_i be the set of objects written by T_i (its outputs). The set of transactions $\{T_i\}$ can run in parallel with no concurrency anomalies if their outputs are disjoint from one another's inputs and outputs:

$$O_i \cap (I_j \cup O_j) = \emptyset \text{ for all } i \neq j. \tag{7.1}$$

7.3.1 Static versus Dynamic Allocation

Early transaction schedulers worked by evaluating Equation 7.1. Each transaction would declare its input-output set, and the transaction scheduler would do the computation comparing the new transaction's needs to all the running transactions. If there was a conflict, initiation of the new transaction would be delayed until the conflicting transactions had completed. The problem with *static allocation* was the difficulty of computing the inputs and outputs of a transaction before it runs. A transaction's behavior, and consequently its data inputs and outputs, is often dependent on the transaction input message. For example, since a banking transaction potentially updates any record of the ACCOUNT table, static allocation would probably reserve the entire table. The locking system cannot tell which particular records will be accessed until the transaction runs. In this case, static allocation would schedule only one such banking transaction at a time. By 1972, this approach had been abandoned for the more dynamic one of looking at the individual actions of the transaction.

In a *dynamic allocation* scheme, each transaction is viewed as a sequence of actions rather than as an input-output set. The requests of each action are scheduled on demand as they occur. When an action accesses a particular object, the object is dynamically allocated to that transaction. For example, when your teller runs a banking transaction, only your bank account record and the other specific records accessed by the transaction are allocated to it. Transactions on different accounts can run concurrently and in isolation.

7.3.2 Transaction Dependencies

A more mechanical view of the dynamic allocation model postulates that transactions are sequences of actions operating on objects. A particular object accepts one action at a time. Each action of a transaction is either a read or a write of an object. To reiterate, the definition of object includes not just storage objects but also display objects (windows, menus, and keyboards) and real objects (printers, drill presses, reactor rods, and doors). Reading such objects implies sensing their states, while writing them implies changing their states.

Objects go through a sequence of *versions* as they are written by these actions. Reads do not change the object version, but each time an object is written, it gets a new version. If a transaction reads an object, the transaction *depends* on that object version. If the transaction writes an object, the resulting object version *depends* on the writing transaction. When a transaction aborts and goes through the undo logic, all its writes are undone. These cause the objects to get new-new versions (that is, the undo looks like an ordinary new update). For example, imagine that there is a record with version 23 having value *A*. If your transaction sets the variable to *B*, the version will increment to 24. If your transaction makes a further update, the version will become 25. If your transaction aborts after that, the record value will be updated back to *A*. Because versions only increase, this undo update will set the version to 26 (not to 23).

This object model is an elegant way of thinking about concurrency. It takes the view that nothing ever changes; rather, new versions of objects are created. Paper-based bookkeeping systems work this way, and some computer systems have been implemented in this way. In such systems, programs can request either the current value of an object or the value of an object as of some time in the past (called *time domain addressing*).

Thinking in these terms suggests a data flow or dependency graph, fragments of which are shown in Figure 7.1. It shows the three possible execution sequences of reads and writes by two transactions, $T1$ and $T2$, operating on versions of an object named *o*. Originally the object has version $\langle o,1 \rangle$, but as it is written it acquires versions $\langle o,2 \rangle$, and $\langle o,3 \rangle$. The corresponding dependency graphs are shown below the execution sequences. In that figure, the middle column shows transaction $T1$ writing version 2 of object *o,* and then transaction $T2$ reading that version. This creates a WRITE→READ dependency between the two transactions.

Figure 7.1 has no READ→READ dependencies, because transactions reading the same version of an object create no dependency on one another. Only write actions create versions and dependencies. The only subtle point in Figure 7.1 is the READ→WRITE dependency case. That dependency states that $T1$ read object *o* before $T2$ altered the object.

A dependency graph can be read as a time sequence. If there is an edge from transaction $T1$ to transaction $T2$, then $T1$ accessed an object later accessed by $T2$, and at least one of these accesses created a new version. In that sense, $T1$ ran before $T2$. In a purely sequential execution of the transactions—running $T1$ to completion, then running $T2$ to completion— all dependency arrows will point from $T1$ to $T2$. But in a parallel execution, dependency arrows can form an arbitrary graph.

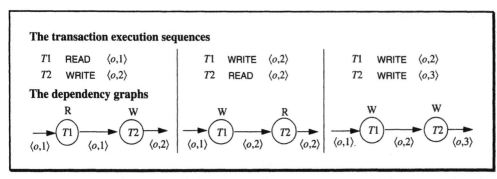

The transaction execution sequences

T1	READ	⟨o,1⟩		T1	WRITE	⟨o,2⟩	T1	WRITE	⟨o,2⟩
T2	WRITE	⟨o,2⟩		T2	READ	⟨o,2⟩	T2	WRITE	⟨o,3⟩

Figure 7.1: The three forms of transaction dependencies. The leftmost column shows transaction T2 writing version ⟨o,2⟩ of object o after T1 reads version ⟨o,1⟩. This READ→WRITE dependency is shown in the graph below the execution sequence. The other two columns show the other two forms of dependency WRITE→READ and WRITE→WRITE.

The main result of the isolation theorems is that any dependency graph without cycles implies an *isolated* execution of the transactions.[1] On the other hand, if the dependency graph has cycles, the transactions were not executed in isolation. This is fairly intuitive: if the dependency graph has no cycles, then the transactions can be topologically sorted to make an equivalent execution history in which each transaction ran serially, one completing before the next began. This implies that each transaction ran in isolation, as though there were no concurrency; it also implies that there were no concurrency anomalies. If there is a cycle, such a sort is impossible, because there are at least two transactions, such that T1 ran before T2, and that T2 ran before T1.

7.3.3 The Three Bad Dependencies

The various ways isolation is violated are characterized by the related dependency cycles. Cycles take one of only three generic forms, diagrammed in Figure 7.2. Each form of cycle has a special name: *lost update, dirty read,* or *unrepeatable read.*

Lost update. Transaction T1's write is ignored by transaction T2, which writes the object based on the original value ⟨o,1⟩. A READ-WRITE-WRITE sequence is shown in the diagram, but a WRITE-WRITE-WRITE sequence forms the same graph and is equally bad. To give a simple example of a lost update: suppose you and I are writing a program together. We both make a copy of the program and change it independently. We then return the program to the program library. If each of us is unaware that the other has updated the program, and if there is no control on updates, then the program will end up with only my changes or only your changes. One of our updates will be lost.

Dirty read. T1 reads an object previously written by transaction T2, then T2 makes further changes to the object. The version read by T1 may be inconsistent, because it is not the final (committed) value of o produced by T2. To continue the programming example, suppose you tentatively install a version of the program in the library, and I use that

---

[1] A *cycle* is any non-null path starting and ending at the same node.

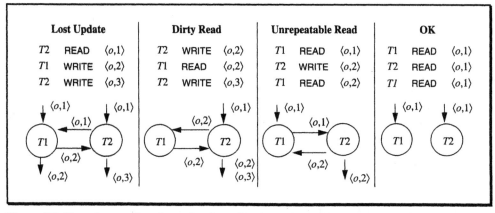

Figure 7.2: Four transaction dependencies. Versions of a single object, o, are shown being read and written by two transactions, $T1$ and $T2$. The kinds of dependencies are WRITE→WRITE (can cause lost updates), WRITE→READ (can cause dirty reads), READ→WRITE (can cause unrepeatable reads), and READ→READ (causes no inconsistency).

program. Then you realize that the program is wrong and reverse the change, creating a new version of the program. My read of your tentative program was a dirty read.

Unrepeatable read. $T1$ reads an object twice, once before transaction $T2$ updates it and once after committed transaction $T2$ has updated it. The two read operations return different values for the object. To continue the program example, suppose I use version 1 of your program, and you later install and commit a new version of it (version 2). If I read your program again, it will be the new version that I read. Thus, my first read was not repeatable.

If there were no concurrency, none of these anomalous cases would arise. As a result, these cases definitely violate the first law of concurrency. Note that the missing case, READ→READ dependencies, cannot cause inconsistency. *The surprising thing is that these three generic forms of inconsistency are the whole story. If they can be prevented, then there will be no concurrency anomalies, and the transaction will appear to run in isolation.* This is the idea behind the isolation theorems.

In exceptional cases, the nonisolated executions in Figure 7.2 may not create inconsistency. But in the general case they may, and we are looking for a general way to prevent inconsistency caused by concurrency. Consequently, the first three kinds of graphs must be prevented. Preventing such anomalies gives the effect of running transactions in isolation (the I of ACID).

7.3.4 The Case for a Formal Model of Isolation

To make more precise statements about the issues of concurrency and recovery, a formal model is required. Because the problems are complex and subtle, it is easy to let the formalism get out of hand (with subscripts on subscripts). The approach here is, rather, to give a precise and formal model for flat transactions with shared and exclusive locks (read and write actions). The model is followed by an informal discussion of degrees of isolation, lock granularity, nested transactions, and optimizations of the basic ideas. The authors believe it is worth the effort to follow the formal part of the development; we attempt to present it simply.

Several equivalent definitions of isolation are useful:

Intuitive. In terms of user transaction properties, the intuitive definition is used to describe the system behavior to application designers and users.

Mathematical. In terms of system execution histories and dependency graphs, the mathematical definition is used to state and prove isolation properties.

Operational. In terms of lock protocols, the operational definition is used to guide system implementations.

First, let's start with the intuitive view given to the programmer using the isolation system.

7.4 Isolation: The Application Programmer's View

The application programmer is given the notion of a transaction that preserves the system invariants. His job is to write such programs, using a book full of actions on system objects (create file, send message, SQL statements). He is told that these actions are all atomic, consistent, isolated, and durable (ACID); that is, they make consistent transformations of the objects they access, and they act as subtransactions. His job is to compose a top-level transaction out of these simple actions. He starts the transaction with a BEGIN WORK statement and declares the end of a successful transaction with a COMMIT WORK statement. Before issuing a COMMIT WORK, a ROLLBACK WORK statement may be issued to undo all changes made by this transaction since the BEGIN WORK.

Transactions have inputs and outputs, but these terms are defined broadly. For example, if the input comes from a user at a terminal, then the user and the terminal are part of the input. The outputs of a transaction are said to be *uncommitted*, or *dirty*, if the transaction has not yet issued COMMIT WORK. A transaction that issues a ROLLBACK WORK has no outputs.

Concurrent execution raises the problem that one transaction may read or write another transaction's dirty data. Using this notion of dirty data, isolation can be defined in one of the following ways:

Isolation: user's definition 1. The transaction processing system may run transactions in parallel, but it behaves as if it has run transactions in sequence. As far as the application programs are concerned, it is as though the transactions were run with no parallelism; the exact ordering of the transactions is controlled by the system. The behavior of the system is equivalent to some serial execution of the transactions, giving the appearance that one transaction ran to completion before the next one started.

Isolation: user's definition 2. This more mechanistic application programming definition states that transaction T is isolated from other transactions if:

(0) T does not overwrite dirty data of other transactions.

(1) T's writes are neither read nor written by other transactions until COMMIT WORK.

(2) *T* does not read dirty data from other transactions.

(3) Other transactions do not write (dirty) any data read by *T* before *T* completes.

Clauses 0 and 1 preclude lost updates, clause 2 isolates the transaction from dirty reads, and clause 3 prevents unrepeatable reads.

These two definitions are almost equivalent.[2] If all transactions observe the rules of the second definition, the following properties apply:

Consistent inputs. Each transaction reads a consistent input state.

Isolated execution. Any execution of the system is equivalent to some serial execution. That is, it is equivalent to an execution with no concurrency and, consequently, equivalent to an execution with no concurrency anomalies.

Durability. If any transaction issues ROLLBACK WORK, or if the system faults and unilaterally issues a ROLLBACK of some uncommitted transactions, then the rolled-back work of the uncommitted transactions may be lost. None of the updates or messages of committed transactions is lost. Database consistency is preserved, and the aborted transaction can be rerun.

The next section offers "proofs" of these assertions.

7.5 Isolation Theorems

After the informal and vague discussion of the previous section, you are probably wishing for a more formal presentation of isolation theorems.[3] To begin, a notation for sequences is introduced. Almost everything in computer science is a sequence: records are sequences of fields, programs are sequences of statements, and executions are sequences of steps. This material, too, relies heavily upon sequences of elements. A sequence of values is represented by a comma-separated list, such as $S = \langle a,b,c \rangle$. Sequences S and S' may be concatenated as $S \parallel S'$. The *i*th element of sequence S is represented by $S[i]$. A subsequence S' of sequence S is represented in a manner similar to set notation by $S' = \langle S[i] \mid \text{predicate } (S[i]) \rangle$.

$\langle$Name, value$\rangle$ ordered pairs are sequences of two elements; the first element is the name, and the second element is the value. As a first use of sequences, the *system state*, S, consists of an infinite set of named objects, each with a value. S is denoted $\{\langle \text{name, value} \rangle\}$.

7.5.1 Actions and Transactions

The system supports *actions* (READ, WRITE, XLOCK, SLOCK, UNLOCK) on these objects, as well as three generic actions (BEGIN, COMMIT, ROLLBACK). READ and WRITE have the

---

[2] Using the notation of Bernstein, Hadzilacos, and Goodman [1987, p. 36], definition 1 is SR (serializable), and Definition 2 is two-phase locking (2PL). sR ⊃ 2PL: some isolation schemes are more general than the locking mechanisms described here.

[3] These theorems are usually called the *serialization theorems*, but the term isolation is used here for consistency with the ACID terminology. The acronym CAPS (consistency, atomicity, persistence, serializability) is an alternative mnemonic.

usual meaning: READ returns the named object's value to the program; WRITE alters the named object's value. Explanations of the other actions' meanings follow.

For the purposes of this model, a *transaction* is any sequence of actions starting with a BEGIN action, ending with a COMMIT or ROLLBACK action, and not containing any other BEGIN, COMMIT, or ROLLBACK actions. Here are two trivial transactions:

T	BEGIN		T'	BEGIN	
	SLOCK	A		SLOCK	A
	XLOCK	B		READ	A
	READ	A		XLOCK	B
	WRITE	B		WRITE	B
	COMMIT			ROLLBACK	

In practice, transactions are actually program executions with branches, loops, procedure calls, messages, and other control flow. For the purposes of this discussion, however, only the "external" sequence of program actions (behavior) is examined. Transactions are represented symbolically by a sequence such as $\langle\langle t, a_i, o_i\rangle \mid i = 1, ..., n\rangle$; this means that the ith step of transaction t performed action a_i on object o_i.

To simplify the transaction model, BEGIN, COMMIT, and ROLLBACK are defined in terms of the other actions, so that only READ, WRITE, LOCK, and UNLOCK actions remain. A *simple transaction* is composed of READ, WRITE, XLOCK, SLOCK, and UNLOCK actions. Every transaction, T, can be translated into an *equivalent simple transaction* as follows:

(1) Discard the BEGIN action.

(2) If the transaction ends with a COMMIT action, replace that action with the following sequence of UNLOCKS:

$\langle$UNLOCK A | if SLOCK A or XLOCK A appears in T for any object $A\rangle$.

(3) If the transaction ends with a ROLLBACK statement, replace that action with the following sequence of WRITEs and then UNLOCKs:

$\langle$WRITE A | if WRITE A appears in T for any object $A\rangle$ ‖

$\langle$UNLOCK A | if SLOCK A or XLOCK A Appears in T for any object $A\rangle$.

The simple transactions equivalent to T and T' above are TS, and TS' (the actions in italics are the substitutes for the COMMIT and ROLLBACK actions):

TS	SLOCK	A	TS'	SLOCK	A
	XLOCK	B		READ	A
	READ	A		XLOCK	B
	WRITE	B		WRITE	B
	UNLOCK	*A*		*WRITE (UNDO)*	*B*
	UNLOCK	*B*		*UNLOCK*	*A*
				UNLOCK	*B*

The idea here is that the COMMIT action simply releases locks, while the ROLLBACK action must first undo all changes to the objects the transaction wrote and then issue the unlock statements. Notice that if the transaction has no LOCK statements, then neither COMMIT nor ROLLBACK will issue any UNLOCK statements. As will be shown, such transaction nor ROLLBACK will issue any UNLOCK statements. As will be shown, such transaction behavior risks violating isolation. It will be shown that a transaction should lock an object before any read or write of the object, and the transaction should not issue any UNLOCKs. It should let COMMIT and ROLLBACK issue the UNLOCKS.

To simplify the notation, *the discussion from here on is in terms of equivalent simple transactions*. The results apply to both simple transactions and to transactions involving BEGIN, COMMIT, and ROLLBACK.

7.5.2 Well-Formed and Two-Phased Transactions

Each lock action of a transaction *covers* certain actions within the transaction. The SLOCK action is intended to cover the transaction's reads. The S in SLOCK stands for *shared*: since readers can concurrently share access to an object without violating isolation. The X in XLOCK means eXclusive lock: this action is intended to cover reads and writes of a transaction and to exclude reads and writes of the object by other transactions. A READ or UNLOCK operation by transaction T on object o is *covered by a lock* if the operation is preceded by T performing an SLOCK or XLOCK action on o, and if there is no intervening UNLOCK action on o. Similarly, a WRITE or UNLOCK operation on o is covered by a lock if it is preceded by an XLOCK on o, and if there are no intervening UNLOCK operations on o.

A transaction is said to be *well-formed* if all its READ, WRITE, and UNLOCK actions are covered by locks, and if each lock action is eventually followed by a corresponding UNLOCK action. This is depicted graphically in Figure 7.3.

A transaction is defined as *two-phase* if all its LOCK actions precede all its UNLOCK actions. A two-phase transaction T has a growing phase, $T[1], ...,T[j]$, during which it acquires locks, and a shrinking phase, $T[j + 1], ...,T[n]$, during which it releases locks.

7.5.3 Transaction Histories

Any sequence-preserving merge of the actions of a set of transactions into a single sequence is called a *history* for the set of transactions and is denoted $H = \langle \langle t,a,o \rangle_i \mid i = 1, ..., n \rangle$. Each step of the history $\langle t,a,o \rangle$ is action a by transaction t on object o. A history for the set of transactions $\{T_j\}$ is a sequence, each containing transaction T_j as a subsequence and containing nothing else. A history lists the order in which actions were successfully completed. For example, if a transaction requests a lock at the beginning of the history but has to wait, and

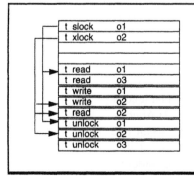

The actions *covered* by the two lock actions are shown as shaded rectangles. The transaction is not well-formed because the READ and UNLOCK actions on object $o3$ are not covered by an SLOCK or XLOCK, and the WRITE action on object $o1$ is not covered by an XLOCK. The transaction is two-phase.

Figure 7.3: A diagrammatic representation of locks covering actions.

is finally granted the lock near the end of the history, that lock request will appear near the end of the history.

The simplest histories first run all the actions of one transaction, then run all the actions of another to completion, and so on. Such one-transaction-at-a-time histories are called *serial histories*. Clearly, serial histories have no concurrency-induced inconsistency, and no transaction sees dirty data.

The definition of histories implicitly defines each action as an ACID transformation of the object state: each action is executed as an ACID step. The results here show how, given an underlying set of ACID actions, groups of actions can be executed concurrently while still providing transaction isolation.

7.5.4 Legal Histories and Lock Compatibility

A history should not complete a lock action on an object while that object is locked by another transaction in a incompatible mode. Consequently, locking constrains the set of allowed histories. Histories that obey the locking constraints are called *legal.* The following table defines the compatibility of lock requests and modes:

Compatibility		Mode of Lock	
		Share	Exclusive
Mode of	Share	Compatible	Conflict
Request	Exclusive	Conflict	Conflict

Defining legal histories more formally, *transaction* t *has object* o *locked in* SHARED *mode at step* k *of history* H, if for some $i < k$, action $H[i] = \langle t, \text{SLOCK}, o \rangle$, and if there is no $\langle t, \text{UNLOCK}, o \rangle$ action in the subhistory $H[i + 1], ...,H[k-1]$. *Transaction* t *has object* o *locked in* EXCLUSIVE *mode at step* k is defined analogously. History H is *legal* if there is no step $H[k]$ of H at which two distinct transactions have the same object locked in incompatible modes.

Figure 7.4 shows three representative histories for the simple transactions *TS* and *TS'* introduced earlier, but renamed *T1* and *T2* respectively. The first history is serial. The second is nonserial because T1 and T2 execute concurrently, but it is legal. The third history is another concurrent history, but is not legal because both *T1* and *T2* have an exclusive lock on object *B* at the same time (this step is shown in bold type in the figure). Note that the combination not shown (serial and not legal) is impossible if each transaction ends with a COMMIT or ROLLBACK statement.

It may appear that this is a centralized view of transactions. What if many computers execute the transactions in parallel? How can such parallel execution be viewed as a single sequential history? There are two answers: (1) Imagine a global, universal clock precise to 10^{-100} seconds. Each action at each machine gets a timestamp from this clock when it completes. These timestamps give a sequential ordering (history) of all the actions. (2) Alternatively, each computer can linearly order its actions into a local history, and when two machines interact by X sending a message to Y, they synchronize their histories so that all X actions prior to the send precede all Y actions after the receive. The resulting partial ordering can be transformed into a global sequential history.

Legal and Serial			Legal and Not Serial			Not Legal and Not Serial		
T1	SLOCK	A	*T2*	SLOCK	A	*T1*	SLOCK	A
T1	XLOCK	B	*T1*	SLOCK	A	*T1*	XLOCK	B
T1	READ	A	*T2*	READ	A	*T2*	SLOCK	A
T1	WRITE	B	*T2*	XLOCK	B	*T2*	READ	A
T1	UNLOCK	A	*T2*	WRITE	B	*T2*	**XLOCK**	**B**
T1	UNLOCK	B	*T2*	WRITE	B	*T2*	WRITE	B
T2	SLOCK	A	*T2*	UNLOCK	A	*T2*	WRITE	B
T2	READ	A	*T2*	UNLOCK	B	*T2*	UNLOCK	A
T2	XLOCK	B	*T1*	XLOCK	B	*T2*	UNLOCK	B
T2	WRITE	B	*T1*	READ	A	*T1*	READ	A
T2	WRITE	B	*T1*	WRITE	B	*T1*	WRITE	B
T2	UNLOCK	A	*T1*	UNLOCK	A	*T1*	UNLOCK	A
T2	UNLOCK	B	*T1*	UNLOCK	B	*T1*	UNLOCK	B

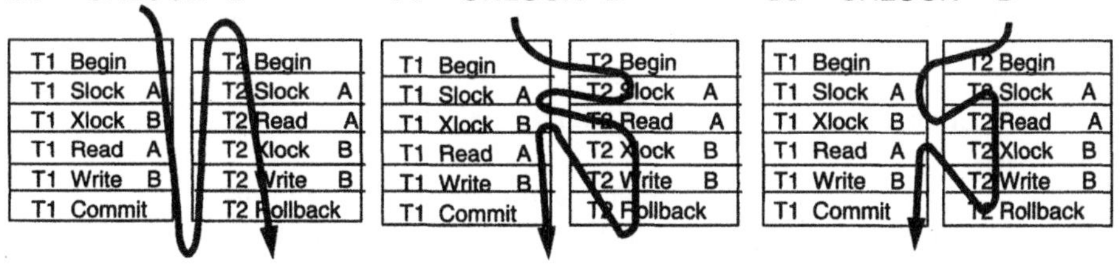

Figure 7.4: Three execution histories of simple transactions *T*1 and *T*2.   Each history was chosen to demonstrate the differences between legal and serial histories. The third history contains an XLOCK action by *T*2 in bold type. That action violates the lock protocol, since *T1* already has B locked. That is why the history is not legal. The diagrams at the bottom show how the history threads the execution steps of each transaction. Note that it is not possible to have a serial history that is not legal.

As a second point, histories are not constructed; they are a byproduct of the system behavior. For example, locking systems only produce legal histories. Histories are mathematical abstractions that allow us to discuss various isolation mechanisms.

7.5.5 Versions, Dependencies, and the Dependency Graph

An initial state and a history completely define the system's behavior. At each step of the history one can deduce which object values have been committed and which are dirty (written data is dirty until it is unlocked). One transaction instance *T* is said to *depend* on another transaction *T'* in a history *H* if *T* reads or writes data previously written by *T'* in the history *H*, or if *T* writes an object previously read by *T'*. Dependencies define the data flow among transactions and are useful in comparing two histories. If two histories have the same dependencies, then transactions read the same inputs and write the same outputs in both histories, thereby making the two histories equivalent. The definition of inputs, outputs, and dependencies needs the notion of object versions introduced in the previous section. The dependency graph will be defined as a labeled, directed graph in which the nodes are

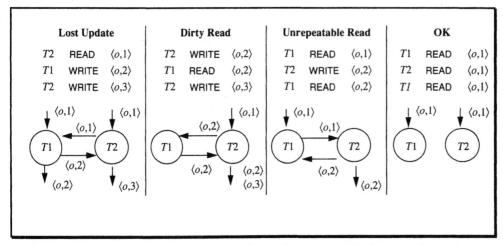

Figure 7.5: The dependencies induced by history fragments. Each graph shows the two transaction nodes *T*1 and *T*2 and the arcs labeled with the object ⟨name,version⟩ pairs. Outgoing read dependencies are not shown (see Exercise 3).

transactions and the arcs are transaction dependencies labeled with the object versions being written or read by the transactions.

The *version of an object* o *at step* k *of a history* is an integer and is denoted $V(o,k)$. Initially, each object has version zero ($V(o,0) = 0$). At step k of history H, object o has a version equal to the number of writes of that object before this step. This is stated formally as:

$$V(o,k) = |\{\langle t_j, a_j, o_j \rangle \in H \mid j < k \text{ and } a_j = \text{WRITE and } o_j = o\}|$$

(The outer vertical bars represent the set cardinality function.)

Each history, H, for a set of transactions $\{T_i\}$ defines a ternary *dependency relation* DEP(H), defined as follows. Let *T1* and *T2* be any two distinct transactions, let o be any object, and let i, j be any two steps of H with $i < j$. Suppose step $H[i]$ involves action $a1$ of *T1* on object o, step $H[j]$ involves action $a2$ of *T2* on o, and suppose there is no WRITE of o by any transaction between these steps (there is no ⟨*T′*,WRITE,o⟩ in $H[i + 1]$, ..., $H[j-1]$). Then DEP(H) is defined as:

$\langle T, \langle o, V(o,j) \rangle, T' \rangle \in$ DEP(H)	if	$a1$ is a WRITE and $a2$ is a WRITE
	or	$a1$ is a WRITE and $a2$ is a READ
	or	$a1$ is a READ and $a2$ is a WRITE.

This definition captures the WRITE→WRITE, WRITE→READ, and READ→WRITE dependencies. The dependency relation for a history defines a directed *dependency graph*. Transactions are the nodes of the graph, and object versions label the edges. If ⟨T,⟨o,j⟩,T'⟩ ∈ DEP(H), then the graph has an edge from node T to node T' labeled by ⟨o,j⟩. Figure 7.5, by repeating Figure 7.2, demonstrates this.

7.5.6 Equivalent and Isolated Histories: BEFORE, AFTER, and Wormholes

Each history defines a dependency relation. Two histories for the same set of transactions are *equivalent* if they have the same dependency relation (DEP(H) = DEP(H')). A history is said to be *isolated* if it is equivalent to a serial history. This use of the word *isolated* is justified in Subsection 7.5.7.

The dependencies of a history define a time order of the transactions. This ordering is denoted by the symbol $<<<_H$, or simply $<<<$, and is the *transitive closure* of $<<<$. It is the smallest relation satisfying the equation:

$T <<<_H T'$ if $\langle T,o,T'\rangle \in \mathsf{DEP}(H)$ for some object version o, or
$\quad (T <<<_H T''$ and $\langle T'',o,T'\rangle \in \mathsf{DEP}(H)$ for some transaction T'', and object o).

Informally, $T <<< T'$ if there is a path in the dependency graph from transaction T to transaction T'.

The $<<<$ ordering varies from one history to another, but all equivalent histories define the same ordering. Each $<<<$ ordering defines the set of all transactions that *run before T*; that is, transactions that directly or indirectly wrote inputs that were read or written by transaction T. Similarly, all the transactions that *ran after T* are the ones that read or wrote objects written by T or are ones that overwrote objects read by T. These definitions are:

$\mathsf{BEFORE}(T) = \{T' \mid T' <<< T \}$
$\mathsf{AFTER}(T) = \{T' \mid T <<< T'\}.$

If T runs in a vacuum—for example, it is the only transaction, or it reads and writes objects not accessed by any other transactions—then its BEFORE and AFTER sets are empty. In this case, it can be scheduled in any way. Things are more interesting when the BEFORE and AFTER sets of T are nonempty. It is particularly interesting when some transaction T' is both before and after another transaction T, that is, when:

$T' \in \mathsf{BEFORE}(T) \cap \mathsf{AFTER}(T).$

Such a transaction, T', is called a *wormhole transaction*, since it ran both in the future and in the past with respect to transaction T. Wormhole transactions are named after the points near black holes that reputedly let one travel arbitrarily in time and space. They get this name because they perform actions before T completes and after T completes. We will later see that a wormhole transaction T' has the property $T' \in \mathsf{BEFORE}(T') \cap \mathsf{AFTER}(T')$ Such transactions T' run before *and* after themselves.

7.5.7 Wormholes Are Not Isolated

Clearly, serial histories don't have wormholes. In a serial history, all the actions of one transaction precede the actions of another; the first cannot depend on the outputs of the second. It turns out that isolated histories have the *unique* property of having no wormholes. A history that is not isolated has at least one wormhole: a pair of transactions T, T' such that $T <<< T' <<< T$. Stated another way, T is BEFORE T' is BEFORE T. Stated yet a third way, if each transaction precedes the other, the execution history probably represents a concurrency anomaly and fails the ACID test.

In graphical terms, if the dependency graph has a cycle in it, then the history is not equivalent to any serial history because some transaction is both before and after another transaction. The first three graphs in Figures 7.2 and 7.5 show such cycles. It is possible to have cycles involving more than two transactions, as is shown in Figure 7.6.

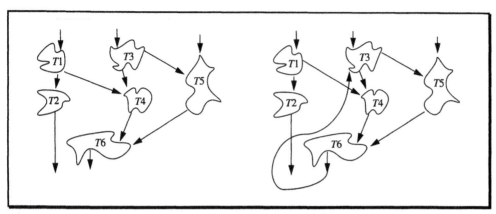

Figure 7.6: The dependencies among a set of transactions induced by two different execution histories. The graph on the left has no cycles and, consequently, no wormhole transactions. It allows the serial history $T1,T2,T3,T4,T5,T6$. The figure on the left shows that the sets of transactions $\{T1,T3\}$ $\{T2, T4,T5\}$, and many other subsets, do not directly interact at all and may therefore be run concurrently without any risk of violating isolation. The graph on the right has two cycles. Transactions $T3$, $T4$, $T5$, and $T6$ are wormhole transactions that ran both before and after one another.

Examine the graph on the left of Figure 7.6. Note that BEFORE($T4$) = $\{T1,T3\}$ and AFTER($T4$) = $\{T6\}$. $T2$ and $T5$ are therefore neither before nor after $T4$. This means that $T2$ and $T5$ can run concurrently with $T4$. Since they do not interact with one another, the actions of these three transactions may be interleaved in an execution history without changing the dependency graph. Put more formally, if <<< has no cycles, it is a partial order of the transactions. A particular history, H, such that <<< = <<<$_H$, implies a total order of the transactions extending the partial order <<<. Two transactions not related by <<< may be arbitrarily scheduled with respect to each other. Equivalent histories could schedule one before the other or schedule them concurrently.

7.5.8 Summary of Definitions

This subsection summarizes the definitions of terms introduced up to this point and, using those definitions, states the theorems of concurrency control. The subsections that follow give proofs of each theorem.

A *transaction* is a sequence of READ, WRITE, SLOCK, and XLOCK actions on objects ending with a COMMIT or ROLLBACK action.

General transactions containing COMMIT and ROLLBACK can be transformed into equivalent *simple transactions* with just READ, WRITE, SLOCK, XLOCK and UNLOCK actions.

A transaction is *well-formed* if each READ, WRITE, and UNLOCK action is covered by a corresponding lock, and all locks are released by the end of the transaction.

A transaction is *two-phase* if it has a growing phase in which it only acquires locks, and then a shrinking phase in which it only releases locks.

A *history* is some merge of the actions of a set of transactions.

A history is *serial* if it runs one transaction at a time.

A history is *legal* if it does not grant conflicting locks to two different transactions at the same time.

Each history defines a *dependency relation* that characterizes the data flow among transactions.

Two histories are *equivalent* if they have the same dependency relation.

A history is said to be *isolated* if it is equivalent to a serial history.

The dependency relation of a history defines an ordering among its transactions, $T <<< T'$, which is read *T ran before T'*.

A *wormhole* in a particular history is a transaction pair in which T ran before T' ran before T.

An important point to note is that *systems do not build histories or dependency graphs.* Rather, these are purely mathematical constructs used to talk about the way systems operate. Histories and dependencies result from purely local scheduling decisions that are made as action requests arrive.

Given the preceding definitions, the basic results of concurrency control are stated as follows:

Wormhole theorem: A history is isolated if, and only if, it has no wormhole transactions.

Locking theorem: If all transactions are well-formed and two-phase, then any legal history will be isolated.

Locking theorem (converse): If a transaction is not well-formed or is not two-phase, then it is possible to write another transaction such that the resulting pair is a wormhole.

Rollback theorem: An update transaction that does an UNLOCK and then a ROLLBACK is not two-phase.

Each of these results will now be stated and proved.

7.5.8.1 Wormhole Theorem

Wormhole Theorem:
A history is isolated if, and only if, it has no wormhole transactions.

Proof: (Isolated => no wormholes). This proof is by contradiction. Suppose H is an isolated history of the execution of the set of transactions $\{T_i | i = 1, ..., n\}$. By definition, then,

H is equivalent to some serial execution history, SH, for that same set of transactions. Without loss of generality, assume that the transactions are numbered so that $SH = T_1 \| T_2 \| \ldots \| T_n$. Suppose, for the sake of contradiction, that H has a wormhole; that is, there is some sequence of transactions $T, T', T'', \ldots, T'''$ such that each is BEFORE the other (i.e., $T <<<_H T'$), and the last is BEFORE the first (i.e., $T''' <<<_H T$). Let i be the minimum transaction index such that T_i is in this wormhole, and let T_j be its predecessor in the wormhole (i.e., $T_j <<<_H T_i$). By the minimality of i, T_j comes completely AFTER T_i in the execution history SH, so that $T_j <<<_{SH} T_i$ is impossible (recall that SH is a serial history). But since H and SH are equivalent, $<<<_H \ = \ <<<_{SH}$; therefore, $T_j <<<_H T_i$ is also impossible. This contradiction proves that if H is isolated, it has no wormholes.

(No wormholes => isolated). This proof is by induction on the number of transactions, n, that appear in the history, H. The induction hypothesis is that any n transaction history H having no wormholes is isolated (equivalent to some serial history, SH, for that set of transactions).

If $n < 2$, then any history is a serial history, since only zero or one transaction appears in the history. In addition, any serial history is an isolated history. The basis of the induction, then, is trivially true.

Suppose the induction hypothesis is true for $n{-}1$ transactions, and consider some history H of n transactions that has no wormholes. Pick any transaction T, then pick any other transaction T', such that $T <<< T'$, and continue this construction as long as possible, building the sequence $S = \langle T, T', \ldots \rangle$. Either S is infinite, or it is not. If S is infinite, then some transaction T'' must appear in it twice. This, in turn, implies that $T'' <<< T''$; thus, T'' is a wormhole of H. But since H has no wormholes, S cannot be infinite. The last transaction in S—call it T^*— has the property $\text{AFTER}(T^*) = \varnothing$, since the sequence cannot be continued past T^*.

Consider the history, $H' = \langle \langle t_i, a_i, o_i \rangle \in H \mid t_i \neq T^* \rangle$. H' is the history H with all the actions of transaction T^* removed. By the choice of T^*,

$$\text{DEP}(H') = \{ \langle T, \langle o,i \rangle, T' \rangle \in \text{DEP}(H) \mid T' \neq T^* \}. \tag{7.2}$$

H' has no wormholes (since H has no wormholes, and $\text{DEP}(H) \supseteq \text{DEP}(H')$). The induction hypothesis, then, applies to H'. Hence, H' is isolated and has an equivalent serial history SH' $= T_1 \| T_2 \| \ldots \| T_{n-1}$ for some numbering of the other transactions.

The serial history $SH = SH' \| T_n = T_1 \| T_2 \| \ldots \| T_{n-1} \| T^*$ is equivalent to H. To prove this, it must be shown that $\text{DEP}(SH) = \text{DEP}(H)$. By construction,

$$\text{DEP}(SH) = \text{DEP}(SH' \| T_n) = \text{DEP}(SH') \cup \{ \langle T', \langle o,i \rangle, T^* \rangle \in \text{DEP}(H) \}. \tag{7.3}$$

By definition, $\text{DEP}(SH') = \text{DEP}(H')$. Using this to substitute Equation (7.2) into Equation (7.3) gives:

$$\text{DEP}(SH) = \{ \langle T, \langle o,i \rangle, T' \rangle \in \text{DEP}(H) \mid T' \neq T^* \} \cup \{ \langle T', \langle o,i \rangle, T^* \rangle \in \text{DEP}(H) \} = \text{DEP}(H). \tag{7.4}$$

Thus, the identity $\text{DEP}(SH) = \text{DEP}(H)$ is established, and the induction step is proven. ◆

The wormhole theorem (serializability theorem) is the basic result from which all the others follow. It essentially says "cycles are bad." Wormhole is just another name for cycle.

The Wormhole Theorem can be stated in many different ways. One typical statement is called the *Serializability Theorem:* A history H is isolated (also called a *serializable*

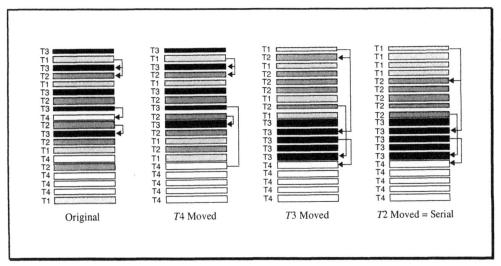

Figure 7.7: An illustration of the induction used in the Wormhole Theorem proof.   The arrows to the right of each history show the dependency graph. Transaction *T*4 is moved to the end, since it is "last" in the dependency graph. The resulting history has the same dependency graph and is therefore equivalent to the first (gives each transaction the same input data). Then the induction applies, allowing the next-to-last transaction *T*3 to be moved to the end of the unsorted subhistory. This repeats until the resulting serial history is produced. In the resulting serial history, the first transaction, *T*1, was the last to finish in the original.

schedule or a *consistent schedule*) if, and only if, $<<<_H$ implies a partial order of the transactions. (Alternatively: if and only if it defines an acyclic graph, or implies a partially ordered set, or . . .).

The induction just considered can be thought of diagrammatically as sorting the actions of the transactions according to the $<<<$ ordering, as in Figure 7.7. In that figure, the original history has four transactions with four dependencies and no cycles in the dependency graph. Note that the dependency graph arrows always point down (forward in time). Transaction *T*4 is the "last" transaction, in the $<<<$ sense. It can be moved to the end of the history without changing the dependency graph. After permuting *T*4 to the end of the history, transaction *T*3 is "last" in the remaining set; hence, it can be permuted to the end of that history without disturbing the dependencies of *T*4 or of *T*1 and *T*2. Once this is done, *T*2 is last in the set and can be permuted to the end. The result is a serial history equivalent to the original. Note that the last step of the original history was an action belonging to the first transaction in the resulting serial history. If there had been a cycle in the dependency graph, then the permutation steps involving those wormhole transactions would not have been possible; moving one of them completely after all the others in the cycle would have broken the cycle and produced a history not equivalent to the original history. It also would have produced dependency graph arrows pointing up in the history (back in time).

The first application of the Wormhole Theorem says that if transactions set locks correctly (are well-formed and two-phase), and if the system schedules locks so that no two transactions are simultaneously granted a lock on an object in a conflicting mode (i.e., the system allows only legal histories), then any execution history will be isolated. Such histories are equivalent to some serial execution. Put briefly, locking correctly done provides the isolation (I) of ACID.

7.5.8.2 Locking Theorem

Locking Theorem:
If all transactions are well-formed and two-phase, then any legal history will be isolated.

Proof: This proof is by contradiction. Suppose H is a legal history of the execution of the set of transactions, each of which is well-formed and two-phase. For each transaction T, define SHRINK(T) to be the index of the first unlock step of T in history H (formally SHRINK(T) = $min(i \mid H[i] = \langle T,\text{UNLOCK}, o \rangle$ *for some object*))[4]. Since each transaction T is non-null and well-formed, it must contain an *UNLOCK* step. Thus SHRINK is well defined for each transaction. First we need to prove

lemma: if $T<<<T'$, then SHRINK(T) < SHRINK(T').

Suppose $T <<< T'$, then suppose there is an object o and some steps $i < j$ of history H, such that $H[i] = \langle T,a,o \rangle$, $H[j] = \langle T',a',o \rangle$; either action a or action a' is a WRITE (this assertion comes directly from the definition of DEP(H)). Suppose that the action a of T is a WRITE. Since T is well-formed, then, step i is covered by T doing an XLOCK on o. Similarly, step j must be covered by T' doing an SLOCK or XLOCK on o. H is a legal schedule, and these locks would conflict, so there must be a $k1$ and $k2$, such that:

$i < k1 < k2 < j$ and $H[k1] = \langle T,\text{UNLOCK},o \rangle$ and
either $H[k2] = \langle T', \text{SLOCK}, o \rangle$ or $H[k2] = \langle T', \text{XLOCK},o \rangle$.

Because T and T' are two-phase, all their LOCK actions must precede their first UNLOCK, action; thus, SHRINK(T) $\leq k1 < k2 <$ SHRINK(T'). This proves the lemma for the a = WRITE case. The argument for the a'= WRITE case is almost identical. The SLOCK of T will be incompatible with the XLOCK of T'; hence, there must be an intervening $\langle T,\text{UNLOCK},o \rangle$ followed by a $\langle T',\text{XLOCK},o \rangle$ action in H. Therefore, if $T <<< T'$, then SHRINK(T) < SHRINK(T'). Proving both these cases establishes the lemma.

Having proved the lemma, the proof of the theorem goes as follows. Assume, for the sake of contradiction, that H is not isolated. Then, from the Wormhole Theorem, there must be a sequence of transactions $\langle T_1, T_2, T_3, ...,T_n \rangle$, such that each is before the other (i.e., $T_i <<<_H T_{i+1}$), and the last is before the first (i.e., $T_n <<<_H T_1$). Using the lemma, this in turn means that SHRINK(T_1) < SHRINK(T_2) < ... < SHRINK(T_n) < SHRINK(T_1). But since SHRINK(T_1) < SHRINK(T_1) is a contradiction, H cannot have any wormholes. ◆

The next result is almost always true; it is false only in the case of degenerate transactions. A transaction is *degenerate* if it does any of the following:

Useless lock: Locks something that it never reads or writes.

Orphan unlock: Unlocks something that it has not locked.

---

[4] Recall that simple transactions replace the COMMIT action of the transaction with the necessary UNLOCKs, and all ROLLBACK actions with the corresponding WRITEs (for UNDOs) and then UNLOCKs. This simplifies the proofs. These results also apply if the transactions contain COMMIT and ROLLBACK actions.

Orphan lock: Ends without unlocking some of its locks (impossible if it ends with COMMIT or ROLLBACK).

The Locking Theorem does not apply to degenerates, but it does apply to all other kinds of transactions.

7.5.8.3 Locking Theorem (Converse)

Locking Theorem (converse):
If a transaction is not well-formed or not two-phase, then it is possible to write another transaction such that the resulting pair has a legal but not isolated history (unless the transaction is degenerate).

Proof: Not well-formed => legal but not isolated. Suppose that transaction $T = \langle\langle T,a,o_i\rangle \mid i = 1, ..., n\rangle$ is not well-formed and not degenerate. Then for some k, $T[k]$ is a READ or WRITE action that is not covered by a lock. The read case is proved here; the write case is similar. Let $T[k] = \langle T,\text{READ},o\rangle$. Define the transaction,

$$T' = \langle\langle T',\text{XLOCK },o\rangle, \langle T',\text{WRITE},o\rangle, \langle T',\text{WRITE},o\rangle, \langle T',\text{UNLOCK},o\rangle\rangle.$$

That is, T' is a double update to object o. By inspection, T' is two-phase and well-formed. Consider the history,

$$H = \langle T[i] \mid i < k \rangle \parallel \langle T'[[1], T'[[2], T[k], T'[3], T'[4]\rangle \parallel \langle T[i] \mid i > k\rangle.$$

That is, H is the history that places the first update of T' just before the uncovered read and the second update just after the uncovered read. H is a legal history, since no conflicting locks are granted on object o at any point of the history. In addition, for some j, $\langle T',\langle o,j\rangle,T\rangle$ and $\langle T,\langle o,j\rangle,T'\rangle$ must be in the DEP(H); hence, $T <<<_H T'<<<_H T$. Thus T is a wormhole in the history H. Invoking the Wormhole Theorem, H is not an isolated history. Intuitively, T will see object o while it is being updated by T'. This is a concurrency anomaly.

Not two-phase => legal but not isolated. Suppose that transaction $T = \langle\langle T,a,o_i\rangle \mid i = 1, ..., n\rangle$ is not two-phase and not degenerate. Then, for some $j < k$, $T[j] = \langle T,\text{UNLOCK},o1\rangle$ and $T[k] = \langle T,\text{SLOCK},o2\rangle$ or $T[k] = \langle T,\text{XLOCK},o2\rangle$. Define the transaction, $T' = \langle\langle T',\text{XLOCK},o1\rangle, \langle T',\text{XLOCK},o2\rangle, \langle T',\text{WRITE},o1\rangle, \langle T',\text{WRITE},o2\rangle, \langle T',\text{UNLOCK},o1\rangle, \langle T',\text{UNLOCK},o2\rangle\rangle$. That is, T' updates object $o1$ and $o2$. By inspection, T' is two-phase and well-formed. Consider the history:

$$H = \langle T[i] \mid i \le j\rangle \parallel T' \parallel \langle T[i] \mid i > j\rangle.$$

This says that H is the history that places T' just after the UNLOCK of $o1$ by T. H is a legal history, since no conflicting locks are granted on object $o1$ at any point in the history. In addition, since T is not degenerate, it must read or write object $o1$ before the unlock at step j and must read or write object $o2$ after the lock at step k. From this, $\langle T,\langle o1,j1\rangle,T'\rangle$ and $\langle T',\langle o2,j2\rangle,T\rangle$ must be in the DEP(H). Hence, $T <<< T' <<< T$, and T is a wormhole in the history H. Invoking the Wormhole Theorem, H is not an isolated history. Intuitively, T sees object $o1$ before it is updated by T' and sees object $o2$ after it is been updated by T'; thus, T is before and after T'. This is a concurrency anomaly.

◆

It would be nice if the Locking Theorem were stronger and read: "A history is isolated *if, and only if,* every transaction is well-formed and two-phase." However, things are not so simple. Consider a transaction that breaks all the rules: it starts with an unlock and ends with a lock. If that transaction runs by itself, there is no problem. Consider the case of a transaction that updates every record in the database without setting any locks. Each update, however, is the null update—it does not change the value of the database but just rewrites the old value. This transaction, which breaks all the rules, can run in any system without creating inconsistency. These are just two of the infinite number of ways to violate the *only if* part of the result. The best the Locking Theorem can say is, "If you break the rules, then someone else may come along next week and get bad information from you or give you bad information." Breaking the well-formed or two-phase rules is considered an antisocial and perhaps even dangerous act, unless you can foretell all the ways the system will be used in the future. The crime may be a victimless one (because no one else is reading the data), but someone may come along next week with a new transaction that changes the situation.

The lack of the *only if* part of the Locking Theorem created a cottage industry that searched for interesting refinements of the theorem. The presentation here distinguishes between reads and writes, but it is possible to have many different kinds of operations that commute in interesting ways. Some of these interesting operators are discussed in Section 7.12.

But back to the basics: the two-phase result states that transactions can release their locks early (before the end of the transaction). The following result says that exclusive locks covering write actions cannot be released before the commit or rollback action without violating the two-phase restriction.

7.5.8.4 Rollback Theorem

Rollback Theorem:
A transaction that does an UNLOCK of an exclusive lock and then does a ROLLBACK is not well-formed and, consequently, is a potential wormhole (unless the transaction is degenerate).

Proof: The proof is virtually trivial. A ROLLBACK action consists of rewriting all objects updated by the transaction, setting their values back to their original states (the undo actions). If the transaction acquired an exclusive lock on object o, and if the transaction is not degenerate, then it wrote object o. The ROLLBACK action will therefore have to WRITE object o again. Because this second WRITE will not be covered by a lock, the transaction will not be well-formed.

◆

It might be argued that the rollback action should reacquire exclusive mode locks on all such unlocked objects. That would make it well-formed, but would violate the two-phase restriction and, in doing so, introduce another potential wormhole.

7.5.9. Summary of the Isolation Theorems

The implication of all these results is that a transaction should:

Be well-formed: it should cover all actions with locks.

Set exclusive mode locks on any data it dirties (writes).

Be two-phase: it should not release locks until it knows it needs no more locks.

Hold exclusive locks until COMMIT or ROLLBACK.

If these rules are followed, there will be no wormholes, and all execution histories will be equivalent to some serial execution history, giving each transaction the illusion it is running in isolation. In addition, rollback will work automatically, without needing to acquire locks and running the consequent risk of creating a wormhole. On the other hand, if any of the above rules are violated, then it is possible that the <<< ordering has a cycle and that the transaction may have inconsistent inputs or outputs.

7.6 Degrees of Isolation

Surprisingly, most systems do not provide true isolation. Originally, this was because implementors didn't understand the issues. Now the issues are understood, but implementors make a compromise between correctness and performance. The typical modern system default is to guard against wormholes caused by WRITE→WRITE and WRITE→READ dependencies, but to ignore READ→WRITE dependencies. This goes under the name *cursor stability* in most SQL systems. The ISO and ANSI SQL standards mandate true isolation as the default, but few vendors follow this aspect of the standard. Rather, they allow sophisticated users to request isolation as an option called *repeatable reads*. They also allow a third option to disable WRITE→READ isolation, called *browse* access, which allows queries to scan the database without acquiring locks and without delaying other transactions.

These options are generally called *degrees of isolation*[5]. The definitions in the previous section were chosen to simplify explanation of these options. The *user's definition* of the four degrees of isolation are:

Degree 0.   A 0° isolated transaction does not overwrite another transaction's dirty data if the other transaction is 1° or greater.

Degree 1.   A 1° isolated transaction has no lost updates.

Degree 2.   A 2° isolated transaction has no lost updates and no dirty reads.

Degree 3.   A 3° isolated transaction has no lost updates and has repeatable reads (which also implies no dirty reads). This is "true" isolation.

The *lock protocols* for the four degrees of isolation are:

Degree 0.   Lock protocol is well-formed with respect to writes.

Degree 1.   Lock protocol is two-phase with respect to exclusive locks and well-formed with respect to writes.

Degree 2.   Lock protocol is two-phase with respect to exclusive locks and well-formed.

Degree 3.   Lock protocol is two-phase and well-formed.

---

[5] The term was originally *degrees of consistency*, but the overloading of the term *consistency* created confusion. *Isolation* is a more descriptive term for the desired property.

The common names for these properties are *anarchy* (0°), *browse* (1°), *cursor stability* (2°), and *isolated, serializable,* or *repeatable reads* (3°). Degree 3 defines isolation as it was explained in the previous section and as it is used in the rest of this book. The concepts and definitions of degree 0, 1, and 2 dependencies easily follow from the idea that 0° ignores all dependencies, 1° is sensitive to WRITE→WRITE dependencies, and 2° is sensitive to WRITE→WRITE and WRITE→READ dependencies. Given these definitions, the idea of (0, 1, 2) degree-equivalent histories is a simple generalization. After that, (0, 1, 2) degree isolation can be defined as 3° isolation was in the previous section. The definition of legal history is unchanged. The basic Degrees of Isolation Theorem follows.

7.6.1 Degrees of Isolation Theorem

Degrees of Isolation Theorem:
If a transaction observes the 0°, 1°, 2°, or 3° lock protocol, then any legal history will give that transaction 1°, 2°, or 3° isolation, as long as other transactions are at least 1°.

For the proof of this theorem, see Gray et al. [1976].

♦

This result says that each user can select the isolation degree appropriate to his transaction without causing other concurrent transactions to malfunction with inconsistent inputs, as long as everybody runs at browse mode or higher (1°). For example, if you are willing to accept dirty data for your query, then by running a 1° transaction you can get your job done more quickly; you won't have to wait for writes by others to be committed, and you won't have to make other transactions wait for you to release locks on data you read.

There is one flaw in mixing isolation levels. A 1° transaction's inputs are 1° isolated, which means the transaction may get dirty reads. Such data may not satisfy the system consistency constraints. If the transaction uses dirty reads to update the database and then commits these updates, other transactions will see inconsistent values and may malfunction. The Degrees of Isolation Theorem assumes that the 1° transaction knows what it is doing, and that any updates it makes satisfy the system consistency constraints. It assumes the transaction is a consistent transformation of the state, even though the transaction may be reading inconsistent data. Given this, most systems reserve 1° isolation (browse mode) for read-only transactions. They abort browsing transactions that attempt to update public data.

7.6.2 SQL and Degrees of Isolation

The lower degrees of isolation allow transactions to acquire fewer locks or to hold the locks for a shorter time. Degree 2 isolation is supported, so that transactions can scan the database without locking too many objects and thereby interfering with others. Consider the SQL code fragment:

```
select count(*)
from emp
where eyes = "blue" and hair = "red";
```

This might scan the whole EMP table looking for such records and never find one. Using 3° isolation, it will hold thousands of record locks or one table lock when the scan completes. SQL system implementors worry that such programs will give them a bad name; unsophisticated users can easily write such programs and lock the whole database. Consequently, some SQL systems automatically release share-mode locks by default after the record or table is read. That is, 2° isolation is the default.

SQL systems actually implement a slightly better form of isolation than pure 2°, and this difference provides the name *cursor stability*. It is very common to see a cursor-based FETCH of a record followed by a free-standing update (by key), or a cursor-based update (Update where current of cursor), as in Figure 7.8. To prevent lost updates, most SQL systems keep a shared lock on the record currently addressed by a cursor.

Figure 7.8 illustrates this: the four programs may look equivalent, but they are not. When executed with pure 2° isolation, the account balance is not locked by the read

---

Bad: 2° Isolation Causes Lost Updates

```
exec   sql select balance
             into :balance
             from account
             where account_id = :id;



balance = balance + 10;
exec sql update account
             set balance = :balance
             where account_id = :id;
```

Good: Cursor Stability Avoids Lost Updates

```
exec sql declare cursor c for
             select balance
             from account
             where account_id = :id;
exec sql open c;
exec sql fetch c into :balance;
balance = balance + 10;
exec sql update account
             set balance = :balance
             where account_id = :id;
exec sql close c;
```

Good: Searched Update is OK 1° or 2°

```
exec sql update account
             set balance = balance + 10
             where account_id = :id;
```

Good: Cursor Stability Avoids Lost Updates

```
exec sql declare cursor c for
             select balance from account
             where account_id = :id;
exec sql open c;
exec sql fetch c into :balance;
balance = balance + 10;
exec sql update account
             set balance = :balance
             where current of cursor c;
exec sql close c;
```

Figure 7.8: Four common programs that look identical but are different. By default, most SQL systems run programs at 2° isolation. This means that the ACCOUNT RECORD in the program fragment on the upper left is not locked when the SELECT statement returns. Therefore, the balance value may be stale data by the time the UPDATE statement is issued. On the other hand, the two programs on the right running with cursor stability keep a lock on the ACCOUNT record between the FETCH and the UPDATE. The program in the lower left is correct, even in 1°, because each SQL statement is an atomic action.

(SELECT), which means the read is not repeatable. All but the stand-alone UPDATE (lower-left corner) can produce inconsistent updates in a pure 2° isolation system. The two program fragments on the right can run correctly with cursor stability, because the cursor keeps a lock on the record currently addressed by the cursor. The program in the upper left is not helped by cursor stability (there is no cursor). This program works fine when tested in isolation, but it may produce inconsistent updates when put into production. It can clobber other transaction's updates as follows: (1) it reads the old balance and is delayed, (2) a second program updates the account to a new balance and commits, and (3) the first program, using the old balance, adds 10 to it and writes the result to the database. That second write overwrites the update of the transaction in step (2). The pernicious thing about this scenario is that all the programs pass acceptance tests when run in isolation, and all the programs run to completion without signaling any error in production. But the net effect is an inconsistent database. This is the sort of thing that 3° isolation prevents.

After studying these programs, you may conclude that systems always should, to quote J. Edgar Hoover, "Give 'em the third degree." But when running such programs on most commercial systems, you have to explicitly ask for 3° to avoid problems like the ones in Figure 7.8. The SQL and SQL2 standards default to full isolation (3°).

The SQL2 standard defines four isolation levels which are set by the statement:

```
SET TRANSACTION ISOLATION LEVEL    [ READ UNCOMMITTED ]
                                   [ READ COMMITTED    ]
                                   [ REPEATABLE READ   ]
                                   [ SERIALIZABLE      ]
```

Read Uncommitted, called browse here, is allowed only for read-only transactions. Read Committed is cursor stability. Repeatable Read is degree 2.9999° isolation (3° without phantom protection; phantoms are explained later in this section). Serializable is called isolation, or 3° here [Melton 1991].

In NonStop SQL a transaction can select the locking protocol on a transaction basis, a table basis, or a cursor basis. Degrees 1, 2, and 3 are supported. DB2 and Rdb support 2° and 3° isolation. As in SQL2, DB2 isolation is selected on a transaction basis.

7.6.3 Pros and Cons of Low Degrees of Isolation

The lower degrees of isolation reduce the time data is locked and reduce the amount of data that is locked, increasing the chances for concurrent execution of different transactions (at the risk of sacrificing consistent inputs and outputs). They do this by releasing locks early (before COMMIT). This gives rise to the notion of *lock duration*. Locks that are released quickly are called *short duration* locks. Locks that are held to the end of the transaction are called *long duration* locks. The uses of durations are discussed in Subsection 8.4.3. Protocols higher than 0° get long duration write (exclusive) locks but short duration read locks, or no read locks at all. Degree 0 goes all the way and even gets short write locks.

Because the ROLLBACK action needs locks to cover its actions, 0° does not support ROLLBACK. For read-only transactions, 0° = 1°; thus, 0° only makes a difference for transactions that update data. Application update transactions need ROLLBACK at restart and in case of application failure. For these reasons, applications are rarely allowed to run at 0°, though certain utilities do run at 0°.

Degree 1 isolation is intended for transactions that need only an approximate picture of the database. It allows them to browse without waiting for any locks; read-through locking (described later) is used to examine uncommitted data without waiting for others to commit

Table 7.9: Summary of isolation degree attributes.

Issue	Degree 0	Degree 1	Degree 2	Degree 3
Common Name	Chaos	Browse	Cursor stability	Isolated serializable repeatable reads
Protection Provided	Lets others run at higher isolation	0° and no lost updates	No lost updates No dirty reads	No lost updates No dirty reads Repeatable reads
Committed Data	Writes visible immediately	Writes visible at EOT	Same as 1°	Same as 1°
Dirty Data	You don't overwrite dirty data	0° and others do not overwrite your dirty data	0°, 1°, and you don't read dirty data	0°,1°,2° and others don't dirty data you read
Lock Protocol	Set short exclusive locks on data you write	Set long exclusive locks on data you write	1° and set short share locks on data you read	1° and set long share locks on data you read
Transaction Structure	Well-formed WRT writes	Well-formed WRT writes and two-phase WRT writes	Well-formed and two-phase WRT writes	Well-formed and two-phase
Concurrency	Greatest: only set short write locks	Great: only wait for write locks	Medium: hold few read locks	Lowest: any data touched is locked to EOT
Overhead	Least: only set short write locks	Small: only set write locks	Medium: set both kinds of locks but need not store read locks	Medium: set and store both kinds of locks
Rollback	Undo cascades can't rollback	Undo incomplete transactions	Same as 1°	Same as 1°
System Recovery	Dangerous updates may be lost and violate 3°	Apply log in 1° order	Same as 1°	Same as 1° or can rerun in any <<< order
Dependencies	None	WRITE → WRITE	WRITE → WRITE WRITE → READ	WRITE → WRITE WRITE → READ READ→ WRITE

their updates and without acquiring any locks that might delay others. The SQL UPDATE STATISTICS statement is a classic use; it counts the approximate number of records in a table and their statistical properties and can therefore run 1°.

Degree 0 transactions get an exclusive lock on data they update, do the update, and immediately release the lock. This prevents a 0° transaction from overwriting uncommitted updates (dirty data) of higher degree transactions. Consequently, each action of a 0° transaction commits the moment it releases its locks.[6] A summary of the attributes of the four isolation degrees is given in Table 7.9.

---

[6] There is a delicate issue with 0°. Implementations of 0° transactions typically do not assure that the update is moved to durable storage at the end of the operation. After all, so the argument goes, if

One odd thing to note in Table 7.9 is that the overheads of 2° and 3° are about the same. When this was first observed, it surprised many people. The 2° cost of releasing and getting locks (especially the coarse-granularity locks discussed in Section 7.8) causes 2° locking to use more processor resources. Degree 3 rarely reacquires a lock and can batch the lock releases at the end of the transaction. Therefore, 3° often uses less processor time than 2°.

7.6.4 Exotic SQL Isolation—Read-Past and Notify Locks

Except for two minor lock ideas, little more need be said about degrees of isolation. *Read-past* locking and *notify* locks are discussed here, because they relate to isolation. The syntax here is hypothetical, but the concepts and mechanisms are available in many systems.

Degrees 0 and 1 isolation are implemented using *read-through* locking: a cursor scanning the database sees uncommitted updates. It is sometimes desirable to skip all uncommitted updates. This is called *read-past* locking, since reads skip over (read past) dirty data rather than wait for the dirty updates to be committed. A read-past cursor only returns records that have no exclusive mode locks set on them.

Read-past locking is easy to implement and has many applications. One is the implementation of sets, bags, and queues. The example of implementing bags is given here. Sets are left as an exercise. A sample implementation of queues was given in Chapter 6.

A *bag*, or *multiset*, is a set with duplicates allowed (sets do not normally allow duplicate members). SQL tables are bags; they allow duplicates.[7] Our bag design uses a single BAG table to store all the elements of all bags (the bag table will be big). Particular bags are named by varchars ("Ripa" and "Strettoia"), and the elements of each bag are also varchars ("Jim", "Andreas", and "Christiane"). Thus, a record in the BAG table is a ⟨name, value⟩ pair, such as ⟨"Ripa", "Jim"⟩, which means that Jim is in the Ripa bag. The SQL table definition is

```
create table BAG (name varchar(100), value varchar(64000));
```

There are two common operations on bags, bag_insert() and bag_get().[8] Andreas and Jim can be inserted into the Ripa bag by

```
insert into BAG values ("Ripa","Andreas");
insert into BAG values ("Ripa","Jim");
commit work;
```

---

the transaction cannot afford to hold a long duration lock, how can it afford a move to durable storage? Rather, it simply runs as a "lazy transaction" that places a redo log record in the log and hopes that some other transaction will force the log. Degree 0 transactions, then, are not necessarily durable. This may be a problem at system restart. At restart, the 0° update may be lost (it is not in the durable log and therefore not redone). A higher-degree transaction that read this update and went on to commit may now have inconsistent information. If that second transaction happened to run on the same log as the first, it probably forced that log to stable storage, and the 0° log records piggy backed on that work, but there is no guarantee of this.

[7] Defining a *unique* key on an SQL table converts it from a bag to a set (no duplicates).

[8] To make the bag-get() operations efficient, a nonunique index would be created on BAG. name by: create index I on BAG(name) not unique;

A random element can be removed from the bag by

declare cursor Ripa on	select value	-- declare a cursor on the bag
	from BAG	
	where name = "Ripa"	
	for update **READ PAST**;	

```
open Ripa;                                      -- fetch and delete a member from the bag
fetch Ripa into :value;
delete from BAG where current of cursor Ripa;
close Ripa;
...etc....                                       -- work on the member and then commit.
commit work;
```

Without the READ PAST option, this program would likely have waited for uncommitted inserts or deletes of others on the Ripa bag to commit. But the program wants just one member of the bag to work on. The program with the READ PAST option will succeed if there are any committed elements in the bag—it skips over any records locked by other transactions. This allows many programs to access a common pool without waiting for one another, and it is but one of many applications of read-past locking.

The example just given also motivates *notify* locks. Suppose the Ripa bag is empty, and the program wants to wait for it to become nonempty. In that case, the program can issue the statement

```
notify    from BAG where name = "Ripa";
```

This statement returns control to the caller when the bag (key range) "Ripa" changes. Notify locks are a kind of trigger. The underlying mechanism creates a lock on a key range (= "Ripa" in this case). This lock request is granted whenever some other transaction releases a lock intersecting that key range. The implementation of notify locks is explained in the next chapter.

7.7 Phantoms and Predicate Locks

The previous sections describe actions as operating on individual objects: they specify the object name and either read or write its value. Applying this model immediately runs into difficulty. Consider the following query.[9]

```
select   *
from     emp
where    eyes = "blue" and hair = "red";
```

---

[9] This was a favorite query of Don Chamberlin, SQL inventor and one of the few red-haired, blue-eyed people in the world.

Either the EMP table is an object and so the SELECT locks the whole EMP table, or records within the EMP table are the lockable objects and the SELECT statement locks all the individual records of EMP that satisfy the query. Suppose the individual record-locking scheme is used. What is to prevent someone else from inserting a new, blue-eyed, red-haired EMP after the read completes? There is no lock on nonexistent records. Similarly, if this query were a DELETE rather than a SELECT, then it would make the records disappear and would have nothing to lock. But at first, such a DELETE statement would be uncommitted; it must therefore prevent other transactions from seeing that the deleted records are gone, and prevent other transactions from inserting new records to replace the deleted ones. Individual record locking requires individual records to lock. Therefore, the DELETE statement must lock the deleted records until it commits.

Such new or deleted records are called *phantoms,* records that either appear or disappear from sets. There is no pure record-locking solution for phantoms. Thus, the obvious conclusion is that transactions must lock the entire EMP table; record locking simply doesn't work.

This is an unacceptable conclusion. Record locking must be made to allow multiple transactions concurrent access to the data. There is an elegant solution to the phantoms problem, called *predicate locks.* It turns out that predicate locks are too expensive, but they are a great way of thinking about things. When it comes to actually doing things, one ends up using simplified predicate locks, called *granular locks.*

Predicate locks work as follows: rather than locking an individual object, a lock request can specify a subset of the database to which the lock applies. For example the statement considered previously would issue the lock statement

⟨ t, slock, emp.eyes = "blue" and emp.hair = "red"⟩.

In general, a transaction, T, could issue a lock like the following:

⟨ t, [slock ǀ xlock], predicate⟩.

Here the predicate is any test on the system state—essentially any WHERE clause from an SQL statement. This generalizes the simple model used in the previous section:

⟨ t, [slock ǀ xlock], object⟩

Two predicate locks ⟨t,mode,p⟩, ⟨t',mode',p'⟩ are *compatible* if:

$t = t'$ (a transaction does not conflict with itself), *or*
both modes are SHARE (shared locks do not conflict), *or*
the predicate (p AND p') is FALSE (no object satisfies both predicates).

For example, the lock

⟨ t , xlock, emp.eyes = "blue"⟩

is compatible with the blue-eye, red-hair lock above, because both locks are set by the same transaction. The lock request

⟨ t', slock, emp.eyes = "blue"⟩

is also compatible with the first request, because the lock modes are compatible. But the following predicate lock is incompatible, because the predicates overlap and the lock modes are incompatible:

⟨ t',, xlock, emp.eyes = "blue"⟩

A predicate lock system can schedule transactions dynamically as follows: each time a transaction requests a predicate lock, the system compares the lock request with the other granted and waiting predicate locks. If the lock request is compatible with all other requests, it is added to the granted set and granted immediately. Otherwise, it is marked as waiting and added to the waiting list. When a transaction ends, the locking system removes that transaction's predicate(s) from the granted set and from the waiting list. It then considers in turn each predicate lock in the waiting list. The scheduler grants each predicate that is compatible with the new granted group of predicates and adds it to the granted set. When it encounters the end of the list, or an incompatible predicate lock in the waiting list, it stops and waits for the next lock or unlock request. If predicate locks are used, no additional locking is required (e.g., no record or page locks are needed).[10]

7.7.1 The Problem with Predicate Locks

As described, predicate locks solve the phantoms problem and provide isolation. But predicate locks have three shortcomings:

Execution cost.   The predicate lock manager has to test for predicate satisfiability as an inner loop of the locking algorithm. Predicate satisfiability is known to be NP-complete—the best algorithms for it run in time proportional to 2^N. This is not the sort of algorithm to put in the inner loop of another algorithm, let alone a lock manager.

Pessimism.   Predicate locks are somewhat pessimistic. Predicates P AND P' may be satisfiable (not provably false), but there may be an integrity constraint C such that P AND P' AND C is not satisfiable. The predicate lock manager is unlikely to understand system integrity constraints. For example, if I lock the mothers in a department and you lock the fathers in the same department, the lock manager may not know that fathers can't be mothers.

Source.   In general, it is difficult to discover the predicates.

For these reasons, predicate lock implementations have not been very successful. A variant of predicate locks, *precision locks*, solves the first two problems. Reads and writes are still covered by set-oriented predicates. In addition, each actual write is covered by an exclusive record lock. When a new set-oriented predicate is requested, it is compared to all record locks held by other transactions. If any of those records conflict with the new predicate, the new predicate lock must wait. Each time a transaction reads or writes a record, the record is compared to all outstanding predicates of other transactions. An update is treated as two writes (old and new record values), and both values are compared to the predicate locks. A read or write action on a record violates isolation if the record satisfies the predicate of another transaction, *and*

> the record is being read, and the conflicting predicate lock is exclusive, *or*
> the record is being written.

If isolation would be violated, the action must be delayed until the other transaction completes. Precision locks are less expensive to implement than predicate locks, and they allow

---

[10] As explained in Chapters 8 and 15, it may be necessary to set semaphores on the physical pages containing the records and access paths, but these semaphores can be released at the end of the operation, they need not be held to the end of the transaction.

greater concurrency. But they have not been used, because they tend to convert waits to deadlocks and because they are still much more expensive than the granular locks scheme described next.

7.8 Granular Locks

Phantoms raise the issue of defining the *lock unit*, the data aggregates that are locked to insure isolation. Candidate units are databases, files, file subsets, records, fields within records, and so on. The choice of lock granule presents a trade-off between concurrency and overhead. On the one hand, concurrency is maximized by a fine locking granule (such as a record). Record locking is good for many small transactions running in parallel. On the other hand, a small locking granule is costly for a complex transaction that accesses a large number of granules. The large transaction would have to acquire and maintain a lock on each granule. A coarse locking granule, such as a file, is convenient for complex transactions. But such a coarse granule would discriminate against the many small transactions that want to access just a tiny part of the file. In addition, the predicate locks discussion suggests that some transactions want to be able to lock predicate subsets of an object. A protocol is needed to satisfy all these needs: it should let batch transactions set a single lock that covers an entire file, while letting interactive transactions lock finer granules.

Predicate locks allow this: each transaction specifies the predicate it wants. But predicate locks (predicate comparisons) are expensive to execute. What is needed is a predicate lock scheme that can set or clear a lock in 100 instructions. The granular lock protocol comes close to satisfying this need.

The idea is to pick a fixed set of predicates—in essence, to precompute the predicate locks. These predicates form a directed acyclic graph with TRUE at the top. Initially, think of the graph as a tree. The finest granules get one predicate each and represent the leaves of the tree (see Figure 7.10). If the system wants record-granularity locks, the leaves of the tree will be predicates that are TRUE for only one record. For example, if the system is thought of as SITEs, FILEs, and named RECORDs, then the lock with finest granularity would be a predicate such as

SITE = "RIPA" AND FILE = "PHONE" AND RECORD = "GIOVANNA "

If a transaction wanted to lock all the Ripa data, it would use the predicate:

SITE = "RIPA".

This all sounds just like predicate locks, and that is the point. Each predicate can be locked in shared or exclusive mode. The trick is that the system has chosen a fixed set of predicates, each predicate is represented by a name, and the predicates are organized into a tree, as illustrated in Figure 7.10. If one predicate $P1$ implies another $P2$, then $P1$ is under $P2$ in the tree. In general, the two predicates are under the predicate $P1$ OR $P2$. All the predicates form a tree when closed under disjunction (OR). The root node is the universally TRUE predicate: the "is in the database" predicate.

7.8.1 Tree Locking and Intent Lock Modes

By following the hierarchical lock protocol, locking a node of the tree in some mode *implicitly* locks all the descendants of that node in the same mode. Locking SITE = "RIPA" in exclusive mode implicitly locks in exclusive mode that site, as well as all files and records below the Ripa node in the lock tree. To lock a subtree rooted at a certain node (e.g., a file at

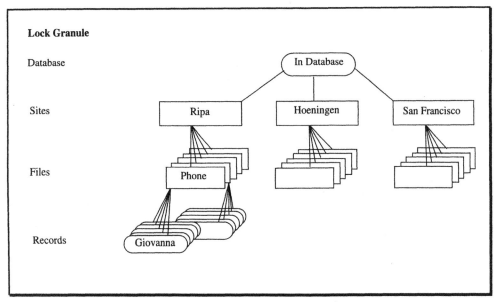

Figure 7.10: A lock hierarchy. Each node of the tree represents a lock covering all its descendants. For example, locking the site Ripa implicitly locks all files and records at that site. To lock the Giovanna record and prevent locks of parent nodes (Phone, Ripa, and In Database), the transaction must first set intention mode locks on the parent nodes.

Ripa) without locking any of the other files at Ripa (or any of the files at other nodes), a transaction must prevent a shared or exclusive lock from being set on the root node and on the Ripa site node. This is best done by inventing a new lock mode, one different from a shared or exclusive mode. This new lock mode, called *intent mode,* represents the intention to set locks at a finer granularity. Setting a record-granularity shared lock on Giovanna consists of the following sequence of lock requests:

```
LOCK   "IN DATABASE"          IN INTENT MODE
LOCK   NODE="RIPA"            IN INTENT MODE
LOCK   FILE= "PHONE"          IN INTENT MODE
LOCK   NAME = "GIOVANNA"      IN SHARED MODE.
```

An intent mode lock on a node (predicate) should prevent other transactions from setting coarse granularity (i.e., shared and exclusive) on that node. The sequence just considered should prevent another transaction from setting an exclusive lock on the Ripa node, but

Simple Compatibility Matrix for Granular Locks				
	Granted Mode			
Requested Mode	**None**	**INTENT**	**SHARE**	**EXCLUSIVE**
INTENT	+	+	−	−
SHARE	+	−	+	−
EXCLUSIVE	+	−	−	−

Table 7.11: The compatibility matrix for granular lock requests. If a lock is requested in one mode and granted to another transaction in a second mode, the lock request can be granted immediately if the two modes are compatible (+). If the modes are not compatible (−), then the new lock request must wait for the first transaction to release its locks.

Compatibility Matrix for Granular Locks						
	Granted Mode					
Requested Mode	**None**	**IS**	**IX**	**S**	**SIX**	**Update**	**X**
IS	+	+	+	+	+	−	−
IX	+	+	+	−	−	−	−
S	+	+	−	+	−	−	−
SIX	+	+	−	−	−	−	−
U	+	−	−	+	−	−	−
X	+	−	−	−	−	−	−

it should allow another transaction to set a shared lock on the Giovanna record, on any other file, or on any other node. This discussion motivates the compatibility matrix of Table 7.11.

This compatibility matrix indicates that intent mode locks are incompatible with (cannot be granted concurrently with) shared mode locks and exclusive mode locks. If one transaction wants to lock at record granularity and another wants to lock the same record at site granularity, then one of the transactions must wait for the other to finish. On the other hand, one site (e.g., San Francisco in Figure 7.10) may be locked in exclusive mode while another (e.g,. Ripa) is locked in intent mode, and files at Ripa are being locked in shared, exclusive, or intent mode.

In a true predicate locking scheme, if one transaction were locking in shared mode at coarse granularity and another were locking in shared mode at fine granularity, the locks would not conflict (share does not conflict with share). The intent mode lock scheme described so far may cause one transaction to wait for another, even though both want shared mode locks. To deal with this problem, intent mode locks are refined into three modes:

IX: Intent to set shared or exclusive locks at finer granularity.

IS: Intent to set shared locks at finer granularity.

SIX: A coarse-granularity shared lock with intent to set finer-granularity exclusive locks—essentially the union of S and IX.

The compatibility among these three modes is motivated by their definitions and the corresponding compatibility that would be allowed by predicate locks. For example, a coarse-granularity shared lock (S) is compatible with a fine-granularity intention shared lock (IS). This logic can be applied to each pair of lock modes to construct the compatibility matrix shown in Table 7.11 (update lock mode is explained in the following subsection).

To give a simple example of granular locking on a tree of locks, Figure 7.12 shows three transactions operating on a lock tree using these lock modes. The figure caption describes the scenario.

The *granularity of locks protocol* for locking on a tree (or DAG[11]) is then defined as follows:

---

[11] This protocol is defined so that it works on a tree and on a directed acyclic graph (DAG). A tree node has only one parent.

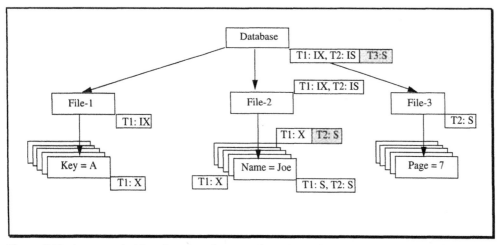

Figure 7.12: An example of setting granular locks in a hierarchy. Locks are set from root to leaf. In this picture, File-1 and File-2 are using record locking, while File-3 is under page-granularity locking. Transaction *T3* wants to lock the entire database in shared mode with a single lock on the database. It is waiting for transactions *T1* and *T2* to complete. Transaction *T1* is using record-granularity locking on File-1 and File-2. Transaction *T2* has locked File-3 in shared mode, using a file-granularity lock. Transaction *T2* also has record-granularity locks on File-2 and, in fact, is waiting for transaction *T1* to release an exclusive lock on one of these records.

Acquire locks from root to leaf.

Release locks from leaf to root.

To acquire an S mode or IS mode lock on a non-root node, one parent must be held in IS mode or higher (one of {IS,IX,S,SIX,U,X}).

To acquire an X, U, SIX, or IX mode lock on a non-root node, all parents must be held in IX mode or higher (one of {IX,SIX,U,X}).

7.8.2 Update Mode Locks

Update mode locks are introduced to avoid a common form of deadlock. A typical construct in programs is to read a record and then rewrite some of its fields based on the values that were read, much in the style of Figure 7.8. In this situation, a shared lock on the record is first acquired to cover the read, and then an exclusive lock is requested to cover the subsequent write. This is fine, unless the record is frequently updated (such records are called *hotspots*). Two different transactions may both read the hotspot at nearly the same time, getting an S mode lock on it. Then they both request it in exclusive mode. That creates a deadlock cycle of transactions waiting for one another. An unpublished study of the uses of System R showed that virtually all deadlocks in that system were of this form. Subsection 7.11.2 discusses how deadlocks can be detected and resolved, but it is much better to prevent them in the first place. Acquiring a lock in UPDATE mode avoids this read-write form of deadlock.

The UPDATE lock mode converts many deadlocks into lock waits. The compatibility matrix for update mode locks is interesting. It is chosen to be asymmetric: update is compatible with share, but share is not compatible with update. This allows the updater to read but delays other transaction readers and updaters, since this transaction is about to update the record.

When an SQL cursor is declared with the clause FOR UPDATE, record locks acquired by the cursor are acquired in UPDATE mode rather than in SHARED mode. If the cursor updates the data, the update mode lock is converted to an exclusive lock, which is held to transaction commit. If the the cursor moves without updating the data, UPDATE mode lock is downgraded to SHARED mode for degree 3 isolated transactions (repeatable read transactions), and released by degree 2 isolated transactions (cursor stability transactions). This downgrading is done to avoid update mode locks delaying other transactions that are scanning the database (see Exercise 16).

7.8.3 Granular Locking Summary

The granular lock protocol provides most of the benefits of predicate locks, while avoiding the cost of predicate comparisons. As shown in subsection 8.4.5, simple locks can be set in about 100 RISC processor instructions (100 is good, 1,000 is slow). Thus, setting and releasing a lock in a three-level lock hierarchy costs about 600 instructions. If, as is typical, several fine-granularity locks are set under a coarse lock (say, five record locks within a file), then the cost of the two coarse locks is amortized across five locks, and the per-lock cost is closer to 250 than it is to 600 instructions. It is typical not to support a "root" lock at all (i.e., not to support a database lock representing the "is in the database" predicate). This further reduces the per-lock cost ($\approx$ 200 ins/lock) by removing one level from the lock hierarchy, but it reintroduces the phantom problem. Exercise 14 discusses this.

To summarize, seven lock modes are recognized:[12]

None. Gives no authority to the lock or corresponding node; represents the absence of a request for a resource.

Intention share (IS). Gives the grantee authority to explicitly set IS and S mode locks at a finer granularity, and prevents others from holding write {X,U} on this node.

Intention eXclusive (IX). Gives the grantee authority to explicitly set IS, IX, S, SIX, U, and X mode locks at a finer granularity, and prevents others from holding coarse-granularity {S,SIX,X,U} locks this node.

Share (S). Gives the grantee read authority to the node and its descendants, and prevents others from holding update-mode locks {IX,X,SIX} on this node or its descendants.

Share and intention eXclusive (SIX). Gives the grantee read authority to the node and its descendants (the equivalent of share authority), and prevents others from holding coarse or update locks {X,U,IX,SIX,S} on this node or its descendants. In addition, it gives the grantee authority to explicitly set IX, U, and X mode locks at a finer granularity.

Update (U). Gives the grantee read authority to the node and its descendants (the equivalent of share authority), and prevents others from holding nonshared locks {X,U,SIX,IX,

---

[12] These are the definitions for lock trees (hierarchical locking). Exercise 17 revises these definitions for arbitrary DAGs.

IS} on this node or its descendants. This mode represents an intention to update the node in the future. To prevent a common form of deadlock, it is not compatible with itself (see 7.8.2).

EXclusive (X). Gives the grantee write authority to the node preventing others from holding locks {X,U,S,SIX,IS,IX} on this node or its descendants. In addition, it gives the grantee authority to explicitly set any mode of lock at a finer granularity.

7.8.4 Key-Range Locking

Granular locks are actually predicate locks. They solve the phantom problem by locking sets of records rather than individual records. The sets can be physical or logical. To give some physical examples, file locks cover the file that would hold the phantom, and page locks cover the physical pages that would hold the phantom. To give an example of logical locks, the set of records can be partitioned into subsets based on some value stored in the records. Typically, this value is a prefix of the record's primary key. If all transactions accessing the records first acquire locks on the record's primary key prefix, then phantoms can be locked by locking their primary key prefixes. This idea is generically called *key-range locking*.

Before elaborating on key-range locking, let us briefly review the phantom problem. Suppose the file has a sorted list of records with key values W, Y, Z. There are four operations of interest on sorted lists:[13]

Read unique.   Read a unique record (say X), given its key.

Read next.   Read the next record, Y, after the record W.

Insert.   Insert record X between W and Y.

Delete.   Delete record Y.

Phantom records with keys X and Y arise in the following cases. If transaction T performs a *read unique* of record X, and it is not found, T must prevent others from inserting phantom record X until T commits. If T is at record W and does a *read next* to get record Y, then W and Y cannot change; in addition, no one may insert a new record (phantom record X) between W and Y, until T commits. If T *deletes* record Y, no other transaction should *insert* a phantom Y, until T commits. In addition, no other transaction should notice that the original Y is missing and that Z is now immediately after X, until T commits.

These examples raise two issues here: (1) the *existence* of records, X and Y in this case, and (2) the *ordering* of records, W,X,Y,Z in this case.

The key-range locking idea is easily explained. A key range is denoted by the first key in the range and by the first key after the range. For example, the key range containing all keys beginning with the letter R is denoted by $[R,S)$. This is all keys k, such that $R \leq k < S$. It is analogous with the notation for intervals of the real line, where $[0,1)$ is the set

---

[13] The idea of key-range locks works for any value-based ordering of unique record values. The discussion here is in terms of sorted lists. Chapter 15 uses these same ideas to control concurrent access to B-tree records.

$\{x \mid 0 \leq x < 1\}$. The key value of the leftmost key of the range is used as the name of the key-range lock.

The key-range lock protocol acquires a lock on the key range before it accesses records in the key range. Because key ranges are granules within files, intent mode locks on the file—and on any coarser-granularity objects—must first be acquired in accordance with the granular lock protocol.

Consider an example. Suppose the set of records is partitioned into three key ranges $[A,N)$, $[N,X)$, $[X,\infty)$. The $[X,\infty)$ includes X and all keys after X. The lock protocol on this example is easy. Assume the transaction already has an intent mode lock on the file. In the cases just given, the *read unique* of X or Y would lock the $[X,\infty)$ range in shared mode—it would request a shared mode lock on key X. The *read next* from W to Y would lock the two key ranges $[N,X)$, $[X,\infty)$—it would request a shared mode lock on keys N and X (notice that there is no record N). The *insert* of record X and the *delete* of Y would both lock the key range $[X,\infty)$—they would request an exclusive mode lock on key X.

Why does this work? If these three key ranges are thought of as predicates, they are simply predicate locks covering the records. Locking the key starting the range is a surrogate for locking the entire range. By using the granularity of locks protocol, and by locking root to leaf, it is possible to get shared, exclusive, or intent mode locks on these sets.[14]

7.8.5 Dynamic Key-Range Locks: Previous-Key and Next-Key Locking

The static approach to key-range locking described in the previous subsection works, but it is not adaptive because there are a fixed number of key ranges. It would be useful to have a key range for each pair of records in the file. Then, as the file grew, the granularity of locks would be refined.

Next-key locking or *previous-key locking* is a variety of key-range locking that assigns a key range to every record in the file. As with static key-range locking, the record keys represent the key ranges. In *previous-key locking*, the transaction requests a lock on the key value of W to lock key range $[W,X)$. The dual of this is *next-key locking* which uses the half-open interval $(W,X]$ to lock anything after W up to X. Previous-key locking is described here.

In the example of Subsection 7.8.4, the initial key ranges for a previous-key locking scheme would be $[A,W)$, $[W,Y)$, $[Y,Z)$, $[Z,\infty)$. After the insert of X, the key ranges would be $[A,W)$, $[W,X)$, $[X,Y)$, $[Y,Z)$, $[Z,\infty)$, that is the $[W,Y)$ range is split into $[W,X)$ and $[X,Y)$. After the delete of Y, the key ranges would be $[A,W)$, $[W,Z)$, $[Z,\infty)$, that is; the $[W,Y)$ and $[Y,Z)$ ranges would merge to form a single range $[W, Z)$.

Dynamic key ranges appear and disappear. This makes the locking protocol more complex than for static key-range locking. Let us go through the cases one by one, using a simple approach (there are *many* refinements of this approach). Again assume that the necessary intent locks (IS, IX, or SIX) have been acquired by transaction T at coarser granularities.

Read unique. If the read unique finds the record X, it gets a shared lock for T on that record key. That lock prevents anyone else from updating or deleting the record until T commits. Actually, since the shared lock on X is a key-range lock on $[X,Y)$, it also

---

[14] For this discussion, assume that at any instant there is only one operation on the file at a time. This can be achieved by having each operation acquire a semaphore on the file for the duration of the operation. Chapter 15 explains how these semaphores can be refined to share and exclusive, and to page granularity.

prevents inserts in that key range. If the record is not found, the read operation must prevent a phantom insertion of X by another transaction prior to T's commit. To do this, the read locks the current key range that would hold X. This key range is named by the existing keys adjacent to the phantom X. If the current set is W,Y,Z, then the read locks the $[W,Y)$ range to prevent a phantom X. This range has the surrogate name W in previous-key locking. The read finds W by looking in the sorted list just prior to where X would be inserted. A shared-mode lock on key W is requested to prevent others from inserting, deleting, or updating any record in the key range $[W,Y)$ until T commits.

Read next.   Consider the case that transaction T is currently reading record W and requests the subsequent record Y in the ordered list. T already holds a lock on W, and thereby holds a lock on the key range $[W,Y)$. This prevents any phantoms from appearing in this key range. All T needs, then, is to request a shared-mode lock on key Y. This implicitly gives it a lock on the key range $[Y,Z)$. (Pop quiz: How is *read previous* different? Answer: Get key previous to W, which is A covering the range $[A,W)$.)

Insert.   Inserting a new record in a key range splits the key range in two. Inserting X into $[W,Y)$ creates two key ranges $[W,X)$, and $[X,Y)$. The locking protocol is interesting. First, the old key range $[W, Y)$ must be locked in exclusive mode to ensure that it is not locked by another transaction. Then, the key range $[X,Y)$ should be locked in exclusive mode. There is a subtle reason for this second lock: if another transaction now reads the $[X,Y)$ range, the access mechanism will see X in the list and attempt to get a key-range lock on $[X,Y)$, rather than on $[W,Y)$. T's lock on $[X,Y)$ causes this second transaction to wait for T to commit.

Delete.   The lock protocol for deleting a record is analogous to that for inserting a record. Delete merges two key ranges. To delete key Y from the sequence W,Y,Z, first lock key Y (key range $[Y,Z)$) in exclusive mode, then lock key W (which is old key range $[W,Y)$, soon to be key range $[W,Z)$) in exclusive mode. When these two locks are granted, perform the delete.

There is one troublesome point: if a key-range lock has to wait to be granted, then when it *is* granted, the key range may have disappeared! Consider, for example, the INSERT statement. Suppose that after the insert, a second transaction tries to read the record previous to Y. In that case it will wait for the $[X,Y)$ key-range lock, which is currently held by the insert transaction. If the insert transaction aborts, the insert will be undone, and the key-range will return to $[W,Y)$. To deal with this, any transaction that waits for a key-range lock should revalidate the key range when the lock is granted. If the key range has changed, the transaction should release the lock and request the lock for the new key range.

To review static and dynamic key-range locking, a sorted list of items is partitioned by a set of predicates $[A,B) = \{\text{record} \mid A \le \text{record key} < B \}$. The name A is chosen as the lock name for key range $[A,B)$. Whenever reading or writing records in the key range, transactions should first acquire a lock on the key range. For static key ranges, these ranges are fixed in advance. For dynamic key-range locking, these ranges are determined by the records in the file. Each record defines the range it is a member of. When key ranges are split or merged by inserts and deletes, both key ranges should be locked. In case of lock waits, the transaction should revalidate the key-range lock when it is granted. If this protocol is followed, phantoms are prevented and transactions have isolated execution.

There are many refinements of the key-range locking ideas. Some of them, notably the use of instant locks and of exotic lock modes, are presented in Chapter 15, on B-tree locking. That discussion derives from Mohan [1990], which has an excellent presentation of the ideas. As a sample implementation, NonStop SQL supports as its default a trade-secret version of previous-key locking. As an option, it also supports key-prefix locking to get coarse-granularity locks on sets of records by setting a short prefix length.

7.8.6 Key-Range Locks Need DAG Locking

Thus far, all locking has been on a tree of locks; each lock had a unique parent, and each record had a unique lock. Let us returning to the famous query

```
select      *
from        emp
where       eyes = "blue" and hair = "red";
```

What key range should we lock in order to lock all the blue-eyed, red-haired people? Suppose that the primary key of this table is employee number. In that case, the obvious key-range lock is employee number in $[0,\infty)$, since hair color has nothing to do with employee number. This locks the whole EMP table. Indeed, if this is all that we know about the table, that is the best that can be done.

But suppose there are indices on eye color and hair color. That is, suppose there are two tables, one sorted by eye color and one by hair color:

```
create table eye_color(eyes char(8),empno int ) primary key (eyes,empno);
create table hair_color(hair char(8),empno int ) primary key (hair,empno);
```

Since these are indices on the EMP table, if red-haired, blue-eyed Don Chamberlin is employee number 1, then

⟨"red",1⟩ is in the hair_color index, *and*
⟨"blue",1⟩ is in eye_color index.

More generally, if you have hair color H, eye color E, and employee number N, then $\langle H,N \rangle$ will be in the hair_color index, and $\langle E,N \rangle$ will be in the eye_color index (see Figure 7.13).

If these indices are kept as sorted lists, the key-range locks are obvious. For example, suppose white is the next hair color after red in the hair_color index. Then $[\langle$"red",0$\rangle$, $\langle$"white",0$\rangle)$ is a key-range lock covering all the redheads. Similarly, if brown is the next eye color after blue in the eye_color index, then $[\langle$"blue",0$\rangle$, $\langle$"brown",0$\rangle)$ is a key range covering all the blue-eyed people. In the interest of simplicity, the following presentation drops the employee numbers and rewrites those key intervals as [red,white), and [blue, brown).

When reading the blondes, the key range [blonde, brunette) is acquired on the hair_color index in shared mode. This, incidentally, is the predicate "blonde" $\leq$ hair < "brunette". It allows others to get exclusive access to brunettes but prevents them from getting exclusive access to any blondes or exclusive access to anyone between blondes and brunettes. When inserting or deleting a record, programs acquire an exclusive key-range lock bounded by the record's two neighbors in each sorted index (the highest key less than or equal to it, and the lowest key greater than it). When inserting the first brown-haired person into, or deleting the

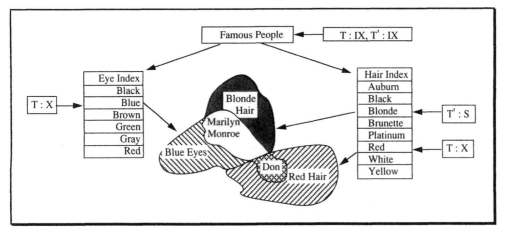

Figure 7.13: An example of setting granular locks in a DAG (directed acyclic graph). Locks are set from root to leaf. In this picture, transaction T has exclusive access to the blue-eyed redheads, while T' has shared access to the blondes (which includes blue-eyed blonde Marilyn Monroe). This shows how granular locks give the effect of predicate locks. This form of locking is often called key-value locking, or key-range locking (if a range of index values are locked). Key-range locks protect against phantoms.

last brown-haired person from, the hair_color index, exclusive locks on the two key ranges [blonde,brown) and [brown,brunette) would be acquired.[15] This prevents others from creating or reading the phantom brown set until this transaction commits. It also stops the readers of blondes, and that's too bad.

To return to the red-haired, blue-eyed example that began the phantoms discussion, key-range locks immediately break the assumption that the locks form a tree. Assume that records about famous people are indexed by only two attributes, one for hair color and one for eye color (see Figure 7.13). Each record will have two parent records (index records) and two parent predicate locks (eye color and hair color). The red-haired, blue-eyed predicate lock will need to lock the red range of the hair_color index and the blue range of the eye_color index. This is not a tree. Consequently, a locking protocol is needed for "trees" whose nodes have two or more parents. Such "trees" are called directed acyclic graphs, or DAGs, and the protocol to set locks on them is called the DAG protocol.[16]

7.8.7 The DAG Locking Protocol

Recall that granular locks were introduced to give the effect of predicate locks. For simplicity, they were first described for a tree of locks rather than for a directed acyclic graph (DAG). If locks are to deal with arbitrary predicates, such as the red-haired, blue-eyed predicate, then they must deal with acyclic graphs. Assuming you are comfortable with the tree

---

[15] The actual locks would be [⟨"blonde",*i*⟩,⟨"brown",*n*⟩) and [⟨"brown",*n*⟩,⟨"brunette",*j*⟩), where *i* is the minimum blonde employee number, *j* is the minimum brunette employee number, and *n* is the employee number of the brown-haired person.

[16] The graph is acyclic because the set of predicates closed under disjunction (= sets closed under union) forms an upper semilattice. Expressed less formally, if set *S* is the union of sets *s1* and *s2*, then *s* is not a proper subset of *s1* or *s2*. Thus, a predicate cannot be a parent of itself in the graph. This means the graph has no cycles.

cate, then they must deal with acyclic graphs. Assuming you are comfortable with the tree protocol, it is very easy to understand the graph protocol, because they are the same! The wording of the tree protocol also applies to the case in which a node has multiple parents. But since it is such a good idea, the protocol is repeated here. The *granularity of locks protocol* for locking on a DAG is

> Acquire locks from root to leaf.
>
> Release locks from leaf to root.
>
> To acquire an S mode or IS mode lock, one parent must be held in one of {IS, IX, SIX, S, X}.
>
> To acquire an X, U, SIX or IX mode lock on a node, all parents must be held in one of {IX, SIX}.

The idea behind the DAG locking algorithm is that

> A directed acyclic graph has *root* nodes (ones with no parents) that correspond to the root of a tree.
>
> Share and update locks on a node require that all nodes on *at least one* path from that node to a root be covered by locks chosen from the set {IS, IX, S, SIX, U, X}.
>
> Exclusive locks on a node require that all nodes on *all paths* from that node to *all roots* be covered by locks chosen from the set {IX, SIX, X}.

The example in Figure 7.13 illustrates these requirements. That graph has a single root node, the set of famous people. The graph has one index with a corresponding set of key-range predicates covering hair color, and a second index covering eye color. Transaction T, presumably written by Don Chamberlin, wants exclusive access to the red-haired, blue-eyed famous people. Another transaction, T', wants shared access to the blonde-haired famous people. The diagram shows the appropriate locks being set for the two predicates.

Examine the diagram. T does, indeed, have exclusive access to blue-eyed red-heads. T' has shared access to all the blondes, including the blue-eyed Marilyn Monroe record. The exclusive lock by T on blue-eyed people does not give it exclusive access to blue-eyed people because there is another path to such people—the hair path. Marilyn Monroe, for example, is a blue-eyed blonde. The exclusive lock by T on blue-eyed people gives T an implicit shared mode lock on all such people. The only subset that has all its parent paths covered by an exclusive lock is the red-haired, blue-eyed subset. In this example, T' can prevent blonde phantoms and T can prevent other transactions from reading or writing blue-eyed redheads.

This solves the phantom problem for keys that are instantiated in the index. To protect against phantom values that are not instantiated (perhaps because the phantoms are being deleted), it is necessary to lock *key ranges*. For example, if T deletes all the blue-eyed redheads and, in doing so, deletes all the redheads, then the additional [platinum,white) hair_color key-range lock would be needed to cover the delete. We hope that this example will encourage you to delve into the following more formal presentation, which defines explicit DAG locks and the implicit locks the explicit locks define on the directed acyclic graph.

7.8.8 Formal Definition of Granular Locks on a DAG

A directed acyclic graph is a finite set of nodes N and a set of arcs A (a subset of $N{\times}N$). A node p is a *parent* of node c, and c is a *child* of node p, if $\langle p,c \rangle \in A$. A node with no parents is a *root*; a node with no children is a *leaf*. A *path* is any sequence of two or more nodes $\langle b_i \mid i = 1, ..., k \rangle$, such that for each $1 \le /i/< k$, $\langle b_i, b_i + 1 \rangle \in A$. Node b is an *ancestor* of node c if b lies on some path from a root to node c. A set of nodes, S, is a *node-slice for node* b if each path from a root to node b contains at least one member of S (such sets can cut node b off from all roots).

For this discussion, pick a directed acyclic graph, N, on which the granular lock protocol is to operate. The lock modes are $M = \{$NULL, IS, IX, SIX, S, U, X$\}$; lock compatibility is defined in Figure 7.11 and represented by the function $C\colon M{\times}M \rightarrow \{Yes, No\}$.

The *explicit locks of a transaction T* are a mapping from nodes to lock modes $\text{LOCKS}_T\colon N \rightarrow M$ indicating what locks have been explicitly requested and granted to a particular transaction, observing the DAG lock protocol. Such a graph must satisfy the following constraints for each node $b \in N$:

If $\text{LOCKS}_T(b) \in \{$IS, S, U$\}$, then either b is a root, or $\text{LOCKS}_T(p) \ne$ NULL for some parent p of b (equivalently $\text{LOCKS}_T(p) \in \{$IS, IX, SIX, S, X$\}$ for some parent p of b). By induction, there is a path from a root to b such that $\text{LOCKS}_T(x) \ne$ NULL for each node x of the path.

If $\text{LOCKS}_T(b) \in \{$IX, SIX, X$\}$, then either b is a root, or $\text{LOCKS}_T(p) \in \{$IX, SIX, X$\}$ for *all* parents p of b. By induction, $\text{LOCKS}_T(p) \in \{$IX, SIX, X$\}$ for all ancestors p of b (on all paths from roots to b).

Having defined the locks explicitly requested by a transaction, the *implicit* locks (locks implied by the explicit locks) can be defined. The implicit locks are just *simple* share mode and exclusive mode locks (S and X) on nodes of the lock graph. There are no intention-mode implicit locks. If LOCKS_T are the explicit locks of some transaction T, the *implicit locks of that transaction are* $\text{IMPLICITLOCKS}_T\colon N \rightarrow M$ defined for each node n of N as:

$\text{IMPLICITLOCKS}_T(b)$	$= X$ if b is a root and $\text{LOCKS}_T(b) = X$, or b is not a root and
$\text{IMPLICITLOCKS}_T(b_i)$	$= X$, for each node b_i in some node slice for b.
$\text{IMPLICITLOCKS}_T(b)$	$= S$ if the previous clause is not satisfied, and
	if $\text{LOCKS}_T(p) \in \{$S, SIX, U, X$\}$, for some ancestor p of b.
$\text{IMPLICITLOCKS}_T(b)$	$=$ NULL otherwise.

This definition captures the idea that an S mode (or U or X mode) lock on any ancestor is enough to prevent another transaction from getting exclusive access to this node; and, conversely that to get exclusive access to a node, a transaction must get an X mode lock on *all members of* a node-slice (a cut set) between the node and all root nodes.

The LOCKS_T and IMPLICITLOCKS_T label the nodes of N with lock modes. We call these labeled graphs the *explicit lock graph* and the *implicit lock graph* of transaction T.

Two explicit lock graphs, LOCKS_T and $\text{LOCKS}_{T'}$, are said to be *compatible* if

$$C(\text{LOCKS}_T(b),\text{LOCKS}_{T'}(b)) = \text{YES for all nodes } b \in N.$$

Similarly, two implicit lock graphs IMPLICITLOCKS_T and $\text{IMPLICITLOCKS}_{T'}$ are said to be *compatible* if

$$C(\text{IMPLICITLOCKS}_T(b),\text{IMPLICITLOCKS}_{T'}(b)) = \text{YES for all nodes } b \in N.$$

Given these definitions, the Granularity of Locks Theorem can be stated. It says that if all transactions follow the DAG locking protocol, and if the explicit locks granted to all running transactions are compatible, then the implicitly granted share and the exclusive mode locks on children of the explicitly locked nodes are also compatible. For example, it implies that transaction T in Figure 7.13 has exclusive access to the Don Chamberlin record and to all other red-haired, blue-eyed people. But it has only a shared mode lock on Marilyn Monroe. Transaction T' also has an implicit shared mode lock on Marilyn Monroe and on all the other blondes. Perhaps surprising is the observation that transaction T has an explicit X mode lock on blue-eyes, which applies to Marilyn, but this lock gives only an implicit S mode lock on her and all other blondes (because the transaction does not have an X mode lock on the eye_color paths to blondes). If you understand this, you get the idea.

7.8.8.1 Granularity of Locks Theorem

> **Granularity of Locks Theorem:**
> If two explicit lock graphs are compatible then their implicit lock graphs are compatible.

Proof. Let L and L' be two explicit compatible lock graphs. Assume, for the sake of contradiction, that their implicit lock graphs I and I' are incompatible. In that case, there must exist a leaf node, b, in both lock graphs such that $C(I(b),I'(b)) = $ FALSE. Examining the function C, either $I(b) = X$, or $I'(b) = X$, and neither of them is NULL. If they were both S, or if one were NULL., they would be compatible. Assume without loss of generality that $L(b) = X$ and $L'(b) \in \{S,X\}$. By definition, there is a node slice Z of b, such that $L(c) = X$ for all nodes c in the slice. Similarly, there must exist an ancestor, d, of b, such that $L'(d) \in \{SIX,S,U,X\}$, and a path, P, from d to a root, such that $L'(e) \neq $ NULL. for all $e \in P$, and another path, Q, from d to b.

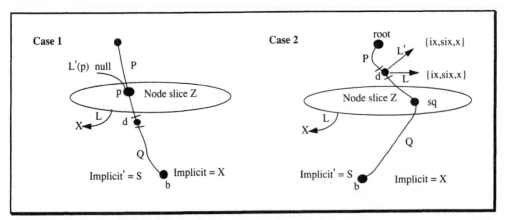

Figure 7.14: The two cases in the proof of the Granularity of Locks Theorem. The two paths P ∥ Q intersect the node slice Z on path P or Q. In either case, there is a contradiction.

By the definition of node slice, the path $P \parallel Q$ to node b must intersect the node slice Z for node b. There are two cases (see Figure 7.14): (1) P intersects Z, or (2) P does not intersect Z, so Q must. Let us consider the cases in turn. In **case (1)**, If path P intersects the node slice Z at node p, then L and L' would be incompatible, since $L(p) = X$ and $L'(p) \neq$ NULL. So, if L and L' are compatible, P cannot intersect Z. Case (1) is therefore impossible. Hence, **case (2)** must hold, and Q intersects Z at some node sq. Since sq is in node slice Z, $L(sq) = X$ and $L(c) \in \{$IX,SIX,X$\}$ for all ancestors, c, of sq. Node d is such an ancestor, since path $P \parallel Q$ intersects S and path P does not. Thus, $L(d) \in \{$IX,SIX,X$\}$. But since $L'(d) \in \{$SIX,S,U,X$\}$, L and L' are incompatible on d, if S intersects path Q. This contradiction shows that case (2) is also not possible. The initial assumption, then, must be false. There cannot be a node b for which the implicit locks are incompatible if the explicit locks are compatible. This establishes the theorem.

♦

7.9 Locking Heuristics

This section covers several miscellaneous topics related to locking. These topics include conversion, escalation, and heuristics for picking lock granularity.

The discussion so far has assumed that a transaction acquires a lock once and in a single mode. What if a transaction requests a lock in shared mode and later in exclusive mode? The desired effect is to leave the lock in exclusive mode. The transaction cannot release the shared lock and then get the exclusive lock, because that would violate two-phase locking. Should the lock be granted in both shared and exclusive modes? A simple answer is that a lock should be granted to a transaction in a single mode. If a lock is held in one mode and requested in a second, then the lock request should be *converted* to the maximum of those two modes in the lattice shown in Figure 7.15. For example, a transaction holding an S mode lock and requesting an S mode lock will end up with an SIX mode lock. The placement of update mode (U) in the lattice is somewhat arbitrary (it could be under SIX). The logic and process of replacing a set of lock modes with their MAX is called *lock conversion*.

Automatic locking systems acquire locks for transactions on demand. They generally default to fine-granularity locking (e.g., record-granularity locking) unless they have a hint

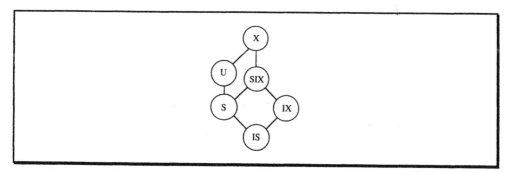

Figure 7.15: The lock conversion lattice. If a lock is held in one mode and requested in a second mode, the request is converted to the max of the two modes in this lattice. For example, if the lock is held in IX mode and requested in U mode, then the request is converted to a request for an X mode lock.

that the transaction will request many locks on a particular set, as in a scan of a large SQL table. In the latter case, they get a single, coarse-granularity lock. The SQL statement[17]

LOCK TABLE T IN [SHARE | EXCLUSIVE] MODE;

is one such hint, and it causes the system to use table-granularity locking. If the system guesses wrong and chooses coarse granularity when fine granularity is needed, then concurrency is limited. Hence, the system tends to err in favor of fine-granularity locks and then adopt coarse-granularity locks on demand.

If the system makes a mistake and uses fine granularity when coarse granularity is appropriate, the transaction will acquire tens, then hundreds, then thousands, then millions of locks. At some point the lock system will run out of storage. Long before that happens, an *escalation threshold* is reached. If the number of locks held by a transaction passes this threshold, the lock manager and the related resource manager execute a heuristic to convert fine-granularity locks to coarse locks. This typically involves converting record and key-range locks to partition or file-granularity locks. The heuristic knows the lock hierarchy. If it finds many S or U mode locks, it looks for an IS lock with a large number of children set in S mode, converts the parent IS mode lock to an S mode lock, and releases all the S mode locks on the children (and descendants) of that parent. If the heuristic finds many X mode locks, it looks for a node slice that covers them, acquires all members of the node slice in X mode, and then releases all locks on the children (and descendants) of the node slice. This process of trading fine-granularity locks for coarse ones is called *lock escalation*. It is described in more mechanical terms in the next chapter (lock implementation).

If the lock system makes a mistake in picking the lock granularity, the mistake is easily corrected. The escalation threshold is usually set at 1,000 locks. Thus, interactive transactions run with fine-granularity locks. If a batch transaction arrives, it runs a little slowly at first, acquiring locks one at a time until it hits the escalation threshold. Then all these locks are automatically converted to a single file-granularity shared or exclusive lock, and the application will not have any additional locking overhead. Some worry that the escalation process may cause waiting or deadlock, but this possibility exists even if the transaction initially issues a sequence of LOCK TABLE statements.

A completely different approach is taken by Rdb. It defaults to file-granularity locks. If there is any contention on the file-granularity lock, each holder of the lock is notified (via a notify lock), and each holder *de-escalates* to finer granularity on demand. This requires each transaction to track the locks it would have needed if it were ever asked to de-escalate. The rationale for this algorithm is described by Joshi [1991].

One final comment on lock granularity. Some systems use only file and page lock granularity. Others use file, area, key-range, page, and then record granularity. Conceivably, one could go all the way to field-granularity locking. Relational systems have normalized records, which tend to put relatively little data in each record. But complex objects are popular in object-oriented systems. Complex objects include sets of records as fields of a single object. This means that finer granularity, or sub-object locking, may be in our future.

Many people have learned the following adage the hard way: *page granularity is fine, unless you need finer granularity*. The virtue of page-granularity locking is that it is very easy to implement, it works well in almost all cases, and it can be used to give phantom pro-

---

[17] Explicit table locking is not in the SQL standard, but it is in most implementations.

tection (by locking the page on which the phantom would have to appear). Perhaps a more compelling argument for coarse-granularity locking is that many simple recovery systems cannot support multiple uncommitted changes by different transactions to objects on the same page. But page-locking systems have a serious problem with hotspots: if all the popular records fit on a single page, then page-granularity locking can create hotspots. Here are three common examples of the pitfalls of page locking.

Dictionaries or repositories often have high-traffic directories that cluster together on a page. Because these directories are actually small, high-traffic read-write databases, they can become hotspots. They frequently demonstrate the problems with page locking.

The debit/credit transaction is typical of an update-intensive database (BRANCH records) that demonstrates main-memory hotspot problems. A 100 tps system has only 100 branch records that occupy only two 8 KB pages. Page locks on such a system will not allow 100 transactions per second to execute.

Similarly, inserting in a sequential file can give page locking systems heartburn, since locking the page containing the end of the file prevents any other transaction from inserting at the end of the file. The sequential insert into the debit/credit HISTORY file catches this performance bug.

7.10 Nested Transaction Locking

Up to this point, our discussion has used the *flat-transaction model*. The assumption has been that a transaction is an atomic unit with no internal structure. As discussed in Chapter 4 this simple view is taken by most older systems (ones built before 1990), but it is unlikely to be the view of future systems.

The simplest generalization of flat transactions is nested transactions without parallelism, called *sequential nested transactions*, or *savepoints*. In such designs, the transaction makes linear progress. Occasionally, it executes a nested BEGIN WORK that starts a new *subtransaction*, often called a *savepoint*. The transaction sometimes does a ROLLBACK to one of these savepoints. The COMMIT WORK of the subtransaction is essentially a null operation. The effects of the transaction are made durable and public only when the top-level transaction invokes COMMIT WORK.

Sequential nested transactions are easily implemented. All subtransactions run under the same trid as the root transaction; locks for the transaction are maintained as a stack or list. When the transaction does a nested BEGIN WORK or COMMIT WORK, that establishes a savepoint in the stack. If the transaction does a ROLLBACK to one of these savepoints, all locks subsequent to the lock in the savepoint are released. This process ignores lock escalations and conversions that may have taken place in the interim, but that is not a problem— the rollback mechanism is safe and simple. Such a rollback mechanism is used by most SQL systems to get atomicity of SQL operations. The design described here is used in System R, R*, SQL/DS, and DB2.

Nested transactions with parallelism among the subtransactions are a nontrivial problem. The parallel subtransactions are each viewed as atomic units (they have A, C, and I, but not D, of ACID). Each subtransaction, therefore, runs in isolation from its siblings. But a nested child transaction can *inherit* locks from its parent transaction; when the child terminates, the parent *anti-inherits* the locks. The design makes the assumption that the parent transaction does not need its locks while the children are active (not a good assumption, since there is no way to enforce it). If the child aborts, the inherited locks are returned to the parent, but locks acquired by the child are released. If the nested transactions are viewed as nodes of the tree, then locks can go down the tree at any time and can go up the tree one level when the child executes the COMMIT WORK statement. The whole tree is called the *transaction family tree*. The *transaction family name* is the transaction identifier (TRID) of the family tree's root.

The challenge in this model is to make inheritance and anti-inheritance efficient—it should fit within the 200 instructions allowed for each lock-unlock pair. Each node of the family tree gets a unique TRID. Each subtransaction gets a new TRID when it does a BEGIN WORK. When a new lock is acquired, it is acquired for that TRID and kept on a list threaded from that TRID. When a TRID aborts, its acquired locks are easily released. Inherited locks are kept in a separate lock list for the transaction. At COMMIT, both inherited and acquired locks are given back to the parent, but at ROLLBACK only inherited locks are returned to the parent. In either case, any siblings waiting for the locks are woken up.

When a transaction requests a lock that is already held by another transaction, the following test is run:

Is the other transaction in the same family?
    If yes, is it an ancestor?
        If yes, inherit
        If no, wait, then inherit.
    If no, wait.

This logic requires that the family membership test be very quick. As a consequence, TRIDs carry both the family name and the subtransaction name. If a lock requestor name matches the family name of some transaction already granted the lock, then the family tree is traced to see if the lock can be inherited from the grantee.

A word of caution: these ideas are still in the conceptual stage. There are many papers on nested transactions, but few systems provide these functions yet. Nesting without parallelism (savepoints) is standard in many systems, but the details of parallel nested transactions are still an area of active research. As explained in the next chapter, there are many open issues on how to combine nested transactions with the many other locking features described in this chapter.

7.11 Scheduling and Deadlock

Resource allocation and scheduling is a generic computer science topic. In transaction processing systems, scheduling consists of controlling the workload (transactions) to minimize response time, maximize throughput, or achieve some other desired property. Very primitive scheduling techniques have sufficed in the past: controlling the degree of multiprogramming (number of active transactions); and time-slicing the execution of each transaction, so that each makes forward progress.

The lock manager is a scheduler. If many processes are waiting for a lock, a scheduling decision is made when the lock becomes available; this decision determines which transactions should continue to wait and which should be granted access to the resource. Traditionally, simple first-come, first-served scheduling has been used.

These simple approaches to transaction scheduling are breaking down as the complexity and diversity of transaction processing applications grow. As a quick fix, most systems have implemented a priority scheduling system, so that interactive transactions get service in preference to batch transactions. Yet locking can confound this scheduling strategy. Locks are another level of scheduling. If a low-priority batch program gets an exclusive lock on a popular file, then all interactive transactions will wait for the batch program to commit. This is another form of the *priority inversion problem* (discussed in Chapter 2, Subsection 2.4.5), in which a low-priority transaction holds a resource needed by higher-priority transactions. The obvious solution is to *preempt* the resource by rolling back the batch program and giving its lock to the interactive programs. This suggests that in the future, lock managers will have to cooperate with transaction processing schedulers. At a minimum, granting locks from the waiting group should observe a priority scheduling discipline.

7.11.1 The Convoy Phenomenon

The perils of FIFO (first in, first out) scheduling often appear in new systems as *convoys*—high-traffic locks that become the dispatcher list. In a convoy situation, the execution of processes in the system is controlled by the processes' passage through these locks or semaphores. The log lock is a frequent source of convoys. Each update generates a log record to be inserted at the end of the log. Such inserts can occur every few thousand instructions. The log lock is held for the duration of the insert, typically a few hundred instructions. Thus, the log lock is utilized less than 10% on a uniprocessor, and less than 100% on a ten-way multiprocessor.

In a uniprocessor, suppose a low-priority process, $P1$, acquires the log lock, and its execution is preempted by a higher priority process, $P2$. The second process will quickly request and wait for the log lock, as will all others, $P3$, $P4$, ..., until the log lock owner, $P1$, is redispatched. The situation is that all processes are in the log lock queue except the low-priority log lock holder, $P1$. When $P1$ is finally dispatched, it completes the update, releases the lock, and, using a FIFO schedule, grants the lock to the next process in the queue, $P2$. Since $P2$ has higher priority, it immediately preempts $P1$ and uses the log lock; it then releases the lock and grants it to the next process in the queue, $P3$. Assuming $P2$ is not preempted by $P3$, $P2$ performs a second update and immediately joins the end of the log lock queue. Now $P3$ will run and join the end of the log queue. These convoys are stable. Once formed, convoys last forever. They are much worse in multiprocessors than in uniprocessors, the case described here. The problem is exacerbated by the observation that lock-unlock is a few hundred instructions while lock-wait-dispatch-unlock is a few thousand instructions. Consequently, when a convoy forms, the application processor load can increase by a factor of from 2 to 10! This is generally viewed as a severe problem.

Once recognized, the problem of convoys is easily solved. The solution has three parts:

(1) Do not schedule hotspot locks on a FIFO basis; rather, wake up everybody who is waiting and let the scheduler-dispatcher decide who should be dispatched and granted the lock.

That means that the convoy queue has been returned to the scheduler-dispatcher queue.[18]

(2) In a multiprocessor, spin (busy wait) on a lock for a few hundred instructions, rather than wait. Spinning is much less expensive than a process wait plus dispatch. If the lock is, in fact, 20% busy and is held for only a few hundred instructions, then it probably will be free before the processor can run through the wait logic.

(3) Do not allow processes holding hotspot locks to be preempted (this is not simple in most systems).

The third part of the solution, no preemption, is desirable but not essential. Several systems have gotten by with just the first two parts.

7.11.2 Deadlock Avoidance versus Toleration

The scheduling problems just described represent only a system slowdown. Deadlock is the ultimate slowdown. In a *deadlock* situation, each member of the deadlock set is waiting for another member of the set. In other words, no one in the set is making any progress, and no one will until someone in the set completes. An easy solution to deadlock is never to wait, but instead to cancel any request that might wait, do a (partial) rollback, and then restart the program. That definitely avoids deadlock, but it may create a *livelock* situation in which each member of the livelock set may soon want to wait for another member of the set, resulting in another rollback and restart. Livelock is actually worse than deadlock, because it is harder to detect and because it wastes resources.

It is possible to avoid (prevent) deadlock. The standard *deadlock avoidance* technique is to linearly order the resources and acquire them only in that order. A deadlock requires a waits-for cycle, and the linear order (or any partial order) avoids such cycles. The next chapter discusses semaphores—simple locks without deadlock detection—which use a linear ordering to avoid deadlock.

For resources such as storage pools, pools of tape drives, and other commodities, the system can ask jobs to *predeclare* their maximum needs and schedule the jobs accordingly. Such deadlock avoidance schemes are used at low levels within systems, but they break down as the layers of abstraction build. The application designer using a fourth-generation language (4GL) has little idea of his program's needs; that is one of the benefits of 4GLs. Any static declaration is likely to be wildly pessimistic (preclaiming the maximum possible). Hence, there has been a strong trend toward dynamic resource allocation on demand. Deadlock is assumed to be a rare event that can be resolved by the transaction rollback mechanism already available for fault tolerance.

Given that deadlocks are allowed to occur, how can the system detect and deal with them? One solution is *timeout*: whenever a transaction waits more than a certain time, declare that something is wrong and rollback that transaction. This is the technique used by IBM's CICS and by Tandem's Encompass and NonStop SQL Systems. When the CICS devel-

---

[18]All semaphores in UNIX have this convoy-avoiding logic. This is a nemesis for many applications because in many UNIX applications, these semaphores are *intended* to act as a scheduler. In some cases, convoys are desirable.

opers were queried a decade ago, they responded that none of their many customers had ever requested a deadlock detector more sophisticated than timeout. It turns out that the following two observations explain this state of affairs:

All systems must ultimately depend on timeout to detect some deadlocks. For example, an application waiting for terminal input or for a lost tape to be mounted may have to be rolled back if it holds resources needed by other applications.

Lock waits must be very rare events. If that is not the case, the system will have poor behavior. Waits cause unacceptably high variance in service times. Systems are designed so that most locks are free most of the time. If lock waits are very rare, then deadlocks are very, very rare (rare squared = $rare^2$). Mechanisms to deal with $rare^2$ events should be simple, cheap, and reliable. Timeout certainly meets these criteria.

Timeout is a very pessimistic deadlock detector. Any long wait will be declared a deadlock. It seems more elegant to detect deadlocks and distinguish between deadlocks and long waits. Perhaps a compromise position is to run a deadlock detector after a transaction times out, just to see if there is a deadlock that can be resolved. If one is found, then a victim can be picked, and the others can continue waiting until they are granted. The next subsection discusses how a simple deadlock detector works.

7.11.3 The Wait-for Graph and a Deadlock Detector

At any instant, the transactions of the system define a directed *wait-for graph*. The transactions are the graph nodes, and there is an edge from transaction T to transaction T' if

T is waiting for a resource held by T', *or*

T will eventually wait for a resource to be granted to T'. That is, they are both waiting for the same resource, and T is behind T' in the waiting list, and their requests are incompatible.

A cycle in the wait-for graph is called a *deadlock*, and the transactions in the cycle are said to be *deadlocked*. When resources are taken from the general class (pooled resources, such as tape drives and sessions; and related resources, such as contiguous blocks of storage), the graph must be labeled with the kind of resource being demanded. Because the discussion here is restricted to simple requests for resources, the arcs of the graph need not be labeled.

If all resource requests are exclusive, and if scheduling is purely FIFO, then a process is waiting for at most one other process, the one ahead of it in the queue, and the wait-for graph has out-degree one (the number of edges pointing "out" from a node is the node's *out degree*). Generally, however, the graph is bushy. Deadlock detection consists of looking for cycles in the graph. One could treat this as a standard transitive closure algorithm, but that would be inefficient, for this graph has some special properties. First, it is sparse (waits are very rare). Second, based on both theory and observation, most cycles are very short. Rather than building the entire graph and doing the transitive closure, then, it is best to use an incremental algorithm.

The lock data structures can be used to build the wait-for graph. Each lock L has two lists, the granted list and the waiting list. Both lists have the form $\langle\langle t_i, m_i\rangle, ...\rangle$, where each t_i is a transaction and each m_i is a lock mode. The edge $T \rightarrow T'$ should be added to the wait-for graph if transaction T in the waiting list and T' in the waiting or granted list meet two conditions: (1) T' is in the granted list or is ahead of T in the wait list, and (2) modes m and m' are incompatible, as computed from the compatibility matrix (Figure 7.11).

Lock conversions are an exception to this construction of the wait-for graph. Transaction T can be both granted and waiting when doing a lock conversion. In this case, T is not waiting for itself.

In addition to the lock data structures, it is convenient to have a quick way of finding all the places a particular transaction is waiting. Therefore, a *transaction wait list*, with an entry for each active transaction, is maintained. All the locks for which a transaction is waiting (typically only one lock) are threaded from its entry in this list. A diagram of the needed data structures appears in Figure 7.16.

A simple deadlock detector builds the wait-for graph from the list of locks and the list of waiting transactions. For each lock with granted set G, and a nonempty waiting list, W, of transactions, the detector proceeds as follows. For each $g \in G$ and $w \in W$, add the arc $\langle w,g \rangle$ to the graph if mode(g) and mode(w) are incompatible. In addition, if w' is behind w in the wait list W, and their modes are incompatible, then add the arc $\langle w',w \rangle$ to the graph. The algorithm then iterates, picking a new lock until all locks with nonempty wait lists have been examined. When this completes, the graph contains the wait-for graph. The graph can be examined for cycles by doing a depth-first search that runs in time proportional to the number of edges. The number of edges can be reduced by more careful construction (see Exercise 28). Section 8.5 describes a simple periodic deadlock detector built in this way.

7.11.4 Distributed Deadlock

Detecting deadlocks in a distributed system uses the same basic idea: look for cycles in a sparse graph. Distributed deadlock detectors, however, must deal with the distributed nature of the transaction wait list. Locks are kept with the objects they protect; for example, if a file

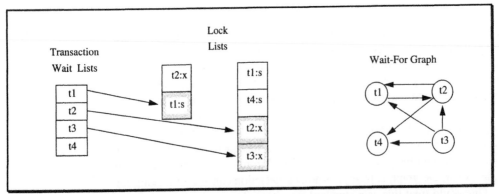

Figure 7.16: Diagram of data structures for transaction wait lists, lock lists, and wait-for graphs. To detect deadlock, it is convenient to have access to the lock lists (both the granted and waiting groups). The elements of the list are transaction identifier and lock mode pairs. In this figure, the waiting lists are shown as shaded boxes. In addition, it is convenient to be able to find where (for which lock) a transaction is waiting. That is the purpose of the transaction wait list data structure on the left. The corresponding wait-for graph is shown at the right. It shows a deadlock between transactions t1 and t2.

is distributed, the locks associated with the fragments of the file are kept with the fragments. There have been proposals to keep the locks somewhere else, but those proposals do not appreciate that locks must be set and cleared in 200 instructions. Thus, each lock exists at a single site (object), and locks are not distributed data structures.

In contrast, the transaction wait list of Figure 7.16 will be distributed. Typically, each node maintains a local fragment of the transaction wait list containing all transactions waiting at that node. The centralized approach to distributed deadlock detection—an apparent contradiction—appoints a deadlock detector for the system. That program must find all the places where a particular transaction, $T1$, is waiting. To do so, a home node is appointed for each transaction. The home node tracks all the places the transaction has visited. When a central deadlock detector runs, it consults a transaction's home node to find which other nodes might have transaction wait list entries related to that transaction. As you can see, this logic is fairly complex for something that deals with rare[2] cases.

A good approach to distributed deadlock detection is called *path pushing*. In that scheme, each node with a wait-for edge pointing to a transaction in a second node traces back from that edge to source transactions; it then sends (pushes) the resulting graph to the target node. The target adds these edges and iterates the logic. If there is a cycle, one or more nodes in the cycle's path will find it. Unlike most distributed deadlock detection schemes, this one was actually implemented. It has the useful property that all two-site deadlocks are detected with one message.

A serious problem arises in a distributed system when only some of the resource managers participate in the deadlock detection. If, for example, an Oracle system is cooperating with a DB2 system, then the deadlock detector has to get information from these two systems. Supposing that these two, in fact, do exchange lock-wait graphs; all it takes to foil any deadlock detector is one nonparticipating resource manager not providing its part of the waits-for graph. This has caused most designers of global (distributed) deadlock detectors to despair. If there were an ISO standard representation of the wait-for graph, and if each resource manager implemented it, then a global deadlock detector could glue the ISO wait-for graphs together. Perhaps that will happen someday; it involves two big *if*s.

Since deadlock detection may be expensive, some systems do *periodic deadlock detection*. Periodically, the deadlock detector calls each resource manager and asks for its wait-for graph. The resource manager can ignore any transactions that have no arcs; otherwise, it returns the complete graph. The deadlock detector composes all these graphs and looks for cycles.

Because the wait-for graph is constantly changing—new transactions are waiting and others are timing out—it is not possible to get a consistent picture of the graph. In particular, the algorithm mentioned above is subject to *phantom deadlocks*, cycles in the graph caused by transient arcs. To give an example, suppose T is waiting for T' to release the log lock mentioned above. Then the local lock manager may report that T is waiting for T' (although this is a very short wait). Suppose, in addition, that T' releases the log lock and then requests access to a server that is currently working for T. The server class manager might report that T' is waiting for T. By composing these two graphs, the deadlock detector will find a phantom deadlock. The good news is that the deadlock detector will not miss any real deadlocks (they are stable).

Once a deadlock is found, it must be broken. The best solution is to find a set of transactions that have minimum backout cost and that break all cycles when they are removed from the wait-for graph. Finding such a set is called *deadlock resolution*. The standard resolution technique is a greedy algorithm that rolls back the least expensive transactions: the ones with the shortest logs. Again, though, this is a scheduling issue that should not be done blindly. If effort is expended to find the cycles instead of just using timeout, then the scheduling decision about who to roll back should be made with equal care. Each resource manager should therefore be consulted about the "value" of the transaction, and then a minimum value cut set can be chosen. That, incidentally adds a few more *ifs* to the ISO standard deadlock detection issue.

To summarize, deadlock detection is an easy systems problem if timeout is used. If an actual deadlock detector is to be built, it must interact with every resource manager and must make a nontrivial scheduling decision. Most system designers have concluded that this involves too much programming to deal with a rare[2] case. Hence, they fall back on timeout plus a simple local deadlock detector that detects some deadlocks.

7.11.5 Probability of Deadlock

The key component of the deadlock discussion is the belief that deadlocks are rare. This is a self-fulfilling prophecy: since systems that frequently deadlock are unusable, application designers will design out the deadlocks. However, there is another way to understand the phenomenon. Deadlocks are rarer than lock or resource waits, because it takes two such waits to cause a deadlock. Any system that waits is also unusable: it will have very high variance in service times. One aspect of application design, then, is to eliminate waits. If there are no waits, there will be no deadlocks. Section 7.12 gives some standard techniques for eliminating waits. Fundamentally, they all minimize the transaction's collision cross section by minimizing the duration of locks.

A very simple model illustrates why deadlock is so rare and also gives a way of estimating the probability a system will experience deadlock. Imagine that a system consists of R records. Then imagine that there are $n + 1$ processes and that each process executes the same transaction profile, consisting of $r + 1$ actions. Each action picks a random record from the set of R records and locks it. At the last step, the transaction commits, releasing all its locks. Each step takes one time unit, unless the transaction has to wait for a lock held by another transaction. In that case, the step completes when the holding transaction commits (second-order effects, such as queues of waiting requests, are ignored). In addition, assume $nr << R$; that is, most of the database is unlocked most of the time.

Given this simple model, what is the probability that a transaction's lock request waits? Because each other transaction holds approximately $r/2$ locks each, and the number of other transactions is n, the probability a single request waits is approximately $PW = nr/2R$. However, a transaction makes r lock requests. The probability that a particular transaction, T, waits in its lifetime is therefore:

$$PW(T) = 1 - (1 - PW)^r = 1 - (1 - \binom{r}{1}PW + \binom{r}{2}PW^2 + \dots + \binom{r}{r}PW^r) \approx rPW = \frac{nr^2}{2R} \qquad (7.4)$$

The high-order terms can be dropped, because $nr << R$, so $PW << 1$.

What, then, is the probability transaction T deadlocks? A deadlock consists of a cycle. The probability T experiences a cycle of length two is the probability that T waits for some $T2$ that waits for T. This is $PW(T)^2/n$, since the probability $T2$ waits for T is $1/n$ times the probability $T2$ waits for someone. The probability of a cycle of length three is the probability that T waits for $T2$ waits for $T3$ waits for T. This is proportional to $PW(T)^3$. In general, the probability of a cycle of length i is proportional to $PW(T)^i$. If the probability of waiting is small (say, less than 0.1), then these high-order terms can be ignored. This suggests that if waits are rare, then cycles are rare[2] and are mostly cycles of length two.

Plugging into these formulae, the probability a transaction participates in a cycle of length two is about

$$\text{Probability a transaction deadlocks} \approx \frac{PW(T)^2}{n} \approx \frac{nr^4}{4R^2} ; \qquad (7.5)$$

This approximates the probability a transaction deadlocks, because most cycles are of length two. Equation 7.5 gives the probability one transaction sees a deadlock. If we look at the overall system (all concurrent transactions) the probability is multiplied by n:

$$\text{Probability any transaction deadlocks} \approx \frac{n^2 r^4}{4R^2} \qquad (7.6)$$

If each transaction has an average execution time of one second, then Equation 7.6 also gives the system deadlock rate (deadlocks per second). Exercise 29 elaborates this discussion.

The simplicity of this model is both its strength and its weakness. The equations just presented, although crude, give a sense of where the problems lie. As transaction sizes grow, the probability of waits goes up as the square of the transaction size (number of lock granules acquired). This is why fine-granularity locking, shared lock modes, browse mode locking, and so on, are important. They all tend to reduce the transaction's collision cross section. Reducing the cross section by a factor of 2 reduces waits by a factor of 4 and deadlocks by a factor of 16. The system-wide rates of transaction waits and deadlocks go up as the square of the degree of multiprogramming (n times the rates of individual transactions). Therefore, as explained in Chapter 6, Subsection 6.4.1, the multiprogramming level must be kept low by the transaction processing monitor and system administrator.

By using browse mode locking, share locks, and fine-granularity locking, application designers can keep the probability of waits and deadlocks small. If a system is experiencing too many deadlocks (or timeouts), the designer must change the design to meet the demand. This is a fairly rare situation. When it arises, though, it is an exciting opportunity to apply these ideas and perhaps invent some new ones. This leads, naturally, to the section on exotics—elegant techniques that minimize lock waits and, of course, consequent deadlocks.

7.12 Exotics

The simplest go-fast technique is to turn off locking completely. Unfortunately, that cannot be done. The system software needs to set short duration locks on its own data structures to traverse them using low-level parallelism, and transaction undo needs degree 1 isolation to reverse updates. For example, it is very hard to examine a B-tree page while some other process is reorganizing the page, moving all the bytes down by five characters. Yet this is what might be happening if the system uses multiprocessors or even multiprogramming without locking. Consequently, the system gets a short-duration shared lock on the page while reading it, and a short exclusive lock on the page while altering it. Hence, even when locking is turned off in browse mode, a substantial number of locks are being acquired by the underlying system to protect itself from inconsistent data structures.

7.12.1 Field Calls

Rather than focusing on ways to turn off locking, most work on concurrency control has focused on reducing the *transaction's collision cross section*, the time-space product of the amount of data the transaction locks and the lock duration. *Field calls* have been the most successful technique to minimize the collision cross section. As will be shown, they can reduce lock durations to less than a millisecond.

A simple example motivates field calls. Inventory control applications have three types of parts, A, B, and C. Type C parts are in the inventory, but no one has used one in years. Most parts are type B; they are used regularly. Then there are type A parts; almost every order involves several type A items. For grocery stores, bread and milk are type A. For chip vendors, RAM chips are type A. For hardware stores, 10 mm nuts are type A. Type A records are hotspots. Each update transaction includes one or more SQL updates to a type A item. Such updates typically have the form:

```
update      inventory
   set         quantity_on_hand = quantity_on_hand - :delta
   where       item = :item;
```

In the grocery store example, an application containing such statements would allow one clerk at a time to sell milk. The others would have to wait until the first clerk commits the sale. Application programmers go to considerable lengths to circumvent this problem, which field calls can solve.

The idea behind field calls is somewhat similar to predicate locks: each *field call* is an action on a specific hotspot record. The action consists of two parts:

A *predicate* ; for example, quantity_on_hand > 100 and
A *transform* ; for example, quantity_on_hand = quantity_on_hand −100

Sometimes no predicate is needed, and sometimes there is no transform. The field call's semantics are as follows: The predicate, if there is one, is immediately tested against the current contents of the record. The test is covered by a short duration share mode lock. This lock is released as soon as the predicate is tested. If the predicate is false, the call returns an error. If the predicate is currently true, the call generates a REDO log record to be performed at transaction commit. The REDO log record contains the predicate and the transform. After the predicate test, the unchanged record is unlocked and made available to others to read and update. Then, at commit (phase 1), all deferred REDO log records of the committing transaction are examined. Shared locks are acquired on predicate-only records, and exclusive locks are acquired on records mentioned in transforms. Each predicate is again tested at commit phase 1, and if the predicate is false, the transaction is rolled back with a predicate violation error. If the predicates are all still true at phase 1, then at commit phase 2, each transform is applied and the locks are freed.

The predicate in the grocery store example was empty (there is no predicate), and, assuming one milk carton was bought, the transform was "subtract 1". If two milks were bought, either a single "subtract 2 field" or two separate "subtract 1" field calls may have been issued. In the latter case, there will be two "milk" records in the REDO list. The milk record will be locked only during the commit of the transaction. Consequently, none of the checkout clerks using cash registers will be delayed (See Figure 7.17).

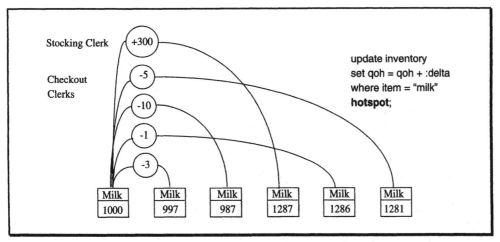

Figure 7.17: A hotspot being updated by several transactions using field calls. Each transaction simply specifies the transformation it wants to apply to the data. In this case, all transactions can run completely in parallel. Conventional locking (or even so-called optimistic techniques) would serialize these transactions.

In the milk example, the predicate is empty because the clerk can see the milk, so it must exist. If this were a telemarketing application, where the clerk cannot see the product, then the update would have the form

```
update      inventory
   set      quantity_on_hand = quantity_on_hand -:delta
   where    item = :item
   and      quantity_on_hand ≥ delta;
```

and the predicate would be quantity_on_hand ≥ delta.

Although field calls were invented in IMS FastPath, they are much easier to understand and use in a predicate-oriented system such as SQL. As first implemented, they had some minor drawbacks. First, if the transaction read a quantity it had updated, the transaction did not see the effects of the update. As a consequence, if the transaction updated the same record n times, the subsequent predicates would not see the changes made by the update. For example, if there are 100 widgets, the telemarketing clerk can execute the UPDATE statement thousands of times in the same transaction, as long as delta is less than 100. The latter problem can be solved either by prohibiting multiple updates if a predicate is declared or, with a little more programming, by applying in order the predicates, then the transforms, at phase 1 of commit. There is no known way to provide consistent reads of hotspot data (but see the discussion of escrow data in the following section).

Note that field calls never have any transaction undo work. If the transaction aborts, the field calls have not made any changes to the database; thus, they are already "undone." Redo of field calls is a little more subtle. Because field call transformations are deferred to phase 2 of commit, it is safest to delay inserting field call transforms into the redo log until the end of phase 1 of commit. If this is done, all the field calls will appear in the redo log at a point when all the hotspot records have been locked and all the predicates validated. In addition, the field transforms will appear in the log in the order that they were applied (rather than the order in which the field calls themselves were issued). For example, IMS FastPath delays adding field-call transformations into the log.

Suppose that the field calls are not delayed in this way, but are inserted in the redo log in the order in which the field calls occur (rather than the order in which the transforms occur). For that to work, all field transforms t, t' of a hotspot record h must commute, in the sense that $t(t'(h)) = t'(t(h))$. To see why this is so, imagine that two transactions T and T' execute the two operations t and t' on hotspot h. Suppose that T did t to h first, placing the redo record for t in the log first, but then T did many other things and consequently committed second (after T'). As a result, the commit order was T' followed by T and the database ended up with h transformed by t', then t (i.e., $t(t'(h))$). Now suppose the system crashed, and the redo logic reconstructed the value of h. It applied the operations in redo order (t followed by t'), producing $t'(t(h))$. If $t'(t(h)) \neq t(t'(h))$, the redo operation will have reconstructed the wrong value. Transforms typically do commute in these applications (e.g., addition and subtraction commute). However, the system should be careful to enforce commutativity. Alternatively, the system can defer the log records during normal processing, as IMS FastPath does, or it can sort them in commit order as part of redo processing.

To summarize field calls, an application programmer or database designer can specify that the field-call logic be used either on a table basis (as part of a CREATE TABLE or ALTER TABLE statement) or on an update statement basis (UPDATE ... HOTSPOT). When accessing hotspot data, updates will not acquire (long duration) locks until commit. Commit may return an error (field call violated) if the update predicate has become false since the field call was issued. Read operations to hotspot data will not see the effect of the deferred updates. In particular, a transaction never sees its own updates.

7.12.2 Escrow Locking and Other Field Call Refinements

A simple refinement of field calls prevents transaction predicate failure at phase 1 of commit, and the consequent transaction aborts. The idea is to preserve the truth of the predicate between the time the transaction first makes the field call and the time the predicate is reevaluated at phase 1 of commit. The idea, which only works for numbers (ordered sets), is illustrated in Figure 7.18. Associated with each hotspot field is a range of values denoted by the closed interval $[m,n]$, meaning that the value of the record is between m and n. If there are no pending field calls on the record, the range is simply $[m,m]$ where m is the current value. When a field call with transform $+x$ comes along, the system maintains the value as $[m,m + x]$. When subsequent predicates are evaluated, they are tested against both the values m and $m + x$. When the transaction commits or aborts, the value becomes $[m + x,m + x]$ or $[m,m]$. In addition, the uncommitted predicates are maintained each time a new field call arrives. That is, if there is a outstanding (uncommitted) field call predicate P, and if the new field call would produce a range $[m',m'']$, then $P(m')$ and $P(m'')$ must be TRUE or the new field call is rejected with error.

The escrow logic described above implies that if the predicate is true when the field call is invoked, it will be true at commit. So deferred transforms will not generate transaction aborts.

It is fairly easy to modify the field call and escrow schemes in order to fall back on conventional locking if degree 2 or 3 consistent reads are present. The idea is that each field call gets and keeps a lock on the hotspot record in a mode (call it F, for field call) that is compatible with F. If a transaction holding an F mode lock tries to read the record, its request for an

S mode lock during normal processing causes the transaction's lock to be escalated from F to S mode; then all the transaction's deferred transforms are applied to the record immediately, and the hotspot logic is suspended for that transaction on this record.

More elaborate proposals to provide read access of hotspot data—while still preserving the hotspot-write logic—center around providing a fuzzy read of the data. The idea is to support two kinds of read operations on hotspots. The first type is a conventional read that returns a value and optionally preserves that value until the reader commits or rolls back (3° isolation). A second type of read, called *escrow read,* preserves the hotspot logic by taking a predicate as input and returning a boolean value as a result; the read promises to maintain the truth of the boolean until the transaction commits or rolls back. By structuring field-call predicates as escrow reads, predicate failure and the resulting transaction rollbacks at phase 1 of commit are eliminated. In fact, this is the typical application of escrow reads. The idea is for the escrow read predicate to be a range predicate (e.g., quantity on hand > 100) and for the data manager to maintain this predicate for the transaction (see Figure 7.18). Of course, the third kind of read is just the degree 1 consistent (dirty) read that gives the most recently written value.

There is one last point that is very interesting, especially since it seems to violate some of the basic theorems. IMS/FastPath applies the transforms at the end of phase 1 of commit and then releases the locks, even before the commit record of the transaction (call it T) has been written to durable media. If the system crashes at this point, T's updates will be lost

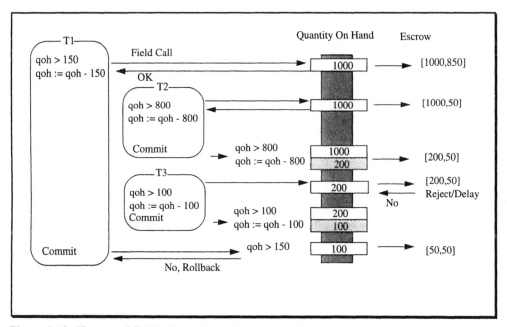

Figure 7.18: The use of field calls and how their semantics change with escrow reads. As the diagram shows, the hotspot milk quantity on hand is unlocked most of the time (dark-shaded area), because field calls are used. Three transactions issue predicates against it, and all three predicates are true when issued. When transaction $T1$ tries to commit, however, its predicate has become false, causing $T1$ to be aborted. In an escrow scheme (shown at the right), the system maintains the truth of the uncommitted predicates. Therefore, it would delay or reject the predicate of transaction $T3$ and would successfully commit transaction $T1$.

when the system restarts from the durable database and durable (disk) log. This means other transactions that may have read T's outputs will have inconsistent information. The trick here is *lazy commit:* IMS FastPath is a centralized system with a single log (or so it thinks). It is the last resource manager in the commit chain; thus, when it gets to the end of phase 1 of commit, it knows that the transaction will commit if the commit record gets to disk (durable media). In addition, it knows that any other transaction, $T2$, that later commits will generate a log record later in this log; consequently, it will have to write T's log records to durable media before $T2$'s record can be written. This is a form of lazy commit by T.

Field call and escrow schemes are still developing (they are only teenagers). They are designed to deal with arithmetic operations on fields of hotspot records. There is a well-known and common problem that they do not solve, the *serial number problem*. Businesses often number events with unique sequence numbers: invoice numbers, employee numbers, or the serial numbers on bonds, stocks, or even dollar bills. Suppose that the application designer wants all of the following properties:

Monotone.   Sequence numbers increase monotonically; that is, if t' commits after t, then sequence(t') > sequence(t).

Readable.   The application receives the sequence number in a host variable before commit.

Dense.   Sequence numbers are dense; no gaps are allowed.

Rollback.   Transactions may roll back.

High throughput.   Tens or hundreds of operations per second must be possible.

Field calls do not help the sequence number problem (they only help updates, not reads). There is no known high-throughput solution to this problem. It is easy to prove that no solution exists (see Exercise 32). The typical advice to the application designer is "change your requirements." For example, Oracle provides a sequence number mechanism that relaxes the monotone and dense restrictions (numbers are not in commit order, and gaps are possible).

7.12.3 Optimistic and Timestamp Locking

One of the interesting things about locking exotics is the vast literature. It is possible for experts to be completely ignorant of some major branch of the field. *Optimistic* schemes[19] are an example. They were invented five years after field calls were being sold on the street and, in fact, are less general than field calls. Optimistic methods differ from field calls in only the following:

The *predicate* is {field = old-value}.
The *transform* is {field = new-value}.

These are rather degenerate predicates and transforms. Applying optimistic methods to the grocery store example, the application would

---

[19] Schemes which lock objects as soon as they are used are called *pessimistic*. The optimistic schemes lock objects only during commit.

(1) Read the current quantity on hand into the application (say, 100).

(2) Propose a new value (say, 99).

(3) At commit, check whether the quantity on hand is still 100; if so, set it to 99.

As with field calls, any check at commit must be done as a two-phase, well-formed transaction covered by conventional locks. Optimistic concurrency control has the same poor throughput as conventional locking on hotspots; in reality, it is worse, since conventional locking would serialize the transactions, causing the clerks to wait for one another, whereas optimistic techniques would let all the clerks' transactions run and then abort all but one of them. Eighty percent of the transactions shown in Figure 7.17 would be aborted by optimistic techniques, and that is not desirable. Labeling this scheme *optimistic* maligns a perfectly good philosophy.

Timestamp schemes are degenerate forms of optimistic concurrency control— degenerate-degenerate field calls. They postulate that all records include a timestamp field that is read as part of the predicate check. The predicate is "timestamp hasn't changed," and the transform always includes the clause "timestamp = CURRENT." Thus, timestamp schemes are slightly worse than optimistic schemes.

Field calls plus escrow reads are the most general go-fast locking technique known. They subsume timestamp and optimistic techniques. Field calls are present in IMS FastPath. To our knowledge, however, they have not yet been implemented in other systems.

7.12.4 Time Domain Addressing

Aside from field calls, there has been one other truly novel idea in concurrency control in the last 20 years—the idea that data never be updated. (Again, most of the work has centered around locking; these are non-locking schemes). When bookkeeping was done with clay tablets or paper and ink, accountants developed some clear rules about good accounting practices. One cardinal rule is double-entry bookkeeping, which makes calculations self-checking and, thereby, failfast. Another cardinal rule is that one never alters the books; if an error is made, it is annotated and a new compensating entry is made in the books. The books are thus a complete history of the transactions of the business.

Early computer systems obeyed these rules. The bookkeeping entries were represented as records on punched cards or on tape. A nightly batch run would output a new master from the old master and the day's activity. The old master was never updated. This procedure was partly the result of good accounting practices, but it also was due to the technical aspects of cards and tape: writing a new tape was easier than rewriting the old one.

The advent of direct-access storage devices (disks and drums) changed that. They made it possible to update only parts of a file. Rather than copy the whole file whenever one part changed, it became attractive, when constructing the new master, to update only the parts that changed. Some designs (notably side files, shadows, and differential files) did not update the old master and therefore followed good accounting techniques. For performance reasons, however, most disk-based systems have been seduced into updating the data in place. Today, this is simply taken for granted.

Update-in-place strikes many as a cardinal sin: it violates accounting practices that have been observed for centuries. It destroys data (the old master), and if data has value, then update-in-place destroys value. There have been several proposals for systems in which objects are never altered; rather, an object is considered to have a history. In such a system, an object is not updated but evolves as information is added. The process consists of creating a new value and appending it to the object history as the object's current value. All the old values continue to exist and can be addressed by specifying any time within the object's life. Object addresses become <name,time>, rather than simply name. Such designs are variously called *time domain addressing*, *version-oriented systems*, or *immutable objects*. It is important to understand that this is the way systems have worked for thousands of years and that update-in-place was a Faustian bargain. Update-in-place makes it easy to find out the current value, but one must hunt through the log to reconstruct the history of the object.

There have been several attempts at implementing time domain addressing, but the best-developed one comes from Dave Reed. The leading examples of these ideas today are Interbase, Oracle, Rdb, and Postgres. In Reed's design, each object has a sequence of values over time. Each value is valid for some time interval. Thus, the history of an object (call it O) can be denoted as

$$\langle\, \langle V0[t0,t1]\rangle\,,\, \langle V1,[t1,t2]\rangle\,,\, \langle V2,[t2,*]\rangle\, \rangle$$

where $V0$, $V1$, $V2$ is a sequence of values, and $t0$, $t1$, $t2$ is an increasing time sequence. This is interpreted to mean that the object was created at time $t0$. Between time $t0$ and $t1$, it had value $V0$. At time $t1$ it was updated to value $V1$, and at time $t2$ the most recent update, $V2$, was made. That is the current value.

Each transaction is assigned a time at which it ran, that is, a time at which all its reads and writes are interpreted. Reading an object, transaction T, assigned to run at time $t3$, gets the value of the object at that time. In the example above, if $t3 \geq t2$, then the object value seen by transaction T is $V2$. Incidentally, such a read extends the validity of the current value of the object to time $t3$. The history of the object is therefore updated to

$$\langle\, \langle V0,[t0,t1]\rangle\,,\, \langle V1,[t1,t2]\rangle\,,\, \langle V2,[t2,t3]\rangle\,,\, \langle V2,[t3,*]\rangle\, \rangle.$$

The object value has not changed, but its history has been extended to the present.

If $t1 \leq t3 \leq t2$, then value $V1$ is returned, and the object's history is not changed at all. On the other hand, if T writes a new value (say, $V3$) to the object, it must be that $t3 > t2$. In that case, the object history becomes

$$\langle\, \langle V0,[t0,t1]\rangle\,,\, \langle V1,[t1,t2]\rangle\,,\, \langle V2,[t2,t3]\rangle\,,\, \langle V3,[t3,*]\rangle\, \rangle.$$

If $t3 < t2$, then T is running in the past and cannot update the object.

In this design, the writes of a transaction and its commitment all depend on a commit record. At transaction commit, the system validates (makes valid and durable) all the transaction's updates by validating the commit record and writing all updates to durable media. At transaction abort, the system simply marks the commit record invalid. This very elegant design unifies concurrency, recovery, and time domain addressing. In addition, it includes a design for nested transactions not described here. Time is implemented as pseudo-time to avoid the problem of clock synchronization among multiple processors.

Reed's work was an excellent Ph.D. thesis, [1978], and there was considerable optimism that these ideas were a breakthrough in the way transaction processing systems should be designed and built. Unfortunately, some implementation problems with the scheme have never been fully worked out. Notable among them are

Reads are writes.   Most reads advance the current date of an object's history and, in doing so, update it. This means that read-only transactions can actually be update intensive.

Waits are aborts.   Much as in optimistic concurrency control, if a locking system causes one transaction to wait for another, the time domain addressing scheme causes one of the two transactions to abort when the timestamps do not match. This seems to preclude long-running batch transactions that do updates, since they will appear to be running in the past by the time they complete, and they will therefore be unable to install their updates.

No granularity.   Timestamps seem to force a single concurrency granularity. There is nothing resembling a lock granularity scheme.

Hotspots.   Frequently updated records, like the milk record in the grocery store, are not helped by version-oriented databases. In fact, read-only hotspots are created with time domain addressing because read operations update the object timestamp and generate log records. No one has proposed the analog of field calls for hotspots.

Real operations and pseudo-time do not make much sense.   If one reads and writes a real device (terminal, thermometer, or whatever), it is read or written at some real time. It is unclear how real time and pseudo-time interact.

Initially, locking schemes were terrible. Many people worked for many years to make locking a workable alternative. One has the feeling that if similar effort had been expended on time domain addressing, there would be a workable scheme today. If, as many believe, updating data is a bad thing, then it is just a matter of time and technology until a workable and economical approach to time domain addressing is found. There are problem domains—such as medical records, engineering drawings, source-code control, and system dictionaries—where version-management is a major issue. System support will be very welcome in these areas. Several commercial systems provide a form of the domain addressing (Interbase, Oracle, and Rdb).

One possible scenario is that time domain addressing systems simply will be used for new and different applications. If that is so, they need not compete with locking systems for performance. It is possible that locking systems will continue to be used for simple, high-update rate applications, while time domain addressing will be used more for complex applications and for historical databases. Alternatively, there may be a synthesis of the two approaches.

Despite the length of this chapter, not all the problems of concurrency control have been solved. There is, in fact, considerable innovation in progress as this book is being prepared.

7.13 Summary

Concurrency is inherent in distributed systems. Yet programs and programmers find it difficult to deal with concurrency and with the interactions among concurrent programs. For that reason, transaction processing systems go to great lengths to create the illusion that each program is running in isolation, while in fact the system is running many independent transactions in parallel against the shared database. The various parts of the transaction processing system usually use locking to provide this illusion.

By acquiring locks on objects before accessing them, and by holding these locks until the transaction commits, it can be guaranteed that the execution of each transaction will have no concurrency anomalies. Refinements of this idea to predicate locks and then to granular locks, allow transactions to dynamically adjust the locking granule and to avoid phantoms. Using the locking and isolation theorems, a transaction processing system can automatically set locks that guarantee isolation.

Reduced isolation levels are one technique for reducing the time-lock cross-section of a transaction. By acquiring fewer locks, or by holding them for shorter duration, the transaction can reduce its impact on others and increase its chances of parallel execution. But this is an area for experts; reduced isolation levels lend themselves to obscure bugs.

When locks are unavailable, some transactions must wait. Waiting creates an interaction between lock scheduling and global scheduling of system resources. These interactions have not been satisfactorily addressed by any system. Deadlock is the ultimate form of waiting, and resolving deadlocks by rolling back a set of transactions is a major scheduling decision. A simple analytic model indicates that waiting and deadlocks rise with the square of the degree of multiprogramming. Here, again, is an interaction between locking and resource scheduling.

Exotic locking techniques have been devised to reduce lock contention. Field calls and escrow reads have been the most successful to date, but time domain addressing schemes may someday stage a comeback.

7.14 Historical Notes

The concurrency control literature is vast. The theoretical foundations are in Karp and Miller's Parallel Program Schemata [1966]. That paper contains all the basic ideas, but it is focused more on determinism than on isolation: the authors thought in terms of parallel computations looking for a single answer (THE answer). The notion that *any* consistent answer would be acceptable was first introduced in the paper by Eswaran et al. [1976]. That paper also pointed out the problem of phantoms and suggested predicate locks to solve the problem. When it was realized that predicate locks would not work very well, the authors of that paper developed the theory of lock granularity. Parallel developments in IBM and elsewhere came to similar conclusions. The IMS developers had implemented a record-granularity lock scheme in 1972 [Obermarck 1980]; a group at General Electric developed similar ideas for the Madman system [Rosenkrantz, Stearns, and Lewis 1977]; and David Lomet developed the notion of atomic actions [1977]. At about the same time, Dieter Gawlick and other IMS developers were faced with serious hotspot problems in large systems; they responded by developing and implementing field calls [Gawlick and Kinkade 1985]. Jay Bannerjee developed the alternate idea of precision locks to solve the difficulties of predicate locks [Bannerjee, Jordan, and Batman 1981]. The idea of key-range locks comes from Kapali Eswaran and Mike Blasgen, but it was never published. The idea was refined and extended by Franco Putzolu, who only writes code—his code appears in IBM's SQL/DS, DB2, HP Allbase, and Tandem's NonStop SQL.

After this fairly intense period of invention, there followed a long period of consolidation. Many were unsatisfied with the Locking Theorem, and there were many attempts to generalize it. In addition, there was considerable activity on problem-specific locking schemes for directory updates, replicated files, and so on. Occasionally, a new concurrency control paradigm, such as optimistic or timestamp, was examined. The consolidation is well summarized in the seminal book by Bernstein, Hadzilacos, and Goodman [1987], which covers all the issues presented in this chapter with considerably more rigor and in considerably greater depth. A precise treatment of the formal results related to the Locking Theorem is fully developed in Papadimitriou [1986]. Together, both books give an excellent picture of the theoretical activity on concurrency control over the last 15 years. Virtually all database systems use variations of the Locking Theorem to provide isolation (consistency) to their clients.

The refinements of key-range locking remain a trade secret. Mohan's papers on next-key locking [1990a; 1990b; 1990c] are excellent, but they are intentionally vague on several critical issues, such as key-range lock escalation and handling end-of-file. To our knowledge, the most sophisticated implementation of the key-range locking ideas is a design of Franco Putzolu and Robert Vanderlinden, found in NonStop SQL.

Unfortunately, field calls have also received little public attention. The early work of Reuter [1982] extended Gawlick's original ideas to include escrow reads. O'Neil extended Reuter's ideas and gave escrow reads their name [O'Neil 1986]. These are the only papers of note on field calls.

The topic of scheduling has fared a little better. Convoys were introduced and "solved" in Blasgen, Gray, Mitoma, and Price [1979]. The priority inversion problem is still folklore [Englert and Gray 1991]. No standard solutions are public. Papers are beginning to appear discussing the relationship between locking and scheduling. On the other hand, the field of deadlock detection has a vast literature that includes operating systems, distributed systems, and database systems. The simple analysis of deadlock given here comes from Gray, Homan, Obermarck, and Korth [1981]. Tay wrote a beautiful thesis that both correctly analyzed and refined the results to apply to a finite number of processors [Tay 1987]. The seminal paper on how to detect deadlocks [Beeri and Obermarck 1981] convinced most of us that deadlock detection in a loosely coupled system is hopeless: it requires too much information. Consequently, most systems do deadlock detection only within the database and use timeout to detect more complex deadlocks. Mike Carey and Alex Thomasian have extensively analyzed and simulated various approaches to concurrency control. See, for example, [Carey 1990] and [Thomasian 1992].

By 1980, there was concern that the flat transaction model was too limited. Since sequential nested transactions were a good idea in System R, it became clear that the transaction concept should be made recursive. Eliot Moss and others on Barbara Liskov's Argus project at MIT get credit for developing the ideas of nested transactions [Moss 1985]. The TABS and then Camelot projects at CMU did the first credible implementation of those ideas. This chapter's presentation of nested transaction locking and family trees is taken from their papers [Eppinger, Mummert, and Spector 1991; Spector et al. 1987].

The idea of time domain addressing has a long history. Davies and Bjork, who wrote the classic papers on transactions, concluded that an immutable database is the correct approach: the Sumerians were right to use clay tablets. Unfortunately, many of Davies' and Bjork's design documents and arguments were never published. The best reference is Bjork [1973] or Davies [1978]. The work of Dave Reed went considerably beyond the Davies-Bjork design and makes essential reading [Reed 1978; Svobodova 1980; Reed 1981]. That work, though promising, had disappointing performance (it was implemented in 1979 on very slow personal computers and even slower optical disks). The Rdb system [Hobbs and

England 1991] gives read-only transactions a timestamped *snapshot* of the database by maintaining a side file of database updates. Snapshots are used to allow read-only queries to run without delaying update transactions. The Postgres system is a next generation database system with a time domain addressing storage model [Stonebraker 1988]. Another promising approach to time domain addressing is being taken by Lomet and Salzberg, who have developed an efficient data structure to store time-indexed objects and have developed concurrency control and recovery algorithms for these new structures [1989a; 1989b; 1990a; 1990b]. They propose data structures that efficiently cluster and access historical data.

Exercises

1. [7.2, 5] Suppose the most efficient way to run transactions is to save them up and run them in batches overnight. Running online transactions concurrently probably has lower throughput than the overnight batch if throughput is measured in transactions per second. True or False: The second law of concurrency seems to favor the batch approach over the OLTP approach.

2. [7.3.2, 5] (a) Suppose a transaction is *read only*; that is, it only reads objects and never writes them. Is there any sense in running such a transaction? (b) Suppose a transaction is *write only*. Is there any sense in running such a transaction?

3. [7.3.2, 10] Figure 7.2 is incomplete; it does not show many of the outgoing dependencies of other transactions on the actions of $T1$ and $T2$. Complete the graph, filling in those dependencies.

4. [7.3.3, 10] It seems that *dirty read* and *unrepeatable read* are the same thing. What is the difference?

5. [7.5.1, 10] The conversion of transactions to simple transactions implicitly took a certain approach to rollback. By repeating history backwards it makes an aborting transaction look like a committing transaction. What is the structure of the resulting transaction?

6. [7.5.4, 10] (a) Are all serial histories legal? (b) If not, give a counter example. If so, prove it.

7. [7.5.6, 15] The original definition of history equivalence did not have version numbers in the definition of dependencies. (a) Define two transactions (each containing two actions) and write two histories for these transactions, such that the histories would be equivalent if one ignored object versions but would not be equivalent if one paid attention to object versions. (b) This issue was not a problem for the original paper, which did not cover degrees of isolation and so was only concerned with histories without wormholes. Prove that for histories without wormholes, the two definitions of equivalence (with and without object versions) are the same.

8. [7.5.8, 15] A different construction for the converse of the Wormhole Theorem (the no wormholes implies isolated) would be to pick T^* such that BEFORE(T^*) = $\emptyset$, and then show that H is equivalent to the history T^*, H'. What is the problem with this construction?

9. [7.5.8, 5] Give an example that violates the *only if* direction of the Locking Theorem. That is, show a history involving non–two-phase or non–well-formed transactions that is isolated.

10. [7.6, 10] Consider the SQL query

```
select avg(salary), sum(salary)/count(*)
     from emp,
```

Where emp is a non-empty table with a non-null integer salary field. What results will this query give with (a) repeatable reads and (b) cursor stability?

11. [7.7, 10] The discussion of predicate locks claims that they often result in spurious waits because the lock manager cannot tell that the predicates are disjoint. The text gave one example that would be run concurrently by precision locks. Give another.

12. [7.7, 10] The discussion of precision locks ended with the statement that they tend to convert predicate lock waits into deadlocks. Give an example of this.

13. [7.8, 10] The discussion of granular locks pointed out that many systems do not explicitly support a root node of the lock hierarchy. This reduces the depth of the lock tree by one, but it raises the problem of phantoms: In Figure 7.12, for example, what phantom problems arise if the database lock is not implemented?

14. [7.8.1, 5] In Figure 7.12, what were the lock requests of *T2*, and where is *T2* now?

15. [7.8, 10] In the discussion of update mode locks, it was mentioned that when a 3° cursor moves, its update mode locks are downgraded to shared mode locks. Why? What would happen if they were not? The compatibility matrix of Figure 7.11 is asymmetric: update is compatible with share but share is not compatible with update. Why was this choice made? Would the matrix be correct if it were symmetric?

16. [7.8, 10] The verbal definition of lock modes works for trees but not for DAGS. Restate the definitions for DAGS.

17. [7.8, 15] Granular locks in a tree lock from root to leaf. Could they lock from leaf to root?

18. [7.8, 5] (a) What does the key-range lock ["A","C") mean? (b) What is the name of the lock? (c) If next-key locking is used, what does the range become when "B" is inserted?

19. [7.8, 15 or project] When reading an existing unique record *X*, next-key locking gets a shared lock on the key *X*. What does this actually lock? Invent a scheme that locks less. Suppose a transaction using next-key locking inserts a thousand records in the key range [bolimia,bolinas), what key range locks does it get? Suppose it deletes a thousand such records. What locks and key ranges will it get?

20. [7.8, 15] In the discussion of key-range locks on a DAG, what locks would be needed to insert a pink-eyed bald person into the list of famous people?

21. [7.9, 5] Figure 7.12 displays the *Locks_T* labeling of the lock tree. Apply the definition of ImplicitLock to the graph of Figure 7.12, labeling each node with its implicit locks.

22. [7.8, 5] In the Ripa phone book there is no entry for computers, just a gap between compressors and concrete. What page lock will prevent a phantom filling this gap? What key-range lock would prevent such a phantom? What predicate or precision lock? In each case, "prove" your answer by showing a histories of locks, reads, and writes.

23. [7.9, 5] In Exercise 20, many locks are acquired. How would escalation deal with them?

24. [7.9, 5] Suppose one cursor of a transaction is pointing at record R and has it in shared mode. Suppose another FOR UPDATE cursor of that transaction also moves to R. (a) What is the new lock mode? (b) When the second cursor moves, what is the new lock mode? (c) Is the degree of isolation relevant here?

25. [7.9, 5] Suppose a lock request costs ≈ 100 instructions. Suppose an SQL cursor scans a million-record table of File-1 in Figure 7.12 with degree 3 isolation, and suppose that the SQL compiler defaulted to next-key granularity locking. How many locks will the transaction acquire? What will be the locking cost (in instructions and in instructions/record)?

26. [7.11, 5] Describe why convoy avoidance is different in a multiprocessor and in a uniprocessor.

27. [7.11, 5] Suppose transaction $t1$ in Figure 7.16 aborts. What does the new figure look like?

28. [7.11, 5] The deadlock-detection algorithm in Subsection 7.11.2 builds the wait-for graph using a set of transactions and a set of locks. It adds an arc, $\langle w,g \rangle$ to the graph if transaction g is in the granted group and transaction w is in the waiting group. The algorithm adds too many arcs to the graph. If lock conversion for transaction g is waiting, this will add arc $\langle g,g \rangle$ ($= \langle w,w \rangle$) to the graph. Such arcs are not needed in the graph. In addition, other arc classes need not be added to the graph. What are those classes?

29. [7.12, 15] Generalize the simple probabilistic model of deadlock to a situation of shared and exclusive locks. Suppose that the fraction of locks that are shared is s. Generalize the equations to the situation in which the processing rate of the system is $1/n$ that is, as the degree of multiprogramming rises, the processing rate of each transaction slows.

30. [7.12, 5] If there is an SQL lottery table

    CREATE TABLE lottery(name char(1) PRIMARY KEY,next int);

    containing a single record named "A" which counts the number of tickets sold, (a) write the field call to update this field. (b) What is the predicate? (c) What is the transform?

31. [7.12, 10] In classic field-call schemes, what degree of isolation does a transaction get when reading (ignoring the fact that a transaction cannot see its own updates)?

32. [7.12, 10] Prove that the sequence-number problem as stated in Subsection 7.12.2 has no solution. Relax one of the restrictions and state a solution for that problem.

Answers

1. False. The second law of concurrency talks about throughput *and response time*. Batch has terrible response time (50,000 second response time, rather than 1 second response time).

2. (a) Probably not; the only thing a read-only transaction can do is slow down other transactions. Since it has no outputs, it cannot write to the database, to other processes, or to terminals. (b) Write-only transactions are very common and useful. They are used to reinitialize objects.

3.

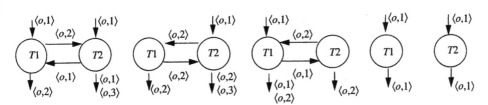

4. Dirty reads read uncommitted data, unrepeatable reads read only committed data.

5. A rollback step becomes a list of all the original writes of the transaction and then a list of unlocks corresponding to the locks. This makes rolled back transactions look like palindromes. This is called logging undos; the undo operations look like ordinary write operations. See Figure 9.16 for example.

6. (a) No. (b) H $=\langle\langle T1, \text{XLOCK}, a\rangle, \langle T2,\text{XLOCK},a\rangle,\langle T2,\text{WRITE},a\rangle\rangle$ is a counter-example. If *T2* and *T2* are well-formed, then any serial history is legal.

7. (a) $t1 = t2 = \langle\text{write } a,\text{write } a\rangle$ H1 $= \langle\langle t1,\text{write } a\rangle,\langle t2,\text{write},a\rangle,\langle t1,\text{write } a\rangle,\langle t2,\text{write},a\rangle\rangle$, H2 $= \langle\langle t2,\text{write},a\rangle,\langle t1,\text{write } a\rangle,\langle t2,\text{write},a\rangle,\langle t1,\text{write } a\rangle\rangle$.

8. The object versions in DEP(H') would not reflect any updates made by T, so in general, DEP(H)$\not\supseteq$ DEP(H')

9. Let T be any transaction. T need not be well-formed or two-phased. The history of T alone (T running without any other transactions) is isolated.

10. The computation may scan the table three times: once for count(*), once for sum(salary), and once for avg(salary). (a) With repeatable reads, each scan will see the same data and so will give give *x,x* for some *x*. (b) With cursor stability, each scan can see a completely different table. So cursor stability can return *x,y* for any *x* and *y*.

11. There are many. Suppose one predicate is salary > 1,000,000,000 and the other predicate is job_code = 'janitor'. Janitors don't make that kind of money; only the company president does. Precision locks would run these in parallel without problems.

12. You and I both lock "eyes are blue" in exclusive mode as a precision lock, and we are both granted. Then we both try to read a blue-eyed record. We will conflict with each other and so deadlock.

13. Phantom files.

14. slock database, slock file-3, islock file-2, slock name="Joe." It is waiting to be granted access to the Joe record.

15. Locks are downgraded so that other scans will not block (recall s incompatible with u). The choice for asymmetry was made for two reasons: (1) to show that asymmetry is possible (and make this exercise), and (2) if it is likely that the update mode lock will, indeed, turn into an update (which it often is in OLTP systems), then new readers should be made to wait for the update to go through. If they are granted, they could delay or starve the updater. The matrix would be correct either way. Updates could be made fully compatible with reads.

16. In essence, the "authority" that each mode gives has to be qualified by the parent mode. In particular, U, IX, SIX, and X require that *all* parents be held in IX or higher, else they should be treated as IS or S mode locks.

17. Probably not. To lock a parent, one would have to first lock all children of that parent. Since leaves appear dynamically (phantoms), this would be difficult. There seems to be no benefit in the leaf-to-root ordering.

18. (a) {record | "A" $\leq$ key(record) < "C"} (b) "A" (c) ["A","B") and ["B","C")

19. (a) It locks the key range[X,Y). By inventing new lock modes one can distinguish record locks from key-range locks. (b) The insert will split the key range into 1,001 key ranges and will get 1,001 locks. The delete will merge the 1,001 key ranges to one and will get 1,001 locks. Most commercial systems have trade-secret algorithms to deal with the problem of acquiring many locks. That problem would be a good research topic for a master's student. You know you have a good solution when you lock exactly what you need to lock, nothing more and nothing less. Pay special attention to inserting records at the end of a key-sequenced file.

20. Exclusive locks on [Auburn,Black), [Bald,Black) hair_color key ranges, and the [Gray,Red) and [Pink,Red) eye_color key ranges.

21.

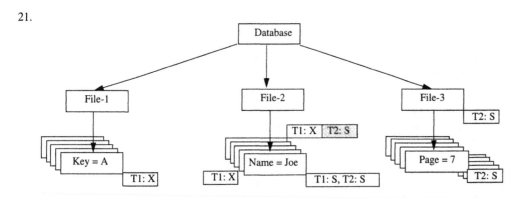

22. Lock the pages holding these two index entries, or lock the key range [concrete, compressor), or lock the predicate name ="computer".

23. Escalation would covert the 1,001 key-interval locks to one table lock. This is a catastrophe, so key-range locking as described is here not workable. Commercial systems, of course, have solutions for this problem, but the open literature does not.

24. (a) Lock is converted from shared to update. (b) If cursor has updated record, exclusive lock; if not, lock is converted to share from update. (c) Not if the degree of isolation is greater than zero.

25. Suppose the lock escalation limit is 1,000. The transaction will get a DB and File-1 lock in intent mode, then it will get 998 record locks and hit the escalation limit. It will then get a coarse grain file lock and release all its record locks. In the end, it will release its file and database locks. This is 1,000 lock-unlock pairs plus an extra convert-lock call. So, the locking cost is 20,100 instructions, and about .02 instructions per record.

26. In a uniprocessor, if a requestor finds that a lock is busy, the lock status will certainly not change until the requestor relinquishes the processor. In a multiprocessor, one of the other processors may be about to release the lock.

27.

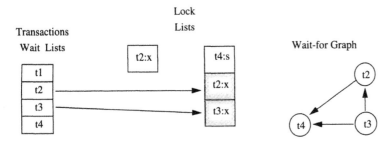

28. If mode(g) is compatible with mode(w), and for all waiting transactions t is ahead of w, mode(t) is compatible with mode(g). Example g has IS; g' has SIX; w is only waiter and wants SIX, then w waits for g' but not g.

29. Let $S = 1 - s^2$. Then $PW = \dfrac{Snr}{2R}$, and $PD = \dfrac{S^2 nr^4}{4R^2}$.

This is shown graphically below. It indicates that contention is cut in half when $s = .75$.

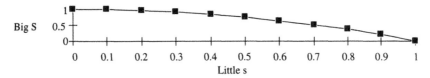

30. (a) UPDATE lottery SET next = next + 1 WHERE name = "A" HOTSPOT; (b) Null. (c) next = next + 1.

31. 2° because the read releases locks immediately.

32. Suppose a batch program gets a sequence number and holds it for a day. The high-throughput requirement means that 10^6 other sequence numbers have been distributed by the time this batch program commits. If the batch program commits, the monotone restriction is violated. If it rolls back, the dense restriction is violated.

A zealous locksmith died of late,
And did arrive at heaven's gate,
He stood without and would not knock,
Because he meant to pick the lock.

ANONYMOUS

8

Lock Implementation

8.1 Introduction

Concurrency control regulates the access of multiple processes or transactions to shared data. Ultimately, this involves multiple processes accessing a piece of data at some location. As explained in the previous chapter, this regulation is usually done with a locking scheme. By organizing locks in a hierarchy, predicate locks with multiple granularity can be simulated. Again, this comes down to acquiring or managing an individual lock. Locks record all the current requests, either granted or waiting, for a named resource. They are a simple data structure with two basic operations, lock() and unlock(), along with support operations that enumerate a transaction's locks, escalate lock requests to coarser granularity, release generic classes of locks, detect deadlocks, and configure the lock system.

8.1.1 About This Chapter

This chapter discusses the details of implementing locks. It begins by developing semaphores—first exclusive, then shared[1]—and then shows how storage blocks can quickly be allocated from a shared pool. Next, the chapter covers the logic of flat-transaction locks and deadlock, including the mechanisms to support savepoints and persistent savepoints. Following these basic topics, the presentation briefly treats the mechanisms needed to support parallel nested transactions. The initial discussion of semaphores is detailed, coming quite close to the bare machine instructions. This gives a sense of how implementations really work and exemplifies the structure of parallel algorithms. When the discussion turns to full-function locks, the presentation is abbreviated, covering only the main ideas and consequent program fragments.

8.1.2 The Need for Parallelism within the Lock Manager

It is possible to implement concurrency control as a *monitor*: that is, all the locking can be done by a serially reusable program with no internal parallelism. In that design, the lock manager acquires an exclusive semaphore on entry and only releases it when the lock

---

[1] Some prefer the term *latch* to the term *semaphore*, because these semaphores allow shared and exclusive access.

manager exits. The exit can be either a return to the requestor when the lock is granted or a call to the operating system wait( ) routine if the request must wait. In the latter case, when some other process releases the needed lock, the lock manager running in the requesting process is woken up—the wait( ) returns—before it reacquires the lock manager semaphore and continues to process the original request.

A lock manager implemented as a single monitor with no internal parallelism is much simpler than a lock manager that has concurrent execution on the lock data structures. Some famous lock managers work this way. For example, the original IMS DL/1 lock manager had a single exclusive semaphore protecting all its data structures. On the other hand, more recent lock managers use fine-granularity locking on the lock data structures: individual semaphores cover each lock. Concurrency within the lock manager, though more complex, is forced by preemptive scheduling, virtual memory, and multiprocessors. The issues can be summarized as follows:

Preemptive scheduling.   If the lock manager running on behalf of a low-priority process is preempted by a higher-priority process, the lock manager in the higher-priority process will be blocked by the semaphore until the lower-priority process is redispatched. This is an example of the priority inversion problem. Finer granularity semaphores reduce the severity of this problem by minimizing the data locked by the low-priority process.

Virtual memory.   Even if there is no preemptive scheduling, the lock manager may run in virtual memory and experience a page fault. In that case, the lock managers of all other processes will be blocked by the lock manager semaphore until this page fault is serviced and this lock manager request completes.

Multiprocessors.   In some applications, the lock manager may consume 10% of the system pathlength and thereby utilize the semaphore 10% of the time. A 10-way shared-memory multiprocessor would saturate such a single semaphore ($10 \cdot 10\% = 100\%$). Finer granularity is essential for multiprocessors.

For these reasons, the locking approaches presented here use fine granularity semaphores.

8.1.3 The Resource Manager and Lock Manager Address Space

Chapter 2 explained that processes can share memory by executing in one address space or by having independent address spaces that have some common shared segments (see Figure 2.8). Locks and semaphores control the execution of a set of processes. It is assumed that all the processes are running on processors with some shared address space segments. These shared segments contain the data as well as the semaphores and locks regulating access to the shared data. Of course, processes and transactions running in a truly distributed system can acquire locks at other nodes, but they do so by calling surrogate processes at the site where the data (and locks) are stored. This discussion therefore focuses on just the local processes (see Figure 8.1).

Each process has an identifier that can be used to name the process. Concurrency control needs one routine that causes a process to wait, and a second routine that allows one process to wake up another (that is, to end the other's wait). The three basic routines to manipulate processes are MyPID( ), wait( ), and wakeup( ). Their interfaces are as follows:

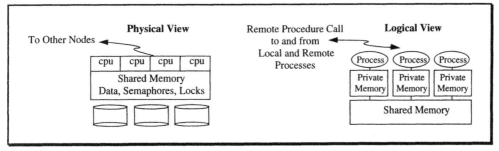

Figure 8.1: Logical and physical views of processes and resource managers sharing memory. It is assumed that a node consists of multiple processors accessing a shared global memory and communicating with other nodes via a network. The operating system abstracts this model to provide processes. Each process executes in an address space with some private memory. Processes typically interact via remote procedure calls, but they may also share segments of a global memory by binding them to segments of the process address space (see Subsection 2.2.1). The database buffers and the locks to regulate access to their data are examples of such memory sharing. Each process executing the database manager code shares these data structures with other such processes at that node.

```
typedef long    PID;                    /* process identifier                                      */
typedef struct  Process{                /* the definition of a process handle                      */
                PID     pid;            /* process identifier                                      */
                PCB *   sem_wait;       /* needed below for semaphores (ignore it right now)        */
                /* other things*/       /*                                                         */
                } PCB;                  /* process control block structure                         */
PID             MyPID(void);            /* returns the caller's process identifier                 */
PCB *           MyPCBP(void);           /* returns pointer to caller's process descriptor          */
void            wait(void);             /* a process can wait to be woken up                        */
void            wakeup(PCB * him);      /* wakes a waiting process.                                 */
```

Given these primitives and two processes, each with the variable him set to the process control block of the other, the following code fragment causes each process to alternately sleep and then wake up the other:[2]

```
while (TRUE) {  wakeup (him);           /* alternately wake up the other process                    */
                wait( );                /* and sleep waiting for a wakeup.                          */
                };                      /*                                                         */
```

The execution model assumes that processes run at arbitrary speed but eventually make progress. A process executing a program may be delayed for a while, but it eventually executes the next step of the program, unless that step is a wait for an event that never occurs (such as a wait in a deadlock). The assumption in this chapter is that processes execute their programs correctly. Any exceptions cause process termination. This, in turn, may cause a backup process to be invoked (if the process is a process pair), or it may cause transaction

---

[2] Implicit is the standard wakeup-waiting logic found in all operating systems; see Tannenbaum [1987].

rollback; it might even cause system restart if the process or the data it controls are especially critical (see Subsection 3.7.3).

8.2 Atomic Machine Instructions

Parallel programs cooperating via shared memory need a way to synchronize their execution. This synchronization can be implemented from the bare load-and-store instructions, with no special help from the hardware. By assigning a cell to each process, and by having each process set its own cell and then poll the others, each process can signal its state to others, using a kind of busy waiting (with $O(n^2)$ execution cost for n sharing processes). However, virtually all modern machines provide some form of synchronization instruction that atomically alters a cell.[3] These instructions range from simple *bit-test-and-set* instructions (ones that atomically perform {if (cell==0) {cell=1; return TRUE;} else return FALSE;}) to more complex instructions that test and set whole words (four bytes)—the so-called *compare-and-swap* instructions explained next. Some machines even offer instructions that directly implement semaphores in hardware. This presentation assumes compare-and-swap instructions defined by the following:

```
/* compare-and-swap (CS) is an atomic transformation of the cell (4-byte word).          */
/* If the cell contains a value equal to old, the cell is set to the new value and TRUE is returned.   */
/* If the cell value is not equal to old, the cell value is unchanged, the contents of old is set to   */
/*     the current cell value, and FALSE is returned.                                      */
Boolean CS(int * cell, int * old, int * new)          /*                                  */
     {if (*cell == *old)  {*cell = *new;    return TRUE; }  /* change cell to new if it equals old.  */
           else           {*old = *cell;    return FALSE;};  /* otherwise read old cell value into old  */
     };                                                /*                                   */
```

Suppose we want to update a shared counter by one. The following code will not work:

```
temp = counter + 1;          /*   unsafe code to increment a shared counter           */
counter = temp;              /*   this assignment may suffer a lost update            */
```

The code is subject to lost updates (see subsection 7.3.3 or Exercise 1 at the end of this chapter). On the other hand, the following code does update the shared counter exactly once:

```
temp = counter;                       /* read the current value of the counter into temp      */
do                                    /* loop until the counter is incremented (until CS is successful)  */
     new = temp+1;                    /* propose a new value for the counter                  */
while (! CS(&counter,&temp,&new) );   /* set cell to value of new unless cell has changed      */
                                      /* if CS failed, temp was set to counter, so repeat      */
```

---

[3] Certain machines optimized for numeric processing provide only a privileged operation to disable interrupts. Since disabling interrupts does not prevent other processors from accessing the memory and does not prevent virtual memory page faults, this design only applies to uniprocessor OS kernels. On such machines, there is usually an (expensive) operating system call that implements compare-and-swap for nonprivileged programs like resource managers.

The compare-and-swap instruction is atomic and isolated in the sense of the ACID transaction properties. It is *atomic* in that it has only two outcomes: the shared data (cell) is changed, or it is not changed. It is *isolated* in that if any two processes execute the instruction on the same cell, it will appear that the instruction of one of the processes' ran first, and the other ran second. In the terminology of the previous chapter, the compare-and-swap instructions can be organized into an isolated history with an acyclic dependency graph. In fact, the instruction has a third behavior: *exception*. It may produce a protection exception (by trying to write read-only data), an addressing exception (by trying to write a nonexistent address, or by acting on a cell that is not word aligned), a parity exception (when a cell is damaged), and many other hardware-related exceptions. In these cases, the behavior of the instruction is usually left unspecified. These exception conditions are discussed in more detail in Subsection 8.3.5. When exceptions are raised, the system initiates an exception handler and, failing that, initiates high-level transaction recovery-restart, using the full ACID mechanisms.

The definition of compare-and-swap in C may be too vague to convey the idea. If so, let us momentarily lapse into machine language. Imagine a register machine with word registers named $R1$, $R2$, and $R3$. The compare-and-swap loop we just considered translates into the following:

```
1            load     R1,&cell     /* get the address of the cell to be atomically altered       */
2            load     R2,cell      /* get the current value of cell                              */
3 loop       add      R3,R2,1      /* get the desired new value R3 = R2 + 1                      */
4            CS       R1,R2,R3     /* compare-and-swap: if *R1=R2 then *R1 = R3 else R2 =*R1     */
5            branch≠ loop          /* if compare-and-swap failed, do it again                    */
```

The compare-and-swap instruction of this program is the only atomic statement. The program "nonatomically" gathers together the contents of registers *R1, R2,* and *R3*, and sends them to the shared memory at address *R1* as a message or bus request. In Figure 8.1, the message is sent to the shared memory box at the left of the picture. Several processors may send a message to the same cell at the same time. The processor marshals the parameters to the instruction, but the instruction's compare logic is executed in the shared memory subsystem (the memory shared by many processors).

Let us return to the C-program definition. The memory executes the compare of old (*R2*) with the value of the cell, and the memory does the replace (with *R3*) if the compare is true. The processor cannot execute the test, because the memory is shared among multiple processors. (There is no single *processor*; rather, there is only a single *cell*.) Even on a uniprocessor, the program may have to repeat the compare-and-swap. If the program is preempted by a higher-priority process at step 4, and if that process alters the cell, then when the original program runs, its compare-and-swap will fail because the value of old has changed. The miscompare will cause *R2* to be set to the cell's current value, and the next time the compare-and-swap executes it will (probably) work. This uniprocessor situation is just as though another process on a different processor had raced for the memory cell and won.[4]

---

[4] Some cache designs allow a processor to lock the memory cell and thereby get the same effect in cache. But even in that case it is the memory subsystem, not the processor, that is making the update atomic.

Given an understanding of how compare-and-swap works, the compare-and-swap double (8 bytes) is no surprise. It, too, is an atomic instruction. The need for it arises in the discussion of semaphores and storage allocation. The compare-and-swap double is defined by the following:

```
/* compare-and-swap (CSD) is an atomic transformation of the cell (8-bytes).              */
/* If the cell currently holds the value old, the cell is set to the new value and TRUE is returned. */
/* If the cell value is not equal to old, then the cell is unchanged, the contents of old is set to   */
/*  the current cell value, and FALSE is returned.                                         */
Boolean CSD(long * cell, long * old, long * new)            /*                              */
    {if (*cell == *old)   {*cell = *new;     return TRUE; }   /* change cell to new of it equals old.  */
         else            {*old = *cell;      return FALSE;};  /* otherwise read old value into old     */
    };                                                        /*                              */
```

8.3 Semaphores

Semaphores derive from the corresponding mechanism used for trains: a train may proceed through a section of track only if the semaphore is clear. Once the train passes, the semaphore is set until the train exits that section of track. Computer semaphores have a get( ) routine that acquires the semaphore (perhaps waiting until it is free) and a dual give( ) routine that returns the semaphore to the free state, perhaps signaling (waking up) a waiting process.

Semaphores are very simple locks; indeed, they are used to implement general-purpose locks. Semaphores have no deadlock detection, no conversion, no escalation, and no automatic release at commit, and they support only two very simple lock modes: shared and exclusive. Semaphore users must avoid deadlock by acquiring semaphores in some fixed partial order (thereby avoiding cycles). In the following discussion, semaphores that support only exclusive mode locking are introduced first. Then semaphores that support both shared and exclusive mode are described.

8.3.1 Exclusive Semaphores

The anchor for an exclusive semaphore is a pointer to a list of processes. This pointer is usually NULL, since most semaphores are usually free. If the semaphore is busy but there are no waiters, the pointer is the address of the process that owns the semaphore. If some processes are waiting, the semaphore points to a linked list of waiting processes. The process owning the semaphore is at the end of this list. Assuming a process can wait for only one semaphore at a time, it makes sense for each process to have a dedicated piece of memory (a structure) that the process can chain into any semaphore wait list. This was the function of the sem_wait field defined as part of the process structure in Subsection 8.1.3. That field is NULL, or it is a pointer to the first process in the semaphore list. This gives rise to the following structures:

```
typedef PCB * xsemaphore;               /* Exclusive semaphore is a list of processes.      */
                                        /*The last process in the list owns (holds) the semaphore.  */
                                        /* All others are waiting in FIFO order.            */
                                        /*The list is linked by the process.sem_wait pointers.  */
/* Xsem_init initializes an exclusive semaphore. Sets it to NULL indicating it is free.      */
void Xsem_init(xsemaphore * sem)        /* parameter is pointer to an X semaphore           */
    {*sem = NULL; return;}              /* set semaphore to NULL pointer and return         */
```

The code to acquire an exclusive semaphore is simple and demonstrates the use of compare-and-swap.:

```
/* Xsem_get acquires access to an exclusive semaphore for the calling process.              */
/* The program adds a pointer to the calling process to the head of the semaphore list and  */
/*      moves the current list head (typically NULL) to MyPCBP()->sem_wait.                  */
/* This adds the calling process to the semaphore wait list if there is one.                 */
/* If the semaphore was not free the process waits for a wakeup.                             */
/* The semaphore is owned by the caller when this routine returns.                           */
void Xsem_get(xsemaphore * sem)         /* parameter is pointer to an X semaphore           */
    {PCB *     new    = MyPCBP();        /* new will be the new value of the sem (me)        */
    PCB *      old    = NULL;            /* guess at old queue head = NULL                   */
    do                                   /* loop until process is on queue (until CS is successful)  */
        new->sem_wait = old;             /* move current queue head to my sem_wait           */
    while ( ! CS(sem, &old, &new));      /* replace queue head with pointer to me            */
    if (old != NULL)                     /* if queue was not null then I'm not yet the       */
        wait();                          /* owner and must wait for a wakeup from owner.     */
    return;                              /* semaphore acquired, return to caller             */
    };                                   /*                                                  */
```

Once a process has acquired a semaphore and has used the resource covered by it, the process should quickly free the semaphore. Typically, no other process is waiting for the semaphore. However, if there is a list of waiters, then the process should scan to the end of the list and wake up the oldest process, thereby granting it access to the semaphore and providing a fair (first in, first out) scheduler. Here is the resulting logic:

```
/* Code to release access to an exclusive semaphore for the calling process.                */
/* Program removes the process from the tail of the semaphore list and if the list is not empty,  */
/*      wakes up the previous process (FIFO scheduling)                                      */
void Xsem_give(xsemaphore * sem)        /* parameter points to an exclusive semaphore       */
    {PCB *  new    = NULL;               /* guess that the new wait list is null             */
    PCB *   old    = MyPCBP();           /* guess that the old list is my process alone      */
    if (CS(sem,&old,&new)) return;       /* if guessed right, return;                        */
    while (old->sem_wait != MyPCBP())    /* if guessed wrong, old is now a non-null wait list  */
        { old = old->sem_wait; };        /* advance to the end of the list                   */
    old->sem_wait = NULL;                /* remove me from the end of the list               */
    wakeup(old);                         /* wake up the process at the end of the list       */
    return;                              /* (note there is one, since list was not null)     */
    };                                   /*                                                  */
```

The key property used by the Xsem_give() routine is the invariant "the list of processes pointed to by the semaphore only grows at its head and is ended by the giver." (See Figure 8.2). The giving process gets a pointer to the current queue head and scans to the queue tail. If new processes are concurrently executing Xsem_get(), they will not modify that section of the queue. Consequently, once the Xsem_give() routine gets the queue pointed to by "old" in the program, each process in that list becomes a waiting process; accordingly, those pointers are not changing.

This is FIFO (first in, first out) scheduling. To avoid the convoys described in the previous chapter, the Xsem_give() routine may simply free the semaphore (set the queue to null) and then wake up everybody in the "old" list. In that case, each of those processes will have to reexecute the Xsem_get() routine. The corresponding "broadcast" convoy-avoiding versions of get and give are as follows:

```
/* Convoy-avoiding semaphore logic: Xsem_get retries, Xsem_give broadcasts.        */
/* Only new logic is commented, other code is the same as before.                  */
void Xsem_get(xsemaphore * sem)              /*                                     */
    { PCB *  new     = MyPCBP();             /*                                     */
    PCB *   old      = NULL;                 /*                                     */
    do                                       /*                                     */
        new->sem_wait = old;                 /*                                     */
    while ( ! CS(sem, &old, &new));          /*                                     */
    if (old != NULL)                         /*                                     */
        { wait();                            /* new logic:                          */
        Xsem_get(sem);                       /* rerequest the semaphore at wakeup   */
        };                                   /* (recursion is for simplicity of presentation) */
    return;                                  /* eventually the semaphore is acquired. */
    };                                       /*                                     */

void Xsem_give(xsemaphore * sem)             /*                                     */
    {PCB * old  = MyPCBP();                  /* eventually the semaphore is acquired. */
    PCB *   new = NULL;                       /* guess that the new wait list is null */
    while ( !CS(sem,&old,&new) );            /* blind free: set semaphore free in all cases */
    while (old != MyPCBP())                  /* scan to end of list, wake up all waiters */
        { new = old->sem_wait;               /* remember the pointer to the next in chain */
        old->sem_wait = NULL;                /* mark current waiter not waiting     */
        wakeup(old);                         /* and wake him up                     */
        old = new; };                        /* advance to next waiter              */
    return;                                  /*                                     */
    };                                       /*                                     */
```

8.3.2 Crabbing: Traversing Shared Data Structures

Often, a data structure is a collection of nodes connected via pointers. Traversing such data structures proceeds by reading a root or anchor record to find the current value of some pointer and then following that pointer to some other record. That second record is then

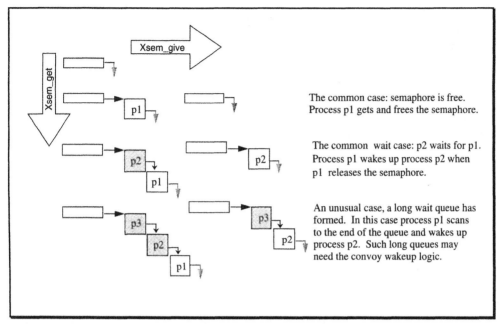

The common case: semaphore is free. Process p1 gets and frees the semaphore.

The common wait case: p2 waits for p1. Process p1 wakes up process p2 when p1 releases the semaphore.

An unusual case, a long wait queue has formed. In this case process p1 scans to the end of the queue and wakes up process p2. Such long queues may need the convoy wakeup logic.

Figure 8.2: Transition diagrams for an exclusive semaphore data structure. Vertical transitions are caused by Xsem_get calls, while horizontal transitions are caused by Xsem_give calls. Usually the semaphore is free, and the path is Xsem_get , Xsem_give . But, if process p2 calls Xsem_get before p1 calls Xsem_give , the wait case occurs. In the rare instance that p1 holds the semaphore for a long time, a long queue of processes can form. In this case, each process will be granted, in FIFO order, and then will wake up its successor (that is, its predecessor in the queue).

examined to find a second pointer. This process continues until the target object has been located.

The simple way to manage such traversals is to have a single exclusive semaphore covering the whole data structure. Unfortunately, this can result in considerable queueing on that semaphore if there are multiple processors concurrently accessing the root. As a result, there is an incentive to have finer granularity semaphores—generally, one per node of the data structure. The root record and even the high-level records in such addressing hierarchies are frequently accessed. Thus, it is important to minimize the time during which these records are locked: the semaphore should be released as soon as possible.

As an example, the B-tree design of Chapter 15 has a semaphore per page of the B-tree. In that design, anyone wanting to find the leaf page containing a particular key acquires a semaphore on the root page, looks up the key to find the address of the next page, gets a semaphore on the next page in the tree, and then releases the root page semaphore. When the program arrives at the leaf, it gets an actual key-range lock on the record or key range covered by the search (i.e., a lock with all the features discussed in the last chapter and later in this chapter). This graph traversal may involve several disk reads; therefore, if the root semaphore were held during the entire traversal, there likely would be a long queue of other processes waiting for the semaphore.

When traversing a shared-pointer structure, it is necessary to keep each pointer stable until it has been used to find and stabilize the next object. The target object is made stable by acquiring its semaphore or lock *before* releasing the semaphore on the source pointer. This is called *crabbing,* by analogy with the way crabs, spiders, and mountain climbers move: they always hang on to the previous point while reaching for the next one. A program that does not crab through a shared-list structure runs the risk of following a pointer to the wrong place. For example, suppose a program gets a semaphore on a B-tree root page, reads a page address in that page, and then releases the semaphore. If the program then accesses the second page based on the address gotten from the first page, the program could go to the wrong page, if another program had run in the interim, deallocated the target page, and recorded the deallocation in the root page. But if the original program retains a semaphore on the root pointer while following it to the page, the semaphore assures that no second program can invalidate the pointer.

8.3.3 Shared Semaphores

The previous chapter explained two generic strategies for minimizing contention: granularity and lock modes. Crabbing explains the granularity issue for semaphores; the lock mode issue is even simpler. Many data structures are read-intensive. Exclusive semaphores would create spurious waits on such data structures, since read operations by different processes can proceed in parallel without violating isolation.

This phenomenon explains the heavy use of shared semaphores within systems. If most accesses to high-traffic structures are reads, then readers should concurrently share the semaphore, and only updaters of the structure need get the semaphore in exclusive mode. A simple implementation of shared semaphores is presented here. This implementation uses a broadcast mechanism to free the semaphore. Doing shared semaphores that guarantee FIFO service is left as (nontrivial) Exercise 8.

A shared semaphore has three components: the mode it is currently in (free, shared, exclusive, waiting), a count of the number of processes granted the semaphore, and a list of processes waiting to be granted the semaphore. Unlike exclusive-mode semaphores, shared-mode semaphores do not record the identity of processes granted access to the semaphore. There is only a count of the grantees. As with exclusive-mode semaphores, the waiters are explicitly recorded in the wait list. The scheduling rule is that if anyone is waiting, then all new requests will wait.

```
enum LOCK_MODE {                          /* lock mode definitions                              */
        LOCK_FREE,                        /* lock is free, the null mode                        */
        LOCK_S,                           /* shared lock mode                                   */
        LOCK_X,                           /* exclusive lock mode                                */
        LOCK_U,                           /* update lock mode                                   */
        LOCK_IS,                          /* intention share lock mode                          */
        LOCK_IX,                          /* intention exclusive lock mode                      */
        LOCK_SIX,                         /* share and intention exclusive lock mode            */
        LOCK_WAIT};                       /* lock is in a wait state                            */
typedef int lock_mode;                    /* mode is one of the lock modes                      */
/* Share + Exclusive Semaphore definitions.                                                     */
typedef struct                            /*                                                    */
    { lock_mode    mode;                  /* mode is free, share, exclusive,                    */
      int          count;                 /* number granted: 0: free, 1: exclusive, ≥ 1: shared */
      PCB *        wait_list;             /* null if none waiting, else, the list of waiting    */
    } semaphore;                          /*  processes chained via process.sem_wait.           */
```

The code to initialize a shared semaphore is simple; it sets the mode to free, sets the count to zero (no one is granted), and sets the wait_list to NULL (no one is waiting).

```
void sem_init(semaphore * sem)        /*                              */
    {sem->mode = LOCK_FREE;           /*   mode is free               */
     sem->count = 0;                  /*   count of grantees is zero  */
     sem->wait_list = NULL;           /*   wait list is null          */
     return;};                        /*                              */
```

Shared semaphores are double words (8 bytes) and therefore need the compare-and-swap double instruction (CSD()) to make the semaphore transformation atomic. The code to request a shared semaphore assumes that the semaphore is initially free. If that is not the case, it hopes that the request is shared and that the semaphore is currently in shared mode with no waiters. Otherwise, the request must wait. When the last holder of the semaphore is done with it, he will free the semaphore (marking it free) and broadcast a wakeup to all waiters. The waiters then resubmit their requests. This is the convoy-avoidance logic.

```
/* sem_get acquires the semaphore in a specified mode (LOCK_S or LOCK_X)        */
/* If the semaphore is free it is acquired immediately.                         */
/* If the semaphore is shared and the requested mode is share and there are no waiters, */
/*    then the semaphore is also acquired immediately.                          */
/*    otherwise the request waits for a wakeup and rerequests the semaphore.    */
/* The corresponding wakeup logic uses broadcast to avoid convoys.              */
void sem_get(semaphore * sem, lock_mode mode)  /*                              */
    {semaphore  new;                  /* new value for semaphore       */
     semaphore  old;                  /* old value for semaphore       */
     PCB *      me = MyPCBP();         /* pointer to requesting process */
     while (TRUE)                      /* repeat until request is granted */
         {old = {LOCK_FREE, 0, NULL};  /* guess old value for semaphore is free */
          new = {mode, 1, NULL};       /* & guess new value has only me granted */
          if (CSD( sem, &old, &new)) return;  /* if semaphore free, this gets & exits */
          /* if compare-and-swap-double failed, it set old to current value of semaphore */
          while (  (mode == LOCK_S) &&  /* if request is shared mode      */
                   (old.mode == LOCK_S) &&  /* and semaphore is currently in shared mode */
                   (old.wait_list == NULL))  /* and no one is waiting         */
              { new.count = old.count + 1;   /* then try to join the shared group, */
                if (CSD( sem, &old, &new)) return; }  /* got it, return success */
          /* Request must wait.                                                 */
          new.mode = LOCK_WAIT;         /* set semaphore to indicate non-null wait */
          new.count = old.count;        /* granted count is unchanged     */
          new.wait_list = me;           /* this process is head of wait list */
          me->sem_wait = old.wait_list;  /* and it points to rest of wait list */
```

```
            /* try to add this process to wait list. If it works fine, wait for wakeup          */
            if ( CSD( sem, &old, &new) )              /* if get on the list                      */
                wait();                               /*    then wait for wakeup                 */
            /* at this point,    either the process just woke up from a wait,                    */
            /*                        or it never got on the wait list because the list changed  */
            /* In either case, the process restarts at the top of the while loop and re-requests */
        }; };                                         /* repeat while loop until request granted  */
```

The release logic (sem_give()) is a little simpler. It broadcasts a wakeup to all the waiters.

```
void sem_give(semaphore * sem)                   /*                                              */
    {semaphore  new = {LOCK_FREE,0,NULL}; /* guess that the new state is free                    */
    semaphore   old = {LOCK_S,1,NULL};        /* guess that the old state is me only S mode       */
    PCB *       him, * next;                   /* pointers used to scan wait list                 */
    if (CSD( sem, &old, &new)) return;        /* free it & return if guessed right               */
    do                                         /* if that didn't work then guessed wrong, compute new */
        { if (old.count > 1)                   /* if I'm not last to leave                        */
            new = {LOCK_S, old.count - 1, old.wait_list};  /* decrement count                   */
        else                                                   /* If I'm last to leave           */
            new = {LOCK_FREE, 0, NULL };                       /* Free the semaphore             */
    while (! CSD( sem, &old, &new));          /* do the CSD and exit loop if it works            */
    if (old.count == 1)                        /* if I was the last to leave and                 */
        { him = old.wait_list;                 /* if there were others waiting                    */
        while (him != NULL)                    /* then                                            */
            { next = him->sem_wait;            /* scan down the wait list                         */
            him->sem_wait = NULL;              /* take him off the wait list                      */
            wakeup(him);                       /* wake him up                                      */
            him = next;                        /* go to next in wait list                         */
        };   };                                /* end of wait list scan                           */
    return;                                    /*                                                 */
};                                             /*                                                 */
```

In a later chapter, it will be convenient to have a bounce-mode semaphore that never waits. It acquires the semaphore immediately, if possible, and returns the outcome to the caller. Its interface follows; the code is left as Exercise 12.

```
Boolean sem_get_bounce(semaphore * sem, lock_mode mode)  /*                                      */
```

This completes the implementation of semaphores and demonstrates the use of the compare-and-swap instructions. The design avoids the delicate issue of allocating storage. Since each process has a dedicated queue element in the process descriptor, the process.sem_wait field, no dynamic storage needs to be allocated. Storage allocation from a shared pool is surprisingly difficult.

8.3.4 Allocating Shared Storage

The standard way to allocate storage quickly is to preallocate a pool of blocks, each of a fixed size. The pool's free blocks are linked together in a list anchored in the pool header. That is, free points to the first free block, and in each free block, block→next points to the next free block. The null pointer ends the list.

Semaphores can be used to control the allocation and deallocation of storage from a storage pool. The manipulation can be protected by a semaphore—say, Pool.Sem—and by bracketing all pool reads or updates with an Xsem_get(&Pool.Sem) and Xsem_give (&Pool.Sem) pair. But storage allocation is so common that a more efficient technique is needed. The following might seem to be a safe way of getting the next block from the pool without using semaphores at all:

```
/* An unsafe way to allocate blocks from a free list                                        */
typedef struct {                      /* definition of a storage block                      */
    struct block * next;              /* pointer to next block if block is in free list      */
    /* and other things*/            /* data contents of block are not relevant here        */
    } block;                          /*                                                     */
static block * free;                  /* global variable is pointer to the free list of blocks. */
                                      /* Allocation and initialization of free list is not shown. */

block * bad_get_block(void)           /* get the next free block from the pool free list     */
    { block *    new;                 /* pointer to next block in list                       */
    block *      old = free;          /* pointer to first block in list                      */
    do                                /* repeat until compare-and-swap works                 */
        { if (old == NULL) panic();   /* ignore empty list case                              */
        new = old->next;}             /* find address of node successor                      */
    while (! CS(&free,&old,&new));     /* replace head with successor, retry on CS failure     */
    return (old);                     /* return address of allocated node                    */
    };                                /*                                                     */
/* give_block returns a block to the free list.                                              */
void give_block(block * freeit) /* return a block to the free list                          */
    { block *    new  = freeit;       /* pointer to block to be freed                        */
    block *      old  = free;         /* pointer to first block in list                      */
    do                                /* repeat until compare-and-swap works                 */
        new->next = old;              /* new free block points at old free list head         */
    while(! CS(&free,&old,&new));      /* replace head with new free block, retry on CS failure */
    return;                           /*                                                     */
    };                                /*                                                     */
```

The give_block() routine is fine, but the bad_get_block() routine has a bug. The invariant assumption in the compare-and-swap instruction of bad_get_block() says,

If free = old, then the next block in the free list after old is new (i.e., free→next = new).

But this "invariant" is sometimes false, as Figure 8.3 shows.

A version of the bad_get_block() code was implemented and ran for several days without problems, getting and releasing blocks at random. The bad scenario never occurred. Still, one is nervous about such code. The logic can be made safe by adding a process ID to the pool header and setting it to the invoker's unique identifier prior to block allocation. The idea is that the caller has a unique identifier (its process ID). If each process that wants to change the list leaves its ID at the head of the list, then other processes can sense that the list has changed and can retry. This is the resulting code:

```
typedef struct {                                    /* freelist is a list of free blocks.                */
        PCB *   kilroy;                             /* id of last process to allocate from the pool      */
        block * free;                               /* pointer to the head of the free list.             */
        } freelist;                                 /*                                                   */
static freelist free;                               /* Freelist allocation and formatting not shown.     */
/* better get_block routine that avoids the problem in Figure 8.3                                        */
block * get_block(void)                             /* get the next free block from the free list        */
    { freelist    new ;                             /* new free list header                              */
    freelist      old;                              /* old header (will point to allocated bock)         */
    do                                              /* loop until block allocated                        */
        { free.kilroy = old.kilroy = new.kilroy = MyPID(); /* guess kilroy was here                      */
        old.free = free.free;                       /* get address of first free element                 */
        if (old.free == NULL) panic();              /* if null, panic                                    */
        new.free = old.free->next;  }               /* find address of node successor                    */
    while ( ! CSD(&free,&old,&new));                /* replace top block with successor in freelist, CS will */
                                                    /* fail if kilroy has changed. retry loop if kilroy changed */
    return (old.free);                              /* return address of allocated node                  */
    };                                              /*                                                   */
```

The invariant used by the compare-and-swap double statement says,

If the value of kilroy is MyPID(), then the list has not changed since the most recent store of MyPID() in the kilroy.

This assertion allows you to prove that the allocated block is, indeed, free and that the freelist pointer does, indeed, point to the next free block.

The locking presentation later in this chapter assumes that pools of blocks have been preallocated, so that a new block can be allocated in a few instructions in the style of the get_block() and give_block() routines. To further accelerate this process, the fields of the free blocks are often preformatted to default values.

8.3.5 Semaphores and Exceptions

If a process fails while holding semaphores, the data covered by the semaphores is suspect—it may be in an inconsistent state. There is no transaction mechanism underneath semaphores to provide transaction backout. Semaphores help provide isolation, but they do not help with the other ACID properties. Consequently, if a process holding a semaphore aborts, the entire subsystem usually is restarted. For example, both the lock manager and the database buffer pool manager heavily use semaphores. If any process executing the locking or buffering code gets an exception that the subsystem cannot handle, then the whole subsystem (locks or buffers) is suspect and should be restarted. This, in turn, is likely to cause a general restart of

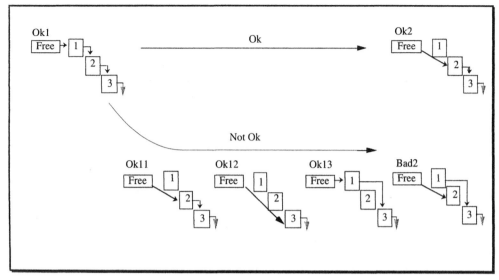

Figure 8.3: An example showing the flaw in bad_get_block(). In the upper part of the figure, process 1 replaces the free pointer with a pointer to node 2 and knows it has allocated node 1. Bad_get_block() assumes that node 1 →next = &node2 if node1 is still at the head of the queue. But that is false, as shown in the scenario producing case OK13. In that case, some other process has allocated nodes 1 and 2, returning node 1 (but not node 2) to the list. This produced state OK13, in which free = &node1, but node1.next = &node3. If the compare-and-swap of process 1 is delayed and executes on state OK13, then state BAD2 (rather than OK2) results. In that state, the free list has been lost, and the pool free pointer points at an allocated node.

all client resource managers and all processes sharing storage with the failing process. The transaction mechanism then comes into play, restoring the system state to the most recent consistent state.

Fault-tolerant systems and disaster recovery systems view such restarts and takeovers as a natural course of events. To these systems, such events are an inconvenience, but nothing more. With a process-pair or backup system present to take over, service may be interrupted for a few seconds. (That time can be reduced to centiseconds if the customer has enough megadollars.)

Conventional systems go to considerable lengths to avoid such restart events, because a restart generally implies an outage of several minutes—two orders of magnitude longer than seconds. Such systems carefully track the semaphores of each process. If a failing process holds no semaphores, then it can be terminated without compromising the shared data; the data is protected by the ACID mechanisms. The transaction manager will clean up any uncommitted updates left behind by the process. On the other hand, if a failing process holds semaphores, then Functional Recovery Routines (FRRs, also called *salvagers*) are invoked to clean up the data and release any semaphores held by the process.

The FRR code intimately understands the failing routine and failing data structures (30% of the MVS kernel is reputed to consist of such recovery code). By examining the semaphores and hints the faulty code left behind, the salvager can tell whether the process holds any exclusive semaphores and whether it is waiting for any kind of semaphore. It can only guess whether a process holds a shared semaphore (the data structure counts grantees but does not list them). Waiting requests and shared semaphores can be released with no problem, but semaphores held in exclusive mode pose a real problem, because they represent data that may be inconsistent. The standard technique, pioneered by AT&T on the Electronic Switching Systems and now common in most big operating systems, is to run integrity checks, called *auditors*, on the data structure. These integrity checks clean up the data structures by relinking doubly linked lists, salvaging free blocks that are not on the free list, and so on. If the data structure passes the test, the failing process's semaphore is released. This is an area of art and faith rather than of engineering. It requires careful analysis, more careful implementation, and even more careful testing and maintenance.

With time, the FRR approach is likely to be replaced by, or combined with, the process-pair takeover approach. Writing and maintaining FRR code is just too expensive for organizations with a finite budgets. It is easier to buy twice as much hardware and use the transaction mechanism to clean up the mess—especially in view of the rising cost of software and falling cost of hardware. Having the ACID properties at the top application level makes it easier to build disaster-recovery nodes. These systems use the concurrency control (isolation) provided by the lock manager and the atomicity provided by the recovery manager.

8.4 Lock Manager

Locks record the current requests for each named resource and schedule access to those resources. This section begins with a discussion of the lock data structures and goes on to show how these structures are used to implement the lock() and unlock() routines. Then the discussion turns to certain details, such as lock escalation, savepoint handling of locks, and the locking aspects of transaction commit, transaction rollback, and system restart.

8.4.1 Lock Names

Naming is one of the more difficult issues the lock manager must face. Each lock has a name, and clients would like those names to be of unlimited length. That may be the correct design, but for performance reasons, names are usually limited to a small, fixed length. This is a typical format for a lock name:

```
typedef struct                  /* definitions for lock names and pointers to them        */
      { RMID   rmid;            /* resource manager identifier (two bytes)                  */
        char   resource[14];    /* object name is 14 bytes interpreted by resource manager  */
      } lock_name;              /*                                                          */
```

The purpose of a resource manager identifier in each lock name should be obvious: it allows the resource managers to have disjoint sets of locks and to pick lock names at will from their own name spaces. Alternatively, each resource manager can have a private set of lock names by having a private lock manager. This definition suggests that all object names fit in 14 characters, but that is highly unlikely. In general, each resource manager must compress, fold, or hash long object names into this smaller unit. If two objects hash to the same lock name, and the two requested modes are incompatible, then the collision may cause spurious waits. If the hash is any good—if it is effective in randomizing names—such spurious waits are not likely; two names will collide with probability $2^{-(8 \cdot 14)} \approx 10^{-34}$. Spurious waits should not cause a problem, for they are just like ordinary waits. The only possible exception occurs if the resource manager is doing deadlock avoidance by acquiring the locks in a certain order. In that case, names should be chosen carefully (recall that the resource manager is doing the hash).

A typical construction of short names can be described by the example of database file, record, and key-range locks. The locks for a partition of the database form a particular lock space. On a DB2 node, all files at that node might be one lock space; on an OS2/EE DB node (an IBM PS2 PC), the lock space is that PC. On a VAX cluster, all the Rdb files might form one space. In a Tandem NonStop SQL system, all the files and records on one disk form a lock space. In each case, the lock space is the scope of the local resource manager.

In the NonStop SQL case, the file server managing a partition of the database (disk) assigns a 2-byte number to each open file or table. There may be many more than 64 K files open in the network, but this is the lock space for a particular file server at a particular node. The other file servers have disjoint lock spaces. Within a file, the server may be doing page locking (4 bytes), record locking (8 bytes), or key-range locking (many bytes). Key-range locks are the only ones that may not fit in the free 10 bytes of lock names (16 minus 2 for RMID, and 4 for file ID). The solution is to hash (fold) each key-range lock down to 10 bytes. If two predicates on the same file have the same hash value and conflicting modes, one may have to wait. If the hash is good, this will be very rare. Similar techniques apply to object-oriented databases.

8.4.2 Lock Queues and Scheduling

Most locks are free most of the time and should therefore occupy no space. A lock that has one or more requests outstanding, however, has a lock header summarizing the lock status and a list of all requests for that lock. Some of the requests have been granted, and some are waiting to be granted—these are called the *granted group* and the *waiting group*, respectively. Granting requests is a scheduling decision that has historically been made FIFO, but that may change with time. FIFO is the simplest *fair* scheduler: no transaction is indefinitely delayed or *starved* while waiting behind other tasks that are granted ahead of it. The FIFO discipline is implemented by placing new transactions at the end of the waiting list.

Each granted group has a summary mode that is the maximum of the modes of the group members, as computed from Figure 7.4 and tabulated in Table 8.4. A new request is compatible with the members of the group if it is compatible with the group mode. Part A of

Table 8.4: Computation of granted group mode from request modes. The entry {U, {S}} means that one U and zero or more S requests are currently granted. In that case, the granted group mode is U.

	Request Modes	Group Mode
	X	X
	{SIX, {IS}}	SIX
	{U, {S}}	U
	{S, {S}, {IS}}	S
	{IX, {IX}, {IS}}	IX
	{IS, {IS}}	IS

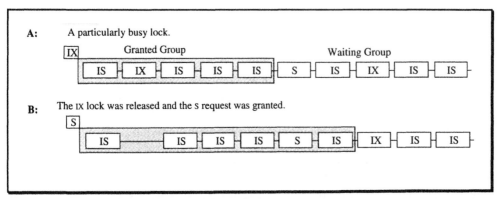

Figure 8.5: Depiction of a particularly popular lock.   The granted group consists of five requests; the waiting group also has five requests. The group mode is initially IX. When the IX mode request is unlocked, the group mode becomes IS and is compatible with the next waiting request; the S mode and IS mode requests join the granted group, and the group mode becomes S. The next waiting request, IX, is incompatible with the granted group and therefore must continue to wait.

Figure 8.5 depicts the queue for a particularly busy resource and shows the requests and their modes. When a new request for the resource arrives, the lock manager appends it to the end of the queue. There are two cases to consider. Either someone is waiting, or all outstanding requests for this resource are granted (no one is waiting). If no one is waiting and the new request is compatible with all grantees, then this request can be granted immediately. In any other case, the request cannot be granted immediately. If waiters exist, then this request must wait if FIFO scheduling is desired. If the requestor is unwilling to wait, then its request is removed from the queue. Otherwise, the request waits either until it is granted, until the wait times out, or until the system declares that the requestor is a deadlock victim. In the latter two cases, the request is canceled, and an error status is returned to the caller. The caller should then initiate rollback.

In the typical case, depicted in part B of Figure 8.5, the request is granted either immediately or after a short wait. An IX mode request departed from the granted group, causing the group mode to become IS. The first waiting request was an S mode request, which is compatible with the granted group. Thus it joined the group, making the group mode S. Similarly, the next mode was compatible and also joined the granted group. But the following request for IX mode is not compatible with the granted group. It will continue to wait for the group mode to return to IS or to FREE.

Lock conversions complicate the notions of granted group and waiting group; they also complicate the scheduling logic. A transaction can be granted a lock in one mode and then request it in another mode. As discussed in the previous chapter and depicted in Figure 8.6, lock conversion computes the maximum of the granted mode and the requested mode. Rerequests are converted to this maximum lock mode.

For example, a lock held in IX mode and then requested in S mode will be granted in SIX mode. The lock conversion matrix derived from Figure 8.4 is given in Figure 8.6. It shows that requesting an IX mode lock and then rerequesting the lock in S mode results in an SIX mode lock. Structuring the lock manager logic as tables (compatibility matrix, conversion matrix, granted group matrix, and so on) allows lock manager clients to invent new lock modes without slowing down the lock manager; all such computations are simply table lookups.

Lock Conversion Matrix							
		Granted Mode					
Requested Mode	None	IS	IX	S	SIX	U	X
IS	IS	IS	IX	S	SIX	U	X
IX	IX	IX	IX	SIX	SIX	X	X
S	S	S	SIX	S	SIX	U	X
SIX	SIX	SIX	SIX	SIX	SIX	SIX	X
U	U	U	X	U	SIX	U	X
X	X	X	X	X	X	X	X

Figure 8.6: Lock conversion matrix. If a lock is granted in one mode and requested in a second mode, the new request is treated as a request for the maximum of the two modes. This matrix derives from Figure 8.4.

Lock conversions need not be compatible with the granted group mode. Rather, a lock conversion needs to be compatible only with the granted modes of *other* members of the granted group. To see this, imagine that the requestor is the only member of the granted group. If the requestor's new request is not compatible with his old request, then it is also not compatible with the granted group mode (his new request might be for exclusive access). However, it is assumed that all of a transaction's requests are compatible with one another. A conversion need only wait until the converted mode is compatible with all requests granted to other transactions.

When conversions are waiting, no new members are admitted to the granted group until all conversions have been granted. After a conversion is granted, the transaction holds the lock in the converted mode. Immediately granting conversion requests and delaying waiting requests is a minor violation of FIFO scheduling.

An example may help clarify this explanation of scheduling conversion requests. In part A of Figure 8.7, the granted group mode is IX, and the second requestor in the group wants the lock in S mode. This translates to an SIX request (the maximum of IX and S); since SIX is compatible with the other granted modes, the request is granted immediately, and the granted group mode becomes SIX (Figure 8.7, part B). The first requestor then wants to convert his request from IS to IX. But IX is incompatible with SIX; therefore, this conversion request must wait (Figure 8.7, part C). In fact, several of the requestors leave the queue (Figure 8.7, part D) before the SIX request is released and the waiting conversion request is granted (Figure 8.7, part E).

8.4.3 Lock Duration and Lock Counts

Two more concepts, *lock class* and *lock count*, are needed before we discuss lock implementation in detail. Chapter 7 introduced the idea of *lock duration*—how long the lock is held. Some locks, called *long duration* locks, are held to transaction commit; others are released at the end of a particular operation and are lumped together as *short duration* locks.

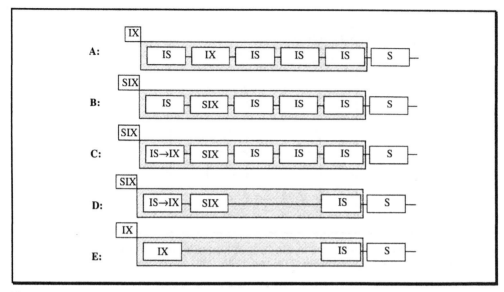

Figure 8.7: The history of a lock. The diagram shows the immediate granting of one conversion request (B), and the extended wait of a second request (C–E) because the conversion was incompatible with other members of the granted group.

Medium duration locks (e.g., the share locks held for cursor stability) are explicitly released; *very long duration* locks are held across transaction boundaries. At the other end of the spectrum, some callers want a combined lock-unlock operation, giving rise to *instant locks*—locks that are held only for an instant.

The possibilities seem endless. The lock manager supports these ideas with the *lock class* construct. Each lock is requested and held in some class. Instant, short, medium, long, and very long are examples of classes. The class names are represented as integers and are accordingly ranked: longer duration locks have larger class numbers. There is an unlock_class() call that will release all of a transaction's locks in a certain class, or all of a transaction's locks in that class and any lower class. This unlock applies to the transaction's locks acquired by a particular resource manager or to all the transaction's locks. Much as with lock modes, there is a kind of *class escalation*. A short lock can become a long lock. If a lock is held in one class and requested in a second, then the resulting class is the maximum of the two. Most of the lock classes are understood only by the resource managers. The lock manager recognizes and acts only on the following lock classes:

Instant. The lock operation immediately calls unlock on requests that are acquired for instant duration.

Long. Any lock in the long class or any class greater than long can be unlocked only by class (that class). Explicit unlock-by-name calls on long locks are ignored. The semantics are that long locks are held to transaction commit.

The actual defines for lock classes are as follows:

```
typedef int lock_class;    /* defines lock classes, also called lock duration          */
enum LOCK_CLASS {LOCK_INSTANT, LOCK_SHORT, LOCK_MEDIUM, LOCK_LONG, LOCK_VERY_LONG};
```

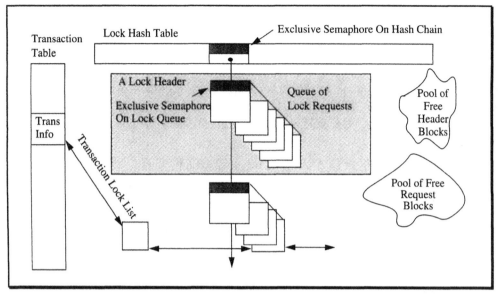

Figure 8.8: Schematic of the lock manager data structures. Lock names hash to a vector of buckets. Each bucket has a chain of locks, and each lock has a queue of requests. Because locks that are free (have no requests) consume no storage, only busy locks appear in the chain. Each transaction's requests are linked on an orthogonal structure, called the transaction lock list, anchored in the transaction table. Preallocated and pre-formatted pools of header blocks and request blocks are maintained to allow quick allocation and formatting of these blocks. The lightly shaded area represents a particular lock. Each hash chain and each lock queue has an exclusive semaphore to regulate access to that structure. The hash-chain semaphore protects access to the chain and to the lock names. The lock header semaphore protects access to other fields of the lock header and to the lock requests in the lock queue of that header.

The last concept is *lock count*. Resource managers may lock an item several times. For example, if multiple cursors belonging to a single transaction all point at the same SQL record, then that record will be locked by each cursor. If all locks have long duration, this is fine. But if locks are released prior to transaction commit, then the SQL resource manager wants a twice-locked record to remain locked after one unlock. That is, if two cursors lock the record and one cursor moves, the other cursor still has the record locked. The lock manager therefore keeps a count of how many times a record has been locked by each requestor. An unlock decrements the count for its requestor. If the count overflows, then the lock is made long duration.

8.4.4 Lock Manager Interface and Data Structures

As explained previously, the lock manager keeps a list of all requests for each lock. Figure 8.8 is a schematic of the lock manager data structures.

Lock hash table. The main lock data structure is the *lock hash table*. Each table entry has a pointer to a chain of locks, each with a name that maps to that hash bucket. Access to the chain and to the lock name field of each lock is protected by an exclusive semaphore located in the bucket header.

Free locks.   Free locks (ones with no outstanding requests or grants) are represented by their absence. That is, if the name lookup gets "not found," then the lock is free.

Lock header.   Busy locks have a *lock header* block that contains the lock name, a pointer to the next lock header in the hash chain, an exclusive semaphore to protect the lock queue, and other header information. The lock header also has some summary information about the lock queue. Free locks have no header or other data structures allocated to them.

Lock requests.   The lock points to a list of *lock requests*, each of which contains a description of the request (owner, mode, duration, and so on), a pointer to the lock header, a pointer to the next request, and pointers needed for the transaction lock list.

Transaction lock list.   The *transaction lock list* is a list of locks held by a transaction. Each list is anchored in the transaction table, where other descriptive information about the transaction is kept. The list enumerates all the locks of the transaction.

Pools.   The *lock header free pool* is a preallocated and pre-formatted pool of blocks for quick allocation. A similar *lock request pool* is also maintained.

Most of these structures have already been introduced. The transaction lock list is used to accelerate generic unlock operations. At transaction commit, it is necessary to find quickly all locks belonging to a transaction (they are all released at phase two of commit or at the end of rollback). In addition, the transaction lock list plays a role in transaction savepoints and in releasing all of a transaction's locks in a certain class (duration). To make it possible to quickly delete elements from the list, it is maintained as a doubly linked list.

Having gone through the detailed implementation of semaphores, we now turn to the implementation of locking at a higher level of abstraction. Locks support three basic calls: lock(), unlock(), and unlock_class(). The externals of these three procedures are described in the following section. Then the underlying data structures are defined. Finally, highlights of their implementations are presented.

8.4.4.1 Lock Manager Externals

A lock request specifies a lock name, a mode (shared, exclusive, and so on), a class (short, long, medium, and so on), and a timeout for waits. In addition, a lock request implicitly names a transaction, and a process. These global variables are the same in many calls; thus, they are not explicitly passed. The lock request returns either OK, timeout, or deadlock. If it returns OK, the lock was acquired. Otherwise, the lock was not acquired, and the request was canceled. In that case, the requestor should initiate rollback.

The necessary parameter types (names, modes, classes, and so on) for locks have already been defined. The resulting interface definition is as follows:

```
enum LOCK_REPLY {LOCK_OK , LOCK_TIMEOUT, LOCK_DEADLOCK, LOCK_NOT_LOCKED};
typedef int lock_reply;
lock_reply lock(lock_name name, lock_mode mode, lock_class class, long timeout );
```

The unlock operations are relatively simple: one unlocks a particular named resource, and the other unlocks all locks belonging to a certain class. Since these ideas have been described previously, the interfaces are presented here with little comment:

lock_reply **unlock(**lock_name **name);**   /*   */

To release all locks in a certain class (duration) or all locks in a class less than or equal to the specified class, the unlock_class() operation is called. The all_le parameter is a boolean and used to control unlocking of all classes below the specified class. In addition, the unlock can be restricted to a particular resource manager if the RMID is nonzero. If it is zero, the specified lock classes of all resource managers are unlocked.

lock_reply **unlock_class(**lock_class **class,** Boolean **all_le,** RMID **rmid);** /*   */

Additional lock complexity comes with transaction savepoints and nested transaction family locking. These topics are deferred until the basic lock manager functions have been explained.

8.4.5 Lock Manager Internal Logic

Given these lock externals, the lock data structures needed to implement the constructs of Figure 8.8 are simple. First, one needs the hash table. The table has a prime number of entries, and hashing is implemented as a remainder of a divide by that prime. Each entry of the table has an exclusive semaphore and pointer that anchors the hash chain. Thus, the structure is

```
#define MAXHASH 97
static struct {                         /* the lock table has MAXHASH entries             */
          xsemaphore  Xsem;             /* each entry is an exclusive semaphore           */
          lock_head *  chain;           /* and a list of all non-null locks with that hash */
          } lock_hash[MAXHASH];         /* allocates the lock hash array                  */
```

It is assumed that the following function computes the hash of a name:

long **lockhash(**lock_name **name);**

The hash chain points to a list of lock headers. Each header has the format

```
typedef struct {                        /* declare of lock header                         */
          xsemaphore   Xsem;            /* semaphore protecting the lock queue            */
          lock_head *  chain;           /* pointer to next in hash chain                  */
          lock_name    name;            /* the name of this lock                          */
          lock_request * queue;         /* the queue of requests for this lock            */
          lock_mode    granted_mode;    /* the mode of the granted group                  */
          Boolean      waiting;         /* flag indicates nonempty wait group             */
          } lock_head;                  /* is the head of a non-null lock queue           */
```

A pre-formatted pool of these blocks is maintained; there is a pair of functions to get one of them from the pool and format it, and a function to put the block back in the free pool. (This formatting is buried in these routines, so that the code here is not full of trivial assignment statements.) These two functions have logic similar to the get_block, give_block routines described earlier. They have the following interfaces:

lock_head * **lock_head_get**(lock_name **name**,lock_mode **mode);**

and

void **lock_head_give**(lock_head * **it**);

Each lock header points to a queue of lock request blocks. Each lock request block represents a granted or waiting request by a transaction. So the request block records all the fancy features discussed so far: modes, conversions, counts, and classes. In addition, the request block is linked on the transaction lock list so that all the lock requests of a particular transaction can quickly be found. Lock requests have a certain status.

```
enum LOCK_STATUS {LOCK_GRANTED , LOCK_CONVERTING , LOCK_WAITING, LOCK_DENIED};
typedef int lock_status;              /* takes on the values in the enumerated type       */
typedef struct {                      /* declare of lock request block                    */
        lock_request *  queue;        /* pointer to next request in lock queue            */
        lock_head *     head;         /* pointer back to head of the queue                */
        lock_status     status;       /* granted, waiting, converting, denied             */
        lock_mode       mode;         /* mode requested (and granted)                     */
        lock_mode       convert_mode; /* if in convert wait, mode desired                 */
        int             count;        /* count of the number of times lock was locked     */
        lock_class      class;        /* class in which lock is held (lock duration)      */
        PCB *           process;      /* process to wakeup when lock is granted           */
        TransCB *       tran;         /* pointer to transaction record                    */
        lock_request *  tran_prev;    /* previous lock request in transaction list        */
        lock_request *  tran_next;    /* next lock request in transaction list            */
        } lock_request;               /* represents a lock request by a transaction       */
```

As with lock headers, a pool of request blocks is maintained; there is a pair of functions to get these blocks from the pool, and one function to return a block to the free pool. They have the following interfaces:

lock_request * **lock_request_get**(lock_head *,lock_mode, lock_class);

and

void **lock_request_give**(lock_request * **it**);

These routines maintain the transaction lock list and format the other fields of the lock request block on the assumption that the lock will be granted to this transaction. Figure 8.9 may help you to visualize these structures. It shows a lock queue with several lock request blocks.

A descriptor is maintained for each transaction at this network node. The transaction descriptor has many fields that are of no interest to the lock manager; but the transaction lock list is anchored in the descriptor. In Section 8.6, the transaction family tree information is also represented by the descriptor. For present purposes, this is the transaction descriptor:

```
typedef struct{                                /*                                                    */
        lock_request *    locks;               /* anchor of transaction lock list                    */
        lock_request *    wait;                /* lock waited for by this transaction (or null)       */
        TransCB *         cycle;               /* used by deadlock detector (see below)               */
        /* stuff             */                /* other transaction information not relevant here     */
        } TransCB;                             /* represents the status of a transaction              */
```

The routine MyTransCBP() returns a pointer to the current transaction descriptor of the process. A transaction can run in many processes, and each process can execute on behalf of many transactions. At any instant, a process is executing for at most one transaction, the MyTransCBP() transaction.

Transaction and process are two independent concepts. The transaction is abstract— essentially a token that labels many locks and log records, as well as the execution steps of many processes. The process is a specific entity. It is the process that waits for a lock, and a process (program) that gets the wakeup when the lock is granted. The computation of a transaction may wait and deadlock, but it is actually some process executing on behalf of the transaction that waits and deadlocks. If there are threads within a process, and the threads wait and are woken up, then the idea is the same; all of these comments apply to threads (lightweight processes within a process) as well as to processes.

Lock() and Unlock() need additional routines to compute the compatibility of lock modes (lock_compat() from Figure 7.10), granted group modes (lock_max() from Figure 8.4), and lock conversion modes (from Figure 8.5). Refer to the figures for descriptions of these routines. With all these preliminaries out of the way, we can now have a look at the short version of the lock() routine.

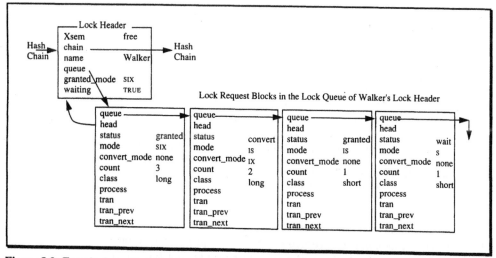

Figure 8.9: Four lock request blocks queued on a lock named Walker. Two requests are granted; one is waiting for a conversion, and one is waiting because the conversion is waiting. To simplify the display, some pointers are not diagrammed. Did the conversion arrive before the waiting s lock request?

```
/* short version of lock code (no conversions, no instant, no notify locks).          */
/* Returns ok, deadlock, or timeout                                                    */
lock_reply lock(lock_name name, lock_mode mode,lock_class class, long timeout) /*      */
    { long          bucket;                    /* index of hash bucket                 */
    lock_head *      lock;                      /* pointer to lock header block         */
    lock_request *   request, * last;           /* this lock request block & queue end  */
    TransCB *        me =MyTransCBP();          /* pointer to caller's transaction descriptor */
    lock_reply       error_num;                 /* error number in failed case          */
    bucket = lockhash(name);                    /* find hash chain                      */
    Xsem_get(&lock_hash[bucket].Xsem);          /* get semaphore on it                  */
    lock = lock_hash[bucket].chain;             /* traverse hash chain looking for lock */
    while ((lock != NULL) && (lock->name != name))  /* with this name                  */
        {lock = lock->chain;};                  /*                                      */
    /* lock is free case:                                                               */
    if (lock == NULL)                           /* if name not found then lock is free. */
        { lock = lock_head_get(name, mode);     /* allocate header and request blocks   */
        lock->queue = lock_request_get(lock,mode,class); /* chain them together         */
        lock->chain = lock_hash[bucket].chain;  /* add lock to hash chain               */
        lock_hash[bucket].chain = lock;         /*                                      */
        Xsem_give(&lock_hash[bucket].Xsem);     /* release hash chain and exit          */
        return (LOCK_OK);};                     /* end & exit of lock free case->>>>>>> */
    /* lock not free case:                                                              */
    Xsem_get(&lock->Xsem);                      /* acquire semaphore on lock queue      */
    Xsem_give(&lock_hash[bucket].Xsem);         /* release hash chain semaphore         */
    for (request = lock->queue; request != NULL; request = request->queue) /* is this a */
        {if (request->tran == me) break; last = request;}; /*conversion (rerequest)?   */
    /* a new request for this lock by this transaction                                  */
    if (request == NULL)                        /*                                      */
        {request = lock_request_get(lock,mode,class); /* allocate lock request block    */
        last->queue = request;                  /* put it at the end of the queue       */
        if ((! lock->waiting) && lock_compat(mode,lock->granted_mode)) /*               */
            /* new request: no wait case (compatible and no other waiters)              */
            { lock->granted_mode = lock_max(mode,lock->granted_mode);/* granted mode    */
            Xsem_give(&lock->Xsem);             /*give up lock semaphore                */
            return (LOCK_OK);                    /* and return to the caller             */
            }                                    /* end & exit of granted new case->>>>> */
        else /* new request: must wait case                                             */
            { lock ->waiting = TRUE;             /* mark this fact in the header status and */
            request->status = LOCK_WAITING;      /* and in the request status            */
            Xsem_give(&lock->Xsem);             /* release the lock semaphore and       */
            wait(timeout);                       /* wait                                 */
            error_num = request->status;         /*                                      */
            if error_num == LOCK_GRANTED         /* if lock granted                      */
                {return (LOCK_OK);}              /* return success (ignores instant locks) */
            if (error_num == LOCK_WAITING)       /* if request still waiting             */
                error_num = LOCK_TIMEOUT;        /* request timed out (wakeup was timer) */
            /* request denied                                                           */
            request->class = LOCK_INSTANT;       /* make sure the unlock will work       */
            unlock(name);                        /* use unlock to release the request    */
            return(error_num);}     /* tell the caller why it failed end & exit of new wait case->>>>>>>> */
                                                 /* end of new request case             */
        }
    /* re-request for this lock by this transaction (conversion case)                   */
    else {/* deal with lock conversions, not handled by this example */}; /*            */
    };                                           /*                                      */
```

The logic in this program does not cover conversions, instant locks, or notify locks, but it does cover most other aspects of a lock manager (timeout, denial of requests, and so on). As is the custom in this text, it does not have the parameter and result testing typical of

---

This page set on tighter interline spacing at authors' request.

defensive programming (which would make the program 30% bigger and no easier to read). In its current form, the program shows how lock headers are allocated, how requests join the queue, and how requests wait. It even shows how requests are denied and release their locks.[5]

The logic required to deal with conversions is not substantially different from the code just provided and is therefore not included. You might try writing it to test your understanding of the data structures. The request must wait if it is incompatible with anyone in the granted group; otherwise, it is identical to the wait case except that the mode must be upgraded, the count incremented, and the class (duration) set to the maximum of the granted and requested class.

The simple lock release case, unlock(), follows. Again, it does not deal with lock conversions but otherwise is fairly complete. Several optimizations have been left out to make the code shorter. One surprising thing is that unlock is slightly more complex than lock. This is true in the full-length program as well. Unlock must deal with more cases having to do with wakeup.

```
/* unlock code, does not handle convert waits.                                                       */
lock_reply unlock(lock_name name)               /*                                                   */
    { long            bucket;                    /* index of hash bucket                              */
    lock_head * lock, * prev = NULL;             /* pointer to lock header block                      */
    lock_request *    request;                   /* current lock request block in queue              */
    lock _request *   prev_req = NULL;           /*Prev lock request block in queue                   */
    TransCB *         me =MyTransCBP();          /* pointer to caller's transaction descriptor        */
    lock_reply        status;                    /* error number in failed case                       */
    /* find the requestor's request                                                                   */
    bucket = lockhash(name);                     /* find hash chain                                   */
    Xsem_get(&lock_hash[bucket].Xsem);           /* get semaphore on it                               */
    lock = lock_hash[bucket].chain;              /* traverse hash chain looking for lock              */
    while ((lock != NULL) && (lock->name != name)) /* with this name                                  */
        {prev = lock; lock = lock->chain;};      /* get next header in chain.                         */
    if (lock == NULL) { goto B;};                /* if name not found then lock is free.              */
    /* found lock, look for request belonging to the caller in the lock queue                         */
    Xsem_get(&lock->Xsem);                       /* acquire semaphore on lock queue                   */
    for (request = lock->chain; request != NULL; request = request->queue) /* find req in queue       */
        {if (request->tran == me) break; prev_req = request;}; /* and set prev_req                    */
    if (request == NULL) { goto A;};             /* if my request not found, then lock free           */
```

---

[5] The program has a delicate feature, which will certainly test the reader's understanding. What happens if there is a race condition between the wait timing out and the lock being granted? In particular, what happens if the status is read saying wait, and immediately afterwards the lock is asynchronously granted to this process? The behavior is correct, but perhaps not desirable. Race conditions like these make designing such code difficult. Since they are rare, they should be dealt with as simply as possible.

```
        /* found it, if >= long class, unlock is a null operation.                          */
        if (request-> class >= LOCK_LONG || request->count > 1) /* if long duration or count > 1,  */
            { request->count = request->count - 1; goto A;};   /* then no release, decrement count */
        /* end of no op cases where nothing changed                                          */
        if (lock->queue == request && request->queue == NULL) /*if mine is only request      */
            { if (prev == NULL) lock_hash[bucket].chain = lock->chain; /* free the lock       */
            else prev->chain = lock->chain;              /* remove it from chain              */
            lock_head_give(lock);                        /* deallocate header block           */
            lock_request_give(request);                  /* deallocate request block          */
            goto B;};                                    /* exit sole owner case ->>>>>>>>>   */
    /* interesting case: granted group not null when this request leaves                     */
        if (prev_req!= NULL) prev_req->queue = request->queue; /* remove my request           */
        else lock->queue = request->queue;              /*                                    */
        lock_request_give(request);                     /* and return it to free list         */
        lock->waiting = FALSE; lock->granted_mode = LOCK_FREE; /* reset lock header           */
        /*traverse lock queue: compute granted group, wake compatible waiters                */
        for (request = lock->queue; request != NULL; request = request->queue) /*             */
            { if (request->status == LOCK_GRANTED)      /* if req granted, add to granted mode */
                lock->granted_mode = lock_max(request->mode,lock->granted_mode); /*           */
            else if (request->status == LOCK_WAITING)   /* if request waiting then            */
                { if (lock_compat(request->mode,lock->granted_mode)) /*if compat with granted */
                    { request->status = LOCK_GRANTED;   /* grant it, upgrade granted mode     */
                    lock->granted_mode = lock_max(request->mode,lock->granted_mode); /*       */
                    wakeup(request->process); }         /* and wake up process                */
                else                                    /* if request is incompatible then FIFO */
                    { lock->waiting = TRUE;             /* implies it and all successors must wait */
                    break; }}                           /* so exit the wakeup loop and return  */
            else {/* convert waits not handled */};     /* this case not handled here          */
            }                                           /* end of loop on lock queue           */
A:  Xsem_give(&lock->Xsem);                             /* release lock semaphore              */
B:  Xsem_give(&lock_hash[bucket].Xsem);                 /* release hash bucket semaphore       */
    return (LOCK_OK);                                   /* return to caller                    */
    };                                                  /* end of unlock code                  */
```

The lock and unlock routines did not deal with lock conversion. There is nothing novel about the lock conversion code beyond what was said in the text: it is just more of the same. It is possible to do a simple deadlock detection inside the lock code (if two conversions form a deadlock), but that seems the only notable thing about the lock-unlock conversion code.

The code just given has only one optimization—it is optimized for simplicity of presentation. In practice, each of the five main lock cases must be fast. These cases are: (lock 1) acquiring a free lock, (lock 2) joining a lock queue with no waiting, (lock 3) rerequesting a lock with no waiting, (unlock 1) freeing a lock, and (unlock 2) freeing a lock request in a still-active lock with no wakeups. The other paths involve wait() or wakeup() and thus are viewed as rare and not performance sensitive. The typical requirement is that each of the frequent lock-unlock pairs should cost less than 300 instruction units—which is hard to do. Typical first attempts are 1,000 instructions per pair. The heavy use of compare-and-swap (up to 8 semaphore operations, and up to 4 pool operations, for a total of 12 uses) is a real problem, since those instructions often are the equivalent of 20 ordinary instructions.

An important optimization is for lock clients (the resource managers) to keep a cache of recently requested locks to minimize their rerequesting the same lock. For example, the cursor code of page-locking systems only calls the lock manager when it crosses page boundaries, rather than calling unlock(page)-lock(page) each time it moves from record to record. It also caches the fine-granularity IS mode or IX mode locks, so that they are requested only once. With a combination of such techniques the lock manager can be kept well below 10% of the application pathlength, which seems to be be the threshold of pain.

8.4.6 Lock Escalation and Generic Unlock, Notify Locks

The management of the pools of lock headers and lock requests has been discussed only briefly. Either the lock request asks the operating system for space as needed within the lock code, or an asynchronous task allocates and formats the blocks. In either case, there needs to be some limit on the number of locks a particular transaction or transaction-resource manager pair can acquire. The lock manager maintains a count of the locks held by the transaction (the length of the transaction lock list). When this count becomes large—say, 1,000 or 10,000 locks—the lock manager attempts *escalation*: the conversion of many fine-granularity locks into a single coarse-granularity lock.

Historically, escalation has been done in an ad hoc way, and perhaps that is the way it will always be. Escalation is something the lock manager must negotiate with the resource manager. The following is an abstraction of the several ad hoc designs we have seen. (No actual system works this way, but one might.) First, a count of locks held per transaction per resource manager is kept. If some transaction–resource manager pair tries to exceed the limit, then the request is denied with an escalation_needed error. The resource manager then needs a way to find all the locks it has for the transaction and to pick a single name that will cover them all (e.g., replace record locks with a file lock). This is the basic routine:

```
struct Buffer {                           /* buffer to get description of transaction's locks   */
        lock_name   name;                 /* name of a lock held by this transaction-rmid pair  */
        lock_mode   mode;                 /* mode in which lock is held                         */
        } buffer [ESCALATION_LIMIT];      /*                                                    */
void locks(rmid,trid, count,buffer);      /* Returns lock names and modes of this rm-trans pair. */
```

Calling the locks() routine allows a resource manager to enumerate the locks of a resource manager–transaction pair, pick a coarser lock, lock it, and then call unlock on the escalated locks. That is escalation.

The unlock() code just given unlocks a particular lock. Resource managers like to deal with sets of locks by class (duration). To do generic unlock, either at end of transaction or at other events, the following routine is provided. It traverses the caller's transaction lock list and calls unlock on each qualifying request.

```
lock_reply unlock_class(lock_class class, Boolean all_le, RMID rmid);   /*                          */
    {lock_head *        lock;                       /* pointer to lock header block                    */
    lock_request *      request, * next;            /* pointers to this lock request block & next      */
    TransCB *           me = MyTransCBP();          /* pointer to caller's transaction descriptor      */
    for (request = me->locks; request != NULL; request = next)      /* for each request               */
        { next = request->tran_next;                /* remember the next one                           */
        lock = request->head;                       /* point at the lock header                        */
        if ( request->class == class  ||            /* if duration matches or if the class is less     */
            (request->class < class && all_le))     /* and the all_le option is chosen then see if     */
        if ( rmid == 0 || lock->name.rmid == rmid ) /* the resource manager id is generic              */
            { request->class = LOCK_INSTANT;        /* or matches. If so set the lock class to         */
            request->count = 1;                     /* instant and the count to 1 and then call        */
            unlock(lock->name);                     /* unlock                                          */
        };   };                                     /* bottom of loop on transaction lock list         */
    return;                                         /*                                                 */
    };                                              /*                                                 */
```

This almost completes the discussion of implementing locks for flat transactions. The one remaining topic is *notify locks*. Recall that some clients want to be notified when the status of a lock changes. Therefore, they request the lock in *notify mode*. This lock mode is compatible with all other lock modes and, in general, acts like the free lock mode. To support notify locks, the lock header is modified with a boolean flag that says, "There is a notify lock in the granted group." When this boolean flag is true, successful unlock operations and conflicting lock operations search the granted group for such notify requests and wake up the corresponding process to notify it that the object may have changed. Otherwise, no special support is needed for notify locks. The VMS lock manager is a good example of this [Snamann and Thiel 1987].

8.4.7 Transaction Savepoints, Commit, and Rollback

A transaction's shared mode locks (S, IS, U) can be released at the end of phase 1 of commit,[6] and all remaining locks, except for very long duration locks, can be released at the end of phase 2. This can be done in one of two ways: (1) Each resource manager can use the generic unlock routine to ask the lock manager to release all the resource manager's locks for that transaction, or (2) the lock manager can join the transaction and thereby get prepare, commit, and abort callbacks from the transaction manager when the transaction changes state. Either approach is valid. The first approach gives the resource manager more control, while the second approach provides a simpler interface to the resource manager.

---

[6] It is difficult to detect the end of phase 1 of commit, since one resource manager may invoke another as part of phase 1. A resource manager may be called to do additional work after that resource manager has voted to commit the transaction. This situation is called *rejoining the transaction* or *reinfecting the resource manager*. This problem argues against releasing any locks during phase 1 of commit.

The lock manager must help support *transaction savepoints*. Recall that transaction savepoints are declared during the serial execution of the transaction. The beginning of the transaction is a savepoint, and the commit of the transaction is another savepoint; there may be others, as well. Typically, the start of each complex SQL operation is a savepoint. Every user input during a conversational transaction can be a savepoint. A transaction can roll back to a savepoint. That is how SQL gets statement atomicity—if anything goes wrong within a complex statement, the SQL executor rolls back to the savepoint that began the statement. The rollback cleans up (undoes) all the statement's work.

At each savepoint, it is necessary to save the transaction state so that the state can be restored later. From a locking perspective, this state restoration consists of unlocking resources acquired since the savepoint and reacquiring locks released since the savepoint. The unlock is optional, but the reacquisition of released locks is essential.

Savepoint unlock is easily implemented, and many designs are possible. A simple one is to insert a dummy lock request block in the transaction lock list at each savepoint. After rollback to a savepoint, all locks after the dummy lock request block in the transaction lock list (except for lock escalations) are released. This design does not handle conversions or escalations, but it releases most new locks.

Reacquiring locks released since the savepoint is more difficult. One design has the resource manager remember, in the savepoint log record, the names of the resources needing such locks. At rollback, the savepoint log record is read and an attempt is made to reacquire the locks. If reacquisition is successful, the rollback to the savepoint is a success. If the locks cannot be reacquired, then the rollback fails, and a further rollback is initiated. In the System R and DB2 approach, the cursor manager rerequests the locks for each cursor when the transaction returns to the savepoint. Similar savepoint designs are present in R*, SQL/DS, Ingres, and presumably other systems. Alternatively, the lock manager could write a log record recording all the locks of the transaction. That is the design used in the recovery management section of this book (Chapters 10–11).

Lock names are a delicate issue. If the lock name of a resource can change over time, then the lock manager cannot safely (correctly) record the lock names in the log. Recall that the lock manager does not understand lock names. It is given a hash of the object name. In the example of how lock names are used (Subsection 8.4.1), lock names included open file numbers. In that design, if a file were unlocked, closed, and then reopened during the transaction's life, the hashed lock name for a record in the file would be different the second time around (it would have a different file number). Only the resource manager understands this. Therefore, the resource manager must either write the lock savepoint records, recording the ⟨name, mode, class, count⟩ of each lock, or implement durable lock names that do not change over time.

8.4.8 Locking at System Restart

Ordinarily, the lock manager has little to do at system restart. It allocates and initializes its data structures and starts accepting lock requests. If periodic deadlock detection is supported, it starts the deadlock detection process.

There are two standard assumptions in classic transaction processing systems that make the lock manager's life much simpler:

(1) Any uncommitted transactions can be aborted.

(2) There are relatively few active transactions (hundreds).

The two-phase commit protocol invalidates these assumptions for systems supporting distributed transactions, since it can leave a transaction *in doubt* at restart—the transaction is neither committed nor aborted. The locks of in-doubt transactions must be reestablished at restart if the transaction outcome cannot be resolved at that point. Transactions may be in doubt for months. They cannot be aborted unilaterally by the system, and there may be many of them.

Reestablishing the locks of in-doubt transactions at restart is much like reestablishing locks for savepoints: each in-doubt transaction is returned to its commit phase 1 savepoint. Only the commit phase 1 locks—the exclusive mode locks and their parents in the lock hierarchy—need to be reacquired. As with savepoints, the resource managers record these locks in a savepoint log record at commit phase 1, or the lock manager writes a log record summarizing all the transaction's locks. These locks are described as a {⟨name, mode, class, count⟩} set. At restart, locks are reacquired for in-doubt transactions.

The presence of in-doubt transactions can take the active transaction count from the realm of hundreds to the realm of thousands, which begins to invalidate the assumption of relatively few active transactions.

8.4.9 Phoenix Transactions

There is considerable interest in designs that allow the state of some active transactions to survive system restarts and, in fact, to persist for days or years. This state is variously called the *transaction context* or *persistent storage*, and the corresponding transactions are known as *long-lived transactions* or *phoenixes*. These are the next logical step in the progression from flat transactions through savepoints and in-doubt transactions. What is desired is the ability to restart such uncommitted transactions after a crash. The techniques for reestablishing the transaction context are discussed in the recovery and transaction monitor sections (Chapters 5–6 and 10–11) of this book. Support for in-doubt transactions brings with it almost complete support for long-lived transactions; very little extra lock code is needed. If savepoints can survive system restarts, then by restarting the application process, the system can reinstantiate the transaction.

Lock restart of in-doubt transactions merely reestablishes the transaction's locks, but the persistent savepoint mechanism is designed to reconstruct the entire transaction state if rollback to that savepoint is requested. Therefore, the combined support of savepoints and in-doubt transactions comes very close to support for phoenixes.

Heavy use of phoenixes will violate the basic lock manager assumption that there are few transactions and relatively few locks. In such a system, the lock manager will have to operate in the realm of 10^5 active transactions and 10^7 active locks. The implementation presented here would certainly crumble under such a load. In fact, the basic premise that most locks are free most of the time might be violated. A system that supports many phoenixes will have to refine the notions of lock compatibility or perhaps take an entirely different approach to isolation. But this seems very far in the future when compared to the primitive state of transaction processing in 1991.

In summary, the lock manager's duties at restart are growing. They used to be nonexistent, but modern lock managers must cooperate in reestablishing the locks of in-doubt transactions and phoenixes. The savepoint mechanism is the vehicle for this.

8.4.10 Lock Manager Configuration and Complexity

The lock manager has minimal configuration parameters. It needs to know the escalation limits for each resource manager. If periodic deadlock detection is done, it needs to know the period. It automatically computes pool sizes for preallocated blocks from the default multiprogramming level and a fraction of the escalation limits. All these values are defaulted so that no configuration is needed. They may be changed to reconfigure (tune) the lock manager.

The whole body of lock code (semaphores and lock routines, along with a deadlock detector and all their startup code), written with all the requisite defensive programming, exception handlers, optimizations, and comments, comes to about 3,000 lines of text—about 1 *KLOC* (thousand lines of code with comments excluded). By hacker standards, this is hardly a large program.

8.4.11 Lock Manager Summary

That's what a lock manager looks like. Starting with semaphores, it builds data structures to track named locks. The locks can be requested in various modes for various durations. A set of tables define lock compatibility and lock conversions. A list of granted and waiting lock requests is kept for each lock. All the locks of a transaction are kept in a list so they can be quickly found and released at commit or rollback.

8.5 Deadlock Detection

Lock waiting can create a *deadlock*—a cycle in which each process is waiting for a lock held by the next process in the cycle. As mentioned in the previous chapter, timeout is the universal deadlock detector and is used by most systems. But it is easy enough to add another deadlock detector in addition to timeout. Such a detector will find deadlocks earlier and perhaps will be more equitable in picking deadlock victims than timeout, which picks a random victim, has been.

The lock data structures have all the information needed to detect deadlocks involving locks. Recall that deadlocks can involve other resources not covered by locking, such as tape drives (or removeable disk drives), communications sessions, servers, terminal input, and so on. Lock-oriented deadlock detection can be *local*, in which case only local deadlocks are sought, or it can be *global,* in which case elements of the wait-for graphs from many nodes (lock or resource managers) are gathered and glued together. In addition, deadlock detection can be *periodic*, or it can be done *on demand* when any requestor waits. The logic for a very simple deadlock detector, a local and periodic one, follows. It does not deal with conversions and assumes that all the lock data structures are static (i.e., it does not acquire semaphores on the lock data structures). To make this deadlock detector work while locks are being acquired and released, semaphores would have to be added to the transaction lock list, and the code would have to acquire semaphores on the transaction lock lists and lock queues as it proceeded.

When a cycle is found, something must be done about it: the deadlock must be resolved. This program merely enumerates the cycles. It is presented to show how simple deadlock detection can be. A real deadlock detector handling all the cases would be 200 lines of code, not 20, but the program is simple to write by most standards. It uses the same ideas and some of the same code found in the lock and unlock routines to decide who is compatible with whom and, consequently, who is waiting for whom.

First, recall the definition of the transaction descriptor:

```
typedef struct {                           /*                                              */
          lock_request *    locks;         /* anchor of transaction lock list              */
          lock_request *    wait;          /* lock waited for by this transaction (or null) */
          TransCB *         cycle;         /* used by deadlock detector (see below)        */
          } TransCB;                       /* describes trans waits for other trans graph  */
```

Using these fields, here is a simple deadlock detector:

```
/* This is a simple deadlock detector that assumes the lock data structures are not changing.   */
/* A depth-first search of the wait-for graph enumerates all cycles (each is found many times)  */
#define NTRANS BIG                          /* define an array of all the transaction       */
TransCB tran[NTRANS];                       /* descriptors. This is the array used by locks */
/* Visit is the recursive routine that visits each waited-for transaction. When visit is called, */
/* trans[].cycle holds a linked list of all transactions in the call chain so far, that is a list of */
/* transactions waiting for this one.                                                           */
void visit(TransCB * me)                    /* me is the transaction being waited for       */
    { TransCB *  him;                       /* him is some transaction me is waiting for     */
    lock_request *    them;                 /* them is a cursor on the lock queue of me      */
    if (me->wait == NULL) return;           /* not in deadlock if me not waiting.            */
    them = ((me->wait)->head)->queue;       /* scan over the lock queue holding me           */
    while (them->tran != me)                /* look at everyone ahead of me in the queue     */
        { if (!compat (them->mode,me->wait-> mode) || /* I'm waiting for him if we are incompatible */
            them->status ! = GRANTED)       /* or if he is waiting                           */
            { him = them->tran;             /* look at his transaction record                */
            me->cycle = him;                /* me is waiting for him                         */
            if (him->cycle != NULL)         /* if he is in the cycle, DEADLOCK               */
                {/*DECLARE DEADLOCK CYCLE HIM waits for ME*/} /*                              */
            else visit(him);                /* if not cycle, look deeper                     */
            me->cycle =NULL;                /* when he returns, remove me from cycle         */
            them=them->queue;               /* examine next in queue                         */
            };                              /* end case he is incompatible with me           */
        };                                  /* end of searching my lock queue                */
    return;                                 /*                                               */
    }                                       /* end of recursive tree search                  */
```

```
/* the deadlock detector                                                    */
deadlock ();                                    /*                          */
    { long i;                                   /* index on tran array      */
    for (i = 0; i < NTRANS; i++) {tran[i].cycle = NULL;}; /* clear the stack */
    for (i = 0; i < NTRANS; i++)                /* for each transaction      */
        visit(&tran[i]);                        /* look for deadlocks        */
    return;                                     /* done.                     */
    };                                          /*                          */
```

Several exercises are built around this example. If the deadlock detector is to be used in a global algorithm, then it must enumerate all the global paths. These paths can be pushed to the next node in the path—a kind of depth-first search—or they can be collected centrally.

In any case, the critical issue for deadlock detection is not detection but *resolution*. How are victims chosen? Timeout picks victims at random; deadlock detection should pick them with more intelligence. Thus, the set of all cycles should be examined, and a low-cost cut set should be found. This, in turn, requires that there be a cost associated with rolling back each transaction. It is easy enough to place such a cost field in the transaction record, but it is not clear how the field should be filled in. Should it contain priority? Log length (undo work)? Seniority? This is an area in which we have no particular advice.

8.6 Locking for Parallel and Parallel Nested Transactions

Chapters 10 and 11 explain how the lock manager supports transaction commit and system restart. Those chapters show that the lock manager has little difficulty supporting savepoints, in-doubt transactions, and even long-lived transactions. Such support is common in production systems today.

The features that really complicate locking are parallelism within transactions and within nested transactions. Nested transactions without parallelism are, in fact, just simple savepoints. Thus, it is parallelism or parallelism-plus-nesting that creates problems. Let us discuss them in turn.

If there is parallelism within a transaction and the transaction is flat in the sense that it has no savepoints or nesting, then the lock manager must be very careful in manipulating the transaction lock list. The code for lock and unlock used the get_lock_request() routine that had the logic to place the request on the transaction lock list. The code would have to use a semaphore to serialize updates to the transaction lock list if there were parallelism within the transaction. The locking section code was designed to deal with processes rather than with transactions, and therefore it can deal with multiple processes executing on behalf of a transaction. On the other hand, the deadlock detector would be made more complex by such parallelism, since all its underlying data structures would be in transit. Of course, parallel applications using the lock manager must also be very careful, since processes within a transaction are not isolated from one another.

At any rate, parallelism without nested transactions is so complex that few are likely to want to use it outside of very limited contexts. Parallel SQL systems, such as Teradata and NonStop SQL, use parallelism either for read-only queries or in very carefully controlled update cases (e.g., parallel index maintenance or parallel updates to disjoint subsets of a table). It is more likely that a system implementing parallel transactions will actually implement some form of parallel nested transactions. In such designs, there is no parallelism within a subtransaction (an atomic, consistent, isolated unit). The whole transaction may have parallelism, but each process within the computation has its own subtransaction. The set of all transactions forms a family tree of transactions. It is easy to invent a scheme that allows each subtransaction to inherit locks from its ancestors in the tree and then to anti-inherit locks when the subtransaction completes. Having spent hours discussing various designs, we concluded that this is well beyond the state of the art. To our knowledge, no one has implemented and used parallel nested transactions in an application system. A single paragraph will therefore suffice to explain a possible design.

Beginning a subtransaction gets a new TRID (transaction identifier), which becomes a child of the currently active transaction of this process. The transaction identifier is augmented to hold the family path, consisting of the family name (TRID of the root record) and the TRIDs of all ancestors of this transaction in the family tree. The lock routine logic looks to see if the caller's family matches the family of some transaction already granted the lock; if so, this is treated as a rerequest for the lock and, accordingly, is not scheduled in FIFO order. Rather, the caller tries to inherit the lock from the family member. If the owner is an ancestor of the caller (in the family tree), then the lock is granted. (Ownership is transferred to the caller by making the trans field of the lock request block point to the caller's transaction record, and by putting the request on the caller's transaction lock list.) If the owner is a family member, but not an ancestor, then the caller must wait for an unlock by that family member (the owner). Thus, the caller queues his request on the family member's lock request and waits. The implicit assumption of this lock inheritance is that if the child is running, the parent is not running and hence does not need the lock. This assumption is invalid for all parallel systems we have seen and used.

The unlock logic is much more subtle. At subtransaction end (subcommit) the child's locks are given to the parent. This means that the parent gets the child's transaction lock list. The simplest way is to fill in the child's trans record with the parent's name. In addition, one or more family-related waiting requests can now be granted. If several such requests are queued, then a scheduling policy should be adopted. We have no clear idea how conflicting requests should be granted—perhaps they should be FIFO, perhaps nearest in tree. On rollback, the logic is similar, except that inherited locks are given back to the parent but newly acquired locks are released. Many of the issues of compatibility, counting locks, conversion, escalation, and lock scheduling for nested transactions have not been worked out. This is a field of active research.

8.7 Summary

This chapter first explained the typical atomic instructions available on most processors (compare-and-swap). It showed how to use those instructions to implement exclusive semaphores, shared semaphores, and a shared storage manager. Then a simple lock manager, which makes heavy use of semaphores, was described in considerable detail. The presentation was designed to convince you that you could write a lock manager and even write a deadlock detector for the centralized case, if you had to.

8.8 Historical Notes

The first multiprocessors, circa 1960, had test and set instructions (e.g., the Burroughs 5000). Presumably, the operating systems implementors worked out the appropriate algorithms, although Dijkstra is generally credited with inventing semaphores many years later. The compare-and-swap instructions first appeared in the IBM System/370. There have been innumerable papers on how to avoid using compare-and-swap, but so far as we know, this is the first attempt to explain how to use it. Of course, the instructions themselves are known to systems programmers the world over. The shared and exclusive semaphore logic is taken from the authors' implementation in System R. The discussion of functional recovery routines and the strategy for handling process recovery is due largely to Bob Jackson; it is implemented within IBM's MVS, although similar techniques were no doubt developed for AT&T's Electronic Switching System.

Many people have implemented lock managers. Those who maintained and supported the resulting code (often a different cast of characters) deserve most of the credit. Even well-designed lock managers have some of the most difficult bugs. If the history of lock managers has one lesson, it is this: *don't get stuck maintaining a lock manager, and if you do, take out all the optimizations and fancy features as a first step*. The lock manager described here derives from one designed by the authors along with Franco Putzolu and Paul McJones. Franco worked out the lock-naming scheme and the savepoint mechanism. Bruce Lindsay maintained it for a while. Bruce fixed the "last" bug in it about 10 years after the first bug was fixed, and just a few months before the lock manager was mothballed. Our explanation of how IMS program isolation works comes from discussions with its author, Ron Obermarck. The Tandem lock manager, implemented by Andrea Borr and Franco Putzolu, provided some guidance on the emphasis in this chapter.

The discussion of parallel nested transactions owes an obvious debt to the Camelot group in general, and to Dan Duchamp in particular, for his chapter on how nested transactions work in the Camelot system [Eppinger, Mummert, and Spector 1991]. The one-paragraph design described here is an abstract of his work.

Exercises

1. [8.1, 5] Write an execution history (in the sense discussed in Chapter 7) showing the lost update problem for parallel executions of the code following fragment.

```
temp = counter + 1;                      /*                                    */
counter = temp;                          /*                                    */
```

2. [8.1, 5] Implement test and set , using compare-and-swap. That is, write a routine that will automatically set a word to TRUE if it is FALSE. If the word is TRUE, the routine does nothing. The routine returns a boolean indicating whether the test and set changed the word.

3. [8.3.1, 5] Two words in two nonadjacent locations cannot be atomically updated with one compare-and-swap instruction. As a simple example, consider the following structure, which tracks the cash balance of each of 10 tellers in a bank branch and also tracks the branch balance, which is the sum of the teller balances:

```
static struct   {   int   sum;          /* the sum of all the tellers cash position       */
                    int   teller[10];   /* teller[i] is the cash position of the i'th teller */
                    }branch;            /* branch table is global to the routine.          */
```

Write the program DebitCredit(int i, int delta) that atomically adds delta to teller[i] and to the branch.

4. [8.3.1, 15] (a) Add the logic for multiprocessor spin logic to Xsem_get. (A spin lock is a lock in which the requestor does not wait, it just reissues denied requests. If the cost of dispatching is high, it may make sense for a shared-memory multiprocessor system to spin for a few cycles prior to waiting.) Do an analytic model to decide what the right spin duration is. *Hint: Postulate an average duration and an average dispatch cost.* (b) New problem: what if the semaphore is a hotspot (has ~ 100% utilization)?

5. [8.3.1, 15] Locking used a FIFO scheduler because that is the simplest fair scheduler. The Xsem code is also FIFO, and thus fair. But the broadcast code to avoid convoys is not fair. Give an example of how one process could "starve" (never be granted the resource). Is this a bad thing?

6. [8.3.2, 5] What is wrong with the following code to scan to the end of a list of pages, each protected by a semaphore? Assume pages may be inserted into and deleted from the list while you are reading it, but assume that the root pointer is never updated. Fix the program.

```
typedef       {   Xsem    sem;          /* Exclusive semaphore to control branch access   */
                  page *  next_page;    /* pointer to next page in the list, or NULL      */
                  char    stuff;        /* ignore this                                    */
                  } page;               /* a semaphore protected linked list of pages     */
page *    root;                         /* the root of the page list                      */
page *    next;                         /* a cursor on the page list                      */
next = &root;                           /* start at the root                              */
while (next != NULL)                    /* scan to the end of the list                    */
    {Xsem_get(&next->sem);              /* get the page semaphore                         */
    next = next->next_page;             /* get the next pointer                           */
    Xsem_give(&next->sem);};            /* release the page semaphore                     */
```

7. [8.3.3, 5] In the implementation of sem_get(), what prevents starvation? Is that what prevents a new share-mode request from being granted immediately if there are other processes waiting?

8. [8.3.3, 15] Change the design of shared semaphores (allowing convoys) to provide FIFO scheduling (or nearly FIFO scheduling) of requests.

9. [8.3.3, 10] Why is crabbing not required as the process that is granting the shared semaphore to the waiters traverses the wait list, waking up each process in turn?

10. [8.3.3, 10] Semaphore code is called frequently. What part of it should be made in line (i.e., no subroutine calling overhead)? In one system, this trick brought the cost of a semaphore get-give from over 150 instructions down to 14, speeding the system up by 25% and reducing the semaphore code overhead from 30% of the pathlength to 5%.

11. [8.3.3, 15] The semaphore logic to avoid convoys by broadcasting creates a kind of lazy busy wait. What are the pros and cons of this broadcast? Is it always a good idea? Do an analytic model to justify your answers.

12. [8.3.3, 15] Write the program for sem_get_bounce() modeled on sem_get(). It acquires the semaphore immediately, if possible, and returns the outcome to the caller. Its interface is

Boolean **sem_get_bounce**(semaphore * **sem**, lock_mode **mode**)   /*   */

13. [8.3.4, 10] Both Xsem_init() and sem_init() did ordinary (nonatomic) stores into the semaphores. What is wrong with that?

14. [8.3.4, 15] Consider the bad_get_block() routine. Assume that there are 100 processes on 100 parallel 1 mips processors that acquire and free blocks at random, but never go below 0 blocks or above 101 blocks. Assume 10,100 blocks have been allocated, so that panic is never called. Assume 1 process runs 1,000 times slower than the others. Do an analysis or simulation to determine the average time between failures of the bad_get_block algorithm.

15. [8.3.4, 15] The good block_get() routine has one problem: starvation. It is conceivable that so many kilroys are around that no CSD ever executes before some other process smashes the kilroy field with its ID. Devise two solutions for this problem.

16. [8.3.5, project] Write a functional recovery routine for the lock manager. That is, if it gets an exception, try to clean up the lock state and the semaphore state. *Hint: Keep careful track of the algorithm state in a special block (called the foot print) so that the exception handler can clean up the state.*

17. [8.4.2, 5] Where do notify locks fit in the graph of Table 8.4?

18. [8.4.3, 5] To make the unlock() code simple, all the semaphore release calls were put at the end (exit). This causes the hash chain to be locked for much longer than is needed. What is the soonest the hash chain can be unlocked in unlock() code?

19. [8.4.3, 5] Find two cases, other than parameter-result checking, where unlock() is not failfast and it should be.

20. [8.4.3, 20] (a) Write the code to allocate and free lock request blocks from a pool. Include code to format them and chain them to the transaction lock list. (b) Modify the code to allow parallel execution of transactions; that is, place an exclusive semaphore on the transaction lock list and modify the code to acquire and release it.

21. [8.4.3, 20] Add the logic to handle conversion requests to the lock() and unlock() code.

22. [8.4, 15] The deadlock detector assumes no data structures are changing. In fact, it is running concurrently with transactions that are changing the lock structures. Modify the declare for the trans structure to include an exclusive semaphore, and modify the code to use that semaphore and the lock-head semaphores. If you can avoid using the hash-chain semaphore, explain why (watch out for unlocks). Try not to hold semaphores on lock queues that are deep in the deadlock detector's stack. In addition, watch out for the following semaphore deadlock: (1) deadlock detector locks transaction lock list, then lock header, (2) transaction locks lock header, then locks transaction lock list (when adding lock to list). Assume throughout that a transaction executes in a single process. Waiting transactions are not executing.

23. [8.4, 10] The deadlock detector presented in the text has a simple notion of waiting: if $t1$ is granted and $t2$ is in the queue, then $t2$ waits for $t1$. This never misses a deadlock but may find some spurious ones. (a) Give an example of such a spurious deadlock, using the standard lock modes. (b) The algorithm may miss some future deadlocks, ones that appear when some waiting requests are granted. Give an example. (c) Refine the wait-for test to detect only situations where $t2$ is really waiting for $t1$. Be aware that this is an area that is very prone to bugs, and so prove that your "optimization" is correct. Ignore conversions.

24. [8.4, 10] Repeat Exercise 23, but this time pay attention to conversions.

25. [8.4, 5] The deadlock detector finds the same cycle many times. What is the simplest way to assure that cycles are found only once?

26. [8.4, 20] Distributed deadlock detectors want to know all paths beginning and ending with network transactions (those which are distributed). Modify the tran table to have a boolean indicating that a transaction is a network transaction, and then modify the deadlock detector to enumerate all such paths.

27. [8.4, project] How should lock escalation and lock conversion interact with nested transactions?

28. [8, 10] What is the relationship between cursor stability in SQL systems and crabbing?

Answers

1.

```
T1   temp = counter + 1;        /*read counter = 100      */
T2   temp = counter + 1;        /*read counter = 100      */
T1   counter = temp;            /*store counter = 101     */
T2   counter = temp;            /*store counter = 101     */
```

2.
```
Boolean TestAndSet(int * flag)
    { int    false = FALSE;     /* we do not want to update the FALSE literal so make a temp   */
    return CS(flag,&false,&TRUE); } /* return the outcome of compare FALSE swap TRUE           */
```

3. Modify branch to have an exclusive semaphore.

```
struct      {    Xsem    sem;            /* Exclusive semaphore to control access to the branch   */
                 int  sum;               /* the sum of all the tellers cash position              */
                 int  teller[10];        /* teller[i] is the cash position of the i'th teller     */
                 }branch;                /* branch table is global to the routine.                */
DebitCredit(int i, int delta)            /* the program to do the atomic update of two fields     */
    { Xsem_get(&branch.sem);             /* get exclusive access to the branch                    */
    branch.sum = branch.sum + delta;     /* update the sum                                        */
    branch.teller[i] = branch.teller[i] +delta;  /* update the teller                            */
    Xsem_give(&branch.sem);              /* free the semaphore now that update is complete        */
    return};                             /*                                                       */
```

4. (a) To maximize throughput, balance dispatch cost against spin cost. If dispatch is more than .5 of duration, then it is best to spin on a dual processor. (b) In that case split the resource, but never spin.

5. A low-priority process is never dispatched and so is starved by the scheduler. Its not a bad thing because it is somebody else's problem—the problem of the low-priority process.

6. The original code did not crab. The correct code is

```
page * prev;                        /* remembers address of previous page                */
next = &root;                       /* start at the root                                 */
Xsem_get(&next->sem);               /* get the page semaphore                            */
while (next != NULL)                /* scan to the end of the list                       */
    { prev = next;                  /* remember previous page so can release sem         */
    next = next -> next_page;       /* get the next pointer                              */
    if ( next != NULL)              /* if there is a next page, get its semaphore        */
            Xsem_get(&next->sem);   /* get its semaphore                                 */
    Xsem_give(&prev->sem);}         /* got it, now can release prev page semaphore       */
```

7. The clause (old.wait_list == NULL) in the while loop. If this clause is dropped, shared requests can be scheduled ahead of waiting exclusive requests.

8. The trick is to examine the wait list. Decide what the new semaphore mode and count are, then come back and do a CSD to that value. When that is done, wake up the grantees, who then proceed without rerequesting the lock. It is not a trivial program but a good exercise.

9. Crabbing is required. The grantor knows that the wait list will not change until he changes it, since all the processes on it are waiting to be woken up. So the grantor has an implicit exclusive lock on those processes. This allows the grantor to read and store him→sem_wait, knowing that no one else will read or write this field.

10. Move the no-wait and no-wakeup cases in line. Wait and wakeup are hundreds of instructions, so procedure call overhead in the remaining out-of-line cases will be dwarfed by OS overhead.

11. Broadcast has increased dispatch overhead, but yes, it is a good idea if convoys are a possibility .

12.
```
Boolean sem_get_bounce(semaphore * sem, lock_mode mode)  /*                          */
    {semaphore     new;                        /* new value for semaphore                       */
    semaphore     old;                          /* old value for semaphore                       */
    old = {LOCK_FREE, 0, NULL};                 /* guess old value for semaphore is free         */
    new = {mode, 1, NULL};                      /* & guess new value has only me granted         */
    if (CSD( sem, &old, &new) ) return TRUE;    /* if semaphore free, this gets & exits          */
    if (    (mode == LOCK_S)       &&           /* if request is shared mode                     */
            (old.mode == LOCK_S) &&                     /* and semaphore is currently in shared mode     */
            (old.wait_list == NULL))                    /* and no one is waiting                          */
            { new.count = old.count + 1;                /* then try to join the shared group,            */
            if (CSD( sem, &old, &new) ) return TRUE;    /* got it, return success                        */
            };                                          /* else cannot acquire semaphore                 */
    return FALSE;                               /* if someone waiting or if incompatible then    */
    }                                            /* return failure, semaphore not acquired        */
```

13. It may not be safe. They should really do compare-and-swap to write the cells if they are to be called in a concurrent environment.

15. (1) Do exponential backoff a la Ethernet (wait for a random time). (2) Replace the kilroy field with a counter that is incremented by every successful allocation. The counter wraps every 2^{32}, and so the algorithm can fail in the old way if: (a) the counter exactly wraps while the process is sleeping ($\approx$ an hour or more), (b) the list header is just like it was before, and (c) the header has a different next pointer. Situation (c) is very likely, but if both (a) and (b) happen to this process, it is so unlucky that it has already been run over by a truck.

17. Since notify locks are compatible with everything else, they could go anywhere. In particular, they could easily go below IS mode locks.

18. In the unlock() code, the hash chain can be freed as soon as the start of the interesting case (granted group not null when this request leaves).

19. If the lock name is not found or the requestor's lock request is not found in the lock list, the requestor should be given an error rather than just LOCK_OK.

22. Only look at waiting transactions so deadlock is not possible. Hash chain semaphore is not needed because **trans** semaphore is held and transaction is waiting.

23. (a) {1IS,2IX}←3S; {3X}←1IS. The deadlock detector thinks this is a cycle, but when 2 completes, 3 will be granted and the cycle will be broken. (b) {1S}←2IX,3X; {3S}←2IX. In this case, 2 and 3 are in

a cycle, but it is based on wait-list order that is not considered by the deadlock detector in the text. (c) If {a}←b,c, watch out for lock_compat(a,c) but not lock_compat(b,c). So b waits for a, and c waits for b. Some students miss the c waits for b case.

24. Not much new here. Check compatibility with conversion mode. The program must consider convert requests as being at the head of the wait list.

25. If a node has already run the visit logic, do not run it again. That is, skip the loop the second time around by keeping a visited flag for each node.

28. When reading data of one cursor to position a second cursor, do not move the first cursor until the position of the second cursor is established. For example, when reading the item-master record to locate the item-detail records, or when following some other parent-child relationship, if the parent cursor moves, both the parent and child could be deleted or changed between the time of the parent read and the time of the child read. If the parent is kept locked by a cursor stability lock, the child cannot change. This is crabbing.

PART FIVE

Recovery

As easy as falling off a log.

9

Log Manager

9.1 Introduction

This chapter explains how the transaction log is read, written, and stored. Since the log is nothing more than a sequential file, one might think that this chapter could be about one paragraph long. But the log is special. Every insert, delete, or update to a transactional object generates an insert to the log. This means that the log can easily become a performance problem, and it also means that the log can get very large.

These size and performance issues make the log a key part of system performance. They create a need for many interesting algorithms to write, archive, and read the log. This chapter surveys the more important of these algorithms. Notable algorithms for expediting writes have names like careful write, serial write, Ping-Pong, group commit, WADS, and staggered allocation. Besides these performance issues, the chapter discusses how much of the log should be kept online and when the older parts of the log should be archived.

9.1.1 Uses of the Log

People who implement logs like to point out that the log knows everything. It is the temporal database. The online sessions, tables, contexts, queues, and other durable objects are just their current versions. The log has their complete histories. It is possible to reconstruct any version of an object by scanning through the log. Oliver North discovered this the hard way when he attempted to destroy his mail and files related to the Iran-Contra Affair. Unfortunately for North, the mail system's log dutifully recorded all his messages as well as his frantic attempts to destroy them. Investigators were able to reconstruct the scenario along with the contents of all those durable objects.

The log was originally used only for transaction recovery. Increasingly, it is being used for broader functions. Corporate auditors evaluating a transaction system may use the log to check that the transformations are correct. If they want to find out how your bank account suddenly got very big, they can check the log to see who updated it and when the updates happened. The log will increasingly be used in this way to provide application-level time-domain addressing of objects.

The log also can be used for performance analysis and accounting. It records when each transaction began, when it ended, and how much write activity it generated. This information can be used to determine system throughput and response time. The information also can be used to generate bills to the clients who invoked the transactions. At a finer granularity, the log can show objects or devices that have very high update activity and are therefore potential bottlenecks.

9.1.2 Log Manager Overview

The log manager provides an interface to the log table, which is a sequence of log records. Each log record has a *header* that contains the names of the resource manager and the transaction that wrote the record, along with housekeeping information understood by the log manager. The bulk of each log record is a *body* containing UNDO-REDO information generated by the resource manager that wrote the log record. The body is not understood by the log manager and is treated as a byte string. The log record body is typically a few hundred bytes but may be a few megabytes.

Each record in the log table has a unique key, called the *log sequence number* (LSN). Given that, the following is a typical definition of the log table, expressed in SQL:

```
create domain LSN            unsigned integer(64);  -- log sequence number (file #, rba)
create domain RMID           unsigned integer;      -- resource manager identifier
create domain TRID           char(12);              -- transaction identifier
create table log_table (
        lsn              LSN,              -- the record's log sequence number
        prev_lsn         LSN,              -- the lsn of the previous record in log
        timestamp        TIMESTAMP,        -- time log record was created
        resource_manager RMID,            -- resource manager that wrote this record
        trid             TRID,             -- id of transaction that wrote this record
        tran_prev_lsn    LSN,              -- prev log record of this transaction (or 0)
        body             varchar,          -- log data: rm understands it
        primary key (lsn)                  -- lsn is primary key
        foreign key (prev_lsn)             -- previous log record in this table
            references log_table(lsn),     --
        foreign key (tran_prev_lsn)        -- transaction's prev log rec is also in table
            references log_table(lsn),     --
        )    entry sequenced;              -- inserts go at end of file
```

The log appears to be an SQL table, so it can be queried using ordinary SQL statements. For example, this is the query to find the records written by a resource manager:

```
select *
from a_log_table
where resource_manager = :rmid
order by lsn descending;
```

To explain the header fields just a little more, the log record header contains the record LSN and the LSN of the previous record. This second LSN is useful in scanning backward through the log. If the previous record is very large (say, a few megabytes) or is in the previous file, it is preferable to go directly to its record header rather than to examine each intervening page or byte. The next LSN can be computed from the length of the body, the header size, and the data page overhead. Thus, no forward LSN is needed. The header also contains the timestamp of the log record to microsecond granularity. This timestamp is useful for *time domain addressing*, or reconstructing an object as of a certain time. It is also useful for debugging and reporting. Each log record header contains the identity of the resource manager that wrote the log record and that will handle the UNDO-REDO work associated with the record. The header also contains the identifier of the transaction that created the log record. Transaction UNDO needs to find the previous record of a particular transaction. Rather than scan the log backward until an appropriate record is found, the log manager stores the LSN of the transaction's previous log record.

9.1.3 The Log Manager's Relationship to Other Services

The log manager provides read and write access to the log table for all the other resource managers and for the transaction manager. In a perfect world, the log manager simply writes log records, and no one ever reads them. But in the event an application, transaction, or system fails, the log is used to clean up the state. In those cases, the transaction manager reads the log and drives the recovery process, returning each transaction-protected object (logged object) to its most recent consistent state.

The log manager maps the log table onto a growing collection of sequential files provided by the operating system, the file system, and the archive system. As the log table fills one file, another is allocated.

Refer to Figure 9.1. The use of the operating system and the file system should be clear: the logs are stored in files. The archive system is needed because logs grow without bound. In general, only recent records are kept online. Log records more than a few hours old are stored in less-expensive tertiary storage (tape) managed by the archive system. Archived log files are eventually discarded; otherwise, the archive would fill up with logs.

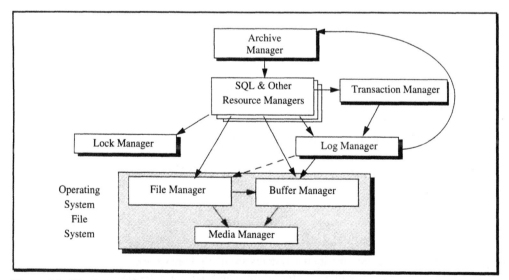

Figure 9.1: The interactions among the various resource managers from the perspective of the log manager.   The arrows show who calls whom. The circularity (the archive manager using the log manager) is dealt with in the text.

9.1.4 Why Have a Log Manager?

Conceptually, then, the log is an entry-sequenced SQL table—each log record header is described by structured fields, while the body is a single VARCHAR field. This is a correct view; it is convenient for applications and utilities to read the log using SQL operations. However, writing the log has several unique properties that give the log manager reason to exist:

Encapsulation. If nothing else, the log manager encapsulates log record headers, assuring that these fields are filled in correctly. Historically, the log manager had only two clients, the database manager and the queue manager. This allowed—even encouraged—an unprotected call interface to the log manager. There is increasing adoption of a clean and protected interface to the log manager, both to improve fault isolation and to provide an interface for new resource managers implementing new durable types. In systems with such an interface, any resource manager can write log records. Consequently, in the design presented here, the log manager encapsulates log records and is the only one actually to write log records. It exports an interface that allows other resource managers to specify the contents of the log record body. The log headers are private to the log manager.

Startup. The log manager helps reconstruct the durable system state at system restart. At restart, almost none of the system is functioning. In particular, the SQL compiler and SQL catalogs are not yet operational. The log manager must be able to find, read, and write the log without much help from the SQL system. This forces the log manager to maintain and use a special catalog listing the physical log files, and to use low-level interfaces to read and write these catalogs and files. The data can be stored in SQL format, but restart operations must be able to access it via record-at-a-time calls.

Careful writes. The log is generally duplexed, and it is written using protocols (serial writes, Ping-Pong writes, staggered allocation, and so on). This is done because the log is the only durable copy of committed transaction updates until the data is copied to durable storage.

Some argue that the need to write long fields (say, several megabytes), the need for high-speed sequential read and insert, and novel locking are major reasons for a special interface to log files. However, many other applications want all these features at the SQL level (notably graphics and free-text applications). Thus, the SQL system should support such an interface to SQL tables. On the other hand, the encapsulation, startup, and careful-write issues are fundamental to the log manager and are the real reasons it exists as a separate entity.

9.2 Log Tables

Simple systems have only a single log table, but distributed systems are likely to have one or more logs per network node. They maintain multiple logs for performance and for node autonomy. With a local log, each node of a distributed system can recover its local transactions without involving the other nodes of the network. Large systems may maintain several logs at one node for the sake of performance. Almost every operation that alters an object generates log data. In systems with very high update rates, the bandwidth of the log can become a bottleneck. Such bottlenecks can be eliminated by creating multiple logs and by directing the log records of different objects to different logs. Generally, the partitioning of object space is physical—each log covers all objects stored on certain disks, at certain nodes, or by certain resource managers. This, in turn, allows those physical media to be independently managed and recovered.

In some situations, a particular resource manager keeps its own log table. This is common for portable systems that try to minimize their use of system services. These resource managers must implement log managers with most of the functions mentioned in this chapter.

Occasionally, a log table may be dedicated to an object for the duration of a "batch" operation. The online reorganization of a table is a typical example. Reorganizing a terabyte file generates about a terabyte of log. If done using parallelism, the operation may last for a day or two; otherwise it could last a month, and the table obviously cannot be taken offline for such a long period. Hence, the old master–new master recovery technique cannot be used. Rather, an incremental reorganization technique must be used, along with a corresponding incremental recovery technique, such as logging. During such operations, a special log table is dedicated to the object so that standard log tables are not cluttered with the traffic from the operation. When the operation completes, the object's normal log records are again sent to the main log. Operations like these, which split and merge logs, create a *two-dimensional log table* rather than a linear log table. A particular log may refer the reader to a second log when the log splits or merges. This two-dimensional structure is hidden when the log is viewed as an SQL table.

For simplicity, this book assumes a single log per transaction manager. When they raise interesting points, multilog issues are treated as digressions.

9.2.1 Mapping the Log Table onto Files

The log is implemented using sequential files. Recently generated files (say, four or five) are kept online and filled one after the other The files are usually duplexed, so that no single storage failure can damage the log. Because the log manager records all these files in the SQL catalogs, the log appears to be an ordinary, duplexed, entry-sequenced SQL table. The two physical-file sequences are often stored in independent directory spaces (file servers) to minimize the risk of losing both directories. Initially, two physical files are allocated. As the log grows, these files fill up, and two more are allocated to receive the next log records. This process continues indefinitely.

The two log files use standard file names, ending with the patterns LOGA00000000 and LOGB00000000, respectively, where the zeros are filled in with the file's index in the log directories. Since there is an algorithm to compute the nth log file name, the log manager need not store the above array. Rather, it need only store the common prefixes of the log file names (directory names) and the index of the current log file. Thus, the log manager maintains a single record to describe each log:

struct **log_files**

```
{   filename    a_prefix;        /* directory for "a" log files    */
    filename    b_prefix;        /* directory for "b" log files    */
    long        index;           /* index of current log file      */
};
```

This information forms the core of a data structure known as the log anchor (see Figure 9.2). The log anchor is cached in main memory and is also recorded in at least two places in durable storage—in two files, typically, so that it can be found at restart. When the anchor is updated in these files, careful writes are used to minimize the risk of destroying both copies of the anchor.

On a system with only one disk (such as a workstation or automated teller machine), it still makes sense to keep a transaction log: transactions furnish complex data with atomic updates. In addition, it makes sense to duplex the log contents and log anchor, since single-block media failures are not uncommon. On a system with native support for duplexed disks (also known as *mirrored disks* or *shadowed disks*) or for other types of reliable disk arrays, the explicit management of the "a" and "b" files by the log manager can be eliminated; the underlying file system provides such management. However, there is still a need for the log manager to request careful writes and a need to explicitly read both copies of the duplexed files at restart.

Both the anchor records and the duplexed log files must mask storage media failures. Duplexing easily masks single failures. The following scenario represents the most

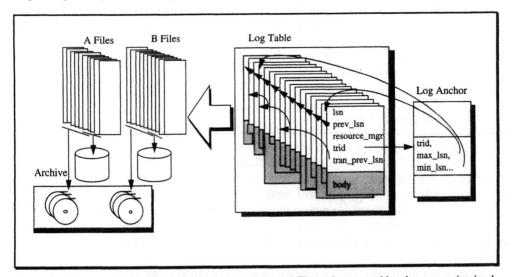

Figure 9.2: The mapping of log tables to entry-sequenced files. Log record headers are maintained by the log manager. The header contains the log record's sequence number (LSN), the name of the resource manager that wrote the record, and the name of the transaction that wrote the record. Each transaction's log records are in a linked "tran_prev_lsn" list to speed transaction backout. The log table is mapped to two sequences of files (the "a" and "b" series). Most log files are in the archive and are used only for media recovery, but recent log files are kept online and are used for transaction backout and system restart.

worrisome double failure. Log "a" fails, and "b" proceeds; then "b" fails and, at restart, "a" is available, but "b" is not. Now the log updates to "b" have been lost, yet the database has advanced past the end of the "a" log. The simplest way to deal with such issues is to triplex or quadraplex rather than duplex, the anchors and log files and then use a majority scheme to resolve any conflicts (see Daniels, Spector, and Thompson [1986]). The statistics from Chapter 3 indicate that the chance of this double failure scenario happening is very slim with modern duplexed disks ($\approx$ 10,000 years mean time to double failure). It is not clear that triplexing the disks will improve the situation, since software and environmental errors are more likely to cause problems that will mask any improvements a triplex disk scheme might buy. Triplexing may be useful for unreliable servers (workstations that come and go), but there is a trend toward storing data on reliable servers in order to reduce the problems of managing programs and data on unreliable private workstations.

9.2.2 Log Sequence Numbers

As explained earlier, each log record has a unique identifier, or key, called its *log sequence number* (LSN). The LSN is composed of the record's file number and the relative byte offset of the record within that file. LSNs are defined by the following typedef:

```
typedef struct {   long    file;        /* number of log file in log directory                */
                   long    rba;         /* relative byte address of (first byte) record in file */
                } LSN ;                 /* Definition of Log Sequence Numbers (LSN)             */
LSN NullLSN ={0,0};                     /* null LSN is used to end pointer chains.              */
```

LSNs can be cast as unsigned, 8-byte integers that increase monotonically, so that if log record A for an object is created "after" log record B for that object, then

```
LSN(A) > LSN(B).
```

This important property of LSNs, *monotonicity*, is used by the write-ahead log (WAL) protocol. Of course, if two objects send their log records to different logs, then their LSNs are incomparable.

Given the record's LSN, the log record can be located quickly using the following scheme. The first word of the LSN, lsn.file, gives the record's file index, NNN, which in turn implies the two file names, a_prefix.logaNNN and b_prefix.logbNNN. As a rule, these are the current log files. The log record starts at byte number lsn.rba of those files (RBA stands for relative byte address). Thus, the relevant file page and offset are easily computed and located.

In summary, then, the log manager implements the log table as two sequences of log files (the "a" and "b" sequence). These files are formatted as ordinary SQL tables. The log file is recorded in the SQL catalog as an SQL table, so that high-level applications can read the log. The SQL log tables look like duplexed-partitioned, entry-sequenced tables. Only the log manager writes the log.

9.3 Public Interface to the Log

Two log read interfaces are provided. The SQL interface is set oriented, returning all records that satisfy a given predicate. The second interface is low-level, record-at-a-time, providing direct access to the log, given the record's LSN.

9.3.1 Authorization to Access the Log Table

Authorization is a major issue when providing access to the log. The log contains a complete history of the database. Read access to a log table implicitly gives read access to all objects covered by that log table. The security system is probably unaware that accessing the log provides an overt read channel into the database. The usual way of handling this problem is to deny log read access to everyone except the transaction manager and the resource manager that wrote the record.

Many users find the information in the log useful for auditing, capacity planning, performance analysis, and in database repair utilities. Thus, it is infeasible to prohibit access to the log. One scheme to control access is to use the SQL view mechanism. Clients can be given read access to SQL view–subsets of the log table. Such views can restrict access to value-based subsets of the log. These SQL views have all the high-level security implicit in SQL.

To minimally deal with security issues for the low-level log interface, the log manager needs to interact with the security system. In doing so, its purpose is to validate the caller's read or write authority to the log table. This is an expensive operation that, therefore, cannot be done on each access to a log record. Rather, an "open-close" interface is provided. The resource manager or client first calls logtable_open() to set a flag indicating that the caller is authorized to make read or insert calls to the log manager. A multitable log design would include the table name in the call. When done, logtable_close() is called to deallocate the descriptor. The relevant prototypes are as follows:

```
enum ACCESS {READ, WRITE};              /* kind of access: read or read-write    */
Boolean   logtable_open( ACCESS access);  /* read access or read&write access      */
void      logtable_close(void);           /* closes log file                       */
```

Once the log is open, log_read() will be able to read all records in the log and log_insert() will be able to add records to the log.

9.3.2 Reading the Log Table

The record-at-a-time log interface is similar to most record-at-a-time file read routines. Because the log record is usually less than 100 bytes, the caller reads the whole thing. Occasionally, the log records are large (say, several megabytes), and the caller may only want to read the log record header or a substring of the log record body. The log_read() routine copies a substring of the log record body into the caller's buffer; in addition, it returns the values of the fields in the log record header. The number of bytes actually moved is returned by the routine. (Error cases are ignored in this exposition.) Here is the prototype for log_read_lsn():

```
/* generic header of all log records                                                            */
typedef struct {      LSN              lsn;              /* lsn of record                        */
                      LSN              prev_lsn;         /* the lsn of the previous record in log */
                      TIMESTAMP        timestamp;        /* UTC time log record was created       */
                      RMID             rmid;             /* id of resource mgr writing this record */
                      TRID             trid;             /* id of transaction that wrote this record */
                      LSN              tran_prev_lsn;    /* prev log record of this transaction (or 0) */
                      long             length;           /* length of log record body             */
                      char             body[];           /* dummy body of log record              */
                      } log_record_header;               /*                                       */
/* Read log record header and up to n bytes of the log record body starting at offset into buffer */
/* Return number of bytes read as function value.                                                */
long log_read_lsn( LSN               lsn,               /* lsn of record to be read              */
                   log_record_header * header,          /* header fields of record to be read    */
                   long              offset,             /* offset into body to start read        */
                   pointer           buffer,            /* buffer to receive log data            */
                   long              n);                 /* length of buffer                      */
```

In addition, the following routine returns the current maximum LSN of the log (essentially, the end of the log):

```
LSN log_max_lsn(void);                        /* returns the current maximum lsn of the log table.     */
```

These two routines are sufficient to read the log in either direction. For performance reasons—especially in a client-server architecture, where each call to the log manager is an expensive message interchange—it is desirable to have a set-oriented interface to the log manager. SQL provides such a set-oriented interface. The set is declared by opening a cursor on the log table and declaring a start position, a scan direction, and a filter predicate. Then a sequence of fetch calls returns the set of qualifying log records; typically, each call returns a buffer full of records. When an end-of-set indicator is returned, the cursor is closed.

Here are two simple programs to count the number of log records of a resource manager. The first program, using SQL, does the job the easy way.

```
long sql_count( RMID rmid)                             /* count log records written by this rmid */
    { long     rec_count;                              /* count of records                       */
    exec sql   SELECT    count (*)                     /* ask sql to scan log counting records   */
               INTO      :rec_count                    /* written by the calling resource mgr and */
               FROM      log_table                     /* place count in the rec_count           */
               WHERE     resource_manager = :rmid; /*                                            */
    return rec_count;                                  /* return the answer.                     */
    };                                                 /*                                        */
```

Now let us do it bare-handed, using the basic log reading routines. The routine opens the log, gets the current LSN, and scans backwards through the log, counting records belonging to the caller's resource manager identifier.

```
long c_count( RMID rmid)                         /* count log records written by this rmid        */
   { log_record_header   header;                 /* structure to receive log record header        */
   LSN          lsn;                              /* log sequence number of next log rec           */
   char         buffer[1];                        /* null buffer to receive log record body.       */
   long         rec_count = 0;                    /* count of records                              */
   int          n = 1;                            /* size of log body returned                     */
   if (!log_table_open(READ)) panic();            /* open the log (authorization check)            */
   lsn = log_max_lsn( );                          /* get most recent lsn                           */
   while (lsn != NullLSN)                         /* scan backward through the log                 */
       { n = log_read_lsn(    lsn,                /* lsn of record to be read                      */
                          &header,                /* log record header fields                      */
                          0L, &buffer, 1L );      /* log record body is ignored.                   */
       if (header.rmid == rmid)                   /* if record written by this RMID then           */
           rec_count = rec_count + 1;             /*    increment count                            */
       lsn = header.prev_lsn;                     /* go to previous LSN.                           */
       };                                         /* loop over LSNs                                */
   logtable_close( );                             /* close log table                               */
   return rec_count;                              /* return the answer.                            */
   };                                             /*                                               */
```

9.3.3 Writing the Log Table

Writing a log record is simple, once the table has been opened for write access. The only parameter is the log record body (the data to be logged). The log manager allocates space for the record at the end of the log. It then fills in the log record header (using the parameters along with the caller's resource manager ID and transaction ID) and adds the record's LSN, the transaction's previous log record LSN, and the current timestamp. Then the log manager fills in the log record body by moving *n* bytes from the passed record. The routine returns the LSN of the resulting log record. Details of this logic are discussed in the next section.

```
/* Write a log record for the calling resource manager and transaction. Return the record's LSN   */
LSN log_insert( char * buffer, long n);                        /* log body is buffer[0..n-1]       */
```

In general, new log records are buffered in volatile storage. If the system fails at this point, all or part of the log record may be lost. When the resource manager wants to assure that the log record is present in durable (nonvolatile) storage, it must call a second routine, log_flush(), specifying an LSN. When this routine returns, all records of the log table up to and including the designated LSN will have been copied to durable storage. As a rule, most of the records have already been written asynchronously by the buffer manager at the request of someone else. If not, the flush will write as many records as possible, so that others can benefit from this single-flush write. Log_flush() has a "lazy" option to allow the log manager either to defer the log write, perhaps waiting for the last page to fill, or to do periodic writes. This is the function prototype:

```
/* assure the designated log record (LSN) is in durable storage and return max durable LSN        */
LSN log_flush( LSN lsn, Boolean lazy);                         /*                                  */
```

9.3.4 Summary

The log manager provides record-oriented read and insert-flush interfaces to log tables. Resource managers use these interfaces to record changes to persistent (recoverable) objects. The transaction manager reads these records back to the resource manager if the transaction must be undone or redone.

With the following three exceptions, record-oriented read and insert-flush interfaces approximate the design of most logging systems:

Data copy.   The interface requires data to be moved between the caller's data buffer and the log; it does not provide a direct pointer to the data area in the log buffer. Using direct pointers has the performance benefit of saving data moves, but it also has several disadvantages. It implies that the caller can directly access the log pages in the log manager's buffer pool and can "fix" pages in the pool. It also implies that the caller has direct read-write access to the log record header and to the representation of the log record body, which may be fragmented across many pages. Direct addressing would violate the log manager's desire to encapsulate the log data. Therefore, general log managers do not support a pointer interface. Traditional log managers for database systems have supported a call-by-reference interface to reduce data movement. That design, however, is not modular and does not extend to untrusted callers.

Incremental insert.   The second unusual thing about the interface is the requirement that the caller provide the entire log body on a single insert call rather than provide it one part at a time. In many situations, the client first builds the UNDO part of the record and then the REDO part, or the caller may have a large (several megabyte) log record to write. In these cases, some log systems allow the caller to allocate the log record and then incrementally fill in the log body, much as the log_read_lsn() interface allows the caller to incrementally read the body. Incremental interfaces can create log records that are incomplete. This may, in turn, create a problem at restart when the resource manager is presented with an incomplete log record. An incremental interface is therefore not provided. The resource manager can use several log records to describe a single operation. That may be a reasonable compromise. There is one other compromise that helps both the client and performance. As the design stands now, there are three data moves: the client must move data to a contiguous buffer, the call to the log manager moves the buffer to the log manager's address space, and then the log manager moves the data to the end of the log (to the file space). By letting the caller specify a set of pointers to data fragments, at least one stage of this data movement can be saved.

SQL representation.   The third novel aspect of this design is allowing SQL read access to the log, something that has not been common practice in the past.

The more typical design dedicates a log manager to a resouce manager and treats the log as part of the resource manager's data, which the resource manager can directly address. The main problem with such a design is that it proliferates logs as resource managers proliferate. Having many logs complicates system management (they must be archived) and reduces performance (they must each be copied to stable memory at commit).

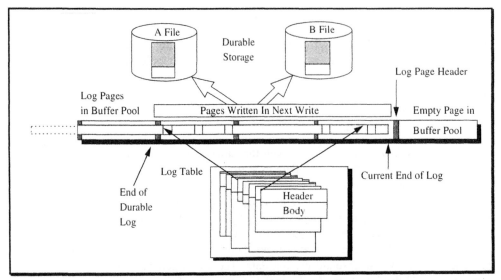

Figure 9.3: Mapping of the log into main memory buffer pool. The last few pages of the log table reside in the disk buffer pool. New records of a log table are inserted into these pages in the standard way. Large records may be fragmented across page boundaries. Each page has the standard layout, which includes a few bytes of header and trailer. When log_flush() of the current LSN is called, the three pages indicated are written to the two disks.

9.4 Implementation Details of Log Reads and Writes

Log files are formatted as entry-sequenced SQL tables. This means that log pages and records have the standard layout (see Chapters 13–15). Each page has a standard header and trailer and contains one or more contiguously stored log records. The log manager fragments records that span pages into units that fit within a page. To simplify the recovery code, records are not allowed to span files. Rather, if the record does not fit within the current file, a small dummy record (alias record) is written to mark the end of the current file; then a new file is allocated, and the new record starts that file. For that reason, there can be "holes" in the log. Larger holes will appear if the log file partitions are allocated to be less than maximum file size (recall that LSNs have the structure ⟨file number, byte offset⟩). Figure 9.3 shows log records being mapped to the pages in the buffer pool. It also shows some record fragmentation, the end of the durable log (log already written to disk), and the end of the current log. Exercises 3 and 4 discuss some other details associated with fragmentation.

Recently read and written log pages are cached in the disk buffer pool. The buffer manager's caching algorithm is aware that the log is read and written sequentially and, consequently, tends to age log pages more quickly than simple least recently used (LRU).

9.4.1 Reading the Log

There is little to say about reading the log. All but the last log record can be read without locking, and the last record cannot be read while it is being updated. There is a semaphore that protects that update. Exercise 6 explores this issue a little further.

The log manager does optimistic reads of most pages: it usually reads only one copy of the duplexed log. As explained in Chapter 3, optimistic reads are dangerous because they run the risk of reading stale data. Log pages are self-identifying; the only undetected fault mode, therefore, would be a case in which one disk was written and the other was not.

The log manager detects this situation by keeping a flag in each page to indicate if the page is full. Since the log is written sequentially, all pages but the last should have the full flag set to true. The last page is buffered in memory most of the time, so that reading usually requires no I/O. When completing a page—writing it out for the last time—the log manager sets the full flag to true and writes the page to both the "a" and the "b" files. When reading a log page, if the full flag of the first read is false, the log manager reads the other copy of the page and uses the "fuller" version if the two are different. This mechanism allows safe optimistic reads.

9.4.2 Log Anchor

The log anchor describes the active status of the log table. It contains the log table name, the array of open files, and various LSNs described below. It also contains a semaphore that serializes log insert operations. The anchor has the following structure:

```
/* anchor record used by log manager as base of addressability                        */
typedef struct {   filename    tablename;      /* name of log table                    */
                   struct      log_files;       /* A & B file prefix names and active file #  */
                   xsemaphore  lock;            /* semaphore regulating log write access */
                   LSN         prev_lsn;        /* LSN of most recently written record   */
                   LSN         lsn;             /* LSN of next record                    */
                   LSN         durable_lsn;     /* max lsn recorded in durable storage   */
                   LSN         TM_anchor_lsn;   /* lsn of trans mgr's most recent checkpoint. */
                   struct {                     /* array of open log partitions          */
                       long    partno;          /* partition number                      */
                       int     os_fnum;         /* operating system file number          */
                       } part [MAXOPENS];       /*                                       */
                   } log_anchor ;               /*                                       */
```

Concurrent access to the end of the log is protected by an exclusive semaphore called the *log lock*. Once a log record is written, it is never changed. Therefore, the only locking needed is that which controls access to the end of the log and the data structures that describe the end of the log. For example, read via LSN need not acquire a lock if the LSN is less than the log's maximum LSN. On the other hand, each write (insert or flush) access to the end of the log acquires the log lock in exclusive mode. To avoid congestion, this lock is never held during an I/O operation. The implementation of the log lock—that is, the implementation of semaphores—was explained in Chapter 8.

9.4.3 Transaction Related Anchors

The transaction manager also keeps a small amount of log information about each live transaction—namely, the first and last log record written by the transaction. Here is the actual data:

```
typedef struct {    TRID        trid;           /* transaction identifier                       */
                    LSN         min_lsn;        /* lsn of its first log record                  */
                    LSN         max_lsn;        /* lsn of its most recent log record            */
                    /* stuff */                 /* many other items not relevant here           */
                    } TransCB;                  /*                                              */
```

Initially, these two LSNs are null. The log manager calls the transaction manager each time it is about to insert a log record. The transaction manager does the following:

```
LSN log_transaction(LSN new_lsn)            /* Tell the TM about a new log record           */
    { TransCB *  trans = MyTransP();        /* pointer to transaction structure             */
    LSN                 prev;               /* tran prev lsn now that new lsn has arrived    */
    prev = trans->max_lsn;                  /* make a copy of the record's lsn.             */
    trans->max_lsn = new_lsn;               /* trans max lsn is this record now             */
    if (trans->min_lsn == NullLSN)          /* if this is the first log rec of this trans    */
        trans->min_lsn = new_lsn;           /*    update min_lsn                            */
    return prev; }                          /* return lsn of previous record                */
```

9.4.4 Log Insert

With the preliminaries out of the way, we can now examine the code for log_insert(). The code presented here is complete for the simple case in which the log record does not span page boundaries or file boundaries. The program acquires the log lock, using the semaphore code; next, using the buffer manager, it fixes the log page in the buffer pool (see Chapter 13), allocates space for the record in the page (using an undocumented routine), and fills in the record. It then updates the log anchor, unfixes the page in the buffer pool, and unlocks the semaphore. When this is all done, the program returns the resulting LSN to the caller.

```
/* Insert a log record in the log. Assumes record fits in current log page. Return record LSN    */
LSN  log_insert( char * buffer, long n)         /* insert a log record with body buffer[0..n]     */
    { pointer          log_page;                /* page in buffer pool where log record starts    */
    log_record_header * header;                 /* pointer to log record header                   */
    LSN                 lsn;                     /* new record's log sequence number               */
    long                part;                    /* log partition index in log_anchor.part array   */
    long                i;                       /* loop index;                                    */
    long                rec_len;                 /* length of log record (logical)                 */
    rec_len = sizeof(log_record_header) + n;    /* compute record length                          */
/* Acquire the log lock (an exclusive semaphore on the log).                                       */
    Xsem_get(&log_anchor.lock);                 /* lock the log end in exclusive mode             */
    lsn = log_anchor.lsn;                        /* make a copy of the record's lsn.              */
/* find page and allocate space in it.                                                             */
    for (part = 0; part <= MAXOPENS; part++)     /* find the file number in the array             */
        { if (log_anchor.part[part].partno == lsn.file) break; }; /*                               */
    if (part == MAXOPENS) panic();              /* not found => bug in log daemon                 */
    log_page = page_fix(log_anchor.part[part].os_fnum,lsn.rba); /* get the page in buffer pool     */
    header = log_record_allocate(log_page,rec_len); /* allocate space in the page                  */
    if (header == NULL) {/*overflow logic*/ };  /* page overflow not shown in example.            */
```

```
/* fill in log record header & body                                                         */
    header->lsn = lsn;                          /* record lsn                                */
    header->prev_lsn = log_anchor.prev_lsn;     /* previous log record in log                */
    header->timestamp = timestamp();            /* timestamp of this record                  */
    header->rmid = ClientRMID();                /* resource manager of this record           */
    header->trid = MyTRID();                    /* trid of this log record                   */
    header->tran_prev_lsn = log_transaction(lsn); /* tell TM and get prev_lsn of this trid   */
    header->length = n;                         /* length of body (a varchar field)          */
    for (i=0; i<n; i++) header->body[i] = buffer[i]; /* copy the log body                    */
    page_unfix(log_page);                       /* release the page in the buffer pool       */
/* update the anchors                                                                        */
    log_anchor.prev_lsn = lsn;                  /* log anchor lsnpoints past this record     */
    log_anchor.lsn.rba = log_anchor.lsn.rba + rec_len; /*                                    */
    Xsem_give(&log_anchor.lock);                /* unlock the log end                        */
    return lsn; };                              /* return lsn of record just inserted        */
```

The code just given handles the straightforward case of writing a log record to a single page. It does not deal with records spanning pages or with records that start in new files (a comment in the code alludes to the page overflow logic). Handling records that span pages is mostly arithmetic: one must subtract the space for each page header and break the record into fragments that will fit on the page. The pages must be allocated, fixed in the buffer pool, formatted, filled in, and then unfixed in the buffer pool. When log_insert() fails to find enough space in a page, it calls another routine to allocate new page(s) in the buffer pool and then adds the log record data to those pages. This causes no I/O, because it is a property of entry-sequenced files that the disk contents of empty pages are irrelevant.

A word of caution about these programs: a real program should validate its input parameters, should not call panic(), should not do linear search of the log-anchor table (for performance it should be hashed), should test for errors on all procedure calls, and should not ignore the limitations of the C programming language.

9.4.5 Allocate and Flush Log Daemons

Allocating a file is time-consuming and involves authorization, space allocation, and even disc I/O. Therefore, log_insert() should not do file allocation as part of normal processing. Rather, a log manager *daemon*, an asynchronous process, allocates files in advance (see Figure 9.4). It wakes up periodically to see if the current file is half full. If so, it allocates the next file. By the time the current file is full, the next file will have been allocated and opened for the log manager. The daemon adds the file descriptor to the log_anchor and updates the log_anchor in durable storage, so that the log manager can find the most recent log files at restart. In addition, it records this new partition in the SQL catalogs.

In simple systems, the buffer manager performs all log writes, either on request or as part of its normal aging of sequentially written files blocks. High-performance systems require a few exotic log-writing techniques and, therefore, routinely appoint a separate process to drive the buffer-manager write logic. In these designs, the movement of data to

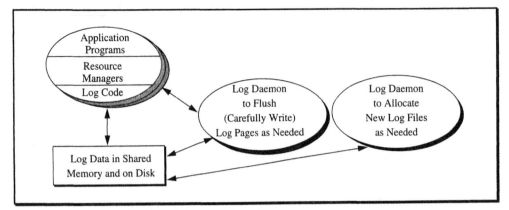

Figure 9.4: A typical shared-memory logging design. The mainline log functions of reading and writing the log are part of the application process, while asynchronous processes manage movement of data to disk and allocation of new log files. In a shared-nothing design, the application, resource managers, and log code would all have separate processes.

durable storage (duplexed disks) is coordinated by an asynchronous process called the *log flush daemon*. A separate process is used because most log writes do not require immediate I/O. The log flush daemon is woken up by flush requests and by periodic timer interrupts. Its goal is to move recent log additions to disk in a way that will not damage data already present in durable storage, and to do so with low overhead and high performance. The correctness goal is discussed first.

9.4.6 Careful Writes: Serial or Ping-Pong

Duplexing the log table guards against most media errors, but it does not necessarily protect against the following scenario. Suppose the last log page on disk contains some good information but is only partially full. Because the next log record will be added to the partially full page, writing the page containing this new record to disk overwrites the old, half-full version of that page on both disks. If there is a processor or power failure during the transfer, both copies of the last page could be damaged by the single write.

The easy solution to this problem is to do *serial writes*; that is, write one copy and, when that completes, write the second copy. Serial writes double the write time, effectively cutting the log write bandwidth in half.[1] This problem is serious enough to warrant careful design. The first observation we can make is that if the page being written is new—that is, if this is the first write to the page—then serial writes are not required, because they will not damage anything on disk if they fail. New pages are written to empty disk slots. The next observation is that at high data rates, there is a real incentive to write full log pages rather than partial log pages, since the partial write will soon be followed by a full write of the same page. The integrity argument is just one more reason for full-page writes. This suggests deferring log writes until a log page is full.

In cases where neither argument applies, one can use the so-called *Ping-Pong algorithm* (see Figure 9.5). Suppose the last page of the log—call it page *i*—is not empty and is about

---

[1] The discussion here is in terms of disks, but these arguments apply to any block-oriented update-in-place persistent storage device.

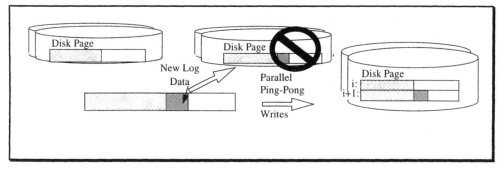

Figure 9.5: Using Ping-Pong parallel writes to overwrite good pages on a duplexed disk. Duplex writes risk destroying data already safely stored in durable storage. Either serial writes or the Ping-Pong scheme can be used to avoid the problem.

to be overwritten by additional data. In that case, write its contents to page $i + 1$ instead. Overwrites now Ping-Pong back and forth between page i and page $i + 1$. When the page is completely full, two writes may be implied: one of page $i + 1$ and a later one of page i. This Ping-Pong algorithm avoids overwriting the most recently written log page and, in doing so, allows parallel writes of the two log files. The Ping-Pong scheme is a good idea for simplex logs as well. Observe that the Ping-Pong scheme is just the careful write scheme in a different context.

With the Ping-Pong algorithm, the last page is always correct in the buffer pool. When reading from disk, however, one must read the last two pages (i and $i + 1$) and accept the one with the larger timestamp.

9.4.7 Group Commit, Batching, Boxcarring

Given that the log is written sequentially and with parallel writes, there is really only one optimization for log writes: write full pages, and write as many pages as possible in a single I/O. Writing the log has fixed overhead associated with dispatching the daemon, preparing and issuing the I/O, and cleaning up after the I/O completes. For small (single-page) writes, this overhead can exceed the cost of doing the actual I/O. A request arriving after the daemon launches the previous request must wait for the old request to complete. This leads to the paradoxical conclusion that, to minimize overhead and maximize throughput, the log daemon should delay writes, effectively resulting in batch processing log writes.

If the log daemon wakes up once every 50 ms and does all the log writing that has accumulated, then it adds 25 ms to the average transaction response time and consumes only a tiny overhead. When this idea is applied to commit flush requests, it is called *group commit*. When it is applied to all forms of requests, it is called *boxcarring* (as in freight trains) or *batching*.

It is possible to automatically adjust the log flush daemon's time delay to optimize throughput. At low loads, there is no delay. At high loads, the delay is balanced to minimize overhead while still improving response time. By delaying writes to get large data transfers (boxcars), the log can exploit the full sequential bandwidth of secondary storage devices. The only disadvantage of delaying flushes is the delay in releasing locks—it makes transactions last longer. For high-traffic locks, this might create contention problems (see Exercises 11 and 15).

Because the log daemon only reads the log pages in the buffer pool, it need not have the log lock when flushing any page except the last. To avoid contention on the log lock, if the last page is not full and must be written, the log flush daemon acquires the log lock, copies the last page to a memory buffer, releases the log lock, and then issues the I/O against the copy of the page. This logic is designed to avoid log lock contention, which is often a system hotspot.[2]

9.4.8 WADS Writes

One additional technique is used by high-transaction rate systems that require minimal latency in writing a disk-based log. They want to begin transferring the log to durable storage right away, without having to wait for the disk to rotate to the point where the current log ends. Here is an easy way to do that with off-the-shelf disks:

Dedicated cylinders.   Dedicate a pair of disks to the log and reserve a cylinder of disk to buffer the end of the log on each of the disks. In IMS, this cylinder and the corresponding algorithm were called the *write-ahead data set* (WADS).

Write anywhere on next track.   Each successive write goes to a different disk track within the WADS. These writes start with the next sector to come under the disk write head. This implies a 0.2 ms latency for disk writes (see Exercise 13).

Write log when cylinder fills.   When all the WADS tracks have been used up, the disk arms move to the actual end of the log and write all the data that has accumulated in the WADS cylinder since the last full write. All tracks in the WADS disk cylinder now are free to accept new write requests.

Read cylinder at restart.   At restart, read the WADS cylinder and add its data to the end of the log if it has not already been placed there.

For a 20-surface disk, the WADS algorithm obtains 0.1 ms latency 95% of the time and 20 ms latency 5% of the time, for an average latency of about 1 ms. If the movement from the WADS is done by a read-ahead daemon, then all requests can achieve the 0.1 ms latency. The WADS algorithm has the additional benefit that since it never overwrites a page (it only writes new pages), parallel writes can be used without fear of destroying good data. With the advent of battery-backup memory and RAM-disks with microsecond latencies, the WADS idea becomes even more attractive. In those designs, WADS resides in the duplexed, low-latency device, while the bulk of the log resides on lower-cost media such as disk.

Once the data has been moved to durable storage, the log daemon updates log_anchor.durable_lsn of the log's descriptor in memory and wakes up any processes that had called log_flush() and were waiting for a write of the LSNs just written. If the anchor has not been updated in durable storage for a long time (several seconds), the daemon then does a careful write of the anchor in durable storage. The durable storage copy of the durable_lsn is merely a hint. It will be recomputed at restart (see Section 9.5).

---

[2] The convoy phenomenon was first observed on the log lock of both IMS and System R. Standard techniques can avoid convoys (refer to Chapter 8, Subsection 8.3.1), but they cannot solve the problems of the lock being 100% utilized. If the log lock becomes too busy, the log should be split into several log tables.

9.4.9 Multiple Logs per Transaction Manager

In a system that supports multiple logs, the transaction manager must be aware of which logs the transaction participates in. The transaction manager uses this information during rollback to find all the transaction's log records and to apply the UNDO operation to each of them. For simplicity, a single log is assumed here, but the more general design is briefly described. In both designs, the log manager informs the transaction manager by invoking log_transaction(LSN) each time a transaction writes a log record (see the log_transaction() and log_insert() code). In the multilog case, log_transaction() needs an additional parameter naming the log table. The first time a transaction writes to a particular log, the transaction manager allocates an entry indexed by that ⟨transaction, log table⟩ pair. Each entry contains the table name and the minimum and maximum LSN (min and max LSN) of that transaction in that table. As with the one-log version of log_transaction() presented previously, the transaction manager returns the NullLSN on the first insert to a table. On subsequent calls, the transaction manager returns the former max_lsn. The log manager uses this returned LSN as prev_lsn in the header of the new log record. The relevant routine has this prototype:

```
LSN log_transaction(filename logtable, LSN new_lsn);
```

The log insert code need only be modified to pass the log table name to the log_transaction() routine.

9.4.10 Summary

The log manager implements reads of the table via SQL. The table is written by a special routine that serializes updates using a semaphore, buffers the writes in main memory, and batches the writes to durable storage.

Some simple techniques are used to minimize I/O requests. First, one asynchronous process preallocates log files; another asynchronous process performs log writes. This write daemon batches log writes, thereby implementing group commit. Writes of the log and of the log anchor follow the careful-replacement rule of not overwriting a valid object unless another copy of the valid object exists somewhere else.

The discussion now turns to using logs and the log manager to help recover the system after a failure.

9.5 Log Restart Logic

As stated earlier, the log manager knows everything; it has the complete history of all objects. The log manager is, therefore, a key component of the restart process. It helps resource managers recover their durable states by remembering their log records, and it helps the transaction manager start up by remembering the LSN of the transaction manager's most recent checkpoint record. This section describes how the log manager prepares for restart and how it behaves when the system restarts.

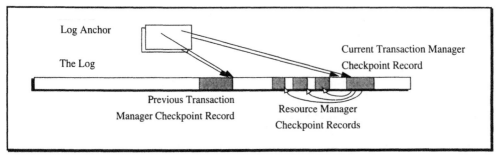

Figure 9.6: The log anchor points to the most recent transaction manager checkpoint record. That record, in turn, points to the most recent checkpoints of each resource manager.

9.5.1 Saving the Transaction Manager Anchor

Almost every resource manager needs an anchor to find its startup information at restart. In addition, the resource manager generally needs log records going back to a certain LSN (called the *resource manager low-water mark*) to actually perform the restart. To avoid many replications of the anchor maintenance logic, the log manager and the transaction manager provide a general-purpose anchor mechanism for the other resource managers. Each resource manager can write a *checkpoint* in the log, consisting of an ordinary log record containing the resource manager's restart information. The resource manager then registers its anchor LSN and low-water LSN with the transaction manager. The transaction manager, in turn, records this information in the transaction manager checkpoint record. Hence, the system only needs to remember the location of the transaction manager's checkpoint record. As shown in Figure 9.6, it is recorded as a field of the log manager's anchor record.

The log_write_anchor() routine updates the transaction manager LSN in the log anchor. It then does a flush of the log up to and including the anchor LSN, followed by a careful update of the log_anchor in durable storage, before returning. Upon return, the transaction manager will be assured that its new anchor is established in durable storage. Thereafter, the transaction manager can call the log_read_anchor() routine to read this anchor, either during normal operation or at restart. The transaction manager can then call log_read_lsn() to read the actual anchor (checkpoint record) from the log. The function prototypes are as follows:

```
void log_write_anchor( LSN anchor);        /* save TM anchor in log anchor
LSN log_read_anchor( void);                /* read TM anchor from log anchor
```

9.5.2 Preparing for Restart: Careful Writes of the Log Anchor

The log manager maintains its anchor in main memory. This anchor describes the log files and the current log end (log_anchor.lsn). The log manager periodically writes out the anchor. This allows it to start at the anchor point in the log and scan a short distance further at restart to find where the log ended at the time of failure or shutdown. The anchor also carries the anchor LSN of the transaction manager. This LSN points to the transaction manager's most recent checkpoint record and allows the transaction manager to recover its state.

The log anchor is a precious thing; it is the root of all addressability at restart. When it is updated in persistent storage, *careful writes* are used to minimize the risk of destroying both copies of the anchor. Here is a typical careful write scheme:

Ping-Pong.   Do not overwrite the most recent anchor record. Rather, store two or more anchor records in each anchor file and write a new record, augmented with the current timestamp.

Independent updates.   Align the records so that the disk transfer that writes one record does not disturb the data in adjacent records. That is, put the records in different disk blocks.

Independent failures.   Place the two files on different media with independent failure modes (e.g., two different file servers).

Accept most recent.   When reading the anchor file, read all copies and use the anchor with the most recent timestamp.

This is essentially the old master–new master recovery scheme applied to anchor records. It guards against all single failures and some double failures.

9.5.3 Finding the Anchor and Log End at Restart

At restart the log manager must find the log anchor. It does so by looking in a special place (two special places, in fact, since the anchor is duplexed): it typically looks at well-known files on well-known disk servers.[3] As explained previously, the log anchor is carefully written so that each update is atomic. Each of the two anchor files has several records, and each record has a timestamp. The log manager reads all these records at restart and takes the one with the most modern timestamp. If the two files disagree, one of the files has stale data. In that case, the log manager updates the stale record to the new version before going on.

Having read and located the log anchor at restart, the log manager must treat certain parts of the anchor with suspicion. Since most updates to the log anchor do not cause it to be copied to persistent storage, the log anchor data may be stale. If so, it must be recomputed from the log files. In particular, the maximum LSN (log_anchor.lsn) must be recomputed. Also, there is an interval between the time the next partition of the log file is allocated and the time the anchor is updated in durable storage; thus, the log manager must also look for the next file in the sequence. If the file is present, it is added to the anchor, and the anchor is updated in durable storage.

Before it can accept any new writes to the log, the log manager must first find the end of the log and clean up its last record. If the WADS algorithm is used, the log manager reads the two copies of the WADS and moves the resulting data to the end of the log. Otherwise, the log manager must search for the end of the log. The log manager scans the log table forward from log_anchor.lsn. The log manager can recognize the end of the log because the last page will be correctly formatted and will have a correct filename, page number, and timestamp.

---

[3] If you are building a recovery manager on a file system that can lose files, then you have two choices: (1) fix the file system or (2) write your own file system using raw disks. "Portable" recovery systems are forced into the second choice. Native recovery systems have considerable leverage with the file system developers once customers lose a few databases. Such events cause the file system to be fixed or the vendor to go under. This discussion assumes that all such vendors have gone under by the time this book goes to press.

The page after that will often have data left over from a different file. If the Ping-Pong write algorithm is used, the transaction manager must consolidate the last two pages of the log.

When the restart logic finally knows where the end of the log is, it may find a fragment of a log record on that page (in fact, the fragment could extend back a few megabytes if it was a monster record). If a record was fragmented across multiple pages, a suffix of the record may not have been written. The safest course then is to invalidate the fragmentary record. This is the only instance of rewriting a log record. The code is very prone to error and must be thought out carefully. For example, if multiple pages are to be invalidated, the last one should be invalidated first so that no valid page ever follows an invalid one.

Once the log manager has reestablished log_anchor.lsn and log_anchor.prev_lsn, it carefully rewrites the log anchor, restarts the log daemons, and begins accepting requests. The first request is likely to be a log_read_anchor() call from the transaction manager. Log manager restart is idempotent; it deals with failures during the restart process by beginning again. Once it has written the new log anchor, it will always restart in that state, no matter how many times it fails thereafter.

9.6 Archiving the Log

The log files are archived to tertiary storage (tape) from the online storage (disk). Online log files are eventually moved to off-line storage; otherwise, the system would fill up with logs. Such system overflows are a common form of system failure. The online logs could simply fill up all the disks, leaving no place to store new data records or log records. Archiving log files is especially important for the design outlined in the next chapter. That design generates log data, called *compensation log records*, as part of UNDO. Transaction rollback and system recovery could be blocked if the logs fill up or if the disks fill up with logs. It is important, therefore, to move log files offline when they are unlikely to be needed. In addition, offline (tape) copies of log files are usually discarded after a few days, weeks, or months.

9.6.1 How Much of the Log Table Should Be Online?

The most troublesome problem in logging is running out of space. The log runs out of space when it has no more space to write the UNDO records involved in aborting transactions and no more space to do a system restart. In this situation, the log can go neither forward nor backward. The log manager wants to avoid this situation *at all costs*. It does so by keeping a running estimate—and a very generous estimate—of how much log would be required to abort each live transaction; this estimate is approximately equivalent to the amount of log consumed by that transaction. In addition, the log manager needs to store the anchors for its resource managers and, accordingly, adds some space for that. It keeps enough log space in *reserve* to cover these needs—the log daemon actually preallocates these files and the space they occupy, so that the log manager knows they will be there when needed. When the log gets near the reserve, the log manager refuses to begin new transactions. This quickly alerts the world to the situation, because all new work stops.

The log manager estimates the rate at which it is consuming log space and informs the operator, as well as the event management system, whenever it gets within one hour of running out of space. This gives the archive system sufficient time to clear space for the log by freeing old copies of the log or by moving something else offline.

It is common to keep enough log online to support the transaction rollback, resource manager failure and restart, and system failure and restart. It is less common to keep online the log needed for archive recovery.

9.6.2 Low-Water Marks for Rollback, Restart, Archive

In discussing how much log should be kept online, it is convenient to have a term for the lowest LSN that each log client needs. These LSNs are generically called *low-water marks*.

To UNDO live transactions quickly, the UNDO log records of live transactions must be kept online. This means the log manager needs to know the minimum LSN of all transactions live in its log. This LSN is

Transaction Low-Water = min(Transaction—>min_lsn).

Call this value the *transaction low-water mark*. At restart, each resource manager will want to return to its anchor record (checkpoint record) in the log and then use the log to REDO changes commited since the resource manager's low water and UNDO uncommitted changes. During normal operation, then, each resource manager declares a low-water LSN that it wants to keep online. As a rule, these LSNs are the checkpoint records of the various resource managers:

Resource Manager Low-Water = min(resource_manager—>low_water_lsn).

The minimum of all these LSNs is the *restart low-water mark*. By not involving any offline log files, the restart low-water mark expedites system restart:

Restart Low-Water = min(Resource Manager Low-Water, Transaction Low-Water).

If all log data back to the restart low-water mark are kept online, then transaction rollback, resource manager recovery, and system recovery can all proceed from the online data.

That covers the online log needs of transaction backout and system restart. *Archive recovery*, sometimes called *media recovery*, consists of recovering a damaged object from an archived copy by applying all subsequent log records to it. Archive recovery has even lower low-water marks, going all the way back to the time the archive copy was made.

For each object covered by the log, the *object's archive recovery low-water mark* is the transaction low-water LSN at the time the most recent archive copy of that object *began*. The minimum of all these LSNs is the *archive recovery low-water* LSN. Typically, the log manager cooperates with the archive system to maintain this information as part of the archive catalogs. The archive low-water mark of each object is kept as an object attribute in the media catalogs. The global archive low-water mark is managed by the archive system. These ideas are diagrammed in Figure 9.7.

In summary, it is common to keep enough log online to support the transaction rollback, resource manager restart, and system restart. This implies keeping the restart low-water mark online. Log files earlier than these LSNs can be archived, and log files earlier than the archive LSN can be released unless one wants to keep a second-level archive (old, old masters as well as old masters).

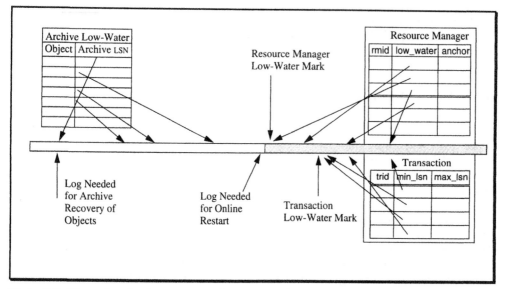

Figure 9.7: The various log low-water marks.   Transaction low-water marks are needed for online transaction backout. Resource manager low-water marks are needed for online system restart. Archive low-water marks are needed for archive recovery. Generally, the resource manager low-water mark is the cutoff point for the online log, and the archive low-water mark is the cutoff point for logs in the archive (older logs are discarded).

Sometimes the archive recovery low-water LSN is kept online. For example, the log that covers the archive catalog should be online so that the archive catalog can be recovered from the online log. This avoids the recursion problem of the log needing the archive catalog to recover the archive catalog.

9.6.3 Dynamic Logs: Copy Aside versus Copy Forward

There are two troublesome design details: hung transactions and hung resource managers. Suppose, for example, that a transaction begins and does not commit for a week. The transaction low-water mark will be weeks old and the online log will fill up the system. Similarly, suppose that a resource manager is broken and cannot be restarted until the code is fixed. Since this could take days, the resource manager low-water mark may be days old.

These problems have plagued system designers since the beginning of logging. The problem will become more acute when support for long-lived transactions—transactions designed to take days, weeks, or even years—is introduced. The standard solution is to abort transactions that exceed a time or space limit, that is, ones that are very old or that span more than 25% of the online log space. The theory is that such transactions are probably hung or are in a loop. Aborting works for online transactions but is not popular. For transactions that are in doubt due to a distributed commit decision, it is not acceptable. For in-doubt transactions, long-lived transactions, and unavailable resource managers, the only alternative is to maintain the relevant log records until the situation is resolved.

One solution to these problems is to involve tertiary storage in transaction backout and system restart; that is, just move the log records offline and keep archive copies of the log. When needed, the log records can be found in the archive. This is a feasible solution.

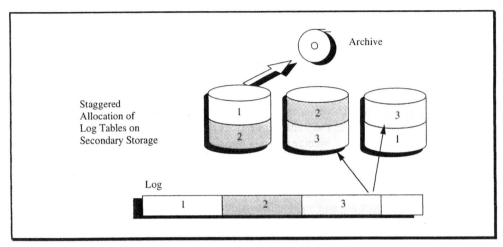

Figure 9.8: Staggered allocation of log files. By using three disks, one disk can be read to archive while the other two are absorbing new log data. This prevents the archive copy from stealing disk arms or disk bandwidth from the online logging. In particular, area 1 can be archived without disrupting the creation of log records in area 3.

A more attractive scheme is to segregate the old log records into one or more special files called the *copy aside log* (or *dynamic log*, after a similar structure maintained by IMS). Special care is needed when archiving a log partition whose records are needed to back out an old transaction or to recover a sleeping resource manager. In such cases, the log records for dealing with these two anomalies are moved to the dynamic log before the log partition is archived and its online storage freed. The premise is that a small fraction of the log records will occupy the dynamic log. When the transaction is committed, the dynamic log space is freed. If the transaction is aborted, its online dynamic log is used for rollback and then freed. When a resource manager is recovered, its dynamic log is also used and freed.

Dynamic logs are another instance of the need, mentioned earlier, for a two-dimensional log. The earlier use was to cover batch programs that might saturate the log. In both the batch case and the dynamic log case, the log manager log_open() routine must be sensitive to the situation and create a cursor on "side" files rather than on the main log.

The Camelot transaction manager moves records forward in the log rather than to a separate dynamic log space. This approach is called *copy forwarding* and *backstopping*.

9.6.4 Archiving the Log Without Impacting Concurrent Transactions

Archiving the log can adversely impact the performance of the log manager by saturating the log device. The archive operation wants to read log data at many megabytes per second. If the file being archived resides on the same disk as the current LSN, then reads and writes to the current log will frequently have to wait for archive transfers and then for a seek to the end of the log. This will be a problem, even if a WADS scheme is used. One solution, called *staggered allocation* (see Figure 9.8), is to dedicate three disks, $D0$, $D1$, and $D2$, to the log table and allocate the ith log files to disks Dj and Dk, where $j = i$ mod 3 and $k = (i + 1)$ mod 3. At any time, only two of the disks receive log information. The free disk has the most recently completed partition. That partition is an ideal candidate for the archive.

9.6.5 Electronic Vaulting and Change Accumulation

With the advent of archive robots (tape librarians, disk jukeboxes, and so on), archive media handling is completely automatic, thereby reducing operator errors in tape handling. Because these devices are typically adjacent to the system, environmental failures (fire, flood, sabotage, and so on) can destroy both the online and archival copies of the data and logs. Consequently, many application systems maintain two archival copies, placing one in a remote site, or *vault*. Transporting these media to the vault reintroduces operator error. A solution is *electronic vaulting*, in which the second archive robot is remote from the system, and the copies are written via high-speed communications lines; duplexed 45 Mb/s ($\approx$ 5 Mb/s) lines are adequate for each pair of read/write stations. Electronic vaulting is becoming common.

A system can easily generate gigabytes of log and archive data each day. When this data must be used to recover a damaged object, it can take a long time to plow through all the log data to find the records needed to reconstruct one broken disk page or other object. Many systems provide offline utilities to compress or cluster log records, thereby speeding up and simplifying object recovery from an archive copy. Compression consists of discarding irrelevant and redundant entries. Typical redundant entries are UNDO data of committed transactions and log records of aborted transactions started after the object was archived. Discarding such entries might compress the data by a factor of two. A much larger compression factor can be obtained by discarding all but the most recent update to an object, or by merging all the updates to a complex object into a single update. Such compression is very specific to the resource manager's logging design.

In addition to compression, the log can be clustered so that all log records applying to a certain object (e.g., page, message queue, B-tree) are physically clustered together. This clustering speeds recovery of individual objects by reducing data movement. The ultimate step is to merge the logs with the archive copies as an alternative to online dumps. All these forms of clustering and compression are generically called *change accumulation*. Change accumulation is most often done as an offline or off-peak activity with spare computing capacity. Clearly, all these techniques are very specific to the resource manager and must be implemented by it. (Recall that the log manager and transaction manager do not understand the meaning of the log record body; that is the job of the resource manager.)

Maintaining a separate replica of the data and applying the logs to it as they are produced is the ultimate form of change accumulation. In fact, that is becoming the common way to provide a disaster-recovery facility for online systems. In such systems, the disaster recovery site has a complete copy of the database and is continuously applying the log to its copy. If the primary system fails, the backup system is ready to take over almost immediately.

At the other end of the spectrum, some applications forego archiving completely; they just keep the online log back to the minimum of the resource manager and transaction low-water marks. This gives transaction protection and system restart but sacrifices archive recovery. The design is popular with small systems that have no tertiary storage. Such systems often keep just one log file and maintain it as a ring buffer, called the *log ring*. In that case, the file number within the LSN becomes a counter of how many times the log has gone around the ring (filled the file).

9.6.6 Dealing with Log Manager–Archive Circularity

The use of the archive system creates a possible circularity: the archive system stores its media catalogs (descriptors of tapes, optical disks, and magnetic disks) as SQL tables with transaction protection. At restart, the recovery and log managers must recover the archive database before the media catalog is readable. If the online archive database is damaged, the recovery system calls on the archive system to find the archive copies of log tapes and the old versions of the archive database. The location of these tapes is described in the media catalogs, the very data structures the system is trying to recover. This circle seems to preclude the use of transactions by the archive system. Indeed, most archive systems do not use the transactional recovery system to protect the integrity of their catalogs.

The circularity can be prevented as follows: (1) At restart, the log manager does not usually read the archive at all, since the necessary log information is generally online. Therefore, unless the archive catalogs have suffered an unrecoverable media error and all online copies have been lost, the log manager can assist in the recovery of the archive catalogs without recourse to any archive data from tertiary storage. (2) If the archive catalogs are physically damaged and require media recovery, then their old state (snapshot) must be restored from offline storage. The system or operators must know where these archive tapes are—the archive cannot depend on itself to recover from amnesia.

Log manager–archive circularity has nothing to do with transactions; it is inherent in *any* design. Once the archive snapshots have been brought online, the online log can be used to bring them up to date. This, in turn, requires that the online log cover all updates since the snapshot of the archive catalogs, and that it have independent failure modes. Since updates to the archive are relatively infrequent (say, one transaction per minute), a log of archive updates covering a week or a month will not be very large. Failures can be made independent by storing these logs on file servers and physical media disjoint from those storing the archive catalogs. Thus, it is indeed possible to implement the archive on top of the SQL system.

9.7 Logging in a Client-Server Architecture

The foregoing discussion is framed in terms of local procedure calls to the log manager. This design is typical of classical centralized systems with one or more processors sharing memory and a collection of disks. If the system is actually a loosely coupled cluster of processors, such as a Tandem Dynabus, a DEC VaxCluster, or one of the many other LAN designs, the issues are largely unchanged. Much as with databases, the performance of cluster systems depends critically on the performance of the underlying message system.

Consider the Tandem system as an example of such cluster systems. Tandem's TMF implements a process-oriented logger that looks fairly "classical." Multiple logs are supported (not as SQL tables, but as unstructured files). Typically, a cluster of up to 16 processors and hundreds of disk servers sends all the log records to a single log server for the entire cluster. Having a single logger is simpler for people to administer and minimizes log space and I/O requirements.

The logger itself is a conventional disk file server—an ordinary process pair with duplexed (mirrored) disks. Each server, of course, uses many special algorithms internally, but it looks rather commonplace to clients. The logger has only two write clients: a file system and an SQL system. Both clients "batch" records to the logger at transaction commit or when they have a full buffer of log records. The clients implement their own sequence numbers, so that they can generate log records locally without sending a message to the log to get an LSN.

The transaction backout process also reads collections of records in batches to minimize messages, but this is, again, merely a low-level buffering mechanism. Most of the code views the log as local. In summary, TMF is a fully distributed logger, but to its clients looks much like a cleanly designed local logger. Clearly, one benefit of an encapsulated interface to the log is that it generalizes nicely to such client-server architectures. The Camelot system has a similar client-server log design, well documented by Eppinger et al. [1991].

9.8 Summary

The log manager implements log tables that are readable by SQL queries. The log manager encapsulates log writing in a set of routines—log_insert(), log_flush(), max_lsn()—that map each log table onto duplexed files. These records subsequently can be read with SQL or with the low-level, record-at-a-time log_read_lsn() routine. Each log record has a unique log sequence number (LSN). LSNs increase monotonically, and the log manager ensures that if LSN(A) < (LSN(B), and LSN(B) is in durable storage, then LSN(A) will also be in durable storage. This is the basic property used by the write-ahead log (WAL) protocol.

Historically, the log has had only two clients, the database system and the queue manager. This created ad hoc interfaces to the log manager. With the advent of extensible systems supporting persistent objects, the log manager must provide a clean and simple interface. This goes hand-in-hand with the DO-UNDO-REDO interface provided by the transaction manager. Besides encapsulating the log, the log manager provides two useful services to other resource managers:

(1) It links the log records of each transaction so that UNDO scans are fast.

(2) It remembers the transaction manager's anchor LSN so that its restart logic is simplified.

Performance is a major issue for the log manager. The log participates in every update to persistent data. Various techniques presented here alleviate the performance problem. Ultimately, if a log becomes a bottleneck, it can be split into multiple logs, each protecting a subset of the objects. Each object (page, record, table, message queue, mailbox, transaction context, and so on) can send its log records to a different log table. In this way, the log need never be a bottleneck. Of course, log partitioning comes at a cost; two logs do about twice as many forces as one log.

To prevent the logs from completely filling online storage, log records below the restart low-water mark are archived to tertiary storage, and records below the archive low-water mark are discarded. A staggered allocation scheme allows the log to be archived without disrupting service. Later chapters explain how to make archive copies of objects without disrupting service.

Using the log to record updates in durable storage can improve performance by converting random updates to the database into sequential updates to the log, thereby reducing the I/O density of an application. Main-memory databases and transactional objects represented in volatile electronic memory are particular beneficiaries of this reduced I/O density.

9.9 Historical Notes

Perhaps the first reference to logging is found in the story of Theseus and the Minotaur. Theseus used a string to UNDO his entry into the labyrinth. Two thousand years later, the Grimm brothers reported a similar technique: Hansel and Gretel discovered that the log should be built of something more durable than bread crumbs (they reported the first log failure). The basic ideas, then, go back a long way. The concepts of logging, LSNs, log duplexing, WAL, and so on were all worked out by 1971, when volatile VLSI memory replaced core memory. Prior to that, the log was stored in nonvolatile core memory, and a log salvager reclaimed it at restart. Ron Obermarck, the author of IMS Program Isolation, and Homer Leonard, one of the designers of IMS queue manager, designed a logging system documented by Gray [1978]. Interestingly, others independently formalized the same ideas at about the same time [Lampson and Sturgis 1979; Lampson 1981; Rosenkrantz, Stearns, and Lewis 1977]. Clearly, it was an idea whose time had come.

The group-commit scheme was invented by Dieter Gawlick and implemented in IMS FastPath in 1976 [Gawlick and Kinkade 1985]. Eight years later, it was independently invented and named [DeWitt, et al. 1984]. Pat Helland, Harald Sammer, Richard Carr, and Andreas Reuter developed the equations to optimize the setting of group commit timers [Helland et al. 1987]. Fault-tolerant logging using process pairs was suggested by the original Lampson-Sturgis paper in 1976 and was worked out by the TMF group over several releases in the early 1980s [Borr 1981; Borr 1984]. The generalization to automatic logging of persistent types within the programming language was worked out by Liskov and others in the Argus system [Liskov and Scheifler 1983; Liskov et al. 1987]. The WADS scheme comes from Gawlick, Gray, Obermarck, and Vern Watts. The staggered log scheme is owed to John Nauman, and the Ping-Pong scheme is owed to Al Chang. The log lock convoy problem was described, and a solution proposed, in Blasgen et al. [1979].

The Camelot group—notably Dean Daniels, Dan Duchamp, Jeff Eppinger, and Al Spector—pioneered *n*-plexing of logs on unreliable servers. They also refined the idea of dynamic logs to include the copy-forward and copy-aside techniques [Daniels, Spector, and Thompson 1986; Eppinger, Mummert, and Spector 1991]. Today, the active work on logging is focused on efficiently sending the log to a second site for electronic vaulting and disaster recovery [Burkes and Treiber 1990; Lyon 1990].

Exercises

1. [9.1,5] Log records have 40 byte header overhead. (a) When is this a problem? (b) How can this problem be ameliorated?

2. [9.2, 10] (a) Given an LSN for a record of N bytes that fits entirely on a page, what file and what byte should I read? (b) What is the answer if the page size is P and there are H bytes of header and T bytes of trailer information on the page? (c) Repeat this for a record that spans two pages.

3. [9.2, 10] The previous exercise implicitly showed how to compute the LSN of the next record after a multipage log record. The text says that log records do not span files. Rather, it says that an *alias* record is put in the log to end one file and then the new record starts in the new file. (a) What should the alias record look like (header and body fields)? Note that a similar aliasing technique is used to create the two-dimensional logs described in the text. (b) What is the prev_lsn of the new record?

4. [9.2, 5] One last LSN hack: the log manager tries not to fragment records across pages so that most LSN reads will access a single page. But if the record is above a certain size, it will be fragmented. If the system will sacrifice 5% to slack, and if pages are 8 KB, then records larger than 400 bytes are candidates for fragmentation. Given such a design, how can you compute the next LSN of a record?

5. [9.2, 5] Just as a refresher, suppose that disks have a 100,000-hour mean time to failure and a 20-hour mean time to repair. And suppose that they are failfast. Ignoring software failures, (a) What is the mean time to failure of a duplexed log? (b) What is the mean time to failure of a triplexed log? (c) What is their availability class? (d) What is a reasonable estimate of the mean time to failure if software is included? *Hint: See Chapter 3.*

6. [9.4, 10] (a) Under what circumstances do readers need the log lock in order to read the log? (b) Should the log lock be a shared semaphore as a consequence? (c) Can you think of a way to avoid the shared semaphore?

7. [9.4, 10] Modify TransCB and log_transaction() as suggested in the text to support multiple logs. Assume a transaction can only participate in MAXLOGS logs.

8. [9.4, 5] Give an example where deferring log writes until the buffer fills will deadlock.

9. [9.4,5] The text said that Ping-Pong writes are especially good for simplexed logs. Why is that?

10. [9.4, 10] Imagine a centralized system with a main memory database and P processors. The system throughput is limited only by the processor speed. Ignore any lock contention. Suppose each transaction executes T instructions. (a) What is the maximum throughput of the system (transactions per second)? (b) Suppose T has two components: W seconds for useful work, and LW seconds for the commit work. A group commit timer adds delay $D/2$ to a transaction but reduces LW to LW/N cpu cycles by batching writes. N is the number of transactions committing in time D. What is a setting for D that maximizes throughput? (c) If average response time must be 1, what value of D maximizes throughput? Assume $1 >> W >> LW$.

11. [9.4, 15] Group commit delays commit requests so that it can batch requests together. The WADS scheme tries to minimize commit response time by eliminating device latency. Does it make sense to use both WADS and group commit? As devices get faster and RAM-disks offer 100 ms latency, is there a need for group commit?

12. [9.4, 5] The WADS discussion claims the device latency is $\approx .2$ ms. Derive that, assuming that disks rotate 60 times a second, sectors are 1 KB, and there are 50 sectors per track.

13. [9.5, 5] In what sense are Ping-Pong writes and careful replacement like crabbing?

14. [9.5, 15] The discussion of group commit mentioned that delaying the release of high-traffic locks may be a problem. (a) Give an example of the problem. (b) One strategy is to release such locks prior to the write of the log (prior to the initiation of the flush requests). Under what circumstances can this be done with no risk of aborting other committed transactions if this transaction happens to abort? (c) In the cases where there is a risk and the application is willing to accept the risk, describe what records the system must keep (and how carefully it must keep them) in order to correctly detect the situation.

15. [9.5, 15] The log restart discussion mentioned that at restart, the end of the log may contain a fragmentary log record. Design a way to "clean up" such fragments.

16. [9.5, 5] Log restart must be idempotent. What does that mean?

17. [9.6,15] The discussion of dynamic logs was vague on the contents of the dynamic log for a hung resource manager. What is it?

18. [9.6, 15] How are the various low-water marks ordered? For example, is the transaction LSN always greater than the restart LSN?

19. [9.6, 15] This exercise explains why change accumulation is a good idea. Suppose the archive recovery of a 1 GB disk will require applying a day's worth of log records to the disk. During the week, about 10^7 log records were written. The log records are each about 100 bytes long, and 1% of them apply to this disk. Consider two scenarios: (a) The week-long log is applied directly to the disk using 100 MB buffer pool. (b) The log is filtered to remove irrelevant records, then sorted (at 10^4 records/second), and then applied to the disk in sequential order. Assume disks have 25 ms service times for random reads or writes, and that the disk can scan the data at 10 MB/s.

20. [9.6, 5] Consider the single-file ring-buffer log design. Suppose the log has n bytes, the low-water LSNs are $\{L_i\}$, and the durable_lsn is L. How much of the ring buffer is free? *Hint: Worry about careful writes.*

21. [9.2, 5] The text explained that the log manager can safely do optimistic reads most of the time. What is the key property of the log that makes this possible?

Answers

1. It may be a problem when the log body is small compared to 40 bytes (say, 8 bytes). (b) Group several log bodies together if possible.

2. In all cases, read file a.prefix.logaNNN, where NNN = LSN.file, or read the "b" version of the file. Let *rba* mean LSN.rba. In case (a), read bytes [rba ... rba + N-1] of that file. (b) The same as (a). (c) Let $Q = P - T - (rba \bmod P)$. Then the first record fragment is [rba ... rba + Q–1], and the second fragment starts at $rba + Q + H + T$ and has $n - Q$ bytes.

3. The alias should be a log record with null trid, null tran_prev_lsn, log manager RMID as the RMID, current timestamp, the current and previous LSN set as usual. The body should indicate to the log manager that on forward scans of the log, this is an alias record and should switch the scan to the next log file. (b) The new log record prev_lsn can point to this alias, or it can point to the prev_lsn of this alias log record.

4. You can't. It is the LSN you compute if the record is big (> 400 bytes) or if the record fits, but otherwise it is the next useful byte of the next page. Without knowing the size of the next record, you have no way of knowing for sure. You guess the computed LSN and then check to see if your guess was right. One way to speed this up is to store the LSN of the next record in the header of each page.

5. (a) $\mathrm{MTTF_{pair}} \approx \dfrac{\mathrm{MTTF}^2}{2 \cdot \mathrm{MTTR}} = 10^{10}/20 \approx 5 \ 10^8$ hours ≈ 10 millennia. (b) $\mathrm{MTTF_{TMR}} \approx \dfrac{\mathrm{MTTF}^3}{3 \cdot \mathrm{MTTR}^2} = 10^{15}/300 \approx 3$ 10^{11} hours ≈ 1000 millennia. (b) $\mathrm{MTTF^{TMR}} \approx \dfrac{\mathrm{MTTF}^3}{3 \cdot \mathrm{MTTF}^2} = 10^{15}/300 \approx 3 \cdot 10^{11}$ hours $\approx 1{,}000$ millennia.

(c) Duplex availability is $10/(5 \cdot 10^8) \approx 2 \cdot 10^{-8}$ so class 7. Triplex is $10/(3 \cdot 10^{11}) \approx 3 \cdot 10^{-11}$ so class 10.

(d) Less than 100 years and less than Class 6.

5. Create view *V42* as   SELECT trid, timestamp, body
                         FROM   log
                         WHERE resource_manager = 42;
   grant SELECT on V42 to Zaphod;.

6. (a) While a log insert is in progress, the last log record, and so the last page(s) of the log, may be inconsistent. If readers are at or below log_anchor.prev_lsn they do not need a semaphore, because those records are not changing. If they want to read log_anchor.lsn, then they need to acquire the semaphore. (b) Maybe, but see (c). There are many ways to allow readers to detect whether the current LSN is valid and to wait for it to become valid if they want to. One simple scheme is for readers to fetch the log_anchor.lsn and then fetch the log lock. If the log lock is zero, the log record is valid. If the log lock is not zero, then log_insert() is working on it. If the readers request the semaphore, it will be granted immediately after the log_insert() completes. It should then release the log lock and proceed to read the completed record. Many other approaches are possible.

7.
```
typedef struct {    TRID          trid;                                          /* transaction identifier                       */
                    struct {  filename    log;                               /* name of log file                             */
                              LSN         min_lsn;                           /* lsn of its first log record                  */
                              LSN         max_lsn;                           /* lsn of its most recent log record            */
                              } logs[MAXLOGS];                               /* an array of high- and low-water marks        */
                    /* stuff */                                             /* many other items not relevant here           */
                    } TransCB;                                              /*                                              */
LSN log_transaction(filename log, LSN new_lsn)                              /* Tell the TMR about a new log record          */
    { TransCB *    trans = MyTransP();                                     /* pointer to transaction structure             */
    int                   i;                                               /* loop index on logs array                     */
    LSN                   prev;                                            /*trans prev log record                         */
    for (i=0; i < MAXLOGS & trans->logs[i].filename != BLANK; i++)  /* search log array for name                            */
        { if (trans->logs[i].filename != filename)                        /* found it                                     */
            { prev = trans->logs[i].max_lsn;                              /* make a copy of the record's lsn.             */
            trans->logs[i].max_lsn = new_lsn;                             /* trans max lsn is this record now             */
            return prev;}                                                 /*                                              */
        trans->logs[i].filename = filename;                               /* new entry, fill in log table name            */
        trans->logs[i].min_lsn = new_lsn;                                 /* trans max lsn is this record now             */
        trans->logs[i].max_lsn = new_lsn;                                 /* trans min lsn is this record now             */
        return NullLSN; };                                                /* prev lsn = NullLSN since this is first        */
```

8. Suppose the system is running a single batch job that has called Commit Work. That job will stall until the buffer fills. But the buffer will not fill until the batch job commits and goes on to the next mini-batch step. This is a kind of deadlock: each is waiting for the other. That is why the log daemon has a ≈ 100 ms timer that causes it to stop waiting for the log to fill.

9. Duplexed logs can use serial writes to avoid corrupting partial log pages. Simplex logs cannot use serial writes, they must use Ping-Pong.

10. (a) Maximum throughput is P/T. (b) D = infinity, so that N = infinity and LW/N is zero. (c) $N = D \cdot P/(W + LW/N) \approx (D \cdot P)/W$. Average response time is $1 = W + D/2 + LW/N \approx W + D/2 + (W \cdot LW)/(D \cdot P)$. This gives $0 = D^2 + D(W - 1) + W \cdot LW/P$. Solving this quadratic for D gives an estimate. This estimate is the work of Carr, Helland, Sammer, and Reuter.

11. Group commit also cuts down overhead by batching requests together. If group commit timers are set much above the device latency (~ 30 ms for disks), it makes little sense to use the WADS. Note that the

biggest group commit savings comes when going from one to two transactions per group (a factor of two). The n'th member of the group saves $1/n$. So unless commit response times or lock duration times are critical, the extra expense of WADS is not needed. Rather, the log flush daemon should be synchronized to the disk rotation and do a group write on every n'th revolution. If durable device latencies approach zero, and if they are inexpensive, then the rational for group commit disappears.

12. The disk head sees $60 \cdot 50$ per second. That is 3,000 sectors per second, or one every 333 microseconds. On the average, you only have to wait for 1/2 a sector, so that is 166 microseconds. That is $\approx$ 2 ms.

13. The analogy may be a little thin, but crabbing does not free one resource until it has used it to acquire a second resource. Careful replacement does not replace one object until there is a second object that is valid.

14. See the discussion of field calls and IMS lazy commit in Chapter 7.

15. The simplest way is to change the header to have the log manager as the resource manager, have a dummy trid, and set the length to the existing length. That will invalidate the fragmentary record. No one but the log manager will ever act on it. This is similar to the alias record created by the log manager when switching to a new log file (see Exercise 3). The other strategy is to try to reclaim the space by invalidating the pages holding the log record (last first), and then writing, discarding the partial log record on the last page containing a valid log record. This must all be done with careful updates to the durable log.

16. If restart fails and the restarts many times, the log anchor must eventually come to the same state.

17. All the log records belonging to that resource manager (with that RMID) from the rm.low_water_lsn to the **log lsn** at failure. In addition, it must include the **low_water lsn** of any live transaction that has log records associated with that RMID, since such transactions must eventually be undone by that resource manager.

18. Archive low-water is less than the others. Restart low-water is less than transaction low-water and resource manager low-water. At a graceful shutdown, the transaction low-water is nil (no live transactions), and the restart low-water is very recent (close to the checkpoint record written by the transaction manager).

19. There are 10^5 relevant log records. (a) In the first case they are random, so they get a 10% hit rate in the 100 MB cache. Consequently, in that case the system does $\approx 2 \cdot .9 \cdot 10^5$ random requests (a read and a write). Each request takes $2.5 \cdot 10^{-2}$ seconds, for a grand total of $4.5 \cdot 10^4$ seconds, or about 12 hours. (b) Scanning the log at 10 MB/s and filtering out the relevant records will take 100 seconds. This will result in 10^5 records that can be sorted in the 100 MB buffer pool in 10 seconds. The log can then be applied to the disk sequentially, reading 50 MB at a time, applying the log, and then writing out the 50 MB. Reading the next 50 MB can be overlapped with processing the previous 50 MB. So in essence, the system must do a 2 GB read and write. At 10 MB/s, this is 200 seconds. So the total time for case (b) is less than 10 minutes, about 100 times faster than the "random" approach.

20. Suppose the log has not wrapped, so that the busy part is between L=min{L_i} and H=log_anchor.lsn. Then if Ping-Pong is used, pages H and $H + 1$ are busy, and the page containing L is busy. So if the page size is P, the free log is bytes $[0 \ldots L - (L \bmod P)]$ and also the segment $[(H + 2P) - (H \bmod P) \ldots n-1]$.

21. Most pages have a "final" value that can be sensed by the writer (in this case, the final value is "full"). If a reader gets a "final" value, it knows the other page has the same value.

Commitment:
It's like bacon and eggs.
The chicken participates.
The pig is committed.

ANONYMOUS

10

Transaction Manager Concepts

10.1 Introduction

This is the first of three chapters on the transaction manager. In this chapter, the external functions of the transaction manager are outlined, and the basic techniques used to write transactional resource managers are presented. The next chapter explains how a transaction manager works. It covers the normal commit and rollback operations and describes system restart, resource manager restart, and recovery from an archival copy. It also shows the algorithms and data structures used to implement these ideas. The third chapter in this group, Chapter 12, presents the advanced topics of optimizations, high availability, heterogeneous transaction managers, chained and lazy commits, and persistent savepoints.

Understanding transaction management is difficult. It is complex when compared to concurrency control's elegant and simple model (see Chapters 7 and 8). The complexity leads to a bag of tricks, each solving some particular problem. The tricks have names like DO-UNDO-REDO, *two-phase commit, force-log-at-commit, fix, WAL, LSN*, and so on. So far, the topic has eluded attempts to simplify the model.

This chapter begins with a brief refresher on the transaction verbs presented in Chapters 4, 5, and 6. The application calls and the resource manager callbacks are quickly reviewed. Then, as a preview of the next chapter, the various recovery scenarios are sketched in Section 10.2, which is necessarily a whirlwind tour. Skip it if you dislike such things.

The remaining sections present techniques used to implement transactional resource managers. The recovery actions of a session manager are described, and a one-bit resource manager is implemented as a step-by-step example. The DO-UNDO-REDO protocol that generates log records and acts on them at rollback and restart is demonstrated. Then, several log record styles are introduced, ranging from physical (byte-oriented) logging to logical (functional) logging. This book recommends a compromise between the two, called physiological logging. The essential techniques used by physiological logging are explained, and the chapter ends with a description of the two-phase commit protocol.

10.2 Transaction Manager Interfaces

The transaction manager does very little during normal processing; it simply gathers information that will be needed in case of failure. Although such failures are rare, the transaction manager nevertheless furnishes the A, C, and D of ACID. It provides the all-or-nothing property (atomicity) by undoing aborted transactions, redoing committed ones, and coordinating commitment with other transaction managers if a transaction happens to be distributed. It provides consistency by aborting any transactions that fail to pass the resource manager consistency tests at commit. And it provides durability by forcing all log records of committed transactions to durable memory as part of commit processing, redoing any recently committed work at restart. The transaction manager—together with the log manager and the lock manager—supplies the mechanisms to build resource managers and computations with the ACID properties.

In the simple case, each network node has a single transaction manager with a single log table that records all the changes to recoverable objects at that node. With the aid of the log manager, the transaction manager records the first and last log record of each live transaction. In addition, each log record has the key of the transaction's previous log record. This gives the transaction manager a linked list of the transaction's UNDO records. To aid system restart, the transaction manager also records transaction state changes and transaction manager checkpoints in the log.

When a client invokes a server (a resource manager), the transaction processing (TP) monitor's transactional remote procedure call (TRPC) either does a domain switch, creates a new server process, or allocates a process from a preallocated pool of server processes. In any case, the TRPC mechanism tells the transaction manager when a new local resource manager joins the transaction.

Each local resource manager sends all its log records to the common log. If an object is distributed among network nodes (e.g., a replicated file), then each fragment sends its log record to a local log (see Figure 10.1). In that sense, the fragment "belongs" to that transaction manager and log.

If a transaction is completely local, then the communication manager does nothing special. The communication manager does, however, detect distributed transactions—either

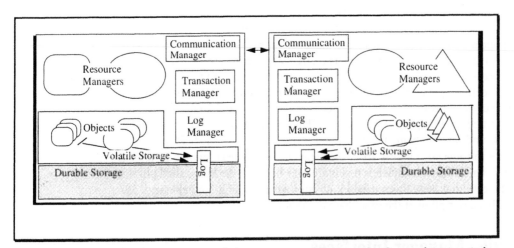

Figure 10.1: The transaction manager and the resource managers cache the persistent state in volatile memory. Changes made to an object are recorded in the log. Most of the log is kept in durable memory. A transaction altering many objects at many nodes can generate log records in many different logs. The transaction manager tracks the resource managers and remote transaction managers used by each transaction. It invokes them at transaction commit and rollback.

remote ones that are visiting this node, or local ones that are about to visit a remote node. When a remote TRID (transaction identifier) first arrives on a session (as a transactional RPC), the communication manager informs the transaction manager about the new TRID. The transaction manager allocates an entry in the live transaction table for this new transaction; this entry has the foreign transaction's name. Conversely, when a session first sends a local or remote TRID to another node, the communication manager informs the transaction manager about it. In this way, the transaction manager knows where foreign transactions came from and which transactions have emanated from this node.

That information is critical for transaction commit and rollback. If the transaction is to be rolled back, then the rollback must propagate to all the associated sessions and nodes. Conversely, when a transaction started at this node wants to commit, the transaction manager must ask all other participating nodes to vote on the commit decision, and it must inform them of the outcome. This logic is clarified in the discussion of distributed transactions and two-phase commit.

10.2.1 The Application Interface to Transactions

Applications declare transactions by bracketing a set of actions with a Begin-Commit or a Begin-Rollback pair. Begin_Work() allocates a trid. Each subsequent action is performed for that transaction by some resource manager as either a local or a remote procedure call. The TRPC mechanism propagates the TRID and informs the transaction manager of all resource managers participating in the transaction.

The TRID tags the transaction's messages, locks, and log records. It is the ACID object identifier. In that sense, the transaction manager is the resource manager for TRIDs. The transaction manager exports the following verbs as an application interface:[1]

```
TRID         Begin_Work(context *);          /* begin a transaction                        */
Boolean      Commit_Work(context *);         /* commit the transaction                     */
void         Abort_Work(void);               /* rollback to savepoint zero                 */

savepoint    Save_Work(context *);           /* establish a savepoint                      */
savepoint    Rollback_Work(savepoint);       /* return to a savepoint (savept 0 = abort)   */
Boolean      Prepare_Work(context *);        /* put transaction in prepared state          */
context      Read_Context(void);             /* return current savepoint context           */

TRID         Chain_Work(context *);          /* end current and start next transaction     */

TRID         My_Trid(void);                  /* return current transaction identifier      */
TRID         Leave_Transaction(void);        /* set process TRID to null, return current id*/
Boolean      Resume_Transaction(TRID);       /* set process TRID to desired TRID           */

enum tran_status { ACTIVE , PREPARED , ABORTING , COMMITTING , ABORTED , COMMITTED};
tran_status  Status_Transaction(TRID);       /* return the status of a transaction identifier */
```

---

[1] Commits can be lazy, savepoints can be persistent, and transactions can be chained. For simplicity, these refinements are ignored in this chapter.

The meanings and uses of these verbs are discussed in Chapters 4, 5, and 6. The implementation of each is discussed in the next chapter.

The typical transaction is just a simple C program that uses a presentation resource manager, such as a persistent X-Windows toolbox, then uses a database resource manager, such as Ingres, and finally commits. Such programs have this form:

```
Begin_Work();
read_window();
do_some_sql();
write_window();
if (ok) Commit_Work();
    else Rollback_Work();
```

For this application, the transaction manager simply implements the three transaction verbs Begin, Commit, and Rollback.

Slightly more sophisticated applications use the Save_Work() verb to *nest* transactions, establishing points of internal consistency within the transaction. Rollback_Work() can return the transaction to an earlier savepoint. Rollback to savepoint zero undoes the entire transaction and is a transaction abort (Chapters 4 and 5 discuss these concepts). Figure 10.2 diagrams such scenarios.

The transaction model can be generalized to parallel nested transactions, but for simplicity, the presentation here is restricted to transactions without parallelism. The lack of parallelism within a transaction vastly simplifies matters. A transaction's execution can be

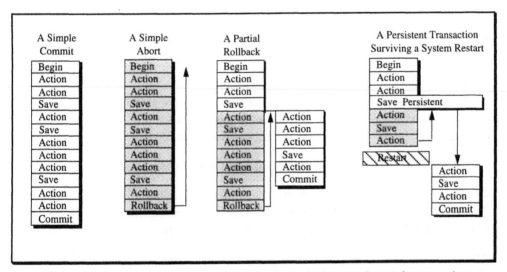

Figure 10.2: The different types of transaction executions. In the normal case, the transaction executes and commits. If the transaction aborts, it either calls Rollback_Work() or is rolled back by the system. In other cases, the transaction does a partial rollback to an intermediate savepoint and then continues forward processing. In some cases, the transaction declares a persistent savepoint. In that event, its state is preserved across system restarts.

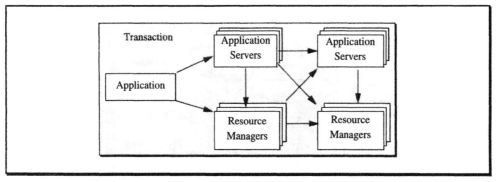

Figure 10.3: Transaction execution forms a call graph, with the transaction beginner at the root. The other participants join the transaction via local or remote procedure calls. They can include application programs or resource managers (SQL, windows, queues, and so on). Only the root can call commit, but any participant can invoke rollback or savepoints and can vote on commit.

viewed as a call graph of all the resource managers and processes participating in the transaction (see Figure 10.3). Because there is no parallelism, only one participant is executing at any given instant. The others are waiting for more requests, for answers, or for the transaction to commit or roll back. The distinguished participant that started the transáction is called the *root*. To simplify application programming, only the transaction root can call Commit_Work().

Transactional RPC messages carry the caller's current TRID. Invoked processes automatically inherit the caller's TRID, rather than call Begin_Work() explicitly. They can call Save_Work(), creating savepoints, and Rollback_Work(), undoing the transaction state to any point prior to the current savepoint.

Normally, there are no transaction rollbacks and no system restarts. Each resource manager accepts requests from the application and operates on the objects it implements. These operations acquire locks and generate log records. The locks and log records are tagged with the TRID generated by the Begin_Work() call. This is illustrated in Figure 10.4.

When the root calls Commit_Work(), the transaction manager invokes each participant, asking it to vote on the consistency of the transaction and to perform any consistency tests that were deferred until the end of the transaction. The database manager, for example, performs any deferred consistency checks, tests referential integrity constraints, executes any deferred triggers, acquires field call locks, and tests the field call predicates. If any of these tests fail, the participant votes no to the commit poll, and transaction rollback is initiated. If all vote yes, the transaction is committed via a second round of calls to the participants (see Chapter 7, Subsection 7.12.1). If any vote no or fail to respond in time, the transaction manager aborts the transaction. During phase 2, participants apply their deferred operations (e.g., field call transformations, lock releases, deferred message deliveries, and real operations) associated with the transaction. This is the two-phase commit protocol later described in detail.

If a participant calls Rollback_Work(), all resource managers participating in the transaction are invoked to UNDO state changes they made for that transaction. If a participant fails, the transaction manager aborts all transactions in which that process participates. A more sophisticated approach is to return to the most recent persistent savepoint. In any case, the transaction manager must detect process failures and act on them.

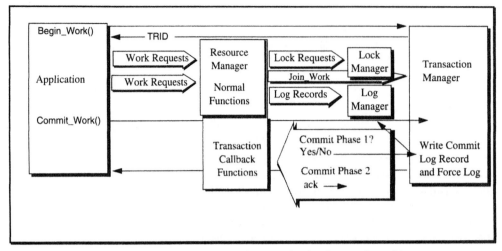

Figure 10.4: The normal, no-failure execution of an application interacting with a resource manager.   The transaction manager generates a trid at Begin_Work(). The TRID tags all work requests, log records, and lock requests. When the application commits, the transaction manager calls the resource manager to vote on the transaction's consistency. If the vote is yes, the transaction manager writes a commit record to the shared log table and forces it to durable media. The transaction manager then tells the participants that the transaction committed.

10.2.2 The Resource Manager Interface to Transactions

Resource managers implemented on top of (that is, using) a persistent programming language or database can act as ordinary application servers. For these simple resource managers, the persistent programming language or database resource manager handles recovery. The simple resource manager is registered with—*installed* in—the TP monitor and exports its methods (entry points). Clients invoke the methods via TRPCs that automatically join the callees to the transaction. The server runs and returns as though it were an ordinary, non-transactional program. Chapter 6 (Section 6.3) gives an example of a queue manager implemented in this way.

More sophisticated resource managers want to vote on transaction commit and to generate log records. Such resource managers export a set of callbacks (entry points) that are invoked by the transaction manager. If any callback is null, it is not invoked. Thus, for example, a resource manager that only wants to be informed about commit would only export that procedure.

When a resource manager is installed, it is assigned a unique resource manager identifier (RMID), and its callbacks are registered. The following callbacks are declared when the resource manager is installed with the transaction manager (see Chapter 6):

Boolean	**Savepoint**(LSN *);	/* invoked when tran calls Save_Work(). Returns RM vote	*/
Boolean	**Prepare**(LSN *);	/* invoked at phase_1 commit. Returns vote on commit	*/
void	**Commit**();	/*called at commit Ø2	*/
void	**Abort**();	/*called at failed commit Ø2 or abort	*/
		/*	*/

void	**UNDO**(LSN);	/* Undo the log record with the specified LSN	*/
void	**REDO**(LSN);	/* Redo the log record with the specified LSN	*/
Boolean	**UNDO_Savepoint**(LSN);	/* Undo savepoint. vote TRUE if can return to savepoint	*/
void	**REDO_Savepoint**(LSN);	/* Redo a savepoint.	*/
		/*	*/
void	**TM_Startup**(LSN);	/* transaction mgr restarting. Passes RM checkpoint LSN	*/
LSN	**Checkpoint**(LSN * low_water);	/* TM taking checkpoint. Return checkpoint LSN,	*/
		/* set low water LSN	*/

Each time a resource manager starts, it calls the transaction manager to identify itself and to initiate its recovery. Once the resource manager's recovery is complete, it can begin offering services. When a particular service is invoked by a transaction, the resource manager is joined to the transaction by the TRPC mechanism, which automatically generates a call of the form

Boolean **Join_Work**(RMID, TRID);   /*   */

This call informs the transaction manager that this resource manager is participating in the transaction. Thereafter, the callbacks will be invoked for savepoint, rollback, prepare, and commit events of that TRID. By joining the transaction, resource managers can vote at phase 1, returning TRUE or FALSE, and be informed at phase 2 of commit. Similarly, they can participate in rollback to a savepoint. They can veto the savepoint by returning FALSE, which means that they want to initiate further rollback to an earlier savepoint. These interactions are diagrammed in Figure 10.5.

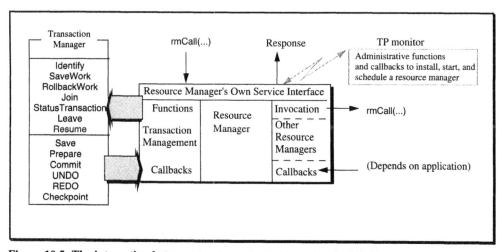

Figure 10.5: The interaction between a resource manager and the transaction manager. The application calls the transaction manager to begin, commit, or abort the transaction. The resource manager calls the transaction manager to identify itself, to join a transaction, to leave it, and to initiate transaction rollback. On the other hand, the transaction manager invokes the resource manager callbacks at savepoints, commit points, UNDO and REDO steps, and at checkpoints.

10.2.3 Transaction Manager Functions

The transaction manager coordinates recovery in case of failure. There are several scenarios to consider.

Transaction rollback. The transaction manager coordinates transaction rollback to a savepoint or cancellation (abort) of the transaction. Such rollbacks and aborts can be initiated by any participant.

Resource manager restart. If a resource manager fails and restarts, the transaction manager presents the log records needed to return the resource manager to its most recent committed state.

System restart. At restart of the computer system, the transaction manager helps recover the durable state of the local resource managers. It also resolves any distributed transactions that were in doubt at the time of the crash or shutdown. This mechanism also implements transaction manager restart.

Media recovery. If an object is damaged, the transaction manager helps the resource manager reconstruct the object using archive copies of the object and the log of all changes to the object since the object was archived.

These cases cover transactions and data within the scope of a single transaction manager. A transaction manager typically protects the transactions at a node or cluster of a network. A transaction involving several clusters will likely involve several transaction managers. These transaction managers may fail and restart independently. They use a two-phase commit protocol to make transaction commitment atomic. If one of the transaction managers fails during this protocol, then additional work will need to be done when it restarts and reconnects to the other transaction managers. When viewed from the failing TM's perspective this is just system restart, but when viewed from the perspective of the other (nonfailing) TMs, it gives rise to one more scenario:

Node restart. Transaction commitment is coordinated among independent transaction managers when one of them fails.

10.2.3.1 Transaction Rollback

The transaction manager performs rollback (see Figure 10.6) by reading the transaction's log backwards (most-recent-first order). As part of the log record header, each log record carries the name of the resource manager that wrote it. Thus, the transaction manager invokes the UNDO() callback of that resource manager and passes it the log record. The resource manager must undo the action that wrote the log record, returning the object to its old state. When the transaction is undone to the designated savepoint, all resource managers are invoked to vote on the savepoint. Is it OK? If they all vote yes, the rollback to savepoint was successful. If any votes no, rollback continues to the next prior savepoint. This continues until savepoint zero is reached, or until all the resource managers vote yes. It is the transaction UNDO protocol later described in detail.

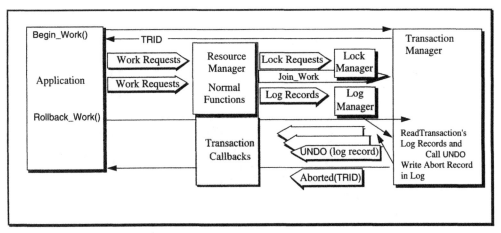

Figure 10.6: Control flow in a transaction abort. At transaction UNDO, the transaction manager reads the transaction's log and passes each record to the resource manager that wrote it. The resource manager is expected to UNDO the action. When UNDO is complete, the transaction manager calls the Abort() entry point of each resource manager and then writes a record in the log, saying the transaction was aborted. Rollback to a savepoint has similar logic.

10.2.3.2 Restart

If a resource manager fails and restarts, or if the node fails and restarts, the transaction manager is responsible for helping each resource manager recover its state. To this end, the transaction manager regularly invokes checkpoints during normal processing. It begins a checkpoint by calling each resource manager and suggesting it checkpoint its state to persistent memory; the transaction manager then ends the checkpoint. This is all in preparation for the unlikely restart event.

At restart, the transaction manager scans the log table forward from the most recent checkpoint to the end. For each log record it encounters, the transaction manager calls the REDO() call back of the resource manager that wrote the record passing the log record. The resource manager must advance the object to the new state represented by applying the changes described in the log record. When this scan is complete, all transactions have been redone. This is the REDO protocol described in Subsection 10.3.1 and Chapter 11, Section 11.4.

Some of the transactions redone at restart may not have committed. Some may have been in progress, while some may have been *persistent* transactions (ones with persistent savepoints). A few may be involved in distributed commit. In the simple case, the uncommitted transactions are undone (see Figure 10.7). In the more complex cases of distributed transactions and persistent savepoints, the transaction manager either preserves the transaction state (persistent) or negotiates with the other transaction managers in the network to resolve the outcome of the in-doubt transactions. This is another aspect of the two-phase commit protocol.

10.2.3.3 Media Recovery

In rare cases, a resource manager loses the online state of an object (e.g., the disk-based copy). In such cases, the current state must be reconstructed from an archival copy of an

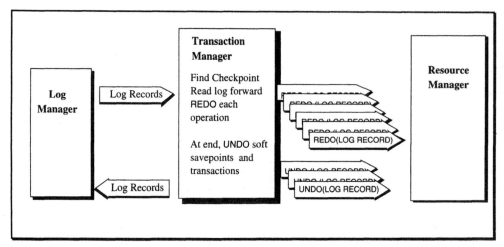

Figure 10.7: Data flow in a system restart. The transaction manager reads the log table to find its restart information. It then scans the log table to the end, redoing all transactions. When the log end is reached, the transaction manager undoes any soft savepoints and any transactions that are uncommitted and not at a persistent savepoint. Finally, it records the current state by writing a new checkpoint to the log table.

object, along with a log of all changes since the archive copy was made. The archiving and restoration of the object are done jointly by the resource manager and the archive system. Once the archived object has been restored, the transaction manager scans the log table for all log records needed to reconstruct the current object state; it then invokes the resource manager's REDO entry point with each such log record. This process, called *media recovery*, leverages the system restart mechanism to recover data from offline copies of the data.

10.3 Transactional Resource Manager Concepts

The preceding whirlwind tour of transaction manager interfaces introduced many terms. This section defines those terms and the algorithms that use them.

10.3.1 The DO-UNDO-REDO Protocol

The *DO_UNDO_REDO protocol* is a programming style for resource managers implementing transactional objects. It recommends that each operation be structured so that it can be undone or redone. That is, each operation on an object, called the DO program, should perform the operation; in addition, it should produce a *log record*. The operation design should also include UNDO and REDO programs. The UNDO program can reconstruct the old object state from the new object state and the log record. Conversely, the REDO program can construct the new object state from the old state and the log record (see Figure 10.8).

The DO_UNDO_REDO protocol contrasts with the nonincremental checkpoint and old master–new master protocols. Those protocols record the old and new values of objects at transaction boundaries, rather than recording the incremental changes a transaction makes to objects.

The contents of log records and the style of programming UNDO and REDO are elaborated in the next subsections. First, however, it is important to understand how log records

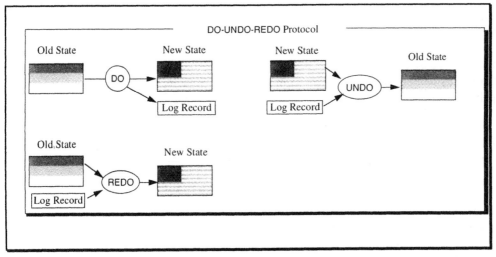

Figure 10.8: A representation of the DO_UNDO_REDO protocol programming style. Each state transformation should generate a log record that can be used to UNDO the operation from the new state or REDO the operation from the old state. Designing an operation using this protocol involves designing the UNDO and REDO programs, along with the log record and the normal DO program.

are used. As a transaction progresses, its update operations generate a sequence of log records. This sequence is called the *transaction's log*. As explained in the previous chapter, resource managers add these records to the common log table. Each record has a unique key, called its log sequence number (LSN). An SQL cursor can be defined on the log table to give just the log records of a transaction:

```
declare cursor for    transaction_log      /*                                            */
        select      rmid, lsn         /* a cursor on the transaction's log          */
        from        log               /* it returns the resource manager name       */
        where       TRID = :TRID      /* and record id (log sequence number)         */
        descending  lsn;              /* and returns records in LIFO order           */
```

The transaction manager can undo the whole transaction by undoing each of its individual actions. To accomplish this, it reads the transaction log and invokes each log record's UNDO operation. Note that the log should be read backwards, undoing the most recent operation first.

```
void transaction_undo(TRID TRID)              /* Undo the specified transaction.             */
  { int    sqlcode;                            /* event variables set by sql                  */
    open cursor transaction_log;               /* open an sql cursor on the transaction log   */
    while (TRUE)                               /* scan trans log backwards & undo each record */
          { fetch transaction_log into :rmid, :lsn;  /* fetch the next most recent log record */
            if (sqlcode != 0) break;           /* if no more, trans is undone, end while loop */
    rmid.undo(lsn);}                           /* tell resource manager to undo that record   */
    close cursor transaction_log;              /* Undo scan is complete, close cursor         */
  };                                           /* return to caller                            */
```

If UNDO to a savepoint were desired, the UNDO could read the record to see if it is the desired savepoint number and if so, stop.

Conversely, at system restart and in archive recovery situations, the transaction manager must ensure that changes made by committed transactions are preserved—that is, *durable*. Since the log records of many transactions are all lumped into the shared log table, the transaction manager reapplies each transaction's updates by performing the following REDO operation:

```
void log_redo(void)                          /*                                                  */
    {declare cursor for the_log               /* declare cursor from start of the log forward     */
                select   rmid, lsn            /* gets resource manager id  log record id (lsn)     */
                from     log                  /* of all log records.                               */
                ascending lsn;                /* in FIFO order                                     */
    open cursor the_log;                      /* open an sql cursor on the log table               */
    while (TRUE)                              /* Scan trans log forwards & redo each record.       */
        { fetch the_log into :rmid, :lsn;     /* fetch the next log record                         */
        if (sqlcode != 0) break;              /* if no more, then all are redone, end while loop   */
    rmid.redo(lsn);}                          /* tell resource manager to redo that record         */
    close cursor the_log;                     /* Redo scan is complete, close cursor               */
    };                                        /* return to caller                                  */
```

Note that REDO is applied in the forward direction: the most recent changes are applied last. REDO proceeds forward in the log (FIFO), while UNDO proceeds backward (LIFO). After REDO has been applied, there may be some transactions that generated log records but did not commit. Such transactions will be undone to their most recent persistent savepoint— the transaction UNDO logic is applied to them. The result is a consistent state: all committed transactions have been redone, and all uncommitted transactions are either still in progress or have been undone.

That describes the basic function of log records. The next subsections discuss the contents of log records and how to write the UNDO and REDO operations.

10.3.2 The Log Table and Log Records

Chapter 9 described a log manager in detail. A brief summary of the relevant externals is included here.

The local log is a table available to all resource managers. The log can be read via either SQL or a low-level, record-at-a-time interface. The log is an entry-sequenced table; thus, each log record's key—the log sequence number (LSN)—is simply a long integer. The log manager encapsulates sequential inserts to the log with the routine

```
LSN     log_insert( pointer buffer, long  n); /* insert a log record with body = buffer[0...n-1]              */
```

Each log record has a standard *header* and a type-dependent *body* that describes the operation that generated it. The header is filled in by the log manager and carries the transaction identifier, the name of the resource manager that wrote the record (the manager that can UNDO or REDO the transaction), and a few other useful fields (see the structure that follows, or see Chapter 9). The log body contains whatever information is needed by the UNDO and REDO operations. Each log record has this header structure:

```
typedef struct {   LSN           lsn;            /* lsn of record                          */
                   LSN           prev_lsn;       /* the lsn of the previous record in log  */
                   TIMESTAMP     timestamp;      /* time log record was created            */
                   RMID          rmid;           /* resource mgr id writing the record     */
                   TRID          TRID;           /* id of transaction that wrote this record */
                   LSN           tran_prev_lsn;  /* prev log record of this trans (or 0)   */
                   long          length;         /* length of log record body              */
                   char          body[];         /* dummy body of log record               */
                 } log_record_header;            /*                                        */
```

DO operations invoke log_insert() to generate such log records. The log manager formats the log record header and manages both the online log and archiving of old logs. The next subsection gives examples of the log record bodies of a particular resource manager and how the DO_UNDO_REDO protocol works in a particular case.

Of course, a resource manager can keep its own log, but it will then have to read the log and orchestrate its own recovery at transaction undo, transaction redo, and system restart. Having a single common log to allocate and archive simplifies system administration. It also simplifies the resource manager—there is less code to write—and improves performance, since all transactions add records to a single sequential log. Portable resource managers, however, may want a private log.

10.3.3 Communication Session Recovery

With the basic concepts of log records and DO_UNDO_REDO in place, we can now discuss the recovery structure of a particular resource manager in more detail. Let us consider the issue of recovering the communication sessions of a communications resource manager. A *session* is a communication pipe between two end points. Sessions are variously called virtual circuits, connections, dialogs, and conversations. Sessions carry messages; either end point can send a message to the other end point. The basic session operations are OPEN, SEND, GET, and CLOSE.

The DO_UNDO_REDO protocol for communication sessions is relatively simple. The recoverable state of a session consists of the two session end points, their sequence numbers (inbound and outbound), as well as any undelivered messages (see Subsection 3.7.4). Since sessions are usually private to the transaction, no locks are involved, and no concurrency issues arise. When a message is sent via a session, the value of the message and its sequence number are logged. When a message is received, a savepoint is established, the sequence number of the received message is logged, and the message is acknowledged. This results in the following structure for the body of a message log record:

```
enum MSGOP {OPEN, CLOSE, GET, SEND}; /* the kinds of session-oriented log records  */
struct message_log_record_body       /* log rec describing a transactional session change */
       { SESSION   session;          /* session name                               */
         MSGOP     operation;        /* send, get, open, close, reset,...          */
         long      seq_no;           /* sequence number of message                 */
         long      length;           /* length of message body                     */
         char      message[length];  /* the message                                */
       };                            /*                                            */
```

The REDO of OPEN() and CLOSE() are the OPEN() and CLOSE() operations themselves. The UNDO of OPEN() and CLOSE() operations are CLOSE() and OPEN(), respectively. The REDO of a SEND() operation consists of resending the message with the original
sequence number. The REDO of a receive operation advances the local inbound sequence
number. The UNDO of a send operation is easy for the sender; it sends a second message that
says "ignore that other message I sent you—the one with sequence number n." Such
messages are called *cancels*. Cancel messages usually travel as new messages with higher
sequence numbers (sequence numbers increase). Since the cancel message is a new message,
it is an example of an UNDO operation generating a log record: the cancel message itself is
treated as an ordinary message and generates recoverable state changes and log records at
the sender and at the receiver. Such log records are called *compensation log records* because
they compensate for the work of a DO operation.

Handling cancels at the recipient is nontrivial, for the cancel must undo the original receive. The typical approach is to use savepoints. Because messages of committed transactions are never cancelled, cancel messages only apply to messages sent and received by an
uncommitted transaction. To prepare for cancels, the recipient establishes a savepoint at
each message receipt. An arriving cancel corresponds to some earlier savepoint. The first
thing the recipient does is to roll back to the savepoint. This returns all recoverable objects
and communication sessions to their state as of the receipt of the original (cancelled) message. Thus, undoing the recoverable message state is fairly easy if transactions are supported. It works nicely for complex communications environments in which all effects are
reversible (computer displays and the like). The difficulty of handling cancellation without a

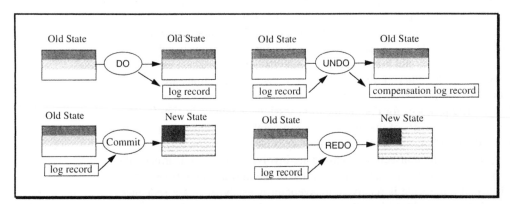

Figure 10.9: A representation of the DO_UNDO_REDO protocol for *real* operations.   The actual
state transformations of real operations—operations that cannot be undone—are deferred to commit.
When the operation is requested, a log record is generated so that the operation can be performed when
the transaction is sure to commit. This log record can also be used to REDO the operation in case the
transaction must be redone from the log at restart. The UNDO operation does not need to change the
state, since UNDO only applies to uncommitted operations. Rather, the UNDO operation merely invalidates the log record generated by the DO operation, probably generating a compensation log record
to cancel the first one. The CLOSE operation is often treated as a real operation, since undoing the
CLOSE involves reopening the session. OPEN is a difficult and quite complex operation involving
authorization, authentication, and much information that may not be present in the session descriptor.
Rather than writing the code to reopen the session, then, the implementer of a communication manager
may find it easier to defer the CLOSE to phase 2 of transaction commit.

transaction mechanism explains, in part, the popularity of transactions in distributed applications: they provide a simple exception-handling mechanism.

10.3.3.1 Real Operations

The discussion of UNDO leaves open the question of how to cancel messages to "real" devices such as printers, drill presses, gas pumps, nuclear reactor rods, and so on. These real operations cannot be undone—that is the definition of a real operation. Consequently, such operations should not be done until the transaction commits; they must be deferred to phase 2 of commit. When the commit decision is made, the "real" messages can be sent. The standard technique for deferring real operations is to generate the REDO log records during normal processing but not to send the actual message. Then, at commit, the REDO log is applied to actually deliver the message (see Figure 10.9). If this approach is taken, message cancellation invalidates the log records of the corresponding deferred operations.

10.3.3.2 Idempotence and Testable

Just as it may not be possible to undo some messages, there can be a problem with resending some messages multiple times (multiple REDOs). That topic is covered in the discussion of fault tolerance (Chapter 3, Subsection 3.7.3), but for the sake of convenience it is repeated here. An operation is said to be *idempotent* if doing it many times is equivalent to doing it once (see Figure 10.10). The term derives from the definition of an idempotent function: $f(f(x)) = f(x)$. The term *restartable* is also used to mean idempotence.

Message sequence numbers make message SEND idempotent. Sending the message many times causes the message to be received at most once, since all later messages arriving with the same sequence number are treated as duplicates and are discarded. However, many physical devices lack a sequence number mechanism to discard duplicates. One alternative is to structure the device interface so that operations are inherently idempotent. For example, the operation "move the reactor rods down 2 cm" is not idempotent. If applied enough times, it will shut the reactor down or blow it up. On the other hand, the operation "move the

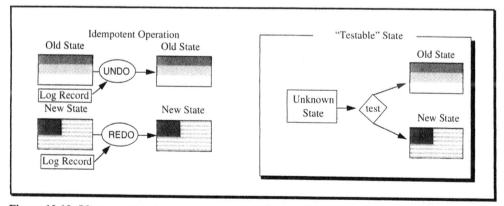

Figure 10.10: Idempotent operation versus testable state. If the UNDO or REDO operation can be repeated an arbitrary number times and still result in the correct state, the operation is *idempotent*. If the old and new states can be discriminated by the system, the state is *testable*. If an operation is not idempotent and the state is not testable, the operation cannot be made atomic; that is, "exactly once" semantics are not attainable.

reactor rods to position 35" is an idempotent operation. If the rods are already at that position, they will not move.

If the device can be designed with idempotence in mind, most operations can be made idempotent. Some devices do not have idempotent operations; in that case, their state must testable. A state is *testable* if the sender can reliably distinguish the old state from the new state. If the state is testable, the sender repeats the loop while(old_state){send} until the new state is attained (this assumes that messages are not arbitrarily delayed). If the operation is not idempotent and the state is not testable, then by definition it is not possible to provide *exactly-once* operations on the device.

10.3.3.3 Summary

To summarize communications recovery, log records are generated by message SENDs, and log records plus savepoints are generated by message GETs. Undoing a SEND consists of sending a cancel message, while redoing a SEND consists of resending the message. Cancel messages cause the receiver to return to an earlier savepoint. In addition, OPEN and CLOSE are inverses of one another; they form the respective UNDO operations for each other. Since OPEN is such a complex operation, CLOSE is often treated as a real operation and deferred until phase 2 of commit. Sending messages to devices that cannot cancel must be delayed to commit. Either messages must be idempotent, or the recipient state must be testable. Table 10.11 summarizes the actions of the sender and receiver at each event of idempotent operations.

Most systems, in fact, do not have very powerful savepoint support; they just abort the transaction (return to savepoint 0) in case of a rollback condition. This definitely cleans things up.

Table 10.11: Summary of session and message recovery actions.   During normal operations, message SENDS generate log records, and receipt of messages generate transaction savepoints. UNDO causes a cancel message to be sent and rolls the transaction back to the corresponding savepoint. REDO causes the message to be resent. Duplicate messages are discarded using a sequence number scheme. Sending messages that cannot be cancelled (real messages) must be deferred to phase 2 of commit.

	Sender	Receiver
DO	log message and sequence number send message	establish savepoint
		log message and sequence numbers
		acknowledge
UNDO	send cancellation (generates log record)	Log cancellation message
		return to savepoint
		acknowledge
REDO	resend message	if not duplicate ⟨normal DO processing⟩
		else just acknowledge
COMMIT	send any deferred (real) messages	do it

Communication sessions raise interesting issues. They illustrate the need for real operations, for idempotent operations, and for operations that generate compensation log records as part of their undo processing. Now, let us turn to the issues of the DO_UNDO_REDO protocol for durable memory objects.

10.3.4 Value Logging

There are many styles of writing log records and the corresponding UNDO_REDO programs for durable data. The simplest technique, called *old value–new value logging,* places the old and new object states in the log record. UNDO and REDO are then trivial: the object need only be reset from the appropriate value in the log record. As an example, if the objects are fixed-length pages of files, then value-log records would look like this:

```
struct value_log_record_for_page_update    /* body for a page value logging scheme   */
    { int     opcode;                       /* opcode will say page update            */
    filename fname;                         /* name of file that was updated          */
    long     pageno;                        /* page that was updated                  */
    char     old_value[PAGESIZE];           /* old value of page                      */
    char     new_value[PAGESIZE];           /* new value of page                      */
    };                                      /*                                        */
```

If the object state is small—for example, a single cell acting as a counter—then value logging is a good design. But if the object is large and the change is small, then the log record often is *compressed* so that it contains only the changed portion(s) of the object. If, for instance, a page of a large file is changed, the log record might contain the page change rather than the old and new values of the entire file object. Similarly, if a single field of a page is changed, the log record for the page might be compressed to the following:[2]

```
struct compressed_log_record_for_page_update /*                                      */
    { int  opcode;                          /* opcode will say compressed page update */
    filename fname;                         /* name of file that was updated          */
    long     pageno;                        /* page that was updated                  */
    long     offset;                        /* offset within page that was updated    */
    long     length;                        /* length of field that was updated       */
    char     old_value[length];             /* old value of field                     */
    char     new_value[length];             /* new value of field                     */
    };                                      /*                                        */
```

One of the nice things about these physical log records is that UNDO and REDO are idempotent. The UNDO operation of a value log record sets the page to the old value. That can be done many times, and it always leaves the page in the "old" state. Conversely, the REDO operation is also idempotent. This may seem trivial, but the logical logging schemes described next need an extra mechanism to achieve idempotence.

---

[2] Since the UNDO and REDO transform one value to a second value, a further compression by a factor of two can be obtained by storing the exclusive OR of the old and new values, rather than both the old and new values. This is often called *transition* logging (see Exercise 9). Care must be taken to ensure idempotence.

10.3.5 Logical Logging

Value logging is often called *physical logging* because it records the physical addresses and values of objects. A second style of logging—called *logical logging,* or *operation logging*—records the name of an UNDO-REDO function and its parameters, rather than the object values themselves. To give an example, an SQL system might record the single log record

<insert op, tablename, record value>

to record the insertion of a certain record in a certain table. This insertion might cause disk space to be allocated for a new file extent or cause other records to move within the page; it might even cause a complex index update (a B-tree split). If the table has indices, each index insert will generate comparable work. In the extreme, the table may have a trigger or integrity constraint that runs a program in response to the insert. Thus, this single "logical" log record could correspond to tens or hundreds of physical log records.

The UNDO of a logical insert action is a logical delete of the record from the table, and the REDO operation is a logical insert of the record in the table. This is another virtue of logical logging; often, the UNDO operation is simply another (preexisting) operation on the object.

Clearly, logical logging is the best approach; the log records are small, and the UNDO-REDO operations are mirrors of one another. As many failed designs have shown, however, there is a flaw in the logical logging approach. Logical logging takes the DO-UNDO-REDO model literally. It assumes that each action is atomic and that in each failure situation the system state will be *action consistent*: each logical action will have been completely done or completely undone.

To see how action consistency is often violated, consider our insert example. What if there had been a failure during the insert? Here is a short list of such failures:

Logical failure.   One of the index inserts tries to create a duplicate on a unique index and initiates rollback.

Limit failure.   One of the index files runs out of space and initiates rollback.

Contention failure.   One of the index inserts encounters deadlock and initiates rollback.

Media failure.   A page of one of the files is damaged and cannot be written, or an index at a remote node is unavailable; the action is rolled back.

System failure.   The system crashes during the action.

In all these cases, the action will be partially complete, and the state will not be action consistent. The UNDO operation will be requested to UNDO states produced by such partially complete actions. In the system failure case, a more or less random subset of the pages in persistent memory will have been updated. Thus, the fundamental problems with logical logging are twofold:

Partial actions.   Partially complete actions can fail and need to be undone. The UNDO of these partial actions will not be presented with an action-consistent state. Partial actions are relatively easy to handle, because they imply that an initial subsequence of the action was done. For example, if steps *A*, *B*, and *C* were involved, then perhaps nothing was done, or perhaps *A* alone was done, or perhaps *A* and *B* were done.

Action consistency.   At restart, persistent media present a state in which the most recent page writes are preserved, and the network presents a state in which all acknowledged messages have been sent. Actions involving a single message or a single persistent write are atomic (all-or-nothing at restart). But complex actions involving several messages or persistent writes are not necessarily atomic. Consequently, UNDO and REDO may not be presented with an action-consistent state at restart. To continue with the partial-action example, if the action involved steps *A*, *B*, and *C*, then *any* subset of {*A*,*B*,*C*} may persist at restart.

10.3.5.1 Shadows

Because logical logging is so elegant and seductive in its simplicity, designers have gone to considerable lengths—solving the partial-action and action-consistency problems—to make it work. The basic idea is to ensure that UNDO and REDO operations need only deal with action-consistent states. To achieve this, a two-level recovery scheme is introduced: a low-level recovery system presents an action-consistent state to a high-level scheme that can then use logical logging. The best developed of these schemes, called *shadows* (see Figure 10.12), deals with the page consistency problem; it turns a page-consistent state into an action-consistent state by keeping a shadow copy—the old value—of each page modified by an action.[3] The shadows are maintained as either a log or a separate page directory structure. If an action aborts, the action's page modifications are discarded, and the pages return to their shadow values. This covers UNDO during normal operation (the partial action problem).

Shadow restart from persistent memory is more subtle; it must solve the action-consistency problem. To do this, the shadow mechanism periodically produces an action-consistent state in persistent memory by creating an *action-consistent checkpoint*. There are many ways to do this, but the most popular has been to periodically action-quiesce the system. No new actions are started, and the system waits for all existing actions to complete. This eventually produces an action-consistent state, unless some action is waiting for a lock. Such long waits are not allowed. At the *shadow checkpoints*, the current state is atomically made persistent: the changed pages are copied to new locations in persistent memory, never overwriting any shadow pages. Then a directory is written, telling where the current version of each persistent page is located, and a new free-space table is written. When the directory write is complete, a single write to persistent memory makes the new directory the current directory, as shown in Figure 10.12. After this write completes, normal work resumes. At restart, the system begins from the most recent shadow-checkpoint state. This presents the UNDO and REDO operations with an action-consistent state at restart.

Performance problems and complexity plague the shadow design just described. Shadow pages force transactions to lock at page granularity, since UNDO is performed by returning to the shadow page. This creates serious problems for hotspots such as the end of sequential files, interior nodes of B-trees, free-space allocation tables, list headers, and so

---

[3] To these authors' knowledge, no one has developed a corresponding shadow scheme to make a message-consistent state an action-consistent state. Consequently, this design does not generalize to distributed applications or databases. If you develop a solution using pure logical logging, make sure it handles this issue, too.

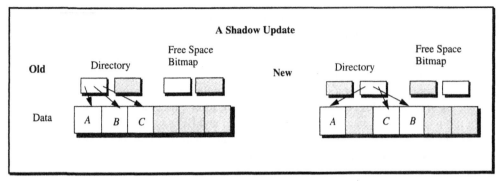

Figure 10.12: Design of a shadow update. Updating a shadow involves writing the new page to persistent memory in a new slot; in the figure, logical page *B* is remapped to data slot 4. A new version of the data free-space bitmap is then written to a new slot, and, finally, a new directory is written to the other slot. The new directory has a newer timestamp. Shaded pages represent free or unused space. At restart, the shadow file system reads both directories and takes the one with the most recent timestamp. This example shows that shadows generally decluster data and convert one random page update into three random persistent memory writes (directory, free space, and data).

on. The action-quiesce for shadow checkpoints is a nuisance, at best. Long-running actions (ones that involve many processor cycles, I/Os, or remote messages) must be broken into shorter actions so that they can be interrupted. In general, actions are not allowed to wait for external events. Lock waits are handled in a special fashion. Without overwriting the old version, the shadow mechanism writes each updated page to a new location, gradually destroying any physical clustering of the pages in a file or database. Little by little, the complexity builds, and the simplicity and elegance of logical logging are lost.

10.3.6 Physiological Logging

A compromise between logical and physical logging has emerged. It uses logical logging where possible. This design is called the *physical-to-a-page logical-within-a-page,* or simply *physiological* logging. These are the ideas that motivate physiological logging:

Page and message actions. Complex actions can be structured as a sequence of messages and page actions. Each message applies to a single session, and each page action applies to a single page.

Mini-transactions. Page and message actions can be structured as mini-transactions that use logical logging. When the action completes, the object (page or session) is updated; an UNDO-REDO log record is created to cover that action. In this sense, these actions are atomic, consistent, and isolated mini-transactions.

Log-object consistency. It is possible to structure the system so that at restart, the persistent state is page-action and message-action consistent. The log can then be used to transform this action-consistent state into a transaction-consistent state at restart.

Each mini-transaction generates a log record for its page or session state change. This is the physical logging part of the design: a log record applies to a particular physical page or a particular communication session. The state transformation of a physical object (page or session) can be represented physically or logically. The term *physiological logging* derives from the use of logical logging to represent the transformation of physical objects. A physiological log record for a table insert would have the following structure:

```
struct physiological_log_record_for_record_insert /*                          */
    { int     opcode;                  /* opcode will say physiological insert   */
    filename fname;                    /* name of file that was updated          */
    long     pageno;                   /* page that was updated                  */
    long     record_id;                /* index of record in page                */
    long     length;                   /* length of record                       */
    char     record[length];           /* record value                           */
    };                                 /*                                        */
```

The insert action might reorganize the page or, if the page is kept sorted, it might cause all the records on the page to be moved. In addition, insert actions typically update the page header and trailer. The fact that the page was reorganized, the header was changed, and so on, are all implicit in this logical log record. By contrast, a physical-physical log record representing the insert of a 100-byte data record could be two pages long: one for the old page and one for the new. In this case, the physiological log record is about 100 times smaller than the purely physical log record.

Complex actions generate a sequence of physiological log records. In addition to the log record describing the table insert, there would be additional log records describing the inserts to the table indices, the updates performed by any triggers, and so on. Figure 10.13 and the following example contrast physiological logging with purely logical logging.

Consider the insert example that had logical log record

⟨insert op, tablename = A, record value = r⟩.

If the table had two indices, and all the index inserts were simple, the corresponding physiological record bodies would be

⟨insert op, base filename = A, page number = 508, record value = r⟩
⟨insert op, index1 filename = B, page number = 72, index1 record value = keyB of r = s ⟩
⟨insert op, index2 filename = C, page number = 94, index2 record value = keyC of r = t ⟩

These records would be generated by the three page actions that updated the data pages of Tables A, B, and C. If overflow processing, B-tree splits, or triggers were involved in the insert, then more pages would be involved and, consequently, more log records would be generated to cover the relevant page changes. (Many more examples of physiological logging appear in Chapter 15's presentation of B-trees.)

Physiological logging has many of the benefits of logical logging. When compared to physical logging, it has small log records. Like logical logging, the UNDO and REDO operations are often similar to other operations. For example, the REDO of a physiological insert log record is almost identical to inserting a record on a page, and the UNDO operation is almost identical to deleting a record from a page.

The fundamental idea of physiological logging is to think in terms of sessions and pages: log records are generated on a per-page or per-session basis. Log records are designed to make logical transformations of pages and sessions.

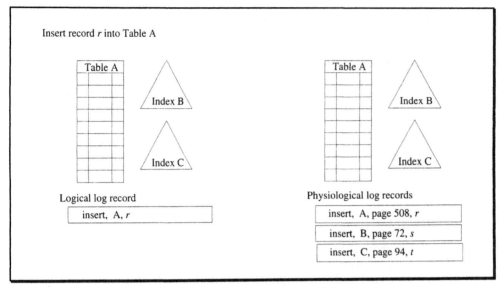

Figure 10.13: Logical logging versus physiological logging. The logical log has only one record per action, while the physiological log gets a log record per updated page (or per sent message). If the action at the left failed after the insert to Table A but before the insert to Index C, then the UNDO or REDO of the action would be difficult, since the state of Index B is unknown, but the current state is clearly wrong. At the right, the complex operation is broken into three separate page actions. If there is a failure between steps A and C, then either log record B exists or it does not. If it does not exist, the action can be undone by simply undoing the A record. If it does exist, then both the A and B records need to be undone. By structuring each page action as a mini-transaction, it is easy to UNDO or REDO complex operations.

Physiological logging presumes pages are *page-action consistent*: It postulates that page transformations change the page and generate a log record, and that complex actions are composed of such page actions. Because the page may be inconsistent during the page transformation and creation of the log record, a semaphore is used to isolate such changes from the view of other transactions. When the page action is complete, and the log record is present in the log, the semaphore on the page can be released. This semaphore logic is called the *fix rule* (defined in Subsection 10.3.7).

To summarize the discussion so far, the DO-UNDO-REDO protocol is a programming style that suggests each state transformation generate a log record that can be used to UNDO or REDO the action. These log records accumulate in a transaction log. The actions of a transaction can be undone by undoing, in turn, each of its actions. In fact, by undoing only some of the transaction's actions, the UNDO can be partial, giving the effect of savepoints. The log records themselves are often physical to a page or session and logical within a page or session—the so-called physiological logging design.

10.3.7 Physiological Logging Rules: FIX, WAL, and Force-Log-at-Commit

At this point, the notion of page-action consistency may still be a little vague. This subsection clarifies that idea and shows how to accomplish it for physiological logging. The discussion falls into two parts: the normal case, in which there are no failures, and the restart case, in which volatile memory has been reset. The normal case, called the *online* case, is covered first. For simplicity, session-message consistency is omitted (see Subsection 10.3.3).

10.3.7.1 Physiological Logging During Online Operation

Resource managers implementing physiological logging must be prepared to UNDO any un-committed action if the transaction aborts. There are many ways to do this, but a particularly stylized way is to provide the following two guarantees of consistency during online opera-tion:

Page-action consistency.   Volatile and persistent memory are in a page-consistent state, and each page reflects the most recent updates to it.

Log consistency.   The log contains a history of all updates to pages.

Taken literally, online consistency would prevent any page updates, since updating a page and generating a log record cannot happen simultaneously. To allow updates, all page changes are structured as mini-transactions of this form:

Mini_trans()
> lock the object in exclusive mode
> transform the object
> generate an UNDO-REDO log record
> unlock the object.

If the system was online-consistent when the mini-transaction started, it will be online-consistent when the mini-transaction completes.

10.3.7.2 The One-Bit Resource Manager

Let us take a concrete example to illustrate the page mini-transaction idea. Imagine a *very* simple resource manager that manages an array of bits stored in a single page. Each bit is either free (TRUE) or busy (FALSE). The resource manager accepts two calls: (1) get_bit(), which gets a free bit for the transaction, makes it busy, and returns the bit index, and (2) give_bit(), which frees the designated bit. Clients of this resource manager can call get_bit() to get the index of a free bit. That bit will be reserved until someone calls give_bit() with that index.

The interesting thing about these bits is that they are transactional. If one transaction gets bit B, other transactions cannot give bit B until the first transaction commits. If the allo-cating transaction aborts, the bit returns to the free state. Therefore, if I call give_bit(i), the bit cannot be given to another transaction until I commit. This is implemented by assigning a lock name of B to the bit with index B (see discussion of the lock() verb and lock names in Chapter 8). The resource manager acquires locks on these bits, and the lock manager ensures that no two transactions get exactly the same bits (locks) concurrently. In addition, these are durable bits; when the system restarts, the most recently committed version of the bit array is reconstructed.

This simple resource manager demonstrates most of the concepts in this book. In partic-ular, it demonstrates semaphores, locks, fix, logging, WAL, and the various resource manager callbacks. Incidentally, this resource manager is the free space manager for disks, the free block-free space manager for files, and it is found in many other applications (see Exercise 18).

The one-bit resource manager takes a dim view of failures: it insists the caller pass it a TRID, and if anything goes wrong in the call, the one-bit resource manager calls Abort_Work() and then returns. The basic data structure it manages is stored in a persistent file named ONEBIT and in a volatile memory structure:

```
struct {                          /* layout of the one-bit resource manager data structure    */
    LSN            lsn;           /* page LSN for WAL protocol                                 */
    xsemaphore     sem;           /* exclusive semaphore regulates access to the page          */
    Boolean        bit[BITS];     /* page.bit[i] = TRUE => bit[i] is free                       */
    } page;                       /* allocates the page structure                              */
```

Changes to this structure are trivial: a bit is set from TRUE to FALSE or from FALSE to TRUE. Accordingly, the physiological log record body is also trivial:

```
struct                            /* log record format for the one-bit resource manager        */
    { int          index;         /* index of bit that was updated                              */
    Boolean        value;         /* new value of bit[index]                                    */
    } log_rec;                    /* log record used by the one-bit resource manager            */
const int rec_size = sizeof(log_rec);  /* the size of the log record body.                      */
```

What do page and log consistency mean for this simple resource manager? First, let us recall two terms introduced in Chapter 7. Data is *dirty* if it reflects an update by an uncommitted transaction. Otherwise, the data is *clean*. Page consistency means that the following conditions have been met:

(1) No clean free bit has been given to any transaction.

(2) Every clean busy bit has been given to exactly one transaction.

(3) Dirty bits are locked in exclusive mode by the transactions that modified them.

(4) The log sequence number (page.lsn) reflects the most recent log record for this page.

For these simple pages, log consistency means that the following condition is met:

(1) The log contains a log record for every completed mini-transaction update to the page.

Consider the simple give_bit(i) routine. To free a bit, the routine must temporarily violate the page consistency. This transformation must be hidden from concurrent executions of give_bit() and get_bit() by other processes. An exclusive semaphore therefore protects access to the page. If every mini-transaction on the page gets the semaphore, and if each mini-transaction makes the page and log mutually consistent prior to releasing the semaphore, then each mini-transaction will observe a consistent page state.

```
void give_bit(int i)                                  /* free a bit                                           */
    { if (LOCK_GRANTED==lock(i,LOCK_X,LOCK_LONG,0))/* get long exclusive lock on the bit      */
        { Xsem_get(&page.sem);                        /* got it, so get the page semaphore          */
        page.bit[i] = TRUE;                           /* free the bit                                         */
        log_rec.index = i;                            /* generate log record saying bit is free    */
        log_rec.value = TRUE;                         /*                                                      */
        page.lsn = log_insert(log_rec,rec_size);      /* write log rec to log table and update lsn  */
        Xsem_give(&page.sem);}                         /* page is now consistent, free semaphore    */
    else                                              /* else lock failed, caller doesn't own bit,  */
        Abort_Work();                                 /*  in that case abort caller's transaction   */
    return; };                                        /*                                                      */
```

This code has all the elements of a mini-transaction. It is well formed and two-phased
with respect to the page.sem semaphore, providing a page action-consistent transformation
of the page. All of the five consistency constraints just outlined are preserved. Give_bit() dirties a bit, but it locks it in exclusive mode for the transaction. It alters a page, but it generates
a log record to undo or redo the update. Note that the lock request has a timeout of zero. If
the lock request is denied, the bit is locked by someone else, and the caller does not own the
bit. Hence, the caller is aborted. (We could just as well have waited for the lock to be
granted, freeing the bit.)

The get_bit() routine is similar but slightly longer, since it must search for a free bit:[4]

```
int get_bit(void)                                     /* allocate a bit to and returns bit index    */
    { int     i;                                      /* loop variable                                       */
    Xsem_get(&page.sem);                              /* get the page semaphore                       */
    for ( i = 0; i<BITS; i++);                        /* loop looking for a free bit                   */
        {if (page.bit[i])                             /* if bit says free, may be dirty (so locked)  */
            {if (LOCK_GRANTED =lock(i,LOCK_X,LOCK_LONG,0));/* get lock on bit            */
                { page.bit[i] =FALSE;                 /* got lock on it, so it was free              */
                log_rec.value = FALSE;                /* generate log record describing update     */
                log_rec.index = i;                    /*                                                      */
                page.lsn = log_insert(log_rec,rec_size); /* write log rec and update lsn            */
                Xsem_give(&page.sem);                 /* page now consistent, give up semaphore    */
                return i; }                           /* return to caller                             */
            };                                        /* else lock bounced(timeout =0), bit is dirty */
        };                                            /* try next free bit,                           */
    Xsem_give(&page.sem);                             /* if no free bits, give up semaphore          */
    Abort_Work();                                     /* abort transaction                            */
    return -1;};                                      /* returns -1 if no bits are available.        */
```

---

[4] As an aside, the lock request here also has a timeout of zero. The get_bit() routine cannot wait
for a lock while holding the semaphore, because that might cause a deadlock.

10.3.7.3 The FIX Rule

Online page consistency is conditional on the page semaphore being free. All the consistency constraints should be prefaced by the clause, "If the page semaphore is free, then. . . ." This acquisition of the semaphore becomes so stylized in accessing an object that it has a name: *fixing the page*. While the semaphore is set, the page is said to be fixed, and releasing the page is called unfixing it.[5]

FIX Rule:

(1) Get the page semaphore in exclusive mode prior to altering the page.

(2) Get the semaphore in shared or exclusive mode prior to reading the page.

(3) Hold the semaphore until the page and log are again consistent, and the read or update is complete.

This is just two-phase locking at the page-semaphore level. The Isolation Theorem, along with common sense, tells us that if the fix rule is obeyed, then all read and write actions on pages will be isolated. A page may be inconsistent while it is fixed; there may be a log record for it that does not match the state of the page, or there may be an update in the page that has no log record. Page updates, then, are actually mini-transactions. The exclusive semaphore on the page prevents other transactions from seeing the page while the transformation is underway. When the semaphore is released by UNFIX, the page should be consistent and the log record should allow UNDO or REDO of the page transformation, as in Figure 10.8.

Some actions modify several pages at once. Inserting a multi-page record and splitting a B-tree node are examples of such actions. As a rule, these actions are structured to get many pages and locks (several FIX steps), then do all the modifications and generate many log records (several LOG and UPDATE steps), and finally UNFIX the pages. The B-tree code in Chapter 15 gives an example. Since semaphores have no deadlock detection, they must be acquired in some fixed order to avoid deadlock. In addition, there can be no lock waits while the semaphore is held; otherwise, a lock-semaphore deadlock might arise. Exercises 18–20 explore this issue.

10.3.7.4 Dealing with Failures within a Complex Action

If page changes are mini-transactions, what happens if the operation gets an error while doing the page update? Who is responsible for the all-or-nothing atomicity of the update? If the error is easily correctable (e.g., insufficient space, duplicate record, and lock timeouts), the operation itself can restore the page to its original state, generate no log data, and then unfix the page. A simple way to provide such undo is to copy the page at the beginning of the action; then, if anything goes wrong with the page action prior to writing the log record, the page action just returns the page to its original value by copying it back. That is analogous to the shadow scheme. Often, incremental undo schemes are used to avoid the cost of making a complete copy of the page.

---

[5] The fix-unfix terminology derives from the related topic of temporarily binding a page to a fixed address in the address space.

In rare cases, the error is so serious that the page cannot be repaired (e.g., the page data structures are incomprehensible and no current copy of the page is available). In such instances, the resource manager should *invalidate* the page and initiate page recovery from persistent memory or archive memory. Most systems provide a scheme for marking a page invalid (the page header discussed in Chapter 13 has such a mechanism). Once the page is invalidated, the operation can roll back to the savepoint and return an error indication to the caller. The recovery of the invalid page will be done by an asynchronous process. Such page invalidation is rare, for the operation normally finds the page in a consistent state and leaves it in a consistent state. Note that the page invalidation is not undone by transaction rollback; it is an example of an unprotected action on a protected object.

Consider how physiological logging handles a failure within a complex action. Each complex action should start by declaring a savepoint. If anything goes wrong during the page action, the operation first makes the page page-action consistent. This mini-UNDO makes the state page-action consistent. The action can then call Rollback_Work() to return to the savepoint declared at the beginning of the complex action. That undoes all recent changes to pages and sessions (database and messages), setting them to their states as of the start of the action. The physiological design, then, vastly simplifies the problem of undoing complex actions that are in progress. Examples of such actions are set-oriented updates within SQL, cascading updates and deletes within SQL, and certain trigger procedures. A savepoint can wrap each such complex action within a subtransaction so that the complex action can be undone if it fails. This is the most widely used aspect of nested transactions.

To summarize: during online operation, page actions provide page consistency even if they fault, and they depend on transaction UNDO to roll back any failed complex operations. Having covered online operation, let us now consider how copies of volatile memory pages can be migrated to persistent memory, and how this information can be used at system restart to reconstruct the consistent state.

10.3.7.5 Physiological Logging at Restart

Page-action consistency at restart has weaker constraints than page-action consistency during online operation. Recall that volatile memory is reset at restart, but that persistent memory retains its state as of the last write. During online operation, the resource manager must generate enough information to allow it to redo any committed transaction updates and to undo any uncommitted updates to persistent memory. In preparation, resource managers implementing physiological logging make the following consistency guarantees at all times; in particular, these guarantees are enforced at system restart:

Page-action consistency. Persistent memory is in a page action-consistent state.

Log consistency. The durable log contains records of all committed updates and all updates to persistent pages.

There are two big differences between these restart consistency guarantees and the online guarantees given in Subsection 10.3.7.1. First, the clause, "each page reflects the most recent updates to it," is missing from the page-action consistency list. This means that the page may be in its original state, containing no updates of any transaction. One thing, though, is assured: if a persistent page has been updated, the log contains a record describing that update. Second, the log may have many newer updates that have not been applied to

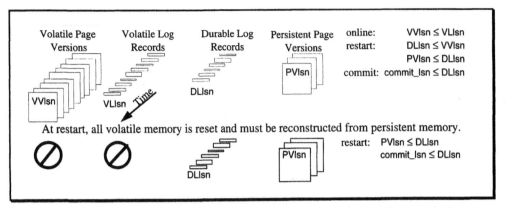

Figure 10.14: The implications of online consistency and restart consistency for a particular page and its log records. Online consistency says that the volatile page is consistent and the volatile log is current (VVlsn ≤ VLlsn). Restart consistency says nothing about the volatile state, but it requires that the persistent page be consistent and that the durable log contain log records for any committed updates to the volatile page and any updates to the persistent version of the page.

persistent memory, but it does not promise to have all the recently written log records. Rather, the durable log is guaranteed to have all committed log records, all records that precede those records in the volatile log, and perhaps some more recent uncommitted updates as well.

Perhaps a picture will help. Figure 10.14 shows the durable log, the persistent versions of a page, the current volatile page, and the log of changes to the page. The figure depicts the evolution of volatile versions of the page, which currently has log sequence number VVlsn. Online log consistency requires that the volatile log contain all log records up to and including VVlsn; that is, VVlsn ≤ VLlsn. Restart consistency ensures that if a transaction has committed with commit_lsn, then that commit record is in the durable log: commit_lsn ≤ DLlsn. In addition, restart consistency guarantees that if version X of the volatile copy overwrites the durable copy, then the log records for version X are already present in the durable log. Put more succinctly, VVlsn ≤ DLlsn.

10.3.7.6 Write-Ahead Log (WAL)

How can a resource manager guarantee these restart consistency properties? The rules are actually very simple. When a volatile page is copied to persistent memory, the resource manager first ensures that the page is consistent by getting a shared semaphore on it—that is, by fixing it. Now suppose the page is written right away, so that version VVlsn replaces PVlsn. If the page had just been updated by a get_bit() or give_bit() operation, it is unlikely that the volatile log record(s) describing the update has been written to durable memory. If the page were written to durable memory before the recent log records, the persistent page would be consistent, but restart log consistency would be violated (PVlsn ≤ DLlsn would be false). If the system failed at that moment, the log record would not yet be in durable memory and, as a result, the update to that page could not be undone at restart. To avoid this situation, the log records of a page must be moved to durable memory prior to overwriting the page in persistent memory. The writer must ensure that the log is ahead of the page. In Figure 10.14, it must ensure that DLlsn ≥ VVlsn. Once this is true, it can overwrite page PVlsn in persistent memory with page VVlsn. This rule is called the *write-ahead log* (WAL) protocol, because it writes an object's volatile log records to the durable log before overwriting the persistent data.

The write-ahead log protocol is typically implemented by calling log_flush(page.lsn) prior to copying the page to durable memory. It frequently happens that the page was updated quite some time back; consequently, the volatile log records for the page were written to the durable log long ago. In these cases, the log_flush() causes no actual I/O. But if the page was updated more recently and has some volatile log records, those records will be copied to the durable log before the data page is moved to persistent memory. If the resource manager is not in a hurry, it can use the lazy option on log_flush() (see Chapter 9).

To see this idea in action, let us look at the one-bit resource manager. Occasionally, the resource manager copies the current volatile version of the page to a persistent file. This is the program:

```
LSN checkpoint(LSN * low_water)       /* copy 1-page RM state to persistent store    */
   { Xsem_get(&page.sem);             /* get the page semaphore                        */
   *low_water = log_flush(page.lsn);  /* WAL force log up to page lsn, set low water mark */
   write(file,page,0,sizeof(page));   /* write page to persistent memory               */
   Xsem_give(&page.sem);              /* give page semaphore                           */
   return NULLlsn; }                  /* return checkpoint lsn (none in this case)     */
```

Once the checkpoint is complete, the copy of the page in persistent memory is current; that is, VVlsn = PVlsn. Checkpoint declares this as the new low_water mark for the one-bit resource manager. At restart, no updates prior to page.lsn need to be redone.

The *write-ahead log protocol* can be stated as the following rules:

Write Ahead Log Protocol:

(1) Each volatile page has an LSN field naming the log record of the most recent update to the page.

(2) Each update must maintain the page LSN field.

(3) When a page is about to be copied to persistent memory, the copier must first ask the log manager to copy all log records up to and including the page's LSN to durable memory (force them).

(4) Once the force completes, the volatile version of the page can overwrite the persistent version of the page.

(5) The page must be fixed during the writes and during the copies, to guarantee page-action consistency.

10.3.7.7 Force-Log-at-Commit

There is one more page-related case to consider: what if no pages were copied to persistent memory, and the transaction committed? If the system were to restart immediately, there would be no record of the transaction's updates, and the transaction could not be redone. This would violate transaction durability. To avoid that, all the transaction's log records are made durable as part of commit. Consequently, at restart the system will be able to redo the transaction. This brings us to one last rule: the transaction's log records must be moved to durable memory as part of commit. This rule is called *force-log-at-commit*.

Implementing the force-log-at-commit logic is simple in the single-log case. When a transaction commits, the transaction manager writes a commit record in the log and requests that the record be made durable by calling log_flush(commit_lsn). The log manager, in turn, makes the log—an entry-sequenced file—durable up to that commit record.[6]

A similar issue was involved in the discussion of message logging: committed messages must periodically be retransmitted until they are acknowledged. This means that such messages and their session sequence numbers must be logged, reconstructed at restart, and resent. Message recovery at restart is, therefore, simply a matter of reconstructing durable memory at restart (the messages and sequence numbers can be represented as durable memory). Message recovery adds no new requirements to the handling of log records and durable memory. It just requires that the transaction's log be moved to durable memory as part of commit.

In summary, then, the physiological logging assumptions of page-action consistency and log consistency require the resource manager to observe the following three rules:

Fix rule.   Cover all page reads and writes with the page semaphore.

Write-ahead log (WAL).   Force the page's log records prior to overwriting its persistent copy.

Force-log-at-commit.   Force the transaction's log records as part of commit.

10.3.7.8 Physiological Logging and Shadows Compared

Recall that shadows had two fundamental problems: (1) undoing failed partial operations during online operation, and (2) reconstructing page-action consistency at restart. Physiological logging is not immune to either problem, but it has a simple solution to each. It solves the partial action problem by establishing a savepoint at the start of each complex action. If a page action cannot complete, the action returns the page to its original state, or at least to a state consistent with the log. This is the mini-transaction idea. Rollback is then initiated to the action savepoint, and the action returns as a null operation.

Physiological logging deals with action consistency at restart by ensuring that (1) only consistent versions of pages are written to persistent memory (the fix rule), and (2) the log records needed to undo or redo an action are present in persistent memory before the new version of the page is present in persistent memory (the write-ahead log protocol and the force-log-at-commit).

Having discussed the rules obeyed by forward processing (the DO step), let us now turn to how physiological logging performs the UNDO and REDO operations.

10.3.8 Compensation Log Records

Many systems use the physiological design. For simplicity, most systems also generate log records during UNDO; these are often called *compensation log records*. This may seem

---

[6] In the case of multiple logs per transaction manager, the force-log-at-commit logic is slightly more complex. The transaction manager tracks the logs containing records of each transaction and the max LSN of each transaction (see the log_transaction() call in Chapter 9). At commit, each participating log manager is invoked to flush these log records to durable storage.

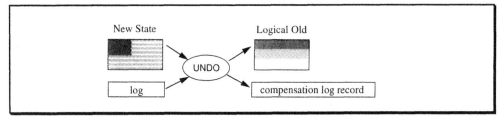

Figure 10.15: The UNDO operation generates a *compensation log record*. This type of log record, which is included in some designs, provides a simple way to invalidate a transaction's rolled-back log records.

surprising, but the UNDO operation (see Figure 10.15) generates a log record that can be used to REDO or UNDO the UNDO operation! Continuing the example of Figure 10.13 (an insert to a base table and to two indices on that table), the UNDO of that insert would generate the following three compensation log records:[7]

⟨delete op, base filename, page number, record value⟩
⟨delete op, index1 filename, page number1, index1 record value⟩
⟨delete op, index2 filename, page number2, index2 record value⟩

Why do systems generate log records describing the UNDO operations? These records just take up space; they are redundant. The discussion of session recovery (Subsection 10.3.3) gave one example of why logging UNDOs is the simplest design. The UNDO of a message-send action sends a cancel message as a brand new message and advances the session sequence number. Having UNDO set the sequence number backwards rather than forward would be dangerous, because sequence numbers are used for duplicate detection. Similar issues arise with logging of page changes.

As the transaction proceeds, it generates log records, and they are added to the end of a shared log table. When the transaction is undone, these log records become invalid. It might seem that the easiest way to invalidate a log record would be to set it to zero or to invalidate the whole batch by inserting a new log record that says "ignore all those records you saw." Indeed, this is approximately what some implementations do. As usual, though, there are complications.

It often happens that the DO-UNDO pair is not *exactly* the identity transformation, especially if logical logging is used. For example, pages frequently carry a monotonically increasing sequence number used variously to record the page version, enforce the write-ahead log protocol, and provide idempotence. This sequence number is usually just the LSN (log sequence number) of the most recent update that transformed the page and is called the *page LSN*.

What should the page LSN become when an action is undone? If subsequent updates to the page by other transactions have advanced the log sequence number, the LSN should not be set back to its original value. Suppose I update a page, setting its LSN from 1 to 2, and then you update the same page, setting its LSN to 3. If I then UNDO my request, should we set the LSN back to 1? Clearly, this should not happen, much as the cancel request cannot safely reset the session sequence number (see Subsection 10.3.3). One design is to set the page LSN to the LSN of a single new log record that says "cancel all those log records." Even

---

[7] Recall that the record-delete operation is used as the UNDO for the record-insert operation.

that design generates a compensation log record—the "cancel" record—but it complicates the UNDO protocol quite a bit, since the one-to-one correspondence between page updates and log records has been lost (it is not a physiological log record).

The solution seems to be for each UNDO operation on a page to generate a compensating log record, so that the page LSN can be advanced to the sequence number of the new UNDO operation. This makes page LSNs monotonic, an essential property for physiological idempotence (the next topic) and for write-ahead log.

The one-bit resource manager illustrates these issues. Remember that get_bit() and give_bit() generate log records and acquire locks. How does the UNDO of one of those operations work? Consider the following simple code, which undoes the operation and generates a compensation log record. Note that it advances the page LSN.

```
void undo(LSN lsn)                                  /* undo a one-bit resource manager operation    */
    { int         i;                                /* bit index                                     */
    Boolean       value;                            /* old bit value from log rec to be undone       */
    log_rec_header header;                          /* buffer to hold log record header              */
    rec_size = log_read_lsn(lsn,header,0,log_rec,big);  /* read the log record into a log_rec[0..big]  */
    i = log_rec.index;                              /* get bit index from log record                 */
    value = ! log_rec.value;                        /* get complement of new bit value               */
    Xsem_get(&page.sem);                            /* get the page semaphore                        */
    page.bit[i] = value;                            /* update bit to old value                       */
    log_rec.value= value;                           /* make a compensation log record                */
    page.lsn = log_insert(log_rec,rec_size);        /* compensation log rec and advance page lsn     */
    Xsem_give(&page.sem);                           /* free the page semaphore                       */
    return; }                                       /*                                               */
```

To summarize the previous paragraphs, compensation logging simplifies the design of physiological logging. With that design, each update to a page or session is accompanied by a log record. If the action is undone, the UNDO looks just like a new action that generates a new log record—a compensation log record.

One implication of this design is that aborting a transaction that produced n log records during forward processing will produce n new log records when the transaction is aborted (undone). In general, the log records of aborted transactions read like palindromes: when redoing them, one redoes the forward processing and then the UNDO processing. See Exercise 22 for a discussion of optimizations related to this.

10.3.9 Idempotence of Physiological REDO

UNDO logging brings us naturally to the topic of making physiological REDO idempotent. Suppose the following physiologic log record were redone many times:

<insert op, base filename, page number, record value>

As will be seen in the discussion of restart (Section 11.4), such repeated REDOs can arise from repeated failures during restart or from restarting from a fuzzy checkpoint. If no special care were taken, this repeated REDO would result in many inserts of the record into the page. The solution to this problem is to adapt the sequence number scheme used to make message SENDs idempotent (see Subsection 10.3.3). The page LSN is used to detect and suppress duplicate REDOs. If page LSNs are monotonic—that is, if UNDOs generate compensation log records rather than use one of the more sophisticated schemes—then the following assertion is true:

> *If* page.lsn $\geq$ log_record.lsn, *then*
> *the effects of that log record are present in the page.*

Given that assertion, the following logic makes physiologic REDOs idempotent:

idempotent_physiologic_redo(page,logrec)
{if (page.lsn < logrec.lsn) redo(page,logrec)};

The first successful REDO will advance the page LSN and cause all subsequent REDOs of this log record to be null operations. As discussed in the next chapter, this key property is all that is needed to make restart based on UNDO-logging idempotent.

Using the more sophisticated schemes—those that do not log UNDOs—gives rise to very subtle logic and even more subtle bugs. Consequently, after considerable experience with invalidation schemes, conventional wisdom is that it is simpler and safer to invalidate a log record by writing an inverse log record. Thus, the compensation-logging approach is taken in this book.

Consider again the one-bit resource manager. Remember that it has get_bit() and a give_bit() routines that generate log records and acquire locks. The following simple code redoes the operation and uses the LSN for idempotence. For good measure, it reacquires the lock associated with the operation.

```
void redo( LSN lsn)                             /* redo an free space operation          */
    { int          i;                           /* bit index                             */
    Boolean        value;                       /* new bit value from log rec to be redone */
    log_rec_header header;                       /* buffer to hold log record header       */
    rec_size = log_read_lsn(lsn,header,0,log_rec,big);    /* read log record               */
    i = log_rec.index;                          /* Get bit index                         */
    lock(i,LOCK_X,LOCK_LONG,0);                 /* get lock on the bit (often, this is not needed */
    Xsem_get(&page.sem);                        /* get the page semaphore                 */
    if (page.lsn < lsn)                         /* if bit version older than log record    */
        { value= log_rec.value;                 /* then redo the op. get new bit value     */
        page.bit[i] = value;                    /* apply new bit value to bit              */
        page.lsn = lsn; }                       /* advance the page lsn                    */
    Xsem_give(&page.sem);                       /* free the page semaphore                 */
    return; };                                  /*                                        */
```

10.3.10 Summary

The discussion of physiological logging introduced many concepts and terms. Let us briefly summarize them here.

Model. Complex actions are structured as a sequence of page and message actions.

LSN. Each page carries an LSN and a semaphore.

Read FIX. Read page actions get the semaphore in shared or exclusive mode.

Write FIX. Update page actions get the semaphore in exclusive mode, generate one or more log records covering the page, and then advance the page LSN to match the most recent relevant log record.

Write-ahead-log. Before overwriting the persistent version of a page, force its log records to durable memory (log_flush(page.LSN)).

Force-log-at-commit. When committing a transaction, force all log records up to the commit LSN.

Compensation logging. When undoing an action, invalidate the log record by generating a compensating log record.

Idempotence. When redoing an action, use the page LSN to achieve idempotence.

That's it! Now you are ready to write your own resource manager. We recommend you start with the two-bit resource manager.

Having discussed the generation of log records, let us look at how to make all the actions of the transaction an ACID unit by exploiting these records. How does commit assure that the transaction is atomic and durable?

10.4 Two-Phase Commit: Making Computations Atomic

During normal operation there are no memory failures, resource manager failures, or system failures; hence, there is no REDO, restart, or media recovery. However, a small fraction of transactions do fail and are aborted, either because an application or a resource manager calls Abort_Work(), or because as part of the commit step, one of the resource managers asserts that the state transformation is inconsistent. Incorrect input data, deadlock, and timeout are typical causes of application-related rollbacks. Violations of integrity constraints (e.g., uniqueness) are typical examples of resource manager–related rollbacks.

When rollback is requested, the transaction manager scans the transaction's log backwards, and for each log record it invokes the UNDO callback of the resource manager that wrote the record. At savepoints, it broadcasts the savepoint number to each resource manager participating in the transaction.

Transactions usually commit rather than roll back. When a transaction is about to commit, each participant in the transaction is given a chance to vote on whether the transaction is a consistent state transformation. If all the resource managers vote yes, the transaction can commit. If any vote no, the transaction is aborted. This is called the *two-phase commit protocol*, because there is a voting phase and, after all the votes are counted, there is an actual commit phase. Prior to the commit phase, the transaction could go either way: it could roll back or it could commit. This protocol is used both in centralized systems (to coordinate the commitment of multiple resource managers), and in distributed systems (to coordinate the commitment of multiple transaction managers). We begin our exposition with the centralized case, because the issues there are a little simpler.

Let us consider some examples that clarify the need for the two-phase commit protocol in a centralized system:

Cancel key. The client may hit the cancel key at any time during the transaction. If there is a cancel message sitting in the input buffer, the communication manager will vote no.

Server logic. A server may require that a certain set of steps be performed in order to make a complete transaction. A mail server, for example, wants a destination list and a message body. An invoice system wants a master record and at least one invoice line item. Many forms-processing systems want several forms to be *completely* filled out. In general, these systems allow the data to be presented in any order. At commit, they check the completeness of the data, and if the data is incomplete, they vote no.

Integrity checks. SQL has the option to defer referential integrity checks to transaction commit. Some mutual integrity checks (e.g., if a.spouse = b then b.spouse = a), must be temporarily suspended; otherwise, such relationships could never be created. These deferred assertions must be checked before commit. If any integrity checks are violated at commit, the transaction changes cannot be committed, and SQL votes no.

Field calls. High-performance techniques, such as the field calls described in Subsection 7.12.1, test predicates and acquire locks at the end of the transaction. They do this to minimize the time locks are held on high-traffic data. It is possible that they cannot acquire the locks or that the predicates are false. In such cases, the resource manager wants to abort the transaction and votes no.

Transactions should be atomic; thus, if any participant (resource manager) votes no, the transaction must be rolled back. If the participant explicitly votes no, it is because the transaction is incorrect. Committing it would violate the consistency of the database. If a *resource manager* votes yes, that resource manager is said to be *prepared* to commit. When all the resource managers have voted yes, the transaction is said to be prepared to commit.

When a resource manager votes yes, it must be able to commit or undo the transaction's changes, even if there is a failure and a restart. This means that after the prepare step, the resource manager cannot require any further processing that is not guaranteed to be successfully completed. It also means that the resource manager's prepared state must be persistent. For example, if the resource manager will need to reacquire locks at restart to reestablish its prepared state, then it should either reacquire locks during REDO (as the one-bit resource manager does), or it should record these locks in a log record written as part of its prepare step, and use this information at restart.

10.4.1 Two-Phase Commit in a Centralized System

How, then, does two-phase commit work in a centralized system? Consider the commitment of a particular transaction—say, transaction 599. When the application invokes Commit_ Work(), the transaction manager executes the commit logic. It needs to know the names of all the resource managers participating in transaction 599.

The first time a resource manager is invoked by a transactional RPC, the TRPC mechanism informs the transaction manager that this resource manager has done some work on transaction 599. TRPC calls the transaction manager, saying "RMID is joining transaction

599." Joining transaction 599 means the resource manager will be informed about the transaction's rollbacks and savepoints and will be asked to vote on the transaction's commit. Some resource managers are "simple"; they represent their data in terms of other resource managers. Most application servers also act like simple resource managers. Such programs do not have to join the transaction; recovery will be performed for them by the transactional resource managers. But other resource managers—such as the persistent programming languages, database systems, and even sophisticated applications—definitely want to vote on the transaction's commitment and, accordingly, join the transaction when they first do work on its behalf.

10.4.1.1 Commit

The TRPC join mechanism assures that, at commit, the transaction manager has a list of resource managers that want to vote on the transaction (resource managers that joined the transaction). The application eventually decides to commit the work performed by all these resource managers on behalf of that transaction identifier. A successful *centralized two-phase commit*, then, consists of the following sequence of steps:

Prepare.   Invoke each resource manager in the list, asking for its vote.

Decide.   If all vote yes, durably write the transaction commit log record.

Commit.   Invoke each resource manager in the list, telling it the commit decision.

Complete.   When all acknowledge the commit message, write a commit completion record to the log, indicating that phase 2 ended. When the completion message is durable, deallocate the live transaction state.

The prepare phase is also called *phase 1* of commit, and the commit phase is called *phase 2*. If any of the resource managers vote no at the prepare phase, the commit fails, and rollback to savepoint 0 is initiated (abort). If all vote yes, the commit step writes a record in the log saying that the transaction committed. This record has the transaction name and the names of all the resource managers that will be invoked at phase 2. When that record appears in durable memory, the transaction is logically committed. If the system fails prior to that instant, the commit step will have failed. If the system fails after that instant, the commit step will be carried forward by the restart logic.

Resource managers can do work and generate log records during the prepare phase. It is quite possible for a resource manager to defer work to phase 1 of commit (SQL triggers can be deferred to phase 1, field calls can generate log records at commit, and so on). In that case, the resource manager performs the work when phase 1 arrives. This added work can cause new resource managers to join the transaction. Eventually, all the resource managers have voted yes, all the transaction's work is done, all the log records have been written, and all agree that the transaction is a consistent-state transformation.

The prepare phase can invoke resource managers after they have already voted to commit. For example, a communication manager might be invoked to transmit replicated data updates to remote nodes after the communication manager had already voted to commit; or, some resource manager might invoke the database manager as part of the prepare step. In these cases, the resource manager might want to reconsider its vote. Thus, during the prepare phase, a resource manager that has already voted may call Join_Work()

again. This places it at the end of the list of voters and will cause it to be invoked a second (or third) time to vote on the transaction. The transaction manager continues to poll this list until everyone on it has voted yes. Once all have voted yes to phase 1, no resource manager can join the transaction.

After phase 1, then, the transaction *could* commit—it is prepared to commit. Now it is up to the transaction manager to make the transaction atomic (all-or-nothing) and durable. The transaction manager does this by writing a commit record for the transaction and then forcing all the transaction's log records to durable memory; this is the force-log-at-commit rule. This action durably records the commit decision in the log.[8] Once the commit record is durable, the transaction is committed. The commit record write is what makes a transaction atomic and durable. If the record is not made durable, the transaction will be undone at restart.

Once this durable write is complete, the transaction manager performs phase 2 of commit by informing each resource manager that the transaction committed. At phase 2, the resource manager knows the transaction is done and can therefore release locks, deliver real messages, and perform other clean-up tasks.

When the transaction manager has informed each resource manager that the transaction is complete, and when each resource manager has completed its commit phase 2 work and informed the transaction manager that the resource manager has completed phase 2, the transaction manager writes a log record saying that the commit is complete. This record, called the *phase 2 completion record*, is used at restart to indicate that the resource managers have all been informed about the transaction. As such, the record can be written *lazy*: that is, it does not need to be immediately forced to durable memory but can piggyback on the write of some other log records. The control flow of two-phase commit is diagrammed in Figure 10.16.

This last point brings up the concept of *lazy commit*. If an application requests a lazy commit, the transaction manager returns control to the application process right after the phase 1 vote is complete. The writes of the log commit record and related log force are done asynchronously as a lazy log write; that is, the record is not immediately forced to durable memory. The commit logic is the same, but forcing the commit record to durable memory is performed by the transaction manager as a separate and deferred task, asynchronous from the application's commit request. A lazy commit can abort; that is, a failure after the commit returns but before the commit record is recorded in durable storage can cause the "committed" transaction to be aborted at restart. So, lazy commit is for those who do not necessarily need durability. The default and common case is *eager commit*, in which all the commit work is done as part of the Commit_Work() invocation.

Commit copies no objects—only log records—to durable memory. In that sense, logging converts random write I/Os to sequential write I/Os. The transaction updates a more or less random set of objects in volatile memory, but these updates generate a sequential stream of log records. The transaction can be made durable by writing this sequence as one durable memory write (e.g., a duplexed disk write), rather than by writing the many individual objects. Since sequential disk write latencies are four times shorter than random writes, this is a

---

[8] If the system supports multiple logs, the transaction manager tracks which logs the transaction participates in and forces each of these logs (to the max_lsn of the transaction in that log) prior to writing the commit record in the master log. The individual resource managers do not need to do any log forcing unless the resource manager has a private log unknown to the transaction manager.

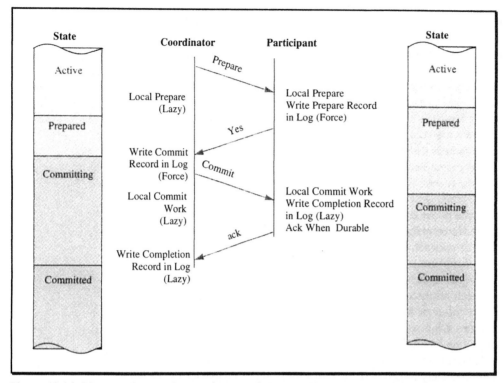

Figure 10.16: Message flows and state changes of the coordinator and participants of the two-phase commit protocol (successful commit). The coordinator sends a prepare message and a commit message. The participant acknowledges each message after performing the local prepare or commit work. These message flows can either be local TRPCs to local resource manager participants or remote TRPCs that flow as messages on a wide area network to remote transaction manager participants.

major benefit.[9] If and when durable electronic memory replaces moving magnetic memory, this benefit will become irrelevant, because electronic memories have very low latency. Nevertheless, one big write will always have an advantage over many little ones.

10.4.1.2 Abort

The discussion up to this point has been in terms of a successful commit. If any resource manager votes no during the prepare step, or if it does not respond at all, then the transaction cannot commit. The simplest thing to do in this case is to roll back the transaction. Alternatively, the commit could return the error to the application and allow it to either correct the problem or call Abort_Work(). The transaction cannot commit so long as one or more of the resource managers is not responding.

Rollback uses the transaction log and the list of resource managers that have joined the transaction. The logic for Abort_Work() is as follows:

Undo. Read the transaction's log backwards, issuing UNDO of each record. The resource manager that wrote the record is invoked to undo the operation.

---

[9] Sequential writes also have at least 10 times more bandwidth (bytes written per second). See the discussion of disks in Chapter 2 for an explanation.

Table 10.17:   The log records of a committed and an aborted transaction.   Commit invoked the two resource managers to prepare, and one of them (rm2) wrote a prepare record containing its locks. Commit then wrote a commit record containing the list of resource managers that participated in the transaction. Aborted transactions have somewhat similar information, but since UNDOs generate compensation log records, each DO step generates one or more uNDO records. The "complete" records indicate that all work associated with the transaction is complete.

Committed	Aborted
begin	begin
DO rm1	DO rm1
DO rm2	DO rm2
DO rm2	DO rm2
prepare rm2 {locks}	UNDO rm2
commit { rm1, rm2}	UNDO rm2
complete	UNDO rm1
	UNDO begin { rm1, rm2}
	complete

Broadcast.   At each savepoint—and, in particular, at savepoint 0—invoke each resource manager joined to the transaction, telling it the transaction is at the savepoint.

Abort.   Write the transaction abort record to the log (UNDO of Begin_Work( )).

Complete.   Write a completion record to the log indicating that abort ended. Deallocate the live transaction state.

The transaction manager can write the abort completion record into the log without waiting for acknowledgments from the participants.

As mentioned in Section 10.2, the log manager keeps the transaction's log records as a linked list: each record contains the LSN of the previous record, making the UNDO scan efficient. The log records of a committed and an aborted transaction are summarized in Table 10.17.

This concludes the description of the two-phase commit protocol in a centralized system. The discussion of restart in the next chapter amplifies some of these points.

10.4.2 Distributed Transactions and Two-Phase Commit

Two-phase commit is used primarily to coordinate the work of independent resource managers within a transaction. It is especially useful for dealing with integrity checks that have been deferred until the transaction is complete (phase 1) and with work that has been deferred until the transaction has finally committed (phase 2). However, two-phase commit is also essential for transactions that are distributed among several nodes of the network and, consequently, among several independent transaction managers.

Recall that each node or cluster in a geographically distributed system has its own transaction manager. This manager coordinates the transactions at that node. Normally, transactions are completely local to that node or cluster and access only local resources. But some transactions may be *distributed*, accessing objects at multiple clusters. In such cases, the transaction is known to several transaction managers. The two-phase commit protocol is used to make the commit of such distributed transactions atomic and durable, and to allow each transaction manager the option of unilaterally aborting any transactions that are not yet prepared to commit.

The protocol is fairly simple. The transaction manager that began the transaction by performing the original Begin_Work() is called the *root* transaction manager. As work flows from one node to another, the transaction managers involved in the transaction form a tree with the root transaction manager at the root of the tree. This is called the *transaction tree*. The commit messages can easily flow on the edges of this tree.

Any member of the transaction can abort the transaction, but only the root can perform the commit. The root transaction manager is the transaction commit *coordinator*, and all other transaction managers are *participants*. The coordinator polls all the participants at phase 1; if any vote no or fail to respond within the timeout period, the coordinator rejects the commit and broadcasts the abort decision. Otherwise, the coordinator durably writes the commit record and broadcasts the commit decision to all the other transaction managers.

For their part, the participants receive the phase 1 PREPARE poll, coordinate the phase one work at their nodes, and respond to the poll with a summary yes or no vote. When a participant responds yes, it and all its local resource managers must be prepared to either commit or abort. The prepared state must be durable. When the participant receives the phase 2 decision (commit or abort), it broadcasts the decision to its local resource managers. When the local RM's reply, it writes a completion record. Once the completion record is durable, the participant acknowledges the commit message from the coordinator. If the coordinator and participant transaction managers somehow lose contact, each repeatedly tries to contact the other until the participant gets the phase 2 message, is able to act on it, and acknowledges it. Rather than polling all the participants, the coordinator typically deals only with its direct children in the transaction tree. They, in turn, poll their children. This abbreviated description summarizes the logic that is next explained in detail.

10.4.2.1 Incoming and Outgoing Transactions

How does a transaction manager first hear about a distributed transaction? There are two cases: the *outgoing* case, in which a local transaction sends a request to another node, and the *incoming* case, in which a new transaction (trid) request arrives from a remote transaction manager or node. In the outgoing case, the local transaction manager is the coordinator; in the incoming case, it is a participant in the commit protocol. Since the incoming case may be a new trid at this node, the transaction manager may have to allocate all the transaction data structures needed to support the trid. The next chapter discusses these structures in detail.

The communication manager helps the transaction manager track distributed transactions when they first travel on a communication session (see Figure 10.18). The communication manager allocates sessions to transactions (trids). When a session first becomes part of a transaction—when the trid first is sent or arrives on the session—the communication manager calls the transaction manager and says,

(a) The communication manager is joining the transaction,

(b) session #32567 to remote transaction manager "ABC" is joining the transaction,

(c) and, this is an outgoing or incoming request (the *session polarity*).

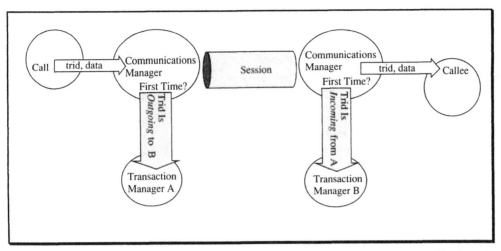

Figure 10.18: How the communications manager helps the transaction manager track distributed transactions. When a trid first flows as a message on a session, the communications manager informs the transaction manager that the transaction is outgoing or incoming; that is, leaving from the local or arriving from a remote transaction manager.

The transaction manager needs to track such transactional sessions, because it will be responsible for coordinating or participating in commit of this trid with the "ABC" transaction manager.

Clause (c) tells the transaction manager whether this trid is outgoing or incoming. If it is outgoing, the transaction manager just adds the session and the remote transaction manager's name ("ABC") to the list of outgoing sessions for that trid. If it is incoming, the logic is more complex. The first question is whether this trid already has visited this node and therefore already has a transaction structure allocated. If not, the transaction manager allocates any needed entries for the trid. Once the relevant transaction control blocks have been allocated, the transaction manager adds the session and the transaction manager's name ("ABC") to the list of incoming sessions.[10] In OSI-TP and X/Open DTP, incoming and outgoing sessions are called *branches*, and this process is called *branch registration*. These brances are the edges of the transaction tree.

The transaction managers involved in a transaction form the transaction tree. The transaction managers are the nodes of the tree, and if there is a new outgoing session from *A* to *B*, the tree has an edge from *A* to *B*. If a transaction manager has both incoming and outgoing sessions, it will be both a participant (on the incoming sessions) and a coordinator (on the outgoing sessions). The commit protocol described above is recursive. Each node of the graph executes the algorithm on its outgoing sessions and reports the results on its one incoming session. Figure 10.19 diagrams the data kept by each of the transaction managers.

---

[10] If the session is from a transaction manager to itself, a so-called *loopback session*, then it will be both incoming and outgoing. Such sessions do not create distributed transactions and, consequently, are not recorded as either outgoing or incoming.

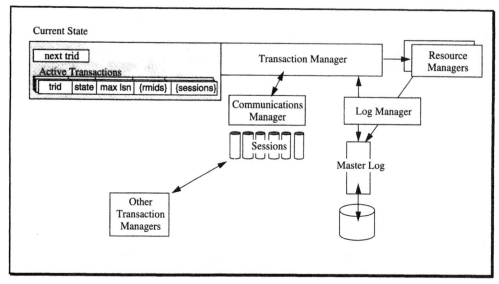

Figure 10.19: The transaction manager has a current state that describes all incomplete transactions in which it is involved. For each such transaction, it keeps the transaction status, a list of the resource managers involved in the transaction, the maximum LSN (most recent log record) of the transaction, and (if the transaction is distributed) a list of the sessions on which the transaction has travelled. Each such session is either outgoing, in which case the transaction manager is commit coordinator for that session, or incoming, in which case the transaction manager is a commit participant. In either case, the session record carries the name of the remote transaction manager.

10.4.2.2 Distributed Two-Phase Commit

The root commit coordinator executes the following logic when a successful Commit_Work() is invoked on a distributed transaction:

Local prepare. Invoke each local resource manager to prepare for commit.

Distributed prepare. Send a prepare request on each of the transaction's outgoing sessions.

Decide. If all resource managers vote yes and all outgoing sessions respond yes, then durably write the transaction commit log record containing a list of participating resource managers and transaction managers.

Commit. Invoke each participating resource manager, telling it the commit decision. Send "commit" message on each of the transaction's outgoing sessions.

Complete. When all local resource managers and all outgoing sessions acknowledge commit, write a completion record to the log indicating that phase 2 completed. When the completion record is durable, deallocate the live transaction state.

The prepare phase has an associated timeout. If some participant does not vote within that time, the coordinator interprets the inaction as a no vote. In addition to the information in the commit record of a centralized two-phase commit, the commit record of a distributed transaction has the list of remote transaction managers who expect a phase 2 commit message (the list of outgoing sessions). The coordinator maintains this transaction's state until all recipients have acknowledged receipt of the commit message. If any participant votes no, if any local resource manager votes no during phase 1, or if anyone fails to respond within a time limit, then the commit coordinator issues a transaction abort. This causes all the participants to get an abort message.

In the case of a successful commit, the participant logic is similar to the coordinator's. When the prepare message arrives, the participant executes the following logic:

Prepare()

    Local prepare.   Invoke each local resource manager to prepare for commit.

    Distributed prepare.   Send prepare requests on the outgoing sessions.

      Decide.   If all resource managers vote yes and all outgoing sessions respond yes, then the local node is almost prepared.

      Prepared.   Durably write the transaction prepare log record containing a list of participating resource managers, participating transaction managers, and the parent transaction manager.

      Respond.   Send yes as response (vote) to the prepare message on the incoming session.

    Wait.   Wait (forever) for a commit message from coordinator.

When the commit message arrives, the participant stops waiting and executes the following commit logic:

Commit()

    Commit.   Invoke each participating resource manager, telling it the commit decision. Send the commit decision on each of the transaction's outgoing sessions.

    Complete.   When all local resource managers and all outgoing sessions acknowledge commit decision, write a completion record to the local log indicating that phase 2 completed.

    Acknowledge.   When the completion record is durable, send acknowledgment of commit to coordinator and deallocate local transaction state.

10.4.2.3 Abort

The previous subsection described the successful commit path. If an abort message arrives from the coordinator at phase 2, if a local resource manager or outgoing session votes no during phase 1, or if the prepare request waits longer than a timeout period, then the participant can abort the transaction and vote no to the coordinator. Subsection 10.3.1 describes transaction_undo(). For the sake of completeness, however, here is the logic for abort:

    Broadcast abort.   Send abort messages on all outgoing sessions.

    Undo.   Scan the transaction log backwards; for each record, invoke the undo callback of the record's resource manager. At savepoint or Begin_Work records, invoke all participating resource managers.

    Complete.   Write a completion record to the log, indicating that abort completed. Deallocate the live transaction state.

If, rather than a full transaction abort, the rollback were to an intermediate savepoint, the logic would be similar. The two exceptions are that (1) the resource managers can veto any savepoint, and (2) the completion record is just a dummy pointer to the previous savepoint. The implementation of rollback to an intermediate savepoint is discussed in the next chapter.

10.4.2.4 In-Doubt Transactions

This subsection concludes the discussion of two-phase commit by mentioning a few final details. If a transaction manager has multiple incoming sessions for a single transaction, the participant should immediately vote yes on all but one of them to break a potential deadlock (see Exercise 30). The participant needs to vote no on only one of them to cause the transaction to abort. Similarly, during phase 2, it can immediately acknowledge all but the last of the commit messages.

A participant transaction manager that voted yes to all its commit requests is said to be *prepared*: it is ready to go either way. If the participant transaction manager fails, or if it loses contact with the coordinator, the participant preserves the transaction in the prepared state until a commit decision is received from the coordinator. While this situation persists (the transaction is prepared but not connected to the coordinator), the participant transaction manager is said to be *in doubt* about the transaction. The in-doubt participant continually polls the coordinator by asking for the transaction outcome. The coordinator will eventually respond with a commit or an abort message. Conversely, the coordinator polls the participant once in a while if the participant has not acknowledged the commit message.

Now consider the coordinator's handling of in-doubt transactions. The coordinator is never in doubt: it makes the decision. If the coordinator gets a query from a participant regarding a transaction and the transaction is not active, prepared, or committing at this node, then the transaction presumably aborted, and its state was discarded. This is the *presumed abort* protocol. If the transaction had committed, the state would have been maintained until all participants and all local resource managers acknowledged receipt of the commit message.[11] The presumed abort—the presumption is that no-record-found means abort—is why the participant sends the acknowledgment message only when the completion state is durable, and why the coordinator records the completion log record only when all commit messages have been acknowledged.

10.4.2.5 Summary of Two-Phase Commit

Transactions go through the state transitions diagrammed in Figure 10.20. Some of the states, such as the prepared state and the persistent savepoint state, are persistent. The two-phase commit protocol ensures that *all* participants eventually get to the same final (durable) state. This is the all-or-nothing atomicity of ACID.

To complete this discussion, let us look at the commit and rollback operations associated with the one-bit resource manager. The one-bit resource manager has no integrity checks at phase 1 and no transaction context beyond the locks it holds for the transaction. The savepoint() and prepare() callbacks are therefore null. At commit and abort, the resource manager must free all the transaction's locks acquired by that resource manager. This is a single call to the lock manager. In the REDO operation, locks were reacquired at each step (see Subsection 10.3.9). If they had not been, then the prepare operation would have to write

---

[11] There are corresponding presumed commit and presumed nothing protocols. If the vast majority of transactions commit, these other protocols have no virtue over presumed abort. Presumed abort saves a forced log write, which would be needed to make the "preparing" and "abort" states durable.

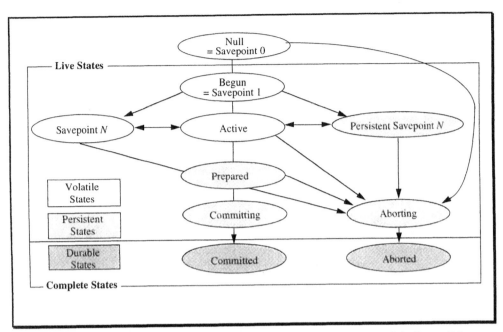

Figure 10.20: The various states of a transaction. Once a transaction starts, it is *live* until it *completes*. Most states are volatile: they do not survive restart. Persistent and durable states survive restart. Durable states are irreversible, while transactions in persistent states can subsequently either commit or abort.

a log record describing the transaction's locks so that they could be reacquired at restart if the transaction were in doubt. Here are the code fragments for the one-bit resource manager callbacks:

```
Boolean savepoint((LSN * lsn)          /* no work to do at savepoint            */
    {*lsn = NULLlsn; return TRUE ;};    /*                                       */
Boolean prepare(LSN * lsn)             /* 1-bit resource mgr has no phase 1 work */
    {*lsn = NULLlsn; return TRUE ;};    /*                                       */
void Commit(void )                     /* commit                                */
    { unlock_class(LOCK_LONG, TRUE, MyRMID()); };  /* in any case release locks & return */
void Abort(void )                      /* commit                                */
    { unlock_class(LOCK_LONG, TRUE, MyRMID()); };  /* in any case release locks & return */
void UNDO_savepoint(LSN lsn)           /* rollback work or abort transaction    */
    {if (savepoint == 0)               /* if at savepoint zero (abort)          */
        unlock_class(LOCK_LONG, TRUE, MyRMID());    /*   release all locks      */
    };                                 /*                                       */
```

10.5 Summary

This chapter first gave a whirlwind tour of transaction manager architecture, showing how a transaction manager allows many resource managers and applications to cooperate in implementing transactions on durable objects. The basic idea is for the transaction manager to allow anyone to join the transaction, and to provide a common log that anyone can write into. Resource managers joined to the transaction are informed about transaction events and are also given transaction log records in an orderly fashion during transaction UNDO and REDO.

The basic DO-UNDO-REDO protocol and the two-phase commit protocol were presented. These two protocols are the key ideas in transactional recovery management. Ancillary to them are the concepts of logging and persistent memory writes. A few logging techniques were explored. The need for idempotence of UNDO and REDO was met by a sequence number scheme, both for pages and for sessions. The need for UNDO led to a discussion of compensation log records and of deferring real operations (e.g., messages to real devices) until phase 2 of commit. We then explored physical, logical, and physiological logging. Physiological logging was presented in detail. A one-bit resource manager demonstrated the ideas of page-action consistency, page semaphores, page LSNs, mini-transactions, write-ahead log (WAL), force-log-at-commit, compensation log records, and REDO idempotence via page LSNs.

Incidental to the logging technique is the idea that changes to durable memory be modeled as mini-transactions on individual pages, along with a log record describing the change. The change is covered by an exclusive semaphore, and the page is fixed in volatile memory during the transformation. Once the page transformation is complete and the corresponding log record is generated, others may read and write the page, and it becomes a candidate for being moved to persistent memory (the fix protocol). This provides page-level atomicity, consistency, and isolation (the ACI of ACID). To provide the D, the movement to persistent memory must observe the write-ahead log protocol, ensuring that the undo-redo log record is written to the durable log prior to overwriting the page in persistent memory. All these techniques explain why the recovery system and the failure model distinguish between volatile and persistent memory. Persistent memory is written carefully.

Discussion then turned to achieving agreement among the resource managers and transaction managers participating in a transaction at commit. The solution turns out to be the familiar wedding ceremony, rechristened by computer scientists as the two-phase commit protocol. It involves a voting phase and then a commit phase. If there are any failures prior to the end of the voting phase, the transaction aborts. This mechanism provides the all-or-nothing atomicity property of ACID transactions.

To recapitulate, then, the transaction manager exports the transaction verbs and orchestrates the protocols that make transactions atomic and durable. The next chapter applies these ideas and shows how a simple transaction manager works.

10.6 Historical Notes

This chapter described the structure and algorithms characteristic of online transaction processing systems. These algorithms were independently developed by many different groups during the 1960s and 1970s, as companies built transaction processing systems. Typically, each group, unaware of the others, thought it had invented something unique and did not want to tell competitors how it worked. Often groups did not even take the time to write an architecture document for themselves. This mentality led to very slow progress in the field; each succeeding generation had to rediscover the ideas within a company, and new companies coming on the scene had to discover the ideas afresh.

The presentation here is colored by the authors' experience within IBM and Tandem. The failure model of volatile and durable memory was implicit in all designs, but Butler

Lampson and Howard Sturgis made it explicit in their classic paper [Lampson and Sturgis 1979].

Physiological logging must go back a long way. We believe Larry Morgan, Sid Kornelis, Ron Obermarck, Tom Sawyer, and Vern Watts invented a form of it associated with IMS around 1969. That system also introduced WAL (there called write-ahead log tape, or WALT) and the corresponding buffer fix and force-log-at-commit logic, around 1973. In the early 1980s, Franco Putzolu and Andrea Borr pioneered the physiological logging ideas applied to B-trees as part of Tandem's DP2 system. Don Haderle, Bruce Lindsay, C. Mohan, and others at IBM developed and widely published a similar, but more refined approach to recovery, called ARIES [Mohan 1989, 1990 a,b,c; Mohan et al. 1989; Mohan and Levine 1989; Mohan et al. 1990; Mohan, Narang, and Palmer 1990; Mohan, Haderle, and Peterson 1990; Mohen and Narang 1991 a, b; Mohan and Pirahesh 1991; Mohan et al. 1991; Mohan and Levine 1992; Mohan et al. 1992].

The DO-UNDO-REDO protocol was built into Warren Teitleman's InterLisp system. That system had an open recovery mechanism—an UNDO mechanism—in the early 1970s. Inspired by that design, the System R transaction manager built in 1975 first used the idea in the database context. System R had an "open" transaction manager and log manager [Gray, McJones et al. 1981]. That log manager was for a database system based on shadows and, as a result, did not face any of the LSN-WAL issues—it just had the inadequate performance inherent in disk-based shadow systems. On the positive side, it introduced the notion of savepoints. To our knowledge, no one has yet implemented persistent savepoints.

The two-phase commit protocol is just contract law applied to computers, so it is difficult to claim that any one individual invented it. The first known instance of its use in distributed systems is credited to Nico Garzado in implementing the Italian social security system in the early 1970s. By the mid-1970s, it had been fairly well analyzed and had been named. Gray included a description in his 1976 notes (published in 1978); that was its first public mention, although it was implemented in CICS by that time. Bruce Lindsay, in his "Notes on Distributed Databases" corrected several errors in Gray's presentation [Lindsay et al. 1979]. Chapter 12 of this book covers some of the many generalizations of the two-phase commit protocol. Mohan and Lindsay [1983] were the first to publish a careful analysis of the message and I/O cost of various commit protocols. They coined the terms *presumed commit*, *presumed abort*, and *presumed nothing*.

The excellent book by Phil Bernstein, Vassos Hadzilacos, and Nat Goodman [1987] was the first comprehensive attempt to organize the whole topic of concurrency control and recovery. It placed the main algorithms used by transaction processing systems in a comprehensive framework.

The idea of having an extensible system and transaction manager has deep roots. The resource manager design described here is modeled on the CICS resource manager interface (RMI). The generalization of recovery to a resource manager structure was inspired by the IBM MVS subsystem interface (SSI)—the structuring mechanism within MVS that lets subsystems coexist. The subsystem interface was not general enough for TP systems such as CICS and IMS. These ideas were worked out by Pete Homan and Earl Jenner for CICS and then applied by Gray, Don Haderle, Bob Jackson, and John Nauman for a product that eventually became the DB2 transaction manager [Dash and Ojala 1984]. In that design, there are many systems implementing persistent objects: notably, IMS queue manager, IMS database manager (DL/1), IMS Fast Path, System 2000, ADABASE, CICS services, DB2, Oracle, Ingres, and so on. Each of these systems acts as a resource manager (a subsystem). It participates in system startup, system shutdown, system checkpoints, and in the various stages of a transaction's life (begin, commit, abort, etc.) [Crus 1974]. That idea is also present in the DECdtm design, in the design of the AT&T Tuxedo, and in the X/Open DTP design.

Exercises

1. [10.2.1, 5] (a) Give a scenario in which a chained transaction will behave differently than an application that does chaining by issuing a commit-begin verb. (b) If a process is in chained transaction mode and it terminates normally, what happens?

2. [10.2.3, 5] Suppose a system has perfect hardware, a perfect environment, and perfect operations, so that the only failures are due to software. Does the recovery system still need to distinguish between volatile and durable memory?

3. [10.3.1, 5] Suppose the UNDO scan were implemented FIFO rather than LIFO. Give an example of a transaction that would be undone incorrectly.

4. [10.3.1, 10] Consider the Sumerian transaction processing system of 4000 B.C. operating on clay tablets, or any more modern version of a system that has no updates, just inserts. Such systems are called *versioned systems* or *immutable object systems*. What is the DO-UNDO-REDO protocol for such systems, and what do the log records look like?

5. [10.3.1, 10] You are assigned to implement a transactional X-Windows Manager, one that resets the windows of a CRT if the transaction aborts because of a power failure or system failure. Suppose the windows contain only text. (a) Describe what information you need about each window in a log record or savepoint record. (b) Are operations on the window idempotent? (c) Are operations on the window testable?

6. [10.3.4–6, 15] Continuing Exercise 5: Describe (a) a physical log scheme for a window, (b) a logical log REDO scheme for a windows system, and (c) a physiological log REDO scheme for a window. (d) Which scheme seems best? (e) Now consider UNDO.

7. [10.3.3, 5] Table 10.11 says to resend the message in order to REDO it. What is the sequence number of the new message?

8. [10.3.4, 10] Some systems split UNDO (old value) and REDO (new value) records into two different logs. What are the pros and cons of this idea?

9. [10.3.4, 10] Another compression scheme mentioned in a footnote for value logging is to use the *exclusive or* of the old and new value. This is called *transition logging*. Explain how it works. Explain how to get idempotence.

10. [10.3.4, 20] If a transaction committed many weeks ago and we are redoing it, do we need to redo the session open and message sends of that transaction?

11. [10.3.6, 15] Write the (a) physical, (b) logical, and (c) physiological log records, DO, UNDO, and REDO routines for both insert and delete of a sorted list of integers stored on a page. Inserts that do not fit in the page can call Abort_Work(). *Hint: See the one-bit resource manager. What locks are acquired?*

12. [10.3.6, 15] Assume the records in Exercise 11 are 100 bytes (rather than integers) and that updates change only 10 bytes. Repeat Exercise 11 for updates. Include the log headers in your answer, so that you can evaluate the size of the log records.

13. [10.3.6, 15] Now repeat Exercise 11 for physiological logging, but this time worry about read-by-value, and read-next record after a given value. *Hint: See the discussion of key-range locking in Chapter 7.*

14. [10.3.5, 5] To test your understanding of shadows, suppose that in Figure 10.12 a new page, *D*, were added to the database after page *C*. (a) What would the new picture look like? (b) How many disk I/Os does this take? (c) What if logging techniques were used?

15. [10.3.5, 5] To further test your understanding of shadows, suppose transaction UNDO is based on shadows rather than on log records. Suppose two uncommitted transactions have updates on the same page and then one aborts. What happens to the other transaction's update?

16. [10.3.5, 10] What are two similarities between shadows and the mini-transactions discussed in Subsection 10.3.7?

17. [10.3.5, 5] To test your understanding of shadows yet again, how can several transactions insert at the end of a sequential file implemented using shadows for UNDO?

18. [10.3.7, 10] It was obliquely mentioned (in Subsection 10.3.7.2) that the one-bit resource manager can be used to manage free space in a file. (a) What is the connection (i.e., what is being managed)? (b) Why does it need to be transactional? (c) Why do the bits need to be locked?

19. [10.3.7, 10] In the get_bit() routine of the one-bit resource manager, a lock is acquired with a timeout of zero. Could something bad happen if the timeout were long?

20. [10.3.7, 15] Imagine a mini-transaction that must update two pages in order to provide consistency. In particular, suppose the sorted list of Exercise 11 involves two pages, and that inserts to page 1 can cause overflow to page 2. (a) What is the semaphore structure of the insert mini-transaction? (b) What log records does it generate? (c) Is there an additional deadlock problem?

21. [10.3.7, 15] Consider the checkpoint() callback of the one-bit resource manager given in the text. (a) Modify it to do a single I/O rather than two I/Os. For extra credit, do it in zero I/Os. (b) Modify it so that the semaphore is not held during a write of the data to secondary memory. (c) Does it make sense to have a shared semaphore?

22. [10.3.8, 15] Assume physiological logging with a compensation logging scheme. (a) If *N* DO records are generated, how many UNDO records are generated? (b) Suppose the transaction rolls back to a savepoint and then goes forward. Can a subsequent UNDO skip over these log records? If not, why not? If so, design a simple mechanism to do it. (c) Can the REDO scan skip over these log records? If not, why not? If so, design a simple mechanism to do it.

23. [10.3, 10] What is the analog to WAL for communication sessions? *Hint: Consider message UNDO.*

24. [10.3, 10] Suppose a page *P* has a boolean flag in it at byte 100. Write a code fragment to update the flag, setting it to the character TRUE using the physiological logging scheme described in this chapter. The code fragment should generate a log record and should obey the fix rule. It will also have to maintain the page LSN.

25. [10.3, 10] Explain why UNDO of the physiological log scheme described in this chapter need not be idempotent.

26. [10.3, 15] Modify the one-bit resource manager prepare() callback to write the transaction's locks into a prepare log record, and write the code to redo the prepare record to reacquire the locks.

27. [10.4, 10] Imagine that someone implemented a presumed abort system, but that the commit co-ordinator failed to wait for acknowledgments to the commit message before writing the commit complete record and deallocating the transaction. Describe a scenario in which the participant would do the wrong thing.

28. [10.4, 10] The wedding ceremony has a minister or a judge. The real estate sale has an escrow of-ficer. The contract has a notary. Why does the two-phase commit protocol allow one of the par-ticipants to be the commit coordinator? Under what circumstances will a third party be involved?

29. [10.4, 5] If there are N transaction managers involved in a transaction, how many messages are sent to commit the transaction?

30. [10.4.2.4, 10] The discussion of distributed two-phase commit explained that the commit graph could be cyclic. (a) Explain this. (b) Can such cycles cause a commit deadlock? (Give an exam-ple.) (c) What simple rule breaks the deadlock (and why)?

Answers

1. (a): If the begin is persistent and if there is a process failure between the commit and the begin, then the chaining design will be reinstantiated at the most recent savepoint (probably the begin). But the commit-begin design will have the application outside a transaction, and so the application will not be automatically restarted. (b) The "last" transaction of each such program will be aborted. If the chaining were persistent, this would roll back to the start of the transaction and then reinstantiate the process. A common bug is to exit and consequently get restarted by the system, and then exit again (and again). To resolve it, there is usually a limit on the number of restarts a transaction is allowed to perform. It seems a special exit verb is needed to explicitly break the chain of transactions.

2. Yes. When the software process (e.g., a database system) fails, its volatile state is corrupt and so must be reconstructed from a durable copy, and the log of changes.

3. Pick any two operations on an object that do not commute. For example, begin; $A = 10$; $A = 20$; rollback; will return A to its original value if done LIFO and will set A to 10 if done FIFO.

4. It depends on the failure model. UNDO consists of removing a clay tablet or compensating for it with a new tablet. DO = REDO consists of adding the tablet to the pile. The log records consist of replicas of the tablets, along with a header giving the *trid* and the other header information dis-cussed in Subsection 10.3.2.

5. (a) A record of old and new window position, attributes, and contents. (b) If operations are logical (e.g., insert text), no; if they are physical (e.g., write bits), yes. (c) No, the state of a CRT is typically not testable, so operations must be made idempotent. If the CRT frame buffer were

persistent (nonvolatile) and were readable by a program, then display operations could be made testable.

6. (a) Record new bitmap (b) Record X-Windows calls and parameters to each call. (c) Record messages to X-Windows server (rather than calls). For both (c) and (d), occasionally take checkpoints and discard the log below the transaction low-water mark. (d) As usual, logical logging uses much less log space, so it is best. Physiological logging seems to have no virtue in this case. (e) Either record the bitmap at each savepoint, or record how to compute it from the current state, or record how to recompute it as a REDO scan: this is UNDO via REDO from the start (or a checkpoint) to a savepoint. If the bitmap is used, it is physical. If the REDO scheme is used, then it is logical. Physiological does not seem to be an asset in this application.

7. The original sequence number of the message.

8. Con: Splitting implies extra complexity and twice as many log headers. Pro: Splitting allows the system to discard the old-value (UNDO) records as soon as the transaction commits. This saves log space. It also solves the copy-aside problem for transactions (see log manager chapter). A compromise is to filter out the undo information as the log is being archived (see change accumulation in Chapter 9, Subsection 9.6.4).

9. The one-bit resource manager used this idea. Store logval = old XOR new. UNDO and REDO are the same: data XOR logval. To get idempotence, store the log sequence number on the page and use the same logic that physiological logging uses to get idempotence of undo and redo. Of course, compensation logging is needed.

10. Maybe. In the simple case, no. A transaction with a commit complete or abort complete record in the log has no remote resource managers waiting for it. However, these completion messages are not found, the remote node may still be waiting for the transaction outcome. If the transaction sets up a computation web and is chained to later transactions that use that web, it may also be essential to reconstruct the session state.

11. Physical log records are a half page long on average, since about half the list gets moved on each insert or delete to keep the list sorted and dense. Logical and physiological log records are the same. They carry opcode (insert or delete) and value. If data records are much smaller than pages, then the logical and physiological log records will be much smaller than physical log records. Lock the value in exclusive mode. Fix the page for update. To avoid deadlock, be sure not to get the lock while holding the semaphore.

12. The physical log record is about one page long (old sorted list, new sorted list after record). The logical and physiological log records are about the same: they are 10 old bytes and 10 new bytes, with a 40-byte record header.

13. There are much fancier schemes, but try this. The semaphore becomes a shared semaphore (not just exclusive). Readers get the semaphore shared, inserters and deleters get it exclusive. Simple key-range locking requires a lock on the next record. Acquiring this lock is delicate: you cannot wait while holding the page semaphore. So bounce-mode locking (timeout = 0) is used, and if that fails, the semaphore is released and then the lock is requested with a long timeout. Once acquired, the caller must reread the page and assure that the next key has not changed. An outline of the insert logic follows:

```
insert: lock new key no wait
           if don't get it rollback work and return
        retry: get the semaphore exclusive
        K = next higher key
        lock K exclusive no wait
        if didn't get it;
               give semaphore
               lock K exclusive long wait
               go to retry
        do the insert, write log record, update page lsn
        give semaphore
```

14. (a)

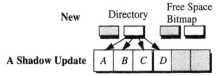

New   Directory   Free Space Bitmap

A Shadow Update | A | B | C | D | |

(b) At least 3. (c) If logging is used, then directory and bitmap need not be forced to disk; one can just force the log records describing the updates. This is an example of using logging to convert random I/O to sequential I/O.

15. The page returns to the shadow (original value), so the second transaction's update is lost and the second transaction must be aborted. If the second transaction has just committed, then this is impossible. To avoid it, shadows use page locking.

16. They both use page locking. They both undo by returning to the old version of the page. It is just that the mini-transactions run in microseconds, while shadow transactions run for seconds or minutes.

17. By using file locking! Only one transaction at a time can insert at the end of such a file. To see this, study the answer to Exercise 15.

18. (a) Files typically have empty blocks, which are managed in this way. A bitmap is kept, and when an empty block is needed, the bitmap is consulted. Conversely, when a block becomes empty, the bitmap is updated to reflect the change. (b) Suppose a transaction deletes many records, empties many blocks, and then aborts. The bitmap should not change. (c) Suppose there were no locks. Then get_bit() could give out a bit freed by an uncommitted transaction that then aborted and undid its give_bit(). This dirty read of the bitmap would cause the block (bit) to be allocated twice. Exclusive locks prevent dirty reads.

19. Yes, deadlock. My get_bit() waits for a lock you hold. Your get_bit() waits for the semaphore. This lock-semaphore deadlock will not be detected by the deadlock detector because semaphores do not participate in deadlock detection (see Chapter 8).

20. (a) There is a semaphore on each page. The mini-transaction gets both semaphores if both pages are affected. (b) Each page change gets a separate log record. So each page gets the LSN of its record. (c) Since the semaphores are acquired in order, there is no new deadlock problem.

21. (a) and (b),

```
LSN checkpoint(LSN * low_water_lsn)              /* copy one-page rm state to persistent memory      */
    { LSN          checkpoint_lsn;               /* my checkpoint lsn                                 */
      char         my_page[sizeof(page)]);       /* local copy of the page                            */
    Xsem_get(&page.sem);                         /* get semaphore to get a consistent page            */
    copy page to my_page;                        /* copy it to local copy                             */

    Xsem_give(&page.sem);                         /* give page semaphore now that we have a copy        */
    checkpoint_lsn = log_insert(my_page,sizeof(my_page));/* write copy of page to log (lazy)            */
    *low_water_lsn = log_flush(checkpoint_lsn);   /* notice: checkpoint_lsn > page_lsn, so flush writes both. */
    return checkpoint_lsn; }                      /* This is my checkpoint lsn                          */
```

Extra credit: Use the lazy option of log flush. The transaction manager (which calls the checkpoint callback) will remember the checkpoint LSN for the one-bit resource manager. This will ease restart. (c) No, a shared semaphore does not make sense since get_bit() and give_bit() need an exclusive semaphore, and checkpoint is rare and fast (given this copy scheme).

22. (a) *N* (b) Yes. At the end of the UNDO, write a savepoint record, *B*, that points to the previous valid savepoint, *A*. When the next undo hits savepoint *B*, it can skip back to savepoint *A*. The net effect of the intermediate records is the null transformation. (c) If the savepoint *A* can be updated to point to savepoint *B*, then the same trick works for forward scans. At REDO of *A*, skip to *B*. Ideas (b) and (c) were implemented in the System R savepoint mechanism (which did not use compensation logging). It used the idea implicit in Figure 10.3, and it was willing to update savepoint records with forward pointers. See also Figure 11.5 and the discussion around it.

23. If the recipient needs an undo message in case of abort, then the sender must write and force a log record describing the message prior to message send.

24. give_bit(100-sizeof(header)).

25. UNDO generates compensation log records.

26. The code is fairly easy, using the locks routine from Chapter 8, Subsection 8.3.4.

```
struct {                                  /* buffer to get description of transaction's locks   */
    lock_name    name;                    /* name of a lock held by this transaction-rmid pair  */
    lock_mode    mode;                    /* mode in which lock is held                          */
    } buffer [BITS];                      /*                                                     */
Boolean prepare(LSN * lsn)                /* one bit resource mgr saves locks at prepare         */
    {locks(MyRMID(), MyTrid(),BITS, buffer);/* Returns lock names and modes                      */
                                          /* belonging to this rmid-TRID pair and puts it in buffer */
    *lsn = log_insert(buffer,BITS);       /* return save point data lsn                          */
    return TRUE;};                        /*                                                     */
```

At REDO of this record, write a loop to lock each name in the designated mode.

27. Suppose the coordinator deallocates the state and then fails. When a participant recontacts the coordinator and asks about the in-doubt transaction, the coordinator will find no record of that transaction and so will presume the transaction aborted. This is the wrong decision.

28. A third party is involved if external authority is needed (marriage) or if there is a lack of trust (real estate). These problems are often lacking in computer systems. If they are present, then a third party is required. See also the discussion of transfer of commit in Chapter 12.

29. Approximately $4(N-1)$, but see the optimization discussion in Chapter 12.

30. (a) and (b) If A has an outgoing session to B and B has an outgoing session to A, then A will not commit until B does, and conversely. (c) Vote yes on all but the *first* incoming session. Discard the automatic sessions from the commit graph and you have a commit tree rooted at the transaction root. It has no cycles.

Software is like entropy.
It is difficult to grasp,
weighs nothing,
and obeys The Second Law of Thermodynamics;
i.e., it always increases.

NORMAN AUGSTINE

11

Transaction Manager Structure

11.1 Introduction

This chapter sketches the implementation of a simple transaction manager. It uses the ideas and terminology developed in the previous chapter. The first section deals with normal processing: Begin_Work(), Save_Work(), Commit_Work(), and the no-failure case of application-generated Rollback_Work(). The remaining sections explain how the transaction manager handles various failure scenarios. The TM prepares for failures by writing checkpoints to persistent memory. At resource manager restart or system restart, the transaction manager reads these checkpoints and orchestrates recovery. Recovery of objects from archive copies is also discussed. The techniques used to replicate data and applications at remote sites are covered in Chapter 12.

The presentation here is simplified by the lack of parallelism within a transaction. Still, this is an open, distributed transaction manager that allows independent resource managers to vote at every step of the transaction and supports persistent savepoints.

11.2 Normal Processing

During normal processing, there are no resource manager failures or system failures. The transaction manager is invoked by applications calling Begin_Work(), Save_Work(), Prepare_Work(), Commit_Work(), Rollback_Work(), and Read_ Context(). In some systems, the Leave_Transaction(), Resume_Transaction(), and Status_Transaction() calls are frequently used. In addition, resource managers invoke the transaction manager with Identify() and Join_Work() calls.

The begin, save, and prepare work calls each establish a savepoint and have the application context as an optional parameter. This context can be retrieved when the application returns to that savepoint. The context typedef says that the context is a variable-length string. The transaction manager does not understand the meaning of the context beyond that.

```
typedef struct { long length; char data[length];} context;  /*context is just data to the TM.          */
```

Each resource manager may also be maintaining some context associated with the transaction. Each context record is understood only by the subsystem that wrote it. For example, the contexts saved by a persistent programming language, a database system, and a transactional windows system all look quite different.

11.2.1 Transaction Identifiers

Most of transaction management and recovery centers around transaction identifiers, *trids*. Thus, it is best to begin by defining them in detail. Within the network, trids must be unique for all time; each identifies some ACID unit of work. In addition, it is convenient for a trid to define which transaction manager created it. That transaction manager is sure to know whether the transaction committed, aborted, or is still in progress. Consequently, each transaction manager is given a unique identifier, or name, and a unique number, or *transaction manager identifier* (here called TMID). This TMID will appear in each trid created by this transaction manager. Each transaction manager, in turn, has a private counter that increments each time it creates a new transaction.

It is possible for a transaction manager to restart with *amnesia*—having lost its logs, it goes through a complete restart. In that case, its trid sequence counter resets to zero. This is never supposed to happen, but it does. To allow other transaction managers to detect amnesia, each transaction manager remembers its *birthday*: the oldest timestamp it can remember. The form of trid that is actually unique is the triple, ⟨birthday,TMID, counter⟩, where TMID is the unique identifier of the transaction manager, and *counter* is its sequence number. This is the form of trids exchanged among transaction managers (i.e., in the network). Hence, the definition of trid:

```
typedef struct {TIMESTAMP  birthday,    /*the earliest time the TM can remember        */
                RMID       tmid;        /*transaction mgr identifier; unique in network */
                long       sequence;    /*8 byte transaction sequence number within tmid */
                char       filler[2];   /*reserved for the future                       */
               } TRID;                  /*trid type definition                          */
```

11.2.2 Transaction Manager Data Structures

The transaction manager, along with the TP monitor, keeps a data structure describing each resource manager that has called Identify(). It also keeps a data structure for each live transaction: its status, its log records, the resource managers joined to it, and the sessions allocated to it. This data structure is diagrammed in Figure 11.1. It is a subset of the data structures shown in Figure 6.7.

When a transaction begins, a descriptor of the transaction (a TransCB) is added to the list of live transactions. Initially, the transaction has no locks and only a begin transaction log record. As resource managers do work for the transaction, the transactional remote procedure call (TRPC) mechanism automatically invokes Join_Work(rmid,trid) for that resource manager. This causes the transaction manager to create a link between the resource manager and the transaction, diagrammed as the RMTransCB in Figure 11.1. As the transaction's log grows, the log manager and the transaction manager maintain the addresses of the first and last log records of the transaction (*min and max LSN*). At savepoints, commit, and rollback, each resource manager in the transaction's RM_list is invoked to perform the next step of the transaction. The rest of this subsection elaborates on the transaction manager data structures and the routines that manipulate them.

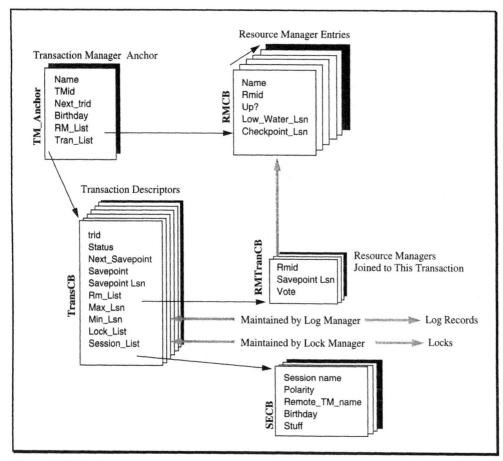

Figure 11.1: The data structures of the transaction manager.   The anchor points to a list of known resource managers, some of which may be down. It also points to a list of live transactions. Each transaction has some status information and a list of resource managers that have joined the transaction. In addition, the transaction points to its first and last log record (maintained by the log manager) and to a list of its locks (maintained by the lock manager). If the transaction is distributed, the communication manager will maintain a list of sessions bound to this transaction.

The transaction manager's root data structure, called the *anchor*, stores a few key values (e.g., the TM name, the next trid, and the birthday), but its primary job is to point to the list of identified resource managers and the list of transactions that resource manager has joined. The anchor's declaration in C is as follows:

```
struct TM_anchor { char      name[BIG];      /*transaction mgr's name (unique in net)   */
                   RMID       TMid;           /*resource manager id of this TM           */
                   TRID       next_trid;      /*the next trid to be allocated by this TM */
                   LSN        ckpt_lsn;       /*lsn of most recent TM checkpoint record  */
                   RMCB *     RM_list;        /*list of resource mgrs known to this TM   */
                   TransCB *  tran_list;      /*list of all transactions known to this TM*/
                   };                         /*transaction mgr's volatile info          */
```

The RM_list is a linked list of all resource managers known to this transaction manager, their names and IDs, their status (up or down), and their pointers to two relevant places in the log. These places are (1) the low-water mark, where this resource manager's REDO should start for resource manager recovery (log records earlier than that are not needed to recover this resource manager's online state), and (2) the log address of the resource manager's most recent log checkpoint record. These two items are clarified later, in Subsection 11.4.3. Here are the relevant fields of each resource manager control block:

```
typedef struct {    RMCB *    next_RMCB;      /*the next resource manager or NULL         */
                    char      name[BIG];      /*the resource manager name                 */
                    RMID      rmid;           /*the rm short name (identifier)            */
                    Boolean   up;             /*status flag says rm is up or down         */
                    LSN       low_water_lsn;  /*min lsn needed for redo scan for this rm  */
                    LSN       ckpt_lsn;       /*lsn of rm's most recent checkpoint record */
          /*  stuff          stuff           /*data used by other subsystems not shown   */
          } RMCB;                             /*describes RM status                       */
```

This structure tells the transaction manager all it needs to know about resource managers. When a resource manager first comes on the scene, it informs the transaction manager of the resource manager callbacks and requests recovery via an Identify() call. Thereafter, the transaction manager invokes the resource manager's callbacks at critical system events (checkpoint, etc.). In addition, once a resource manager has identified itself, it can invoke Join_Work() for a transaction. This causes the transaction manager to inform the resource manager about all subsequent events related to that transaction. These events include savepoints and rollbacks as well as participation in the prepare, commit, and abort steps of the transaction. Chapter 6 explained that the Identify() call also calls the TP monitor, to allocate structures needed for transactional remote procedure calls (TRPCs) to the resource manager.

The transaction manager keeps a description of each active transaction—transactions that have not completely committed or aborted. Each description, called a TransCB, carries the trid and transaction status. It also records the current and next savepoint numbers. It might seem that these would be simply X and $X + 1$, but that would ignore rollback. Savepoint numbers do increase monotonically. Begin_Work() creates savepoint 1, and each successive Save_Work() increments next_save_pt. If a transaction was at savepoint 98 but has just rolled back to savepoint 7, then it has two relevant savepoint numbers: the current savepoint (7) and the next savepoint (99). Both these savepoint numbers, then, are recorded in the transaction description. In addition, it is convenient to have a quick way to find the transaction's current savepoint record, so that the application can restore its context. This hint is stored in the save_pt_lsn.

As discussed in Chapter 9, the transaction descriptor also stores the min_lsn and max_lsn of log records created by the transaction. Min_lsn bounds how far back in the log an UNDO scan of this transaction may go; it is the transaction low-water mark. The max_lsn says where to start the UNDO scan for Rollback_Work(). As the transaction's log grows, the log manager and the transaction manager maintain the min_lsn and max_lsn field of the transaction via the log_transaction() routine explained in Section 9.4.

The lock manager uses the transaction descriptor to keep a list of all locks held by a transaction. Each time a transaction gets a lock, the new lock request block is chained to the lock header and to the transaction lock list (see Figure 8.8). Of course, the transaction descriptor has a list of all resource managers joined to the transaction and all sessions allocated to the transaction. Given those hints, it should be easy to read the declaration of the transaction control block:

```
enum tran_status { ACTIVE , PREPARED , ABORTING , COMMITTING , ABORTED , COMMITTED};
typedef struct  {   TransCB *      next;          /*the next tran entry in the list              */
                    TRID           trid;          /*the trid of the transaction                  */
                    tran_status    status;        /*active, prepared, committing, aborting..     */
                    long           next_save_pt;  /*next savepoint number                        */
                    long           save_pt;       /*current savepoint number                     */
                    LSN            save_pt_lsn;   /*lsn of current savepoint log record          */
                    LSN            max_lsn;       /*trans most recent log rec (see chap 9)       */
                    LSN            min_lsn;       /*first log record of this transaction    "    */
                    RMTranCB *     RM_list;       /*list of resource mgrs joined to this trans   */
                    SECB *         ses_list;      /*list of sessions that are part of this trans */
                    pointer        lock_list;     /*locks of this transaction.                   */
                    pointer        wait;          /*lock waited for by this transaction (or null)*/
                    long           timeout;       /*timeout interval for lock waits (see chap 8) */
                    TransCB *      cycle;         /*used by deadlock detector              "     */
                  } TransCB;                      /*                                             */
```

The global list of all the resource managers (RMCBs) was given previously. Not all resource managers, however, participate in each transaction. The TransCB.RM_list enumerates all resource managers that have joined the transaction. Each element of the list, an RMTransCB, describes the resource manager, its vote on prepare, and its most recent savepoint context. The following is, therefore, the basic structure of entries in the resource manager list:

```
typedef struct {  RMTransCB*    next;          /*next resource mgr joined to this trans     */
                  RMID          rmid;          /*id of this resource manager                */
                  Boolean       prepared;      /*rm is prepared to commit                   */
                  LSN           save_pt_lsn;   /*lsn of RM's last savepoint record          */
                } RMTransCB;                   /*describes a rm joined to a trans           */
```

At each savepoint, each interested resource manager is invoked via its Savepoint() callback to optionally write a savepoint record in the log. The returned LSN is recorded in RMTransCB.save_pt_lsn. The transaction may later be returned to that savepoint by an application rollback or by a system restart that reestablishes that persistent savepoint. When such events occur, the resource manager is expected to restore its state as of that time; its savepoint record can help it do so. The UNDO_Savepoint(LSN) and REDO_Savepoint(LSN) callbacks to the resource manager pass the LSN returned by the original Savepoint() callback.

The communication manager maintains the list of sessions allocated to this transaction. New TRPCs allocate sessions to the transaction. When the transaction commits, the sessions continue to exist, but they are no longer associated with the transaction. These sessions carry messages among the processes performing the transaction, track distributed transactions, and are used to perform the two-phase commit protocol. Each entry in the session list has this format:

```
typedef struct {   SECB *      tran_next_ses;        /*the next session of this transaction or NULL        */
                   char        name[BIG];           /*the session name                                   */
                   Boolean     incoming;            /*session polarity (incoming or outgoing)            */
                   char        him[BIG];            /*name of the TM at the other end                    */
                   TIMESTAMP   birthday;            /*birthday (timestamp) of remote TM                  */
          /*       stuff            ***/            /*many other things                                  */
                } SECB;                             /*describes a session allocated to a trans           */
```

The development here also postulates a set of addressing routines that lets the caller find its control blocks. These are the addressing routines for transactions:

```
TRID         MyTrid(void);        /*returns transaction identifier of caller's process      */
TransCB      MyTrans(void);       /*returns a copy of caller's transaction control block     */
TransCB *    MyTransP(void);      /*returns pointer to caller's transaction control block    */
```

Given these global structures, the logic of the Begin_Work(), Commit_Work(), Save_Work(), and Rollback_Work() can be discussed. Before doing that, however, let us describe the very simple housekeeping routines, such as MyTrid(). This should help provide some groundwork for the basic data structures and how they are used.

11.2.3 MyTrid(), Status_Transaction(), Leave_Transaction(), Resume_Transaction()

Recall that at any instant, each process may be executing in the scope of some transaction. That is called the *process-transaction identifier*. A process can use the following code to ask what its current trid is:

```
trid MyTrid(void)                                   /*return current trid of calling process              */
   { TransCB *   mytranp = MyTransP();              /*pointer to caller's transaction control block       */
   if ( mytranp != NULL ) return mytranp->trid;     /*return his trid if he has one                       */
   else return NULLTrid;}                           /*no trid if caller has no control block              */
```

The status of any transaction can be queried. If the transaction is currently live (active, prepared, aborting, or committing), then a record of it will be found in the TM_anchor.tran_list. In those cases, the following code will work for Status_Transaction():

```
tran_status Status_Transaction(TRID trid)          /*return status of named transaction            */
    { TransCB *  it = TM_anchor.tran_list;         /*pointer to list of live transactions          */
    while (it != NULL)                             /*scan list looking for the named trid          */
        {if (it.trid == trid) return it.status;    /*if found, return its status                   */
        it = it->next; }                           /*else go to next in list                       */
    return ?;}                                     /*didn't find it, see text for what's next      */
```

On the other hand, if the transaction aborted or committed, then it will not be present in the list, and the log or another data structure must be consulted. The simplest design is to run the following SQL query on the log table:

```
select max(lsn)
from log
where trid = :trid;
```

If the max(LSN) comes back zero, then there is no record of the transaction (max of the empty set is zero). In that case, it must have aborted—this is the presumed abort protocol. If the record comes back nonzero, then it is the transaction completion record, because it is the last record the transaction wrote. The completion record can be read to see if the transaction committed or aborted. That describes the logic for Status_Transaction(). Exercise 3 discusses some optimizations of it (systems do not typically scan the log in this way).

The implementation of Leave_Transaction() and Resume_Transaction() is straightforward. Recall that if a process running under one transaction identifier wants to begin a new transaction or work on another one, it must first *leave* its current transaction. It can then begin the new transaction, work on it, leave it, commit it, or issue a rollback. At any point, it can *resume* the previous transaction. This allows programmers to write multi-threaded server processes that work on multiple trids, perhaps having a separate internal thread for each one.

Leave_Transaction() is trivial to implement; it simply sets the process trid to NULLTrid. Resume_Transaction() is more difficult. A process can only resume trids that it has left. Thus, the transaction manager maintains such a list and updates it each time a transaction is left by the process, is committed, or is aborted. Resume_Transaction() searches this list and, if the trid is present, makes it the current TransCB of the process. The necessary process structure is not shown here, but the field PCB.TAsToDo in the process control block is shown in Chapter 6, Section 6.2.2.

11.2.4 Savepoint Log Records

From the transaction manager's perspective, every transaction event is a kind of savepoint. This can sometimes be a difficult concept to grasp. Begin is a savepoint (numbered 1), and transaction completion is a savepoint. Some savepoints, notably prepare and abort, are persistent, but they are otherwise all alike. They all have similar log records as well.

Treating all savepoints in the same manner simplifies the code and easily provides for persistent savepoints. The reason is as follows: the two-phase commit protocol requires that the prepared-to-commit state be persistent. That means that each resource manager must be able to reinstantiate its prepared transaction context if the system fails and restarts. After phase 1 of commit, every resource manager has established a persistent savepoint. If the system fails before the transaction finally commits, the resource manager is able to reinstantiate the prepared transaction state: the prepared-to-commit state is a persistent savepoint. If that mechanism exists for commit, why not make it available for long-running and for chained transactions? In that sense, then, persistent savepoints come for free.

Savepoint records all have a record type, a savepoint number, a flag showing if the state transition is persistent, and then a list of resource managers and sessions involved in the transaction at this point. All that is followed by the application context passed by the state-change call. Begin, save, prepare, rollback, commit, abort, and complete all write such records. The structure of a savepoint log record is as follows:

```
enum SAVE_PT_TYPE
        { begin, save, prepare, commit, abort, commit_complete, abort_complete};
typedef struct {
        SAVE_PT_TYPE    record_type;        /*begin, save, prepare, commit, abort, ..      */
        long            save_pt_num;        /*the number of the savepoint: 1, 2, ...       */
        tran_status     status;             /*trans committed, aborted, prepared,...       */
        Boolean         soft;               /*flag says savepoint is soft or persistent    */
        long            num_RM;             /*number of resource mgrs joined to this tran  */
        RMTransCB       RM[num_RM];         /*the names and status of each joined rm       */
        long            sessions;           /*the number of sessions joined to this tran   */
        SECB            session[sessions];  /*names, sequence numbers and polarities       */
        context         it;                 /*application context at savepoint.            */
    } TM_savepoint;                         /*generic format of a savepoint record         */
```

11.2.5 Begin Work()

The logic for Begin_Work() is to allocate a new transaction identifier, add an entry in the transaction table, and format the entry to reflect savepoint 1. The transaction manager then writes a begin transaction log record that causes the log manager to set the min and max LSN pointers in the transaction entry to that log record. The log manager maintains the LSN fields, and the lock manager maintains the trans->lock_list. If the transaction wants to establish a persistent savepoint (one that will survive restarts), then the Begin_Work() request forces the log record to persistent memory. The last step is to set the process transaction identifier to this trid. From this point until the process commits, aborts, or leaves the transaction, all work done by this process and all RPCs it issues will be tagged with this trid.

```
TRID Begin_Work(context * it, Boolean soft)      /*                                       */
    {TransCB *        trans;                      /*the transaction's descriptor           */
    TRID              him;                         /*the new trid                           */
    TM_savepoint   save;                          /*the savepoint record to be written     */
    if (MyTrid() != NULLTrid) return(NULLTrid);   /*insist it not have one already         */
    him = TM_anchor.next_trid;                    /*give him the next trid                 */
    TM_anchor.next_trid.sequence++;               /*increment next trid                    */
    (MyProcessP())->trid = him;                   /*make this the process trid             */
      /*allocate and format the transaction control block                                 */
    trans = malloc(sizeof(TransCB));              /*allocate a trans entry and             */
    trans->next = TM_anchor.tran_list;            /*add transaction to transaction list    */
    TM_anchor.tran_list = trans;                  /*                                       */
    trans->trid = him;                            /*set his trid                           */
    trans->status = ACTIVE;                       /*status is active                       */
    trans->save_pt = 1; trans->next_save_pt = 2;  /*at savepoint 1, next is 2              */
    trans->RM_list = trans->lock_list = trans->ses_list = NULL;  /*no sessions, locks, resources yet  */
      /*format and write the begin transaction (= savepoint 1) log record.                */
    save.record_type = begin;                     /*set log record body type               */
    save.save_pt_num= 1; save.soft = soft;        /*format savepoint record                */
    save.num_RM = save.sessions = 0;              /*only TMs joined now                    */
    copy(save.it, it, it.length);                 /*add his context                        */
    trans->save_pt_lsn = log_insert( save, sizeof(save));  /*write begin tran log rec, section 9.4  */
                        /*shows how log_insert() updates min and max lsn                   */
    if (!soft) log_flush(trans->max_lsn,FALSE);   /*force log if persistent begin.         */
    return(him);                                  /*return his trid to him.                */
    };                                            /*                                       */
```

The transaction manager is the resource manager owning commit, prepare, savepoint, and abort savepoint records. This savepoint log record and all other log records written by the transaction manager use the resource manager identifier of the transaction manager, TMID, in the log record header. This means that the transaction manager invokes (recursively) its own UNDO and REDO entry points when this log record is undone or redone. In that way, the transaction manager acts like any other resource manager during UNDO and REDO as described in Subsections 11.2.9 and 11.4.2.

11.2.6 Local Commit_Work()

Committing a transaction is a simple matter. The resource managers vote by being invoked at their Prepare() callbacks. The outgoing sessions vote by being sent Prepare() TRPCs and then replying with a yes or no vote. If all vote yes, the transaction is prepared to commit. The commit call writes a commit record (savepoint record) and forces it to persistent memory. The commit operation then broadcasts the commit decision to the local resource managers and to the remote sessions via the Commit() TRPC. When they all respond, the transaction manager writes a completion record in the log and deallocates the transaction control block. The overall logic for Commit_Work() is roughly this:

```
Boolean Commit_Work(context * it, Boolean lazy)  /*                                            */
    { if Prepare_Work()                          /*try to prepare transaction,                 */
        commit();                                /*if successful prepare, then do phase 2 work  */
    else                                         /*if not successful                           */
        Rollback_Work(0);                        /*abort the transaction (undo all its work).   */
    };                                           /*                                            */
```

Figure 11.2 gives a schematic presentation of one round-trip data flow. The two-phase commit protocol has two such flows.

To illustrate this essential logic, fairly detailed pseudo-code for Commit_Work() is shown next. The code uses the syntax rmid.Prepare() to mean that the designated resource manager (rmid) is being invoked via a TRPC at its Prepare() callback. The same syntax is used to invoke other transaction managers participating in the transaction. The syntax TM.Prepare() invokes that transaction manager at the other end of an outgoing session at its Prepare() callback. The next section explains the remote callbacks in more detail. Guideposts in the flow are printed in boldface.

```
Boolean Commit_Work(context * it, Boolean lazy)         /*Root commit coordination logic            */
    {TransCB *         trans = MyTransP();               /*ptr to process's transaction descriptor   */
    TM_savepoint       save;                             /*savepoint record to be formatted          */
    long               save_num;                         /*the savepoint number                      */
    Boolean            vote;                             /*vote of a remote TM on Prepare()          */
    RMTransCB *        rm;                               /*resource managers joined to this trans.   */
    SECB *             session;                          /*sessions allocated to this transaction.   */
    if (MyTrid() == NULLTrid) return(0);                 /*insist it have a transaction              */
    for each rm in trans->RM_list,                       /*for each resource mgr joined to trans,    */
        {rm->prepared =rmid.Prepare(&rm->save_pt_lsn))   /*ask it to commit the transaction          */
        if (!rm->prepared)                               /*if resource manager votes no,             */
            { Abort_Work();                              /*then abort the transaction                */
            return FALSE;};}                             /*return false                              */
    for each outgoing session in trans->ses_list         /*for each outgoing session in the trans's list */
        {vote = TM.Prepare(void);                        /*do remote Prepare() TRPC to remote TM     */
        if (! vote or timeout)                           /*if any vote no or timeout                 */
            { Abort_Work();                              /*then abort the transaction                */
            return FALSE;};};                            /*return false                              */
    trans->status = PREPARED;                            /*enter prepared state                      */
    save_num = trans->save_pt ++;                        /*increment the savepoint                   */
    save.record_type = commit;                           /*set log record body type                  */
    save.soft = FALSE;                                   /*commit state is durable                   */
    save.save_pt_num = save_num;                         /*format savepoint record                   */
    copy(save, trans->RM_list);                          /*record resource managers joined           */
    copy(save, trans->ses_list);                         /*record sessions joined                    */
    copy(save.it, it);                                   /*add his context                           */
    trans->save_pt_lsn = log_insert( save, sizeof(save)); /*write prepare log record                 */
    log_flush(trans->max_lsn, lazy);                     /*force log if not a lazy commit            */
```

```
trans->status = COMMITTING;                     /*enter committing state                        */
for each rm in trans->RM_list,                  /*for each resource mgr joined to trans,        */
    { if (rmid.Commit( ))                       /*ask it to commit the transaction              */
        { deallocate rmid from transaction;};   /*if OK then deallocate rmid control block      */
      else   {rm_commit(&rm);};};               /*if rm does not respond, tell TM               */
for each outgoing session in trans->ses_list    /*for each outgoing session in the trans's list */
    { TM.Commit();                              /*tell remote transaction manager to commit     */
      if (! timeout) { free session; }          /*if acked then free session from trans         */
      else          {session_failure(&session);};};  /*if timeout, give session to TM to handle */
if (  trans->RM_list == NULL &&                 /*if all rms complete (deallocated) and         */
      trans->ses_list == NULL)                  /*if all outgoing sessions committed (freed)    */
    {  trans->status = COMMITTED;               /* then enter committed state                   */
     save.record_type = commit_complete;        /*set log record type to say trans completed    */
     log_insert( save, sizeof(save));           /* write completion record lazy                 */
     dequeue and free trans structure;}         /*deallocate trans control block, we are done   */
(MyProcessP())->trid = NULLTrid;                /*process has no trid now                        */
return TRUE;                                     /*return the resulting savepoint num            */
};                                               /*                                              */
```

The Prepare() invocations ask the resource managers to vote on the transaction consistency. The resource manager must perform any deferred integrity checks; if the transaction does not pass checks, the resource manager votes no. Because a resource manager can invoke other resource managers during the prepare step, it is possible for new resource managers and new sessions to join the transaction at this time. In addition, a resource manager or session that voted yes to the prepare may subsequently be invoked by another resource manager to do more work. In this case, the invokee calls the transaction manager and asks for a second vote—that is, it rejoins the transaction. The transaction manager makes sure that all "new" resource managers and sessions have voted before it computes the outcome of the prepare step. This logic is implicit in the pseudo-code just given.

The program for Commit_Work() leaves one issue vague: how are errors handled during phase 2 of commit? If a session or resource manager does not respond during the prepare

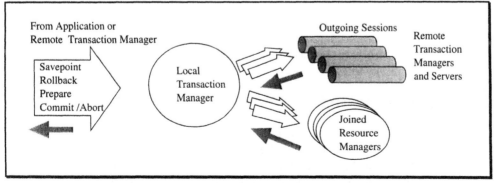

Figure 11.2: Data flow at commit.   A transaction manager gets a message from a remote transaction manager (via an incoming session) or from the application, requesting to take a savepoint, initiate rollback, or participate in commit. It passes this request to each outgoing session of the transaction and to each local resource manager joined to the transaction.

phase, the transaction manager simply calls Abort_Work(). If a failure occurs during phase 2, the transaction manager must eventually deliver the message and get a response from the resource manager or the remote transaction manager. The code given just signals this situation by calling rm_commit(RMTransCB) or session_failure(session CB). In these cases, the Commit_Work() code returns to the caller without having completed the transaction; that is, no completion record is written, and the transaction control block is not deallocated. These routines—rm_commit() and session_failure()— are TRPCs that run *asynchronously*. The caller continues to execute, and the callee is responsible for completing the transaction. The code for session_failure() is executed by an independent process and reads approximately as follows:

```
void session_failure(SECB * session)    /*persistently send Commit() TRPC to remote TM    */
    { TransCB *      trans = MyTransP();  /*ptr to process' transaction descriptor          */
    Boolean          timeout = TRUE;      /*flag says TRPC timed out                        */
    TM_savepoint     save;                /*completion record to be formatted               */
    RMID             TM= session->him;    /*name of remote TM to receive commit() callback  */
    while( timeout)                       /*repeat TRPC until acknowledged                  */
        { TM.Commit( );};                 /*tell remote transaction manager to commit       */
     free session;                        /*if acknowledged then free session from trans    */
     if ( trans->RM_list == NULL &&       /*if all resource managers complete (deallocated) */
         trans->ses_list == NULL)         /*and if all outgoing sessions committed          */
         { trans->status = COMMITTED;     /* then enter committed state                     */
         save.record_type = commit_complete;  /*set log rec type to say trans completed     */
         log_insert( save, sizeof(save)); /*write completion record lazy                    */
         dequeue and free trans structure;};  /*deallocate trans control block, we are done */
     exit();                              /*process is complete, terminate process          */
     };                                   /*                                                */
```

Subsection 11.2.7 discusses the programs executing at the other end of this failed session. Besides these programs, the remote participant can also try to resolve the in-doubt transaction by sending Status_Transaction() messages. Eventually, these two TMs will connect, and the process will terminate. The code for rm_commit() is discussed with resource manager recovery (Subsection 11.4.3.); for now, let us consider the programs executed by a remote transaction manager as part of the commit protocol.

11.2.7 Remote Commit_Work(): Prepare() and Commit()

The Commit_Work() code of Subsection 11.2.6 is for the transaction root—the application process and the transaction manager that began the transaction. If the transaction involves several transaction managers, only one of them is the root. The others receive a pair of TRPCs via each incoming session. The participant transaction managers are invoked by their communication managers, first to perform the Prepare() and later to perform Commit(). These look like ordinary local callbacks. Figure 11.3 illustrates this idea.

Participant transaction managers export two routines that perform the two phases of commit. Since these routines are very similar to the two parts of the Commit_Work() routine shown in the previous subsection, the code is not repeated here. Only the differences are explained.

Prepare() performs the first half of Commit_Work(), as described in Subsection 11.2.6, with the following differences. Prepare() does not have a context parameter; it writes a savepoint log record of type *prepare*; and, just prior to the statement in Commit_Work() that sets the transaction status to committing, the routine returns TRUE to the caller.

Commit() continues where the Prepare() ended in Commit_Work(), as described in Subsection 11.2.6. It sets the state to committed and completes the transaction. Ignoring failures, that is all there is to the Prepare() and Commit() routines. The use of TRPC considerably simplifies both the local and the distributed protocol.

Only one problem remains: what happens if one of the two session end points fails? Looking at Figure 11.3 again, what happens if the root fails, or if the right-most participant fails? Let us consider the two cases in turn.

If the participant fails, the root session_failure() routine mentioned in the previous subsection continues to invoke the participant's TM.Commit() until the participant replies. As explained in the discussion of transaction manager restart (Section 11.4), if the root fails—or if any T M with an active session_failure() routine fails—the transaction manager will reinstantiate that process at restart. Thus, session_failure() is executed by a persistent process (see Chapter 3), which means that eventually the participant will execute and reply to the

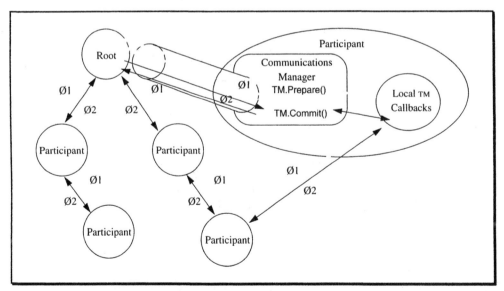

Figure 11.3: The commit graph of a distributed transaction. The root commit coordinator broadcasts the phase 1 (Ø1) and phase 2 (Ø2) messages on its outgoing sessions. Each participant transaction manager gets one TRPC to Prepare() and a second TRPC to Commit(). Locally, these TRPCs are invoked by a communications manager process. A participant that has outgoing sessions sends these TRPCs on its sessions prior to replying. The large oval at right shows a particular incoming session and the communication manager invocations of the local transaction manager callbacks. A participant with many incoming sessions can immediately reply yes to all but one of them, thus ignoring the others.

session_failure(), and the entire transaction will complete. This covers the case of failure of the participant transaction manager.

Participant transaction managers handle resource manager failures and outgoing session failures in the same way the root does, with one exception. In a pure presumed-abort design, the participant cannot acknowledge the commit—that is, return from the TRPC—until the transaction has completed. Consequently, the session_failure() and rm_commit() calls cannot be asynchronous; they must complete before the transaction manager responds to its parent. This may be a problem if some resource manager or outgoing session fails: the commit completion could be delayed for a very long time.

Two design alternatives allow the Commit() call to return early: (1) write a persistent "committing" savepoint record in the local log and reinstantiate the Commit() call if the local system restarts, or (2) assume that the Status_Transaction() can determine the outcome of committed transactions at restart by polling the root. The Status_Transaction() design is chosen here; that is, it is assumed that the transaction manager will be able to answer the Status_Transaction() question many years into the future, perhaps by asking the root or perhaps by examining the log. With that design, the session_failure() and rm_commit() calls can execute asynchronously with respect to the caller.

The cases just discussed cover all the participant transaction manager failures. But what if the root fails? In that event, the participant is prepared to commit but is in doubt. As explained in Section 11.4, if the failure happens after the commit record is present in the durable log (after the log force), root restart will initiate a session_failure() process to assure that the participant executes phase 2 of commit. This handles most in-doubt transactions.

If the failure happens before the commit record is durable, the root transaction manager may have no record of the transaction, since all the transaction's records may have been in volatile memory. The transaction will have aborted at the root transaction manager, but the participant transaction managers may not get an Abort() callback from the root because the root has no record of the transaction. In this case, the prepared participant will wait in doubt forever unless something is done.

To handle such in-doubt transactions, prepared participants periodically issue TM.Status_Transaction(trid) callbacks to the parent transaction manager. These calls can also be directed to the transaction root or to any other participant. If the call gets no response, the transaction manager is still in doubt about the transaction outcome. If the call gets a response, the transaction manager can act on it, executing either the phase 2 Commit() callback or the Abort() callback. This again behaves as an asynchronous process trying to resolve in-doubt transactions. Here is the rough pseudo-code for this program:

```
void coordinator_failure(SECB * session)     /*send Status_Transaction() to coordinator        */
    tran_status      outcome = prepared;      /*says TRPC timed out or this has trans status     */
    RMID             TM= session->him;        /*remote TM to receive status callback             */
    while( outcome not in {committing, aborting})  /* repeat TRPC until acknowledged            */
        { outcome = TM.Status_Transaction(MyTrid());};  /*ask remote TM about outcome          */
    switch (outcome)                          /*based on reply, decide action                    */
        { aborting:     Abort();      break;   /*if answer is committing, commit it              */
          committing:   Commit( );    break;}; /*if answer is aborting, then abort it            */
    exit();                                   /*process is complete, terminate process           */
    };                                        /*                                                 */
```

We have now covered all the failure cases of transaction commit. To summarize, each committing node invokes the Prepare() callbacks of all local transaction managers on outgoing sessions. If all respond yes, the commit record is written, and a second round of Commit() callbacks is issued. If any respond no to the first round of callbacks, the transaction is aborted. If any failures happen during the second round, persistent processes are created to resolve the in-doubt participants. Having covered the basic begin-commit case, let us now consider savepoints and rollback.

11.2.8 Save_Work() and Read_Context()

The previous discussion was intentionally vague concerning exactly what goes into savepoint records. This is because in normal forward processing, begin-prepare-commit does not read savepoint records, it just creates them. Now that we are about to discuss Read_Context() and Rollback_Work(), the contents of savepoint records become more important.

Many resource managers and many sessions participate in a savepoint. Each may write its own savepoint information in the log. Thus, a savepoint is actually a sequence of savepoint log records consisting of the transaction manager's record, the communication manager's records, and the records of other resource managers joined to the transaction—such as the context manager, the queue manager, the database system, or the persistent programming language. Figure 11.4 shows the general structure of savepoint records in the transaction log.

At a savepoint, the transaction manager first invokes each resource manager participating in the transaction at the resource manager's Savepoint() callback by asking it to freeze-dry its state into a savepoint log record and, as a result, return the LSN of that record. Each resource manager does whatever is needed to allow it to return to this savepoint in case of UNDO or REDO.

If the resource manager's state changes generate incremental log records, then the REDO/UNDO scans will reconstruct the resource manager's state, and no extra log records will need to be written at a savepoint. This was the case with the one-bit resource manager introduced in the previous chapter. Hence, its savepoint and prepare codes were empty.

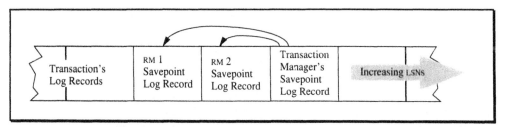

Figure 11.4: Structure of savepoint records in the transaction log. Each transaction savepoint record written by the transaction manager records the log sequence numbers of the savepoint records written by the various resource managers for this transaction. These records are used to reinstantiate the transaction state at this savepoint if the transaction rolls back to this savepoint due to an application failure or system restart. Transaction prepare and commit records are themselves persistent savepoints; thus, this structure also applies to transaction prepare, commit, and abort records.

Many resource managers do not log each state transition incrementally; rather, they summarize their state transitions at the save and prepare steps. For example, database read operations typically do not generate log records; consequently, the states of read cursors must be recorded at each savepoint. Similarly, lock and unlock calls do not generate log records; the status of the locks acquired by a resource manager must therefore be recorded at phase 1 of commit and at persistent savepoint records. The transaction manager itself does not log changes to its TransCB structure. Rather, when a transaction reaches a savepoint or a commit point, the transaction manager writes a log record containing the list and status of resource managers and sessions associated with the transaction. In general, frequently changing data use the checkpoint-restart scheme embodied in writing periodic log records (savepoint log records), rather than the incremental logging scheme that generates one or more log records per action. When the transaction returns to the savepoint, the savepoint data are used to reset the object state. Exercise 26 in Chapter 10 gives an example of the prepare record holding the locks of the one-bit resource manager.

Once all resource managers return from their Savepoint() callbacks, the transaction manager increments the savepoint number, and writes a savepoint log record describing all the resource managers and sessions joined to this transaction (as well as the application context passed as a parameter). If the savepoint is persistent, the transaction manager forces the log. The new savepoint number is returned to the application.

Hiding in this logic is the mechanism to establish savepoints within distributed transactions. The Savepoint() callback of the communication manager causes it to send a Savepoint() TRPC on all its outgoing and incoming sessions, thereby establishing the savepoint for the entire transaction tree (see Exercise 5).

There is great similarity among the programs for Save_Work(), phase 1 of Commit_Work(), and the final phases of Rollback_Work(). Of course, each of these procedures calls its associated resource manager callbacks—for example, Savepoint(), Prepare(), and Abort()—and each sets the savepoint record type to a different value; otherwise, the logic is the same. To reinforce this point, the code for Save_Work() is repeated here:

```
int Save_Work(context * it, Boolean soft)          /*savepoint logic                              */
   {TransCB *      trans = MyTransP();             /*ptr to process's transaction descriptor      */
   TM_savepoint    save;                           /*savepoint record to be formatted             */
   long            save_num;                       /*the savepoint number                         */
   RMTransCB *     rm;                             /*rms joined to this transaction.              */
   SECB *          session;                        /*sessions allocated to this transaction.      */
   Boolean         vote;                           /*summary of rm votes on savepoint             */
   if (MyTrid() == NULLTrid) return(0);            /*insist it have a transaction                 */
   save_num = trans->next_save_pt + +;             /*next savepoint number                        */
   for each rm in trans->RM_list,                  /*for each resource mgr joined to trans,       */
         if( ! vote = rmid.Savepoint(&rm->save_pt_lsn ))  /*ask it to take a savepoint            */
            { Abort_Work();   return 0;};           /*if votes no, abort and return zero           */
      for each session in trans->ses_list          /*for each session in the trans's list         */
         { vote = TM.Savepoint(save_num);          /*do TRPC to remote TM asking it to save       */
            if (timeout || ! vote ) { Abort_Work();  /*if any times out or votes no, then          */
                  return 0;};};                     /*abort the trans & return savepoint zero      */
```

```
trans->save_pt = trans->next_save_pt++;        /*advance savepoint                            */
save.record_type = save;                       /*set log record body type                     */
save.save_pt_num = save_num; save.soft = soft; /*format savepoint record                      */
copy(save, trans->RM_list);                    /*record resource managers joined              */
copy(save, trans->ses_list);                   /*record sessions joined                       */
copy(save.it, it);                             /*add his context                              */
trans->save_pt_lsn = log_insert( save, sizeof(save)); /*write savepoint log record            */
if (!soft) log_flush(trans->max_lsn, soft);    /*force log if not a soft savepoint            */
return save_num;                               /*return the resulting savepoint num           */
};                                             /*                                             */
```

An application can read its current savepoint context by calling Read_ Context(). This routine reads the savepoint log record (via a log_read(MyTransP()->save_pt_lsn,...) extracts the context from the end of that record, and returns it to the caller. Beyond that, there is not much to say about either Save_Work() or Read_Context(). Let us therefore consider Rollback_Work().

11.2.9 Rollback_Work()

Having discussed the logic for forward transaction processing, we now look at the logic for transaction rollback. This is an UNDO scan back through the log. The rollback can return to any previous savepoint. When the UNDO scan reaches the requested savepoint, the transaction manager polls each resource manager, asking it to reinstantiate that savepoint. If a resource manager cannot reinstate that savepoint, the UNDO scan proceeds to the previous savepoint. Ultimately, the UNDO scan reaches a savepoint that each resource manager can agree to, or it reaches savepoint 0, that is, a complete UNDO of the transaction. Resource managers are not allowed to veto savepoint 0. Hiding in this UNDO code is the UNDO of distributed transactions. At each savepoint, the session manager is invoked to UNDO that savepoint. This generates an UNDO_Savepoint() callback on all incoming and outgoing sessions. (For a mechanism to prevent cycles in this process, see Exercise 5.) For example, in Figure 11.3, if any resource manager at any of the five nodes in that network calls Rollback_Work(), then all the other nodes of that transaction graph and all participating resource managers at all nodes will vote on the destination savepoint. The code is as follows:

```
long Rollback_Work(long target_savepoint)     /*                                             */
   {TransCB *    trans = MyTransP();           /*ptr to process' transaction descriptor       */
   TM_savepoint save;                          /*savepoint record to be formatted             */
   LSN          lsn;                           /*LSN used for undo scan                        */
   RMID         rmid;                          /*rmid extracted from log record               */
   log_record_header header;                   /*buffer to hold log record header             */
   Boolean      abort = FALSE;                 /*indicates UNDO failure so abort trans        */
   if (MyTrid() == NULLTrid) return(0);        /*already aborted                              */
   lsn = trans->max_lsn;                       /*get lsn of last log record                   */
```

```
/*the UNDO scan back through the log                                                          */
while (lsn != NULLLSN)                    /*undo scan through log                             */
    { log_read(lsn,&header,save,sizeof(save));   /*read the log record header                 */
    rmid = header.rmid;                   /*extract resource manager id                       */
    rmid.UNDO(lsn);                       /*invoke him to undo the log record                 */
    if (timeout II error) abort = TRUE;   /*on undo step fail, initiate trans abort           */
    if (  ! abort &&                      /*if no undo failures (all undos worked) &          */
        trans->save_pt <= target_savepoint &&   /*if trans is at or below target savepoint    */
        trans->max_lsn == trans->save_pt_lsn )  /*and if current savepoint reestablished      */
        return trans->save_pt;            /*then return success                               */
    lsn = header.tran_prev_lsn;           /*else undo incomplete, continue undo               */
    };                                    /*bottom of undo scan loop                          */
/*End UNDO scan back through the log, at savepoint 0, so abort trans                          */
for each rm in trans->RM_list,            /*for each resource mgr joined to tran,             */
    rm.Abort();                           /*ask it to abort                                   */
for each session in trans->ses_list       /*for each session in the trans' list               */
    TM.Abort();                           /*send an abort TRPC to TM at other end             */
format abort_complete savepoint record;   /*of session                                        */
log_insert abort_complete savepoint record;   /*write an abort completion record in log        */
deallocate TransCB;                       /*deallocate transaction control block,             */
(MyProcessP())->trid = NULLTrid;          /*process has no trid now                           */
return 0 ;                                /*return savepoint zero.                            */
};                                        /*                                                  */
```

How to implement this mechanism is clear; how to use it is less clear. As an example of a curious situation, the root of the transaction tree in Figure 11.3 established savepoint 1. If a leaf of the tree rolls back to savepoint 1 then the computation should return to the root process. After all, at savepoint 1, no other process was even part of the transaction. But the way the routines are defined, control returns to the process that called Rollback_Work(). In practice, savepoints are used in a controlled way, and these problems do not arise (see Chapter 4, Subsection 4.7.3 and Section 4.9, and Chapter 16, Subsection 16.7.3).

If a resource manager or session fails during an UNDO scan, the rollback operation causes the transaction to abort: the transaction will not be able to establish a unanimous vote on any savepoint (this is the purpose of the abort flag in the code). Transactions involved in a resource manager that is down cannot commit; therefore, unless the transaction is at a persistent savepoint, it is aborted. Clearly, this approach could be improved. The abort operation completes without the participation of the down resource manager. When the down resource manager is recovered, the UNDO-REDO protocol allows the resource manager to reconstruct its most recent consistent state. All transactions in which it was actively involved either will have been returned to their most recent persistent savepoint or will have aborted.

The code for rollback has one interesting feature, the UNDO of savepoints. Such UNDOs are actually executed by the transaction manager's UNDO routine. That routine reads as follows:

```
void UNDO(LSN lsn)                                          /*UNDO a transaction savepoint                  */
   {TransCB *        trans = MyTransP();                    /*ptr to process' transaction descriptor        */
   TM_savepoint save;                                       /*savepoint record to be undone                 */
   TRID            him =MyTrid();                            /*his trid                                       */
   RMID            rmid;                                     /*rm id extracted from log record               */
   RMTransCB *      rm;                                      /*rms joined to this transaction.               */
   SECB *           session;                                 /*sessions allocated to this transaction.       */
   log_record_header header;                                 /*buffer to hold log record header              */
   Boolean          vote=TRUE;                               /*summary vote of resource managers             */
   log_read(lsn,&header,save,sizeof(save));                 /*read the log record                           */
   trans->save_pt = save.save_pt_num;                       /*set current savepoint number                  */
   for each rm in trans->RM_list,                           /*for each rm joined to tran,                   */
       { if (rm is in save)                                 /*if rm participated in the savepoint then      */
           rm->save_pt_lsn = save.RM.save_pt_lsn;           /*reset save_pt_lsn from savepoint              */
       else    rm->save_pt_lsn = NULLlsn;                   /*else set save_pt_lsn to null.                 */
       vote= vote && rmid.UNDO_Savepoint(rm->save_pt_lsn);} /*ask it to return to savepoint                 */
   for each session in trans->ses_list                      /*for each session in the trans' list, send and */
       vote = vote && TM.UNDO_Savepoint(trans->save_pt);    /*UNDO TRPC to remote TM                        */
   if (vote)                                                /*if all vote yes on the savept, its established*/
       { trans->max_lsn = header.tran_prev_lsn;             /*point to previous savepoint record.           */
       trans->save_pt_lsn = log_insert(save,sizeof(save));} /*establish this savept by                      */
   return;};                                                /*writing new one (clone)                       */
```

The code is rather dull, but two details are of interest. First, the code reads the savepoint record and reestablishes the state of each resource manager by getting the RMtransCB.save_pt_lsn current at the time of the savepoint. This is the LSN of the savepoint record the resource manager wrote at the time of that savepoint. That LSN is passed to the resource manager as part of the UNDO_Savepoint() callback.

Second, if a transaction returns to savepoint *S*, a new savepoint record is written by the transaction manager just prior to the end of the UNDO scan. This record is a copy of the original savepoint record. In particular, it has the *same* tran_prev_lsn (the third-to-last line of the program does this). Subsequent UNDOs of the transaction will skip all intervening records, since they have already been undone and since the tran_prev_lsn of the new savepoint record points past them. Figure 11.5 illustrates this skipping. The shaded records are matching DO-UNDO pairs. Thus, if the transaction is to be undone during normal processing, the shaded records can be skipped. In addition, since all the shaded records are redone at restart, the UNDO of the shaded records can also be skipped at restart. This is easily accomplished, as the program shows.

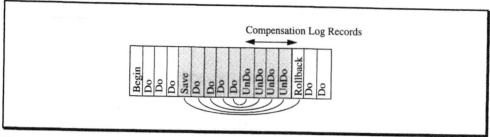

Figure 11.5: The log records generated by a rollback to a savepoint. When a transaction rolls back to a savepoint, the rollback record can point to the previous savepoint. Future UNDO scans can skip the shaded records, since they cancel one another out.

11.3 Checkpoint

Checkpoint is used to speed restart in the unlikely event of a resource manager or node failure. At restart, all volatile memory is reset—this is the definition of volatile memory. The most recent committed state must be reconstructed from records kept in persistent memory. In theory, restart could go back to the beginning of the log and redo all work since then. After a few years, restarting such a system would take a few years. But restart should be fast; ideally, restart would have no work to redo.

Checkpoints are used to quickly reestablish the current state. A *checkpoint* is a relatively recent persistent copy of the state that can be used as a basis for restart. Checkpoint frequency is a performance trade-off: frequent checkpoints imply quick restart, but they also imply much wasted work because each checkpoint is unlikely to be used. Each checkpoint is superceded by the next checkpoint. The checkpoint is only needed and *used* at restart. At that, only the most recent checkpoints are used.

The process pairs described in Chapter 3 (Subsection 3.7.3) checkpoint many times a second, because they want quick takeover times. Large database systems routinely checkpoint every few minutes. If REDO proceeds much faster than normal processing, restart from such checkpoints should complete in a minute. One strategy is to control checkpoint frequency by log activity; for example, checkpointing every time the log grows by a megabyte, or by 10,000 records.

Since volatile memory is lost at restart, any committed updates to volatile memory that appear in the durable log but not in persistent memory must be redone. To reestablish the state of persistent and prepared transactions, their log records must also be redone: their locks must be reacquired and their other state changes reestablished. Any uncommitted transactions must be undone. In general, each resource manager has some state that it must recover before it can accept new work. Each resource manager, then, places requirements on how far back in the log the restart REDO logic must go. These are generically called *low-water marks*.

Chapter 9 (Section 9.6) introduced the notion of low-water marks. Now would be a good time to review that section. Briefly, the transaction low-water mark is the minimum LSN of any live transaction present in the log. If the transaction called rollback right now, or if the system restarted, the UNDO scan would require the log back to this LSN. The resource manager low-water mark is the minimum LSN needed by any resource manager to redo its work; that is, it is the LSN of the oldest update not present in a persistent copy of the object.

Also explained in Chapter 9 (Section 9.5) are the log manager routines to save a pointer to the transaction manager's two most recent checkpoint records. The routines have the interface

void	**log_write_anchor**(LSN anchor);	/*record TM anchor in log anchor	*/
LSN	**log_read_anchor**(void);	/*read TM anchor from log anchor	*/

The transaction manager anchor (checkpoint record), in turn, points to the checkpoint records of the resource managers. Figures 9.6 and 9.7 illustrate these ideas.

Resource managers keep their low-water marks close to the current LSN by periodically copying volatile memory objects to persistent memory. This operation is called *resource manager checkpointing*. Typically, such flushing is done as a low-priority background activity, so that updates are reflected in persistent memory within a few minutes. If the low-water mark becomes too old (say, more than 5 minutes), then the priority of the flush task is increased, and it may become a foreground activity.

11.3.1 Sharp Checkpoints

Some systems periodically checkpoint the entire state of volatile memory to persistent memory as a synchronous operation. That brings the resource manager low-water LSN up to the current LSN. Such events are called *sharp checkpoints*. As memories become large, sharp checkpoints become infeasible because they imply moving gigabytes and, consequently, denying service for a period of seconds.

To demonstrate checkpoints, let us generalize the one-bit resource manager described in the previous chapter. Assume that it manages an array of *1,000* pages of bits, rather than just 1 page. Here the get_bit(i) and free_bit(i) programs have to compute the page number (i/BITS) and then operate on bit (i *mod* BITS) within that page. Each page continues to have a semaphore and a page.lsn. Beyond the more complex bit addressing, the logging and semaphore logic is unchanged. Recall that the one-bit resource manager had the following checkpoint code:

LSN **checkpoint**(LSN * low_water)	/*copy one-page rm state to persistent memory	*/
{ Xsem_get(&page.sem);	/*get the page semaphore	*/
*low_water = log_flush(page.lsn);	/*WAL: force log up to page lsn, set low-water mark	*/
write(file,page,0,sizeof(page));	/*write page to persistent memory	*/
Xsem_give(&page.sem);	/*give page semaphore	*/
return NULLlsn; }	/*return checkpoint lsn (none in this case)	*/

A sharp checkpoint of 1,000 such pages would proceed as follows:

(1) Get the exclusive semaphores on each of the 1,000 pages.

(2) Observing the write-ahead-log protocol, copy all 1,000 pages to persistent memory (disk).

(3) Set the resource manager low-water LSN to current durable LSN.

(4) Release all 1,000 semaphores.

This is an easy program to write, but it denies service for at least 1 second, while all the semaphores are held and all the I/Os are performed. A more fundamental problem with sharp checkpoint is that it may fail. If it fails when only half the pages have been copied out, then half the pages may be inconsistent with the others. The sharp checkpoint therefore needs two copies in persistent memory; each checkpoint overwrites the oldest copy. (This is an example of shadows.) The simple idea of a sharp checkpoint has turned into a substantial space and complexity problem.

11.3.2 Fuzzy Checkpoints

Fuzzy checkpoints write changes to persistent memory in parallel with normal activity. They do not disrupt service. Fuzzy checkpoints get their name from the fact that the collection of checkpointed pages may not be mutually consistent—the checkpoint may be fuzzy in time, since it was taken while the objects were changing. Each page will be consistent, though. The state is page consistent but not action consistent or transaction consistent.

A fuzzy checkpoint is made into a sharp checkpoint by applying to it all the log records generated during the checkpoint. This operation is an implicit part of restart.

Using the one-bit resource manager example of the previous subsection, a fuzzy checkpoint of the 1,000 pages would execute the one-page checkpoint logic for each of the 1,000 pages. This does not deny service to any page for very long, and it accepts mutual inconsistency among persistent pages from the start (the write-ahead-log protocol will resolve this inconsistency at restart).

What is the log low-water mark for such a fuzzy checkpoint? It is the minimum LSN containing a log record that may need to be redone after this checkpoint completes. The low_water_lsn is the LSN current at the time the fuzzy checkpoint began. Nothing prior to that needs to be redone, but someone may update the first page immediately after its semaphore is freed by the checkpoint and that new update will have to be redone. This is the REDO low-water mark. The UNDO at restart must go back to the min LSN of all transactions active when the checkpoint began. The minimum LSN is the UNDO low-water mark.

Such checkpoints are called *fuzzy* because the pages are each checkpointed as of some time between the LSN at the end of the checkpoint and the low_water_lsn. By starting at the low-water mark and redoing all subsequent updates, all the pages are converted to a sharp (current) picture of memory. Idempotence is the key property needed to allow fuzzy checkpoints. Because the update may already be in persistent memory, the approach of starting with a pessimistic "low" LSN and working forward on a fuzzy checkpoint works only if redoing an operation many times is the same as doing it once. As explained in Chapter 10, Subsection 10.3.9, the use of LSNs plus physiological logging makes REDO idempotent.

There are many optimizations of this idea. Here are just few of them: (1) The optimization shown in Exercise 21 of chapter 10, which avoids holding the semaphore during an I/O by copying each page to a buffer, then releasing the semaphore and performing the I/O. (2) Each page can carry a bit indicating it has been updated since it was last read from or written to persistent memory. Initially, the bit is false, and each checkpoint sets the bit false; each update sets the bit true. Checkpoint need only write updated pages. (3) Chapter 2 pointed out that sequential writes have much higher bandwidth than random writes. Thus, checkpoint may want to write out many contiguous pages at a time, rather than just one at a time. (4) Rather than writing all the checkpointed pages out in a burst, the fuzzy checkpoint can spread the writes across the checkpoint interval by adding a delay between each write. The delay time is approximately the checkpoint interval divided by the number of writes needed to perform the checkpoint. These and other optimizations are discussed in Subsection 11.4.6 and in Chapter 13.

That completes the preliminaries. We can now proceed to a fairly simple description of the transaction manager checkpoint logic.

11.3.3 Transaction Manager Checkpoint

Checkpointing is orchestrated by the transaction manager. The decision to take a checkpoint can be driven by time or by log activity. The goal is to minimize REDO time. Not much can be done about UNDO time, since that is determined by how many transactions are aborted at restart and how much work each of those transactions has done. The number of bytes added to the log since the last checkpoint is a measure of how long REDO will take. Thus, every few minutes—or every few megabytes of log activity—the transaction manager initiates checkpoint.

Each time the transaction manager decides a checkpoint is needed, it invokes each active resource manager to record the resource manager's current volatile state in a checkpoint log record. The resource manager returns the LSN of this checkpoint record, as well as its low-water LSN. The function prototype for such callbacks is

LSN **Checkpoint**(LSN* low_water); /*TM checkpointing. Return checkpoint & low water LSN   */

The one-bit resource manager provided an example of such a callback. It has no checkpoint state and, accordingly, returns NULLlsn as its checkpoint LSN, but it does return a low-water LSN. The buffer manager discussed in Chapter 13 gives a more complete example of a checkpoint callback.

The transaction manager's checkpoint logic is as follows:

Checkpoint callbacks.   In parallel, invoke each resource manager to take a checkpoint.

Write checkpoint record.   When all up resource managers reply with their LSNs, write a TM_checkpoint record in the log and force it to durable memory.

Save the checkpoint LSN.   Ask the log manager to copy the LSN of the checkpoint record to durable memory.

In the interest of simplicity, this chapter ignores the semaphores needed to prevent the transaction manager data structures from changing while they are being traversed. It is enough to say that these semaphores are held for short periods and do not disrupt normal system services.

The TM_checkpoint record has all the information needed to reconstruct the data structure shown in Figure 11.1. It contains the transaction manager anchor (TM_anchor), a description of all installed resource managers (the RMCB list), and a description of each live transaction.[1] Restating this in more programmatic terms, the TM_savepoint record nicely describes transactions, and the RMCB nicely describes installed resource managers. The checkpoint record can be declared as follows:

---

[1] The transaction manager does not record the transaction lock list. The transaction's locks are controlled by the resource managers that acquire the locks.

typedef struct {	SAVE_PT_TYPE	record_type;	/*this is a CHECKPOINT record type	*/
	TM_anchor	anchor;	/*contains anchor info of TM	*/
	LSN	low_water;	/*low-water mark of	*/
	long	num_RM;	/*number of resource mgrs installed	*/
	RMCB	RM[num_RM];	/*the status of each installed rm	*/
	long	num_trans;	/*the number of live transactions	*/
	TM_savepoint	trans[num_trans];	/*their descriptions	*/
} **TM_checkpoint;**			/*format of a checkpoint record	*/

The transaction manager's pseudo-code for checkpoint is

```
void TM_Checkpoint(void)                                /*TM invokes checkpoint                  */
  { TM_checkpoint tm_checkpoint;                         /*The checkpoint record to be written    */
  LSN          checkpoint_lsn;                           /*LSN of checkpoint record to be written */
  LSN          low_water = log_max_lsn();                /*start with current durable log as best lsn */
  RMCB *rm;                                              /*Installed resource manager description */
  for each "up" rm in TM_anchor.RM_list                  /*Invoke each "up" resource manager at   */
      rm->checkpoint_lsn = rmid.Checkpoint(&rm->low_water_lsn);  /*checkpoint callback       */
      if ( fail )                                        /*if the resource manager fails to respond */
          rm->RMup = FALSE;                              /*mark it down if it fails to respond else */
      else low_water = min(low_water,rm->low_water_lsn); /*add lsn to the global low water        */
  /*now all rms have checkpointed, write the TM_checkpoint record                                 */
  copy TM_anchor to tm_checkpoint;                       /*remember TM anchor                     */
  TM_checkpoint.low_water =low_water;                    /*global low water of RMs and TM         */
  for each rm in TM_anchor.RM_list                       /*remember all installed rms             */
      copy RMCB to tm_checkpoint;                        /*                                       */
  for each trans in TM_anchor.tran_list                  /*Remember all live trans, their joined  */
      copy its TransCB, RMTransCB, SECB to tm_checkpoint; /*RMs and their sessions                */
  TM_anchor. checkpoint_lsn = log_insert(tm_checkpoint); /*add the ckpt record to the log         */
  log_write_anchor(TM_anchor.checkpoint_lsn);            /*ask log mgr to force log and remember   */
  return;                                                /*checkpoint LSN                         */
  };                                                     /*checkpoint complete                    */
```

If a resource manager has failed, or if it fails to successfully write the checkpoint record within some time limit (say, 30 seconds), then the checkpoint operation declares that resource manager to be down, and the checkpoint will complete without it. Such failed resource managers will go through resource manager restart (discussed in the following section). In addition, if the resource manager's low-water mark is too old (less than the previous checkpoint), the resource manager is marked as down.

The whole checkpoint process ordinarily takes less than a second and generates a few tens of kilobytes of log data. While a checkpoint is being taken, the system is continuing to process transactions and do other work. Should a system failure occur during the checkpoint, restart would begin from the previous checkpoint. Once the TM_checkpoint record is written and recorded by the log manager as the checkpoint anchor, restart will begin from this point.

In summary, then, the transaction manager periodically invokes each resource manager to take a checkpoint. The resource manager records its current state and its low-water mark. The transaction manager then writes a checkpoint record summarizing the state of all transactions and resource managers. It saves a pointer to this checkpoint record with the log manager. At restart, the transaction manager will read its checkpoint record, and REDO will begin from the checkpoint low-water mark.

11.4 System Restart

Many systems make distinctions between different types of restarts: *hotstart* starts from an active state (something like a takeover), *warmstart* starts from persistent memory, and *coldstart* starts from the archive. Hotstart is included in the discussion of disaster recovery and fault-tolerant commit protocols (Chapter 12, Section 12.6). Warmstart is called *restart* here and is described in this section. Coldstart from an archive copy to the current state or to some previous timestamp state is discussed along with archive recovery (Section 11.6).

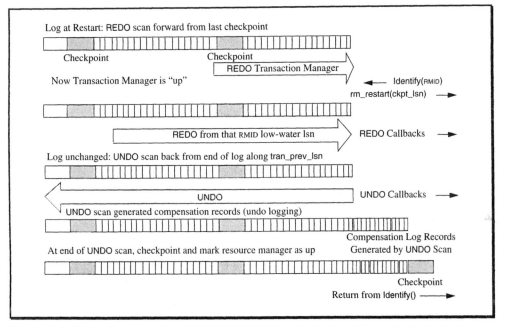

Figure 11.6: The logic for system restart.   Restart first reads the most recent checkpoint and scans forward to the end of the log to reconstruct the transaction manager's state. The transaction manager is then up. It waits for a resource manager Identify() and begins recovery of that resource manager. Recovery consists of giving the resource manager its most recent checkpoint record, then performing a REDO scan from the resource manager's low-water mark. When the REDO scan completes, the transaction manager initiates an UNDO scan of each live transaction back to its most recent persistent savepoint (or to the beginning of the transaction). This UNDO work may generate log records. The resource manager should acquire any transaction locks needed at commit phase 1 or at persistent savepoints. Transactions that are prepared to commit are reinstantiated in this way. When UNDO is complete, the transaction manager marks the resource manager as up, takes a checkpoint, and returns from the Identify() call. The resource manager is then up. Many resource managers may be recovering concurrently.

The logic for system restart is diagrammed in Figure 11.6 and is explained in the figure legend. The overall recovery plan is for the transaction manager to first recover itself, rebuilding the data structures shown in Figure 11.1. Once that is complete, resource managers invoke the transaction manager via Identify() to request recovery. The transaction manager reads them the log, performing first a REDO scan and then an UNDO scan for any actions that are uncommitted or not persistent. Then the transaction manager marks the resource manager as up and returns from the Identify() call. The following subsections explain first the transaction manager restart, then resource manager restart.

11.4.1 Transaction States at Restart

The discussion of restart needs a generic classification of transaction states at restart (see Figure 11.7):

Completed.   The transaction committed or aborted and wrote a completion record in the durable log. All resource managers have been informed about the transaction. Incomplete transactions are generically called *live transactions*.

Completing.   The commit or abort decision has been made and the commit record has been written to the log, but some of the transaction's resource managers may not yet have received the phase-2 invocation.

Persistent.   The outcome of the transaction is in doubt, either because it is a "prepared" distributed transaction with a remote commit coordinator or because the transaction is at a persistent savepoint. In either case, the transaction cannot yet be committed or aborted. Completion of this transaction is dependent on the remote commit coordinator or the application that established the persistent savepoint.

Active.   The transaction has done some work but has not established a persistent savepoint. In this case, the transaction is aborted at restart.

11.4.2 Transaction Manager Restart Logic

At system restart, the TP monitor starts the log manager, the transaction manager, and other installed resource managers. The TP monitor invokes the rm_Startup() callbacks of each such resource manager. When started, the transaction manager first asks the log manager for the LSN of the most recent checkpoint log record. That checkpoint record describes the transaction manager's data (the control blocks in Figure 11.1) as of the checkpoint. Using this, the transaction manager reestablishes its tables of installed resource managers and live transactions. It then brings these tables up to date by scanning the log forward, reading transaction log records. When it sees a begin transaction log record, it allocates a TransCB; when it sees a commit_complete or abort_complete log record, it deallocates the associated TransCB. When it sees any other type of savepoint record (save, prepare, commit, or abort record) it updates the TransCB and the lists of joined resource managers and sessions allocated to that transaction. This is the code to perform the REDO of a single transaction manager log record:

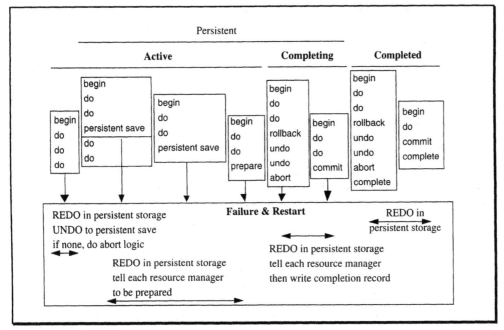

Figure 11.7: The various transaction states at restart. Most transactions are completed. Most of the rest (the live ones) are active, having begun recently. They were doing work when the failure occurred. A few of the transactions were either at a persistent savepoint or were part of a distributed transaction and were in the prepared state. The shaded actions are undone at restart.

```
void REDO(LSN lsn)                                /*REDO a transaction manager log record          */
    {TransCB *    trans;                          /*ptr to process' transaction descriptor         */
    TRID          him;                            /*his trid                                        */
    TM_savepoint save;                            /*savepoint record to be redone                   */
    log_record_header header;                     /*buffer to hold log record header                */
    log_read_lsn(lsn,&header,save,sizeof(save));  /*read the log record                             */
    him = header.trid;                            /*extract trid that wrote log record              */
    switch (save.record_type) {                   /*depending on type of savepoint record           */
        begin:                                    /*at begin transaction,                           */
            allocate a TransCB for him;    break;  /*   create a TransCB for this transaction        */
        save: prepare: commit: abort:             /*at any savepoint,                               */
            { trans = &TransCB of him;            /*connect to that trid environment                */
            copy save to trans;                   /*   set TransCB from savepoint record            */
            copy save to trans->RM_list;          /*   set each RMTransCB from savept record         */
            copy save to session_list; break;}    /*   set each SECB from savepoint record           */
        commit_complete: abort_complete:          /*at any completion,                              */
            deallocate him Trans structure; break;/*deallocateTransCB or this transaction           */
        default::}                                /*ignore any other record types                   */
    return;}                                      /*operation redone                                */
```

Transaction manager restart invokes the above REDO routine for every durable transaction record written after the checkpoint. At the end of this REDO scan, the transaction manager has a list of all transactions that have not completed. Then, for each transaction that is in doubt at restart, the transaction manager launches a process that executes the coordinator_failure() routine (see Subsection 11.2.7) to resolve in-doubt transactions during normal processing. That process persistently asks the remote coordinator (transaction manager) for the status of the transaction and acts on the result. Similarly, for each outgoing session of a committing or aborting transaction, the transaction manager creates a process that executes session_failure() to persistently send the Commit() or Abort() decision to the participant at the other end of the session.

After a transaction manager failure, the transaction manager at restart may not know about the last few trids it created. The trid counter is only made persistent at checkpoints (see Section 11.3). Recent transaction identifiers may have been sent to other nodes. To avoid duplicate trids, the transaction manager at restart advances the sequence counter well beyond any such unrecorded trids. There is little more to say about the following code for transaction manager restart.

```
void Transaction_Manager_Restart(void)                          /*TM Restart code                              */
    {TM_checkpoint      tm_checkpoint;                           /*TM checkpt record to be read from log        */
    LSN                 checkpoint_lsn;                          /*LSN of that record during redo               */
    RMID                rmid;                                    /*rmid wrote log record being redone           */
    TRID                trid;                                    /*trid is author of a log record               */
    LSN                 lsn;                                     /*address of log record during redo scan       */
    int                 sqlcode;                                 /*sql indicator, nonzero means error           */
    log_record_header header;                                   /*header of log record, needed for read        */
    checkpoint_lsn = log_read_anchor();                          /*get TM checkpt addr from log mgr             */
    log_read_lsn(checkpoint_lsn,header,tm_checkpoint,sizeof(tm_checkpoint));  /*read checkpoint             */
    TM_anchor.checkpoint_lsn = checkpoint_lsn;                   /*set anchor checkpt lsn to that checkpt       */
    TM_anchor.next_trid =                                        /*set next trid to the checkpt trid            */
        tm_checkpoint.TM_anchor.next_trid + BIG;                 /*plus BIG number to avoid duplicate trids     */
    declare cursor for the_log                                   /*a cursor from the start of the log forward   */
        select    rmid, trid, lsn                                /*get rm id, trid, log record key (lsn)        */
        from      log                                            /*of all log records.                          */
        where     lsn > :checkpoint_lsn                          /*after checkpoint                             */
        order by lsn ascending;                                  /*in FIFO order                                */
    open cursor the_log;                                         /*open the sql cursor on the log table         */
    while (TRUE)                                                 /*Scan log forward & redo each TM rec          */
        { fetch the_log into :rmid, :trid, :lsn;                 /*fetch the next log record                    */
        if (sqlcode != 0) break;                                 /*if no more, then redone, end loop            */
        Resume_Transaction(trid);                                /*assume the identity of that transaction      */
        if (rmid = TMID) TMID.REDO(lsn);                         /*If TM wrote it (begin, commit... ) REDO it   */
        else Join_Work(rmid,trid);                               /*just in case, join this rmid to that trans   */
        log_transaction(lsn);};                                  /*advance tran.max_lsn                         */
    close cursor the_log;                                        /*Redo scan is complete, close cursor          */
    TM_Checkpoint();                                             /*Write a checkpoint for good measure.         */
```

```
For each completing transaction              /*For each completing transaction,          */
    for each outgoing session                /*create a process to send commit/abort      */
        session_failure(&session);           /*   on each outgoing session.               */
For each in doubt transaction                /*For each in-doubt transaction, create      */
    coordinator_failure(&session);           /*   a process to ask coordinator about it.  */
};                                           /*Transaction Manager Restart complete       */
```

After executing this code, the transaction manager is up. It has a current `TransCB` structure for every transaction that has not completed. It knows what sessions those transactions have and what resource managers are joined to them. It has launched persistent processes to resolve distributed transactions that are committing or are in doubt. It is now ready to help recover the local resource managers.

Because checkpoints are relatively frequent, transaction manager restart usually scans less than a megabyte of log before it is available for operation. This sequential scan completes in less than a second.

11.4.3 Resource Manager Restart Logic, Identify()

At system restart, the TP monitor starts all resource managers at their rm_Startup() callbacks. As described in the previous subsection, the transaction manager comes back to life by reading its checkpoint record and performing a REDO scan of the log since that checkpoint. While this is happening, each resource manager is doing some of its own startup work: opening files, setting up its process structure, and perhaps even running its own recovery using a private log. Once this initialization is done, the resource manager calls transaction manager Identify() to declare itself ready for recovery.

The identify call waits on a semaphore within the transaction manager until transaction manager restart is complete. Then, if the resource manager is simple—that is, if it has no callbacks—the Identify() call marks the resource manager as up and returns. The resource manager is then ready to offer services. Some resource managers keep their own logs and perform their own recovery. Such resource managers only need to resolve in-doubt transactions at restart—they have no records in the common log. The more interesting case of a sophisticated resource manager that generates log records in the common log and participates in transaction commit is shown in Figure 11.8.

The transaction manager coordinates the recovery of a sophisticated resource manager via a sequence of callbacks. First, it invokes the resource manager's rm_restart(checkpoint_lsn), passing the most recent checkpoint LSN of that resource manager (RMCB.checkpoint_lsn). Then the transaction manager performs a REDO scan of the log from the resource manager's low-water mark, invoking rmid.REDO() for each log record written by that resource manager. At the end of the REDO scan, the transaction manager searches the list of live transactions for ones joined to that resource manager. The transaction manager calls rmid.Commit() for each committing transaction. If any are aborting, it initiates an UNDO scan. When this work is complete, the Identify() call marks the resource manager as up and returns to the resource manager.

Let us now step through the key parts of this recovery scenario a little more slowly. The transaction manager REDO scan from the resource manager's low-water mark forward to the end of the log passes any log records of the down resource manager to that resource manager's REDO() callback:

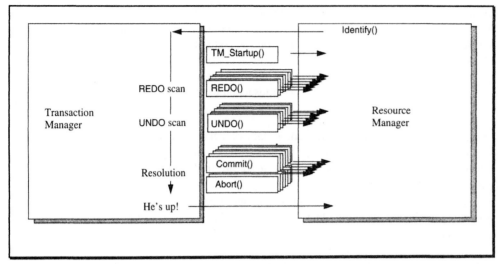

Figure 11.8: The restart recovery of a resource manager.   The resource manager calls Identify(), which first generates a callback telling the resource manager the address of its most recent savepoint log record. Then the resource manager is sent a list of records to redo. After this, it is presented with a list of records to undo and a set of transactions to either commit or abort. When all this is complete, the resource manager is marked up, and the Identify() call returns.

```
REDO_recovery(RMID rmid, LSN rmid_low_water_lsn)        /*logic to recover a "down" rm        */
    { declare cursor rm_recovery                        /*cursor to scan the log             */
        select   lsn, trid                              /*returning next lsn and trid        */
        from     log                                    /*                                   */
        where    rmid = :rmid                           /*of this rm between low-water        */
        and      lsn ≥ :rmid_low_water_lsn              /*and crash                          */
        order by lsn ascending;                         /*towards end of log                 */
    exec sql open rm_recovery;                          /*open the cursor                    */
    do { exec sql fetch rm_recovery into :lsn, :trid;   /*loop to get next log record of this */
        if (sqlcode ! = 0) break;                       /*keep going to end of log           */
        Resume_Transaction(trid);                       /*establish that transaction context */
        rmid.REDO(lsn);                                 /*resource manager and to redo it    */
        } while (TRUE);                                 /*keep going to end of log           */
    exec sql close rm_recovery;                         /*close the cursor                   */
    }                                                   /*                                   */
```

This completes the REDO scan. At the end of this scan, the resource manager will have redone the work of all completed and live transactions. It will have reestablished the savepoints of all transactions that have not yet completed. The transaction manager then searches for any transactions joined to this resource manager (any **RMTransCBs** of this RMID). If there are no such transactions, or if all of them are in doubt or at a persistent savepoint, then recovery is complete. In that case, the transaction manager marks the resource manager as up and returns from the Identify() call.

If, on the other hand, there are committing or aborting transactions, then recovery is not yet complete. In that event, the committing transactions are handled first. For each committing transaction this resource manager has joined, the recovery manager invokes the following routine:

```
void rm_commit(TransCB * trans, RMTransCB * rm)      /*send Commit() TRPC to rmid                       */
    { TM_savepoint   save;                           /*completion record to be formatted               */
    RMID            rmid = rm->rmid;                  /*remote TM to receive Commit() callback          */
    Resume_Transaction(trans->trid);                 /*establish that transaction context              */
    rmid.Commit( );                                  /*tell remote TM to commit                        */
    deallocate RMTransCB;                            /*RM no longer joined to transaction              */
    if (   trans->RM_list == NULL &&                 /*if all rms complete (deallocated)               */
           trans->ses_list == NULL)                  /*and if all outgoing sessions committed          */
        { trans->status = COMMITTED;                 /*then enter committed state                      */
        save.record_type = commit_complete;          /*set log rec type to say trans completed         */
        log_insert( save, sizeof(save));             /*write completion record lazy                    */
        dequeue and free trans structure;}           /*deallocate trans control block, done            */
    return;                                          /*process is complete, terminate process          */
    };                                               /*trans committed for this rm                     */
```

That resolves any committing transactions. If there are no aborting transactions, then recovery is complete. Otherwise, an undo scan of the log is needed to reverse the changes of aborting transactions. The scan goes to the min_lsn of all transactions joined to this resource manager. The UNDO scan is straightforward:

```
UNDO_recovery(RMID rmid, LSN min_lsn)  /*logic to UNDO a "down" resource manager      */
    { declare cursor undo_recovery                       /*cursor to scan the log                        */
        select    lsn,trid                               /*returning next lsn                            */
        from      log                                    /*                                              */
        where     rmid = :rmid                           /*of this resource manager                      */
        and       lsn ≥ :min_lsn                         /*starting at high-water mark                   */
        order by lsn descending;                         /*down to first trans begin lsn.                */
    exec sql open undo_recovery;                         /*open the cursor                               */
    do { exec sql fetch undo_recovery into :lsn, :trid;  /*loop to get rm's next log record              */
        if (sqlcode ! = 0) break                         /*stop when no more records                     */
        if (Status_Transaction(trid) in {aborting,aborted} )   /*If trid aborting or aborted             */
            {Resume_Transaction(trans->trid);            /*establish that transaction context            */
             rmid.UNDO(lsn);}                            /*invoke down resource manager to UNDO it       */
        } while (TRUE);                                  /*keep going to min trans lsn                   */
    exec sql close rm_recovery;                          /*close the cursor                              */
    }                                                    /*                                              */
```

When the UNDO scan is complete, the transaction manager removes the resource manager from the RM_list of all these aborting transactions. If that causes any transactions to complete, the logic of rm_commit() is used to write a transaction completion record in the log and deallocate the transaction. Once all that is done, the Identify() call marks the resource manager as up, and returns.

There are many fine points associated with resource manager restart, but a major one concerns who needs whom. If one resource manager needs another in order to restart, there must be some way for the first to wait for the second to recover. The Identify() call gives an example of this situation. It allows other resource managers to wait for the transaction manager to restart. Similarly, the log_read_anchor() call allows the transaction manager to wait for the log manager to start. This staged recovery must be part of the client resource manager design.

If there is a failure during resource manager restart, the whole restart procedure starts over from the beginning. The idempotence of REDO scans allows such restarts.

11.4.4 Summary of the Restart Design

The preceding two subsections explained how the transaction manager reconstructs its state at restart from the most recent checkpoint and from the durable log records since that checkpoint. Once it has restarted, the transaction manager helps other resource managers restart as they invoke Identify(). This simple design has a REDO scan from the low-water mark, followed by an UNDO scan. The transaction manager orchestrates these scans, helping the resource manager to remember its checkpoint to resolve in-doubt transactions. The next two subsections describe alternate designs for resource managers and for transaction manager restart. The final subsection rationalizes why the REDO-UNDO approach works when combined with physiological logging.

11.4.5 Independent Resource Managers

The design described in Subsection 11.4.3 assumes the resource manager is using the common log and wants help in reading that log. There may be resource managers that keep their own logs or that have their own ideas about performing recovery. Such resource managers want only one thing from the transaction manager: they want it to coordinate the transaction commitment. They would rather do their own recovery. They want only Prepare(), Commit(), and Abort() callbacks, as well as support for Status_ Transaction(). With those primitives, they can write their own logs and recover their own states.

Portable systems often maintain their own logs and, therefore, take this view. Such a system first recovers its own state at restart with a private REDO scan, which calls Status_Transaction() to resolve incomplete transactions. It typically uses a private log to do this. Then it invokes Identify() to get the Commit() and Abort() callbacks for transactions that are committing or aborting. It uses the Commit() callbacks to trigger phase-2 commit work and completion of the transaction. Abort() callbacks trigger a private UNDO scan. Once these tasks have been performed, the resource managers are marked up, and the Identify() calls return.

11.4.6 The Two-Checkpoint Approach: A Different Strategy

In the decentralized recovery design presented in Subsections 11.4.2 and 11.4.3, each resource manager is recovered independently and asynchronously. This simple design was chosen because it unifies system restart (Section 11.4) and resource manager restart (Section 11.5). The same logic is used if the resource manager failed for internal reasons while the system was operating, or if it failed because the whole system failed.

All this is great, but there is one problem with the design. If *n* resource managers need recovery at restart, the transaction manager scans the log $2n + 1$ times: once for itself and twice for everybody else (a REDO scan and an UNDO scan). Why not piggyback all these scans and have just two scans to recover everybody? To be sure, that is a good idea—it is what many systems do, and it was the original design used in this book—but the centralized design was not presented here because it is a little longer and a little more complex. Here is the basic idea (see Figure 11.9).

At checkpoint, the transaction manager insists that each resource manager's low-water mark be more recent than the last transaction manager checkpoint. This is called the *two-checkpoint rule*: no low-water mark is more than two checkpoints old. Thus, a REDO scan from the second-to-last checkpoint will redo everybody. Note how well this interacts with the fuzzy-checkpoint strategy mentioned in Subsection 11.3.2. It allows the fuzzy checkpoint to spread its writes over an entire checkpoint interval, thereby avoiding any bursts of write activity.

At restart, the transaction manager goes back two checkpoints and restores its state. It waits for everybody to call Identify() and for them to respond to the rm_restart() callback.

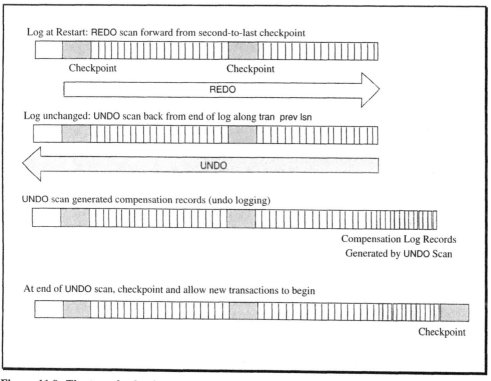

Figure 11.9: The two-checkpoint approach to restart.   In this scheme, all resource managers are recovered in two log scans. First, the TM reads the second-most-recent checkpoint and scans forward from there to the end of the log, redoing all log records. It knows that this checkpoint is below the low-water mark of all up resource managers. Then, it initiates an UNDO scan of each live transaction back to its most recent persistent savepoint (or to the beginning of the transaction). This UNDO work may generate log records. Transaction locks are reacquired at persistent savepoints. Transactions that are prepared to commit are reinstantiated in this way. The transaction manager then takes a checkpoint and declares all resource managers recovered.

Then it performs a global REDO scan, invoking the rmid.REDO(lsn) of every log record after the restart checkpoint. Actually, it can suppress such calls if the rmid.low_water_lsn is greater than the log record LSN.

After this REDO scan, all up resource managers have recovered their states, and all the completed transactions have their effects reflected in the volatile state. The transaction manager then begins the UNDO of all live transactions back to their most recent persistent savepoint. The UNDO scan generates compensation log records and eventually completes, but it could take a very long time if some transaction has done a huge amount of work without establishing a persistent savepoint. If the UNDO scan lasts more than a few minutes, new checkpoints may be taken by the transaction manager. Eventually, all live transactions are returned to their most recent persistent savepoints. Aborted transactions have been undone, and transactions that are prepared or are at a persistent savepoint are reinstantiated: in particular, their locks have been reacquired. At this point, a new checkpoint is taken, and the transaction manager allows new transactions to begin.

Once normal service is started, the transaction manager resolves distributed transactions as described in Subsection 11.4.2.

11.4.7 Why Restart Works

The restart and REDO logic seems quite simple, but it would not work correctly without all the mechanisms described in Chapter 10. The FIX protocol assures that the persistent store is page consistent. The write-ahead-log protocol ensures log consistency; that is, it ensures that the log records needed to UNDO any uncommitted changes in persistent memory are also present in the durable memory log. The force-log-at-commit rule ensures that the log records of any committed transactions are present in persistent memory. Page log sequence numbers (LSNs) make REDOs of physical and physiological log records idempotent, so that restart can fail and restart arbitrarily many times and still produce the correct result.

Table 11.10 is a case analysis of why persistent memory recovery indeed reproduces the most recent atomic and consistent memory state. Consider any transaction and any page update by that transaction. The transaction may or may not have committed; the update may or may not be persistent (the persistent page may be old or new), that update corresponds to a log record; and the log record may or may not be durable. This gives rise to the eight possibilities cataloged in Table 11.10 and discussed individually in the following paragraphs.

Let us step through the cases one by one. If the transaction is committed, then the log record must be durable (force-at-commit), and the transaction will be redone. Cases 1 and 2, then, are precluded by force-at-commit. If the page update is volatile (not persistent) and the log record is durable, then restart will redo the update as part of the REDO scan. Therefore, case 3 is handled correctly. If the persistent page is already updated, the REDO idempotence will leave the page in the correct state. Case 4, too, is handled correctly. This, incidentally, is quite important, since restart itself may crash and need to start again. Restart will eventually succeed, and when it does, the page update may have been redone many times. Idempotence means that all these REDOs will leave the page in the correct state.

The logic for committed transactions applies equally well to in-doubt transactions and to transactions with persistent savepoints. Each of these transactions will have its persistent state restored—all their persistent updates will be done and all their locks will be reacquired.

Table 11.10: A case analysis of the restart state of a transaction's outcome, the state of its log record, and the state of the page in persistent memory.

Case	Transaction	Log record	Persistent Page	Why Recovery Works
1	committed	volatile	old	impossible: force-log-at-commit
2			new	impossible: WAL + force-log-at-commit
3		durable	old	REDO makes it new
4			new	REDO idempotence
5	aborted	volatile	old	no record at restart (implicit UNDO).
6			new	impossible: WAL
7		durable	old	REDO then UNDO
8			new	REDO idempotence + UNDO

Now let us consider the aborted transaction case. The transaction's persistent memory updates must be undone unless the transaction *already* was undone and wrote an abort completion record. The recovery scheme presented here redoes all persistent transaction records found in the log: committed ones and aborted ones. After this REDO scan, the incomplete transactions are undone. If the transaction's rollback record (the undo_begin record in Figure 10.17) was recorded in the log, then the restart logic realizes that the transaction was aborted and all its changes were reversed by the REDO scan. If the abort completion record was found in the log, then nothing more need be done to abort the transaction; all of its changes to persistent state and the network have been undone as part of the REDO scan. If the aborted transaction has no completion record, the transaction manager carries out the abort completion, informing all the transaction's local resource managers and outgoing sessions, and then writes the abort completion record. This is done as an asynchronous task by the transaction manager.

If, on the other hand, the transaction was not yet aborting, then transaction UNDO is initiated as though this were an active transaction. If the log record is volatile, then it will not be present at restart. WAL assures that the corresponding page update will also not be present in persistent memory. Thus, in case 5 UNDO is not needed, since the update itself was lost. The whole purpose of WAL is to prevent case 6. Case 7 is the standard UNDO case: the persistent update is undone. Case 8 is quite interesting; it explains why UNDO need not be idempotent in this design. The REDO scan will redo the update before UNDO is called to reverse the update. As a result, at restart (and during normal processing) UNDO will never be presented with an "old" state. Since the system state has been reconstructed using the log REDO, the "online" transaction UNDO logic can be used. The only special feature about UNDO at restart is that no locks are held or acquired except at a persistent savepoint that survives restarts.

11.4.8 Distributed Transaction Resolution: Two-Phase Commit at Restart

The previous subsection explained why REDO and UNDO eventually produce the most-recent committed local memory state, once the outcome of the transaction is known. Now, consider the logic for resolving in-doubt transactions. If the transaction manager is the root coordinator for a transaction that has not completed—one that was committing or aborting—it tries to complete the transaction by notifying the local resource managers and by sending the commit decision to all of the transaction's outgoing sessions. The root transaction manager is never in doubt about the outcome of the transaction, because it makes the decision.

For transactions that are aborting, the commit coordinator can write the abort completion record in the log and deallocate the transaction structure once the local resource managers have responded. As a consequence of the presumed-abort protocol, the commit coordinator does not have to remember that it aborted the transaction. The absence of any record of an in-doubt transaction implies that the transaction aborted. On the other hand, if the transaction committed, the coordinator must wait for an acknowledgment from all participants before it can claim the transaction is complete.

The participant's logic is similar. It repeatedly sends inquiries to the coordinator (say, once a minute), asking the status of in-doubt transactions. If no reply is received, it tries again. Eventually, the coordinator responds with the commit or abort message. When this happens, the participant resumes its commit or abort logic and completes the transaction.

There is one case that should never happen, but it does: the commit coordinator is reset, and the transaction manager fails and cannot recover its state. This is considered a disaster and is called *amnesia*. How can the system sense amnesia and deal with it? As explained in Subsection 11.2.1, each transaction manager remembers its *birthday*, the day its logs began and the day its memory began. When a transaction manager is reset, it gets a new birthday. Transaction managers cooperating in a distributed transaction exchange birthdays as part of the commit protocol. If at restart the transaction manager's birthday does not match the birthday it had when the commit started, then something is terribly wrong. The birthday mechanism detects transaction manager failures; it is up to system administrators to resolve any transactions involved in such a failure. Transactions that are in doubt and get a birthday mismatch should remain in doubt and send diagnostic messages to the system administrators. This is quite similar to the logic used by heuristic commit and operator commit (see Chapter 12, Section 12.5).

11.4.9 Accelerating Restart

Restart speed is critical. If restart takes twice as long, unavailability doubles. Chapter 3 pointed out the need for short repair times to provide high availability. The main techniques for speeding up restart are to minimize the work needed at restart (e.g., checkpointing); to perform the restart work incrementally (e.g., recover the most critical resources first); and to perform the restart work in parallel, using all the processors, memory, disks, and communications lines at once.

Incremental restart has many variants. Each resource manager can be recovered independently. If some resources are more critical than others, they can be recovered in priority order. If it is difficult to recognize this priority, the redo log can be sorted by resource and redo can be performed on demand—when the objects are accessed. The data that new transactions want to access will typically be the same as the data accessed a few moments ago—indeed, the transactions may even be identical if the clients are resubmitting work that was interrupted by the restart. So restart will probably have to recover the data in use at the time of the restart.

The redo scan must be performed prior to accepting new work on a resource. At the end of the REDO scan, locks are held on all resources held by incomplete transactions. New transactions can be processed against the database while the UNDO scan is proceeding.

Parallelism offers the greatest opportunities for speedup. Each resource manager can be recovered in parallel, and, in fact, each resource can be recovered in parallel. Exercises 13 and 14 explore these ideas.

11.4.10 Other Restart Issues

The discussion of restart mentioned the two-checkpoint rule: no resource manager should have a low-water mark more than two checkpoints old. This rule limits the REDO work. Similar problems arise with UNDO: undoing a transaction that has been generating log for an hour could easily take an hour. If the transaction establishes persistent savepoints, then restart only needs to undo back to the most recent one. If these savepoints are frequent, the UNDO work will be limited to a few seconds or minutes. At the time this book is being written, no system supports persistent savepoints. To avoid the problem of long restart times, the application programmer must issue frequent commits; this involves converting a batch program to a sequence of *mini-batch transactions*. In general, systems that want to limit restart times must abort any transaction that would take more than a few seconds to undo. Obviously, this adds considerable complexity to application programming and system operation. It is probable that the rationale for adding persistent savepoints to transaction processing systems will ultimately come from the benefits persistent savepoints provide for quick restart.

To support online UNDO, the log manager must keep the log records of all live transactions online. If a live transaction is a year old, the log manager must keep a year of log online. There are three schemes to deal with this situation:

Abort.   Abort any transaction that spans more than N megabytes of log.

Copy-forward.   Copy the transaction's log records forward in the log.

Copy-aside.   Copy the transaction's log records to a side file.

The abort scheme is commonly used today, but it does not support persistent long-lived transactions—ones that last for weeks. Chapter 10 discusses the implementation of copy-forward and copy-aside (also called a *dynamic log*, after a comparable mechanism in IBM's IMS program isolation facility). Exactly the same issues come up with resource managers: if a resource manager is down, its low-water mark will be very old. In this case, the transactions cannot be aborted completely, because the resource manager is needed to carry out the rollback. Consequently, resource manager recovery forces a copy-forward or copy-aside scheme for all log records belonging to a resource manager that is down. Because the volume of log data could be quite large in these situations, a copy-aside scheme is preferable.

11.5 Resource Manager Failure and Restart

Supporting the independent failure of various resource managers within a system is one of the key fault-containment techniques of transaction systems. If one resource manager fails, it should only affect the transactions using that resource manager and the objects managed by that resource manager.

A resource manager can fail unilaterally, declaring itself to be down and requesting restart. Alternatively, the transaction manager can decide that the resource manager is broken because it is not responding to transaction commit requests, UNDO requests, or checkpoint requests. In such cases, the transaction manager marks the resource manager as down and denies it permission to join transactions until it has completed a recovery step.

When a resource manager first fails, all live transactions using that resource manager are aborted. Transactions that are prepared, are committing, or are at a persistent savepoint are not aborted, but rollback is initiated on the others. Of course, the down resource manager is not called for the UNDOs of these transactions, because it is not servicing requests. Consequently, the abort completion records for these transactions cannot be written (they require that the down resource manager be consulted). All other resource managers go through their UNDO logic, and after the rollback is complete, the effects of the transactions have been undone for all the up resource managers.

When the down resource manager is ready, it asks to be recovered by invoking the transaction manager via an Identify(rmid) call. The transaction manager then recovers the resource manager, as explained in Section 11.4 (see Figure 11.8). It does a REDO scan from the low-water mark, then an UNDO scan for aborted transactions. Once the REDO scan is complete, the resource manager is considered to be up. If there is a failure during resource manager restart, the whole restart procedure starts over from the beginning. The idempotence of REDO scans allows such restarts.

Resource manager restart is, therefore, quite similar to ordinary restart. The previous subsection discussed copying log records of down resource managers to a side file (the copy-aside logic) so that the online logs need to extend back only a day or a week. The copy-aside logs allow a resource manager to be down for longer periods without causing the online logs to overflow.

11.6 Archive Recovery

If the online version of an object in persistent memory is damaged in some way, it can often be recovered from an archive copy of the object and from the log of all updates to the object since the copy was made. For example, if the online copy of a page somehow gets a double failure (both disks fail), or if the software somehow damages it, then the page might be recovered by starting with an archive copy of the page and redoing all changes to it. Since the logic for this is identical to the REDO scan at restart, such archive recovery is virtually free.

Moving a copy of an object to the archive is called *taking a dump* of the object. If the dump is made while the object is being updated, then it is a *fuzzy dump*. This terminology is an exact analogy to the terminology used for checkpoints. Fuzzy dumps are used in the same way as fuzzy checkpoints. Each archive object has a *REDO LSN:* the LSN at which the

REDO scan should begin. This is the LSN that was current when the fuzzy dump began. Updates after the REDO LSN may not be reflected in the fuzzy dump.

The REDO LSN is recorded as an attribute of the object's fuzzy dump descriptor. Archive recovery of an object, then, consists of the following:

Archive_Recovery
> Get exclusive access to the object.
> Replace it with the value of its fuzzy dump (archive copy).
> REDO all changes to the object from its REDO LSN to the current LSN.
> UNDO any uncommitted changes to the object.

This logic is virtually identical to resource manager recovery, except that it is restricted to a single object (the resource manager itself is functioning regularly). If there is a failure during archive recovery, the whole process begins again.

To complete archive recovery, the entire log (all the way back to the REDO LSN) must be brought online. Since the scan is sequential, the archived sections of the log can be retrieved a gigabyte at a time (or in some smaller unit), and once they have been applied to the object, the online copies can be discarded. The archive copy of the log continues to exist. An archived object also has an *UNDO LSN* that is the min LSN of any transaction that might have to be undone against the object (see Figure 9.7). In the absence of long-lived transactions, the UNDO LSN is a few hours old, while the REDO LSN is days or weeks old. This, again, is a consequence of logging undos: any UNDO logging needed for complete transactions (aborted or committed) will be encountered by the REDO scan. If long-lived transactions are supported, the UNDO scan places no extra requirements on the online log—those transactions need to have their log records online anyway, in case they need to be aborted. Presumably, their "old" log records have been moved to a copy-aside log.

There are various schemes to accelerate archive recovery: the log can be sorted by resource manager and by object, so that only the log records for the relevant object need be scanned. In addition, the object's log can be sorted so that duplicates are eliminated. All these optimizations are generically called *change accumulation.* They are elaborated in Chapter 9, Subsection 9.6.5.

Occasionally, the online copy of an object is so damaged that the system administrators want to go back to the way it was yesterday. When that happens, the whole system state is set back to a previous version. In the typical scenario, a new program with a serious bug is installed. The program manages to contaminate most of the database before the operations staff discovers the situation. Management decides to recover the state as of the time the buggy program was installed. Most recovery systems provide a mechanism to recover the system state (or an object's state) to a certain timestamp. *Recover-to-a-timestamp* aborts all transactions that committed after that timestamp. It can be implemented as forward recovery (REDO from the archive) or backward recovery (UNDO from the current state). Recover-to-a-timestamp violates the durability of committed transactions. In particular, the local parts of any distributed transactions that were committed are now aborted. To allow other transaction managers to detect this situation, the recover-to-a-timestamp operation gives the transaction manager a new birthday (see Subsection 11.2.2). In addition, the transaction manager can detect the trids and transaction managers of distributed transactions that were reversed and generate an exception report.

Archive recovery is the last hope of recovering the data. If it fails due to a bug, the data is lost until the bug is fixed. Thus, it is dangerous to use exactly the same programs for system restart, resource manager restart, and archive recovery. If the code has a bug in it, all three attempts at recovery will fail in exactly the same way. To deal with this problem, some systems employ design diversity (see Chapter 3, Section 3.6): they implement archive recovery as a logical REDO. The basic design is to notice that the physiological log records contain all the information needed for a logical REDO or logical UNDO. Hence, a separate archive recovery program can be written. This program first uses physiological logging to make an action-consistent state from a fuzzy checkpoint—that is, recovery to a timestamp just after the end of the checkpoint. Once this state has been reconstructed, a logical REDO of the log from that timestamp forward can be performed. This is an example of fault tolerance through design diversity. Logical archive recovery has failure modes different from those of physiological recovery.

11.7 Configuring the Transaction Manager

The transaction manager has relatively few configuration parameters. At coldstart it is given a name and number, which it uses to identify itself to other transaction managers in the network, and a resource manager identifier, which it uses to identify itself in subsystem calls. It is also given the name of its master log and the name of its TP monitor. Thereafter, logs can be added and resource managers can be registered with it.

The transaction manager can be adjusted to take checkpoints more or less frequently (a configuration parameter discussed in Section 11.3) and to have one or another attitude about heuristic abort (see Chapter 12, Subsection 12.3.1).

The transaction manger's reporting interface displays the current status of each transaction and each resource manager. Historical reports about committed transactions can be generated from the log tables using the SQL query processor.

11.7.1 Transaction Manager Size and Complexity

Despite the length of this chapter, the structure of the transaction manager is quite simple. Most of the actual recovery work (UNDO and REDO) is inside the resource managers themselves. In fact, the code to write log records and to undo and redo operations typically makes a resource manager about 50% larger.

A basic transaction manager that provides savepoints, archive recovery, and distributed transactions can be written in about 10,000 lines of code. Industrial-strength transaction managers are often 10 times that size. The bulk of this additional code is in areas such as managing archive dumps, generating exception reports, and automating operations tasks. Still, that makes the transaction manager much smaller than an industrial-strength database system or operating system, which would occupy about a million lines of code.

11.8 Summary

The transaction manager implements the transaction verbs and coordinates both transaction commit and transaction rollback. In addition, it helps the resource managers checkpoint their state and reconstruct their state at restart or from the archive.

The transaction manager design presented here is open (extensible). It anticipates the proliferation of transactional resource managers such as database systems, persistent programming languages, TRPC mechanisms of various stripes (SNA LU6.2, OSI/TP, X/OpenDTP, etc.), persistent queue managers, and specialized applications that have their own ideas about recovery.

Chapter 10 covered the basic ideas needed to supply the A, C, and D aspects of ACID transactions. This chapter described how those ideas are embodied in a simple transaction manager. It showed first how commit works and then how rollback and rollback to a savepoint work in the no-fault situation. In essence, this was simply the DO-UNDO protocol.

The discussion then turned to checkpoint-restart. Checkpoints are written to accelerate restart. At restart, the system reads the log and uses the DO-UNDO-REDO protocol to redo all the work of committed transactions. Then uncommitted transactions are resolved, either by aborting them or by returning them to their most recent persistent savepoints.

Finally, the issues of resource manager restart and archive recovery were covered. As it turns out, the techniques used for these two problems are the same as those for online restart. This is no accident, since minimizing the size and complexity of the recovery mechanism is a conscious goal; simple things work. Chapter 12, Section 12.5 will show how this same mechanism provides disaster protection by replicating the objects at two or more sites.

Exercises

1. [11.2.1, 5] How does the birthday detect amnesia?

2. [11.2.2, 5] Suppose the transaction manager stores all its anchor structures in non-volatile RAM so that its data structures are persistent and atomically updated (a neat trick). What would change about its restart logic?

3. [11.2.3, 10] (a) Design a set of optimizations that will make most Status_Transaction() calls quick. (b) What about distributed transactions?

4. [11.2.7, 5] In the discussion of Figure 11.3 and the Commit() callback, it was stated that in a pure presumed-abort protocol, the participant cannot acknowledge until all its outgoing sessions and joined resource managers have responded yes to the Commit() callback. Why? Give an example of what might go wrong if the participant responds early.

5. [11.2.8, 10] The presentation of Save_Work() broadcasts the Savepoint() callback on all incoming and outgoing sessions. (a) What is wrong with this idea? (b) How can it be fixed to work?

6. [11.2.9, project] Rollback lets a process roll back over savepoints it never saw. A process that joined the transaction at savepoint 100 can roll the transaction back to savepoint 50. A process needs to abort the transaction, so it must roll back to savepoint 0. Come up with a set of rules that allow abort (rollback to savepoint 0) but also prevent an application from rolling back to a point that it never saw. *Hint:* Think in terms of a persistent programming language.

7. [11.2.9, 5] Using the ideas and tools discussed in Subsection 11.2.9, implement Abort_Work().

8. [11.2, 10] Consider a transaction manager that uses multiple logs. What needs to change about the design of Save_Work(), Commit_Work() and Rollback_Work()?

9. [11.2,15] Consider a resource manager that maintains its own log (it does not use the system services log). What does it do at each of the prepare, commit, UNDO_ Savepoint, and abort callbacks? How does it handle restart?

10. [11.2, 5] What exactly is the logic for lazy commit? What needs to be synchronous with the caller and what can be deferred?

11. [11.2, 5] The discussion of commit processing was vague on the logic for chained commit. Assuming that resource managers want to preserve context across the commit point, how does the nonchained commit logic described in this chapter change?

12. [11.3.2,10] Suppose your resource manager is doing fuzzy checkpoints in a system that enforces the two-checkpoint rule. Suppose it manages a 1 GB volatile storage pool caching data in a 1 TB persistent store. Also suppose that a 10 KB page is updated at random every millisecond. (a) After 5 minutes, what fraction of the pages have been updated? Using the statistics for disks from Chapter 2, how many disks are needed to service these writes if the disks are written (b) at random, (c) sequentially?

13. [11.4,15] This chapter assumed that there is no parallelism within a transaction. Suppose that were false; suppose that a database system supported parallel processes reading and updating different parts of the database. To what extent could UNDO be run as parallel processes?

14. [11.4,15] Repeat Exercise 12 for restart.

15. [11.6,15] The discussion of recovery-to-a-timestamp was vague on exactly which log records are ignored (not redone). What is the answer?

Answers

1. If the TM can only remember back to 10 A.M., then any transactions or sessions with earlier birthdays will have been forgotten. By comparing the transaction or session birthday with the current birthday, a remote TM can detect that this TM has forgotten those objects.

2. It could avoid the redo scan to rebuild the data structures. It would just mark all RMs as down. It would still have to create processes to resolve committing, aborting, and in-doubt transactions. It would still have to service Identify() calls.

3. (a) (1) Keep a hash table or B-tree of all transactions that aborted since restart (many fewer abort than commit). (2) Checkpoint this table and, at restart, update it to include the "big" gap introduced by restart, and all transactions that aborted lately. If the table is too large, hash it into a bitmap for quick negative answers. (b) For distributed transactions, cache the answers locally (both commit and abort), but go to the root commit coordinator to find the answer.

4. If the participant responds early, the coordinator may deallocate the transaction state and so presume that the transaction aborted (in a pure presumed-abort protocol). If the participant fails and restarts, it would then abort the transaction. But we assume here that the coordinator will respond correctly to a Status_Transaction() call, so early replies cause no inconsistency.

5. (a) The broadcast will, in turn, cause a broadcast on all incoming and outgoing sessions. The algorithm will never terminate. (b) This is a standard problem called flooding. The usual way to flood a system is to never send exactly the same callback on the same session (in either direction). So each callback will travel on each session exactly once.

6. The use of multilevel transactions prevents a subtransaction from returning to savepoints it cannot name. See Chapter 4, Subsection 4.7.3 and Section 4.9, and Chapter 16, Subsection 16.7.3.

7. Rollback_Work(0);

8. The transaction manager must track all the logs containing records generated by a particular transaction. At the savepoint of a transaction, the TM must write a savepoint record in each participating log. At the prepare of a transaction, the TM must force all participating logs before forcing the master log. At UNDO, it must UNDO all the participating logs. At restart, it must perform a REDO-UNDO scan on all logs.

9. At each event, it must replicate the recovery manager logic. It must force logs at commit and write savepoint records at savepoint, prepare, commit, and abort. At restart, it must execute its own UNDO=REDO scan as a slave to the master log. That is, when the restart scan invokes Abort() for a transaction, the resource manager must do the abort using its private log. Similarly, it must commit if it gets an Commit() invocation, and so on.

10. The phase-1 work that tests for consistency needs to be synchronous. The actual force of the log record and the phase-2 work can be done asynchronously. The premise is that failures are very rare, so the transaction will probably commit if it gets to the end of phase 1. The only case that would prevent commit would be a transaction manager restart.

11. The prepare call must have a flag indicating that the commit is chained. The phase-1 savepoint record of each resource manager must include data needed to reinstantiate either the phase-1 state or the state at phase-2. The phase-2 logic of each resource manager resets the transaction context to the context as of the begin of the next transaction. The begin transaction log record points to these dual-function log records. At restart, if the transaction is committed and the chaining is persistent, the restart logic calls each resource manager to reinstantiate the process/transaction context from the most recent savepoint record.

12. (a) 5 minutes = 300,000 ms, which is 300,000 updates to 100,000 pages. So almost all pages are updated. (b) Must write 100,000 pages in 300 seconds, so 333 pages per second. Using the data from 2.2.1., and random access disks, this is ≈10 disks. (c) Using sequential access disks, this is 3.3 MB/s, which is the bandwidth of 1 disk.

13. First, each node can undo a distributed transaction in parallel. Within a node, if physical or physiological logging is used, one can run the recovery of each page as a parallel stream. That is, UNDOs of two log records can proceed in parallel if they apply to disjoint resource managers, objects, or pages. In general, if the UNDO work can be partitioned so that no partition depends on data from other partitions, then UNDO can be split and run in parallel for each partition. The UNDO work must be synchronized at target savepoints. For example, UNDO of each log may proceed in parallel if there are multiple logs covering different data partitions.

14. The answer is the same. The restart logic can split one or more logs into N streams. Each stream can run the restart logic in parallel, synchronizing only at persistent savepoints.

15. Ignore all log records belonging to transactions with commit records greater than that timestamp. Redo all other transactions. Write a "special" checkpoint log record at the end of the log and undo all transactions that committed after the timestamp or did not complete.

Decay is inherent in all complex things.
Strive on with diligence.

THE BUDDHA'S LAST WORDS

12

Advanced Transaction Manager Topics

12.1 Introduction

This chapter discusses features present in some modern transaction managers. First, it discusses how heterogeneous transaction managers can interoperate and how portable resource managers can be implemented. Then it shows how the process-pair technique can be applied to make transaction managers highly available. Next, the issue of transferring commit authority from one transaction manager to another is discussed. Transfer of commit benefits both performance and system administration.

Discussion then turns to transaction commit performance issues. First, the performance of the standard protocol is analyzed for both message and I/O costs. Earlier chapters described several commit optimizations, and a few more are described here. The chapter ends with a discussion of disaster recovery systems that can mask environmental, operations, and transient software failures.

12.2 Heterogeneous Commit Coordinators

As networks grow together, applications increasingly must access servers and data residing on heterogeneous systems, performing transactions that involve multiple nodes of a network. Frequently, these nodes have different TP monitors and different commit protocols.

This raises the issues of interoperability and portability. Applications want to interoperate in several different modes. Some want to issue transactional remote procedure calls (TRPCs); others want to establish peer-to-peer transactional sessions with other TP systems. In addition, portable applications and resource managers need a standard transaction manager interface so that they can be moved easily from one operating environment to the next.

If each transaction manager supports a standard and open commit protocol, then portability and interoperability among them are relatively easy to achieve. Today, there are two standard commit protocols and application programming interfaces:

IBM's LU6.2   as embodied by CICS and the CICS application programming interface

OSI-TP   combined with X/Open Distributed Transaction Processing.

CICS is a de facto standard. Virtually all TP monitors can interoperate with it to some degree. The X/Open standard is newer, but it has the force of a de jure standard. Both standards are likely to proliferate in the years to come.

12.2.1 Closed versus Open Transaction Managers

Some transaction managers have an *open commit protocol*; which means that resource managers can participate in the commit decision, and the commit message formats and protocols are public. The transaction manager described in Chapters 10 and 11 fits this description, so it is open. The standards listed in Section 12.2 are also open. CICS, DECdtm, NCR's TOPEND, and Transarc's transaction manager are open. Transaction managers are evolving in this direction, but the evolution is not yet complete.

Historically, many commercial TP monitors had a *closed commit protocol* in that resource managers could not participate in commit (there were no resource manager callbacks), and the internals of commit were proprietary. The term *closed TP monitor* is used to describe TP systems that have only private protocols and therefore cannot cooperate with other transaction processing systems. Unfortunately, several popular transaction processing systems are closed—among them IBM's IMS and Tandem's TMF. There is considerable commercial pressure to open them up; we guess they will soon become open.

If a TP monitor is open and obeys some form of the two-phase commit protocol, then it is possible to implement a gateway that translates between the TP monitor protocol and one of the standard open protocols. Subsection 12.2.3 shows how, using this technique, ACID transactions involving multiple heterogeneous TP monitors can be constructed. On the other hand, it is virtually impossible to implement general ACID transactions involving closed TP monitors and other monitors. The key problem is atomicity: the closed transaction manager can unilaterally abort any transaction, even though the others decide to commit.

The next few subsections describe the issues involved in writing gateways between one of the standard protocols and the local protocol. The need for a standard protocol is obvious. If there are 10 different transaction managers in the world, then building a special gateway between each pair of them requires building 90 different gateways (e.g., each of the 10 TMs must have 9 gateways to others). If a standard interchange protocol is used, only 10 gateways need be built. This explains the enthusiasm for interoperability standards.

12.2.2 Interoperating with a Closed Transaction Manager

It is almost impossible to write a gateway for a closed transaction manager. Some special cases can provide atomicity to distributed transactions involved with a closed transaction manager. If a set of open transaction managers shares a transaction with a *single closed* transaction manager, then the open transaction managers can achieve atomicity by letting the closed transaction manager be the commit coordinator. The idea is for each open transaction manager to enter the prepared state and then ask the closed transaction manager to commit. In the normal case, where there is no failure, the closed commit coordinator will quickly come to a decision to commit or abort. In these cases, the open transaction managers will promptly be informed and commit or abort as appropriate.

In the single-closed-TM case, the only problems arise when one of the transaction managers fails. If there is a communication failure or a failure of any of the transaction managers, there must be a way to atomically (all-or-nothing) resolve the in-doubt transaction. Because the closed transaction manager is the commit coordinator, it must support an interface that returns the status of any current or past trid (the Status_Transaction() call described in the previous chapter). The status will be one of {active, aborting, committing, aborted, committed}. The open transaction managers can periodically poll the closed transaction manager gateway to find out the status of any in-doubt transactions.

Typically, the closed transaction manager does not provide such a Status_Transaction() TRPC. Rather, a gateway to the closed transaction manager must implement this function. The simplest way for the gateway to maintain this information is to keep a transaction-protected file of all the successful trid's {active, prepared, committing, and committed}. The gateway process inserts each trid into this file when the trid first arrives at the closed transaction manager. If the transaction commits, the trid will be present in the file. If the transaction aborts, the trid will be missing from the file. If the transaction is live, the trid record in the file will be locked. By reading the record via the trid key (with a bounce-mode locking), an open transaction manager (or the gateway) can determine whether the closed transaction manager committed the transaction, aborted it, or still has it live. This logic is similar to the Status_Transaction() logic mentioned in section 11.2.3.

The scheme works only for transactions involving a single, closed transaction manager. Section 12.5 will explain that this technique is an application of the last transaction manager optimization.

12.2.2.1 Closed Queued Transaction Monitors

If the transaction manager is closed *and* supports only a queued interface, then things are even more difficult. IMS and Tuxedo were originally queued-only transaction managers, but now both support a form of direct processing. The problem with queued systems is twofold: (1) since conversational transactions are impossible, all requests to the transaction manager must be deferred to phase 1 of commit; (2) the queued transaction system acknowledges the input message and then processes it asynchronously. Queueing complicates both the application and the gateway.

The application may be able to tolerate closed-queued TP monitors by sacrificing consistency while still attaining atomicity and durability. To do so, requests are classified as *inquiry requests* (ones that do not change the server's state) and *update requests* (ones that do change the server's state). Each request to a closed-queued TP monitor must be implemented as a separate transaction at the closed system—queued TP monitors do not support conversational transactions. Given this restriction, the application can send the closed TP monitor many inquiry requests and defer all update requests to phase 2 of commit.

In this design, inquiry requests give degree 1 isolation answers rather than the degree 3 isolation of ACID transactions. This lower degree of isolation results from each closed transaction releasing its locks when it commits and replies.

Update requests to the closed TP monitor must be treated as real operations. That is, the updates are deferred (by the application) until commit. The application must complete all processing on all the open transaction managers and get them to enter the commit state. Then, during phase 2 of commit, the application repeatedly sends the sum of all the update requests to the queued TP monitor gateway. This request invokes another part of the application, called the *rump*, that runs in the closed system. The rump does all the deferred updates, then commits and responds to the application on the open system (see Figure 12.1).

If the closed TP monitor successfully performs the rump, it will respond to the open part of the application, and atomicity plus durability will be achieved. If the rump aborts, then it must be retried. The application keeps resending the rump message until the rump is performed successfully. This might cause the rump to be processed more than once, and that would also be bad. The usual technique to achieve idempotence (exactly once processing of the rump) is to assign a unique identifier to each rump—the original trid is a good choice. The rump maintains a table of the processed trids; let us call it the DONE table. The rump has the following logic:

```
deferred_update(int id, complex_type list_of_updates)        /* rump logic for closed TM        */
    {Begin_Work();                                           /* start a new transaction          */
    select count(*) from done where id = :id;                /* test to see if work was done     */
    if not found then                                        /* if not done                      */
            do list_of_updates;                              /*   then do the list of updates.   */
            insert into done values (:id);                   /* flag transaction done            */
    Commit_Work();                                           /* commit update and flag           */
    acknowledge;                                             /* reply success to caller          */
    }                                                        /* in both cases.                   */
```

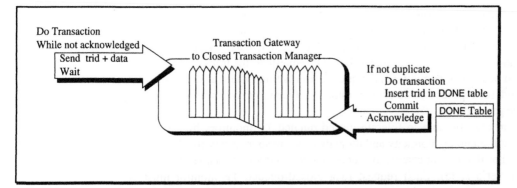

Figure 12.1: Logic for a gateway to a closed transaction manager. Such a gateway cannot provide all the ACID properties, but it can durably apply updates from an open transaction manager to a closed one. The gateway processes the updates as a second transaction executed as part of phase 2 of the ACID transaction. To achieve idempotence, the gateway maintains a list of done transactions in the closed system. The insertion of the trid in the DONE table is an atomic part of the deferred processing by the closed system. In this way, the update is done exactly once.

The use of rump transactions is not elegant, but it allows open transaction managers to interoperate with closed-queued transaction managers. Typical applications of this technique involve maintaining a duplicate database in which updates to the master file must be sent to a slave copy on an old system with a closed transaction manager. This is a short-term problem; in the long term, the LU6.2 and OSI-TP standards will force all TP monitors to become either open or obsolete.

12.2.3 Writing a Gateway to an Open Transaction Manager

The problems in writing a gateway between two open transaction managers that have slightly different communications protocols and two-phase commit protocols mostly concern name translation, full duplex–half duplex conversion, and so on. The recovery issues are relatively minor. Within the scope of the transaction manager issues, some problems lie in translating the fancy features of one or another protocol. One protocol might only support chained transactions or might not support transfer-of-commit, heuristic abort, and so on. These problems can be eliminated by a simple rule: the gateway doesn't support or accept any features not supported by the local transaction manager. Given that extreme view, the gateway's logic is as follows (refer to Figure 12.2).

The gateway acts as a resource manager. It joins any transactions that pass through the gateway; it participates in both phase 1 and phase 2 of commit; and it participates in transaction savepoints, rollback, and abort.

A gateway sees two kinds of transactions, *incoming* and *outgoing*. An outgoing transaction is one that originated here and is being sent elsewhere; this node will be the commit coordinator for the transaction with respect to the outgoing session. Conversely, if a transaction request arrives on an incoming session, then the transaction originated elsewhere, and this node is a participant rather than the coordinator. The logic and issues for the two can be treated separately.

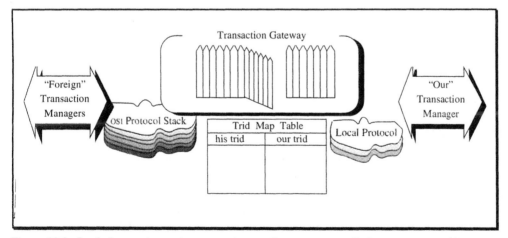

Figure 12.2: Logic for a gateway to an open transaction manager. Such a gateway provides ACID properties for transactions that span the two transaction managers. It translates between the foreign commit protocol and the local commit protocol. It acts as a transaction manager in both worlds: it is capable of starting transactions and, consequently, of creating new trids. It also acts as a resource manager for outgoing transactions.

12.2.3.1 Outgoing Transactions

Let us first consider an outgoing transaction. The gateway notices that this transaction is new to it and therefore joins the transaction, acting as a resource manager by issuing Join_Work() to the local transaction manager. Next, the gateway must send the outgoing request to the foreign transaction manager. The outgoing request must be tagged with a foreign trid correlated to this local trid by the gateway. As a rule, foreign and local trids have different formats; for example, LU6.2 trids are different from OSI-TP trids. Thus, the gateway must be able to invent new foreign trids, complete with a birthday, transaction manager ID, and sequence number ID. This, in turn, means that the gateway must act as a foreign transaction manager. It can use a private log file or even the local database manager to implement much of this logic. Assuming it uses the local transaction manager and database, the gateway maintains a recoverable table of the two trids:

```
create table trid_map (    his_trid   char(32) unique,
                           my_trid    char(12) unique;
                    );
```

When an outgoing transaction first goes out, the gateway invents a foreign trid for the transaction and makes an entry recording the two trids in this table, all under the scope of the local trid. The entry will be made durable when the local transaction commits. At that time, the gateway gets a Prepare() callback from the local transaction manager and forwards it on the session to the foreign transaction manager. If a yes vote comes back from the foreign transaction manager, the gateway votes yes; otherwise, it votes no to the prepare request. Similarly, the gateway is invoked at phase 2 and sends the phase 2 commit message; it does not acknowledge the phase 2 callback until the remote commit coordinator responds. This is very similar to the standard logic for a resource manager at commit.

If the local transaction aborts, the gateway gets an Abort() callback from the local transaction manager, since the gateway has joined the transaction. In this case, the gateway sends an abort message on the outgoing session to the foreign transaction manager.

At restart, the remote transaction manager may ask the gateway for the transaction outcome. To determine the status of the transaction, the gateway, using the presumed-abort logic, can simply issue this query:

```
translate: select my_trid
           into :my_trid
           from trid_map
           where his_trid = :trid for browse access;
```

If the answer is "not found," then there is no record of the transaction, and it must have aborted—this is presumed abort. If the transaction did not abort, then the record will be locked if the transaction is still in doubt (that is why browse-mode locking was used). If the record is returned, it has the added benefit of translating the foreign trid to the local trid. The transaction manager uses this trid to invoke the Status_Transaction() verb exported by the local transaction manager:

```
trans_status Status_Transaction(TRID);
```

The gateway calls this routine, passing the local trid (my_trid) returned by the translate() step. If the inquiry routine returns "prepared," then the transaction is still in doubt, and the gateway must ask again later. Otherwise, the returned status is either commit, committing, abort, or aborting. In any of these cases, the gateway returns the status to the remote transaction manager.

12.2.3.2 Incoming Transactions

The gateway logic for incoming transactions is similar, but it places more demands on the local transaction manager. In the outgoing case, the gateway acted as a simple resource manager to the local system and as a full-blown transaction manager to the remote system. For incoming transactions, the gateway acts as the local commit coordinator, and the local transaction manager must accept Prepare(), Commit() and Abort() messages from it. This can be done in two ways. The gateway can masquerade as a communication manager and simulate the messages and protocols of a peer remote commit coordinator. Alternatively, the transaction manager can export procedures to implement these functions. The masquerade approach is described here.

To handle foreign incoming transactions, the gateway must act as a local transaction manager (as opposed to a foreign TM). It gets a unique name and maintains a local durable trid counter. Thus, the gateway can generate trids in the format of the local transaction manager. When the gateway gets an incoming foreign trid, it invents a local trid and executes a local Begin_Work() to insert this record in its trid_map table. It then sends the local trid via a session to the local TP monitor as an incoming transaction request. The TP monitor views this as an incoming transaction, allocates a local server for the transaction request, and replies.

To the remote transaction manager, the gateway is acting as a transaction participant; to the local TP monitor, it is acting as coordinator. When a request arrives, the gateway does protocol translation, tags the request with the local trid, and forwards it on the local session. When the Prepare() request arrives, the gateway sends the prepare message (tagged with the local trid) via the session to the local TM. The gateway passes the reply back to the remote commit coordinator. Commit() and Abort() logic are similar. The restart logic is only slightly more complex. When the transaction manager restarts, it polls the gateway (via a session) about any in-doubt transactions coordinated by that gateway. The gateway looks up the local trid in its trid_map table and sends the inquiry about the foreign trid to the appropriate remote transaction manager. The gateway then passes the reply back to the local transaction manager.

To summarize, the gateway is acting as a transaction manager in both protocol networks. For example, it is acting as an LU6.2 transaction manager in an IBM-CICS network and as an OSI-TP transaction manager in an X/Open AT&T Tuxedo network. It translates the commit/abort messages between these two networks and translates the trids as well.

12.2.3.3 The Multiple Entry Problem

Although this design works in most cases, it has the flaw that if a foreign trid enters the local system many times via different sessions, it will get a different local trid each time. This problem can be fixed by testing the trid_map table before allocating a new trid. A more serious problem is that the trid may enter many different gateways of the same subnet. For example, it might enter the Visa net via the London and the San Mateo gateways. Detecting this situation is more difficult, but the problem is not serious. It can result in a transaction deadlocking with itself, but it will not result in incorrect execution. No good solution—that is, no efficient solution—to this problem is known.

12.2.4 Summary of Transaction Gateways

In summary, if all TP monitors are open, it is possible to write simple gateways to inter-connect them and provide ACID transactions that span heterogeneous TP monitors. If a transaction involves at most one closed TP monitor that supports direct communication with the application (not just queued communication), then by making that transaction manager last in the commit chain, ACID transactions can be implemented. Updates involving multiple closed TP monitors or queued TP monitors must be treated as real operations and probably must sacrifice the consistency and isolation properties, attaining only atomicity and durability.

12.3 Highly Available (Non-Blocking) Commit Coordinators

Up to this point, our discussion has focused on reliability. How can one build a highly available transaction manager—one that continues operating after a processor or com-munication link fails? The obvious solution is to duplex memory and processors, as de-scribed in Chapter 3.

The first step is to make the log manager highly available. It can operate as a process pair that duplexes each log file. By doing this, the log manager can tolerate any single fault. If a processor fails, the backup process in another processor takes over almost instantly, without interrupting service. If a disk or a disk write fails, the log manager can mask the failure by reading the remaining disk. Concurrently, it can repair the failed disk by replacing it with a spare and then copying the log information from the good disk to the new disk. This is a straightforward application of the ideas set forth in Chapter 3, Section 3.7.

The transaction manager should also use process-pair techniques to tolerate hardware faults and transient software faults. The transaction manager's persistent state is recorded in the log anchor or in log checkpoints, so that it benefits from the log manager's fault tolerance. The transaction manager's volatile data structures (e.g., the list of resource managers and sessions involved in a transaction shown in Figure 11.1) should be managed as a process pair. That is, these tables should be recorded in two process address spaces on separate computers, and the state transitions of these tables should be synchronized via process-pair checkpoints (see Figure 12.3). This is a standard application of the process-pair concept.

Commit coordinators implementing a process-pair scheme are called *non-blocking*, because they are not blocked by a failure. A blocking commit coordinator—one imple-mented as a single process—could be unavailable for hours or days. In that case, all in-doubt transactions coordinated by that transaction manager remain in doubt (blocked) until the coordinator returns to service.

Non-blocking commit coordinators are common in fault-tolerant systems and are much discussed for distributed systems. In fault-tolerant systems, there is a primary process and a

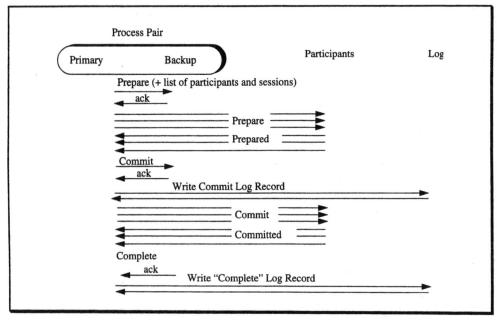

Figure 12.3: Message flows for a non-blocking commit coordinator. A non-blocking commit coordinator acts as a process pair that checkpoints its state to a backup process. If the primary process fails, the backup takes over and continues the commit operation. As explained in Chapter 3, takeover can have a latency of 10 ms if the processes are LAN-connected.

backup. If the primary fails, the backup senses the failure and takes over. The key property of these systems is that the backup process can tell when the primary commit coordinator process has failed. Given this assumption, applying duplexed storage and process pairs to make a fault-tolerant commit coordinator is straightforward.

Distributed systems generally have a different fault model. In a distributed system, if two processes cannot communicate, the problem could be a failed process or a failed session (a broken wire). The latter case is called a *network partition failure*. If network partitions are possible, non-blocking protocols for distributed transactions require that the transaction be coordinated by three or more nodes; these protocols allow a majority of the nodes to declare a minority to be failed. Unfortunately, the most common case of a distributed transaction involves just two nodes. There, the non-blocking algorithms do not apply: if there is a failure, one node cannot form a majority. Consequently, non-blocking protocols are rarely used in distributed systems. Rather, fault-tolerant nodes are used with fault-tolerant (duplexed) communication sessions. Alternatively, practical recovery systems postulate that they can distinguish between network partitions and node failures; they usually ask the operator to decide (see Section 12.6).

An alternative to the process-pair design for non-blocking commit is for the coordinator to broadcast the list of participants at phase 1 of commit as part of the prepare message. Then if the coordinator fails, the participants can contact one another. If any got a commit decision from the coordinator, they can all act on it. If none got a commit decision, then they must either wait or transfer the commit coordinator authority to another participant, which is delicate. This non-blocking protocol can be made to work, but is more complex than the process-pair design and does not help in the common case of two-node transactions.

12.3.1 Heuristic Decisions Resolve Blocked Transaction Commit

There has been considerable concern about the implications of the two-phase commit protocol forcing participants to wait forever for a decision. While the participant waits, resources are locked, queued messages are in doubt, and a client is waiting for a response. Two additional mechanisms are commonly used to resolve in-doubt transactions being coordinated by a failed commit coordinator: *heuristic commit* and *operator commit.*

Heuristic commit has the participant transaction manager make a heuristic decision about the status of an in-doubt transaction when the coordinator fails or when contact with the coordinator is lost. These are some typical heuristic decision criteria:

> Always commit.
> Always abort.
> Always commit deposit transactions.
> Always commit transactions of less than $1,000.

When such decisions are made, the transaction manager records the transaction state as *heuristically* committed or *heuristically* aborted. These become new persistent states (see Figure 10.20). When the commit coordinator later contacts the participant transaction manager to announce the real commit decision, the local transaction manager compares it to the heuristic decision. If they agree, great! If they disagree, the local transaction manager tells the commit coordinator and the operator that there is a *heuristic commit/abort mismatch.* At that point, it is up to humans to clean up the situation.

In a related vein, the system operator is given a command to *force* an in-doubt transaction to commit or abort. If that transaction is holding resources that prevent the system from doing useful work, this command is essential to get the system moving again. The operator decision is treated much like the heuristic decision. If it later disagrees with the decision of the commit coordinator, an *operator commit/abort mismatch* diagnostic is sent to both the coordinator and the local operator.

Operator abort may appear to be more rational than heuristic abort. But, in fact, the operator rarely has much information when making the commit/abort decision. He knows the transaction identifier and perhaps can deduce the names of the local server program and the remote commit coordinator, but that is not much information. The application administrator is probably in a better position to make a decision; that person, however, may not be present at the crisis. Thus, the heuristic abort decision is often no worse than an operator abort decision.

In either case, if the operator or heuristic decision results in a later mismatch between two nodes, then system administrators must resolve the transaction at each site. This resolution mechanism must be part of the application design. Just giving the operator a list of trids that do not match will not be much help in resolving the situation. The trids must be correlated with application-level concepts, such as users and application programs.

12.4 Transfer-of-Commit

It is nice to be the commit coordinator for a transaction. The coordinator always knows the status of the transaction; it is never in doubt. A participant, on the other hand, may remain indefinitely in doubt about a prepared transaction. Consequently, everyone wants to be the commit coordinator.

By default, the beginner (transaction manager) is the commit coordinator. There are two reasons why it is sometimes desirable to transfer the commit coordinator responsibility from the beginner to another node participating in the transaction:

Asymmetry.   The client may not be as reliable as the server. The transaction commit coordinator should be one of the most reliable nodes in the transaction tree.

Performance.   Transferring commit can produce much better performance.

The asymmetry argument arises when a gas pump, ATM, or workstation starts a transaction (does a Begin_Work()) and then makes one or more requests to servers running on system pairs. The servers are much more reliable than the client.

Consider the case illustrated in Figure 12.4. You buy some gas from Arco using a Wells Fargo Bank (WFB) system. The gas pump is in Death Valley, California, and is attached to Wells Fargo's Los Angeles data center. The transaction debits your account in San Francisco, but you don't have enough money in it; the overdraft causes a debit of your Visa credit card account in London. The nodes involved in the transaction are diagrammed in Figure 12.4. The problem is that WFB does not trust the gas pump to coordinate the transaction commitment. Similar issues apply to other peripheral clients, such as workstations or sensors in distributed applications. The solution is to transfer the commit coordination responsibility from the peripheral processor to another transaction participant, which is presumably more reliable or trusted.

Figure 12.5 illustrates the performance benefit of transfer-of-commit. Suppose the client has performed all the work it needs to do for the transaction and is prepared to commit if the

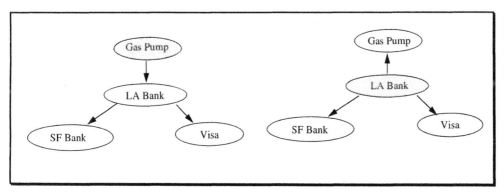

Figure 12.4: Transfer-of-commit for asymmetry.   The servers do not trust the client (a gas pump) to be the commit coordinator for the transaction. Thus, the server becomes the commit coordinator. The arrows in the figure designate session polarity.

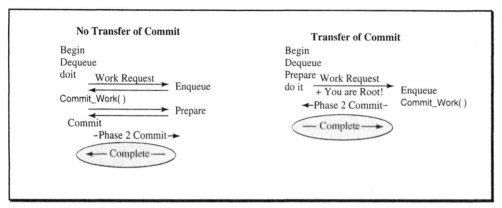

Figure 12.5: Transfer-of-commit for performance.   These examples show the performance benefit of transfer-of-commit. Both examples dequeue an element from a queue at one node and enqueue it at a second node. The message flows are diagrammed. In the case at the right, the client did a Prepare() before sending the enqueue request to the server. Accordingly, there are only two synchronous messages, rather than the five shown at the left. The messages in gray are completion messages that travel asynchronously and can be piggybacked on other traffic. In particular, the next request from the client can carry the completion message in the transfer-of-commit case.

server will do some more work for the transaction. For example, moving a message from one recoverable queue to another consists of a Begin_Work() plus a dequeue at one node, and an enqueue plus a Commit_Work() at the other node. If the first node executes Prepare() before sending the request to the second node, the second node can make the commit decision. This reduces message flows by a factor of two in the simple case.

The logic involved in transferring commit responsibility is easy in the design described in Chapter 11. Recall that all transaction managers participating in a transaction form a tree (or a directed acyclic graph). The beginner of the transaction is the root of this tree. All the transaction's sessions at that transaction manager have outgoing polarity. That transaction manager could transfer commit to any of its neighbors in the tree by simply reversing the polarity of a session between itself and one of them. Then the child would be the root of the tree. How is the polarity reversed? It is easily done by changing the local polarity to incoming and sending a message to the other end saying "you are the root." This can be done at any time prior to making the commit decision (assuming the presumed-abort protocol is used). When the server gets the "you are the root" message on a session, it changes the polarity of that session from incoming to outgoing. This same idea is used in the last resource manager optimization of nested commit. See Section 12.5.

Is it really that simple? Almost, but there are a few nasty problems. Suppose the client calls two servers. If neither server trusts the client, the servers have a problem: both of them want to be the root. Also, the transaction's trid carries the root transaction manager's name. As a last resort, participants can consult the root transaction manager to see what the outcome of the transaction is. What if the root is relatively untrusted? The proposed solution to both problems is for the prepare message to be extended to include the name of the new transaction root. In this way, a server can judge the reliability of the root commit coordinator and vote no if the root seems inadequate. In addition, the new commit root should remember the outcome of any such transactions for a long time (say, a day or two). This logic is currently being considered for the OSI-TP standard.

12.5 Optimizations of Two-Phase Commit

Since Nico Garzado's first implementation of two-phase commit in 1970, most work on commit protocols have been optimizations. The performance of the protocol can be measured in any of three dimensions:

Delay. The elapsed time to make the commit decision.

Message cost. The number of messages that must be sent.

Write cost. The number of forced disk (durable storage) writes.

Of course, delay is correlated with message cost and write cost. The standard way to reduce delay is to do things in parallel: for example, broadcasting the prepare message to all participants in parallel, rather than asking them one at a time. The coordinator broadcasts the Prepare() and Commit() callbacks to the joined local resource managers in parallel; in addition, it broadcasts these callbacks to the remote (outgoing) sessions with remote transaction managers in parallel (see Figure 12.6). If the transaction tree is deep, then parallelism can be improved if the coordinator directly sends messages to all coordinators. This, however, may not be possible if there are gateways involved (doing trid translation) or if the two transaction managers have no session in common. That is about all there is to say about delay. However, there is a lot to say about reducing message cost and write cost.

In general, if N transaction managers and L logs are involved, the transaction commit will involve $4(N-1)$ messages and $2L$ log writes. Since there is usually 1 log per site, we can assume for the rest of this discussion that $N = L$. The messages are *prepare, prepared, commit,* and *committed.* The log writes are *commit* and *complete* or *prepare* and *complete.* The committed message and the complete log write can be lazy, since they do not add to the delay and do not cause resources to be held longer than needed. Suppose W is the minimum delay for a synchronous log write, and M is the minimum delay for sending a message to another transaction manager. The minimal delay for a one-node transaction to reach phase 2 of commit is $L \cdot W$, the delay for the log writes. These minima do not account for any processor delays or for the necessary variability that arises as more resource managers are added. But they give a sense of relative costs and delays.

To discuss distributed transaction commit costs and optimizations, the notion of the *transaction tree* is needed. Recall that, in general, the incoming-outgoing sessions among transaction managers form a directed graph. This graph can be pruned to a tree by discarding incoming sessions to nodes at which the transaction was already established when the incoming session was first started, as shown in the rightmost example in Figure 12.6. In that illustration, the root and the leftmost leaf both have incoming sessions that are not needed for the commit protocol. The transaction tree is a spanning tree rooted at the transaction root and connecting all participating transaction managers.

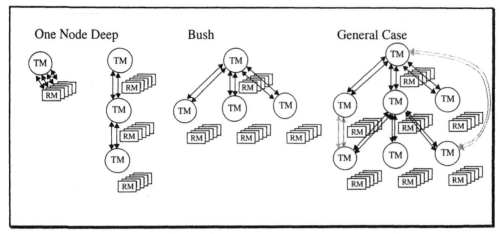

One Node Deep   Bush   General Case

Figure 12.6: A variety of transaction trees. The one-node transaction has several resource managers (RMs) joined to the transaction. The transaction manager (TM) is broadcasting the prepare and commit callbacks to each resource manager. (The other illustrations do not show these resource manager callbacks.) The second transaction tree is deep; not all nodes are connected to the root TM. The third tree shows a four-node transaction with three TMs directly connected to the root. The fourth diagram shows the general case. Two nodes (transaction managers) have received calls for this transaction after the transaction was already started at the node. These extra links are discarded to form the transaction tree.

Suppose the transaction tree has height H. Then, the minimum root delay to reach phase 2 of commit for a distributed transaction is $H(2M + 2W)$ if parallelism is used. This equation is computed as follows. For a tree of height 1, the delay is the sum of:

(1) The delay to broadcast the prepare message (M),

(2) The delay at each participant to prepare and write a prepare record in the log (W),

(3) The message delay for the participant to respond (M), and

(4) The coordinator delay in writing the commit record (W).

When the tree is deep, the participant must wait for its subparticipants, which adds another $2M + 2W$ for each layer of the tree.

The minimal leaf participant delay to reach phase 2 of the commit has 1 additional message delay, or $H(3M + 2W)$. If parallelism is not used, the minimum root delay for commit is $2M(N - 1) + N \cdot W$.

12.5.1 Read-Only Commit Optimization

The first and perhaps most important optimization is called the *read-only* optimization. It means that the participant has no work to do at commit and so does not need a Prepare(), Commit(), or Abort() callback for this transaction. The term is a misnomer: Chapter 8 explained that read-only transactions should use two-phase locking and hold locks until phase 2 of commit; thus the read-only optimization should, in fact, be called the *degree 1 isolation optimization*—the participant is not keeping any locks on resources it has read.

This optimization applies to individual resource managers and to whole subtrees of the transaction tree. If a remote transaction manager and all its outgoing sessions have no work to do at commit, then the transaction manager can declare this fact (declare itself "read-only") and so avoid any transaction completion work. A slight variation occurs if the resource manager or remote node has only phase 1 or only phase 2 work to do. In these cases, half the messages can be saved. In general, the read-only optimization saves four messages per node and one synchronous log I/O per transaction manager. A true read-only transaction which provides complete isolation has only phase 2 work—it must release locks at Commit() or Abort().

12.5.2 Lazy Commit Optimization

A second important optimization is *lazy commit* (as opposed to *eager* commit). In lazy commit, all messages and disk writes are piggybacked on other message or log-write traffic. To deal with the unlikely case that there is no other such activity, the lazy commit will be converted to an eager commit after a time period (e.g., a second). Lazy commit has the same savings as the read-only optimization in that it costs no extra messages or disk I/O. Of course, it has the worst delay cost, and if multiple logs are involved, lazy commit may not be atomic because each log is written independently. That is why eager commit is the default. Lazy commit is an extreme form of group commit, already discussed in Chapter 9, Subsection 9.4.7.

12.5.3 Linear Commit Optimization

A third optimization, called *linear commit,* or *nested commit,* is just an application of the transfer-of-commit design discussed in Section 12.4. The idea is to arrange the transaction managers in a linear order, with each first preparing, then transferring commit authority to the next in the chain. The last in the chain then becomes the root, writes the commit record, and propagates the commit decision back up the chain. Each participant goes through phase 2, simultaneously passing the message back up the chain. When the commit message reaches the end of the chain, a completion record is written; then a completion message is sent back down the chain. At each node, this completion message generates a completion log record. After the completion log record is written, the message passes down the chain. If the tree is a simple chain of length H (i.e., $H = N-1$), the minimum root delay to reach phase 2 is $2M(H) + N \cdot W$, and the overall delay is $3M \cdot H + 2 \cdot W$. Linear commit, then, has bad delay but good message cost: $2M(N-1)$ or $3M(N-1)$ versus 4M(N-1).

That is the theoretical analysis, but there is an important special case: $N = 2$. In the common two-node case, the linear commit algorithm has the same delay as the general algorithm, and it saves a message as well. *Therefore, in the $N = 2$ case, linear commit should always be used*, unless the client is afraid to transfer commit authority to the server (i.e., it doesn't trust the server). Since this argument applies when the system knows that the next prepare message goes to the last transaction manager, it is often called the *last transaction manager optimization*, or sometimes the *last resource manager optimization*.

One can mix the general (4*N* messages) commit protocol with the linear (3*N* messages) commit protocol. But, of course, the commit coordinator must be prepared and must have

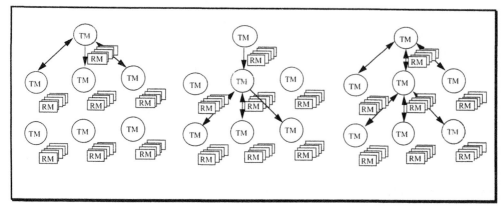

Figure 12.7: Message flows in a transfer-of-commit. Transfer-of-commit from the root to the transaction manager is shown at the lower right. The first two diagrams show the prepare step followed by the transfer-of-commit (shown as a heavy arrow). This saves 2 of the 12 messages needed to commit the transaction using a standard commit protocol.

prepared the rest of its commit subtree before transferring commit authority to the last one of its subtrees. An example of this mixing is shown in Figure 12.7.

Two other optimizations associated with transaction commit are discussed elsewhere in this book. Group commit appears in Chapter 9, and the presumed-abort optimization is explained in Chapter 11. Transfer-of-commit was discussed in Section 12.4. Having discussed performance, let us consider schemes that make a system super-available by replicating it at two or more sites.

12.6 Disaster Recovery at a Remote Site

As shown in Chapter 3, environmental and operations faults are a major source of system outages. The simplest technique that masks such faults is replication of hardware, data, and applications at two or more geographically distributed sites. If one site has an operations or environmental failure, the other site is not likely to have the same failure. In addition, there is evidence that these designs mask some software failures.

System-level replication is an area of active research and development. As this book is being prepared, many special systems are in operation and a few general-purpose designs are being used. Therefore, the presentation here focuses on the simple case and on basic concepts. It also shows how the transaction concept and the disaster recovery system ideas dovetail. This connection is not surprising, since transactions are intended to make distributed computations atomic and durable.

The disaster recovery idea is clear: use *system pairs* rather than just process pairs. Each client is in session with two systems. When one of the two systems fails, the other system continues the transaction, either completing the commit and delivering the messages or aborting the incomplete transaction and restarting the transaction. To the client, the pair looks like a single system. The key property of these systems is that the application is unaware that it is running on a system pair; little or no special programming is required. There is a close analogy between this idea and the idea of process pairs discussed in Chapter 3, Section 3.7.

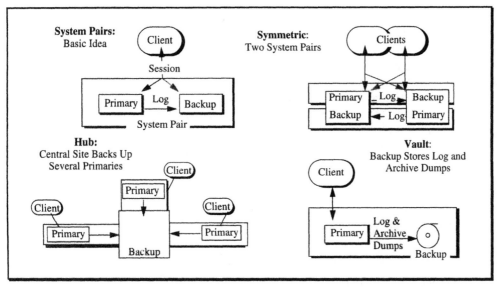

Figure 12.8: Some configuration options for system pairs. Each transparent rectangle represents a computer system; shaded rectangles represent system pairs. Presumably, the systems are geographically remote, so that they can tolerate environmental faults. Each system pair has a primary and a backup. All data, programs, and sessions are duplicated at the primary and the backup. The primary sends a copy of its log records to the backup. If the primary fails, the backup continues servicing the client, much as with process pairs.

System pairs can be configured in many ways. Figure 12.8 illustrates the most common designs. The simplest design is to have a single system pair: a *primary system* and a *backup system*. The backup is sometimes called a *hot standby system*. The data, applications, and sessions are all duplicated at the backup. The client is in session with both the primary and the backup. Ordinarily, the client sends requests to the primary, and log records generated at the primary are sent to the backup and applied to its state. The backup is continually doing the restart REDO scan, applying the log records to the session state and to the durable storage state.[1] When the primary fails, the backup takes over almost instantly. The network is up, the resource managers are up, and the database is current. The backup completes the REDO scan and then rolls each application back to its most recent persistent savepoint. It then concurrently completes any committing or aborting transactions and starts accepting work from the network. Typically, the takeover requires a few seconds or minutes; by that time, the clients are becoming impatient. It is essential that the takeover complete before the network begins to time out and disconnect from the systems.

In the basic system pair design, the backup is wasted if the REDO scan does not consume most of the backup system's resources. In these designs, the backup is often used to run other applications while it is tracking the primary. The backup can offer fuzzy read-only query service (degree 1 isolated) to the backup database for decision support applications. It can run utilities that ordinarily run on the primary, such as archive dumps

---

[1] This design, in which restart is a pure REDO scan followed by an UNDO scan, is one of the benefits of compensation logging.

and log change accumulations. The backup can also be used for other applications. When the backup becomes the primary, these lower-priority activities are suspended.

A *symmetric* arrangement of system pairs is possible if the application and data can be partitioned into regions such that most transactions access only one region. In this arrangement, each network node acts as primary for one region and backup for another. Regional banks, distributors, hospitals, governmental agencies, and phone companies all have been able to exploit this symmetric design. If the application is not partitionable, then the symmetric design will cause most transactions to involve requests to multiple network nodes. The cost of these remote requests in both time and processing power will likely be unacceptable. In such cases, the single primary-backup design will be more efficient.

Any pairing of systems accomplishes a symmetric design. In an n-node network, each node becomes primary for $1/n$ of the database and the backup for another fraction of it. Another design has a central, very large, and very reliable hub with many satellites. The hub is the backup for the satellites. The main point is that any directed graph can be used as the pairing mechanism.

Another design alternative applies the log spooling technique to achieve high durability rather than high availability. The primary sends a copy of its log and archive dumps to a remote electronic vault that can be used to reconstruct the database at a (much) later time. Support for vaulting is a consequence and an extra benefit of the basic design.

System pairs are a kind of replicated data system. However, they differ from replicated data systems in two key ways:

No partitions.   System pairs assume the backup can reliably tell if the primary is unavailable (perhaps with operator assistance).

Replicate programs, network, and data.   The backup system replicates applications and the network connections, as well as the data.

These two criteria are essential to allow the backup system to perform takeover and deliver service when the primary fails.

12.6.1 System Pair Takeover

On demand, the backup can become the primary. The primary system operator can use a SWITCH command to gracefully transfer control. This command causes the primary to stop accepting new work, finish all completing transactions, and then place a SWITCH record in the log. After that record goes into the log, the old primary becomes the backup of the pair. The old backup becomes the primary when it processes the SWITCH record. This takeover is used for operations on the primary, such as installing new software and doing hardware or software maintenance. It is even used when moving the primary to a new building.

The unscheduled switch is more interesting. In a local cluster where the computers are connected via many reliable LANs, it is a safe assumption that if the backup cannot communicate with the primary, then no one can, and the primary is unavailable. This is the assumption underlying the process-pair design of Chapter 3. But if the processors are geographically remote, it is much more difficult to distinguish between a WAN partition and the failure of the primary node. When log records stop arriving from the primary, it could be because the network failed or because the primary failed. There is no simple way for the backup to distinguish these two cases. In the case of a broken network, called the *network partition case*, the backup should not take over; the primary is still operating. But when the primary actually fails, the backup must take over, and quickly. This problem has plagued the distributed database community for decades. It all comes down to a majority vote, but with only two systems, there is no majority. The system-pairs design solves the problem by giving the operator the third and deciding vote. If someone can replace this person with a robot, so much the better.[2]

In such ambiguous cases, the operators of the primary and the backup consult one another and decide that the primary is dead. If the primary is still up, it is told to stop accepting new work and to abort all active transactions. The backup is told that it is the primary. The new primary (old backup) continues the REDO scan to the end of its input log. At that point, all live transactions have had their recoverable state redone in the backup system, which now becomes the primary system. The transaction manager then reestablishes the prepared and persistent transactions and undoes any work that is not persistent.

To expedite this UNDO scan, no transaction should do very much work between persistent savepoints. That is, if a transaction has done one hour of forward processing, it may well take an hour to undo the work. If that same batch transaction is broken into many mini-batch transactions or into a transaction with many persistent savepoints, the backup system can reestablish the most recent persistent savepoint at takeover. To do so, it undoes the transaction back to that savepoint, reacquires the transaction's locks, and then begins offering service.[3] This results in much higher availability, because it minimizes the repair time for a fault.

The new primary now informs the local applications that they are now primary and should start accepting work from the network. At the same time, it initiates tasks to complete any transactions that are committing or aborting.

12.6.2 Session Switching at Takeover

Now let us turn to the issue of the session pairs and the client's management of messages arriving from the system pairs. In Figure 12.9, the client either is very intelligent or is attached to an intelligent front-end processor. In either case, things look the same to the system pair: both the primary and the backup system have a session with the client. The client application sees the system pair as a single logical session to a single logical system. This logical session is implemented by a *session pair*. Each of these two sessions can go to a

---

[2] In some designs, the communications processors that front-end the primary can sense and communicate the primary failure to the backup. There are many communications processors and they are richly connected to the primary, the backup, and the network. Therefore, a partition can likely be detected by a majority of them. However, they cannot announce a network partition. If all lines between the primary and backup fail, the backup is sometimes forced to guess the situation: did the network fail, did the primary fail, or did both fail? In the VAXcluster, a disk controller may be given a vote to resolve a 2-processor situation.

[3] This book originally described a design that tried to reconstruct the locks of all live transactions at restart. But there were too many problems with that design. The best we could do was to reconstruct the locks of persistent savepoints including prepared transactions. IMS/XRF does reconstruct locks at takeover and so quickly offers service to new transactions.

process pair at the fault-tolerant hosts; thus, the client can actually be in session with four server processes that act as a single logical process. The front-end processor, or some fancy software in the client, converts these multiple physical sessions into one highly available logical session, masking the complexity of session pairs from the client application. Let us call this software or hardware the client's *clerk*. The clerk's logic is based on session sequence numbers stored by the clerk. These sequence numbers detect lost and duplicate messages travelling on the primary session and correlate messages retransmitted on the backup sessions.

The session pair is managed as follows: the clerk sends all messages to the primary of the system pair via the primary session. During normal processing, the backup session is idle at the clerk; the backup maintains the status of the primary session's outbound messages and sequence numbers by reading the log records (refer to Chapter 10, Subsection 10.3.3, on recoverable sessions). At takeover, the backup resends the oldest unacknowledged message on each client session. This logic is part of the backup communication manager that tracks the status of each session. The backup communication manager deduces these messages from the log. The messages travelling on the backup sessions implicitly tell the clerks that the backup has become the primary. The previous message has the previous message sequence number and, consequently, synchronizes the backup session to the sequence numbers of the new primary. If the sequence numbers do not match up, standard session recovery can be used to synchronize them (see Subsection 10.3.3).

This logic clearly places a burden on the clerk (client): it must have a durable store for its session sequence numbers. That is why the typical design uses fault-tolerant front-end processors for the system-pair clients, as diagrammed at the right of Figure 12.9. This clerk-system-pair logic is exactly the session-pair logic for process pairs in the fault-tolerant model, as described in Chapter 3, Subsection 3.7.4.

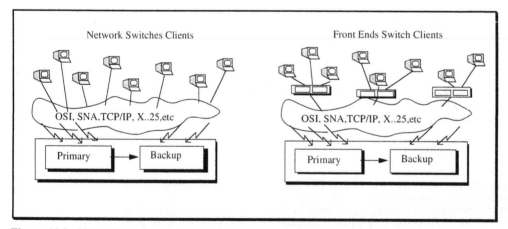

Figure 12.9: Network vs. front end switching.   When the primary of a replicated system fails, the backup takes over. Both the primary and the backup must be in session with the client or with a system that interfaces to the client. In the case on the left, there is no control for duplicate messages. Therefore, the client itself must have the logic to durably store the session sequence numbers and to manage the duplexed sessions. In the figure at the right, a local processor attaches to the client and manages the duplex-session logic.

12.6.3 Configuration Options: 1-Safe, 2-Safe, and Very Safe

There are several ways to configure system pairs. They can be configured for high throughput, high availability, or high integrity. These three options are respectively called *1-safe*, *2-safe*, and *very safe*. The difference centers around transaction commitment. If a transaction's commit response is returned to the client before the commit record arrives at the backup, the transaction might commit at the failed primary but be aborted by the backup after takeover. Such transactions are called *lost transactions*. The three designs trade better response time or availability for the risk of lost transactions. The three options, depicted in Figure 12.10, are as follows:

1-safe. In a 1-safe design, the primary transaction manager goes through the standard commit logic and declares completion when the commit record is written to the local log. In a 1-safe design, throughput and response time are the same as in a single-system design. The log is asynchronously spooled to the backup system. This design risks lost transactions.

2-safe. When possible, the 2-safe design involves the backup system in commit. If the backup system is up, it is sent the transaction log at the end of commit phase 1. The primary transaction manager will not commit until the backup responds (or is declared down). The backup TM has the option of responding immediately after the log arrives or responding after the log has been forced to durable storage. The 2-safe design avoids lost transactions if there is only a single failure, but it adds some delay to the transaction commit and consequent response time.

Very safe. The very safe design takes an even more conservative approach: it commits transactions only if both the primary and the backup agree to commit. If one of the two

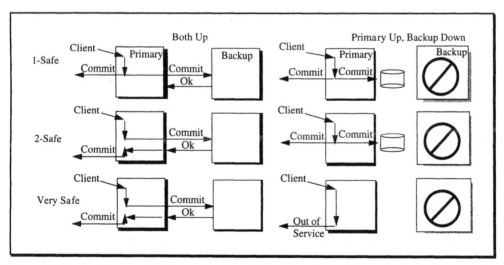

Figure 12.10: 1-safe versus 2-safe versus very safe handling of commit. A 1-safe design responds to the client after the primary commits. A 2-safe design gets a backup acknowledgment of the commit, unless the backup is down. If the backup is down, 1-safe and 2-safe are the same. Very safe refuses to commit work unless both the primary and the backup are able to record the commit record.

nodes is down, no transactions can commit. The availability of such systems is worse than the availability of a single system; however, very safe avoids lost transactions unless there are two site disasters. Although some systems offer very safe as an option, these authors know of no one who uses it.

The 1-safe design has the virtue of supplying high availability with a few lost transactions. When the primary returns to service, it is possible for the two systems to compare logs and report on any lost transactions. This is similar to the heuristic and operator commit decisions discussed earlier.

If the system is configured as 1-safe, transactions may not be durable and distributed transactions may not be atomic, because commitment at the primary does not assure commitment at the backup. If the primary fails, the transaction may be committed at some nodes but aborted at others. In the distributed case, the commit protocol sends messages to the other nodes as part of the commit; as a result, there is little performance justification for 1-safe distributed transactions. If distributed transactions are 2-safe, the consistency and commit issues are just the standard two-phase commit and fault-tolerant (non-blocking) commit designs.

The rationale for 1-safe designs is that 2-safe causes unacceptable delays. System pair designs generally postulate dual high-speed communication lines between the primary and the backup. It is assumed that these dual lines can tolerate any single communication line failure. The lines have round-trip latency of less than 100 ms and bandwidth of 100 KB per second, making the net latency of a transaction with 10 KB of log about 200 ms. For most applications, this added delay is imperceptible. Consequently, most system pairs are configured as 2-safe systems. They provide the ACID properties, high availability, and high reliability.[4] They also have no lost transactions. Given the declining cost and increasing bandwidth of communications lines (as described in Subsection 2.2.3), it seems likely that by the year 2000, only 2-safe designs will be used.

12.6.4 Catch-up After Failure

The discussion of takeover is almost complete, but one issue remains. When a failed system is repaired, how can it return to service? The fundamental idea is that a backup system redoes the log from the time the system failed; once the repaired system has caught up with the current log, it can assume the role of an active backup.

In a very safe design, there is no real catch-up: since both systems are in the same state, there is no catching up to do. Rather, there is just a system restart once the failed system is ready to return to service.

In a 2-safe design, the current primary is saving all the log records needed by the backup until the backup is repaired and the communication link(s) between the primary and backup are repaired. Then the primary sends all recent log records to the backup, which applies them to its state as part of the REDO scan. Once REDO is complete, the backup declares itself *caught up* and assumes the role of a functioning backup. Should there then be a failure, the backup can switch to being the primary. A failure of the backup during catch-

---

[4] In the near term, the common use of slow (64 Kb) communications lines and the high cost of communications software ($\approx$ 10 instructions per byte) encourage 1-safe designs. But as processors and communication lines become faster, the 2-safe design will dominate.

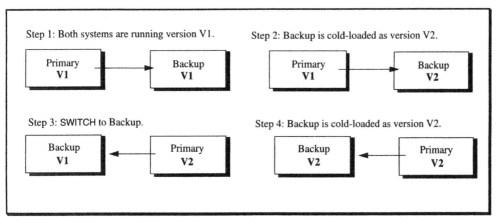

Step 1: Both systems are running version V1.   Step 2: Backup is cold-loaded as version V2.

Primary **V1** → Backup **V1**   Primary **V1** → Backup **V2**

Step 3: SWITCH to Backup.   Step 4: Backup is cold-loaded as version V2.

Backup **V1** ← Primary **V2**   Backup **V2** ← Primary **V2**

Figure 12.11: System pairs can be used to install new versions of software. The diagram shows how a new (upward-compatible) operating system version can be installed without interrupting service to the clients. Similar techniques can be used for hardware maintenance and upgrades, database reorganization, and even environmental changes, such as system moves.

up just extends the catch-up work. A failure of the primary during catch-up is treated as a double failure and interrupts service.

Catch-up for 1-safe designs is more complex. If the backup failed and the primary continued service, then there is no inconsistency, and the catch-up is just like the 2-safe design. If the primary fails in a 1-safe design, the backup will take over with the risk of some lost transactions—transactions that committed at the failed primary but were not committed at the backup. When the primary is repaired and wants to return to service, it must try to bring its state into synchrony with the new primary. This means undoing any lost transactions. Lost transactions can be detected by comparing the logs of the primary and backup systems. Once detected, the backup undoes those transactions and announces the lost transactions to the system administrator. Once this is complete, the backup can proceed with catch-up.

12.6.5 Summary of System Pair Designs

System pairs protect against environmental faults by being geographically dispersed. Weather, utility outages, and sabotage are unlikely to fault both systems at the same time. In addition, system pairs having two sets of operators protect against many forms of operator fault. They allow systems to be taken offline for software or hardware maintenance and even for physical relocation of the systems. Figure 12.11 gives an example of installing new upward-compatible software without interrupting service. Similar techniques apply to database reorganization and some other logical changes.[5] To tolerate physical and logical reorganization, the log records must be made more logical than the simple physiological log scheme described in Chapter 10, (Subsection 10.3.6). The log records must represent the abstract transformations of the data if they are to be applicable to databases that have been reorganized. Devising such a scheme is an active area of database research today.

---

[5] Here, *upward-compatible* means that the changes can understand objects in the "old" format, since the persistent data and messages will continue to have that format.

12.7 Summary

The previous three chapters developed the concepts and techniques of transaction managers, explaining how they deliver atomicity, consistency, and durability (the ACI of ACID). This chapter focused on exotic features present in some of the more modern transaction managers. First was openness, the ability of one vendor's transaction manager to interoperate with that of other vendors; next was the ability to write portable resource managers against a standard transactional API. CICS has an open transaction manager (based on the SNA/LU6.2 protocol and CICS API). Since CICS is the best-selling TP monitor, all others are more or less forced to interoperate with it. This, in turn, forces them to support an LU6.2 gateway and, in doing so, become open. This openness will be accelerated by the adoption of the ISO/TP and X/Open DTP standards. They will force most vendors to implement such gateways and standard resource manager interfaces to their systems.

The next exotic topic was fault-tolerant, or non-blocking, commit coordinators. This turned out to be a simple application of process pairs. The commit coordinator becomes a process pair, checkpointing its state to the backup at critical points of the commit protocol.

Next, the issue of transfer-of-commit authority was discussed and shown to be a simple matter of reversing the polarity of sessions. Transfer-of-commit also had the benefit of saving messages, yielding the linear commit protocol. That led to a general discussion of commit performance. Of the several optimizations covered, the three key techniques were read-only optimization, parallelism, and the linear commit protocol.

The chapter ended with the topic of disaster recovery systems, introducing the concepts of system pairs, 1-safe, 2-safe, and very safe. This is an area of active research, but it promises to yield the next order of magnitude in system availability. It neatly handles environmental, operations, and hardware faults. In addition, it can mask some software faults.

12.8 Historical Notes

As far was we can tell at this writing, it was Nico Garzado who invented the two-phase commit protocol while implementing a distributed system for the Italian social security department. He had to solve the atomicity problem and, in doing so, invented the protocol. He told his friends about it, and gradually word of the problem and its solution spread. By 1975, the problem was well understood, and papers began to appear describing elaborations of the protocol.

Most of the more modern work on transaction processing algorithms belongs in this exotics chapter; the basics covered in the previous chapters were well understood by 1975. There have been many attempts to write gateways to closed transaction managers, and the gateway section reflects the folklore of those attempts, as well as the architecture implied by the ISO-TP and X/Open DTP designs.

Alsberg and Day [1976] introduced the idea of system pairs but seem not to have developed it much beyond that paper. Dale Skeen [1981] is credited with inventing the definition and algorithms for non-blocking commit coordinators in distributed systems. Tandem shipped such a transaction manager (working as a process pair) several years earlier. Andrea Borr is credited with that part of the design [Borr 1981].

Optimization of the two-phase commit protocol is a cottage industry. It was done quietly for several years, but as others rediscovered, named, and published the algorithms, the original inventors stepped forward to claim credit. The situation with Skeen and Borr is just one example of that phenomenon. The root problem here has been the considerable financial value of these optimizations. The original CICS commit mechanism had the linear commit optimization (the last transaction manager optimization) and a read-only optimization in which participants could vote on reply. The design of that protocol was largely the work of Pete Homan. Bruce Lindsay did a careful study and explanation of two-phase-commit protocol optimizations in his class notes [Lindsay et al. 1979]. Both Lampson [1979] and Gray [1979] published an analysis showing how to minimize commit messages by having the coordinator or the participant remember its state. This provides one-, two-, three-, and four-message commit protocols. Presumed abort was not well understood until Mohan and Lindsay clearly showed the log-force trade-offs among the various optimizations [Mohan and Lindsay 1983]. Section 12.5 of this book derives from their analysis. The group commit protocol [Gawlick and Kinkade 1985] and many other logging optimizations invented by 1975 were not described in the open literature because of their clear commercial value. In fact, the logging chapter of this book (Chapter 9) contains the first public description of some of them. The discussion of transfer-of-commit follows the design of Rothermel and Pappe [1990].

Disaster recovery systems offer a fertile ground for new algorithms and promise much higher availability. Several groups are actively pursuing these designs: the RDF group at Tandem, typified by Lyon [1990]; the IMS group at IBM, typified by Burkes and Treiber [1990]; the RTR group of Digital [Digital-RTR 1991]; and a group at Princeton, typified by Garcia-Molina and Polyzois [1990]. It is fair to say that disaster recovery and generalized transaction models (sagas, contracts, etc.) are the most active areas of transaction processing research. The presentation in Section 12.6 borrowed heavily from the ideas and terminology of Tandem's RDF group.

Exercises

1. [12.2.1, 5] How does the discussion of the closed transaction managers relate to (a) the last transaction manager optimization, and (b) transfer-of-commit?

2. [12.2.2.1, 5] Why is it so much harder to build a transaction gateway to a queued transaction processing system?

3. [12.2.3, project 30] Assuming you have access to a local SQL database system, write a gateway to the transaction manager described in the Chapter 11. The gateway should do trid translation and should handle the Prepare(), Commit(), Abort() callbacks from the local transaction manager and from the remote one.

4. [12.2.3, 10] The discussion of the gateway for an open transaction manager mentioned that if the same trid visited a node twice from two ports, it might get two trids and deadlock with itself. Explain the scenario, and say why it will result in abort rather than inconsistency.

5. [12.3, 10] (a) How many messages are added to the commit protocol by a non-blocking commit coordinator? (b) Why are the acknowledgment messages needed?

6. [12.3, 10] Heuristic commit and abort resolve in-doubt transactions in an ad hoc way. Why bother with two-phase commit if failures are handled in this way?

7. [12.5, 10] Consider the following commit tree, with each node representing a transaction manager with one log. What is the optimal mix of parallel and linear commits? What is the minimum message cost commit strategy and what is the minimum root delay message strategy?

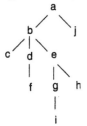

8. [12.6, 10] This exercise requires an understanding of Chapter 7. (a) Give an example of a transaction execution that is read-only with respect to a resource manager, but that will not be ACID if the read-only commit optimization is used for this resource manager. (b) Repeat the exercise, replacing the term RM with TM.

9. [12.6, 10] This exercise requires an understanding of the chapters on isolation. Suppose reads are allowed on data at the backup of a 1-safe or 2-safe disaster recovery site. What kind of isolation is provided to the reader?

10. [12.6, discussion] You have just sold a disaster-recovery system to a customer. Unfortunately, he read Chapter 3 after he signed the contract, and he discovered that operator errors are a major source of system failures. In addition, operators are expensive. So he has decided to eliminate operators. You have been offered a cost-is-no-object contract to replace the operator with a robot. The robot must decide when the primary system is down, and command the system to switch to the backup. You, of course, can prove that no such robot can be built, but you take the money anyway. What do you do next?

11. [12.6, 15] Some systems run two copies of the same application on one physical computer. If one copy of the system fails, the other takes over and continues offering service. For example, CICS has such an option. Explain when this is a good idea.

Answers

1. The scheme of making the closed transaction manager last is the same as the last transaction manager optimization and transfer-of-commit.

2. Queued systems do not allow conversational transactions. So the gateway cannot easily track the progress of the transaction between the request and the commit steps.

4. Suppose your organization has an SNA/CICS network with nodes all over the world. Suppose my organization has a DECNet/DECdtm network with nodes around the world. Suppose that your computation enters my network at a DECdtm↔LU6.2 gateway at the San Francisco node and at the Stuttgart node. Then the two entry points (gateways) will assign different trids to your one SNA/CICS trid. These two trids will have two independent process trees in my network and will behave like independent transactions. In particular, they will wait for one another if they try to lock the same database record. So, this may result in deadlock. They may both commit or both abort, but they will not see inconsistent information or make inconsistent transformations of the state.

5. (a) Two message pairs. (b) The acknowledgments are not needed if one only wants single-fault tolerance, but they give a degree of double-fault tolerance (primary fails and message is lost).

6. Good question! Some argue that 2-phase commit handles the 3% of the transactions that abort; it allows resource managers to vote at commit and allows distributed transactions to do unilateral abort on timeout. Since node failures are so rare, how they are handled is not much of an issue. Perhaps only 100 transactions in a million will be mishandled in this way, and the heuristic decision will guess right on half of those. The rest can be cleaned up by people if anyone cares. Well, that is the answer. Now you decide.

7. Minimum root delay time = fully parallel
   Cost: 36 messages, 10 synch and 10 asynch log writes.

   Root delay is $8M + 5L$.
   Minimum Cost: Use Linear on path $a \rightarrow b \rightarrow e \rightarrow g \rightarrow$. Use parallel-general on the others.
   Cost: $(4(5) + 3(4)) = 32$ messages + 10 synch and 10 asynch log writes.
   Root delay is $16M + 8L$.

8. (a) The read-only optimization implies that the resource manager has no work to do at commit. This, in turn, implies the transaction is not using two-phase locking. Imagine a transaction, T, that reads a data item, A, in one RM, and reads an item, B, in another RM. A second transaction, $T2$, can read and change B and then A in the interval between $T1$'s two reads because $T1$ has no long-term locks. The resulting history has a wormhole and so is not isolated (see Subsection 7.5.8.3) (b) Replace RM with TM in answer (a).

9. Degree 1 isolation; the reader gets the equivalent of browse-mode locking at the primary. If the reader acquires locks on the data, it may prevent an updater at the primary from being able to commit. In a 1-safe scheme, this will lead to inconsistency of the primary and the backup. On a 2-safe system, it will cause the primary site transactions to abort or time out. In either case, it is a bad idea to allow anything more than browse-mode access to data on the backup site.

10. (1) Take the money and run to Rio de Janeiro (and change your name). (2) Take the statistical approach used by fault-tolerant systems. Install many communications links between the two sites, so that the following assertion is likely true:

    If he can't talk to me, he can't talk to anybody.

    Then install an *I'm Alive* program at each site. If the *I'm Alive* messages stop arriving, the other site is dead. In that case, the robot sends a kill message on all links to it, and after a discreet time (say, 50 ms), assumes authority over the network.

11. It is a good idea when hardware (processor and memory) or communications are very expensive (it saves buying a separate computer), and when a major source of failure is software above the operating-system level. This scenario is typical of "mainframes" today and is likely to be typical for the first half of the 1990 decade. It is not true of cluster systems such as those from DEC, Tandem, Teradata, and others. It is also particularly appropriate for transaction processing systems like CICS, which have no fault containment (the TP monitor and all applications run in one address space with no protection among them). Again, such TP monitor designs are not likely to prosper in the next decade.

PART SIX

Transactional File System: A Sample Resource Manager

"On a clear disk you can seek forever."

FOLKLORE

13

File and Buffer Management

13.1 Introduction

This is the first of a series of chapters explaining the implementation of one of the most important resource managers in a transaction processing system: the *file manager*. The purpose of the file manager is to organize data kept on durable external storage such that it can easily be processed by other resource managers and by application programs. The degree of "ease" is limited, of course, but a file manager facilitates processing of external data by means of several useful abstractions:

Device independence.   The file manager turns the large variety of external storage devices, such as disks (with their different numbers of cylinders, tracks, arms, and read/write heads), RAM-disks, tapes, and so on, into simple abstract data types. These abstract data types, depending on the file organization, support certain access operations, such as read and write, on objects like bytes or records.

Allocation independence.   The file manager does its own space management for storing the data objects presented by the client.[1] Thus, for a given set of objects—that is, for a single file from the client's perspective—the file manager can employ one or many storage devices, controlled by one or several nodes in the network; it may even store the same objects in more than one place (replication).

Address independence.   Whereas objects in main memory are always accessed through their addresses, the file manager provides mechanisms for associative access. Thus, for example, the client can request access to all records with a specified value in some field of the record. Support for associative access comes in many flavors, from simple mechanisms yielding fast retrieval via the primary key up to the expressive power of the SQL select statement.

These abstractions are not implemented in one stretch; that is, associative access typically is not built directly on the bare metal, whether a magnetic disk or other media. Rather, there is

---

[1] Here and in the following, the other resource managers and application programs that use the file (resource) manager are referred to as *clients*. This emphasizes the execution model implicit in the abstract model of a TP system on which this book is based.

a layering of abstractions, with the external storage media at the bottom and content-addressable files at the top. In between, there are simpler files with less flexibility and functionality, but the interfaces to these simple abstract data types are available as part of the file management system.

The following chapters are organized according to the abstraction hierarchy in a typical file manager[2]. The present chapter discusses the lowest level, called *basic file system*, which is little more than an abstract device. The basic file system leaves no choice of objects that can be accessed; they are always *blocks* with a fixed length.

Chapter 14 then describes methods to allow more flexibility with respect to the objects that can be grouped into one file. For example, the application may want to treat the entire file as a simple byte string (unstructured), or it may view the file as a collection of *records* or *tuples* (these two terms are used synonymously). All records in a file have the same logical structure, but the instances can have different lengths. Most of Chapter 14, therefore, deals with the problem of how to map records and fields onto blocks, and with the aspects of different file organizations (except for associative access).

Associative access is the topic of Chapter 15. That chapter describes in detail the two most important techniques for associative access: *hashing* for fast single-record access via a primary key, and *B-trees* for associative access of single records and for sequential access to sets of records via unique and nonunique attributes. The chapter makes the point that finding a dynamic, adaptive data structure for associative search in large files is only one part of the problem. In the context of transaction processing, one also has to consider how these data structures can be given the ACID properties, and how their (negative) impact on concurrency can be kept within reasonable limits. Chapter 15 presents a kind of synopsis of the entire book in that it employs many of the techniques explained earlier (in particular, those on isolation, logging, and recovery) to demonstrate the implementation of a fairly complicated resource manager.

13.2 The File System as a Basis for Transactional Durable Storage

This section is a brief presentation of why files are used to organize and access storage in a manner that is different from the way main memory works. The arguments used define a road map for the contents of this chapter.

13.2.1 External Storage versus Main Memory

The organization of external storage, as opposed to internal (main) memory, is determined by five aspects:

Capacity. Main memory is usually limited in its addressing capabilites to a size that is some orders of magnitude smaller than what large databases need. External storage therefore provides the large storage capacities that are required.

---

[2] *Typical* in the sense that the same abstractions and functional characteristics can be found in many existing file systems, irrespective of any implementation details.

Economics. Even if the addressing limitations were removed, main memory technology (DRAM) would not be appropriate for large databases, because its cost per byte is still considerably higher than for magnetic disks. Thus, external storage holds large volumes of data at reasonable cost. The aspects of memory economics are illustrated in Figure 2.3 of Chapter 2.

Durability. Main memory is volatile. If the system crashes because of a power failure, it is restarted with complete amnesia as far as main memory is concerned. However, all persistent objects, such as catalogs, databases, the log, and so on, must be durably stored. Making DRAM durable is possible to a certain degree (by using battery backup), but it adds to the cost per byte, and in database applications, large volumes of data need to be kept in durable storage. External storage devices such as magnetic or optical disks are inherently durable and therefore are appropriate for storing persistent objects. Another facet of durability is the issue of safety. After a crash, recovery starts with what is found in durable storage. Hence, durable storage must be updated in such a way that no matter when the crash occurs, its contents can be consistenly reconstructed. For example, a pointer to some record must not be written to durable storage if the record is not at the storage location indicated by the pointer. This problem is discussed under the name of *careful update* or *careful replacement*.

Speed. External storage devices are some orders of magnitude slower than main memory; as the name suggests, they are also further away from the CPU. As a result, it is more costly, both in terms of latency and in terms of pathlength, to get data from external storage to the CPU than to load data from main memory.

Functionality. Data cannot be processed directly on external storage: they can neither be compared nor modified "out there." For data to be processed, they must first be transferred into main memory. The interface to transfer data between external storage and main memory is very simple when compared to a machine's instruction set.

As the discussion of memory economics indicates, there are significant differences among the technologies used to build main memory, and the same observation holds for external storage. As a consequence, real systems have no simple distinction between main memory and external storage; rather, they employ a *storage hierarchy*. It is recast from Chapter 2 for our present purposes in Figure 13.1.

The path from the top to the bottom of the pyramid is the path from expensive storage to cheap storage, from low latency to high latency, from volatile storage to durable storage. Note that main memory, looked at more closely, reveals a similar hierarchical structure: registers, first-level cache, second-level cache, and main memory. But since the only parameters that change in this hierarchy are speed and cost, this detail structure is not considered in the discussion that follows.

The question of how to interface external storage to main memory is obviously concerned with finding a "good" compromise between the five aspects just listed. Such a compromise is determined by the balance between the advantages of external storage (high capacity, low cost, durability) and its disadvantages (high latency, no processing capabilities). As will become clear in the following chapters, the key trick—especially to avoid the penalties of high latency—is to access external storage asynchronous with active

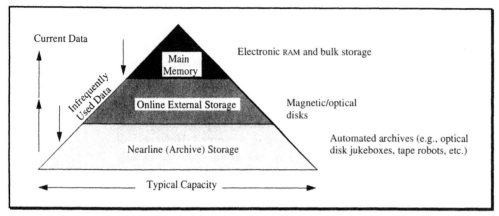

Figure 13.1: A storage hierarchy. The hierarchy reflects the stepwise compromise between speed, cost, capacity, and durability of the different storage media. The top of the pyramid is close to the processor; the storage used there is very fast but also expensive and volatile. Each layer down the pyramid is slower, cheaper, and has higher capacity than the previous one—and most of them are non-volatile.

transactions: do it when there is nothing else to do, so to speak. But in a number of situations, there is no choice: first, if the data to be processed resides on external storage, that data has to be brought into main memory, because this is the only way it can get to the CPU. Second, if some portion of data has to be made durable (say, a log record), it must be moved from main memory to external storage. File organization is very concerned about avoiding such situations whenever possible.

To understand the options in interfacing external and internal storage, let us assume a highly simplified processor model. All comparisons, computations, and modifications can be performed only on data stored in registers. To move data back and forth between registers and main memory, there are two instructions:

load reg-no, mem-addr
store mem-addr, reg-no

These instructions define the diameter of the CPU's horizon. In real-memory operating systems, the number of memory boards in the cabinet determines the maximum value of mem-addr; there is no point in generating a higher address than there are bytes in the real (physical) memory.

Virtual memory is a way around this limitation. Each process can generate addresses independent of the size of real memory. The operating system's virtual memory manager simulates the additional storage space required by "parking" on external storage devices (mostly magnetic disks or RAM-disks) those data objects that temporarily do not fit into real memory. To do that, the operating system's memory manager uses a basic file system much like the one described in this chapter. The details of how this works are irrelevant at the moment. Let us just consider the effect: with such a basic file system, the CPU's horizon is limited by the maximum address it can generate, that is, by the number of bits in mem-addr.[3]

---

[3] For simplicity, we assume that the virtual memory manager has unlimited quantities of external storage at its disposal.

Given the fact that the majority of current processor architectures have a maximum of 32 bits for memory addresses, which makes the horizon 4 GB wide, it is clear that large databases are way beyond the addressing capabilities of such a CPU. As a consequence, there must be a mapping mechanism between main memory and external storage that is even more powerful than the virtual memory technique. This is what the file system is for.

As mentioned earlier, external storage is presented to the application programs and resource managers *not* as a variety of devices, but as files with permanent, unique names. Files can grow and shrink during their lifetimes; each file is a collection of objects, such as bytes, records, or blocks. All objects within one file are of the same type. The criteria by which a specific object in a file can be accessed depend on the *file organization*, a subject that is discussed in Chapter 14.

Given this abstract view of external storage as a collection of files, there are three structurally different methods to make them accessible in main memory. These methods are illustrated in Figures 13.2–13.4.

The first method, called *read/write mapping*, which is depicted in Figure 13.2, is by far the most common. A large majority of existing systems use read/write mapping, and the file concept supported by all procedural programming languages implicitly assumes this technique. Files and main memory are treated as completely foreign address spaces with different operational characteristics. Elements (objects) of a file must be copied (read) into main memory explicitly. Depending on the file type and the organization, the unit of transfer can be a single byte or a string of bytes, a record, or containers–such as blocks–which reflect the physical properties of the external devices. This is explained more carefully in the discussion that follows.

In general, the order of the objects in a file need not be correlated to the memory locations into which these objects are copied. As Figure 13.2 shows, different objects can be

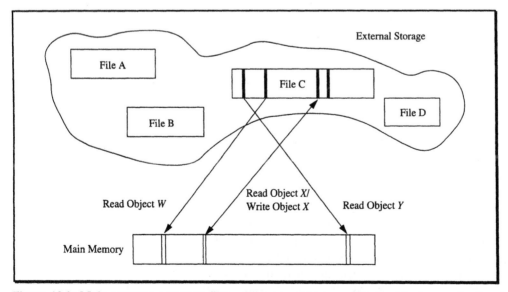

Figure 13.2: Main memory access to files. Files are made accessible in main memory by two operations: a read, which copies an element of a file into a specified area in main memory, and a write, which copies the modified file element back from main memory to external storage. At different points in time, different elements can be copied into the same memory location (this is not shown).

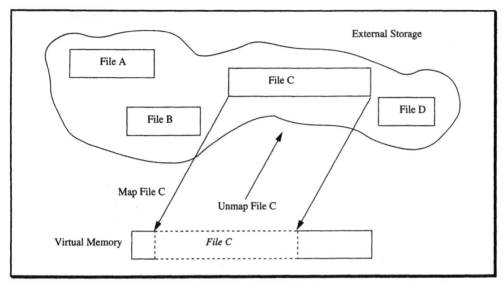

Figure 13.3: Mapping a file into memory. A file is made accessible by mapping it entirely into a contiguous portion of virtual memory. Of course, this implies copying the file contents. From then on, the objects in the file are accessible by machine instructions; that is, they can be treated like any other main-memory data structure.

copied into the same memory location—at different points in time, of course. An object is put into a file by copying a portion from main memory (a write). Since main memory, on one hand, and the files in external storage, on the other, have incompatible address spaces, a subtle problem arises: if a program reads, say, record x into memory location A, does some processing, and later on (re-)writes the same record x from memory location B, things work just fine. Reading some file object x into a memory location does not "tag" this piece of memory as the holder of x in the sense that x can only be rewritten from that location. However, a write operation to x can use any memory address, and whatever is written from there defines the new contents of object x in that file. Thus, it is the client's responsibility to make sure that the file system's read and write operations are applied to the proper memory locations.

Figure 13.3 illustrates a technique called *memory mapped files*, which achieves a tighter coupling between the file address space and the virtual memory address space. A file is made accessible by the map_file operation (see Chapter 2), which copies it *as a whole* into a contiguous region in main memory.[4] From then on, the file contents can be accessed by machine instructions; that is, there is no difference between the objects in the file and any other main-memory data structure.

Note that, in contrast to the read-write technique, each file object remains bound to the memory address it has been mapped to for as long as the file remains mapped to main memory. In other words, if part of the memory that contains the mapped file is modified, the object that corresponds to that location is effectively modified as well.

Again, however, there is a subtle twist: machine operations modify only the *mapped image* of the file, which is volatile because it is stored in virtual memory. For the

---

[4] This limits the maximum size of one file to less than the maximum memory size the system can handle.

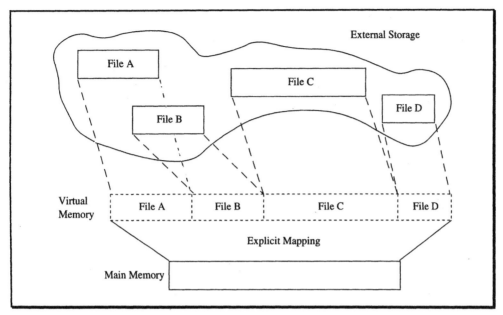

Figure 13.4: The virtual memory approach. It assumes that the processor can generate sufficiently long addresses to locate all the databases the system may have to handle during its lifetime—say, 64 bits. Each file, upon creation, is given a unique address in the (extended) virtual memory (its start address), and it expands in contiguous addresses from there. All files, program objects, catalogs, and so on are handled in the same way. Consequently, the processor can refer to any such object by presenting the proper virtual address. Of course, the translation of such a long virtual address into a real main memory address requires explicit mapping between main memory and external storage devices.

modifications to become durable, the file has to be unmapped, or at least the memory pages have to be copied to external storage. This operation not only frees the region in virtual memory allocated to the file but also has to transfer all changes that have been applied to it back to the durable external storage media. Without any refinements, then, a memory mapped file can stay in memory for a long time. All changes to it remain volatile, and at certain intervals these changes are transferred to external storage to make them durable. Based on the discussion of the properties of the disk write operation (see Chapter 4), it should be easy to see that the process of making changes to a memory mapped file durable during the unmap_file operation is, in itself, not atomic. Rather, considerable effort is required to achieve atomicity for such a complex operation.

In comparison, the read-write technique allows much finer control over the process of making changes durable. It is completely up to the application program to decide when to invoke the write operation.

Memory mapped files are even used for special purposes, such as loading executable programs from libraries stored in files on external memory, in systems that otherwise use the read-write technique.

The third approach, depicted in Figure 13.4, combines memory mapped files with the idea of virtual memory. It is based on the assumption that the processor can generate addresses that are *many orders of magnitude* larger than the 32-bit addresses mostly used today. For example, with an address range of 64 bits ($\approx 10^{19}$), there are enough addresses to locate each byte in a database of 10^7 terabytes. (By the way, storing such a database would require 10^{10} disk drives with 1 GB each, or more than two disk drives per person on planet Earth; this is just another way of saying that such an address space is large enough to store each object of the system's database in its own location once and for all, without any need to replace other objects for space reasons.)

The functional principle is very simple. Each object (e.g., a file, a program, or a table) is assigned an address in the extended virtual memory, which basically is the start address from which it extends contiguously in the address space. This address is never changed. As a result, there is a strict binding, which cannot be altered by a program, between addresses and object.

There are a number of consequences of extended virtual memory. First, all objects in the system can equally be accessed via their addresses by normal machine instructions; a local program variable can be handled in exactly the same way as, say, a record in a database. This is why this scheme is often referred to as *single-level storage*. Second, there must be a mechanism to make the extended virtual storage durable, because it contains databases and other persistent objects. This is a major difference from the virtual memory provided by an OS. Third, just having longer addresses does not make this scheme work. The real, physical main memory does not grow accordingly, and for all the reasons outlined, the large portions of the database are still on external storage devices. Consequently, an implementation that translates the very long virtual addresses into real main-memory addresses must use the services of a basic file system to exchange data between main memory and external storage. A conventional virtual memory manager does that, too; but its job is much simpler, because it does not have to worry about durability, recovery, and other issues that are indispensable for a transaction processing system. And finally, not all objects must be accessible from all process address spaces for security reasons. So depending on the architecture, there has to be a bind step similar to the map_file operation, or capabilities have to be used (see Section 13.5).

13.2.2 The External Storage Model Used in this Book

In accord with virtually all current transaction processing systems, the discussion in this book is restricted to the read-write technique for file handling. But there is more to this decision than just majority consensus. It will become clear as this chapter progresses that both file mapping and single-level storages have to be implemented on a simple read-write file system. These techniques are abstractions rather than implementation alternatives in their own rights—there is no magic. Our assumption, therefore, can be rephrased as follows: the more abstract file handling methods, as shown in Figures 13.3 and 13.4, hide from the system's client the necessity of transferring data between main memory and external storage, whereas the simple read-write technique offers a low-level abstraction that allows just that: transferring data between main memory and external storage.

We will see later that the virtue of this simpler interface is the direct control it allows over which data objects are read and written *and when* they are read and written: this is particularly important when it comes to implementing the A (atomicity) and D (durability) of ACID. Chapter 8, on lock implementation, demonstrates the importance for transaction systems exercising control over their critical resources in a very flexible and efficient way; that is why they need low-level primitives such as semaphores for process synchronization. The same is true for the file manager: because of the large difference in latency between main memory and external storage,[5] performance can be impaired badly if the data transfer is not carefully adjusted to the specific reference characteristics of a transactional file or database system. Therefore, transactional file managers build on top of low-level interfaces to external storage devices, because these interfaces allow for more fine tuning.

Now that we have defined the type of file system interface to be used, let us also assume a specific structure for the memory hierarchy, the elements of which are shown in Figure 13.1. One must clearly understand that this structure is totally dependent on the storage technologies available. A design that is adequate for current disk-based configurations probably has to be changed if large SSDs (solid state devices) are used. And if holographic memories ever become useful, a completely different storage architecture might be needed.

One of the interesting issues is the intensity of traffic between main memory and external storage. Chapter 2 mentions that the cost per MB of main memory will approach that of magnetic disks; thus, we might expect main memories to become large enough to hold an entire database.

However, the memory requirements of many applications continue to grow at a higher rate than the main memory size of a typical system, which means that the *relative* portion of data that can actually be kept close to the processor is shrinking. Yet due to the effect of locality—the tendency for recently used data to be re-referenced by later operations—the increase in absolute memory size will result in more and more of the *currently* needed data being kept in main memory. This, in turn, can speed processing considerably, assuming that the overall increase in storage demand is primarily due to archiving and "just not throwing things away." On the other hand, people thinking about multimedia databases, including voice and digital images, hold that the amount of active data grows in proportion to the total storage available. Thus, getting these data to the processor fast enough will remain a problem.

These mixed expectations are reflected in the two opposing architectural camps described in Chapter 2: the "disks forever" faction and the "main memory and tapes" confederation. For the reasons explained, the chapters on file system implementation assume the first scenario. The first subsumes the second, and it is more demanding on the data management architecture. It asks for high bandwidth between main memory and disks, as does the second one, but it also requires fast selective access to single objects on disk, which the second prognosis assumes to be a rare operation. And, finally, the first scenario is a simple extrapolation of the way current systems work.

A key property of the storage hierarchy we have described is *inclusion*: for each data object handled in main memory, there is a corresponding place in the online external storage, and for each object at the online external level, there is a place in the nearline (archival) storage. Since data can only be processed if they reside in main memory, and since they only can get there from the online storage,[6] they must be allocated dynamically as follows: all data with a very high probability of re-referencing must be kept in main memory; all data with high probability of re-referencing should be kept in online storage; and only the rest can migrate to the nearline storage. This is exactly what the five minute rule in Chapter 2, Section 2.2 quantifies.

---

[5] As Figure 2.3 shows, the latency of main memory access is about four orders of magnitude shorter than a random disk access. This is often referred to as the *access gap*.

[6] Here we only consider data that already exists in the system. New data coming in through some kind of terminal shows up in main memory first and then percolates down the storage hierarchy. But, of course, for any such "new" data item the inclusion property must hold, too.

Obviously, caching only makes sense if references to data objects are not uniformly distributed across the entire database. On the contrary, storage economics require the vast majority of data to be passive in that they can be moved to archival storage and never (or only very rarely) be touched again. All empirical evidence indicates that this is true. There is a small percentage of active or current data that needs to be close to the processor, and there is a large (and continuously growing) portion of data that reflects past states of the system and therefore will be referenced only under very special circumstances, such as restoration of previous states, analysis of old versions, or the like. Examples are very easy to find: I am interested in the *current* state of my account and in the debit or credit I am making right now; a debit that was done two months ago could only be of interest if I had the impression that something was wrong with it. Likewise, the flight reservation record for the flight to my destination today or tomorrow is very relevant to me; the flight reservation record of yesterday's flight is quite definitely obsolete.

For each application, then, the structure of the database and the types of applications it supports determine which data items are active and how fast they age. A popular rule of thumb, the 20/80 rule, holds that 20% of the data get 80% of all references, and the remaining 80% of the data get only 20% of the references, which is to say that the reference frequency of the active data is 16 times higher than the frequency of the passive data. Very few systematic studies of this phenomenon (which everybody in the field knows to be true) have been done so far. But the available measurement results indicate that the 20/80 rule is by far too pessimistic. There seem to be many applications that can be more appropriately characterized by, say, a 1/99 rule. This is a good thing, because a cache with an 80% hit rate yields very poor performance (see Chapter 2, Section 2.2.).

Of course, a file manager does not "know" about the application-specific criteria of which data are active and which are not. The data are distinguished by observing the actual reference pattern and by interpreting it under the principle of locality, which has already been mentioned in Chapter 2. This principle can be stated in two (complementary) ways:

Locality of active data.   Data that have recently been referenced will very likely be referenced again.

Locality of passive data.   Data that have not been referenced recently will most likely not be referenced in the future.

This principle explains why storage hierarchies work. It is not a law of nature, though; that is, decisions based on it can be wrong. But being wrong in that context just means being less efficient by either wasting expensive (higher-level) storage on stale data or by moving data to a lower level before they actually become obsolete. It is explained later in this chapter how additional information about the actual future use of data objects can be utilized to improve the performance of the memory hierarchy.

Since latency of disk storage is $\approx 10^4$ times higher than that of main memory, locality of reference not only helps to optimize the decision of which data to remove from main memory and when to do so, but it also guides the physical organization of external storage. The key point is that disks transfer blocks at a much higher rate if the blocks are accessed in physically sequential order rather in a sequence of random block read operations; this is because arm movement is such a slow operation. A typical disk supported by an adequate I/O subsystem can sustain a data rate of 3–5 MB/sec, provided it is allowed to move its arm monotonously in one direction. With random block accesses scattered across the whole disk, the response time for reading one block of, say, 8 KB is about 20 ms; that is, at the saturation point one gets 400 KB/sec out of that same disk. Hence, if it is known in advance that there will be substantial locality of reference among data spread out over multiple blocks, it is important to put these data into physically adjacent blocks; this is the principle of clustering described in Chapter 2, Section 2.2.

A further consequence is that one has to find storage allocation schemes on disks that will turn most access patterns at the higher layers of the system into physically adjacent disk accesses. This seems to contradict the notion of data independence. In some respects it indeed does, but then the notion of "clean" layering, with separation of concerns, and so on, is often at odds with performance requirements.

13.2.3 Levels of Abstraction in a Transactional File and Database Manager

The last convention we need to establish in order to get a proper perspective on the organization of the following three chapters has to do with the levels of abstraction inside the file system. This should not be confused with the storage levels shown in Figure 13.1. Their separation is determined by technological and economic considerations.

The levels of abstraction in the file system, on the other hand, are guided by the principles of data abstraction and module design. Figure 13.5 gives an overview of the abstraction levels found in current transaction processing systems and relates them to the storage pyramid. Let us briefly discuss them by proceeding from the bottom up.

The archive manager is concerned with data that most likely will not be referenced again, or that will be referenced only very infrequently, and under special circumstances. Examples of this activity are writing the incremental dump of the database and copying the REDO log records from the online log to the archive log. These data are only needed for media recovery, an infrequent event. The operations of the archive manager are mostly asynchronous to all active transactions, which means they should interfere as little possible with the online activities. Since the operations are asynchronous, they can be optimized for throughput. The archive manager's basic task is to copy data from the online external storage to archival storage as fast as possible.

Note that the pyramid metaphor is slightly misleading: according to our assumptions, there is no way of transferring data directly between these two storage layers. Online storage, as well as nearline storage, is just external storage from the processor's perspective, and it is thus treated in the same way. In other words, if anything has to be transferred to or from archival storage, it has to go through main memory. Thus the archive manager has to use the block-oriented file system interface to access the online storage, just like the other components residing higher in the abstraction hierarchy. But it also has to use the specific interfaces of the archival devices, which are not considered in detail here. It should suffice to say that because of the need to optimize for throughput, the archive manager operates at a device-dependent level. For that reason, its implementation is not discussed here beyond its relation to the log manager, as explained in Chapter 9.

Next come the media and file managers. For the purposes of this book, we assume that they manage magnetic disks. The media manager abstracts a simple data structure from the disk geometry—that is, from cylinders, tracks, slots, and from functional components such as arms, heads, and so on. It hides these mechanical aspects of disk drives and presents the contents of disks as arrays of blocks, which are called *files*. Blocks have a fixed length and can be read and written.

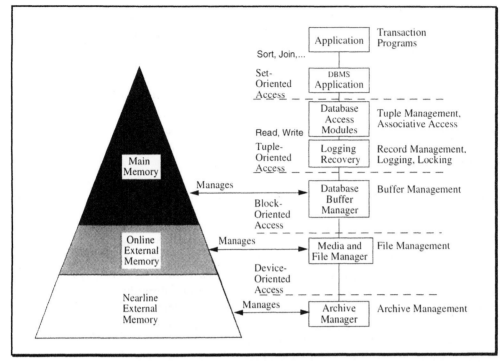

Figure 13.5: Components of the physical storage organization in a transactional database system. Applications use interfaces that provide set-oriented, associative access to the data, such as SQL. The interface is implemented on top of a tuple-oriented (record-oriented) file system, which includes logging and recovery to achieve the A and D of ACID. These services, in turn, are implemented on top of the buffer manager, which is a sort of file-oriented virtual memory manager. It handles the read-write-oriented file system and makes sure that the objects maintained by the higher layers (tuples, access paths, and so on) are addressable by machine instructions in main memory. The buffer manager uses a basic file system that manages the online external devices, such as disks. The archive manager moves data with very low probability of referencing from online storage to nearline storage—and back, if needed.

The file manager, furthermore, abstracts general linear address spaces from disk volumes; in particular, it allows its clients to reference files, that is, arrays of blocks, without having to know which volume a certain block is stored on. The file manager presents files as collections of blocks, and it maps these blocks to the (block-structured) disks according to its own strategies. The operations it provides to the user layer are essentially the same as those of the media manager: a block, identified by a number that is unique within a file, can be read and written.

The main client of the block-oriented file system is the *buffer manager*, the explanation of which occupies most of this chapter. The buffer manager's main purpose is to make life easier for the modules implementing the higher layers; that is, the more abstract objects. Rather than having each of them deal with the simple file interface, the buffer manager creates the illusion of having the entire database addressable in main memory. As we will later see, this does not achieve the conceptual simplicity of single-level storage, but it has some of its flavor.

The modules using the buffer manager interface in turn create another read-write–style file system interface, but this time with records (tuples) as the units of reference. Records can be longer or shorter than blocks, and they can be accessed either associatively or by some ordering criterion.

As Figure 13.5 shows, this is also the level where the measures for atomicity, isolation, and durability are implemented. The SQL abstract data type is built on top of that file system, and the application finally uses SQL plus transactions to manage its durable objects.

One must understand that Figure 13.5 shows an abstraction hierarchy, not an invocation hierarchy. Of course, an application can directly invoke database services. We will later see that database access modules can directly access the buffer manager's interface, and so forth. But this is not the point. Rather, the figure illustrates the correspondence between storage layers and the abstraction of accessible objects in the system model upon which the file management chapters are based.

This chapter talks about the media and file manager and about the buffer manager. The first aspect is fairly simple and therefore can be kept short. The fundamental question is, How can simple files that appear as arrays of blocks be mapped onto magnetic disks with their specific geometric properties? The second aspect, buffer management, is much more subtle. Among the many problems here are: how can objects on external storage be accessed in main memory without requiring the use of the basic file system for each component? How is durability managed without going across the very slow external storage interface too often? How can files be shared among concurrent activities? How can external file handling be optimized by exploiting locality?

13.3 Media and File Management

This section gives a more precise definition of the basic file system mentioned. The basic file system presents external storage devices to its clients in a device-independent way. It extracts a collection of variable or fixed-length records from the cylinders, tracks, and so on, which one would have to be aware of when working directly on a disk. There is little functionality beyond this device independence; in particular, there is typically no notion of consistency or atomicity at this layer. Presented here are the implementation techniques for a very simple, low-level file system, including space management on disk and dynamic allocation and extension. Although it may seem very primitive, this is fairly representative of a large class of existing file systems.

13.3.1 Objects and Operations of the Basic File System

At the level of the basic file system, each file is an array of *blocks*. A block is a fixed-length string of bytes.[7] For simplicity, we assume that all files of the basic file have the same fixed block length; this is quite reasonable, because disks come pre-formatted into fixed-size slots. Within each file the blocks are numbered contiguously, starting with 0. The number of blocks associated with a particular file can grow and shrink dynamically, disk space permitting.

---

[7] Currently, 8 KB is a typical block length. As the bandwidth between main memory and disks increases, blocks lengths will grow. Some high-throughput disk systems for special applications already use block lengths of 64 KB and more.

There is often some confusion with regard to the terms used when talking about disk accesses. To avoid the overhead of explaining these terms every time they are used, let us define them once and for all. There are three related concepts:

Blocks. These are the objects of the basic file system. The read and write operations described later are executed in units of blocks. This is not say that each physical transfer operation involves only one block; but whatever goes across the I/O interface will be *multiples of blocks*.

Pages. Pages are introduced formally in Chapter 14. They are the units into which the virtual address space maintained by the buffer manager is organized. A page is part of the database's address space. The contents of a page are stored in a block (the page and the block are the same size); a block in a file either contains the image of a page or it has no valid contents at the moment.

Slots. These are the units into which the surfaces of a disk are divided. A slot is the physical location that can store a block on a track. Its coordinates reflect the disk geometry. In other words, when a block is written, it is written to its corresponding slot. Conversely, when a block is read, it must be read from its slot. There are disk subsystems with very small slots (512 bytes, for example), which means an 8 KB block spreads out across 16 such slots. Since this variant does not introduce any new aspects, we will assume slots that are large enough to hold one block.

For the file organizations we will describe, these distinctions are hardly ever necessary. A block normally is tied to one slot; thus, both terms can be used interchangeably. Likewise, a page is always stored in the same block, so that saying "a page is written to a file" should not cause any problems. There are some exceptions, though. The shadow page algorithm, which is explained in the Subsection 13.5.1.3, requires a careful distinction between blocks and slots; but this is pointed out explicitly. Whenever there is no warning, the reader can rest assured that the terms can be treated as synonyms.

Now let us define the generic data structure of a block at the basic file system layer:

```
#define     EIGHTK 8192
typedef     unsigned int FILENO;
typedef     unsigned int BLOCKID;
typedef     struct  {  int          flip       /* write check pattern - front      */
                       FILENO       fileno;    /* no. of file the block belongs to */
                       BLOCKID      blockno;   /* relative block no. within the file */
                    }  BLOCKHEAD;              /*                                  */
typedef     struct  {  BLOCKHEAD    header;    /* header of block with redundant   */
                                               /* data for sanity checks           */
                       char         contents[EIGHTK-sizeof(header)-2]; /*          */
                                               /* payload of the block             */
                       int          flop;      /* write check pattern - back       */
                    }  BLOCK, *BLOCKP;         /*                                  */
```

The header declared here is rudimentary: it simply makes the point that there is a header and that part of it is used for making the block self-identifying and fault tolerant (to a small degree). A more complete header is introduced in Chapter 14, when a typical page layout for file systems is presented. For the moment, two observations will suffice:

First, blocks are stored to be self-identifying by keeping the FILENO and BLOCKID in the block header. Typically, the BLOCKID is a relative number within the file; whether the FILENO is unique within the system or just within a disk or a group of disks is not relevant for our purposes. But whatever the domain of its definition, FILENO is a unique name for the file as long as it exists. One can view it as a numerical shorthand for the (usually much longer) filename. Even if both FILENO and BLOCKID are restricted to the data type short int (i.e., 2 bytes each), blocks of 8 KB give us a maximum address space of 2^{45} ($\approx 32 \bullet 10^{12}$) bytes. This may not be enough for truly large future systems, but on the other hand, none of the current systems manages 32 TB (32,000 disk drives), so the simple design is at least reasonable. Of course, fields such as FILENO and BLOCKID are redundant, but so are all safety measures. In case of a disaster—a failure from which recovery is not possible by using the normal transaction mechanisms—it might be necessary to try to reconstruct the file system (or parts of it) from what is found on disk. And under such circumstances, it is useful if the contents of a slot says what it is.

The two fields flip and flop help to check if a block was written to disk completely or if the operation was interrupted by a crash, a power failure, or whatever. Under normal conditions, both fields have identical values; upon each write operation, the contents of both fields are inverted. A read operation checks if (flip == flop) and panics if this is not the case. Note that block sizes are increasing and continue to do so as disk capacities, recording densities, and controller bandwidths increase. But writing a block is by no means an atomic operation, and a failure in the middle of a write operation may leave the block damaged in a way that goes unrecognized, even by the parity check. That could cause the database to be corrupted beyond recoverability and, thus, should be prevented at all costs. The flip-flop mechanism is a simple way of doing this. Another method is to compute a checksum from the block contents and store it in the header. After the read, the checksum is recomputed from what actually arrived in main memory, much the way messages are made testable and (partially) recoverable in communication systems. However, the checksum approach is computationally more expensive, and for the typical failures a disk drive can produce, the flip-flop technique is quite appropriate.

The operations of the basic file system can be defined as a set of function prototypes. Parameter allocparmp for the create function specifies how large the newly allocated file has to be. A declare for this parameter is given in Subsection 13.3.2; for the moment, it is sufficient to remember that it specifies the file size.

```
enum     STATUS = {OK, FAILED};          /* success or failure from the file routines    */
typedef  char *      filename;           /* the file name is a character string          */
typedef  struct { }  FILE;               /* a file handle the structure of which is       */
                                         /* irrelevant for the present purposes           */
typedef  FILE *      FILEID;             /* pointer to file handle                        */
typedef  char        ACCESSMODE;         /* read (R) or update (U)                        */
int      blockcount;                     /* contains a number of blocks to read           */
STATUS   create(filename,allocparmp)
         /* creates and allocates the new file based on the specified space request.      */
         /* operation may fail because of authorization or due to lack of space.          */
```

```
STATUS delete(filename)
        /* deletes the file and de-allocates all space it had. may fail if the filename is invalid or      */
        /* if user is not authorized to that operation.                                                     */
STATUS  open(filename,ACCESSMODE,FILEID);
        /* opens an existing file in the desired access mode. operation returns a file handle.              */
        /* operation may fail because of invalid file name, missing authorization, illegal                 */
        /* access mode specification, etc.                                                                  */
STATUS  close(FILEID)
        /* closes an open file. operation may fail if handle is invalid, i.e. file was not open.            */
STATUS  extend(FILEID,allocparmp)
        /* extends an existing file by a specified amount. may fail because of invalid                      */
        /* handle, lack of space, or missing authorization.                                                 */
STATUS  read(FILEID,BLOCKID,BLOCKP)
        /* reads a disk block with the specified number into a block buffer in memory                       */
STATUS  readc(FILEID,BLOCKID,blockcount,BLOCKP)
        /* reads a certain number of disk blocks starting at the block with the specified                   */
        /*number into memory. Blocks are transferred into contiguous addresses,                             */
        /* starting at then one specified in BLOCKP.                                                         */
STATUS  write(FILEID,BLOCKID,BLOCKP)
        /* writes a disk block with a specified number from a block buffer in memory                        */
STATUS  writec(FILEID,BLOCKID,BLOCKP)
        /* writes a certain number of disk blocks starting at the block with the specified                  */
        /* number. a contiguous portion of memory is transferred, starting at the the                       */
        /* address in BLOCKP.                                                                                */
```

The interfaces to these functions contain the functionality required for organizing the access to disks. Direct access is the minimum; the functions that read and write a number of blocks with adjacent block numbers into contiguous portions of memory are useful extensions that exploit the fact that disks provide the highest throughput when arm movement is kept minimal; that is, when the access proceeds sequentially. So if data can be clustered into adjacent blocks, then the readc() and writec() functions allow access to this group of blocks in one piece.

Note the difference between FILENO and FILEID: the first one uniquely identifies the file for the duration of its existence; the second one is valid only while the file is open. As a matter of fact, FILEID is just some kind of address that points to the open control block, and its only purpose is to make references to an open file fast.

Of course, the access functions also have to perform security checks to make sure that the user issuing the access request is authorized to perform it. In what follows, this is not discussed in detail. The typical implementation of such security measures is based on access control lists as described in Chapters 2 and 6 (Sections 2.4 and 6.5), so there is not much new here. Also note that typical application programs do not use that interface to the file system; they rather do C— or COBOL—I/O, for example.

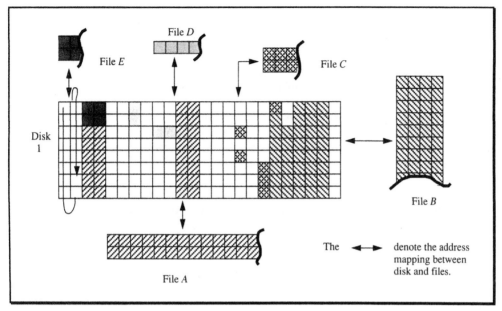

Figure 13.6: Mapping files with fixed-length blocks onto disk. The center of the figure represents a disk as an ordered set of fixed-length slots. The columns can be viewed as tracks, and a group of adjacent tracks as cylinders. The twisted arrow indicates the counting order of the slots.

13.3.2 Managing Disk Space

The first problem is to consider how block numbers of a file get translated into physical disk and slot addresses. These addresses eventually consist of quadruples of the type ⟨disk-id, cyl-no, track-no, slot-no⟩. In our simplified scheme, a slot is a container for one block. Figure 13.6 illustrates the situation. Note that this is already an abstraction from the real layout of slots on a disk.

There are five files of different sizes, the blocks of which are numbered according to some rule. There is usually an n:m relationship between disks and files: one disk can hold (parts of) many files, and one file can be spread across many disks. Files normally grow; at the moment they are created it is hard to estimate how large they will get. Files can shrink as well; that is, they can release space on disk that was previously allocated to them. The effect of all this is shown in Figure 13.6. Contiguous blocks (according to the counting scheme of the file) are not necessarily mapped to contiguous slots on disk. Groups of slots belonging to the same file are scattered across the whole disk. Not even relative ordering of addresses need be maintained. If a and b are block numbers in file D, and $a < b$, then it is quite possible that slot number(a) > slot number(b).

For the general case, then, there is no simple, global mapping function {blocks} $\rightarrow_m$ {slots}. As the examples of files C and D show, it is possible that the mapping has to be done explicitly for each single block. This will be the case when the system allocates space for files in units of single slots: every time the file needs a new block, a free block is found and assigned to the file. But, obviously, such a technique becomes expensive as files grow to the size of 10^5 to 10^6 blocks, especially since the mapping information has to be stored somewhere. Other mapping techniques give groups of contiguous slots to one file for holding contiguous blocks. Deferring the question of how to translate block numbers into actual physical disk addresses for the moment, the allocation problem can be put as follows:

Initial allocation. When a file is created, how many contiguous slots should be allocated to it? If the application knows how big the file is going to be, that information can be used. But for a general-purpose system, it is essential to have a good strategy, even if no hints from the application are available, or if they turn out to be grossly wrong.

Incremental expansion. If an existing file grows beyond the number of slots currently allocated, how many additional contiguous blocks should be assigned to that file? Again, information from the application may be used, but it can be as wrong as the first guess. Moreover, how many expansions can be added to a file ?

Reorganization. When and how should the free space on the disk be reorganized? Reorganization refers to the process of merging fragments of free slots in order to get groups of free slots of maximum size.

These issues are discussed together with the related problem of address translation for four different mapping techniques. All cases assume that there is a component keeping track of which slots on a given disk are free. The information about which slots are free is kept on the disk itself. There are a few basic strategies to do this, none of which is particular to disks. One is a linked list technique that chains (groups of) free slots, starting from a directory entry. Another possibility is to keep a bitmap with one bit per slot indicating whether it is assigned to a file or not. With this method, it is fairly easy to find groups of adjacent free slots. The overhead is minimal, as the following simple calculation shows. Assume a 1 GB disk (2^{30} bytes). With 8 KB slots, the disk has 2^{17} slots, which is how many bits are required. Since one slot has 2^{16} bits, 2 slots are sufficient to hold the entire free-space information.

One aspect of disks that is related to space allocation but is not considered in detail has to do with media failures on the disk itself. Assume there is a defect in the recording material somewhere on the surface of the disk. This normally has the effect that for the slot located in the area affected, some bits always come out the same no matter what was written, or they appear to be random noise. Without any provisions, this would imply the loss of the entire disk, because one of the slots cannot be used any more. A typical solution to this problem looks as follows [Tandem 1991]: Each cylinder of a newly installed disk has a number of spare slots at the end of the cylinder. Initially, these slots are not addressable; that is, the basic file system mapping blocks to slots does not "see" these slots. The cylinder appears to be slightly smaller than it is. If one of the slots in the cylinder goes bad, it is implicitly remapped to a spare slot; its slot address remains the same, but the physical location on disk changes. Note that this does not mean that the *contents* of the slot are automatically recovered; to the client of the disk the situation still looks like a media failure. But the gain of this scheme is that some media recovery manager can write the correct contents of the slot to the old slot number and thus make the disk consistent again.

If all spare slots in a cylinder are used up, the whole cylinder is remapped to a spare cylinder at the end of the disk. The data structures needed for this remapping are kept in predefined locations on the same disk. All this is transparent to the basic file system. Increasingly, the disk controller itself does this remapping, called *sparing*.

The following subsections will describe different schemes for blocks onto slots, as they can be found in current operating systems.

13.3.2.1 Static and Contiguous Allocation

Static and contiguous allocation is the simplest allocation technique. At file creation time, the total number of blocks the file is ever allowed to have is allocated at one time in contiguous slots. This makes address translation easy. Let s_b be the slot holding block number 0 of that file, then block number k is stored in slot $s_b + k$. The only mapping information needed is the complete address of the first slot and the total number of blocks in that file.

This scheme is particularly attractive because it efficiently supports both block-direct access and sequential access; note that, due to the contiguous allocation, one can guarantee that logically sequential equals physically sequential.

Since such files cannot grow, they cannot shrink either. The free-space administration, therefore, is straightforward: when the file is created, the requested number of contiguous blocks is allocated (or the allocation fails). But from then on, until the file is deleted, there are no structural changes.

Considering all its properties, static allocation at the file level is the obvious choice if a whole disk is to be assigned to one file, because then growth is not an issue, nor is reorganization or fragmentation. Database systems by third-party vendors (i.e., those not directly tied into a specific operating system) prefer such file organizations for creating "raw" or "virtual" disks, which they then manage by their own rules.

13.3.2.2 Extent-based Allocation

Extent-based allocation is geared toward files that are allowed to grow and shrink dynamically. The assumption is that it is not possible (for cost or other reasons) to allocate the maximum of all future space requirements at file-creation time. Therefore, it must be possible to extend the file incrementally and to remove space allocated to it at run time. The basic idea is to do multiple contiguous allocations. The file gets space in chunks of contiguous slots called *extents*; the first chunk is usually called the *primary allocation*, the others are *secondary allocations*. See Figure 13.7.

The directory entry for one such file contains, among other things, an array describing the current space allocations for that file. Each entry points to the disk containing the chunk; note that one unit of allocation always must fit on one disk. The next sub-entry points to an extent directory for that disk, which in turn points to the first slot of that extent. The reason for not keeping the slot address in the file directory is twofold. For space reorganization on a disk, it is necessary to move extents around in order to get large groups of contiguous free slots. With the indirect address, reorganization can be kept transparent to the directory, thus reducing the number of entries to be updated. Also, while an extent is moved, it must be locked to protect it from concurrent accesses. Identifying extents by a simple name, like ⟨volume-id,extent-index⟩, makes it much easier to create a lock name.

In the third sub-entry, the accumulated number of blocks for the file (up to and including that extent) is stored. Thus, if an access request is issued to block number x, one can do a linear search, a binary search, or whatever to determine directory index i such that curr_alloc[i].accum_length is the smallest value $\geq x$. Unless x exceeds the maximum block

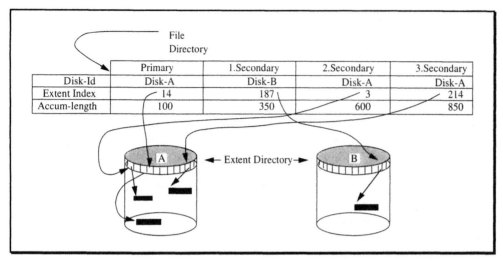

The table shown within the figure:

	Primary	1.Secondary	2.Secondary	3.Secondary
Disk-Id	Disk-A	Disk-B	Disk-A	Disk-A
Extent Index	14	187	3	214
Accum-length	100	350	600	850

A ← Extent Directory → B

Figure 13.7: Sample directory entry for a file with four extents. The file directory points to a (small) array with three fields per entry. The first entry describes the primary allocation, the other entries describe each secondary allocation. The first field per entry says on which disk the respective extent is allocated. The second one contains the index of an array local to that disk, which, in turn, points to the first slot of the extent. The third field contains the maximum block number of the file that is mapped into the respective array.

number currently allocated, block x is stored in the extent entry i points to, in slot number $(x - \text{curr\_alloc[i].accum\_length[i} - 1] - 1)$ relative to the first slot.[8] Compared to the total pathlength for a block-oriented I/O operation, which is in the order of 10^3 instructions, the overhead for address translation is negligible. There are a number of optimizations like address caching, which assume that the next access to a file will be in the same extent as the previous one and thereby avoid the overhead for searching through the directory, but this will not be discussed in detail.

Space allocation in extent-based file systems is generally done using parameters passed to the file system when the file is created or expanded, respectively. The create() function specifies the size for the primary allocation, which then is assigned completely to this file. File expansion works in the same way, based on parameters specifying the requested secondary allocation size. The setting and style of these parameters is very different from one system to the next. For example, the VSAM access method supports a primary and secondary size specified at file creation time. The extend() function is invoked implicitly. That is typical of most other commercial file systems. Assuming extent-based allocation, the declare of parameter allocparmp for the create function looks as follows:

```
struct allocparm
    {    Uint          primary;       /* initial allocation request
         Uint          secondary;     /* subsequent allocation request
         float         growth;        /* increase factor for subsequent allocations
    } ;
struct allocparm * allocparmp;
```

---

[8] Of course, if x is in the primary extent, no accumulated length is taken from the directory.

A comparison between static allocation and extent-based allocation shows that static allocation has no advantage other than the simplicity of its address translation. Extent-based allocation can easily achieve the same effect—if so desired—by using a very large primary allocation. But furthermore, extent-based allocation can handle large files even if the number of contiguous free slots is smaller than what is required for the file. Static allocation always needs its disk space in one chunk. Extent-based allocation can also handle files larger than one disk in a straightforward manner; static allocation would need substantial modifications to do that.

The problem of actually finding the required number of contiguous slots on disk is identical to the problem of managing a free space heap in main memory; thus, all the options developed in that area apply. Most media managers, whether in operating systems or in database systems, use the "first fit" approach to find a suitable extent. They also do periodic reorganization to clean up external fragmentation. UNIX systems tend to avoid external fragmentation by providing extents of uniform length. A "logical volume" in AIX version 3, for example, is implemented using extent-based allocation with chunks of equal size [Misra 1990]. As is well known from heap management, this increases the risk of internal fragmentation unless the extents are very small, which then means a huge number of extents for large files. (See the next subsection for details.)

13.3.2.3 Single-Slot Allocation

Single-slot allocation is extent-based allocation with a fixed extent size of one slot. In other words, each block of the file gets its own slot, irrespective of where the others are. This scheme was used by the original UNIX file system, with the following implementation: the file directory contains the i-node, which is an array of 13 pointers (let us call it slot_ptr) to slots on the disk. Now slot_ptr[0] to slot_ptr[9] hold the slot IDS of blocks 0–9; slot_ptr[10] points to a slot holding all pointers, which point to the next n slots (for blocks 10 to $n + 9$). The value of n depends on the slot size; it is 128 for the original UNIX system. The next directory sub-entry, slot_ptr[11], points to a slot with n pointers, each of which points to a slot with n pointers, holding the slot addresses of the next n^2 blocks in total. It is easy to imagine what slot_ptr[12] contains. Free space is obtained from the head of a linked list of unused blocks; this is no problem, since the allocation scheme does not depending upon physical contiguity.

The algorithm described provides addressability for $10 + n + n^2 + n^3$ blocks, but through an extremely unbalanced tree. Slot addresses for the first 10 blocks are found in the directory entry of that file. For the next n they are stored down the tree one level; for the next n^2 they are two levels down; and for the majority of block numbers, assuming a large file, they are three levels down. However, this scheme was designed explicitly for applications where most of the files are small, as they are in typical time-sharing applications. Assuming 8 KB pages, files of up to 80 KB can be addressed using the i-node only, which, according to some empirical studies, cover more than 98% of all files.

For very large files, however, random access performance gets poor because of the skew in the addressing structure. One could think instead of using more balanced search structures such as B-trees, or simply a linear array with one entry per block number. But that would not avoid the problem of having to go through considerable overhead for each and every block access, which is unacceptable for database systems. Note that in these systems, block accesses should be very cheap and fast because all "real work" of file management, tuple management, access path maintenance, and so on, is built on top of that. It obviously makes no sense to spend any I/O operations just on determining the slot address of a block, which, after it has been read (another I/O), turns out to be the wrong one because it does not contain the requested tuple, entry, or whatever.

UNIX, meanwhile, has given up this allocation scheme and uses extent-based allocation instead—mostly because it has to provide a reasonable platform for database systems.

Two conclusions can be drawn from this discussion:

(1) Space allocation must use a technique that allows for very fast address translations from block numbers into disk addresses: "very fast" means no I/O.

(2) Space allocation should be done in (possibly) large units of physically adjacent disk blocks in order to support fast sequential access. Of course, this is only a problem for large, database-sized files.

13.3.2.4 Buddy Systems

This class of algorithms allows only certain predefined extent sizes. To avoid going into too much detail, only the version where the number of blocks per extent always is a power of 2 will be considered. An extent is said to be *of type i* if it contains 2^i contiguous slots. Addressing is particularly easy in this scheme, because the lowest slot number of an extent of type i is $f \cdot 2^i$ for integer $f \geq 0$, assuming that the first slot has number 0. Free extents of the same size are linked together in a free list, and space allocation works from this list. When a **create()** command is executed with some primary allocation request p, the free list is checked for extents of the type $t = \lceil \log_2 p \rceil$. If no such extent is available, the free list for the next bigger type is inspected.[9] Let us assume that there is a free extent of type $t + 1$. According to the definition, it is two times the size of the one requested. Since it is contiguous, it can be split up into two extents of the desired size; that is, the larger one is taken out of its free list, one half of it is used for allocation, and the other half is linked to the free list of type t.

Conversely, when a file is deleted, all its extents must be given back to the free lists. But adjacent free extents must be merged into larger free extents, because otherwise most extents would quickly end up being decomposed into extents of type 0. Thus, if an extent E of type i is freed, this triggers a check of whether its *buddy B* is also free. The address of the buddy can easily be determined: since the extent is of type i, the low order $(i - 1)$ bits of its starting address are 0. If the ith bit of the starting address of E is 0, B is the right neighbor (in the order of increasing addresses); otherwise, it is the left neighbor. Note that the notion of a buddy is symmetric: B is the buddy of E, and E is the buddy of B. Consequently, whenever an extent and its buddy are both free, both are made one extent of the next-larger type. If the buddy of this newly established extent is free, the merging is repeated. This continues until no free buddy is found. Whatever gets collected in this manner is linked to the appropriate free list. Figure 13.8 illustrates the principles of buddy allocation.

The buddy system is attractive for a number of reasons. First, reclaiming unused space by the method just outlined requires only logarithmic time in the worst case, and in most practical situations it will be constant time. In contrast, the techniques described so far have costs proportional at least to the number of extents. Splitting a large extent into smaller ones is equally cheap. Second, each allocation requirement can be fulfilled down to the precision

---

[9] For reasons of practicality, there is always a maximum extent size that can be handled by the buddy system.

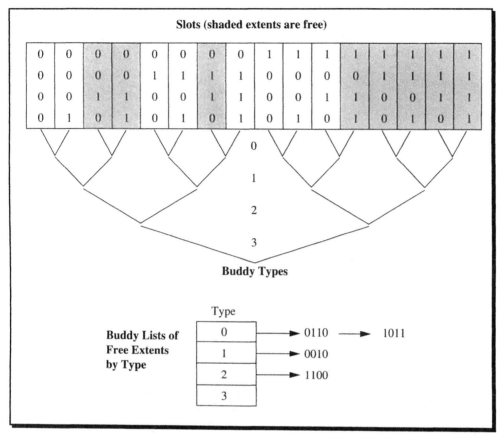

Figure 13.8: The buddy system. The binary buddy system organizes slots into extents the sizes of which are powers of 2. As the figure shows, this creates a simple mapping from the binary representation of the slot number on extent types this slot can belong to, and vice versa. Extents that can be combined into the next-larger extent type are called buddies. This is indicated by the binary tree. The figure shows a number of allocated extents and some free extents. Assume slot 0101 gets deallocated. It will go into the free extent chain of type 0; although its neighbor slot is free, they cannot be combined into an extent of type 1 because they are not buddies. If, however, slot 0111 were deallocated, it would be merged with its buddy 0110 to form a free extent of size 1.

of one block: just take the binary representation of the number of blocks requested, and if there is a 1 in position i, allocate an extent of that type—assuming, of course, that such an extent is available. In real implementations, one usually limits the number of extents per file allocation to some reasonable value v; that is, the amount requested is rounded up to the next higher value with exactly v 1s in its binary representation. Third, this technique lends itself naturally toward automatic space allocation for dynamically growing files. If a file is created with no size requests, a good strategy with the buddy system is to proceed as follows: at first, the file gets an extent of one slot; if it grows, it gets two slots; if it keeps growing, it gets four slots, and so on. This is essentially the method described for sizing secondary extents; the system responds to file extensions with the allocation of increasing portions of space. If more information on the file type is available at creation time, a higher initial value might be chosen.

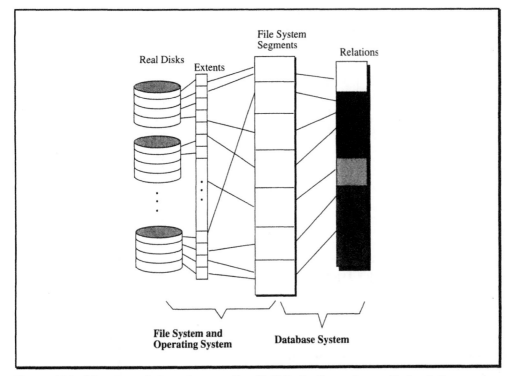

Figure 13.9: Mapping relations down to "real" disks in three steps. Each relation can be decomposed into a number of fragments; each fragment is mapped onto exactly one file fragment (segment). Each file fragment, in turn, can be mapped to an arbitrary number of extents.

However, buddy systems are susceptible to external fragmentation. If too many small extents that are not buddies are allocated, then it may become impossible to allocate large extents. Hence, the space on disk must be compressed periodically to make sure the small extents are next to each other, which minimizes fragmentation. But then, this problem has to be solved for each allocation technique. Even with the 2-block bitmap, one would have to devise some strategy for garbage collection to make sure allocations can, on the average, be made in large chunks—so why not use the buddy system, even if the actual bookkeeping is done in a 2-block bitmap?

13.3.2.5 Mapping between Different Address Spaces

The discussion so far has focused on space allocation on disk: the aspect of managing physical storage media. The goal is to support the concept of block-oriented files, but in order to keep them flexible in size, an intermediate layer of abstraction called *extents* is required. As was shown, the size of an extent can vary from one slot to the entire file; the different allocation strategies are basically determined by which types of extents one considers. Essentially, this two-step abstraction is sufficient to provide a platform for implementing logical files—files where tuples, catalogs, logs, indices, and so on are stored. The resulting structure is shown in Figure 13.9.

This scheme is sufficient for supporting all aspects of a tuple-oriented file system, as will become clear in this and in the following chapter. Fragments of a relation are the units

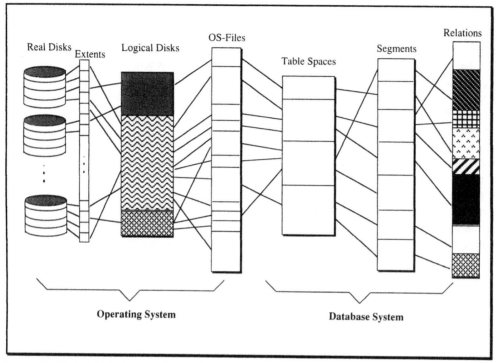

Figure 13.10: Multiple layers of mapping and space allocation in the operating system and the database system. If the operating system uses multiple layers for mapping its files onto physical disks, and the database system, in turn, maps relations onto files in multiple steps to achieve flexibility and independence of limitations in the operating system's file system, the resulting mapping scheme can be fairly complex. It is important to note that each step does the same thing: mapping groups of block-sized containers to other such groups. Each step needs its own free space administration, data structures for address translation, and so forth.

of distribution; that is, each fragment can be stored in a different node, in a file that is local to that node. The buffer manager (see Section 13.4) manages the movement of pages between an individual disk and a main memory buffer pool.[10]

In some systems, mapping of relations down to physical storage is typically much more complex. This is to say there are many more layers of abstraction between the physical disk and the tuple in a relation, and each layer comes with its own space allocation, administration tables, and so forth. A typical situation is depicted in Figure 13.10.

Figure 13.10 shows what would happen if Oracle ran on AIX version 3. At least two of the seven layers that "support" the tuples in this scenario are redundant. They merely redefine the concept of contiguous storage space over and again under new names, creating overhead and the need for additional administration. Note that each mapping has to be done explicitly, and that the mapping strategies need to be compatible. Apart from the inherent overhead, such sequences of mapping and remapping of storage space make it unnecessarily hard (if not impossible) to preserve the logical sequence of tuples in their physical ordering on disk.

---

[10] There are designs for buffer managers in distributed database systems allowing for remote buffering, but such variations are not considered in this book.

Now if this is so obvious, why do many database systems use that kind of "Babel" mapping? There are basically two historical reasons. First, many of the older file systems allow only very limited flexibility in terms of file expansion. Therefore, if the database wants its relations to be more dynamic, it must provide an additional layer where the creation of new files, the addition of new disks, and so on, are kept transparent to the higher layers. The second reason is closely related to the first: an independent database vendor wants his system to be widely portable, and thus it is a safe decision to build a storage manager that assumes only the minimum functionality of all target file systems.

In this book, we do not want to burden ourselves with historical legacies and the shortcomings of inadequate mapping schemes. It is therefore assumed that the operating system and the database system mean the same thing when they say *file*; this reduces the number of mappings to the configuration illustrated in Figure 13.9.

Clearly, some amount of space allocation has to be done for mapping relations onto files. But in the scheme used for the rest of this book, this simply amounts to allocating space in a file (fragment), which, in turn, will negotiate its needs with the basic file system.

13.3.3 Catalog Management for Low-Level File Systems

As we have already seen in the discussion on extent-based allocation (Subsection 13.3.2.2), the mapping of address spaces and the maintenance of free space information requires some auxiliary data structures that also have to be stored in durable memory. They are part of the overall system catalog, which is required for all kinds of name binding and address translation. Typically, file system catalogs are organized as a hierarchy. This hierarchy can reflect the file name structure, as in most operating systems; the layering of object classes, as in ADABAS; or it can simply be a search tree over the set of file names. More detail will be presented in the discussion of mapping relations onto the basic file system.

The basic file system needs three very simple types of structures, which should be fast and easy to maintain. The first one describes the current allocation of a file and must allow for fast access via FILEID. Assuming extent-based allocation, the declaration for a file entry looks like the following:

```
#define maxextents 1000
struct     basic_file_descriptor              /* structure of information to be kept about a file    */
    {   FILEID        fileno;                  /* internal identifier the external name is bound to   */
        char          filename[];              /* external file name                                  */
        unsigned int  partition_#;             /* for partitioned files, partitions are numbered      */
        int           version_#;               /* version counter (not used here)                     */
        allocparm     spacerequest;            /* specifies primary & second. extents                 */
        unsigned int  curr_no_extents;         /* how many extents are currently allocated            */
        struct                                 /* descr. of allocated extents                         */
            {   char             diskid[];      /* on which disk is the extent                         */
                unsigned int ext_#;             /* index in extent table on disk                       */
                unsigned int accum_length;      /* accumulated length from prev. extents               */
            } curr_alloc[maxextents];           /* size of that extent                                 */
    };                                         /*                                                     */
```

There is one parameter, partition_#, which has not been discussed so far. Since a full explanation of distributed files is given in Chapter 14, for the moment the following remark should be sufficient: a file can be distributed in that it holds a fragment of a relation, other fragments of which are stored in other nodes (or on other disks). Such a file, which structurally is a complete file in itself, is called a *partition*, and the fact that other partitions exist is kept in the file catalogs at the next-higher mapping layer.

As the function prototypes defined in Subsection 13.3.1 suggest, the binding of the file name to the internal file number is done at open time. Whether the filename stored in the structure just given is the full external name or just the lowest-level suffix in a name hierarchy does not matter here. Essentially, the file descriptor is itself a record in a file. There is a recursion in this definition, which has to be broken somewhere because it does not make sense to try to access the file descriptor file in order to find out where the file descriptor file is. Thus, the catalog files are anchored at predefined locations and organized in a predefined format; otherwise, they use the same file access methods as the rest of the system. It is just that their addresses are not determined using the normal binding mechanism, which needs the catalog.

The other two data structures are bound to the physical disks, where they are also stored in predefined locations. One is the bitmap for keeping track of which slots are assigned and which are free; there is no need to declare a simple structure like that.

Finally, there is an array describing the extents on that disk:

```
#define xt_per_disk BIG
struct     extent_entry                         /*                                          */
           {   long int        first_slot;      /* where does the extent start              */
               unsigned int    xt_length;       /* how many slots does the extent have      */
           };                                    /*                                          */
struct     extent_entry extent_table[xt_per_disk]; /* table of all extents on disk          */
/* if first_slot == 0 the extent number is currently not assigned                           */
/* note that this table will span a number of contiguous slots                             */
```

A file is created once and used many times; one has to insert many records to fill an extent. Consequently, catalog operations are rare. Thus, at open time, after the authorization checking has been done, the file system only keeps a small portion of the file descriptor, namely the information required for address translation. All the static interpretation of the descriptor and the related extent tables has already been done; in particular, the ext_# entries of the descriptor are replaced by the current values of these entries in the extent_table. Hence, a given block number can be translated into a slot number with minimal delay.

There is one important observation here. Let us assume a file is expanded by another extent. Obviously, all three data structures have to be modified during this operation: the slots given to the new extent have to be marked as "not free" in the bitmap; the extent entry for the new extent has to be filled; and the reference to the new extent must be added to the basic_file_descriptor. The fact that all these data structures must be mutually consistent at all times means especially that their copies on durable storage must be consistent when the system is brought up or restarted after a crash. Using only the block-oriented access functions, this cannot be guaranteed. No matter how the three data structures are written to disk (and they are generally in three different blocks), a system crash can interrupt that sequence at any point. Now imagine that a new extent has been allocated; the system crashes; and the basic_file_descriptor and the extent_table were written, but the free slot bitmap was not. Hence, after restart the system will find the old bitmap, and the slots that have already been given to an extent will eventually be allocated twice.

File systems in operating systems go through great pains to prevent such situations from happening. This will not be discussed in detail because transactions are a generic solution to the problem, but one principle applied here is useful in many other situations. Here is the basic idea:

The principle is called *careful replacement*, and it encompasses a number of rules. Some of them, like the Ping-Pong scheme, are explained in Chapter 9. Another rule says that related data structures must be written in the inverse order of the read sequence. Therefore, in a hierarchical structure, where reading proceeds from the top down, modified (related) entries must be written from the bottom up in order to avoid the inconsistencies mentioned.

In our example, it works as follows: first write the free slot bitmap, then the extent_table, then the basic_file_descriptor. It is easy to see that with such a protocol multiple allocations or invalid references after an allocation cannot occur. All these data structures being shared, space allocation and deallocation also has to use locking in order to avoid concurrency anomalies, but let us ignore this at the moment. Exercise 13.11 deals with the deletion of a file, which means that all space allocations are freed. The consequence of this simple protocol is obvious: whenever the careful replacement sequence is interrupted, slots are left marked as "allocated," although the allocation is forgotten about by the higher levels and will therefore be repeated, using up other slots. This is not exactly right, but it does not cause integrity problems for the application, as was the case in the first scenario. The lost slots can be reclaimed during reorganization, which has to be done anyway for compacting the free space on disk. There are, of course, many improvements of this basic scheme. The most popular method is to use two slots on disk for each directory block, and to write them alternately at each modification; a version number that monotonically increased (see the declaration of basic_file_descriptor) tells which is the current version. If a write sequence is interrupted, one can then discard the incomplete new state and switch back to the previous version, which is in the alternate slots. The most elaborate version of this careful replacement scheme is the shadow page algorithm (see Subsection 13.5.1), which has been designed for databases but has clear performance disadvantages over the recovery techniques described in detail in this book. The only thing to understand for the moment is this: maintaining file descriptors, even at the lowest level of the system, requires more than one block to be written atomically when the structure is updated—a requirement that causes considerable problems, unless transaction support can be used at that level. It is interesting to note that all operating systems are moving toward logging to make catalog update operations atomic actions.

13.4 Buffer Management

As shown in Figure 13.1, the database buffer is the mediator between the basic file system and the tuple-oriented file system. The buffer manager's main purpose is to make the pages addressable in main memory and to coordinate the writing of pages to disk with the log manager and the recovery manager. It should also minimize the number of actual disk accesses for doing that.

The presentation of buffer management techniques in this section is organized into four parts. First, there is an overview of what the buffer manager has to do and what technical constraints have to be considered. The second part translates this into implementation, showing the basic data structures and the C code for the most frequent operations with the buffer manager. The third part describes the relations of the database buffer to the log and the recovery managers. The final part presents a list of optimizations that can be used to improve the basic design described in this book.

13.4.1 Functional Principles of the Database Buffer

To understand the fundamental issue in buffer management, we should consider Figure 13.9 again. It shows that a relation can be mapped onto many files (each file containing data of one relation only), and that each file is viewed as a set of equal-sized pages, which can be accessed according to different criteria depending on the file organization. As will be explained in detail in Chapter 14, all the database access modules (those responsible for providing associative access, implementing joins, etc.) operate on the basis of page abstractions. Each tuple is located by specifying the identifier of the page in which it is stored, and the offset within that page. A page identifier has the following structure:

```
typedef  struct                              /* makes it easier to talk about page nos.    */
       {   FILENO          fileno;           /* file to which the page belongs              */
           unsigned int    pageno;           /*page number in the file                      */
       }   PAGEID, *PAGEIDP;
```

The page numbers grow monotonically, starting at 0, within each file. Note that this does not refer to the tuple-oriented file system, which is described in the next chapter. For the moment, it is sufficient to say that each page of that file system is the contents of the block with the same number in the corresponding basic file; thus, there is a static 1:1 relation between pages and blocks.[11] It should therefore create no confusion when throughout the section on buffer management both terms are used interchangeably.

The database access modules, then, reference their objects by addresses that are tuples of the type ⟨PAGEID, offset⟩. For executing instructions on such objects, however, the objects must be located in some process's virtual memory; moving pages between a disk and the buffer pool is the buffer manager's basic function, which is illustrated in Figure 13.11.

The buffer manager administers a segment in virtual memory, which is partitioned into portions of equal size called *frames*. Each frame can hold exactly one page. Compared to many existing systems, this is a simplification. Real buffer managers can be more complex in the following ways:

Buffer per file.   Rather than just one storage area for mapping pages into virtual memory, one such segment per file could be used.

Buffer per page size.   If a system uses different page (and block) sizes, there is usually at least one buffer for each page size. Mapping pages of different sizes onto a buffer with

---

[11] This assumption rules out mapping schemes such as shadow pages, differential files, and so on, all of which require the same page to be stored in different blocks of the underlying basic file system. But since these mapping schemes are not seriously considered in this book, the assumption can safely be made, and it helps to simplify the presentation.

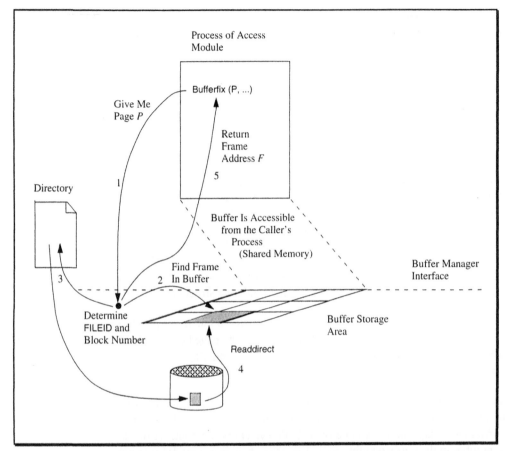

Figure 13.11: The buffer manager as a mediator between the file system and the access modules. The buffer manager provides addressability of pages in files by translating the PAGEID into a FILEID and a block number using the system catalog. It then accesses the basic file using the readdirect interface and puts the page into a storage area that it manages—the database buffer. The caller gets back the starting address of the page in the database buffer address space. Steps 3 and 4 are needed only if the page is not currently in the buffer pool storage area.

only one frame size (which would have to be the size of the smallest page) creates space allocation problems identical to those of allocating extents on disks. This would make buffer operations unnecessarily expensive; thus, having a buffer for each page size is the obvious solution. Since for the purpose of this book only one page size is assumed, this needs no further consideration.

Buffer per file type. There are files like indices (see Chapter 15), which are accessed in a significantly different way from other files. Therefore, some systems dedicate buffers to files depending on the access pattern and try to manage each of them in a way that is optimal for the respective file organization. Subsection 13.4.4 discusses the degree to which the buffer management can react to the access patterns, even if there is only one global buffer.

None of these variations contains any aspects of buffer management that would not show up with a single buffer. They provide more flexibility in administering and tuning the system, but they also add more complexity, which this book tries to avoid as far as possible. The database buffer, then, can be declared as a simple data structure:

```
/* these declarations are needed to illustrate the basic buffer functions (fix a page,      */
/* unfix a page, flush a page)                                                               */
#define  buffersize   MANY            /*                                                     */
#define  hashsize     PRIME           /*                                                     */
struct                                /*                                                     */
    {   PAGE_HEADER        page_header; /* header of a page in a file                        */
        char               page_body[]; /* payload of the page                              */
    }   bufferpool[buffersize];         /* fixed size is assumed for the buffer             */
```

Of course, some additional data structures are needed for administrative purposes, but this is deferred to the next subsection. As Figure 13.11 shows, the interaction between the higher-level modules and the buffer manager works as follows: the module finds that it needs access to something stored at offset O in page P. Since the offset is a relative address to the page, it need not be passed to the buffer manager; the module, therefore, calls it with P as the parameter. The buffer manager then goes through the following logic:

Search in buffer. Check if the requested page is in the buffer. If found, return the address of this frame—let it be F—to the caller. This requires a fast associative access to its bufferpool (this is demonstrated in the next subsection).

Find free frame. If the page is not in the bufferpool, check if there is a frame that currently contains no valid page.

Determine replacement victim. If no such frame exists, determine a page that can be removed from the buffer (in order to reuse its frame). Of course, it is crucial to pick a page that is not likely to be needed right after it is removed from the bufferpool. If no page can be removed, panic.

Write modified page. If the page to be replaced has been changed while in buffer, write it to its block on disk, using the write-ahead log (WAL) protocol, as described in Chapter 10, Section 10.3. If it was not changed, it can simply be overwritten.

Establish frame address. Now it has been determined which frame will hold the requested page. Denote the start address of the frame as F.

Determine block address. Translate the requested PAGEID P into a FILEID and a block number. This is done using the file catalog and the basic file descriptor. With the mapping conventions introduced in the previous section, this translation is trivial. Check if the file is open. Read the block into the frame selected.

Return. Return the frame address F to the caller.

Note that opening the file has been made a separate function that is not executed by the buffer manager. The main reason for that is that open() does things (and needs parameters) that are very different from the normal bufferfix() and therefore should not be inside something else. For example, open() has to check authority, check if other opens have to be made (partitioned files), check the validity of the access plan, and so on. Details will be explained in Chapter 14.

At first glance, the buffer manager logic might create the impression of something very similar to a read operation in a file system. But for what follows, it is important to understand the differences between a conventional file buffer and a database buffer. First, the caller is not returned a copy of the requested page into his address space; rather, he gets back an address in the buffer manager's domain to access the page there. This is necessary, because in large systems the database system runs in several processes, each of them servicing a number of transactions at the same time. Since transactions running in different processes might have to access—and might have to change—tuples in the same page, there must not be multiple copies of this page in different address spaces. Figure 13.12 shows what would happen if two processes each had a "private" copy of a page, applied changes to it, and tried to write it back to the database later on.

The second difference between the interface to a normal file system and the buffer manager interface is the fact that, as a consequence of a request for a page, other pages (probably not related to the transaction issuing the request) can be written. In other words, it is not the access module that issues a write command to the buffer; typically, the buffer manager's clients just request addressability for a page. Then they go ahead and do their processing, which may or may not result in a modification of the page. If the page is

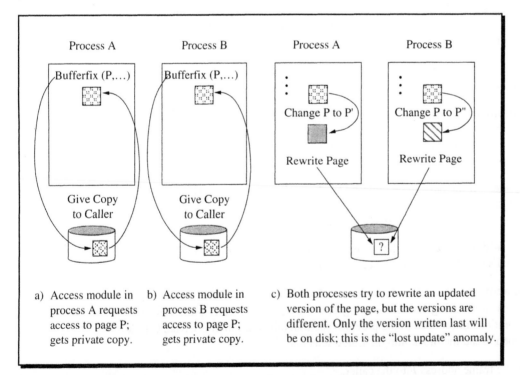

a) Access module in process A requests access to page P; gets private copy.

b) Access module in process B requests access to page P; gets private copy.

c) Both processes try to rewrite an updated version of the page, but the versions are different. Only the version written last will be on disk; this is the "lost update" anomaly.

Figure 13.12. An illustration of the "lost update" anomaly. Giving private copies of pages to different database processes while allowing parallel updates in pages causes inconsistencies in those pages. Typically, only the updates of the process that writes last are reflected in the database; the others are lost—hence the name. Therefore, the buffer manager has to make sure that operations on pages have at least the ACI of ACID. Whenever a transaction commits, any page updates it has caused must be made durable.

modified the buffer manager must be informed, but it will essentially decide by its own criteria when the modified page is written back to the file.

Let us summarize what has been determined so far. The buffer manager provides:

Sharing.   Pages are made addressable in the bufferpool, which is an area of shared virtual memory accessible to all processes that run the database code.

Addressability.   Each access module is returned an address in the bufferpool, denoting the beginning of the frame that holds the requested page.

Semaphore protection.   Many processes can request accesses to the same page at the same time; the buffer manager gives them the same frame address. The synchronization of these parallel accesses in order to preserve consistency is not the buffer manager's problem. It has only to provide a semaphore per page that can be used for implementing locking protocols. See Chapter 8 for details on semaphores.

Durable storage.   The access modules inform the buffer manager if their page access has resulted in an update of the page; the actual write operation, however, is issued by the buffer manager, probably at a time when the update transaction is long gone.

To handle all this via the very simple buffer fix/unfix interface, more information needs to be exchanged than just a PAGEID and an address in the bufferpool. In the following, we assume that all service requests to the buffer manager refer (via a pointer) to a *buffer access control block*; its declare looks like this:

```
typedef struct
    {   PAGEID          pageid;        /* id of page in file                        */
        PAGEPTR         pageaddr;      /* base address of page in bufferpool        */
                                       /* this entry is set by buffer manager       */
        int             index;         /* record within page (used by caller)       */
        semaphore *     pagesem;       /* pointer to the semaphore for the page     */
        Boolean         modified;      /* flag says caller modified page            */
        Boolean         invalid;       /* flag says caller destroyed page           */
    }   BUFFER_ACC_CB, *BUFFER_ACC_CBP;   /* control block for buffer access        */
```

This control block tells the caller what he has to know for accessing the requested page in the buffer. PAGEID is the name of page he wanted access to, and it is just echoed back. The pageaddr is the pointer to the frame in the bufferpool that contains the page. The variable index is there for the caller's convenience; there he can keep a local identifier (local to the page) for the object in the page that he is accessing. The pointer pagesem contains the address of the semaphore that can be used for negotiating access to the page by concurrent transactions. The modified switch is initialized to FALSE; the client sets it to TRUE whenever he has done any updates to the page. The invalid switch, eventually, is initialized to FALSE. It may happen, however, that for some reason the caller fails to function properly (bugs in the access module, for example). The transaction must then be aborted, and the buffer manager must be informed that the page contains garbage. This is indicated by setting the switch to TRUE.

Invalid pages are an interesting issue. As long as it is only the buffer pool version that is corrupted, then recovery can be done from the older (but valid) version on disk. If, however, the present module just finds out that the page was left invalid by some previous corruption, and the invalid state was written to disk, then UNDO most likely will not work. The only way to restore a transaction-consistent version of the page is to initiate a dynamic media recovery. In other words, the broken page must be recovered from the archive log, together with all the REDO logs written since then.

The call that fills in the buffer access control block is defined by this function prototype:

```
Boolean     bufferfix (PAGEID pageid, LOCK_MODE mode, BUFFER_ACC_CBP * address);
/* returns TRUE if the page could be allocated, FALSE otherwise. if it is allocated the    */
/* address of the 1st byte of the page header in the buffer pool is returned in           */
/* BUFFER_ACC_CBP. The fix count is increased by 1. There is no check if the transaction  */
/* already has a fix on that page. The semaphore protecting the page is acquired in the   */
/* requested mode (shared or exclusive)                                                   */
```

Semaphores are needed because, in general, multiple instances of the database code run in parallel (in different processes). These multiple threads of control can, of course, access the same page simultaneously, with one trying to insert a tuple while the other one tries to remove it, or both trying to use the same segment of free space in the page for a new tuple, or whatever. At any rate, the problem is that a sequence of related updates to a page has to be made before the page as such is again in a locally consistent state. Note that concurrency control only helps that problem if the granule of locking is an entire page. But since this is a bad idea, at least for high-traffic pages such as access paths, catalogs, and so on, semaphores must be employed to achieve mutual exclusion when accessing pages in the buffer. The underlying idea is that of page action consistency, as explained in Chapter 10, Section 10.3.

The buffer manager therefore grabs the semaphore on the client's behalf before returning the page address. The further correct use of the semaphore, however, is completely up to the caller.

The name *bufferfix* hints at a problem in this kind of page mapping that has been ignored so far. Remember that the caller at the interface gets a frame address in the bufferpool, which he can use from now on. All accesses to objects in the page will be normal machine instructions using pageaddr as a base address. In other words, the buffer manager does not know if and when its clients actually work with the pages. But it needs some information about that because, as was explained previously, it has to remove pages from the buffer in order to make room for new allocation requests. This cannot be done in an uncoordinated fashion, though, because then the situation depicted in Figure 13.13 could arise.

Clearly, if the transactions only tell the buffer manager which pages they want to access, then after a short time the whole bufferpool will fill up with pages requested on behalf of some transaction. For the next request, the buffer manager will have to replace one of the pages currently stored in the bufferpool, which creates the addressing problems shown in Figure 13.13. Transaction X is informed that its page P is stored in a certain frame. It gets the pointer to the frame and works in P, using that base address. If later on the buffer manager decides to give the same frame to another requestor and store page Q in it, then two processes will hold a pointer to the frame: one assuming (correctly) that Q is stored in this place, and one assuming (incorrectly) that P is stored there. This problem can be solved in a number of ways, some of which are subjects of the exercises at the end of this chapter. Database systems typically use the FIX-USE-UNFIX protocol, which works as follows:

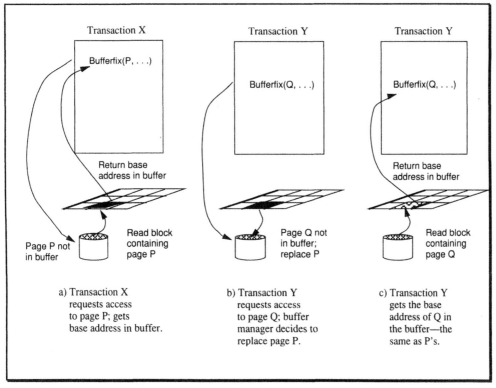

Figure 13.13: Uncoordinated page replacement in the buffer. Such replacement potentially invalidates the addresses used by higher-level access modules. So the buffer manager must be able to make guarantees as to the validity of page addresses in the buffer pool.

FIX. The client requests access to a page using the bufferfix interface. As the name suggests, the page is fixed in the buffer; that is, it is not eligible for replacement.

USE. The client uses the page with the guarantee that the pointer to the frame containing the page will remain valid.

UNFIX. The client explicitly waives further usage of the frame pointer; that is, it tells the buffer manager that it no longer wants to use that page. The buffer manager can therefore UNFIX the Page, which means the page can potentially be replaced.

The interface for unfixing a page is defined by the following function prototype:

Boolean   **bufferunfix** (BUFFER_ACC_CBP);
/* returns true if the page could be unfixed, FALSE otherwise. if the unfix is possible, the fix   */
/* counter is decreased by 1. If the transaction has multiple fixes on the page, it must issue   */
/* the corresponding number of unfix operations. Note that the parameter is the address of   */
/* the buffer access CB.   */

Several concurrent transactions can share concurrent read access to a buffer page at the same time. In that case, each transaction is given the same pointer to the bufferpool (see

Figure 13.11), and each transaction fixes the page. Now, if one transaction unfixes the page again, the page does not become eligible for replacement until all transactions that fixed it have called the bufferunfix() routine. Thus, the buffer manager must count the number of outstanding fixes on a page.

The consequence is that an access module using the buffer interface must make sure that for each bufferfix() there is a corresponding bufferunfix(). It is easy to see that if a client issued, say, three subsequent fix requests to the same page (these could be different modules each making sure that the page is really addressable) and then invoked bufferunfix() only once, the buffer manager would assume that there are still two access modules needing that page. In other words, the buffer would soon be clogged with irreplaceable pages.

This suggests that all modules operating at the buffer manager interface must strictly follow the FIX-USE-UNFIX protocol, with the additional requirement of keeping the duration of a fix as short as possible. Therefore, even if a module "knows" that it might need access to a page again later on, it is best for it to unfix that page as soon as it starts working on another page and to rerequest the first page whenever some pointer refers to it again. These basic rules for accessing the durable storage implemented by the buffer manager are summarized in Figure 13.14.

The additional advantage of the FIX-USE-UNFIX protocol is that the access modules do not have to keep track of which pages they have already touched and which they have not; every time a page number is found that is different from the one currently used, the bufferfix routine is called. As a consequence, the FIX/UNFIX operations are among the most frequently used primitives in a database system, and thus should be very fast.

With these two operations, the basic interface between the buffer manager and its clients is defined. Two additional operations are needed during normal processing. The first one is very similar to the bufferfix function and is defined by the following function prototype:

```
Boolean      emptyfix(PAGEID pageid, LOCK_MODE mode, BUFFER_ACC_CBP address);
/* returns TRUE if the page could be allocated, FALSE otherwise. The function requests an      */
/* empty page to be allocated in buffer. the identifier of the empty page has to be provided   */
/* by the caller. the buffer manager formats the page header with the PAGEID and returns a     */
/* pointer to the buffer access CB like bufferfix.                                             */
```

According to the abstraction hierarchy introduced in the previous section, the free-space administration for tuples and other logical objects is done above the layer of the basic file system and, therefore, above the buffer manager. Consequently, the buffer manager's clients keep track of which page is used and which is free. Whenever an empty page is to be accessed, the buffer manager must provide a frame for it; yet there is, of course, no point in reading this page from disk. This is the main reason for having a separate function for that case. Note that just as with bufferfix(), there must be a corresponding unfix for each emptyfix().

Whenever a page that was modified in the bufferpool by a successsful transaction is to be replaced, it must be forced to durable storage (disk) before it can be removed from the bufferpool. Since the basic file system is not accessible to the higher-level modules, they cannot issue a write operation. This has to be done by the buffer manager; consequently, there must be an interface for telling him to so. The function prototype for it is very simple:

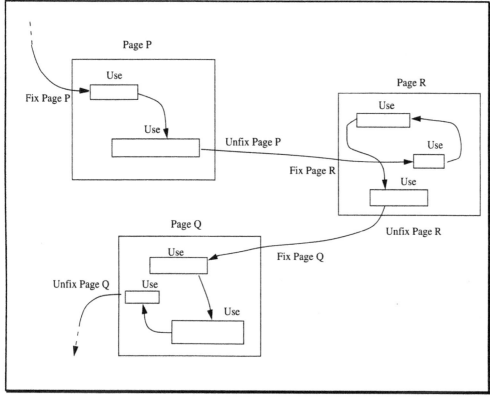

Figure 13.14: Access to pages in durable storage following the FIX-USE-UNFIX protocol. A page is fixed as long as access to it is required; then it is unfixed again. Note that the strict sequence shown here is not mandatory. There are situations, however, where it is necessary to keep a fix on a page when access to the next page is requested. This technique is called *lock coupling*, or *crabbing*.

Boolean   **flush** (BUFFER_ACC_CB);

```
/* returns TRUE if page was written to the file, FALSE otherwise. The page is written to its    */
/* block in the file, the modified field in the buffer control block is set to 'N', and the page  */
/* remains in the buffer. This function can be called by any client. The buffer manager will      */
/* acquire a shared semaphore on the page while writing it.                                       */
```

13.4.2 Implementation Issues of a Buffer Manager

This section develops some of the basic data structures and algorithms needed for implementing a typical buffer manager. The major portion is taken up by a C program that implements the bufferfix routine and some of the administrative functions it needs. After that, some general design options for buffers are discussed.

As stated in the previous section, the database buffer is essentially an array of frames, each of which can hold one page. The algorithms on that array must provide:

Fast access. Given the PAGEID, the proper entry in the bufferpool must be located quickly, or it must be decided that the page does not reside in buffer.

Correct control information.   The buffer manager must transparently maintain the control blocks that are given to the client, including semaphores and free-space counters.

Locality. The buffer manager must collect enough information to pick a "good" page for replacement.

Cooperation with recovery manager.   The buffer manager has to provide the information required by the transaction manager (checkpoint data, minimum page LSNs, and so on—this will be covered in the next section).

Efficient file access.   The buffer manager must drive the underlying basic (block-oriented) file system.

To meet these requirements, the basic data structures must be augmented by a number of administrational data structures, which are briefly introduced in the following.

13.4.2.1 Data Structures Maintained by the Buffer Manager

Of course, the key data structure maintained by the buffer manager is an array of frames; this array is called the *bufferpool*. A division/remainder hash function (divide by prime P) coupled with hash chaining is used for associative access to the bufferpool via PAGEID. There must be an array of P pointers to buffer control blocks. Each buffer control block contains all the information about a page in the bufferpool, and each has a forward pointer to the "next" control block belonging to the same hash class. Furthermore, there is an array that holds indexes of the buffer pool array. It is used to keep track of which frames are unused (do not hold valid page images) at the moment. Of course, other data structures could have been chosen, but using arrays makes the subsequent presentation of algorithms simpler—the topic of this section is buffer management, and not clever tricks on fancy data structures. So the bufferpool, together with its infrastructure, looks as follows:

```
#define  buffersize   MANY
#define  delta         SMALL
#define  hashsize      PRIME
#define  MAXLSN        VERY_LARGE_VALUE          /* this is to represent the maximum LSN      */
                                                 /* that could be returned from the log       */
                                                 /* manager. needed to initialize a field     */
                                                 /* based on which a minimal LSN is to be      */
                                                 /* determined.                               */
/* the bufferpool array is statically allocated. each entry contains storage space for one page.   */
struct
    {   PAGE_HEADER     page_header;     /* header of a page in a file        */
        char            page_body[];     /* payload of the page               */
    }   bufferpool[buffersize];          /* fixed size is assumed for the buffer   */
struct
    {   Uint            free_index;      /* index of a free frame             */
    }   free_frames[buffersize];         /* table of free frame indexes       */
Ulong       no_free_frames;              /* current number of free frames     */
semaphore   free_frame_sem;              /* semaphore to protect operations on */
                                         /* the free_frames list              *
```

The next group of declares comprises the administrative data structures to access the bufferpool and to keep track of how the pages have been used, if they are currently fixed by a transaction program, if they have been modified, and so on. This information is kept in the *buffer control block*. Buffer control blocks are kept in an array that is associatively addressed via the PAGEID, using the hash mechanism mentioned previously. The control blocks are also threaded together in least recently used order (this is called the *LRU chain*), for reasons that are explained later in the chapter.

```
/* Template for a control block that is linked to the hash-table entry. It contains all the    */
/* administrative data about the page in the bufferpool it refers to. The buffer access control */
/* block that is given to the caller is loaded from the information in the buffer control block. */
typedef     struct
    {       PAGEID          pageid;         /* no. of page in buffer (0 = no page)           */
            FILEID      *   in_file;        /* handle of file where page is stored           */
            Uint            frame_index;    /* buffer pool index where page now stored       */
            semaphore       pagesem;        /* semaphore to protect the page                 */
            Boolean         modified;       /* TRUE if page is modified, FALSE else          */
            int             fixcount;       /* number of page fixes                          */
            LSN             forminlsn;      /* LSN of first fix for update since page        */
                                            /* was read into the bufferpool                  */
            BUFFER_CBP      prev_in_LRU;    /* previous page in LRU - chain                  */
            BUFFER_CBP      next_in_LRU;    /* next page in LRU - chain                      */
            BUFFER_CBP      next_in_hclass; /* hash overflow chain forward pointer           */
    }       BUFFER_CB,  *   BUFFER_CBP;
/* statically allocated hash table for accessing the buffer via PAGEID                           */
struct
    {   semaphore       class_sem;          /* each entry is protected by a semaphore        */
                                            /* while being used                              */
        BUFFER_CBP          first_bcb;      /* pointer to first control block                */
    } buffer_hash[hashsize];
BUFFER_CBP  mru_page;                       /* pointer to cb of most recently used page      */
BUFFER_CBP  lru_page;                       /* pointer to cb of least recently used page     */
semaphore   LRU_sem;                        /* semaphore protecting the LRU - chain          */
BUFFER_CBP  free_cb_list;                   /* pointer to the first element in the           */
                                            /* list of free buffer control blocks            */
Uint        no_free_cbs;                    /* contains the current number of free           */
                                            /* buffer control blocks                         */
semaphore   free_cb_sem;                    /* semaphore to protect operations on            */
                                            /* the list of free control blocks               */
```

The buffer access control block was introduced in the previous section, so the declare need not be repeated here. But we need some administrative add-ons to control the dynamic allocation and deallocation of buffer access control blocks. The corresponding set of declares looks as follows:

```
BUFFER_ACC_CBP  free_acc_cb_list;              /* pointer to the first element in the     */
                                               /* list of free buffer                     */
                                               /* access control blocks                   */
Uint            no_free_acc_cbs;               /* contains the current number of free     */
                                               /* buffer access control blocks            */
semaphore       free_acb_sem;                  /* semaphore to protect operations on      */
                                               /* the list of free access ctrl blocks     */
```

Since the buffer manager handles all the accesses to the block-oriented file system, it has to maintain a data structure of the files that are currently in use. We do not declare them, though, for two reasons: first, they are straightforward, and second, the code examples do not contain explicit file access operations.

Figure 13.15 gives an overview of how the buffer manager's central data structures hang together.

13.4.2.2 Initialization of the Buffer Manager

At system startup, the buffer manager's data structures must be initialized such that all the integrity constraints implied by their definitions are met. These initializations must be completed before the buffer manager can service client requests.

First, the bufferpool itself (which is assumed to be a statically allocated array, for simplicity) must be made consistent by marking all frames and semaphores as free.

```
Uint    i;
/* the bufferpool itself need not be initialized because if all its frames are declared free,  */
/* the actual contents of the frame is irrelevant.                                             */
for (i=0; i<buffersize; i++)                   /* initialize all frames                   */
     { free_frames[i].free_index = i;   };     /*                                         */
no_free_frames = buffersize ;                  /* enter all frames into list of free frames */
initsem(free_frame_sem);                       /* initialize the free list semaphore      */

mru_page, lru_page = NULL;                     /* set LRU - anchor to indicate that       */
                                               /* the chain does not exist                */
initsem(&LRU_sem);                             /* initialize the semaphore for the        */
                                               /* LRU - chain as free                     */
```

Next, the control blocks must be made consistent with the data structures they refer to, and the linked lists chaining together control blocks must be set up. There are three groups of control blocks that need to be initialized by the buffer manager. First, there is the buffer_hash table for the associative access to the bufferpool, together with the buffer control blocks that provide access to the frames through the hash table. Second, there are the buffer access control blocks, which are given back to the caller as a result of a bufferfix or emptyfix operation; and third, there is the list of open files. But note that the buffer manager *allocates* the access control blocks and only returns a pointer to the caller. Since the code is very similar for all types of control blocks, only the allocation of the buffer_hash table and the buffer control blocks will be presented.

```
Uint               i;                                    /*                                    */
/* the hash table for associative access via PAGEID is initialized by setting the anchor       */
/* pointers to the chains of buffer control blocks to NULL (no instance in this hash class)     */
/* and by setting up the semaphores (free).                                                     */
BUFFER_CBP    new_cb;                                    /*                                    */
for (i=0; i<hashsize; i++)                               /*                                    */
          { buffer_hash[i].first_bcb = NULL;             /*                                    */
            Xsem_init (& buffer_hash[i].xsemaphore; };/*                                        */
new_cb = alloc(sizeof(BUFFER_CB));          /* allocate the first control block                */
free_cb_list = new_cb;                      /* and store the address in the anchor             */
i = 0;                                      /*                                                 */
while (i < buffersize + delta)              /* a few more CBs than buffer frames               */
          { new_cb -> pageid = 0;           /* indicate that the control block does            */
            new_cb -> frame_index = -1;     /* refer to a valid page                           */
            sem_init (& (new_cb -> pagesem)); /* initialize the semaphore for the page         */
            new_cb -> prev_in_LRU = NULL;   /* initialize the chain pointers for               */
            new_cb -> next_in_LRU = NULL;   /* maintaining the LRU chain                       */
            /* the other fields are initialized when the control block is used for             */
            /* representing a page in bufferpool.                                              */
            if (i == (buffersize - 1))                   /* check if last control block        */
              {   new_cb -> next_in_hclass = NULL;}  /* end of control block list              */
            else                                         /*                                    */
            {   new_cb -> next_in_hclass = alloc(sizeof(BUFFER_CB)) ; /*                        */
                new_cb = new_cb -> next_in_hclass;                   /*                         */
          };                                        /* allocate the next control block and link it to */
          i++;                              /* the previous one via the hash chain pointer     */
      };                                    /*                                                 */
no_free_cbs = buffersize + delta;           /* for each frame in the buffer there needs to     */
                                            /* be a CB, so this counter is a sanity check      */
sem_init  (& free_cb_sem);                  /* set the free list semaphore in free state       */
```

All this code assumes, of course, that the startup phase is executed in single-user mode. If this were not the case, all the actions on the shared data structures would have to be protected by semaphores.

13.4.2.3 Implementation of the bufferfix Routine

Due to the simple design used for our presentation, the number of buffer control blocks is fixed by the parameter **buffersize**, so there is no need to dynamically allocate or deallocate these control blocks. On the other hand, the number of both the open file control blocks and the buffer access control blocks can vary within wide margins at run time, which is why they are maintained as linked lists. The buffer manager allocates and frees them as required. But again, this is a simplifying assumption. A hash table like the one used to translate PAGEIDs into addresses of buffer control blocks would be much more efficient, but since this does not add any new aspect, it is not considered in the following discussion.

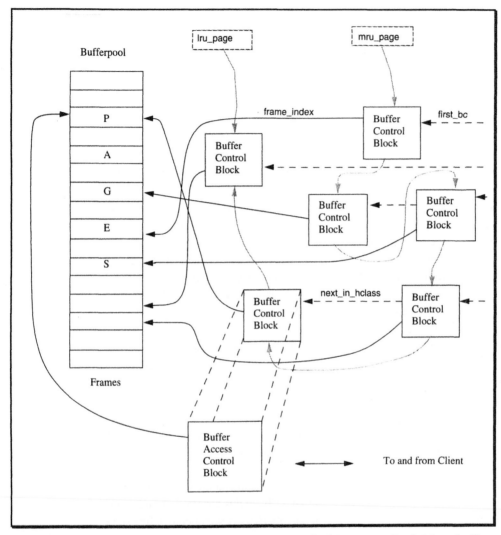

Figure 13.15: Graphical overview of the data structures required to manage the database buffer. The different pointers and pointer chains are distinguished by different textures of the arrows. For an explanation, refer to Subsection 13.4.2.2

The buffer access control blocks should not be allocated and freed on demand, because they are required and released at a very high rate (with each fix/unfix); it is therefore crucial for this operation to be fast. Accordingly, the buffer manager preallocates a number of them (say, 3 • buffersize) and then just works from its own free list. Only if this list gets exhausted will the buffer manager have to allocate more, which from then on are also kept in the buffer manager's free list.

All operations on the free lists for control blocks must follow the protocol for concurrent allocation of free blocks, which is explained in detail in Chapter 8 Section 8.3. To understand the implications for buffer management, the reader should become familiar with the get_block() and give_block() routines described there. For the sample implementation in this section, there are a number of routines with the same logic for maintaining the free lists; the function prototypes for them look like this:

```
BUFFER_CBP        get_bcb()
/* returns the pointer to the next free buffer control block and maintains the free list anchored    */
/* at free_cb_list.                                                                                   */
void              give_bcb(BUFFER_CBP)
/* returns a buffer control block to the free list                                                    */
BUFFER_ACC_CBP get_acb()
/* returns the pointer to the next free buffer access control block and maintains the free list       */
/* anchored at free_acc_cb_list.                                                                       */
void              give_acb(BUFFER_ACC_CBP)
/* returns a buffer access control block to the free list                                             */
```

In addition, a number of service routines that are not interesting enough to be spelled out completely in C are required; they will also be introduced by their prototype declaration only.

```
Uint              hashpage(PAGEID)
/* this routine takes in a PAGEID and returns the corresponding hash class value for                 */
/* accessing the buffer_hash table. The return value is between 0 and hashsize-1.                     */
HANDLE            find_filecb(PAGEID)
/* this routine takes in a PAGEID, from which it extracts the FILEID. It searches the open file       */
 /* list for that file. If not found, the file is opened and a new control block is appended to the   */
/* list. The handle to the file is returned.                                                          */
LSN               log_max_lsn()
/* This call to the log manager returns the highest lsn currently used.                               */
```

These preparations are sufficient to present the code for the bufferfix routine; note that the access functions to the basic file system described in the previous subsection are used without further comment.

```
Boolean bufferfix(PAGEID pagein, LOCK_MODE mode, BUFFER_ACC_CBP address)
    {    Uint           hash_index;              /* hash index computed from the PAGEID          */
         BUFFER_CBP     next_bcb;                /* pointer to buffer control block              */
         FILEID         file_handle;             /* needed for the block-oriented file sys.      */
         BLOCKID        blockno;                 /* pages are read from and written to blocks    */
retry:   hash_index = hashpage(pagein);          /* determine hash class of requested page       */
         sem_get(&(buffer_hash[hash_index].class_sem),LOCK_S);
                                                 /* protect class by exclusive semaphore         */
         next_bcb = buffer_hash[hash_index].first_bcb; /* initialize search in hash chain        */
         while (next_bcb != NULL)                /* as long as there are allocated cbs ...       */
             {   if (next_bcb -> pageid == pagein)   /* is there a cb for the requested page?    */
                     { if (!sem_get_bounce (&(next_bcb -> pagesem), LOCK_S))   /* is x-sem on page?  */
                         { if (next_bcb -> frame_index = = -1)       /* page is being brought in  */
                             {sem_give (&(buffer_hash[hash_index].class_sem));    /* return class sem */
                             goto retry; } ;      /* another process reads the page, retry        */
                         }                        /* normal exclusive semaphore                   */
```

```
            else {sem_give (&(next_bcb-> pagesem));};              /* return test semaphore      */
            goto p_found;}                                         /* page is in buffer          */
        else                                                      /*                            */
            {    next_cb = next_cb -> next_in_hclass; }; /* follow hash class chain            */
    };                                                            /*                            */
/* page not in bufferpool. Before it can be read, a free frame in the bufferpool must be found  */
/* or a page must be replaced.                                                                  */
        next_bb = locate_page(pagein, hash_index);                /* get page in bufferpool     */
/* Now the requested page is in buffer and the control block for it is pointed to by next_bcb.  */
p_found: if   (mode != LOCK_FREE)                 /* caller wants a semaphore to be set         */
        {   if   (mode == LOCK_S)                 /* caller wants shared semaphore              */
                {   sem_get(&(next_bcb -> pagesem),LOCK_S); }   /* grab shared semaphore        */
            else                                                  /*                            */
                {   sem_get(&(next_bcb -> pagesem),LOCK_X);       /* grab exclusive semaphore   */
                next_bcb -> fixcount = 1;/* there is one fix on that page                        */
                if   (next_bcb -> forminlsn == MAXLSN) /* first update fix ?                     */
                    next_bcb -> forminlsn = log_max_lsn(MYLOG);
                                               /* tag page control block by curr. end-of-        */
                                               /* log of MYLOG - the log file underneath         */
                };                             /*                                                */
        };                                     /* semaphore handling complete                    */
    if   (mode == LOCK_FREE II mode == LOCK_S)     /* no exclusive semaphore requested           */
        (next_bcb -> fixcount)++;                  /* increase fix count on page                 */
/* the fields of the buffer access control block are initialized by either copying the global   */
/* values from the bcb, or by setting them to default values                                     */
        address = get_acb();                          /* allocate a new access control block    */
        address -> pageid = next_bcb -> pageid;       /*                                         */
        address -> pageaddr = &(buffer_pool[next_bcb->frame_index].page_header); /*              */
        address -> pagesem = &(netx_bcb -> pagesem); /*                                          */
        address -> index = -1;                        /*                                         */
        address -> modified = FALSE;                  /*                                         */
        address -> invalid = FALSE;                   /*                                         */
        sem_give  (&(buffer_hash[hash_index]. class_sem));                                       /*    */
        return(TRUE);     /*since there is no error checking,sample routine always succeeds      */
    };
```

The program just given contains the invocation of an ancillary subroutine called locate_page, which requests an empty buffer frame from another subroutine, get_frame. The requested page is read into this frame by locate_page, and the buffer control block is initialized. The pointer to the proper buffer control block is returned. The code of this subroutine is shown next.

```
BUFFER_CBP    locate_page(PAGEID ThisPage, Uint hash_index)
    {  BUFFER_CBP      next_bcb;              /* pointer to buffer control block      */
       RETCODE         retcode;               /* return code from subroutines         */
       int             frame_no;              /* frame number of new block            */
```

```
        sem_get (&free_cb_sem, Lock_x);              /* protect chain of free bcbs                    */
        next_bcb = free_cb_list;                     /* grab free bcb; no error handling              */
        free_cb_list = next_bcb-> next_in_hclass;    /* modify anchor                                 */
        no_free_cbs --;                              /* decrease free bcb counter                     */
        sem_give (&free_cb_sem);                     /* return bcb-chain semaphore                    */
        file_handle = find_filecb(ThisPage);         /* get the pointer to the file to read           */
        blockno = ThisPage.pageno;                   /* block number equals page number               */
        sem_get (&(next_bcb->pagesem), Lock_x);      /* protect bcb while page is not there            */
        next_bcb -> frame_index = -1;                /* indicate page is being brought in             */
/* now the new control block can be initialized                                                       */
        next_bcb -> pageid = ThisPage;               /* store number of requested page                */
        next_bcb -> in_file = file_handle;           /* remember file handle for writing              */
        next_bcb -> modified = FALSE;                /* page is not modified                          */
        next_bcb -> fixcount = 0;                    /* page was just read; fix will be applied later */
        next_bcb -> forminlsn = MAXLSN;              /* initialized to largest possible LSN           */
                                                     /* will be set to a real LSN upon update fix     */
/* now the control block is linked to the chain of the hash class                                     */
        hash_index = hashpage(ThisPage); /* compute hash class of requested page                      */
        sem_get(&(buffer_hash[hash_index].class_sem),LOCK_X); /* grab excl. sem.                      */
        if   (buffer_hash[hash_index].first_bcb == NULL)   /* if hash class is empty ...              */
            { buffer_hash[hash_index].first_bcb = next_bcb;
            next_bcb -> next_in_hclass = NULL;
            }                                        /* put pointer to new CB in hash table           */
        else                                         /* there is at least one entry in the hash class */
            { next_bcb -> next_in_hclass = buffer_hash[hash_index].first_bcb;
              buffer_hash[hash_index].first_bcb = next_bcb;
            };                                       /* make new control block first in chain         */
        sem_give (&(buffer_hash[hash_index].class_sem));   /* release class x-semaphore               */
                                                     /* paging is now protected by excl. sem on new page bcb */
        frame_no = get_frame ();                     /* get frame with page in it                     */
        retcode = read (file_handle, blockno., & (bufferpool [ frame_no]. page_header));
                                                     /* read block into frame                         */
        next_bcb -> frame_index = frame-no;          /* page is there!                                */
        sem_get (&(buffer_hash [hash_index].class_sem));   /* get S-semaphore on hash class           */
        sem_give (&(next_bcb -> pagesem));           /* release sem on new page                       */
        return (next_bcb);                           /* return control block pointer to caller        */
/* note that the semaphore on the hash synonym chain is kept; will be returned by bufferfix.          */
        };
```

The routine locate_page in turn invokes get_frame. The purpose of this subroutine is to either find an empty frame in the bufferpool or to empty one by replacing a page. It returns the template of a buffer control block that points to the frame_index of the empty frame. Note that the code for this routine is more involved than one might expect from the simple description of its task.

```
int  get_frame();
     {   BUFFER_CBP    next_bcb, temp_bcb;        /* pointer to buffer control block        */
         Uint          frame_no, hash_index;      /* number of free frame & hash index      */
         PAGEPTR       pageaddr;                   /* pointer to address in bufferpool       */
         LSN           fromlog;                    /* needed to invoke the log flush routine */
         PAGEID        pageid;                      /* pageid of replacement victim           */
         sem_get(&free_frame_sem,LOCK_X);          /* protect array of free frames           */
         if    (no_free_frames > 0)                /* are there any free frames?             */
               {    frame_no = free_frames[no_free_frames-1].free_index; /* get frame no.    */
                    no_free_frames--;              /* decrease free frame counter            */
                    sem_give(&free_frame_sem);     /* release sem. on free frame array       */
                    return(frame_no); }            /* return new frame with number           */
         sem_give(&free_frame_sem);                /* there is no unused frame in bufferpool */
         sem_get(&LRU_sem,LOCK_X);                 /* protect LRU chain                      */
         next_bcb = lru_page;                      /* start with the LRU page                */
         while    (next_bcb != NULL)               /* try the next page in the LRU chain     */
                  {    pageid = next_bcb -> pageid;  /* remember id of replac. candidate     */
                       hash_index = hashpage(pageid);  /* compute hash class of cand. page  */
                       sem_get(&(buffer_hash[hash_index].class_sem),LOCK_X); /* protect class by */
                                                    /* X semaphore                           */
                       if    (next_bcb -> pageid != pageid) /* has page been replaced?       */
                             {    sem_give(&(buffer_hash[hash_index].class_sem)); /* give up page */
                                  goto next_younger; }      /* try younger one               */
                       if    (!sem_get_bounce(&(next_bcb->pagesem),LOCK_X) || /* get sem on   */
                             next_bcb->fixcount > 0)   /* but do not wait (avoids deadlock)   */
                             {    sem_give(&(buffer_hash[hash_index].class_sem)); /* if failed to get */
                                  goto next_younger; }     /* sem or page was fixed: try younger one */
                       take control block out of LRU chain;
                       sem_give(&LRU_sem);          /* release LRU chain                      */
                       take control block out of hash synonym list;
                       sem_give(&(buffer_hash[hash_index].class_sem)); /* rel. sem. on hash cl. */
                       if    (modified)             /* does page contain updates ?           */
                             {    pageaddr = &(buffer_pool[next_bcb->frame_index].page_header);
                                                    /* determine address of page             */
                                  fromlog = log_flush(pageaddr->safe_up_to,FALSE); /*         */
                                                    /* force log up to LSN of last update    */
                                  write block back to file; } /* after log: write block (this is WAL) */
                       frame_no = next-bcb-> frame_index;   /* save index of freed frame      */
                       return freed bcb to chain of unused bcbs
                       sem_give(&(next_bcb->page_sem); /* release sem. on page                */
                       return(frame_no);           /* return cb for emptied frame            */
next_younger:          next_bcb = next_bcb->prev_in_LRU;    /* go back in LRU chain           */
     };         };                                 /* no error handling; end of routine      */
```

The routine get_frame() returns a pointer to a buffer control block that is empty except for the entry frame_index(). This entry must refer to an empty bufferpool frame into which the requested page can be read. Note that the other entries of the buffer control block need not be initialized by get_frame; the convention simply says that they do not contain relevant information.

The routine first checks the list of unused frames, that is, frames not containing valid page images. This can be the case after a transaction has been aborted. Pages modified by an aborted transaction that have not been written to disk during the transaction's lifetime are simply discarded: their control blocks are removed from both the hash synonym list and the LRU chain; the frames are marked as free.

If there are no free frames, one must be freed by replacing another page—called the *replacement victim*. The sample implementation uses the "least recently used" heuristic to determine which page to replace. To support access to the buffer control blocks in least recently used order, the active buffer control blocks are threaded together in a doubly linked list with an anchor at the beginning (mru_page) and at the end (lru_page). The latter pointer refers to the control block of the page that has not been referenced for the longest time of all pages. Once the page to be replaced has been determined, the buffer manager checks whether or not that page has been updated while in buffer (modified entry). If so, the page must be written back to its position in the file. But before that, the corresponding log entries must be on durable storage. This is achieved by calling the log_flush routine, which gets the LSN as a parameter that pertains to the most recent update in the page (safe_up_to).

The interesting aspect of get_frame is its use of semaphores. First, it tries keep the number of semaphores held simultaneously as low as possible. In most phases, it holds at most one semaphore. However, when it comes to finding a replacement victim and actually replacing it, things get a little more complicated. First, a shared semaphore on the LRU chain is needed, because the linked list is to be processed back-to-front until a page is found that no transaction currently needs, and that therefore can be replaced. The rationale behind the logic of the get_frame routine is as follows (we proceed along the LRU chain, starting with the least recently used page):

Get the pageid out of the current page under consideration. Get an exclusive semaphore on the hash class (that is, on the chain linking the hash synonyms of that pageid); the semaphore must be exclusive because the control block is going to be removed from the synonym list. Next, check if the current control block still contains the pageid that was seen there when coming via the LRU chain. This check is necessary because another instance of the buffer manager could be doing the same thing concurrently; if that invocation of get_frame is a little faster, the control block is changed next time we look at it.

This check could be made unnecessary by requesting a semaphore on the page as soon as the pointer to the control block has been obtained through the LRU chain. However, we still would need the semaphore on the hash class, and then an undesired situation would arise: the get_frame routine would request semaphores in the sequence control block first, hash class second. Now, if the bufferfix routine requests semaphores in inverse order, there would be the potential of deadlocks between these two. To avoid this, get_frame proceeds in the same order as bufferfix.

One more detail: the exclusive semaphore on the buffer control block is requested in bounce mode only. This is to say, if the page suggested by the LRU chain has another semaphore (that is, is being used by another transaction), we do not want to wait for it to become available (it would then be one of the most recently used pages anyway); rather, we consider the next-younger page from the LRU chain.

Also note that the routine does not hold a semaphore while doing I/O—except for the semaphore on the empty control block of the page that has been replaced.

13.4.2.4 Remarks on the Other Buffer Manager Routines

The remaining routines, in particular emptyfix() and bufferunfix(), are not spelled out in C because the data structures to be maintained are the same as in the bufferfix routine, and the problems with respect to synchronization via semaphores are identical.

There is one thing worth noting: changing a page's position in the LRU chain is part of the bufferunfix routine; that is, as soon as a page is unfixed, it becomes the most recently used page. This requires its control block to be removed from its current position in the linked list and reinserted as the first element, pointed to by mru_page. One might expect this to happen as part of the bufferfix routine, that is, at the moment of reference, and indeed, that would work just as well. Empirical studies indicate that the page fault rate in the buffer is the same for both schemes. The reason for picking our design is that the bufferfix routine can be kept shorter this way.

In order to change a control block's position in the LRU chain, an exclusive semaphore must be requested on LRU_sem. Again, one must be careful to avoid deadlocks. Remember that get_frame() first gets a shared semaphore on LRU_sem, then requests a semaphore on the hash synonym chain, and finally requests a semaphore on the page in bounce mode. The bufferunfix routine is invoked in a situation where a semaphore on the page is held by the client (unless bufferfix() had been called with the LOCK_FREE option). If bufferunfix() now requests a semaphore on the LRU chain, it obviously proceeds in inverse order compared to get_frame. The analysis of this situation with respect to potential deadlocks is the subject of Exercise 17.

13.4.3 Logging and Recovery from the Buffer's Perspective

In what has been described so far, the buffer manager appears to be completely autonomous in handling the incoming requests. In particular, the decision of *which* (modified) page is written back to disk *when* seems to be left to the buffer manager, which can use LRU heuristics (or something else) to potentially optimize overall system performance. If our discussion were referring to a "normal" (non-transactional) file buffer, this would be perfectly satisfactory. In a transaction system, however, the buffer manager must make sure not to violate the ACID properties; this requires some synchronization with both the log manager and the transaction manager. We do this by applying the ideas outlined in Chapter 10, Section 10.3.

According to our assumption, each page is statically mapped to a block on disk: in other words, each time the page is written back to disk after modification, the old state of that page is lost, as far as the disk block is concerned.[12] On the other hand, if a transaction modifies a page and then commits—implying its results are durable—and the buffer manager has not yet written that page to disk, a subsequent crash will leave a file system with a block containing the old (invalid) state of the page. Therefore, if the buffer manager decides to

---

[12] Of course, the underlying file system that provides the block interface is assumed not to have any transaction-oriented recovery facilities of its own.

Table 13.16: The buffer manager's role in preserving transaction atomicity and durability. The possible outcome of a transaction having updated two pages, *A* and *B*. The assumption is that the transaction has either aborted or committed, and later on the system crashes. The column at the far right indicates the state of the database after that crash. In only two out of eight cases does that database have the right contents. At the time of crash, a page is either "in buffer," or "on disk." If "in buffer," then after the crash only the (old) state is available. If "on disk," then only the (new) state is available.

State of Transaction *TA*	Page *A*	Page *B*	State of the Database
Aborted	In Buffer (Old)	In Buffer (Old)	Consistent (Old)
Aborted	In Buffer (Old)	On Disk (New)	*Inconsistent*
Aborted	On Disk (New)	In Buffer (Old)	*Inconsistent*
Aborted	On Disk (New)	On Disk (New)	*Inconsistent*
Committed	In Buffer (Old)	In Buffer (Old)	*Inconsistent*
Committed	In Buffer (Old)	On Disk (New)	*Inconsistent*
Committed	On Disk (New)	In Buffer (Old)	*Inconsistent*
Committed	On Disk (New)	On Disk (New)	Consistent (New)

write a modified page belonging to an incomplete transaction, atomicity can be violated; if it does not write the modifications of a committed transaction, durability is in jeopardy. The possible scenarios are illustrated in Table 13.16.

A transaction will eventually be in one of two states: aborted or committed. If it modifies two pages, and if there are completely autonomous replacement decisions by the buffer manager, then any of the eight constellations shown in Table 13.16 can occur. Only the first one and the last one comply with the atomicity rule in that no changed page is written in the abort case, and all of them are written in the commit case. Considering the fact that writing a single page is not an atomic operation (and writing a group of pages is even less atomic), it is obvious that the log manager must collect sufficient information during normal processing to enable the recovery component to put the database (which, after the crash, will most likely be inconsistent) back into the consistent state determined by the outcome of the transaction.

In the second case, for example, the log must contain information about the old contents of page *B* in order to overwrite the incorrect new state on disk. In the fifth case, the log must contain the *new* values of both page *A* and page *B* in order to write the result of the committed transaction to the database during restart, and so forth.

But, of course, the problem is not as simple as Table 13.16 suggests. This table shows all possible situations at one glance; complete information is given, making trivial the task of figuring out what needs to be done. In a real system, however, there is no indication of which case of the scenario has to be handled: each page in the database is a "new" page with respect to the transaction that created its current contents, and at the same time it is an "old" page from the perspective of the transaction that is going to modify it. In other words, there is no flag on the pages in the database that distinguishes old states from new states (as assumed for simplicity in the scenario). The buffer contents are also lost after a crash; even the information about *which pages* the buffer contained at the moment of the crash is not easily available.

A "brute force" approach for coping with this situation would work as follows:

Whenever a page is going to be modified (a bufferfix request with an exclusive semaphore is issued), write its old contents to the log (*old* value, or *before image*). When the page is unfixed, write its current contents to the log (*new* value or *after image*). Obviously, this creates a lot of traffic to the log. First, the usual granule of updating is a tuple or just an attribute within a tuple; writing the whole surrounding page to the log therefore includes a large amount of data that has not been modified at all. Second, new values are written even if it is unclear whether or not the transaction will eventually commit, and if a page is modified repeatedly, then a corresponding number of unnecessary intermediate old value/new value pairs are written. Let us consider the first problem for a moment.

Assume the transaction in the scenario of Table 13.16 has inserted tuples t_1 and t_2 into pages A and B, respectively. Since the other parts of the pages remain unchanged, there is no point in writing these unmodified parts to the log for the sake of being able to recover transaction *TA*. Rather, it is sufficient to remember that transaction *TA has inserted tuple t_1 into page A*, and so on. Having an entry like $\langle TA,$insert$,t_1,A\rangle$ allows recovery of transaction *TA* in both directions by one of the following:

Reapplying the operation to the page in case its version in the database does not contain the tuple, and the transaction has committed.

Applying the inverse operation to the page in case its version in the database contains the tuple, and transaction *TA* has been aborted.

Again, however, in considering just this one page, the four cases shown in Table 13.17 must be distinguished.

Table 13.17: Recovery operations applied to the wrong states of a page. If the recovery operation is not synchronized with the state of the page to be recovered, such operations generally result in an inconsistent database.

State of Transaction TA	State of Page A In Database	Result of Recovery Using Operation Log
Aborted	Old	Wrong Tuple Might Be Deleted
Aborted	New	Inverse Operation Succeeds
Committed	Old	Operation Succeeds
Committed	New	Duplicate Of Tuple Is Inserted

The table illustrates the fact that if an operation is to be applied to an operand, the operand must have the right value in order for the operation to produce a correct result. Here the assumption is that operations (together with some parameters, such as transaction identifiers and tuples) are applied to pages. Now let us look at the first row of Figure 13.17. Attempting to recover from the crash (which left transaction *TA* incomplete and having to be aborted), executed the inverse operation to the original insert. However, page *A* actually is in the old state; that is, it does not contain tuple t_1. One might think that it should be easy to check if the tuple is actually there; if not, then nothing needs to be done. But, as will be explained in the next chapter, tuples are usually identified by pointing to "the *n*th entry in that page." Clearly, in this scenario that could be a different tuple, and the recovery would leave the database in an inconsistent state. The last row of Figure 13.17 illustrates the inverse situation: here tuple t_1 is inserted into page *A*, although page *A* already contains that tuple. Again, though, given the usual mechanisms for identifying tuples, this cannot be detected locally.

The result is that in order to guarantee the correct execution of recovery actions during restart, the buffer manager and the log manager have to exchange information at run time that indicates whether a given log entry should be applied to a page in the database. The simplest way to do this is to assign a *state identifier,* or *version number,* to a page and to record with each log entry the value of the state identifier of the page to which it refers. During recovery, the state of the page found on disk can then be compared with the state recorded with the log entry. This shows whether the log entry refers to the current state of the page, to an older one, or to a more recent one.

The mechanism used for characterizing states by an unambiguous, monotonically increasing value is the log sequence number (LSN). Each entry that is added to the log gets such a number, which is higher than all LSNs issued before, and for all practical purposes it can be guaranteed that these numbers will never repeat. Since it is reasonable to assume that there is one global log per system, the LSN mechanism creates globally unique version numbers for all the objects in the database.[13]

The interplay between the buffer manager and the log manager, based on the LSN mechanism, is illustrated in Figure 13.18.

Log records are assigned their LSNs, and the state of a page *relative to the log* is documented by storing the LSN of the most recent log record generated for that page in the page header; this is the resource managers' responsibility. Of course, it is implemented by modifying the page header entry every time a new log record is created for that page. Whenever the page is written, it automatically takes the LSN of its latest log record with it. At recovery time, there is a simple way of deciding which log records need to be applied to the state of a page found on disk:

Rollback (UNDO).   Only log records with an LSN less than or equal to the page LSN need to be applied in reverse chronological order for removing a transaction's updates.

Commit (REDO).   Only log records with an LSN higher than the page LSN need to be applied in chronological order for repeating all the transaction's updates to the page.

Of course, for this method to be correct, all the relevant log records must be written to durable storage prior to overwriting the page in durable storage; this is necessary to make

---

[13] The case of multiple logs was discussed in Chapters 9 and 10.

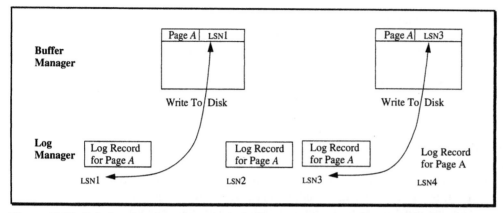

Figure 13.18: Relating the state of a page in buffer to the log records describing the updates performed on the page via the log sequence number. The state of a page on disk is recorded by storing the LSN of the most recent log record pertaining to that page every time the log manager writes the page to disk.

recovery from durable storage possible. As explained in Chapter 10 (Section 10.3), there are three rules governing the interaction between the buffer manager, the log manager, and the recovery manager that take care of these LSN dependencies: the fix rule, the write-ahead-log rule, and the force-at-commit rule. One should keep in mind, however, that these rules essentially constrain the buffer manager's autonomy of *when* to write *which* page to disk.

The previous discussion refers to the general case of buffer and log management, without any additional constraints. Some buffer managers, however, restrict themselves to a smaller class of protocols. The reason is either to simplify the implementation or to optimize system performance in special situations. The rest of this section presents some of the most relevant variations and considers their potential for large transaction systems.

13.4.3.1 Steal versus No-Steal Buffer Management

A page with modifications by a transaction that has not yet committed is a dirty page until either commit or rollback processing for that transaction has been completed. The buffer manager can either distinguish dirty pages from clean pages when deciding which page to remove from the bufferpool, or it can ignore the update status of a page. In the latter case, the buffer manager uses a *steal* policy, which means pages can be written (stolen) from the buffer even if the transaction having modified the pages is still active. The alternative is the *no-steal* policy, in which case all dirty pages are retained in the bufferpool until the final outcome of the transaction has been determined. The steal policy implies that rollback of a transaction requires access to pages on disk in order to reestablish their old state. With the no-steal policy, on the other hand, no page on disk ever has to be touched when rolling back a transaction: either a page is allowed to be written, in which case it must be clean, or it has to stay in the buffer. Consequently, no log information for UNDO purposes will be needed.[14] At first glance the no-steal policy may appear always to win, because it avoids some overhead during rollback processing; the price is, however, a bufferpool that has to be large enough for accommodating all the dirty pages of all concurrent transactions. This is

---

[14] Rolling back a transaction during normal processing is also facilitated by the no-steal policy: all pages modified by such a transaction are simply marked "invalid" by the buffer manager.

generally infeasible for long (batch) transactions. Moreover, it enforces page locking, which is a bad idea.

13.4.3.2 Force versus No-Force Buffer Management

Force versus no-force has to do with writing clean pages from the bufferpool. The simple question here is: who decides, and when, that a modified page is written to disk? There are two basic approaches:

Force policy. At phase 1 of a transaction's commit, the buffer manager locates all pages modified by that transaction (if the buffer manager employs a steal policy, some of the pages might already have been written), and writes (forces) the pages to disk.

No-force policy. This is the liberal counterpart. A page, whether modified or not, stays in the buffer as long as it is still needed. Only if it becomes the replacement victim will it be written to disk.

The force policy has an obvious advantage during restart. Since writing is initiated during commit processing, the situation after a crash is simple: if a transaction is successfully committed (indicated by a commit completion record on the log), then, by definition, all its modified pages must be on disk. Conversely, if all its pages are not on disk, then the transaction cannot be committed. In other words, the force policy avoids any REDO recovery during restart. Why not, then, use it as the standard buffer management policy? One could continue to argue as follow:

Each modified page must be written back to disk sooner or later; thus, forcing the page at commit is just fine, and even more so because forcing at commit facilitates restart. This conclusion ignores one important performance aspect, which is illustrated in Figure 13.19.

The figure focuses on just one page in the bufferpool (page *A*), which is special in that it is frequently accessed *and modified* by different transactions. Due to the high access frequency, the page is kept in buffer by the replacement algorithm for a long time. As the scenario shows, the page is written eight times, once for each transaction commit; this is what the force policy implies. With the no-force policy, the page will *not be written at all* until the buffer manager decides that it has to be replaced. Note that there is no way of trading database I/Os for log I/Os. Log records have to be written no matter what policy is used for commit processing. The reason is that the recovery manager must also be able to cope with the loss of storage media such as disks; it obviously is no help to force a transaction's updates to disk if this disk is destroyed by a head crash shortly thereafter.

Let us summarize what has been established so far. The force policy simplifies restart, because no work needs to be done for transactions that committed before the crash; that is, it avoids REDO. The price for that is significantly more I/O for pages that are modified more than once during their life span in the bufferpool. Typically, these are pages holding catalog information, access paths, address tables, and so on. As main memory sizes increase, so will the size of the bufferpool, which means more pages will stay in the buffer for a longer time. This increases the probability of multiple updates to one page and therefore makes the force policy even less attractive.

But even without considering multiple page updates, no-force is preferable over force for the following reason: forcing the pages updated by a transaction during commit processing means a sequence of fairly expensive operations (disk writes), which are *synchronous* with the commit process. In other words, the transaction will not be completed

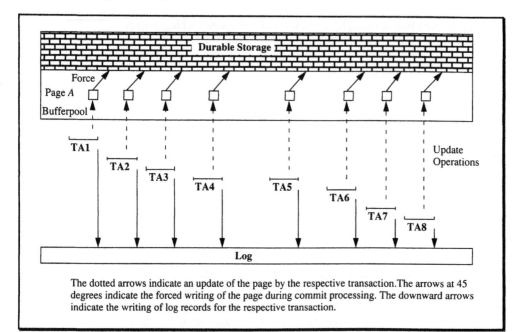

The dotted arrows indicate an update of the page by the respective transaction. The arrows at 45 degrees indicate the forced writing of the page during commit processing. The downward arrows indicate the writing of log records for the respective transaction.

Figure 13.19: The problem of "hotspot" pages. The scenario illustrates the implications of the force policy for pages that are modified at high rates by subsequent transactions without being moved out of the bufferpool in the meantime.

before the last write has been executed successfully, and response time may be increased significantly as a consequence. With no-force, the only synchronous write operation goes to the log, and the volume of data to be written is usually about two orders of magnitude less. All page writes from the buffer can be done asynchronously, and for keeping response times low it is generally desirable to design a system such that all expensive operations can be executed without anybody actually waiting for them to complete.

The argument in favor of no-force sounds plausible, but note that with the buffer manager design introduced so far, it actually is a fake argument. It is true that with the no-force policy there are no synchronous write operations from the bufferpool at commit. But with the demand paging scheme described previously, a modified page will be written as part of a page replacement operation triggered by a bufferfix request of some other transaction. Since the page requested cannot be read until the modified page has been written successfully, there is still somebody waiting synchronously for that write operation—it just is somebody else. Therefore, in order to capitalize on the performance gains through asynchronous writing that is inherent to the no-force policy, some additional measures are required. These are described in the next subsection.

Ignoring the necessity of logging for media recovery for the moment, one might think of avoiding log records entirely by combining the no-steal and the force policies. It is left as an exercise (Exercise 15) for the reader to demonstrate why this is not possible.

13.4.4 Optimizing Buffer Manager Performance

The buffer manager described previously, together with the sample implementation of some function modules, will work correctly in the sense that the interface specifications are met.

However, it will not work efficiently, except for very small databases with low transaction rates. This subsection identifies some of the major performance problems with the simple design and presents better solutions.

13.4.4.1 Checkpointing

The first group of problems follows directly from the observation that no-force is superior to force, especially if multiple updates to a single hotspot page occur. Restarting the system after a crash under the no-force policy means the following:

There is no guarantee that any page on disk contains the most recent consistent state according to the ACID paradigm. Thus, all log records pertaining to that page with a higher LSN than the disk page LSN must be reapplied to the page in chronological order before normal operation on the database can be resumed. As long as only a limited number of pages have to be recovered, this is all right. But how can these pages be identified? According to the ACID rules, log records must be applied *to all pages modified by committed transactions and not written to disk, and to all uncommitted updates written (stolen) to disk.* As Figure 13.19 (assuming a no-force policy) suggests, there can be pages which, due to their high access frequency, are never written from the bufferpool (for replacement) and in which the updates of many transactions accumulate over time. Put the other way around, the disk image of these pages will soon be very outdated. Recovering such a page at restart requires going back in the log to the disk LSN of the page.

Using no-force together with this design may imply that a page has not been written since the last startup; restart recovery may therefore have to process all the log since the previous system startup. Obviously, this is unacceptable, because the more reliable the system is (that is, the longer the interval between two subsequent crashes), the more expensive restart becomes.[15] And there is yet another, related problem: at restart, there is no information about which pages were in the bufferpool at the moment of the crash, that is, which are the candidates for recovery. Recovery must therefore assume that any page could have been in the buffer and, accordingly, consider all REDO records found in the log. Whether they actually have to be applied depends on the page LSN and the log record's LSN.

Checkpointing minimizes these problems, assuming that only a small number of pages have to be recovered to the current state during restart and assuming that pages are written from the buffer to disk at regular intervals. This guarantees that only a fixed portion of the log has to be considered for REDO purposes, independent of how long the system has been up and independent of the number of updates applied to a page in the bufferpool.

Chapter 11 describes in detail how checkpointing is orchestrated by the transaction manager, how all the resource managers registered with the transaction manager are asked to participate in a checkpoint, and how this information can be used at restart. For the current discussion, it is sufficient to consider only the two resource managers of interest in this chapter, namely the buffer manager and the log manager. The basic checkpoint algorithm works as follows:

Quiesce the system.   Delay all incoming update DML requests until all fixes with exclusive semaphores have been released. This guarantees that all pages are locally consistent, assuming all higher-level modules make proper use of the FIX-USE-UNFIX protocol.

---

[15] Keeping a log over arbitrary amounts of time also hurts performance.

Flush the buffer. Write all modified pages to disk. Note that no page is replaced in the buffer; pages are just copied to durable storage, and the modified flag is reset. Of course, the WAL protocol applies here, as usual.

Log the checkpoint. Write a record to the log, saying that a checkpoint has been generated, and force the log. If there is a subsequent crash, restart can rely on the fact that all updates that occurred before the most recent checkpoint will be on durable storage; that is, all log records that have to be applied for REDO will have LSNs higher than the checkpoint LSN.

Resume normal operation. The bufferfix requests for updates that have been delayed in order to take the checkpoint can now be processed again.

This technique definitely solves the problem of pages that stay in the buffer for a long time and receive many updates. There is still no information about which pages were in the bufferpool at the moment of the crash, which means that the entire log from the recent checkpoint has to be processed. But if checkpoints are taken at reasonable intervals (5 to 10 minutes is a typical figure), the total number of records to be processed will be within acceptable limits, unless the application is very large.

Let us analyze the performance of this checkpoint mechanism. Assume a bufferpool of 40 MB and a block length of 8 KB; the buffer therefore contains 5,000 pages. With a reasonable share of update transactions, about 50% of all pages will have been modified by the time a checkpoint is taken. The cost of writing 2,500 pages to disk depends on how this is performed. In the worst case, the buffer manager does a sequential scan through the bufferpool and writes each page that has the modified flag set. With an average access time of 15 ms per block write, the total time for taking a checkpoint is > 37 sec. In other words, the system is unavailable for more than half a minute every 5 or 10 minutes. This is not acceptable behavior.

There are some obvious ways to improve the performance of checkpoint. All the pages that have to be written to the same disk could be sorted by block numbers to decrease the amount of disk arm movement. Another option is to write to many disks in parallel, so that the elapsed time is only the maximum of what has to be written to one disk, rather than the sum over all disks. But even if all these tricks were applied (and few real database systems actually do that), checkpoints of the simple type we have described will hold up operations an unacceptably long time.

There are a number of techniques that prevent checkpoints from interrupting service. One tries to write modified pages independent of the replacement strategy, as a background activity. In that case, whenever a checkpoint is taken, there will only be few pages to write. Another technique does not quiesce the whole system. Rather, the checkpoint is taken on a page-by-page basis, spreading the activity across the checkpoint interval. Yet another technique is based on the observation that, at least with current buffer sizes, pages with high update frequencies (as shown in Figure 13.19) are rare—but they are the reason why checkpoints have to be taken in the first place. The basic idea behind indirect checkpoints is shown in Figure 13.20.

Rather than writing *pages* to the *database*, the buffer manager writes its "table of contents" to the *log*; that is, it writes the PAGEIDs of the pages stored in the bufferpool at checkpoint time. In addition, it records the modified flag, because only changed pages have to undergo recovery at restart. This tells precisely which pages must be considered for

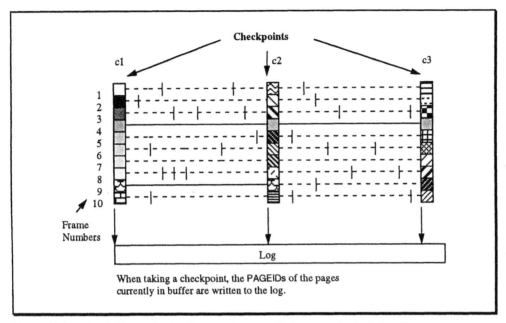

When taking a checkpoint, the PAGEIDs of the pages
currently in buffer are written to the log.

Figure 13.20: The indirect checkpointing scheme. Each texture in the buffer frames represents a different page in the buffer. The vertical bars denote page replacement in the respective frame. A heavy, solid line indicates that this page has remained in the buffer for an entire checkpoint interval.

REDO, but it does not specify how far back the log must be scanned for log records. To understand the issue, look at checkpoint c2 in Figure 13.20; ignore frames 4 and 9 for the moment. When a crash occurs between c2 and c3, the buffer manager will know at restart which pages were in the buffer at the moment of c2. If their modified flag was set, then REDO recovery may be necessary, because the buffer manager cannot tell whether any of the pages have been written to disk after c2 and before the crash.

Which log records, then, are required? Since no page is written during checkpointing, log records older than the recent checkpoint are required, too. This is the major difference from the direct checkpoint scheme. For example, the page in frame 5 has been brought into the bufferpool right before the checkpoint was taken, whereas the page in frame 2 has been in the buffer for a much longer time. The relevant range in the log varies accordingly. A simple policy would be to process all log records since the next-to-last checkpoint—c1, in this example (note that the pages in frames 4 and 9 are still being ignored). But this is a worst-case assumption, and it is fairly simple to do better than that. At each checkpoint, the buffer manager also records the low-water LSN, which is the LSN of the oldest update to a page in buffer that has not yet been written to disk. The implementation examples in Subsection 13.4.2 demonstrate how the low-water mark is determined. When a page is read into the bufferpool, the variable forminlsn in its associated control block is set to a high value (MAXLSN). When the first bufferfix request is issued for a page with an exclusive semaphore, the buffer manager assumes that it will be modified and sets forminlsn to the current LSN. Then the oldest page to be considered for REDO is the one with the minimum of all instances of forminlsn . Note that this has to be done at bufferfix time. Checking the modified flag at bufferunfix and then setting forminlsn would not work, because then the update log records describing the modifications would already have been written, and with a lower

LSN. The range of log records to be considered for REDO during restart is bounded by the buffer low-water mark.

The two special cases in frames 4 and 9 have been ignored so far. These are pages that have remained in the bufferpool for more than one checkpoint interval, and if they have been updated they are exactly the type of pages that potentially make restart very expensive. Left to themselves, they would basically freeze the low-water LSN, with all the implications that have been discussed before. Therefore, an indirect checkpointing scheme has to identify such pages and treat them separately. The obvious way to do so is to compare the buffer table of contents of two subsequent checkpoints and see if any pages have not been replaced. If so (and if the modified flag is set), write them to disk. Of course, one can also tolerate a latency of 2, 3, ... checkpoint intervals, depending on how far one is willing to go back in the log. Empirical observations show that modified pages remaining in the buffer for more than a checkpoint interval are only a small percentage of the pages that have to be written with direct checkpoints. In other words, indirect checkpoints drastically reduce the amount of time the system is in limbo for checkpoint processing.

The basic logic of indirect checkpoints can now be summarized as follows:

Record table of contents.   Write the list of PAGEIDs, flags, and so on, to the log.

Compare with previous checkpoint.   See if any modified pages have not been replaced since the last checkpoint.

Force lazy pages.   Schedule the writing of those pages during the next checkpoint interval.

Determine low-water mark.   Find the LSN of the oldest still-volatile update; write it to the log.

Write "Checkpoint done" record.   Completion of checkpoint processing is written to the log; the log is forced.

Resume normal operation.   Process all requests to the buffer manager normally.

There are many further tricks and optimizations to reduce both the range and the duration of what has to be quiesced for checkpoint processing; to discuss them, however, would involve a level of detail beyond the scope of this text. See Chapter 11, Section 11.3, for some of these tricks.

13.4.4.2 Pre-Fetching and Pre-Flushing

Pre-fetch and *pre-flush* denote a whole range of pragmatics intended to increase the amount of work that is done asynchronously by the buffer manager and by related processes in order to speed up the most important operation, the bufferfix request. Rather than going into any detail, we will just present some of the ideas behind the algorithms.

Pre-fetching tries to capitalize on locality by hypothesizing that if a transaction has accessed page i, there is a good chance that it will also access page $i + 1$ and, therefore, read it before there is a bufferfix request for it. Now this may seem like a wild guess, but especially with small page sizes, it is good way of emulating larger page sizes with significant performance improvements as MVS, Guardian, UNIX, and others have demonstrated. If the buffer manager observes the access behavior of its client transactions and has found that some transaction has requested pages $i, i + 1, i + 2,...$ or $i, i - 1, i - 2, ...$, then the hypothesis of further sequential references is well founded, and pre-fetching can be done in larger units than just pages. It is worth noting that, especially in relational databases, sequential scans of that type can be found very often; for example, for join processing or for evaluating a SELECT clause for which there is no adequate access path.

In general, pre-fetching uses heuristics of some sort to extrapolate the future reference behavior of a transaction. The better the heuristics, the higher the performance gain. But there is one case in which a fairly accurate estimate of the "future" references is possible, simply because in that situation parts of the recent history have to be repeated. Consider the restart based on indirect checkpoints, as described in Subsection 13.4.4.1. The checkpoint entry in the log specifies log records for which pages with LSNs between the low-water mark and the checkpoint have to be considered. Now, if log records are processed starting at the low-water mark during restart, the bufferpool will initially be empty, and each relevant page has to be brought in explicitly through a buffer fault. This is the worst-case scenario described for direct checkpoints.

It obviously is more efficient to "prime" the buffer by pre-fetching the pages listed in the checkpoint record before the log records are processed. For large applications, this may still not be enough. With a checkpoint interval of a couple of minutes and very high transaction rates (> 100 transactions/sec), the set of pages found in the buffer at checkpoint time and the set of pages that were actually in buffer at system crash do not have a large intersection. If this is the case, priming the buffer based on the checkpoint table of contents might turn out to be overhead, because most of the pages that are pre-fetched will be replaced by the ones actually needed.

The solution to this problem is to log all page read operations. Note that this creates only marginal overhead during normal processing, generating a few extra log records. The log records are very short, and there is no need for forcing them. This means that they just travel to the durable log with whatever is being written anyway, and the only effect is a slight increase in the data volume that goes to the log. This is how the additional information on the log is used during restart:

Get the checkpoint table of contents. Read the list of PAGEIDs; no reading of pages at that point.

Scan the log for page read records. Starting at the checkpoint, the log is scanned in chronological order until the end. Each page read record is processed by modifying the current table of contents.[16]

Prime the bufferpool. The table of contents created at the end of the scan is a precise picture of what was in the bufferpool at the moment of the crash. The pages that were only read will probably still be needed after restart (locality), and the modified ones are those for which REDO recovery has to be performed.

Of course, in each of these phases, the transaction manager does additional things, but they are not the subject of this chapter. The page read records can also be used to reduce the

---

[16] If the replacement strategy used by the buffer manager is deterministic, it can be applied in the same way during restart. If it is not, the page read records must contain additional information about which page was replaced.

duration of quiescing the system during checkpoint processing. This optimization is part of a database buffer design described by Lindsay and others in [Lindsay et al. 1979].

Pre-flushing is the technique that allows exploiting the performance potential of the no-force policy. If pages are written as part of the bufferfix operation, triggered by a replacement decision, then this is synchronous with the transaction waiting for the bufferfix to complete. If a page is written during checkpoint processing, this is synchronous with all transactions (or at least those that are blocked by the checkpoint). The idea of pre-flushing is to write a modified page at times when there is nothing else is to do and, in particular, when no activity is waiting for the page.

The basic implementation works as follows: there is a process (or a group of processes, depending on the number of CPUs around the same main memory) that can access the bufferpool but work independent of the "main line" buffer manager. This process monitors the age of modified pages in the bufferpool; the age is measured by the difference between the page's value in forminlsn and the current LSN. Pages falling behind a defined threshold are asynchronously written by the housekeeping process. Of course, the process must acquire an exclusive semaphore on the pages it wants to write.

Pre-flushing modified pages is a typical background activity. However, if the priority of the process is too low (and the bufferpool is too large), pages might still age faster than they are flushed from the buffer. Then the system will be back in a state where most page replacements result in a synchronous write. Of course, whenever a page is written, its forminlsn entry in the buffer access control block is reset to MAXLSN.

13.4.4.3 Cooperation with Transaction Scheduling

In relational systems using non-procedural DML, the access plan generated by the compiler and the optimizer contains a fair amount of information about the reference pattern that will be generated by a transaction. Some hints of that category are:

This relation will be scanned sequentially.

This is a sequential scan of the leaves of a B-tree.

This is the traversal of a B-tree, starting at the root.

This is a nested-loop join, where the inner relation is scanned in physically sequential order.

Assuming there were a way of communicating these hints to the buffer manager, how could it exploit them?

Consider the start of a sequential scan of a relation. According to the simple design presented in this chapter, a buffer manager processes bufferfix requests one by one and does not consider any dependencies between them. Thus, if a transaction starts to read page i, then page $i + 1$, and so forth, the following effect will be observed (independent of pre-fetching): in general, the buffer manager uses LRU or some other age-dependent replacement strategy. For the moment, let us assume LRU. Then the page that was read most recently along the sequential scan will be at the top of the LRU chain. The requesting module processes the page and then requests the next one, which in turn becomes the most recently used page. The previous page, although it will definitely not be used again by that transaction, will remain in buffer for quite a while, slowly percolating down the LRU stack.

After a while, the buffer will be cluttered with "useless" pages, thereby increasing the fault rate for the other transactions. A sequential scan of a file might read 40 MB in a minute, thereby completely confusing the least recently used algorithm.

So if the buffer manager is informed by its client about a sequential scan (or if it detects sequential behavior by itself), it must make sure to not use the standard LRU replacement strategy. There are two options how to do this. One is to basically stick with LRU replacement but to "age" pages more quickly if they have been read as part of a sequential scan. The other one is to allocate buffer space not globally—as was assumed so far—but to give each client a share of the the total bufferpool that is adequate for its current reference pattern. In case of the sequential scan, it would be sufficient to give one or two frames to the access module doing the scan; within these two frames, the sequentially referenced pages can simply replace each other.

The latter idea can be extended to other reference patterns. Assume a join where the inner relation is small—say, 10 pages. The query optimizer has decided to do a nested loop join, where for each tuple of the outer relation the inner relation is scanned in physically sequential order. This is fine if the small relation fits into the buffer completely: each page of the buffer must be read once and then is available in the bufferpool for the rest of join processing. But now consider Figure 13.21.

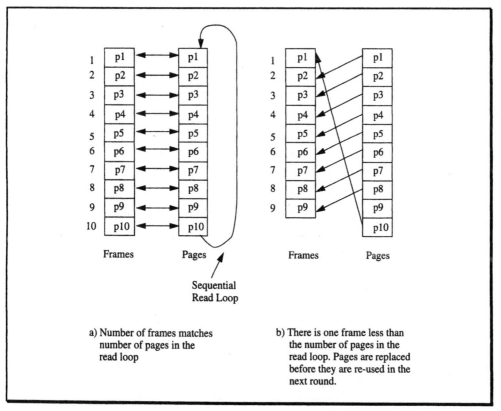

a) Number of frames matches number of pages in the read loop

b) There is one frame less than the number of pages in the read loop. Pages are replaced before they are re-used in the next round.

Figure 13.21: Buffer replacement in support of nested-loop joins. For pages referenced in sequential order in a loop, the loss of just one buffer frame can result in a 100% page fault rate in the bufferpool.

The left side of Figure 13.21 shows the good case: pages are read once and stay in buffer. The right side of the figure describes the scenario in which there is one less frame available for that transaction than the total size of the inner relation. Assuming LRU, the interesting observation is that the page fault rate in the read loop now is not "a little higher" than in the first case; it may go up to 100%. As the figure shows, after 9 pages have been referenced, page p10 is requested. This causes the least recently used page, p1, to be replaced. If, according to the nested-loop pattern, p1 is referenced next, it creates a page fault and effectively replaces p2, because this is the least recently used page, and so on. Clearly, without additional measures on part of the buffer manager for supporting special reference patterns, the resulting performance would be poor.

The general conclusion can be put as follows: whenever the type of reference pattern is known in advance, and if the number of frames required for that pattern can be estimated with reasonable precision, this information should be communicated to the buffer manager. If the buffer manager cannot reserve the required number of frames for that transaction (like the 10 frames in the example above), then processing of the transaction should be delayed. This will yield bad response time for that transaction, but otherwise the page fault rate in the buffer would increase globally, and everybody would observe bad response times. This is the basic idea behind the "hot set" model described in Sacco and Schokolnick [1986].

13.4.4.4 Reducing Administration Overhead

The sample implementation of parts of the bufferfix operation demonstrates the hidden cost that is caused by buffer management. A number of tables and administrational data structures need to be maintained, there must be some kind of space allocation, and most of these maintenance functions access shared data structures. Consequently, semaphores must be used very carefully, because otherwise the bufferfix and bufferunfix calls would create tremendous bottlenecks in the system.

Now this implementation contains almost no optimizations. The only data structure that is not mandatory for the buffer manager to work correctly is the LRU chain. Its purpose is to make a "good" guess of which page to replace in case a frame must be emptied, and empirical studies show that among all heuristics that do not exploit knowledge about the future reference behavior (see Subsection 13.4.4.3), LRU is fairly close to the optimal page fault rate. In other words, it is desirable to have something like an LRU replacement strategy in the buffer manager.

But if you consider the implementation, there is also an undesired effect. To maintain the pages in reference order, the LRU pointers of the respective control blocks must be updated for each reference. Since these are updates, they must be protected by exclusive semaphores. Assume there are three pages, which are very frequently read by many concurrent transactions. The pages themselves only need to be protected by shared semaphores, because the transactions just read them. However, each read operation moves the page to the top of the LRU chain, which means three pointers must be modified—under the protection of an exclusive semaphore. Even though the pointer readjustment is not a long piece of code, the fact that the control blocks of some of the most popular pages are exclusively held very frequently (even though the pages are simply read, which can go on at arbitrary levels of concurrency) causes a potential problem, which becomes more serious as machines get faster.

For the virtual memory manager of an operating system, this problem is much more serious. From his perspective, each instruction is a reference (the equivalent to a **bufferfix** operation), so there is obviously no way he can maintain an LRU chain unless this would magically be done by the hardware. Operating systems instead use a scheme that has a performance similar to LRU, but is much cheaper to implement. It is usually called *clock algorithm* or *second chance*. It works as follows (we use the buffer manager terminology).

The frames are assumed to be in cyclic order. This is simple to achieve; just order them by frame numbers and let the first one follow the last in the sense of modulo-addressing. The page in each frame has a reference bit that is set to TRUE each time a bufferfix operation is executed for that page. There is one central pointer, *P*, that points to a frame; let it point to frame *f* at the moment. This, by the way, is the frame out of which the most recent replacement was done.

Now assume a page has to be replaced. Pointer *P* is advanced "clockwise," which is to say it is set to (*f* + 1 mod buffersize). Then the reference bit of the page in that frame is examined. Ignoring the case of empty frames without a page in them, these are the rules defining the clock algorithm:

Bit set.   Clear reference bit and advance pointer.

Bit cleared.   Replace page in that frame.

Obviously, this strategy is much simpler than LRU, and it requires no exclusive semaphore on administrative data structures for page references. One might object that now the pointer *P* is a potential hotspot, but this is not the case. First, it is moved only for page replacement, not at every reference. And second, the update can be done with one CSW operation.

It is interesting to reconsider the optimization proposals in Subsection 13.4.4.2 from this perspective. Since they exploit more information, more data have to be gathered at run time, which might lead to more complicated data structures and more contention. It therefore requires careful analysis and measurement to find out if a clever strategy to predict the future references really gains anything, or if the data structures for its implementation just cause more conflicts among concurrent transactions.

For large database bufferpools (> 100 MB) any heuristic support might be unnecessary. Empirical studies [Effelsberg and Haerder 1984] show that beyond a certain buffer size, the locality set becomes so large that random replacement works just as well as any heuristic strategy. So future database systems will probably adopt that method, which alleviates the need to maintain any data to support the replacement decision. This minimum cost replacement combined with asynchronous pre-fetching and pre-flushing, plus some hints about the working set size of a transaction that can be determined at compile time (and therefore need minimum maintenance at run time), will keep the page fault rate at a tolerable level even for very large databases. On the other hand, one can argue that the clock algorithm is just as simple as random replacement, but it has better worst-case behavior.

13.5 Exotics

As mentioned in the beginning of this chapter, a large variety of methods exists for moving data back and forth between main memory and external storage. Since the majority of current (transaction processing) systems uses the read-write technique, all the others have been relegated to the exotics section. This does not mean they are generally inferior or less suited for transaction processing; with new storage technologies, the picture may change significantly.

The various techniques to be considered here have tried to improve on different aspects of simple read-write files, depending on what the designers thought to be important. There are two categories that have received particular attention.

The first category has to do with the issues of atomicity and error recovery. As noted before, writing a block to disk is not an atomic operation, and making each individual write atomic is unacceptably expensive. Consequently, the state of the database after a crash must be considered incorrect with respect to all integrity constraints with a scope larger than one page, and a crash may even leave blocks on disk unreadable. A whole family of techniques subsumed under the name of *side file* tries to avoid the unpleasant consequences of the block write interface, thereby making recovery simpler, at least at the conceptual level.[17]

The second category has already been mentioned in the introduction to this chapter: the single-level store. With new machine architectures using long (64-bit) addresses, this concept might become much more important than it is now. A brief discussion of the pros and cons is therefore presented here.

13.5.1 Side Files

The name *side files* conveys the basic, simple idea: objects are not modified "in place"; rather, the new value is written to a new location that was previously unused. As long as the transaction having performed the updates has not yet committed, the old object versions are available at their old locations. Consequently, nothing needs to be done in case the transaction aborts or the system crashes. Since all updates are written "to the side," a failure interrupting a block write cannot cause any problems, because the old version is still available in a different location. At commit time, all references to the old object versions must be replaced by references to the new ones. The critical problem is how to make this transition from the old object versions to the new versions atomic. It needs to be atomic, of course, because otherwise some of the objects modified by a transaction could be referenced in their new states, while the others are still in their old states—a violation of the isolation property.

Put in this brief way, the idea sounds rather vague and not simple at all; several questions are raised: What is an object? What is a reference to an object? How can the new location be determined? And so on. But at the level of the block-oriented file system, things can be kept quite easy. This the list of requirements to be met when applying the side file idea to the block-oriented file system:

Update. A modified block is never written back to the slot it was read from. Rather, it is written to an empty slot in the side file. Conventional file systems, in contrast, do "update in place."

Versioning. After the new version of a block has been written to the new slot, both the old and the new version are kept available. The duration of that depends on which particular side file technique has been chosen (see below).

---

[17] There are systems such as Rdb which use side files as a means to support versions (time domain addressing). That aspect is not considered in this chapter.

Addressing.   Because of versioning, there needs to be an explicit mapping of the block numbers used at the file system interface to the slot numbers on disk. Note that with the basic file system described at the beginning of this chapter, this mapping is a static 1:1 relationship. The side file concept, however, implies that a block due to updates is stored in a different slot than before. In particular, while there are two versions, two different slot numbers are associated with one block number. This is illustrated in Figure 13.22.

Propagation.   At some point, the new version of the block becomes the only (current) version, which means the old version is given up. As was pointed out, this must happen in an atomic, recoverable way.

The problem of mapping block numbers to slot numbers is closely related to the problem of choosing empty slots for modified blocks. Let us gradually develop a solution by proceeding from a very simple and inefficient approach to a more elaborate one. For simplicity, assume two files, as in Figure 13.22: the original file and the side file. Of course, at the read-write interface there is only *one* file, but its implementation uses two sets of slots, which are referred to by these names.

13.5.1.1 A Simplistic Approach to Using Side Files

The naive method works as follows: each block read operation first looks in the side file to check if the most current version of the block is there. If not, it must be in the original file, from which it is read. For both files, there must be a mechanism that determines which slot

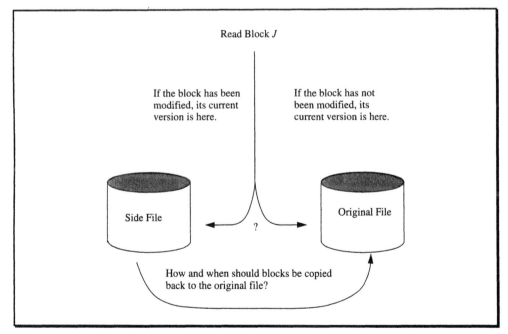

Figure 13.22: Addressing blocks using the side file concept.   With the side file technique, each block can be stored either in one slot on disk (its home slot in the original file), or in two slots (the old version in its home slot, the new version in a slot of the side file). For good performance, it is critical to have a fast way of deciding where to look for a requested block.

to look in for a given block; for the moment, it is sufficient to assume that some such address translation is done. The block write operation must distinguish two cases: if the block was read from the original file (which means there was only one version of the block), a free slot in the side file is found, and the block is written to that slot. If the block was already in the side file, it is rewritten to this very same slot—the number of versions per block never exceeds two.

After a while, the contents of the side file are copied to the original file; the side file is empty after that. This process of copying the new block versions needs some additional remarks. First, it must be done in regular intervals in order to avoid too large a discrepancy between the original and the side file. Note that in case of a crash, the side file is thrown away, and restart begins with what is in the original file. On the other hand, copying should not be done too frequently, because it is expensive. Thus, the copying interval basically is determined by load balancing considerations, weighing the overhead during normal processing against the risk of higher expenses at restart. Second, copying can only be done with an action-consistent database, because each update action potentially affects more than one block, and it must be guaranteed that a consistent state is copied to the original file.[18] The virtues that this has for logging and recovery are described in Chapter 10. Third, copying the side file can be made atomic simply by repeating it in case it should get interrupted by a crash (copying blocks is an idempotent operation).

There is a little twist here: most of the time, the side file has to be thrown away after a crash. Only if the crash happened while copying the sidefile to the original must the process be repeated. Hence, there must be a way to recognize at restart that copying was in progress. Exercise 20 asks the reader to design an algorithm that makes the copy process crash resistant and, thereby, truly atomic.

13.5.1.2 The Differential File Algorithm

Differential files are an implementation of the side file concept that is very close to the simplistic approach just outlined. But while the first method requires two block read operations for all blocks that are not in the side file (and, given the periodic emptying of that file, the majority of blocks at any given instant are in the original file only), the differential file algorithm uses an elaborate scheme to decide whether or not a block is in the side file at all. It is based on probabilistic filters and works as follows (see Figure 13.23).

There is a bit vector M maintained by the differential file manager, which contains a "large" number of bits compared to the number of blocks that are modified on the average between two subsequent copies of the side file to the original file. Assume the vector has $m = 10^5$ bits. After the side file has been copied successfully, the bit vector is set to FALSE. In addition to that, there is a set of hashing functions that take a block number as a parameter and produce an integer between 1 and m as a result. The actual number of hashing functions depends in a nontrivial way on the update frequency and the length of the copy interval. For the present discussion, it is sufficient to assume hash functions H_1 through H_f.

Now consider block j, which gets modified for the first time since the side file was last copied. The write block operation puts the block into a slot of the side file. Furthermore, for

---

[18] In principle, one could copy at any time. But then the side file concept would achieve the same inconsistent database states after a crash as a conventional file system, so there would be no point in paying the higher costs of keeping a side file.

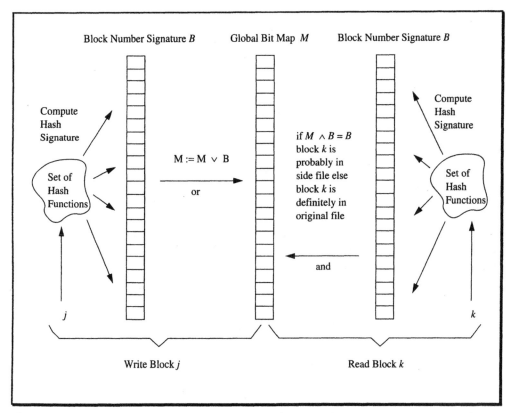

Block Number Signature *B*   Global Bit Map *M*   Block Number Signature *B*

Compute
Hash
Signature

Compute
Hash
Signature

$M := M \vee B$

or

if $M \wedge B = B$
block *k* is
probably in
side file else
block *k* is
definitely in
original file

Set of
Hash
Functions

Set of
Hash
Functions

and

j

k

Write Block *j*   Read Block *k*

Figure 13.23: Block addressing with the differential file method. Whenever the new version of a block is written to the side file, its block number is turned into a binary signature by means of a set of hashing functions. The central bitmap *M* collects all signatures of all modified blocks. When reading a block, its signature is compared to *M*; if not all bits of the signature are set in *M*, the block cannot be in the side file.

each of the hash functions, the following assignment is made (*j* still denotes the number of the modified block): $M[H_i(j)] = \text{TRUE}$.

It should be easy to see what that does. As shown in Figure 13.23, the hash functions applied to the block number define another bit vector, *B*, of length *m*, in which those bits are set to TRUE, whose index is the result of one of the hash functions. *B* is referred to as the signature of block *j*. The operation makes sure that all bits set in *B* are also set in *M*, which formally is a bit-wise disjunction of *M* and *B*. *M* thereby accumulates the signatures of all modified blocks.

The rest is straightforward. If a block *k* is to be read, the addressing issue comes up: is its current version in the side file, or is there only one version in the original file? To decide that, the signature of *k* is computed, using the hash functions. Then the conjunction of the signature *B* and *M* is determined. If the result is equal to the signature—that is, if all its set bits are also set in *M*—then block *k* has *probably* been written to the side file. One cannot be sure for the following reason: the bits in *M* corresponding to the bits in *k*'s signature have been set either by block *k* being written to the side file, or by a number of other blocks whose signature bits happen to cover those of *k*'s signature being written. On the other hand, if some bits of B are not set in M, then it is clear that k's signature has not been ORed to M, which means block k is in the original file only.

Apart from the CPU cycles required to compute the signatures and make the comparisons, then, the only access overhead here is due to read accesses to the side file for blocks that, in fact, do not have a new version there. Mathematical analysis shows that, for reasonable assumptions with respect to update frequencies, length of copy intervals, and so on, the probability of such useless accesses to the side file can be kept in the 10% range.

13.5.1.3 The Shadow Page Algorithm

Even if the number of unnecessary read operations can be kept low, the differential file technique as described in Subsection 13.5.1.2 suffers from a major performance penalty: the necessity to explicitly copy the side file back into the original file causes a large amount of additional I/O, and because of the requirement to copy action-consistent states only, there can be no update actions during the copy process. The shadow page algorithm tries to overcome that problem to a certain degree. It still uses the basic idea of writing changed blocks "to the side," but there is no longer a static distinction between side file and original file. Rather, there is only one block-oriented file, and each slot in that file can be in any of three states:

Empty. Currently, the slot holds neither an old nor a new version of a block, so it can serve as a side file slot if required.

Current block image. The slot contains the version of a block for which no update has been performed recently. At the moment, therefore, the slot is part of what was called the original file.

New block image. The slot contains the updated version of a block for which the old version exists in some other slot.

Again, the role of slots can change dynamically. This obviously requires some additional data structures to keep track of which block is where and the contents of each slot. The following paragraphs give a brief description of the approach taken in the shadow page algorithm (see Figure 13.24).

As Figure 13.24 shows, the mapping between block numbers and slot numbers is done via the *page table*. It is an array with one entry per block[19] of the file; each entry contains the number of the slot that holds the current image of the respective block. If the block has not yet been allocated, the entry contains a NULL pointer. The slots are organized as an array, using a fixed or extent-based allocation scheme as described for the basic file system. In addition, there is a bitmap with one bit per slot, indicating whether or not the corresponding slot currently holds a block image or not. In other words, a slot is marked "free" in the bitmap if its number does not occur in an entry of the page table. Both the page table and the bitmap are stored in reserved slots on disk.

---

[19] Note that the data structure is called *page table,* although it is indexed by the block number. This should not cause confusion, because we use the terms *page* and *block* interchangeably. But since the literature on the shadow page algorithm calls the data structure for address mapping *page table,* we use the same term.

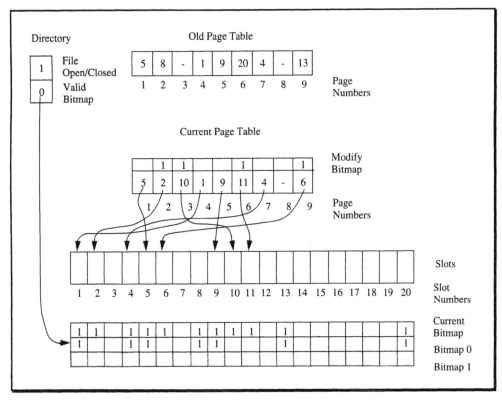

Figure 13.24: The shadow page algorithm. The algorithm uses a level of indirection between block numbers and slot numbers. The page table is indexed by the block number and contains the number of the slot holding the current image of the page. Since two versions of the page table are kept until the next globally consistent state is reached, any block writes to new slots can be rendered undone by simply returning to the old version of the page table, which contains no references to the new slots. The same two-version scheme is applied to a bitmap that says which slots are free and which are taken.

A file using the shadow page scheme is either closed for update (which means that no write operations are allowed on it), or it is open for update. Its current state is recorded in a data structure called *directory* in Figure 13.24; this data structure is part of the file descriptor explained in this chapter. A file that is closed for update always is in an action-consistent state; after it has been opened for update, it can be closed again only when an action-consistent state is reached. The time between opening the file for update and closing it again is called an *update interval*.

Let us now assume a file that is is about to be opened for update. There is one instance of the page table and one instance of the bitmap consistently describing the allocation of blocks to the slots. The file is marked as "closed" in the directory. When a file is opened, a complete copy of the current (action-consistent) state of the page table is first written to another reserved area on disk (this is called *old page table* in Figure 13.24). The bitmap is copied into main memory; this can be done even for very large files. The in-memory version is called *current bitmap* in Figure 13.24. As a last step, the file is marked as open for update; this means toggling the corresponding bit in the directory and writing the directory back to disk in an atomic fashion, using the stable write method described in Chapter 4.

While the file is open, the current page table, which is the one used to actually translate block numbers into slot numbers, is augmented by an additional data structure with one bit per entry of the page table. Initially, all bits are are set to FALSE; as soon as the corresponding block is modified, the bit is set to TRUE. This is how the data structure keeps track of which blocks have been modified (and thus relocated to a new slot) during the current update interval.[20] Whether this data structure, which is called *modify bitmap* in Figure 13.24, is kept as a separate array or whether the bits are sub-entries of the page table entries makes no difference.

Let us now assume the following declarations:

BLOCKID	block_no, slot_no;	/* since the shadow page algorithm turns	*/
		/* block numbers into slot numbers, two	*/
		/* names for the same concept are needed	*/
BLOCKID	current_page_table [LARGE];	/* page table as described above	*/
Boolean	modify_bit_map [LARGE];	/* tags modified blocks	*/
FILEID	this_file;	/* name of a file	*/
BLOCKP	to, from;	/* buffer for one block	*/

A block read operation with a given block_no is effectively executed as a slot read operation of the following type:

```
read (to, this_file, current_page_table [block_no])
```

The block write operation has to go through some additional logic:

```
if    (! modify_bit_map [block_no])
      {    slot_no = get_free_slot;
           current_page_table [block_no] = slot_no;
           modify_bit_map [block_no] = TRUE;
      };
      write (from, this_file, current_page_table [block_no]);
```

Here, get_free_slot is a routine that delivers the number of a free slot and sets the corresponding bit in the current bitmap to mark it as taken. Thus, a block is written to a new slot after the *first time* it is modified within an update interval. All subsequent modifications of the block are written to the same new slot. Figure 13.24 shows the contents of the data structures after the blocks with block numbers 2, 3, 6, and 9 have been modified.

Now, how is action consistency in the presence of crashes achieved with the shadow page algorithm, given the fact that the blocks of the file, as well as the blocks containing the page table, are physically written according to some buffer replacement policy, and that an update action typically changes more than one block?

First, consider the case of a crash in the middle of an update interval. Upon restart, the file directory, which says the file was open for update when the crash occurred, is read. Recovery can then be performed by executing the following steps:

---

[20] Actually, the shadow page algorithm assumes two bits per block number for this additional data structure, the second one noting whether the new value of the block has already been propagated to the archive log file. This is ignored in our discussion.

Restore page table. The "old page table" is copied into the location of the current page table, thereby restoring the block number mapping at the beginning of the update interval. This step is idempotent.

Restore bitmap. Nothing needs to be done, because the current bitmap was entirely kept in main memory.

Change directory. The directory switch is set to "closed for update," and the corresponding block is written using a stable write operation.

As a result, the file is returned to the state it was in at the beginning of the update interval. Note that the contents of the modified blocks are not actually removed from the new slots they were mapped to; restoring the page table and the free space bitmap simply makes sure these new slots do not correspond to any valid block number and are marked free.

There are two reasons why, after a certain number of block changes, the update interval must be completed: First, the amount of work lost in case of a crash must be contained; and second, the system should avoid running out of free slots. Closing a shadow page file for update has to be an atomic action. This is to say that either all updates applied to it during the update interval must be correctly mapped to disk, or the file has to return to the state at the beginning of the update interval by means of the procedure just sketched; there is no other way to guarantee an action-consistent file in the presence of system crashes. The steps required to close a shadow file atomically are almost mirror images of the steps executed at restart after a crash:

Force block bufferpool. All modified blocks that have not yet been written to their new slots are forced to disk.

Force page table. All blocks of the current page table that have not been written to their place on disk are forced. Note that the old page table remains unchanged.

Force bitmap. After successful completion of the update interval, the slots containing the old images of changed blocks must be given up. In other words, the bitmap describing the overall new state of the file must mark them as free. As a result, the entries in the current bitmap corresponding to old block images must be set to 0 before writing the current bitmap to disk. This can be done efficiently using an ancillary data structure, which, for simplicity, is not introduced here. The key point is that the contents of the current bitmap do not overwrite the bitmap on the disk from which they were loaded at open time. Which disk the contents were loaded from is noted in the directory. As Figure 13.24 shows, there are two bitmaps on disk, bitmap 0 and bitmap 1, written in an alternating fashion. If the variable valid_bit_map indicates the bitmap used at open time, the current bitmap is written to the other bitmap, that is, the one with index (1 <u>exor</u> valid_bit_map).

Change directory. The entry valid_bit_map is set to the alternate value to point to the new valid free space bitmap; the file switch is set to closed. The directory block is written using a stable write operation.

It is easy to see that all the updates performed during the update interval will not take effect until the last step has been successfully executed. If anything goes wrong along the way, the restart procedure takes the file back to the previous state. Thus, the problem of writing a large number of modified blocks to disk atomically is reduced to writing one block (the directory) to disk atomically; this is what the stable write mechanism does. But the basic idea is the same for all the data structures involved: as long as the state transition to the new consistent state has not been completed, there must be a copy with the old (consistent) values in some other place on disk; hence, the name of the shadow page algorithm.

13.5.1.4 Summary of Side File Techniques

As explained in Chapter 10, side file techniques, and the shadow page mechanism in particular, allow logical logging at the level of, say, SQL commands. Side files provide an action-consistent database on disk even after a crash, which, in turn, means writing sets of pages in a pseudo-atomic manner. Consequently, each side file mechanism comes with a crash recovery mechanism that guarantees action consistency; based on that mechanism, a logical logging scheme can then do transaction-oriented recovery. Despite the elegance and compactness of logical logging, with current disk and memory technology, that technique cannot make up for the inherent disadvantages of side files. Let us summarize the salient points of the problems of side files in large databases, using shadow paging as an example.

First, there needs to be a page table that translates block addresses into slot addresses. For large files, these tables cannot be guaranteed to fit completely into main memory. As a result, they are read and written on a per-block basis, thus increasing the average cost of a block read operation. Second, reallocating blocks upon modification destroys data locality (clustering of data on disk), thereby increasing the number of (expensive) random block I/Os. And third, the necessity of periodically closing the file to get rid of shadows and to definitively install the new versions of blocks adds significantly to the cost of normal processing. Note that closing a file (and reopening it) as just described effectively creates a checkpoint. However, since the purpose of the file organization is to create an action-consistent version on disk, this is a *direct* checkpoint, requiring all modified blocks, all modified portions of the page, and the whole bitmap to be forced to disk. This creates a flurry of synchronous I/O activity, and the file is down for update operations during that period. All things considered, these drawbacks outweigh the advantages of logical logging.

13.5.2 Single-Level Storage

The notion of single-level storage was sketched briefly in the beginning of this chapter. It extends the idea of a virtual address space as it can be found in all modern operating systems in the following way: the operating systems' virtual storage extends the amount of *main memory* a process can use to the maximum address that a machine instruction can have; in a 32-bit architecture, this sets a limit of 4 GB. Single-level storage both generalizes and modifies this concept of virtualization in two important ways:

Durable storage.   Rather than just making main memory appear larger than the system's actual physical main memory, the virtual address space comprises everything: files, programs, libraries, directories, databases—you name it. All these things are given their portions of the virtual address space and thus can be unambiguously referred to by a virtual address. This is why only a single (level) storage is needed.

Shared address space.   Address spaces of 2^{32} bytes are too small to hold everything on a system. Removing this boundary by using longer addresses creates another problem:

once objects are given a fixed address in a large address space, process address spaces must, in principle, be shared rather than disjoint, as they are in current operating systems. As was mentioned in Chapter 2, there is a way of selectively sharing address spaces by requesting that certain segments of address space *A* be mapped to the same portion of physical memory as a corresponding segment of another address space *B*. But clearly this is a kludge and has nothing to do with a shared virtual address space. The single-level store is inherently shared, simply because everything is in it. Since all processes (potentially) can create any address in that global address space, all things in that storage are (potentially) shared. The question of which processes are allowed to access which portion of the storage is thus decoupled from the addressing mechanism; this is an issue of access control and security, just like file access control in conventional systems.

The most obvious implication of single-level storage is that the distinction between main memory and external storage is blurred in the sense that everything appears to be data structures in the (virtual) main memory. The most obvious question is how that can be made to work efficiently.

This being the "exotics" section, we will not enter a detailed discussion of all the topics involved. Rather we present the main points of a commercially available implementation of the single-level storage, using IBM's AS/400 system as an example.

Figure 13.25, which is borrowed from Clark and Corrigan [1989], shows the major ingredients of the single-level storage scheme in the AS/400. At the center lies the (single-level) virtual storage, which defines the scope of the system's world. Virtual addresses at the user level are 64 bits long. The operating system and the underlying hardware are designed to provide the user with an object-oriented environment.[21] Consequently, the virtual storage contains *objects*, which, loosely speaking, means code and data encapsulated into a named entity. Note that objects are not addressed like ordinary (passive) data; rather, they are referenced by invoking one of the *methods* (services) they implement. To implement a service, an object can employ other objects, and so on. Typical objects are *files*, which consist of data made accessible by the operations allowed for the respective file type. User *programs* (applications) can be viewed as objects, too. They typically support one method: execute. A database relation is an object, exporting SQL operations. An account is an object, which supports the methods create, debit, credit, inquire, delete, and a few more; it probably uses the relation object for its implementation. This should be enough to get the idea.

So the system at the user level provides basic services to create objects. At the moment of creation, an object is permanently mapped into virtual storage. That means it is assigned a contiguous portion of the address space, in which all its data and the code will reside. Figure 13.25 shows two examples. Another class of services allows access to an object, that is, to execute one of its methods. To do that, the system loads the portion of virtual storage given to the object into main memory and starts executing at the appropriate location. So essentially, all the virtual storage is kept on durable storage and is transparently paged in and out by the system on demand. The entire main memory serves as a buffer for the virtual storage maintained on disk.

---

[21] If you are not familiar with the ideas of object orientation, you do not have to stop reading now. The explanations of the storage handling mechanisms should still be understandable. However, a certain understanding of object-oriented systems is required to appreciate the consequences of such a machine architecture. An explanation is beyond the scope of this book.

At the user level, each object is identified by an MI (machine interface) pointer containing its virtual address. Special hardware support makes sure that such pointers can only be used for addressing; they can neither be read nor manipulated at the user level. This will be explained in more detail in a minute.

Of course, inside the object, in the code implementing the methods, the same virtual address space is visible. All addresses used here refer to the portion of address space assigned to the object at creation time. At run time, these addresses must be converted into real memory addresses. The mechanisms to do that are similar to the dynamic address translation used in operating systems to convert virtual into real addresses. This part of the implementation is referred to as *CPU addressing mechanism* in Figure 13.25.

External storage management is the component that maps the virtual storage space onto the external storage devices, that is, onto the set of blocks available on disk. It is the only system component to issue read and write operations at the block level. Consequently, it is also responsible for allocating disk space to new objects—note that for each virtual address in use, there must be a place on disk to which it is mapped to. Free space management is done using a binary buddy scheme like the one described in Subsection 13.3.2. The translation of virtual addresses into disk block addresses relies on directories, which are implemented as search trees similar to the B-tree scheme that is explained in detail in Chapter 15.[22] Every time an object is referenced after some time of inactivity (that is to say, when it is not in main memory), its MI pointer is dereferenced using the search tree structure. From then on, of course, address translation is much faster because translation look-aside techniques are used. (As an aside: the buffer hash table used for the sample implementation of the bufferfix operation is the software version of a hardware translation look-aside buffer.)

External storage management also tries to balance the load on disk by judiciously assigning space to new objects. For small objects (≤ 32 KB), the disk is chosen by a randomized round-robin scheme. For larger objects, the disk with the largest percentage of free blocks is chosen. Apart from that, the disks can be divided into separate pools such that certain objects can only be allocated in certain pools. This allows the system administration to keep objects with a high amount of sequential traffic, such as the log, on their own disks, preventing the disk arm from being moved back and forth by other object references, which would deteriorate the log performance.

An optional feature of the external storage manager is storing parity information of disk blocks on other disks, thus allowing the reconstruction of any broken disk from the other disks—a technique that has come to be called RAIDS [Patterson, Gibson, and Katz 1988]. The basic idea is to combine the blocks of n disks by the exclusive or function and store the result on the $(n + 1)$ disk. In this system, n ranges from 3 to 7. Similar concepts are used in disk arrays to improve availability.

Main memory management interfaces real memory to external storage. Its basic strategy is demand paging combined with an LRU replacement scheme, much like the buffer management algorithms described in this chapter. It also applies some of the optimizations mentioned, namely:

---

[22] The AS/400 obviously uses a tree variety called *binary radix tree* rather than multi-way search trees. But since these binary trees are balanced at the page level, the difference is negligible for the present purposes. Readers interested in the whole story are referred to Chapter 15 and to the literature that goes with it.

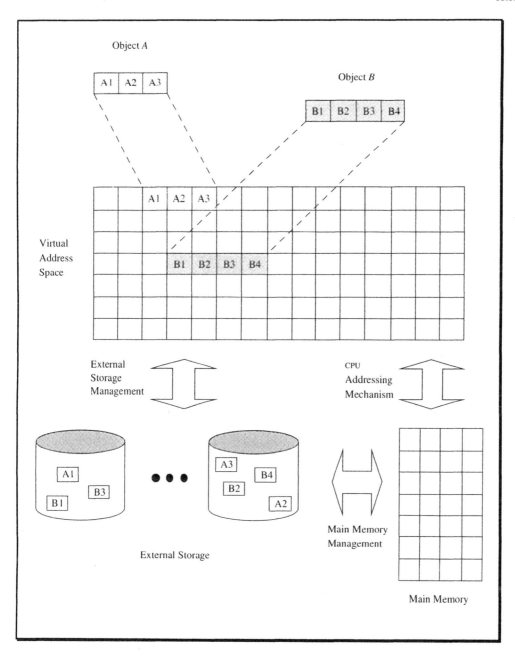

Figure 13.25: An overview of the components involved in implementing the single-level storage abstraction in the AS/400 system. All objects are permanently allocated in a very large virtual address space. Their virtual addresses are mapped onto real memory addresses by the CPU addressing mechanism. The mapping between virtual memory segments and durable storage on disk is handled by external storage management. Buffer management for making objects that are being processed in main memory is done by main memory management. [Source: Clark and Corrigan 1989]

Pre-fetching.   A group of (clustered) pages can be brought into main memory prior to the actual reference to the object.

Empty pages.   This is the optimization embodied by the emptyfix operation.

Obsolete pages.   Depending on the object type, heuristics can be applied to identify pages that are not likely to be rereferenced in the near future; these are moved to the end of the LRU chain.

Buffer types.   The user can define different bufferpools, such that each application and system task will be serviced from one pool only. This is to prevent, say, batch jobs from dominating the buffer at the expense of interactive applications. See the discussion of the pros and cons of application-specific buffer pools.

In addition, there are more detailed optimizations that we will skip for the sake of brevity.

Making a single-level storage scheme viable (from a performance perspective) and secure requires carefully designed architectural support in both the hardware and the low-level system software. A simple scheme of the interface layering used in the AS/400 is shown in Figure 13.26.

To summarize, then, single-level storage is an old, recurring, attractive idea. It has a number of convincing advantages, and it is very hard to make it work properly with high performance. It may turn out to be the Wankel engine of computer architecture. Unlike side files, which have clear disadvantages, single-level storage is much harder to judge. So let us just restate the critical issues and then try a conclusion.

Basic concept.   Having just one address space in which all objects can be kept (forever, if necessary) is certainly a great conceptual simplification. It provides on a system-wide scale what buffer management does for the higher-layer modules in a database system.

Language support.   The impedance mismatch between relational database systems and tuple-oriented programming languages is an old observation. In the same vein, there is an impedance mismatch between classical programming languages and single-level storage. One can compile such languages to a machine interface supporting single-level storage, but the power of the concept cannot be harnessed properly.

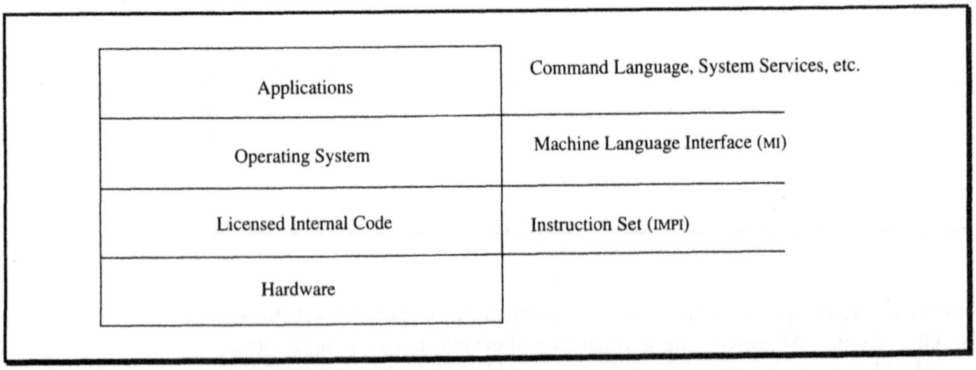

Applications	Command Language, System Services, etc.
Operating System	Machine Language Interface (MI)
Licensed Internal Code	Instruction Set (IMPI)
Hardware	

Figure 13.26: Interface layering in the AS/400 system.   The AS/400 system uses layered machine language interfaces to allow for hardware protection of its single-level storage addresses. These addresses are set and maintained by the "licensed internal code" at the IMPI (internal microprogrammed interface) layer, whereas the operating system itself is implemented on the higher-layer machine interface (MI), which has no operations to modify address pointers.

Address translation. Translating addresses from a very large address space into disk locations for paging purposes is more expensive than in "normal" virtual memory operating systems. Therefore, associative search structures, which—depending on the type of address space—will be accessed with a high degree of concurrency, must be maintained efficiently. Chapter 15 gives an idea of which problems have to be solved in that area.

Replacement. Since in single-level storage, paging comes as part of the machine's main-memory architecture, all the optimizations sketched previously must be applied, including pre-fetching, pre-flushing, and so on. In the AS/400 system, for example, this is achieved by (among other things) mapping an object—that is a piece of code together with a variable number of data—into adjacent addresses, which in turn are mapped onto adjacent disk blocks. Since references in that system are object-specific, the whole object (cluster) can be loaded upon the first reference. This is a version of pre-fetching. Another example is the operating system AIX, version 3, which maps files into virtual memory (this is a "weak" variant of single-level storage). Depending on the file organization, predictions of the future references can be used to optimize page replacement.

Durability. This is is probably the hardest part. Since all objects are mapped onto the single-level storage, the system accepts responsibility for durable objects. But what exactly does this responsibility cover? If machine instructions are executed on a durable object, when is this main memory update mapped to durable storage? (This is similar to the problem in some file systems, where a write operation, even if it completes successfully, cannot be trusted to really have written anything to disk, for example.) If the decision is bound to a write instruction in the application program, this basically moves (part of) the burden to the programmer—consider the mismatch described previously. If one tried a more transparent and efficient solution, based on logging as described in this book, this would require all components using durable objects to understand the logging protocols and make provisions for their own recovery. In case of programming languages, this would get us back to the topic of persistent languages. Just considering this short laundry list, one can appreciate the complexity of the problem. An interesting design of transactional virtual memory based on logging is described by Eppinger [1989]. Even though that design does not readily carry over to the design of a single-level storage manager of a general-purpose system, it contains a number of technical arguments of why a solution might be feasible.

So here comes the conclusion, which is more of a personal hyphesis than a technical analysis. Given the idea's great simplicity, single-level storage will certainly not be discarded just because of the hard problems associated with it; the fact that there were some spectacular failures before makes it even more attractive. Judging from some recent developments (AS/400, AIX, Camelot, HP9000), developers obviously have not given up yet. If this is so, and if future systems are inherently transaction-oriented down to the very operating system (the key thesis of this book), then there is good chance for these future systems[23] to be equipped with single-level storage.

---

[23] Computing history already knows about a future system with single-level store. This system was not a big success—most likely because it was not transactional.

13.6 Summary

The basic file system is the mediator between *main memory*—which is fast and volatile, and in which data must reside to be accessible to the CPU for processing—and *external memory*, which is slow and durable, and which has virtually unlimited capacity. The trade-off between these two types of memory is dictated by economic considerations; that is, performance requirements have to be weighed against the cost for achieving them. The guiding principle here is locality, which says that objects that have been used recently have a high likelihood of being used again; and conversely, objects that have not been referenced for a while will probably continue being unused.

This chapter presents things from a simplified perspective: main memory is assumed to have just one level, and the same assumption is made for external memory; that is, archiving is not considered. Since magnetic disks are the dominating technology for online external storage, the discussion is restricted to the problem of how to access and manage external storage on disks efficiently. The model presented here is very close to all actual implementations. The disk is formatted into slots of a fixed size (typically 2 KB to 8 KB), and these slots are addressed in terms of the disk geometry. The basic file system abstracts files, which are simple arrays of fixed-length blocks, from these slots and makes sure that blocks get efficiently mapped onto slots, which means space allocation and garbage collection are included. Blocks in files are accessed simply by relative block numbers, without having to be aware of any details of the disk geometry.

The buffer manager makes blocks that are stored on disk accessible to modules implementing higher-level database functions, such as access paths, scans, and so on. In doing so, the buffer manager must be aware of the ACID properties of the transactions requesting access to blocks. The reason is simple: all processing results reflected in the block contents are volatile unless the block is forced to disk, or unless there is sufficient redundant information in the log to reconstruct the most recent transaction-consistent state of the block, should this ever be necessary. On the other hand, for performance reasons, the buffer manager tries to avoid I/O operations whenever possible.

The behavior of the buffer manager with respect to transaction atomicity and durability is defined by a number of protocols that regulate which data have to be written in which order, and when. In relation to the log manager this is the write-ahead log (WAL) protocol. In relation to the transaction manager, these are the different propagation strategies (force/no-force), and in relation to the recovery manager the buffer manager establishes savepoints in order to limit the amount of REDO work after a crash.

Another problem is the fact that the blocks made accessible by the buffer manager are shared by many concurrent transactions. To mediate these concurrent (and potentially conflicting) access requests, the buffer manager control access to blocks by semaphores. The duration of address stability for a block in the bufferpool is regulated by the FIX-USE-UNFIX protocol.

The decision of which blocks to keep in the bufferpool for how long is based on the locality assumption and a number of heuristics for predicting the system's future reference behavior; one of the most popular heuristics is LRU, implemented as "second chance."

This chapter's final section presented two methods for managing external storage that are significantly different from those discussed in the main part of the chapter. Side files have adopted a strategy for updating blocks that does not primarily involve the log, but is a mix of old master–new master techniques and logging. It is argued that these methods are fundamentally inferior for performance reasons.

Single-level storage attempts to extend the notion of virtual memory as it is used in operating systems to arbitrarily large address spaces with durable data. Some of the implementation issues involved have been discussed—especially those related to address translation and binding. The general assessment is that single-level storage is a great idea that will probably replace current architectures once the performance problems have been solved—which still requires a good amount of work.

13.7 Historical Notes

File and buffer management are straightforward technical applications of methods people have been using for millennia to organize their lives and businesses. The Sumerian scribes to whom we owe so much did not record their database on a gigantic wall without any substructure; rather, they used uniform-size clay tablets, which were grouped by some contextual criterion such as county, year, or subject. Thus, the Sumerians invented records (tablets) and files (groups of tablets with something in common). Of course, the technology of external storage media evolved; clay—which had superseded stone—was replaced by papyrus, which got replaced by paper, which finally got replaced by rust. People also came up with structured records (see Chapter 14), which are commonly known as forms. They devised means to speed up access; think of the alphabetic dividers in file hangers. All these are refinements of the same basic idea.

The main idea behind buffering is to exploit locality. Everybody employs it without even thinking about it. A desk should serve as a buffer of the things one needs to perform the current tasks.[24] What I will have to touch frequently should be within reach, for the rest, I will have to perform a physical access; that is, stand up and walk to the shelf. Production lines are optimized by buffering parts and tools—note that in this case, pre-fetching rather than demand paging is used. Examples can be found everywhere.

In the context of computers, files came into the picture when operating systems were introduced—at about the time of the so-called third generation, in the mid-1950s. Before that, computers used to be programmed "on the bare metal"; real memory was real real memory, and external devices were real external devices.

Buffering the way it was described in this chapter came later. The normal way of handling external devices was to have a file buffer, which in case of a block-oriented file would be a portion of memory large enough to hold one block. Now if block 1 is to be accessed, it is read into this buffer. If it gets modified, it is written back right away. Then block 2 is accessed, overwriting block 1 in the file buffer. Then block 1 is accessed again, which means it needs to be read again—and so on. Of course this is inefficient, but it is a style of thinking about file accesses that is suggested by conventional programming languages.

To fend off the speed difference between main memory and external storage, double buffering was introduced for writing, especially for sequential files. Assume there are two buffer frames, *A* and *B*. As soon as buffer *A* is filled, a write operation is initiated that asynchronously transfers *A* to the file. The application program is "switched" to buffer *B* and can continue filling it. During the next round, the roles are reversed, and so on.

---

[24] Andreas's desk probably doesn't, but that's a different story.

This is still state-of-the-art in the majority of operating system–supported file systems. Buffering on a larger scale, as described in this chapter, was employed by database systems with their "leave me alone" attitude toward the operating system, and by systems providing either memory-mapped files or single-level storage.

The aspect of durability was mostly ignored in the early file systems for a simple reason: at that time, main memory was built from magnetic cores and thus was pretty durable. So writing to main memory was just as good as writing to disk from a recovery perspective. The only relevant difference was that main memory was small (64 KB was considered plenty) compared to those huge disks with their 10 MB. Consequently, restart after a crash could pick up the most recent state of the process from main memory. It could not do that indiscriminately, because a bad control block might have been the reason for the crash, but at least the data were there. IMS actually had a scavenger routine that looked at the database buffer after restart to see if it was any good and, if so, performed a "warm" start.

Many database systems, although they used global buffering to improve performance over simple file buffers, at some point were caught cold by the rapid growth of main memories and the resulting increase in buffer sizes applications would use. The reason was that early implementations of database buffers used sequentially linked lists as look-aside data structures to check if a block was in buffer. This is acceptable for very small buffers, but as they grow, the linear increase in search time for each buffer reference costs more than is gained by higher hit rates.

The rest of the development toward current file systems and database buffer implementations followed that path, although it was not until the late 1970s that the underlying concepts were investigated and described in a systematic way. The papers about the implementation of System R and Ingres were the first to discuss the issues of a database buffer from a performance perspective and, of course with respect to the recovery issues incurred by the transaction paradigm [Astrahan et al. 1981; Blasgen et al. 1979; Gray 1978; Lindsay et al. 1979; Stonebraker et al. 1976].

At the same time, attention was brought to the fact that there was a considerable mismatch in concepts between databases and operating systems with respect to resource scheduling, file management, recovery, and some more issues. These were summarized in some frequently cited papers [Stonebraker 1981; Stonebraker 1984; Traiger 1982c]. They had considerable impact on the database community, much less on the operating systems community. But at least Stonebraker's papers explained to a wider audience why the standard UNIX file system is utterly inadequate for databases from both a performance and a recovery perspective. The result was the introduction of raw disks into UNIX—exactly what the guys who want to be left alone need.

In parallel to that, file systems became more flexible, more versatile, and more complex. The most notable example is IBM's VSAM under the MVS operating system. It provides a wide variety of functions and optimizations, many more than we will even mention in this book. It has associative access, and data sharing, and recovery—but it does not speak transactions, and therefore all the database systems running on MVS have to do their own thing all over again.

It is an interesting observation that there are very few transactional file systems yet; in the commercial domain, Tandem's Guardian and DEC's RMs are the only notable exceptions. IBM's UNIX-style operating system for the RS/6000, AIX 3.1, purportedly uses transactions to protect its update operations on the file system directory. It therefore is one of the few UNIX implementations that will not lose files due to a crash. However, it does not give transactions to the file system's user, and so it is not a transactional file system in the full meaning of that term.

An interesting approach was taken in a research project, Camelot, where a conventional operating system (Mach) and file system were extended by a virtual memory manager with transaction semantics. In contrast to the single-level storage idea, this does not require hardware support or larger addresses. It will be interesting to see the influence on real products. The reader is referred to Eppinger [1989] and Eppinger, Mummert, and Spector [1991] for details.

Single-level storage has a fairly long history, with a number of failures in the beginning. Two systems that have become famous for their great designs and high ambitions, the Burroughs B5000 and Multics, among other things tried to implement single-level storage. They also were capability-based (*object-oriented*, to use the modern words), used high-level machine languages, believed in late binding, and exhibited many more innovations like these. The other aspect they had in common was low performance, which is why they ultimately failed. In retrospect, this did not prove the inapplicability of the ideas; it just demonstrated that on machines with .3 MIPS, multiple layers of dynamic abstraction are not affordable.

After machines had become fast enough to make the trade-off between a clean design on one hand and performance on the other worth considering, some implementations of single-level storage appeared. They have been around for circa 10 years: IBM's System /38; its successor, AS/400; and HP's MPE operating system on the 9000-series (Precision Architecture).

Memory-mapped files have been used in all operating systems implicitly, without making the mechanism generally available. Load modules are a typical example. The main memory databases in IMS FastPath can also be viewed as an application of the mapping idea. MVS selectively maps files into the *hyper space*, and AIX 3.1 maps each file at open time. In the latter case, this only has consequences for the system implementation itself, because it is a UNIX implementation with all the standard file operations.

This chapter was a very brief description of the low-level issues in file management, with a focus on the database buffer manager, which is typically not covered in much detail in textbooks on file systems. On the other hand, such books contain more material about subjects such as file design, performance estimates, security, and so on, that have been mentioned just briefly or not at all in the present chapter. For further readings on file systems see Salzberg [1988] and Wiederhold [1977].

Exercises

1. [13.2, 10] Name three issues that a single-level storage scheme must support, which are not considered by today's virtual memory managers in operating systems.

2. [13.2, 10] Find at least five examples for the principle of locality in everyday life.

3. [13.2, 20] Based on your knowledge of database systems and how they work, where is locality (in terms of locality of references in the bufferpool) most likely to occur? (Name at least three different types of local reference behavior.)

4. [13.2, discussion] There is a RAM-based storage technology that is frequently called something like "extended storage," and that tries to bridge the gap between disks and main memory. It has the

following characteristics: units of transfer are pages of 4 KB to 8 KB, the bandwidth is 1 GB/sec, and the storage is made durable by battery backup. Remember that a typical read or write access to disk proceeds in the following steps:

(1) Process calls operating system to initiate I/O operation.

(2) Process gets suspended for the duration of the I/O.

(3) When the operation completes, the process becomes "ready for execution" again.

(4) Sometime later, the process is resumed.

How would you interface an extended storage to the application program? Would you use the same interface as for disk I/O and just benefit from the faster access times (no arm movement, no rotational delay, higher bandwidth), or are there additional things to be considered? Assume a 100 MIPS CPU and explain how you would use a storage device with the properties explained here.

5. [13.2, 10] What are the key arguments in favor of the "main memory and tapes" prognosis of system storage architecture?

6. [13.3, discussion] A block on disk has its FILENO and its BLOCKID stored in the header as a provision for fault tolerance. Do you see any potential problem with this?

7. [13.3, 30] With the extent-based allocation, periodic garbage collection of free slots on the disk has to be performed once in a while to prevent the available extent from getting too small. Design an algorithm for this task that is fault tolerant (not necessarily ACID) and that has minimum impact on the transactions executing concurrently. *Hint: Try to do the space reorganization incrementally.*

8. [13.3, 20] Assume a 40 GB file with single-slot allocation. Each slot is 8 KB long; a pointer has 8 bytes. Allow 20 bytes per slot for bookkeeping. If this file is accessed randomly using stochastically independent block numbers with uniform distribution, what is the average number of slots that must be read for translating a block number into a disk address? (Count the directory holding slot_ptr. [] as one slot.) How many slots are needed for the addressing tree?

9. [13.3, 25] Construct an allocation pattern for files, using the buddy system in which all extents contain only one slot and no merge is possible. What is the minimal space utilization for which such a pattern can be constructed? Whatever your answer is, prove that it is minimal.

10. [13.3, 30] Read the documentation on MS-DOS and find out how its file system handles space allocation on disks. Which of the categories established in Section 13.3 does this scheme belong to? What are the performance characteristics?

11. [13.3, 20] Assume the block-oriented file system with the data structures that have been declared in Section 13.3. Explain how these structures must be written according to the principle of careful replacement after a file has been deleted. It is important that you also specify exactly how blocks are written for newly allocated files. Remember: the scheme must under all circumstances avoid multiple allocation of the same slots.

12. [13.4, 10] The task of a buffer manager is comparable to that of a virtual memory manager in an operating system. As is explained in Section 13.4, the buffer manager's interface needs the fix/unfix brackets to function properly. There is no equivalent for that at the interface to the virtual memory manager. Why?

13. [13.4, 10] The explanation of why different page sizes make life more complicated for the buffer manager was a bit vague. Explain precisely what is different in that environment from the sample implementation presented in this chapter.

14. [13.4, 20] The text briefly mentions invalid pages. What must be done upon bufferunfix() when the invalid flag is set? Is it sufficient to just discard the page and mark the frame as free, or is there something else that needs to be done—except for starting online media recovery for the broken page?

15. [13.4, 20] The no-steal policy guarantees that no transactions need to be rolled back at restart, so no log records are required for reestablishing *old* states of pages. The force policy guarantees that no REDO work for completed transactions needs to be done at restart, so no log records are required for bringing pages up to the *new* state (ignoring the problem of media recovery for the sake of argument). Does that mean a combination of the two policies will avoid the necessity of keeping a log? If not, what is wrong with the idea? *Hint: Remember that writing a single page is not an atomic operation; then consider what it means to write a set of pages; that is, all pages that have been modified by some transaction.*

16. [13.4, 25] Consider a transaction abort during normal operation, with the buffer manager using a no-steal/no-force policy. Due to no-steal, all pages modified by the transaction are still in the bufferpool when abort is initiated. One could think of doing the abort by simply discarding the pages in buffer, that is, by tagging the corresponding frames as empty. What is wrong with this simple approach under the assumptions made? Design an extension that would allow the buffer manager described in this chapter to exploit the properties of no-steal for normal abort processing at least in some situations.

17. [13.4, 30] Write the code for the bufferunfix routine. Use the interface prototype declared in Section 13.4, and do the following things: make the page that gets unfixed the most-recently-used page; that is, put its control block at the head of the LRU chain—unless, of course, the page comes back with the invalid flag set. Ignore the case of invalid pages. Then decrement the fix counter and release any semaphore the client may have on the page. Note that the client, while holding the page, may have given back and reacquired semaphores on the page at his leisure. When requesting semaphores on critical data structures, make sure you do not run the risk of semaphore deadlocks. Look at the order in which the bufferfix routines request and release their semaphores.

18. [13.4, 20] Consider a very simple case of pre-fetching at the interface to the basic file system: whenever a read operation is issued to a block with block number j, then j and $n - 1$ subsequent blocks with numbers $j + 1, ..., j + (n - 1)$ are transferred as part of the same read operation. (Here we ignore track and cylinder boundaries as well as extent sizes.) Compute the elapsed times for sequential scans reading N blocks, starting at block number 0, with n varying between 1 and 8. If the read operation of block 0, for example, has completed, then the pages mapped into blocks 1, ..., $n - 1$ are already in buffer, so no read requests have to be issued for them. The next read operation will be directed toward block n. The sequential scan issues bufferfix requests for *pages* 0 to $N - 1$. Assume that the disk arm is moved to a random position between subsequent block read operations on behalf of the scan. Therefore, the following parameters can be used to estimate processing times: mean time for arm movement: 16 ms; mean time for rotational delay: 8 ms; time for transferring *one* block: 1 ms. Note that the exercise hinges upon the assumption that blocks with adjacent numbers are always mapped to adjacent slots.

19. [13.4, 10] Let us assume a buffer with n frames, on which 1 transaction is operating. After the n frames have been filled with pages, the page fault ratio drops to 0; the buffer manager uses a pure LRU replacement strategy. If the same transaction were run on a buffer with $n - 1$ frames, the

page fault ratio would be 100%. Which type of access pattern could create such a surprising result?

20. [13.5, 25] The simple version of the side file technique and the differential file require periodic copying of the side file to the primary file. This has to be atomic. The text has explained that it is idempotent, which is not sufficient to make it atomic in the presence of crashes. Design a scheme that makes the copy process atomic. *Hint: Go back to Chapter 4 and look at the methods to make single block write operations atomic.*

Answers

1. (1) Lifetime assignment of addresses in virtual address space to objects, (2) durability of objects in the address space (which includes recovery), (3) sharing of the single-level storage among all process address spaces (which includes synchronization and security issues).

2. (1) The stores you shop in, (2) the friends you visit, (3) the type of things you do at any given time of day, (4) the food you prefer, (5) the opinions you hold.

3. (1) Assume a relation scan: after a tuple in page p has been accessed, it is very likely that the next tuple in the same page gets accessed, too. (2) When a certain number of insert transactions are active, the page(s) holding the free space information of the respective file are accessed at least twice for each individual insert operation. See Chapter 14 for details. (3) If there are hotspots in the application, such as the tuple for the last flight out of New York to San Francisco on Friday night, there will be a high frequency of reference on these hot spots.

4. The key issue to consider here is when it makes sense to switch synchronous read/write operations in the sense that the process holds on to the processor while the I/O is going on. The rationale for suspending the process in current system is the very long latency of disk storage compared to the processor speed. Now if the latency can be reduced to a few thousand instruction equivalents (rather than more than 1 million instruction equivalents for a disk read in case of a 100 MIPS processor), it might be cheaper to let the process wait while holding the CPU, because now the I/O operation is in the same price range as a process switch.

5. Main memory will be large enough to hold all active data; durable storage is needed for logging and archiving only, both of which are sequentially written. Hence, tapes (of whatever technology) are most appropriate.

6. The tuple ⟨FILENO,BLOCKID⟩ must be unique throughout the system as long as the block exists somewhere (maybe on an old archive tape) and has a chance chance of being re-referenced.

7. In the following, we ignore all optimizations for the garbage collection process; the only concern is fault tolerance. At the beginning of the reorganization process, there are collections of slots (extents) that are currently allocated to a file, and collections of slots that had been allocated to a file in the past but have been declared free in the meantime. Reorganization can be performed incrementally by copying allocated extents into free extents one by one. So we can restrict our discussion to the problem of how to use up one free extent such that the repeated execution of this process will move the entire free space to the end of the disk. Consider the following scenarios, showing the beginning of the disk, with the disk directory in the first slots. Allocated extents are shaded gray, free extents are white.

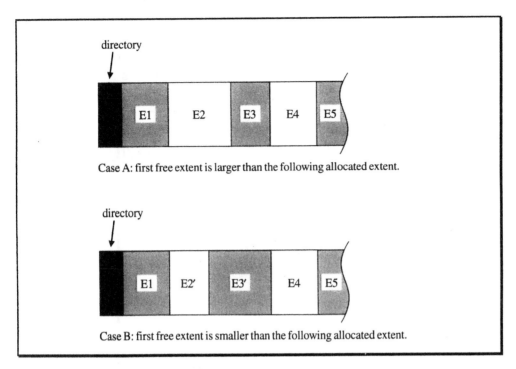

Case A: first free extent is larger than the following allocated extent.

Case B: first free extent is smaller than the following allocated extent.

The first free extent is E2 (we are looking at Case A first). It is followed by an allocated extent that comprises fewer slots than the free one. Here, copying requires the following steps: (1) Set an exclusive lock on the free space map in the directory. (2) Copy the slots from E3 into E2. (3) Modify the entries in the free space map accordingly. (4) Set an exclusive lock on the directory. (5) Change the base address of extent E3 (it now starts where E2 started before). (6) Write the free space map to disk. The trick here is that there are two locations on disk for the free space map, which are written alternately. (7) Write the directory to disk. We assume that the affected part of the directory fits into one block, which is written using a stable write operation (see Chapter 4).

Case B is more difficult in an environment where we cannot assume transaction support. Steps 1 and 2 are performed exactly as in Case A, up to the point where the free space in E2' is used up. However, there are still slots in E3' that must be moved. Assume a crash occurs at that moment. After restart, the disk comes back with the old directory, where E2' is marked free, and where all slots of E3' contain their proper contents. But if we continue copying slots from E3' to E2' and crash sometime after that, the disk will be inconsistent: The directory still says E2' is free and E3' is allocated, but now slots at the beginning of E3' have been overwritten by slots from E3' with higher addresses. For careful replacement to work, the following steps must be taken at the moment the last slot of E2' is used up: (2.1) Set an exclusive lock on the directory. (2.2) Set a flag on the entry for extent E3', saying how much has been copied and that it is "in transit." (2.3) Do a stable write for the directory. Then proceed as in Case A.

8. The file has 4,882,813 blocks. A block can hold 1,021 pointers. If we assume the I-node as described in the text, we get the following addressing structure: 10 blocks can be directly addressed via the I-node, the next 1,021 block accesses go through one indirection, the next 1,043,472 block accesses go through two indirections, the remaining 3,839,341 block accesses go through three indirections. So the average number of block accesses per random access (including address translation) is:

$$A_{avg} = (10 \cdot 1) + (1021 \cdot 2) + (1{,}043{,}472 \cdot 3) + (3{,}839{,}341 \cdot 4)/4{,}882{,}813 = 3.7867.$$

9. The obvious answer is to have alternating slots at the lowest level: one slot free, one slot allocated. This yields 50% utilization. One could suppose that utilization gets lower when groups of two adjacent free slots are arranged such that they are neighbors but not buddies. The following illustration shows that this results in a 50% utilization, too.

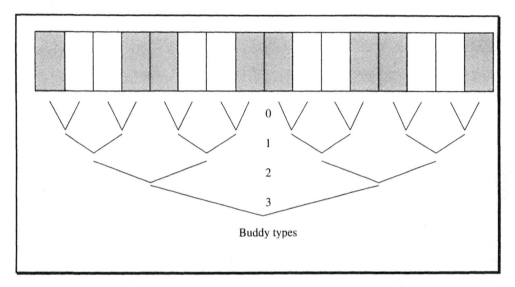

Buddy types

11. The answer to this exercise can easily be obtained by applying the principles explained in the answer to Exercise 7.

12. The operating system (with some support from the hardware) checks *before each machine instruction* whether the required pages (the page holding the instruction and the page containing the data, in case the instruction references a memory location) are in real memory.

13. If page sizes are different, the replacement problem gets more complicated. Assume a bufferfix operation for a page that currently is not in the bufferpool. Making sure that there is a frame in which to put the requested page requires more than just picking a replacement victim. The buffer manager must try to replace a page that is at least as long as the one that is to be fixed. If there is no such page in the bufferpool, things get even more complicated. Either two or more pages must be replaced to make room for the new one, but now locality is not an issue anymore because these pages must be picked according to the criterion that they are stored in adjacent buffer frames. Another possibility is to replace pages strictly based on locality estimates and do garbage collection in the bufferpool after that to make sure the free space is contiguous. No matter which method is used for replacement, periodic garbage collection has to be performed anyway to reduce space fragmentation in the bufferpool. Garbage collection, of course, requires exclusive semaphores on all affected portions of the buffer and thus potentially causes wait situations for concurrent transactions.

14. Since the page is invalid, UNDO is not guaranteed to work. So recovery means that some older consistent state of the page must be rolled forward by applying REDO logs from all complete transactions before the page got invalidated. If the page on disk is consistent, this is the starting point for the REDO pass. If, however, the page got replaced while the transaction that corrupted the page was active, it might be better not to rely on its contents. So one must check the page LSN of the page version on disk and see if any log records of the failed transaction pertaining to that

page exist in the log. If this is the case, the transaction updated the page before declaring the page data structure invalid, and that state was written to disk. In that case, it is safer to acquire the most recent version of the corrupted page from the archive and start REDO recovery from there. This recovery path is longer, but it starts from a version of the page that is trustworthy—in contrast to the page version on disk.

15. In order to implement the force policy, all dirty pages must be written during commit processing. While they are being written they are still dirty, so the buffer applies the steal policy. The inverse argument is also correct: If you want to implement no-steal, nothing must be written before commit completes, which implies no-force. If you want both force and no-steal, you have to implement some kind of shadow page algorithm that does the atomic write for each transaction commit. This can be done, but it is very expensive.

16. This is a strong hint rather than a complete answer: The problem is that a page P containing updates by an incomplete transaction $T1$ may at the same time contain updates by a committed transaction $T2$. So P is dirty from $T1$'s perspective, but clean from $T2$'s point of view. If $T1$ aborts, simply discarding page P from the bufferpool would also discard $T2$'s updates, thus corrupting the database.

18. Ignoring CPU time, we have to model the fact that every N/n bufferfix requests a physical I/O operation is necessary, transferring n blocks. So the elapsed time as a function of n can be estimated as:

$$T_e(n) = (N/n) \bullet (16 + 8 + 1 \bullet n)$$

$$= N \bullet (24/n + 1).$$

Assuming $N = 10,000$, one can calculate the effect of pre-fetching. If $n = 1$, we get $T_e(1) = 250$ sec; for $n = 8$, the estimate is $T_e(8) = 40$ sec.

19. Read Subsection 13.4.4.3.

20. A simple solution works like this: In the primary file, there are two blocks containing counters for the side file copies that have been applied to the primary file. These counters are increased monotonously. During normal operations, both blocks—let us call them B and E—contain identical values. If the side file is to be copied, block B is written with the next higher value of the counter. Then all blocks are copied back from the side file to the primary file. Once this is complete, block E is written with the new counter value. During restart after a crash, both blocks, B and E, are read. If they contain identical values, the primary file is consistent. If the values differ, the copy process was interrupted by a crash and must be repeated.

Let's look at the record.

ALFRED E. SMITH,
Campaign Speeches, 1928

14

The Tuple-Oriented File System

14.1 Introduction

The basic file system described in Chapter 13 provides the foundation for managing large quantities of *tuples* (or *records*, as they are called in traditional file systems) in a flexible and efficient way. Tuples can be of either fixed or variable length, and the tuple-oriented file system has to provide six fundamental types of service:

Storage allocation. It has to store tuples into the blocks supported by the underlying block-oriented file system, which includes space allocation.

Tuple addressing. It has to make the tuple addressable from other parts of the database; that is, each tuple must be given a stable identifier, and there must be an efficient access path to the tuple via that identifier.

Enumeration. There must be a fast access path from one tuple of a relation to the "next" tuple, thus making it possible to enumerate all tuples of a relation.

Content addressing. The tuple must be made accessible via the contents of its attributes.

Maintenance. It must be possible to delete existing tuples and sever all ties to this tuple that might exist in other parts of the database.

Protection. There must be some basic support for security, such as storing the tuples in encrypted form, or content-sensitive access control.

Since the techniques to implement these functions are complex, this chapter is organized into five major sections. Section 14.2 describes how pages have to be organized to store tuples efficiently. This includes the problems of tuple addressing and free space management. Section 14.3 discusses addressing, storing, and all related issues for *a single tuple*. Section 14.4 builds on top of this and contains a description of the most common ways tuple-oriented files are organized; that is, it presents how sets of tuples stored in a file of the underlying basic file system can be maintained. It starts by introducing the notion of a *scan*, which provides navigational access to the tuples in a file based on various ordering criteria.

Section 14.5 concludes the chapter with a brief discussion of "exotic" topics—exotic, at least, from the perspective of this book.

You will notice that there are no "Historical Notes." This not because there is no history of file management. There is quite a bit of it; we have not just made things up. However, the present chapter is a transition on the way from the basic, block-oriented file system to files with associative access (Chapter 15), which is what database systems really need. So all the file management issues are still relevant in the next chapter, and the account of the evolution of the key techniques is deferred to its end.

14.2 Mapping Tuples into Pages

This section describes the methods for structuring pages, for allocating storage space to tuples, and for generating stable tuple identifiers. But before getting into the details, the basic terminology needs to be established. According to the mapping scheme in Figure 13.6, the tuple-oriented file system builds on top of the basic file system; in other words, tuples are mapped into blocks. In the literature, there are subtle terminological distinctions between tuples, tuple representations, and records, that read something like this:

A *page* contains a number of *records*, and each record is the physical representation of a *tuple*, or of an entry in a table, or of some other object maintained by the tuple-oriented file system. These tuple-oriented files are implemented on top of the basic file system, which provides access to fixed-length *blocks* organized into extents of variable size.

As explained in Chapter 13, the distinction between slots, blocks, and pages can be ignored in most circumstances. The same is true for the distinction between records and tuples. Of course, at the file-system level, the records may contain fields such as pointers and length counters, which are not visible at the SQL level. On the other hand, because a record "implements" a tuple at the physical storage layer, there is a close relationship between the two concepts. Consequently, the two terms are assumed to be synonyms for the purposes of this chapter. Since this is so, *tuple* and *record* are used interchangeably.

Likewise, the terms *file* and *relation* are not meticulously distinguished. The previous chapter made the point that the easiest way to map relations onto files contains one step (Figure 13.10). A relation can be fragmented into a number of files, but each *file* manages tuples of one *relation* only. In that sense, both terms can be used interchangeably in most places. The situation is different when multi-relational clustering is considered, but then the necessary terminological distinctions will be made.

14.2.1 Internal Organization of Pages

Since all file organizations have the common task of mapping tuples into pages, they must first organize pages so that tuples can be stored and retrieved efficiently.[1] In the examples that follow, pages are assumed to have a standard page header, according to this definition:

---

[1] This seems to suggest that a tuple is always stored entirely in one page. For the discussion in the first part of this chapter, this is true. Later on, we will describe techniques that permit storing tuples that are (potentially) longer than one page.

```
/* These declares establish a data type "page," together with an identifier for its instances.      */
typedef  struct                                    /* makes it easier to talk about page numbers      */
       {   FILENO          fileno;                 /* file where the page lives                        */
           uint            pageno;                 /* page number within the file                      */
       }   PAGEID,         PAGEIDP;
/* A page can contain information of different categories, although usually any given page            */
/* contains data of one type only. The following enumerated type describes the different              */
/* types of data structures that have to be handled by the tuple-oriented file system.                */
/* The enumeration only serves as an example to illustrate the following discussions. It is           */
/* by no means complete.                                                                              */
enum PAGE_TYPE   { DATA, INDEX, FREESPACE, DIRECTORY, CLUSTER, TABLE };
/* The values of PAGE_TYPE have the following meaning (all the concepts referred to are               */
/* elaborated in this chapter and in Chapter 15):                                                     */
/*   DATA           page contains tuples of exactly one file (relation)                               */
/*   INDEX          page contains the node of an index  file (see chapter 15)                         */
/*   FREESPACE      page contains parts of a freespace management table                               */
/*   DIRECTORY      page contains meta data about this file or other files                            */
/*   CLUSTER        page contains tuples of more than one relation                                    */
/*   TABLE          page contains table with administrative data (e.g. addressing)                    */
/* This enumerated data type is used to distinguish the different states a page can be in             */
enum PAGE_STATE {VALID, INVALID, INDOUBT, SHADOW};
/* The following structure defines the standard header of each page. note that it has the             */
/* block data structure around it (see Figure 14.1).                                                  */
typedef  struct
           PAGEID          thatsme;               /* identifies the page                              */
           PAGE_TYPE       page_type;             /* see description above                            */
           OBJID           object_id;             /* internal id of the relation,index,etc.           */
           LSN             safe_up_to;            /* page LSN for the WAL-protocol                    */
           PAGEID          previous;              /* often pages are members of doubly                */
           PAGEID          next;                  /* linked lists                                     */
           PAGE_STATE      status;                /* used to mark the contents of the page            */
                                                  /* (valid,in-doubt,copy of something,etc.)          */
           int             no_entries;            /* number of entries in page dir (see below)        */
           int             unused;                /* number of unused bytes which are not part        */
                                                  /* of contiguous freespace                          */
           int             freespace;             /* number of contiguous free bytes for              */
                                                  /* payload                                          */
           char            stuff[];               /* will grow                                        */
       }   PAGE_HEADER, *   PAGE_PTR;
```

Most database systems, in fact, use much longer page headers than this, and in many cases the layout varies with the file organization. But these complexities are not needed to describe the functional principles. Figure 14.1 illustrates the relationships between slots (on disk), blocks, and pages at the physical level.

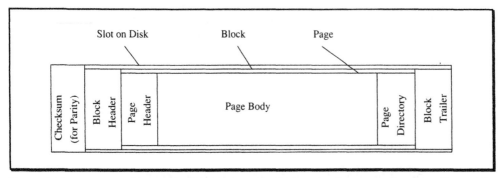

Figure 14.1: A page and its surrounding structure. The page has its own header and trailer, and it is surrounded by a block with another header and trailer. Around that comes the slot, with yet another header. The various headers contain administrative data and redundancy for error-checking recovery that is used and maintained by the respective layer in the system. Note that slots are the objects handled at the device and channel layer, blocks are handled by the basic file system, and pages are maintained by the tuple-oriented file system.

Since a page can hold entries of different types (attribute page_type), each of which can be of variable length, each page needs a local page directory to manage storage and retrieval of the entries. The simplest way to do this is to have an array that contains as many entries as there are records in the page, and that points to the beginning of these records. Details of this addressing scheme are described in Figure 14.2. An *array* is a fixed data structure. If it was allocated inside a page with the maximum number of records that might occur in a page, much space would be wasted in the case of long records (fewer of them fit into a page).

Figure 14.2 illustrates the typical solution to that problem. The header is always at the beginning of the page (low address), and the tuples are inserted right after it in increasing address order. The page directory is indexed backwards; that is, the first entry occupies the highest page address, the second entry comes in the next-lower address, and so forth. This method of two stacks growing toward each other is commonly used whenever different dynamic data structures have to be allocated in the same linear address space; for example, in operating systems, to allocate code and data segments in a process address space.

As the page fills up, tuples and their respective page directory entries grow toward each other, and free space management in the page has to make sure that they do not overlap. Since, according to this scheme, the page directory is a variable-size array, the number of active entries must be kept somewhere. One way is to have an entry in the page header containing the current number of records in the page (no_entries in our declaration), which also is the number of entries in the page directory. Another method would be to put a NULL pointer after the last valid directory entry, but this would leave sequential search of the directory as the only viable access method. However, as is shown later on, binary search is important in many cases, for performance reasons. Since this requires the number of entries to be known in advance, we chose this design.

The declaration of the page directory looks as follows:

```
struct
      {    char    not_needed[PAGESIZE];        /* covers the whole page         */
           Uint    offset_in_page[];            /* offset of a tuple in the page */
      }    PAGE_DIR, *    PPAGE_DIR;
```

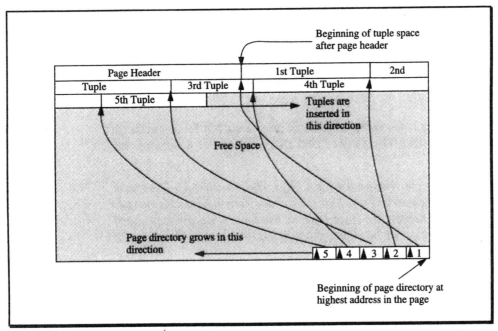

Figure 14.2: A common technique to allocate two dynamic data structures in the same address space. Tuples are inserted from the beginning in increasing address order; the directory grows in the opposite direction, expanding from the highest address in the page, toward the middle. In this example, it is assumed that the page header contains the information about how many valid entries there are in the directory.

This declaration probably looks a bit strange at first, because the array representing the directory is preceded by a dummy declaration the size of the entire page; in other words, the directory is declared "behind" the page. This is a trick which, though some people might call it dirty, is nevertheless commonly applied: negative addressing. An array normally extends in the forward direction (increasing addresses), using positive values for the indices. However, it can quite as well be allowed to expand backwards by using negative index values.[2] The base address of the directory, then, is the first byte after the page, and the first entry starts at that address minus 4. In general, the offset of the ith tuple in the page is found in PAGE_DIR.offset_in_page[$-i$]. The offset values themselves are relative offsets from the beginning of the page; therefore, entries of type Uint will be sufficient even for large pages.

Note that the internal organization of a page we have described is a simplified version of what many database systems actually have implemented. Some systems, however, do not have a page directory at all. Rather, they do sequential search through the page to locate a tuple. These systems were typically designed at times when page sizes of 2 KB were considered large, so that a page would hold only a few tuples. But with page sizes of 64 KB and more, searching through a page sequentially may carry a serious performance penalty.

Other systems, such as Rdb and UDS, for example, allow more complex data structures in a page than just tuples or index tables. Consequently, the page directories hold more information per entry than merely the offset. But in this subsection we focus on methods to

---

[2] Of course, there are programming languages supporting that, but C, which is used throughout this book, in principle does not.

store short tuples (shorter than a page), and for that purpose the directory structure is adequate. More complicated issues, such as tuple overflow, management of very long tuples, and so on, are discussed later in this chapter.

Besides locating an entry, page management must also keep track of which portion of the page is actually free; that is, in which area inside a page a new entry can be stored. There are four different occasions that affect the free space in a page:

Inserting a single tuple.   This is the online transaction processing (OLTP) scenario. A transaction issues a single INSERT command, and there is no reason to assume that more tuples will follow suit.

Deleting a tuple.   A single tuple is deleted from a page, thereby increasing the total amount of unused bytes. But note that this does not automatically increase the number of *useful* bytes in the page, because the space freed by that tuple is usually surrounded by other tuples and therefore cannot be allocated contiguously together with the rest of the free space.

Updating a tuple.   In most database systems, tuples of the same relation can vary in length, which means that an UPDATE operation can make them shrink or grow.

Bulk loading of tuples into a relation.   This is typically done after creating a new relation, or while processing large quantities of data in a batch. Think, for example, of order entry applications. The characteristic is that the system knows in advance that many tuples of a certain relation will have to be inserted.

Reorganizing.   Occasionally, pages of a file must be (locally) reorganized to make sure the unused bytes in the page are located contiguously "in the middle," between the tuples and the directory. To compress out holes, tuples must be moved toward the beginning of the page, and unused directory entries must be filled.

Note that bulk deletes have not been distinguished as a separate category. It would be easy to do that.

Because techniques to administer free space in a page vary considerably, only the most basic criteria are described here. The following enumerates the aspects to be considered:

When a tuple shrinks during update, it remains in its place, and the header variable unused is increased by the number of bytes freed. If the tuple grows, three different cases must be distinguished:

Simple.   The value in freespace is larger than the new length of the tuple. In that situation, the old space is freed (increase unused), and the tuple is reinserted after the current last tuple.

Complex.   The value in freespace is not large enough, but freespace + unused + (old length of tuple) is. For reasons that will become obvious later in this chapter, a tuple should be kept in the page in which it was originally stored; in this case, a local compaction is performed.[3] This means relocating all tuples within the page such that all the *unused* space, along with the space occupied by the old version of the tuple, is moved

---

[3] If the extended tuple is the current last tuple in the page, this can be given special treatment.

behind the last tuple and therefore becomes free space. If there is a hole large enough to accommodate the new tuple, this can be handled as a special case to avoid the (expensive) compaction.

Impossible. The extension of the tuple cannot be accommodated in the page. Depending on how tuples are represented internally (see Section 14.3), there are two solutions: (1) relocate the extended tuple to another page, or (2) keep as much of the tuple as possible in the old page and move attributes that do not fit into another page (fragmentation).

When deleting a tuple, its length is added to unused. If the ratio unused/freespace exceeds a predefined threshold, internal garbage collection is initiated.

To insert a new tuple, a page is chosen with enough free space so that the tuple can be stored completely without fragmentation. Again, this assumes we are dealing with *short* tuples, which are typical of most existing database systems. If no such page exists, an exception must be raised, because the file is about to run out of space. The way of handling this differs from system to system: (1) garbage collection must be done in all pages in order to exploit whatever storage space is left, or (2) the file must be extended if possible, or (3) a new file must be allocated for that relation. But this goes beyond space management in one page; the matter is discussed in more detail in the next subsection.

Bulk inserts are easy to handle if an appropriate number of empty pages is available in the file. Tuples are inserted sequentially into the empty pages. Most load operations have a parameter called PCTFREE (or something similar) that specifies which portion of the storage space in a page should not be used *during loading*. There are several reasons why this is a good idea. First, if there is some slack, then tuples can grow without having to be relocated to another page. Second, there are file organizations (see Section 14.4) where the storage location of a tuple depends on its key value. In that case, it is mandatory to leave some space during loading, because all tuples expected to be inserted later on will be mapped to the same set of pages, and there should be enough space to accommodate them.

14.2.1.1 Summary

The internal organization of pages has to meet the following requirements: it must be able to accommodate entries of different types, provided the entries are shorter than one page. A page must have a local directory to manage entries of variable length for two reasons. One is faster addressing, the other reason is to support binary search on the set of entries in a page. And finally, page administration must keep track of the free space in a page and be able to reorganize the entries in case of local fragmentation. The reason is that there is a strong incentive to keep entries in the page in which they have originally been stored, even if they expand after modification.

14.2.2 Free Space Administration in a File

Subsection 14.2.1 considered managing free space *inside a page*. This subsection covers the problem of tracking free and unused space in an entire file. As we will see later on, the various file organizations need different types of free space management; this section therefore simply presents the methods available, independent of file type.

To illustrate the problem, consider a SQL INSERT statement. The new tuple is converted into its internal representation, and once the space required to store it has been determined, the question becomes: in which page should the tuple be stored? There are file organizations where the page to store a tuple is determined by an attribute value in the tuple (see Section 14.4), but for now, assume the tuple can be stored anywhere. Obviously, there has to be a quick way to find a page with sufficient free space to store the tuple.

In current systems, there are typically two ways to handle this problem; one is a *free space table*, and the other is a *free space cursor*. Both are explained briefly in what follows, without referring to any particular implementation.

14.2.2.1 Free Space Table

The free space table is similar to the method used to keep track of free blocks on a disk. As Figure 14.3 shows, it is an array stored at predefined locations, with one entry per page of the file; the entry contains the current amount of free space in that page. Assuming that one page can hold e such entries, and that there is no need to keep free space information about the table pages (they are, by definition, always 100% full) the number of free space table pages F for a file with a total number of P pages is determined by:

$$F \cdot e \geq P - F$$

This is to say that there must be at least as many entries as there are pages not used for the free space table. Allocating all F table pages contiguously as a cluster at the beginning of the file is a bad idea, although it is actually done this way in a number of systems. As one can easily see, there is no easy way to expand the free space table as the file grows. In order to maintain the addressing scheme, the file would have to be reorganized completely— which is clearly not acceptable.

A more flexible method is shown in Figure 14.3. There is one table page, followed by e data pages; then comes the next table page, followed by another e data pages, and so on. This scheme can be extended as the file grows.

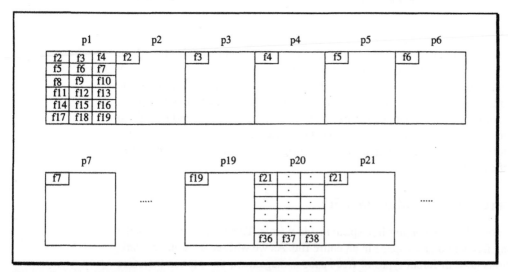

Figure 14.3: Implementation of data structures to maintain information about the amount of free space in each page. The first page is used for the free space table; it is followed by as many data pages as can be managed by the free space page; then comes another free space page, followed by the second portion of data pages, and so forth.

The value of F depends on both the page size S (which is assumed to be an integer power of 2 in the following) and the length of one entry E. E, in turn, is determined by the granule of free space allocation. Some consequences of that are discussed in Exercise 2.

The simplest type of free space administration is to distinguish empty pages from those containing some data; in that case, E is one bit long. The table to keep track of which slots on a disk are free and which are assigned to an extent is an example. The one-bit resource manager, the implementation of which is discussed in Chapter 10 to demonstrate the use of the transaction manager's interfaces, is also based on that scheme. It is instructive to go back and reconsider this sample implementation. Comparing the code with the apparently simple idea illustrated in Figure 14.3 gives a sense of what it means to add such a simple data structure to a page-structured file, provided the operations on that file are to be transaction protected. Section 14.4 contains a more detailed discussion of the locking and logging requirements for keeping free space tables consistent with the respective pages.

14.2.2.2 Free Space Cursor

When considering the functional requirements at the tuple level, it becomes clear that there is no real need for a redundant data structure with the free space information of *all pages* in the file. What is needed is a good guess of where the next tuple could be inserted. Figure 14.4 shows the basic idea.

Instead of a table, this scheme requires two pointers in the file catalog. One points to the page that is the "current point of insert"; the other is the anchor of a chain of empty pages. Space allocation is very simple: as long as the tuple to be inserted fits into the "current" page, it goes there. If this page fills up, the next empty page is taken from the chain and becomes the new current point of insert. If a page becomes empty because of deletes or reorganization, it is chained behind the anchor. The discussion of locking implementation in Chapter 8 uses a similar algorithm to demonstrate the use of semaphores; in that case, it is used to maintain free pages in main memory.

Note that updates to the empty page chain and the respective catalog entries must be transaction protected. A simple example of an operation using the free space cursor is presented in Subsection 14.4.3.

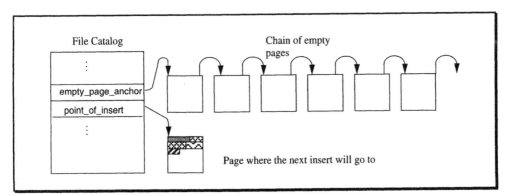

Figure 14.4: Maintaining free space in a file through a free space cursor. In this scheme, a list of empty pages is maintained, and the current point of insert is remembered. When the page that defines the current point of insert fills up, another page is claimed from the empty page list.

14.2.2.3 Summary

Free space administration in a file is needed to quickly answer the question: Here is a new tuple; where should it go? Apart from this standard service, free space information is also required to decide if and when a global reorganization of the file should be performed, or if a file expansion is needed.

There are two popular techniques. One is a table that contains one entry per page; this provides exact, up-to-date information about the space occupancy in the entire file. It requires, though, a transaction-protected update of the table information for each insert and delete operation, and for each update that changes the tuple size.

The second technique has less overhead but does not maintain exact global information about space occupancy. It maintains a list of empty pages and remembers the current point of insert. It is particularly suited for two types of files: first, it works well if tuples are inserted sequentially "at the end"; these are the entry-sequenced files. Second, it is adequate for files where the location of a tuple is determined by attribute values rather than by space occupancy. These file types, called key-sequenced, typically just request empty pages from the free space manager; the rest is done by the algorithms maintaining the specific file structure.

14.2.3 Tuple Identification

In database systems, tuples are not just stored; there is a very elaborate infrastructure for managing the tuples and the various (value dependent) relations among them. To do this, there need to be identifiers for tuples that

Distinguish them from other tuples, and

Locate a tuple via this identifier with minimum overhead.

The first point may seem a bit far-fetched, given the fact that relational database systems come with the explicit requirement for a primary key in each relation. However, applications frequently need to store tuples that are identical in all attributes, yet are different tuples. In other words, the fact that these two identical things exist must be stored in the database. They could generate their own keys in some way, but it is certainly more convenient to rely on the system to provide an identifier and simply use that. Moreover, application-generated keys generally are long and of variable length, whereas system-internal identifiers can be kept short and of fixed sized. The system must guarantee uniqueness and stability for these implicit attributes, that is, for the internal identifiers.

The second point is more obvious. On each relation, there are a number of secondary indices, that is, key-sequenced files and hashed files implementing associative access "to that tuple"; the methods for doing that are presented in Chapter 15. These files need some way of pointing to the tuples in the base relation. Such pointers must be unambiguous, and they must provide efficient access to the tuple.

There is yet another reason for a stable tuple identifier. Crash recovery and archive recovery are both based on the recovery log. The log entries describe operations on tuples. The system must be able to unambiguously relate log entries to the objects in the database. Therefore, the temporal range of available log files also determines when and under which circumstances an identifier of a deleted object can safely be reused.

Tuple identification can be done in four different ways, each of which is explained in the following. Independent of which of these techniques is actually used, the tuple identifier has an external structure that is defined by the following declaration:

```
typedef  struct
    {   NODEID         at_node;        /* node where the tuple is located      */
        FILEID         in_file;        /* to which file does it belong         */
        TUPLENAME      local_id;       /* this is the value identifying the tuple */
                                       /* relative to the file in_file         */
    }   TUPLEID,  * TUPLEIDP;
```

This declaration makes the point that a tuple is identified through a three-layer hierarchy: first, there is a NODEID pointing to the node in a distributed system where the tuple is stored. Second, the file within that node is specified through FILEID. And, finally, the tuple is given a unique name within that file.

The first two components of the tuple identifier are concerned with naming files in a distributed system and therefore are not discussed here. The techniques to be described differ only in the way they generate unique tuple names (hence, the italics entry in the declaration). However, the fourth technique, primary keys, also generates tuple names that are not necessarily local to a file or a node. Having node-independent primary-key values is a great advantage for referencing tuples in a distributed system.

14.2.3.1 Relative Byte Addresses (RBAs)

The byte address of the first byte of a tuple in a file, consisting of the PAGEID and the offset relative to the beginning of the page, is certainly unique for each tuple.[4] It is a fast access path, because it directly points to the beginning of the tuple. The only problem is that it is not stable for most file organizations; one reason is that tuples may have to be relocated because they grow as a result of an update. Also, there are file organizations where the storage position is determined by attribute values; a change in these values necessarily requires the tuple to be moved. An addressing scheme that causes a change of tuple identifiers in all such situations can safely be ruled out.

14.2.3.2 Tuple Identifiers (TIDs)

This scheme gets efficient access comparable to physical addresses but is more stable over time. The basic idea is illustrated in Figure 14.5.

Case A is the simple case. The tuple name consists a page number (7446 in the example) and an index to the directory in the page. The directory entry points to the offset relative to the page of the first byte of the tuple. This allows for free relocation of the tuple within the page, without affecting the tuple identifier.

Tuples can move to other pages when they are updated or when the pages are reorganized. As shown in case B, moved tuples simply leave a "forwarding address," which has the same structure as a tuple identifier, in the original page. This level of indirection is hidden by the DBMS as part of the TID lookup procedure.

---

[4] This is only true under certain assumptions: tuples are not fragmented, space allocation guarantees that there is no overlap among tuples, and tuples are never moved (pages are never compressed).

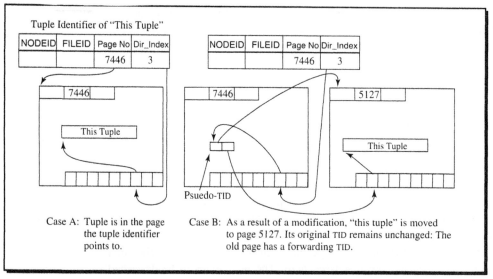

Case A: Tuple is in the page the tuple identifier points to.

Case B: As a result of a modification, "this tuple" is moved to page 5127. Its original TID remains unchanged: The old page has a forwarding TID.

Figure 14.5: The TID addressing scheme. Case A shows the situation in which "this tuple" has not yet been relocated. Case B demonstrates how "this tuple" is found after relocation via a forwarding address stored in its original page. Note that the pseudo-TID contains only pageno and dir_index; the implicit assumption is that relocation is done in the same file and the same node specified in the external TID.

The complete structure definition for a TID-style tuple identifier looks like this:

```
typedef struct
    {   NODEID        at_node;      /* node where the tuple is located          */
        FILEID        in_file;      /* to which file does it belong             */
        PAGEID        in_page;      /* tuple is stored in this page/file         */
        Uint          dir_index;    /* index of the tuple's directory entry      */
    }   TUPLEID,    * TUPLEIDP;
```

For tuples that have moved, two page accesses are needed to accomplish a tuple access. If the tuple moves again, the forwarding chain does not continue to grow, though; it keeps its old TID, and the forwarding address is changed. This is no problem because, as was mentioned above, it has not been exposed to any module outside the tuple-oriented file system. However, relocation is not transparent from a performance perspective; tuples residing in the page to which their TIDs point can be retrieved twice as fast as "moved" tuples. Thus, depending on the percentage of such tuples, the file may have to be reorganized to consolidate TIDs and actual storage locations. Reorganization, however, is a serious problem, for the reasons outlined next.

Cost

Reorganizing large parts of the database is a long and expensive affair. Assume a file of 100 GB ($\cong 100 \cdot 2^{17}$ pages), where 10% of all tuples have been relocated. The number of pages that have to be modified in order to "repair" the relocation effect (delete the forwarding address, give new TIDs to the relocated tuples, and change all references to those tuples based on the old TIDs) depends on parameters such as distribution of tuples over pages, number of tuples per page, and so on. If, on average, there are 80 tuples per page, then the probability of *most pages* being affected by the reorganization is quite high. But to illustrate the problem, assume that 25% of the pages need to be modified. If each update costs 20 ms (the pages must be read and written back to the database), the elapsed time for the reorganization can be estimated as follows: $T_{reorg} = 100 \cdot 2^{15}$ (25% of the pages) $\cdot \, 20 \cdot 10^{-3}$ (update time per page in seconds). This yields 2^{16} seconds, or almost a day.

Without additional optimizations, such as processing pages from different disks in parallel, the actual performance is likely to be worse. The calculation makes the "hidden" assumption that one knows beforehand which tuples have been relocated; however, the only way to find that out is to read the entire file sequentially. The costs for modifying other access paths that have used the old TIDs were ignored, and so on. But even this rough estimate illustrates the expenses incurred by readjusting the addressing scheme. Of course, such overhead is acceptable only if reorganization can be done as a background activity.

Log Dependencies

As mentioned, reorganization assigns new TIDs to relocated tuples. The physiological logging scheme, however, only works if the TIDs appearing in the log are still valid in the database. There are two ways to cope with this dependency. The first method is similar to the checkpointing technique described in Chapter 13. Before starting the reorganization, a shared lock is acquired on the table. Of course, each individual TID change must be covered by exclusive locks to avoid inconsistent access by concurrent readers. This is one application of the SIX lock mode. It guarantees that no log entries will have to be applied to the state of the database that is going to be created by the reorganization. The output of the reorganization goes to a different file, which replaces the original file after reorganization is completed—a method similar to the old master–new master scheme, or to the differential file technique. Its main disadvantage is that it makes the relation unavailable for updaters for a long time.

The second method is to run the reorganization in parallel to normal processing, protected by transactions. This means, of course, that the TID modifications have to be logged and that the modified entries of the page directories must be locked exclusively according to the two-phase locking protocol. What happens, essentially, is that each relocated tuple is deleted from its old page and inserted into the page to which it has been relocated with the new TID. A more detailed analysis of how to reorganize TIDs on the fly,[5] the costs for doing it this way, and the anomalies this can cause for non–two-phase transactions is beyond the scope of this book. Comparing the two techniques, however, the second is much the better one.

Note that the remark about dynamic TID reorganization being a sequence of tuple deletes and reinserts is not quite accurate; Exercise 5 deals with some of the reasons.

14.2.3.3 Database Keys

Database keys are an indirect addressing scheme that avoids the necessity of reorganizing tuple identifiers: all identifiers, once assigned, remain stable for the lifetime of the tuple. This addressing scheme is part of the DBTG data model and is also used in other database systems (ADABAS, for example). The idea is illustrated in Figure 14.6.

---

[5] One of our reviewers took the challenge and came up with the design of an algorithm for dynamically reorganizing TIDs [Salzberg and Dimock 1991].

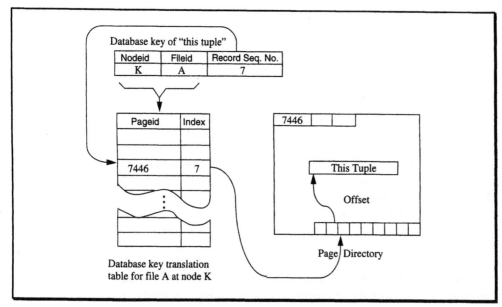

Figure 14.6: Indirect addressing scheme using a database key. The database key is a record sequence number, which is translated into a page address by means of a translation table that must be allocated in contiguous memory.

Upon insert, each tuple (record) is assigned a sequence number that is unique within that file or relation. Record sequence numbers start at one, and the next tuple to be inserted gets the highest current number plus one. For each file, there is an array stored in contiguous pages with as many fixed-length entries as there are tuples expected to be stored in this file. This array is called the *database key translation table*, and its first byte is pointed to from the file catalog. At each moment, entry i of the translation table points to the page where the tuple with sequence number i is stored; it also contains the index of the directory entry pointing to the tuple. In essence, the entries of the database key translation table are TIDs according to the previous scheme.[6]

Tuples can move inside a page. If they are relocated to another page, the database key remains stable, and the respective entry in the translation table is modified. This leaves the addressing structure unchanged, making it unnecessary to reorganize the identifiers. In a sense, the translation table represents a data structure with permanent forwarding addresses for all tuples.

Accessing a tuple with sequence number i always requires two steps:

(1) Locate the page of the translation table containing entry i; this is trivial, since the starting address is fixed, and the table is stored contiguously.

(2) With the pointer found in entry i, locate the page containing the tuple.

This technique is generally more expensive than the TID mechanism, because for large files the translation table cannot be assumed to completely reside in the database bufferpool.

---

[6] This is a convention to keep the presentation simple. Many actual implementations of the database-key scheme only store the page number in the translation table (no directory index).

Consider the following case: let the file have a total size of 10^{10} bytes. If the average length of a tuple is 100 bytes and each entry in the translation table is 4 bytes long, the translation table comprises $4 \cdot 10^8$ bytes, or $5 \cdot 10^4$ pages with a page size of 8 KB. Assuming a bufferpool of 3,000 pages (24 MB), the chance of finding the right page of the translation table in buffer upon random retrieval is low. If, however, a file of the same size has tuples with an average length of 2 KB, there are only $2 \cdot 10^7$ tuples, which yields a translation table of $2.5 \cdot 10^3$ pages. Now the probability of finding the right table page is significant. Assuming that per tuple, 4 different pages are accessed; this means that on the average 1/4 of the bufferpool contains pages of the translation table. With the numbers given here, 750 table pages will be in the bufferpool at any instant, yielding an expected hit ratio of .30—for purely random access. The average number of I/O operations for accessing via the database key is therefore 1.7, whereas there are 1.1 I/O operations for each random access via a TID, provided 10% of the tuples have been relocated.

Given that we analyzed the scenario with fewer tuples, this seems to be a clear argument against database keys. But things are not that simple, because the database key mechanism is not just like the TID technique with all tuples relocated. Our estimate assumes random access across the entire file. This is not a very typical access pattern. More realistically, one finds strong locality of access, which means certain groups of tuples are accessed frequently, while others are not. If this is the case, the hit rate for the translation table increases drastically, whereas the access cost of the TID mechanism depends on the number of relocated tuples only. Another issue is sequential retrieval along a sorted list of tuple identifiers. As will become clear in Chapter 15, such lists are maintained for secondary indices. In that case, the hit ratio on the translation table comes very close to 1 (unless the adjacent database keys in the sorted list are very far apart), whereas TID access will still have its 10% miss ratio. And finally, in order to make a complete comparison, one has to take into account that the low number of 10% relocated tuples is not free; it is maintained by periodic reorganizations, the cost of which must be compensated over the access operations between two such reorganization points. And note that the probability of a tuple overflowing, and thus the frequency of reorganizations, increases as the average tuple length grows in proportion to the page length. It is quite conceivable that there are situations in which the stability of database keys outweighs their potential performance loss for random retrieval.

14.2.3.4 Primary Keys

By definition, each file always has a unique primary key, which is either supplied by the user (through the corresponding clause in the CREATE TABLE statement) or is generated by the system. The following are typical primary keys:

For a relation.   Identifying attributes, TIDs, database keys, and so on. Note that a TID can be viewed simply as an identifier for a tuple, without using the addressing mechanism described above. If there is a different way of relating the identifier with the physical location of the tuple (as described in this paragraph), then relocation is handled differently, too.

For an index.   An index entry of the B-tree variety (see Chapter 15, Section 15.4 for details) can be identified by the key value concatenated with a sequence number that distinguishes multiple occurrences of that key value, in case the key is not unique. Instead of the sequence number, the primary key of the respective relation can be used.

For a sequential file.   If the sequential file is organized such that new tuples are appended at the current end-of-file only (this is the entry-sequenced organization described in Section 14.5), then a timestamp or a sequence number can serve to identify a tuple. Note that an LSN is a sequence number that serves as a primary key for the log file entries.

For a hash file.   A tuple in a hash file (see Chapter 15, Section 15.3 for details of this technique) is normally identified by the value of its primary key attribute, which serves as the argument to the hash function. Since hash-based addressing does not work well for nonunique attributes, distinguishing multiple occurrences of the same value is not an issue.

For a relative file.   In a relative file, tuples are identified by the relative tuple number within the file. Whether this relative number has any meaning in terms of the application is not an issue at the current level of abstraction.

Tuple identification mechanisms based on primary keys are very important for a variety of reasons. The first thing is that the system be able to guarantee the uniqueness of primary keys and other attributes that have been declared unique. In other words, when a new tuple is inserted, it must be possible to decide quickly whether another tuple with the same primary key value already exists. Referential integrity constraints restrict the existence of tuples in one relation based on the primary key values of another relation, which also calls for an efficient mapping mechanism from a key value to a tuple. Depending on the application and its workload characteristics, it might be important to store tuples sorted by their primary key, or to cluster tuples based on key values.

All this illustrates that tuple addressing schemes using synthetic identifiers such as TIDs or database keys are not adequate for all types of references to and among tuples. For that reason, database systems provide a fast, associative access path for each relation via its primary key.

There is, however, an important distinction to be made here. The typical implementation in modern database systems uses either TIDs or database keys as *internal* tuple names and builds everything else on top of that. Access paths for primary keys are treated just like any other access path for other arbitrary attributes. The point is that—given an associative access via the primary key for each relation—internal addressing mechanisms would be obsolete. Whenever a reference to a tuple has to be made (for an integrity constraint or for a secondary access path), its primary key value is used, and the associative access path is used to dereference this pointer. It is easy to see that this kind of addressing meets all the stability requirements: since a primary key value is bound to the identity of a tuple, that key value is a valid reference to the tuple as long as the tuple exists. Being completely independent of all physical aspects, the tuple can be relocated arbitrarily without affecting its identification mechanism. In parallel and distributed database systems, where many references cross node boundaries, this property is particularly important.

14.2.3.5 Summary and Miscellaneous Remarks

We can now summarize the pros and cons of the different addressing schemes and conclude with a recommendation of the optimal technique. Some remarks will be made along the way, indicating which other roles can be assigned to an addressing mechanism in a real system.

The TID mechanism allows free relocation of tuples while keeping the identifier stable. Access is fast, provided the number of relocated tuples is small ($\leq 10\%$). To maintain reasonable performance, the mechanism must be supported by an efficient online reorganization facility for the TIDs of relocated tuples.

With database keys, tuples can be relocated freely without the need for reorganization. On the other hand, there is one more level of indirection for each access.

Many people consider addressing tuples via their primary keys to be too expensive. As is explained in the next chapter, dereferencing a primary key pointer using a B-tree structure typically costs three to four *page* accesses, depending on the size of the relation. Locality considerations show that two to three of these accesses should be buffer hits in virtually all cases, so this leaves one or two physical block accesses, which is about the same number as for the TID scheme and the database key technique. Now consider an associative access via a *secondary* key, which is implemented as a B-tree–like search structure in all database systems. Mapping the secondary key value to pointers to those tuples with the desired attribute value requires a traversal of the search tree, which also costs some four page accesses. Assume 50 tuples are qualified; that is, the search tree produces 50 tuple identifiers. The costs for dereferencing these 50 tuple pointers with each of the three techniques described can easily be estimated:

TID. With 10% relocated tuples, a total of 55 physical block accesses are required.

Database key. Depending on how far apart the database keys in the "qualified" list are, the number of physical block accesses ranges between 51 and 100.

Primary key. Depending on the locality at the level below the root (this has to do with how far apart the primary key values are), the number of physical block accesses ranges between 51 and about 102.

So assuming a bufferpool that is sufficiently large in proportion to the primary key B-tree (to achieve a good hit ratio), tuple addressing via primary keys costs about as much as the physically-oriented techniques. It gets more expensive, though, if the hit ratio goes down.

Before making a judgment based on that rough cost estimate, however, we have to appreciate that primary key addressing has important advantages in several other respects: first, since associative access via the primary key is needed anyway, no additional addressing mechanism must be implemented; the associative access path determines the tuple's storage location and allows retrieval as well. Furthermore, if the primary key is an attribute designated by the application, it will not contain administrative detail such as nodeid and fileid. Thus, a tuple can move freely from one node to another without having to change the tuple identifier, which would be necessary for all the other addressing mechanisms. Primary keys as the basis of tuple identification and addressing achieve a higher level of data independence than do other identification schemes that are oriented toward the physical file organization. In centralized systems, this is not important; but in a distributed system, it is a clear advantage to have an addressing scheme that remains stable even if tuples move among nodes. And, finally, addressing tuples through an associative access path avoids any reorganization beyond what is required to maintain the access path itself. As we will see, these access paths, if used properly, allow all maintenance operations to be done online.

All things considered, the advantages of the primary key addressing technique outweigh its higher cost, especially since there are many tricks to reduce the overhead for the majority of operations.

An interesting trick is to use two pointers rather than one: the first one is the primary key, which is always correct but may be more expensive to use. The second one is a *guess*, or a *probable position pointer*—there are many different names. Essentially, it has a TID structure and points to the page and index entry where the tuple was and probably still is, unless it was relocated since the pointer was used last. This provides fast access, but the guess may be wrong. Dereferencing now works as follows: take the guess pointer and see if the tuple is really stored at the position it points to. If it is, everything is fine, and the access costs are as low as for the TID scheme with no relocation. If the tuple is not stored at the position the guess pointer points to, forget the guess and follow the primary key access path. This will definitely locate the tuple. Depending on the access right of the transaction executing the operation, the result of the primary key access can be used to update the invalid guess and make it valid—for the time being. The basic advantage is that any relocation that does not change the primary key need not adjust any references to the tuple.

Such optimizations may reduce the number of physical block accesses required for the primary key addressing scheme, but the price is a higher CPU pathlength. Whether the net balance is positive depends on many parameters such as hit ratios, access frequencies, frequencies of tuple relocation, and so forth. No general recommendation can be made.

14.3 Physical Tuple Management

Representing an SQL tuple in a page requires a number of different mechanisms, depending on the type of relation the tuples belong to and the domains on which the attributes are defined.

Internal representation of attribute values.   The fields of the SQL tuple have to be mapped onto some internal representation, which must provide at least as much precision as the SQL datatype. Fields of varying length may or may not be compressed, NULL values must be distinguished from valid instances, fields of length 0 must be distinguished from those having the NULL value, and so on. These are the considerations for "short" attribute values (those not exceeding the size of one page). For "long" attributes, additional mechanisms are required.

Tuple mapping.   The internal representations of the field values of the same tuple must be arranged such that retrieval of any single value is equally fast, and that updates modifying the length of attribute value are not restricted. In addition, it must be possible to add new attributes to an existing relation without having to reorganize all the tuples that have been stored before. Again, we will first consider the problem for short tuples fitting into one page.

Long tuples.   In case a tuple can grow beyond page boundaries—either because of a large number of attributes or because some attributes can have very long values—tuple fragmentation across multiple pages must be supported. The mechanisms to be discussed in that category still assume normalized relations; that is, each attribute has at most one value.

Complex tuples.   Some database systems (for example, those in the object-oriented domain) need to support complex tuples. These are tuples of relations that are not necessarily in first normal form; in other words, the attribute values can be structures, repeating groups, or entire sub-relations. Tuples of that type require additional mapping techniques.

Security. The storage mechanism must support encrypted representation of field values, if required.

The following subsections describe in some detail a number of implementation techniques for each of these tasks. The focus is on the commonly used methods in real systems, rather than on exotic algorithms. The discussion makes use of some simple data structures that should help in understanding how SQL tuples work. These data structures implement the very core of an internal schema description; they are presented here for ease of understanding rather than for performance.

14.3.1 Physical Representation of Attribute Values

The fields of a stored tuple contain the encoded representation of the attribute values the application program has supplied through the SQL interface (CREATE, INSERT or UPDATE commands). It must support all the data types allowed for attributes in an SQL table. The SQL standard contains no encoding rules for its data types (with the partial exception of INTERVAL and DATETIME), and in many cases explicitly leaves it to the implementor to define maximum precision, length, and other parameters constraining the representation. Under these circumstances, finding an internal encoding scheme for the attribute values is not as obvious as one might think. To understand this issue, consider the following representations in which an attribute value can occur:

External representation (E).   This is the way attribute values are presented at an interactive SQL interface. Typically, these are strings of bytes based on ASCII or EBCDIC code, depending on the environment. For the current discussion, it is sufficient to assume that this representation is a complete and correct image of the respective SQL data type.

Program-internal representation (P).   If SQL is embedded into a programming language, the database attributes are dynamically bound to variables of this language, and the attribute values are therefore represented in the data types the language supports. That, of course, varies from language to language. For example, the SQL data type varchar is represented in C as a zero-terminated string, whereas in COBOL it is a string with a length field in front of it.

Field encoding (F).   This is the way in which the attribute is stored internally in the database.

With these different levels of representation, there have to be a number of mapping functions, as illustrated in Figure 14.7.

If e is an instance of representation E, p is an instance of P, and f is an instance of F, then some trivial invariants should be preserved; for example:

$$m_{EP}(m_{PE}(p)) = p, \; m_{PF}(m_{FP}(f)) = f, \; m_{FE}(m_{EF}(e)) = e.$$

Of course, the inverse invariants must hold, too. The same must be true for a three-step mapping. For example:

$$m_{\mathrm{FE}}(m_{\mathrm{PF}}\ m_{\mathrm{EP}}(e))) = e.$$

The SQL standard does not exactly specify these equality rules; it only contains some informal remarks about exception conditions to be raised in case the mapping is not possible for certain values or data types. It should be obvious, however, that a system without such mapping invariants would be fairly useless.

In addition, it must be guaranteed that the operations on attributes (comparison, arithmetic calculations, aggregation, sórting) yield the same results in all representations. The semantics of the operations are defined at the data model level; that is, with reference to E. If that is not possible, the values have to be transformed into an appropriate representation *before* carrying out the operation.

All these requirements imply that all three representation schemes should have the same expressive power. This is to say that there should be a 1:1 mapping between all instances of the respective layers. However, this is not the case in typical implementation environments. There is, for example, a datatype DATETIME at the SQL level (E), but there is no corresponding type in programming languages like C, COBOL, and many others (P). On the other hand, FORTRAN supports REAL numbers with quadruple precision, which SQL may not. More examples can easily be found. The same problem occurs at the level of internal tuple representation. Since each implementation of the tuple-oriented file system is written in some programming language, the types available at level F are those supported by that language; that is, not all types required by E have a direct counterpart at the internal layer. (As an aside, this is one facet of the so-called *impedance mismatch* between SQL and programming languages, observed by the object-oriented community.)

Under such circumstances, it does not make much sense to maintain three distinct repre sentation schemes, as sketched in Figure 14.7. All exisiting database systems, rather, simplify matters by one of the following methods:

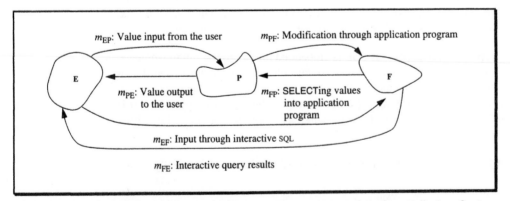

Figure 14.7: Mapping functions between different value representations for attributes of a tuple.   There are three representation domains of attributes in a relation: the external representation (E) on the screeen, on a form, and so on; the database representation (F); and the representation used by the programming language in which the database management system (or the application, for that matter) is implemented (P). All three representation domains can have different data types, different value ranges, different comparison operators, different consistency constraints, and so forth. Of course, for each attribute, there exists—in principle—the abstract domain, which may be different from all three domains mentioned. Since the specification of this abstract domain is not yet part of the SQL standard, it is omitted from the discussion for simplicity.

F ≅ P. This approach tries to take as much as possible from the run-time system of the implementation language. Of course, the available support varies from language to language, but the consequences are the same in each case. An SQL datatype that has a matching counterpart in the language is internally represented in that encoding, which, in turn, is determined by the machine-internal conventions for data representation. The datatypes not supported by the language are implemented by the tuple-oriented file system and cast into a related type in the programming language. For example, the SQL type DATETIME is cast into an ANSI character representation of the date. As a consequence, the mapping invariants mentioned previously do not hold for all datatypes: at the SQL level, one can manipulate date or time intervals (comparison, subtraction), but it is not possible to do the same thing in the programming language in which the application is written. The internal implementation of such extra types is mapped from and to E, but not to P.

F ≅ E. This is a more radical approach. Since the implementation language cannot provide all the datatypes required anyway, the tuple-oriented file system uses only two very basic types: characters and binary integers. The rest is implemented at level F, according the system's own conventions, and is explicitly mapped from and to E and from and to F (as far as possible). Oracle is a typical example of this approach. For all the numeric datatypes that can be declared at the data model interface, there is one internal representation, namely, a somewhat unconventional floating point scheme. It is a byte string of variable length with the following structure: the first byte contains both the sign and the exponent of the number in standard encoding. The bytes after that contain the digits of the number in base 100 notation with an offset of 1; all numbers are normalized.

Both approaches have their pros and cons. The first technique stores most of the data—numerical data in particular—the way they are delivered (and expected) by the usual programming languages the database has to cooperate with. This is efficient, but it implies certain machine dependencies. Considering subtleties such as Big Endian versus Little Endian, it generally is not possible to move data in their internal representation from one machine to another, even if the same database system runs on both machines.

The second approach is much more machine independent. The representation for numerical values is both neutral and safe in that its potential precision exceeds that of all common programming languages. It can be mapped into all specific floating point representations of any given machine. It also avoids "anomalies" like the binary representation of −1 being larger than the binary representation of 1 when compared as ASCII byte strings—and this is just one example of mismatches between the different representation domains. On the other hand, the F ≅ E approach *has to be mapped*, because no machine uses exactly that representation, and additional run-time overhead is therefore incurred.

One special problem of representing attribute values deserves explicit treatment: how can NULL values be represented? Note that this is another example of incomplete mapping between the different layers of representation. SQL allows NULL values for each datatype, but programming languages have no corresponding notion and therefore cannot handle them directly. For the reasons mentioned previously, NULLs and their semantics have to be implemented by the tuple-oriented file system. One could try to use some "reserved" value to express NULL, but that would have to be a different value for each datatype, and the solution is generally clumsy. Consequently, NULL values are represented independent of the datatype by making appropriate adjustments to the data structures used to map tuples into pages. This is described in Subsection 14.3.3.

14.3.2 Physical Representation of Short Tuples

Before explaining the implementation techniques for short tuples, we need to define some control blocks that contain the schema description. That is, we need to describe which relations have been defined, what their attributes are, which datatypes the attributes have, and so on, in a form that is adequate to support query processing at the tuple level.

According to the SQL standard (and in agreement with many existing relational systems), the schema description that is provided by the application using the SQL command CREATE is stored as tuples in a number of system-owned catalog relations, such as the following:

ACCESSIBLE_TABLES.   This relation contains one tuple per relation in the system (including the system-owned relations); its declare follows.

TABLE_PRIVILEGES.   This relation contains one tuple per access right granted to a user on a relation using the SQL command GRANT.

ACCESSIBLE_COLUMNS.   This relation contains one tuple per attribute for each relation described in ACCESSIBLE_TABLES. It describes datatype, length, consistency constraints, and so on. The declaration follows.

There are four more system-owned schema relations: COLUMN_PRIVILEGES, CONSTRAINT_DEFS, CONSTRAINT_COLUMNS, and DOMAIN_DEFINITIONS; since their contents are not required for the description of tuple representation, they are not presented in detail.

The declaration of ACCESSIBLE_TABLES and ACCESSIBLE_COLUMNS, according to the SQL standard, looks like the following:

```
/* L is an implementor-specified integer not less than 18                          */
CREATE TABLE accessible_tables
          ( owner               CHARACTER VARYING  (1)  NOT NULL,
            table_name          CHARACTER VARYING  (1)  NOT NULL,
            table_type          CHARACTER (1)           NOT NULL,
                  CHECK         (table_type IN ('T','V') ),
            PRIMARY KEY         (owner, table_name)
          );


CREATE TABLE accessible_columns
          ( owner               CHARACTER VARYING (1)  NOT NULL,
            table_name          CHARACTER VARYING (1)  NOT NULL,
            column_name         CHARACTER VARYING (1)  NOT NULL,
            data_type           CHARACTER VARYING (1)  NOT NULL,
                  CHECK         (data_type IN        ( 'CHARACTER',
                                                       'INTEGER', 'SMALLINT',
                                                       'DATE,'TIME',
                           /* here comes the rest of SQL data types              */
                                 )
          ),
```

data_length	INTEGER NOT NULL DEFAULT 0,	
data_precision	SMALLINT NOT NULL DEFAULT 0,	
data_scale	SMALLINT NOT NULL DEFAULT 0,	
datetime_precision	CHARACTER VARYING (1) NOT NULL DEFAULT ",	
nullable	CHARACTER (1) NOT NULL	
	CHECK (nullable in ('Y', 'N')),	
domain_owner	CHARACTER VARYING (1),	
domain_name	CHARACTER VARYING (1),	
PRIMARY KEY	(owner, table_name, column_name),	
FOREIGN KEY	(owner, table_name) REFERENCES accessible_tables,	
FOREIGN KEY	(domain_owner, domain_name) REFERENCES domain_definitions	

);

For performance reasons, these schema relations are not used at run time by the modules implementing tuple and attribute access. Rather, a compiled version of these relations in the form of C structures is used to access the data; they contain the same fundamental attributes as the schema relations, plus some run-time data that are explained in the following. These compiled versions are created either at system startup or when a relation is accessed by an application for the first time. They are typically stored in the schema tables as *binary large objects* (BLOBs). The control blocks compiled from the schema descriptions are to relations what the open control blocks are to files, as described in the previous chapter.

The ACCESSIBLE_TABLES relation is compiled into the following structure (in the following, it is assumed that only tuples describing base tables—TABLE_TYPE == 'T'—are considered):

```
#define nrelations MANY
#define nattributes MANY
struct      relations
{      Uint        relation_no;              /* internal id for the relation             */
       char        relation_name[ ]          /* external name for error messages         */
       char    *   owner;                    /* user id of the creator                   */
       long        creation_date;            /* date when it was created                 */
       PAGENO      current_point_of_insert;  /* free space administration is done        */
       PAGENO      empty_page_anchor;        /* using the free space cursor method       */
       Uint        no_of_attributes;         /* how many attributes in relation          */
       Uint        no_of_fixed_atts;         /* how many fixed-length attributes         */
       Uint        no_of_var_atts;           /* how many variable-length attributes      */
       struct      attributes  *  p_attr;    /* pointer to the attributes array          */
};
```

```
/* Depending on the mapping scheme, there will be additional fields in the relations control block.       */
/* Array of records for describing the relations declared in that schema. It is filled from the            */
/* TABLES table at open time. Whenever a new relation is defined or an existing one is                     */
/* modified, it has to be updated accordingly. In the following, the index for relation_cat will           */
/* be omitted.                                                                                             */
struct    relations      relation_cat[ ];

/* Record structure describing an attribute of a relation. Not all references to other description         */
/* tables are actually used in the following examples. The entries are filled from the TABLES              */
/* and COLUMNS relations at open time. Whenever a new relation is defined or attributes are                */
/* added to (dropped from) a relation, they have to be updated accordingly.                                */
struct attributes
       {    Uint         relation_no;            /* this assumes a normalized repres.                       */
            char *       attribute_name;         /* external name of the attribute                          */
            Uint         attribute_position;     /* index of the field in the tuple (1,2,...)               */
            char         attribute_type;         /* this encodes the SQL-type definition                    */
            Boolean      var_length;             /* is it variable_length field ?                           */
            Boolean      nulls_allowed;           /* can field assume NULL value ?                           */
            char *       default_value;          /* value other than NULL that is to be                     */
                                                 /* assumed if none is stored in a tuple                    */
            Uint         field_length;           /* maximum length of field; specified in                   */
                                                 /* declaration or implicit to datatype                     */
            int          accumulated_offset;     /* will be explained with the mapping algorithms           */
            Uint         significant_digits;     /* for data type FIXED                                     */
            char *       encryption_key;         /* in case you want to store the value                     */
                                                 /* encrypted                                               */
            char *       rest;                   /* further information on the attribute                    */
       };
```

Depending on the mapping scheme, there will be additional fields in the attributes control block. For each existing relation, an array of the attributes structure is allocated. The attribute descriptions are stored in their ordinal sequence. The pointer *p_attr in relation_cat points to the array pertaining to the respective relation. In the following code examples, the base pointer for attribute_cat will be omitted because the discussion is restricted to one relation. Its declare looks like this:

```
struct attributes attribute_cat[nattributes];
```

Figure 14.8 gives an overview of the relationship between these control blocks and the actual tuple representations in a page. The declarations here have been restricted to what is needed to discuss the techniques for physical tuple representation. Their use will be demonstrated by explaining the techniques for retrieval of a specific attribute value in a given tuple. The sample code uses the variable names of the control blocks already declared. One should note, though, that in some systems nothing even remotely similar to these structures exists. There is the external (SQL) catalog, and the rest is directly compiled into the access plans.

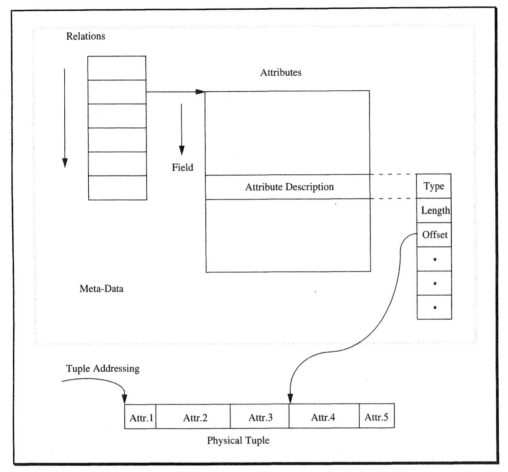

Figure 14.8: Structure of the schema description in relational databases. The run-time control blocks compiled from the schema relations contain all the information needed to "interpret" a physical tuple or to compute the proper offset within a tuple where the value representation of an attribute begins. The relations control block is the anchor for an array containing descriptive information about all the attributes in all relations. For each attribute, a row in the attributes array relates the external name to the ordinal number of the attribute within the relation (and thus within each tuple, for most of the mapping schemes). This is important, because SQL sometimes explicitly refers to the sequence of attributes in a relation. Furthermore, the row describes the attribute's datatype, the attribute's (maximum) length, its default value, and so on. In the simplest case, it says at which offset relative to the beginning of the tuple the attribute value starts; this allows fast retrieval of the attribute value, given that the begin address of the tuple has been determined by the addressing mechanism (as described in Subsection 14.2.3).

However, assuming such a compiled catalog makes the presentation of the algorithms much more convenient.

We start by discussing the mapping of short tuples; according to the usual terminology, these are tuples that fit into a single page, whatever the size of a page may be. Most database systems have been designed for applications where tuples are short in that sense; in fact, some systems still do not allow storing tuples that exceed page size. Consequently, many algorithms and storage structures are designed to work well under that assumption. Because the support for long tuples is generally an add-on to the basic structure of short tuples, it makes sense to separate discussions of these issues. The solution to spanning tuples across page boundaries is described separately (see Subsection 14.3.2).

A physical representation technique for short tuples must make a number of decisions, the parameters of which involve storage consumption, implementation cost and complexity, extensibility and ease of reorganization, pathlength, and so on. There is no best strategy, a systematic way of describing and modeling the various approaches is a basis for picking the right strategy under given constraints. Here are the fundamental questions:

Reorganization.   Should reorganization of the data structure, such as adding a new attribute to an existing relation, be easy?

NULL values.   Should fields containing NULL values be stored or suppressed?

Variable length.   Should the tuples be stored with variable or fixed length?

Compression.   Should compression be done on fields with variable length?

Spanning.   Should growth of tuples across page boundaries be easy?

It will be instructive to compare the algorithms that follow with respect to these criteria. The basic set of techniques to be analyzed is graphically represented in Figure 14.9. The examples are based on a simple table definition:

```
CREATE TABLE     DEMO_REL     (    F1   CHAR(3)    NOT NULL,
                                   F2   VARCHAR(20),
                                   F3   NUMERIC(10,2),
                                   F4   INTEGER,
                                   F5   NUMERIC (6, 7),
                                   F6   VARCHAR (15) );
```

There is a prefix to each tuple, which is conceptually the same for each tuple representation. For some file organizations, however, not all fields of the prefix have to be stored explicitly, because their contents can be derived from the context.

Also, note that the prefix elements relation_id and TUPLEID are normalized in most practical cases. The former, relation_id, can be eliminated by adopting the convention of storing just one relation per file. The latter, TUPLEID, is redundant because the page number, concatenated with the index of the page-directory entry pointer to the tuple's begin address, is the tuple identifier—assuming the TID mechanism is used. But these are simple optimizations; there are a number of implementations that allow tuples of different relations to be stored in the same page (for clustering); then each tuple must be self-identifying to a certain degree. But apart from that, the given structure simply repeats the "defensive" style that has already been introduced for blocks and pages; they, too, are equipped with a prefix that contains their identity.

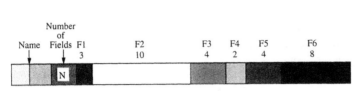

A: Fixed length for all fields in the record.

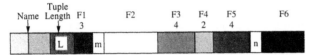

B: Mix of fixed-length and variable-length fields. Variable-length fields are preceded by a length field that has a fixed length.

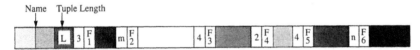

C: Composition of variable-length fields. Each field value comes with a length field and an attribute indentifier. Total length field at the beginning.

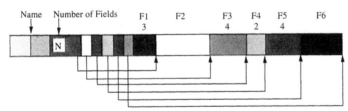

D: Composition of fixed-length fields and variable-length fields. Tuple prefix contains an array of pointers to the end of each field value.

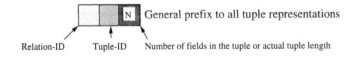

Figure 14.9: Different techniques for mapping a tuple into a page. The attribute names and field lengths hovering above the tuples are obtained from the attributes control block. The other information is explicitly stored in the tuple and must be determined at run time.

As mentioned earlier, SQL allows an existing relation to be extended by adding another attribute to it. Assume the relation DEMO_REL declared previously had some 10^6 tuples, and then the command ALTER TABLE DEMO_REL ADD COLUMN F7 is executed. Trying to change all existing tuples as a consequence of that command would cause a major reorganization effort and therefore could not be executed online. But this is not necessary. By definition, the value of the new attribute is NULL for all tuples that were stored before the attribute was declared.[7] The storage mechanism, therefore, has only to make sure that F7 is returned with the NULL value for "old" tuples when they are accessed after the ALTER command.

The solution to this is very simple. Adding the new attribute causes a modification of the catalog structures; in particular, no_of_attributes in relation_cat is increased by one, and the index of F7 in attribute_cat will be that value. All existing tuples will have a value in no_of_fields that is (at least) one less than the new no_of_attributes. The following convention can therefore be made:

When a tuple is accessed, and the index of the requested attribute in attribute_cat is higher than no_of_fields in the tuple's prefix, then the NULL value is returned for that attribute. Obviously, this works for multiple extensions of a relation.

For the sample implementations of the tuple representation mechanisms, the following assumptions are made:

(1) Length fields do not include their own length, because the field is fixed at whatever the implementation has chosen. It is 1 byte in many "old style" databases, some LONG FIELDs come with a 2-byte length field, or one could make it 4 bytes to be on the safe side—if 4 GB are considered safe.

(2) The implementations assume their input parameters to be set to correct values; in the following sample implementations, they are passed in the variables rel_index, att_index, and tuple_begin.

(3) The algorithms return two result variables, value_begin and actual_length.

(4) Other parameters, such as datatype, are retrieved from attribute_cat as needed.

These are the declares of the input parameters:

```
Uint    rel_index;        /*index in relation_cat of the relation the tuple belongs to     */
char    *tuple_begin;     /* points to the beginning of the tuple accessed (prefix)        */
                          /* the page containing the tuple is in buffer and fixed          */
                          /* the tuple has been located by one of the mechanisms           */
                          /* described in 14.1                                             */
Uint    att_index;        /*index of the entry for the requested attribute in attribute_cat */
```

The output parameters are declared to be:

---

[7] According to the SQL standard, a newly defined attribute can have either the NULL value or some explicitly specified default value. To keep things simple, the following discussion assumes the NULL value only. But note that this is no restriction. All the schemes proposed would work with the default value as well, because it is stored in the catalog.

```
char     *value_begin;        /* pointer to first byte of the field value (lowest address byte)    */
                              /* NULL if there is no value for that attribute                       */
int      actual_length;       /* length of the field value. for fixed length fields, this is a      */
                              /* copy from attribute_cat; stored length otherwise. −1 if there       */
                              /* is no attribute value.                                              */
```

Let us now briefly review the four techniques for tuple representation shown in Figure 14.9. The conclusion of this discussion will be an "optimal" algorithm for storing short tuples, a sample implementation of which is spelled out in C.

14.3.2.1 Fixed-Length Fields, Fixed-Length Tuples

Using fixed-length fields only makes for the simplest algorithm. All fields are stored in the sequence in which they are declared in the CREATE statement, at the maximum length that was specified. There is no need for storing any administrative information with the data. The advantage of the fixed-length fields, fixed-length tuples approach is that the template for the physical representation of the tuple can be compiled at schema-definition time. Whenever a tuple is accessed, the base pointer of the template has to be set to the beginning of the tuple, and all attribute values can be found at a fixed offset from there. To support this simple off-set addressing, the end of each field relative to the beginning of the tuple is stored in the variable accumulated_offset in attribute_cat.

Access to all attributes within a tuple is equally fast. Since all attributes are allocated with the maximum length, updates can never extend a tuple, which can cause relocation in mapping schemes that use variable-length fields.

There are some obvious drawbacks: if there are many variable-length character fields, this scheme wastes lots of space. Making fields unneccessarily long increases storage costs, which one might be willing to sacrifice for the sake of a simple (and therefore less error-prone) implementation; it also means that there will be fewer tuples to the page. Therefore, more disk accesses are required for reading a given number of tuples, compared to a scheme that can compress variable-length fields. Note that this argument holds for all aspects of physical storage organization: when comparing the performance of two structures, *A* and *B*, the one that results in a higher *page pathlength* (i.e., the number of pages touched for an average access operation) carries a performance penalty. It may be negligible, but the effect still has to be considered.

The approach just described does not allow for tuples to span across page boundaries. Even if one ignores page headers for the moment, the first byte of page *P* will generally not follow the last byte of page *P* − 1 *in the address space the access modules work in*, because pages are mapped into buffer frames individually; thus, adjacent pages in the database address space will be stored in nonadjacent buffer frames. In other words, if a tuple were mapped according to the fixed-length scheme to span two pages, it would not be possible to access all its fields by an offset relative to the tuple's start address in the address space of the access modules.

14.3.2.2 Variable Fields with Preceding Length Fields

Length counters in front of variable-length fields try to save space by storing variable fields with their actual length, using a classical chained data structure. As in the previous case, the fields are stored in the sequence they were declared in the catalog; for fixed-length fields, the length information is taken from the directory. The variable-length fields come with a preceding length field, which itself has a fixed, system-specific length. Note that for such attributes, the length field must be there, even if the attribute has been assigned the NULL value (see the discussion of NULLs below). The scheme allows, however, for a length field with value 0, which is immediately followed by another length field or by a fixed-length field.

The basic procedure for determining the position of a field value is straightforward: start at the beginning of the tuple; for each attribute preceding the one to be retrieved, add the field length either from the catalog or from the length field. For each length field, add 1. This algorithm is correct, but inefficient. The major problem is that for each tuple access, one has to add up things that do not change from one access to the next, namely, the length contributions of the fixed-length fields. That can easily be done at compile time, but the catalog structure attribute_cat would have to be extended to accommodate that solution. Here is the basic idea:

First, there is an entry var_length distinguishing fixed-length fields from variable fields. What is needed in addition is a "forward chain" among the entries in attribute_cat, pertaining to the same relation that links all entries describing variable-length fields. Then the following definition can be made: the entry accumulated_offset contains the sum of the lengths of all fixed-length fields either *since the previous variable length field* or *since the beginning of the tuple*, respectively. With these provisions, retrieval only needs to add up the lengths of the variable-length fields it has to cross on its way through the tuple; the contributions of the fixed-length fields are compiled into the catalog.

Like the fixed-length scheme, this storage structure implies some restrictions. First, field values must be stored in the order the attributes were declared in the CREATE TABLE statement, which, in the simplified catalog structure used for the code examples, is directly mapped onto the indices of the array catalog_cat. Second, tuples cannot exceed one page for the same reasons explained in Subsection 14.3.2.1: the starting address of a field value is determined by adding offsets to the starting address of the tuple, but neighboring pages will not have contiguous addresses in the address space where the instructions shown previously are executed. This problem is solved by the next storage structure.

14.3.2.3 Sequence of Self-Identifying Attributes

Making fields self-identifying is the most flexible of all mapping mechanisms for fields of tuples. It makes no implicit assumptions about the ordering of attribute descriptions in the catalog being the same as the order of stored values in the tuples. Each field comes fully equipped with a length field and an internal identifier for the attribute. This identifier could be the value of att_index, under which the respective attribute is listed in attribute_cat.

Retrieval is almost as simple as in the first scheme because there is no distinction between fixed-length and variable-length attributes. In the first scheme, all fields are stored with fixed length; here, all attributes are stored as variable-length fields, even if all occurrences have the same length. The advantage is that the same storage structure can be used for all instances.

There is a price for this simplicity. No pre-compiled addressing information from the catalog is used; rather, the entire tuple is scanned sequentially, which means the data structure is *interpreted*. The access cost for a field value increases in proportion to its distance from the beginning of the tuple. A NULL value usually requires the whole tuple to be scanned before it is determined to be NULL.

Besides simplicity, self-identifying attributes have some other advantages, too. The scheme allows for easy extension and reorganization. NULL values do not require any special treatment; they are simply represented by not storing the attribute ID at all. Therefore, adding a new attribute to a relation is trivial. Having self-identifying attributes also helps in spanning tuples across page boundaries. The reasons are twofold. First, since the address of each field instance must be computed at run time anyway, it does not change the structure of the algorithm if some more logic is added to allow the address of the next field to be in another page. Second, consider a tuple spanning two pages. One page, P_a, will be the one the tuple identifier points to and will contain the first group of fields; the other page, P_b, will contain the remaining fields. With the first two schemes, apart from the addressing problems, some additional logic would be required to make sure that the fields in P_b are counted correctly (remember, the convention is that they appear in the order of declaration). Self-identifying fields pose no problem, because no matter where in the tuple they occur, they carry their unique identifier with them.

The most important point to make here results from comparing the three techniques introduced so far. Essentially, they represent the transition from compilation to interpretation, as far as addressing within a tuple is concerned: with fixed-length fields, all field offsets can be obtained from the catalog (they are pre-compiled). The second scheme uses pre-compiled offsets for everything between two variable-length fields, but it requires adding up the contributions of all segments bounded by a variable field at run time. The last scheme is purely interpretive in that all offsets are determined by reading the length fields at run time.

The obvious problem is to find a storage scheme that supports at least variable-length fields and dynamic extension, but at the same time avoids any run-time interpretation of data structures other than those of the requested field. This is discussed in the next subsection.

14.3.2.4 Prefix Pointers to the Fields

Scenario D in Figure 14.9 illustrates the basic idea of prefix pointers to the fields. Since pre-compilation of addresses requires entries of fixed length, and since the fields themselves can have varying length, some other type of entry is needed to serve as a "moderator" between the addressing mechanism and the field containing the actual values.

In the simple, unoptimized version, this is done by defining a prefix array after the standard prefix for each tuple. That prefix array contains one pointer per field—again, in the order the attributes have been declared. This pointer holds the offset of the *first byte after the value* of the respective attribute; that is, it points to the end of the field. This convention has two advantages. First, the beginning of the first field is known anyway, since it starts right after the pointer array. And second, the difference between two successive offset pointers is the length of the field the second one belongs to; thus, there is no need for explicit-length fields in front of variable fields. Note that NULL fields are not stored at all; their offset pointer just has the same value as the previous offset pointer.

The addressing information is essentially obtained by accessing an array with the index of the attribute requested. It is the array of pointers (following the prefix) that serves as a rudimentary catalog for the tuple. The only notable difference from the first scheme is the computation of the offset difference, which is required for this technique and which, of course, cannot be pre-compiled. This marginal run-time overhead could be removed, too, but then the length of variable fields would have to be stored explicitly in preceding length fields, as in the second scheme.

Dynamic schema extension by adding new attributes works exactly as it does in the other schemes. The prefix variable no_of_fields says how many attribute values are in a tuple, and this is how many prefix pointers there are. The convention, therefore, is that all fields for which there is no prefix pointer (at the end of the array) implicitly have the NULL value.

14.3.2.5 A Consolidated Storage Structure for Short Tuples

The only drawback of the scheme using prefix pointers is a certain amount of redundancy. Since there is a prefix pointer for *every* field, the length of each fixed-length field is effectively repeated in all tuples. And this is not just redundancy: the unnecessary increase in tuple length reduces the number of tuples per page and therefore causes more page accesses for any given operation on that relation. But there is a way to preserve all the nice properties of that algorithm and at the same time to get rid of the prefix pointers for fixed-length fields. It basically is a combination of the first scheme (fixed-length only) with the prefix pointer technique. Figure 14.10 shows the layout of the optimized data structure.

The data structure consists of four parts: the prefix, a portion containing all the fixed-length fields, a pointer array for the variable-length fields, and a portion containing all the variable-length fields. This obviously requires the fields to be rearranged from the order in which they were declared. Remember that the index position of the attribute entries in attribute_cat is assumed to increase according to the declaration order in the CREATE TABLE statement. To allow for a rearrangement, there is the entry attribute_position. It specifies at which position in the tuple the corresponding field value will be stored.

Since the tuple contains separate portions for fixed-length and variable-length fields, the following convention is made: for a fixed-length field, attribute_position refers to the fixed portion; for a variable field, it refers to the variable portion. In the prefix, there are counters saying how many fixed- and variable-length fields the tuple contains; from relation_cat, it is known how many attributes of the respective categories have been declared; thus, dynamic

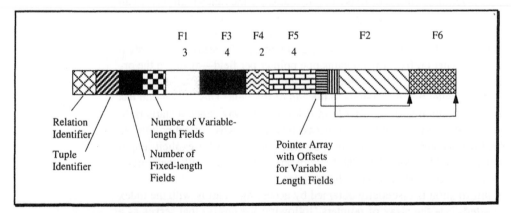

Figure 14.10: Optimized mapping scheme for tuples with fixed and variable-length fields. Fixed-length fields are stored at the beginning of the record, and the length information is obtained from the directory. Variable-length fields are stored after the fixed-length part, with a pointer array preceding the actual values. For both types, there is a field in the header of the record containing the number of instances of each field type.

extension of a relation can be handled in the usual way. Note that with this scheme a relation can be arbitrarily extended by either fixed-length or variable-length fields without having to modify any stored tuples. Addressing of the fixed fields is completely pre-compiled, and the length is copied from attribute_cat; variable fields are handled as in the fourth scheme.

The declare of the tuple prefix (no normalization of relation_id and so on) for this technique looks as follows:

```
#define pre_length 26                                /* length of tuple prefix                         */
#define pointer_length 4                             /* length of a pointer field                      */
struct      tuple_prefix
     {      Uint           relation_id;               /* index of relation entry in relation_cat        */
            TUPLEID        tuple_id;                  /* identifier of this tuple; TID assumed           */
            Uint           no_fixed_fields;           /* number of fixed-length fields in tuple          */
            Uint           no_var_fields;             /* number of variable-length fields in tuple       */
            Uint           offset_var_part;           /* offset of first variable-length field           */
     };
struct      tuple_prefix * ptuppre;
struct      pointer_array
     {      Uint           field_offset[]; };          /* array of offsets of variable-length fields      */
struct      pointer_array * ppa;                      /* base address of pointer array                   */
Uint        type_index;                               /* field is the nth fixed- or var.-length field    */
```

Based on these preparations, together with the set of input and output parameters already declared, retrieval of a specific field value in a predetermined tuple can be implemented as follows (note that the attribute indices are assumed to start at 1):

```
type_index = attribute_cat[att_index-1].attribute_position;       /* determine position from catalog      */
if    (!attribute_cat[att_index-1].var_length)                    /* is it fixed-length field?            */
      {      if      (type_index > no_fixed_fields)               /* is the field stored in that tuple?   */
                     {      value_begin = NULL;                    /* return the "no value" setting        */
                            actual_length = -1;}
                     else                                          /* there is a value for the  attribute  */
                     {      value_begin = tuple_begin+pre_length+   /* set pointer to offset relative to   */
                            attribute_cat[att_index-1].accumulated_offset;       /* the beginning of tuple */
                            actual_length = attribute_cat[att_index-1].length_or_offset;   /* copy length  */
      };              }
else                                                              /* field has variable length            */
      {      if      (type_index > no_var_fields)                 /* is the field stored in that tuple?   */
                     {      value_begin = NULL;                    /* return the "no value" setting        */
                            actual_length = -1;
                     else                                          /* there is a value for the  attribute  */
                     {      ppa = offset_var_part;                 /* make array addressable               */
                            if    (type_index == 1)                /* first field was requested            */
                                  value_begin = offset_var_part;   /* copy offset of field value           */
                            else                                                        /* field with index > 1 was req.*/
                                  value_begin = field_offset[type_index- 2];            /* beginning of this field      */
                            actual_length = field_offset[type_index-1] - value_begin;   /*  field length   */
      };          };
return;
```

As the code shows, the amount of address and length computation done at run time is reduced to a minimum. The pathlength of the fixed-length scheme is lower still, but its potential space overhead incurs a lot of indirect pathlength due to extra I/O, so the consolidated scheme is better overall. One could object that the entry offset_var_part in the tuple prefix is redundant because it can be derived from the catalog, but in order to keep the sample code simple, this design was chosen. With respect to the problem of compilation versus interpretation, it makes no difference.

Note that the code example illustrating one storage mechanism is highly simplified. It locates only one field value, whereas in a real system many attribute values normally are to be read from the same tuple per access. Of course, in that case all the preparatory operations should be performed only once. This can easily be achieved by assuming att_index, *value_begin, and actual_length to be arrays rather than scalars, with the indices being specified in the sequence in which the field values are stored. Other aspects that have been ignored are access control (Is the requester entitled to read that field?) and encryption of field values.

14.3.2.6 Summary

This subsection has discusssed the techniques for mapping records into pages, assuming that the total length of the tuple representation does not exceed page size. The key criteria of the comparison were (1) the flexibility in representing variable-length fields, (2) the adaptability to schema extensions such as adding new fields, and (3) the speed of access to individual fields in a record. If the tuple representation is made self-documenting to a certain degree, especially by storing the number of occurrences of fixed-length and variable-length fields in each record, adapatability can be achieved by comparing these counters with the current status of the record type (relation) that is described in the catalog. Representation of variable-length fields relies either on individual-length fields per attribute value or on prefix pointers to the end of each value. From a performance perspective, the solution using prefix pointers is preferable, because it allows most of the address computations to be done at compile time, whereas the individual-length fields in front of each attribute value require the interpretation of the tuple at run time.

14.3.3 Special Aspects of Representing Attribute Values in Tuples

This subsection briefly discusses two additional issues of how to structure a tuple. The first problem, representing NULL values, is mandatory in order to comply with the SQL standard; the other one is a performance optimization for a typical situation in key file organizations.

14.3.3.1 Representing NULL Values

From what has been established so far, the only scheme for storing tuples that lends itself easily toward representing NULLs is the sequence of self-identifying attributes. The absence of an attribute entry in the tuple says that the attribute is NULL. It is clear, however, that this scheme has performance problems. Representing NULLs in the other schemes is not that simple. At some points it was argued that length zero indicates the NULL value for the corresponding field. But this is not completely correct for two reasons.

First, only variable fields have a length field, but fixed-length fields can be NULL, too. Remember that the conclusion of Subsection 14.2.1 was that a combination of fixed and variable fields is the optimal storage scheme for short tuples. Second, length zero does not imply NULL for data type VARCHAR. According to the SQL standard, an attribute of that type which has been assigned a string of length zero is *not* NULL.

So a representation method for NULL values is needed. Introducing more special cases makes the implementation unnecessarily complex. A simple, neutral, and more flexible approach is to put a prefix at the beginning of the tuple with one bit per field (modulo the fields not represented in the tuple; see Subsection 14.3.1), not just for the variable ones. If the bit is set, the field contains a valid value; if not, it is NULL.

14.3.3.2 Representing Multi-Field Keys

Certain fields in a file can serve as *keys*, that is, as criteria for associative search or for storing (retrieving) records in sorted order. Associative access and related subjects are discussed later, so for the moment it should be sufficient to accept that comparing the values of fields in a record with other values is a frequent operation that should be carried out efficiently.

Let F_i denote some field of a relation, and C_i a constant value; then in the simple case, comparisons such as $F_i = C_i$ or $F_i < C_i$ must be performed when searching and sorting. As long as only one field is involved, this is trivial: assuming that F_i has the same datatype as C_i, the type-specific comparison operator is used, and that is it. But now consider the case of multi-field comparisons. An example of this is $\{F_1 \| F_2 \| ... \| F_n\} < \{C_1 \| C_2 ... \| C_n\}$; here $\|$ represents the concatenation operator, the exact definition of which is given two paragraphs from now. The < relation holds if there is an index k between 1 and n such that $F_i < C_i$ for all $i < k$, and $F_k < C_k$. One obvious way to test the < relation would be a loop, in which the comparison is done field by field according to our definition. This has two disadvantages: first, most machine architectures have instructions that allow for the comparison of byte strings up to 255 bytes; a field-wise comparison does not exploit this feature and therefore loses efficiency. Second, as will become obvious in Chapter 15, proceeding field by field often implies a separate index on each field, which is much slower than using just one index—provided there is a way to carry out the multi-field comparison as *one* comparison.

Assume each field (potentially) is a variable-length field. By $L(F_i)$ we denote the actual length of field F_i. One could then expand each field value to the maximum length of its datatype and concatenate the resulting fixed-length byte strings. If the same is done with the C_i, two byte strings of equal length can be compared, which is trivial. However, if the maximum lengths of the underlying datatypes are large (say, 64 KB), then this is not feasible. So the question is how to concatenate the mutiple field values into *one* string such that (1) only the actual length of each field value is represented, and (2) the right ordering is achieved when comparing the resulting strings. Consider the problem by determining just how the information in F_1 and C_1 must be encoded as part of the one byte string. Assume that $L(F_1) = 18$, and $L(C_1) = 23$. If we just append the length of the field (as a fixed-length binary) to the field value, then the byte string comparison will come out wrong: the 18 bytes of F_1 are compared to the first 18 bytes of C_1 (assume for the sake of argument that they are equal so far), but then the binary-coded length bytes of F_1 are compared to the next one or two value bytes of C_1, which will result in the wrong ordering. So the concatenation scheme must make sure that value bytes are always compared to value bytes, and length fields are always compared to length fields—while still allowing each field value to have its individual (varying) length.

Here is the idea that was first published by Blasgen, Casey, and Eswaran [1977]. (The description is restricted to fields of type VARCHAR). Assume a fixed value $s < 255$. Then as a first step, each field F_i is turned into a field F_i' by appending so many bytes with binary zeros to it that $L(F_i')$ is the smallest multiple of s larger or equal to $L(F_i)$. Then, as the second step, F_i' is divided into segments of length s, and after each segment a byte with all ones is inserted. After the last segment, however, a byte is inserted which contains the value $L(F_i') - L(F_i)$ in binary coding. These $(L(F_i') + L(F_i')/s)$ bytes represent the value of F_i in the resulting byte string. If the concatenation of the F_i as well as of the C_i is prepared this way, it is easy to see that both byte strings can be compared from left to right as though one attribute value, and the ordering will come out correctly according to previous definition. For field values with an average length less than 100 bytes, the optimal value of s is between 5 and 8.

14.3.4 Physical Representation of Long Tuples

Tuples can be long for two reasons: they may have many attributes, and some of the attribute values may be very long.

The first case is largely ignored by current database systems. The usual advice for cases where this might be a problem is to either do a vertical partitioning into many relations (which can then be VIEWed together, if needed), or to do an over-normalization of the relation, or to place all the many attributes in a single VARCHAR field. This problem is briefly reconsidered in the discussion of storage structures for complex tuples, but for the moment discussion is restricted to the problem of storing long attribute values.[8]

The reasons why short attributes and long attributes are treated separately are partly historical, partly technical. Early database systems supported either fixed-length fields or variable fields with a 1-byte-length field. Those systems also typically restrict the tuple size to one page. Our discussion of techniques for mapping short tuples hints at the problems that arise when tuples span page boundaries: space allocation gets more complicated, offset addressing of fields works only relative to the tuple fragment in a page, and so on. Since early database applications did not support very long tuples, such restrictions made perfect sense from both an implementation and an economic point of view.

Over the years, however, vendors have concluded (with a little help from their users) that this is not enough. But changing the storage structure such that the data structures for tuples are no longer bound to pages is a major effort. It may require redesign of several parts of the system, including logging and recovery. Furthermore, a versioning scheme for the database files is required if the new code is to support "old" databases (those created before the data structures were changed). As a result, many vendors decided to pursue the following mixed approach: the basic mapping scheme for tuples is not changed, but some special support for very long attributes is provided: a new datatype is introduced, LONG CHARAC-

---

[8] There are systems such as Informix, Rdb, and Sybase supporting long attributes. These remarks pertain to "classical" database systems that act as resource managers in the majority of today's OLTP systems.

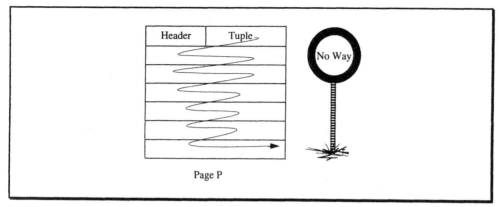

Figure 14.11a: Storing tuples contiguously in one page.   The maximum tuple size is restricted to the maximum page size. So if longer tuples need to be stored, the underlying basic file system must first support pages of adequate length.

TER, or LONG FIELD, or simply VARCHAR(n) with *n* being larger than 255. They are often generically referred to as binary large objects (BLOBs).

Some of the older systems essentially upgraded the previous limitations to a slightly larger scale. Their LONG attributes come with 2-byte-length fields, which is the maximum physical record size file systems have supported for many years. Some newer systems adopted a more radical attitude towards long attributes, but first let us describe the established technology.

Since the techniques for accommodating attribute values of up to 64 KB are simply extensions of the basic ideas just presented, there is no need to discuss them at the same level of detail. The basic ideas are sketched graphically in Figures 14.11a–d.

14.3.4.1 Long Pages

The first technique presents nothing new. As with the short tuples, each tuple is confined to a page. The only difference is that these pages can get as large 32 KB or 64 KB in order to provide the capacity for longer tuples and/or long attributes. Since page sizes are growing anyway with the increasing bandwidth of disk subsystems, this may be standard in the near future (Figure 14.11a); DB2 is a typical example of this approach.

14.3.4.2 Separate Pages for Long Fields

Figure 14.11b shows a technique that is influenced by the idea of long fields being different in respects other than just length. They might be accessed less frequently, and the reference pattern might be different from ordinary attributes, too.[9]

The tuple body is stored as a short tuple, and the field value at the position of the long attribute is a pointer to its value. This pointer refers to a page that only holds long fields. Depending on the addressing scheme, it can be part of a different file. One can decide, for example, to store the tuple body (which is assumed to have a high reference frequency) in 8 KB

---

[9] In fact, most database systems featuring long attributes severely restrict the use of these fields. The long fields typically cannot be indexed, used in a WHERE clause, used in GROUP BY, used in a sub-query, used in expressions, and so on. In DB2, a table with a long attribute cannot be ALTERed to get a new attribute.

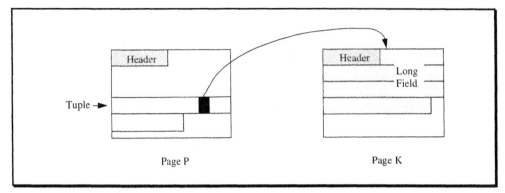

Figure 14.11b: Storing long fields in separate pages. The maximum size of long fields is restricted to the maximum page size. If this is too narrow a restriction, either the page size must be increased or the long field must be decomposed into, say, an array of long fields, each of which can then extend to the size of a page. Of course, the latter option puts the burden on the application program.

pages, which are handled by the standard buffer manager. The long fields, depending on their expected size, can be stored in a file with a 32 KB page size or more, handled by a dedicated long-field resource manager. This is particularly important if a long field is a special object such as, say, an X-ray image that is stored on a different medium (optical disk) than the rest of the relation.

If it happens that these long attributes are accessed less frequently than the rest of the tuple, this technique will maintain the performance of normal transaction processing although the tuples—from the application's point of view—have long fields. This is a major difference from the first technique.

14.3.4.3 Overflow Pages

At first glance, the third technique looks like a straightforward extension of the second one, but it behaves differently. The idea is to store the whole tuple as one object, as in the normal case, but to let it span page boundaries and even become longer than one page. If this happens, the scheme implements some kind of logical page expansion, as is illustrated in Figure 14.11c.

Assuming a normal file organized into pages 0, 1, ..., $p - 1, p, p + 1, ...s$, a tuple t is stored in page p as long as it fits there. Now if t grows (for example, by getting a long-field value), page p is expanded by chaining additional pages p', p'', and so on, to it. Initially, these overflow pages only contain data of tuple t. If later on another tuple l in page p exceeds the available size, the options are to either make use of the larger logical page size of p, or relocate tuple l.

The overflow pages p', p'', ..., can potentially come from a different file. For example, the base file can be key sequenced, while the overflow file is entry sequenced. This allows for dynamic storage reorganization in order to keep the overflow chains short and fragmentation small. Often the overflow file is on optical disk or other such media.

Let us take a simple example as an illustration. Assume the file out of which $p, p + 1, ...,$ are taken consists of pages 8 KB long. If tuple t is already 30 KB long at the moment it is inserted, the first small fragment will go into p; for the rest, p' will be allocated out of a 32 KB page pool. If, on the other hand, t was initially small, so that it was completely contained in p, and it overflows later by just a couple of kilobytes, then p' should come from a pool with

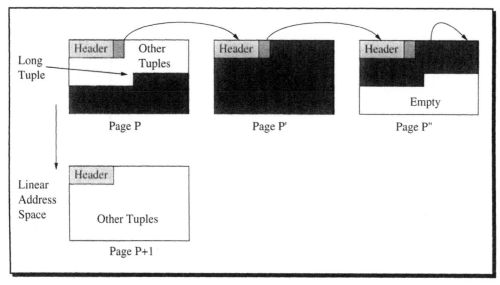

Figure 14.11c: Allowing a physical page to expand by chaining overflow pages to it. A page is expanded "sideways" by chaining empty pages to it. This can continue as long as there are more empty pages, but without additional measures, access performance deteriorates badly as the overflow chain grows.

smaller pages. Conversely, if the overflow chain has grown over time, and all its members are small pages, then it can be reorganized such that it only contains one large p'. By declaring short attributes first in a relation and long attributes last, one can get the same performance benefits that were mentioned for the previous technique. With the overflow file on, say, optical disk one can focus the short, high-traffic attributes on magnetic disk and put the BLOBs on nearline storage.

Overflow pages are also used by some systems to support value-based clustering of tuples from different relations (see Subsection 14.6.1). In this case, each of the tuples may be short, but the total length of all tuples belonging to the same cluster may well exceed the length of a page. Separate pages for long fields and overflow pages are (approximately) the techniques used in Informix, Rdb, Sybase, and other systems to handle long fields.

14.3.4.4 Tuple Fragmentation

The last variant also views a tuple as a linear sequential object; that is, no attributes are explicitly removed and represented by pointers. Since, according to the assumptions, there will generally not be sufficient contiguous storage space for one tuple in a page, the tuples are simply decomposed into fragments, each of which is stored in one page (Figure 14.11d). To reduce overhead, a page contains at most one fragment of a tuple. The fragments of each tuple are threaded together by a (doubly) linked list. Normally, a tuple is fragmented at attribute boundaries, but long attribute values can be cut off at any point.

Note that this storage scheme is also usable for short tuples if their *aggregate* length exceeds one page, or if the tuple no longer fits into the page to which it was originally assigned because of updates.

The difference between this technique and the previous is obvious: the method shown in Figure 14.11c does expansions on a per-page basis, whereas here the fragments form a tuple-

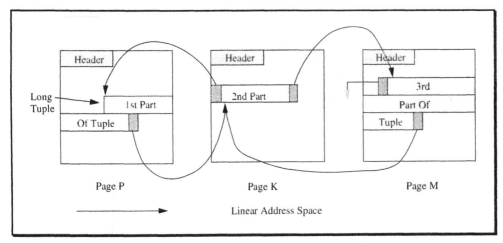

Figure 14.11d: Partitioning the long tuple across many pages. Rather than expanding the page, as in the previous scheme, only those tuples that become too long get overflow pointers into other pages, where fragments of the tuple are stored. With long overflow chains, access to the "rear" part of such a tuple will be slow.

specific overflow chain. If a system does already support spanned tuples, there is no need for an additional mechanism to cope with long fields. The drawback, compared to the previous methods, is that the number of fragments can get very large if the pages for fragments holding large attributes are simply taken from the normal address space's page pool. Since BLOBs are large, tuples would be "diluted" in the file, which increases the number of page accesses and reduces the buffer ratio. To avoid that, one has to distinguish the causes for fragmentation and assign pages from a different pool to hold long fields; see the description of the second method (Subsection 14.3.2.2) for the performance arguments.

14.3.4.5 Summary

The simplest way to cope with long tuples is to keep the conventional technique of confining a tuple to a page and just increase the page size to accommodate longer tuples. Of course, this only works within the limitations of "reasonable" page sizes. What is reasonable depends on both the block sizes supported by the basic file system, and on the variance in tuple lengths. If most tuples are short but a few can grow up to some 100 KB, then it would not be a good idea to use, say, 1 MB as the uniform page length, because each random access to a short tuple would drag a large amount of other tuples into the bufferpool, most of which are probably not needed at all.

The more flexible schemes use overflow handling. In one approach, the tuple is fragmented into as many parts as are required, and each part is stored in a different page. The fragments are either threaded together as a list, or there is a "header" tuple (fitting into one page), which contains all the short attributes and pointers to the long attributes. A different approach maintains the illusion of a contiguous address space per tuple—no matter how long—by logically growing the pages. This is achieved by chaining overflow pages to the original page as needed. Depending on whether the tuple is long because it has BLOBs or because it has many (short) attributes, one or the other technique is preferable. If the attributes of a relation are very different in length and access characteristics, the first approach lends itself naturally, especially because some of the long attributes might be stored on different media. If the tuple is just longer than a page but still needs to be accessed as one entity, the second approach is obviously better.

There are many variations to the techniques just sketched. To mention just one, Rdb partitions BLOBs into segments (segmented strings) and allows each of those segments to be updated individually. All such optimizations, however, do not add anything fundamentally new to the issue of storing long fields.

14.3.5 Physical Representation of Complex Tuples and Very Long Attributes

Up to now, tuples were assumed to be instances of normalized relations; that is, each attribute was allowed to have exactly one value (including NULL). This assumption holds for classical relational systems, but it does not hold for either CODASYL-type database systems or for extensions of relational systems to support the object-oriented style; in such extensions, attributes in one relation can be other relations, some attributes of which are relations again, and so on. The main difficulties center on data models, query languages, query optimization, and so forth. Mapping such complex tuples onto linear address spaces is not very different from the techniques described previously. Therefore, the discussion that follows only mentions a number of typical representation methods and points out which of the mapping schemes they use in principle. Of course, each scheme allows for endless variations and optimizations, mixing with other schemes, and such like.

14.3.5.1 Multi-Valued Attributes and Repeating Groups

Before the relational model determined that repeating groups were bad for you, they were implemented in all of the "old-style" database systems. Most such systems used the mapping technique with preceding length fields (see Subsection 14.3.1). A multi-valued attribute was stored as a variable-length attribute, but the length field at the beginning specifies the *number of occurrences* in the repeating group. Each occurrence, then, was either a fixed-length value, a variable-length value, or another multi-valued field.

Although relational systems do not support repeating groups as part of the data model, they are used internally[10] for different purposes, such materializing joins and storing TID lists in secondary indices (see Chapter 15). One of the techniques for long fields (overflow pages) described in the previous chapter could also make use of repeating groups. Rather than organizing the overflow pages into a doubly linked list, one could represent the long attribute as a repeating group in the tuple body, the elements of which point to the pages holding parts of the long field. This is essentially the segmented string approach mentioned in Subsection 14.3.4.5.

14.3.5.2 Sets and Relation-Valued Attributes

The term *set* refers to CODASYL sets, the named 1:*n* relationship between records of different types. In the object-oriented community, there are either non-first-normal-form relations

---

[10] There is an interesting corollary: since relational databases do not support multi-valued attributes, applications tend to "masquerade" such attributes as VARCHARs. Then it may happen that these VARCHAR attributes, used to mimic repeating groups, are internally mapped onto repeating group structures.

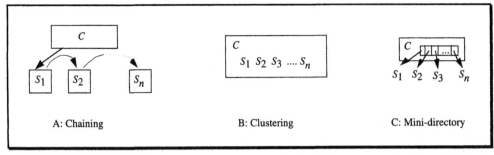

Figure 14.12: Three data structures for representing relationships among tuples from different relations.   The first technique, *chaining*, relies on pointers to thread related tuples together. *Clustering* expresses the relationship by physical neighborhood within a defined environment, say, a page. The *mini-directory* is clustered with the parent tuple and forms an array of pointers to the related child tuples.

or complex objects; in either case, the requirement is to refer to a subset of tuples of relation A as *one attribute value* in another relation B.[11] No matter what the data model calls it, one tuple must be addressable from a varying number of other tuples, which may or may not have the same properties.

Consider some complex tuple C; it has a relation-valued attribute A, the instances of which are the elements of a tuple set S_i. There are three ways to map this relationship onto pages, which are illustrated in Figure 14.12.

The first technique is *chaining*. In the stored version of C, the value of A is a pointer to the first tuple of the set, S_1. S_1 in turn points to S_2, ..., up to the last element related to C. Whether the ordering of the S_i matters to the application is not an issue here. Chaining can be combined with each mapping technique. All the system has to do is introduce additional attributes (which are not visible to the data model) that contain the pointers and thus maintain the relationship at the storage structure layer.

The second method is *clustering*. As in the previous case, the value stored for A in C's physical representation points to some S_1. But now space is allocated such that all S_i related to C are stored in the same page. If there are too many of them, the page is expanded logically, using overflow pages as described in Subsection 14.3.2. Of course, this technique is applicable only once per set of S_i; that is, if the same class of tuples S is a member in a second complex relationship, this one cannot be mapped by clustering—unless the system supports redundancy at the physical tuple level.

The file organization called *cluster files* has been designed to support multi-relation clustering of tuples (see Section 14.4).

The third method is often referred to as *mini-directories*. In the simplest version, the value stored for A in C's physical representation is a repeating group containing pointers to all S_i related to C. It can also be the case that A is just a single pointer to a separate structure referring to the S_i. In the latter case, this structure could then contain additional information, such as access paths.

---

[11] With recursively defined complex objects, it is possible for a relation to have as attribute values subsets of itself, but since this does not change things at the storage structure level, we will ignore it.

14.3.5.3 Very Long Attributes

Very long tuples can have values up to some 100 MB. They can contain data such as documents, books (including figures), digital images, and video and sound recordings. It is quite likely that such attributes will be both retrieved and updated differently from conventional attributes. The SQL update operation, for example, only allows attributes to be modified as a whole; that is, the SET clause specifies a complete new value for the field. Assuming very long fields, however, it is more likely that such fields will be changed in some parts (think of editing a book), that new data will be appended, and so on. The same holds for retrieval: rather than putting the name of the attribute in the SELECT list and getting back the whole 50 MB chunk, one would rather scan through the data sequentially in smaller portions. The key idea, then, for storing very long attributes is to treat them like complex objects with a specific structure and access primitives based on that structure (browsing through a book, playing digital voice, frame-to-frame access to a movie, etc.). The tuple itself contains a mini-directory for such attributes, with all the addressing information required to retrieve the components of the very long value. Space allocation is done by the database system.[12] The basic technique for storing very long attributes is an elaboration of the method shown in Figure 14.11c, using entry sequenced files.

However, handling very long attributes is an active research topic, and there are many other designs in the literature. Some are intended to provide more flexible addressing modes for components of the long field; others aim at efficient space allocation, and so forth. The Exodus design [Carey et al. 1986] uses the principle of single-page allocation for managing the storage space of very long fields (or complex objects). From a storage manager's point of view, the long object is simply a long, uninterpreted byte string. The byte string is partitioned into pages, and a B-tree is established over these pages (that is, the data pages are the leaves of the B-tree). The key for the B-tree is the byte position inside the long object. So each entry in a non-leaf level node has the form (count, page no.), where *count* denotes the number of the highest data byte that is contained in the sub-tree covered by that entry. (For details about B-trees, see Section 15.3.) The identifier of such a long object points to the root of the B-tree via which the long object is accessible. So essentially, this scheme also is a variation of the mini-directory technique shown in Figure 14.11c; but as the size of the object grows, the directory itself will not be particularly "mini" any more. The problem with the Exodus scheme, as with all single-slot schemes, is the loss of sequentiality at the disk level.

The design proposed for the Starburst system [Lehman and Lindsay 1989] instead uses extent-based allocation, with the extents organized into a buddy system. The attribute stored in the primary relation is very much like the basic_file_descriptor described in Chapter 13. Of course, there are a number of optimizations and compression tricks to reduce the storage requirements for the descriptor, but its structure is an array of extent addresses. The Starburst design limits the size of the descriptor to 255 bytes; with a maximum buddy size of 8 MB, this allows for long fields of up to 400 MB.

---

[12] Depending on the type of the very long attribute, there can be specific space allocation requirements. For example, if it contains digital audio, space should be allocated in physical contiguity to avoid hiccups caused by disk arm movement when the recording is retrieved. Of course, it is hard to get 10 GB contiguously, but for the application mentioned, it would be nice to have 1 MB chunks.

Note that the system log can be viewed as a sequence of such long attributes in a system relation. Its implementation is prototypical of the simple approach to very long attributes: a linked list of related entries in an entry sequenced file.

14.3.5.4 Summary

Representing complex objects requires the mapping of (large) hierarchical data structures onto page-structured files. All the established techniques apply: linked lists, search trees, and clusters of different types. There is an interesting aside here. It does not really summarize Subsection 14.3.5, but since there are no historical notes in this chapter, this is its appropriate place.

All the problems of mapping complex data structures were investigated thoroughly for pre-relational database systems of the hierarchical and network varieties. The CODASYL proposal for a data storage description language (DSDL) contains a rich set of mapping techniques—much more than most modern database systems use. The problem with the old-style databases was that they exposed many aspects of the storage structure to the application through their navigational interfaces. Since the relational model was the antithesis to hierarchical and network data models, it effectively relegated most of the more complex storage structures to the Hades of obsolete lore. Now that the necessity of supporting complex objects is widely recognized, there will be a renaissance (or rediscovery) of these techniques, at least for object-oriented database systems.

14.4 File Organization

File organizations determine the mechanisms used to *retrieve the tuples* in the file, based on their attribute values, or on their absolute (relative) position, or on both; and to *find the insert location* within the file for a new tuple.

Of course, viewed from an SQL perspective, all tuples are alike in that the same statements of the data manipulation language (DML) can be executed on them. But for different relations, one can choose different styles to manage the tuples. It is quite obvious that not all relations belonging to an application are accessed in exactly the same style. As an example, take the debit/credit transaction discussed in Chapter 4. The ACCOUNTS relation is accessed randomly (read and modified) via the account number, whereas the HISTORY relation is inserted sequentially at the end. These significantly different access patterns have to be supported (in the sense of performance optimization) by adequate file organizations. A file organization is called adequate (for a given application) if it yields short pathlength and few page accesses for the given workload.

Customers of the tuple-oriented file system are *access plans*.[13] An access plan is a program generated by the SQL compiler; this program implements an SQL statement at a lower, procedural level. The languages used at that level are typically procedural programming languages, plus the operations provided by the tuple-oriented file system. These operations depend to a certain degree on the file organization. The decision of which file organization to pick for a relation to get the best performance possible is part of *physical database design*.

---

[13] Of course, sophisticated application programs might use the tuple-oriented file system directly. But since from the perspective of this book there is no advantage for an application using the tuple-oriented file system rather than SQL, we will consider access plans only.

It is important to understand that the tuple-oriented file system is very different from the basic file system, with respect both to the objects it manages and to the way it is used.

The *basic file system* implements media management. It provides read-write access to blocks based on relative block numbers. It is used by the buffer manager, who opens and closes the files and moderates the access requests issued on behalf of all transactions in the system.

The *tuple-oriented file system* is used in a different style. It is opened by the modules implementing the access plans. Thus, there can be multiple opens of the same tuple-oriented file at the same time. At open time, it is specified which attributes and which tuples are to be accessed in which order for that plan. One might say that, by opening the access plan, a view on the tuples in that plan is established. That view must, of course, be compatible with the file organization; in turn, it presents the contents of the tuples in a way most adequate for the access plan.

The tuple-oriented file system does not *directly* implement relational operators. Rather, it provides a set of single-tuple operations, which are the basis for the next-higher layer to implement the access path primitives. The operations we will describe next can be grouped into two categories:

Administrational operations.   These are create, delete, open, close, grant, revoke, alter, and drop. Since they are independent of the file organization, they are described separately.

Access operations.   For each file organization, of course, there is read-, an insert-, and an update-operation. Others that may be supported depend very much on the file organization and therefore are described in the respective subsections.

In order not to overload the presentation with too many control block declarations, the interfaces to the tuple-oriented file system are explained informally rather than with function prototypes complete with parameters.

14.4.1 Administrative Operations

Out of the four administrative operations, only create and open are discussed here. The others are irrelevant for our purposes and are ignored in the following discussion.

Create.   At file creation, all parameters required to allocate data at block level must be supplied. If the file is to contain tuples of a relation, the first thing it needs is the description of the tuple fields. In addition, the create operator needs information about the following aspects of the new file:

File organization.   This parameter depends on what the tuple-oriented file system actually supports. It might, for example, specify that the file is to be organized sequentially, or that it is to support keyed access, or that random is required. The remainder of Section 14.4 gives an overview of file organizations typically found in current operating systems, although none of them supports all file types.

File location.   This parameter says at which node or disk pool the file is to be stored. The default is the node where the create operation is executed. The default disk pool depends on the authentication identifier of the client.

File partitioning.   As will be explained in Section 14.6, some systems allow a file to be fragmented into a number of partitions. This can be done for both load balancing and availability. If partitioning is requested, it must be specified upon creation, and each partition must be given a location.

Block size.   This is a parameter to be passed down to the basic file system. If different block sizes are possible, the most appropriate one (from a performance perspective) must be selected at creation time.

This is the essential set of parameters. Most systems have additional options for the create operation, such as locking granularity, logging requirements (should an archive log be kept for that file), and replication (should copies of the file be transparently stored in two places). However, the following discussion does not make use of any of these.

Since the SQL standard does not contain any specifications about the physical level—where the tuple-oriented file system is allocated—there is no standard way of describing and storing the additional file parameters we have listed. Of course, it is easy to add them to the system catalog relations as attributes, just like the record description quoted from the standard manual. Rather than inventing an arbitrary, ad hoc notation, we use an example of a CREATE TABLE statement in the syntax of NonStop SQL [Tandem-SQL 1991]; this is standard SQL plus the physical parameters needed for feeding the tuple-oriented file layer.

```
CREATE TABLE      \a.$b.c.accounts  (          /*This describes the logical relation          */
          account_number    pic x (10),
          account_balance    decimal (12,2),    /*                                              */
          rest               character (80),    /*                                              */
          PRIMARY KEY        account_number     /*                                              */
                             ),                  /* The test table about the file in which the relation  */
                                                 /* is stored                                    */
          CATALOG            \a.$b.cat,         /* spec. the node to store the file             */
          ORGANIZATION       KEY SEQUENCED,     /* file organization                            */
          BLOCKSIZE          4096,              /* for the basic file system                    */
          AUDIT,                                /* please keep a log                            */
          MAXEXTENTS         16,                /* for the basic file system                    */
          EXTENTS            (100,100),         /* see basic file descriptor                    */
          PARTITION          (                  /* which fragments are there                    */
                    \a.$c.catalog \a.$b.cat start key "0000008000",
                    \x.$b.catalog \x.$z.cat start key "0000016000",
                    \x.$c.catalog \z.$z.cat start key "0000024000",
                    \y.$b.catalog \y.$b.cat start key "0000032000"
          );
```

This description assumes a 1:1 correspondence between a relation in the database and a file at the tuple-oriented file layer, which stores the tuples of that relation. Many systems actually use that kind of mapping. In case one file can contain tuples of different relations (see the "clustered" file organization), file creation and table definition cannot be as closely coupled as in the case of NonStop SQL. Note that the assumption of a 1:1 correspondence does not mean files and relations are the same thing. The present section is concerned with the organization of files (physical objects), into which relations (logical objects) are mapped.

Note that many of the parameters can be changed while the file exists, either directly or via reorganization. Of course, parameters such as blocksize are hard to change; one basically has to unload and reload the data into a new file with the desired blocksize. Also, many systems do not allow to remove an attribute, or to change its type.

The open operation binds a program to a relation. The program points to the relation it wants to open by the external name of the relation; if the operation is successful, the open returns, among others things, a file handle of the file where the relation is stored. As described with the basic file system, the handle is not the system-internal identifier of the file, but an index to an array where the operating system keeps track of its open files. Note also that the only component that has to know about open is the buffer manager. Since files can have different organizations and, therefore, different functional characteristics, the open statement must get more parameters than just the file name and must return more than a mere file handle. The parameters to be passed with the open request include:

User/program. The authentication identifier of the subject requesting the file to be opened. This information is required for authorization and security checking.

Access type. Will the file be read, updated, or both? This is also required for checking the requester's privileges.

Access mode. This parameter says whether the file will be accessed randomly, or sequentially, or via an access path—if the file organization allows any choice at all.

Access predicate. If only tuples fulfilling a predicate are to be accessed, this predicate has to be passed with the open.

Access mode and access predicate are especially required to specify the access via scans (or cursors); this aspect is explained in Subsection 14.4.2.

The program that has issued the open request needs enough catalog information about the file to access it correctly. This includes:

File timestamp. This is the timestamp of the last modification of the file description. Since transaction programs are often pre-compiled, their code is valid only if the files they access have not changed their characteristics since the compilation was done. There are different ways of checking this. One is to assign a so-called *valid bit* to each compiled access plan. It is set to *valid* at the moment of compilation. Each file maintains references to all access plans that depend on it, and whenever a file description is modified (new attributes, other partitioning, etc.), the valid bits of all dependent access plans are set to *invalid*. Another method is to use timestamps, as suggested here. Each access plan stores the time when it was compiled, and upon open it checks the file timestamps of all files it depends on. If the file timestamp is not smaller than the timestamp of the access plan, the plan is invalid. Once a plan has been found to be invalid, it must be recompiled at open time.

Other partitions. If a relation is partitioned, the program having issued the open must know about the other partitions and open them, too. If some partition cannot be opened—for example, because the node holding the partition is unavailable—this should not abnormally terminate the overall open. Typically, the program will try and run with the partitions that are available. Only if data from an unavailable partition are needed will the program return an error. In such cases, the transaction may have to be rolled back.

Secondary indices.   If secondary indices have been defined for the relation to be opened, and the program needs them either for accessing the tuples or because it performs updates that affect the indices, these index files must be opened, too. In case the index file is not available, there are two cases to be considered: (1) The access plan needs the index only for fast retrieval; in that case, the plan can be recompiled dynamically to work without the index. (2) The program updates the file; for consistency reasons, this is not possible without having access to the index, so replication is not possible.

Figure 14.13 contains a brief summary of the the open logic.

Note that the file descriptor that is used when opening the file, and that is returned to the requesting module, is *not* the catalog description in relational source code. Referring to this representation at open time would require an interpretation of all catalog entries pertaining to that file; this would be unacceptably slow. To speed up the opening process and all further references to the file, a *compiled* version of the file description is produced when the file is created (or every time its characteristics are modified). For fast local access, this compiled file descriptor is stored with every partition. The relational source code can be kept in one place, that is, at the node where the file was created. The compiled file descriptor contains, in a simple internal format, all parameters that are required for accessing the file at run time. The structures relation_cat and attribute_cat, used in Section 14.3, give an idea of what such a descriptor looks like, although they have been extended by a bit in order to simplify the presentation.

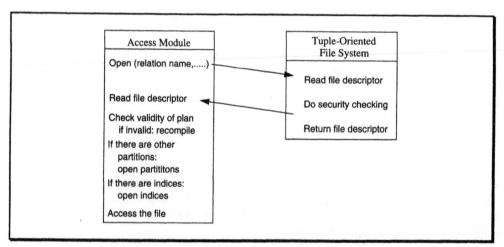

Figure 14.13: Opening a relation mapped into a file of the tuple-oriented file system.   When access to a relation mapped into the tuple-oriented file system is needed, an open request is submitted to the file system. The file system performs security checks and—if successful—returns a compiled file descriptor. The database access module must then check the version number in the file descriptor to see if its own access plan is still based on the latest version of the file. If so, processing can continue; otherwise, the access plan must be recompiled.

14.4.2 An Abstract View on Different File Organizations via Scans

Accessing tuples stored in files with different organizations is a primitive operation when viewed from those layers of a database system that have to support high-level, non-procedural languages such as SQL. Query translation and query optimization cannot be discussed in this book, but the description of scans should give an idea of how file organization and other low-level detail are hidden from the access modules when creating the access plans for complex multi-relation queries.

As a motivation, let us start with an intuitive explanation of what a query optimizer and the corresponding compiler have to do. Given an SQL statement with joins, selection predicates, group by clauses, and sort order specifications for the result tuples, the compiler's problem is to translate the statement into operations on the existing tuples stored in their respective files, such that the specified query result is computed. The optimizer's problem is to determine the most efficient sequence of operations that can produce that result. Consider the following simple example:

```
select   R.x, S.y
from     R,S
where    R.k = S.f and R.b < 12;
```

This is a join of two relations, R and S, via the primary key of R and a foreign key of S, with some additional restriction on R. The query optimizer has determined[14] that the fastest way to answer the query is to read S sequentially, and for each tuple of S to read all relevant tuples of R (those with R.b < 12) to find the one with the matching value in k. This is the so-called "nested loop" technique, and it is adequate if R is small enough to completely fit into the bufferpool for the duration of the query.

Somewhere in the system, therefore, a module (let us call it *NLJ*) exists to implement the nested loop join algorithm for arbitrary relations. It issues tuple requests according to its outer loop/inner loop scheme, does the matching, and inserts the join results into a temporary relation that might be the input for further processing steps—depending on the overall query. The question now is: how does *NLJ* read its input tuples, given the large variety in file organizations, and given the fact that its input might be the intermediate result of a previous sub-query?

One possibility would be to implement *NLJ* such that it can handle all file organizations, issuing the right versions of read operations, writing its results in the proper style, and so on. But then, this is just one module, implementing one join technique. For other join techniques, there are other modules, and, of course, there are more operators than joins that have to be implemented, too. If all the different implementations of the operators in an SQL command had to deal with full complexity of file organization and physical tuple representation, the result would be highly redundant code, which would be hard to maintain.

14.4.2.1 The Definition of a Scan

This is where the idea of *scans* comes in. A scan is fundamentally an SQL statement on one relation. For retrieval purposes, it does everything a **select** operation (without the group by

---

[14] The methods used to generate possible access plans and to estimate their performance are beyond the scope of this book.

clause) on a single relation can do: project on certain attributes, suppress tuples that do not fulfill the selection predicate, and sort the tuples by the values of some attributes. Furthermore, a scan can be used to insert, delete, and modify tuples in any position of the retrieval sequence. A scan, then, is a way of opening a file in a more abstract and powerful way than by using the operations of the tuple-oriented file system directly. It is more abstract because the file organization can be ignored, and it is more powerful because the access operations that can be executed on a scan are even more flexible than the intersection of the access operations of all file organizations described in this chapter. There is a close correspondence between scans at the tuple-oriented file level and cursors at the SQL level; this will be examined in Subsection 14.4.2.6. Let us now define a scan and its properties more precisely.

A scan is a logical access path for the tuples of some relation R. It allows retrieval of tuples in a procedural fashion and in a sequence that depends on the definition of the logical access path. Whether this access path is supported at the physical layer by an index or by some other kind of storage structure is irrelevant for the definition of a scan. The definition of a scan has five components:

Relation name. This specifies the relation from which the tuples are to be processed by the scan.

Order criterion key. A scan always delivers the tuples of its base file in some well-defined sorted order; the attribute(s) by which the tuples are sorted are the *key* of the scan. The key can consist of a single attribute in the file, or concatenation of attributes (see Subsection 14.3.3.2), or it can be a system-internal attribute reflecting the physical storage location of the tuple, such as the tuple identifier.

Range condition. This condition refers to the same set of attributes as the order criterion; it specifies the lowest key value (start key) and the highest key value (stop key) to include in the scan. In other words, it simply specifies a value range within which the tuples are to be selected. The range can be open or closed on both ends, that is, the lower boundary can be specified as "start-key > k_0" or "start-key $\geq k_0$"; correspondingly, the stop key can be included or not.

Filter. The filter specifies which attributes (fields) have to be returned by the scan. In addition, it may contain a selection predicate on attributes other than the scan key. The tuples returned must then fulfill the predicate, plus they must match the range condition.

Isolation criterion. Specifies whether the operations on the scan are to be protected by degree 1, 2, or 3 isolation. This is derived from a corresponding clause in the SQL declare cursor statement.

Except for the relation name, all parameters are optional. As stated earlier, this is very similar to the clauses in a select statement. However, while a select statement can be viewed as a function that is defined on relations and produces a relation as its result, a scan is an operator that provides procedural, tuple-at-a-time access to relations. Thus, in addition to the parameters already mentioned, each active scan has a scan pointer which points to the current position of processing.

14.4.2.2 Operations on a Scan

To establish a scan on a relation, the scan has to be opened. The open_scan command contains as its parameters the options listed in Subsection 14.4.2; it returns a handle that identifies this scan among all others in the system. All subsequent operations referring to the scan have to pass the handle to specify which scan they refer to.

Once a scan is open, the tuples can be retrieved with the next_tuple operation; again, a scan defines a procedural interface. The retrieval operation changes the position pointer in the same way the file pointer is changed when reading a sequential file.

The current tuple (this is the one the scan pointer points to) can be modified or deleted. It is also possible to insert a tuple, but its position in the scan is completely determined by the new tuple's value in the scan key attribute(s)—provided it matches the range condition and the filter predicate. In other words, inserts are independent of the scan pointer, and vice versa.

14.4.2.3 Scan Pointers

According to the assumptions sketched in Subsection 14.4.2.1, access via a scan is governed by the scan key. So once a tuple has been located, the scan pointer points to that key value, and the sort order determines what the next (and the previous) key value is. If, however, the tuple the scan pointer refers to is deleted, it is not so obvious which value the scan pointer has. But let us explain the use of the scan by proceeding from the simple case (read access) to the complicated case (update).

As long as a scan pointer is used for read access only, the rules that govern the relationship between the pointer and the sequence of next_tuple operations are trivial. After opening the scan, the pointer is located before the tuple with the minimum key value; after retrieval, it points to the tuple with the current key value; and after retrieving the last tuple in the sequence, it points after the maximum key value.

As soon as update operations are allowed on the tuples accessed via a scan, the situation becomes more complicated. What happens, for example, if a tuple is modified such that its position in the scan changes according to the order criterion?

To define unambiguously the effects of the scan operations on the scan pointer, four different scan states are distinguished, as illustrated in Figure 14.14. Normally, the scan pointer is AT a key value, which is the current tuple's value in the scan key attribute(s). Since the scan moves sequentially from one key value to the next one, the state of the scan pointer is always AT a key value—except for two special cases. When the scan is opened, the scan pointer is BEFORE the start key value; after the scan has been exhausted, the scan pointer is AFTER the stop key value. Of course, this definition assumes that the scan proceeds in ascending key order. If the tuples are accessed in descending key order, the definition must be reversed. When the scan is closed, the pointer is said to be in the NULL state.

It is easy to see that these states cover all situations that can arise when navigating over a sequence of key values. Since the next_tuple operation only refers to the result of the previous operation, no reference history needs to be remembered; the four states introduced here allow all possible outcomes to distinguished.

The next step is to specify how the state of the scan pointer changed, given its current state and the operation on the scan, that is, the mapping,

{old state of scan pointer, operation} → {new state of scan pointer, result}.

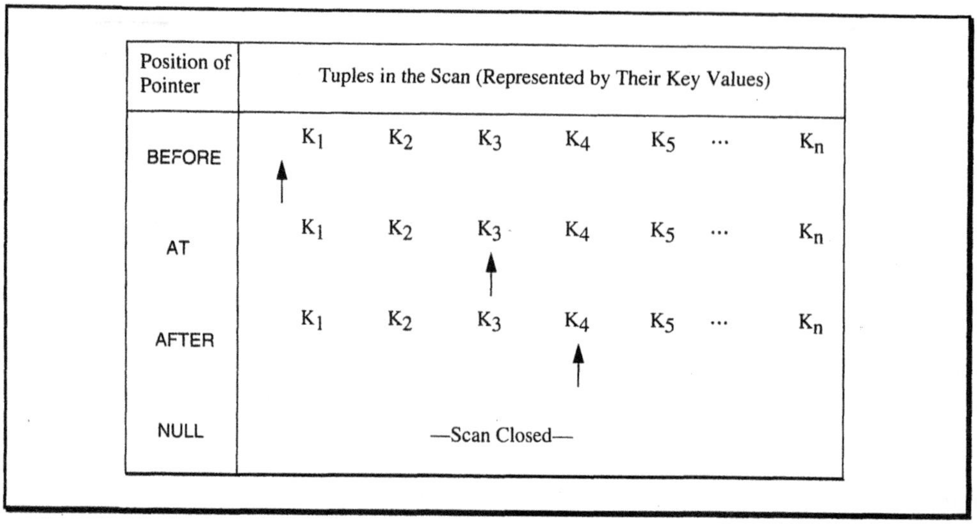

Position of Pointer	Tuples in the Scan (Represented by Their Key Values)
BEFORE	K_1 K_2 K_3 K_4 K_5 ... K_n ↑
AT	K_1 K_2 K_3 K_4 K_5 ... K_n ↑
AFTER	K_1 K_2 K_3 K_4 K_5 ... K_n ↑
NULL	—Scan Closed—

Figure 14.14: The role of the scan pointer. A scan pointer can be in four different states. After the scan has been opened, the scan pointer is BEFORE the start key value. As the tuples are accessed, the scan pointer is AT the corresponding key value. After the scan is exhausted, the pointer is AFTER the stop key value. The NULL state of the pointer corresponds to a closed scan.

14.4.2.4 Transition Rules for the Scan Pointer

Most of the scan state transition rules have to do with the effects of update operations on the scan. For example, if an update operation modifies the scan key value in the current tuple, which changes the tuple's position in the scan, what happens to the tuple, and what happens to the scan pointer?

There are many similar cases, and, in general, there is no single right answer. However, for each constellation there must be a clear definition of what happens; otherwise, the system would not produce predictable answers. For brevity, we avoid religiously going through all the combinations of states and operations; rather, we focus on the interesting cases and try to convey the idea of how scan pointers are handled. In principle, each implementation can adopt its own conventions—as long as they are consistent.

To explain things as simply as possible, let us assume a transaction T_1 operates on a scan S_1. At the same time, other transactions T_i may use (and update) tuples in the file S_1 is defined on—but, of course, not via the scan S_1. It is also possible that T_1 uses other scans S_j that partially intersect with S_1, that is, one or more of those S_j are defined on the same files as is S_1.

First, whenever an operation cannot be executed and returns an error code, the state of the scan pointer remains unchanged. Second, consider the case of the tuple S_1 is currently AT being deleted. This can either be done by T_1 or by another transaction T_i, if S_1 has been opened with isolation degree 1. In either case the scan pointer of S_1 remains unchanged; that is, it is still AT the key value of the deleted tuple. Of course, if T_1 subsequently tries to refer to the CURRENT tuple of the scan without executing a next_tuple operation before, an error code is returned.

Update operations are straightforward. Clearly, if the update does not affect the tuple's position in the scan, the tuple assumes its new value, and the scan pointer remains unchanged. If the update affects the scan key attribute(s), then the tuple moves to the location in the scan determined by the *new* key value, whereas the scan pointer remains AT the *old* key value.

Note that updating the attributes that constitute the scan key may cause problems, which are generally referred to as the *Halloween syndrome*. An example is illustrated in Fig. 14.15. The transaction using the scan updates key value K_4. The update increases the key value, moving the tuple forward in the scan order. When the transaction reaches the same tuple (now with value K_4'), it updates it again, moving it still further ahead in the scan order. If there is no range condition, this will go on until the key attribute overflows. Therefore, when generating access plans, database systems are very careful about not using scans the scan keys of which would be modified by the access plan.

Note that the Halloween syndrome could also occur if the update transition rule said that the scan pointer moves to the position of the new key value.

14.4.2.5 Implementation Aspects of Scans

This brief subsection only mentions the issues of interest in implementing scans, rather than discussing the solutions in detail. Issues specifically related to *index* scans are covered extensively in the next chapter.

It is important to understand clearly that a scan is not another file organization, or a file system on top of the tuple-oriented file system. It simply describes the state of processing the tuples in a file on behalf of some transaction program. For one transaction, there can be multiple active scans on the same file at the same time; and, of course, different transactions can open scans on the same relation concurrently. The whole purpose of scans is to provide

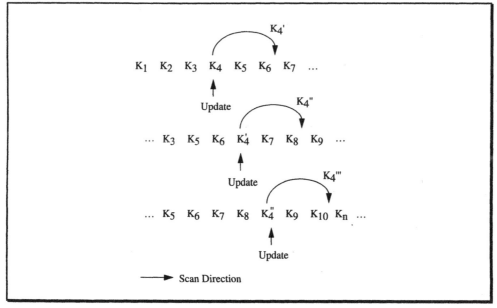

Figure 14.15: Updating a tuple in a scan. A tuple update affecting the scan key attribute may have an indirect impact on subsequent operations. This can result in reaccessing tuples that have been visited before and updating them again. This can cause the *Halloween* anomaly.

those parts of the system that implement the access plans for complex queries with a uniform interface to tuples in one relation, independent of the particular file organization.

For each scan, there is a control block containing all the parameters required to access the respective file according to the specification of the scan. Without going into any technical detail, the structure of a scan control block looks like the following:

```
enum SCAN_STATE { TOP, ON, BOTTOM, BETWEEN, NIL };
                                /* data type for the five different scan states              */
typedef  struct
    {   Uint            scanid;       /* handle for scan; returned by open_scan               */
        TRID            owner;        /* which transaction uses the scan                      */
        FILE      *     fileid;       /* handle of file the scan is defined on                */
        char      *     scan_key;     /* specification of scan key attribute(s)               */
        char      *     start_key;    /* lower bound of the value range covered by the scan   */
        char      *     stop_key;     /* upper bound of the value range covered by the scan   */
        char      *     filter;       /* qualifying condition for all tuples in scan          */
        Uint            isol_degree;  /* specifies the locking policy for the tuples accessed via the scan */
        SCAN_STATE      scan_state;   /* state of scan pointer                                */
        char            scan_key[ ];  /* value of the scan key the scan is before, at, or after */
    }   SCANCB,         * SCANCBP;
```

For simplicity, it is assumed that the key attribute names and the various qualifying conditions are kept as character strings. This, of course, would require them to be interpreted upon each access via the scan, whereas in real systems they are kept in a pre-compiled form for performance reasons. That issue, however, can be ignored here.

A scan, by definition, is based on a scan key. So the first requirement is that the next_key operation can be implemented such that the tuples can be accessed in ascending or descending order of the scan key. If the scan key is a physical attribute referring to the physical storage location, such as a TUPLEID, then this is trivial. Since TUPLEIDs are designed as efficient internal access paths, there is no difficulty in accessing tuples in TUPLEID order.

If the scan key, however, involves external attributes (fields) of the file, such as employee_no, part_no or whatever, an efficient access path along these attributes must either exist or must be created temporarily in order to support the scan. One possibility is an index on the scan attribute; if such an index has been created as part of the physical database design, it can be used for the scan. Since the implementation and maintenance of indexes is the topic of Chapter 15, we will not pursue this aspect here.

If using an index is no option for some reason, then the scan has to be materialized. That means a copy of the file underneath the scan is created. This copy contains all tuples of the file qualifying according to the range condition and the filter; the tuples are stored in scan order, which means the next_key operation can be implemented by a sequential read operation on the temporary file.

Depending on the file organization of the file the scan is defined on, one of the options has to be chosen. The properties of the various file organizations are explained in Subsections 14.4.3 to 14.4.6.

As the control block declare shows, a scan has different degrees of isolation (see Section 7.6). In BROWSE mode (degree 1), the tuple a scan is AT can be deleted by another transaction, so any subsequent references to the current tuple will cause an error. If the scan is processed with degree 2, the tuple the cursor is AT cannot be affected by another transaction—this is what the name CURSOR STABILITY refers to. However, at degree 2, tuples that have been accessed by the scan before can still be deleted or updated by other transactions. To protect against such interferences, the cursor must be opened with degree 3.

Note that these considerations only apply to interferences among different transactions working on the same file. A tuple pointed to by the scan pointer of scan S_1 can still disappear even at isolation degree 3, if the transaction using S_1 deletes that tuple using another scan S_2. But, of course, what a transaction does to its own tuples is completely the responsibility of that transaction.

Scans are the ideal basis for implementing key-range locks, as explained in Chapter 7, Subsection 7.8.4. This does not say key-range locking should be used for all scans. If the scan key is an internal physical attribute, such as a TUPLEID, locking a value range between two subsequent TUPLEIDs could only prevent new tuples from being inserted into the range of the scan; otherwise, such a value has no meaning to the user of the scan.

If, on the other hand, the scan key is an attribute of the file (relation), then using the key-range locking technique helps to avoid the phantom anomaly with respect to the scan. When processing the typles in ascending key order, previous key locking is the obvious choice; otherwise, next-key locking is more adequate.

The aspects of implementing key-range locks on an index scan are discussed extensively in Chapter 15, Section 15.4.

14.4.2.6 The Relationship between Scans and Cursors

As was mentioned at the beginning of Subsection 14.4.2, there is a close correspondence between scans as an abstraction of the tuple-oriented file system and SQL cursors. It is important to understand, though, that the two concepts are not identical.

We do not want to start a detailed discussion of SQL cursors and the options that can be applied, so let us just mention some of the differences. First, a scan is defined on one file of the tuple-oriented file system only; it is an abstract procedural interface to a file. A cursor, on the other hand, can be declared with any legal select expression, including multiple joins and grouping operations. One can imagine the result of such a complex select statement being materialized in a temporary file on which a scan is then used to retrieve the result tuples. But that does not establish equivalence between a complex select cursor and a scan. It is quite possible to produce the result of, say, a join on the fly (without materializing it), while the application still sees a cursor. And, of course, cursors on a complex query result are generally not updatable, whereas a scan in principle can always be updated. Second, SQL adopts the convention that updates applied to the tuples in a cursor do not become accessible *via the cursor* until the cursor is closed. This clearly reflects the notion of a materialized copy on which the cursor operates.

The third point is closely related to the second one: if the select expression of the cursor contains an "order by" clause (and remember that in our definition a scan is always solved by the scan key), then the cursor is read only—simply because an update in the sort attribute(s) would not be reflected in the tuples. The only advantage of that convention is that it avoids the Halloween anomaly at the application level.

There are also similarities between scans and the currency indication that are visible at the programming interface to DBTG-style network database systems, or to hierarchical databases à la IMS. It would be interesting to explore the differences and equivalences between these concepts, but that is outside the scope of the present chapter. The important issue is this: we have introduced scan as a system-interval abstraction to the tuple-oriented file system; that is, scans are used by access plans, which in turn are generated by the SQL compiler. But even though a single-relation select statement may be mapped to an equivalent scan, it is important to understand that the usefulness of a scan as an internal interface does not automatically transfer to scan-like external, procedural programming interfaces.

14.4.3 Entry-Sequenced Files

The rest of this chapter presents the access operations for six different file organizations. To get an idea of what is coming, refer to the "road map" in Figure 14.16 (Figure 2.13 is a simpler version). Each file organization supports a certain type of scan in that it organized tuples sorted by some physical or logical attribute. If a scan with that attribute as the scan key is needed, then the readpos operation directly implements the next_key operation.

The name *entry-sequenced files* says it all: tuples are appended to the file. The result is a sequential file that reflects the order in which the tuple arrived. This file organization is clearly geared toward fast sequential access to the entire table for both reading and writing. The sequential reading part is obvious: all pages of the file except the last will be filled with tuples (some of which may have been deleted), and if the block-oriented file system preserves the ordering of pages at the disk level, the file can be accessed with the maximum speed the disk will allow. Writing is a one-way process: the insertion point is advanced at every insert, and no space lying behind the current end-of-file will ever be reused. Given the same assumptions as for reading, then, the file can be written at maximum channel speed, too. The log file is a typical entry-sequenced file. We will use the entry-sequenced file organization to illustrate the implementation of tuple access operations in a transactional

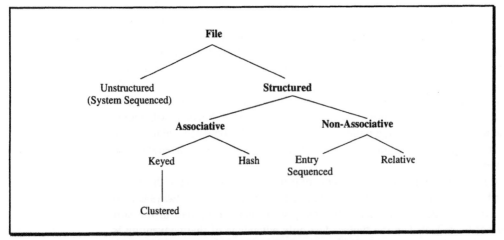

Figure 14.16: An overview of the most frequently used file organizations. The description in this and the next chapter mostly is concerned with the organization and implementation of structured files.

context by C-code fragments. The reader is invited to go through these code examples carefully, because they illustrate how the interfaces to the buffer manager, the log manager, and the lock manager are used to give simple file accesses the ACID properties. The description of other file organizations does not go to the same level of detail; rather, it refers back to the entry-sequenced organization as far as logging and locking is concerned.

14.4.3.1 The insert Operation

Free space in an entry-sequenced file is handled by a free space cursor, which at any instant is the end-of-file pointer. Initially, all pages are in the free page chain,[15] and the current_point_of_insert entry in the file descriptor points to the end of the file. Since tuples are always appended, the value of freespace in the page header must be large enough to put a tuple into the page. If it is not, the next empty page is claimed, and the remaining free space in the previous page goes unused. The basic logic of inserting a tuple into an entry-sequenced file is illustrated in the piece of (pseudo-) code that follows. The directory is assumed to fit into one page; the TID of the inserted tuple is returned to the caller.

As the code illustrates, the modification to the page at the current end-of-file, caused by the insert of the new tuple, is logged; the page is tagged with the LSN returned by the log manager; and an exclusive lock is acquired on the new tuple before the semaphore on the page is released. The implementation assumes physiological logging; that is, it records the fact that a tuple, represented as a byte string according to some storage structure, has been inserted into that page with a certain TID (see Chapter 10, Section 10.3).

Note that the directory entry, in case it is modified because a new end-of-file page needs to be allocated, is not handled by a lock. During the modification, it is protected by an exclusive semaphore; the modification itself is logged as afterimages for the affected catalog entries, saying that there are new values for the end-of-file page and the next free page. However, no lock is held on the modified entries, and the semaphore is released as soon as it has been determined that a proper place for the insertion of the new tuple has been found.

That means the ACID rules are interpreted in a very particular way with respect to the free space data in the catalog (and in the data pages, for that matter). When releasing the semaphore, the updates on the free space cursor are committed to other transactions, which now can go ahead and insert into the new page. If the transaction having caused the new end-of-file page to be allocated aborts, the directory update obviously must not be undone. The transaction must only delete its tuple from the page (thereby probably leaving a hole in the page), but the directory entries keep their values as though the transaction had committed. The same holds for undoing the uncommitted transaction as part of restart recovery after a crash. This is why the log record for the space allocation contains REDO information only: there will not be an UNDO of updates on these directory entries under whatever circumstances. To make sure the directory information gets properly redone even after a crash, the log record must not have the TRID of the initiating transaction. Rather, a new transaction (nested top-level transaction) is started to cover the update of the end-of-file pointer.

---

[15] Since no page that has been removed from the empty page chain will ever appear again, there is no need to actually maintain a chain. It is sufficient to know that the next empty page after p is $p + 1$. But conceptually (and for ease of presentation) the set of empty pages will be treated as a chain.

```
Uint                 timeout=1000;                              /*                                              */
BUFFER_ACC_CBP  pacb_data, pacb_dir;                            /* BACB of data and directorypage               */
PAGEID               curr_poi, new_poi,directory_page;          /* curr/new point of insert, dir-page           */
PAGEPTR              data_p, dir_p;                             /* pointer to required pages                    */
Uint                 tuple_length;                              /* length of tuple to be inserted               */
TUPLEID              tupleid;                                   /* TID of new tuple                             */
lock_name            ThisTID;                                   /* lock name for new tuple                      */
LSN                  LogPosition;                               /* returned from calls to the log               */
TRID                 NewTRID, OldTRID;                          /* for starting nested top-level transaction    */
bufferfix(directory_page,ex_sem,&pacb_dir);                     /* fix the directory page with excl. sem.       */
bufferfix(curr_poi, lock_x,&pacb_data);                         /* fix the current end-of-file page             */
data_p = pacb_data -> pageaddr;                                 /* get data page address in buffer              */
if   (data_p -> freespace < tuple_length + 4)                   /* space for tuple + directory entry?           */
     {   bufferunfix(pacb_data);                                /* NO: unfix data page                          */
         dir_p = pacb_dir -> pageaddr;                          /* get directory page address in buffer         */
         new_poi = dir_p -> relation_cat ->
                        empty_page_anchor;                      /* next empty page end-of-file                  */
         if   (new_poi == NULL) panic ;                         /* file has run out of space                    */
         OldTRID = MyTrid();                                    /* save current transaction id                  */
         Leave_Transaction ();
         New TRID = Begin_Work ();                              /* initiate nested top-level transaction        */
         curr_poi = new_poi;                                    /* use new end-of-file page                     */
         bufferfix(curr_poi,ex_sem,&p_acc_cb);                  /* fix new empty page                           */
         data_p = pacb -> pageaddr;                             /* get page address in buffer                   */
         new_poi, dir_p -> relation_cat -> empty_page_anchor =
                        data_p -> next;                         /* next page in chain is new anchor             */
         prepare log record ['advance-EOF',directory_page, curr_poi,new_poi];
         LogPosition=log_insert(log_record, length);            /* log directory change                         */
         dir_p->safe_up_to = LogPosition;                       /* note log entry LSN in directory page         */
         Commit_Work(NULL,TRUE);                                /* commit nested top-level transaction          */
         Resume_Transaction(OldTRID);                           /* continue original transaction                */
     };  /* it is assumed that the length of the new tuple ≤ capacity of an empty page                           */
bufferunfix(pacb_dir);                                          /* release fix on directory page                */
data_p-> no_entries = data_p -> no_entries + 1;                 /* add new entry in page directory              */
data_p -> offset_in_page[- (data_p -> no_entries)] = PAGESIZE - (data_p-> freespace); /*comp.offset             */
copy physical representation of tuple;
prepare tuple identifier in tupleid;
data_p -> freespace = data_p -> freespace -  tuple_length - 4;/* adjust freespace counter                       */
prepare log record ['insert',curr_poi,TID,tuple data];
LogPosition=log_insert(log_record, length);                     /* log tuple insert into page (physiological)    */
data_p->safe_up_to = LogPosition;                               /* set page LSN for WAL protocol                */
make lockname in ThisTID from tupleid and MyRMID();
```

```
switch   (lock(ThisTID,LOCK_X,LOCK_LONG,timeout))     /* long excl. lock on new tuple        */
         {   case    LOCK_OK:                          /* lock granted                        */
                     bufferunfix(pacb_data);           /* unfix page with new tuple           */
                     return(This TID);                 /* return to caller successfully       */
             case    LOCK_TIMEOUT:                     /* request timed out                   */
                     do something about it (try again);
                     if it times out repeatedly: panic();   /* this should not happen         */
             case    LOCK_DEADLOCK;                     /* cyclic wait occurred               */
                     panic(); };                        /* this should not happen             */
```

   This style of handling the end-of-file information in an entry-sequenced file is not mandatory. One could as well protect the directory entries by a long lock, and thereby achieve the standard ACID properties. A discussion of this issue is the subject of Exercise 13.
   As a result of the operation, the assigned TID is passed to the client.

14.4.3.2 The readpos Operation

This readpos operation exploits the insertion order of the tuples, that is, it implements a scan in timestamp order. If new pages are allocated in ascending order, the TIDs will increase accordingly. Opening the file for sequential reading establishes a *cursor*, which is specific for that open. The cursor has the datatype TUPLEID and points to the last tuple that was accessed using that open. Depending on whether the tuples are to be accessed in ascending or descending temporal order, the cursor is initialized to point before the first tuple or behind the current end-of-file, respectively. The basic logic is sketched in the pseudo-code that follows. For simplicity, it is assumed that the page that was allocated first for this file has page number 1. Of course, this code is simpler than the implementation of the insert operation. It basically scans the directory entries in a page (remember that a 0-offset in the directory denotes a deleted tuple), and once a page is exhausted, the scan follows the next pointer in the page header, via which the free page chain had been maintained and which, after insert, can be kept to thread the occupied pages in entry-sequenced order. A shared semaphore is requested when the scan first touches a page, and it is kept until the read sequence proceeds to the next page. Of course, when a tuple is returned to the client, the semaphore is released. Exercise 15 investigates the question of why keeping the semaphore while the transaction is scanning a page is necessary.
   Note that this discussion of the readpos operation is greatly simplified. It just covers the basic case of reading tuples sequentially in insert order and keeping them locked until end of transaction. As is shown in Section 14.5, access modules implementing SQL operators need more flexibility when accessing tuples through a procedural interface. Entry-sequenced files are particularly easy because of the guarantee that tuples can only be inserted behind the current end-of-file. One must also understand that the explanation of acquiring locks in a tuple-by-tuple fashion along the scan just covers the basic protocol. Of course, in a real implementation there will be means to escalate the lock granule to larger units such as pages or files in case too many individual tuple locks are requested; see Chapter 8 for details. But unless the query optimizer determines up front that large-granularity locks should be used, each sequential reading scan will start out requesting tuple locks.

```
/* this example assumes the file has been opened for sequential access in ascending order   */
Uint                    timeout = 1000;
TUPLEID                                             /* this cursor is returned by the open     */
                        old_cursor;                 /* function; initialized depending on the  */
                        new_cursor;                 /* access order                            */
TUPLEID                                             /* used for locating the next tuple        */
typedef        char *   TUPLEP;                      /* result returned by retrieval operation  */
TUPLEP                  tuple_begin;
BUFFER_ACC_CBP          pacb;                        /* pointer for buffer access control block */
PAGEPTR                 data_p;                      /* pointer to data page                    */
lock_name               ThisTID;                     /* lock name for new tuple                 */
Uint                    TupleOffset;                 /* tuple position within page              */
Boolean                 RC;                          /* from buffer manager                     */
new_cursor = old_cursor;                            /* save old cursor value                   */
if   (new_cursor.in_page == NULLTID)                /* cursor in initial state ?               */
    {   new_cursor.pageno = 1;                      /* page that was allocated first           */
        RC = bufferfix(new_cursor.in_page,sh_sem,&pacb);  /* fix first page for reading         */
        data_p = pacb -> pageaddr;                  /* get page address in buffer              */
        new_cursor.dir_index = 0;                   /* first tuple has index -1.               */
    } ;
while   (TRUE)                                       /* search the next page(s)                 */
    {   while    (new_cursor.dir_index < page_ptr -> no_entries) /* more entries in page        */
            {    new_cursor.dir_index++;            /* get next directory entry                */
                 TupleOffset = offset_in_page[ - new_cursor.dir_index];   /* where is tuple?    */
                 build ThisTID from TupleOffset , page no., etc.     /*                         */
                 make lock name from ThisTID and MyRMID;             /*                         */
                 switch   (lock(ThisTID,LOCK_S,LOCK_LONG,timeout))   /* request read lock       */
                        {    case    LOCK_OK:  ;     /* lock granted                            */
                             case    LOCK_TIMEOUT:   /* request timed out                       */
                             case    LOCK_DEADLOCK;  /* cyclic wait occurred                    */
                             rollback transaction;   /* transaction must be aborted             */
                        };
                 tuple_begin = page_ptr + TupleOffset;      /* locate tuple pointed to by entry */
                 if   (offset_var_part == 0)     continue;  /* this tuple was deleted           */
                 old_cursor = new_cursor;                   /* remember current position        */
                 return TID to caller for processing;
            };                                       /* at this point a page has been exhausted */
        new_cursor.in_page = data_p -> next;         /* move to next page                       */
        if   (new_cursor.in_page == NULL)  break;    /* end of file has been reached            */
        new_cursor.dir_index = 0;                    /* first tuple has index -1                */
        RC = bufferunfix(pacb);                      /* release previous page                   */
        RC = bufferfix(new_cursor.in_page,sh_sem,&pacb); /* fix next page for reading           */
        data_p = pacb -> pageaddr;                   /* get page address in buffer              */
    };                                               /* end of loop over pages in the file      */
invoke logic for closing the file and return NULLTID;
```

14.4.3.3 Other Operations on an Entry-Sequenced File

The remaining operations need not be covered as extensively as insert and readpos, because they are very similar. So the following is a brief sketch of the operations' properties.

The readid operation

Tuples in an entry-sequenced file can be retrieved "directly" using the TID (see Section 14.2). The sequential structure that is imposed by the way tuples are inserted only refers to the correlation of insertion order and address ordering in the file. Since the underlying basic file system supports direct block access, there is no problem in implementing access operations that use this mechanism, provided the block (i.e, page) number is known. Since the TID mechanism relies on a combination of page numbers and directory indices, direct addressing is easy. Locking is simple: the page the TID points to is fixed with a shared semaphore. If the tuple exists, a shared lock is requested for it. If the tuple does not exist (directory entry = 0), no lock on the TID is needed, because the TID cannot suddenly appear phantom-like because of the entry-sequenced organization. Likewise, there cannot be forward TIDs.

The update operation

Modification is limited in entry-sequenced files. Although tuples generally have variable length, an update cannot increase the tuple size, because according to the entry sequence definition, a tuple cannot be moved to another location within the file. Tuple expansion is therefore prohibited for entry-sequenced files (unless it can be accommodated within the current page). On the other hand, records can shrink and even disappear (see what follows). The page with the tuple to be modified is fixed with an exclusive semaphore; the tuple (TID) is locked exclusively; the log record is generated (old value, new value) and inserted; the page is updated (the tuple part and the page LSN); and finally, the page is unfixed.

The delete operation

The delete operation is particularly simple in entry-sequenced files. Remember that, due to the way tuples are inserted, there is no way freed space can be reclaimed. This implies that unused directory entries cannot be reused, which in turn means TIDs belong to a tuple as long as it exists; after the tuple has been deleted, the TID will never be assigned to any other tuple. Consequently, there is no need to modify the page structure when a tuple is deleted. Security requirements notwithstanding, the physical representation can stay where it is, and the page directory can remain unchanged. One only has to mark the tuple deleted. Using the storage structure described in Subsection 14.3.2.5, this can be done by setting the entry offset_var_part of the tuple prefix to 0. The sequence of fix, lock, and log operations is the same as in case of tuple update.

14.4.4 System-Sequenced Files

As the name suggests, the tuple-oriented file system has complete control over where the tuples of system-sequenced files are stored; additional information such as insert order is not maintained. Tuples are inserted wherever the free space administration points. Space freed by deleted tuples can be reclaimed either directly or after reorganization (see Section 14.3).

Tuples can be accessed via their tuple identifiers or by reading the entire file in block-sequential order. The operations listed next are those directly supported by *system-sequenced files*.

The insert operation

As mentioned, the place for a new tuple is determined by the tuple-oriented space allocation. If the free space table is used, a free space table page is fixed in buffer with an exclusive semaphore. The entries are scanned by requesting an exclusive semaphore in bounce mode. If the request bounces, try the next entry until a table entry is locked for update. If the amount of free space described by this entry is not sufficient, release the semaphore and continue the scan. Once an entry with enough free space has been determined, generate a log record saying that the amount of "tuple length" is subtracted from the entry. Modify the entry and the page LSN of the free space table page. Then fix the data page pertaining to the free space entry in buffer with an exclusive semaphore. Release the semaphore on the free space table page. Inserting the tuple is straightforward. The header entry no_entries is increased by one, and the corresponding directory entry is set. This establishes the TID of the new tuple. A long exclusive lock is requested for the new TID. A log record is prepared that describes the insert of that tuple with the new TID into the page (physiological logging). The tuple is copied into the page, and the free space counter is decreased. The semaphore on the data page is released, and the exclusive lock on the free space table page is returned. The file system passes the TID assigned to the new tuple to the client.

The fact that the exclusive semaphore on the data page as well as the exclusive lock on the free space table entry are released before end of transaction must be considered carefully: it means that the update operations on the page and table data structures are treated as subtransactions according to the multi-level transaction model. Now the transaction manager described in this book does not support multi-level transactions (or nested transactions), so all the log records are written with the TRID of the application-level transaction. This is acceptable, provided the resource managers participating know what to do in case of rollback: since they have no nested transaction mechanism underneath, they must request and release their locks properly and make sure the operations are undone in a semantically correct way. If, for example, the insert operation is undone later on, it may be that the free space entry must not be increased. Another transaction may have inserted a tuple into the same data page, so removing the first tuple increases unused, but not freespace.

The readid operation

The readid operation works almost exactly as for entry-sequenced files: based on the TID, the page is fixed in buffer with a shared semaphore; a shared lock is requested for the tuple; and the offset of the tuple prefix is returned to the client. There are but two differences: first, in case there is no tuple with the specified TID, a shared lock on that TID must be requested anyway, because with the autonomous free space administration in system-sequenced files, a new tuple with that TID might well occur while the read transaction is still going on (phantom). Second, if the entry found in the page is just a forwarding TID, this pointer must be followed by repeating the whole operation with the new TID. The same fix and lock protocol applies. The shared semaphore on the page the original TID points to can be released.

The update operation

If the update does not alter the tuple's length, it works exactly as in the entry-sequenced file organization. If the tuple length changes, there are three cases to be considered: first, the tuple stays in its old page; second, it is moved to another page, and a forwarding TID is installed in the old page; third, the tuple must be moved to another page, but it had been "exiled" before, so it must be completely removed from its current page and the forwarding TID in the original page must be changed.

Consider the simple case first. Assuming the free space table technique, an exclusive semaphore is requested on the table page containing the entry for the page in which the modified tuple is stored. Then the data page is fixed with an exclusive semaphore, and the tuple is locked exclusively. A log record is prepared that contains the tuple's old and new values; it is inserted into the log. The actual update is performed. Depending on whether the tuple grew longer or shorter, either the header entry unused or freespace, or both,[16] must be modified. If the freespace entry is not modified, the semaphore on the table page is released. Otherwise, an exclusive lock is requested on the proper free space entry. A log record for the entry modification is generated, and the entry is modified in the same way it was in the page. Then the semaphore on the table page is released. At the end, the semaphore on the data page and the lock on the free space entry are released.

The case where the tuple needs to be exiled is slightly more complicated. The update of the page where it was stored proceeds as in the previous case—think of the tuple shrinking from its old size to the size of a forwarding TID. The free space table should be handled in a different fashion, though. Imagine the transaction performing the update aborts; in this case, the tuple is reverted to its original length, which means it can return to its home page. To make sure there is still enough space in that page, the lock on the free space entry must be held till end of transaction. Finding a new page for the (longer) tuple and storing it there is identical to the insert operation, so effectively both algorithms must be combined (note that an exclusive lock on the new, internal forwarding TID must be acquired, too) to implement an update operation that forces a tuple out of its current page.

The third case is an extension of the second one; rather than two data pages, it involves three, the third one being the tuple's original data page that holds the forwarding TID. The fix, lock, and log sequence on that page is the same as for any other modified data page; its free space counter remains unchanged.

The delete operation

The delete operation is handled like an update with the tuple size shrinking to zero without affecting other pages. So the steps for locking and logging are not repeated. The reference to the tuple in the page directory is removed; this implicitly invalidates the tuple identifier. The tuple length is added to the entry unused in the page header. Unless the tuple was the last one in the page (empty space behind it), this leaves the freespace counter and the header entry no_entries unaffected. For the reasons explained with the update operation, the free space entry must be kept locked until end of transaction. Should the freespace counter change, the free space table is modified as described for the update operation. The storage space in the page occupied by the physical tuple representation is normally not modified. Only if either security or privacy constraints require *physical* deletion will it be set to binary zeroes, or

---

[16] Even if a tuple in the middle of the page shrinks, which only affects unused, this may have side effects. As was mentioned, a local page reorganization can be triggered if unused/(freespace + 1) exceeds a predefined threshold.

something equivalent. Of course, all the problems with forwarding TIDs can occur when deleting a tuple as well; since there is nothing new, the discussion is omitted.

The readpos operation

Since the system-sequenced file organization does not maintain any predefined order among the tuples, the only sequence that can be followed for readpos scanning the file is physical neighborhood. So the reading sequence starts with the first page (lowest page number) and reads all the tuples in that page in the order of the directory entries (see example for entry-sequenced files); then it proceeds to the page with the next higher number,[17] and so on. The locking protocol is essentially the same as for entry-sequenced files. Since the ordering criterion is page numbers, the semaphore on page p can be released before the semaphore on page $p + 1$ is acquired—there is no way a new page could get "in between." For the same reason as was explained for the readid operation, the TIDs corresponding to all directory entries in a page (between 1 and no_entries) must be locked in shared mode, even if they contain the value 0, which means they belong to a deleted tuple. Otherwise such an entry could be reused for inserting a new tuple between tuples that were returned as part of the reading sequence—these would be *phantom* tuples.

Note that phantoms can still occur within a series of readpos operations implemented in the way we have sketched—unless a file lock is obtained. According to the algorithm developed for entry-sequenced files, the shared semaphore on a page is released as soon as the current position of reading moves out of that page. All the tuples in the page are read-locked, though. However, if the page still has some free space, a concurrent insert operation may store a new tuple into it (increasing no_entries), thereby creating a potential phantom for the reading transaction. Keeping the semaphore on the pages is no remedy, because that would jam the bufferpool with obsolete pages up to the point where no free frames are left. A possible solution would be to acquire a shared lock (not semaphore!) on the corresponding free space table entry of each page that is read; this would prevent new tuples from being inserted into the page. There are a number of straightforward optimizations (such as special lock modes for free space table entries), which are beyond the scope of this book.

14.4.5 Relative Files

Relative files are arrays of tuples. They require the file to be pre-formatted up to the current end-of-file. Pages assigned to a relative file must be contiguous (that is, there must be no gaps in the sequence of page numbers; the set of pages can well be mapped to multiple extents), and each page is divided into k slots of fixed length, which is determined by the maximum tuple size to be stored. This creates a one-dimensional array of slots,[18] the ordinal of which runs from 0 to $(k \cdot P)-1$, where P denotes the number of pages for the file. Tuples can then be efficiently accessed via the ordinal, which is called the *relative* tuple number.

Page management is simple for relative files because of the fixed format. Since all slots have equal length, free space management has only to keep track of which slots are free and which are not. In order not to change the overall page layout, the page directory can be used for that. The offsets stored in the directory entries for the other file organizations are only

---

[17] If the free space table mechanism is used, those pages in the page address space that hold free space table segments must be skipped when reading the file sequentially.

[18] This use of the term *slot* must not be confused with the slots that denote the units into which disks are pre-formatted.

needed if the records have variable length. Since in relative files they are stored in fixed-size slots, the record offset can simply be computed from the ordinal; the directory entries can now hold the *actual* length of the records in the slots. Length 0 indicates a free slot, as with system-sequenced files. Of course, in that case the tuple length need not be stored in the tuple prefix. The page layout for relative files is illustrated in Figure 14.17.

Relative files are the tuple equivalent of block-oriented files. Just assume that slots are of page length; then the functionality is exactly that of a block-oriented file, only at a higher level of abstraction.

Description of the access operations can be kept short, because in most cases we can draw on the explanations given earlier for other file organizations. To keep things simple, we assume free space administration is done via a free space table, the entries containing the *number of free slots* per data page.

The readid operation

Strictly speaking, there are two system identifiers for a tuple in the relative file organization: the relative tuple number (RTN) and the TID. Since one can be transformed into the other by a simple formula, it is sufficient to consider access via the RTN only. First, it is checked whether the page for the given RTN (this is $\lfloor RTN/k \rfloor$) is beyond the current end-of-file. If so, the tuple does not exist, but a read lock on the RTN must be kept in order to prevent phantoms. Otherwise, the access operation is identical to the corresponding operation in system-sequenced files.

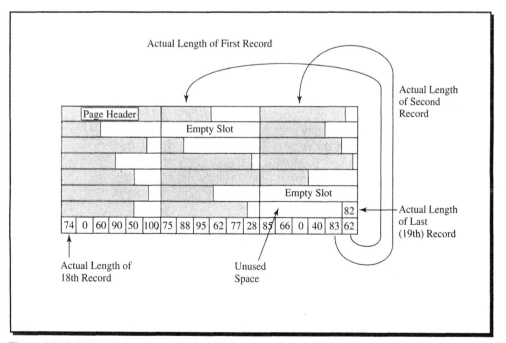

Figure 14.17: Internal page organization for a relative file. After the page header follows an array of fixed-size slots. The page directory also has a fixed number of entries, which is determined by the total page length and the length of the slots.

The readpos operation

This function is defined similarly to the corresponding function in entry-sequenced files. The ordering of tuples is now imposed by the ordinal, that is, by the RTN. Note that sequential access along the relative tuple number is also block sequential (assuming that pages are synonymous to blocks), and therefore can achieve high throughput. The fix and locking protocols are the same as for the readpos operation in system-sequenced files. The only minor difference lies in the fact that phantoms cannot occur even without special locking protocols on the page header, simply because the number of directory entries is fixed, and a sequential reading pass acquires shared locks on all of them.

The insert operation

For relative files, this operation comes in four different styles, depending on how the location for the new tuple is determined. Let us briefly characterize each of them.

insert at.   The insert comes with the *exact* RTN. If the corresponding slot is free, the tuple is inserted; otherwise, the operation fails. The fix, lock, and log protocols for both data page and free space table page is the same as described for the insert operation in system-sequenced files.

insert near.   The insert comes with an RTN and requests the tuple to be inserted *near* that original position. The free space table page is fixed with an exclusive semaphore, and an exclusive lock is requested on the specified entry in bounce mode. If the request fails, another request is issued for neighboring entries, "spiraling" around the denoted position. Should this search leave the free space, the semaphore is released, and the procedure is repeated for the next page, depending on the search strategy. The slot corresponding to the first succeeding lock request is taken for insert. The rest is identical to the previous case. The RTN corresponding to the chosen slot is returned to the client.

insert at end.   This call mimics the entry-sequenced organization. The tuple is inserted into the next slot after the current last tuple (that is, the one with the highest RTN). If there is still room in the current "high page," the operation proceeds exactly as insert at. If the high page is exhausted, a new one must be allocated. This means the end-of-file counter in the directory must be advanced, an empty page must be fixed in buffer where it is formatted according to the definition of the relative file organization. In the free space table, the entry corresponding to the new page must be initialized. The lock and log protocols are basically the same as for the other insert operations; the only difference is that additional locks and logs are required for the file directory page. The RTN corresponding to the receiving slot is returned to the caller.

insert anywhere.   This operation works just like the insert into a system-sequenced file. All explanations given there apply.

The update operation

Tuples can be updated arbitrarily, as long as their resulting length is less than the slot length. When creating a relative file, the slot size must be chosen such that the maximum expected tuple length can be accommodated. If there is no reasonable estimate for the maximum tuple length, there are two options: either allow tuples to be fragmented (see Section 14.3), or pick another file organization. Due to the properties of relative files, update operations cannot change the free space counter for the page, nor can a tuple be exiled—the slots in the pages are all the same size. So the fix, lock, and log protocols are the same as for entry-sequenced files.

The delete operation

The delete operation only requires the directory entry pertaining to the slot to be set to 0, unless security considerations call for erasing the tuple's slot. According to the definition, each delete operation modifies the free space entry corresponding to the page. So the fix, lock, and log protocol is the same as for insert at, except that the lock on the free space entry must be held until end of transaction.

14.4.6 Key-Sequenced Files and Hash Files

The file organizations described so far are non-associative in that the storage location of a tuple is not determined by the contents of any attributes. Associative access, on the other hand, is characterized by the existence of a mapping:

$$\text{tuple.attribute value(s)} \rightarrow \text{location in file.}$$

Note that such a mapping implies a mapping from the attribute value(s) to the TID. The attribute values determining the tuple's storage location are usually *primary keys* of the respective relation.[19] The main advantage of such a file organization is, of course, the fast access to each tuple, given the value of the key attribute. Depending on how the associative mapping is actually done, the operations on key-sequenced and hash files, respectively, come with slightly different properties. The description of the access operations to associative files is kept brief, because implementation of the mapping functions from attribute values to storage locations is the subject of Chapter 15. In particular, no locking and logging issues will be considered, because they critically depend on the mapping algorithms and the data structures used by them. The following is just to give an impression of where associative access operations differ from those described earlier in this subsection.

The readid operation

This operation works exactly as it does in the other organizations.

The insert operation

Upon insert, the mapping function is applied to the key attributes of the new tuple; it yields the page number where the tuple is to be stored. Of course, the key attributes must not contain NULL values, because then the result of the mapping function might be undefined. The position inside the page depends on the type of the mapping function. For hash files, the tuple can be stored wherever free space is available; key-sequenced organization also determines the location within the page. When the insert operation is complete, the TID of the tuple is determined implicitly.

---

[19] In principle, both file organizations could be used with attributes that do not identify a tuple. But for reasons that will become more evident in the next chapter, this makes little sense in general.

The readkey operation

The client supplies the value of the key attribute(s), and the operation returns the tuple with the specified key value; if it is a primary key, exactly one tuple is returned. If no tuple with the specified key value exists, an error code is returned.

The readpos operation

This operation is defined differently for hash files and for key-sequenced files. Key-sequenced files store tuples in sorted order of the key attribute. Therefore, the position for reading the next or previous tuple is defined with respect to that sort order. In hash files, no such ordering exists.[20]

The update operation

Tuples can be modified arbitrarily. They can shrink or grow, and the aspects for handling that are exactly the ones described earlier in this chapter. The only special case to be considered is the modification of the key value. Since this value determines the storage location of the tuple, it has to be deleted from its current page and inserted into the page that the mapping function computes for the new attribute value.

The delete operation

The reference to the tuple is removed from the page directory, and its length is added to the unused space counter.

14.4.7 Summary

The key point of Section 14.4 was that the tuple-oriented file system implements the notion of files on top of something that has already been described as a file system of its own, namely the basic (block-oriented) file system of Chapter 13. Whether files are really implemented in this strict way, with separate file names, opens, and so on at each level is not the issue here; what is important is the abstraction of tuples, with their different access operations, from blocks with relative addressing.

The section started out by explaining which administrative aspects are relevant for the tuple-oriented file system. This is particularly important, because it is this level that makes persistent storage available to "normal" applications. So security issues such as authentication and authorization must be handled here. There must also be provisions to inform modules that have statically been bound to the file (database access modules) about changes in the file structure or allocation.

Then we described scans as an abstract procedure interface to to tuple-oriented file system. The similarities between scans and SQL cursors were briefly considered.

The major part of the section was devoted to describing different file organizations, namely entry-sequenced, system-sequenced, relative, and associative files. The file organization determines three important aspects of tuple management: first, where the tuple is stored upon insert; second, according to which criteria a tuple can be retrieved; and third, to which degree a tuple can grow after it has been inserted. This latter aspect also has to do

---

[20] The CODASYL DML, however, calls for a readpos operation on such files, and the definition says that the next tuple that was mapped into the same page (bucket) as the previous one is to be returned—although its key value may be completely different.

with the question of whether or not space in the file that has become free after the deletion of tuples can be reused.

Each access operation was explained with respect to the use it makes of the data structures supporting the file organization, and with respect to the fix, lock, and log protocols that are required in order to make these operations protected actions. It became clear that the sequence and duration of page fixes and semaphores must be carefully adjusted in order to prevent phantoms, and in order to make sure operations can be undone in case of a transaction abort. This is particularly important for delete operations. It was also demonstrated that nested top-level transactions are useful for maintaining catalog information such as free space entries.

Most of the file organizations described here allow to retrieve tuples by system-internal criteria only, such as position, tuple identifier, or relative tuple number. The last subsection points out that there are file organizations supporting associative access via attribute values. But there has been no detailed discussion of this subject, because all of Chapter 15 deals with it.

14.5 Exotics

Since this chapter describes only the very basic concepts of a tuple-oriented file system, many special aspects, optimizations, implementational constraints, and so on, have to be left out. Three topics are mentioned briefly, though, because they help to give a better perspective on many existing systems and some of their inherent limitations and problems.

14.5.1 Cluster Files

All the file organizations described so far are assumed to contain records (tuples) of one type only; the tuples can vary in length, but they can be interpreted using the same schema-entry. For performance reasons, it may be desirable to cluster tuples *of different files* along the value of some common attribute. If the expected load is such that a join over this attribute is to be done frequently, storing tuples that will be joined together in the same page will clearly speed up that operation. As a matter of fact, storing tuples in such a file is a materialization of that join. Whether two or more relations are involved in the cluster makes no difference. The CODASYL-type database systems use clustered files as an implementation of the LOCATION MODE VIA SET; this means that the member records of a set have to be stored in the same page as the owner record. Some relational systems (Oracle, for example) provide similar options at the storage structure layer.

Since clustering depends on attribute values, it fundamentally calls for the structure of a key-sequenced file. One way of looking at it is to have different relations organized into key-sequenced files that use the same set of pages for storing their tuples. One only has to make sure that the same value of the clustering attribute from different relations is mapped to the same page. Note that, in general, the *name* of the cluster attribute will be different for different files.

If one page per distinct value is not large enough to hold all tuples with that value, the page is logically extended in the way that has been described for very long attributes; that is, by chaining overflow pages to it. But then the desired effect of fast access to *all* members of one cluster rapidly deteriorates with the number of overflow pages. There cannot even be fast sequential access to all tuples of a cluster with many overflow pages, since they are generally not immediate neighbors of each other. The problem, then, of whether or not to use a cluster file for materializing joins has to be handled judiciously. Note that in case of a 1:*n* join, a simple key-sequenced file for the large relation over the join attribute will achieve value clustering of all the *n* tuples.

Because of the value-dependent clustering, the storage location of the tuples on the *n*-side of the join is determined by the value in the clustering attribute. One can put it the other way: for each distinct value in the cluster attribute, there is one page (with as many overflow pages as needed); whenever a tuple's value in the cluster attribute changes, the tuple must be relocated.

The directory of a cluster file has to distinguish between the tuples of different relations; this can be done using the entry data_id (see Section 14.2). Since all the access functions of the tuple-oriented file system are bound to a single file type, they will not be different for cluster files. If a system supports cluster files, it will also have some specific access routines for them, but this topic is beyond the scope of this text. Example of cluster files of this sort can be found in many CODASYL database systems, for example, UDS, and in Oracle, to name one from the relational camp.

14.5.2 Partitioned Files

One file can be decomposed into a number of disjoint partitions according to some criterion that can be checked at the tuple level. A typical way of partitioning a file, key-range partitioning, is illustrated in Figure 14.18.

Remember that, according to the mapping scheme introduced in the previous chapter, a relation can be made up from several fragments. These fragments are mapped to the parti-

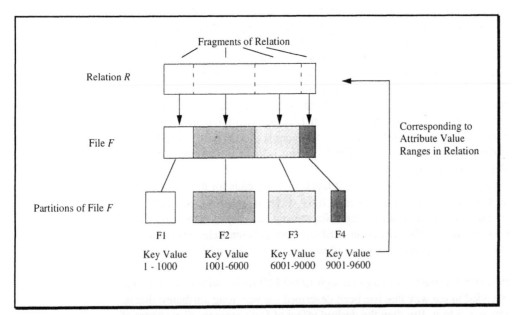

Figure 14.18: File partitioning by key ranges of attribute values in the relation. Partitioning of a file can be done for load balancing across disk arm, for data allocation in a distributed database, or for supporting locality of reference to keep data close to where they are needed most frequently.

tions of the file that, as a whole, contains the representation of the relation. Defining fragments can be done in many different ways. The following are some them:

Key ranges. Based on the primary key of the relation, value ranges are defined, and each fragment contains all tuples whose key value is in the respective value range.

General predicates. Rather than restricting the fragmentation criterion to the primary key, one can define a characteristic predicate for each fragment. Then all tuples for which the defining predicate holds are elements of the fragment. If this is to work with partitioned files, though, it must be guaranteed that the predicates establish a complete partitioning of the set of tuples; that is, for each potential tuple, there must be exactly one fragment to which it belongs. The reason is that if no predicate were fulfilled, the tuple could not be stored; conversely, if more than one predicate could hold a tuple, the storage scheme would require the handling of replication, which is a completely different issue.

Origin. The fragments can be defined by the nodes storing the fragments; thus, each tuple goes to the local fragment.

The fragmented relation is then mapped onto a partitioned file, and each partition holds exactly one fragment. Note that this is very different from simply assigning the fragments to unrelated files. To understand that, consider the following situation: a tuple of relation R has key value 800 and therefore belongs to the first fragment. An update changes this value to 7530; that is, it now belongs to the third fragment. This, by the way, is the same situation that was described for associative file organizations. If the fragments were simply mapped to independent files, then additional logic would be needed to determine that the tuple under consideration must be removed from the file holding the first fragment, and that it has to be inserted into another file instead.

Partitioned files are designed to cope with exactly this situation. As described in Section 14.4, the file catalog contains the information that there are other, related partitions, and each partition has complete information on how the other partitions are defined.

Partitioning a file is done for different reasons:

Load balancing. If large relations receive more traffic than a single disk drive or a file server can handle, then the data can be partitioned and assigned to different drives.

Distribution. In a distributed DBMS, it is important to have fragments of a relation stored in different nodes. Mapping the relation to a partitioned file and keeping the file at the respective nodes does that.

Addressing. Very large relations can contain more than a single file can hold; note that some operating systems still have a limit of 1 GB per physical OS-level file. Since each partition of a partitioned file (viewed in isolation) is a separate file in itself, partitioning is a means to expand the address space that is available for storing a relation.

14.5.3 Using Transactions to Maintain the File System

All structural operations that maintain the file organization or the page data structure are normally protected by the transaction that issued the respective update DML operation. Obviously, there are operations that require updating more than one page to bring the file structure back into a consistent state. Consider, for example, the insert operation into an entry-sequenced file; once in a while, this requires advancing the end-of-file pointer, which is stored in the file descriptor. Of course, the file descriptor must also be recovered to a consistent state after, say, a crash, and therefore all updates on it must be transaction protected.

Trivial as this sounds, it is not. Consider an application where most transactions just insert into an entry-sequenced file. This results in much traffic on the end-of-file pointer. Assuming the isolation techniques described in this book, there will be many transactions requesting an exclusive lock on the file descriptor because they may have to advance the end-of-file pointer. This will serialize transactions updating this object, and, consequently, many transactions will wait. Throughput will be low, and response time will be high—just the opposite of what is desired. The general conclusion is that yes, catalogs and other administrative data structures must be ACID objects, but for performance reasons they require specialized synchronization techniques.

As long as all structural updates are done within the domain of the transaction-protected file system, things are essentially under control. However, in many existing systems, the tuple-oriented file system sits on top of a basic file system provided by the operating system, which does not know what a transaction is. This creates situations where at some point the execution leaves the sphere of control that the transaction provides and continues unprotected for a while. An example is the creation of a new extent for an existing file. This is what happens in that case:

The transaction execution is suspended at the point where the basic file system is invoked with the expand operation. This operation is performed according to its own specification, making itself recoverable by careful replacement, intention lists, or whatever. If the system crashes at that point, the transaction will be recovered in its domain, and the basic file system will, independently, perform its own recovery. If the expansion was successful, the thread of control is resumed inside the transaction. Now, if this transaction is rolled back later on, there is no effect on the creation of the new extent; the basic file will retain its larger size as though the transaction had completed successfully. The contents of blocks in the new extent will be recovered correctly, though, because the modules responsible for that run under transaction protection.

Clearly, this is not a pleasant situation. A clean solution would be to have transaction protection at all layers of the system. If nested transactions were available to encapsulate administrative operations, such as creating new extents, matters would be further simplified. But as it stands now, the only reasonable place to talk about transactions in the file system is the "exotics" section—in a book on transaction processing.

14.5.4 The Tuple-Oriented File System in Current Database Systems

This subsection is merely an introduction to the ideas behind transactional record managers. Many commercially available database systems, especially those from independent vendors, do not maintain exactly the division of labor represented in the previous Chapters 13 and 14. In particular, many systems do not explicitly use the notion of (tuple-oriented) files and file organizations. Rather, they talk about access paths, location modes, and so forth. The reason is fairly simple: because file systems in different operating systems are very different, building on top of them would either constrain the operational basis of the DBMS, or tremendous effort would be required to adapt it to the various platforms. The largest common denominator among file services is the block-oriented access described in Chapter 13.

As a result, many database systems use this interface to the operating system's file system and do everything else for themselves. They do their own free space administration; that is, they have system-sequenced files as the basic file organization. On top of that, they build other organizations, such as hash files and key-sequenced files, even if the the "underlying" file system has something similar.

These pragmatic issues create a great deal of terminological confusion. Apart from them, however, the functional principles laid out in these chapters are the same everywhere.

14.6 Summary

This chapter discussed the issue of mapping records, or tuples, onto a page-structured file system and making them accessible by different criteria. Most of the descriptions made an assumption that is typical of the majority of current database systems, namely that tuples are shorter than one page.

The chapter began by explaining the basic mapping issues. First, the internal layout of a page was described. It is determined by some obvious requirements. The data structures should be simple: that is, they should not impose much overhead on the operations on tuples; they should be flexible enough to support different tuple representation techniques; and they should allow for an easy internal reorganization of the page. Next, the techniques for administering free space in a page-structured address space were surveyed. And finally, the problem of tuple addressing was explained in some detail. The point is that tuple identifiers should be stable for the duration of the tuple's existence, that they should allow the tuple to be relocated freely within the file, and that they should also support the migration of the tuple to another node in a distributed system. It was argued that primary keys as internal tuple identifiers are the best match for these requirements—provided they can be kept sufficiently short.

Then it was shown how tuples can be represented in a page, such that variable length fields are accommodated, NULL values are supported, dynamic schema modifications (adding new fields to the file) are supported without calling for reorganization, and retrieval is equally cheap for any field in the tuple. It was shown that the optimal design consists of a combination of redundant data in the tuple and compiled information in the catalog. The tuple contains a header that has the number of fixed-length and variable-length fields *in that tuple*, followed by all the fixed-length fields, followed by an array of pointers pointing to the current end of each variable-length field.

These techniques apply to short tuples. Storing long tuples requires additional mechanisms, such as tuple or page overflow. If tuples that are not in (at least) first normal form are to be handled, more complicated data structures such as linked lists, clusters, or search trees must be introduced.

The third section described the notion of a scan, plus three file organizations—namely entry-sequenced, system-sequenced, and relative files—in some detail. The properties of associative files (hash and key-sequenced) were sketched. The focus of this section is on the use of the buffer interface and the lock and log protocols needed to implement the access operations in a transactional way. In particular, it was demonstrated how nested transactions and nested top-level transactions can be used to increase concurrency on central data structures such as the free space table.

Finally, the more remote aspects of cluster files, file partitioning, and the use of transactions to maintain the file system were briefly surveyed.

Exercises

1. [14.2, 20] Consider a free space administration based on free space tables as described in Section 14.2. In contrast to what was described in the chapter, assume the updates on the tables' entries were not logged. Thus the entries are correctly recovered if a transaction aborts during normal operation, but this may not be the case after a crash. Can the free space table be kept usable under those circumstances? How can it be prevented from deteriorating completely? *Hint: Each page has a local free space counter, which is always correct.*

2. [14.2, 10] Assume the free space table method. If an entry contains the number of free bytes in the corresponding data page, then for 8 KB pages, 13 bits are needed, which means the entry will usually be 2 bytes. Can you administer pages of that size with only 1 byte per free space table entry?

3. [14.2, 10] The free space cursor technique will achieve a space utilization that—on the average—is lower than the free space table. Why is that?

4. [14.2, 10] Consider the free space cursor technique. When a new file is created, all its pages can be considered empty. Is there a way to avoid explicitly chaining all these pages together as members of the empty page chain, which would require each page to be written?

5. [14.2, 20] The text says that reorganizing TID incrementally during normal operation is not exactly the same as deleting the tuple with its old TID and reinserting it with a new one. What are the differences?

6. [14.3, 25] The SQL command ALTER TABLE x ADD COLUMN c extends the schema definition of an existing relation by one attribute. This chapter has discussed methods for minimizing the impact of that operation on tuples that have been stored before the extension of the relation. Of course, there is also an ALTER TABLE x DROP COLUMN c, which removes an attribute from an existing relation. Design implementations of that operation (based on the storage structures defined in this chapter) that have the same property of leaving all the tuples unchanged until they are explicitly modified the next time. How does your algorithm affect the read operations for field values shown? What would happen if a new attribute were added after another one had been removed, using your algorithm? Can these schema modification operations be interleaved arbitrarily?

7. [14.3, 10] Assume a length field for variable-length attributes with a fixed size of 1 byte. How can you store values longer than 255 bytes in such a variable-length attribute?

8. [14.3, 30] Find out exactly how Oracle stores numerical values and analyze this scheme carefully. Make a comprehensive feature list to answer questions such as: how can values in that representation be sorted? *Hint: Normal system sort utilities do not understand this special representation.*

9. [14.3, discussion] Compare the various techniques for storing long tuples (described in Section 14.3) with respect to the amount of locking that is needed to access a long tuple.

10. [14.3, discussion] Compare the various techniques for storing long tuples (described in Section 14.3) with respect to the ease and speed of processing many such tuples sequentially.

11. [14.3, 10] The summary about techniques for storing long tuples says that using 1 MB pages just to store (rare) long tuples is a bad idea. The arguments for that are not completely elaborated. What are the relevant aspects and assumptions here? What about locality?

12. [14.2, 14.3, 14.4, 25] Consider the operation of garbage collection within a page. It is usually triggered by a DML operation that is part of a user transaction. What kind of locking and logging has to be done for such an operation? What is the most adequate transaction model?

13. [14.4, 10] Consider the implementation of the insert operation of an entry-sequenced file, as described in Section 14.4. The data page is protected by a semaphore while the insert is being processed; after that, only the new tuple is locked. If the end-of-file page is advanced, this modification is protected by a nested top-level transaction. Which undesired consequences can arise?

14. [14.4, 20] Consider the implementation of the insert operation of an entry-sequenced file, as described in Section 14.4. It suggests physiological logging be used to record the operation. What does that mean for REDO processing after a crash? Describe precisely how insert operations must be redone, and what the critical issues are.

15. [14.4, 20] Consider the implementation of the readpos operation of an entry-sequenced file, as described in Section 14.4. While the transaction is reading in a page, a shared semaphore is kept on it. Since the file is entry-sequenced, there can be no insert "behind the transaction's back," so one might argue that the semaphore need not be held while the transaction is processing a tuple. Do you see a reason why the semaphore must be held?

16. [14.4, 10] Consider the implementation of the readpos operation of an entry-sequenced file, as described in Section 14.4. When moving from one page to the next, the first page is unfixed, and then the next one is fixed. This implies that the number of the next page does not become invalid between these two operations. Why is this so?

17. [14.4, 10] The text suggests that no modification of free space information is necessary when deleting a tuple from an entry-sequenced file. Why?

18. [14.4, 20] Consider the implementation of the insert operation of a system-sequenced file, as explained in Section 14.4. The text says that the semaphore on the free space page must be held until the semaphore on the data page is granted. Why is this necessary?

19. [14.4, 10] The text says that the free space entry must be locked long when deleting a tuple from a system-sequenced file. Explain why.

20. [14.4, 25] The basic retrieval operation of a relative file is to locate a record via its RTN, which points to a page and an index in that page. But the retrieval algorithm only works if the pages involved have the appropriate format. One way to guarantee this is to explicitly format all the pages up to a certain point (end-of-file) at the moment of file creation. Later on, the highest page in which a tuple has been stored becomes the current end-of-file. Can you devise a scheme that requires only those pages that actually contain records to be formatted? *Hint: pages will be accessed randomly with this file type, and whenever a page is read, one must be able to decide if it has the right format or if it has never been used before (for that file). You may come up with a scheme that is not as safe as the conventional solution; discuss the risks.*

21. [14.4, 20] For all the update operations explained in Section 14.4, modifications of the free space table entries were handled by a nested top-level transaction. In case a transaction aborts, the updates on the table entries can be undone during the undo operation for the tuple in the data page— note that the free space table contains redundant information. Why is it still necessary to log the update of the free space entry?

Answers

1. Consider the free space table entry pertaining to page *P*. If upon insert it turns out that the actual free space in the page is less than what the table entry says, the entry can be corrected. If the table entry contains too small a value compared to the actual free space in the page, the page may

never get visited by an insert, and thus the space remains unused. That problem can only be discovered by periodic housekeeping transactions.

2. Adopt the convention that free space is not counted in units of bytes, but in units of 2^5 bytes. Then with counters of 1-byte length we can administer $2^8 \cdot 2^5 = 2^{13}$ bytes.

3. The free space cursor technique does not reclaim partially free pages.

4. After file creation, one can adopt the convention that the page with the next higher number is the next free page. Only after the page with the highest number has been allocated must the policy be changed. Even while the initial policy is used, one can establish a free page chain of those pages that are explicitly returned as empty. The directory for the file must contain an entry saying which is the current policy for finding the next free page.

5. This is a strong hint rather than a complete answer. Implementing reorganization by using the original delete and insert operations would cause all the additional activities bound to these operations to take effect: ingrity constraints would be checked, deletes might be cascaded, triggers would fire, and so forth. Obviously, all this is not necessary.

6. A simple solution is to keep the entry for the dropped attribute in the directory for the relation and mark it as deleted. Then this attribute does not influence the attribute count at the SQL level, but it must be counted internally when determining how many prefix pointers are there, and so on. With that scheme, adding new attributes and deleting old ones can be arbitrarily interleaved. Without further optimizations, this solution has a strange property: In order to keep the storage structures consistent, the system must automatically insert prefix pointers for the deleted attributes into the internal representations of those tuples that are inserted *after* the attribute was dropped.

7. See the answer to Exercise 2.

11. Pages of 1 MB would cause performance problems for at least two reasons. First, reading a page of that size from a conventional disk would cost about 1 second. Second, updates in a page must be covered by exclusive semaphores. Now if such a page contains short tuples (100 bytes), each update temporarily renders 10,000 tuples inaccessible to other transactions. The first problem might be solved by disk arrays; the second problem remains.

12. Assuming that for garbage collection most portions of the page have to be modified, page logging is the most effective way to prepare for recovery. Consequently, a page lock is required. The reorganization should be covered by a nested transaction.

13. Holes in the data page can occur, which—because of the entry-sequenced organization—cannot be reclaimed.

14. The key point is that REDO makes sure tuples are inserted into the same pages as during original execution, even if that means leaving pages (partially) empty during REDO. The reason is that TIDs are handed back as a result of the insert operation, and so they must also be redone. Since they depend on page identifiers and directory entries in the pages, the requirement cited results.

15. Even without considering the phantom problem, the reading transaction depends on the page data structure being consistent. This means, in particular, that the value of no_entries in the page header is consistent with the page directory. To make sure that this does not change without notice—be it because of an inserter or because of a deleting transaction that aborts—the reader must hold a shared semaphore.

16. Storage space is not reused in the entry-sequenced organization, so pages never get reallocated.

17. See the answer to Exercise 16.

19. Without the long lock on the free space entry, another transaction might claim the space in the corresponding page, thus making UNDO of the tuple delete impossible—or at least very difficult.

20. There is no safe method. The point is that without initial formatting, one has to decide after reading a page whether or not it has been touched before. This must be done based on the information found in the page. So one must define a *signature* that distinguishes pages in the relative file from any other pages. The signature is written with the page after it has first been touched. So upon reading, the page is checked for the signature: if it is correct, one assumes that the page has been formatted before; if the signature is not found, the page is touched for the first time and needs formatting. The residual risk of this approach is that a page that has not been touched before accidentally contains the signature's bit pattern. One can make it safer by using more bits, but one cannot rule out misinterpretations. If all bit patterns are assumed to occur with the same probability, then a residual risk of, say, 10^{-15} requires $15 \cdot \log_2 10$ bits (approximately 50 bits). Whether or not that risk is acceptable is a difficult design decision. Note that it is lower than the chance of a disk writing a block to a different address than the one specified without signalling an error. But then, this will be discovered upon the next read of the overwritten slot—and individual risks do add up.

21. The data pages are written independently from the free space table pages, and so there might the situation that no UNDO is necessary on the data page, but the free space entry needs to be recovered.

. . . only God can make a tree.

JOYCE KILMER

15

Access Paths

15.1 Introduction

The discussion of key-sequenced files in Chapter 14 mentioned that tuples can be stored and retrieved based on the *value of their primary key attribute*, rather than on internal administrative data such as TIDs, free space counters, and so on (see Figure 14.13). This is a special case of the more general problem of associative access (or *content addressability*, as it is sometimes called). In non-procedural languages like SQL, queries are expressed by specifying a predicate for the tuples that qualify for the result set. In other words, the system is not asked to retrieve tuples based on information about their storage location; rather, it has to find all tuples the attribute values of which fulfill certain conditions (the selection predicate).

In principle, associative accesses could be realized by sequentially scanning the database as often as the structure of the query requires. For very complicated queries, this may actually happen. But for simple selection predicates, which have to be processed very frequently (e.g., "Find attribute BALANCE from the tuple for ACCOUNT_NO. 123456"), this would be unacceptably slow—even for in-memory databases. Therefore, the system needs mechanisms for handling at least the most frequent types of associative access more efficiently than by doing a sequential search. The class of algorithms and data structures designed for translating attribute values into TIDs, or into other types of internal addresses of tuples having those attribute values, is called *access paths*.

Depending on what kind of selection predicate is to be supported, the techniques for content addressability vary widely. Even ignoring the numerous designs for associative access by means of specialized hardware, the number of access path structures reported in the literature is too large to be described in this book. Just mentioning them all would require an entire chapter. This is not a problem, however, because today's transaction processing systems get by with a very small number of different types of access paths, all of which are introduced in some detail here.

The reasons for the striking difference between the number of *suggested* algorithms on one hand and the number of *implemented* ones on the other are discussed in the historical notes at the end of this chapter. Readers interested in content addressability will find some references there to the literature on designs different from the ones in this section. It is a safe assumption, though, that the basic techniques presented in this chapter will be at the core of future transaction systems. The degree to which the merging of transaction systems with ob-ject-oriented programming models will encourage the use of additional (type-specific) ac-cess paths remains to be seen.

The basic techniques a system has to provide for content addressability can be divided into three categories: primary key access, secondary key access, and multi-table access.

Primary key access.   A tuple of a relation must be retrieved efficiently via the value of its primary key or, for that matter, via the value of any other unique attribute. This can be achieved by integrating the access path mechanism with the storage allocation at the tu-ple level. Key-sequenced files and hashed files both are examples of that approach, where the physical storage location of a tuple is determined by its primary key value. In the simplest case, primary key access paths support selection predicates of the type (key-attribute = const); that is, they produce exactly one result tuple, provided the value exists in the database. A more general form is the range query on the primary key attribute ($const_1 \leq$ key-attribute $\leq const_2$), the result of which is a set of tuples.

Secondary key access.   This type of access path provides the same functionality just de-scribed, for *nonclustered* attributes, which may not be unique. Since even in the simple case of an equality predicate more than one tuple may qualify, secondary access paths do normally yield result *sets*.

Multi-table access.   Tuple access is often based on relationships between different tuples, both of the same and of different relations. For example, all orders placed by a given customer have to be found, all components of a certain part must be modified, and so on. Such relationships can be hierarchical (1:1 or 1:*n*) or complex (*m:n*). Hierarchical and network database systems feature data models that explicitly allow such relation-ships (mostly of the 1:*n* type); they also maintain relationships among tuples in special access path structures, such as multi-table clusters, pointer arrays, multi-table indices, pointer chains, and so on. In SQL systems, relationships among tuples cannot be de-clared in the data model; rather, they have to be computed by a join operation. Of course, such joins could be "materialized" in access path structures, just as in network database systems, but few of the current SQL systems do that. Multi-table access paths are not discussed in detail in this text. To get an idea of the techniques to be used, the reader is referred to the options for implementing complex tuples described in Chapter 14 (Subsection 14.2.3). The focus of this chapter is on single-relation access paths; some of the more general techniques are briefly surveyed in Section 15.6.

Note that associative access is just the basic primitive; additional functionality is re-quired to retrieve tuples in sorted order of the primary key attributes. More complex selec-tions are computed by combining the results obtained from simple access paths or, in the ex-treme case, by using the *default access path*, which is a sequential scan of the entire relation. Section 15.6 (on exotics) contains references to algorithms designed for more complex pred-icates.

15.2 Overview of Techniques to Implement Associative Access Paths

Associative access on a single relation can be supported by two types of access paths that use fundamentally different approaches to solving the problem of translating attribute values into tuple addresses. These approaches, which yield different functionality, are generally referred to as *hashing (key transformation)* and *key comparison*. This chapter describes the most prominent instances of these two classes of algorithms. But before going into the details, let us briefly characterize the basic ideas underlying each class.

Hashing   is based on the idea of using the primary key value as a parameter to a function, which returns the storage location of the tuple as a result. This is the very principle of hashing, and it has a number of interesting properties. If the transformation function can be kept simple—that is, if it does not need large data structures with search paths and routing data—then the access cost to retrieve a tuple via its key is minimal: take the key value, do some arithmetic, and find the tuple at the address delivered by the function. Ideal hash algorithms allow for *one-access retrieval*, which is to say that only the page holding the tuple needs to be read when accessing via the primary key. The functional principle of simple hashing is to relate the key value of a tuple and the page number in which it is stored, through a predefined function; because of this, simple hashing is not just an access method, but also a file organization technique. (This was explained in Chapter 14.) As such, it needs page address spaces with special properties, as will become obvious during the detailed decription. Hash-based access paths support only queries of the type (key-attribute = const). They do not efficiently support range predicates such as key-attribute between A and B. The attribute used for hashing typically is a primary key of the relation, but can also be used for nonunique attributes.

Key comparison   comprises all methods for maintaining a dynamic search structure on the set of values in the key attribute. These values (or compressed versions of them) can be organized into tables, lists, trees, and so on, depending on the amount of data, the type of search operations to be supported, and the storage size that is available for maintaining the search structure. If such a technique is used for a primary access path, the entire tuple can be stored in the search structure (see Section 14.4.5, on key-sequenced files, in Chapter 14); otherwise, it will contain pointers to the tuples (e.g., TIDs). Sorting a file along some attribute and keeping it sorted under updates is a very simple example of a search structure based on key comparison—in this case, it is a sequential sorted list of tuples. If records are clustered within blocks according to the key attribute values, searching and scanning in sorted order can be performed efficiently.

As mentioned, the suggested algorithms for maintaining dynamic search structures abound. This chapter contains the detailed description of just one, the B⁺-tree. The term B⁺-tree is suggested in Comer [1979]; it denotes a variety of B-trees that have all the tuples (or references to the tuples) in the leaf nodes. Since in this chapter there is no risk of confusion with other membes of the B-tree family, we will simply call them B-trees. B-trees are, for all practical purposes, so much more important than all the other access path structures that the bias of focusing this chapter on them is justified. Except for the brief remarks in Section 15.6, we will only provide pointers to the literature on the popular and fertile field of search algorithms.

Access paths based on B-trees support *equality queries* and *range queries*, and they allow retrieving the tuples in sorted order of the attribute(s) on which they have been defined.

It should be noted that hashing (key transformation) and key comparison are not strictly complementary in that a specific algorithm belongs to either one or the other category. The two concepts, rather, denote the end points of a spectrum, and a given access mechanism can well have aspects of both. The transition from one class to the other essentially depends on the amount of context used by the transformation function. If it needs but one built-in constant, like the basic hashing technique, it is a pure key transformation. However, if the function operates on a large table or other type of data structure, it can easily adopt key comparison techniques. The algorithms explained in this chapter represent key transformation and key comparison in "pure" versions.

There is yet another thing to note before undertaking the descriptions of typical access path structures in transaction systems: textbooks on algorithms and data structures usually deal with the problem of how to search efficiently *in memory*. This assumption is important, because it implies that access to all portions of the search structure are equally expensive. If that is true, the efficiency of the algorithm is determined by the number of such accesses, which, by and large, depends on the number of comparisons necessary to find a given value in the search structure. Perfectly balanced binary trees are very efficient in that respect. It is well known, however, that it is expensive to keep binary trees perfectly balanced under updates. Thus, there is whole greenhouse of trees that are not-so-well balanced, are easier to maintain, and still deliver acceptable performance.

Many of these results lose their significance, though, as soon as the amount of data to be maintained exceeds the confines of main memory. The reason for this is very simple. Consider a 20 MIPS machine. A comparison of the cost for in-memory processing with the cost for an I/O operation yields the following estimate:

The response time of a disk to an average random block read operation is about 25 ms, which is equivalent to 500,000 instructions. The operating system will charge some 2,000 instructions for the I/O, but this is negligible in comparison. Furthermore, the process doing the I/O is suspended and reactivated some time after the operation is completed, adding to the total cost of instruction equivalents. If, therefore, a search structure can be constructed that permits trading, say, 10,000 instructions for one I/O operation, then this obviously is a good trade-off. In general, one has to design algorithms such that a good balance between I/O, CPU-cost, and messages is achieved. But for random accesses (that are typical of associative access paths), I/O dominates the total cost so clearly that in the following we just count I/O operations to measure performance.

The key criterion, then, for search structures on external memory is to minimize the *number of different pages* along the average (or longest) search path. Note that this number of different pages is not equal to the number of actual I/O operations required for a search. There is still the database buffer pool, where it is hoped that some of the pages will already be available. But the fundamental argument is that by reducing the number of different pages for an arbitrary search path, the probability of having to read a block from disk is reduced. The next sections will help to further clarify this issue.

15.2.1 Summary

Associative access to a relation in the simplest case means retrieving a tuple via the value of its primary key, or a set of tuples via the value of any other attribute. Here the selection criterion is equality of the attribute value with a search value. Another type of associative access delivers the tuples of a relation in sorted order of some attribute; the *range query* retrieves only tuples between a given start value and a stop value. From these basic access types, more complex ones can be built. For example, rather than an attribute value being compared to a predefined constant, it could be compared to the attribute values of other tuples. If these tuples belong to other relations, the associative access path effectively is a materialized join.

Algorithms to implement associative access come in two flavors. The first one, hashing, supports access based on value equality only; it uses a transformation function that turns the attribute value into a page address where the tuple can be found. The second one, B-trees, is based on a dynamically maintained search structure that hierarchically decomposes the entire value space into smaller value spaces, such that the page where the tuple with a requested value must be stored can be determined with a small number of comparisons.

The key performance criterion for both classes of algorithms is to minimize the number of pages required to handle any access operation.

15.3 Associative Access by Hashing

Hash files are designed to provide fast access to one tuple via an attribute or a concatenation of attributes. Of course, the TUPLEID does just that, but it is a system-generated, internal identifier, which normally does not have any significance for the application.[1] The attribute used for hash file access is an *external* attribute; that is, one that has been declared for the relation in the CREATE TABLE statement; account number and social security number are examples. As in hash-based memory organizations, there has to be a function to transform the attribute value into a file address, where the tuple will (most likely) be found. The function prototype for a hash-base file access can be declared as follows:

```
PAGEID      hash(FILEID fileid,char *keyvalue, int keylength)
/* fileid contains the internal name of the file into which the tuple has to be hashed.          */
/* keyvalue and keylength refer to the primary key of the tuple.                                 */
```

Note that the function returns a PAGEID rather than a TUPLEID. There are three reasons for that. First, the content-oriented access mechanism should work independently of how tuples are made accessible in the lower layer of the file system. The second reason has to do with the functional characteristics of typical hash algorithms (discussed in Subsection 15.3.2). And third, given a page where the tuple is stored, the construction of the corresponding TUPLEID is simple.

But, of course, merely specifying a function prototype and assigning data types to the variables does not say anything about how to actually *implement* the hash function used to achieve a one-access retrieval. The explanation of the basic procedures distinguishes two steps: first, *folding* is introduced. It is required to turn the key value—which can be a

---

[1] Strictly speaking, in a truly data-independent system, the application has no access to the TUPLEID. But there are a number of systems supporting system attributes (e.g., ROWID), which the application can read but not modify.

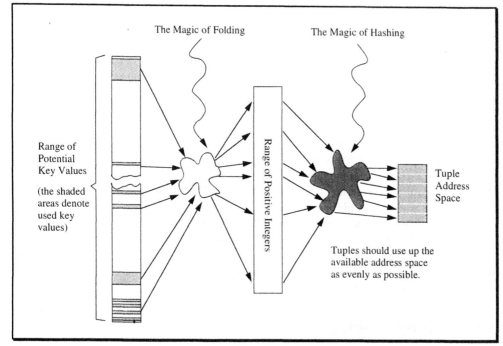

Figure 15.1: The two steps required for hash-based associative access: folding and hashing. Key values usually come from a large domain, in which the actual values are not evenly distributed. First, they have to be converted into a numerical representation (folding). Then the numerical value is transformed into a valid address from the tuple address space. In this address space, utilization must be high, and tuples must be evenly spread across the available locations.

character string of arbitrary length, or a timestamp, or a concatenation of attributes of different types—into a value of a numeric datatype, typically a positive binary integer. This is the prerequisite for the second step, where an arithmetic transformation is used to turn the numeric value produced by the first step into a page number of the hash file. Figure 15.1 illustrates this two-step procedure.

15.3.1 Folding the Key Value into a Numerical Data Type

Folding is shown in the left-hand side of the figure. The instances of the key are taken from a domain that is (in the general case) *much* larger than the number of tuples in the relation. The distribution of instances across the domain is very uneven, and there may be large parts of the potential value range that will never be used. Moreover, the instances of the key attribute(s) may be non-numeric; they may actually be of mixed types in case of concatenated attributes.

The hash function to be applied in the second step, however, requires a numeric value—more specifically, a positive integer—as its argument. So folding has to convert whatever domain the application key value comes from into a positive integer. Whether it is a 4-byte or an 8-byte integer normally depends on what the underlying machine architecture can handle efficiently. A typical folding technique that is used in many database systems is shown in Figure 15.2.

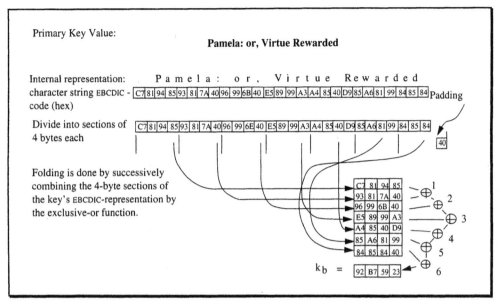

Figure 15.2: Folding long key values into a 4-byte representation which can be interpreted as a positive integer. The key value is considered a byte string, which is partitioned into segments of 4 bytes. If the last segment is shorter, it is padded with bytes containing some standard value (zeroes, the character representation of blank, or whatever). The segments are then combined by EXCLUSIVE OR. The resulting 4-byte bit pattern is then interpreted as an unsigned binary integer.

The example assumes alphanumeric key values, as we would find them in a relation about, say, English novels. Internally, each letter is encoded in one byte, and the value itself is organized as a string with varying length (see Chapter 14). Starting with the first byte, the string is now cut into 4-byte segments; if the total number of letters is not a multiple of 4, the necessary number of padding characters is added.[2] Then the first segment is combined with the second one by an exclusive OR; the result is XOR-ed with the third segment, and so forth. The resulting 4-byte bit pattern is interpreted as an integer number k_b. The outcome of this sequence is viewed as an *unsigned* binary integer, so the whole value range of 2^{32} is utilized. Thus, any string of arbitrary encoding can be folded into a positive 4-byte integer, considerably facilitating the design of the subsequent hashing function.

Since folding, like hashing itself, is a theme with endless variations, our example should not be mistaken as the only applicable method. Some remarks will point to the most important issues to be considered; we lack the space, though, to give the subject a thorough treatment.

First, any method that reduces a given key value to the number of bits allowed for a positive integer in a reproducible fashion could be used for folding. For example, we could simply take the first 31 bits, or 31 bits from the middle, or the first, fourth, and seventh bit, and so on. Such a scheme, however, loses information in that not all bits of the internal representation of the key value influence the resulting numeric value. The main reason for combining the 4-byte segments by exclusive OR is to exploit all the information contained in the key value.

---

[2] What is used for padding—whether blanks or something else—is insignificant.

Second, we should note that even an exhaustive scheme like the one we have shown may not be optimal for certain types of key value domains because it tends to repeat patterns in the encoding scheme, which in themselves do not contain any information to distinguish between different key values. Take the method illustrated in Figure 15.2, and consider key values consisting of strings of unpacked decimal numbers in EBCDIC[3] representation. A 4-byte segment written in hexadecimal notation looks like X'FnFnFnFn'. Here n is a wildcard character representing arbitrary digits between 0 and 9. If two such segments are XOR-ed, the result looks like X'0n0n0n0n'. The next round of exclusive OR produces the pattern X'FnFnFnFn', and so on. Thus, the fact that in unpacked numeric digits the upper half of the byte contains a constant value is neatly preserved during folding. The effect is that half of the 4 bytes contain no information that is used to discriminate key values. Fixing the scheme so that unpacked numbers get more relevant bits into the final value is obvious, but it is just as straightforward to come up with another pattern in the key values for which a different fix would be optimal. The problem of patterns in the key values will be reconsidered in Subsection 15.3.2.2, when discussing the hashing functions.

Third, folding—establishing a simple hash function in itself—suffers from the same fundamental problem as all hash functions: since the domain of key values is larger than, say, 2^{32} values, there are many potential key values that are mapped onto the same unsigned integer value. This may lead to a phenomenon called *collision*, which is explained in detail in the following subsection. To keep the probability of this undesired event as low as possible, it is essential for the folding procedure as well as for the hashing function to exploit all the information in the original key value, and to generate results where all the bits are set to 0 and 1, respectively, with equal probability. In other words: although it is true that any method delivering the required number of bits *could* be used for folding, only carefully designed algorithms will yield good performance.

15.3.2 Criteria for a Good Hash Function

Let us start by reconsidering the problem of shrinking domains from the original key values, via the intermediate unsigned integers, to the tuples to be ultimately addressed. Here we assume that in the typical case many fewer than 2^{32} tuples are kept in the hash file.

The key values, especially in database applications, are often taken from a very large domain; that is, the key has many digits. Think, for example, of part numbers, location names, person names, or timer values. If a primary key is defined over a domain with 15 decimal places, there are 10^{15} ($\approx 2^{50}$) *potential* instances; of course, there will be many fewer actual instances. If the key values occurring in the existing tuples were evenly distributed over the entire domain, then mapping them into the tuple address space would be simple: dividing the key value (its numerical representation) by the ratio between the number of potential values and the maximum number of tuples expected would yield a good approximation of the tuple's location in its address space. The tuple with the lowest key value would get address 1, the one with the next-higher value would get address 2, and so on.

As Figure 15.1 shows, however, actual key values are all but evenly distributed; thus, the simple scheme does not work. The requirements for a general hash function can

---

[3] Similar problems arise for the ASCII representation as well.

therefore be restated more precisely in the following way: a good hash function H has to map primary key values, which are very *unevenly distributed* over a large value range, into a tuple address space that is much smaller (proportional to the number of existing tuples), such that the resulting addresses are *evenly distributed* over the address range.

The critical issue is that although H cannot define a general 1:1 mapping (due to the different sizes of the two domains), we would like it to *effectively produce* such a mapping. The simple reason for this requirement is that the tuple address space, by definition, is large enough to hold all the tuples expected to occur in the relation, and, therefore, the number of different existing key values is the same as the number of addresses to be generated. As a result, the number of values actually fed into the hash function is identical to the cardinality of the result set. Viewed from that perspective, there is no reason why the mapping should produce collisions. The potential collisions could be restricted to those key values that do not occur in the first place. But, again, there is no information about which values will (or will definitely not) occur, and—like any other attribute—key values can change over time. Thus, the only reasonable requirement is to keep the number of collisions as small as possible, independent of the key value distribution.

15.3.2.1 The Image Set of the Hashing Function

Before introducing actual hash functions, we briefly justify the choice of page numbers as the result of a hash function (see the function prototype declare at the beginning of this section). As you are probably aware from hashing used in main memory (see Chapter 8, for example), units of uniform size are addressed by a hash access method, be it table entries, pointer arrays, or whatever. Since tuples have varying length in general, they cannot be addressed directly by a hash function. There are, however, other units of storage organization one can consider as bases for addressing: bytes, blocks, tracks, cylinders, and so on. Given that the basic file system introduced in Chapter 13 has blocks as the only units of transfer between disk and main memory, we restrict the discussion to the comparison between bytes and blocks as the units of addressing for hash-based access.

Bytes (relative to the beginning of the file) are not a good choice as the units of addressing, because of the accompanying complex free space administration in case of varying length tuples. This leaves blocks (or *pages*, as we call them at this level) as the obvious alternative. In the context of hashing, a block is often called a *bucket*. The term suggests the critical property: a bucket is a fixed-size page that is long enough to hold *many* tuples. Apart from the fact that this fits nicely into the overall file system architecture that has a block-oriented file system underneath, there is another advantage to the bucket concept: since hashing only determines in which page a tuple has to be stored, the internal organization of the page can be decided upon by different criteria. It is shown later on that this degree of freedom is quite valuable.

With this, we can define the properties of a general hash function as follows:

K_b, the folded key value, varies between 0 and $2^{32} - 1$. Assume that B pages have been allocated for the hash file. Then hash function H is a mapping

$$H: \{0...2^{32}-1\} \rightarrow \{0...B-1\}.$$

Of course, the page numbers produced by H are relative page numbers to the beginning of the relation. Our definition of H has two immediate consequences:

Contiguous allocation.   The *pages* used for the hash file must be allocated contiguously in one chunk,[4] because they are addressed by contiguous numbers, starting from the beginning of the file.

Fixed size.   Since the image set of H must be defined in advance, all the pages of the file must be allocated at file creation time. B cannot be changed later on without modifying the hash function. Modifying H, of course, means that the file must reorganized with respect to all the existing tuples. So hashing of the sort described in this section is based on the assumption that the total number of tuples can be estimated with reasonable accuracy, and that the file size remains stable over a long time.

If these restrictions strike you as too rigid, you might want to read Section 15.6, which describes a variety of hashing called *extensible hashing* that allows H to be modified on the fly, such that the image set is increased without invalidating the addresses of any existing tuples.

Given these properties of the hash function, it is clear that upon insert the storage location for the new tuple must be determined by H. This implies the following steps:

Determine the bucket.   Apply H to the folded key value, K_b; let j ($0 \le j \le B - 1$) be the result. The page number of the first page allocated to the file is S.

Check the bucket.   If page $(S + j)$ has enough free space to accommodate the tuple, the tuple is stored there. Even if other tuples (with different key values) are stored in the same page (bucket), this is no problem, because they can be distinguished independent of the hash function by using appropriate search mechanisms inside the page (see Subsection 15.2.4). Only when the remaining free space in page $(S + j)$ is insufficient to hold the new tuple is there a *collision*. (How to proceed in that case is discussed later.)

Let us first consider some typical hashing functions.

15.3.2.2 How to Find a Hash Function

There is no way of systematically *constructing* hashing functions. A number of different types of functions have been explored, and they proved to work more or less satisfactorily for certain types of applications. The problem of turning irregular key value distributions into smooth uniform address value distributions (this is what the term *hashing* refers to) is mostly investigated empirically. A thorough analysis of even simple functions requires profound number-theoretical considerations.

Hash functions that are used in practice can be divided into six categories, only one of which is subsequently described in any detail:

Division/remainder (Congruential hashing).   This is the simplest, cheapest, and most popular hashing scheme. The numerical value produced by folding, k_b, is divided by B. The remainder of this division is the page number where the tuple is stored, that is, $H(K_b) = K_b \bmod B$.

---

[4] Strictly speaking, it need not be just one chunk. One can easily use the extent scheme described for space allocation on disk in Chapter 13 to provide more flexibility for hash files, but this would not introduce any new aspects.

Nth power. K_b is taken to the nth power, and from the resulting bit string (which comprises $n \cdot 31$ bits) $\log_2 B$ bits are taken from the middle.[5] B must be power of 2, and the selected bits, interpreted as a positive integer, denote the page number.

Base transformation. The value of k_b is represented in a number system with base r, which must be different from the base in which the original key was expressed. Some appropriately chosen middle digits of that representation are then used for determining the page number.

Polynomial division. This is the technique used for computing cyclic redundancy checks in data communications. The bit pattern of the key value (no folding) is divided by a generator polynomial, and the remainder is the relative page number. The major drawback of this technique is its higher cost compared to the congruential technique.

Numerical analysis. This is a euphemism for user-specific hashing. If the rules for generating the primary key values are known, they can be exploited to compute better hash functions than any of the generic mechanisms. Whether this is done using tables with value ranges or by some other means depends on the properties of the key domain.

Encryption. Feed the original key (folded into blocks) into a standard encryption algorithm, such as data encryption standard (DES), and take the appropriate number of middle bits to encode the page number.

In the following, we will briefly describe hashing based on the congruential technique. If folding is assumed to do its own thing, there is but one parameter for the function: B, the number of buckets. The question now is how to determine B, given the two parameters that must be known at file creation time, namely T, which is the expected number of tuples, and F, which denotes the average number of tuples that can be stored per page. Note that F in general is not an "exact" value; rather it is computed by dividing the page size by the average tuple length.

The obvious answer is to compute B as

$$B = \lceil T/F \rceil.$$

This, however, will yield a poor hashing function because it easily reproduces patterns that are in the original key (or in K_b, for that matter). For example, B should not be even because then if K_b is even, so is the remainder, and vice versa. The hash function would reproduce patterns in the key values, which it definitely should not. B also should not have factors which might have significance to the application. The reason for that is easy to understand.

Assume $B = x \cdot y$. Ignoring the process of folding for simplicity, assume the key values are made up according to the rule $k_i = k_0 + i \cdot y$. According to the definition, the page number is computed as $H(k_i) = (k_i \bmod B)$. The rest is simple arithmetic:

$$H(k_i) = k_i \bmod B = (k_0 + i \cdot y) \bmod (x \cdot y)$$
$$= k_0 \bmod (x \cdot y) + (i \cdot y) \bmod (x \cdot y)$$

The first term of the right-hand side is independent of i, so let us call it r_0. The second term can be simplified by removing the common factor, which yields

---

[5] There are many variations on which bits to select. It should be neither the high-end nor the low-end bits, though, because they do not depend on all the bits of k_b.

$H(k_i) = r_0 + i \bmod x.$

This is an important result. It states that in situations like those just assumed, only a fraction of the available bucket numbers (namely B/y) will actually be generated by the hash function—certainly not a very uniform distribution. Therefore, the general recommendation is to make B a prime in order to avoid anomalies. Database systems usually let the database administrator decide whether he wants to provide his own hash function or let the system choose one. Selecting the system option generally means the congruential technique, with the number of buckets determined according to the following rule:

$B = \text{next\_higher\_prime}(\lceil T/(F \cdot 0.8) \rceil);$

The reason for the *load factor* 0.8 is discussed in the following subsection.

It is interesting to note, though, that even prime divisors can yield very uneven distributions of bucket numbers under special circumstances. Exercise 2 deals with such a case.

15.3.2.3 Estimating the Probability of Page Overflows Due to Collisions

If B was just made of the next higher prime of T/F, then each page would have to be filled up almost completely to capacity in order to accommodate all the tuples. This, in turn, would require the hashing function to produce an almost ideal uniform distribution of key values over page numbers—which should not be expected to happen. The best one can hope for is that each application of the hash function will produce any of the B page numbers with equal probability—which is not identical with filling all pages up to exactly the same level. The question is then, How much "slack" must be provided in each page to allow for most of the address collisions to be handled locally, that is, not to cause a page overflow?

Let us investigate this problem by sketching an analytic model that describes the mapping of tuples into pages using a hash function with good randomizing properties.

F was introduced to denote the average number of tuples (with average length) per page. If more pages are allocated in order to avoid filling them all up completely, only $L = F \cdot U$ tuples will be in each page on the average, where U is the load factor, or the page utilization. Again, note that all these are values averaged across all the B pages. To set up the analytic model, we ignore the necessity to make B a prime number and simply calculate B as

$B = \lceil T/(F \cdot U) \rceil.$

An ideal hash function transforms the primary key values such that each bucket number from 1 to B is generated with equal probability (uniform distribution of the addresses over the address domain). Assume for the moment that such a hash function is used. To understand how the model works, assume $F = 1$ for the moment (this implies $U = 1$, of course). In this minimal case, the probability for each page number to be produced is $1/T$, an overflow occurs as soon as a bucket gets more than 1 tuple.

In the general case, the probability for any page number to be generated by the hash function, given a key value, is $1/B \approx (F \cdot U)/T$, and a collision requires more than F tuples to be mapped to the same page. Which collision probability is lower, the one for the large number of small pages, or the one for the smaller number of pages that can hold up to F tuples?

Without going into any detail, we can observe that the process of mapping tuples into pages can be modeled by a binomial distribution. Given the uniform probability $1/B$ for each page, the probability of an arbitrary page receiving t tuples is estimated by computing the probability of exactly t matches and exactly $(T - t)$ misses. This yields

$$P(t) = \binom{T}{t} \cdot \left(\frac{1}{B}\right)^{t} \cdot \left(1 - \frac{1}{B}\right)^{(T-t)}$$

For an arbitrary page, the collision probability is then defined as

$P_{\text{coll}} = 1 - \Sigma_{i \le f} \ P(i).$

In the general case, T and B are large numbers; thus, the evaluation of this formula is not straightforward. Table 15.3 shows some estimates based on our model. It does not give the values for P_{coll}; rather, it says how many *additional* buckets (beyond the one whose address is generated by the hash function) must be checked before a free place for the tuple is found. These additional buckets are required for overflow handling, which is explained later in this section. The key observation here is that the number of additional buckets increases quite rapidly as a function of the overflow probability.

The table shows clearly that the number of overflows drops drastically as the bucket size grows. Note that the load factor, U, is a global parameter of the file. It says which portion of the available storage space is used to store the T tuples, independently of the page size. Hence, each line in Table 15.3 describes files with a constant storage overhead $(1 - U)$ and different page sizes. The left column is the minimal case.

There is no optimal bucket size—at least not in terms of this model: the larger, the better. This makes it look as though the best case is exactly one bucket with the size of the entire file. By definition, there cannot be any overflows. But note that this is an artificial solution: it says only that all tuples will be stored in that file, which is trivial, and leaves completely open the question of how to organize the tuples within the file, which is the purpose of an access path. Therefore, in real implementations, buckets typically are pages, the units of transfer between main memory and external storage; this is what the function prototype of the hash function says. The average number of tuples L per bucket is then determined by the ratio between the page size on one hand *and* the average tuple size and the

Table 15.3: Average bucket utilization and resulting number of overflows in hash-based access methods. If a tuple cannot be stored in the bucket whose address is computed by the hash function, additional accesses to overflow buckets are required. This table shows the average number of additional accesses per tuple if the hash file is accessed with randomly selected key values (uniform distribution). The average length of the overflow chain is displayed as a function of the page size and the page utilization. This table is based on computations in van der Pool [1973].

Page Utilization	Maximum Number of Tuples Per Page (Bucket)						
	1	2	3	5	10	20	40
.50	0.500	0.177	0.087	0.031	0.005	0.000	0.000
.60	0.750	0.293	0.158	0.066	0.015	0.002	0.000
.70	1.167	0.494	0.286	0.136	0.042	0.010	0.001
.80	2.000	0.903	0.554	0.289	0.110	0.036	0.009
.85	2.832	1.316	0.827	0.449	0.185	0.069	0.022
.90	4.495	2.146	1.377	0.777	0.345	0.144	0.055
.92	5.740	2.768	1.792	1.024	0.467	0.203	0.083
.95	9.444	4.631	3.035	1.769	0.837	0.386	0.171

utilization on the other hand. For an average tuple length of 200 bytes and 8 KB pages, a bucket capacity of a little less than 40 results. Assuming a utilization of .8, this means overflow rates around 1% (according to Table 15.3). Such numbers are quite acceptable, because they say that more than 95% of tuples will be found in the first page accessed, and only for the rest must additional pages be searched.

Let us make it 95%, just to roughly estimate the average access time. If one page access costs 20 ms then the average cost per associative access with a hashing function as we have described costs

$$\text{Cost}_{access} = .95 \bullet 20 \text{ ms} + .05 \bullet 40 \text{ ms} = 21 \text{ ms}.$$

Caveat: These estimates are based on the assumption of an *ideal hash function*, which produces uniformly distributed addresses. Since real hash functions very rarely exhibit this ideal behavior, the number of collisions in the parameter range specified here will be higher. It largely depends on the application, the way key values are generated, and so on. Before deciding to use a hash-based access method for a vey large file, it is advisable to do a careful analysis of the key domain, the expected instances, and their behavior with respect to a number of available hashing functions.

15.3.2.4 Hashing for Nonunique Attributes

All the previous considerations implicitly or explicitly were based on the assumption that hashing is applied to a unique attribute. This is why the estimation of an appropriate value for B could be based on the expected size of the relation only.

Now in principle, hash-based access paths can be used for nonunique attributes as well, provided the restriction of hashing to exact-match queries (key-attribute = const) is acceptable to the application. But for such attributes, the collision problem potentially gets much more serious. With unique attributes, collisions are caused by imperfect hashing functions mapping too many *different* key values to the same address. In the case of nonunique attributes, however, there are multiple occurrences of the same key value in the tuples to be addressed; and of course, the same key value is always mapped to the same address. So even if the hashing function achieves an ideal uniform distribution of the key values over the address range, the question of how many page overflows will occur is determined by the distribution of the attribute values over the tuples. If, for example, one particular attribute value occurs very often, then all these tuples are mapped to the same page, which means there will be many tuples overflowing from that page.

Let us briefly analyze the behavior of hashing with nonunique attributes. The variables are used as defined previously; an additional parameter is V, which says how many different values the nonunique attribute that is used for hash-based access can assume *at maximum*. Remember that B denotes the number of buckets in case of a unique hash key. By B' we will denote the number of buckets used for the hashing scheme with a nonunique attribute. Now one has to distinguish three cases:

$V \approx T$.   This is the case of a nonunique attribute that is *almost* unique. Think, for example, of the attribute "Title" in a relation about novels. There are different novels with the same title, but that does not happen too often, so the few collisions can be tolerated. In that situation, all the considerations of primary key hashing apply.

$V \geq B$.   There are more different values than pages are needed to store the tuples in the normal case—maximum utilization and all other aspects considered. That means the hash function will actually generate all the allocated page numbers, and if the value distribution is sufficiently uniform, there should not be too many overflows. One should, however, include one additional aspect into the considerations of which B' to choose. On top of the criteria already explained, one should make sure that the following holds: let n be defined as $n = \lfloor V/B \rfloor$. Then, rather than using B, a modified B' should be chosen according to the equation $B' = $ next_higher_prime($\lceil V/n \rceil$). To see why that is so, assume we had $V = B + D$, with $D \ll B$. Now if the hash function is good and the attribute values are uniformly distributed, then all B pages have the same probability—upon each insert—to receive a tuple, except for D pages, which have twice the probability and thus are susceptible to early overflow. So if the original estimate for B' does not meet the criterion, one should adjust B' in order to make D as small as possible. Of course, the page utilization is implicitly reduced, but that "waste of space" is justified by maintaining the performance characteristics of the hash-based access path.

$V < B$.   This is the problem case. There are not enough values in the key attribute to generate all the page numbers needed to store the tuples. If V is close to B, though, performance may still be acceptable, because page utilization is not dramatically increased if only a small portion of pages do not receive any tuples. In that case, one has to check Table 15.1 with a utilization of $(T/(V \cdot F))$ rather than $(T/(B \cdot F))$.

If V is not close to B, there are two options: first, one can decide not to use hashing for that access path. Second, one can try to reduce the required value of B, such that the second constellation we have described is achieved. This can be done by *increasing the page size* (if that is feasible), thereby increasing F. Or one can modify the file organization such the actual tuples are stored elsewhere (maybe with a different file organization), and the hash pages only contain pointers to the tuples. Then B must be calculated with the F resulting from the shorter entry length (pointer vs. tuple), and for typical tuple lengths this will result in a reduction of the estimated value of B by a factor of 20–30. But then, of course, each tuple access via the hash attribute costs two page accesses at minimum (no overflows): one to the hash page to find the TID, and one to the page with the tuple via the TID.

One must understand clearly that the estimates for $V \geq B$ and $V < B$ are valid only if the value distribution of the hash attribute is not heavily skewed. If significant skew has to be expected, hashing is not the proper access path technique to use. Then B-trees are the method of choice.

15.3.3 Overflow Handling in Hash Files

This subsection describes the basic strategies to cope with overflow situations—more specifically, with methods to store tuples that are mapped by the hash function to pages with insufficient free space to accommodate them. Since in hash files the storage location of a tuple is determined by the tuple's value in the hash attribute, overflow handling must also consider retrieval; overflow tuples cannot be stored in the pages to which their attribute value maps, but they have to be retrieved by a subsequent exact-match query specifying that value. The discussion is restricted to the data structure issues; all the problems related to synchronization and recovery are ignored. These issues are discussed in some detail in the second major portion of this chapter, on B-trees.

To keep things simple, we assume that all the pages required by the hashing function have been allocated contiguously somewhere in the file, starting at page number S. For reasons that will become obvious during the discussion, we will also assume that there are more (empty) pages in the file, not necessarily located right behind the hash pages, that can be requested individually if more space is needed.

Given these prerequisites, consider the generic overflow situation: a new tuple is to be stored. Its key value, K, is folded, and then $H(K_b) = p$ is computed. Page p, however, is full, and so in order to keep the file operational, another page q has to be found, such that (1) q can accommodate the tuple, and (2) the tuple will be found again when a retrieval operation with (attribute $= K$) is performed.

15.3.3.1 Finding Space for Overflow Tuples

In general, there are two different approaches: *internal* and *external collision handling*. The distinction between internal and external collision handling refers to the set of B buckets. There are two alternatives when more space is needed for a tuple that cannot be stored in its home bucket: one is to search other buckets (among the B buckets that have been allocated); this is the *internal* strategy. The other is to request new pages that are not among the B primary hash buckets; this results in addresses beyond the range of B buckets. Of course, these new pages cannot play any role in the hash algorithm; this is why this variant is called *external strategy*.

The external method is simpler and, therefore, is presented first. It is very similar to the technique for storing long tuples in overflow pages, described in Chapter 14 (Section 14.2). The basic idea is sketched in Figure 15.4. A bucket that overflows because more tuples are hashed into it than it can hold is simply expanded by requesting a free page (of the same or a different file) and chaining that page to the overflowing bucket. The addresses of overflow pages can be chosen freely by the free space administration. If an overflow page overflows, another free page is chained to it, as needed. In case overflow pages become empty, they can be returned to the free space manager; note that empty buckets (hash pages) cannot be returned.

The advantage of external overflow handling is its simplicity and general applicability. It also allows the hash file to grow beyond the size of $(B \cdot F)$ tuples, but, of course, at the cost of deteriorating performance as the load factor approaches 1. Even if the file does not grow beyond the size that was originally estimated, space utilization decreases with each allocation of an overflow page, because more pages are needed to store the same number of tuples. From a performance perspective, however, this is an advantage: if some of the $(B \cdot F)$ tuples reside in overflow pages, the load factor of the B primary buckets is lower than it would be otherwise, and so is the overall overflow probability.

Internal collision handling keeps all tuples within the originally allocated B buckets. Thus, in case a tuple t with key value K does not fit into its home bucket, it is necessary to determine some other page that still has enough free space to store it. The problem is to compute an alternate bucket address such that upon retrieval, the tuple t can be found in the alternate bucket without sequentially searching the whole file. And then, of course, a page holding overflow tuples from other pages can get full; in that case, its own tuples may have to be stored in other pages.

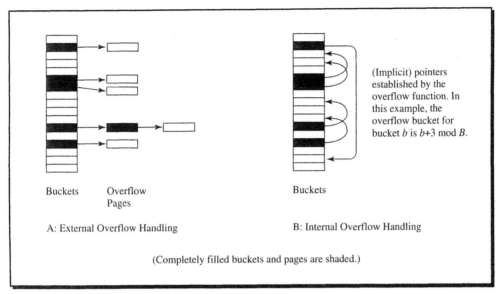

A: External Overflow Handling

Buckets   Overflow
Pages

B: Internal Overflow Handling

Buckets

(Implicit) pointers
established by the
overflow function. In
this example, the
overflow bucket for
bucket b is $b+3$ mod B.

(Completely filled buckets and pages are shaded.)

Figure 15.4: External versus internal methods for overflow handling in hash file organiza-tions. External collision handling chains overflow pages behind those buckets that have overflowed from the primary area. This can be viewed as extending the size of a bucket as needed by assigning more pages to it. This decreases the overall space utilization whenever an overflow page is allocated. Internal overflow handling only uses the original buckets in the primary area. In case of a bucket over-flow, a search strategy is used to determine another bucket that can accommodate the tuple from the overflowed bucket. This keeps space utilization high, but it increases the collision probability of those buckets, which—in addition to their "own" tuples—have to keep overflow tuples from other buckets.

The basic idea here is to supplement the initial address computation, using a hash func-tion H, by an iteration of alternate addresses according to the following scheme:[6]

page-no$(K,i) := H(K) + O(K,i); \quad O(K,0) = 0$

The iteration starts with $i = 0$, that is, with the bucket number suggested by the hash function. If this bucket is full, i is set to 1 and the overflow function is evaluated. This yields the first alternate address page-no$(K,1)$. If this bucket is also full, the iteration $i = 2$ is com-puted, and so forth, until either a suitable bucket is found or the last iteration ($i = B - 1$) has failed, at which point the free space in the file is exhausted.

The overflow function O is typically a linear or quadratic function of the iteration vari-able i. In simple cases, it is independent of the key value; that is, it has the structure

$O_1(i) = a \bullet i + c$, or $O_2(i) = a \bullet i^2 + b \bullet i + c \mod B$,

respectively. Coefficients a and b are predefined constants.

15.3.3.2 Retrieving Overflow Tuples

So far, we have discussed how to find alternate pages for tuples in case of overflow. Let us now consider the consequences of these techniques for retrieval. The problem obviously is the following: since upon insert a tuple can have been stored in virtually any page down the overflow chain, upon retrieval one needs a criterion to decide how far the overflow chain must be checked to find the tuple—or to know for sure that a tuple with the specified key

---

[6] $k(r)$ again denotes the value of the record's key.

value does not exist. Note that the latter result (establishing the nonexistence of a given key value) is also needed for insert if the hash-based access method is to support a unique attribute. There are a large number of options for maintaining the overflow chains in order to keep retrieval times short, but this is not the place to discuss them in detail. We will only present some key ideas and then let the reader consider the consequences of the different implementation techniques with respect to the transaction-related aspects, such as locking and recovery. There are some exercises at the end of this chapter dealing with such problems.

External overflow handling is quite simple in that respect. If the bucket page (see Figure 15.4) has no forward pointer to an overflow page, then no overflow chain exists and retrieval has to consider only the tuples in the bucket page. Otherwise, if the tuple with the requested key value was not found in the bucket page (or if hashing is done on a nonunique attribute), then the overflow page must be read. Here the same considerations apply: if it has no forward pointer, it is the end of the overflow chain.

Internal overflow handling provides no immediate indication as to whether there are tuples belonging to the respective hash bucket page somewhere down the overflow chain, in case a requested key value is not found. So some additional information must be maintained to say whether overflows have occurred from a given bucket, and how far search for overflow tuples must be extended. Optimizing retrieval of overflow tuples with internal overflow handling is an interesting problem.

15.3.4 Local Administration of Pages in a Hash File

The third implementation problem to be mentioned briefly is the local administration of buckets. How should the tuples be stored in a bucket page? More specifically, how should the search for a tuple with a given key value be organized? Remember that the hash function only points to the bucket page. The next step after reading this page is always a search within the page. For retrieval it has to be determined if the requested tuple is in the bucket, and for insert a location in the page has to be found; this may involve overflow handling.

The simplest method is to insert the tuples starting with the beginning of the page. This, however, means sequential search through the page for each tuple access. With large page sizes, this can be unacceptably expensive. Thus, the local organization of the bucket has to feature a data structure to allow for an efficient search for a given key.

The obvious choice for such a structure is the page directory introduced in Chapter 14. Even if the tuples have variable length, the directory can easily be organized such that it has fixed-length entries, including the values of the hash keys. Then sequential search can be performed on the directory rather than the tuples, which is more efficient. One can improve on that by applying binary search on the directory entries, thereby reducing the number of comparisons needed to locate a tuple significantly, especially if the bucket size is large.

The second possibility is another round of hashing: the bucket is partitioned into (a prime number of) sub-buckets, into which the tuples are hashed using an appropriate local hash function, and in which sequential search is performed. In this case, only internal collision handling can be used. There is an obvious way of combining these two options; its elaboration is left to the reader.

15.3.5 Summary of Associative Access Based on Hashing

This subsection summarizes the properties access methods based on hashing have with respect to organizing large files. Referring to the discussion in Chapter 14, this is the list of access operations on a hash-based file. (We only consider those operations that are influenced by the hash mechanism; standard functions such as retrieval via the TID are omitted). We also ignore most of the the problems related to logging and locking, because these issues are discussed in considerable detail in Section 15.4 on B-trees, where they are more complicated and therefore their analysis is more instructive.

readkey. This function is what the whole file type is designed for. As described for insert, the bucket address is computed using the hash function. Then the whole bucket has to be searched for the tuple with the specified attribute value; as mentioned, different methods for searching can be used. If no entry is found, and if there are overflow tuples for that bucket, alternate buckets or overflow pages have to be searched. From a transaction processing perspective, the only interesting aspect of the readkey operation is the way isolation is achieved. At the tuple level, a shared lock is acquired on the key value to protect against phantoms. At the page level, semaphores are used to protect the access path. Since there is a little more to it than just requesting and releasing semaphores as the pages are traversed, let us consider retrieval in a hash-based file organization in a little more detail. For the following discussion, we assume external overflow handling.

First, the shared lock on the requested key value is acquired. Next, the primary bucket address is computed using the hash function. With a shared semaphore, a bufferfix request is issued for the bucket page. The page is scanned for the requested tuple under the protection of the semaphore. In case the tuple is not found and there is an overflow page, the readkey must crab over to the overflow page—and from there to the next overflow page, should that be necessary.

As was explained in Chapter 8, *crabbing* means holding a semaphore on one control block until the semaphore on the *next* control block has been acquired successfully. Hence, the readkey procedure must hold on to the semaphore on the bucket page while it issues a bufferfix request for the overflow page, again with a shared semaphore.

The potential problem here is that the procedure crabs from one *page* to another page. Since the overflow page may not be in the bufferpool, this means an I/O is performed while a semaphore is held on the bucket page. Normally one tries to avoid that under all circumstances. Let us assume, though, that crabbing is considered acceptable with shared semaphores. For the insert operation, however, we have to find a way of crabbing without holding an exclusive semaphore for the duration of an I/O operation.

insert. The hash function is applied to the attribute value; the bucket pointed to by the hash function is read. If the hash attribute is unique, there must be a test if the value to be inserted is already there. This may include searching alternate buckets or overflow pages. If the value already exists, reject the insert. If the value does not exist, store the tuple (if it is the primary key access path) or the pointer to the tuple (if it is a secondary access path). Whenever possible, store it in the home bucket. Otherwise, use the collision handling technique to find another page. Here is the detailed list of steps, assuming external overflow handling.

First, an exclusive lock is requested for the key value to be inserted. Next, the address of the bucket page is computed using the hash function. From now on, we have to distinguish two cases: if the hash attribute is unique, the readkey operation must be executed for the new value to check for a uniqueness violation. If there is no violation, or if the hash attribute is not unique in the first place, the actual insertion can be done. Let us begin our considerations at this point.

An exclusive semaphore is acquired on the bucket page. If there is enough free space in the bucket to hold the new tuple, the insert operation can be completed by writing a physiological log record saying that this tuple was inserted into that bucket page, and by copying the physical tuple into the page.

If the bucket page cannot accommodate the tuple, then either an overflow page has already been chained to the bucket, or that must be done. For simplicity, let us assume there is an overflow page. The key problem now is how to crab over to the overflow page without running the risk of doing I/O while holding an exclusive semaphore.

One could think of crabbing to the proper page that can accommodate the new tuple under the protection of a shared semaphore, and converting the semaphore from shared to exclusive on that. The problem with this approach is that two or more transactions could try to do this at the same time, thus creating a semaphore deadlock.

A viable solution works like this: store the LSN of the bucket page and release the semaphore. Issue a bufferfix request for the overflow page with no semaphore. This ensures the page is *fixed* in the bufferpool, but since the semaphore is not acquired in inverse order, semaphore deadlock is avoided. Then, start the search for a place to insert over again; that is, acquire an exclusive semaphore on the bucket page, and crab over to the overflow page. There is no risk this time, because the overflow page is guaranteed to be in the bufferpool.

Of course, there is the marginal chance of either the bucket page or the overflow page having changed while those pages were not covered by a semaphore. In this case, all semaphores and buffer fixes must be returned, and the entire insert operation must be retried (except for the lock on the key value).

update.   This works as it does for the other file types, with two exceptions: if a tuple is expanded such that it exceeds the free space in the page, overflow handling will result. If the attribute on which the hash access is based gets modified, the tuple is relocated within the file. It therefore has to be deleted from its current bucket and reinserted with the new attribute value into the corresponding bucket.

delete.   First, the tuple has to be located, so the retrieval logic must be applied. This time, however, an exclusive semaphore on the bucket page is required, and the hash key is locked in exclusive mode. If there are overflow pages for that bucket page and the file design assumes shortening of overflow chains by relocation of tuples, all the affected pages and relocated tuples must also be protected by exclusive semaphores and locks, respectively. All considerations about avoiding I/O while holding an exclusive semaphore apply.

A well-designed hash access path provides associative access to a *single tuple* via its primary key at little more than one page access per tuple. This is as close to the minimum as is reasonable. But, as with all these incredibly good prices, some restrictions apply, and the drawbacks that all static hashing mechanisms have should be taken into account.

First, one must have a good idea about how large the file will become, and space must be assigned to such a file in contiguous pages. Moreover, when using the standard hashing algorithm, the file cannot be extended beyond the number of buckets initially assigned without having to re-hash all the tuples. Of course, with external overflow handling, the file can basically become arbitrarily large, but access times will become unacceptable as soon as a significant portion of tuples reside in overflow pages. So one must overestimate the number of tuples expected. This is only feasible for stable relations—those that will neither grow nor shrink drastically during a significant time of system usage.

Second, hash algorithms do not preserve the sort order of the original key value domain; that is, they cannot be used for range queries. When hashing on a nonunique attribute, multiple occurrences of the attribute value are hashed into the same bucket, substantially aggravating the collision problem.

Hash files are applicable where performance requirements call for the "one access retrieval" property, and where all the resulting limitations are justified by that. The access path presented in Section 15.4 is much more general in terms of functionality and applicability, at a (slightly) higher price for each of the access operations.

15.4 B-Trees

B-trees are by far the most important access path structure in database and file systems. They are a variety of *multi-way trees*, which are so named because each node has many successors; this differs from the classic binary tree, in which each node has at most two successors. The key property of B-trees is that each possible search path has the same length, measured in terms of nodes. Because the number of key comparisons per node may vary widely, we get different instruction pathlengths for different search paths. But in terms of the dominant performance criterion—pages—a B-tree is always perfectly balanced, and it is fairly easy to keep it balanced under arbitrary update operations. It will be shown in the next subsections that B-trees have some additional advantages with respect to their locality behavior (something the buffer manager is interested in), and that they lend themselves naturally to parallel operations, a feature that is important for concurrency control.

15.4.1 B-Trees: The Basic Idea

Each node in a B-tree is a page. There are two types of nodes: the *leaf nodes*, which contain the data (tuples, for example) in which to search is the purpose of the B-tree, and the *index nodes*, which contain no data but hold routing information to guide the search for a given key value.[7] The basic structure of a B-tree index node is is given by the following declare:

```
Uint              F;                  /* max. number of entries in an index node    */
struct                                /*                                             */
    {   char *    K;                  /* value of dividing key                       */
        PAGEID    P;                  /* pointer to other node (page)                */
    } index_node_structure[];         /* array of key value-pointer pairs            */
```

In the following text, when referring to the data structures in the B-tree nodes, we will use the subscript notation for the entries rather than C-style. So we will use K_i rather than $K[i]$.

Each index node contains a sorted sequence of keys $K_1 \leq K_2 \leq \ldots \leq K_F$, which divide the search space covered by that node. Each key value K_i is followed by a pointer P_i to a succes-

---

[7] This distinction vanishes in the special case of a tree consisting of one node only. But since such trees are rare, we do not consider that explicitly.

sor of that node containing further information about all keys K_j, such that $K_i \leq K_j < K_{i+1}$. Information about all key values larger than or equal to K_F is contained in the sub-tree pointed to by P_F. Likewise, further details about key values less than K_1 are found in the sub-tree pointed to by P_0. The parameter F is called the *fan-out* of the index node; since it is usually the same for all nodes (they are mapped to pages of the same length), one also refers to F as the fan-out of the tree.

Note that the structure just declared contains an additional key value field, K_0, right at the beginning. Given the definition that all key values less than K_1 can be found in the sub-tree referred to by P_0, this field is not really needed. It is present, though, in most existing B-tree implementations because the node-internal data structure becomes simpler that way: rather than having a pointer and then an array of pairs ⟨key value, pointer⟩, one now has a regular array ⟨key value, pointer⟩ throughout. This avoids the treatment of special cases and other complications in the implementation. K_0 contains the lowest possible value of the key domain, so every possible instance is larger or equal to that, which keeps the formal properties of the index node structure intact.

All the interior nodes contain just this type of routing information, that is, dividing keys and pointers to lower-level nodes where more detailed information can be found. The leaf-level nodes have essentially the same structure, but instead of pointers to other nodes they contain the data that is organized by the B-tree.

The term *data* can have two different meanings, depending on what the B-tree is used for:

Access path.   This is what this chapter is primarily about. One can assume that the tuples of the relation are stored elsewhere, that is, in another file with some arbitrary file organization. This implies that the B-tree is used to implement a secondary access path to these tuples, based on the value of the attribute(s) on which the B-tree is defined. In that case, the data in the B-tree leaves are pointers to the tuples—TIDs, for example. So a B-tree can index an entry-sequenced, a relative, a hashed, or a B-tree table.

File organization and clustering.   As was discussed in Chapter 14, the key-sequenced file organization relies on B-trees to determine the place where the tuples are stored in the file. In that case, the data entries in the B-tree leaves are the tuples themselves rather than pointers to them. This clusters records with adjacent key values together on the same page and in the same storage area. But note that even then, each tuple can be accessed independent of the B-tree via its TID—provided the system uses a TID mechanism for its internal purposes.

So the structure of a leaf node is an array of pairs ⟨key value, data⟩. Again, the entries are stored in ascending key sequence. Note one important difference: whereas in an index node the key value of the first entry (K_0) has no significance, it is important in the leaf nodes. Given the previous definition, K_0 in a leaf simply is the lowest key value in that node; that is, the key value belonging to the tuple that sorts first in the node's key sequence. Since the data field in general has a different length from the pointer field in the index nodes, the maximum number of entries in a leaf node differs from the capacity of an index node; in the following, we use the parameter C to denote the capacity of a leaf node.

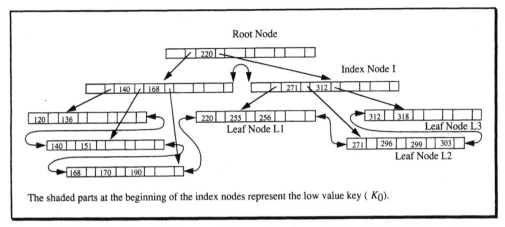

Root Node

Index Node I

Leaf Node L1

Leaf Node L3

Leaf Node L2

The shaded parts at the beginning of the index nodes represent the low value key (K_0).

Figure 15.5: Example of a small B-tree. This example shows a B-tree of height 3. Index nodes have a capacity of five entries, leaf nodes can hold up to four entries. The root node points to two intermediate index nodes, which in turn point to a total of six leaf nodes. The leaf nodes are threaded together in key sequence order.

15.4.1.1 Searching in a B-Tree

Before going into the details of the access functions, let us try an intuitive approach to understanding how the B-tree algorithm works in principle. For the sake of simplicity we assume that the tuples are stored as data in the tree; this makes it easier to talk about what happens in the different steps. We also restrict ourselves to B-trees on *unique* attributes, for the moment.

Consider a retrieval operation, searching for the tuple with attribute value = *s*, by looking at the example in Figure 15.5. Searching always starts at the root, which has the structure of an index node. Let *m* denote the index of the entry with the highest key value currently stored in a node ($m \le F$). There are only two cases to consider:

$s \ge K_m.$ Follow pointer P_m to the relevant sub-tree.

Otherwise.   Follow pointer P_j such that $K_j \le s < K_{j+1}.$

If the node the pointer leads to is an index node, apply the same procedure again. Finally, this leads to a leaf node. Either the tuple whose key attribute has the value of *s* is in this leaf node, or it does not exist in the file. In all cases, seaching inside the nodes is done using binary search, interval search, or some other efficient method, as discussed in detail later.

A range query of the type *s* ≤ attribute value ≤ *t* is *not* processed by explicitly generating all possible values between *s* and *t* and traversing the tree with each of them—that would be expensive, as was already explained for hash-based access paths. Rather, range queries exploit the fact that a B-tree induces a total ordering of its leaf pages, which is equivalent to a sorted order of the key values in the file. The complete analysis of this is the subject of Exercise 6, but here are the basic arguments: assume an arbitrary leaf node *N*, which is pointed to by pointer P_i in the corresponding index node; let *i* be neither 0 nor the highest index currently used in that index node. Then N has a right neighbor H, which is the leaf pointed to by P_{i+1} in the same index node that covers N. In the same vein, N has a left neighbor L, which is the leaf node pointed to by P_{i-1}. According to the definition of the B-tree, all the key values in N are larger or equal to those in L, and the key values in R are larger or equal to those in N.

So the leaves covered by one index node represent a sorted list of the portion of key values they contain. Since by the very same arguments one can define a total ordering of the index nodes immediately above the leaf level (applying the neighborhood definition recursively up to the root level), one gets a total ordering of *all leaves* such they contain the key values in ascending sequence. In order to utilize that sort order, the leaves are chained together from left to right by bidirectional links. This is shown in Figure 15.5.

Processing the range query [s:t] consists of two steps: first, go down the B-tree searching for the lower boundary of the interval; that is, proceed as though the exact match query attribute value = s was to be answered. The tuple located that way is the first qualified tuple for the query; assume it has index j in the leaf node. Second, process all tuples in the same leaf with indices greater than j, checking that their key value does not exceed t, the upper boundary of the query range. When the last tuple of the leaf is processed and t has not yet been reached, follow the pointer to the right-hand neighbor, and resume sequential processing with the first tuple. Continue until either the upper boundary is reached or the last leaf has been processed.

Of course, one can just as well proceed from the upper boundary down to the lower boundary if the tuples are to be produced in descending order, but this does not add any new aspects.

That is all there is to searching in a B-tree. Given that the access path structure is established as shown in Figure 15.5, the algorithms obviously are very simple.

15.4.1.2 Inserting into a B-Tree

The question, of course, is how the B-tree structure is maintained under update, how pointers are kept consistent, how tree balance is guaranteed, and the like. Let us describe the basic mechanism for adding tuples to a B-tree by referring to the example in Figure 15.5. Some very special cases will not be covered, but the presentation should give an idea of how maintenance of a B-tree works in the majority of cases.

Consider a simple insert first; assume a tuple with key value 240 is added to the file. First, a normal search is performed to locate the leaf page where—according to the structure of the B-tree—a tuple with that attribute value should be placed. This leads to leaf page L1. This leaf has 3 entries at the moment, so the new tuple can be inserted without problems, provided the tuple fits into the remaining space. The tuple is sorted into its proper place (it becomes the second entry), which means that all entries with a higher key value must be shifted one place up. No other maintenance is required. Since the search for attribute value 240 has already led to this page, it is guaranteed that subsequent retrieval operations will find the tuple via its key value.

Now apply the same procedure to the insertion of a tuple with key value 280. Searching in the tree leads to leaf page L2, but this page already has the maximum number of entries. In this situation, a so-called node split is performed. The idea is illustrated in Figure 15.6.

First, a new, empty page is allocated; it is called Ln in the figure. Note that this can be any page from a pool of empty pages in the file. This is the same situation as allocating a

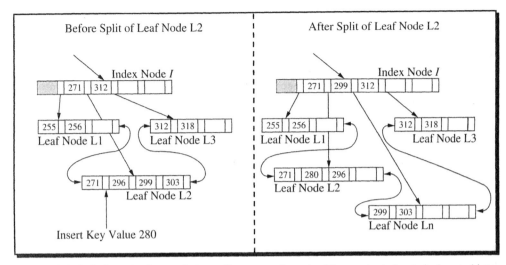

Figure 15.6: Splitting a leaf page that overflows upon insert. If a new tuple has to be inserted into a leaf page that already holds the maximum number of entries, this leaf page is split into two leaf pages: the old one, and a newly allocated page. The existing entries are distributed across the two pages; one gets the lower half, the other one the upper half of the tuples. The dividing key between these two pages is propagated up to the index page that holds the pointer to the split page.

hash overflow page. Then the upper half of the entries in the full page are moved to Ln. Now both pages hold half their capacity of entries. Of course, the forward and backward pointers between neighboring leaf nodes must be maintained according to their specifications.

The next aspect that needs consideration is the fact that where there was one page (L2), now there are two. But right now, there is only one pointer to L2 from the corresponding index node *I*. A pointer to Ln is needed in the index node, together with a dividing key that separates the value range stored in Ln from the value ranges of the adjacent leaves.

Given our definitions, it is easy to figure out how that can be achieved. Ln's value range is bounded by the split point at the low end and by what bounded L2's value range before the split at the high end. So the dividing key is Ln's low key, and this value, together with a pointer to Ln, must be inserted as a new entry into the index node that already points to L2. According to the rules, it will be sorted between the entry with the pointer to L2 and the current next entry. This is also shown in Figure 15.6. One can easily convince oneself that with this new dividing key, all structural requirements of the B-tree are fulfilled and the value ranges of the leaf nodes are correctly bounded.

After the split is complete, the new tuple is inserted into one of the two pages resulting from the split (L2, in the example), depending on which page the key value of the tuple belongs to.

15.4.1.3 Growing a B-Tree

Performing a split operation according to the description just given can lead to another problem: since the entry with the new dividing key has to be moved up to the index node, it can happen that the index node is full, and therefore the new entry finds no place. In this case, as part of the overall operation, the index node is split exactly as was described for leaf nodes: a new page is allocated, the index entries are evenly distributed, and the dividing key is propagated up the index node at the next-higher level. This process stops as soon as an index page is reached that has room for the dividing key being propagated up from below.

It can happen, though, that such an index split escalates up to the root node. Now if the root is full and a new dividing key has to be accommodated, the root has to be split. Clearly, this cannot be handled in exactly the same manner as described before, simply because there is no higher level to which the dividing key can be propagated. Without going into details, the steps to be taken for a root split are presented next. (Let R be the page number of the root.)

First, two new pages are allocated; call them I1 and I2. Then move the lower half of the root entries from R to I1, the upper half from R to I2. Now that R is empty, move the dividing key between I1 and I2 to R. It becomes the value of K_1. Finally, let P_0 point to I1 and P_1 point to I2.

As one can see, the procedure works almost like an index node split. The major difference lies in the fact that the page that held the root node *before* the split is also the root node *after* the split. The reason is that the name of the root is stored in many different places in the system, such as the catalog, the access plans, and so on. Since each operation on a B-tree has to start at the root, it is a good idea to actually identify the tree by the number of its root page. But if this is done, the root had better not change.

If you think about the maintenance operations presented so far, you will notice that all split operations leave the height of the tree unchanged—except for the root split. This is a very important point for the following reason: a root split establishes a new root, and therefore all possible search paths in the tree are now one page access longer than they had been before. Since each B-tree starts out perfectly balanced, namely with just one node, this also means that all operations changing its height *leave* it perfectly balanced. This structural robustness is one of the great virtues of B-trees.

15.4.1.4 Deleting Tuples from a B-Tree

Just considering the way insert operations work, it is guaranteed that no node in the B-tree is less than half filled. This minimum space utilization of 50% is usually quoted in textbooks. But in order to maintain that guarantee, there must be a matching definition of the delete operation. Let us briefly look at this.

Deleting a tuple starts with a tree traversal to locate the tuple. Assume it is stored in the entry with index i in the leaf page N. The entry is deleted, and all entries with indices $> i$ are moved down one rung. If the occupancy of the leaf page does not drop below 50%, this is all there is to do. It is important to understand that even if the tuple with the key value that serves as the dividing key at the index level is deleted, there is no impact on the index node. The entry in the index node just specifies a certain value range for the leaf, and this value range cannot be exceeded by the delete operation. It can happen that a leaf does not contain a tuple with a key value equal to the lower boundary of its value range. This observation has an important consequence. The dividing keys in the index nodes need not be taken from the set of key values in the tuples; all that must be guaranteed is that they correctly guide the search operations down to the key values in the leaves. It is shown in Subsection 15.4.2 how this fact can be exploited to increase the fan-out of a B-tree.

Now assume the node occupancy of node N drops below 50% as a consequence of a delete. In that situation, the textbook definition of B-trees calls for a merge of the underflowing leaf with its, say, right-hand neighbor H in order to keep up the minimum occupancy of all nodes. As Subsection 15.4.2 will demonstrate, the attempt to keep node occupancy high is motivated by more than just concerns about storage costs. Obviously, the number of entries that are actually stored in an index node—that is, its average fan-out—determines the number of lower-level nodes covered by it. So the higher the fan-out, the fewer index nodes are required for a given number of leaves. And the smaller the number of index nodes, the shorter the way to the root. In other words, when the fan-out is high, the height of the tree is low—and the height is the key performance measure for a B-tree. So worrying about underflowing nodes is completely justified.

However, the approach of merging adjacent pages upon underflow has a number of problems. For example, if the right-hand neighbor of N is just half-filled, it would underflow itself by giving tuples to N. To cope with that one might fill up N anyway, and then treat the underflow of H. This may, in the extreme case, leave the right-most leaf without a neighbor to merge with. Another possibility is to move the tuples of N and H into one node and release the page that got emptied by this action. A third possibility is to include the left-hand neighbor, L, of N and distribute the tuples of L, N and H evenly across two nodes, releasing one page as a result.

All these possibilities are fairly complicated. Furthermore, assume an underflowing node is merged into one node with its right neighbor that is just 50% full: it is clear that two insert operations (in this key range) later, the node resulting from the merge has to be split again. One also has to take into account that merging is an expensive process, involving at least three nodes. The synchronization measures required to maintain isloated execution of such an operation can significantly reduce parallelism on the B-tree, which is strictly undesired because such search structures tend to be used by many transactions concurrently. Now one could object that the same holds for insert operations, but there is a critical difference. In case of a node overflow, there is nothing one can do but split the node. So the high price must be paid in order to keep the tree operational. In case of an underflow, there is no problem with the tree functioning as specified. Therefore, the question is whether the expensive process of restructuring (by merging) should be done even though it is not necessary. Given that database relations in general do grow rather than shrink (in the long run), a temporary underflow will be "healed" by subsequent inserts sooner or later.

Most practical implementations of B-trees do not merge nodes upon underflow. They allow nodes to be emptied completely and only return pages that are no longer needed. This, of course, must be done in a way that keeps the B-tree structure correct: consider a delete operation that removes the last entry from a page. In analogy to the insert operation, one has to remove the corresponding entry from the index node pointing to the page and then return the page to the free space. The double links to the left and right neighbors must be shortcut across the removed node. If the index node becomes empty as a result, it is handled in the same way, going recursively up the levels just as splits propagate up the tree. This can eventually result in shrinking the tree by giving up a root that has only one child node.

There is an interesting subtlety at this point: giving back collapsed nodes with all the structure maintenance required need not be done as part of the delete operation in the first place. Even if a leaf node or an index node is completely empty, the tree is structurally intact and therefore functions as specified.[8] This gives the possibility of telling asynchronous system transactions check the B-tree once in a while and remove all the empty nodes. And even

---

[8] Of course, the implementation of the retrieval and insert operations must be able to handle nodes with no entries.

this operation can be divided into a number of asynchronous steps: if an empty leaf node has been removed, there is no need to also remove an index node that consequently becomes empty *as part of the same operation*; the tree is still structurally intact. So one can first remove collapsed leaves at leisure, then proceed to the first index level, and so on. That has the advantage of keeping delete operations cheap; futhermore, one can schedule such housekeeping activities at times where system load is low, so the impact of the necessary structure modifications is less severe. Some systems actually operate their B-trees this way.

B-trees implemented according to the textbook definition have a minimum occupancy of 50% and an average occupancy of 69%. Recent analyses [Johnson and Shasha 1991b] have shown that B-trees that let nodes become empty are not drastically worse in terms of space utilization. In the stable state (number of inserts equals number of deletes), space utilization is about 40%. At 60% inserts and 40% deletes, space utilization is 60%. The key point is that—according to these analytic results—performance of the no-merging scheme is much better (fewer access conflicts because of structure maintenance operations, and therefore higher concurrency on the tree) than the merging scheme. So these analyses confirm what implementations have opted for all along. We will return to some of these estimates in Subsection 15.4.2 on performance aspects.

15.4.1.5 B-Trees for Nonunique Indexes

So far, all the explanations have been put as though the B-tree was defined on the primary key attribute, and the data in the leaves were the tuples themselves. This is the case of a key-sequenced file organization. But, as was mentioned before, there are other options: the B-tree attribute(s) can be nonunique, and the data stored in the leaves can be pointers to the tuples that are stored elsewhere. These pointers can be any of those described in Chapter 14; this just depends on the design of the tuple-oriented file system. If a B-tree is used in that manner, it is called a *secondary index*.

If the B-tree is defined on nonunique attributes, this means the same attribute value (potentially) occurs in many tuples, or—put the other way—there are multiple references in the leaves belonging to the same attribute value. Figure 15.7 shows the three different methods that can be used to represent these multiple references per attribute value.

The first method is to simply ignore the fact that the attribute is nonunique. For each tuple in the file, there is a leaf-level entry consisting of the attribute value and the pointer to the tuple. According to the definition of the B-tree, entries with the same attribute values are sorted next to each other, in ascending order of the tuple identifier, which can be the primary key. The great advantage of this scheme is that B-trees for nonunique attributes are not special in any respect; all the machinery already explained can be used without modification. The disadvantage, of course, can be seen in the fact that the same attribute value is stored repeatedly, thus requiring more space in the leaves, which creates more index nodes and eventually makes the tree higher than it needs to be.

The second technique tries to avoid the storage overhead by changing the layout of the leaf pages. Now each attribute value is followed by a variable-length sorted list of tuple identifiers. Although these are not particularly complicated data structures, the modification introduces additional logic (and thus additional complications) into the B-tree code. The lists of tuple identifiers can grow longer than one leaf page, so there must be a way of handling such overflows. Either the surplus pointers are stored in the right-hand neighboring leaf, or overflow pages for leaves are introduced, as in the case of hash files. In any case, the property of having one logical entry be completely stored in one page cannot be maintained. All

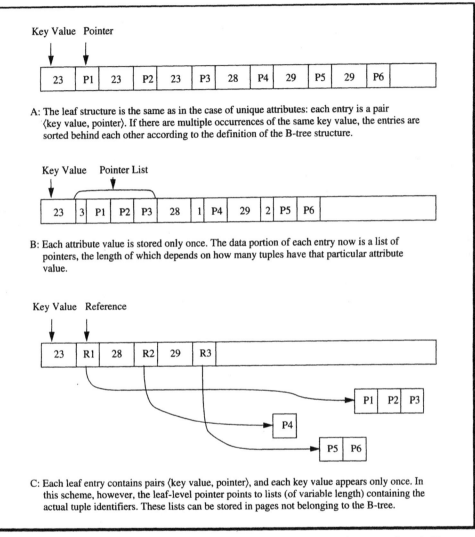

Key Value   Pointer

A: The leaf structure is the same as in the case of unique attributes: each entry is a pair
⟨key value, pointer⟩. If there are multiple occurrences of the same key value, the entries are
sorted behind each other according to the definition of the B-tree structure.

Key Value   Pointer List

B: Each attribute value is stored only once. The data portion of each entry now is a list of
pointers, the length of which depends on how many tuples have that particular attribute
value.

Key Value   Reference

C: Each leaf entry contains pairs ⟨key value, pointer⟩, and each key value appears only once. In
this scheme, however, the leaf-level pointer points to lists (of variable length) containing the
actual tuple identifiers. These lists can be stored in pages not belonging to the B-tree.

**Figure 15.7: Three different leaf page layouts for B-trees implementing secondary indices on
non-unique attributes.** The three variants differ in two aspects: first, are the multiple occurrences of
the same attribute value stored only once, or is there one occurrence for each tuple? Second, does each
leaf page entry have a fixed or a variable structure? This has to do with the way to represent the
varying number of tuple pointers belonging to one attribute value. The three layouts represent different
balances between storage overhead, access cost, and homogeneity in B-tree handling.

this is aggravated by the fact that these data structures are accessed and manipulated concurrently.

The third variant combines both approaches. Each attribute value appears only once,
and there is only one pointer per leaf node entry; the tree looks like it implements a primary
key access path. The pointers, however, point to variable-length sorted lists of tuple
identifiers that are maintained elsewhere. One can actually use the techniques for tuple
representation (see Chapter 14) to handle these lists, so they have TIDs—it just happens that
they are not visible schema objects but system-internal tuples. Note that the B-tree manager

would not have to know about this at all. All it does is store the fixed-length data portion of the leaf entries. The component using the B-tree, however, has to know whether these pointers point to database tuples or to some internal data structures.

Looking at how B-tree access paths are implemented in real systems, one finds (among the many similarities) two different philosophies with respect to handling nonunique attributes. One camp has it that—from a B-tree perspective—there is no such thing as a nonunique attribute. Either the B-tree is defined on a primary key, in which case the attribute values are unique and there is exactly one data field to go with each of them (tuple or tuple identifier), or the attribute values are not unique but the concatenation of attribute value and tuple identifier is unique and can be fed into the B-tree just like a primary key.[9] In the latter case, it is completely up to the client of the B-tree manager to know and understand what the key values and the data fields mean and how they have to be used. The advocates of the unique-value approach claim the uniformity of mechanisms in the B-tree manager as the decisive advantage.

The other camp claims that it is important for the B-tree manager to understand the differences between unique and nonunique attributes for two reasons: first, the data structures containing the tuple references can be optimized for each case, which, of course, means a substantial amount of extra code. But the proponents hold that the potential gain in performance is worth the additional complexity. Second, the optimal strategies for synchronizing concurrent operations on B-trees depend on whether the attribute is unique or not. It is possible to use one synchronization method for both cases, but then the level of concurrency in case of nonunique attributes will not be the level that could be achieved by exploiting the fact that there can be multiple occurrences of the same attribute value. There is a detailed discussion of this issue in Subsection 15.3.4.

Of course, each system designer swears by his own approach and has all the good reasons for it. It is probably impossible to find an abstract position from which to compare both views and decide that one is better than the other. Apart from many optimizations one can apply in each design, there are important criteria that cannot be quantified easily, such as the uniformity of the first approach (unique attributes only) as opposed to the additional complexity of the second one. Readers may want to consider this problem for themselves, because it is a very good illustration of what it means to judge the merits of an algorithm (or a local optimization of an algorithm) from a more global, system-architecture perspective.

15.4.1.6 Miscellaneous Remarks

So far, all the problems related to concurrency and recovery have been ignored. They are covered in subsequent subsections. In addition, two of the access functions, readkey and insert, will be explained in detail by means of C programs using the page structures, synchronization primitives, and so on, defined earlier in this book.

It is important to understand that access path structures such as B-trees are implicitly maintained by the database system once they have been declared. They are transparent to the application; that is, from the SQL programming interface, access paths are not visible. However, if several indices have been declared for a relation, then each insert or delete of a tuple in that relation will automatically result in maintenance operations on each of the index

---

[9] Note that this view results in a B-tree with an empty data portion in the leaf nodes, because what is the data from the perspective of the B-tree user is declared as part of the key to the B-tree manager to obtain unique values only.

structures.[10] This is the positive way of putting it. One might take a different perspective and say that each access path increases the cost of update operations because of the implicit index maintenance. So the decision of whether or not to create an index has to weigh the speedup of retrieval against the slowdown of update.

15.4.2 Performance Aspects of B-Trees

There are two parameters that matter for B-trees serving as primary or secondary access paths in database systems. The first parameter is the height, H, which is the number of pages that must be searched from the root to the leaf page holding the requested tuple. The second parameter is the size, S, of the B-tree, or the number of pages required to store it.

The formulae for estimating these parameters can be derived by some straightforward calculations. The parameters required are defined as follows:

N.   Number of tuples in the database.

F.   Maximum number of entries in an index node; by F^* we denote the average number of entries in an index node.

C.   Maximum number of entries in a leaf node; by C^* we denote the average number of entries in a leaf node.

k.   (Average) length of a key value.

t.   (Average) length of a tuple.

p.   Length of a pointer or a tuple identifier.

B.   Effective storage capacity of a page (page size minus length of administrational data).

u.   Average node occupancy; we assume the same average occupancy for both leaf and index nodes.

Given these definitions, it is clear that the following equations hold:

$$C^* = \lfloor (B/(k + t)) \times u \rfloor \qquad \text{(key-sequenced file)}$$
$$C^* = \lfloor (B/(k + p)) \times u \rfloor \qquad \text{(secondary index not using primary key)}$$
$$F^* = \lfloor (B/(k + p)) \times u \rfloor$$

Let us start with a model for H. To store N tuples, $\lceil N/C^* \rceil$ leaf pages are required, with C^* being determined by the type of B-tree. Each index node can point to F^* successors, so the first level above the leaves has $\lceil \lceil N/C^* \rceil /F^* \rceil$ index nodes. These must be pointed to by index nodes of the same size at the next level, which goes on until the number of index nodes required at the next level drops to one—this is the root. In other words, calculate how often $\lceil N/C^* \rceil$ can be divided by F^* until the result is less than 1; this is the height of the B-tree.

---

[10] Update operations only affect a B-tree index if they change the value of the key attribute. In this case, the update effectively means to delete the tuple from its old (key value–dependent) position and insert it into the new position.

Table 15.8: Numerical evaluation of formula 15.3 for key-sequenced files and secondary indices. The number of tuples N that can be accessed via a B-tree of height H is shown for some reasonable values of H. The increase in storage capacity of the tree when going from one level to the next is also displayed.

H	Key-sequenced file ($C^* = 43$)		Secondary index ($C^* = 300$)		
	N(max)	Increase	N(max)	Increase	
2	12,900	—	90,000	—	
3	3,870,000	3,857,100	27,000,000	26,910,000	
4	1,161,000,000	1,157,130,000	8,100,000,000	8,073,000,000	
5	348,300,000,000	347,139,000,000	2,430,000,000,000	2,421,900,000,000	Use disk partitioning beyond this

$$H = 1 + \lceil \log_{F^*}(\lceil N/C^* \rceil) \rceil \tag{15.1}$$

The total size of a B-tree in units of pages is estimated using the same arguments, just the other way around: first look at each level of the tree and calculate the number of entries in the respective nodes. Then add up the numbers. This yields

$$S = \Sigma_i (F^*)^{i-1}, \quad 1 \le i \le H \tag{15.2}$$

Note that this formula is just an estimate that tends to be too high. (Can you see why that is?) The derivation of an "exact" formula is left as Exercise 5.

Table 15.8 shows a numerical evaluation of the B-tree performance characteristics for both key-sequenced files and secondary indices. The environmental parameters have been set as follows: $B = 8,000$ bytes; $k = 10$ bytes; $t = 100$ bytes; $p = 6$ bytes; $u = 0.6$. This yields the following parameters for formula 15.1: $F^* = 300$, $C^* = 300$ (secondary index), $C^* = 43$ (key-sequenced file). As a matter of fact, Table 15.8 is not an evaluation of formula 15.1, but of a transformed version that says how many entries can be maintained in a tree of height H. It is derived from formula 15.1 by simple arithmetic:

$$N = C^* \times F^{*(H-1)} \tag{15.3}$$

Considering formula 15.1—and the equivalent expressions for the maximum and the average height—it is obvious that the height of a B-tree can be reduced in two ways: first, the argument to the log function, $\lceil N/C^* \rceil$, can be reduced, which means decreasing the number of leaves. With the number of tuples being invariant, this, in turn, means increasing C^*. The second option is to increase the fan-out F^* of the index nodes. Let us consider both options in turn.

15.4.2.1 Reducing the Number of Leaf Pages

If the same number of tuples is to be stored in fewer leaf pages, there are two possibilities to consider. The trivial option is to increase the size of a leaf page; let us rule this out for the following discussion. The other possibility is to shorten the data in the leaf pages—that is, the key values, or the tuples, or the pointers to tuples. Since key compression will be discussed as a method for increasing the fan-out, let us focus on shortening the data portion of the leaf node entries.

If the B-tree under consideration is a secondary index already, there is little one can do because tuple identifiers cannot be shortened significantly. Without considering general data-compression techniques as they are used, for instance, in communications, there is only one interesting question: given the complete freedom of choice, should the tuples be organized as a key-sequenced file, or should they be stored elsewhere and the access path for the primary key be organized as a secondary index? Which gives faster access for equality queries? Of course, if the tuples are frequently accessed in sorted order of the primary key, then the key-sequenced organization is the right choice. But for the sake of argument, let us consider random access to one tuple via the primary key as the typical load.

Since a tuple is, on the average, x times longer than a pointer, a tree that has tuple identifiers in the leaves rather than in tuples has fewer leaf pages and, therefore, probably fewer levels. On the other hand, there is an extra page access for each tuple because the leaves only hold TIDs, that is, pointers to the tuples. Let the average cost for a tuple access via the TID be 1.1 page accesses. In order to find out if the smaller tree outweighs the additional page accesses, we have to make the following calculation. (For convenience, we drop the integer brackets.)

$$1 + \log_F *(N/(x \times C^*)) + 1.1 \leq 1 + \log_F *(N/C^*). \tag{15.4}$$

In this formula, the C^* for the case of embedded tuples (key-sequenced files) is used. This transforms into

$$1.1 \leq \log_F *x \tag{15.5}$$

In other words, to break even, the reduction factor x must be larger than the average fan-out. Unless the average fan-out is fairly small or the tuples are long (greater than 1 KB for a fan-out of 200), the additional page access via the tuple identifier is not compensated by the height reduction of the tree. Estimates such as these are an important part of physical database design.

15.4.2.2 Increasing the Fan-out

There is nothing to be done about the structure of the interior nodes, which are strictly determined by the way the B-tree works. The only way to increase F^* is to compress the key values K_i. This can be done using two facts:

Prefix compression. The keys are sorted along some collating sequence, so that rather than storing the whole key in each entry, we can try to store the difference only to the previous one. How the difference is computed depends on the datatype and the internal representation.

Suffix compression. The index nodes do not actually need the complete key values; all they need is sufficient information about the keys further down the tree, in order to direct the tree traversal to the right successor node at each level.

Compression is most effective with long key values, such as names or other alphanumeric attributes. The basic techniques for shrinking long alpha strings such as B-tree entries will be demonstrated by using the Lucca phone book as an example (the Ripa phone book is just too small).[11] Assume the phone directory is to be represented as a key-sequenced relation with the name as the search key. In the Lucca area, there are approximately 46,000 telephones. With an average of 100 bytes per tuple and 8 KB pages (assuming the average page utilization of 69%), there are 55 tuples per leaf page, or 837 leaves. To further simplify things, assume that only the last name is used as a search key and that key values are stored with fixed length in the interior nodes.[12] If 40 bytes are allowed for a name, and if each pointer is 4 bytes long, there will be an average of 125 used entries per interior node. The tree will be three levels high; the root holds about six key values. To get an impression of how key values might be compressed in that B-tree, let us first look at what the entries in the root will look like, and then consider an arbitrary leaf.

For the Lucca phone book, the discriminating keys in the root would have to divide the name space into seven roughly equal-sized partitions. Thus, according to the value distribution (and according to the real phone book), there would be the following entries: Bertolucci, Copelletti, Gambogi, Lucchesi, Paganucci, Ristoranti. The differences between these values, whether they were computed using exclusive OR on the binary representation or by some other means, would not yield any compression, because the entries are not alphabetically close; that is, they differ in each digit.

Now, consider the second entry (see Figure 15.9). It says that the lowest key value in the successor node pointed to by its right pointer is *Copelletti*. If the search key is smaller than that (but larger than *Bertolucci*), search has to proceed along the left pointer. In the actual phone book (1990 edition), the highest value in the interior node referenced by that left pointer is *Cooperativa*. Since the dividing keys just serve as routers, it is sufficient to store the prefix up to the first character that distinguishes between both values—*Cop*, in this case. It is easy to see that all search paths will still work out correctly. This technique is called *suffix compression*, and it is particularly attractive for the higher-level nodes of a B-tree, where usually just a few prefix digits are enough to distinguish between two adjacent successor nodes.

Next, consider an arbitrary leaf node. There, we can find the following key values: Manino, Manna, Mannari, Mannarino, Mannella, Mannelli, and so forth. These entries are alphabetically close, and the idea of storing differences, rather than full key values, can be used as a compression technique. One variant of this is called *prefix compression*: it requires each key value to be stored as a tuple of the following form: ⟨length_of_prefix,key_suffix⟩. The first component says how many prefix characters of the previous value are identical; the second component has the rest of this key value; that is, the part that differs from the previous value. Thus, if *Man* is the prefix for all entries in the sample leaf page, the sequence of stored values would look like this:

⟨3,"ino"⟩⟨3,"na"⟩⟨5,"ri"⟩⟨7,"no"⟩⟨4,"ella"⟩⟨7,"i"⟩

Typographically, this does not look shorter at all. But note that the prefix length can be encoded in 1 byte. As a result, the version using prefix compression comprises 20 bytes, compared to 43 bytes for the uncompressed values.

---

[11]   That may need an explanation: the B-tree section was compiled during our first writing assignment, in a small village in northern Tuscany called Ripa. The next larger town is Lucca, a famous spa.

[12]   This assumption agrees with the page layout used for the sample implementation later in this chapter. It is used to facilitate efficient search methods inside a page, like binary or interval search.

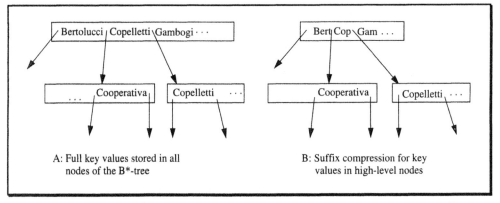

A: Full key values stored in all
nodes of the B*-tree

B: Suffix compression for key
values in high-level nodes

Figure 15.9: Using suffix compression to increase the fan-out of high-level index nodes. Key values in high-level nodes can be truncated from the right (for keys of type char) as long as they correctly distinguish between the high key value of the node the left pointer refers to and the low key value of the node the right pointer refers to.

For interior nodes, especially those at lower levels, both schemes can be combined. Thus, we can take advantage of both alphabetic proximity and the fact that less than the whole key has to be stored. Since the details of that compression technique are rather complicated, we will restrict ourselves to a sketch of the idea by means of yet another phone book example. Consider the following sequence of names: Cresti, Crestoli, Cricca, Cricco, Cricorian, Crimaldi. If these were discriminating keys in an interior node, the constant prefix *Cr* would not help distinguish between successors, and, on the other hand, we only would have to encode suffix characters of the suffixes up to the point where they differ. Since the common prefix goes up to the point where the values start to differ, there is actually not much left to store. Using the notation introduced previously, the sequence of dividing keys in the interior node looks as follows (*Crest* is assumed to be stored at the beginning of the node):

$$\langle 5, \text{``i''}\rangle\langle 5, \text{``o''}\rangle\langle 2, \text{``icca''}\rangle\langle 5, \text{``o''}\rangle\langle 4, \text{``o''}\rangle\langle 3, \text{``m''}\rangle$$

Systems using combined prefix and suffix compression report impressive savings in storage space. In several applications, even long alphanumeric key values could be reduced to an average of less than two bytes per B-tree entry. A detailed explanation of key compression techniques is presented by Bayer and Unterauer [1977].

15.4.2.3 Miscellaneous Heuristics

So far, it looks as though the compression techniques presented are a must. In the example, they would have reduced the height of the B-tree by one. But there are some penalties. First, update operations are more expensive because the prefix differences with the neighbors have to be recomputed upon each insert and delete. The prefix compression scheme has an even more serious drawback: since each key value is made up from the explicitly stored piece and a portion of the previous value, in order to read the nth value in a node, all the preceding $n - 1$ values have to be scanned explicitly. This necessity of searching the page sequentially becomes increasingly unattractive as page sizes grow. For large pages, binary search or interpolation search yields much faster results, but these techniques require the key value to be determined through direct access. There is no such problem with suffix compression.

Prefix compression can be modified such that each stored piece of a key value refers to a global prefix that is the same for the whole page. For very long alphanumeric keys, this will still yield good compression results—at least at the leaf level. It is extremely difficult to weigh the storage savings and the potential height reduction through compression against the additional pathlength incurred by the compression algorithms. Some systems provide the administrator with modeling tools to support the decision process, but these models tend to have many parameters for hard-to-estimate things like value distributions. As a simple rule of thumb, we can say that for short search keys (8–10 bytes) whose values are evenly distributed over the domain, one should use either no compression or, for large files, only suffix compression.

Some minor performance considerations are related to the distribution of tuples in case of a split. The standard textbook policy requires 50% of the tuples to be in the old page and the rest in the new page. That is the only way to guarantee that each page (except for the root) is at least half full. Assume, however, that the tree will be filled by sequential loading in sorted order; such loading then achieves the minimum utilization, because after a split, the node with the lower key values will never get any new entries. Consequently, it might be better to leave a higher percentage of tuples in that page.

Yet another variant tries to optimize for the search inside a page, using the interpolation method. Rather than dividing the tuples in the overflowing node into equal sized partitions, this variant splits them at the key value closest to the mean value of the highest and the lowest key in the set, so that the *key range* in one resulting page is equal to that in the other.

Now we have discussed performance optimizations of a B-tree without having specified precisely how performance is measured.

What, then, is the performance of a B-tree? As was emphasized at the outset, the key figure of merit is its height, H. But that does not mean H I/O operations for each access. Consider a very frequently used B-tree, one that implements the primary access path for a relation on which, say, 60 transactions per second operate.[13] Each access will start at the root, giving this page a very high access rate. Since the buffer manager tries to keep in memory those pages that are busy, the root page will certainly always be there—no I/O is required. Each search path then forks out to the next level, choosing among $F + 1$ pages at maximum, and on the average less than that. Assuming a fan-out of 400, this means that each access operation goes to any of these 400 pages with equal probability. Consequently, each such page has an access frequency of 60/400, or about one access in 6.7 seconds. According to the five-minute rule, such pages should clearly be kept in memory; again, there is no I/O. It is easy to see that pages at all lower layers have a negligible access frequency and therefore will most likely not be found in the buffer. In summary, with a reasonably large buffer, a B-tree with height H requires $(H - 2)$ I/O operations for a random readkey access. Considering the size of files that can be stored with four-level trees, this is a surprisingly low figure. Note that this is even a pessimistic estimate in that it assumes that the root has the maximum number of children—or the average number, depending on how one wants to interpret to value 400. But quite often the root has fewer entries than that. Remember that at the moment a B-tree grows, the root has but two children, and it will get more only if splits percolate up to the root from the leaf level, which is a rare event. So there are long periods in the history

---

[13] We consider such an environment because some of the assumptions needed for the estimate will not hold for B*-trees that are only rarely used. But then, if they are only rarely used, one I/O more or less will not matter much.

of a B-tree where the root has very few entries; if that is the case, the number of I/O operations for a random read access can safely be estimated as (H − 3).

15.4.3 Synchronization on B-Trees: The Page-Oriented View

When implementing a B-tree, there is more to consider than merely the maintenance of the data structures. B-trees are often used by concurrent transactions retrieving through this access path and performing updates that change it. In particular, there will be queries that use only the index and do not touch any tuples; as an example, consider a query of the following type:

```
select count(*)
from relation_a
where attribute_x > 15;
```

Operations on a B-tree must have the same ACID properties that are required for tuple operations. The isolation protocols, consequently, have to preserve serializability; on the other hand, they should be designed such that waiting of transactions on the B-tree is minimized. The other aspect has to do with the related problems of logging and recovery. Insert operations can cause significant changes of the tree structure if the split function has to be invoked. What does that mean for the structure of the B-tree if such an insert is just part of an ongoing transaction, which later on may abort? And if the transaction commits, how can its effects on the tree be made recoverable? We will discuss these issues in some detail.

Considering isolation first, the ground rule is to reduce both the number of locks and their holding time as much as possible for all B-tree operations. An intuitive argument why it is not necessary to lock the whole tree structure goes as follows: if the B-tree is used to implement a key-sequenced file, then the tuples in the leaf pages will be protected by long locks. The higher levels are just redundant search structures (they can be reconstructed from the tuples at any time); thus, they are necessarily consistent with the state defined by the tuples. In other words, if the operations on the tuples are serializable, then so are the implicit operations on the tree. Furthermore, the redundant search structure can be exploited to achieve isolation where simple tuple locking is sufficient, namely, in case of phantoms. If the tree only implements a secondary access path, then it is fully redundant, and the same arguments therefore apply. Note that this is an informal interpretation of the DAG protocol described in Chapter 7, Subsection 7.8.7. It is therefore sufficient to assume that transaction serializability is guaranteed through the locks on the primary objects, the tuples. Phantom protection is achieved by key-range locking, which was introduced in Section 7.8. All operations on the B-tree data structures will be protected by shared and exclusive semaphores, which are released as soon as the routing information in a node has been exploited (or modified).

The retrieval case is simple. First, the root is protected by a shared semaphore. It is then searched for the pointer to follow. A shared semaphore is acquired for the successor page, and the semaphore on the root is released. This is the crabbing technique introduced in Chapter 8, which we already used in the explanation of the access operations in hashed files (Subsection 15.3.5). The tree traversal proceeds in this style until the leaf level is reached. From then on, while the semaphore is still held, an additional synchronization technique takes over (it is described in Subsection 15.4.4). If the readkey operation is to retrieve just a single tuple (unique index), no further semaphores will be needed. If, however, a sequential scan is started—for example, for retrieving all tuples with key values greater than v—then at some point it may be necessary to continue the read scan in the adjacent leaf node. Moving from the current leaf node to the next leaf node also uses the crabbing technique, but in this case some tricky interdependencies with concurrency control have to be considered.

For inserts, the optimistic principle is adopted. It says that most likely no split of the leaf page where the tuple is inserted will occur. If this probability is low, then the probability of a split at the next-higher level is lower by a factor of $1/(F^* + 1)$, and so on. Initially, then, no exclusive semaphores are used on interior nodes when traversing the tree for inserting a tuple. Insert initially uses the same procedure as described for retrieval to determine the location of the insert. While going down, the sequence of nodes from the root to the leaf is stored in a list. At the leaf page, an exclusive semaphore is acquired. If no split is necessary, the page data structure is updated and the semaphore is released. However, if the leaf page needs to be split, another optimistic assumption is made: the path to the leaf node has not changed in the meantime. Thus, the exclusive semaphore on the leaf page is released, and the stored path is retraced, this time acquiring exclusive semaphores for each node; these, in turn, will get modified as a consequence of the split at leaf level. Note that split operations at higher levels can only occur as a consequence of a leaf split. For each node, two things must be checked:

(1) Has the path changed since the read traversal for locating the insert position (i.e., have the path pointers changed)? This check is done by remembering the page LSN during the first traversal and comparing it to the current page LSN when going down the second time.

(2) Is the successor node completely full? If not, release the exclusive semaphore on all higher-level nodes and proceed. If so, keep the exclusive lock and proceed. Clearly, a node that is not completely full (call it N for the moment) need not be split, even if a new entry is inserted into it by a split of one of its children. Thus, if N will not split, none of its predecessors in the hierarchy will be modified, which means there is no point in keeping exclusive semaphores on them.

As a result, all nodes from the leaf upward that are completely full, plus one level above, will be protected by an exclusive semaphore. The split can now be performed as described; then the semaphores are released. The reason for releasing the exclusive semaphore on the leaf page before starting the second traversal is to avoid deadlocks on the B-tree. This protocol follows the algorithm described by Bayer and Schkolnick [1977].

Delete works exactly like insert, except for the case of a leaf page underflow, which may require a merge of adjacent pages. From the discussion of how to protect the tree selectively in case of a split, it should be obvious that a merge can become even more complicated if the pages to be merged are children of different parents. Many systems therefore restrict the merging of leaf pages to siblings and leave the merging of interior nodes to reorganization utilities, which get an exclusive semaphore on the root.

15.4.4 Synchronization on B-Trees: The Tuple-Oriented View

The following discussion rephrases some of the arguments presented in our discussion of isolation concepts (Chapter 7). This time, however, the discussion places special emphasis on how to keep operations on B-trees consistent (i.e., isolated) while allowing for highly concurrent access to this commonly used search structure. The presentation in this section

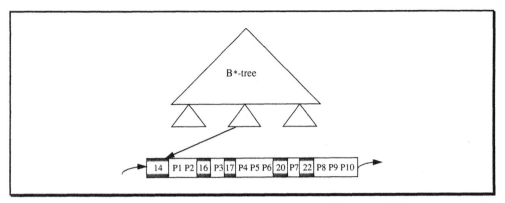

Figure 15.10: Avoiding phantoms by key range locks. Locking index entries is a means to avoid phantom anomalies among concurrent transactions. The example shows a nonunique index with numeric key values. The P1, P2, . . . in the leaf node are assumed to be pointers (TIDs) to the qualifying tuples.

closely follows Mohan's description of a key-value locking scheme [Mohan 1990a]. It is called *key-range locking* in earlier work, and we use this terminology because it is more descriptive.

We have observed that no locks (as opposed to semaphores) are needed on the B-tree, which only contains redundant information. In addition, we want to exploit the search structure to achieve phantom protection, which looking at the tuple alone cannot do. One way to avoid phantoms (described in Chapter 7) is to hold *long locks on key ranges* of an index on the relation. By doing so, it is possible to check whether a search key value relevant to an ongoing transaction is about to appear or disappear. The basic idea is illustrated in Figure 15.10.

Assume transaction $T1$ has read all the tuples with key value 17; then, tuple locking alone would not prevent another transaction, $T2$, from inserting a new tuple that also has 17 as a value in that attribute. However, if the tree entry associated with key value 17 is locked for reading, $T2$ would be serialized behind $T1$. The reason is that—as explained in Subsection 7.8—locking the key value 17 implicitly locks the value *range* [17, 20).

Note that range locking also supports some obvious query optimizations: if a transaction just asks for the total number of tuples with key value 17, then there is no reason to actually lock and access the tuples themselves. The query can be answered using the index alone. However, without key-range locking, the tuples would have to be locked in order to keep the transaction isolated—and even that would not prevent phantoms.

Given this basic motivation of key-range locking, the question is how to implement these locks. The simplest possibility would be to extend the locks to the entire node; that is, to lock the *page* holding the value range for read or update, rather than the entry. Creating key-range lock names would be easy in that case, but for concurrency this would clearly be unacceptable.

The rest of the discussion, then, is based on the assumption that key-range lock names are tuples of the following structure:

⟨table name, index name, key value⟩.

The following explanation of the tree locking scheme based on key-range locks builds on the description of range locking in Chapter 7.

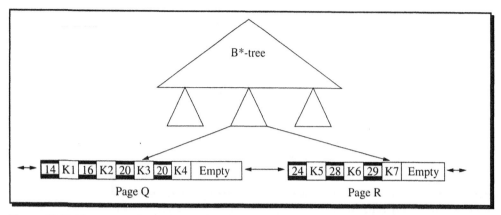

Figure 15.11: Two successive leaf pages in a B-tree. This scenario is used to illustrate the most important issues of the key-range locking protocol for B-trees.

15.4.4.1 The Key-Range Locking Protocol

Before we discuss the use of key-range locking for retrieval and update operations, let us briefly recapitulate the assumptions about the underlying B-tree structure and the notation.

First, we adopt the view of having unique index entries only. For all secondary indexes, each index entry (value) has the following structure:

<attribute value, tuple identifier>

As was mentioned before, the tuple identifier could well be a primary key value. Figure 15.11 illustrates this design. The numbers represent values of the index attribute, and k1, k2, . . . represent primary key values. Second, we adopt the previous key convention introduced in Chapter 7, Subsection 7.8: by locking key value V, we assume the half-open interval $[V, X)$ to be locked implicitly; here X stands for the next-higher key value found in the index. This is why the term *key-range locking* is more appropriate than *value locking*.

When talking about values and value ranges, we refer to the pair notation introduced previously. So the values V, X, etc. to be locked could be pairs <attribute value, tuple identifier>, or they could be just attribute values.

Let us now describe the key-range locking protocol for the following operations: exact-match query, range query, insert of a new tuple, deletion of an existing tuple. Since we have adopted the entry structure of <attribute value, tuple identifier> to make sure there are unique entries only, even exact-match query effectively is a range query for all but unique indexes. Retrieving all tuples with key value = c means searching the interval (<c, $-\infty$>, <c, $+\infty$>). Here $\pm \infty$ represents the high and low values of tuple identifiers. The basic locking protocol using the key-range concept is the following: find min k such that the index entry <c, k> exists at the leaf level of the tree. Let us denote this entry as <c, k_1>. Get a shared lock on the value <c, k_1>. This, by definition, covers the range up to—but not including—<c, k_2>, where k_2 is the next-higher tuple identifier of a tuple with key value c. Proceed in this manner until the first entry <x, k> with x > c is found.

This works and—as will be shown for the insert operation—it prevents phantom tuples with key value c from appearing while the read transaction is active. The problem is that a value lock is needed for each tuple: remember that the tuples themselves must be locked, too. This is where prefix locking comes in. We exploit the structure of the entry and request a shared lock on the *attribute value only*. By definition, this covers the interval $[\langle c, k_{min}\rangle, \langle c_n, k_{min}\rangle)$, where c_n is the next higher attribute value after c. This is exactly what is needed for phantom protection. With this modification, only *one* value range lock is needed for the exact-match query. But of course, the update locking protocols must be designed such that retrieval operations using prefix locking will be isolated correctly.

Range queries of the type $c_1 \leq$ key value $\leq c_2$ do not pose any new problems. Key range locks in S mode are acquired for all value intervals $[c_1, W), [W, X), \ldots [Z, c_2), [c_2, c_3)$, where c_3 is the next-higher attribute value after c_2. So the number of key range locks required is equal to the number of existing values *between* c_1 and c_2, plus two. Now consider the update operations, that is, the insertion and deletion of a single tuple. Since they act on single tuples, these operations primarily are concerned about whole entries, that is, about ⟨attribute value, tuple identifier⟩ pairs rather than prefixes. But since retrieval operations mostly use prefix locking, the update operations must protect the prefix value ranges, too. This is done by using the hierarchical lock protocol introduced in Chapter 7. Here is how it works for B-trees.

Consider the insertion of a tuple with index entry $\langle c, k_n\rangle$. The new entry falls into some prefix interval delimited by c_1 and c_2 with $c_1 \leq c$, and $c_2 > c$. Concurrent retrieval transactions would not see c, of course, but they might try to lock prefix c_1, thereby covering the range $[\langle c_1, k_{min}\rangle, \langle c_2, k_{min}\rangle)$. To prevent the phantom value c from appearing, two key-range locks are needed for the insert: an instant IX lock on c_1, and X lock on c. The instant IX lock makes sure no other transaction is reading or updating in the key range that is split by the insert. The X lock on prefix c makes sure the new interval, whose existence depends on the new tuple, is protected until commit. Of course, if $c = c_1$, then only the instant IX lock is needed.

Looking at the example of Figure 15.11 should make this clear. If a new tuple $\langle 17, k8\rangle$ is to be inserted, then an instant IX lock on attribute value 16 guarantees that no transaction is using the interval [16, 20). The newly established interval [17, 20) is protected by an X lock. On the other hand, if a new tuple $\langle 20, k9\rangle$ is inserted, an IX lock on value 20 makes sure that no concurrent readers are present in the interval [20, 24). Using IX locks has the additional advantage that multiple inserters for the same attribute value, that is, for the same prefix, can proceed concurrently.

The locking discipline for delete operations is straightforward, given the previous considerations. Since a delete operation may collapse an attribute value interval, it must make sure the adjacent intervals are protected properly. To appreciate the problem, assume the tuple $\langle 28, k6\rangle$ is deleted from leaf page R in Figure 15.11. Now consider the deletion of an arbitrary tuple with entry $\langle c, k_d\rangle$. First, find the *next-lower entry* in the index; let this entry be $\langle c_1, k_e\rangle$. If $c = c_1$, then protect the key range by a long IX lock on the key value c. If $c_1 < c$, then request a long X lock on c_1 and a long X lock on c. The rationale for the protocol is the same as for insert: as long as the update happens within an already existing key range, this can go on concurrently (on different entries), as long as no readers are affected. As soon as the update affects the key range structure, it must be covered by an X lock.

Table 15.12 summarizes the key-range locking protocol.

15.4.4.2 Value Locking and Beyond

Note that even the "final" design is not an optimal design by any measure. Looking at Table 15.12, one can easily convince oneself that further refinements are possible. For example,

Table 15.12: Overview of the steps in key-range locking on B-trees. The protocols described also help in avoiding the phantom anomaly under certain circumstances.

Operation	
Retrieval (k = c)	Get a semaphore on leaf page; get s lock on key range defined by largest existing value c_1 with $c_1 \leq c$; hold lock until commit.
Retrieval $c_1 \leq k \leq c_2$	Get s semaphore on first leaf page; get s lock on key defined by largest existing value c_3 with $c_3 \leq c_1$; proceed sequentially along leaf level; request key range s lock for each new attribute value up to and including c_2; do careful crabbing across leaf pages; hold s lock until commit.
Insert $\langle c, k_n \rangle$	Get x semaphore on leaf page; find largest existing value c_1 with $c_1 \leq c$; request instant IX lock on c_1; request long x lock on c.
Delete $\langle c, k_d \rangle$	Get x semaphore on leaf page; find largest existing value c_1 with $c_1 \leq c$; request long IX lock on c; else request long x lock on c and c_1.

consider an exact-match query, that is, a readkey operation with the predicate (key-value = const). If a tuple with the specified values does not exist, then the table suggests acquiring a long S lock on the previous existing value. However, if it is clear from the SQL statement that the transaction only asks for that one value—that is, no further probing in the adjacent value interval will happen—then phantom protection is not needed. That means, in turn, a long S lock on the (nonexisting) key value const is sufficient to provide isolation for the transaction.

Readers interested in this quite complicated but challenging subject are invited to investigate the subject on their own—after having read the relevant literature, of course. The last word on how to control concurrency on B-trees optimally has not been spoken yet.

15.4.5 Recovering Operations on B-Trees

We have mentioned that the operations on a B-tree such as traverse and split are only protected by short semaphores. Although we can rest assured that transaction execution will be equivalent to a serial schedule, there are some subtle problems when considering transaction rollbacks or crashes. Since the interior nodes are not protected by locks, after each split (as long as the transaction having caused the split has not committed), the nodes will be in a state produced by an incomplete transaction—a state that might be revoked. On the other hand, this state is made available to other transactions, which may commit before the transaction that caused the split decides to roll back. Offhand, this is not isolated. Let us illustrate this by the example in Figure 15.13.

Transaction $T1$ causes a leaf page to be split, and $T2$ inserts a tuple in the new page resulting from the split. Now consider what happens if $T2$ commits and after this, while $T1$ is still active, the system crashes. How can the B-tree be recovered correctly in that situation?

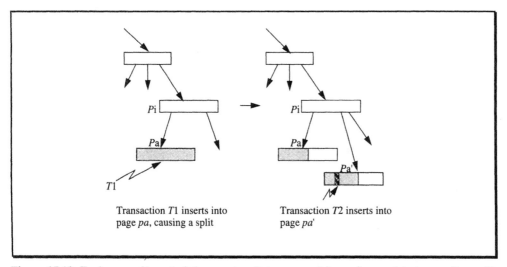

Transaction $T1$ inserts into page pa, causing a split

Transaction $T2$ inserts into page pa'

Figure 15.13: Early commitment of changes to a B-tree caused by an incomplete transaction. If the split operation on a B-tree is considered an "open" subtransaction in a multi-level transaction scheme, then concurrent transactions may use the new nodes resulting from the split. The question then is, What happens to T2 if the transaction T1 having triggered the split aborts?

15.4.5.1 Physiological Logging on B-Trees

The discussion on logging in Chapter 10 argues in favor of physiological logging because it is a compromise between logical and physical logging. Assume that the version of the B-tree on disk has the state of *Pa before* the insert by T1. Of course, there is no image of *Pa'* on disk. Assume further logging is done as described in Subsection 10.3.6. The payload portion of a log entry has to comprise the following data:

```
struct B_tree_log_data
    {    PAGEID      pageno;         /* number of page holding the B-tree node       */
         char        rec_type;       /* says if it is an operation on the tree or a node   */
         char        operation;      /* says if it is insert or delete, update        */
         char        parenthesis;    /* needed for cleaning up the end of the log     */
         int         dir_index;      /* directory index of entry in B-tree-node       */
         Ulong       keyvalue;       /* old/new key value of entry                    */
         int         entry_length;   /* length of the entry affected by operation     */
         char        entry[];        /* data part of the entry (old and new value)    */
    };
/* for simplicity assume that key values have fixed length, so the same log format               */
/* can be used for leaf and non-leaf entries.                                                    */
```

The contents of such a log record can be used for either UNDO or REDO recovery, depending on the state of the transaction. The distinction between operations on the tree and on single nodes will become obvious during the subsequent discussion. For the moment, let us consider operations on interior nodes only. They are of the type create a new node, insert this entry into the node, remove this entry from the node, and so on.

In our example, recovery has to use the log information to redo $T2$, and to undo $T1$. Given the sequence of events, the log will contain the following entries for the two transactions:

T1: A log record for the new entry in Pi inserted by $T2$; log records for the entries that were removed from Pa and a log record describing the allocation of a new node (page Pa'). There may be more log records for changed entries in free space administration tables, but this is ignored.

T2: A log record describing the new entry in Pa' inserted by $T1$.

If these log records are applied without considering the structural properties of a B-tree, it is easy to see that independent of whether the UNDO for $T1$ happens before the REDO of $T2$ or the other way around, recovery will produce incorrect states of Pa and Pi. Moreover, the log record containing the REDO information for $T2$ points to a page, which is declared free by $T1$'s UNDO information. Thus, the B-tree will be left in an inconsistent state; this should not be too surprising, because updates caused by an incomplete transaction ($T1$) have been committed early to other transactions, which subsequently use them for further updates.

A solution to this problem stems from the observation that the B-tree structure is a redundant search structure. It is, therefore, unimportant what its *actual physical structure* is; that is, which pages contain a certain node, whether or not a split or a merge has occurred, and so on. The important guarantee is that all search operations be executed correctly. This is to say that after recovery from a system crash, the B-tree must *behave* such that all the updates of committed transactions—and none of the aborted transactions—are reflected. There is no requirement saying that it must look exactly as it would have looked without the crash. This observation implies an additional degree of freedom. Now an incomplete transaction can be undone by simply *executing the inverse operation*. Whether this brings the tree back to its previous node structure is irrelevant, but the invalid tuple will disappear (or the deleted one will reappear, depending on the original operation). In the scenario of Figure 15.13, it is obvious that this will work for transaction UNDO during normal operation. The question is how to make the tree consistent in terms of its own operations so that the inverse operations can be executed.

15.4.5.2 B-Tree Recovery Based on Physiological Log Data

The structure of the log records need not be changed; they only have to be used in a slightly different way during recovery. This difference is very simple indeed: if the transaction has to be *rolled back* (UNDO), then no physical undo in the node pages is done; rather, the inverse operation is carried out. This is what the log records describing the operation on the whole tree are used for: if a key value was inserted into the tree, then the inverse operation means deleting it from the tree, and vice-versa. There will be no attempt to individually reverse the effects the original operation had on the nodes of the tree. Rather, the tree is accepted as it is now, and the inverse operation is executed as though it were a normal operation. On the other hand, if the transaction has to be *redone*, then recovery simply repeats the page modifications recorded in the log. Note that the degree to which the tree can be left "as is" depends on the original operation the inverse of which is executed during recovery. If the original operation was an insert causing a split, then the tuple is removed by recovery, but the split is not reversed. If, however, the original operation was a delete resulting in a merge, then the insertion of the tuple upon recovery will most likely trigger a split.

Since the recovery of the B-tree is based on UNDO *operations*, all changes applied to the data structure must first be redone independently of whether the corresponding transaction is successful or not. If the new states resulting from update operations on the B-tree are redone completely up to the moment of the crash, then the tree is structurally consistent; that is, all B-tree operations can be executed on it. From that point on, the UNDO operations logged for the incomplete transactions can be executed. It is therefore critical that the following sequence of log entries be maintained:

(1) Cover all B-tree operations with semaphores on all affected pages.

(2) Whenever a logical update is applied to the B-tree, a log record with the logical UNDO operation must be moved to the log.

(3) While the update operation is being performed (remember that the entire split path is protected by exclusive semaphores), physical REDO log records are moved to the log for each page that is modified.

(4) After all REDO records are safely in the log, the exclusive semaphores can be released.

In this way, it is guaranteed that any transaction that uses the modified entries in the B-tree will have its log records behind those that make the modifications recoverable.

To understand how that works, consider the example of Figure 15.13 again. The critical observation is that all relevant log records will be in the log before the insert *T2* begins, because *T2* cannot have finally committed before this transaction's commit record was forced to the log, thereby forcing the redo logs and all of *T1*'s logs pertaining to the split operation that occurred earlier. In other words; if *T1* calls abort, recovery either bumps into a semaphore held on *Pa'* by *T2* or else finds that part of the B-tree to be structurally consistent, which means the delete operation for its entry is possible. Should the reason for *T1*'s abort be a crash of the system, then the pages affected by the updates can be redone, because *T2*'s commit has made sure that all relevant REDO information is on the log. So the scheme works under all circumstances.

Recovery for a B-tree, then, is done in two phases:

Phase1. Go *forward* through the log up to its current end, applying all REDO records to the tree.

Phase2. Go *backward* to the Begin of transaction record of the oldest incomplete transaction, executing the UNDO operations on the tree for all losers along the way.

There is a subtle detail in this protocol. Looking at Figure 15.13, assume the system crashes after the log records for the UNDO operation and the REDO entries of *Pi* and *Pa* have been written; however, the writing of REDO records for *Pa'* was interrupted by the crash. Following our protocol will result in an inconsistent B-tree, thereby preventing the UNDO operation from running successfully. But this is not a big problem, because it can only occur at the "fuzzy end" of the log. All that is required is a means for detecting whether all log records pertaining to a tree update have been written. The simplest way to do so is to write an *open parenthesis record* before the UNDO operation is moved to the log and to write a *close parenthesis record* after the last REDO record.[14] Then, upon restart, check whether for any transaction there is an open parenthesis that has not been closed. If so, each B-tree page mentioned in the log records must be checked to see if it already contains the changes recorded in the log (compare the LSNs). If this is the case, the changes are *physically* undone; that is, the REDO log entry is used to UNDO the B-tree entry it describes. It is easy to see that this is possible, because at the time the log records were written, the changed portion of the B-tree was still protected by exclusive semaphores. As long as they have not been released, the REDO log entries can be used as UNDO log entries as well. The UNDO operation is, of course, ignored for open parentheses. This clean-up scheme works as long as there is no parallelism within a transaction. It is left to Exercise 8 to modify the clean-up scheme such that it can also accommodate intra-transaction parallelism.

15.5 Sample Implementation of Some Operations on B-Trees

This section illustrates the implementation of a B-tree by presenting the details of two of its key functions, readkey and insert, including the split operation. The algorithms are expressed in pseudo-code and in C, depending on what is assumed to be obvious and what requires (from our perspective) some more elaboration. But note that even the C-code programs must not be mistaken as a real-life implementation of a B-tree; the entry structure has been simplified considerably to avoid the complications resulting from variable-length entries, since this is not specific for the functional principles of B-trees. For the same reason, most of the error checking and logic for special cases has been omitted. The main purpose of the programs is to illustrate unambiguously how the data structure of a B-tree is used and maintained, and how various components of the system—the B-tree manager, the record manager, the log manager, the buffer manager, and the lock manager—interact in its implementation.

15.5.1 Declarations of Data Structures Assumed in All Programs

Let us start by declaring the variables and data structures needed. These declarations, in turn, refer to other declarations, such as page headers, log records, buffer control blocks, and so on, which have been discussed earlier. Here is the list of basic variables and control blocks needed.

```
#define keylen 8          /* key length in bytes/fixed for simplicity        */
#define fanout 200        /* maximum number of entries per interior node     */
#define dirlen 4          /* length of an entry in the leaf page directory   */
#define max_depth 10      /* maximum depth of the B-tree                     */
```

---

[14] Of course, these need not be explicit log records of their own. By definition, the UNDO operation record opens the parenthesis, and the last redo log record gets an additional flag saying that it closes it.

```
typedef struct                                     /* structure of an interior node            */
    PAGE_HEADER page_header;                        /* layout of a page header                  */
    {   PAGEID              parentp;                /* pointer to parent node                   */
        int                 busyentries;            /* how many entries are used?               */
        struct                                      /* an entry in a B-tree node contains       */
            {   Ulong       keyvalue;               /* key value and a pointer to a child       */
                PAGEID      thatway;                /* address of node containing entries ≥ keyvalue */
            } one entry[fanout];                    /* entries of the node                      */
    } INTNODE, *INTNODEP;                           /*                                          */
/* note the simplifying assumption of an interior node being an array of fixed-length  values  */
typedef struct                                     /* structure of a leaf node                 */
    {   PAGE_HEADER         page_header;            /* see the type definition                  */
        char                page_space[];           /* contains the leaf entries, i.e. the array */
                                                    /* of key values and records or TIDs        */
    } LEAFNODE, *LEAFNODEP;                         /*                                          */
```

The parameters used to invoke the B-tree routines, and the result variables returned, are described by the following declarations:

```
typedef                                            /* node of a B-tree                         */
    {   PAGEID              root;                   /* pointer to the root                      */
        int                 height;                 /* height of the tree being accessed        */
        FILEID              index_on;               /* file which is indexed by this tree       */
        char                stuff[];                /* other things                             */
    }   BTREE, *BTREEP;                             /* parameters describing the B-tree to be accessed */
RMID    tree_mgr;                                   /* name of "this" B-tree-manager  is assigned by */
                                                    /* the TP-monitor at system start-up time.  */
TRID    trid;                                       /* name of the transaction doing the insert op. */
struct  {   PAGEID          hereiwas;               /* page along the search path               */
            LSN             lsn_seen;               /* lsn of page along the search path        */
            Boolean         x_sem_set;              /* used in the insert routine to remember   */
                                                    /* which nodes have an exclusive sem.       */
        }   searchpath[max_depth];                  /* stores search path through the tree      */
Boolean     value_found;                            /* specified key value was found in tree    */
lock_name   range_lock;                             /* lock name for lock manager when using    */
                                                    /* the key range locking protocol           */
```

Access to the nodes in a B-tree is assumed to be implemented in two subroutines; these are not spelled out in C because they do not contain any aspects that are interesting from a transaction processing perspective. The first one, pagesearch(), gets as parameters a pointer to a page in buffer and a requested key value. It returns the index of an entry in the page according to the following convention: if the page is an index node, the index denotes the entry that contains the proper pointer to the next-lower layer in the traversal sequence. If it is a leaf page, the index denotes the entry that either contains the specified value (if it is present), or the entry that would have to receive that value in case of an insert. The prototype declare is given here:

```
int pagesearch(PAGE_PTR node, Ulong searchkey)
/* node:         address of node page in buffer. It is assumed that the page is already fixed and   */
/*               protected at least by a shared semaphore.                                          */
/* searchkey:    key value whose position in the B-tree page has to be determined.                  */
/* This routine finds the entry for a given key value in a leaf or the successor pointer in an      */
/* intermediate node. No assumptions are made as to the search strategy applied. It could be        */
/* sequential in the simplest case. With the above declarations of the node structures using        */
/* arrays of fixed-length entries, binary search or interpolation search could be used as well.     */
```

The second routine, getvalue, serves two purposes: first, it simply returns the key value from a leaf page, given its index. Second, it finds the maximum key value currently stored in a node and returns both that value and its index in the page.

```
Ulong getvalue(PAGE_PTR node, int position, int * maxpos)
/* node:        address of node page in buffer. It is assumed that the page is fixed and protected  */
/*              least by a shared semaphore.                                                        */
/*position:   ≥0: index of the entry whose key value has to be retrieved                            */
/*            <0: says that the maximum key value in the page has to be determined                  */
/*maxpos:     pointer to int variable that receives the index position of the maximum value         */
/* the routine getvalue gets the address of a page and the index of an entry and returns the        */
/* value of the search key of this entry. If a negative index is passed, it returns the maximum     */
/* value in this page and its current index.                                                        */
```

In what follows, these routines are used without further explanation. Exception handling is omitted. Since the results they produce are fairly obvious, the discussion of B-tree implementation should be understandable without any additional functional details.

15.5.2 Implementation of the readkey Operation on a B-Tree

The readkey() function has to go through some logic having to do with the file descriptor, cursor management, and so on; these details are omitted here. For simplicity, it is assumed that the root page number of the tree and its height have already been determined from the file descriptor. With this, an internal routine, readbt(), is invoked. This routine will also be used by the insert function to determine the insert position. It returns the pointer to the buffer access control block of the page with the entry—that page is fixed and protected by a semaphore. It also returns the index of the entry with the key value or the index of the entry after which the search key value would have to be inserted; this parameter is passed via the index entry of the buffer access control block in the parameter list.

The return code of readbt() is FALSE if no match was found, TRUE if a match was found. For simplicity, it is assumed that the tree implements a unique index; there is no checking if more than one entry matches the search argument. We also ignore the special case of a single-page tree, where leaf and root coincide.

Since a full B-tree implementation with all provisions for synchronization, recovery, and so forth, is a fairly complex piece of code, the following explanation is based on pseudo-code rather than C-code, used in the previous chapters. The pseudo-code is close to C, though, whenever the use of an interesting data structure or interface is discussed. Otherwise, the statements are high-level references to explanations that are given in Section 15.4. Code that is at the C level is printed in the same font as the other C code in this book; for the pseudo-code, the text font is used.

The pseudo-code implementing the traversal of a B-tree in order to determine the page and index position of an existing key value, or the insert position of a new key value, follows the next paragraph. Except for getvalue(), the routine invokes a number of lower-level services: bufferfix(), bufferunfix(), and pagesearch().

Since the pagesearch() routine has not been spelled out completely, we must explain the meaning of the index in the leaf page that is returned in its buffer access control block. If the requested key value is found, it is the index of the entry containing that value. If searchkey is not found, the index points to the entry with the next-higher key value. We must also consider the situation in which searchkey is larger than any key value in the tree; in that case, there is no next page to crab to. This is taken care of by some reserved value representing "infinity," that is, a value larger than any legal value of the index attribute domain. This value can also be used for next-key locking. Again, this technique is assumed without further explanation. The problems that can arise when crabbing along the leaf level are discussed in Subsection 15.4.4.3.

```
/* This routine searches the B-tree for a given key value. It returns TRUE if the entry with the   */
/* specified value exists, FALSE otherwise.                                                         */
/* Furthermore, it sets the pointer to the buffer access control block of the page with the proper leaf node.  */
/* This is the node where the specified key value is stored or where it has to be inserted. The appropriate    */
/* entry index is also set in the buffer access control block. Finally, the routine stores the page numbers    */
/* and lsns of the nodes touched when traversing the B-tree.                                        */
Boolean readbt(tree, searchkey, purpose, leafptr, pathptr)
        BTREE               tree;           /* tree to be searched                         */
        Ulong               searchkey;      /* search argument                             */
        char                purpose;        /* R for reading, I for insert, D for delete   */
        BUFFER_ACC_CBP *    leafptr;        /* pointer to buffer acc. control block ptr of */
                                            /* node with the requested entry               */
        searchpath[]        * pathptr;      /* pointer to search path                      */
        {   PAGEID          nextint = tree.root;    /* search starts here                  */
            int             depth_counter = 1;      /* level count of root is 1            */
            int             right_pos;              /* index of entry investigated        */
            BUFFER_ACC_CBP  left_leg, right_leg;    /* anatomy of the crab                */
```

```
        BUFFER_ACC_CBP      result_node;              /* used to return resulting CB address        */
        Boolean             outcome;                  /* result of function calls                   */
        while(depth_counter < height)                 /* descending from root to parent of leaf     */
           {  outcome = bufferfix(nextint,sh_sem,&right_leg); /* get page into buffer and set sem.   */
              pathptr->searchpath[depth_counter].hereiwas = nextint; /* store path                   */
              pathptr->searchpath[depth_counter].lsn_seen = right_leg.pageaddr->safe_up_to;
                                                       /* store page  LSN                            */
              path_ptr->searchpath[depth_counter].x_sem_set = FALSE;/*clear switch                   */
              if   (depth_counter > 1)
                   outcome = bufferunfix(left_leg);    /* unfix parent node                          */
              right_pos = pagesearch(right_leg->pageaddr,searchkey); /*get entry index               */
              nextint = (right_leg->pageaddr) -> oneentry[right_pos].thatway;
              left_leg = right_leg;                    /* hold on to current node                    */
              depth_counter = depth_counter + 1;       /* proceed to next level                      */
           };
   /* the correct leaf node has been reached; find out what to do with it                            */
      if    (purpose == "R")                           /* this is the read case                      */
              outcome = bufferfix(nextint,sh_sem,&right_leg);  /*get shared sem for read             */
      else
              outcome = bufferfix(nextint,ex_sem,&right_leg);  /*exclusive for update                */
      outcome = bufferunfix(left_leg);                 /* leave node and unfix page in buffer        */
      leafptr->result_node = right_leg;
      right_leg->index = pagesearch(right_leg->pageaddr,searchkey);
                                                       /* move leaf address and index of             */
                                                       /* the (closest) entry for search             */
                                                       /* argument to result parameter               */
      return (getvalue(right_leg->pageaddr,right_leg->index) == searchkey);
                                                       /* set return code according to               */
                                                       /* specification                              */

}
```

15.5.3 Key-Range Locking in a B-Tree

The readbt() routine is not all that is required to implement the readkey() access, although it does most of the work. The rest has to do with error handling, which is omitted here, and locking, which needs some explanation. According to the protocol explained in this chapter (see Table 15.12), the retrieved key value has to be locked in S mode in case the value was found. Otherwise, the enclosing key range must be locked by locking the next-lower value to avoid phantoms. To do this, we assume another ancillary routine that makes lock names from key values in accord with the declares in Chapters 7 and 8. The function prototype looks like this:

```
lock_name   makelockname(PAGEID root, Ulong keyvalue)
/* This routine is invoked with two parameters: the pageid of the tree's root page to uniquely    */
/* identify the tree, and the key value to be locked. The method used to make up the lock          */
/* name is irrelevant here. In general, some type of folding is used. The routine returns a result */
/* of type lock_name. The component rmid of this type is set by calling the function MyRMID.       */
lock_reply      range_lock_result;              /* return code from lock request routine            */
value_found = readbt(tree, keyvalue, 'R', &curr_leaf, &searchpath);       /* invoke traversal       */
range_lock = makelockname(tree.root, getvalue(curr_leaf->pageaddr,curr_leaf->index));
                /* Generate lock name for key value. Note that according to the definition of the tree, this */
                /*will either be the requested value or the next higher one depending on what value_found */
                /* says. In either case, the right lock can be requested with this name. This ignores the  */
                /* special case of searchkey of searchkey being larger than the highest key in a page.     */
range_lock_result = lock(range_lock, LOCK_S, LOCK_MEDIUM, 0);
                /* request the lock on the value or on the next key in shared mode, as a medium lock      */
                /* (might be kept for cursor stability only), and with a timeout of 0 to avoid actually waiting */
                /* for the lock.                                                                          */
switch   (range_lock_result)
        {   case    LOCK_OK:                    /* lock was acquired successfully                   */
                    return to the calling routine;   /*                                             */
            case    LOCK_TIMEOUT:               /* some other transaction has the lock              */
                    release semaphore on leaf page;  /* for reasons explained above, one must not   */
                                                     /* wait for lock while holding a semaphore     */
                    request lock with long timeout;  /* now we can really wait for the lock         */
                    re-acquire semaphore on the leaf; /* make sure page remains stable              */
                    check that the leaf has not       /* this is done using the page lsn that       */
                        changed in the meantime;      /* is stored in searchpath                    */
                    if it has changed:                /* the case of a modification of the page     */
                        see if it is still the right page; /* while the TA is waiting for the lock is */
                        else restart readbt;          /* not covered in detail                      */
            case    LOCK_DEADLOCK:              /* lock not granted :deadlock                       */
                    invoke rollback for TRID; };  /* transaction is rolled back                     */
```

The preceding calls demonstrate the mainline logic used to access a B-tree and to synchronize these accesses using the next-key locking protocol introduced in Subsection 15.4.4. Of course, subsequent lock requests on the tuple pointed to by the B-tree must also be issued, but since these issues have nothing to do with B-tree management, they are ignored here.

The use of the timeout parameter in the invocation of the lock manager needs some explanation. As discussed earlier, one should not wait for a (potentially long) lock while holding a page semaphore. With the interfaces to the lock manager introduced in Chapter 8, there is no clean way to avoid this. We need bounce mode locks to achieve the desired effect: a lock request is issued, and it returns immediately with an indication if the object is already locked by another transaction. Issuing the lock request with a timeout interval of zero gives bounce mode locking, and that is why this trick is used here. If the transaction accessing the B-tree actually has to wait for the lock, it first gives up the semaphore, then requests the lock again (this time with a reasonable timeout), and, of course, has to verify that the leaf page has not changed while the transaction was waiting for the lock. This verification is done by comparing the leaf page's LSN with the LSN of the same page after it has reacquired the semaphore. If the LSN has changed, the page must be reanalyzed. It can be the case that the desired entry is still in the page—the intermediate update has affected another entry. If this is so, processing proceeds normally. Otherwise, the client has to give up and retry the retrieval operation by going through readbt again.

Note that in case the lock is successfully acquired, the translation still holds a semaphore on the leaf page. The actual code hiding behind the phrase "prepare the results" must make sure that the lock gets released properly and the page is unfixed. If the key value was not found, the implementation may also decide to release the read lock on the next key, depending on what kind of read operation the transaction is executing. It was shown in Section 15.4 that there are situations where it is safe to proceed in that fashion.

15.5.4 Implementation of the Insert Operation for a B-Tree: The Simple Case

The routine that inserts a new tuple (or a reference to the tuple) into a B-tree structure first calls readbt to get the leaf page required and the index position in the page where the new tuple has to go (see Subsection 15.5.3). The readbt() routine ensures that there is an exclusive semaphore on the leaf node page and returns the path from the root to the leaf in the structure searchpath, which is passed via the variable pathptr in the parameter list. The function prototype declaration of this routine looks like the following:

```
/* This routine inserts a new reference to a tuple into a B-tree which is assumed to implement    */
/* a unique index. It invokes readbt to determine the location of the key value in the search     */
/* structure. It then attempts to do a local insert in the leaf node determined by readbt( ). If the */
/* node is full, the split leaf routine is invoked to extend the B-tree structure.                 */
RETCODE    insert(tree, newkey, newdata)        /*                                                 */
    BTREE           tree;                        /* tree in which to insert                         */
    Ulong           newkey;                      /* key of new tuple                                */
    TUPLEID         newdata                      /* pointer to the tuple to be inserted             */
```

For the reasons mentioned previously, all aspects related to handling the actual tuple are ignored here, because they are largely independent of the properties of the B-tree access path structure.

We present the implementation of the insert() routine as a sequence of code blocks. The explanation of the implementation issues starts with the simplest case, which is the insertion of the new entry somewhere in a leaf page; that is, special cases such as the new entry being the highest value in a leaf are ignored. Given this standard path through the insert logic, we will then consider some more complicated situations, such as page splits. Again, all the following considerations are based on the assumption that the B-tree implements a unique index and that the tuples are stored somewhere else; that is, the tree only contains TID references to the tuples. The logic for the simple case looks like this:

```
/* start of insert()                                                                    */
lock_reply        value_lock_result;            /* return code from lock request routine    */
LSN               next_lsn;                      /* LSN of new log record                    */
char      *       log_record;                    /* storage area from where to write the log */
access catalog;                                  /* preparatory actions                      */
set parameter values;                            /*                                          */
value_found = readbt(tree, searchkey, 'I', &curr_leaf, &searchpath); /* invoke traversal     */
/* The leaf page is now protected by an exclusive semaphore. Next it has to be checked whether an insert of */
/* searchkey is legal, i.e. if no entry with that value exists already. In thatcase, the insert operation is terminated.*/
if    (value_found == TRUE)                      /* value exists: uniqueness violation       */
      {    outcome = bufferunfix(curr_leaf);      /* unfix leaf page                          */
           report failure of insert to caller;   /* terminate this invocation                */
                                                  /* note this does not imply a TA abort      */
/* There is one detail: in order to report a uniqueness violation, it must be made             */
/* sure that the duplicate value really is a committed value. So an s-lock must be requested    */
/* if the lock is granted and the entry is still there, then the insert must be rejected as above */
      }                                           /*                                          */
else                                              /* value does not exist: insert possible    */
      {    value_lock = makelockname(tree.root,   /*                                          */
                         getvalue(curr_leaf->pageaddr, /*                                     */
                         curr_leaf->index));      /* generate lock name for previous key      */
                                                  /* case of index pointing beyond            */
           highest key in page is ignored.                                                      */
           if    (lock(value_lock,IX_LOCK,LOCK_INSTANT) != LOCK_OK) /* try to get instant      */
                                                  /*IX-lock on previous key value             */
                 {    exception handling;         /* this is the case that waiting for        */
                      details are omitted;        /* a lock while holding a semaphore         */
                 };                               /* must be avoided                          */
           value_lock = makelockname(tree, root,  searchkey); /*make lock name for new key     */
           if    (lock(value_lock,X_LOCK,LOCK_LONG) != LOCK_OK) /* request long X-lock on new key */
                 {    exception handling;         /* if this lock cannot be granted,          */
                      abort transaction;          /* something strange must be going          */
                 };                               /*on (should not occur in principle)        */
           if    ( there is room in the leaf for new entry) /* insert affects this leaf page only */
                 {    log_record=[PAGEID of leaf, /* prepare a log record that contains        */
                             new  entry];         /* the ID of the leaf and the entry data    */
                      nextlsn = log_insert(log_record, /* write physiological log record; it is */
                             sizeof(log_record)); /* logical to the page                      */
                      insert entry into leaf page; /* put new entry into its proper place     */
                                                  /* inside the leaf page                     */
                      (curr_leaf->pageaddr)->     /* note LSN of corresponding log            */
                             safe_up_to = nextlsn; /* record in leaf page                     */
```

```
            outcome = bufferunfix(curr_leaf);      /* unfix leaf page                */
        };                                         /* end of normal insert case      */
    else                                           /*                                */
        {   do node split;    }                    /* this is the complicated case   */
    return(0);                                     /* return to caller               */
};                                                 /* end of insert routine          */
```

Let us now consider the case of an insert that requires a leaf to be split. To keep the discussion simple, the code is restricted to a leaf split only. This is justified by the fact that splitting an intermediate node requires the same essential steps as splitting a leaf node—with the exception of the root.

15.5.5 Implementing B-Tree Insert: The Split Case

The first thing that needs to be done is to protect all the nodes that will be affected by the split with exclusive semaphores. When it is discovered that a page must be split, only the leaf to be split has such a semaphore. This must be released, because the search path is revisited top-down based on the entries in searchpath, and we want to avoid deadlocks among transactions requesting semaphores. Once the nodes to be updated are covered by semaphores, the actual split can be performed and, finally, the semaphores can be released. The pseudo-code portion for the leaf node split implementing the techniques described in Subsection 15.4.1 is presented on the next page (the previous declares are assumed without repeating them).

This piece of code needs some additional comments. First, the idea of releasing the exclusive semaphores on those interior nodes that are not affected by the split rests on a critical asumption: one must be able to tell whether or not the discriminating key being propagated from the lower layer fits into the node before one actually knows which discriminating key that is. If all keys have fixed length (which, for simplicity, was assumed here), this is trivial. If their keys have variable length (and if key compression is used), then it is not possible, in general. If it is not possible to safely decide whether or not an interior node has to be split, then either the entire search path (including the root) must be protected by an exclusive semaphore, or semaphores must be acquired bottom-up during the split processing, which requires means to detect deadlocks involving both locks and semaphores.

Second, it must be noted that there is a subtle problem with the ancillary routine getfreepage that returns the PAGEID of an empty page in the file holding the B-tree. Free page administration is typically done by the tuple-oriented file system, which probably is a different resource manager than the B-tree manager. Consequently, it does its own logging. If it does log the allocation operation in the conventional manner, then there is a problem if the transaction in which the split occurs is later rolled back. The B-tree manager logically undoes the insert but does not revert the split; the file manager, however, would do its part of the rollback, which implies claiming the empty page again. On the other hand, if the file manager does no logging and the transaction crashes early, empty storage might be lost. Therefore, a cooperation between the two components is needed; this cooperation can be defined in different ways. One possibilty is to give the authority for free page management to the B-tree manager; this means that from the file system's perspective, the B-tree manager claims all the space right away and keeps track of which pages are used and which are not. Then, there is no problem in recovering allocation operations according to the scheme introduced here. Another possibility is to enclose the allocation operation (done by the file system) and the log write for the allocation (done by the B-tree manager) into one common, nested top-level transaction. Then, two things can happen: either the page is allocated and the B-tree manager's log record for it is written, which means it can explicitly return that page if the closing parenthesis is missing after a crash; or the nested top-level transaction fails, in which case normal UNDO will take care of recovery.

```
BUFFER_ACC_CBP        modnode[max_depth];              /* nodes affected by the split          */
PAGEID                newnode;                         /* new leaf node for split              */
BUFFER_ACC_CBP        newnodecbp;                      /* buffer access cb for new node        */
int                   split_up_to;                     /* highest level affected by split      */
searchpath[tree.height].hereiwas = curr_leaf->pageid;  /* store leaf address in path           */
searchpath[tree.height].lsn_seen = leafadd.pageaddr->safe_up_to; /* store leaf page lsn        */
searchpath[tree.height].x_sem_set = FALSE;             /* clear switch                         */
outcome = bufferunfix(curr_leaf);                      /* to avoid deadlocks when acquiring    */
                                                       /* semaphores on higher-level nodes     */
split_up_to = 1;                                       /* split might propagate up to root     */
for  (i=1; i<=tree.height; i++)                        /* re-traverse search path              */
    {   outcome = bufferfix(searchpath[i].hereiwas,ex_sem,&modnode[i]);/* get page in buffer and set x-sem. */
        if   (searchpath[i].lsn_seen != (modnode[i]->pageaddr)->safe_up_to)
                                                       /* page has changed since traversal     */
            {   check if page is still on the path;    /* does it still cover the value interval? */
                if so: keep it and remember new lsn;   /* path need not be changed             */
                otherwise: give up the search path and start the insert    /*search path       */
                        operation again by traversing the tree; };      /* invalidated          */
/* The current node is part of a valid search path to the insert value.  Most of the X          */
/* semaphores acquired are not needed, because the split only  propagates up to the first interior node */
/* that is not completely full. All semaphores above that point can be released.                */
        if   (node has room for one more key)          /*check if this node will overflow       */
            {   release all nodes above that one       /* no sem. on nodes that need           */
                store level in split_up_to             /* not be modified                      */
    };          };                                     /*                                      */
fix right neighbor of leaf with excl. semaphore;       /* will be affected by split. if fix fails, */
                                                       /* release path and re-visit searchpath */
/* we do not consider the case of a root split. Now all the nodes from the leaf up to the first */
/* interior node with enough space are protected by an exclusive semaphore.                     */
if   (lock(range_lock,IX_LOCK,LOCK_INSTANT) != LOCK_OK)
    {   exception handling;                            /*since semaphore on the leaf was       */
        details are omitted; };                        /* released, need  previous key  instant lock */
write log record [tree, curr_leaf->pageid, 'Split Begin'];  /* write opening parenthesis       */
newnode = getfreepage((curr_leaf->pageaddr)->fileid);  /* request free page to split the leaf  */
write log record [tree, newnode, 'Alloc Page'];        /* log the allocation of the new page   */
outcome = emptyfix(newnode,ex_sem,&newnodecbp);        /*fix new page in buffer with  X sem    */
```

```
initalize page header;                                    /* set page header according to def.        */
chain new page between leaf and old right heighbor;       /* maintain leaf level chaining             */
write log record for chaining new page;
move entries from old leaf to new leaf;                   /* do the actual entry splitting            */
write log record [tree, newnode, curr_leaf->pageid, list of new entries];
                                                          /* log copy of entries betw. leaf nodes     */
modify parent of old and new leaf;                        /* propagate discr. key to parent           */
write log record [tree, searchpath[tree.height-1].hereiwas, new entry];
                                                          /* log propagated key                       */
write log record [tree, curr_leaf->pageid, 'Split End'];  /* close parenthesis on log                 */
tag all modified pages with lsn of 'Split End' log record; /* record the WAL information              */
release all pages except the leaf receiving the new key;
do normal insert (no split case);                         /* see above description                    */
```

The point about the code here has to do with splitting higher-level nodes. In our example, the operation "modify parent" is assumed to affect only one node. In general, however, it would have to call the split routine recursively, until the level recorded in split_up_to is reached. For each split operation on the way, the same logic is applied. A new opening parenthesis is written to the log, identifying the page to be split; all the log records pertaining to that split are recorded the same way; and so on. In effect, the log will contain nested parentheses, and the insert is complete only if the outer closing parenthesis is found.

15.5.6 Summary

The implementation section has presented (pseudo-) code pieces to illustrate the application of the guiding principles for implementing transactional resource managers: the use of semaphores and logging to perform consistent, isolated, and atomic page changes; the combination of low-level locks (semaphores) and key-range locks to achieve high concurrency on a popular data structure such as a B-tree; the combination of physical REDO and logical UNDO to reduce lock holding times.

15.6 Exotics

Considering which access paths are actually used in real transaction processing systems, the vast majority of algorithms proposed in the literature must be classified as exotic. This may be a bit unfair though, because the decision about which access mechanisms to include in a system is influenced by many criteria, many of which are nontechnical. Given the fact that B-trees provide the optimal balance between functionality and cost, the question usually is, What else?

The obvious answer is that something with the best performance is needed; this favors a decision for static hashing. Beyond hashing and B-trees, it is not trivial to identify requirements that justify the implementation costs of yet another associative access path technique. It would have to be a performance requirement or a functional property that neither hashing nor B-trees can fulfill properly, because no new access path will be implemented in a real system if it is just slightly better under some special circumstances. To appreciate that, the reader should rethink the whole discussion on B-trees. It demonstrates that using an access method in a general-purpose transaction system means *much more* than just coding the search algorithms. The additional transaction-related issues, such as synchronization and recovery, can turn out to be more complicated than maintaining the search structure itself. And furthermore, for each new access method, there must be an extension of the SQL compiler and optimizer to decide when to use this type of access path and to generate code for it.

New access methods, then, will only be justified (and implemented) if there are applications with performance requirements that neither static hashing nor B-trees can meet, or if there is a requirement for types of associative access that exceed the capabilities of B-trees.

This section briefly presents access methods designed for such cases. Each algorithm is described briefly, just to get the idea across. Each subsection also contains some remarks about the applications that need access paths.

15.6.1 Extendible Hashing

Extendible hashing provides exactly the same functionality as the static hash algorithms described in Section 15.3, with one exception: the number of hash-table buckets can grow and shrink with usage. Essentially, it can start out as an empty file with no pages, grow to whatever is needed, and shrink. The pages need not be allocated in contiguous order; rather, they can be requested and released one by one, just as for B-trees. The performance of extendible hashing for single-tuple access via the primary key is not as good as static hashing, but it is still better than B-trees.

The basic idea is simple. Since pages can be allocated and deallocated as needed, the hashing function cannot produce page numbers (or an offset thereof). There has to be an intermediate data structure for translating the hash results into page addresses, and the question is how to make this auxiliary structure as compact and efficient as possible.

A very simple data structure, well-suited for random access, is the array. Static hashing, in fact, uses an array of buckets. Extendible hashing, for the sake of flexibility, employs one level of indirection and instead hashes into an array of pointers to buckets.[15] This array is called *directory*. Of course, the array has to be contiguously allocated in memory, but since the array is much smaller than the file itself ($\approx 0.1\%$), it is less of a problem to make a generous allocation in the beginning. The basic mapping scheme is shown in Figure 15.14. This illustration explains why pages need not be allocated in a row and why allocation can change over time. However, it says little about *how* dynamic growing and shrinking is actually handled. To present this in more detail, some preparation is needed.

The bit string produced by the hash function is called S in the following. The directory grows and shrinks as the file does, but its number of entries is always a power of two. The directory is always kept large enough to hold pointers to all the pages needed for storing the tuples in the file. At any point in time, each entry in the directory contains a valid pointer to an allocated page. Assume the directory has 2^d entries. Then, for a given key value, d bits are taken out of S from a defined position. The resulting d-bit pattern is then interpreted as a positive integer, that is, as the index to the directory table. The pointer in that entry points to the page holding the tuple. There is no overflow handling comparable to the methods for static hashing. Extendibility takes care of that, as we will soon see.

Based on these definitions, let us now explain the key steps of extendible hashing by means of an example. For simplicity, the hashing function is cut short: the binary represen-

---

[15] The derivation of the algorithm in the original paper by Fagin et al. [1979] is completely different, but this is what it boils down to.

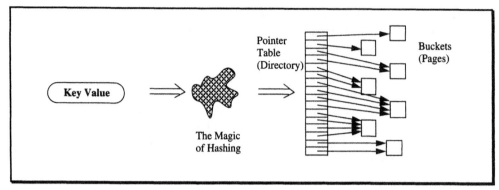

Figure 15.14: The basic idea of extendible hashing. Extendible hashing maps the key value into an array of pointers by means of a hash function. These pointers refer to pages holding the tuples. The pages are allocated and freed depending on the actual storage requirements.

tation of the numerical key value is used as the bit string S. The example starts at a moment when the directory has $2^3 = 8$ entries (see Figure 15.15).

The convention adopted for addressing the directory of 2^d entries is the following: given the bit pattern S, take the d rightmost bits interpreted as a binary integer and examine the corresponding directory entry. This is why the directory always contains 2^d entries, with integer d. Since by definition each entry contains a valid pointer, each hashed key will be routed to a bucket page where either the corresponding tuple is found or the decision can be made that the value does not exist. Figure 15.15 contains the example for key value 37. Now try the same thing with 41. Its binary representation is 101001_2; thus the three low-value binary digits to consider are 001, which leads to entry 1, pointing to a bucket with key values 1 and 25. Therefore, no tuple with key value 41 is stored in the file.

Looking at Figure 15.15 a bit closer reveals some more detail. There is a number associated with each bucket, and there are some buckets with two pointers going to them. With a larger directory, there could be more pointers to the same bucket, but the number of pointers directed at any bucket will always be a power of two; the reasons for that will soon become obvious. The number going with each bucket is called *local depth* (as opposed to d, the global depth). Let b_j denote the local depth of an arbitrary bucket j, and let $\#p_j$ be the number of pointers directed at j from the directory ($1 \le \#p_j \le d$). Then the following invariance holds: $b_j = d - \#p_j + 1$.

A more intuitive interpretation is the following: the local depth says how many bits of S are actually needed to decide that the key value must be in that bucket. Because d is its maximum value, the local depth can never be larger than the global depth. But it may well be lower, which is the case for all buckets to which more than one pointer is directed. Consider, for example, the entries with indexes 2 and 6. Their binary representations are 010_2 and 110_2, respectively. The bucket both entries point to contains 50, which is characterized by 010; as well as 22, the last bits of which are 110. Effectively, then, this bucket holds all keys with 10 as the *last 2 bits*; whether the next bit is 0 or 1 is irrelevant. This is what "local depth = 2" refers to.

How does update work with extendible hashing? The normal case is straightforward. Assume a new tuple with key value 24 is to be stored. Its three relevant bits are 000. First, a normal retrieval is done. The bucket pointed to by entry 0 only contains key value 40; thus,

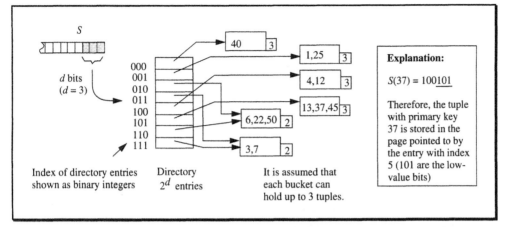

Figure 15.15: Starting configuration of an extendible hashing file with a directory of eight entries. The bits for determining the directory entry pertaining to a given key are taken from the hash result right to left (low- to high-order bits).

24 is not a duplicate. Since there is enough space in the bucket, the tuple with key value 24 is stored, and the insert operation is completed.

The next case is demonstrated by assuming that a tuple with key value 34 is inserted. Its three *index bits* are 010; that is, it is directed to a bucket with local depth = 2. Because this bucket cannot accommodate another tuple, a file extension must be performed—remember that there are no overflow buckets. Since the local depth of the affected page is smaller than the global depth, this amounts to a simple bucket split, as it is illustrated in Figure 15.16.

What is key here is that two pointers are pointing to the overflowing bucket (or 2^n, in general). Since this routes too many tuples to the bucket, another bucket is installed, and the tuples are distributed over these two buckets. To distinguish between the two buckets after the split, one more bit from S is considered; note that the local depth of the overflowing bucket is smaller than the global one. As a result, the local depth of each of the buckets resulting from the split is one higher than the local depth of the bucket before the split. Accordingly, the criterion for deciding which tuple goes to which bucket is different from the one used in B-tree splits. Consider Figure 15.16: the two buckets resulting from the split will have one pointer each (shown as shaded arrows), corresponding to the directory entries 010_2 and 110_2, respectively. Therefore, the tuples must be assigned to the buckets by the following rule: let b_1 and b_2 be the buckets resulting from a split and i_1 and i_2 be the indices of the directory entries holding the pointers to b_1 and b_2. Then all tuples from the old bucket (including the new one that caused the split) whose index bits are equal to i_1 are assigned to b_1. The index bits of the others will necessarily be equal to i_2; they therefore go to b_2.

The locking and logging issues are straightforward for the operations described so far. Locks are acquired for the tuples, and the required access paths are protected by semaphores. For recovery purposes, the same physiological logging design is used as was described for B-trees. So the insert (or delete operation is logged in the beginning, and all the subsequent page maintenance operations are logged physically for REDO (note that the directory is mapped onto pages, too).

In case of a bucket split as illustrated in Figure 15.16, there is a potential for semaphore deadlock. Assume transaction T_1 comes via directory entry 010_2 to the page before the split,

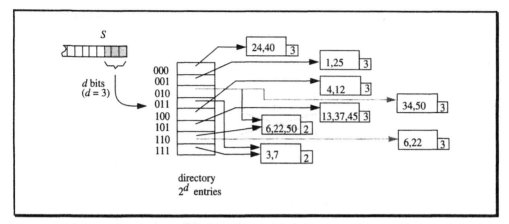

Figure 15.16: Insert into an extendible hash file, causing a bucket split. In this case, the bucket that is split was pointed to by two pointers. Consequently, there is now one pointer for each bucket resulting from the split. The directory structure remains unchanged.

protecting its path with exclusive semaphores. Transaction T_2 comes via entry 110_2, trying to insert into the same page. Now T_2 waits for a semaphore on the page, whereas T_1 waits for a semaphore on directory entry 110_2 to perform the split. In order to avoid such deadlocks, there must be additional rules about when a transaction must not wait for a semaphore. We will not discuss that issue here.

This gives an idea of how the file can grow, given a directory with 2^d entries. But now assume a tuple with key value 61 is to be inserted. Its index bits are 101, the corresponding bucket has local depth = 3, and it is full. Another bit cannot be appended to the left to distinguish two buckets after a split, because the directory itself is addressed by only three bits. Before the bucket can be split, therefore, a larger directory must be built. Its number of entries must be a power of two, so its current size is simply doubled. This implies that the global depth d is increased by 1 (the next bit from S left of the ones currently used is included). As a consequence, all buckets have a local depth smaller than the (new) global one and, therefore, the split algorithm can be applied.

This whole procedure is illustrated in Figure 15.17; its left-hand side is a cleaned-up version of Figure 15.16.

The question of how to double the directory and what to put into the new entries is simple. Since the bits from S are included with increasing exponents, an entry with the old number *xyz* will now turn into two entries with number *0xyz* and *1xyz*. Of course, all key values that up to now had index bits *xyz* will remain unchanged; that is, for locating them, the string *xyz* is sufficient. Therefore, both new entries will contain the same pointer, the one that was stored in entry *xyz* in the old directory. Since this consideration applies to all entries, doubling the directory means the following: a copy of the old directory is placed directly behind its highest entry. The resulting table with twice the number of entries is the new directory.[16] Note that when doubling the directory, the whole directory must be locked exclusively until the operation is completed. This is not comparable to the situation of a root split in a B-tree. Whereas even in a large B-tree at most five to six pages are modified during an insert causing a root split, doubling the directory of an extendible hashing file with

---

[16] There is a variant of extendible hashing in which the index bits are taken from S left to right. This implies another method for doubling the directory.

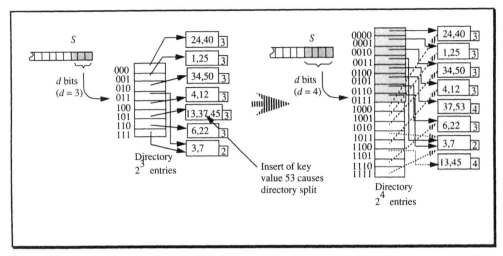

Figure 15.17: Extending the file structure by increasing the size of the directory. If a bucket that is pointed by just one pointer needs to be split, additional pointers must be created. This is done by using an additional bit from the key value's hash signature, which means the number of entries in the directory—and thereby the number of available pointers—doubles.

10^6 pages means that some 6 MB must be copied explicitly—potentially causing substantial I/O along the way.

In Figure 15.17, the old directory portion is shaded; the new one is not. The copied pointers are indicated by shaded arrows. The figure also contains the result of the bucket split that originally triggered the directory split. The resulting buckets are represented by shaded boxes; of course, after the bucket split is completed, both buckets have the new global depth as their local depth.

The performance of the extendible hashing scheme is fairly easy to estimate. For simplicity, let us concentrate on retrieval operations. The additional cost for inserts only depends on the frequency of splits, which in turn is influenced by how much the file grows compared to the original space allocation. Because the frequency of directory splits decreases exponentially as the file grows, this should not be a cost factor.

There are always two steps for retrieving a tuple (not counting the hash function): first, access the directory to find the bucket pointer; then read the bucket page. As long as the directory completely fits into main memory (into the buffer), each retrieval is one page access—the minimum cost. Assuming 4 bytes per entry and 4 KB pages, then with a 1 MB buffer space for the directory, a 1 GB extendible hash file can be maintained, allowing for one-access associative retrieval.

This sounds pretty attractive, but there are some hidden problems that will surface as soon as a real implementation is considered. We will list just a few of them. The estimate yielding the 1 GB file is based on the assumption that each pointer in the directory goes to a different bucket. Of course, this is only the case if the index bits of the key values in the file are uniformly distributed. If the hash function does not produce a uniformly distributed bit pattern, those parts of the directory corresponding to the more frequent bit patterns will experience a higher frequency of splits. This, in turn, means the directory will be larger than it had to be to address the given number of buckets. And note that the directory doubles each time *one bucket* is about to exceed the global depth. It does not help if the local depth of the others is way below that value. In other words, for hash value distributions with a noticeable bias, there will quickly be a directory that is relatively large compared to the number of buckets it manages. Once the bucket entries can no longer be kept in buffer, additional page accesses are required for reading the needed portion of the directory. In the worst case, each tuple access requires two page accesses. This is worse than static hashing, and it is not much better than B-tree performance (if at all), considering that the top two levels of a B-tree can be kept in buffer. The question, then, of whether the additional flexibility provided by extendible hashing is worth the effort from a performance perspective critically depends on the quality of the hash function.

Another problem is shrinking an extendible hash file. If a bucket becomes empty, its pointer can be redirected, but deciding whether or not the directory can be cut in half requires additional bookkeeping. It should also be clear that each structural change of the directory is a complex operation, rendering the file inaccessible for quite some time.

And, finally, there is the question of how to map the directory onto disk. A small directory fitting into main memory is not a problem, but what about large ones that have to be paged just like any other data structure? The speed of the algorithm is due to the fact that, based on the index bits, the bucket pointer can be located at almost no cost. If this is to translate to a disk-based directory, then the directory must at any point in time be stored in consecutive pages. If one does not want to allocate space for the largest directory possible, what happens at a directory split?

15.6.2 The Grid File

The grid access method addresses a functional limitation inherent in all the techniques described so far: symmetric access via multiple attributes. Consider the B-tree algorithm and assume that a relation is to be associatively accessed using the values of two attributes, A and B. The queries can be of any of the following types: $(p_1(A,B))$, $(p_1(A) \text{ con } p_2(B))$, $(p_1(A))$, $(p_2(B))$. Here pi denotes predicates defined over the respective attributes, and con is a logical connector, such as and, or, exor.

There are two possibilities for supporting such B-trees queries:

Two B-trees. A B-tree is created for each of the two attributes, and the (partial) predicate referring to A is evaluated using the tree on A; the same applies to the (partial) predicate on B. This produces two partial result lists with TIDs that then have to be merged or intersected, depending on the type of con.

One B-tree. A B-tree is created for the concatenated attribute $A \parallel B$ or $B \parallel A$. The query predicates are then evaluated using the value combinations in the tree.

Detailed analysis reveals that neither variant works for all query types. The first one has the problem of employing two access paths. This is substantially more expensive than using just one adequate access path; the necessity of maintaining partial result lists and storing them for final processing further adds to the complexity of this solution. But even if all this were acceptable, it is clear that a query with a simple predicate like $(A > B)$ cannot be supported by having two separate B-trees.

Creating a B-tree over the concatenation of both attributes reduces the cost for query processing in some cases, but there are also query types that do not benefit from such an access path. The predicate $(A > B)$, and all variations thereof, is one example. But there are even more trivial cases. Assume the B-tree has been created for $A \parallel B$; this tree can then be used for answering the query $(A < \text{const})$, but it is useless for $(B < \text{const})$.

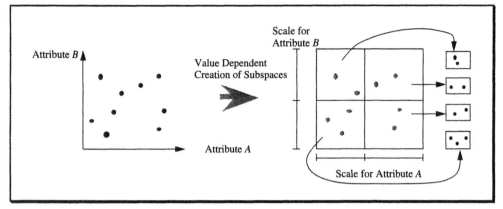

Figure 15.18: The basic idea of the grid file technique. Tuples are thought to be points in a two-dimensional space, the axis of which is established by the search coordinates. This space is divided into subspaces by planes, such that each subspace holds approximately the same number of tuples. For each subspace, there is a pointer in the directory pointing to a page with all the tuples in the respective subspace.

Maintaining separate trees for all types of attribute combinations in all permutations solves some of the retrieval problems, but it adds unacceptable costs to the update operations. Considering the arguments already given, it is obvious that for n attributes, virtually all $n!$ attribute concatenations would have to be turned into *a B-tree* in order to get symmetric behavior with respect to range queries on arbitrary subsets; this is certainly not a reasonable scheme.

What is needed, then, is an access path to allow efficient associative access in an unbiased fashion, based on n attributes with queries of the types shown for the special case of two attributes. For simplicity, all the following presentations are also restricted to two attributes, but a generalization to n attributes is not difficult.

The grid file is one of the most thoroughly investigated access methods for symmetric multi-attribute access in large files. The best way to introduce the basic idea is to use the metaphor of a point set in a plane. Each attribute is an axis in a euclidian space. The tuples have well-defined values in the search attributes A and B; thus, each tuple corresponds to the point in the plane having the tuple's attribute values as its coordinates. This is illustrated in Figure 15.18.

There are two evident reasons why such a "tuple space" cannot be used directly for storing the tuples: first, it has at least two dimensions, whereas the page address space is one-dimensional; second, the n-dimensional tuple space has clusters as well as unused regions, whereas the utilization of the storage space should be uniformly high. But as Figure 15.18 suggests, the arrangement of the points in the plane (sticking to the two-dimensional example) contains enough information to decide for which regions (subspaces) storage space must be allocated, where the density of tuples is high, where no tuples are, and so on.

Given the point set shown at the left-hand side of Figure 15.19, and given pages which can hold up to three tuples, we can replace the plane with a two-dimensional array of pointers, as shown on the right-hand side. Each of the four cells contains exactly one pointer to a page where the actual tuples are stored; the shaded points in the cells merely indicate which of the tuples of the point set on the left are in the pages to which the pointers refer.

The key point of the grid file concept is the following: as Figure 15.18 shows, the subspaces called cells are not of equal size in terms of the attribute dimensions, although each of them contains one page pointer. The criterion for determining the cell sizes is the number of points in the cell. In other words, the limits between neighboring cells along each dimension are adjusted such that biases in the value distribution are compensated. In value ranges with high tuple frequencies, the sides of the cells are smaller; ranges with fewer tuples allow for larger cells.

Since the value space is divided by parallel planes to the axes, the dividing points for each dimension can be stored separately in an array called *scale*. Each scale corresponds to one attribute dimension, and it contains the values of that attribute where a dividing plane cuts through the value space, thus creating the cells. It is assumed that each scale array contains the dividing points in ascending order; that is, the larger the index, the larger the attribute value. The data structures required for the two-dimensional case can be declared as follows:

```
#define MAXBOUND 1000          /* maximum number of cell boundaries along one dimension    */
#define DIMENSIONS 2                       /* number of search attributes supported         */
Ulong      scales[DIMENSIONS][MAXBOUND];   /* scale vectors for each dimension              */
PAGEID     cells[MAXBOUND][MAXBOUND];      /* two dimensional array of page pointers        */
```

Note that these declarations serve only the purpose of illustrating the functional principles of the grid file. In a real implementation, scales would probably not be defined as a two-dimensional array, because the number of cell boundaries along the different attribute-dimensions may vary widely. The array of page pointers cells cannot be kept in main memory for large files. Consequently, there must be some way of mapping the array onto pages; this is discussed later in this subsection. (See also the remarks on maintaining the directory for extendible hashing in Subsection 15.6.1.) By the way, the cell array is often referred to as the *directory* of a grid file.

Given these data structures, it is easy to explain how retrieval works with a grid file. Let us start with an exact-match query, which is also referred to as *point search* when talking about multi-attribute search structures. A point query has a search predicate of the type ($A = c_1$ and $B = c_2$). In terms of the point set metaphor, this means that the tuple corresponding to the point in the plane with the coordinates (c_1, c_2) has to be retrieved. The basic steps are illustrated in the piece of code that follows (note that all concurrency control on the scales, index arrays, and cells is omitted).

Thanks to the simplifications explained previously, the code skeleton for retrieval is surprisingly small. It stops in a situation comparable to the moment when the right leaf node in a B-tree is located: the page accessed through bufferfix is the one where the tuple with the specified search must be stored, if it exists. Locating the actual tuple requires a subsequent search in the page.

The generalization from point search to interval search along arbitrary dimensions is obvious. Search intervals are defined by specifying the coordinate *ranges* along each dimension, rather than single coordinate values. Accordingly, for each dimension, a cell index *range*, rather than a single index, is determined from scales. And finally, cells is accessed with all possible combinations of the cell indexes within the relevant ranges. This yields a set of page numbers completely covering the subspace defined by the range query. It is illustrated in Figure 15.19. The indexes of the two scale vectors are explicitly shown in the figure, for ease of reference.

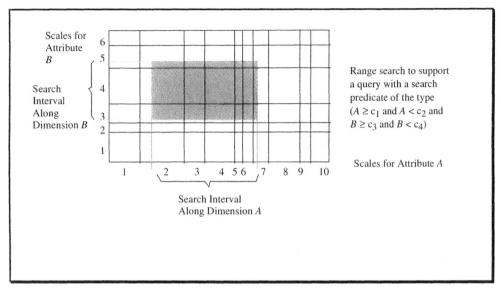

Figure 15.19: A range search in a grid file. Such a search means accessing all pages whose associated subspaces overlap with the search subspace.

```
int       cell_index[DIMENSIONS];        /* index for addressing the cell-array            */
Ulong     c[DIMENSIONS];                 /* search coordinates                             */
int   i,j;                               /* index variables                                */
PAGEID subspace_page;                    /* page number holding tuples from the sub-space  */
                                         /* where the point with the coordinates specified in c[] lies. */
BUFFER_ACC_CBP grid_page;                /* CB pointer for accessing the page in buffer    */
/* it must be checked that both coordinates, c[1] and c[2] are in the valid range between the */
/* minimum and maximum value of the respective dimension. This is omitted for simplicity.    */
for (i=0; i<DIMENSIONS-1; i++)           /* do this for each dimension of the space        */
    {      j=0;                          /* initialize index for boundary values           */
           while (c[i] > scales[i][j]) j++;  /* locate first boundary value >= the         */
                                         /* coordinate along that dimension                */
           cell_index[i] = j;            /* this is the boundary index for cell  for that dim. */
    };
subspace_page = cells[cell_index[0]][cell_index[1]];   /* get address of page holding tuples */
                                         /* from the relevant sub-space                    */
bufferfix(subspace_page,sh_sem,grid_page);  /* get page into buffer for read access        */
```

Given the specified search ranges, the scale for attribute-dimension A says that cells must be accessed with the first index varying between 2 and 7; the scale for B prescribes an index range between 3 and 5. Therefore, the access to all tuples potentially falling into the search rectangle requires the following actions:

```
int i,j,k;                                      /* index variables                                */
BUFFER_ACC_CBP  grid_pages[];                   /* array of page CB pointers for the result set   */
                                                /* of the range query                             */

k=o;
for (i=2; i<=7; i++)
    for (j=3; j<=5; j++)
        {       subspace_page = cells[i][j];    /* fetch page pointer for sub-space               */
                bufferfix(subspace_page,sh_sem,grid_page[k]);
                                                /* get next relevant page into buffer             */
            k++;
        };
```

Because the whole business of updating a grid file—especially inserting new tuples—is fairly complex, we will only explain the principles involved. The key issues are that grid files are dynamic (pages are allocated and freed as needed) and that the subdivison of the scales into value ranges for determining the cell boundaries has to be *dynamic*. In other words, there is no prearranged cell structure (this would make things very easy); rather, the boundaries of the cells are adjusted according to the value distributions of the tuples in the file. As an example, assume more tuples are inserted into the scenario of Figure 15.18. These tuples are given names, for ease of reference. Figure 15.20 illustrates the aspects of updating a grid file.

As always, insertion begins with a retrieval operation (a point search for a grid file) to locate the page where the tuple to be inserted has to go. If the page can accommodate the tuple, the tuple is stored there, and no other data structures are affected. In the example, this is the case for tuple *t*1. If, however, the page is full, its contents have to be distributed across two pages, and the addressing scheme has to be adjusted accordingly. This is similar to how extendible hashing works.

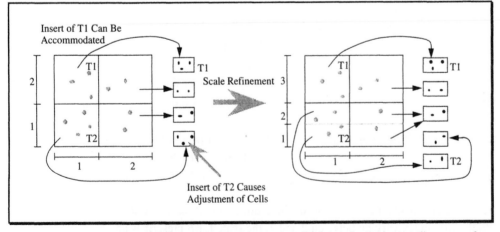

Figure 15.20: Extending a grid file by splitting data pages.   This is reflected in a readjustment of at least one of the scales. Since the coordinates of the dividing points are stored in the scales in ascending order, the structure of these arrays must be readjusted, too.

The directory of a grid file has a page pointer for each subspace, the limits of which are determined by the scales. If a page has to be split, two pointers are needed; that is, the subspace entry in the directory must also be split. As Figure 15.20 shows, the critical subspace with cell indexes (1,1) is split along the vertical dimension (shaded line). As a consequence, all cell entries with indexes (*,1) turn into two entries with indexes (*,1) and (*,2). Except for the split cell, all other cell contents are simply copied; this is also shown in the illustration.

Along the dimension that was chosen for the split, all index values above the point of split for existing cells must be increased by one. This requires special techniques for efficiently maintaining the multidimensional directory, discussion of which is beyond the scope of this short introduction.

If a page becomes empty, its pointer in the directory can be redirected to a neighboring page. *Neighborhood* is defined along any of the dimensions. If an entire subspace along one dimension becomes empty, no entries for it are needed in the directory, and the scale for that dimension can be reduced accordingly. This is the inverse of the process shown previously.

There are a number of difficult problems associated with an efficient implementation of the grid file scheme for a general-purpose transaction system. Splitting is much more complex than shown in our example. The first question concerns which dimension to split along in case of a page overflow. There are different options, depending on how much information about the state of neighboring cells is included. The really tricky issue, however, is how to maintain the (large) directory on disk efficiently. As was demonstrated, the directory is a dynamic, n-dimensional array, and each split operation means that $(n - 1)$-dimensional subarrays are inserted at the split position. Such an operation should not imply a total reorganization of the whole directory. Furthermore, it would be desirable to store the pages associated with neighboring subspaces within a narrow address range. Such a clustering should be maintained under update.

And then, of course, there is the problem of synchronization on a grid file. Which locking protocols are needed for the scales, the directories, and so forth? Is the value locking technique used for B-trees applicable?

Assuming that all these problems can be solved, grid files yield a constant cost of two page accesses for a single-point retrieval. This assumes that the scales can be kept in buffer which is reasonable because they normally comprise just a few KB. Then, one access is required to find the directory page for the subspace in which the point lies, and one access goes to the data page. The performance characteristics and the functional principle are very similar to the extendible hashing scheme. One difference is that extendible hashing is one-dimensional, whereas the grid file supports multidimensional access. Another difference is that extendible hashing relies on a hashing function (hence the name) to produce uniform access frequencies to all directory entries; the grid file employs the scales for the same purpose. And the last, but important, difference is that the directory of an extendible hashing file is much simpler to maintain (and therefore to implement) than the multidimensional directory of the grid file.

15.6.3 Holey Brick B-Trees

Holey brick B-trees (hB-trees) address the same problem as grid files: symmetric multi-attribute search on large files. Just like grid files, they support both exact-match queries and range searches along arbitrary subsets of the attributes on which the search structure is de-

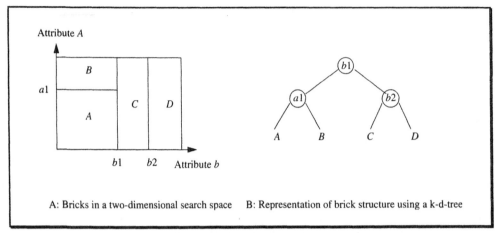

A: Bricks in a two-dimensional search space   B: Representation of brick structure using a k-d-tree

Figure 15.21: Structuring a 2-dimensional search space using a k-d-tree. Each node in the tree corresponds to an attribute value of one of the search dimensions. The order in which the dimensions are used for searching is either predetermined, or it is made dependent on the actual decomposition structure of the search space. The latter version is used here.

fined. But whereas grid files rely on a multidimensional array that actually resembles the structure of the search space, hB-trees (as their name suggests) are much more akin to B-trees as they have been described in this chapter. It makes an interesting exercise to compare these two radically different approaches to the same problem. But let us first illustrate the basic idea behind hB-trees.[17]

The name holey brick B-trees intuitively conveys its idea. Each node in the tree corresponds to a rectangular k-dimensional subspace of the total search space (assuming the search structure has been defined on k attributes of the file). These subspaces are referred to as *bricks*. In contrast to similar search structures, where this correspondence is strict, a node in an hB-tree generally describes a brick from which smaller bricks may have been removed. This means that the bricks into which the search space is decomposed can have "holes"—hence the name of the access path structure. Like a B-tree, an hB-tree grows from the leaves to the root. The leaves contain the data, whereas the higher levels consist of index nodes.

When speaking of hB-trees, we have to distinguish carefully between two types of tree structures. One is the overall structure of the hB-tree; that is, the way its index and data nodes are tied together. This is taken from the K-D-B-tree (K-D stands for k-dimensional), a B-tree generalization for k attributes. This method was introduced by Robinson [1984], and its principle will become clear during the following description. The second type of tree structure is the k-d-tree [Bentley 1975], which is used to internally organize the entries of the index nodes in an hB-tree. Let us first sketch the ideas behind a k-d-tree.

A k-d-tree is a binary tree that structures the search via k different attributes. Its principle is illustrated in Figure 15.21. A node in a k-d-tree represents an attribute value. If the search key value is less than the node value, search proceeds to the left, otherwise it proceeds to the right.[18] So far, this is exactly how a binary tree works.

---

[17] This section closely follows the original paper on hB-trees [Lomet and Salzberg 1990b].

[18] In hB-trees, in order to guarantee minimum fan-out per index node, the convention of whether equality of the comparison is on the left-hand or right-hand side is individually adjusted for each node in the k-d-tree. This optimization is ignored in the following.

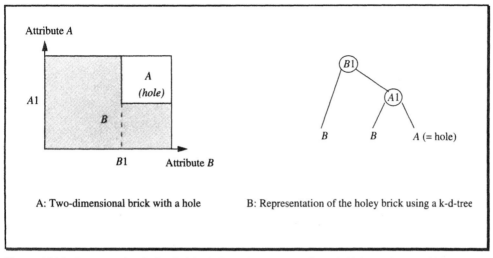

A: Two-dimensional brick with a hole   B: Representation of the holey brick using a k-d-tree

Figure 15.22: Representing holey bricks using a k-d-tree. The "trick" is to allow multiple leaves of the k-d-tree to reference the same subspace. A hole is a region of the search space that is not referenced by any leaf.

However, in a conventional binary tree, each node represents a value of the *same* attribute; in a k-d-tree, on the other hand, subsequent nodes along a search path can represent values of different attributes. The simplest rule to cope with this is to use the k attributes in a fixed order. Therefore, if the tree is defined on $k = 3$ attributes (a, b and c), then the root node contains a value of a, its two successors contain values of b, their successors contain c values, then comes a again, and so forth. This is simple but potentially inefficient, because at a certain level it forces the use of an attribute even if the subspace considered at that level need not be partitioned along that dimension. For example, in Figure 15.21, subspaces C and D are defined by values of b only; attribute a is not relevant for them. Thus, a more sophisticated scheme for the k-d-tree permits using along any search path, that attribute for the next node that yields the most efficient partitioning of the remaining subspace. As Figure 15.21 shows, this may result in the same attribute being used repeatedly. Since with that convention, a node's distance from the root allows no conclusion as to which attribute the node represents, another scheme is sometimes used: each node except for the value must also carry an identifier of the attribute to which it belongs. In what follows, that second scheme is assumed.

As shown in Figure 15.22, the representation of holey bricks by generalizing the k-d-tree technique is straightforward. The conventional search structure is based on the assumption that each node defines a partitioning of the subspace it represents along one dimension, and all dependent nodes further subdivide *that partition*; here, however, multiple nodes can point to the same partition. When you look at Figure 15.22, the consequences become obvious: in a conventional k-d-tree, the left pointer of the node representing $a1$ would have to point to a separate subspace, thus partitioning the right-hand region of the search space. However, since this portion of the region, together with the left-hand part of the search space, establishes the subspace B, from which the hole A has been removed, the pointer refers to B, too.

So much for the introduction of the data structures used in the index nodes of an hB-tree. Let us now consider overall organization of an hB-tree. This is where the need for holey bricks comes in. As mentioned, the structure of an hB-tree is similar to a K-D-B-tree. K-D-B-trees are much like B-trees in that they are balanced, the data is in the leaves only, and so on. But while each index node in a B-tree describes the partitioning of a region of a one-dimensional search space into disjoint intervals, an index node in a K-D-B-tree describes the partitioning of a region of a *k*-dimensional search space into *k-dimensional* subspaces. For each subspace, a lower-level index node is pointed to, describing the partitioning of that subspace into even finer granules, down to the leaf level.

Up to this point, we have described exactly what the hB-tree does. The difference lies in the techniques used to maintain the tree structure during update. When an index node has to be split in a K-D-B-tree, one attribute (dimension) is picked, along which the subspace represented by that node is divided into two. In other words, the old subspace is completely partitioned along a $(k - 1)$-dimensional hyperplane. There are two problems with this approach:

Uneven partitioning. Depending on the location of the tuples in *k*-space, it may not be possible to find a single-dimension partitioning that yields even distribution of the entries across the two nodes resulting from the split.

Cascading spilts. B-trees have the property that splits are always propagated bottom-up: as a result of a node split, its parent node may have to be split. But splitting an index node has no impact on any of its child nodes. In K-D-B-trees, however, the method of splitting along one dimension causes splits to cascade down the tree to child nodes (and maybe to their children) to adjust for the new setting of subspace boundaries.

The hB-tree uses a different split strategy. It allows a node to be split along more than one dimension in order to avoid both of the problems just mentioned. As a consequence, however, one must be able to cope with holes in the subspaces represented by the index nodes. Since the representation of holey bricks is based on multiple nodes pointing to the same successor (see Figure 15.22), this may result in one index node having more than one parent. Strictly speaking, then, we would have to talk about "hB-DAGs," but since we will not go into any detail with respect to mutiple parents, the notion of trees is used throughout this section.

To understand the following description of the operations on hB-trees, we have to appreciate the global layout of this search structure, which is depicted in Figure 15.23. The leaves of the k-d-trees in the index nodes point to lower-level nodes in the tree. More than one pointer can reference the same successor node, and these multiple references of the same lower-level node can come from different higher-level index nodes. In each k-d-tree, holes that have been extracted from the region described by the node are tagged (* in the figure). The data nodes also contain k-d-trees to guide the local search, but here the leaves are the actual tuples (or pointers to the tuples, for that matter). Note that in the general case, a leaf of a data node k-d-tree can represent many tuples, namely all those falling into the subspace denoted by that node in the k-d-tree.

Searching in an hB-tree is straightforward. Let us briefly consider the two types of access operations supported by such a search structure.

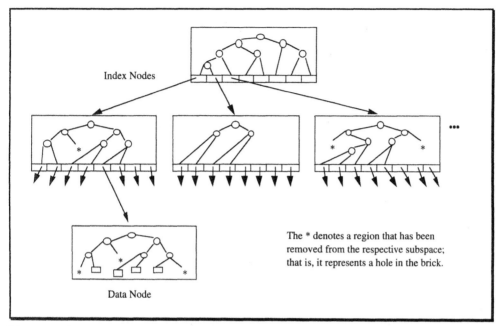

Index Nodes

Data Node

The * denotes a region that has been
removed from the respective subspace;
that is, it represents a hole in the brick.

Figure 15.23: Global structure of an hB-tree.   The index nodes contain k-d-trees, the leaves of
which represent pointers to lower-level nodes, that is, to other index nodes or to data nodes. Each local
k-d-tree describes a region in k-space, from which subspace may have been removed. This is indicated
by * in the figure. The data nodes also contain (small) k-d-trees, but in this case the leaves are
(collections of) records in the file.

Exact-match query.   The k attributes of the tuple(s) to be retrieved must be equal to the
values of the k-vector specified for the search operation. Starting at the root, the k-d-tree
is used in its standard way. Depending on which attribute the k-d-tree node represents,
one compares the respective search value and proceeds along the vector that belongs to
the "=" case. This produces a pointer to a lower-level node, which is processed in the
same way, and finally one gets to the data node with the qualified tuple.

Range query.   This requires following many search paths in parallel. Consider a k-d-tree
node pertaining to attribute a. If the value it represents is larger than the upper bound of
the range in that dimension (or smaller than the lower bound), then one need only
follow the left (or right) pointer. Otherwise, if valid data lies in both directions, both
pointers must be followed. The same argument applies recursively down to the data
nodes.

Update operations follow the same general logic as B-trees; this is explained by considering the insert of a new tuple. First, an exact-match query is performed to determine the insert location. If the tuple fits into the data page, the insert is complete; no structural modifications are necessary.

The specific properties of an hB-tree become relevant when a node split is necessary.
For brevity, we do not discuss all the variants and special situations that have to be consid-

ered. Rather, we focus on some typical scenarios to demonstrate the principles of splitting nodes that contain k-d-trees describing holey bricks.

At the core of the split algorithm lies the observation that it is always possible to achieve a worst-case split ratio of 1:2, no matter what the value of k, provided the split can involve more than one attribute.[19] When a page needs to be split, therefore, one first checks to see if a split at the current root of the node's k-d-tree would partition the entries in the page in a ratio of 1:2 or better. If that is the case, the node is split at the root. The left sub-tree forms one new node, the right sub-tree the other one. If the old node (before the split) represented a complete brick (no holes in it), then there was just one reference to it from an index node. In that case, the old root node must be propagated up to the index node to augment its k-d-tree. If, however, the old node already had holes, then the split may not require any key values to be propagated up the hierarchy; only the adjustment of some pointers is necessary (have them point to the right sub-tree in the new page, rather than in the old one).

If the root node does not achieve the 1:2 split ratio, there must be one sub-tree accounting for more than two-thirds of the entries in the node. Going down this sub-tree produces the first of two possible outcomes (the second will be considered shortly).

Split at lower sub-tree. In the large sub-tree, a node is found, one of whose sub-trees accounts for less than two-thirds and more than one-third of the entries. Then the k-d-tree, and thereby the hB-tree node, is split at this point. This is illustrated in Figure 15.24.

The node to be split (node r) represents a holey brick. Splitting at the node for attribute $b1$ gives the required split ratio, so the left sub-tree of that node is removed. Since it contains only one portion of data, the new node (node u) can, for the moment, do without any local k-d-tree. The removal of the sub-tree is marked in node u by the tag representing a hole in the appropriate branch. In other words, the split has caused the brick described by node r to get a new (bigger) hole. The example also illustrates that in cases where the discriminating attribute's values are already present at higher levels, a split may result in mere pointer adjustments in the index.

Note also that the local k-d-trees resulting from the split are generally reduced to the minimum number of nodes required to represent the remaining region in space. This may also result in the removal of hole references (see node u).

Split at leaf. If no sub-tree with the required property is found, then one of the leaves must account for more than two-thirds of the entries; this can only occur in data nodes. In that case, the data in that leaf must be redistributed. According to the split ratio property mentioned earlier, it is always possible to determine a hole lying at a corner of that subspace, such that the ratio of entries in the hole and in the remaining brick is 1:2 or better. The attribute values defining that corner must be propagated up to the index level. An example in two dimensions is shown in Figure 15.25.

The tree structure of the data node and its index node is assumed to be the same as in the previous example. However, we now consider the case in which no sub-tree accounts for a number of entries that lie between one-third and two-thirds of the entries in the page. As-

---

[19] Remember that the standard split strategy of a B-tree yields a split ratio of 1:1 (within the precision of integer arithmetic).

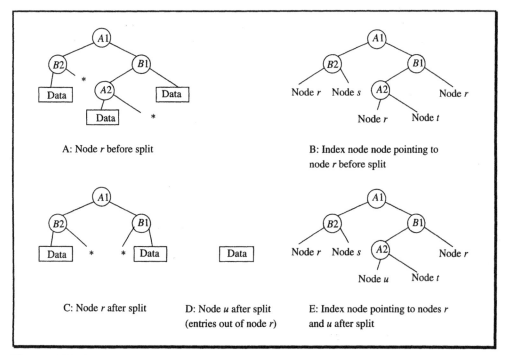

Figure 15.24: Splitting a data node at a sub-tree of the local k-d-tree. This scenario assumes that splitting node *r* at the root of its local k-d-tree would not yield the required 1:2 split ratio, but that splitting at the node representing attribute *b*1 has that effect. As a result, node *r* keeps the right sub-tree of the split node and the nodes above that. The new node, *u*, gets the left sub-tree (which is collapsed) because it contains only one portion of data. In the index tree, only pointer adjustments are done.

sume the data portion in the high-value branch of *b*1 has more than two-thirds of the entries. This brick must be partitioned, and, as we have seen, there is always a corner hole to remove from the brick such that both the removed part and the remaining part of the node to be split hold between one-third and two-thirds of the entries. Figure 15.25 shows the result of the split, assuming that the removed part was actually sliced off the large subspace along dimension *a* at point *a*3. As in the previous scenario, the removed data portion goes to a new page (node *u*); being the only portion in that node, it needs no k-d-tree for the moment. The new node in the k-d-tree of node *r* is propagated up to the index node.

As an aside, assuming $a1 < a2 < a3$ and $b1 < b2$, we find that the holey brick described by node *r* now has become holey to the degree that it is noncontiguous. In other words, the holes separate the remaining parts of the subspace that actually contain data maintained in that node.

To keep this discussion short, we do not elaborate on exactly how nodes resulting from a split are propagated up to the index nodes; what happens in case of multiple parents; and so forth. The material presented so far should be sufficient to convey the idea.

The hB-tree structure is interesting for a number of reasons. First, it is a generalization of the well-established B-tree access path, and some of its organizational principles can be applied without any changes. It guarantees a fixed minimum node utilization, even with the worst-case data distribution. This is its major difference from the grid file, for example, which works well only if the data points are evenly distributed in the search space, and

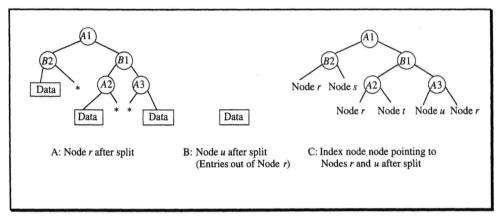

A: Node *r* after split

B: Node *u* after split
(Entries out of Node *r*)

C: Index node node pointing to
Nodes *r* and *u* after split

Figure 15.25: Splitting a leaf of a k-d-tree inside a data node. The initial configuration of the trees is the same as in Figure 15.25, but now it is assumed that the data portion in the high-value branch of *b1* contains more than two-thirds of the entries in the page. Then the node is split along dimension *a* at point *a3*. The data portion pointed to by the left branch of that split point goes to the new node, *u*. The split node in the k-d-tree (*a3*) must be propagated up to the index node, which means this tree has to be modified, too.

which can deteriorate badly if that is not the case. A consequence of the one-third minimum node occupancy is a limit on the height of the hB-tree. For a given file, the hB-tree should come out only slightly higher than a B-tree. This is partly due to the lower (minimum) node utilization and partly due to the fact that the number of entries per node is lower for an hB-tree in the first place, because information about *k* attributes (rather than one attribute) has to be maintained. Analytic models show that an hB-tree with just one dimension has a performance comparable to that of a B-tree.

A consideration of synchronization and recovery techniques for hB-trees is beyond the scope of this discussion. Even these brief explanations, however, should convey the fact that this is an altogether different story.

15.7 Summary

Associative accesss paths have to serve two basic functional requirements: first, exact-match queries have to retrieve all tuples whose value in a given attribute (or set of attributes) is equal to a specified search key value. Second, range queries must be supported to retrieve all tuples whose attribute values are elements of a specified search interval (range). Support of such queries basically implies the possibility to access tuples in sorted order of the attributes defining the boundaries of the query range.

Exact-match queries are supported by hashing. The functional principle can be characterized as follows: upon tuple insert, take the value of the attribute that will subsequently be used for exact-match queries (typically this is the primary key) and transform it (by arithmetic computations) into a relative page number of the file where the tuple is to be stored. For retrieval, the same procedure is applied, too, so the page to be read from disk can be directly computed from the attribute value. Complications such as skewed value distributions in the relation and collisions resulting from that notwithstanding, hashing provides single-page access behavior, which is the absolute minimum for random single-tuple access for the architecture assumed in this book. Whenever very fast random access to single tuples via the primary key (think of account numbers, credit card numbers, and so on) is the dominating performance criterion, hash-based access is an option. It has serious drawbacks, though. Range queries are not supported, exact-match queries via nonunique attributes are possible only within narrow limits, and the size of the relation must be stable over time (and known in advance).

Apart from hashing, which lives in some sort of an ecological niche, the dominating species among the associative access paths in today's databases is the B-tree. It is a multi-way search tree with a number of very attractive features. First, it meets all the functional requirements mentioned. Second, its performance characteristics are predictable precisely, because the tree is at any point in time perfectly balanced in terms of the number of nodes that have to be visited upon retrieval from the root to any leaf. Its absolute performance is very good, depending of course, on a number of application-dependent parameters and design options. Roughly speaking, a random single-tuple access via a B-tree requires between $(H - 3)$ and $(H - 2)$ I/O operations, where H is the height of the tree, which—for the fast majority of applications—ranges between 4 and 5. For range queries and sequential retrieval in sorted order, the overhead incurred by the tree structure is much smaller. If the B-tree is used to implement a secondary index via a nonunique attribute, the performance characteristics are almost the same.

Since the B-tree is ubiquitous in databases, it is an extremely well-investigated data structure. There are numerous designs aimed at optimizing its performance with respect to concurrent transactions reading and updating data via the same B-tree, and at the same time guaranteeing isolated execution for each transaction using the tree. These protocols get fairly complicated, because they have to make clever use of the semantics of the tree structure and its operations. It is instructive to study both the synchronization and the recovery protocols, because they provide isolation without being serializable in the classical sense.

Mighty as the B-tree may be, there are applications that require more than it can provide. Typical examples are symmetric multi-attribute search operations and retrieval operations that refer to spatial criteria such as *neighborhood*, *overlap*, and so on. Once applications in that area are important enough to justify the implementation of dedicated database functions, new associative access paths such as grid files, hB-trees, and others may become relevant. A similar observation holds for access structures supporting complex objects that are typical of object-oriented databases. It is interesting to observe, though, that the most promising of these "new" search structures more often than not are close relatives of the B-tree.

15.8 Historical Notes[20]

The history of access paths, like many other aspects of transaction systems, is a story of rediscovering the same few principles over and over again. Both fundamental techniques—key transformation and key comparison—have been in use in many areas of human activity for at least 200 years, probably much longer than that.

---

[20] The major portion of this section was guest-authored by Betty Salzberg. Her thorough knowledge of the field and her constructive suggestions on how to put it into perspective are gratefully acknowledged.

Indexing is ubiquitous. Since it requires some kind of alphabet for which a sort order can be defined, preliterate societies most likely had little to do with it. After that, however, the idea is applied in many guises. Large libraries, for example, use multi-level indexing. There is an index for the different rooms, one for the shelves in each room, and one for the boards in one shelf. The boards represent the leaf level, where a search in an ordered set has to be performed.

Another application—one that is is not so old—is phone books. Of course, they essentially have a one-level index; here you are literally operating at the leaf level. But phone books do key compression in much the same way described in this chapter. (Look at the upper-left and upper-right corners of a page and see what kind of reference key is printed there.)

Hashing bears an interesting resemblance to the way the human memory works (or pretends to work). Many techniques for improving the capabilities of one's memory (especially the quality of recall) are based on the trick of associating the information to be remembered with something else, something familiar; these are called mnemonic devices. Upon recall, the access to the familiar thing is easy (page number), and associated with it comes the information requested. As in the technical environment, the performance of such techniques critically depends on the quality of the "hash function."

Now let us close in on the much narrower domain of databases and transaction systems. The descriptions of many of the basic algorithms can be found in one of *the* classics of computer science, Knuth's *The Art of Computer Programming* [1973]. Understandably, however, this work gives no consideration to the issues related to maintaining such structures on external storage, and to synchronization and recovery.

One of the earliest attempts to implement multi-level indexes was the index-sequential access method (ISAM) in the OS/360 operating system. The original version was far from the flexibility of B-trees, though, because the index structure was bound to the geometry of magnetic disks. There was a master index pointing to directories, each directory had an index pointing to tracks, and each track had an index pointing to records. It actually was not as simple as that, but this is the basic idea.

The elaboration of what finally came to be known as B-trees was carried out in the mid-1960s in different places and, of course, in isolation. The database management system ADABAS, the development of which started at about that time, from the very beginning made massive use of dynamic multi-level indexes. As a matter of fact, each ADABAS database is something like a "supertree," in that all existing access paths are linked into a higher-level tree, with the catalog on top of all that. Probably for confidentiality reasons, there is no precise description of which algorithms are used, how locking and recovery are done, and so on.

The first concise paper—and the most famous one—about the B-tree is by Bayer and McCreight [1972]. Most of the subsequent literature is based on the concepts presented there, although many of the contemporary implementations were done without the implementors having seen them.

Over the years, the ISAM access method was made more and more device independent and gradually turned into VSAM, which is (among others) a full-blown implementation of B-trees, with key compression and everything else. As part of the operating system, VSAM does not know about transactions. The reader should by now be able to appreciate what it means to keep a data structure consistent after crashes without the benefits of a log, a recovery manager, and so on. VSAM has its very own mechanisms for fault tolerance, which have not been described in this book. Fundamentally, they are an elaborate version of careful replacement.

The development of relational databases brought about another round of B-tree implementations. The system implementation on the large scale is fairly well documented [Astrahan et al. 1981; Haderle and Jackson 1984; Tandem Database Group 1987; Stonebraker et al. 1976]. Yet the details of how the access paths actually work have never been published.

There have been several general expositions of B-trees. The best-known is the survey article by Comer [1979]. Textbooks on file structures usually have an explanation of B-trees. Many of the performance formulas worked out in this chapter, for instance, can also be found in [Salzberg 1988]. Salzberg's book also covers linear hashing [Litwin 1980], bounded extendible hashing [Lomet 1983], grid files, hB-trees, an optical disk access method, external sorting, and relational joins.

Papers suggesting ways to improve the general B-tree algorithms (to increase fan-out, for example) have also been published. The handling of variable-length keys and use of key compression within B-tree nodes was presented by Bayer and Unterauer [1977] and Lomet [1979]. The use of multi-page nodes for leaves is investigated in Lomet [1988] and Litwin [1987]. Having larger leaf nodes can decrease the number of disk accesses. Using partial expansions [Lomet 1987] can increase the average space utilization in leaves, also improving on the number of disk accesses. Having larger index nodes [Lomet 1981; 1983] can increase the fan-out.

In the late 1970s and in the 1980s, a number of academic researchers published papers on concurrency in access methods. These papers, in general, do not consider such system issues as whether I/Os occur while locks are held, what happens on system failure, and so forth. They concentrate on making search correct while insertions and deletions are in progress. Usually there is an implicit assumption that system failures do not occur. Some of the earlier papers on concurrency in tree structures include work by Bayer and Schkolnick [1977] which contains the safe node method used in this chapter, [Lehman and Yao 1981; Ellis 1980; Kung 1980; Kwong 1982; Mandber 1982; and Ford 1984]. The work reported by Sagiv [1986] extends the work of Lehman and Yao to include restructuring. The paper by Shasha and Goodman [1988] gives an integrated description of the principles involved in most of the concurrency algorithms.

Two recent papers [Srinivasan 1991; Johnson 1991] analyze the performance of concurrent B-tree algorithms. Both conclude that the Lehman-Yao method performs best.

In contrast, most of the work on actual implementations of B-trees in commercial systems has never been published. For example, Mike Blasgen, Andrea Borr, and Franco Putzolu have written several B-tree implementations and may very possibly know more than anybody else about how it must be done, but they have never written papers about it.

Implementors of commercial systems have had to consider system failure and recovery, the length of time locks are held (whether I/O or network communication occurs during the time locks are held), lock granularity and lock mode, and the complications of key-range searching and its susceptibilty to the phantom anomaly. These constraints led to a different perspective, which decisively shaped this text but which has been largely invisible to the academic community. Until the papers of Mohan and his colleagues at the Database Technology Institute at IBM's Almaden Research Lab began to appear, it was not possible for people not active in commercial implementation to gain this perspective.

Mohan and his colleagues have published a series of papers on a design for recovery, access path management, and concurrency control called ARIES. A number of these are cited in the references. In particular, the ARIES/KVL paper [Mohan 1990a] is the basis for the discussion of the tuple-oriented view of B-tree synchronization in Subsection 15.3.4. Other papers dealing with B-trees include ARIES/IM [Mohan and Levine 1989] and Mohan et al. [1990]. These papers are very detailed and are difficult to read, but they are worth the effort.

Hashing has been used in almost every component of operating systems, database systems, compilers, and so forth, from the very beginning. Look, for example, at the sample implementations of a lock manager in Chapter 8 and of a buffer manager in Chapter 13. Every book on elementary data structures describes the use of hashing for implementing content addressability in main memory. These mechanisms have been applied to file organization in many database products and other types of data administration software. Some of the earliest implementations of that type have been bill-of-material processors (BOMPs), which essentially used two access paths: hashing for associative access via the part number, and physical chaining for maintaining the "goes into" relationship. Many of these special-purpose packages have been the precursors of general-purpose database systems (IMS and TOTAL, for example).

But generally, the hashing technique used was static hashing with some kind of collision handling, as described in this chapter. When hashing is used in commercial products, this is likely to be how it is done even though it will require massive reorganization when the data collection grows, and even though many suggestions for dynamic hashing have been made in the literature.

In Subsection 15.5.1, we have seen one such suggestion—extendible hashing—as described in Fagin et al. [1979]. An improvement on this basic design, which prohibits the index from growing too large to be kept in main memory is found in Lomet [1983]. An alternate suggestion is linear hashing [Litwin 1980]. Several suggestions for improving linear hashing can be found Larson [1980; 1982; 1983; 1988].

Concurrency in linear hashing is treated in Ellis [1985], and Mohan discusses both concurrency and recovery Mohan [1990c]. Ellis [1982] covers concurrency in extendible hashing. In spite of all this work, these suggested dynamic hashing schemes have not yet been implemented in any commercial products. This would contribute to the suspicion that B-trees, which do not need massive reorganization and which can handle range queries, have been judged adequate for most applications.

Classical applications in banking, inventory control, flight reservation, and so forth need fast access to one tuple by primary key, and efficient access to a small number of tuples via a secondary key. B-trees do satisfy these requirements with sufficient performance. Nonstandard applications such as computer-aided design, geographic databases, biology databases, process control, and artificial intelligence have other requirements. They may need to cluster records by several attributes. They may deal with complex objects—a part together with all its component parts is a good example. So file organizations supporting value-dependent clustering is certainly needed for systems adequately supporting these applications.

New types of indexes have been proposed, especially for applications dealing with geometric data of some sort. In this chapter we have seen the grid file [Nievergelt, Hinterberger, and Sevcik 1984] and the holey brick tree [Lomet and Salzberg 1990b]. Other promising spatial indexes include the R-tree [Guttman and Stonebreaker 1984] and z-ordering [Orenstein 1984].

Although both Salzberg [1986] and Hinrichs [1985] have proposed concurrency control methods for the grid file, these methods do not treat system failure and are somewhat complicated due to the non-local splitting in grid file systems. Also, as with most published work on concurrency in access methods, other system issues (range locking, I/Os while locks are held) are not addressed. Work is ongoing for implementations of concurrency and recovery for holey brick trees.

The simplest spatial index to implement is the z-ordering method, so this is the one most likely to appear in a database management system. For z-ordering, one merely interleaves the bits of the attributes of the key and then places the interleaved bit string in a B-tree. The already developed concurrency and recovery algorithms for B-trees can then be applied. The question of range locking is interesting, for the spatial (rectangular) ranges do not correspond to the linear ranges of the interleaved key. In fact, how to make such rectangular range queries efficient has been the subject of several papers [Orenstein 1986; 1989].

In addition, there have been suggested temporal indexing systems [Lomet and Salzberg 1989a; 1990a] and indexing systems for object-oriented databases [Bertino 1989; Maier 1986]. Object-oriented systems are in great demand and are not as efficient as one would like, so there is sure to be more activity in this area.

Summarizing then, the B-tree is still ubiquitous. Almost every database management system, even single-user microcomputer DBMSs, has them. For large transaction systems, sophisticated concurrency and recovery methods have been developed. Static hashing is sometimes used, but it must be reorganized because it cannot adjust to growth. Dynamic hashing schemes have been proposed but have not been installed. New applications have promoted investigations into spatial indexing, complex object indexing, and temporal indexing. It remains to be seen if any of these new indexes will be integrated into a transaction system such as described in this book.

Exercises

1. [15.3, 15] Consider a hash file with h buckets, each of which has a capacity of f tuples. Ten percent of the buckets have 1 overflow bucket, which is 30% full on the average. There are no multiple overflows. In total, there are T tuples. When doing a series of readkey operations with randomly selected key values, how many page accesses are needed on the average to locate the tuple? For the initial calculation, assume that only existing key values are used. Then refine the model to include $p\%$ of values that are not found in the file. Before formalizing the model, make sure you have made explicit all necessary assumptions about value distributions, and so forth.

2. [15.3, 20] When using the division/remainder technique for hashing, even with B chosen to be the next-higher prime, very nonuniform distributions of the hash addresses generated can occur. One typical case is a value of B that is close to the base of the number system in which the key values are expressed. Try to find a mathematical explanation for that case. *Hint: assume 4-digit numerical key values represented as unpacked (EBCDIC) numbers. Consider what happens if* $B = 257 = 2^8 + 1$.

3. [15.3, 25] In the text, the explanation of external overflow handling says that an overflow page is chained to the overflowing bucket; if there is an overflow in the overflow page, another page is chained to it, and so on (see Figure 15.5). This scheme has an obvious problem: the number of page accesses at a position with many overflows grows linearly, and performance can deteriorate rapidly. Can you come up with a scheme that requires, at most, two page accesses, even in case of

multiple overflows in the same hash class? Compare your scheme and the simple version described in the text with respect to the following criteria: limitations imposed on the number of tuples that can be handled; speed of retrieval of an existing tuple; number of page accesses required to decide that a tuple does not exist; cost of deleting a tuple; methods to release an overflow page that is no longer needed.

4. [15.3, 25] Retrieval of tuples in a hash file with internal collision handling is not as trivial as it might look. Consider a readkey operation with key value k_1. If it is not found in the bucket suggested by the hash algorithm, this does not say that no such tuple exists; it might be in some alternate bucket. Now with the external method, it is easy to tell if one has to access an overflow page: it depends on whether or not there is a pointer to it. For the internal method, without additional information it is not possible to tell whether the requested key is in bucket-number(r,1), bucket-number(r,2), etc. As a matter of fact, with the naive implementation, one has to go through all iterations up to $B - 1$ to decide that k_1 does not exist. Design an implementation for internal collision handling that keeps retrieval cheap (especially consider the detection of nonexisting key values). Weigh the improvements for retrieval against the additional costs for update operations.

5. [15.4, 10] The estimate of the size S of a B-tree derived in Section 15.4 is too high in the average case. Why?

6. [15.4, 25] Prove that when the tuples in the leaf nodes of a B-tree are read left to right through all the leaves, they will be retrieved sorted by the search key attribute. *Hint: First define precisely what it means if leaf page* a *is left of (or right of) leaf page* b.

7. [15.4, 20] Assume a B-tree with large nodes (32 KB or more). For efficiency, it is desirable to avoid searching for key values sequentially. However, schemes like binary search or the interval search need table structures with fixed-size entries to work on. Given that the B-tree has to support varying-length keys, how can you still apply one of the efficient search algorithms? (*Hint: Padding the key values up to a (fixed) maximum size is not a solution.*)

8. [15.4, 30] Design a clean-up algorithm for the "fuzzy end" of the log during restart recovery, which works even if there is parallel execution of actions within a transaction.

9. [15.4, 40] Write the core of the delete function for a B-tree; that is, the parts operating on the data structures. Leave out the logic for file directories and related issues. The implementation should be able to do merging of siblings at the leaf level. Design protocols for locking and logging which follow the same train of reasoning that was presented for insert.

10. [15.4, 20] Typical relational databases currently do not support system-maintained replication of relations. Do you see a way to achieve n-fold replication of an arbitrary relation anyway, including the guarantee that all updates are atomically applied to all copies? (*Hint: Writing a program at the application level is not a solution.*)

11. [15.4, project] This exercise asks you to work out the details of a novel synchronization technique on B-trees. The basic idea is laid out, and the most important aspects to consider are mentioned. But apart from that, you are invited to apply the considerations used in Section 15.4 in order to come up with a correct and efficient synchronization protocol. No such protocol has appeared in the literature.

Here is the basic idea. Assume that the B-tree implements an access path for a unique attribute. In many applications, bulk inserts occur at one point of the key value interval. This is to say that a couple of thousand tuples are inserted between two already existing tuples. The most prominent degenerate case is the bulk insert at the end of the value range, but the same phenomenon can happen at any point of the spectrum.

With the techniques presented so far, individual key ranges will be locked. But after 1,000 inserts, lock escalation strikes—which means the whole tree—is locked exclusively. But this is clearly an overkill: given that the file is key-sequenced, one can safely let other parts of the tree be accessed by other transactions. The trick is to apply key-range locking to the index levels as well.

12. [15.6, 20] Consider a two-dimensional grid file with T tuples. Try to roughly estimate the size of the directory in two cases: first, assume the attribute values of the tuples in the two dimensions to be randomly distributed over the two-dimensional parameter space. Second, consider a strong correlation between the two dimensions; to simplify things, assume that all value combinations are along the main diagonal of the plane. Each directory block can accommodate B TIDs of tuples in the base relation. *Hint: Start from the fact that the directory is a two-dimensional array. Try to estimate the probability of a directory block to have any TIDs. From that, derive the necessary size of the directory.*

Answers

1. Assume all have the same number of tuples, namely the average number of $0.3 \bullet t$. Further assume the other pages also have the same number of tuples, which can be computed by subtracting the number of tuples in overflow buckets and overflow pages from the total number of t. Finally assume that each tuple has the same reference probability.

   The total number of tuples in buckets that have overflowed plus the associated overflow pages is $0.1 \bullet h \bullet 1.3 \bullet t$. Whenever an overflow bucket is hit, the probability is .25 that the tuple is in the overflow page; therefore, the average number of block accesses, provided an overflow bucket is involved, is 1.25. For all the other buckets, exactly one block access is required. So the average number of block accesses can be calculated as

   $$B_{avg} = 1 \bullet ((T - 0.13 \bullet h \bullet t)/T) + 1.25 \cdot ((0.13 \bullet h \bullet t)/T)$$

   If T is 80% of the storage capacity, that is, if $(h \bullet t)/T = 1.25$, then a specific value can be calculated: $B^{avg} = 1.2094$. Doing the corresponding calculation for the case of $p\%$ references to nonexisting value is straightforward. The only modification required is that in case a request for a nonexisting value hits an overflow bucket two block accesses are required.

2. See the detailed discussion of this problem in Knuth [1973], Vol. 3.

3. The solution is simple: rather than using the forward chain along the overflow pages, maintain a pointer array in the primary bucket. Entry one points to the first overflow page, entry two to the second one. Without further measures, this does not speed up retrieval, because one still would have to search all overflow pages for a requested tuple. (With the pointer array, one could read all overflow pages in parallel, but let us ignore this.) But if one chooses the number of entries in the pointer array to be a prime number, then the key value can be re-hashed locally, and then the maximum number of block accesses is two, even if there are more overflow pages for a bucket. Of course, this scheme does not grow arbitrarily. If the pointer array is used up, then no more overflow pages can be allocated to the bucket. In other words, if the first overflow page overflows, then reorganization is necessary.

4. The key problem is to determine if a given bucket has overflowed in the first place, and if so, how many alternate buckets are used. The solution is very similar to the solution to Exercise 3.

5. Because the root has significantly less than 50% utilization most of the time.

7. The only thing that is necessary is that the entries in the page directory pointing to the tuples in the page are arranged according to ascending key order. So the binary halving is done on the directory entries. They have uniform length, because they only contain page-internal offsets. Binary search determines the next offset; use the offset to get to the tuple with the key value. Compare this key value to the search argument, and based on the outcome decide how to continue the binary search.

8. Without parallelism inside a transcation, one knows that log entries for opening and closing parentheses pertain to operations on the same B-tree. With parallelism, one has to additionally keep track of which B-tree index the parenthesis records belong to, because they will be interleaved arbitrarily on the log. Recovery must be able to maintain separate parenthesis stacks for each B-tree the transaction may have worked on in parallel to determine what must be undone physically, and what must be undone physically before a logical UNDO is possible.

10. There is no clean way to do it, but a kludge. If you define an B-tree index on a relation with a key that consists of a concatenation of all attributes, then the leaf level of this B-tree will contain replicas of all tuples (together with pointers to the original tuples), and the system will automatically maintain the consistency of the relation.

11. This is not a complete algorithm, but the information provided should be sufficient to complete the project. Applying key-range locking to the index level means this: If the inserted tuples fill a whole leaf page, then rather than keeping key-range locks for all these tuples, the whole value range in that page can be protected by acquiring a key-range lock on the entry of the index node that holds the pointer to the leaf with the inserted tuples. So far, so simple. The critical issue is that normally index nodes are not subject to key-range locking, so other transactions do not look for them and consequently do not respect them. Because key-range locks at the index level only make sense in special situations such as bulk inserts, one normally does not want to cope with them.

A mechanism to inform ongoing transactions about the fact that index-level key-range locking is in effect for a certain page can be designed as follows: each buffer access control block of a B-tree page, from the leaf level up, contains a control field with the following information: (1) Flag: this page is protected by a higher-level key-range lock. (2) Flag: this page protects lower-level pages with key-range locks. (3) Counter: number of key-range locks held on this page.

There is a problem with page replacement of pages participating in the index-level key-range locking protocol. Unless the control field were made part of the page and thus written to disk in case of replacement, the information that at the moment a different locking protocol is in effect would be lost. Writing it to disk as part of the page, on the other hand, would require such a page to be brought into the bufferpool again just to release a key-range lock. The easiest way to get around these difficulties is to fix all pages participating in index-level key-range locking in the bufferpool while the protocol is in effect. As soon as the counter in the control field returns to 0, the normal protocol can be used again.

Another important problem to consider is the following: Assume one leaf page is filled with newly inserted tuples, and the transaction proceeds to request an exclusive key-range lock on the corresponding entry of the index page. From now on, all references going through this index node must acquire a proper key-range lock (normally an intention lock) before going down to the leaf level. But what about those concurrent transactions (other than the inserting transaction) that have already used this index node to proceed to their leaf? These transactions do only have key-range locks at the leaf (i.e., tuple) level, but now it must be ensured that whatever they got is not in conflict with whatever somebody else may acquire later on at the index level. One option is to check all children of the index node to see if there are key-range locks at the leaf level and then install the appropriate index-level locks. This, however, may result in a high number of (unnecessary) I/O operations. A more feasible design is this: for all entries in the index node (other than the entry covering the leaf with the inserted tuples), acquire an IX lock *for the bulk insert transaction*. This lock is compatible with whatever other transactions may have locked at lower levels, simply because we know that none of these other transactions has an index-level key-range lock on this node. Hence all these other transactions could have acquired on the index node, had they known about the index-level key-range locking protocol, is an intention mode of some sort, which is compatible with IX. Requesting this intention mode for the inserting transaction also takes care of the case that later on the insert transaction will need further X-mode key-range locks in the same index node. The corresponding problems related to delete operations can be solved using this set of ideas.

12. Let us just consider the abnormal case where both attributes are strictly correlated. If the block size is 8 KB and if we can hold 1,021 pointers in one block (see exercise 8 in Chapter 13), then for a grid file of 40 GB there must be 4,783 directory blocks along the main diagonal. As a consequence, the total size of the directory is $4,783^2 = 22,877,089$ blocks. Given the block size of 8 KB, the directory comprises more than 187 GB, more than four times the size of the original—not a very attractive property.

PART SEVEN

System Surveys

It is not the critic who counts, not the man who points out how the strong man stumbled, or where the doer of deeds could have done them better. The credit belongs to the man who is actually in the arena; whose face is marred by dust and sweat and blood; who errs and comes short again and again; who knows the great enthusiasms, the great devotions, and spends himself in a worthy cause; who, at best knows in the end the triumph of high achievement; and who, at worst, if he fails, at least fails while daring greatly, so that his place shall never be with those cold and timid souls who know neither victory nor defeat.

TEDDY ROOSEVELT

16

Survey of TP Systems

16.1 Introduction

This chapter provides brief sketches of a few transaction processing systems. The systems have been chosen to give readers a sense of the commercial products that actually exist today; they exemplify many of the ideas presented in previous chapters. The sketches are careful to emphasize the interesting aspects of each system. They are not intended to compare the relative merits of systems.

Much of this presentation is historical, showing how the systems evolved over time. A typical transaction processing monitor and its infrastructure reflect the efforts of hundreds of people over several decades—thousands of person-years. Seen in this context, each is on the scale of a small Gothic cathedral. Any short sketch is likely to hide as much as it reveals.

Our criteria for picking systems was fairly simple. We picked the most popular ones, and we picked standards (LU6.2 and X/Open DTP) that we believe will define the behavior of future systems. The number of systems was also limited by the size of the chapter. Database systems, even though they provide transactions at the programming interface, are not considered. Database managers are viewed as resource managers in a transaction processing system.

16.2 IMS

IMS is the dominant database and data communication (DB/DC) system in use today—it has most of the data. It began in the late 1960s as an inventory tracking system for the U.S. moon landing effort. At that time, the hardware model was a half-mip processor with about 100 KB of memory, a few disk drives, and a cloud of remote keyboards, card readers, and printers as peripheral devices.

Prior to IMS, the processing model was largely an old master–new master tape-based approach. Online updates to indexed files was considered an advanced concept. Identical information was replicated in many files; access to data was through local or remote card reader/printers and batch jobs. IMS introduced an integrated DB/DC system. From the start, IMS provided a uniform programming interface to both the database and to terminals. The fundamental data model was that items consist of a rooted hierarchy of data segments—the

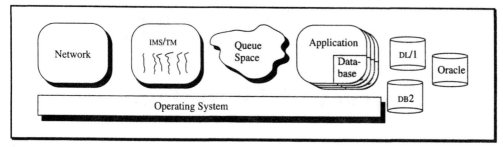

Figure 16.1: The overall structure of IMS. The operating system provides basic services to the network, the transaction manager, and the applications that use the IMS database. The rounded boxes represent processes. Not all the helper processes are shown. A small amount of terminal context is maintained by threads in the IMS/TM address space. This context is used to drive presentation services as well as input/output message switching. IMS maintains applications as one or more server classes driven via recoverable queues. The applications make calls to the IMS database system (DL/1) that runs as a protection domain of the application process. This gives protection and parallelism to application processes.

hierarchical data model. IMS applied this data model to both the terminal interface and the database interface.

Today, the typical IMS system has thousands of terminals distributed around the world, driving a large multiprocessor system with a disk-based database in the 100 GB range. There are only about 10,000 such systems, but they form the core transaction processing systems of virtually all large corporations.

It is a tribute to the original design, and to the IMS developers, that the system was able to evolve. The evolution is continuing. When this chapter was written, IMS was being repackaged as a transaction monitor and separate database, and the transaction monitor, network, and operating system were adopting support for a transactional RPC mechanism (LU6.2/APPC).[1]

IMS has two major parts: (1) IMS/TM (Transaction Management),[2] the transaction monitor that includes scheduling, authorization, presentation services, and operations functions; and (2) IMS/DB, better known as DL/1, a database system supporting a hierarchical data model. Applications running as servers in IMS usually access DL/1 databases, but they can also access other resource managers (e.g., DB2 and Oracle) and other operating systems services. As shown in Figure 16.1, applications can even access the network directly, thereby allowing remote procedure calls [IBM-IMS 1991].

16.2.1 Hardware and Operating System Environment

IMS is interesting in that it takes the *use-the-operating-system* approach rather than the *replace-the-operating-system* approach. IMS uses operating system processes, scheduling and protection, operating system files, program management (loading and binding), and operating system authorization. This is in contrast to CICS (discussed in Section 16.3.), which uses a single operating system process (address space and task) and then implements each operat-

---

[1] This interface is inherently a peer-to-peer protocol, but applications generally use it as a client-server TRPC (see Subsection 16.3.4, or Chapter 2, Subsection 2.4.1).

[2] This was called IMS/DC (Data Communications) until 1990.

ing system function specially within the address space. CICS implements its own processes (tasks, threads) within the address space, has its own program loader and binding, has its own scheduling and memory management, and so on. Each of these CICS functions is simpler and faster than the corresponding general-purpose operating system function. The IMS approach uses more hardware resources (i.e., more processor instructions and more bytes of memory), but it is more general and gives greater functionality than a single-process approach. The CICS approach makes it more portable across operating systems.

Let us use an example to contrast the two approaches. The IMS applications in Figure 16.1 operate in their own operating system processes. Thus, they can call any operating system service and are protected from one another. The failure of one application will not affect the others. By contrast, in Figure 16.5, all the applications run inside the single CICS process (address space). Each application runs as a thread in this address space, which is a single protection domain; as a result, each application can crash the others. A CICS application calling the operating system is making the request with the authority of CICS; if it calls DEALLOCATE FILE, that call is authorized as though it came from the CICS process. Applications in CICS should therefore not make direct calls on the operating system. This prohibition is enforced administratively; the CICS administrator reads any programs that are installed in the system he administers. This human filter occasionally allows dangerous programs into the system.

IMS runs only on the MVS operating system, which, in turn, runs on variants of the IBM 370 processor family (4300, 9370, 3090, System/9000, etc.). At a minimum, one of these systems has a processor, a main memory, some controllers, and a few disks. Figure 16.2 shows the other end of the spectrum: a collection of 16 MVS systems all sharing a terabyte disk farm of about 500 disks. Each MVS system controls up to six processors, a main store of about a gigabyte, and a page-addressable electronic swapping store of about 10 GB. In

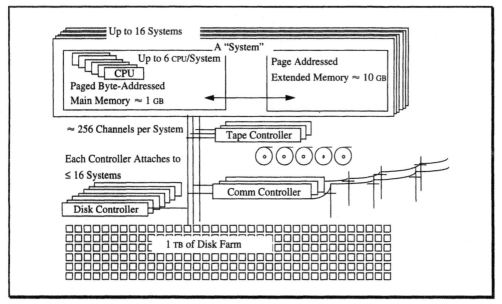

Figure 16.2. A large IBM hardware configuration. Many systems can share a common pool of disks and tapes. Up to 16 systems can be attached to the disk pool. Each system supports a section of the network.

addition, the system can access a pool of disk, tape, and communication controllers. Each of these controllers can be attached to up to 16 MVS systems, and each is an impressive processor in itself. For example, disk controllers have up to a gigabyte of electronic storage (to cache disk data) and contain one or more processors rated at 50 mips.

MVS provides a single-system image to processes running in a system. *Tasks* (the MVS term for processes) are the unit of dispatching, and each task runs in some address space. MVS and the hardware offer an efficient resource manager interface called *cross-memory services,* or more commonly, XA, for *cross-address space.* This mechanism allows an application to invoke a resource manager running in a different protection domain (address space). XA allows a process to efficiently switch from one address space to another, thereby protecting the resource manager from bugs in the calling application. The IMS database (DL/1) and the SQL database (DB2) both act as resource managers within a single MVS system. The subsystem and XA interfaces are public, allowing other subsystems (e.g., the Oracle database system) to act as resource managers.

MVS provides IMS with basic I/O services for peripherals. A basic file system, called VSAM, provides support for disks, file allocation, and simple access methods (unstructured, entry sequenced, relative, and keyed). It does not provide locking or recovery. The operating system is extended by many subsystems (resource managers) offering batch, time-sharing, networking, archiving, database, and transaction processing services. The operating system itself is increasingly being integrated with a repository (system dictionary) built atop the DB2 database system.

The focus here is on IMS and how IMS extends the operating system to support transaction processing. Thus, these other features are ignored.

16.2.2 Workflow Model

IMS originally adopted queued transaction processing as its basic computational paradigm. In this model, a message arrives containing a transaction code and a block of data. The transaction code is a short acronym for the transaction, like DBT to indicate a debit transaction. IMS/TM keeps a context descriptor for each known terminal or client. Based on this context descriptor and the transaction code, IMS/TM does presentation services on the input data, converting it to a hierarchical-data record. This data record is inserted into a queue for later processing by a server. Since these queues are recoverable objects, the insert generates a commit. Once the input message is formatted, inserted in the queue, and the insert is committed, IMS/TM acknowledges the input. The input message is then processed asynchronously.

Each input queue represents a service—all messages in the queue are similar. A server class is associated with each queue. All members of a server class are identical application programs running as standard operating system processes. These servers have the following typical structure:

```
read from queue space
do application logic and database work
insert reply in queue space
commit (spelled SYNC in IMS)
```

IMS/TM preallocates servers as part of startup or reconfiguration based on operator command. As the load changes, a server class may grow or shrink. The creation of servers may be periodic (e.g., once a day) to obtain the effect of batch processing. Having a preallocated pool of reusable server processes waiting for input from the network amortizes the process creation cost across many transactions and dramatically reduces the response time for each request. This *wait-for-input* style of processing was added to IMS in the mid 1970s and is usual today.

A server class (and its servers) may offer many services; that is, it may be able to accept input from several queues. An IMS scheduler assigns queued input messages to servers based on user-specified queue parameters, such as servers-per-queue, message priority, and threshold queue depth.

Each application (server) waits for something to appear in queue space, then processes the message and replies by inserting the result(s) in queue space. The application uses DL/1 (Data Language/1) to manipulate both the hierarchical records in queue space and the hierarchical records in the database. Thus, DL/1 is the universal language for both IMS/DB and IMS/TM.

While queued processing has some drawbacks, one of the benefits provided by IMS is that messages from a program can be sent to other programs (servers) in the same or different systems as separate transactions. The application interface for sending and receiving these messages is the same as for sending and receiving messages to and from terminals. Insert enqueues a message; delete read dequeues a message.

The IMS queue manager is a resource manager with a completely different recovery strategy from that of DL/1. Since the queue manager deals with real operations, it defers all updates to phase 2 of commit. The fact that these two resource managers had to cooperate forced IMS to pioneer a (centralized) implementation of the two-phase commit protocol.

Applications can also make SQL calls to DB2, Oracle, or Teradata; can make operating system calls to MVS; and can even make remote procedure calls to other systems using the MVS support for RPC provided by the network (see the discussion of program-to-program communication in Section 16.3). All these calls are implemented by XA (cross memory) calls, which provide a uniform interface to the caller and allow the callee to run in a protection domain (address space) separate from the caller. Unlike most domain switch mechanisms that require thousands of instructions, the MVS domain switch is equivalent to less than 100 instructions.

When the output message is committed (when the server calls SYNC), IMS/TM formats the output message and presents it to the terminal. When the terminal acknowledges the output message, the message is deleted from queue space and the delete is committed.

As described, processing an IMS transaction actually consists of three ACID transactions: (1) insert in queue space, (2) do work, and (3) deliver response. This model captures the needs of most applications, provides excellent message integrity (exactly-once processing and at-least-once delivery), and has some real benefits for scheduling. But the queued transaction paradigm makes conversational and distributed transactions quite difficult. The queued model also has a significant performance cost, since each request generates three commit steps.

To save the two extra commits, IMS offers an *Expedited Message Handling* option, which inserts the input message in queue space without acknowledging it to the terminal or client. The application then runs, consuming the input message and generating a reply. This is all part of one transaction (ACID unit). IMS/TM then delivers the output message to the client and gets the next input message. This is the transaction flow of expedited message handling (see Figure 16.3):

deliver previous response
get next input
process input
generate response
commit

Expedited message handling solves the performance problem of pure queued processing (replacing three commits with one) while still maintaining output message integrity. Output messages are delivered at least once, because the queues are durable. The use of sessions and session sequence numbers eliminates duplicates and, in doing so, yields exactly-once processing of input messages and exactly-once delivery of output messages.

To ameliorate the conversational and distributed transaction processing limitations of a queued processing model, IMS supports two transaction routing mechanisms: (1) an IMS proprietary protocol called Multiple Systems Coupling (MSC) that routes messages among IMS systems, and (2) an "open" protocol called Inter-System Communication (ISC) that will forward an input message to another IMS system, to a CICS system, or to another vendor's system (e.g., DEC, Tandem, Unisys). The forwarding logic is based either on the input transaction code or on a user-written subroutine that analyzes the message and forwards it to the other site. Once launched at the remote IMS/TM node, the application is free to access the local IMS/TM queue space and to call on other local resource managers. There is no support for conversational transactions, but there is excellent support for pseudo-conversational transactions and for transaction context. For example, terminal-related "scratch-pads" are persistent DL/1 data objects that can travel with a transaction request routed to any

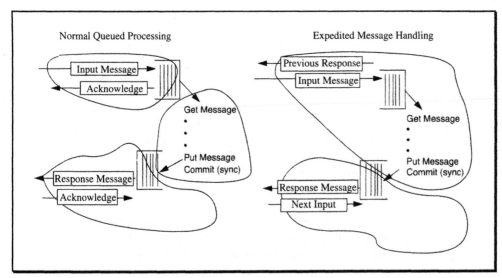

Figure 16.3: Asynchronous message processing versus Expedited Message Handling.   IMS queued messages may be immediately acknowledged, then processed at a later time. This gives rise to three ACID transactions shown as shaded areas in the left part of the figure. If the transaction response time is short and has a single output message, then the response message can acknowledge the previous input message, and the next input message can acknowledge the response. As shown in the figure at the right, this Expedited Message Handling reduces the number of ACID transactions per input by a factor of three.

connected IMS system. The application may suspend and resume conversations based on these scratchpads.

In addition to message-driven programs, IMS also supports access to resource managers from interactive sessions—the MVS Time Sharing Option (TSO) programs—and from batch programs. Many utilities run in this background batch mode. These programs have access to IMS services, including the databases (DL/1, DB2, etc.) and queue space.

IMS has always supported an extensive set of *exits* that allow user-written programs to participate in key steps of the transaction processing system. For example, users can write exits to route transactions, encrypt records, handle errors, or simulate Extended Recovery Feature (XRF) takeovers.

16.2.3 Program Isolation

IMS pioneered many of the concepts presented in this book. The IMS developers are credited with inventing logical views of data, write-ahead logging, the use of LSNs for idempotence, change accumulation utilities, active disk sharing, main storage databases, and field calls (escrow operations). They are also credited with early implementations of record locking and two-phase commit. There is only space here to highlight a few of those ideas.

An IMS DL/1 application declares at compile time what record types it will access and whether the access is for read or for read and write. The initial implementations of IMS did *intent scheduling*, which means they did record-type locking. If two programs updated the same record type, then they would not be scheduled concurrently. This is equivalent to table-granularity locking for relational systems. By 1970, this was clearly inadequate for online systems, and record-granularity locking was added. The chosen implementation provided shared and exclusive record locks with a kind of degree 2 isolation (cursor stability). At the same time, the recovery system was rewritten to include two logs: a REDO log for restart recovery and an UNDO log (called the *dynamic log*) for transaction backout—in this era the REDO log was duplexed on tape, while the dynamic log was simplexed to disk. Two resource managers wrote to the REDO log: the database system, IMS DL/1, and the queue space manager, IMS/TM. These two resource managers each used a different recovery strategy. The database manager used the force-at-commit protocol, flushing all dirty pages at phase 1 thereby avoiding the need for any redo in case of a restart. DL/1 pioneered the use of log sequence numbers for UNDO-REDO idempotence and the use of write-ahead logging. On the other hand, the queue manager used a very modern UNDO-REDO strategy, generating any needed log records at phase 1 and initiating message delivery at phase 2. It used compensation logging to clean up in case of transaction abort. This whole package, called IMS Program Isolation, was delivered in about 1974.

Today, IMS logging is disk-based, with tape used only for archival storage. The dynamic log has merged with the online log to reduce I/O at commit. Group commit is also supported, as is the write-ahead dataset to minimize log write latency (see Chapter 9, Subsection 9.4.7). Extensive utilities are provided for fuzzy dump, incremental recovery of data, and change accumulation of logs to minimize restart time.

16.2.4 Main Storage Databases and Field Calls

IMS users found simple record locking inadequate for high-volume transaction processing systems. In the mid-1970s, the IMS group set the goal of performing 100 transactions per second (tps) on a 370/168 dual processor (about 5 mips). Doing this required much streamlining of code and some new algorithms. The result, called IMS FastPath, introduced group commit, field calls, main-storage databases, and expedited message handling.

In essence, IMS FastPath implemented a new database system with its own data manipulation language and its own recovery system. It became the third resource manager in the IMS family. Traditional DL/1 calls are supported on this database, but the high-performance option was to use *field calls* (escrow operations). When the field call is issued, the predicate is tested and a log record is generated. At phase 1 of commit, a lock on the record is acquired, and the predicate is again tested. If all predicates pass, the transforms are applied and the locks released—all as part of phase 1 of commit. This is an application of the last-resource-manager optimization. Notice that FastPath does not implement true escrow locking that avoids aborts at phase 1 of commit (see Chapter 7, Section 7.12).

FastPath also introduced grouped commit to batch the log writes of many transactions into a single pair of log writes. The main-storage database had an interesting recovery strategy: there was no UNDO logging for field calls (only a REDO log). At system checkpoints, the main storage database is written as a fuzzy dump Ping-Ponged to one of two copies of itself. At restart, the most recent good copy is read into memory, and then a REDO scan of the log is run. IMS FastPath also has an insert-only database (Data Entry Data Base/Sequential Dependents) that has deferred updates with only a REDO log. Consequently, FastPath itself is a pure deferred-update, REDO-only resource manager. In the end, the FastPath group came very close to its goal, achieving about 97 tps on a 370/168 dual processor system in 1976.

16.2.5 Data Sharing

Demands for IMS performance grew much faster than either processor or software speedups. Shared memory multiprocessors were one solution to this problem. Over time, IBM delivered two-way, then four-way, and then six-way shared-memory multiprocessing. But this did not keep pace with demand. As a result, IMS allowed two different IMS systems running on different MVS systems to access and update a disk-resident database shared between the two systems (see Figure 16.2). That means that either system can update a particular page of the database and that the log records for a particular page may be found in the logs of two different systems. Only traditional DL/1 data can be shared in this way; queue space, main storage databases, sequential dependents of data entry databases, and DB2 databases cannot be shared in this way.

This idea of sharing data between multiple semi-independent recovery systems is generically called *data sharing*. It gives rise to many interesting locking and recovery problems. IMS uses page-granularity locks to regulate page consistency among IMS systems. These locks are provided by the inter-system resource lock manager (IRLM), sometimes called the *global lock manager*. Locking is done on names, but a hash of the name is used for performance reasons. IRLM supports shared and exclusive locks. There is a token that allows the token owner to propose updates to the shared hash table; the hash table is replicated at each system. The token, along with new lock requests, circulates in the system several times a second.[3] When the local lock manager needs a lock on a shared object, it hashes the lock name. There are three cases:

---

[3] This "pass-the-buck" algorithm may soon be replaced by a simpler and more general algorithm.

(1) Hash item is already reserved by this system.

(2) Hash item is reserved by others; in this case, add the reservation request to token buffer.

(3) Hash item is free; in this case, add the reservation request to token buffer.

When the token arrives with the new hash table and requests, the local lock manager tries to release any requested but conflicting hash entries and then tries to grant any new requests. This means that if a request is granted, both systems know about it. The lock manager then passes the token, new hash table, and new requests to the peer system.

This algorithm has been shown to perform well in many cases. If each system has good locality of reference, then each system acquires a subset of the hash buckets for "its half" of the database. Only occasionally does a transaction have to ask the other system for a lock. See Section 16.5.4 for the VAX cluster approach to data sharing.

The IRLM logic for handling system failures is complex. If one system fails, then all pages covered by the hash table elements locked exclusively by that system must remain locked until the system's transactions are recovered. This is why IRLM takes such a conservative approach to updating the hash table, insisting the peer system know about any new hash entries prior to granting them. Since DL/1 uses force-at-commit for the shareable resources, only transaction UNDO is needed. The logs are shared-disk resident, which makes it possible for the peer system to run recovery on the failed transactions. Once these transactions are reversed, the IRLM hash table entries of the failed system can be cleared. For media recovery, the journals of the two systems are merged in an equivalent of timestamp order.

16.2.6 Improved Availability and Duplexed Systems

IMS systems are generally big systems. As a consequence, they are constantly changing. Terminals and communication lines are being added or moved, disks are added, files grow, database fields and record types are constantly being added, application programs are added and repaired, and so on.

As late as 1980, making any such change to an IMS system required shutting the system down and restarting it with the new configuration. Over the decade of the 1980s, considerable effort went into allowing the system to grow and change while it was operating. This capability is generically called *online change*. At present, almost any aspect of an IMS system and of the operating system (MVS) and network (VTAM) can be changed while the system is operating. This may sound prosaic, but it did more than anything else to improve the availability of IMS.

A second major change aimed at improving IMS availability had to do with error handling. Originally, IMS was failfast. It had little error masking logic. As systems grew to support thousands of components, this created the problem that a failure anywhere could fail the entire system. For example, if 1 disk containing a file fragment was unavailable, then the entire file was marked unavailable, even though the 500 other disks containing fragments of the file were still available. If a page of a file was invalid, then the file was treated as invalid. IMS adopted several tactics to deal with this. (1) It allowed some data files (DEDBs) to be replicated (up to seven ways) in order to mask hardware faults. (2) It limited the granularity of failure by introducing the idea of data unavailability. Rather than marking a whole file as unavailable or invalid, only the missing parts (pages) were so marked. The rule was this: If a data item and its access path are there, then the program should be able to access the data; if the data item is not there or is invalid, the program should be informed and should be allowed to skip that "hole" in the data so that it can process the remaining data. (3) In a related vein, if a page write fails, IMS remembers the altered page via an internal mechanism, until media recovery is convenient. As a consequence of these approaches, a batch reporting program that scans a terabyte database may encounter a few invalid pages, but it can still process all the available information. Today, most other "big" database systems adopt a similar approach. This approach to missing data is particularly important for distributed systems, where some node or disk of a large distributed file may be unavailable.

IMS also masks faults by using a system pair mechanism. As the fault analysis in Chapter 3 pointed out, most unscheduled outages are due to software, environment, or operations mistakes. A cost-is-no-object solution would build two systems in two locations with two operations staffs, in the style of Tandem's RDF (see Subsection 16.4.3). Short of that, one would like two independent IMS systems in the same location. That is approximately what IMS/XRF (IMS Extended Reliability Feature) provides [IBM-IMS-XRF 1991].

In IMS/XRF there are two IMS systems operating approximately as system pairs (see Figure 16.4). There is only one copy of the database that resides in the pool of disks shared between the primary and the backup. Both the primary and the backup systems are in session with all active terminals. The terminal controllers see these sessions as a primary session and a backup session. The user at the terminal is unaware of the session pairs—the session pair logic is in the local terminal controller.

During normal operation, the primary IMS system performs as usual, and the terminal communicates only with the primary session. The backup system is a clone of the primary. It has all its server classes set up, is maintaining its data structures, and is generally pretending to be the primary, but without doing any actual work. The backup system is constantly performing many REDO "recovery" actions on its state, as though the backup were performing

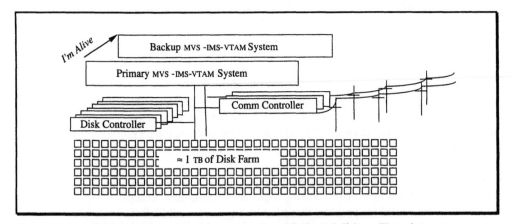

Figure 16.4. IMS/XRF provides a form of system pairs with shared disks. The primary IMS system modifies the database and generates log records. It continually sends *I'm Alive* messages to the backup system that is maintaining a copy of the system state by reading the disk log as it is generated. Both the primary and the backup have access to the disks and terminals. The primary is active, while the backup is passively tracking the primary's state changes. They are both in session with the terminals. If the primary fails, the backup aborts any active transactions and then continues the work. At takeover, the terminal (controller) must resolve duplicate messages (one from the primary session and one from the backup session) by using sequence numbers. The terminal user does not need to reenter any messages and is unaware of the switch. This is the standard process pair logic.

restart after a failure of the primary system. All the backup sessions are idle. The backup system scans the disk log and performs (redoes) any log records that would change the backup main memory state. Disk database recovery is only performed at takeover. As a result, the backup system state is fairly current with the primary.

IMS/XRF might be called a *hot standby system*. The backup carefully tracks the state of the primary in order to minimize takeover times. It tracks descriptor loading into pools, pre-allocates server classes, and tracks their growth. It tracks and performs authorization checks and file opens needed by the database. It tracks all terminal and intersystem sessions, message queues, and scratchpads. It also tracks locks, so that the backup can resume normal processing in parallel to transaction rollback at a takeover.

IMS/XRF uses three surveillance mechanisms to detect primary failure: (1) the primary sends *I'm Alive* messages to the backup via a communications session, (2) the backup looks for log records arriving on the shared disks, and (3) the backup looks at a special "heartbeats" on the restart dataset (indicating that the primary is checkpointing). Based on administrator-specified time limits, surveillance will trigger automatic takeover. The system designer can put the operator in the loop by setting the time limits very high.

When the backup decides that it is the new primary, the backup instructs the disk controllers to reject disk requests from the primary until the takeover is complete. This stops the primary from further accessing and updating the database and assures that the primary knows that a takeover has happened. In this case, the new primary completes the REDO scan and then begins an UNDO of any uncommitted transactions. Once REDO is complete, the backup system sends out an *I'm Here* message on the backup sessions that now become primary. If the terminal was expecting a response from the primary, it will now get that response from the backup session. The fact that input messages and output messages are recorded in recoverable queue space ensures that each acknowledged input message will be processed at least once and each committed output message will be delivered at least once. The use of sequence numbers and the coordination of sequence numbers between the primary and backup sessions ensures that the messages will be delivered and processed *exactly* once.

The whole issue of takeover is a subtle one. It has implications for the network (the backup session logic) and for the operating system. From the operating system point of view, when the backup becomes primary, its behavior changes radically. Instead of consuming almost no resources, it will suddenly be using huge quantities of processor, memory, I/O, and network resources. The operating system does scheduling based on recent history. At takeover, history is no guide to the future. Thus, MVS supports an interface that allows the backup system to suddenly say something to the effect of "Give me ⟨list of resources⟩ right away!" From the network point of view, the load changes radically, and the network must be aware of the session pairs and their more elaborate sequence number logic. This is an area of rapid evolution.

16.2.7 DB2

DB2 is IBM's implementation of SQL on its mainframes. It acts as a resource manager for either IMS, CICS, or programs running without any transaction monitor. From the transaction processing point of view, DB2 implements a no-steal buffer manager, with write-ahead log. It has a private log (not shared with the transaction monitors). Locking is done at page and sub-page granularity, and DB2 supports the IRLM interface. As of 1991, DB2 does not support data sharing among MVS systems. CICS provides a DB2 XRF facility (but IMS does not). DB2 has excellent utilities for change accumulation and for recovery.

16.2.8 Recent Evolution of IMS

By 1991, IBM had substantially generalized IMS. The data communications and transaction processing components of IMS had been renamed IMS/Transaction Management. The database component was packaged as a resource manager. The operating system and networking software have been extended to support the invocation of transaction programs (MVS/APPC) but do not yet support SYNCPT (ACID). A remote duplicate database facility, RRDF, was added to IMS; it is similar in style to the RDF facility described in Subsection 16.4.3.6.

IMS supports many application generators, software engineering tools, and administrative tools. Much of the evolution has been in the area of these higher level capabilities, and in system management.

16.3 CICS and LU6.2

CICS is the most popular transaction processing monitor, while LU6.2 is an IBM de facto standard transactional session protocol. This section first sketchs the structure and functions of CICS. It then gives a brief overview of LU6.2 and how it is used by CICS.

16.3.1 CICS Overview

The original (1968) implementation of CICS has been ported to the many derivatives of OS/360 and of DOS/360 (e.g., MVS and DOS/VSE), and it has also been implemented on OS/2, AS/400, and UNIX.

The early success of CICS was largely due to the approach it took toward the operating system. CICS and all its applications run in a single common operating system address space (see Figure 16.5). A single operating system process runs the entire CICS system, its applications, and its services. CICS makes minimal demands on the operating system and is therefore highly portable from one operating system to another. CICS services are typically 10 times less expensive than the corresponding operating system service. For example, CICS can create a process (thread) in less than 1,000 instructions and can dispatch a thread in less than 500 instructions. Few general-purpose operating systems can match these numbers. CICS achieves this performance at the expense of generality. For example, the processes have no protection, and the scheduler is a simple uniprocessor scheduler.

A second reason for the popularity of CICS has been its openness to other subsystems (resource managers). Early on, each database system vendor discovered that he could install his product as an "application" in the CICS environment, thereby coupling a database system with a TP monitor. As a consequence, CICS quickly had many different database systems attached to it (notably DL/1, System 2000, Mark IV, Adabase, and Cullinet).

At first these attachments were fairly ad hoc, often running inside the CICS address space. This led to real fault diagnosis and containment problems. The single CICS address space contained CICS, the database systems, and the applications. If there was a software

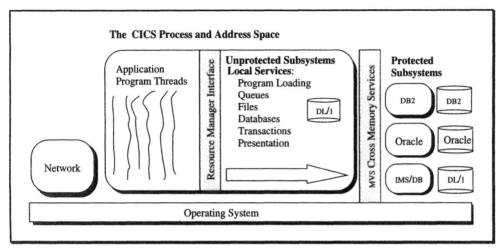

Figure 16.5: CICS runs all applications and services inside one address space. Resource managers may opt to run as part of the address space (in this example, it is DOS DL/1) or in a separate address space. All applications run as threads within the address space. CICS services and all resource managers are accessed via the resource manager interface.

bug, the address space would fault, and it was difficult to diagnose the source of the problem. In addition, the database products learned more and more about CICS internals and began to read and modify CICS control blocks (which are all visible in the address space). When the next version of CICS changed the definitions of these control blocks, the database products failed in exotic ways.

CICS developed a resource manager interface, so that subsystems could have a clean and well-designed interface to its services. The resource manager interface has two aspects: (1) the CICS-RM calls that are used to start, stop, and recover the resource manager, and (2) the application-RM calls that are used to invoke the resource manager. Initially, this applicaton-RM mechanism was intended for resource managers that cohabit the address space with CICS. With time, the resource manager interface was generalized, allowing resource manager stubs in the CICS system to invoke protected resource manager processes, either via interprocess communication or via cross-memory services (XA). This interface allows resource managers to run in separate address spaces, improving fault containment and security.

The resource manager concept evolved from CICS to be the basis for structuring DB2, and it eventually became the structuring concept for X/Open DTP (see Section 16.7). It is a key structuring concept for operating systems.

CICS was also the first commercial system to offer transaction-protected distributed computing. The CICS Inter-System Communication model evolved into what became part of IBM's standard protocol for program-to-program communications. This protocol is variously known as SNA LU6.2 or APPC (for Application Program to Program Communication). LU6.2, in turn, was the inspiration for OSI-TP, an ISO standard for transaction commit protocols.

The CICS application programming (API) interface for Inter-System Communication has not been widely adopted. IBM has four other APIs to LU6.2, giving a grand total of five! The other four are (1) CPI-C (Common Programming Interface-Communications), the SAA standard that derives from the VM/370 design and also exists in OS2/EE, (2) APPC/PC, an interface implemented on MS/DOS, (3) MVS/APPC, and (4) a variant of APPC for the AS/400.

16.3.2 CICS **Services**

CICS is a self-contained programming environment. It provides operating systems services, database services, presentation services, authorization, and a debugging environment. Many application generation systems have been built atop CICS to automate aspects of the development and maintenance process [IBM-CICS 1991].

From the programmer's viewpoint, CICS offers the following features:

Presentation services. These map logical input-output messages to and from device-specific formats. For example, a logical message can be sent to almost any terminal type, and CICS will produce the appropriate physical message and deliver it to the device.

Session services. These provide an open() { read() I write() } close() interface to allow a transaction program to converse with intelligent devices or processes.

Storage. CICS provides two different storage managers: *temporary storage* and *transient data*. These two storage managers are high-performance databases optimized to store terminal context or queues of input or output messages.

Temporary storage objects are optionally transaction protected; this means that object changes are logged to a journal, and the object is reconstructed at a system restart. Temporary storage is used to pass data among programs. CICS provides resource managers for terminal and transaction context, transaction routing, and even queues of transaction requests being routed to other nodes. These resource managers implement their objects in temporary storage.

Transient data is a different storage manager with its own recovery mechanism. Its major clients are various queue managers provided by CICS. Transient data supports either no recovery (unprotected object), transaction recovery (logical recovery), or redo of all logged operations (physical recovery). Transient data provides access to external storage devices (tapes, spool files, and even printers).

Files. A simple database system with sequential, indexed, and direct file access is provided by CICS as a service. Files may be transaction protected or not. Locking is at record granularity, degree 2 isolated, and it uses timeout for deadlock detection.

Transaction management. CICS registers resource mangers, allows them to join transactions, and informs them of significant transaction events (commit, rollback). It resolves in-doubt transactions at restart. It coordinates system startup, shutdown, and transaction termination.

Journals. CICS uses journals for recovery. Consistent with CICS's open design, applications can create new journals and can read and write journals. At restart, CICS optionally invokes a program, passing it the journals of aborted transactions. This allows applications to perform recovery at restart.

Recovery. CICS supports three forms of recovery: transaction abort, system shutdown and restart, and system crash and restart. CICS recently (1991) added support for recovery from an archive copy, which allows media recovery if the online version of the system is damaged. Prior to this addition, CICS queues and files were occasionally lost. CICS supports a hot standby system, XRF, in the style of IMS (see Subsection 16.2.6).

Program management.   Transaction application programs are registered with CICS; thereafter, they can be invoked by clients. CICS manages the linking, loading, and execution of such programs. Programs are written so that many threads can execute a program concurrently. Programs can invoke (call) one another directly or can put messages in queues to invoke a second program (transaction) asynchronously.

Threads.   When a new request arrives (from a client or a queue), CICS first authorizes the request and then creates an execution thread to process the request. Each thread has a priority (sum of operator and program priority). CICS schedules threads with a non-preemptive priority scheduler. If the request arrives via LU6.2, it may carry a TRID, and the new thread will be part of the calling transaction.

Authentication and authorization.   Both a password and a challenge-response mechanism are offered by CICS to authenticate clients. Once a client is authenticated, it is given a subset of 24 security classes (class 1 is "public"), as specified in a security table. For example, a particular client might get security class set {1, 5, 9, 11, 22}. Each application program and each other object has a security class. The client must have that class in his set in order to access the object. CICS optionally allows a third party to perform authentication.

These are the native programing features of CICS. Almost all these resource managers allow the customers to add logic to the resource manager in the form of exits. For example, the file system has exits to allow the customer to add new hash algorithms for associative lookup and to add encryption for data security. In addition, CICS offers an operations interface to configure and operate the system, as well as a trace and debug facility to allow programers to test their programs. Also, the resource manager interface connects CICS to myriad database systems (notably DL/1, SQL/DS, and DB2 from IBM).

16.3.3 CICS Workflow

CICS is a direct transaction processing system. When a message arrives from a terminal, CICS examines the message header and the terminal descriptor to determine the name of the transaction application program to be run; either the header or the terminal descriptor can specify the name. CICS then checks to see if the client is authorized to run the transaction application program. If not, the security violation is logged, and the request is rejected with an error message. If the client has authority to run the transaction application program, a thread is created to run the associated program, and the terminal (client) is marked as "owned" by that thread. The thread, which is passed the input message and terminal name, runs under the security class of the authenticated user. All accesses to objects are checked against the client's security class.

The application program can act on the request and reply, interact with the client as a conversational transaction, or simply queue the request for later processing and return to the client. If the application program accesses protected (transactional) objects, then the transaction must eventually commit (called *syncpoint* in CICS) or abort. All resource managers involved in the transaction can use CICS journals or can keep a private journal for logging. All the resource managers that have joined the transaction will be invoked by the CICS recovery manager at commit and abort. When the application program exits to CICS, the output message is delivered.

The application program makes requests to CICS services and to other resource managers. All these calls fall in the scope of one transaction, called a *logical unit of work* in CICS.[4] These transactions offer both database integrity and message integrity.

CICS message integrity works as follows: If a transaction is protected, then the first input message and all output messages are logged. Sending the last output message is deferred to phase 2 of commit. At restart, the last output message of committed transactions will be resent if it has not been acknowledged. In addition, the first input message will be reprocessed if the transaction was aborted and if the logged input message survived restart. This logic is comparable to the IMS message integrity mechanism.

CICS queues are quite interesting. A queue can be directed to either a program or a terminal. Terminal-related queues buffer output messages directed to busy terminals. Program-related queues cause a transaction program to be invoked whenever a queue becomes too full (so-called *trigger queues*) or whenever a certain time has elapsed (*interval-control queues*). Program-related queues can also be used to invoke batch programs.

CICS application programs can call host operating system services directly, but these calls must all be non-blocking (they must not call the operating system wait routine). If the call did block, that would block CICS and the entire address space. CICS is multiplexing this process among all the different threads. Since most operating systems offer very few non-blocking services, the application should call CICS, and CICS, in turn, will simulate the operating system service. Any waits involved in the service will allow other threads to execute. If the operating system offers inexpensive multi-threading, operating systems facilities can be used, but to date the performance of general-purpose thread interfaces have been unacceptable.

16.3.4 CICS Distributed Transaction Processing

The discussion so far has focused on a single CICS system. In fact, CICS often runs in a distributed configuration. Each CICS system manages a partition of the database and of the terminal network. Transactions in one CICS system either can be routed to another system or can do remote procedure calls to services or applications in another system.

The simplest configuration is to have multiple CICS systems running as processes on a single operating system. These CICS processes communicate via operating system calls based on shared memory. This memory-to-memory communication is typically much more efficient than the corresponding LAN or WAN communication through an SNA network (5,000 versus 25,000 instructions per message pair). This shared-memory configuration is called Multi-Region Operation (MRO).

MRO allows a big CICS system to be decomposed into smaller ones, resulting in better fault containment. As a rule, each organization gets a separate CICS system. Debug and program test get a separate system. Often batch and online application programs are segregated into separate systems so that online applications can be given high (operating system) priority, while batch applications are given low (operating system) priority. The main problem with decomposing a CICS system into many regions is that managing and operating two re-

---

[4] Logical unit of work (LUW), meaning transaction, has nothing much to do with SNA Logical Units like LU6.2, meaning a transactional session, or LU3, meaning a character-oriented CRT session. *Logical unit* is another overloaded term.

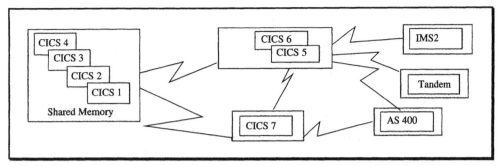

Figure 16.6. CICS distributed transaction processing options. Multiple CICS systems can cohabit the same machine and communicate via memory-to-memory messages provided by the operating system; this is called Multi-Region Operation (MRO). Alternatively, CICS systems in multiple computers connected by IBM's WAN protocol (SNA LU6.2) allow CICS to access remote systems and even IMS (or non-IBM) systems; this is called Inter-System Communication (ISC).

gions is about twice as hard as managing and operating one region. In addition, the programmer must be aware of which data is in which region, since CICS does not provide location transparency. Rather, if an object (file, queue, application) is remote, then the local administrator must give it a local alias, and the local program must access the remote object via the local alias. Maintaining the aliases is a manual and error-prone task.

If CICS systems are not co-located, then a LAN or WAN communications protocol must be used. CICS uses IBM's SNA LU6.2 protocol to communicate with other CICS systems. Because the definition of LU6.2 is public, any other system can masquerade as a CICS system. In Figure 16.6, several different systems are participating in the CICS network. When CICS systems communicate using LU6.2, the configuration is called Inter-System Communication (ISC).

The application programming interfaces to MRO and ISC are identical and are generically called Distributed Transaction Processing (DTP). The application gets transparent access to remote resources (queues, files) by accessing local objects that are actually aliased to remote objects. Remote program access is a send/receive model and, therefore, is different from the local call/return model of local programs. This difference gives rise to a trichotomy of distributed transaction processing:

Transaction routing. Based on a transaction code (or queue, or user-written procedure), an input message can be routed to an application on another system for processing. A *relay* application acts as the surrogate to pass messages between the client and the application server.

Function shipping. By setting up aliases, CICS operations on temporary data, queues, terminals, and files are converted to transactional remote procedure calls that are executed at remote systems. The calls are sent to a *mirror*, a CICS-supplied transaction program that reissues the request as a local request (see Figure 16.7). The fact that the mirror is remote is hidden from the caller. Communication with the mirror is via an LU6.2 session.

Program-to-program communication. Also known as *peer-to-peer communication*. If an application wants to invoke a remote application program as part of this transaction, it must ALLOCATE the remote application program and then either SEND it data,

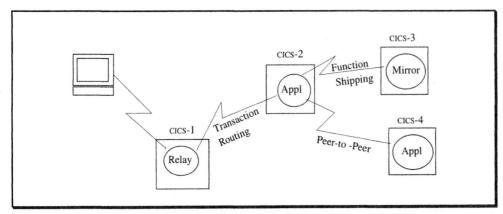

Figure 16.7: Transaction routing, function shipping, and peer-to-peer communications in CICS. Transaction routing uses a relay transaction to mediate between the application and the terminal if the application is remote. Function shipping uses a mirror application to execute CICS operations on remote objects. The mirror receives a TRPC from the application and invokes the operation locally. Peer-to-peer communication is used when the application consists of two or more user-written programs that cooperate to execute the transaction.

RECEIVE data from it, or CONVERSE with it (a combined SEND & RECEIVE). Once the application is complete, it calls SYNCPT, and the remote application may vote on the syncpoint. This program-to-program communication model is based on LU6.2 (see Subsection 16.3.5).

Program-to-program communication is the subject of the next subsection. There is little to say about transaction routing, but there are a few issues surrounding function shipping. If the remote system does not support the two-phase commit protocol, then CICS is forced to use the last-resource-manager trick to allow that system to become the commit coordinator. This means that only one such "closed" system can participate in a transaction. CICS uses this technique to allow applications to access IMS systems. A CICS transaction can atomically update many CICS systems and at most one IMS system as part of one transaction.

CICS uses a heuristic commit mechanism to resolve in-doubt transactions. In case the commit blocks due to a node or network failure, each transaction has the option to heuristically commit, abort, or wait. The default is to heuristically abort. A second option is to heuristically commit if the transaction is in doubt. A third option is to do it right, that is, wait for the coordinator to resolve the transaction. This requires keeping uncommitted updates locked until the session is recovered and the coordinator announces the outcome. This option is available in one special case: transactions involving no MRO and consisting entirely of inserts and deletes to temporary storage queues. The queued work waits for the coordinator to resolve the transaction. As it stands, the default commit logic of CICS does not provide atomicity in case of failures; rather, it simply detects inconsistency at restart if the heuristic decision does not match the coordinator decision.

16.3.5 LU6.2

LU6.2 provides transactional peer-to-peer communication between applications running under two transaction managers (typically CICS). In IBM's networking terminology, there are physical units (PUs, or boxes), and logical units (LUs, or programs). CICS, for example, is a logical unit. Some logical units have no standard personality; one speaks to them with a raw, session-level protocol, the so-called LU0. Other logical units have a very specific personality. For example, LU1 is a printer, and LU2 is an IBM 3270 CRT display with its forms-oriented input-output program. The original LU6 was a protocol invented by CICS long ago to describe its personality as a TP monitor. The protocol was revised in 1980, and the result is called LU6.2 [IBM-LU6.2 1991].

Each TP monitor and terminal in the network has a unique name, called its LU name. The name has the general format network.node. A typical name for a CICS system running on Bruce Lindsay's AIX (UNIX) workstation might be IBM_Almaden.Lindsay. A typical name for a CICS system running on a server machine at Yorktown might be IBM_Yorktown.TestCICS.

Transaction programs are registered with the TP monitor. Suppose the debit/credit transaction were registered under the transaction program name DebitCredit at the server CICS system. Then a program running under CICS at Bruce Lindsay's workstation could invoke that program by executing the CICS verb[5]

```
EXEC CICS   ALLOCATE DebitCredit @ IBM_Yorktown.testCICS.
            DATA "this is the startup string"
            USERID "Bruce Lindsay"
            PASSWORD ...
            RETURNING sessionid;
```

This operation has many effects. It sends a message from Almaden to the named LU at Yorktown to establish a session to that server. The message carries the client authority (a password, or the first step of a challenge-response protocol), the name of the desired service (DebitCredit), and many other parameters. The server authenticates the client, looks up the service name (transaction program name), checks the client's authority to access the service, forks a process (thread) executing that service, registers the incoming trid (passed in by the client) with the local transaction manager (a CICS component), joins the server to the transaction, and then dispatches the server with one parameter pointing to the first message and another pointing to the LU6.2 session connecting the server thread to the client. On the client side, the ALLOCATE sets up the client half of the session and returns a session ID to the client, so that the client can now send messages to the server.

Both the client and server are now executing. If this is a context-free RPC-style call, the server can execute the following code:

```
status = do_debit_credit(input message);    /* execute DebitCredit transaction          */
                                             /* it will access & update the database based on */
                                             /* the input params.                        */
if ( status = OK)                            /* if updates are successful,               */
    EXEC CICS SEND DATA                      /* send rpc response                        */
        SESSION sessionid                    /*    via session (=conversation) to client */
        DATA rpc_reply;                      /*    here is the actual data message       */
EXEC CICS RETURN                             /* tell CICS that server is done            */
    COMMIT status;                           /* status has commit decision:              */
                                             /* false: starts abort of client transaction */
                                             /* true: causes node to enter prepared state */
```

---

[5] In the interest of exposition, we are taking some liberties with the EXEC CICS syntax.

On the client side, following the ALLOCATE step, the code might read:

```
EXEC CICS PREPARE TO RECEIVE       /* get ready to read the server        */
    SESSION sessionid;             /*    via the new session              */
EXEC CICS RECEIVE DATA             /* issue the read                      */
    SESSION sessionid              /*    via the new session              */
    DATA data                      /*    here is the server data          */
    STATUS status codes;           /*    and status codes                 */
if (!status)                       /* if server aborted the transaction   */
    goto panic;                    /*    then panic                       */
update local data based on reply   /* else perform local part of transaction */
EXEC CICS SYNCPT;                  /* and initiate commit                 */
```

This example shows how CICS is routinely used to get a very efficient TRPC mechanism. The server is created, runs, prepares to commit, and replies—all as part of one message pair. In fact, this message flow piggybacks on the ALLOCATE message flow. A second round of messages is needed to execute the syncpoint logic (to send the commit decision to the server).

This example is quite simple and shows how well-suited LU6.2 is to the TRPC protocol. The real strength of LU6.2, however, lies in its use as a peer-to-peer protocol. If our Debit-Credit server had not returned, but rather had just done an EXEC CICS PREPARE TO RECEIVE, the client and server would be in session. They could converse by sending one another data. Finally, one of them could initiate commit by invoking SYNCPT. That would initiate an optimized version of the two-phase commit protocol on the transaction tree (all transactional sessions connected directly or indirectly to the transaction).

Something quite novel about this peer-to-peer protocol is that either side can initiate commit, and all participants (so long as they have not deallocated the session) get to vote on the commit. That is, the participants include all resource managers joined to the transaction at any node, as well as all transaction programs that have not already DEALLOCATED (already voted yes). When a transaction program invokes SYNCPT, that message is sent on every conversation attached to the transaction program. Thus, each neighbor gets a TAKE SYNCPT message. This repeats until all vote yes. In addition, CICS is collecting votes from local resource managers joined to the transaction.

SNA sessions are quite expensive to allocate, much as processes are quite expensive to create. Consequently, CICS tries hard never to allocate a session. Rather, it keeps pools of preallocated sessions to various other LUs. When an ALLOCATE request arrives, CICS tries to customize a preexisting session (setting up the server and some parameters) rather than allocate a whole new session. This gives rise to a distinction between *sessions*, which are bidirectional communication pipes between LUs, and *conversations,* which are transactional sessions between a client and server application program thread. These low-cost, high-function sessions are called *dialogs* in OSI-TP.

The LU6.2 servers usually support some standard services: process creation, queue operations, flat file operations, DL/1 operations, and SQL operations. Particular TP systems extend things in other ways. For example, CICS has the mirror and relay services. Of special interest is a service called CNOS (for Change Number Of Sessions). This little program started out as a way for one CICS system to negotiate with its neighbor on the size and polarity of the preallocated session pool used for conversations. Gradually, CNOS grew in function to include almost all CICS configuration parameters. In particular, it supports the following operations:

Install a new transaction program.

Read and alter the access control list on a transaction program.

Read and alter CICS startup and load control parameters.

Resolve in-doubt transactions and heuristic decisions at reconnect.

Because CNOS is just a service, any suitably authorized client can manage all the CICS systems in a large network by invoking CNOS programs at the nodes to be managed.

This discussion has glossed over many LU6.2 features. Since the focus here is on transactions, it is important to mention that each conversation is optionally transactional. Each conversation has one of three syncpoint levels specified when it is allocated:

Sync Level 0.   No message integrity beyond sequence numbers to detect lost or duplicate messages.

Sync Level 1.   Support for the CONFIRM-CONFIRMED verbs that allow client and server to do end-to-end acknowledgment.

Sync Level 2.   Support for the SYNCPT verb that provides ACID properties across distributed transactions.

Most implementations of LU6.2 do not support Sync Level 2. The IBM implementations on CICS and VM/370 are exceptions to this rule: they do support the SYNCPT verb.

16.4 Guardian 90

Guardian 90 is Tandem Computer's name for a market basket of products that together constitute a transaction processing system. These products include a message-based operating system (Guardian) with an integrated transaction manager (TMF), a server class manager and teleprocessing monitor (Pathway), a database system (NonStop SQL), and a WAN network (Expand). Tools for application development and operations are built atop this base. In addition, there is a large collection of gateways to other communications protocols (e.g., SNA, OSI, TCP/IP). In fact, these communications protocols constitute the bulk of the software [Tandem 1991].

Guardian 90 is unique in the following ways:

Message based.   It is a commercially available message-based operating system.

Transactional operating system.   It integrates transactions into the operating system kernel.

Server classes.   It supports direct (as opposed to queued) transactional interfaces to server classes.

Geographic distribution.   It supports server calls in a WAN distributed system.

Process pairs.   It supports process pairs for high-availability execution.

Transactional process pairs.   It combines process pairs with transactions.

16.4.1 Guardian: The Operating System and Hardware

Perhaps the best way to understand Guardian 90 is to take a historical view of its development. Initially, Guardian was a message-based distributed operating system supporting process pairs. The system came with some distinguished process pairs to act as device drivers for disks and communications lines. The basic configuration is shown in Figure 16.8.

The application of Figure 16.8 is commonly a program with this psuedocode:

1. read input from terminal
2. read and write database
3. write result to terminal.
4. goto 1

The first step is a remote procedure call (RPC) to the communications server process to read a terminal line (window). The second step consists of one or more RPCs to the disk servers that, in turn, implement a record management interface similar to that described in Chapter 15. The third step generates an RPC to the communication server to write the window.

To make the application fault tolerant, it is written as a process pair, and each application RPC is preceded by a checkpoint message to the backup application process (these checkpoint messages can be reduced). Message sequence numbers make the requests idempotent (see the discussion of process pairs in Chapter 3, Subsection 3.7.4.3).

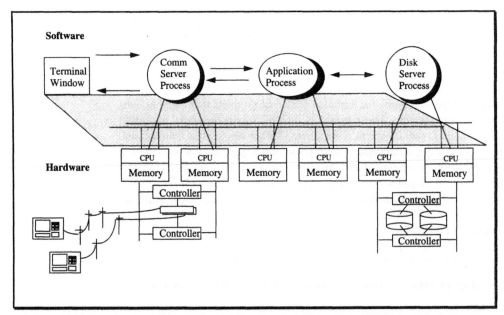

Figure 16.8: The basic structure of the Guardian operating system running on T16 hardware.
The T16 consists of a cluster of up to 16 processors connected via dual 160 Mb/s LANs (for simplicity, only 6 processors are shown). Each processor has one or more channels attached to one or more dual-ported controllers (only 4 channels and controllers are shown here). Each controller, in turn, attaches to one or more devices. At the software level (upper half of the figure), process pairs acting as device drivers externalize disk devices and communication lines; the backup process of the pair is shaded. The application process pair manipulates files and terminal windows by sending messages to the disk and communication server processes.

This message-based approach to a WAN, called Expand, evolved from Guardian; it lets a process communicate with any process in the entire network as though it were local to the cluster. The only restrictions on processes are that the backup of a process must be in a different processor on the same LAN as the primary process, and that a device driver must be in a processor electrically connected to the device. Otherwise, processes can be freely distributed in the cluster. For example a name server or other application process can be placed in any processor.

16.4.2 Pathway, Terminal Context, and Server Class Management

The process-pair approach to fault tolerance was a great advance in availability, although it required considerable sophistication on the part of the application programmer. As the complexity of applications grew, however, the complexity of process pairs began to exceed the powers of even the best programmers. As a simplification, *automatic* process pairs were introduced by the interpretive programming language SCOBOL. SCOBOL automatically generates checkpoint messages whenever they are required by the backup process to take over from the primary (as a rule, just prior to any RPC).

Since SCOBOL is an interpreter, and since it adopts a very conservative checkpointing strategy, it has a large performance penalty (about 1:100). However, SCOBOL's performance penalty was ameliorated by using it less and by making a virtue of its interpretive nature

To reduce the use of SCOBOL, applications are split into SCOBOL clients and native language servers, such as COBOL, Pascal, C, or FORTRAN servers. The servers run at full speed and are not process pairs; the clients run slowly, but they are fault tolerant and maintain the terminal context. In case of a fault, the client reissues the most recent server RPC. This only works if all server operations are idempotent.

To exploit the interpretive nature of SCOBOL, observe that many SCOBOL programs can safely be run as threads in a single operating systems process. Since each thread is running an interpretive language, the context and state of each thread is protected from all others. The SCOBOL interpreter offers *safe* threads (in contrast to CICS, which offers threads in a process that can destroy another thread's state). The use of SCOBOL multiplexes many terminals or input streams down to a few operating systems processes. These threads, in turn, make requests to pools of server processes programmed in conventional programming languages.

To obtain protection among server applications, each server runs as a single application process. SCOBOL multiplexes between the clients and these pools of servers.

The system implementing this design is called Pathway [Tandem-Pathway 1990]. Pathway has a monitor process pair that creates the clients and servers (server classes). The clients are SCOBOL executor processes. The servers are programmed in any convenient language. The server classes have a minimum population and a maximum population. If the load on the server class increases, the monitor expands the server class up to the maximum population. When the load decreases, it shrinks the class. If processors fail and servers are lost from the class, then new servers are created to replace the lost processes. The success of this design depends on the assumption that all servers are context free, that is, all requests are a single message (RPC).

Pathway clients, called Terminal Control Programs (TCP) are multi-threaded. They have one thread dedicated to housekeeping functions (listening to the monitor for inquiries and commands), but most of the threads are running SCOBOL applications. There are often 100 terminals or workstations multiplexed down to a single TCP. Such a TCP has 101 threads.

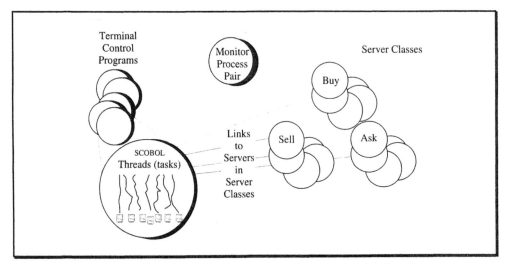

Figure 16.9: A Pathway system with three server classes (ask, buy, and sell).   The monitor process pair does dynamic load balancing by allocating links from clients to servers and, when necessary, growing or shrinking the server classes. Servers are not process pairs, but the clients (Terminal Control Programs) run as threads coded in a persistent programming language (SCOBOL) that manages the process-pair logic and multiplexes many persistent terminal contexts onto a single operating system process.

Each application thread has a context consisting of the SCOBOL execution stack (which includes the current state of the terminal window). The program can read and write its terminal and can RPC to any server. The RPC logic is interesting: TCPs have *links* to servers. A link is a preallocated, preauthorized session to a server. The TCP manages links as a list. On the first call to a server class, the TCP asks the monitor process for the name of a member of that class. The monitor returns such a name (perhaps creating the process first). Thereafter, the client sends all its RPCs for that server class to that server. If a second thread does an RPC to a server class while the link is busy, the TCP asks the monitor for a second link. In this way, a TCP can get many links to the same server class. When making a request, the TCP searches the link list in the order the links were granted. The TCP uses the first free link—the first one not currently used by another thread. This tends to create an unbalanced load on servers; some get many requests, others get none. The monitor tracks the outstanding links and uses them as a measure of the load on the server class. This is a very crude form of dynamic load balancing.

Pathway also supports an operator interface that allows server classes to be defined or redefined while the system is operating; this interface also provides performance statistics on the clients and servers. Much of Pathway code is dedicated to presentation services necessary in supporting many terminal types, from character-mode typewriters to a variety of formatted block-mode displays (notably IBM 3270 and the like) and, more recently, workstations that perform most of the presentation services and issue formatted RPC requests to the terminal control programs.

Pathway, in contrast to CICS and IMS, uses application threads programmed in SCOBOL to perform presentation services and to control the global transaction application flow. These threads execute in a TP monitor process much as CICS threads do. Application server steps are programmed in procedural languages like COBOL and C, combined with SQL. These programs execute as services in server classes. Their execution is tied to the client threads via the transaction atomicity mechanism. The structure of these server classes and servers is analogous to the structure of IMS servers or CICS transaction programs.

16.4.3 Transaction Management

Pathway still had a major problem: it provided availability, but it did not provide ACID execution properties. If a client failed, and the backup process rerequested the operation of a new server, then the database state could be inconsistent unless all server operations were idempotent. If a server failed during an operation, the situation was even more complex. Application programmers developed ad hoc techniques to deal with these exceptions. Each application programmer was implementing his own transaction mechanism for idempotence, isolation, and the DO-UNDO-REDO protocol. There was little hope that COBOL programmers, or even software gurus, could get this right.

Consequently, in 1980, a transaction mechanism was added to the message system and to the disk (database) servers. This transaction mechanism, called TMF (Transaction Monitoring Facility), allows any collection of processes in the LAN or WAN to participate in an ACID transaction [Tandem-TMF 1991]. Clearly, the transaction mechanism itself has to be fault tolerant and distributed. In addition, some processes, like the TCP, may be involved in several transactions at once (each terminal thread can start a transaction); consequently, the transaction mechanism must support multi-threaded processes. These requirements were unique at the time and gave rise to the following design.

16.4.3.1 Application Programming Interface to Transactions

Any process can begin a transaction at any time by calling the subroutine

trid = BeginTransaction();

This allocates a new transaction identifier and assigns it to the calling process. The process can commit this transaction by calling

status = CommitTransaction(Wait);

and abort it by calling

status = AbortTransaction(Wait);

The wait flag indicates whether the caller wants the commit or abort to be synchronous. If the wait flag is false, then the application can later call

status = StatusTransaction(trid);

to determine whether the transaction committed, aborted, or is still in the process of committing or aborting. In addition, there is a way to wait for a change in the status of any transaction associated with the process. Only the root can call commit; any participant can invoke abort.

Since a process can start many transactions or be in many transactions, the operating system maintains a list of all the transactions each process participates in. At any instant, only one of these transaction identifiers is *active* for the process. The application process can make another trid in the process list active by calling

status = ResumeTransaction(trid);

When a client invokes a server, a TRPC message is sent to the server. The Guardian message system appends the client trid to the message. The receiver's message system extracts this trid and appends it to the trid list of the server processes. When the server actually reads the message, the trid is implicitly made active. The following logic, then, either commits the inserts of both the client and the server or aborts both of their operations:

Client	Server
BeginTransaction();	
Exec SQL insert into T values (1,2,3);	
status = ServerCall(server, data)	
	read(data);
	Exec SQL insert into T values (3,4,5);
	reply(sqlcode)
if (status != OK) CommitTransaction();	
else AbortTransaction();	

When a process checkpoints to its backup, the current list of transactions is included in the checkpoint, so that both members of the process pair are participants in the transaction. The SCOBOL programming language does an excellent job of managing the recovery of such process pairs. It maintains two copies of the context of an idle client. When a client starts a new transaction, the SCOBOL interpreter makes a copy of the terminal context and works with that. If the transaction aborts, or if the primary process fails, the terminal context is returned to its initial state (both the primary and backup have a copy of this). At transaction commit, the new context is checkpointed to the backup, and then CommitTransaction() is issued. If the commit succeeds, the old context is discarded; if it fails, the new context is discarded. Thus, the terminal context is a persistent transactional object that can tolerate transaction, process, or processor failures. This logic in SCOBOL gives the application high availability (process pairs) and ACID execution (transactions). In addition, process pairs provide reliable message delivery to the terminal, since the process pair will continue sending the message to the client until the message is acknowledged.

16.4.3.2 Resource Manager Interface

This transaction mechanism was designed to be used by a single resource manager, the database server (disk processes). TMF is not an open transaction manager, so applications cannot participate in the two-phase commit protocol.

Each disk is externalized as a server class that manages the disk; these are the resource managers. The server classes accept file requests and SQL requests for the data on that disk. A client SQL library manages distributed SQL objects (multiple disks at multiple nodes) and manages RPCs to do index and directory maintenance as the fragment of a distributed object changes. The net effect of this design is that each disk server manages the locks and implements the DO-UNDO-REDO protocol for data on that disk.

When a disk server gets a request from a transactional client, the server joins the transaction. This raises the server's "flag" in phase-1 and phase-2 bit vectors kept for that transaction in that processor. Thereafter, the resource manger (disk server class) will be invoked at abort and at phase 1 and phase 2 of commit for that transaction.

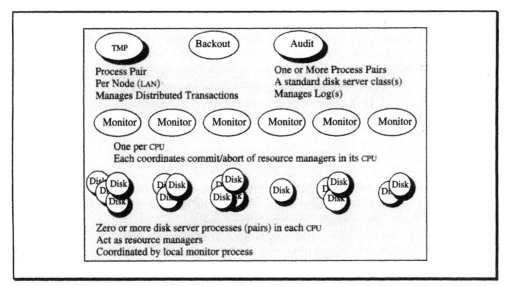

Figure 16.10: The core processes of a Tandem cluster. Each processor has a monitor process that coordinates the commit and abort of resource managers (disk servers) in that cluster. The TMP process global to the cluster pair handles distributed transaction commit and abort, receiving requests on incoming sessions and sending inquiries and replies on outgoing sessions, as in Chapter 11. The audit disk process is just an ordinary disk server that records log files. Backout processes are dynamically created to drive transaction undo in case a transaction aborts. They are persistent; if they fail, they are recreated and restarted. Process pairs are shown as shadowed circles in the diagram.

The disk server class caches the most recently used parts of the database in a main memory buffer pool. If this pool is large enough, the server can keep the whole database memory resident. It uses the two-checkpoint strategy to flush the cache to disk on a periodic basis.

The disk servers support both *audited* (transaction protected) and *unaudited* (not transaction protected) files. Unaudited files are used to store temporary files or to store data that uses the old master–new master recovery scheme (e.g., program files).

For transactional files, the disk servers implement fine-grain locking with three degrees of isolation (browse = $1°$, stable reads = $2°$, and repeatable reads = $3°$). The locks apply at record, key-range, or fragment (part of table) granularity. Shared and exclusive locks are supported with escalation and conversion logic in the style described in Chapter 8.

The disk servers generate log records as the transactions update the data. All these log records are generated by the server in a local buffer. This means that the log records do not get a log sequence number right away. The disk server maintains a local, monotonic sequence number, called the Volume Sequence Number (VSN). Each log record generated by the server gets a new (bigger) VSN that acts as a surrogate for the LSN in page headers and in the UNDO-REDO idempotence logic. In addition, the system uses a logical UNDO–physical REDO scheme (similar to the recovery scheme described in Chapter 15) to allow fine-granularity locking.

At phase 1 of transaction commit, or when the log buffer fills, the log records are sent to a disk server that stores the log for that disk (perhaps itself). Since the server is a process pair, the log buffer is first sent to the backup process and then to the logger (audit disk process).

The combination of transactions and process pairs was a big performance improvement. One checkpoint message at transaction commit (or buffer fill) routinely replaces 5 or 10 checkpoint messages in the non-transactional design. In addition, the use of write-ahead log made almost all disk writes asynchronous. One benefit of converting from a checkpointing strategy to a transactional strategy was to reduce disk I/O and checkpoint messages by a factor of 3, and message bytes by a factor of 5. This resulted in an overall throughput improvement of 40% [Borr 1984]. As a result, transactions actually improved performance while providing more functionality.

16.4.3.3 Log Manager

Any disk can store TMF recovery logs. The log files themselves are "ordinary" unstructured files. Generally, each cluster has only a single logger and, consequently, a single log, but it is possible to have multiple logs per system. This feature, however, is rarely used.

The logger accepts a batch of log requests from a disk server, appends them to the log, and then replies to the server. The logger has various utilities to archive stale logs and to retrieve them if media recovery is required.

16.4.3.4 Recovery Manager

The local transaction (LAN) transaction abort case is discussed first. Any participant of a transaction can call AbortTransaction(). This spawns a backout process, which flushes the log buffers of all disk servers and initiates an UNDO scan of the log. The UNDO scan sends UNDO log records to the disk processes that created them. Each disk server uses the log record to undo the operation, then it generates a compensation log record. When backout is complete, the backout process broadcasts to all resource managers (disk servers) that they may release the transaction locks, and then writes a final abort record in the log.

Only the root process—the process that called BeginTransaction()—can commit the transaction. When it calls commit, a proprietary non-blocking, two-phased, grouped presumed-abort commit protocol is executed. The transaction management system has a surrogate process, called the *transaction monitor*, in each processor. The CommitWork() call wakes up this process in the local processor, and if the call has the NoWait option, then the local monitor executes the commit asynchronously to the client; otherwise the client waits for the outcome. Call this the *root* monitor.

The root monitor first broadcasts the phase 1 message to all monitors (up to 15 others) on the cluster. Now each of the monitors invokes all resource managers in its processor that have joined the transaction. Each resource manager can vote yes or no. If all vote yes, the monitor responds yes to the root monitor; otherwise it responds no. When all responses are in, the monitor tallies the votes. If they are all yes, it checkpoints the decision to the monitor in the *next* processor. If the root processor fails, the *next* one continues the commit after this point (prior to this, it would abort the transaction). This allows the next monitor to take over in case the primary fails and, in doing so, makes the protocol non-blocking. The root then synchronously writes a commit record to the *master* log. Actually, these writes are buffered by a group commit scheme if the transaction rate is above a certain threshold (about 20 tps). The root monitor then proceeds through phase 2 of the commit.

This is a fairly accurate description of the commit protocol. There are a few more optimizations, but the basic flow is as described.

Now consider a transaction that is distributed beyond the LAN (the 16-processor cluster). Somewhere in each cluster there is a well-known process pair named the TMP

(Transaction Monitor Process). When a trid first leaves a cluster, the TMP is informed via an extra message sent by the message system. When a trid first enters a cluster, the TMP is informed by an extra message, and it becomes the local recovery manager for that transaction. At that point, the TMP tells the monitors in each local processor that the transaction has begun, and they each allocate a descriptor for the transaction. If the trid, in turn, is sent out to other clusters, this TMP is informed of the destination node. So, the TMP has one incoming session (where the trid came from), and zero or more outgoing sessions (where the trid was sent). This is quite similar to the transaction manager design described in Chapter 11.

The root LAN TMP has only outgoing sessions. Thus, the TMPs form a spanning tree of the clusters visited by the transaction. This tree implies a parent-child relationship among the TMPs for each transaction.

Given this information, the commit logic is a standard two-phase, presumed-abort commit protocol, as described in Chapter 11. Each TMP acts as a transaction manager (TM) and broadcasts the phase 1, phase 2, or abort messages to its children and then waits for acknowledgment. This broadcast floods a spanning tree of participating nodes with the transaction messages. It does not broadcast to the entire WAN: messages are broadcast on the LAN (cluster) and are multicast on the WAN. Since each TMP is a process pair, and since the network is single-fault tolerant, the commit and abort protocols are non-blocking.

If any process of the transaction calls abort, then the local TMP broadcasts the abort to its parent and child TMPs. If the TMP notices that the parent node of a live transaction has failed, the TMP unilaterally broadcasts an abort to all child TMPs and to all local resource managers participating in the transaction.

At system restart, the recovery manager launches a process that does a standard REDO-UNDO scan of the log. Disk servers that are unavailable at restart (due to hardware or software failures) are treated as unavailable resource managers. There is no copy-forward or copy-aside logic. Restart can recover a subset of the disk servers. Before a disk process can resume service, all its in-doubt transactions must be resolved. This resolution is either via contact with the commit coordinator or via operator command. If the commit coordinator is not available, the resolution can be via operator command. Heuristic decisions are not yet supported. This means that if the commit coordinator is unavailable, the disk server is unavailable, or the operator must force the transactions to commit or abort. The TMF developers report that no customer has complained about this limitation.

When a server becomes available at a later time, an independent REDO-UNDO scan is initiated for it. Online dump (fuzzy dump) of disks and files to an archive device, redo to a timestamp, and redo from an archive copy of a file or disk are all supported. No change accumulation utility is supported.

16.4.3.5 Failure Scenarios

If the root process of a transaction fails, or if any resource manager (disk server or TMP) involved in the transaction fails, then the transaction is aborted. This approach views processor failure as rare (processor MTTF > 10^7 seconds) and, accordingly, takes a simple approach to resolving such cases.

If a disk device fails, the mirrored disk masks the failure. If a disk server fails due to either hardware or software, the process pair of the server in an adjacent processor takes over the disk devices and orchestrates the undo of any in-progress transactions involved in that server.

If both disk devices of a mirrored pair fail, redo from an archive copy is supported. If the failure is localized to a file, other files on the disk can be accessed during this recovery—a file fragment (partition) is the unit of failure and of recovery. Failures of one file or disk do not affect the availability of other files or disks. If both devices of a pair fail, all that data is unavailable until the devices, and then the individual files, are repaired. If this disk pair is one part of a large database, access to other parts of the database is possible while this part is being recovered.

16.4.3.6 Disaster Recovery and Data Replication

To mask environmental, operations, and software faults, data can be replicated automatically at a second site. The Remote Duplicate Data Facility (RDF), allows the database administrator to designate that certain files be replicated at two sites [Tandem-RDF 1990]. At any instant, one site is the primary and the second is the backup for any specific file fragment (see Figure 16.11). Only the primary copy can be updated. A process pair at the primary, called the *extractor*, continually scans the log, looking for updates to the primary fragments. The extractor sends these log records to the node storing the duplicate fragments, where a second process pair, called the *receiver*, stores the log on a local disk and maintains a state table for each live and recently committed transaction. If there is no activity, the primary sends *I'm Alive* messages to the backup every few seconds so that, at takeover, the backup knows the approximate time of failure. An updater process is dedicated to each disk with a replicated object. The updater applies all committed updates to the duplicate file at the backup. Updates are applied in log order, so that the consistency of the primary is reflected in the backup. In the terminology of Chapter 12, this is a 1-safe disaster recovery facility. Read-only access to the secondary data is supported.

If the backup fails, or if all communication links to the backup fail, the primary saves the log and spools it to the backup at a later time. Upon primary failure, a human operator instructs the backup to assume primary responsibility. Typical application takeover times are measured in minutes.

Tandem's RDF allows the data to be remote, while IBM's XRF insists that the primary and backup systems have shared disks. Both provide 2-safe execution; RDF, in addition, offers 1-safe execution. This limits XRF's ability to mask environmental and operations faults. In this sense, XRF is more like a process-pair design. On the other hand, XRF provides appli-

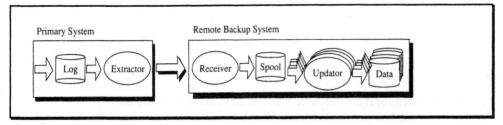

Figure 16.11: The structure of a Remote Duplicate Data Facility. An extractor scans the log of the primary for logical log records that apply to objects replicated at the backup. The extractor sends this subset of the log to the backup system, where a receiver adds the records to the log and caches the status of each transaction. An updater process is associated with every disk holding a replicated object. Each updater scans the log, looking for relevant updates. If the update applies to a new transaction, the updater asks the receiver if the transaction committed. The receiver replies when the transaction outcome is known. Updaters do a logical redo of any committed transactions, in log order.

cation duplication and message integrity, whereas RDF simply provides data duplication. The user of RDF must design the application switch-over to the backup system; a Pathway system must already be configured and connected to the clients in the style of XRF's backup LUs, or the system pairs of Chapter 12. In addition, the surveillance and takeover mechanisms of XRF are more sophisticated and more automated. In late 1991, IBM announced a new product, RRDF, which seems to add many of the RDF features to XRF.

This is an area of intense development. As you read this, it is likely that most TP systems will have evolved to support 2-safe execution and will provide other important features.

16.4.4 Other Interesting Features

Recently Pathway has evolved to support transactional RPCs from a more diverse client base. The first step was PathSend(), which allows any Guardian process to RPC to a Pathway server class. Prior to that, only SCOBOL programs could RPC to a server class. PathSend() has given rise to the TCP-of-the-month club, since now anyone can write a TCP. Such user-written client multiplexors are called MCPs (message control programs). The next step is to support this PathSend() interface from "foreign" systems such as MS/DOS, MVS, OS/2, and UNIX. This is in addition to the more standard, but less convenient, RPC mechanisms provided native to each of those systems. All of these RPC mechanisms funnel through an MCP process.

Since TMF is a closed recovery manager, only very limited ACID properties can be guaranteed in these heterogeneous environments. Essentially, TMF must act as the last resource manager in any ACID transaction.

A second major thrust of the system (from the viewpoint of transaction processing) has been to make the disk servers support an SQL interface. The initial implementation of SQL was explicitly geared to online transaction processing, and it demonstrated that relational systems could deliver transaction performance comparable to network-data model and hierarchical-data model database systems. The major effort here was to push the SQL operations as close to the data as possible (this is very important in a message-based system) and to use the "standard" locking and logging techniques used by other transaction processing systems. Surprisingly, most earlier relational systems used file or page locking and fairly primitive logging techniques.

16.5 DECdta

DECdta is the generic name for Digital's distributed transaction processing architecture in both the VAX/VMS and UNIX environments. The mainstream of these products is represented by ACMS, a transaction processing monitor running on both the VMS and UNIX operating systems. On VMS, other components of DECdta include DECdtm, a transaction manager integrated with the VMS operating system, and the VMS distributed lock manager integrated with the operating system.[6] In addition, several resource managers have connected to transaction managers. Notably, Rdb and Oracle (SQL database systems), DBMS (a network database system), and DECq (a queue manager) act as resource managers to DECdtm, giving transaction atomicity to multisite or multiresource manager transactions.

---

[6] Other transaction processing environments include DECIntact, which is structurally similar to CICS, Digital Standard Mumps, and RTR (described later in this chapter).

There are several novel things about the DECdta architecture. These novelties are best understood by first understanding Digital's approach to system architecture. DEC prides itself on networking computers, from workstations to mainframes. At first, these computers were homogeneous, all running the VMS operating system and all executing the VAX instruction set. The machines were connected into clusters via high-speed links, and clusters were connected via slower, wide-area links into a network. Since 1985, this architecture has had to interoperate with workstations running VMS, MS/DOS Windows, UNIX, OS/2, and MacOS, and it has had to interoperate with UNIX and IBM host systems. Support of this heterogeneous environment is Digital's current focus. One consequence of this is DECdta, a uniform transaction processing interface for all environments (VMS, UNIX, and to some extent MS/DOS Windows, OS/2, and MacOS).

Rather than survey the DECdta architecture vision, this section looks at what actually exists today. In particular, it examines ACMS, DECdtm, and the VMS lock manager, and how resource managers use them.

16.5.1 ACMS's Three-Ball Workflow Model of Transaction Processing

Application Control and Management System (ACMS) is the centerpiece of Digital's transaction processing [DEC-ACMS 1991]. ACMS and DECdta adopt a novel approach to structuring applications: the so-called *three-ball model*, in which presentation services, transaction workflow, and applications run in three separate processes, usually depicted as balls (see Figure 16.12). The *one-ball model* is typified by CICS, which runs everything in one process at one place. IMS, Pathway, and most other transaction processing systems adopt a *two-ball model*, in which terminals attach directly to a transaction processing front end that does presentation services and global transaction flow control. This model is particularly suited to a "big" host supporting many "dumb" terminals. The two-ball model can have many servers and many front-end processes, as is the case with Pathway, but there are only two kinds of processes: clients and servers.

The ACMS three-ball approach to transaction processing evolved from a workstation and minicomputer environment. It is geared more to intelligent terminals (workstations) than to mainframes with dumb terminals. Dumb terminals are attached to ACMS by interfacing the terminals to a terminal server that is a general-purpose computer. The terminal server performs presentation services so that each terminal appears to be intelligent.

The ACMS application flow has the following general pattern:

get input data,
begin an ACID unit (transaction)
invoke servers and converse with terminal
change terminal context,
display output data,
commit,
go on to next step gathering input.

In IMS and CICS, the state of this flow is implicitly stored in a terminal-related context record in the database. In Pathway, the logic and state of this flow are represented by a thread executing a SCOBOL program for the terminal. ACMS is similar to Pathway in that it offers a programming language to define the transaction workflow. The language, called Structured Task Definition Language (STDL), has the usual variables, assignment,

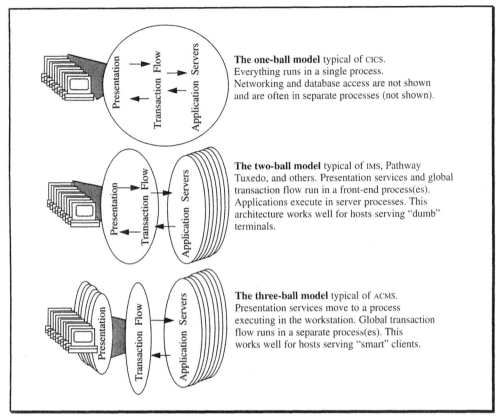

The one-ball model typical of CICS. Everything runs in a single process. Networking and database access are not shown and are often in separate processes (not shown).

The two-ball model typical of IMS, Pathway Tuxedo, and others. Presentation services and global transaction flow run in a front-end process(es). Applications execute in server processes. This architecture works well for hosts serving "dumb" terminals.

The three-ball model typical of ACMS. Presentation services move to a process executing in the workstation. Global transaction flow runs in a separate process(es). This works well for hosts serving "smart" clients.

Figure 16.12: The one-, two-, and three-ball models of transaction processing. ACMS uses the three-ball model, which is especially convenient for workstations or intelligent clients. All the balls (processes) can execute on the same processor, but they typically execute on different processors in order to exploit clusters of multiprocessors.

conditionals, loops, subroutines, and so on. In addition, it provides verbs to begin and end transactions and to invoke presentation services and application processes via RPCs. STDL is a fourth-generation language that is interpreted by the application execution controller at run time. It is a transactional programming language: uncommitted updates to program variables are reset if the transaction aborts. This provides the ACI properties to the terminal context stored as variables. STDL is not a persistent programming language; variables are not durable: if the STDL process fails, the terminal context is lost.

ACMS heavily overloads the term *task*—in ACMS, everything is a task, and all tasks are composed of tasks. The key language is the task definition language. This overloading leads to considerable confusion. For the purposes of the discussion here, imagine that a task is a program (written in STDL) controlling an external device (window or gas pump), and invoking services of servers. It is the program controlling the application workflow of a particular client.

The task, written in STDL, mediates between presentation services and context-free application servers. Each client (workstation or terminal) has a dedicated STDL thread that manages the terminal context, declares transaction boundaries (begin, commit, or rollback), and invokes servers as needed.

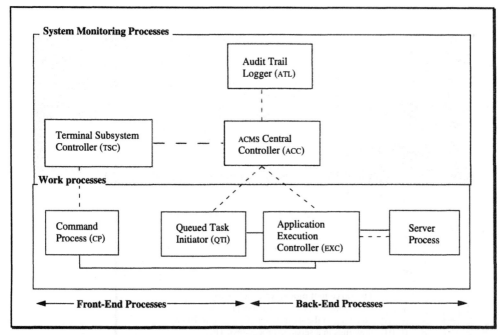

Figure 16.13: Process ensemble of an ACMS environment. The drawing shows only process types; that is, some of the boxes can be instantiated more than once. For example, there can be more than one TSC process, more than one EXC process, more than one server process, and so on. In a distributed system, the process structure is split into a front-end part and a back-end part, as indicated in the figure. If the ACMS system is split as a front-end–back-end system, processes on the left run on the front end, while the others run on the back end; ATL and ACC run on both sides.

Figure 16.13 gives an overview of the ACMS process structure. The ACMS Central Control (ACC) process is responsible for bringing up and reconfiguring the entire ACMS environment based on configuration data stored in the CDD/Plus repository. The Terminal System Control (TSC) processes manage the terminals that are "owned" by ACMS and perform DECforms presentation services for those terminals. The terminal and user context are stored and managed by a dedicated thread in an application execution (EXC) process. There can be many EXC processes, each managing a subset of the terminal network (CPs). Each thread executes an STDL program for its terminal. These threads invoke services as needed.

It is possible for an entire ACMS system (all three kinds of balls) to run on a single node, but it is more usual for the presentation services to run on a workstation. The presentation services process can either support a single dedicated workstation, or it can perform presentation services for a group of dumb terminals or "foreign" workstations (PCs, UNIX boxes, Macintoshes). It the latter case, it runs in a process on a small, inexpensive VAX that acts as a terminal concentrator.

An STDL application can communicate with remote terminals and invoke remote servers as if they were local. This capability, based on a proprietary transactional TRPC mechanism, allows the presentation services (forms and menu handling) to run on a workstation front end, while the "real" processing on files and databases is done on a back-end system. The back end can be a VAXcluster multiprocessor, or even an IBM host. Presentation services are handled by special ACMS components (DECforms or others), which support definition of panels, forms, menus, and so forth.

Servers are commonly written in COBOL, C, Ada, or FORTRAN, but any language can be used. According to the separation of work, a server process cannot do any terminal I/O. It can, however, do file and database I/O. Servers are invoked by TRPCs from the EXC process. The ACMS Central Controller (ACC) dynamically grows and shrinks the number of servers in a server class as the load increases or decreases.

Servers are assumed to be single-threaded and context free. All of ACMS's system processes are multi-threaded. Except for the ACC and the ATL, there can be more than one process of each type per system.

ACMS resource allocation dynamically decides how many processes and of which type are needed to handle the current workload. ACMS attempts to balance the workload among EXC and server processes in a VAXcluster.

Normally, servers are allocated to tasks by the EXC in units of steps; that is, after completion of a step, the server process is given to another task. This requires the servers to be context free. If there is any context, it must be passed from one step to the next via workspaces. For conversational transactions that must maintain database context, such as locks and database cursors, workspaces are insufficient. In that situation, the only solution is to bind the task to a server process. As a consequence, this server remains statically attached to the task in phases where exchange steps are executed, that is, across terminal I/O.

The tasks described so far are *direct* tasks in that they interact directly with the front end. ACMS also supports queued transactions, which are requests for running a certain task at a later time. These requests are put into an ACMS system queue, whence they are scheduled for execution by a special component of ACMS. Operations on the task queue are protected by system transactions. By using DECdtm to coordinate ACMS queue updates and application updates to databases, the queue update operations become part of a user transaction that accesses a database. This provides exactly-once processing of each queued request.

All components administered by ACMS are described in a central, active repository called Common Data Dictionary/Plus (CDD/Plus). This includes display forms, programs, RPC input and output message formats, and server class definitions.

16.5.2 ACMS Services

ACMS runs as an application on top of VMS. It uses the VMS lock manager and the VMS transaction manager (DECdtm); it also uses DECforms for presentation services and the Digital repository, CDD/Plus, to store its definitions and configuration information. In this respect, ACMS is one of the few TP products to integrate with the host repository system. ACMS uses the VMS file system (RMS) and DEC's database systems (Rdb/VMS and DBMS) as resource mangers. ACMS uses RMS files to do logging and request queueing. Several resource mangers have been integrated with ACMS, notably Adabase, Informix, Ingres, Oracle, and Sybase.

The types of services provided by ACMS are briefly characterized here:

Presentation services. ACMS provides virtual terminal support for a wide range of terminals. Terminal input and output are abstracted into forms that serve as the only interfaces between terminals and application programs (and between different applications as well). Forms are defined with a screen painter and are translated by presentation services into a screen and application-message interface. Presentation services are generally offloaded to the front end. The front-end command process executes the DECforms code to gather forms-oriented input data then sends it to the ACMS execution process. When results are returned, the DECforms code displays the data as an output form.

Context. Transaction context is maintained by the STDL thread local storage. Updates to this storage are logged. In addition, ACMS provides a local queue mechanism for request queueing and provides access to DECq as well.

Recovery. ACMS STDL threads can begin, commit, and abort DECdtm transactions. In addition, the STDL interpreter is informed by the transaction manager if the transaction is unilaterally aborted. In the abort case, the ACMS returns the STDL thread to the transaction context as of the start of the transaction. At system restart ACMS recovers, or reestablishes, the software components of its configuration—the process environment and the terminals "owned" by ACMS, the files, and so on. This is to say, after a crash the control blocks are reestablished to set the environment for the application to resume its work. The terminal context does not survive failure or restart. Certain ACMS processes represent single points of failure: if they fail, the entire ACMS system must be restarted.

Program management. ACMS uses the VMS source-code control environment and the repository to manage presentation service programs, STDL programs, and server application programs written in conventional languages (COBOL, C, Ada, FORTRAN, Pascal, etc.). Procedures to be executed as ACMS steps can be written either as programs in conventional programming languages or as VMS command procedures. The executable code is stored in VMS libraries.

Threads. Providing threads is ACMS's main business. For each task group (a number of functions bound together as one executable image), it creates a number of processes and routes function requests to an idle process of the appropriate type. The number of processes per server type can be limited at system startup time, but within the limits, ACMS can vary the number of active processes depending on the load. Requests are transparently routed to remote nodes if the server processes are not locally available.

Authentication and authorization. Authentication is based on passwords. The authorization to invoke a service is kept in access control lists stored for each user in the repository. Note that employing different processes for different server types provides strict isolation among applications.

Cluster load balancing. ACMS grows and shrinks server classes as the load changes. It distributes the load among the nodes of a VAXcluster.

Workflow. ACMS provides direct, conversational, and queued transaction processing. It also supports the notion of workflow. The basic execution unit is a task, which, in turn, is a sequence of steps. The step structure of a task and the workflow relationship among tasks is described in STDL.

Figure 16.14 shows an association between the structure of a general TP monitor, as it was introduced in Chapter 5, and the components of ACMS.

16.5.3 ACMS Summary

ACMS integrates presentation services, program management, access control, process multiplexing, request queueing, file (database) management, and system administration. Its main purpose is to route requests to servers in a distributed environment and to ship responses back; DECdtm is used to coordinate transaction commitment.

ACMS keeps information about all the object types it controls in a central, active data dictionary. ACMS cooperates with VMS-based database management systems distributed over multiple nodes connected either via DECnet or through a VAX Cluster. ACMS provides distributed transactions either through remote-database access or via remote servers (function shipping or application program-to-program communication). It supports the three-ball model of execution.

ACMS provides the user with a two-layer programming environment. The elementary processing steps (single server executions) are implemented using a conventional programming language. These steps are "threaded" together into larger units of work and are embedded into the ACMS environment using a dedicated programming language (STDL), which contains elements for event-oriented programming.

The emphasis today in ACMS is to better integrate with heterogeneous systems (notably a move to UNIX) and to better support desktop application development tools. Additional information on ACMS can be obtained from the manuals [DEC-ACMS 1991]. The Winter 1991 issue of the *Digital Technical Journal* gives more detail on the distributed transaction architecture, on ACMS, and on other DECtp topics.

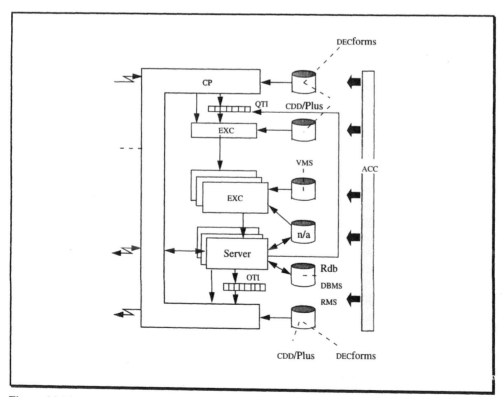

Figure 16.14: ACMS viewed in terms of the taxonomy of Chapter 5. The figure relates the model used in Figure 5.8 to the process types of ACMS. This may facilitate the comparison of the conceptual description with a real system.

16.5.4 VMS **Transaction Management Support**

The VMS operating system provides some unique services relevant to transaction processing. These services are briefly described in this subsection. Initially, VMS was seen as a time-sharing system. But with the advent of personal computers and distributed computing, VMS nodes are increasingly acting as communications gateways or as application server nodes. In response, the VMS architects have added clusters, disk shadowing, locking, and transactions to the VMS architecture. It is their contention (similar to the contention of the MVS and Guardian architects) that support for TRPC properly belongs in the operating system. By providing such support, transaction processing applications offer improved performance, reliability, and operability. This subsection surveys the transaction-related aspects of these VMS features.

16.5.4.1 VAXclusters

The VAXcluster fits the shared-disk model of Figure 2.8. A cluster usually consists of many nodes (197 is the largest known cluster). Each node has memory, communication devices, disks, tapes, and from one to six processors sharing the memory and devices. There are two kinds of nodes in the cluster: VMS nodes running services and applications, and Hierarchical Storage Controller (HSC) nodes, which provide high-performance, high-availability access to pools of shared disk managed by the HSC. A VMS node can service file requests from other cluster nodes to disks attached to the serving node; thus, HSCs are not required for disk sharing. Cluster nodes are connected to one another by multiple links (either Ethernet, FDDI, or a proprietary link).

The VAXcluster provides two desirable properties:

Modular growth.   A computer system can grow by adding more processor, storage, and communication devices. There is no need to scrap the old computers and buy a newer, faster model.

Fault containment.   Each node of the cluster fails independently. If a node or path fails, other members of the cluster can still offer access to the shared data and devices.

VMS does not support a software process-pair notion,[7] but a cluster's clients can attach to the cluster (alias) and will be assigned to a node of the cluster. This switching service is performed both by terminal servers and by the ACMS system. If one node fails, ACMS restarts the missing servers and EXCs in the remaining nodes of the cluster as part of its availability and load balancing activity. These mechanisms are called *failover* in VMS.

VMS and the HSC both implement disk duplexing (and triplexing) to tolerate disk media failures. These are called *shadow-sets* in VMS. Interestingly, the shadows can be stored anywhere in the cluster. Since by using high-speed communications links, clusters can span a metropolitan area network, it is becoming common for applications to duplex disks across multiple sites. In this way, if one site fails, the other site can still offer access to the data. This is a basic form of system pairs described in section 12.6 [Davis 1991; Snamann 1991; Shah 1991].

---

[7] A duplexed VAX, the VAXft provides hardware support for process pairs. Its design masks any single hardware fault.

16.5.4.2 DECdtm

DECdtm is a distributed, two-phase commit coordinator built into the VMS operating system. Its structure is very similar to that of the X/Open DTP model and to the transaction manager presented in Chapter 11. It has a TM at each node, which generates globally unique transaction identifiers. It provides an application programming interface to start, commit, or abort a transaction. These calls may be asynchronous to allow multi-threaded clients. Abort of a transaction can be requested by any participating resource manager and node at any time. Commit can only be requested by the process that started the transaction.

DECdtm provides a resource manager interface to allow resource managers to join a transaction and, in turn, informs the joined resource managers of the transaction's commit and abort events. At present, ACMS, DECintact, Rdb, DBMS, RMS, RALLY, and DECq act as resource managers.

Communication managers can register incoming and outgoing transaction identifiers from other DECdtm transaction managers. This allows transactions to be distributed in a VAXcluster or in a DECnet wide area network.

DECdtm uses a classic two-phase, presumed-abort, non-blocking commit protocol. It offers a one-phase commit protocol (the last-resource-manager optimization discussed in Chapter 12) if the transaction involves only a single resource manager.

As a rule, each node of a VAXcluster has a DECdtm process and a log. A cluster may consist of tens of processors and hundreds of disks. Due to the cluster connection topology, one can assume that the cluster will not be partitioned. Thus, if one node of the cluster fails, active transactions involving that node can be aborted by DECdtm running on another node, once a new quorum is formed. If the node running DECdtm fails, another node will be elected to perform this recovery based on the failed TM's disk log. This effectively makes DECdtm a non-blocking commit protocol. The VMS lock manager (described next) is used to detect and manage this failover.

DECdtm implements the basic functionality required to run flat distributed transactions. DECdtm also provides a log interface that is used by the transaction manager. The log interface is not published and so is not yet accessible to resource managers. In contrast to TMF, which has one or two logs per cluster, DECdtm has one log per node of the cluster, and a log per resource manager.

After a failure, DECdtm recovers its own state. Each resource manager is responsible for restarting and recovering itself. DECdtm tells any resource manager the outcome of any transaction registered at that node. This is similar to the logging and recovery designs described in Chapters 9 and 11.

DECdtm is a classic example of a transaction manager imbedded in a distributed operating system. Everything else—process management, message handling, persistent state, TRPC—must be provided by other components. Laing, Johnson, and Landau [1991] give a more complete description of DECdtm.

16.5.4.3 VMS Lock Manager

The VMS lock manager controls a coherent lock database for all processes executing in a VAXcluster. The lock manager has two levels of abstraction: (1) a connection manager, which determines a quorum of nodes attached to the cluster, and (2) a lock manager, which manages requests for locks as long as this node is a member of the quorum.

Each node of the cluster has a connection manager. Each connection manager knows two numbers: the cluster quorum count and the local vote count. Workstations might have a vote count of 0 or 1, while a highly-reliable VAXft server might be given a vote count of 10. The connection managers of a cluster try to contact one another in order to form a quorum (enough votes to constitute the quorum count). Each connection manager is in session with connection managers at all other "up" nodes of the cluster. Each occasionally broadcasts an *I'm Alive* message to the others. If a new node appears, or if no *I'm Alive* messages appear from a node for a while, the connection managers attempt to form a new quorum. To do this, one connection manager proposes a quorum, then all the others go through a bounded-time, two-phase commit protocol to agree to the quorum.

The lock manager at a node rejects all calls unless this node is part of the current quorum or a new quorum is in the process of forming. The lock manager provides access to named locks in one of five modes (corresponding to S, X, SI, IX, and SIX). Locks are owned by processes (not transactions), because the lock manager predates transactions (DECdtm). The lock manager detects deadlock via a depth-first search similar to the algorithm described in Chapter 8, Section 8.5.

The lock manager supports hierarchical locks and notify locks. Most lock manager clients use it in a simple way. It is commonly used to detect processor failure, for example. But the SQL database system Rdb uses the lock manager in very sophisticated ways. First, it uses the hierarchical locks to do *de-escalation*, rather than escalation (see Chapter 8, Subsection 8.4.6 for a discussion of escalation). Rdb tends to lock very large granules in shared or exclusive mode. When making these requests, it provides an exception handler, called an Asynchronous System Trap (AST). If another process requests the lock in an incompatible mode, the lock manager invokes the exception handler, and Rdb gives up the coarse lock after acquiring finer granularity locks; for example, it will give up a file lock for an area lock, or give up a page lock for a record lock. Rdb's use of this mechanism is described by Joshi [1991].

The lock manager is easy to understand operating on a single node. Making the lock manager work in a cluster, however, is a neat trick. In order to minimize message traffic, the lock hierarchy is actually a forest of trees. Each lock tree is *mastered* at some node; this means that all requests for that tree are managed by that node. Other nodes make RPCs to that node when requesting or releasing locks in that tree. The node making the most requests to locks in a tree eventually becomes the master of the tree. If there is no sharing within a lock tree, no network messages are required, and the lock manager can perform a pair of lock-unlock operations in about 600 instructions. If the lock is mastered remotely, then the pair is about seven times more expensive.

The lock manager at each node of the quorum maintains a directory of which nodes are currently mastering active trees. At node failure, after a new quorum is established, the remaining nodes must recover the locks that were mastered by the failed node. This mechanism is described in Snaman and Thiel [1987].

16.5.4.4 Rdb/VMS and Other Resource Managers

Application programs typically contain calls to resource managers provided by Digital or by other vendors. Digital's most popular database system is Rdb/VMS, an SQL system [DEC-Rdb 1991]. Other database systems include Informix, Ingres, Oracle, Sybase, and Unify, among others. Each of these systems predates DECdtm, the transaction manager integrated with VMS. So, each of these systems is an independent transaction manager. Rdb and Oracle have added the ability to participate in DECdtm transactions, so that a transaction begun by an STDL (Structured Task Definition Language) program can run a global transaction involving many Rdb and Oracle databases.

Rdb is an interesting SQL system in itself. It has both deferred and immediate triggers. It supports the entire SQL2 referential integrity model. RdbExpert is a expert system that analyzes the way the database is used and proposes an optimized physical database design. Rdb is integrated with the repository (CDD/R); in fact, CDD/R is implemented as an Rdb application. The Rdb data distributor provides remote snapshots of data. VIDA collects data from DB2 and other foreign databases. A library of remote procedure calls provides SQL access and tools to desktop clients. BLOBS (binary large objects) support multimedia applications by storing large records, up to several gigabytes each, as part of the database in tertiary storage. It has B-trees, hashing, clustering of records from different tables on a single page, and many other go-fast features [Hobbs and England 1991].

More relevant to this book is the Rdb approach to providing ACID transactions on data. Rdb operates in a VAXcluster. The VAX provides each process with four protection domains. The application operates in one of these domains, and Rdb operates in another. The application can call Rdb with a domain switch rather than a process switch, so Rdb calls are inexpensive compared to the RPC (process switch) calls typical of more primitive operating systems. Rdb caches the pages of the database needed by an application process in a buffer pool local to that process. Since each Rdb process is caching in this way, the VMS lock manager is used to regulate page accesses among the processes. Rather than the escalation scheme described in Chapters 7 and 8, Rdb uses a de-escalation scheme, defaulting to file granularity locking and then refining locks as needed to record granularity. This approach is optimized for the case in which relatively little contention occurs [Joshi 1991].

Rdb logging is novel: it keeps three logs. It keeps a common REDO log, called the *after image journal*, for each database. In addition, each application process keeps a private UNDO log, called a *before image journal*. The UNDO log is only needed for transaction aborts. When the transaction commits, the contents of the UNDO log are discarded. Rdb observes a write-ahead log protocol, so that if the process or processor fails, another process in the cluster can abort the transaction by applying the failed process' UNDO log to the database. As described so far, there is no way to take a fuzzy dump of a Rdb database, since aborted transaction updates might be present in the archive copy, but the UNDO log records would not be present in the log.

Rdb has one additional mechanism that allows read-only transactions to get a *snapshot* of the database. The database is partitioned into storage areas, and Rdb keeps a snapshot log of changes to each area. This log holds the old values of records updated in that area. Each read-only transaction runs as of some time, called the transaction's timestamp. Each record is also timestamped by its most recent update. Read-only transactions look in the snapshot file to find the old version of the record if the online version is newer than the transaction's timestamp. This is a form of time domain addressing. The archive dump process uses this snapshot mechanism to take a transaction-consistent copy of the database.

16.5.4.5 Data Access: Data Sharing versus Partitioning

The original VAXcluster concept was to allow any client to access any shared device in the cluster; this is the data sharing model described in Subsection 16.2.5. Shared disks are just as accessible as local disks, and shared communications servers are just as accessible as local servers. The VMS lock manager is used to coordinate read-write access to these shared objects. In a time-sharing environment, the shared disks become file servers, and the clients cache the files they use in their local memories. In these time-sharing environments, there is very little concurrent read-write sharing of files. In a database or transaction processing environment, there is often intense read-write sharing of files by all processors in the cluster. This sharing creates a heavy load on the shared-disk design. The IMS discussion earlier described this as data sharing. Paradoxically, as IMS moves toward data sharing, the VAXcluster is moving away from it and toward a shared-nothing model in which clients make TRPC requests to servers that manage a local partition of the database.

As explained in Chapter 4, this time-sharing mode of use is being augmented by a client-server paradigm. In that model, client requests are sent as RPCs to servers, which, in turn, perform some operations on the data. STDL programs act as servers to their remote clients. The STDL programs then act as clients when they invoke application servers. The application servers may, in turn, act as clients to other system services; for example, they may act as clients to DECdtm and to the lock manger.

With this change, *device sharing* is giving way to *server sharing*. In device sharing, clients send low-level read-write requests to devices. For example, to update a record, the client would somehow find the page holding the record, fetch that page into its address space, modify the page, and then return the page to the device. In a server-sharing design, the client sends a TRPC update request to a server, which alters the data. The server-sharing design has two advantages over device sharing when accessing shared data:

Control.   The server encapsulates the data and can control the kinds of updates that can be made to the data. The client likes the encapsulation, since it makes programming easier. The data-owner likes the encapsulation, because it means that no client can corrupt the data by manipulating the underlying pages.

Performance.   Rather than moving page-sized messages around, the server-sharing design moves very small messages (RPCs). This saves network bandwidth and also saves the processor instructions needed to move large messages.

With this shift in focus, and with the realization that much of the shared active data is resident in electronic memory, the VAXcluster is increasingly migrating to a partitioned data model in which not all data is directly accessible at all nodes. Rather, a partition of the shared data is managed by a server class at a particular node of the VAXcluster. All access to that data goes through that node. In this partitioned model, there are no distributed locks: all the locks for the partition are mastered at one node. There is still distributed deadlock detection, and the lock manager's connection manager is still used to detect and orchestrate failover (to form a new quorum). At node failure, the server class and its responsibility for the partition moves to another node of the cluster.

These servers use a native resource manager (like the Rdb SQL database system) to store their data. They advertise their TRPC services via ACMS, and they depend on ACMS for the environmental services of a transaction monitor: startup, authorization, load balancing, TRPC, and the other environmental services described in Section 16.4 and in Chapters 5 and 6.

16.5.5 Summary of DECdta

Until recently, VMS and the VAXcluster were geared to acting as device and application hosts to terminals and workstations. Since 1985, there has been a distinct trend toward supporting TRPC and a client-server model of computing. This trend includes the support of transactions and locks in the operating system, the support of failover and long-distance shadowing, and most important, the support of a three-ball model of transaction processing, in which a multi-threaded executor multiplexes client requests among servers distributed in a cluster.

16.5.6 Reliable Transaction Router (RTR)

Digital's Reliable Transaction Router (RTR) provides high-availaiblity execution for distributed and heterogeneous servers and resource managers.[8] Conventional TP systems aim for atomicity; RTR tries to successfully execute each request even if parts of the underlying system fail. Put another way, RTR never aborts a transaction unless the transaction asks to be aborted. Since RTR applications generally involve several closed resource mangers (e.g., Oracle plus Rdb plus IMS plus . . .), RTR aims to execute each request at least once. It is up to the application designer to write servers as idempotent operations, and to write compensation operations in case some one server aborts.

In many respects, RTR is a conventional transaction processing system. It uses the three-ball model: clients send transactional RPCs to routers that, in turn, invoke one or more servers. RTR code located in the client reliably delivers requests to routers. In that sense the requests are transactional RPCs. Clients can be in workstations (MS/DOS, Mac, UNIX, VMS); routers must be on VMS; and servers can be on VMS, UNIX, or MVS.

The router maintains, together with the RTR-code in the clients and servers, highly available sessions to clients and servers. Client and server applications do not see any details of the network layer; rather they communicate via recoverable sessions. Link failures are completely masked by RTR. Even failed routers are replaced transparently.

The router has no application code—it is table driven. Using the request message's service identifier, the router looks in its configuration tables to see which servers should receive this message. Typically, a request is routed to serveral servers in parallel. The routers manage server classes and balance the load among members of each server class. RTR maintains a request queue for all servers of the same class. Each class may be distributed in the network, but all requests to that class must come through the router that manages that class.

The routers act as commit coordinators. A transaction originating at a requestor can employ an arbitrary number of servers. Therefore, atomic commit processing becomes an issue. As discussed in Chapter 12 (Section 12.4), the clients are not the best place to put the coordinator, so the router performs the commit coordinator function.

A server is an application process that waits for request messages from routers. It then acts upon these messages to perform database updates, using resource managers such as Rdb or RMS. RTR's control does not extend to those resource managers. RTR informs the servers about transaction state changes (Begin, Commit, Abort), but the server is responsible for invoking the proper verbs of its resource managers. In this sense, each server is a resource manager.

Each RTR server class typically services a data partition. The partitioning key can be made part of the service ID, and thus requests get automatically routed to the right server class, without the servers having to program the distribution logic. This gives a scaleable design in which new partitions can be added.

---

[8] This material is based discussions with RTR's lead architect, Paul Shrager, and on [DEC-RTR 1991].

A multi-cast mechanism allows clients and servers to announce events to interested groups. Each such message is tagged by a class, and recipients can subscribe to certain classes. These messages need not be transaction protected.

RTR has some unique high-availability features. *Spare servers* are transactional process pairs. The primary server receives and processes requests; the spare server runs on another node of the same VAXcluster but does not receive any requests while the primary is up. When the primary fails as detected by the VMS connection manager (see Subsection 16.5.4.3), the spare server receives the current and all subsequent requests to the pair. Since the spare is running in the same VAXcluster, it can access the data managed by the primary and continue to offer service. This is the standard process-pair approach.

Shadow servers go one step further in trying to provide uninterrupted service—they provide duplexed execution. While a spare is normally inactive, a shadow server is running in parallel to the primary on a copy of the data. The shadow is not restricted to the same VAXcluster; it can be anywhere in the network. Both processes receive the request, and both execute it on their copies in lock step. This is tricky, though: two shadow servers running against two databases might have different execution order. So both servers must execute in full isolation (degree 3 isolation), and the shadows must commit in an order specified by the router. This limits the throughput and response time of such servers.

If a router fails, its sessions are transparently switched to another router without the applications being affected. Messages of all active transactions are remembered by both clients and servers, in case they need to be replayed.

If a router fails during commit, affected clients and servers initiate a cooperative termination protocol that selects a new coordinator and finishes the transaction. When a server node fails, any transactions that had not been committed at the time of failure are replayed to the servers from a log, upon node restart. This replay has pros and cons. On one hand, from the client perspective, it looks like the transaction just continues running; on the other hand, without idempotent servers, the results of the replay can be different from the original invocation.

In summary, RTR provides a high-availability TRPC mechanism. It distributes work for load balancing, modular growth, and fault tolerance. The three-ball model allows easy reconfiguration, some of which is transparent to the application. RTR is not a full-blown TP system in the sense defined in Chapter 5. It provides a call interface to application programs. It does not yet have a repository, presentation management, or application-development tools. There are no preferred resource managers; anyone can participate. From that perspective, RTR is more like a transaction manager in the sense of X/Open (see Section 16.6).

16.6 X/Open DTP, OSI-TP, CCR

As discussed in Chapter 2, Section 2.7.4, the International Standards Organization (ISO) has defined a standard protocol that allows transaction processing systems to interoperate. This protocol has two parts: Open System Interconnect–Transaction Processing (OSI-TP) and a second standard, Open Systems Interconnection–Commit Control and Recovery (OSI-CCR). Together they define formats for global transaction identifiers and define standard two-phase commit message formats and a corresponding protocol [OSI-TP 1992; OSI-CCR 1990]. This commit protocol operates atop the OSI six-layer communications protocol stack but otherwise is very similar to the LU6.2 that operates atop IBM's SNA protocol stack [IBM-LU6.2 1991].

These ISO-OSI standards do not define any programming interfaces; they simply define message interfaces to allow computers to interoperate. A standard application programming interface is needed to allow application programs, resource managers, or transaction managers to be ported and recompiled from one system to another. X/Open has a subgroup defining such application programming interfaces: X/Open Distributed Transaction Processing (X/Open DTP). This group has defined the concept of application program, transaction manager, resource manager, and communication manager. It has defined standard interfaces among them so that portable applications can be written. The X/Open standard is intended to allow a transaction manager to use proprietary commit protocols internally and to use the OSI-TP protocols when interoperating with transaction managers written by other vendors. These programming interfaces allow portable applications and portable resource managers.

The terminology and presentation in this book borrow heavily from the OSI-TP and X/Open terminology and concepts. Conversely, those standards capture the core algorithms implemented by most transaction processing systems as described in this book. These standards provide a fitting ending for the book. As the book goes to press, OSI-CCR is an approved international standard, and OSI-TP has just been approved as an international standard. The X/Open DTP standard has some core components that are quite stable, while other aspects are rapidly evolving [X/Open-DTP 1991]. The most controversial parts of the X/Open DTP design are the attempts to define a TP monitor environment (servers and services) and the debates over the relative merits of transactional remote procedure call (TRPC) and peer-to-peer (PTP) communication. At present, both approaches are represented in the standard. There is considerable debate about how communications managers should fit into the standard. We have simplified or ignored these issues in order to stay within the limited space available here. In addition, X/Open working documents are confidential. We have had to base this presentation on a year-old snapshot.

X/Open adopts the structural model familiar from previous chapters. There is a transaction manager component that registers transactions and manages their atomic commitment. In X/Open, that is all the TM does; this is in contrast to the transaction manager described in Chapter 11, which both manages transaction commit and drives recovery (UNDO-REDO). The X/Open model postulates that each resource manager (RM) has its own log and its own recovery manager. The X/Open transaction manager can be briefly characterized by the following property list:

Commit protocol.   Uses a two-phase, presumed-abort commit protocol.

Rooted.   Only the root can commit the transaction.

Optimized.   Supports the read-only optimization.

Heuristic.   Supports heuristic decisions.

Branches.   Supports subtransactions, but the transaction aborts if any branch aborts.

Chain-option.   Transactions can be either chained or explicitly started.

Timeout is used to limit transaction execution time and action execution time.

OSI/TP protocols may be used when communicating with foreign TMs.

X/Open allows applications to provide transactional application servers (processes) that offer transactional services. Services can be remote procedure calls or full-duplex, peer-to-peer connections (in the manner of OSI/TP dialogs). The RPC and PTP connections can be transactional or not. The RPCs can be asynchronous or not. X/Open has no clear notion of server class. Server configuration is vendor specific. External communication can be via an X/Open-provided RPC or PTP mechanism, or via a communication manager-specific protocol (e.g., DECnet, LU6.2, Encina over TCP/IP).

The structure of X/Open can best be explained by first looking at the local case of a single application program process executing an application involving several local resource managers. Once this simple case is understood, the discussion of a distributed application can proceed as an extension of the basic model.

16.6.1 The Local Case

The presentation in Chapters 3 through 15 relied heavily on remote procedure call to allow transaction managers and resource managers to be in processes and processors different from the process executing application programs. The X/Open design is largely in terms of application programs statically bound to a transaction manager and to resource managers executing as domains of a single process. The X/Open standard talks in terms of compiling and linking all these programs together as part of creating the application process.

The application first calls tmopen() to connect to the transaction manager. Thereafter, it may call tmbegin() to begin a transaction, tmabort() to abort it, tmcommit() to commit it, and tmsync() to chain a new transaction (tmcommit() plus tmbegin()). The application disconnects from the transaction manager by calling tmterm(). These routines comprise the local aspects of the so-called *TX interface*, the interface between a client application and its local transaction manager.

Each resource manager residing in the process provides a list of callbacks to the transaction manager. These callbacks, called the *resource manager switch*, are defined when the process image is constructed (at process bind or link time). This is a fairly static approach to procedure binding. Many different resource managers can be bound into the process by providing their respective switch vectors. These TM to RM callbacks are as follows:

xa_open()	/* called when process starts TM (driven by tmopen())	*/
xa_close()	/* called when process ends connection with TM (driven by tmterm())	*/
xa_start()	/* tells RM it has joined a new transaction or resumed an old one	*/
xa_end()	/* tells RM to leave() this trid (it may resume() later)	*/
xa_prepare()	/* tells RM to prepare to commit (phase 1 of commit)	*/
xa_commit()	/* tells RM to commit (phase 2 of successful commit)	*/
xa_rollback()	/* tells RM to rollback a transaction	*/
xa_complete()	/* allows TM to poll or wait for the RM to complete an asynchronous operation	*/
xa_recover()	/* asks RM for its current list of in-doubt and heuristically resolved transactions	*/
xa_forget()	/* tells RM to forget an in-doubt transaction that the RM resolved heuristically	*/

As might be inferred from the names, this TM-RM interface is generically called the *XA interface*. Many of these XA calls should be familiar from previous chapters. The RM switch carries the RM name; it also has a flag indicating whether the resource manager automatically joins all transactions in this process, or whether it only joins some of them. This is called *static* or *dynamic registration*. If static registration is requested, each new transaction in the process generates an xa_start() call to the RM. Another switch flag indicates if the RM is willing to perform asynchronous operations that return to the TM immediately. The TM can use these operations to increase parallelism in commit and abort operations. The xa_complete() callback allows the TM to wait or poll for the RM's completion of such asynchronous operations.

At xa_open() the TM calls the RM, asking for its list of in-doubt or heuristically resolved transactions. For each in-doubt transaction for which the TM knows the outcome, it calls the xa_commit() or xa_abort() callback. For transactions that were heuristically resolved, the TM calls xa_forget() once it has dealt with that transaction. The TM performs no explicit operations on transactions still in doubt with respect to the TM; they remain in doubt with respect to the RM.

Here, then, is the simple control flow of a new process executing a single transaction against a single resource manager that statically registers with, or joins, all transactions:

Application Calls to TM	TM Calls to RMs		
tminit()		/* application asks TM to init itself	*/
tmopen()		/* application asks TM to start all local RMs	*/
	xa_open()	/* TM opens RM and	*/
	xa_recover()	/* asks RM for in-doubt transactions	*/
	xa_commit, xa_abort, xa_forget	/* resolves RM transactions	*/
tmbegin()		/* application begin a transaction	*/
	xa_start()	/* TM tells RM it has joined trans	*/
application calls		/* application calls RM to do work	*/
tmcommit()		/* application calls TM to commit work	*/
	xa_end()	/* TM tells RM to complete trans	*/
	xa_precom()	/* asks RM to prepare	*/
	xa_commit()	/* informs RM that commit worked	*/
tmterm()		/* application disconnects from TM	*/
	xa_close()	/* TM disconnects from RM	*/
exit()		/* application exits	*/

If the RM switch indicates that the resource manager dynamically joins transactions, then the tmbegin() would not call the resource manager, and the resource manager would call gtrid_reg() upon its first invocation by each new transaction. This is the equivalent of Join_Work() in Chapters 10 and 11. A resource manager can request the read-only optimization at switch time, or can request it dynamically as the transaction progresses by unregistering, or unjoining, the transaction.

The X/Open DTP transaction identifier design is inherited from the rather strange OSI-CCR design. OSI-CCR and X/Open trids are called *global transaction identifiers*, or gtrids. The curious thing is that each TM participating in a transaction creates a different gtrid for the transaction, and each resource manager can optionally get a unique gtrid—each different gtrid is called a branch of the transaction. Global trids, then, are not really global after all! If any gtrid aborts, all related gtrids must abort; consequently, they should not be confused with transaction savepoints or with nested transactions. One can think of the gtrid of the transaction root as trid of the whole transaction, but generally none of the other TMs ever hear about this gtrid.

Since gtrids are big (requiring 32 bytes to store them and 64 bytes to display them), they probably contain lots of extra information (such as a branch identifier). Consequently, applications are not allowed to look inside gtrids. The transaction manager provides interfaces to compare, hash, and display gtrids.

The discussion up to this point has been in terms of processes. In fact, X/Open DTP is heavily geared to multi-threaded processes. The X/Open specifications use the term *thread* almost exclusively—each thread participates in only one transaction at a time, but the entire process contains many such threads.

16.6.2 The Distributed Case: Services and Servers

X/Open defines the notions of servers and services. The specification is a little vague on how these are defined to the TP monitor. There is some discussion of priorities and of administrative functions, but the overall design is incomplete. For example, there is no notion of configuring a server class.

Two types of server are recognized:

Peers use some native peer-to-peer communication mechanism unknown to the TM.

Servers provide a *service*, which is a process (thread) managed by the TM. Servers provide either *TRPC services*, meaning that the call is context-free and has a single response message, or they provide *conversational* services. If a service is conversational—that is, if it maintains client context—then it must use an X/Open peer-to-peer communication protocol to communicate with the client. The protocol is reminiscent of LU6.2. X/Open does not support the concept of a context-sensitive TRPC.

For servers (TRPC or conversational), the TM acts as the main routine for the server. It polls for input messages, manages the transaction identifier, and invokes the service. This is very much in the spirit of TP monitors.

Clients invoke TRPC services by using the X/Open tmcall() routine. This routine provides two buffer areas: a request message and a reply message buffer. Parameter marshalling is not defined. If the call crosses heterogeneous systems, data translation of requests and replies may be required, but this is not a part specified by the X/Open DTP protocol. These points are mentioned here to underscore the preliminary nature of the design.

It seems likely that applications will use other TRPC and peer-to-peer protocols. The X/Open and OSI-TP standards are well positioned to allow such protocols to register outgoing and incoming trids. This mechanism is called *branch registration* in OSI-TP, and its application programming interface is called the XA+ interface (or CM interface) in X/Open DTP. It is very similar to the CM-TM interface described in Chapter 10, Section 10.4.2.

16.6.3 Summary

X/Open DTP and OSI-TP together define a way for heterogeneous TP systems to interoperate. Several systems compliant with the architecture are being built—notably TOPEND from NCR and Tuxedo from USL. It seems likely that as the standard evolves, these programming in-

interfaces will become a common part of all TP systems, much as the UNIX library has become a standard part of most operating systems.

16.7 Other Systems

This section contains brief descriptions of other transaction systems that implement already-described concepts. As explained in Section 16.1, no statement about quality, relevance, or whatever, should be derived from the fact that a system is included here.

16.7.1 Universal Transaction Manager (UTM)

UTM is a subsystem of the BS2000 operating system that runs on SNI (Siemens-Nixdorf) mainframes. It is a TP monitor that supports request/response style processing in cooperation with Siemens database systems (UDS and Sesam) as well as some third-party DBMSs, such as ADABAS and Oracle. Its basic version runs on a single system (shared-memory multiprocessors). The distributed version, UTM-D, contains a distributed two-phase commit coordinator based on the SNA protocol LU6.1, which allows it to interoperate with CICS.

UTM implements an interface standard called KDCS, defined by a number of German manufacturers and public administrations for "open" TP monitors. Since KDCS never gained wide acceptance, it is ignored in the following discussion. UTM has a process structure similar to that of CICS; all applications run in one address space.

UTM provides the following services:

Presentation services. UTM provides presentation services in much the same way the other systems do. A forms handling system (FMS) provides a simple screen painter, allows a hierarchy of panel definitions, and so on. It uses the operating system's virtual terminal support.

Storage. UTM maintains five different types of memory that can be accessed by the transaction programs. Some are private to a program invocation, while others are shareable among concurrent activities. Storage areas may be transaction protected (durable, logged, and the other ACID properties). Another distinction is that some storage areas are transient, while others are durable and are mapped to external storage automatically by the system.

Files. UTM does not provide general file support. The only exception is a logging facility described next. Applications can access the two database systems, UDS and Sesam.

Journals. Application programs are provided with an interface to a user log file to support application-specific and/or terminal-specific recovery. The basic system support is transaction protection for all updates on that log file. However, this log file is for diagnostic pruposes only; it is not used for recovery.

Recovery. UTM provides ACID protection for the program storage areas, messages, request queues, and database resource managers. Recovery is based on a variant of shadow paging and REDO logging.

Program management. Transaction programs and their associations with panels are maintained by UTM in its own libraries. For a program to become part of an application, it must explicitly be checked in with the system. There is no way to simply "RPC" to a server that happens to be around somewhere.

Threads. UTM offers a server class mechanism. Transaction programs belonging to one application are linked together, and the resulting code (which also contains a connection module to UTM) can be loaded into multiple processes to form a server class. Each process runs a single transaction to completion. It becomes free as soon as it returns the response. Multiplexing among the (identical) processes is done by the UTM system that runs as a subsystem of the operating system. It has its own protected address space. The application connection modules transfer control to UTM by a special supervisor call. The transaction programs running in the application processes are essentially context free. If there is context, however, the application programmer has a number of choices about where to keep it: in the database, in the user log file, or in one of the recoverable storage areas.

Authentication and authorization. Terminal users logging onto the system must authenticate themselves with a password. In addition to that, terminal badge readers are supported. Authorization is based on a lock-key concept. Terminals, transaction programs, and databases can be assigned a variable number of "locks." In addition, users, terminals, and transaction programs can be given "keys." Whenever a key matches a lock, the user can use a terminal, the user can execute a program, a program can be called from a terminal, or a program can access a database. All this is part of system generation that produces the application code and the corresponding UTM catalog entries.

Workflow. UTM supports both interactive and queued transactions. The queues are transaction protected. It uses the last-resource-manager optimization if the application uses only one database system (which is typically the case). In the multi-resource manager cases and for distributed transactions, however, UTM goes through the full two-phase commit protocol.

Another version of UTM is available on the UNIX sold by SNI, called SINIX. That version supports the X/Open XA interface and so is an open transaction manager. It has been interfaced to the Informix database system. The material presented in this subsection is based on [Sattler 1989] and [Siemens 1989].

16.7.2 ADABAS TPF

ADABAS TPF is produced by Software AG and is part of their software environment that comprises the database system ADABAS, the fourth-generation language (4GL) programming environment NATURAL, the TP monitor COM-PLETE, and NET-WORK as the communication system in a distributed system.[9] TPF runs under IBM's MVS and DOS/VSE operating systems. Its process model is similar to CICS; the systems and applications all run in a single address space.

---

[9] The material presented in this subsection is based on [SoftwareAG 1988; SoftwareAG 1989].

The services provided by ADABAS TPF can be characterized as follows:

Presentation services. ADABAS TPF provides presentation services in a number of ways. One is the integration of NATURAL that comes with screen pointers, report writers, graphics support, and so on. Since TPF also interfaces to other TP monitors (CICS, for example), applications can go through their presentation managers.

Storage. Except for the storage areas through which screen messages are received and sent, TPF does not support any specific storage types. The discussion of threads (below) explains how transaction context is managed.

Files. Since TPF applications are written in either conventional programming languages or the NATURAL 4GL environment, standard file access is supported through normal interfaces. Additionally, TPF has its own virtual file support, called SD (sequential direct) files. These files can be created and deleted dynamically, and they can exist for the duration of an application program or be declared durable. Whether updates on SD files are transaction protected or not could not be concluded from the documentation.

Recovery. TPF ties into ADABAS as its supporting database system, as does NATURAL. All catalog information, forms descriptions, and so on, are kept in ADABAS files. Since that system also runs in a distributed environment (called ADANET) and uses a distributed two-phase commit protocol, this part of the system is ACID protected. Applications are recovered to the screen menu associated with the last successful commit for that application or user.

Program management. TPF does its own program management, using special libraries for executable code. At run time, it keeps in-memory libraries with the most popular programs to avoid loading code from external storage whenever possible.

Threads. TPF has a unique way of doing thread management. It uses multiple operating system processes—some of them for its own work, plus one process for each active transaction. Rather than providing the application with a temporary storage area in which to keep its state while there is no process associated with it (during terminal interaction, for example), TPF frees the process by rolling out the state of the thread and rolling it back in later. As an optimization, threads used very heavily can be rolled out to a designated storage buffer rather than to disk. Each application process runs under its own, separate storage protection key; the system processes have yet another protection key.

Authentication and authorization. These functions are based on passwords and access control lists maintained by TPF itself and NATURAL, if this component is used. In addition, operating system-specific security features such as RACF can be used.

Workflow. As in other systems described before, workflow can be specified indirectly by defining chains and hierarchies of panels.

TPF supports both interactive transactions and queued transactions; the latter are referred to as *batch transactions*. It also has an integrated message switching facility, which uses transaction-protected message queues. Furthermore, it allows applications to invoke operating system-specific services, such as the spooling system, remote job entry, and some others.

16.7.3 Encina

The Encina transaction processing system from Transarc Corporation is appearing as this book goes to press.[10] Encina is designed to use the threading, communication, naming, and security of the Open Software Foundation's Distributed Computing Environment OSF-DCE. It is also being ported to non-UNIX operating systems. Encina has a set of core services quite similar to those described in Chapters 6–15 of this book.

The Encina lock manager is similar to that described in Chapter 8. It provides a more general form of lock name (a two-level name space of up to 512 characters) and provides nested-transaction locking with several forms of inheritance and anti-inheritance. It keeps lock counts on a per-subtransaction basis but does not provide automatic lock conversion.

The Encina log manager is similar to that described in Chapter 9, but Encina's log manager takes a more flexible approach to log archiving. Each record type may be directed to a different archive stream.

The Encina transaction manager is similar in spirit to, but much more elaborate than, the one described in Chapters 10 and 11. Encina supports nested transactions and commit dependencies among them. Encina provides the interfaces and structure outlined by the evolving X/Open Distributed Transaction Processing specification. Where the interface is vague, Encina takes the interesting approach of implementing all the alternatives and allowing the customer to select the desired behavior.

The Encina recovery manager performs a REDO-UNDO scan of the log at restart and invokes the resource manger callbacks to drive their REDO and UNDO at restart (similar to the design described in Chapter 11, Subsection 11.4.3). The same mechanism is used for transaction abort and for media recovery. Encina does not provide support for savepoints, but it does support nested transactions.

Encina includes a volume manager that maps segments of multiple physical disks to one logical disk. The volume manager can be instructed to duplex physical disks so that the logical volume is highly available. This is similar to the disk duplexing described in Chapter 3, Subsection 3.7.2 and Chapter 13, Section 13.2. A block-oriented buffer manager provides read and write operations on logical volumes. The volume and buffer manager design is similar to that described in Chapter 13.

Encina's Structured File System provides records within files. It is implemented using the lock, transaction, recovery, and volume services just described. The design is similar to that discussed in Chapters 14 and 15. Files can be entry sequenced, relative, or keyed (B-tree). Files can have secondary indices. Hashed indices are not directly supported. When opening a file, the client can specify the degree of isolation: browse, cursor stability, or repeatable read. Updates to files are covered by logging techniques similar to those described in Chapter 15. Encina supports both system restart recovery and media recovery of the files. An online fuzzy dump is supported, but all reorganization is done while the files are offline.

A queue manager is promised for a later Encina release.

The Encina transaction monitor acts as a broker for transactional remote procedure calls arriving from clients. Trids are tagged onto each TRPC as Encina routes messages from clients to servers. Security is based on the DCE Kerberos design for authentication, end-to-end encryption for privacy, and the DCE user/group database. Load balancing is done by a combination of randomization and DCE RPC queueing.

---

[10] Transarc made prerelease versions of the Encina manuals available to the authors. Jeff Eppinger helped in the preparation of this subsection.

System configuration is performed via UNIX, DCE, and Encina tools. Encina does not come with a repository or database system. It has been interfaced to X/Open compliant database systems such as Oracle and Informix.

The Encina transaction monitor supports a DCE RPC gateway for communication to the non-IBM world, an SNA-LU6.2 gateway for communication to the IBM (CICS, IMS, AS/400) world, and an X/Open gateway for integration of other resource managers. These gateways permit multisite heterogeneous transactions and the integration of commercial database systems into an integrated transaction processing system. Heuristic commit, transfer-of-commit, read-only, and many other optimizations are supported. The X/Open XA gateway maps Encina transaction identifiers to X/Open trids. When nested transactions are used, each subtransaction receives a new branch identifier. This approach does not work for LU6.2, so nested transactions cannot travel on those links.

Transarc is proudest of its Transactional-C programming environment. Transactional-C is an extension to the C programming language that facilitates writing transactional clients and servers. The extensions are partly syntactic, using C macros, and partly an extensive library of procedures to manipulate transactions and transactional storage. The basic syntatic extension is to allow the declaration of transactions, subtransactions, and exception handlers. It eliminates the explicit calls to begin and commit a transaction.

```
#include <tc/tc.h>                                           /* A simple transactional C program.     */
inModule("helloworld")                                       /* (copied from Transarc's manuals)      */
void main()                                                  /* All this boilerplate can be ignored.  */
{    int i;                                                  /*                                       */
     inFunction("main");                                     /*                                       */
     initTC();                                               /*                                       */
     for ( i = 0; i < 10; i++) {                             /* do the following step 10 times        */
         transaction{                                        /* start a transaction (could be nested) */
             printf("hello world - transaction %d\n", getTid());  /* print out trid                   */
             if (i % 2 )                                     /* abort odd transactions                */
                 abort("odd transactions are aborted");      /* the abort message will be saved       */
         }                                                   /* implicit transaction completion       */
         onCommit                                            /* go here if transaction commits        */
         printf("Transaction committed \n"0;                 /*                                       */
         onAbort                                             /*                                       */
         printf("Transaction aborted. \n");                  /* go here if transaction aborted        */
}    }                                                       /*                                       */
```

This syntax has many variations. A transactional storage manager tracks allocated storage and frees it if the transaction aborts. No persistent programming storage is provided directly in Transactional-C; when a process fails, its state is not reinstatiated. Applications can use files, queues, databases, or other transactional resource managers for persistent storage.

Transactional-C is designed for multi-threaded programming. Each thread of a multi-threaded process may have a separate transaction identifier. Threads may be created with a syntax like

```
concurrent  {
            subTran <block>
            • • •
            subTran <block>
            }
       onCommit   <block>
       onAbort    <block>
```

There are many variations on this syntax and a concurrent for loop. Threads may also be created by calling a system library routine. Transarc has gone to considerable effort to make the libraries thread-safe. This allows multiple threads to call the same library routine at the same time without confusing the global variables of that library. Encina provides several synchronization mechanisms for threads within a process. Beyond the lock manager, there are two exclusive semaphore mechanisms: mutexes and condition variables.

In summary, Encina is a new TP system based on the emerging OSF-DCE standard. Its extensive use of DCE services, its support for nested transactions, its Transactional-C programming environment, and its support for the X/Open DTP standard distinguish it from other TP systems. For more information on Encina see Transarc-Encina [1991].

16.7.4 Tuxedo

The Tuxedo system is a transaction monitor and database system designed to run on the UNIX operating system.[11] Tuxedo was originally built by AT&T, but today it is a product of UNIX System Laboratories (USL), an AT&T subsidiary [USL-Tuxedo 1991]. In the 1970s, an AT&T group wanted a high-availability system. Rather than buy two mainframes for failover, they opted to buy several minicomputers and build their own TP system. So, Tuxedo was born.

Tuxedo has evolved rapidly since its product introduction in 1983. Originally, it was a two-ball queued-transaction processing monitor. Today it provides a three-ball model with queued, direct, and conversational transaction processing. It balances server classes across a cluster or even a WAN, and it provides extensive connectivity options, both to workstations and to database and application servers.

Tuxedo has two independent components. System/T is a transaction monitor providing an administrative interface, a transaction manager, application development tools, and communications managers to terminals, workstations, and hosts. System/D is a SQL database system which acts as a resource manager for System/T. These two components can be bought separately, much as IMS/TM and IMS/DB are separate products. Many database vendors combine the Tuxedo transaction manger (System/T) with their own database systems, and offer the result as a complete transaction processing system. Similarly, System/D can be integrated with any transaction manager supporting the X/Open XA model.

The middle-ball of the Tuxedo system is a transaction router. This contrasts to Pathway and ACMS and is more like IMS or RTR. Each logical processor executing System/T has a *bridge* process that receives all incoming requests and forwards outgoing requests to other

---

[11] This section benefited from conversations with Randall MacBlane of USL.

Tuxedo systems. The bridge receives input messages and sends output messages via the UNIX (System V), message queueing facility. Messages are mapped to queues based on information in a shared-memory *bulletin board* managed by the Tuxedo system. The bulletin board information and the message source and contents determine the message destination. The data in the bulletin board records the local and remote servers available to perform the service, the server queue, the utilization of these servers, and other statistical information. All communication among client-server, server-server, and resource managers is routed by the bulletin board.

A set of servers at a node can share a single queue, automatically balancing the load within a local server class. If the server class is distributed among multiple nodes in a network, the bridge process uses a round-robin scheduling policy to distribute the load among servers. The bridge process sends the message to the next (in the round-robin) bridge process. That process places the message in the local server queue.

If the client and server are in the same logical processor (e.g., can share memory), the bridge process is not needed. The client's Tuxedo library routines access the shared memory and insert the message directly in the server's queue. A server may, in turn, invoke another local or remote server by calling the library routines. These routines insert a message in another server queue, passing the transaction identifier along with it. The bridge process is needed only to receive a message from a remote client or send a message to a remote server.

System/T executes presentation services in front-end processes. When supporting low-function terminals, these processes run on either the host or a terminal concentrator and multiplex many forms-oriented terminals into the system. Tuxedo provides a tool for designing and executing forms-oriented data capture and display front-end processes.

When supporting a workstation or other high-function client (e.g., another computer), presentation services run as a library inside a workstation or client machine. In the latter case, the process is any application program written with the local development tools; for example, Hypercard on an Apple, VisualBasic on MS/DOS, and perhaps C++ on a UNIX workstation. The Tuxedo client library allows workstation (or other host applications) to submit remote procedure call or conversational (peer-to-peer) transactions to a System/T node. These libraries allow clients to declare transaction boundaries and also provide extensive conversion routines to translate between the client and server data types. They give the client a flat-transaction model, but they give many commit options (e.g., synchronous, asynchronous, lazy).

Servers in the server class communicate with clients through a set of library routines that read the next message in the input queue. Tuxedo provides a server shell that deals with startup, shutdown, and other systems issues. The application programmer includes the application code (service) as a subroutine of this shell. When a message arrives for that service, the shell calls the application program. This gives the effect of a transactional RPC. Application responses are also managed by the shell. Output messages are placed in queues. These messages may cause other servers to be invoked. The queue approach provides server scheduling and load balancing at the transaction level.

A monitor/administrative process starts, grows, and shrinks server classes. It also provides an administrative and operations interface.

Tuxedo supports a gateway to LU6.2. Only outgoing requests are supported and sync point is not supported, so multi-node transactions cannot atomically commit. This minimal LU6.2 support allows System/T to send requests to most other transaction processing systems (notably IMS, CICS, Pathway, and ACMS). An OSI-TP gateway is promised soon after the OSI-TP standard is approved.

System/T is an open transaction manager. It supports a resource manager interface, distributed transactions, and many optimizations of the two-phase commit protocol. It uses a presumed-abort protocol. It supports the group-commit, transfer-of-commit, lazy commit, read-only, and last-resource-manager optimizations. It also supports heuristic decisions. System/D provides, in addition to SQL, a network-model database manager (DBTG), with transaction protected files, fuzzy dump, online recovery, and media recovery. Either SQL or the DBTG system can be used to build other transactional resource managers.

Since Tuxedo has been in use for over a decade, it has a rich set of administrative and operations tools. The system startup configuration comes from a file rather than a repository. Most system parameters can be changed while the system is operating. Servers and server classes can be added and altered, priorities changed, and the performance monitored.

Tuxedo was the prototype for the X/Open Distributed Transaction Model. Tuxedo contributed the prototypes for the XA and conversational peer-to-peer interfaces to X/Open. The X/Open application programming interface to transactions—the TM interface—evolved directly from the corresponding Tuxedo interface.

Tuxedo has been ported to most UNIX systems. It is leading the move to the X/Open DTP interface. All the popular UNIX database systems have been interfaced to it as resource managers (Informix, Ingres, Oracle, System D, and Unify). The popularity of Tuxedo is growing quickly as this book goes to press. Further information on Tuxedo can be found in [USL-Tuxedo 1991; Andrade, Carges, and Kovach 1989; Hasselgrave 1990].

16.8 Summary

This chapter has taken a very narrow perspective on each of the systems presented. The manuals describing each system are several feet thick. We have ignored many key features. In particular, application development tools, administrative interfaces, performance, and system scaleability were not discussed. Those are the very areas where the systems are evolving most rapidly.

The narrow view of this chapter comes from its focus on using transactions as a way of structuring distributed computations. The commercial systems discussed show both the great progress that has been made in this area, and the gap between what we can buy and what we can imagine. Table 16.15 summarizes the systems from that narrow perspective. Note that all the systems are limited to flat transactions without even savepoint support. While only some of them provide message integrity (ACID message delivery), support for distributed transactions is good, and the openness of these systems is improving. But there is still only limited support for high-availability options such as non-blocking commit and system pairs.

Transaction processing techniques have come a long way since the Sumerians first started recording transactions on clay tablets. But there are still a few more algorithms to discover and programs to write before the ultimate system is built.

Table 16.15. A feature summary of the transaction attributes of some commercial TP systems.

	IMS	CICS	Guardian	ACMS	X/Open
Transaction Model	flat chained	flat chained	flat explicit	flat explicit	flat both
Atomicity/Durability					
Multiple DB resource managers	yes	no	yes	yes	maybe
Message integrity (exactly once)	yes	some	no	no	maybe
Clients					
Terminal support	many	many	many	many	?
Intelligent clients	many	many	many	many	?
Processing Models					
Direct	yes	yes	yes	yes	maybe
Queued	yes	yes	yes	yes	maybe
Conversational	no	yes	yes	yes	yes
Routing	yes	yes	appl	appl	appl
Application Execution					
Protected from faults of other applications	yes	no	yes	yes	maybe
uses multiprocessors	yes	no	yes	yes	maybe
Useability/Manageability					
Integrated with repository	some	some	some	yes	no
Integrated with CASE tools	no	yes	no	yes	maybe
Application generators	some	many	some	some	maybe
Integrated with workstation tools	some	some	some	some	maybe
Open					
Resource manager interface	yes	yes	no	yes	yes
Communication manager Interface	no	yes	no	yes	yes
Distributed					
Transaction routing	yes	yes	application	application	yes
Function shipping	no	yes	yes	maybe	maybe
TRPC	no	yes	yes	yes	yes
Context-Sensitive TRPC	no	yes	yes	yes	no
Peer-to-peer	no	yes	yes	yes	yes
Commit					
Two-phase presumed abort	yes	yes	yes	yes	yes
Open	no	yes	no	yes	yes
Non-blocking?	no	no	yes	yes	maybe
Optimizations	group, nested, etc.	nested	group, nested, etc.	read, nested	nested
Availability					
Application scales in a cluster	no	no	yes	yes	maybe
Hot standby	XRF	XRF	process pair	no	no
System pairs	no	no	RDF	no	no

PART EIGHT

Addenda

17

References

Abbott, R. J. (1990). "Resourceful Systems for Fault Tolerance, Reliability, and Safety." *ACM Computing Surveys.* **22**(1): 35–68.

Adams, E. (1984). "Optimizing Preventative Service of Software Products." *IBM Journal of Research and Development.* **28**(1): 2–14.

Agha, G. A. (1987). *Actors: A Model of Concurrent Computation in Distributed Systems.* Cambridge: MIT Press.

Aho, A. v., J. Ulman, and J. Hopcroft. (1987). *Data Structures and Algorithms.* Computer Science and Information Processing. Reading, MA: Addison-Wesley.

Alsberg, P. A., and J. D. Day. (1976). *A Principle for Resilient Sharing of Distributed Resources.* 2nd International Conference on Software Engineering. 562–570.

Anderson, T., ed. (1985). *Resilient Computing Systems.* 2 vols. New York: John Wiley and Sons.

Anderson, T., and P. A. Lee. (1981). *Fault-Tolerance Principles and Practice.* Englewood Cliffs, NJ: Prentice Hall.

Anderson, T., and B. Randell. (1979). *Computing Systems Reliability.* Cambridge: Cambridge University Press.

Andrade, J. M., M. T. Carges, and K. R. Kovach. (1989). *Building a Transaction Processing System on UNIX Systems.* UniForum, San Francisco.

Anon-Et-Al. (1985). "A Measure of Transaction Processing Power." *Datamation.* **31**(7): 112–118.

Astrahan, M. M., M. W. Blasgen, D. D. Chamberlin, K. P. Eswaran, J. Gray, P. P. Griffiths, W. F. King, R. A. Lorie, P. R. McJones, J. W. Mehl, G. R. Putzolu, I. L. Traiger, and V. Watson. (1976). "System R: A Relational Approach to Database Management." *ACM TODS.* **1**(2): 97–137.

Astrahan, M. M., M. W. Blasgen, D. D. Chamberlin, J. Gray, P. P. Griffiths, W. F. King, R. A. Lorie, P. R. McJones, J. W. Mehl, G. F. Putzolu, D. R. Slutz, H. R. Strong, P. Tiberio, I. L. Traiger, and B. Yost. (1979). "An Overview of System R: A Relational Database System." *IEEE Computer.* **13**(4): 43–55.

Astrahan, M. M., M. W. Blasgen, D. D. Chamberlin, J. Gray, W. F. King, B. G. Lindsay, R. A. Lorie, J. W. Mehl, T. G. Price, G. R. Putzolu, M. Schkolnick, P. G. Selinger, D. R. Slutz, H. R. Strong, I. L. Traiger, W. B. Wade, and R. A. Yost. (1981). "System R: An Architectural Overview." *IBM Systems Journal.* **20**(1): 41–62.

Avizienis, A. (1989). *Software Fault Tolerance.* IFIP 11th World Computer Congress. 491–498.

Avizienis, A., P. Gunningberg, J. P. J. Kelly, L. Stringini, K. S. Tso, and U. Voges. (1985). *The UCLA Dedix System: A Distributed Testbed for Multi-Version Software.* 15th FTCS. 126–134.

Avizienis, A., H. Kopetz, and J. C. Laprie. (1987). *Dependable Computing and Fault-Tolerant Systems.* New York: Springer-Verlag.

Bancilhon, F., W. Kim, and H. F. Korth. (1985). *A Model of CAD Transactions.* 11th VLDB. 25–33.

Bannerjee, J., J. Jordan, and R. Batman. (1981). *Precision Locks.* ACM SIGMOD. 194–206.

Barghouti and Kaiser. (1991). "Concurrency Control in Advanced Database Systems." ACM *Computing Surveys.* **23**(3): 269.

Bartlett, J. (1981). *A NonStop™ Kernel.* 8th ACM SIGOPS SOSP. 22–29.

Bayer, R., and K. Elhardt. (1984). "A Database Cache for High Performance and Fast Restart in Database Systems." *ACM TODS.* **9**(4): 503–525.

Bayer, R., and E. M. McCreight. (1972). "Organization and Maintenance of Large Ordered Indexes." *Acta Informatica.* **1**(3): 173–189.

Bayer, R., and M. Schkolnick. (1977). "Concurrency of Operations on B-Trees." *Acta Informatica.* **9**(1): 1–21.

Bayer, R., and K. Unterauer. (1977). "Prefix B-Trees." *ACM TODS.* **2**(1): 11–26.

Beeri, C., P. A. Bernstein, N. Goodman, M. Y. Lai, and D. E. Shasha. (1983). *A Concurrency Control Theory for Nested Transactions.* 2nd ACM SIGACT-SIGOPS PODS. 45–62.

Beeri, C., and R. Obermarck. (1981). *A Resource Class Independent Deadlock Detection Algorithm.* 7th VLDB. 166–178.

Bell, C. G., and A. Newell. (1971). *Computer Structures: Readings and Examples.* New York: McGraw-Hill.

Bentley, J. L. (1979). "Multidimensional Binary Search Trees in Database Applications." *IEEE SE.* **5**(4): 333–340.

Bernstein, P. A., W. T. Emberton, and V. Trehan. (1991). "DECdta: Digital's Distributed Transaction Processing Architecture." *Digital Technical Journal.* **3**(1): 10–17.

Bernstein, P. A., and N. Goodman. (1984). "An Algorithm for Concurrency Control and Recovery in Replicated Distributed Databases." *ACM TODS.* **9**(4): 596–615.

Bernstein, P. A., N. Goodman, E. Wong, C. L. Reeve, and J. B. Rothnie. (1981). "Query Processing in a System for Distributed Databases (SSD-1)." *ACM TODS.* **6**(4): 602–625.

Bernstein, P. A., V. Hadzilacos, and N. Goodman. (1987). *Concurrency Control and Recovery in Database Systems.* Reading, MA: Addison-Wesley.

Bernstein, P. A., M. Hsu, and B. Mann. (1990). *Implementing Recoverable Requests Using Queues.* ACM SIGMOD. 112–122.

Bernstein, P. A., D. W. Shipman, and J. W. Rothnie. (1980). "Concurrency Control in a System for Distributed Databases (SDD-1)." *ACM TODS.* **5**(1): 18–51.

Bertino, E., and Kim W. (1989). "Indexing Techniques for Queries on Nested Objects." *IEEE Transactions on Data and Knowledge Engineering.* **1**(2): 196–214.

Biliris, A. (1987). *Operation Specific Locking in B-Trees.* 6th ACM PODS. 159–169.

Birrell, A. D., R. Levin, R. M. Needham, and M. D. Schroeder. (1982). "Grapevine: An Exercise in Distributed Computing." CACM. **25**(4): 260–274.

Birrell, A. D., and B. J. Nelson. (1984). "Implementing Remote Procedure Calls." ACM TOCS. **2**(1): 39–59.

Bitton, D., D. J. DeWitt, and C. Turbyfill. (1983). *Benchmarking Database Systems: A Systematic Approach.* 9th VLDB. 8–19.

Bitton, D. and J. Gray. (1988). *Disc Shadowing.* 14th VLDB. 331–338.

Bjork, L. A. (1973). *Recovery Scenarios for a DB/DC System.* SJCC. 142–146.

Bjork, L. A., and C. T. Davies. (1972). "The Semantics of the Preservation and Recovery of Integrity in a Data System." IBM General Products Division, TR 02.540.

Blasgen, M. W., R. G. Casey and K. P. Eswaran. (1977). "An Encoding Method for Multifield Sorting and Indexing." *CACM.* **20**(11): 874–877.

Blasgen, M. W., and K. P. Eswaran. (1977). "Storage and Access in Relational Databases." *IBM Systems Journal.* **4**(8): 363–374.

Blasgen, M. W., J. Gray, M. A. Mitoma, and T. G. Price. (1979). "The Convoy Phenomenon." *ACM Operating Systems Review*. **13**(2): 20–25.

Bloom, B. H. (1970). "Space/Time Tradeoffs in Hash Coding with Allowable Errors." *CACM*. **13**(7): 422–426.

Borr, A. (1981). *Transaction Monitoring in Encompass [TM]: Reliable Distributed Transaction Processing*. 7th VLDB. 155–165.

———. (1984). *Robustness to Crash in a Distributed Database: A Non Shared-Memory Multi-Processor Approach*. 10th VLDB. 445–453.

Brinch Hansen, P. (1970). "The Nucleus of a Multiprogramming System." *CACM*. **13**(4): 238–250.

———. (1973). *Operating System Principles*. Englewood Cliffs, NJ: Prentice Hall.

Burkes, D. L., and R. K. Treiber. (1990). *Design Approaches for Real-Time Transaction Processing Remote Site Recovery*. 35th IEEE Compcon 90. 568–572.

Carey, M. J., D. J. DeWitt, J. E. Richardson, and E. J. Shekita. (1986). *Object and File Management in the EXODUS Extensible Database System*. 12th VLDB. 91–100.

Ceri, S., and G. Pelagatti. (1984). *Distributed Databases: Principles and Systems*. New York: McGraw-Hill.

Chamberlin, D., A. Gilbert, and R. Yost. (1981). *A History of System R and the SQL/Data System*. 7th VLDB. 456–464.

Chamberlin, D. D., M. M. Astrahan, W. F. Kung, R. A. Lorie, J. W. Mehl, M. Schkolnick, P. G. Sellinger, D. R. Slutz, W. B. Wade, R. A. Yost. (1981). "Support for Repetitive Transactions and Ad Hoc Queries in System R." *ACM TODS*. **1**(6): 70–94.

Chamberlin, D. D., M. M. Astrahan, W. F. King, R. A. Lorie, J. W. Mehl, T. G. Price, M. Schkolnick, P. G. Selinger, D. R. Slutz, W. B. Wade, and R. A. Yost. (1976). "SEQUEL 2: A Unified Approach to Data Definition, Manipulation, and Control." *IBM Journal of Research and Development*. **20**(6): 560–575.

Chamberlin, D. D., J. Gray, and I. L. Traiger. (1975). *Views, Authorization, and Locking*. 1975 ACM National Computer Conference. 425–430.

Chamberlin, D. D., P. P. Griffiths, J. Gray, I. L. Traiger, and B. W. Wade. (1978). Database System Authorization. In *Foundations of Secure Computing*. Orlando, FL: Academic Press.

Chang, A., M. F. Mergen, R. K. Rader, J. A. Roberts, and S. L. Porter. (1990). "Evolution of Storage Facilities in AIX Version 3 for RISC System/6000 Processors." *IBM Journal of Research and Development*. **34**(1): 105–109.

Cheng, J. M., C. R. Loosley, A. Shibamiya, and P. S. Worthington. (1984). "IBM Database 2 Performance: Design, Implementation, and Tuning." *IBM Systems Journal*. **23**(2): 189–210.

Chou, H., and D. Dewitt. (1985). *An Evaluation of Buffer Management Strategies for Relational Database Systems*. 11th VLDB. 127–141.

Chrysanthis, P. K., and K. Ramamritham. (1991). ACTA: The SAGA Continues. *Transaction Models for Advanced Database Applications*. San Mateo, CA: Morgan Kaufmann.

Chrysanthis, P. K., and K. Ramamritham. (1990). *ACTA: A Framework for Specifying and Reasoning about Transaction Structure and Behavior*. ACM SIGMOD. 194–203.

Clark, B. E., and M. J. Corrigan. (1989). "Application System/400 Performance Characteristics." *IBM Systems Journal*. **28**(3): 407–423.

CODASYL. (1978). "Report of the CODASYL Data Description Language Committee." *Information Systems*. **3**(4): 247–320.

Codd, E. F. (1970). "A Relational Model of Data for Large Shared Databanks." *CACM*. **13**(6): 377–387.

———. (1982). "Relational Database: A Practical Foundation for Productivity." *CACM*. **25**(2): 109–118.

Comer, D. (1979). "The Ubiquitous B-Tree." *ACM Computing Surveys.* **11**(2): 121–137.

Cooper, E. C. (1982). *Analysis of Distributed Commit Protocols.* ACM SIGMOD. 175–183.

Cooper, T. (1989). *IBM OS/2 Extended Edition Database Manager (API) and Query Manager Version 1.1.* GC24-3399-00. White Plains, NY: IBM.

Copeland, G., T. Keller, and M. Smith. (1992). Database Buffer and Disk Configurating and the Battle of the Bottlenecks. *High Performance Transaction Processing Systems.* Springer-Verlag Lecture Notes in Computer Science. New York: Springer-Verlag.

Cristian, F. (1991). "Understanding Fault-Tolerant Distributed Systems." *CACM.* **34**(2): 56–78.

Crus, R. A. (1984). "Data Recovery in IBM Database 2." *IBM Systems Journal.* **23**(2): 178–188.

Daniels, D. S., A. Z. Spector, and D. S. Thompson. (1987). "Distributed Logging for Transaction Processing." *ACM SIGMOD Record.* **16**(3): 82–95.

Dash, J. R., and R. N. Ojala. (1984). "IBM Database 2 in an Information Management System Environment." *IBM Systems Journal.* **23**(2): 165–177.

Date, C. J. (1988). *A Guide to the SQL Standard.* 2nd ed. Reading, MA: Addison-Wesley.

Date, C. J., and C. J. White. (1988). *A Guide To DB2: A User's Guide to the IBM Product IBM DATABASE 2 (a Relational Database Management System for the MVS Environment) and its Major Companion Products QMF, AS, CSP, etc.* Reading, MA: Addison-Wesley.

Davies, C. T. (1972). "A Recovery/Integrity Architecture for a Data System." IBM General Products Division, TR 02.528.

——— (1973). *Recovery Semantics for a DB/DC System.* SJCC. 136–141.

———. (1978). "Data Processing Spheres of Control." *IBM Systems Journal.* **17**(2): 179–198.

Davis, S. H. (1991). "Design of VMS Volume Shadowing Phase II: Host-Based Shadowing." *Digital Technical Journal.* **3**(3): 7–15.

Dayal, U., M. Hsu, and R. Ladin. (1990). *Organizing Long-Running Activities with Triggers and Transactions.* ACM SIGMOD. 204–214.

———. (1991). *A Transaction Model for Long-Running Activities.* 17th VLDB. 113–122.

DEC-ACMS. (1991). *VAX ACMS*
  Getting Started, AA-EV63D-TE
  Quick Reference, AA-LD80C-TE
  Installation Guide, AA-N686H-TE
  Introduction, AA-LD79C-TE
  Concepts and Design Guidelines, AA-PFVCA-TE
  Writing Server Procedures, AA-N691F-TE
  Managing Applications, AA-N689F-TE
  Writing Applications, AA-LC14C-TE
  Application Definition Utility, AA-U715F-TE
  Systems Interface Programming, AA-EA12E-TE
  TP System Case Study: Database and Application Development, AA-NF67A-TE
  AVERTZ Application Overview, AA-PHG1A-TE
  Master Index, AA-PFVDA-TE
  Littleton, MA: Digital Equipment Corporation.

DEC-Rdb. (1991). *DEC Rdb/VMS*
  Getting Started with Rdb/VMS, AA-PJC8A-TE
  Glossary and Master Index, AA-PJC8A-TE
  Guide to using SQL, AA-JM33E-TE
  SQL Reference Manual, AA-JM32E-TE
  Guide to Distributed Transactions, AA-PCU6B-TE
  Guide to Database Design and Definition, AA-N034F-TE
  Guide to Database Maintenance, AA-N035F-TE
  Guide to Databse Performance and Tuning, AA-PJC7A-TE
  Guide to Using SQL/Services, AA-ND79C-TE

SQL Reference Manual, AA-JM32E-TE

RMU (utilities) Reference Manual, AA-PJC5A-TE

Installation Guide, AA-N032K-TE

Nashua, NH: Digital Equipment Corporation.

DEC-RTR. (1991). *DEC Reliable Transaction Router (RTR) for VMS*

Application Programmer's Reference Manual, AA-PWGA-TE

Installation Guide, AA-PHWJA-TE

System Manager's Manual, AA-PHWHA-TE

Marlboro, MA: Digital Equipment Corporation.

DeWitt, D. J., R. H. Katz, F. Olken, L. D. Shapiro, M. Stonebraker, and D. Wood. (1984). *Implementation Techniques for Main Memory Database Systems.* ACM SIGMOD. 1–8.

Dijkstra, E. W. (1965). "Solution of a Problem in Concurrent Programming Control." *CACM.* **8**(9): 569.

———. (1968). "Co-Operating Sequential Processes." In *Programming Languages.* London: Academic Press.

Duquaine, W. V. (1992). *What's Right and What's Wrong with Client Server Models.* Proceedings of *High Performance Transaction Processing Systems.* Monterey, CA.

Effelsberg, W., and T. Haeder. (1984). "Principles of Database Buffer Management." *ACM TODS.* **9**(4): 560–595.

ElAbbadi, A., D. Skeen, and F. Cristian. (1985). *An Efficient Fault-Tolerant Protocol for Replicated Databases.* 4th AMC PODS. 215–229.

ElAbbadi, A., and S. Toueg. (1986). *Maintaining Availability in Partitioned Replicated Databases.* 5th ACM PODS. 240–251.

Ellis, C. (1980). "Concurrent Search and Inserts in 2-3 Trees." *Acta Informatica.* **14**(1): 63–86.

———. (1982). *Extendible Hashing for Concurrent Operations and Distributed Data.* ACM SIGMOD. **1**: 106–115.

———. (1985). *Concurrency Control and Linear Hashing.* ACM PODS. **1**: 1–7.

———. (1987). "Concurrency in Linear Hashing." *ACM TODS.* **12**(2): 195–217.

Enbody, R. J., and H. C. Du. (1988). "Dynamic Hashing Schemes." *ACM Computing Surveys.* **20**(2): 85–113.

Englert, S., and J. Gray. (1991). "Performance Benefits of Parallel Query Execution and Mixed Workload Support in NonStop SQL Release." *Tandem System Review.* **6**(2): 12–23.

Englert, S., T. Kocher, J. Gray, and P. Shah. (1991). "The NonStop SQL Release 2 Benchmark." *Tandem System Review.* **6**(2): 12–23.

Eppinger, J. L. (1989). Virtual Memory Management for Transaction Processing. Ph.D. diss., CMU-CS-89-115, Carnegie Mellon University.

Eppinger, J. L., L. B. Mummert, and A. Z. Spector. (1991). *Camelot and Avalon: A Distributed Transaction Facility.* San Mateo, CA: Morgan Kaufmann.

Epstein, R., M. Stonebraker, and E. Wong. (1978). *Distributed Query Processing in a Relational Database System.* ACM SIGMOD. 169–180.

Eswaran, K. P., J. Gray, R. Lorie, and I. L. Traiger. (1976). "The Notions of Consistency and Predicate Locks in a Database System." *CACM.* **19**(11): 624–633.

Fagin, R., J. Nievergelt, N. Pippenger, and H. R. Strong. (1979). "Extendible Hashing: A Fast Access Method for Dynamic Files." *ACM TODS.* **4**(3): 315–344.

Ferrari, D. (1978). *Computer Systems Performance Evaluation.* Englewood Cliffs, NJ: Prentice Hall.

Ford, R., and J. Calhoun. (1984). *Concurrency Control Mechanisms and the Serializability of Concurrent Tree Algorithms.* ACM Symposium on Principles of Database Systems. **1**: 51–61.

Frank, A. (1981). *Application of DBMS to Land Information Systems.* 7th VLDB. 448–453.

Fu, A., and T. Kameda. (1989). *Concurrency Control for Nested Transactions Accessing B-Trees.* 8th ACM PODS. 270–285.

Garcia-Molina, H. (1982). "Reliability Issues for Fully Replicated Distributed Databases." *Computer.* **15**(9): 34–42.

———. (1983). "Using Semantic Knowledge for Transaction Processing Databases." *ACM TODS.* **8**(2): 186–213.

Garcia-Molina, H., and C. A. Polyzois. (1990). *Issues in Disaster Recovery.* 35th IEEE Compcon 90. 573–577.

Garcia-Molina, H., and K. Salem. (1987). *Sagas.* Proc. ACM SIGMOD. San Francisco. 249–259.

Gawlick, D., and D. Kinkade. (1985). "Varieties of Concurrency Control in IMS/VS FastPath." *IEEE Database Engineering.* **8**(2): 3–10.

Gifford, D. K. (1979). *Weighted Voting for Replicated Data.* 7th SOSP. 150–162.

Gifford, D. K., and N. Glasser. (1988). "Remote Pipes and Procedures for Efficient Distributed Computation." *ACM TOCS.* **6**(3): 258–283.

Good, B., J. Gray, P. Homan, D. Gawlick, and H. Sammer. (1985). *One Thousand Transactions Per Second.* 35th IEEE Compcon 85. 96–101.

Grady, R. (1989). "Dissecting Software Failures." *Hewlett-Packard Journal.* **40**(2): 57–63.

Gray, J. (1978). "Notes on Database Operating Systems." In *Operating Systems: An Advanced Course.* Springer-Verlag Lecture Notes in Computer Science. Vol. 60. New York: Springer-Verlag.

———. (1979). *One, Two, Three, and Four Message Commit Protocols.* Pala Mesa Workshop on Reliable Distributed Computing.

———. (1980). "A Transaction Model." In *ICALP 80: Automata, Languages, and Programming.* Springer-Verlag Lecture Notes in Computer Science. Vol. 85. Berlin: Springer-Verlag.

———. (1981). *The Transaction Concept: Virtues and Limitations.* 7th VLDB. 144–154.

———. (1986). *Why Do Computers Stop and What Can We Do about It.* 5th Symposium on Reliability in Distributed Software and Database Systems. 3–12.

———. (1987). "Transparency in Its Place." *UNIX Review.* **5**(5): 42–53.

———. (1988). *The Cost of Messages.* 7th ACM PODC. 1–7.

———. (1990). "A Census of Tandem System Availability between 1985 and 1990." *IEEE Transactions on Reliability.* **39**(4): 409–418.

———. (1991). *The Benchmark Handbook for Database and Transaction Processing Systems.* The Morgan Kaufmann Series in Data Management Systems. San Mateo, CA: Morgan Kaufmann.

Gray, J., P. Homan, R. Obermarck, and H. Korth. (1981). "A Strawman Analysis of the Probability of Waiting and Deadlock in a Database System." IBM San Jose Research Laboratory, RJ 3066, February.

Gray, J., R. A. Lorie, G. R. Putzolu, and I. L. Traiger. (1976). "Granularity of Locks and Degrees of Consistency in a Shared Database." In *Modeling in Data Base Management Systems.* Amsterdam: Elsevier North-Holland.

Gray, J., P. R. McJones, M. W. Blasgen, B. Lindsay, R. A. Lorie, T. G. Price, G. R. Putzolu, and I. L. Traiger. (1981). "The Recovery Manager of the System R Database Manager." *ACM Computing Surveys.* **13**(2): 223–242.

Gray, J., and G. R. Putzolu. (1987). *The Five Minute Rule for Trading Memory for Disc Accesses and the 10 Byte Rule for Trading Memory for CPU Time.* ACM SIGMOD. 395–398.

Gray, J. P., P. Hansen, P. Homan, M. Lerner, and M. Pozefsky. (1983). "Advanced Program-to-Program Communication in SNA." *IBM Systems Journal.* **22**(4):

Guttman, A., and M. Stonebraker. (1984). *R-Trees: A Dynamic Index Structure for Spatial Searching.* ACM SIGMOD Conference on Management of Data. Boston, June. 47–57. Also in Stonebraker's *Readings in Database Systems.*

Gyllstrom, P. O., and T. Wimberg. (1992). "STDL: A Portable Transaction Processing Language." In *High Performance Transaction Processing Systems*. Springer-Verlag Lecture Notes in Computer Science. New York: Springer-Verlag.

Haderle, D. J., and R. D. Jackson. (1984). "IBM Database 2 Overview." *IBM Systems Journal*. **23**(2): 112–125.

Hagmann, R. B. (1986). "A Crash Recovery Scheme for Memory-Resident Databases." *IEEE TOC*. **35**(9): 87–96.

———— (1987). *Reimplementing the Cedar File System Using Logging and Group Commit*. 11th ACM SIGOPS SOSP: 155–162.

Hammer, M., and D. Shipman. (1980). "Reliability Mechanisms for SDD-1." *ACM TODS*. **5**(4): 431–466.

Härder, T., and A. Reuter. (1983). "Principles of Transaction-Oriented Database Recovery." *ACM Computing Surveys*. **15**(4): 287–317.

Härder, T., and K. Rothermel. (1988). "Handling Hotspot Data in DB-Sharing Systems." *Information Systems*. **13**(2): 155–166.

Haskin, R., Y. Malachi, W. Sawdon, and G. Chan. (1988). "Recovery Management in QuickSilver." ACM TOCS. **6**(1): 82–108.

Helland, P. (1985). "Transaction Monitoring Facility." *Database Engineering*. **8**(2): 9–18.

————. (1989). "The TMF Application Programming Interface: Program to Program Communications, Transactions, and Concurrency in the Tandem NonStop Computer System." Tandem Computers, TR 89.3.

Helland, P., H. Sammer, J. Lyon, R. Carr, P. Garrett, and A. Reuter. (1987). "Group Commit Timers and High Volume Transaction Systems." In *High Performance Transaction Systems*. Berlin: Springer–Verlag.

Hesselgrave, M. R. (1990). *Considerations for Building Distributed Transaction Processing Systems on UNIX System V*. Uniforum, San Francisco.

Highleyman, W. H. (1989). *Performance Analysis of Transaction Processing Systems*. Englewood Cliffs, NJ: Prentice Hall.

Hinrichs, K. H. (1985). The Grid File System: Implementation and Case Studies of Applications. Ph.D. diss., Institut für Informatik, ETH, Zurich.

Hobbs, L., and K. England. (1991). *A Comprehensive Guide to Rdb/VMS*. Maynard, MA: Digital Press.

Horst, R., and J. Gray. (1989). *Learning from Field Experience with Fault Tolerant Systems*. International Workshop on Hardware Fault Tolerance in Multiprocessors, University of Illinois, Urbana, 77–79.

Howard, J. H., M. L. Kazar, S. G. Menees, D. A. Michols, and M. Satyanarayanan. (1988). "Scale and Performance in a Distributed File System." ACM TOCS. **6**(1): 51–81.

IBM-CICS. (1991). *Customer Information Control System /Enterprise Systems Architecture (CICS/ESA)*
General Information , GC33-0155
Processing Overview, SC33-0673
Installation, SC33-0663
System Definition, SC33-0664
Customization, SC33-0665
Resource Definition, SC33-0666
Operations, SC33-0668
CICS-Supplied Transactions, SC33-0669
System Programming Reference, SC33-0670
Application Programming Guide, SC33-0675
Application Programming Reference, SC33-0676
Application Programming Primer (COBOL), SC33-0674
Sample Applications Guide, SC33-0731

Distributed Transaction Programming, SC33-0783
Intercommunication Guide, SC33-0657
Recovery and Restart Guide, SC33-0658
Performance Guide, SC33-0659
XRF Guide, SC33-0661
RACF Security Guide, SC33-0749
Communicating with CICS OS/2, SC33-0736
Hursley Park, Hampshire, England: IBM.

IBM-IMS. (1991). *Information Management System (IMS)*
General Information, GC26-4275
Installation, SC26-4276
System Definition, SC26-4278
System Administration, SC26-4282
Operations Guide, SC26-4287
Operations Reference, SC26-4288
Application Programming, SC26-4279
Data Communication Administration, SC26-4286
Database Administrator's Guide, SC26-4288
Database Recovery Control: Guide, SC26-4287
Database Recovery Control: Logic, SC26-4293
Programming Guide for Remote SNA Systems, SC26-4186
Program Logic Manual, SC26-4294
Utilities Reference, SC26-4629
Master Index and Glossary, SH20-9085
San Jose, CA: IBM.

IBM-IMS-XRF. (1991). *IMS Extended Recovery Facility (XRF)*
Planning, GC24-3151
Implementation, GG24-3152
Technical Reference, GG24-3153
Operation and Recovery, GG24-3154
San Jose, CA: IBM.

IBM-LU6.2. (1991). *System Network Architecture (SNA) Logical Unit 6.2 (LU6.2)*
SNA Concepts and Products, GC30-3072
SNA Technical Overview, GC30-3073
Transaction Programmer's Reference Manual for LU6.2, GC30-3084
Formats and Protocol Reference Manual for LU6.2, SC30-3269
Formats and Protocol Reference Manual: Architectural Logic, SC30-3112
Reference: Peer-Protocols, SC31-6808
Research Triangle Park, NC: IBM.

IBM-MVS-APPC. (1991). *MVS Application Program-to-Program Communications (APPC/MVS)*
Application Development, Writing Transaction Programs for APPC/MVS, GC28-1112
Planning, APPC Management, GC28-1110
APPC/MVS Handbook for the OS/2 System Administrator, GCGC28-1133
San Jose, CA: IBM.

IBM-SAA. (1991). *System Application Architecture (SAA)*
An Overview, GC26-4341
Common Programming Interface: Summary, GC26-4625
Common Communications Support: Summary, GC31-6810
Communications Reference (CPI-C), SC26-4399
Database Reference (SQL), SC26-4348
Repository Reference, SC26-4684

Resource Recovery Reference, SC31-6821
Concepts of Distributed Data, SC26-4417
Writing Applications: A Design Guide, SC26-4362
(see Overview for C, COBOL, FORTRAN, presentation, dialog, . . .)
San Jose, CA: IBM.

Ioannidis, Y. E., and E. Wong. (1987). *Query Optimization by Simulated Annealing.* Proc. ACM SIGMOD. San Francisco. 9–22.

ISO-SQL. (1986). *Database Language SQL.* ISO document ISO/TC97/SC21/WG3 N117 or ANSI document ANSI .X3.13–1986.

———. (1991). *Database Language SQL, an ISO Standard*
SQL1 (1986), X3-135-1986
SQL1 Adendum (1989), X3-135-1992
SQL2, ISO/IEC 9075:1992
SQL3, ISO X3H2-91-254
New York: ANSI.

Jain, R. (1991). *The Art of Computer Systems Performance Analysis: Techniques for Experimental Design, Measurement, Simulation, and Modeling.* New York: John Wiley & Sons.

Jarke, M., and J. Kock. (1984). "Query Optimization in Database Systems." *ACM Computing Surveys.* **16**(2): 111–152.

Johnson, B. W. (1989). *Design and Analysis of Fault Tolerant Digital Systems.* Reading, MA: Addison-Wesley.

Johnson, T., and D. Shasha. (1991a). "B-Trees with Inserts and Deletes: Why Free-at-empty Is Better than Merge-at-half." Courant Institute of Mathematical Sciences, New York University, November 11.

———. (1991b). "The Performance of Concurrent B-Tree Algorithms." University of Florida New York University, October 3, 1991.

Joshi, A. (1991). *Adaptive Locking Strategies in a Multi-Node Data Sharing Model Environment.* 17th VLDB. 181–192.

Joshi, A. M., and K. E. Rodwell. (1989). "A Relational Database Management System for Production Applicaitons." *Digital Technical Journal.* **1**(8): 99–109.

Karp, R. M., and R. E. Miller. (1966). "Properties of a Model for Parallel Computations: Determinacy, Termination, Queueing." *SIAMJAM.* **14**(6): 1390–1411.

Kernighan, B. W., and D. M. Ritchie. (1988). *The C Programming Language.* Prentice Hall Software Series. Englewood Cliffs, NJ: Prentice Hall.

Klein, J. (1991). *Advanced Rule Driven Transaction Management.* 36th IEEE Compcon 91. 562–567.

Klein, J., and A. Reuter. (1988). *Migrating Transactions.* Workshop on the Future Trends of Distributed Computing Systems. 512–520.

Knuth, D. E. (1973). *The Art of Computer Programming.* Reading, MA: Addison-Wesley.

Kohler, W. H., Y. P. Hsu, and T. K. Rogers. (1991). "Performance Evaluation of Transaction Processing Systems." *Digital Technical Journal.* **3**(1): 45–57.

Kramer, S. N. (1963). *The Sumerians: Their History, Culture, and Character.* Chicago: University of Chicago Press.

Kronenberg, N., H. Levey, W. Strecker, and R. Merewood. (1987). "The VAXcluster Concept: An Overview of a Distributed System." *Digital Technical Journal.* **1**(3): 7–21.

Kumar, V. (1989). "Concurrency Control on Extendible Hashing." *Information Processing Letters.* **31**(1): 35–41.

Kung, H. T., and P. L. Lehman. (1980). "Concurrent Manipulation of Binary Search Trees." *ACM TODS.* **5**(3): 339–353.

Kwong, Y. S., and D. Wood. (1982). "Method for Concurrency in B-Trees." *IEEE TOSE*. **8**(3): 211–223.

Laing, W. A., J. E. Johnson, and R. V. Landau. (1991). "Transaction Management Support in the VMS Operating System Kernel." *Digital Technical Journal*. **3**(1): 33–44.

Lamport, L. (1978). "The Implementation of Reliable Distributed Multiprocessor Systems." *Computer Networks*. **2**: 95–114.

Lampson, B. W. (1974). "Protection." *ACM Operating Systems Review*. **8**(1): 18–24.

———. (1979). *Sandwich Commit Protocols*. Pala Mesa Workshop on Reliable Distributed Computing.

———. (1981). "Atomic Transactions." In *Distributed Systems—Architecture and Implementation: An Advanced Course*. Lecture Notes in Computer Science. Vol. 105, New York: Springer-Verlag.

Lampson, B. W., and H. E. Sturgis. (1979). "Crash Recovery in a Distributed Data Storage System." Xerox Palo Alto Research Center.

Laprie, J. C. (1985). *Dependable Computing and Fault Tolerance: Concepts and Terminology*. 15th FTCS. 2–11.

Larson, P.-Å. (1980). *Linear Hashing with Partial Expansions*. 6th International Conference on Very Large Databases. **1**: 224–232.

———. (1982). "Performance Analysis of Linear Hashing with Partial Expansions." *ACM TODS*. **7**(4): 566–587.

———. (1985). "Linear Hashing with Overflow-Handling by Linear Probing." *ACM TODS*. **10**(1): 75-89.

———. (1988). "Linear Hashing with Separators: A Dynamic Hashing Scheme Achieving One-Access Retrieval." *ACM TODS*. **13**(3): 366–388.

Lehman, P. L., and S. B. Yao. (1981). "Efficient Locking for Concurrent Operations on B-Trees." *ACM TODS*. **6**(4): 650–670.

Lehman, T. J., and M. J. Carey. (1987). *A Recovery Algorithm for a High-Performance Memory-Resident Database System*. ACM SIGMOD. 104–117.

Lehman, T. J., and B. G. Lindsay. (1989). "The Starburst Long Field Manager." IBM San Jose Research Laboratory, RJ 6899 (June).

Leu, Y., A. K. Elmargarmid, and N. Boudriga. (1990). "Specification and Execution of Transactions for Adavanced Database Applications." Purdue University, CSD-TR-1030.

Leu, Y., A. K. Elmargarmid, and M. Rusinkiewicz. (1989). "An Extended Transaction Model for Multidatabase Systems." Purdue University, CSD-TR-925.

Lindsay, B. G. (1980). Single and Multisite Recovery Facilities. *Distributed Databases*. Cambridge: Cambridge University Press.

Lindsay, B. G., P. G. Sellinger, C. Galtieri, J. Gray, R. A. Lorie, T. G. Price, G. F. Putzolu, I. L. Traiger, and B. W. Wade. (1979). "Notes on Distributed Databases." IBM San Jose Research Laboratory, RJ 2571(33471),

Liskov, B. (1987). "The Argus Language and System." Chapter 7 in *Distributed Systems—Methods and Tools for Specification: An Advanced Course*. Berlin: Springer-Verlag.

———. (1988). "Distributed Programming in Argus." CACM. **31**(3): 300–312.

Liskov, B., D. Curtis, P. Johnson, and R. Scheifler. (1987). "Implementation of Argus." *ACM SIGOPS*. **21**(5): 111–122.

Liskov, B., S. Ghemawat, R. Gruber, P. Johnson, L. Shira, and M. Williams. (1991). "Replication in the Harp File System." *ACM Operating Systems Review*. **25**(5): 226–238.

Liskov, B., and R. Scheifler. (1983). "Guardians and Actions: Linguistic Support for Robust Distributed Programs." *ACM TOPLAS*. **5**(3): 381–404.

Litwin, W. (1980). *Linear Hashing: A New Tool for Files and Tables Addressing*. 6th VLDB. 212–223.

Litwin, W., and D. Lomet. (1987). "A New Method for Fast Data Searches with Keys." *IEEE Software* **4**(2): 16–24.

Lomet, D. B. (1977). "Process Structuring, Synchronization, and Recovery Using Atomic Actions." *ACM SIGPLAN Notices.* **12**(3): 128–137.

———. (1979). *Multi-Table Search for B-Tree Files.* ACM SIGMOD. **1**: 35–41.

———. (1981). *Digital B-Trees.* 7th International Conference on Very Large Databases. **1**: 333–343.

———. (1983a). "Bounded Index Exponential Hashing." *ACM TODS* **8**(1): 136–165.

———. (1983b). *A High-Performance Universal Key Associative Acess Method.* ACM SIGMOD **1:** 120–133.

———. (1987). "Partial Expansions for File Organizations with an Index." *ACM TODS.* **12**(1): 65–84.

———. (1988). "A Simple Bounded Disorder File Organization with Good Performance." *ACM TODS.* **13**(3): 525–551.

———. (1991b). "MLR: A Recovery Method for Multi-Level Systems." DEC Cambridge Research Lab, CRL 91/7, July.

Lomet, D. B., and B. Salzberg. (1989a). *Access Methods for Multiversion Data.* ACM SIGMOD. 315–324.

———. (1989b). *A Robust Multiattribute Search Structure.* 5th International Conference on Data Engineering. 296–304.

———. (1990a). *The Performance of a Mutiversion Access Method.* ACM SIGMOD. 353–363.

———. (1990b). "The hB-Tree: A Multiattribute Indexing Method with Good Guaranteed Performance." *ACM TODS.* **15**(4): 625–658.

———. (1991). "Concurrency and Recovery for Index Trees." Cambridge Research Laboratory, CRL 91/8, August.

Long, D. D. E., J. L. Carrol, and C. J. Park. (1990). "A Study of the Reliability of Internet Sites." UC Santa Cruz, TR UCSC-CRL-90-46, September.

Lorie, R. A. (1977). "Physical Integrity in a Large Segmented Database." *ACM TODS.* **2**(2): 91–106.

Lynch, N. A. (1983). "Multilevel Atomicity: A New Correctness Criterion for Database Concurrency Control." *ACM TODS.* **8**(4): 484–502.

Lyon, J. (1990). *Tandem's Remote Data Facility.* 35th IEEE Compcon 90. 562–567.

Maier, D., and J. Stein. (1986). *Indexing in an Object-Oriented DBMS.* Workshop on Object-Oriented Database Systems. **1:** 171–182.

Mandber, U., and R. E. Ladner. (1982). Concurrency Control in a Dynamic Search Structure. *ACM Proceedings on Database Systems.* Boston: Association for Computing Machinery.

Maxion, R. A., and F. E. Feather. (1990). "A Case Study of Ethernet Anamolies in a Distributed Computing Environment." *IEEE Transactions on Reliability.* **39**(4): 433–443.

McGee, W. C. (1977). "IMS Structure, Database, Batch, Data Communications, and Transaction Processing (in 5 parts)." *IBM Systems Journal.* **16**(2): 84–168.

Melton, J. (1989). *Database Language SQL 2 and SQL3 (ISO-ANSI working draft).* X3H2-89-252 and ISO DBL FIR-3.

Merrett, T. (1988). "Dynamic Multipaging in Even Less Space." **17**(4): 56–61.

Meyer-Wegener, K. (1988). *Transaktionssysteme.* Leitfäden der Angewandten Informatik. Stuttgart: Teubner Verlag.

Misra, M. (1990). *IBM RISC System/6000 Technology.* Austin, TX: International Business Machines Corporation.

Mohan, C. (1989). "ARIES/LHS: A Concurrency Control and Recovery Method Using Write-Ahead Logging for Linear Hashing with Separators." IBM Almaden Research Center, March.

————. (1990a). *ARIES/KVL: A Key-Value Locking Method for Concurrency Control of Multiaction Transactions on B-Tree Indexes.* 16th VLDB. 392–405.

————. (1990b). *Commit_LSN: A Novel and Simple Method for Reducing Locking and Latching in Transaction Processing Systems.* 16th VLDB. 406–418.

————. (1990c). "ARIES/LHS: A Concurrency Control and Recovery Method Using Write-Ahead Logging for Linear Hashing with Separators." IBM Almaden Research Center, November.

————. (1992). "A Cost-Effective Method for Providing Improved Availability During DBMS Restart Recovery After a Failure." In *High Performance Transaction Processing Systems.* Springer-Verlag Lecture Notes in Computer Science. New York: Springer-Verlag.

Mohan, C., D. Haderle, B. Lindsay, H. Pirahesh, and P. Schwarz. (1992). "ARIES: A Transaction Recovery Method Supporting Fine-Granularity Locking and Partial Rollbacks Using Write-Ahead Logging." *ACM TODS.* **17**(1): 94–162.

Mohan, C., D. Haderle, and A. Peterson. (1990). "ARIES/IM/PD: A Concurrency Control Index Management Method Using Write-Ahead Logging and Pseudo Deletes of Keys." IBM Almaden Research Center, Research Report, in preparation 1990.

Mohan, C., D. Haderle, Y. Wang, and J. Cheng. (1990). *Single Table Access Using Multiple Indexes: Optimization, Execution, and Concurrency Control Techniques.* International Conference on Extending Database Technology. 29–43.

Mohan, C., and F. Levine. (1989). "ARIES/IM: An Efficient and High Concurrency Index Management Method Using Write-Ahead Logging." IBM Almaden Research Center, RJ 6848, August.

————. (1992). "ARIES/IM: An Efficient and High Concurrency Index Management Method Using Write-Ahead Logging." ACM SIGMOD.

Mohan, C., and B. G. Lindsay. (1983). *Efficient Commit Protocols for the Tree of Processes Model of Distributed Transactions.* 2nd ACM PODC. 76–88.

Mohan, C., B. Lindsay and R. Obermarck. (1986). "Transaction Management in the R* Distributed Database Management System." *ACM TODS.* **11**(4): 378–396.

Mohan, C., and I. Narang. (1991a). *Recovery and Concurrency Control Protocols for Fast Intersystem Page Transfer and Fine-Granularity Locking in a Shared Disc Transaction Environment.* 17th VLDB. 195–208.

————. (1991b). "ARIES/SD: A Transaction Recovery and Concurrency Control Mechanism for a Shared Disc Environment." IBM Almaden Research Center, Research Report, forthcoming.

————. (1992). *Algorithms for Creating Indexes for Very Large Tables without Quiescing Updates.* ACM SIGMOD.

Mohan, C., I. Narang, and J. Palmer. (1990). "A Case Study of Problems in Migrating to Distributed Computing: Page Recovery Using Multiple Logs in a Shared Disc Environment." *IBM Research Report,* RJ 7343, March.

Mohan, C., I. Narang, and S. Silen. (1992). "Solutions to Hot Spot Problems in a Shared Disc Transaction Environment." In *High Performance Transaction Processing Systems.* Springer-Verlag Lecture Notes in Computer Science. New York: Springer-Verlag.

Mohan, C., and H. Pirahesh. (1991). *ARIES-RRH: Restricted Repeating of History in the ARIES Transaction Recovery Method.* 7th International Conference on Data Engineering.

Mohan, C., H. R. Strong, and S. Finkelstein. (1983). Method for Distributed Transaction Commit and Recovery Using Byzantine Agreement within Clusters of Processors. 2nd ACM PODC. 89–103.

Moss, J. E. B. (1981). "Nested Transactions: An Approach to Reliable Computing." MIT, LCS-TR-260.

———. (1985). *Nested Transactions: An Approach to Reliable Distributed Computing.* Boston: MIT Press.

Moss, J. E. B., B. Leban, and P. K. Chrysanthis. (1986). *Finer Grained Concurrency for Database Cache.* Fourth Data Engineering Conference. 96–103.

Mourad, J. (1985). *The Reliability of the IBM MVS/XAOperating System.* 15th FTCS. 93–98.

Needham, R., and M. Schroder. (1978). "Using Encryption for Authenticaton in Large Networks of Computers." *CACM.* **21**(12): 993–999.

Nievergelt, J., H. Hinterberger, and K. C. Sevcik. (1984). "The Grid File: An Adaptable, Symmetric Multi-Key File Structure." *ACM TODS.* **9**(1): 38–71.

Obermarck, R. (1980). "IMS/VS Program Isolation Feature." IBM San Jose Research Laboratories, RJ 72879 (36435), July.

Oki, B. M., B. H. Liskov, and R. W. Scheifler. (1985). *Reliable Object Storage to Support Atomic Actions.* Symposium on Operating Systems Principles. 147–159.

O'Neil, P. E. (1986). "The Escrow Transactional Method." *ACM TODS.* **11**(4): 405–430.

———. (1992). "Promises." In *High Performance Transaction Processing Systems.* Springer-Verlag Lecture Notes in Computer Science. New York: Springer-Verlag.

Orenstein, J. A. (1986). *Spatial Query Processing in an Object-Oriented Database.* ACM SIGMOD. **1:** 326–336.

———. (1989). *Redundancy in Spatial Databases.* ACM SIGMOD. **1:** 295–305.

Orenstein, J. A., and T. Merrett. (1984). *A Class of Data Structures for Associative Searching.* ACM SIGMOD Symposium on Principles of Database Systems. **1:** 181–190.

Orfali, R., and D. Harkey. (1990). *Client-Server Programming with OS/2 Extended Edition.* New York: Van Nostrand Reinhold.

OSF-DCE. (1990). "OSF Distributed Computing Environment Rationale." Cambridge, MA: Open Software Foundation.

OSE-CCR. (1989). *Open Systems Interconnection: Commit, Concurrency Control, and Recovery (OSI-CCR)*
Model, ISO IS 9804-1
Service Definition, ISO IS 9804-2
Protocol Specification, ISO IS 9804-3
New York: ANSI.

OSI-TP. (1992). *Open Systems Interconnection–Distributed Transaction Processing (OSI-TP)*
Model, ISO IS 10026-1
Service Definition, ISO IS 10026-2
Protocol Specification, ISO IS 10026-3
New York: ANSI.

Ozsu, T., and P. Valduriez. (1990). *Principles of Distributed Database Systems.* Englewood Cliffs, NJ: Prentice Hall.

O'Neil, P. E. (1990). "Escrow Promises." University of Massachussetts, TR 90-3.

Papadimitriou, C. H. (1986). *The Theory of Database Concurrency Control.* Rockville, MD: Computer Science Press.

Patterson, D. A., G. Gibson, and R. Katz. (1988). *A Case for Redundant Arrays of Inexpensive Disks (RAID).* ACM SIGMOD. 109–116.

Patterson, D. A., and J. L. Hennessy. (1990). *Computer Architecture: A Quantitative Approach.* San Mateo, CA: Morgan Kaufmann.

Pease, M., R. Shostak, and L. Lamport. (1980). "Reaching Agreement in the Presence of Faults." *JACM.* **27**(2): 228–234.

Peinl, P., A. Reuter, and H. Sammer. (1988). *High Contention in a Stock Trading Database: A Case Study.* ACM SIGMOD. 260–268.

Peterson, R. J., and J. P. Strickland. (1983). *Log Write-Ahead Protocols and IMS/VS Logging.* 2nd PODC. 216–243.

Polyzois, C. A., and H. Garcia-Molina. (1992). "A Generalized Disaster Recovery Model and Algorithm." In *High Performance Transaction Processing Systems.* Springer-Verlag Lecture Notes in Computer Science. New York: Springer-Verlag.

Pradhan, D. K. (1986). *Fault Tolerant Computing: Theory and Techniques, Vols. 1 and 2.* Englewood Cliffs, NJ: Prentice Hall.

Pu, C. (1992). "Generalized Transaction Processing." In *High Performance Transaction Processing Systems.* Springer-Verlag Lecture Notes in Computer Science. New York: Springer-Verlag.

Rahm, E. (1992). "Use of Global Extended Memory for Distributed Transaction Processing." In *High Performance Transaction Processing Systems.* Springer-Verlag Lecture Notes in Computer Science. New York: Springer-Verlag.

Ramakrishna, M. V., and P.-Å. Larson. (1989). "File Organization Using Composite Perfect Hashing." *ACM TODS.* **14**(2): 231–263.

Randell, B., P. A. Lee, and P. C. Treleaven. (1978). "Reliability Issues in Computer System Design." *ACM Computing Surveys.* **10**(2): 123–165.

Reed, D. (1978). "Naming and Synchronization in a Decentralized System." MIT, LCS TR 205.

———. (1981). "Implementing Atomic Actions on Decentralized Data." *ACM TOCS.* **1**(1): 3–23.

Reed, D., and L. Svobodova. (1981). "Swallow: A Distributed Data Storage System for a Local Network." In *Local Networks for Computer Communications.* New York: North Holland.

Rengarajan, T. K., P. M. Spiro, and W. A. Wright. (1989). "High Availability Mechanisms for VAX DBMS Software." *Digital Technical Journal.* **1**(8): 88–98.

Reuter, A. (1982). *Concurrency on High-Traffic Data Elements.* 1st ACM PODS. 83–92.

———. (1986). *Load Control and Load Balancing in Shared Database Management Systems.* International Conference on Data Engineering.

———. (1989). *ConTracts: A Means for Extending Control Beyond Transaction Boundaries.* 3rd International Workshop on High Performance Transaction Systems.

Reuter, A., and U. Schmidt. (1992). "Transactions in Manufacturing Applications." In *High Performance Transaction Processing Systems.* Springer-Verlag Lecture Notes in Computer Science. New York: Springer-Verlag.

Rivest, R., E. Shamir, and L. Adleman. (1978). "A Method for Obtaining Digital Signatures and Public Key Cryptosystems." CACM. **21**(2): 120–126.

Rosenkrantz, D. J., R. D. Stearns, and P. M. Lewis. (1977). "System Level Concurrency Control for Distributed Database Systems." *ACM TODS.* **3**(2): 178–198.

Rothermel, K., and C. Mohan. (1989). *ARIES/NT: A Recovery Method Based on Write-Ahead Logging for Nested Transactions.* 15th VLDB. 337–346.

Rothermel, K., and S. Pappe. (1990). *Open Commit Protocols for the Tree of Processes Model.* 10th International Conference on Distributed Computing Systems. 236–244.

Rubenstein, W. B., M. S. Kubicar, and R. G. G. Cattell. (1987). *Benchmarking Simple Database Operations.* ACM SIGMOD. 387–394.

Sacco, G., and M. Schkolnick. (1982). *A Mechanism for Managing the Buffer Pool in a Relational Database System Using the Hot Set Model.* International Conference on Very Large Databases.

Sacco, G. M., and M. Schokolnick. (1986). "Buffer Management in Relational Database Systems." *ACM TODS.* **11**(4): 473–498.

Sacks-Davis, R., A. Kent, and K. Ramamohanarao. (1987). "Multikey Access Methods Based on Superimposed Coding Techniques." *ACM TODS*. **12**(4): 655–696.

Sagiv, Y. (1986). "Concurrent Operations on B*-Trees with Overtaking." *Journal of Computer and System Sciences*. **33**(2): 275–296.

Saltzer, J., D. Reed, and D. Clark. (1984). "End-to-End Arguments in System Design." *ACM TOCS*. **2**(4): 277–288.

Salzberg, B. J. (1986). "Grid File Concurrency." *Information Systems*. **11**(3): 235–244.

———. (1988). *File Structures: An Analytic Approach*. Englewood Cliffs, NJ: Prentice Hall.

Samet, H. (1984). "The Quadtree and Related Hierarchical Data Structures." *ACM Computing Surveys*. **16**(2): 187–260.

Sattler, H. (1989). *Transaktionssystem BS2000. (In German.)* Munich: Siemens AG.

Schek, H. J. and M. Scholl. (1986). "The Relational Model with Relation Valued Attributes." *Information Systems*. **11**(2): 137–147.

Schmuk, F., and J. Wyllie. (1991). "Experience With Transactions in Qucksilver." *ACM Operating Systems Review*. **25**(5): 239–253.

Schnieder, F. B. (1983). *FailStop Processors*. IEEE COMPCON. 66–70.

Schulze, M., G. Gibson, R. Katz, and D. A. Patterson. (1989). *How Reliable is a RAID*. 34th IEEE COMPCON 89. 118–123.

Scrutchin, T. (1987). *TPF: Performance, Capacity, and Availability*. IEEE COMPCON.

Serlin, O. (1990). *TPC Benchmark A™*. Los Altos, CA: ITOM International..

Shah, J. (1991). *VAXclusters: Architecture, Programming, and Management*. New York: McGraw-Hill.

Shasha, D., and N. Goodman. (1988). "Concurrent Search Structure Algorithms." *ACM TODS*. **13**(1): 53–90.

Shasha, D. E. (1984). *Concurrent Algorithms for Search Structures*. PhD Thesis, Comp. Sci. Dept. Harvard Univ., TR-12-84.

Siewiorek, D. P., and R. S. Swarz. (1982). *The Theory and Practice of Reliable System Design*. Bedford, MA: Digital Press.

Siwiec, J. E. (1977). "A High-Performance DB/DC System." *IBM Systems Journal*. **16**(2): 169–195.

Skeen, D. (1981). *Nonblocking Commit Protocols*. ACM SIGMOD. 133–142 (Also available in Stonebraker's *Readings in Database Systems*).

Snaman, W. E. (1991). "Application Design in a VAXcluster System." *Digital Technical Journal*. **3**(3): 16–26.

Snaman, W. E., and D. W. Thiel. (1987). "The VAX/VMS Distributed Lock Manager." *Digital Technical Journal*. **5**(3): 29–44.

SNI. (1989). *Universeller Transaktionsmonitor UTM (SINIX): Verteilte Transaktionsverarbeitung*. Munich: Siemens AG.

SoftwareAG. (1988). *ADABAS TPF: Introduction Manual*. Darmstadt, Germany: Software AG.

———. (1989). *ADANET Distributed Processing Facility*. Darmstadt, Germany: Software AG.

Spector, A. Z. (1991). *Open, Distributed Transaction Processing with Encina*. International Workshop on High Performance Transaction Systems. Monterey, CA.

Spector, A. Z., J. L. Eppinger, D. S. Daniels, R. Draves, J. J. Bloch, D. Duchamp, R. F. Pausch, and D. Thompson. (1987). "High Performance Distributed Transaction Processing in a General Purpose Computing Environment." In *High Performance Transaction Systems*. Berlin: Springer-Verlag.

Spector, A. Z., and P. M. Schwarz. (1983). "Transactions: A Construct for Reliable Distributed Computing." *ACM Operating Systems Review*. **17**(2): 18–35.

Speer, T. G., and M. W. Storm. (1991). "Digital's Transaction Processing Monitors." *Digital Technical Journal*. **3**(1): 18–32.

Spiro, P. M., A. M. Joshi, and T. K. Rengarajan. (1991). "Designing an Optimized Transaction Commit Protocol." *Digital Technical Journal.* **3**(1): 70–78.

Srinivasan, V., and M. J. Carey. (1992). "On-Line Index Construction Algorithms." In *High Performance Transaction Processing Systems.* Springer-Verlag Lecture Notes in Computer Science. New York: Springer-Verlag.

Stonebraker, M. (1979). "Concurrency Control and Consistency of Multiple Copies of Data in Distributed Ingres." *IEEE SE.* **5**(3): 188–194.

———. (1981). "Operating System Support for Database Management." *CACM.* **24**(7): 412–418.

———. (1984). "Virtual Memory Transaction Management." *ACM Operating Systems Review.* **18**(2): 8–16.

———. (1986). "The Case For Shared Nothihng." *IEEE Database Engineering.* **9**(1): 610–621.

———. (1988a). "The Design of the Postgres Storage System." In *Readings in Database Systems.* San Mateo, CA: Morgan Kaufmann.

———, ed. (1988b). *Readings in Database Systems.* San Mateo, CA: Morgan Kaufmann.

Stonebraker, M., E. Wong, P. Kreps, and G. Held. (1976). "The Design and Implementation of Ingres." *ACM TODS.* **1**(3): 189–222.

Strickland, J., P. Uhrowczik, and V. Watts. (1982). "IMS/VS: An Evolving System." *IBM Journal of Research and Development.* **21**(4): 490–510.

Svobodova, L. (1979). *Reliability Issues in Distributed Information Processing Systems.* 9th FTCS. 9–16.

———. (1980). "Management of Object Histories in the Swallow Repository." MIT, LCS TR 243.

———. (1981). *A Reliable Object-Oriented Data Repository for a Distributed Computer System.* 8th SOSP. 47–58.

Tamminen, M. (1982). "The Extendible Cell Method for Closest Point Problems." *BIT.* **22**(1): 27–41.

Tandem. (1991). *Tandem Products*
Introduction to NonStop Systems, 16207
Product Overview, 84055
Summary of Technical Publications, 58967
Cupertino, CA: Tandem Computers Inc.

Tandem Database Group. (1987). NonStop SQL: A Distributed High Performance, High Availability Implementation of SQL. In *High Performance Transaction Systems.* Berlin: Springer-Verlag.

Tandem-Pathway. (1991). *Pathway Transaction Processing System*
Introduction to Pathway, 82339
System Management Guide, 39864
Management Programming Commands, 31199
Management Programming Messages and Events, 31200
PATHCOM, 31005
Application Programming Guide, 39544
Screen Cobol Reference Manual, 20356
Introduction to Pathmaker, 84070
Pathmaker Programming Manual, 27449
Cupertino, CA: Tandem Computers Inc.

Tandem Performance Group. (1988). *A Benchmark of NonStop SQL on the Debit Credit Transaction.* ACM SIGMOD. 337–341.

Tandem-RDF. (1991). *Remote Duplicate Database Facility (RDF™)*
System Management, 40595
Cupertino, CA: Tandem Computers Inc.

Tandem-SQL. (1991). *NonStop SQL*
> *Introduction, 82332*
> *Introduction to Data Management, 15873*
> *Language Reference, 39634*
> *Conversational Interface Manual, 22978*
> *Programming Guide, 82327*
> *Programming Reference Manual, 84258*
> *Installation and Management, 20263*
> Cupertino, CA: Tandem Computers.

Tandem-TMF. (1991). *Tandem's Transaction Monitoring Facility (TMF)*
> *Introduction, 12014*
> *Programming Guide, 22935*
> *Programming Manual, 84065*
> *Management and Operations Guide, 18680*
> *Management and Operations Manual, 84065*
> *TMFCOM Manual, 15755*
> Cupertino, CA: Tandem Computers.

Tanenbaum, A. S. (1987). *Operating Systems: Design and Implementation.* Englewood Cliffs, NJ: Prentice Hall.

Tay, Y. C. (1987). *Locking Performance in Centralized Databases.* Orlando, FL: Academic Press.

Teng, J. Z., and R. A. Gumaer. (1984). "Managing IBM Database 2 Buffers to Maximize Performance." *IBM Systems Journal.* **23**(2): 211–218.

Thomas, R. H. (1979). "A Majority Consensus Approach to Concurrency Control for Multiple Copy Databases." *ACM TODS.* **4**(2): 180–209.

Thomasian, A. (1992). "High Performance Distributed Transaction Processing." In *High Performance Transaction Processing Systems.* Springer–Verlag Lecture Notes in Computer Science. New York: Springer-Verlag.

Traiger, I. L. (1982a). "Virtual Memory Management for Database Systems." *IBM San Jose Research Laboratory*, RJ 3489 (41346), May.

———. (1982b). "Virtual Memory Management for Database Systems." *ACM Operating Systems Review.* **16**(4): 26–48.

Traiger, I. L., C. A. Galtaire, J. Gray, and B. G. Lindsay. (1982). "Transactions and Consistency in Distributed Database Systems." *ACM TODS.* **7**(3): 323–342.

Transarc-Encina. (1991). *Encina Transaction Processing System*
> *TP Monitor, TP-00-D146*
> *Monitor: Programmers Guide, TP-00-D078*
> *Transactional-C Programmers Guide and Reference, TP-00-D347*
> *Using the Transarc Toolkit: Guide to Transaction Processing System Development, TP-00-137*
> *Toolkit Executive, Reference Manual, TP-00-D539*
> *Toolkit Server Core, Reference Manual, TP-00-D540*
> *Structured File Server, Programmer's Guide, TP-00-D170*
> *Structured File Server, Programmer's Reference, TP-00-D223*
> *Base Development Environment, TP-00-D509*
> Pittsburgh, PA: Transarc Corp.

Tullis, N. (1984). "Powering Computer-Controlled Systems: AC or DC?" *Telesis.* **11**(1): 8–14.

USL-Tuxedo. (1991). *Tuxedo System Transaction Manager, Release 4.0*
> *System/T, order no: 308-366.1*
>> *Product Overview*
>> *Application Development Guide*

       Transaction Manager Administrator's Guide
       Transaction Manager Programmer's Guide
       Transaction Manager Reference Manual
       Transaction Manager Master Index
    System/D order no: 308-363.1
       Product Overview
       Application Development Guide
       Database Manager Administrator's Guide
       Database Manager Programmer's Guide
       SQL User's Guide/Reference Reference Manual
       ESQL User's Guide/Reference Reference Manual
       Database Manager Reference Manual
       Report Writer User's Guide
       Database Manager Master Index
  Summit, NJ: UNIX System Laboratories or Prentice Hall, Englewood Cliffs, NJ: Prentice Hall.

van der Pool, J. A. (1973). "Optimum Storage Allocation for a File with Open Addressing." *IBM Journal of Research and Development.* **17**(2): 106–114.

Veklerov, E. (1985). "Analysis of Dynamic Hashing with Deferred Splitting." *ACM TODS.* **10**(1): 90–96.

von Neumann, J. (1956). Probabilistic Logics and the Synthesis of Reliable Organisms from Unreliable Components. *Automata Studies.* Princeton, NJ: Princeton University Press.

Walter, B. (1984). *Nested Transactions with Multiple Commit Points: An Approach to the Structuring of Advanced Database Applications.* 5th VLDB. 161–171.

Watanabe, E. (1986). "Survey on Computer Security." Tokyo: Japan Information Development Corporation (JIPDEC), March.

Weber, R. O. (1990). "Coordinating Computerized Theatrical Cues." *Theater Design and Technology.* **26**(4): 47–50.

Weikum, G. (1987). "Principles and Realisation Strategies of Multi-Level Transaction Management." Technical University of Darmstadt (Germany), DVSI-1987-T1.

Wiederhold, G. (1977). *Database Design.* International Student Edition. New York: McGraw-Hill.

Wong, E., and K. Youssefi. (1976). "Decomposition: A Strategy for Query Processing." *ACM TODS.* **1**(3): 223–241.

X/Open DTP. (1991). *X/Open Common Application Environment*
    Distributed Transaction Processing: Reference Model
    Distributed Transaction Processing: The XA Specification
  Reading, Berkshire, England: X/Open Ltd.

Yelavich, B. M. (1985). "Customer Information Control System: An Evolving System Facility." *IBM Systems Journal.* **24**(3/4): 264–278.

18

Interface Declarations

/* General Declares */

```
typedef int *          pointer;                         /* untyped pointer                        */
typedef Boolean         (* procedure) (pointer);        /*dummy                                   */
typedef long           TIMESTAMP;                       /*                                        */
typedef char *         filename;                        /*                                        */
typedef int            RMID;                            /***dummy**                               */
typedef char              RMNAME;                       /***dummy**                               */
typedef pointer        RMQUEP;                          /*dummy                                   */
typedef pointer        RMTA_CBP;                        /*TransCBP? or RMTransCBP?                 */
typedef pointer        RMPR_CBP;                        /*dummy???                                */
typedef pointer        RMNO_CBP;                        /*dummy???                                */

typedef long           RETCODE;                         /* return code from subroutine calls      */
```

/* Preliminaries */

```
typedef long           NODEID;                          /* dummy****                              */
typedef long           HANDLE;                          /* dummy****                              */
RMID                   NULLLRMID =0;                    /* used to end pointer chains.            */
typedef struct {       long     file;                   /* number of log file in log directory    */
                       long     rba;                    /* log record's relative byte address (first byte) */
                                                        /* in file                                */
              }LSN ;                                    /* Def. Log Sequence Numbers (LSN)        */
LSN                    NULLLSN = {0,0};                 /* used to end pointer chains.            */
typedef struct { long length; char data[length];} context;  /* context of an application or RM   */
typedef     { TIMESTAMP          birthday;              /* birthday of TM                         */
              RMID               tmid;                  /* TM resource manager id                 */
              long               sequence;              /* transaction sequence number            */
              char               filler [2];            /* reserved for the future                */
            } TRID;                                     /* global transaction identifier          */
TRID                   NULLTrid = {0,0};                /* null TRID                              */
```

/* Process */

typedef long PID;		/* process identifier	*/
PID	NULLPID = 0;	/* null process id to end pointer chains	*/
typdedef struct Process * PCBP;		/* pointer to a process control block	*/
typdedef struct Process {		/* describes a a server class process	*/
	PID	pid;	/* process no. provided by the basic OS	*/
	RMID	InstanceOf;	/* this is the process' own server class	*/
	RMID	RunsIn;	/* current process RMID	*/
	RMID	ClientID;	/* RMID of client having invoked RunsIn	*/
	TRID	WorksFor;	/* current trid of the process	*/
	Boolean	busy;	/* Is process servicing a request ?	*/
	Uint	priority;	/* current process priority	*/
	PRTA_CBP	TAsToDo;	/* pointer to list of suspended transactions	*/
	PRRM_CBP	IMayUse;	/*RMs. callable via domain switch	*/
	PCB *	sem_wait;	/* used for semaphore waits	*/
	} PCB;		/* process control block	*/
PCB	MyProcess(void);		/* returns a copy of caller's process CB	*/
PCB *	MyProcessP(void);		/* returns a pointer to caller's process CB	*/
PID	MyPID(void);		/* returns the caller's process identifier	*/
void	wait(void);		/* a process can wait to be woken up	*/
void	wakeup(PID him);		/* wakes a waiting process.	*/

/* Session */

typedef struct Sessions *SECBP;		/* pointer to a session control block	*/
typedef struct Session { char	name[BIG];	/* transactional session name	*/
char	him[BIG];	/* name of transaction mgr at other end	*/
TIMESTAMP	birthday;	/* birthday (timestamp) of remote TM	*/
TRID	trid;	/* transaction currently riding on session	*/
Boolean	incoming;	/* session polarity (incoming or outgoing)	*/
PID	Initiator;	/* ID of process that initiated the binding	*/
NODEID	InitNode;	/* node where the initiator resides	*/
PID	OtherEnd;	/* ID of the bound side of the session	*/
NODEID	BoundNode;	/* node where the bound process runs	*/
HANDLE	handle;	/* session handle used by comm. mgr	*/
SECBP	tran_next_ses;	/* next session used by this transaction	*/
/* stuff	*stuff; */	/* many other things	*/
} SECB;		/* transactional session control block	*/

/* Compare-and-Swap */

```
Boolean CS(int * cell, int * old,  int * new);          /*                                    */
Boolean CSD(long * cell, long * old, long * new);       /*                                    */
```

/* Semaphores */

```
enum LOCK_MODE {                          /*  lock mode definitions                   */
                LOCK_FREE,                /*  lock is free, the null mode             */
                LOCK_S,                   /*  shared lock mode                        */
                LOCK_X,                   /*  exclusive lock mode                     */
                LOCK_U,                   /*  update lock mode                        */
                LOCK_IS,                  /*  intention share lock mode               */
                LOCK_IX,                  /*  intention exclusive lock mode           */
                LOCK_SIX,                 /*  share + intention exclusive lock mode   */
                LOCK_WAIT};               /*  lock is in a wait state                 */
typedef int  lock_mode;                   /*  mode is one of the lock modes           */

typedef PCB * xsemaphore;                 /* Exclusive semaphore a list of processes  */
void     Xsem_init(xsemaphore * sem);     /* initialize an X semaphore                */
void     Xsem_get(xsemaphore * sem);      /* acquire an an X semaphore                */
void     Xsem_give(xsemaphore * sem);     /* free an exclusive semaphore              */

typedef  struct    {   lock_mode   mode;        /*  mode is free, share, exclusive,       */
                       int         count;       /*  number granted                        */
                       PCB *       wait_list;   /*  list of waiting processes             */
                   } semaphore;                 /*       chained via process.sem_wait.    */
void    sem_init(semaphore * sem);              /* initialize a shared/exclusive semaphore */
void    sem_get(semaphore * sem, lock_mode mode); /* acquire access to a  shared/exclusive sem */
void    sem_give(semaphore * sem);              /* give up control of a shared/exclusive sem */
Boolean sem_get_bounce(semaphore * sem, lock_mode mode);   /* acquire access to a shared sem */
                                                /* if not available, do not wait.         */
                                                /* Return boolean indicating success      */
```

/* Locks */

```
typedef struct    { RMID   rmid;                          /* resource manager identifier (two bytes)      */
                  char resource[14];                      /* object name is  interpreted by RM            */
                  } lock_name;                            /* definitions for lock names                   */
enum LOCK_CLASS                                           /* defines lock classes,  (lock duration)       */
   {LOCK_INSTANT , LOCK_SHORT , LOCK_MEDIUM , LOCK_LONG , LOCK_VERY_LONG};
typedef int lock_reply;                                   /* status of  lock(), unlock(), unlock_class()  */
enum LOCK_REPLY {LOCK_OK , LOCK_TIMEOUT, LOCK_DEADLOCK, LOCK_NOT_LOCKED};        /*       */
LOCK_REPLY    lock(lock_name name, lock_mode mode, LOCK_CLASS class, long timeout);   /*      */
LOCK_REPLY    unlock(lock_name name);                     /*    unlock                                    */
LOCK_REPLY    unlock_class(LOCK_CLASS class, Boolean all_le, RMID rmid);         /*      */
```

/* Transaction manager */

```
struct TM_anchor { char           name[BIG];        /* transaction mgr's name (unique in net)    */
                  RMID            TMid;              /* resource mgr id  of this TM               */
                  TRID            next_trid;         /* next trid to be allocated by this TM      */
                  TIMESTAMP       birthday;          /* time of TM start (or  cold start).        */
                  LSN             checkpoint_lsn;    /* lsn of TM's most recent checkpoint        */
                  RMCB *          RM_list;           /* list of resource mgrs known to this TM    */
                  TransCB *       tran_list;         /* list of all transactions known to this TM */
                  };                                 /* transaction mgr's volatile storage info   */
enum tran_status { ACTIVE , PREPARED, ABORTING , COMMITTING , ABORTED, COMMITTED};
typedef int       savepoint;                         /* savepoint number                         */
typedef struct {  TransCB *      next;              /* the next tran entry in the list           */
                  TRID           trid;              /* the trid of the transaction               */
                  tran_status    status;            /* active, prepared, committing, aborting..  */
                  savepoint      next_save_pt;       /* next savepoint number                    */
                  savepoint      save_pt;            /* current savepoint number                 */
                  LSN            save_pt_lsn;        /* lsn of current savepoint log record       */
                  LSN            max_lsn;            /* most recent log record of this trans      */
                  LSN            min_lsn;            /* first log record of this transaction      */
                  RMTranCB *     RM_list;            /* list of resource mgrs joined to this trans */
                  SECB  *        ses_list;           /* list of sessions that are part of this trans */
                  pointer        lock_list;          /* locks of this transaction.               */
                  pointer        wait;              /* lock waited for by transaction (or null)  */
                  long           timeout;            /* timeout interval for lock waits          */
                  TransCB *      cycle;             /* used by deadlock detector (see below)     */
                  } TransCB;                         /*                                          */
```

```
typedef struct    {    RMTransCB *    next;         /* next resource mgr joined to this trans        */
                       RMID           rmid;         /* id of this resource manager                   */
                       Boolean        prepared;     /*RM is prepared to commit                       */
                       LSN            savept_lsn;   /* LSN returned by last savepoint callback       */
                  } RMTransCB;                      /* describes a RM joined to a transaction        */
TRID              MyTrid(void);                     /* returns process' transaction identifier       */
TransCB           MyTrans(void);                    /* returns copy of  transaction CB               */
TransCB *         MyTransP(void);                        /* returns pointer to transaction CB        */
RMID              Identify( RMID);                  /* declare RMID wants recovery from TM           */
Boolean           Join_Work(RMID, TRID);           /* declare RMID wants to join TRID               */
TRID              Begin_Work(context *, Boolean persistent); /* begin a transaction                 -*/
void              Abort_Work(void);                 /* rollback to savepoint zero                    */
Boolean           Commit_Work(context *, Boolean lazy); /* commit the transaction                   */
savepoint         Save_Work(context *, Boolean persistent);   /* establish a savepoint              */
savepoint         Rollback_Work(savepoint);        /* return to a savepoint                          */
Boolean           Prepare_Work(context *);         /* put transaction in prepared state             */
context           Read_Context(savepoint);         /* return savepoint context                      */
TRID              Chain_Work(context *);            /* end current and start next transaction        */
TRID              MyTrid(void);                     /* return current transaction identifier         */
TRID              Leave_Transaction(void);          /* set process trid to null, return              */
                                                    /* current id                                    */
Boolean           Resume_Transaction(TRID);        /* set process trid to desired trid              */
tran_status       Status_Transaction(TRID);        /* return status of a transaction identifier     */
```

/* Log Manager */

```
enum ACCESS {READ, WRITE};
LSN         log_insert( char * buffer,  long n);    /* insert a log rec with body buffer[0..n-1]    */
LSN         log_flush( LSN lsn, Boolean lazy);      /* force log  (up to LSN) to durable storage    */
Boolean     logtable_open( ACCESS access);          /* read access or read&write access             */
Boolean     logtable_close(void);                   /* closes log file                              */
long        log_read_lsn(                           /* read a log record given the record LSN       */
                  LSN           lsn,                 /* lsn of record to be read                     */
                  log_record_header  header,         /* receives header fields of record             */
                  long          offset,              /* offset into body to start read               */
                  char *        buffer,              /* buffer to receive log data                   */
                  long          n);                  /* length of buffer                             */
LSN         log_max_lsn(void);                       /* return current max lsn of the log table.     */
LSN         log_transaction(LSN new_lsn);            /* Tell the TM about a new log record           */
void        log_write_anchor( LSN  anchor);          /* record TM anchor in log anchor               */
LSN         log_read_anchor( void);                  /* read TM anchor from log anchor               */
```

```
struct log_files { filename   a_prefix;                /* directory for "a" log files                */
                   filename   b_prefix;                /* directory for "b" log files                */
                   long       index;                   /* index of current log file                  */
                   };                                  /*                                            */
typedef struct {        LSN         lsn;               /* LSN of record                              */
                        LSN         prev_lsn;          /* the LSN of the previous record in log      */
                        TIMESTAMP   timestamp;         /* UTC time log record was created            */
                        RMID        rmid;              /* id of RM writing this record               */
                        TRID        trid;              /* id of transaction that wrote this record   */
                        LSN         tran_prev_lsn;     /* prev log record of this transaction (or 0) */
                        long        length;            /* length of log record body                  */
                        char        body[];            /* dummy body of log record                   */
                   } log_record_header;               /* generic header of all log records          */
typedef struct {   filename    tablename;             /* name of log table                          */
                   struct      log_files;             /* file prefix names and current fnum         */
                   xsemaphore lock;                    /* semaphore for log write access             */
                   LSN         prev_lsn;               /* LSN of most recently written record        */
                   LSN         lsn;                    /* LSN of next record                         */
                   LSN         durable_lsn;            /* max LSN recorded in durable storage        */
                   LSN         TM_anchor_lsn;          /* lsn of TM's most recent checkpoint         */
                   struct {                            /* array of open log partitions               */
                       long     partno;                /* partition number                           */
                       int      os_fnum;               /* operating system file number               */
                       } part [MAXOPENS];              /*                                            */
                   } log_anchor ;                      /*                                            */
```

/* Resource Manager */

```
RMID        MyRMID(void);                    /* returns process current RMID               */
RMCB        MyRM(void);                       /* returns copy of caller's RM CB             */
RMCB *      MyRMP(void);                       /* returns pointer to caller's RM CB          */
LSN         Checkpoint(LSN * low_water);       /* TM checkpointing. Returns checkpoint       */
                                               /* low water LSN                              */
void        rm_Shutdown();                     /* invoked at system shutdown.                */
Boolean     Savepoint(LSN *);                  /* invoked at Save_Work(). Returns RM vote    */
LSN         Prepare(LSN*);                     /* invoked at Ø1 commit. Returns commit vote  */
void        Commit(Boolean);                   /* invoked at Ø2 commit/abort:                */
                                               /* param=commit decision                      */
void        UNDO(LSN);                          /* Undo the log rec with the specified LSN    */
void        REDO(LSN);                          /* Redo the log rec with the specified LSN    */
Boolean     UNDO_Savepoint(LSN);               /* Undo a savepoint. vote TRUE if can         */
                                               /* return to it                               */
```

```
void              REDO_Savepoint(LSN);              /* Redo a savepoint. vote TRUE if can      */
                                                    /* return to it                            */
void              TM_Startup(LSN);                  /* tran mgr restarting. Passes RM          */
                                                    /* checkpoint LSN                          */
typedef struct ResMgr *RMCBP;
typedef  struct ResourceManager{                    /* describes installed resource manager    */
            RMNAME       rmname;                     /* global name of the resource manager     */
            RMID         rmid;                       /* the RM short name  (identifier)         */
            Boolean      RMLocal;                    /* indicates RM available at the local node */
            pointer      acl;                        /* access control list to authorize requests */
                                                     /* see explanation in Section 6.5         */
            int          priority;                   /* process priority of this RM            */
            Boolean      RMactive;                   /* is RM is activated?                    */
            Boolean      RMup;                        /* is resource manager  is up or down    */
            Boolean      UpAfterREDO;                 /* can RM operate normally after REDO    */
                                                     /*  recovery has completed                */
            int          QueueLength;                 /* number of requests waiting for that   */
                                                     /* server class.  queue information refers */
                                                     /* to node-local server class only        */
            RMQUEP       waiters;                     /* RM request queue                      */
            RMQUEP       end_of_chain;                /* last waiting request; append here     */
            RMTA_CBP RMTA_chain;                      /* list of Xactions RM is currently  working for */
            RMPR_CBP     RMPR_chain;                  /* list of  processes allocated to this RM */
            RMNO_CBP     RMNO_chain;                  /* list of  nodes running this RM        */
            procedure    rm_Startup;                  /* invoked at restart                    */
            RMID         rmid;                        /* resource manager identifier            */
            LSN          checkpoint_lsn;              /* anchor lsn of this resource manager   */
            LSN          low_water_lsn;               /* min lsn needed to recover this RM     */
            procedure    rm_Shutdown;                 /*invoked at system shutdown.            */
            RMCBP        next_RMCB;                    /* next in list of RM control blocks     */
            } RMCB;                                    /* resource manager control block        */
```

/* Buffer Manager */

```
/* template for the access control block a pointer to which is given to the caller          */
typedef      struct
    {  PAGEID        pageid;              /* pageid for sanity                       */
       PAGEPTR       pageaddr;            /* pointer to address in bufferpool        */
       int           index;              /* record within page (set by caller)      */
       semaphorep    pagesem;            /* pointer to semaphore-structure          */
       boolean       modified;           /* flag says caller modified page          */
       boolean       invalid;            /* flag says caller destroyed page         */
    }  BUFFER_ACC_CB, *BUFFER_ACC_CBP;   /* control block for buffer access         */
```

```
boolean     bufferfix (PAGEID pageid, SEMTYPE mode, BUFFER_ACC_CBP address);
```
/* returns TRUE if the page could be allocated, FALSE otherwise if it is allocated the address of the 1st byte   */
/* of the page header in the buffer pool is returned in BUFFER_ACC_CBP. The fix count is increased by 1.   */
/* There is no check if the transaction already has a fix on that page. The semaphore protecting the page   */
/* is acquired in the requested mode.   */

```
enum SEMTYPE { EX_SEM, SH_SEM, NO_SEM };
```
/* This type definition is used for telling the buffer manager which kind of semaphore to grab for the   */
/* requestor of a page. Depending on the type of request, the semaphore will be set in the specified   */
/* mode upon return.   */

```
boolean     bufferunifx (BUFFER_ACC_CBP);
```
/* returns true if the page could be unfixed, FALSE otherwise. if the unfix is possible, the fix counter   */
/* is decreased by 1. If the transaction has multiple fixes on the page, it must issue the corresponding   */
/* number of unfix operations. Note that the parameter is the address of the buffer access CB.   */

```
boolean     emptyfix(PAGEID pageid, SEMTYPE mode, BUFFER_ACC_CBP address);
```
/* returns TRUE if the page could be allocated, FALSE otherwise the function requests an empty page to be   */
/* allocated in buffer. the identifier of the empty page has to be provided by the caller. the buffer manager   */
/* formats the page header with the PAGEID and returns a pointer to the buffer access CB, like bufferfix.   */

```
boolean     flush (BUFFER_ACC_CB);
```
/* returns TRUE if the page was written to the file, FALSE otherwise. the page is written to its block in the   */
/* file, the modified field in the buffer control block is set to 'N', and the page remains in the buffer.   */
/* This function can be called by access module, by the log manager, the recovery manager, and by the buffer   */
/* manager itself. the buffer manager will set a shared semaphore on the page before writing it.   */

/* Page Headers */

/* these declares establish a data type "page", together with an identifier for its instances.   */
```
typedef     struct                                  /* makes it easier to talk about page numbers    */
    {   FILENO      fileno;                         /* file where the page lives    */
        uint        pageno;                         /* page number within the file    */
    }   PAGEID,   *   PAGEIDP;
```
/* a page can contain information of different categories, although usually any given page contains data of   */
/* one type only. The following enumerated type describes the different types of data structures that have to   */
/* be handled by the tuple-oriented file system. The enumeration only serves as an example to illustrate the   */
/* following discussions. It is by no means complete.   */

```
enum PAGE_TYPE    { DATA, INDEX, FREESPACE, DIRECTORY, CLUSTER, TABLE };
/* the values of PAGE_TYPE have the following meaning (all the concepts referred to are elaborated in this   */
/* chapter and in Chapter 15):                                                                               */
/*   DATA            page contains tuples of exactly one file (relation)                                     */
/*   INDEX           page contains the node of an index  file (see chapter 15)                               */
/*   FREESPACE       page contains parts of a freespace management table                                     */
/*   DIRECTORY       page contains meta data about this file or other files                                  */
/*   CLUSTER         page contains tuples of more than one relation                                          */
/*   TABLE           page contains table witrh administrative data (e.g. addressing)                         */
/* this enumerated data type is used to distinguish the different states a page can be in                    */
enum PAGE_STATE {VALID, INVALID, INDOUBT, SHADOW};
/* the following structure defines the standard header of each page. Note that it has the block data structure */
/* around it (see Figure 14.1).                                    */
typedef  struct
        PAGEID          thatsme;                /* identifies the page                            */
        PAGE_TYPE       page_type;              /* see description above                          */
        OBJID           object_id;              /* internal id of the relation,index,etc.         */
        LSN             safe_up_to;             /* page LSN for the WAL-protocol                  */
        PAGEID          previous;               /* often pages are members of doubly              */
        PAGEID          next;                   /* linked lists                                   */
        PAGE_STATE      status;                 /* used to mark the contents of the page          */
                                                /* (valid,in-doubt,copy of something,etc.)        */
        int             no_entries;             /* entriy count  in page dir (see below)          */
        int             unused;                 /* count  of unused bytes which are not           */
                                                /* partof contiguous freespace                    */
        int             freespace;              /* number of contiguous free bytes for payload    */
        char            stuff[];                /* will grow                                      */
    }  PAGE_HEADER, *   PAGE_PTR;               /*                                                */


typedef struct
    {  char    not_needed[PAGESIZE];            /* covers the whole page                          */
       Uint    offset_in_page[];                /* offset of a tuple in the page                  */
    }  PAGE_DIR, *   PPAGE_DIR;


typedef  struct
    {  NODEID      at_node;                      /* node where the tuple is located                */
       FILEID      in_file;                      /* to which file does it belong                   */
       TUPLENAME   local_id;                     /* this is the value identifying the tuple        */
                                                 /* relative to the file in_file                   */

    }  TUPLEID,   * TUPLEIDP;
```

19
Glossary

1-safe system pair.   A *system pair* configuration in which the client is sent the commit response as soon as the primary has committed the transaction. It risks *lost transactions*.

2-safe system pair.   A *system pair* configuration in which the client is not sent the commit response until the backup of the system pair has acknowledged the transaction commit or the backup has been declared down. It prevents *lost transactions*. See also *very safe system pair*.

2PC.   A common abbreviation for *two-phase commit*.

2PL.   A common abbreviation for *two-phase transaction locking*.

Abort.   Terminating a transaction and undoing all its actions.

Aborted.   Said of a transaction, action, or object version if its parent transaction has aborted. See also *active, in-doubt, committed*.

Aborting transaction.   A transaction that is executing a rollback to savepoint 0. All its effects on durable storage will be undone.

Abstract data type.   Implementation technique based on information hiding. Objects are made available to the outside world via the interface operations they export. Internal representation is hidden and has no bearing on the result of the operations. Prerequisite for hierarchic decomposition. Plays important role for the use of *nested transactions*.

Access control list (acl).   An authorization mechanism associated with an object. Each access control list entry has ⟨authid, rights⟩ pairs or ⟨groupid, rights⟩ pairs. When the object is accessed, the list is checked to see whether the client is authorized to perform the operation on the object.

Access path.   A data structure and algorithm that efficiently retrieves tuples according to a specified criterion. Typical criteria are: sorted by attribute A; all tuples with attribute B = const; all tuples in insert order; and so on. The simplest access path is a sequential *scan* of all tuples in that relation. More powerful and efficient access paths are hash tables, *B-trees*, and other search structures. Access paths must be maintained during update in order to remain consistent with the base relation.

Access time.   The *response time* of a memory device to a read or write request.

ACID.   The basic transaction properties of *atomicity, consistency, isolation,* and *durability*.

Acknowledge (ack).   To reply to a message, indicating that it arrived correctly (and perhaps was processed correctly).

Application Control and Management System.   A TP monitor from DEC.

ACMS.   See *Application Control and Management System*.

Action.   A step of a *transaction*. Typically, an invocation of a *resource manager*.

Active. Said of a transaction, action, or object version if its (parent) transaction has not yet started to commit or abort. See also *in-doubt, committed, aborted*.

ADABAS. Database product offered by Software AG. Its data model is neither relational nor network nor hierarchical. It offers a low-level call-interface on top of which either view can be implemented. The internal structure is a tree of key-sequenced files.

ADABAS-TPF. A TP monitor offered by Software AG for distributed transaction processing in an *ADABAS* environment. It is a functional subset of the COM-PLETE TP monitor.

ADABASE Transaction Processing System. A transaction processing and database system sold by Software AG for IBM computers.

ADANET. Distributed version of the *ADABAS* database system. It supports distributed transactions, including the management of replicated data. It is not an open system, though, in that only components of the same system family can participate in distributed transaction processing.

Address space. The directly addressable memory of a process, typically segmented and partially shared with other processes.

ADT. See *abstract data type*.

After image. *Log record* of a data object after a *protected action* has been applied to it. See also *before image*.

All-or-nothing. Casual characterization of a *flat transaction*, which either executes completely or not at all. Used synonymously for *atomic*.

Alpha test. The first application-level test of a product in a waterfall development methodology. This testing is usually done by a few customers who trade early access to new product features for the risks and inconveniences of using immature software. See *waterfall development*.

Amnesia. If a transaction manager forgets about some transactions it has committed, the transaction manager has amnesia. This should not happen. Other transaction managers can detect amnesia by remembering the transaction manager *birthday*. The birthday advances at each amnesia event.

Anchor. The root of addressability for some body of code. Typically the main *control block* of a subsystem.

API. See *application programming interface*.

APPC. See *Application Program-to-Program Communication*.

Application (software). Software that transforms a generic computer system into a system which solves some specific problem. For example, software to implement a hospital patient-care records system.

Application Control and Management System (ACMS). DEC's transaction management system. It has been implemented on the VMS and UNIX operating systems

Application Peer-to-Peer Communication or **Application Program-to-Program Communication.** An application programming interface to IBM's LU6.2 transactional RPC and TM-TM interface.

Application programming interface (API). An interface used by application programmers. Languages like FORTRAN, C, and SQL are APIs. Subroutine libraries like X-Windows, the UNIX run-time library, and X/Open DTP are also APIs. The term is usually used with communications standards to contrast the API and the FAP (formats and protocols).

Application Program-to-Program Communication (APPC). Ambiguously, the application programming interface and the communication protocol used by IBM's LU6.2 protocol to provide transactional peer-to-peer half-duplex sessions between two resource managers or, more generally, between any two application programs. Originally, Advanced Peer-to-Peer Communication. See also *Common Programming Interface for Communications* (CPI-C) and *application program-to-program communication.*

Archive.   A memory (storage) that is used for long term memory. It typically has very low cost/byte of memory, but also very long access time. Sometimes the archive is geographically remote to preserve a copy of the data from environmental failures.

Archive copy.   A copy of an object made at some time in the past, and that can be used to reconstruct the object via *archive recovery.*

Archive low-water mark.   For an archive copy, the lowest log sequence number (LSN) needed by archive recovery to transform the copy to the current version. Typically, the LSN that was current at the time of the copy. For the system as a whole, the archive low-water is the minimum of all archive low-water marks.

Archive recovery.   Recovery of a current version of an object from an archive version of it. The recovery often involves using a log to redo any recent changes to the object.

ASAP queue (as soon as possible).   A queue for which requests are serviced as soon as a server can be allocated to the request, in contrast to *timed* and *threshold* queues.

Association.   The OSI term for a *session.*

Associative (file access).   Accessing the records in a file by content, or key value, rather than by record address. See also *direct file access, key of a record,* and *key sequence.*

At least once.   Guarantee to perform an operation at least once—perhaps multiple times in case of intermediate failures. See *at most once* and *exactly once.*

At most once.   Guarantee to perform an operation at most once—perhaps zero times. Messages sent without provisions for error handling have at-most-once semantics. See *at least once* and *exactly once.*

ATM.   See *automated teller machine.*

Atomic.   For transactions, all-or-nothing. Either all actions happen or none happen.

Atomic action.   Any action that either delivers the specified result or—in case of an error—leaves all parts of the system unaffected. See *all-or-nothing.*

Atomicity.   See *atomic.*

Auditor of data structures.   A program that examines the consistency of a data structure and either corrects inconsistencies or marks the data structure invalid. See *salvager.*

Authenticate.   To establish the identity of (authid of) a person or process by some form of shared secret, or by the authority of an authentication server.

Authentication server.   A trusted server that manages an authentication *domain.* All clients in that domain advertise their authorization identity via that server. The server securely publishes these *authids* to other members of the domain and, indirectly via other authentication servers, to processes in other authentication domains.

Authid (authorization identifier).   An identifier that represents the identity of a person or process and so is input to the authorization test. See *authorize.*

Authorize.   To test whether a client (*authid*) is allowed to perform a requested operation on an object.

Automated teller machine (ATM).   Specialized terminals used by banks to dispense and deposit money or checks. They create many service requests to transaction processing systems. They perform *real actions*, the control of which is a major issue in transaction design.

Availability class.   The number of leading nines in the availability figure for a system or module. More formally, if the system availability is A, the system class is $\lfloor \log_{10}(1/(1-A)) \rfloor$.

Availability of a module. The fraction of the time that a module delivers service. Formally *MTTF/(MTTF + MTTR)*.

Availability of a system.   The fraction of the time that a system performs requests correctly and within specified time constraints.

B-tree.   An associative file access structure that provides keyed and key-sequenced sequential access to data. B-trees cluster records with similar keys together. B-trees are so called because they balance the search tree depth so that all accesses take only a few (less than 4) page accesses to find a record.

Backstopping.   See *copy forward*.

Backup process.   In a *process pair*, the backup process waits passively until the *primary* process of the pair fails. At that point, the backup process assumes the state, identity, and responsibility of the primary. When the primary is repaired, it becomes the new backup.

Backup site.   A second computer site used to provide *disaster recovery*.

Backward error recovery.   To recover from an error by returning to an earlier correct state and then resuming the computation. See also *error recovery* and *forward error recovery*.

Bandwidth.   Characteristic of communication links. Defines how many data can be transferred per unit of time. Typical measures are Mb/sec and MB/sec.

Base relation.   In a relational database, a relation the *tuples* of which are explicitly stored in a *file*. This is the opposite of a virtual relation, called a *view*.

Batch.   A qualitative term meaning to process many jobs as a single group and to process them asynchronously. Such an approach amortizes the set-up costs of the batch across many jobs, and so likely has lower overall cost, but typically gives longer average response time for each job. A batch transaction is one that accesses many records (millions) or runs for a long time (minutes). Batch is often contrasted with *direct* or *online transaction processing*.

Bathtub curve.   The fault rate curve typical of modules that have high *burn-in* failure rates and high *wear-out* failure rates, but relatively low failure rates during mid-life operation. See Figure 3.9.

Before image.   *Log record* of a data object before a protected action is applied to it. See also *after image*.

Begin Work.   The SQL verb to start a transaction. See also COMMIT WORK, ROLLBACK WORK.

Benign bug.   A software fault that rarely causes a failure. See *Bohrbug*, *Heisenbug*, and *virulent bug*.

Birthday.   The timestamp of a transaction manager's most recent coldstart. It is used to detect *amnesia*.

Block.   Unit of data transfer between main memory and disk.

Blocking commit coordinator.   A *commit coordinator* that may fail and so prevent the resolution of *in-doubt* distributed transactions for a long time. See also *non-blocking commit coordinator*.

Bohrbug.   A software fault that causes a failure every time the program executes that piece of code. See *Heisenbug*.

Bolinas.   Town north of San Francisco where the role of TP monitors was clarified once and for all.

Bounce locking.   To request a lock be granted immediately if possible. If waiting is required, the request is immediately denied and bounces back to the caller.

Bounce mode lock. A lock request that will bounce (will cancel rather than wait) if the requested lock is not available.

Boxcarring. To batch a collection of records together in order to amortize the fixed cost of processing them among several operations.

Branch. An ISO-TP term for transactional session.

Branch registration. An ISO-TP term to describe the *communications manager's* (CM's) notification of the *transaction manager* concerning an *incoming* or *outgoing trid*. Branch registration declares a new node in the *transaction tree*.

Broadcast. To send the same message to every node of the network.

Browse mode locking. A locking scheme that allows readers to see uncommitted data (dirty data). This is *degree 1 isolation*. See *cursor stability* and *repeatable reads*.

Buffer manager. The resource manger that moves pages between disk and the primary-memory buffer pool.

Buffer pool. A set of main memory pages used to cache currently and recently used disk pages. The buffer pool is typically volatile rather than durable storage.

Burn in. The early stages of a module's lifetime. Failure rates are typically high during this period, and so modules are typically burned in by the manufacturer and then tested prior to being sold to customers. See also *wear out*.

Byzantine faults. Faults that include arbitrary, even malicious, behavior on the part of the modules. Most fault models assume a much more restricted set of fault behaviors, for example *failfast module* behavior.

Cache. A subset containing copies of the frequently accessed parts of a larger (*main or secondary)* memory. If the cache has short *access times* and high *hit ratios*, then most requests can be serviced by the cache, thereby giving the illusion of a fast memory.

Callback. A procedure exported by a server, used to notify the server of significant events (such as shutdown, cache invalidation, transaction commit/abort, and checkpoint).

Cancel. To send a *message* requesting that a previous message be ignored.

Careful write or careful replacement. Updating two or more copies so that at any time, at least one of the copies is correct. Subsequent readers examine all copies and pick the correct version by accepting the one(s) with the highest *timestamp*.

Catch-up. When one of a *process pair* or *system pair* fails, the failed component must be repaired and then must perform catch-up to synchronize its state with the current state of the *primary process* or *system*.

CDD/Plus. See *Common Data Dictionary/Repository*.

CDD/R. The new name for CDD/Plus. See *Common Data Dictionary/Repository*.

Centralized. An adjective for designs, architectures, and organizations. It implies a single point of control, knowledge, processing, or storage. Contrast with *distributed*.

Centralized transaction. A transaction involving a single *transaction manager*.

Chained transaction. A sequence of transactions, one immediately following the other, perhaps with resources transferred from one transaction instance to the next, and perhaps with persistence so that a system failure will not break the chain.

Challenge response. An authentication protocol in which one process picks a random number, encrypts it with a shared secret key, and challenges the other process to produce the decrypted value.

Change accumulation. To reduce the size of a *log file* by sorting it by object, then merging duplicate updates to the object into a single transformation from the original state to the current state.

Checkpoint. A copy of a state, or the act of making such a copy. In the event of a failure, the restart logic will return to this checkpoint state, then attempt to recover the most recent consistent state, and then continue the computation.

Checkpoint a system. The transaction manager periodically invokes each resource manger to write a checkpoint record to the log. Then the transaction manager writes its own checkpoint record and records the checkpoint LSN with the log manager. This information will be read at system restart to reconstruct the system state.

Checkpoint message. In a *process pair*, the messages sent by the *primary process* to the *backup process*, describing changes in the primary process' state. These messages are often combined with *I'm Alive* messages.

Checkpoint record in the log. A log record written by a resource manager, that allows it to reconstruct the resource manger state after a failure.

Checkpoint-restart process recovery. A form of reliable execution that periodically stores the process state in persistent storage. If the process fails, the recovery mechanism restarts the process, which then refreshes its state from durable storage and continues the computation.

Checkpoint state. Either the process state written to durable storage by a *checkpoint-restart process,* or the state sent from the *primary process* to the *backup process* of a *process pair*.

Checksum. A mechanism to detect data corruption. Any algebraic function of a data byte string produces a checksum. This value is stored with the data, and when the data is later received as a message or read from storage, the checksum is recomputed from the data. If the checksum has changed, the data has changed. Data *parity* is the simplest checksum.

CICS. See *Customer Information Control System.*

CIM. See *computer integrated manufacturing.*

Class. See *availability class.*

Client. A process that makes a request to another process.

Client-server. A relationship between two processes in which one makes a request to the other. It is possible for the server to, in turn, make a request to the client and so reverse the roles. See also *peer-to-peer.*

Closed transaction manager. A transaction manager that does not provide resource manager callbacks (for transaction commit, abort, or savepoint) and does not allow a *transaction gateway* to be implemented on it. See *Open Transaction Manager.*

Cluster of data. A collection of records placed together in a block of memory so that when one record is accessed, the related records will also be retrieved. Data clustering is the basis of the *principle of locality.*

Cluster of processors. A collection of processors, their peripherals, and software, which all behave like and are managed as a single computer. Typically, the processors are connected with high-bandwidth lines and are located in one place to get low communications latency.

CM. See *Communications manager.*

Coarse granularity. See *granular lock*.

CODASYL. Stands for Committee on Data System Languages. Standards body that defined a standard for database systems, access languages, and styles for embedding these languages into conventional programming languages (COBOL in particular), based on the network data model.

Commit. The declaration or process of making a transaction's updates and messages visible to other transactions. When a transaction commits, all its effects become public and durable. After commitment, the effects of a transaction cannot be automatically reversed.

Commit coordinator. In the two-phase commit protocol, the process that collects the votes from the participants, makes the commit decision, and informs all the participants of the outcome. Transaction managers act as commit coordinators.

Commit LSN. The *LSN* of the transaction's commit log record.

Commit participant. In the two-phase commit protocol, a process that votes on the commit of a transaction. More generally, any process or resource manager participating in a transaction.

Commit phase 1 (Ø1). The first phase of the two-phase commit protocol. In this phase, each participant is polled about transaction commitment and prepares to commit. If all vote yes, the coordinator commits the transaction.

Commit phase 2 (Ø2). The second phase of the two-phase commit protocol, during which the participants complete the transaction commitment.

Committed. Said of a transaction, action, or object version if its parent transaction has successfully performed the commit protocol. See also *active, in-doubt, aborted*.

Committing transaction. A transaction in phase 2 of commit; it has decided to commit, but commit has not completed.

COMMIT WORK. The SQL verb to commit a transaction. See also BEGIN WORK, ROLLBACK WORK.

Common Data Dictionary/Repository (CDD/R). The repository used by Digital transaction processing (ACMS), database (Rdb), software development (Cohesion), and presentation services (DECforms) as a common repository for system definitions and for dependencies among system components.

Common Programming Interface for Communications (CPI-C). A callable application programming interface IBM has defined for its LU6.2 transactional RPC and peer-to-peer protocol. CPI-C is the SAA standard way of invoking transactional sessions in LU6.2.

Communications manager (CM). A resource manager that manages transactional communication sessions. Among other things, the communications manager informs the *transaction manager* of *incoming* or *outgoing trids* travelling on sessions provided by that communications manager. In the X/Open Distributed Transaction Processing model, any networking software that acts as a resource manger.

Compare-and-swap (CS(), CSD()). Atomic machine instructions that replace a cell with a new value if it contains the old value. If the cell does not contain the old value, the operation does nothing more than return a FALSE.

Compatibility of lock modes. Two lock modes are compatible if they can be granted concurrently without violating the isolation properties.

Compensating transaction. In *multi-level transactions, sagas,* and *ConTract's,* a transaction that is explicitly designed to semantically reverse the effects of another (committed) transaction. Must be used whenever automatic rollback is not possible because results have been committed early.

Compensation. Once a transaction has committed, its effects cannot be automatically reversed. To correct any mistakes of a committed transaction, a *compensating transaction* must be run.

Compensation log record. A log record generated by an *undo* operation.

COM-PLETE. TP monitor offered by Software AG. It runs on IBM operating systems and complements the *ADABAS* database system.

Complete transaction. A transaction that has completed its commit or abort work.

Completing transaction. A transaction that is in the process of either *committing* or *aborting*. The decision has been made, but the work is not yet complete.

Computer integrated manufacturing (CIM). Integrating the design, planning, scheduling, and manufacturing of a product as one continuous activity. The computer representation of the design, schedule, inventory, and work-in-progress allows better management control and allows optimizations like *just-in-time inventory control*.

Concurrency. Simultaneous execution of independent (and possibly competing) programs, processes, transactions, and so on.

Concurrency control. Techniques that allow transactions to execute concurrently while still providing *isolation* among the transactions. Locking is a typical form of concurrency control.

Configuration (management). The interconnection of software and hardware modules. Configuration management includes the difficult task of managing and merging many versions of software modules. It also includes management of system load among processors, communications lines, and memory devices.

Connection. A synonym for *session*. Often implies the server context associated with a client.

Connectionless server. A *context-free* server.

Consistency constraint. A predicate on data which serves as a precondition, post-condition, and transformation condition on any transaction. *Foreign keys* and *unique keys* are typical consistency constraints.

Consistent. Correct. Data should satisfy certain properties called the *consistency constraints*. Data transformations (transactions) should preserve these properties and satisfy some additional transformation constraints (e.g., no checks for more than 1 m$ will be honored). Transactions are designed to obey and preserve consistency constraints.

Context (transaction). See *transaction context*.

Context-free server. A server that maintains no client state (*context*) between requests. Context free servers are easy to program and have quick restart, but they require the client to pass its context to the server on each request. Contrast with *context-sensitive server*.

Context-sensitive server. A server that maintains client state (*context*) between requests. Because they must manage the client state, context-sensitive servers are more difficult to program than context-free servers. They typically have longer restart times because they must recover the client context, but they generally have better performance in the no-fault case. Contrast with *context-free server*.

ConTract. A two-level transaction structure in which the top-level transaction is a persistent computation that initiates and coordinates flat transactions.

Control block. The generic name for an instance of a data structure.

Conversation. The binding of a preallocated session to a client-server pair in the LU6.2 protocol. Conversations are called *dialogs* by OSI-TP. Conversation is also the IBM term for a transactional session (used in APPC).

Conversational transaction. A transaction (transactional server) that has several message exchanges with a client as part of processing the transaction. This is in contrast to transactions that have a single input message in and a single reply message. See also *context-sensitive server*.

Conversion of a lock. When a lock is rerequested in a new mode, the granted mode is converted to the maximum of the previously granted mode and the newly requested mode.

Convoy. A performance problem that arises when many requestors queue for a frequently accessed resource in FIFO order. As soon at the requestor releases the resource, it rerequests it and joins the end of the FIFO queue. This situation is stable. Once a convoy forms it is unlikely to dissipate.

Coordinator. See *commit coordinator*.

Copy aside. To copy the log records of a transaction or resource manager to a side file so that the space they occupy in the online log can be reclaimed and the restart low-water mark advanced. See also *copy forward, dynamic log*.

Copy forward. To copy the log records of a transaction or resource manager to the current end of the log so that the space they occupy in the online log can be reclaimed and the restart low-water mark advanced. See also *copy aside, dynamic log*.

Cost (price). The monetary value of an item, usually measured as the 5-year cost of ownership. Within a company, cost is the internal price—often two to five times lower than the external price.

Covered action. A read action of transaction T on an object E is covered by a lock if T holds a shared lock on E when performing the action. A write action is covered if T holds an exclusive lock on E.

CPI-C. See *Common Programming Interface for Communications*.

Crabbing. A way of traversing data structures that are protected by *locks* or *semaphores*. When following a pointer to an object, do not release the semaphore on the pointer until a semaphore has been acquired on the target object. Otherwise, the pointer may change in between the read of it and the examination of the target object.

Crash. A failure, typically a major one, requiring a denial of service. A synonym for system *failure*.

Crash recovery. Recovery from a system failure, as contrasted to recovery from transaction failure (ROLLBACK), or recovery from media failure (archive recovery). Also called *online recovery*.

CS() or CSD(). See *compare-and-swap*.

Cursor. An SQL object that enumerates the records in a set (in an SQL select statement that defines the set) and allows the caller to update or delete the current element addressed by the cursor.

Cursor stability. A form of transaction isolation that assures that the record currently addressed by the cursor is not dirty. When the cursor moves to a new record, the previous one may be updated or deleted by another transaction. Such later updates may violate the *repeatable read* property and violate isolation. Cursor stability is approximately *degree 2 isolation*.

Customer Information Control System (CICS). The world's most popular transaction processing system. IBM makes it. It runs on most IBM operating systems and has been reimplemented by several third parties to run on non-IBM operating systems.

Cycle in a graph. A non-null path in a graph in which the first and last nodes are the same.

Cycle time. The time between client requests. The sum of *think time* and *response time*.

DAG. See *Directed Acyclic Graph*.

DAG locking protocol. A locking protocol that allows transactions to lock objects at *coarse granularity* (large objects) or at *fine granularity* (small components of a large object) by organizing locks into a DAG where coarse-granularity locks are above the fine-grain locks they subsume. Locking is done from root to leaf. Transactions accessing large quantities of data use coarse-grained locks, while small transactions use fine-grained locks to minimize contention.

Database key (DBK). Logical sequence number used to identify *tuples* in a *file*. It is also an addressing mechanism in that the sequence number indexes a table that contains a pointer to the page where the tuple is stored. This identifier is stable under relocation and so requires a level of indirection to dereference a database key.

Data control language (DCL). Language used to define the security and transaction aspects of data and programs. The authorization, transaction, and locking verbs of SQL are in this category.

Data definition language (DDL). Language used to define the database schema, that is, the relations, attributes, and so on, or the record types, fields, set types—depending on the data model. In relational systems à la SQL, the DDL is part of the uniform database language, using the same syntax and execution model. In "old style" database systems à la CODASYL, the DDL is completely different from the *data manipulation language* (*DML*) and can be used only as input to a utility, rather than for interactive commands. See *data manipulation language* and *data control language*.

Datagram. A *message* that does not travel on a *session*. Session open messages are datagrams. Datagrams are much less expensive than setting up a session to send a single message.

Data Language/1 (DL/1). The common application programming interface provided by IMS to both database records and network messages. The data model is a hierarchy of records. Renamed IMS/DB in 1990.

Data manipulation language (DML). Language used to access the contents of a database and to modify it. In relational systems à la SQL, it is part of the uniform database language. In "old style" database systems à la CODASYL, it is a separate language that has a different syntax and usage characteristics from the languages used for schema definition (*DDL*) or system administration.

Data partitioning. As opposed to a *data sharing* approach, data partitioning assigns one processor and server class in a cluster to access a particular data item directly. Access to the data from other processors, and, in fact, from processes in that "owning" processor, must invoke the server class via a transactional remote procedure call. This is the typical style of Tandem systems and of newer VAXclusters.

Data sharing. As opposed to a *data partitioning* approach, data sharing allows any processor in a cluster to access the data directly. This is the typical style of old VAXclusters and new IBM clusters.

Data storage description language (DSDL). In the *DBTG* database model, a language used to describe the physical schema that implements a given logical schema. Hardly implemented in any *CODASYL*-style database system.

DBK. See *database key*.

DBTG. Stands for Database Task Group. Subcommittee of the *CODASYL*, responsible for the network data model and the set of access and administration languages to go with it. See *DDL, DML, DSDL*.

DB2.   An SQL system available on MVS from IBM. It acts as a resource manager to IMS and CICS.

DCE.   See *Distributed Computing Environment.*

DCL.   See *data control language.*

DDL.   See *data definition language.*

Deadlock.   A situation in which each set of processes or transactions is waiting for another member of the set. These processes will not advance unless one process stops waiting. In this situation, one of the transactions must *rollback.*

Deadlock avoidance.   To avoid *deadlock* either by linearly ordering resources and requesting them in that order, or by predeclaring requests.

Deadlock detection.   An algorithm or process that looks for deadlocks either by finding cycles in the *wait-for graph* or by *timeout.*

Deadlock resolution.   To end a *deadlock* by denying some of the resource requests of some of the waiting processes in the deadlock cycle. These processes are expected to release their resources so that others can proceed.

Debit/credit.   A transaction profile that was the prototype for the *TPC-A* and *TPC-B* benchmarks. It contains the skeleton of an application program that does a debit or credit on an account record (and the related updates on other records) in a banking environment.

Decay (Storage).   Storage devices gradually lose parts of their data. This process is called decay.

DECdta.   Digital's Distributed Transaction Architecture. A three-ball model of transaction processing in which transaction flow is defined by a STDL program that declares transaction boundaries, manages the transactional client context, services client transactional RPCs, and invokes servers in server classes.

DECdtm.   A transaction manager integrated with the VMS operating system by DEC.

DECforms.   Digital's user interface design and presentation service, used by the ACMS transaction monitor.

DECintact.   A transaction processing system available from DEC.

Decrypt.   To convert an encrypted item to its original form by using a decryption algorithm and a secret key. See *encrypt.*

DECtp.   Approximately synonymous with *DECdta*, Digital's transaction processing architecture.

Defensive programming.   A programming style in which each software module checks the consistency of its input parameters, internal data structures, and the results returned by subroutines and servers it calls. If an inconsistency is detected, the module raises an exception. Defensive programming makes software modules *failfast modules.*

Deferred action.   Technique to give *real actions* the flavor of *protected actions* by deferring their execution to the point where it is certain that the surrounding transaction will commit.

Degenerate transaction.   In *isolation* theory, any transaction that *locks* something that it never reads or writes, or unlocks something that it has not locked, or ends without unlocking some of its locks (impossible if it ends with COMMIT, ROLLBACK).

Degree 0 isolated transaction.   Protected from overwriting *dirty data.* Lock protocol is *well-formed* with respect to writes.

Degree 1 isolated transaction.   Protected from lost updates. Lock protocol is *two-phase* with respect to exclusive locks and *well-formed* with respect to writes.

Degree 1 isolation. A low degree of transaction *isolation,* which allows reading of *dirty data.* Such access is sometimes allowed to programs that want a fuzzy view of the data without waiting for or slowing down other transactions that are changing the data. Often called *browse mode locking.*

Degree 2 isolated transaction. Protected from *lost updates* and *dirty reads.* Lock protocol is *two-phase* with respect to exclusive locks, and *well-formed.*

Degree 2 isolation. An intermediate degree of transaction *isolation,* which prevents *dirty reads* but allows a transaction to see the committed updates of other transactions that ran after this transaction. It holds read locks for shorter duration than does degree 3 isolation. This is often called *cursor stability,* and it is the default in many SQL products.

Degree 3 isolated transaction. Full *isolation,* protected from *lost updates, dirty reads, unrepeatable reads* and *phantoms.* Lock protocol is two-phase and well-formed.

Degree 3 isolation. A high degree of *transaction isolation,* which prevents dirty data reads or unrepeatable reads. The ISO SQL default. Often called *repeatable reads* or serializable.

Degrees of Isolation Theorem. If a transaction observes the $0°$, $1°$, $2°$, or $3°$ lock protocol, then any legal history will give that transaction $0°$, $1°$, $2°$, or $3°$ isolation so long as other transactions are at least $1°$.

Dense faults. Faults that occur more frequently than expected. *N-fault tolerant* systems tolerate N faults within a *repair window.* If there are more than N such faults, the system usually cannot tolerate them.

Dependency. If *transaction t1* reads or overwrites an object *version* written by transaction *t2,* then *t1* is said to depend on *t2.* There are three forms of dependency READ→WRITE, WRITE→READ, and WRITE→WRITE.

Dependency graph. A graph depicting the *dependencies* in a transaction execution *history.* The transactions are the nodes of the graph. There is an edge from *t1* to *t2,* labeled by the object *version* if *t2* depends on that object version generated or used by *t1.*

Descriptor. A synonym for *control block.* A record or struct describing some object.

Design diversity. A *fault tolerance* technique that uses N modules that have the same *specification,* but independent designs (implementations). *N-version programming* is an example of design diversity.

Dialog. The binding of a preallocated *session* to a client-server pair in the OSI-TP protocol. Dialogs are called *conversations* by LU6.2.

Diameter of a network. The propagation distance between nodes of the network. Clusters have diameters measured in meters, wide area networks have diameters measured in hundreds of kilometers. Due to the finite speed of light, this distance determines the propagation delay of messages.

Direct file access. To address a record of a file by its file address rather than associatively by the record value. See *associative file access.*

Direct transaction. A transaction request that is processed immediately by a *server* rather than being put in a message queue for later service. Direct transaction processing is typical of *online transaction processing, conversational transaction* processing, and of *client-server* computing. See also *queued transaction processing.*

Directed Acyclic Graph (DAG). A graph in which edges between nodes are directed (source and target) and a graph which has no *cycles.*

Dirty data. Data that has been updated by an uncommitted transaction and so should not be read by other transactions wanting a consistent view of the data. When the transaction commits, the data becomes clean (no longer dirty).

Dirty read. Reading a dirty, that is uncommitted, version of data. *Degree 2 isolation* prevents dirty reads.

Disaster recovery. To recover from the loss of a computer site (due to fire, flood, or operator error). Typically, this involves switching to a second computer located at a separate site.

Disaster recovery site. A place and computer used as backup for some primary computer in case *disaster recovery* is needed.

Disk. A memory device that rotates a platter of memory media past an electronic read-write head. Disks have cost/byte, cost/access, and access times intermediate between electronic memory and tapes.

Distributed. An adjective for designs, architectures, and organizations. It implies no single point of control, knowledge, processing, or storage. Contrast with *centralized*.

Distributed Computing Environment (DCE). A collection of extensions to UNIX to facilitate the construction of distributed applications. The extensions include two name servers, a time server, an authentication server, a file server, and a remote procedure call mechanism. Surprisingly, no transaction mechanism is included.

Distributed transaction. A transaction involving multiple *transaction managers*.

Distributed Transaction Processing (DTP). A term used by both X/Open and CICS to describe architectures supporting distributed transactions. These architectures define the interaction among transactional applications (APs), transaction managers (TMs), resource managers (RMs), and communications managers (CMs).

DL/1. See *Data Language/1*.

DML. See *data manipulation language*.

Domain (authentication). A set of authorization identifiers (people and processes) managed by an authentication server.

Domain (database). In database systems, and in the SQL standard, a data domain is a datatype. It has a name, a type, a set of integrity constraints, and a set of comments. Values in a column of a table are drawn from such data domains.

Domain (protection). Processes execute in some protection domain: an address space within a process, which is protected from programs executing in other address spaces of that process. For example, the kernel of the operating system usually has an address space that subsumes the process address space.

DO-UNDO-REDO protocol. An incremental recovery protocol in which each action of a transaction generates one or more log records (the DO step). If the transaction aborts, the log records are used to UNDO the transaction. If the transaction commits and the system fails, the log records may be used to REDO the transaction.

DSDL. See *data storage description language*.

DTP. See *Distributed Transaction Processing*.

Duplex. To configure two copies of a module performing a service in parallel. Duplex modules can be used to construct failfast modules and highly reliable modules.

Duplexed write. Application of the duplex principle to disks. Each *block* is written to two addresses, so that a failure to read one will not result in a loss of the block.

Durability. See *durable*.

Durable. State that survives failures and that has transactional update semantics. Durable memory is contrasted with *volatile memory,* which is reset at system restart, and *persistent* memory, which is not volatile but does not necessarily have transactional update semantics.

Magnetic memory is persistent; when combined with a transactional database, the memory is durable.

Durable LSN.   The highest log sequence number found in durable storage. Log records with higher log sequence numbers will be lost if the system fails.

Duration of lock.   The length of time a lock is held.

Dynamic Allocation.   Assigning resources to requestors on demand. See *static allocation*.

Dynamic log.   A log of *undo* records kept as a side file. Undo records are not needed once a transaction commits, and so many systems segregate them to a separate file.

Eager commit.   To write a commit log record and *force* it to durable storage. Eager commit is the default. See also *lazy* commit and *group* commit.

ECC.   See *error correcting code*.

Effective error.   A synonym for failure. Recall that *fault* causes *error* causes *failure*.

Electronic memory.   Memory based on integrated circuits. Registers, *cache*, *main* memory and *RAMdisc* are typically electronic. *Disk* and *tape* are typically based on magnetic media (not electronic). Unless supported by battery backup power, an electronic memory is *volatile*. See also *magnetic memory*.

Electronic vaulting.   To send archive copies and archive logs to a remote site electronically, rather than transporting the data physically (on disks or tapes).

Encapsulation.   A synonym for modularity. A module hides its internal mechanisms and has a simple external behavior. As such, it is said to encapsulate, or hide, its internals.

Encina.   The transaction processing monitor provided by Transarc Corporation. It is largely based on UNIX DCE but has also be ported to other environments. Encina is reputed to be the Greek goddess of transaction processing.

Encrypt.   To secure data from forgery or unauthorized disclosure by transforming the data with some reversible encryption function using the data and an *encryption key*. A decryption function, given the data and another key, reconstructs the data. But without the key, the encrypted data is incomprehensible.

Encryption key.   The secret value (key) used by an *encryption* algorithm to customize the encryption step. Decryption is very difficult without knowing the encryption key or the public key corresponding to the encryption key.

Endpoint of a session.   One of the two processes that use a session to communicate messages.

End-to-end.   A holistic argument, algorithm, or design that takes a global view of the problem. For example, end-to-end fault tolerance design must consider *system delusion*. End-to-end detection of error in messages can use a *checksum* generated at one end and recomputed at the other end to detect errors at any intermediate stage. Such end-to-end error detection may make intermediate checks redundant and wasteful.

Entry sequence.   A file organization in which records are added to the end of the file. This organization is often called a *sequential file*.

Equivalent history.   Two transaction execution histories for a set of transactions are the same if they have the same dependency graph.

Error.   A defect in a hardware or software module. See also *effective error*, *fault*, and *failure*.

Error correcting code (ECC).   A redundant piece of information stored with data. It acts as a checksum to detect corrupt data, and also contains enough information to correct some errors. Electronic memory, for example, often has a double error detection and single error correction ECC on each 32 bits of data. Error correcting codes for messages and storage are typically much more powerful; they can correct bursts of errors in the data.

Error recovery.   Any mechanism or procedure that *repairs* a faulty module or system, either by returning to an earlier state (*backward error recovery*) or by computing an new correct state (*forward error recovery*).

Escalation of a lock.   When a transaction acquires many fine-granularity locks, the lock manager or resource manager may escalate to a coarser granularity, replacing the fine locks with a single coarse lock. For example: replacing many record locks with a single file lock.

Escrow locking.   A generalization of field calls that avoids predicate aborts at *commit phase 1* by maintaining a range of values during normal processing. See *field calls*.

Exactly once.   Guarantee to perform an operation exactly once. Property of messages handled by a transactional message system. Operations that are part of committed *ACID* transactions are performed exactly once. See *at least once* and *at most once*.

Exclusive access.   A mode of access to an object that precludes concurrent access by other transactions to the object.

Exclusive mode lock.   A lock mode that covers write actions and that delays other transactions from concurrently reading or writing the object. See also *covered action*.

Expedited Message Handling.   An option in IMS FastPath, which converts it from a queued transaction processing system to a nonconversational direct transaction processing system in which the response to one message acknowledges the receipt of the previous message.

Explicit file access.   Accessing a *file* with explicit open, read, write, or close verbs rather than implicitly, by mapping the file to memory and then using the processor byte read and write instructions. See also *memory mapped file*.

Exponential failure rates.   The fault rates of modules typically obey a negative exponential distribution ($e^{-\lambda t}$), giving the probability of no *failure* prior to time t. This distribution is *memoryless*.

Failfast.   The failure characteristics of a *failfast module* or *failfast voter*.

Failfast module.   A module that either functions correctly or raises an exception and stops until it is repaired.

Failfast voter.   A voter on the outputs of an *n-plex* set. It emits the majority output of functioning modules. If a module is failfast and fails, the failfast voter ignores that module until it is repaired. If a module miscompares with the majority, the voter declares that module failed and ignores it until the module is repaired. The *MTTF* of a failfast voter is typically greater than the MTTF of the individual modules. By contrast, the MTTF of a *failvote* voter is typically less than the MTTF of the component modules.

Failover.   A synonym for takeover, used to describe the change in path or device ownership after a failure.

Failstop.   A synonym for *failfast*.

Failure.   A situation in which the observed behavior of a module or system deviates from the specified behavior of that component.

Failure rate.   The rate at which a large population of items in that class fails. The reciprocal of the *mean time to failure*.

Failvote.   A voter on the outputs of an *n-plex* set, which takes the majority outputs of all modules. The *MTTF* of a failvote voter is typically less than the MTTF of the individual modules. By contrast, the MTTF of a *failfast voter* is typically more than the MTTF of the component modules.

FAP. See *formats and protocols*.

Fault. A defect in a *module*, which may cause an *error*, which manifests itself as a *failure*.

Fault avoidance. To avoid *faults* by correct construction of system components.

Fault isolation. Containing the effects of a *fault* within a module, rather than propagating the fault to other modules in the system. See also *granularity of failure*.

Fault tolerant. To mask module failures so that system service is not interrupted. See also *N-fault tolerant*.

Field. A structured record is broken into substructures and eventually into individual fields with no components. Database records, message records, programming language structures, and display screens all use the same concept.

Field call. A technique for updating *hotspot* data. A field call consists of a predicate and a transform. The predicate is checked at the time of the call and at commit. If the predicate is false, the call (and transaction) aborts. If the predicate is true at *phase 1 of commit*, locks are acquired and the transform is applied at the start of *phase 2 of commit*. This minimizes the time the resource is locked. See *escrow locking*.

FIFO (first in first out). A simple scheduling discipline in which requests are processed in order of arrival, in contrast to *priority* scheduling.

File. A collection of *records*, often with the same format and organized for efficient access. See *structured file, associative* (file access), *direct file access, hash, sequential file, entry sequence, key sequence, explicit file access, memory mapped file*.

File lock. A *coarse-granularity* lock covering all records in a file.

File manager. The resource manager that allocates files in secondary storage and provides either direct read-write file access, or provides service to the buffer manager or memory managers that implicitly map secondary storage files to primary memory.

Fine granularity. See *granular lock*.

First Law of Concurrency. Concurrent execution should not cause application programs to malfunction.

Fix a page. To get shared or exclusive access to a page or object for a short period of time. This is generally accomplished by acquiring a semaphore. See *fix rule*.

Fix rule. Cover all page reads and writes with the page semaphore.

Flat transaction. A transaction with no *subtransactions* or *savepoints*.

Flow control. To limit the rate at which work flows through a system, and thereby prevent congestion.

Flush. To move data from faster, more-expensive storage to slower, cheaper storage.

Force. To copy data from *volatile memory* to *persistent memory*.

Forced commit or abort. See *operator commit or abort*.

Force-log-at-commit. Force the transaction's log records as part of commit.

Foreign key. A relationship between two tables or files. *Field* values in one file may be chosen from the key values of a second file. For example: part numbers in INVOICE records are chosen from the *parts* table. So parts.partno is a foreign key for invoice.partno. Often, *referential integrity constraints* are checked by the database system when records are inserted or altered. If the check fails, the operation is aborted. These integrity checks are typical consistency constraints.

Formats and protocols (FAP).   The message formats and protocols for exchanging these messages, so that two or more systems can interoperate and perform a desired function. For example, ISO-TP is a FAP.

Forward error recovery.   Error recovery that masks a *failure* by constructing a new correct state rather than returning to an old state. *Error correcting codes* are examples of forward error recovery, while checkpoint-restart is an example of *backward* error recovery.

Fragment.   A subset of the records of a file that satisfy some predicate. File fragments are the units of partitioning and replication.

Free list.   A list of objects that are currently not used and can be quickly allocated.

FRR.   See *functional recovery routine.*

Functional Recovery Routine (FRR).   Data auditor and *salvager* routines found in IBM's MVS operating system. These routines are exception handlers that try to recover the state of a process or data structure.

Function Shipping.   A synonym for *transactional remote procedure call.* The calls are sent to a *mirror*, a transaction program that reissues the request as a local request (see Figure 16.7). In *CICS* it means sending actions on remote objects to the sites owning the objects. More generally, in a distributed computer system it refers to sending the function (operation) to the data server rather than bringing the raw data to the function (client). Only the answers to the operation are sent to the client. It contrasts with *peer-to-peer* communication and with *transaction routing.*

Fuzzy checkpoint.   An incremental copy of an object, made in several units over a period of time. The fuzz is the time duration of the copy. The checkpoint can be made *sharp* by applying a *REDO* or *UNDO* scan to the object.

Gateway.   Any program that translates between one protocol and another. See, for example, *transaction gateway.*

GB.   Gigabyte (10^9 bytes).

General commit protocol.   A four-message commit protocol that sends a pair of prepare messages and a pair of commit messages. Contrast to the *linear commit protocol.*

Granted group of a lock.   A list of all the transactions granted access to the lock. Each list entry has the transaction name, the *mode* of sharing granted to the transaction, the lock *class* (*duration*), and a count of how many times the lock has been requested by that transaction. See also *waiting group of a lock.*

Granularity of failure.   The design goal that *failures* should affect small parts (granules) of the system. Fault isolation tries to limit the effects of a failure to a module or to a small number of modules. A synonym for *fault isolation.*

Granularity of Locks Theorem.   If transactions follow the 0°, 1°, 2°, or 3° *DAG locking protocol*, they may lock at any granularity they choose and still observe a 0°, 1°, 2°, or 3° *isolated history.*

Granular lock (granularity of a lock).   A locking unit. The *DAG* and *hierarchical lock protocol*s allow transactions to lock at coarse granularity (large objects) or at fine granularity (small components of a large object).

Greenwich Mean Time (GMT).   See *Universal Coordinated Time.*

Group commit.   To batch a group of commit requests as a single log write to durable storage, thereby amortizing the write cost across many transactions and allowing the system to use the full bandwidth of the log device.

Guardian 90. An operating system offered by Tandem Computers for its *shared nothing* machine architecture. The system has an integrated transaction manager (TMF) and TP monitor (Pathway).

Halloween problem. Famous bug in a query optimizer that was discovered on Halloween eve. It had to do with an *SQL* operation of the type update R set $x = x +$ const. The faulty optimizer found there was an index on attribute x, so it decided to use an index scan for the update. Of course, all the tuples upon update were relocated "downstream," where they were updated again, and so on, until infinity or overflow—whatever came first.

Hardware. Physical devices such as processors, memory, and communication gear (wires, fibers, switches).

Hardware fault tolerance. To tolerate hardware *faults* via hardware design. *ECC*, *pair-and-spare*, and *TMR* are examples.

Hash. An associative access technique that maps the key via a hash function uniformly among a partitioned set of hash buckets. A key search consists of hashing the key to a bucket address and then examining the small hash bucket for records with the desired key.

Heartbeat. A synonym for *I'm Alive* message.

Heisenbug. A transient software fault that rarely causes a failure when executed. Typically, the bug disappears (does not cause an failure) if observed. See also *Bohrbug*, *virulent* bug, and *benign* bug.

Heterogeneous network. A network involving computers that have different administrative interfaces, different application programming interfaces, different data representations, or different communications protocols. In contrast, see *homogeneous network*.

Heuristic commit or abort. To unilaterally make the commit or abort decision about in-doubt transactions when the coordinator fails or contact with the coordinator fails.

Hierarchical lock. The *DAG locking protocol*, when implemented on a *tree* rather than on a general directed acylcic graph.

History. In the theory of *isolation*, a history is a list of the order in which a transaction's actions completed. See also *serial history, isolated history, legal history, equivalent history*.

Hit ratio. For a memory cache, the ratio between cached data accesses and all accesses. See *miss ratio*.

Hoagland's Law. The magnetic areal density increases by a factor of 10 every decade.

Homogeneous network. A computer network that contains only one variety of computers and software (e.g., one brand of TP system, one brand of operating system, and one brand of processors.) Contrast with *heterogeneous network*.

Höningen. Town in the Palatine Forest, famous for its amazingly reliable power supply, its virtually unlimited access to Riesling, and its literacy in transaction processing.

Hotspot. Any point of contention in a system. A frequently updated record or any other performance bottleneck.

Hot standby. See *disaster recovery site*.

Idempotent operation. An operation f on an object o such that $f(o) = f(f(o))$. In other words, the operation may be repeated many times on an object and it will either transform the object to the desired state or will leave the object in the desired state.

Identify a resource manager. When a *resource manager* first starts, it identifies itself to the *transaction manager*, performs resource manager recovery, and then offers service. See also *install a resource manager*.

***I'm Alive* message.** The *primary* of a *process pair* regularly sends an *I'm Alive* message to its *backup process*, telling it that the primary is still functioning. If such messages do not arrive for a long time, the backup assumes the primary has failed and initiates *takeover*.

Immutable object. A synonym for *time domain addressing*.

Implicit lock. In *hierarchical lock* protocols, setting locks on coarse *granules* gives implicit locks on the finer granularity objects. For example, an explicit file lock gives implicit locks on the records of the file. See *granular lock (granularity of a lock)*.

IMS. See *Information Management System*.

IMS Data Base (IMS/DB). The database system packaged with IMS. Formerly called DL/1.

IMS Extended Recovery Feature (IMS/XRF). A system pair mechanism in which two adjacent *IMS* systems share disks. If one system fails, the second system aborts uncommitted transactions, completes committing ones, and continues to offer services.

IMS Transaction Management (IMS/TM). The transaction processing, transaction management, logging, recovery, and presentation services components of IMS. Formally called IMS/DC.

Incoming session. See *incoming trid*.

Incoming trid. A transaction identifier, and hence a transaction, that is arriving on a communications session for the first time. In this situation, the communications manager owning the session informs the transaction manager about the incoming trid so that the transaction manager can coordinate the commitment of the new transaction at this node. See also *outgoing trid*.

Incompatibility of locks. See *compatibility of lock modes*.

Independent events. The assumption that the probability of one event is not affected by the occurrence of the other. For example, media failures of two different disks are considered independent events.

Index. A file structure used for *associative* access. *Hashing* and *B-trees* are the most popular index structures.

Indexed sequential. The file organization called *key sequenced* files in this book.

In-doubt. Said of a transaction, action, or object version if the commitment of its parent transaction is controlled by a transaction manager that cannot be contacted, so that the decision is in doubt. See also *active, committed, aborted*.

Information Management System (IMS). A transaction processing monitor from IBM, based on the DL/1 hierarchical data model for application access to database and data communications.

Informix. A portable SQL system available on many platforms. It is often a resource manager to the local TP system.

Ingres. A portable SQL system available on many platforms. It is often a resource manager to the local TP system.

Install a resource manager. When a *resource manager* is defined to the system as a *server class*, it is installed with the *Transaction Processing Monitor (TP monitor)*. The resource manger *TRPC calls*, *callbacks*, and execution parameters are defined at this time, and the resource manger is assigned a unique identifier (*RMID*).

Instant duration lock. A lock that is released as soon as it is granted. Such locks are used for *browse mode* access to data. See *lock duration*.

Instant locking. To request that a lock be granted and then immediately released. Such locks query whether some other transaction holds the lock in an incompatible mode.

Integrity constraint. See *consistency constraint.*

Intentions list. A synonym for a *recovery* log, typically written by an application to do its own undo or redo recovery.

Intent mode lock. Any of a set of lock modes used in a hierarchical or DAG lock protocol to signal intent to lock at finer granularity. See *IS, IX, SIX* mode locks.

Interoperation. The interaction of two computer systems. Computer standards are defined to allow vendors to build computers and software that will interoperate with all other computers that observer the standard. Ethernet, X.25, and OSI are examples of such standards. Interoperation and *portability* are orthogonal goals of standards. Interoperation standards are defined by *formats and protocols (FAP)* specifications.

Interprocess communication (IPC). Any mechanism or action that allows two processes to communicate. This includes shared memory, datagrams, sessions, and messages. Frequently, the term is used to mean the low-level and very efficient message system offered by the operating system to processes in a cluster.

Inter-System Communication (ISC). A feature of *CICS* and *IMS* that allows distributed transaction processing: *transaction routing, peer-to-peer* communication, and *function shipping.* Since ISC is based on a published protocols (notably *LU6.2*). Transaction processing systems from other vendors can originate or receive these distributed transactions.

Inter-system resource lock manager (IRLM). A lock manager that arbitrates among lock requests from many systems on up to two MVS nodes. It is used by IMS to regulate access to shared disks.

Invariant. A predicate that is always true of some program or system. A synonym for *consistency constraint* or *integrity constraint.*

IPC. See *interprocess communication.*

IRLM. see *inter-system resource lock manager.*

ISC. See *Inter-System Communication.*

ISO (International Standards Organization). The international body that defines computer (and other standards). It subsumes the United States standards body NIST (National Institute of Standards and Technology, formerly NBS, or National Bureau of Standards). ISO is not related to the industry consortia such as X/Open.

Isolation. See *isolated.*

Isolated. The property that two transactions running in parallel have the illusion that there is no concurrency. It appears that the system runs one transaction at a time. So a transaction is isolated from the uncommitted updates of others (so-called *dirty data*), and the transaction has *repeatable reads.* (See also *degree 1 isolation, degree 2 isolation, degree 3 isolation.*)

Isolated history. A transaction execution *history* equivalent to a *serial history.* Such histories have no *wormhole* transactions and give each transaction an *isolated* execution.

IS mode lock. A *lock mode* used in a *hierarchical* or *DAG lock protocol* to signal intent to request *shared mode locks* at finer granularity.

IX mode lock. A *lock mode* used in a hierarchical or DAG lock protocol to signal intent to request *exclusive or update* mode locks at finer granularity.

Join a transaction. When a resource manager does work on behalf of a transaction, it becomes a *participant* in the transaction and joins it.

Joy's Law. Sun Microsystems processors get twice as fast every year.

Just-in-time inventory control. An approach to manufacturing which predicts when parts and assemblies will be needed. The parts and assemblies are scheduled to arrive just-in-time so that inventory is minimized. This saves space and capital but requires reliable planning and reliable suppliers.

K. Kilo meaning $2^{10} \approx 10^3$. This is slightly more than a k.

k. Kilo meaning 10^3.

KB. Kilobyte (10^3 bytes).

Key of a record. One or more fields of a *record* used for *associative* access to the record. *Unique keys* are used for record identity, nonunique keys are used for record clustering and approximate search. A record may have many keys, and some of the keys may be supported by an *index* for quick access.

Key of encryption. See *encrypt*.

Key-range lock. A *granular lock* that covers all records in some key range of a sorted list. See also *next-key locking*.

Key sequence. A file organization designed for *associative* access, which arranges records in key order so that related records are clustered together and so that *sequential access* to the *record* will return the records in sorted order.

KISS. A design rule: Keep it simple, stupid!

Last-resource-manager optimization. An optimization that allows the last resource manager or transaction manager in a commit tree to become the commit coordinator and thus save one message flow. See *linear commit protocol*.

Latch. A simple lock mechanism, here called a *semaphore*.

Latency. The time between the initiation of a request and the start of its processing. Disk latency is the time before the data arrives at the read head, communications latency is the speed-of-light delay of the wire. See also *response time*.

Latency of a fault. The time between the occurrence of an error and the time that it causes a *failure* (becomes *effective*).

Latent fault. A fault that has caused an *error*, but has not yet been detected or caused a *failure*.

Lazy commit. To write a commit log record but not *force* it to durable storage. See also *eager commit*. The commit call may wait for another to force the log, or it may return immediately. Either the commit record will be forced by a later transaction or the record will be lost. To assure the ACID properties, the transaction outputs (e.g., the commit response to the client) should not be immediately delivered.

Lazy log force. To wait for some other transaction or service to *force* the log.

Leaf of a graph. In a directed graph, any node with no outgoing edges.

Leave a transaction. To stop working on behalf of a transaction.

Legal history. A transaction execution history in which no two distinct transactions were simultaneously granted an *incompatible* lock on an object. *Locking* systems only allow legal histories. See *compatibility of lock modes*.

LIFO (last in first out). A push-down stack. The most recent addition is the first to leave.

Linear commit protocol. A commit message scheme for $N + 1$ transaction participants, that uses $3N$ rather than $4N$ messages, at the expense of longer delays. In the special case of $N = 1$, it is always superior to the general commit protocol. The last-resource-manager optimization uses this protocol.

Livelock. As contrasted to *deadlock*, two programs repeatedly wait for one another, time-out, and then wait again.

Live transaction. A transaction that has not yet completed. Such transactions may be in the *active, prepared, committing, aborting* states. See also *complete transaction.*

Load balancing. To distribute the offered load evenly among a set of servers.

Local Area Network (LAN). A small diameter network, typically about 1 km, which has high bandwidth and low latency. Faster than a *MAN* and slower than a cluster. See *cluster of processors.*

Lock. Either the data structure (the lock) that regulates access to a resource, or the verb (to lock) that reserves access to a resource. Locks are the standard way to achieve transaction *isolation.* A lock request may wait if it is incompatible with other requests, or the request may immediately *bounce.* If the request waits, it may later be *denied* due to timeout or *deadlock.* Once granted to the requestor, shared or exclusive possession of the lock signals to other transactions and processes the requestor's interest in the resource. See *semaphore* and *unlock.*

Lock class. See *lock duration.*

Lock compatibility. See *compatibility of lock modes.*

Lock conversion. See *conversion of a lock.*

Lock duration. The length of time a *lock* is held. Durations range from *instant* (release as soon as granted), to *long* (release at end of transaction), to *very long,* or maintained across *chained transactions.*

Lock escalation. See *escalation of a lock.*

Lock manager. A body of code that provides operations to acquire and release locks. It schedules lock waiting and detects deadlocks.

Locking Theorem. If all transactions are well-formed and two-phase, then any legal history will be isolated. Converse: If a transaction is not well-formed or not two-phase, then it is possible to write another transaction such that the resulting pair is a wormhole.

Lock mode. Lock requests carry a mode, denoting the kind of resource access desired by the requestor and the degree of sharing the transaction is willing to tolerate. *Shared, exclusive, update,* and *intent* are typical lock modes.

Lock wait. If a lock request is incompatible with the grantees, or if someone else is already waiting for the lock, then this request will wait until the lock can be granted.

Log file. A physical file supporting the log table.

Log force. To *force* all log records up to and including a certain *LSN* to persistent storage.

Logged write. Technique to make block write operations to disk *protected actions* by writing a *before image* of the modified *block* to a log before replacing it on disk.

Logical logging. A transaction logging scheme in which log record bodies have the function and its parameters needed to undo or redo the operation; for example, a database insert might just have the new record value (but not the detailed information about index updates and triggers). See also *physical logging* and *physiological logging.*

Logical Unit (LU). An IBM term for a session endpoint.

Logical unit of work (LUW). An IBM (SNA) term meaning transaction.

Logical Unit 6.2 (LU6.2). Ambiguously, the FAP and API of IBM's communications protocol used for program-to-program communication. It includes two-phase commit protocol. It is the proprietary version of OSI-TP.

Log lock. A semaphore regulating insert activity on the log.

Log manager. The body of code and the subsystem that manages the log table.

Log record. A record appearing in the system log. Typically, the record is written by some resource manager on behalf of some transaction, as part of an update operation by the resource manager. The record has a header describing the record, and a body that allows the resource manager to either undo or redo the operation.

Log sequence number (LSN). The primary key of a log record. Since a *log table* is implemented as a sequence of *entry-sequenced* files, the LSN is the file sequence number and then the byte offset (*relative byte address*) of the record in that file.

Log table. A logical *entry-sequenced* table containing *log records*. The table is implemented as a growing sequence of log files. Write access to the table is controlled by the log manager, but there may be SQL read access to the table.

Long duration lock. A lock that is released at transaction commit. Such locks are used for chained transactions. See *lock duration*.

Long-lived transaction. A transaction that starts but does not complete for a long time (hours, days, months). See also *saga*.

Lost transaction. In a *1-safe system pair*, if the primary system commits the transaction and replies to the client before the backup system receives the commit message, then at takeover the transaction may be aborted at the backup (it may be lost). *2-safe* and *very safe system pair* designs avoid lost transactions.

Lost update. If transaction $T1$'s update to an object X is overwritten by another transaction, $T2$ based on an earlier version of object X, then $T1$'s update to object X is said to be lost. *Degree 1 isolation* prevents lost updates.

Low-water mark. A generic term indicating a minimum value. See, for example, *restart low-water mark, archive low-water mark, transaction low-water mark*.

LSN. See *log sequence number*.

LU6.2 (Logical Unit 6.2). A transactional peer-to-peer or RPC protocol defined by IBM by a FAP *formats and protocols* specification. This protocol has been widely implemented by IBM and other vendors. Its design was the basis for the ISO transaction processing standard definition.

LUW. See *logical unit of work*.

M. Mega, meaning $2^{20} \approx 10^6$. This is slightly more than a m.

m. Mega, meaning 10^6.

Magnetic memory. Memory devices based on the storage of information on magnetic or magneto-optic media. Such devices move the media to an electronic read-write station in order to access it. Consequently, magnetic media have long access times but attractive cost/byte. Magnetic media are *persistent*. *Disks* and *tapes* are typical magnetic memory devices. See *electronic memory*.

Main memory. The large, byte addressable electronic memory attached to a processor. It comes below cache and above RAMdisc in the memory hierarchy.

Main memory database. A database that resides in electronic storage close to the processor.

Main storage database. See *main memory database*.

MAN. See *Metropolitan Area Network*.

Marshalling. See *stub*.

Mask an error. A processes or mechanism that tolerates an error and prevents it from causing a *failure* at a higher level of abstraction. *Error correcting codes* and *duplex* disks are mechanisms that mask storage module failures.

Max LSN of a transaction.   The maximum *log sequence number* of a transaction.

MB.   Megabyte (10^6 bytes).

Mb.   Megabit (10^6 bits).

Mean time to failure (MTTF).   The average time to the next failure of the module.

Mean time to repair (MTTR).   The average time needed to repair a faulty module.

Media manager.   A resource manager that provides block-oriented access to secondary and tertiary storage (disk and tape). The media manager controls the placement of data and provides a simple block read, block write interface to the data independent of the device geometry or charactreristics.

Media recovery.   To recover from a storage media failure. See *archive recovery*.

Memory.   Any device that stores information and allows a processor to read and write that information.

Memoryless.   Failure rates are typically assumed to be memoryless. Intuitively, a distribution is memoryless if history has no effect on the current distribution. For example, if module failures are memoryless with one year MTTF, then if a module has been operating for three years without failure, its MTTF today is still one year.

Memory mapped file.   A *file* that is mapped to a *segment* of an *address space*. Reading and writing the *n*th byte of the segment implicitly reads and writes the *n*th byte of the file. See also *explicit file access*.

Message.   A data object sent from one process to another. See also *session* and *datagram*.

Metropolitan Area Network (MAN).   A network spanning less than 100 km. In contrast to *Wide Area Networks*, MANs have low latencies and higher bandwidths. But MANs are slower than *Local Area Networks*.

Mini-batch.   A style of batch programming that breaks a large job into many smaller steps (transactions) so that the job does not lock large parts of the database, and so that in case of failure only the most recent work will be lost and need to be redone.

Mini-transaction.   A *subtransaction*, used in this book to refer to page actions and message actions related to *physiological logging*.

Mirror transaction.   In the function-shipping mode of distributed transaction processing, a server application running at a site remote from the client. When a client requests an operation on a resource near the mirror, the mirror application performs local operations that mirror the client's request.

Mismatch (operator or heuristic).   If an *in-doubt* transaction is resolved by a *heuristic* or *operator* commit or abort decision, and later the commit coordinator announces a different commit or abort decision, the situation is called a mismatch.

Miss ratio.   The fraction of cache accesses which cannot be satisfied by the cache. See *hit ratio*.

Mode of lock.   The degree of sharing allowed by a *lock* request or allowed by the sum of the granted requests. Modes are *shared*, *update*, *exclusive*, and a range of *intent* modes (*IS, IX, SIX*).

Module.   A self-contained unit of service and failure within a system. Both hardware and software are composed of modules. Most modules are, in turn, composed of submodules.

Monitor (as a serialization primitive).   A program guarded by an exclusive semaphore. Also called a serially-reuseable-program. There is at most one execution instance of a monitor at any time. All other invocations wait for the current invocation to complete.

Monotone.   Said of a sequence that always increases or always decreases.

Moore's Law.   Electronic memories get four times bigger every three years.

MRO.   See *multi-region operation.*

MS/DOS (Microsoft/Disk Operating System).   A single-user operating system running on most (75 million at last count) PCs.

MTTF.   See *mean time to failure.*

MTTR.   See *mean time to repair.*

Multicast.   To send the same message to a specific list of addresses. See also *broadcast.*

Multiple Virtual Systems (MVS).   The large operating system for large IBM computers.

Multiprocessor.   A computer system consisting of several processors, either with global memory or in a cluster.

Multi-region operation (MRO).   The use of multiple CICS systems on one operating system to get protection among applications (there is little application protection within a CICS system), and to exploit multiprocessors (CICS uses only one or two processors at a time). MRO provides a convenient and efficient communications among co-located CICS systems through distributed transaction processing.

Murphy's Law.   A design rule: Whatever can go wrong will go wrong, at the worst possible time, and in the worst possible way.

MVS (Multiple Virtual Systems).   The operating system controlling most large IBM machines (it is the heir to OS/360). It pioneered the subsystem interface.

n-**fault tolerant.**   A design that tolerates (masks) up to *n* faults within a *repair window.* The most common case is *single-fault tolerance.*

n-**plex.**   A design that combines *n* copies of a *module* with one or more voters in order to provide a single *failfast, reliable,* or *available* super-module. See *failfast voter, reliability, availability of a module.*

n-**version programming.**   A *software fault tolerance* technique that combines *n* independent implementations of the same *specification.* The outputs of the *n* programs are compared by a voter, which emits the majority output.

Name server.   A process that maintains a database of names and addresses. Servers can register their names and addresses with the name server, and clients can ask for a server's address by name.

NATURAL.   A 4GL programming environment for *ADABAS.* It comprises report generators, graphics support, and presentation management that is also used by Software AG's TP monitors.

Nearline memory.   As opposed to *offline memory* with access times of hours or more, nearline memory has access times measured in seconds or minutes. *Online* memory has access times measured in milliseconds.

Nested commit.   See *linear commit protocol.*

Nested toplevel transaction.   A transaction initiated by another transaction to perform some work that should not be undone even if the initiating transaction aborts. Examples: allocating a new extent, splitting a B-tree page. This concept was originally introduced under the name of "nested toplevel action."

Nested transaction.   A transaction that either has *subtransactions* or is a subtransaction of some nested transaction. See *toplevel transaction, flat transaction.*

NET-WORK.   Session manager for Software AG's distributed databases and TP monitors. It builds on top of IBM's system software, for example on VTAM and CICS.

Network.   The hardware and software that allow processors and processes to communicate. The software that implements interprocessor naming, *interprocess communication, datagrams, sessions,* and session *messages.*

Network partition.   See *partition of a network.*

Next-key locking.   A variant of *key-range locking* in which the key ranges are defined by records in the file. The key range is locked by locking the key of the left (or right) record in each range.

Node.   A *network* source or destination processor, cluster, or system.

Non-blocking commit coordinator.   A *commit coordinator* implemented as a process pair, which can resolve *in-doubt* distributed transactions even if one process or communication line fails. See also *blocking commit coordinator.*

NonStop SQL.   The distributed SQL system implemented by Tandem Computers. It acts as a resource manager to TMF.

Nonvolatile.   *Persistent memory.*

Notify locking.   A lock request mode for an object, which informs the requestor when some other transaction locks or unlocks the resource.

Offline memory.   Memory with access times measured in hours.

Old master–new master recovery.   A recovery scheme that produces a new copy of the state from an old state. The old state is never changed. In the next cycle, the new master acts as old state (old master). This recovery scheme is typical of periodic batch updates of a master file. See Figure 3.1.

Old value–new value logging.   A logging scheme in which log records contain the old and new values of a transformed object.

Oltp.   See *Online transaction processing.*

Online memory.   Memory with access times of 30 ms or less.

Online recovery.   See *crash recovery.*

Online transaction processing (oltp).   Processing of transactions while the client waits, as opposed to queued or batched transactions, which are processed at a later time.

Open transaction manager.   A transaction manager that provides resource manager callbacks (for transaction prepare, commit, abort, or savepoint) and allows a *transaction gateway* to be implemented on it.

Operating system (basic OS).   The software that manages the hardware. Creates and schedules *processes,* creates *address spaces,* provides *interprocess communication (IPC),* creates names for local objects, and authorizes and authenticates users. Keeps its own *repository* (directory) of files, libraries, etc. Provides block-oriented files plus security at the file level. Turns wires into *sessions* with other nodes in the network, *authenticates,* and does error checking on sessions. Naming at this level is physical in that node names, ports, etc. are used. The basic operating system knows nothing about *transactions.*

Operation logging.   A synonym for *logical logging.*

Operator commit or abort.   A form of heuristic commit in which the system operator forces in-doubt transactions to commit or abort.

Optimistic locking.   A degenerate form of field call in which the predicate is value == current_value, and transform is value = new_value. See *timestamp locking, field call,* and *escrow locking.*

Optimistic reads. When data is stored in *N* failfast storage modules, it may be sufficient to read a single copy of the data. The only risk is *stale data.* That is, the data in the storage module may not be the most current version of the data present in other modules.

Oracle. A portable SQL system available on many platforms. It is often a resource manager to the local TP system.

OSI (Open Systems Interconnection). The generic name for all the communications standards defined by ISO (the International Standards Organization).

OSI-ACSE. The ISO definition of *sessions* (called *associations*).

OSI-CCR (Open Systems Interconnection–Commit Control and Recovery). The ISO definition of the two-phase commit protocol on a single session. CCR is subsumed by OSI-TP.

OSI-ROSE (Remote Operations Services). The ISO definition of a simple RPC mechanism.

OSI-TP (Open Systems Interconnect–Transaction Processing). The ISO definition of transaction identifiers and of the two-phase commit protocol in a commit tree.

Outage. A system failure that causes a scheduled or unscheduled denial of service.

Outgoing session. See *outgoing trid.*

Outgoing trid. A transaction identifier, and hence a transaction, that is leaving on a communications session for the first time. In this situation, the communications manager owning the session informs the transaction manager about the outgoing trid, so that the transaction manager can coordinate the commitment of the transaction with the transaction manager at the other end of the session. See also *incoming trid.*

Page. A unit of storage, allocation, and data transfer.

Page-action consistent. In *physiological logging*, a page is page-action consistent if it satisfies its internal consistency constraints, and if the *page LSN* reflects the most recent update.

Page logging. A logging scheme that records the old and new value of a page each time it is changed.

Page LSN. In *physiological logging*, a *log sequence number* stored on the page, which is the key of the most recent log record for an update to that page.

Page semaphore. In *physiological logging*, a shared or exclusive semaphore that controls reading and writing the page. See also *fix rule.*

Pair-and-spare. A module four-plexing scheme in which two *failfast* pairs are combined with a *failfast voter.* Each pair acts as a spare for one other.

Parallel execution. An execution structure in which several processes and or processors work on the same problem at the same time (concurrently). Contrast to *sequential execution.*

Parent transaction. A transaction having *subtransactions.* In a *nested transaction*, a *parent* may be a *subtransaction* of a higher level *parent.* The top-level *parent* is called *root transaction.*

Parity. A simple one-bit *checksum* of a block of data; even parity is a boolean that is true if the block has an even number of binary ones in the data.

Participant. See *commit participant.*

Partitioned data. A file that is broken into fragments, and the fragments are stored at different locations. See also *replicated data.*

Partition of a file or table. To decompose a file or table into disjoint sets (partitions) and store the partitions on different devices, perhaps at different locations. Typically, the partitioning is transparent to the user of the file or table.

Partition of a network. A situation in which two or more network *nodes* cannot communicate (they are partitioned).

Password. A secret pattern shared between a client and server, which authenticates the client to the server.

Path in a graph. A sequence of nodes chosen from a graph such that each node of the sequence is directly connected to the next node in the sequence.

Pathway. The transaction processing system implemented by Tandem Computers.

Peer-to-peer (PTP). A symmetric relationship between two communicating processes. In contrast to the 1:1 request-reply model of *client-server,* peer-to-peer communication allows the two endpoints to have a 1:*n*, *n*:1, or *n*:*m* message exchanges. Typically, though, a peer-to-peer protocol is used as a request-reply client-server protocol. PTP communication is defined both by LU6.2 and as a mode of use in LU6.2, where it is called *program-to-program.*

Persistent. State or memory that survives failures. Persistent memory contrasts with *volatile memory,* which is reset at system restart. It also contrasts with *durable* memory, which is persistent and, in addition, has transactional update semantics (the ACID properties). Magnetic memory is persistent; when combined with a transactional database, the memory is durable. See *volatile memory.*

Persistent process. A *process pair* where the *backup process* is stateless. At *takeover*, the backup is in the null state. When combined with *transactions*, persistent processes give highly available program execution.

Persistent programming language. A programming language that allows some data items to be given the persistent attribute. In this case, the process will be reinstantiated and the persistent items reconstructed after a process or system failure. If transaction semantics are added, the persistent objects take on the ACID transaction properties. A database language like SQL is a persistent programming language, but increasingly, persistent versions of "conventional" languages such as C++ are being built. See *durable* and *transactional programming language.*

Persistent savepoint. A savepoint (named point in the execution of a transaction) that may be reestablished at system restart if the transaction is incomplete. The TP monitor, transaction manager, and resource managers will attempt to reconstruct the transaction's most recent persistent savepoint if the transaction was not yet committed.

Phantom. A record that appears or disappears from a set after a transaction reads the set. If the transaction rereads the set and sees the phantom, then reads are not *repeatable* and the execution is not *isolated.*

Phase 1 of commit. See *commit phase 1.*

Phase 2 of commit. See *commit phase 2.*

Physical logging. A transaction logging scheme in which log record bodies have the old and new value of some physical object at some address; for example, *page logging.* See also *logical logging* and *physiological logging.*

Physiological logging. A cross between *logical logging* and *physical logging.* Each log record applies to a single page or session, and in that sense it is physical. Records are logical within the physical object. The *fix* and *WAL* rules are used to keep the log and page consistent.

Piggyback.   A generic term used to connote the packaging of one operation with a second so that the fixed-cost of the operation is paid by the second. For example, acknowledgment messages may be piggybacked on data message traffic.

Ping-Pong write.   A form of *careful replacement* used in writing sequential files. The write of page i goes to page $i, i + 1, i, ...$ until the page is full. The final write is to page i. Alternatively, if there are two copies of an object, the most recent version may be written to the oldest copy, so that there is an old master and a new master version of the object. If the write fails, the old master is still valid.

Pipe.   A communications *session* between two processes.

Portable.   A program or design that may be easily moved from one computer to another, or one computer architecture to another. Application programming interfaces are designed to provide portability. See *interoperation*.

Precision lock.   A form of *predicate locking* in which all object reads and writes are compared to the precision locks of this and other transactions. The object must be covered by a precision lock of the reader/writer and must not be covered by an incompatible precision lock of another transaction. See also *covered action*.

Predicate lock.   A lock request that carries a *lock mode* and a predicate describing the object(s) the lock applies to. Two predicate lock requests are incompatible if their predicates are mutually satisfiable and if their lock modes are incompatible.

Preempt.   To take a resource away from its current owner rather than *wait* for the owner to relinquish it.

Preemptive scheduling.   As opposed to FIFO scheduling, preemptive scheduling is a priority-driven scheme that runs the highest priority requestor as soon as it demands service. All lower priority clients are preempted, and their resource grants rescinded.

Prefetch.   See *read ahead*.

Prepared transaction.   To test and vote on the consistency of the current transaction, and to record a transaction's updates to durable data so that the transaction can either commit or abort, even if there is an intervening failure.

Prepare-for-commit.   See *commit phase 1*.

Presumed abort.   An optimization of the two-phase commit protocol that does not force the coordinator's prepare log record, thereby saving a synchronous I/O. At restart, if no record of the transaction is found, it is safe to presume the transaction aborted.

Presumed nothing.   An two-phase commit protocol that forces the coordinator's prepare log record. At restart, if no record of the transaction is found for an in-doubt transaction, it indicates a failure of the transaction manger. The presumed abort protocol is generally used in preference to presumed nothing.

Price.   See *cost*.

Primary key.   In relational databases, the primary key uniquely identifies each *record* of the *table*, and which gives quick access to the *file*.

Primary process.   In a *process pair*, the primary process performs the service and *checkpoints* state changes to the *backup process*. When the primary fails, the backup becomes the new primary.

Principle of locality.   The premise of *cache* management: recently used data is likely to soon be used again.

Priority.   An integer rank associated with a process or request, indicating the class of service it should receive in preference to other processes and requests.

Priority inversion. The situation that arises when a high priority server processes a request from a low-priority process at high priority In this situation, the low-priority work may preempt the execution of higher priority work.

Process. The software version of a processor: something executing a program in an address space.

Processor. A device that executes programs, transforms memory, and sends signals on wires.

Process pair. Two *processes* providing a highly available service. The *primary process* services requests and *checkpoints* its state changes to the *backup process*. Should the primary fail, the backup assumes the role of the primary, thus giving the effect of a fault-tolerant or *persistent process*. Process pairs mask hardware and transient software failures. A pair of processes can act as a client or a server.

Program-to-Program Communication (PTP). See *peer-to-peer communication*.

Protected action. Any action in a system having all of the *ACID* properties. In particular, it can be undone and redone. See also *unprotected action* and *real action*.

Protection domain. Processes execute in some protection domain: an *address space* within a process, which is protected from programs executing in other address domains of that process. For example, the kernel of the operating system usually has an address space that subsumes the process address space.

Protocol. A set of rules that specify the behavior of autonomous processes in a communications standard. If you send me this, I should do that. *OSI-TP* and the *two-phase commit* protocol are classic examples of simple protocols. Protocols are generally defined by a state machine (decision table) and a set of actions for each state transition.

PTP. See *peer-to-peer communication*.

Queue. A simple data structure for managing the time-staged delivery of requests to servers. Queue elements may be sorted in priority order or in *FIFO* order. Clients insert items in the queue and servers remove items from the queue, either as soon as possible (ASAP queues), or in a batch (*threshold queues*), or periodically (*timer queues*).

Queued transaction processing. Processing transactions by placing incoming requests in queues that are serviced in priority order by servers. Queueing is convenient for batch transaction processing and for priority scheduling of transactions. See also *direct transaction* processing.

RAID (Redundant Arrays of Independent Disks). A spectrum of designs for n-plex storage modules, which uses some of the modules either in duplex mode or to store an *error correcting code* for the other storage modules. See Patterson, Gibson, and Katz [1988].

RAMdisc. A memory device built from nonvolatile electronic memory, which offers a block-oriented read-write interface to data. So a RAMdisc behaves like a disk with small ($\approx 10\ \mu s$) latency.

Random access. As opposed to *sequential access*, the next address of a random access pattern could be anywhere in the address space or file.

Rapid prototyping. See *spiral development*.

RBA. See *relative byte address*.

Rdb/VMS. An SQL system available on VAX/VMS from Digital Equipment. It acts as a resource manager to DECdtm.

Read-after-write. Technique to protect *block* write operations against *transient errors* by reading the block immediately after it is written and comparing the result to what was supposed to be written.

Read ahead. When the system senses *sequential access* patterns, it anticipates the next read by issuing it before the read is requested.

Read-only optimization. An optimization of the two-phase commit protocol that allows a participant to avoid the Prepare() and Commit() callbacks by declaring that it has no work to do at commit.

Read-past locking. A locking protocol for SQL cursors. It skips over *dirty data*, returning only committed values to the application.

Read-through locking. A locking protocol for SQL cursors, which reads *dirty data*. See also *read-past locking*.

Real action. Action that affects the real world and is hard or impossible to *undo* or compensate for after it has been executed. (For example: launching a missile, drilling a hole.)

Real operation. An action of a transaction that cannot be undone. Real operations must be deferred to *commit phase 2*.

Record. The basic unit of retrieval, update, and insert in a *file*. Objects within files.

Record lock. A *fine-granularity* lock covering a particular record or tuple in a file or table.

Recovery. The process of masking a fault. In transaction processing systems, the mechanism to *abort* transactions while the system is operating, the mechanism to *restart* the system and recompute the most recent committed state after a system outage, and the mechanism to recover objects from *archive* copies should the online version of the object be lost.

Recovery blocks. An exception-handling mechanism integrated with a block structured programming language. Each program module (block) has a postcondition that is tested on exit. If the condition is violated, the process state is returned to the state as of the beginning of the block, and an alternate program is run, typically an earlier version of the program.

Recovery to a timestamp. To apply a redo scan forward to some time and then undo all transactions not committed at that time. The result is the consistent state as of that time. Using such a state violates transaction durability.

Redo an action or transaction. To reapply committed or in-doubt actions of transactions. To transform an object from its old value to its new value.

REDO scan. Reading of the system *log file* in FIFO order, applying each log record to the *persistent* state either for *online recovery* or for *archive* recovery.

Referential integrity constraint. A consistency constraint based on a *foreign key,* which declares that field values in one file must be key values in another file.

Relative byte address (RBA). In an unstructured file or an *entry sequence* file, the address of a byte or group of bytes relative to the start of the file, using zero as a base.

Relative file. A file organization in which records have consecutive record numbers and they are addressed by record numbers. An array of records. See *direct file access*.

Relative Record Number (RRN). See *relative tuple number*.

Relative tuple number (RTN). In *relative files*, tuples are numbered consecutively throughout the file. Since each page has the same number of fixed-length slots for tuples, the relative tuple number unambiguously identifies the page and the slot within the page where the tuple is stored.

Relay Transaction. In the transaction routing mode of distributed transaction routing, a local transaction that forwards messages to the remote server and forwards responses back to the client.

Reliability. The probability that a module will meet its specification, quantified either as the module *mean time to failure,* or the reciprocal of that, the *failure rate*.

Reliable Transaction Router (RTR). A TP system offered by DEC. It provides high availability by routing client requests to multiple heterogeneous servers. If some servers fail (rather than abort), RTR commits the transaction and replays the request at a later time. RTR acts as a commit coordinator among heterogeneous closed transaction managers and resource mangers.

Remote procedure call (RPC). A procedure call that either invokes a local procedure or, if the server is remote, invokes the remote server via a message and returns the server reply message to the caller as though it were the result of a local call. The caller of the procedure cannot tell whether the server is local or remote. Similarly, it may appear to the server that the caller is local. RPC is a way of structuring client-server interactions.

Repair. The transformation of a faulty module or system to a correctly functioning system in a correct state.

Repair window. A period during which a system or module is being *repaired*. The repair window typically lasts for *MTTR* time units. *N-fault tolerant* systems can only tolerate *N*-faults within a repair window.

Repeatable read. One aspect of transaction *isolation*. If a transaction reads the same item twice without updating it in the interim, the read should return the same value (be repeatable). Repeatable reads require holding read locks to the end of the transaction rather than releasing them at the end of the read operation. Repeatable read is a synonym for *degree 3 isolation*. See *cursor stability*.

Replicated data. A file or file fragment that stored at (replicated at) several locations. See also *partitioned data*.

Repository. A database describing all the components of the system. Each resource manager maintains a catalog of its objects as a database. The union of all these catalogs is called the repository.

Resource. A generic term meaning some valuable object, either a piece of data or a piece of hardware.

Resource manager (RM). A subsystem that manages some transactional objects. The resource manger typically offers services to applications or to other resource mangers. A transactional database system, a transaction queue manager, a transactional session manager, and a transactional persistent programming language all act as a resource manager. See *transaction manager*.

Resource manager identifier (RMID). A short, unique identifier used to name a *resource manager*.

Resource manager interface (RMI). In this book, the term for the interface between the transaction manager and the resource managers. X/Open DTP calls it the XA interface. The application interface to the resource manager has no generic name. Each resource manager (LU6.2, Oracle, Ingres, Informix, Rdb, queue manager, etc.) has its own private application programming interface.

Resource manager low-water mark. The lowest log sequence number (LSN) needed by the transaction manager to recover the durable state of a resource manager, should it fail. For the system as a whole, it is the minimum of all resource manger low-water marks.

Response time. The time between the submission of a request and the receipt of the reply. Typically measured from the start of the request to the end of the reply. The 90% response time typically used in transaction processing systems is the smallest time greater than the response time of 90% of the transactions.

Restart. The recovery process after the failure of a resource manager or a transaction processing system.

Restartable operation.   A synonym for *idempotent operation*.

Restart low-water mark.   The oldest log record needed to perform *restart* if the system were to fail. Typically, it is the minimum of the *transaction low-water mark* and the *resource manager low-water mark*.

Resume a transaction.   To assume the trid of a transaction the process previously left. See *leave* a transaction.

Ripa.   Town in Tuscany that is famous for its staggering prices and its literacy in *transaction processing*.

RM.   See *resource manger*.

RMID.   See *resource manager identifier*.

Rollback.   To undo the effects of a transaction by a complete *abort*, or to partially undo back to a *savepoint*.

Rollback Theorem.   An update transaction that does an unlock and then a rollback is not two-phase.

ROLLBACK WORK.   The SQL verb to abort a transaction. See also *COMMIT WORK, BEGIN WORK.*

Root.   In a *tree* (graph), the unique node with no parent. More generally, in a directed graph, any node with no incoming edges.

Root of a transaction.   The first *process* or *protection domain* to work on a transaction. In many designs, only the root can call Commit_Work(). See also *participant*.

Root transaction.   *A* transaction that started a *nested transaction*. All other transactions in that nested transaction are direct or indirect *subtransactions* of the root. Of all transactions in a nested transaction, only the root has all the *ACID* properties.

Round robin scheduling.   The recurring version of FIFO scheduling. Each member of the group is scheduled in turn. When the entire group has been scheduled once, the cycle repeats.

RPC.   See *remote procedure call*.

RTN.   See *relative tuple number*.

RTR.   See *Reliable Transaction Router*.

S Mode lock.   See *shared mode lock*.

Saga.   A recoverable chain of individual transactions. See also *long-lived transaction*.

Salvager.   An exception handling program that heuristically repairs faulty data. See also *auditor of data structures, fault*.

Savepoint.   A named point in the execution of a transaction. In case of failure, the transaction may roll back to one of these savepoints and reestablish the transaction state as of that point. Savepoints may be *persistent*.

Scan.   Capability to process *tuples* (*records*) in a file sequentially (one tuple at a time), in some predefined order and with a filter that screens out irrelevant tuples. Processing tuples includes retrieval, insert, update, and delete.

Schedule.   In isolation theory, a common synonym for *history*.

SCOBOL.   The persistent programming language used within Tandem's Pathway transaction processing system to define global transaction flow. It is a derivative of COBOL, with presentation services, transaction, and RPC verbs added.

Secondary memory.   As opposed to *cache* or *main memory*. Typically disk or RAMdisc.

Second Law of Concurrency. Concurrent execution should not have lower throughput or higher response time than serial execution

Sector. A physical block of memory on a disk track. The minimum unit of disk I/O.

Segment. A section of an address space corresponding to some *memory mapped file*. The unit of *address space* sharing.

Semaphore. A high-performance but low functionality locking mechanism used inside resource managers. Compared to *locks*, semaphores have no symbolic names, only shared and exclusive mode access, no escalation or conversion, no deadlock detection, and no automatic release at commit.

Sequence number. A counter used to detect duplicates and missing elements. Each update, message, action, or item gets the next sequence numbers. Since sequence numbers are dense (no gaps) and unique, they can detect missing or duplicate elements.

Sequential access. A memory access pattern in which subsequent memory access addresses increase or decrease in steady increments. This is the preferred access pattern for magnetic storage devices.

Sequential execution. An execution structure in which only one process works on a problem. Contrast to *parallel execution*.

Sequential file. See *entry sequence*.

Serial history. A transaction execution *history* that runs one transaction to completion before beginning the next transaction.

Serializable. In isolation theory, a common synonym for *isolated history*.

Serial write. A form of careful replacement of two data copies. The write of the second copy does not begin until the write of the first copy has completed. In this way, there is always one valid copy.

Server. A process offering some service and either driven by *RPC*, a *session*, or a *queue*.

Server class. A collection of one or more server processes offering the same service. The TP monitor typically grows and shrinks the server class as the load changes.

Session. A point-to-point connection between two processes offering *peer-to-peer* communication. *Messages* sent on sessions carry *sequence numbers* so that lost or duplicate messages can be detected. Messages may also be *encrypted* by a session key to prevent forgery or disclosure. Sessions may also reserve communication bandwidth and so allow a degree of *flow control*.

Session pair. A single logical *session* implemented as pair of sessions to a *process pair* or to a *session pair*. If the *primary* process or system fails, subsequent messages and replies are sent via the backup session.

Shadows. A memory-recovery mechanism in which copies of the old value of pages or objects are maintained as a shadow state. If the transaction aborts, the state returns to the shadow state. If the transaction commits, the shadow state is discarded and replaced by the new state.

Shadow Set. The DEC term for a duplexed or triplexed disk.

Shared global. A computer architecture in which a collection of processors share secondary or tertiary memory, in contrast to *shared memory* and *shared nothing*.

Shared memory. Memory *segments* shared between two processes or processors. When used to describe a computer architecture, a design in which several processors share a consistent picture of main memory. See also *shared global* and *shared nothing*.

Shared mode lock.   A lock request that allows others to concurrently share access to the resource, in contrast to an *exclusive mode lock* request.

Shared nothing.   A computer architecture in which all memory is private to processors, and processors communicate only via communications lines. See also *shared global*.

Sharp checkpoint.   A copy of an object or state. It is completely consistent, as contrasted with a *fuzzy checkpoint*.

Short duration lock.   A lock that is held for the duration of a transaction step (e.g., a message or a database operation). See also *instant* and *long duration locks*.

Simple Transaction.   In the system sense, an interactive transaction that has a single input-output message pair and a few (less than 100) resource manger calls. In the mathematical development of *isolation* theorems, a transaction that has all its begin, commit, and rollback actions replaced with the necessary write and unlock actions.

Single-fault tolerant.   A design that will *mask* any single *fault* but cannot generally tolerate two faults within a *repair window*.

SINIX.   *UNIX*-style operating system offered by SNI. It is the platform for the first TP monitor (*UTM*) that became commercially available in the *UNIX* world.

SIX mode lock.   A lock mode that combines *IX* and *shared mode locks*.

SMOP.   Simply a matter of programming. Casual way of saying that things should be clear enough to not need any further explanation.

SMOW.   Simply a matter of writing. That's what this book was.

SNA (System Network Architecture).   IBM's network architecture. See *LU6.2*.

SoC.   See *sphere of control*.

Software fault tolerance.   As opposed to *hardware fault tolerance*, a mechanism that masks software faults either by *design diversity* (*N-version programming*), or by instant repair (*process pairs*).

Sort.   To order a collection based on some ordering predicate.

Sorted list.   A list in which successive elements are sorted on some criterion.

Specification.   A description of the correct behavior of a module or system. Behavior is faulty if it departs from the specified behavior. See *fault*.

Sphere of control (SoC).   Model to describe the behavior of complex applications in time under conditions of concurrency and failures. A SoC encloses an atomic action, controlling the commitment of its updates and monitoring any dependencies from other spheres of control that arise through the use of uncommitted data. Spheres of control are typically nested in other spheres of control.

Spin lock.   A lock requested in bounce mode, which, if it is busy, the client immediately rerequests. The requestor is said to spin on the lock until it is freed. If the system is a shared-memory multiprocessor, and if the lock is rarely busy, and if spinning is MUCH cheaper than waiting and being redispatched, then spin locks are a good idea. But that is a lot of ifs. See also *wait* lock.

Spiral development.   A development methodology in which the application is first quickly prototyped. The design is then evaluated and redesigned. Based on this new understanding, a more refined implementation is produced, and it again is evaluated and redesigned. Eventually, the result of this effort is directly shipped to the customer, or the result can be fed to a *waterfall development* effort, either as a specification or as a product to pass through quality assurance and the later stages of a careful development process.

SQL.   An ISO standard relational database language defined in 1986.

SQL2. An extension to SQL, which became a standard in 1992. It added degrees of isolation, read-only transactions, deferred integrity checks, standard catalogs, and a client-server naming and error scheme, among other things.

Stable storage. A synonym for *persistent* memory.

Staggered allocation. A way to allocate log partitions to three disks, so one disk is idle and can be used for archive while the other two disks are busy receiving new log data. This idea works for any sequential file.

Stale data. If stored data should have been written, but the write operation failed and left the data unchanged, then the stored data is said to be stale. See also *optimistic reads*.

Startup. The process of starting a computer system after a graceful shutdown, as opposed to *restart*, which is resuming execution after a *failure*.

Stateless server. See *context-free server*.

Static allocation. Preassigning resources to requestors based on their predeclared demands.

Structured file. As opposed to an unstructured file, which is just bytes, a structured file is a collection of records.

Structured Task Definition Language (STDL). The persistent programming language used by DEC's ACMS transaction manager to define global transaction flow. In addition to a conventional programming language, it has verbs to invoke presentation services, define transaction boundaries, and invoke services of servers.

Stub. Part of the *RPC* mechanism. The stub is a piece of code on both the client and the server. It is responsible for converting the caller's parameters into the callee's format (client makes it right), or vice versa (server makes it right). The stub also does parameter marshalling; for example, taking the (converted) parameter values and arranging them into a string of bytes that is then passed to the message system for sending across the session.

Subtransaction. Transaction that is nested under a higher-level transaction. Of the *ACID* properties, it has *atomicity*, *consistency*, and *isolation*, but it is not durable. Even after a subtransaction has locally committed, it can be rolled back due to the abort of the *parent transaction*.

Sybase. A portable *SQL* system available on many platforms. It is designed to support the client-server style of computing. It was the first commercially available *SQL* system to provide a *prepare-for-commit* call to the application. It allows the application to participate in the *two-phase commit*.

Synchronization point. See SYNCPT.

Sync Level 1. An LU6.2 term meaning the session has support for the CONFIRM-CONFIRMED verbs that allow client and server to do end-to-end acknowledgment.

Sync Level 2. An LU6.2 term meaning the session has support for the SYNCPT verb that provides ACID properties across distributed transactions via two-phase commit.

Sync Level 0. An LU6.2 term meaning the session has no message integrity beyond sequence numbers to detect lost or duplicate messages.

Syncpoint. An IBMism for *Commit Work*.

SYNCPT. The way IBM spells "commit" in CICS and IMS. It stands for synchronization point and is spelled syncpoint. Since these systems adopt the chained transaction model, a synchronization point both commits the current transaction and starts a new one.

System. A generic term that generally means a complete entity. For example, a node of a network, a self-contained resource manager (database system), or a more globally the whole thing (solar system).

System delusion. A failure mode of transaction processing systems in which the computer system is functioning perfectly, but the computer's representation of reality is so far from the truth that there is no incentive for users to trust the system's information or to correct the system data. Transaction processing systems are bi-stable. If the system is accurate, users have an incentive to repair mistakes in data and the system is self-correcting. If the system is deluded, this user incentive is missing, mistakes are not repaired, and the system state drifts further and further from reality.

System dictionary. See *repository*.

System pair. A pair of computer systems which are geographically remote, have different operators and perhaps different designs, but which implement the same service. The *primary system* provides the service and informs the backup system of state changes. When the primary fails, the *backup system* continues the service. System pairs tolerate most environmental, operations, maintenance, and hardware faults. They also tolerate some software faults.

Table. The SQL and relational database word for *file*.

Table lock. A *coarse-granularity* lock covering all records in a file.

Takeover (of a process pair or system pair). The mechanism whereby the *backup* of the *process pair* assumes *primary* responsibility for the pair when the primary fails.

Tape. A memory device in which data is stored on a linear media. Sequential transfer rates are typically good, but random access times are typically measured in seconds or minutes.

TB. Terabyte (10^{12} bytes).

Testable operation or state. If it is possible for a program to decide whether or not the effect of an operation has been achieved without having to redo the operation, the operation is said to be testable.

Think time. The time between the receipt of a reply and the submission of the next request.

Thread. A process or lightweight (inexpensive) process.

Threshold queue. A message *queue* that schedules servers based on some threshold size of the queue (e.g., start a server when there are 10 elements in the queue), in contrast to a *timed queue* or an *ASAP queue*.

TID. See *tuple identifier*.

Time domain addressing. An approach to transactional storage and update in which each object has a sequence of versions. Each version is valid from the time it is created until the time it is replaced with a more modern version. Transactions can either read and write current values or they can run in the past, reading values as of some previous time.

Timed queue. A *queue* for which requests are serviced periodically (e.g., overnight) in contrast to *ASAP queue* or *threshold queue*.

Timeout. The limit on the time a requestor is willing to wait for a resource. When the wait time exceeds the timeout, the request is canceled.

Time slice. In a time-shared or multiprogrammed operating system, a process is scheduled to execute for a time quantum or time slice. If the process consumes the entire time without waiting, the process will be preempted and another process will be scheduled for execution by the CPU.

Timestamp. A reading of the clock in terms of *Universal Coordinated Time*.

Timestamp locking. A degenerate form of field call in which the predicate is: object_timestamp < transaction_timestamp, and the transform is object_timestamp = transaction_timestamp and value = new_value. See *field call* and *escrow locking*.

TM.   See *transaction manager.*

TMF.   See *Transaction Monitoring Facility.*

TMR.   See *triple modular redundancy.*

TOPEND.   A TP monitor offered by NCR on its UNIX systems.

Toplevel transaction.   A transaction that is not nested within any others. The commitment of *nested transactions* depends on the commitment of the toplevel transaction.

Topological sort.   To *sort* a collection based on the ordering implied by a directed graph.

TPC (Transaction Processing Performance Council).   A consortium of about 50 TP vendors and large users, which defines performance metrics for transaction processing systems. These benchmarks are called TPC-A, TPC-B, and so on.

TPC-A.   A simple update intensive transaction consisting of a message in, message out, and four database calls. Most of the database is in main memory. The TPC-A tps rating is the number of transactions the system can run giving 90% of them less than 2-second response time. Terminals have 10-second cycle time ($\approx$ 9 think time) The cost/tps is the 5-year cost of ownership (hardware, software, and maintenance) divided by the tps rate. The system cost includes the cost of terminals, modems, and all associated software: everything but the communications wires.

TPC-B.   The TPC-A benchmark with the network hardware and software removed. TPC-B performance numbers are typically three times higher than TPC-A numbers, and cost/tps numbers are typically seven times lower.

TPF.   See *transaction processing facility.*

TPOS.   See *transaction processing operating system.*

TP monitor.   See *transaction processing monitor.*

tps.   See *transactions per second.*

Transaction.   An *ACID* unit of work (atomic, consistent, isolated, and durable).

Transactional programming language.   A programming language in which some variables have the *ACID* properties. If the application invokes ROLLBACK, these variables are reset to their previously committed state. If the variables are shared with other processes, updates to the variables by independent transactions are isolated. If the program, process, or system fails, at restart the process and program is reinstantiated, and the variables are set to their most recently committed state. Stored procedures in database systems are typically written in such a transactional programming language.

Transactional remote procedure call (TRPC).   Simple *remote procedure call*, extended by the features required to give the computation the transactional ACID properties. A TRPC makes the callee a *participant* of the caller's *transaction*, it implies *server class* management and *commit* coordination among all participants.

Transaction context.   State that is private to an instance of a *transaction*. It can consist of very different types of data: local variables of the *transaction program*, *locks* held by the *transaction*, *cursor* positions established by the *transaction*, *file* control blocks, *sessions* established by the *transaction*, and so on.

Transaction gateway.   A process or program that translates incoming transactions and transaction identifiers to the local names and protocols, and translates outgoing transactions and transaction identifiers to the foreign protocols.

Transaction identifier (trid).   A fixed-length identifier that uniquely identifies the transaction in the network. The transaction identifier is unique for all time. It will never be reused.

Transaction low-water mark. The lowest *log sequence number (LSN)* needed by the transaction manger to recover the transaction. For the system as a whole, it is the minimum of all *varchars.*

Transaction Monitoring Facility (TMF). The transaction manager integrated with Tandem's Guardian operating system.

Transaction manager (TM). Creates *transaction identifiers (trids)* and tracks which resource managers participate in the transaction. Provides the transaction application programming interface (begin, commit, savepoint, rollback). Orchestrates the transaction *commit, savepoints, checkpoints*, etc. Also orchestrates *rollback, crash recovery, archive recovery*, and state restoration of persistent applications.

Transaction message. An input *message* received by a TP monitor, which invokes a transaction program and starts a transaction. See *transaction program.*

Transaction Processing Facility (TPF). A high-performance, low-function transaction management system from IBM. Developed in the 1960s by the airline industry, TPF was variously called SABER and ACP. It runs as its own operating system and supports a primitive file system and basic program and I/O services. The huge investments by the airlines in assembly-language TPF programs assures its existence into the next millennium.

Transaction processing monitor (TP monitor). Name for a class of products typified by *CICS, ACMS, Pathway*, and *Tuxedo*, which provide a transaction execution environment on top of conventional (basic) operating systems. Roughly speaking, TP monitors encompass the functionality of both the *transaction processing operating system* and the *transaction processing services.*

Transaction processing operating system (TPOS). An extension of the basic operating system that makes processes, messages, files, and sessions transactional (objects with ACID properties). Provides a transaction-oriented *remote procedure call (RPC)* mechanism. Creates *transaction identifiers (trids)*; provides a global *log* interface; supports *isolation* via a *lock manager*; manages *savepoints, checkpoints,* and persistent program (transaction) state; and handles the *commit* process. Maps processing requests (coming in from a *client* via RPC) to processes running the proper *server* code. For that, it has to manage durable *queues, server classes*, and *threads* (lightweight processes). Does request *authentication* and scheduling. Keeps a repository with all the components of the *transaction processing system* it is responsible for. Restarts and recovers the transaction processing system after a crash. All in all, it provides a *resource manager interface (RMI)* so that the transaction processing system can be extended by including arbitrary new services which adhere to the transaction paradigm.

Transaction processing services (TRAPS). Provides the programming environment for transactional applications. This includes a full range of high-functionality resource managers like an *SQL* database system, *flow control* mechanisms (also known as *long-lived transactions*), provisions for very high availability (disaster protection, a generic invocation mechanism for remote servers, including name binding). It also includes operations interfaces, *monitoring, load balancing*, security mechanisms, *configuration management.* Presents the application programmer with the notion of an arbitrarily reliable (and available) machine that performs only atomic state changes at (almost) any level of abstraction. Provides development and test tools to go with that execution paradigm.

Transaction processing system. Name for the whole system—hardware, software, procedures, rules, and users—needed to design, implement, and operate a transaction processing application. Specifically, it comprises the following abstraction layers: *hardware*, basic operating system, *transaction processing operating system, transaction processing services,* and *applications*. Online transaction processing systems (OLTP systems) are a special case application requiring high throughput of interactive transactions.

Transaction program. A program registered with a *TP monitor* to serve some class of transaction input messages. When such messages arrive, the TP monitor starts a process executing the program, and sends the message to the process.

Transaction routing. Based on a transaction code, destination queue, or user-written procedure, a transaction input message may be routed to an application on another transaction processing system. A relay application running at the local node acts as the surrogate to pass messages between the client and the remote application server.

Transactions per second. A throughput rating. This term is often used in conjunction with the standard transactions defined by the *TPC (Transaction Processing Performance Council)*. Often, the rating implies the maximum number of transactions that can be processed by the system while 90% of the transactions' response times are less than 2 seconds.

Transaction tree. A distributed transaction involves sessions among several transaction managers. The sessions that first established the transaction at each transaction manager form a tree rooted at the transaction beginner.

Transfer of commit. To transfer the transaction's commit authority from the *beginner* to some other transaction manger. Both *linear commit* and the *last-resource-manager* optimizations are examples.

Transid (transaction identifier). A synonym for *trid*.

Transient error. An error, fault, or failure that is repaired immediately. Timing errors are often transient. Transient errors often are intermittent, meaning that they reoccur.

Transition logging. A logging technique that stores the exclusive (or XOR) of the old and new value, thereby reducing the size of the log record.

Tree (a graph). A connected directed graph in which each node except the *root* or has exactly one parent.

Trid (transaction identifier). A globally unique identifier for a transaction.

Triple modular redundancy (TMR). A triplexing scheme in which the voter compares the outputs of three modules and accepts the majority value. See *N-plex*.

Triplex. See *triple modular redundancy*.

TRPC. See *transactional remote procedure call*.

Tuple. The SQL and relational database word for *record* in a *file*.

Tuple identifier. Mechanism used to identify *tuples* in a *file* such that the identifier can locate the tuple with a minimum number of page accesses and that it remains stable if the tuple is relocated to a different page. It explicitly points to the page where the tuple was originally inserted and provides a forwarding mechanism to handle relocation.

Tuxedo (System/T). A transaction processing monitor from AT&T and now from UNIX System Laboratories (USL).

Two-checkpoint recovery. A two-pass recovery scheme that begins a redo scan two checkpoints back in the log and *REDO*es the updates of all resource managers. Then it performs a single *UNDO SCAN* to *UNDO* uncommitted updates.

Two-checkpoint rule. No resource manager low water mark can be more than two checkpoints old. This is needed if the two-checkpoint recovery scheme is used.

Two-phase commit (2Ø commit, 2PC). A protocol that allows a set of autonomous processes or agents to eventually all commit or all abort. Most transaction mangers offer to act as the coordinator in a two-phase commit protocol. Variants of the protocol are found in LU6.2 and OSI-TP.

Two-phase transaction locking (2PL). A transaction is two-phased if it never locks an object after unlocking some object. The name comes from the fact that such transactions have a growing phase during which they acquire locks, and a shrinking phase during which they release locks. The shrinking phase is usually phase 2 of the two-phase commit protocol. Aside from this connection, there is no connection between two-phase locking and *two-phase commit*.

TX. In X/Open DTP, TX is the name of the application programming interface between the application and the *transaction manager*. It allows portable transaction applications. It includes verbs to begin, commit, and abort a transaction.

U mode lock. See *update mode lock*.

Undo. To reverse an uncommitted action or transaction. To return an object to its old value.

Undo log. A log consisting entirely of records need to undo transactions. See also *dynamic log*.

UNDO scan. An LIFO scan of a *transaction log* or of the *system log* in which all uncommitted updates are undone. Used by Rollback_Work() and by system restart.

Unfix a page. To release the *page semaphore*.

Unique key. A record key such that no two records of the file may have the same key value. Unique keys are used for object identity; non-unique keys are used for record clustering and approximate search

Unit of work. The SQL and LU6.2 term for *transaction*.

Universal Coordinated Time (UTC). The clock. It is accurate to microseconds or better, is monotonic, and never repeats. Also known as Greenwich Mean Time (GMT).

UNIX. An operating system from AT&T, widely used for workstations and LAN servers.

Unlock. The act of one transaction releasing its ownership of a *lock*.

Unprotected action. Action in a system that lacks the *ACID* properties. Distinguished from *real actions* by the possibility to compensate for them by executing *compensating (trans)actions*. See also *protected action*.

Unrepeatable read. If two successive reads of the value of object *X* by transaction *T* return two different versions, and if *T* did not update *X* in the interim, then the reads are said to be unrepeatable. *Degree 3 isolation* , also known as *isolation*, gives repeatable reads.

Update mode lock. A *lock mode* used to signal intent to update an object. Like *exclusive mode*, it delays other transactions from concurrently reading or writing the object. It is used to prevent deadlocks on frequently updated objects (*hotspots*).

UTM. A TP monitor offered by SNI.

UTM-D. Distributed version of the *UTM* TP monitor. It supports distributed transaction processing using the *LU6* protocol.

Validation. A fault avoidance technique that tests hardware for correct operation and tests designs for correct implementation of the specification before the system is placed in operation.

Value logging. A synonym for *physical* logging. See also *logical logging*, *physiological logging*.

Varchar. In the SQL language, a variable length character string.

VAX. The computer architecture and the computers built by DEC to run the VMS operating system.

VAXcluster. A collection of VAX/VMS computers that act as a single computer. Within a cluster, all nodes can access all devices, and sets of processing and storage devices offer high-availability services. If a node or device fails, others continue to offer the service. To clients, the cluster is the unit of service and availability.

Version. As objects change, each successive object is a new version. A transaction reads or writes a particular version of an object.

Very long duration lock. A lock that is not released at transaction commit. Such locks are used for *chained transactions*. See *lock duration*.

Very safe system pair. A *system pair* configuration in which the client is not sent the commit response until the backup of the system pair has acknowledged the transaction commit. See also *2-safe system pair*.

View. In a relational database, a virtual relation that has the same syntactic structure as a *base relation*, but the *tuples* of which are not given explicitly—rather, they are derived from existing tuples via a so-called view definition. Whether the tuples of a view are stored (materialized view) or whether they are derived at run time is a matter of implementation.

Virulent bug. A software fault that affects a system more than once, as contrasted to a *benign bug*. See also *Heisenbug* and *Bohrbug*.

VMS. An operating system from DEC, which includes native support for the *DECdtm* transaction manager.

Volatile memory. Memory that is reset at system restart and so must be recovered from *persistent* or *durable* memory.

WADS. See *Write Ahead Data Set*.

Wait. If a resource is unavailable, a transaction or process may wait for it to become available. See also *bounce locking*.

Wait-for graph. A graph of which processes or transactions are waiting for which other processes and transactions. The edges of the graph are labeled with the resource that is desired by the waiter. A cycle in the graph indicates a *deadlock*.

Waiting group of a lock. A list of all the transactions waiting for access to the lock. Each list entry has the transaction name, the mode of sharing granted to the transaction, and the lock *class* (*duration of lock*). See also *granted group, mode of a lock*.

Wakeup waiting. If a process is waiting for an interrupt or signal, it may test the flag and then call wait(). If a wakeup arrives between the test and the call to wait(), the process might miss the event and sleep forever. So the wait() routine remembers if there are any pending signals and gives the wakeup waiting return in this case.

WAL. See *write-ahead log*.

Waterfall development. A development methodology that divides work into many stages. The stages are requirements, specification, design, unit-test, integration, quality assurance, alpha-test, beta-test, production (gamma test), maintenance, and retirement. Contrast to *spiral development*.

Wear out. The *failure rate* of modules increases as they age. This process is called wear out.

Well-formed transaction. A transaction is well formed if each action is covered by a lock. Read actions require a shared mode lock, and write actions require an exclusive mode lock. Well-formed transactions also unlock all locks as part of *commit* or *rollback*.

Wide Area Network (WAN).   A large diameter network, typically more than 100 km, that has relatively high latency due to switching and propagation delays. Contrast to a *MAN* or *LAN*.

Work.   The SQL term for a transaction is *unit of work*. See *BEGIN WORK, COMMIT WORK, ROLLBACK WORK*.

Wormhole.   In a transaction execution history, any transaction that did not execute in isolation. Based on the dependencies among transactions implied by the history, such transactions ran before and after some transaction. This time travel gives wormholes their name.

Wormhole Theorem.   A history is isolated if and only if it has no *wormhole* transactions.

Write Ahead Data Set (WADS).   A low-latency, disk-based cache of recent log writes. Log writes go to this low-latency cache to speed commit and log force.

Write-ahead log (WAL).   Force the page's log records prior overwriting its persistent copy.

XA.   In X/Open DTP, XA is the application programming interface between the resource manager and the transaction manager. It allows portable transactional resource mangers.

XA+.   In X/Open DTP, XA+ is the TM-CM (transaction manager–communications manager) interface that allows the *communications manager* to inform the *transaction manager* about *outgoing* and *incoming trids*.

X mode lock.   See *exclusive mode lock*.

X/Open.   A consortium of UNIX vendors who are defining portability standards for the UNIX environment. They predate and compete with the American Posix group.

X/Open Distributed Transaction Processing (DTP).   A distributed transaction processing architecture, based on OSI-TP, for a distributed two-phase commit protocol. The architecture defines application programming interfaces and interactions among transactional applications (APs), transaction managers (TMs), resource managers (RMs), and communications managers (CMs). Transaction managers interoperate on distributed transactions by using the OSI-TP formats and protocols.

XRF.   See *IMS Extended Recovery Feature*.

Index

Units and Performance Figures
(Price and performance figures based on 1991 estimates)

Magnitude	Name	Abbreviation	Unit	Abbreviation
$10^{18} \approx 2^{60}$	exa	e, E	bit	b
$10^{15} \approx 2^{50}$	peta	p, P	byte (8 bits)	B
$10^{12} \approx 2^{40}$	tera	t, T	bits per second	bps
$10^{9} \approx 2^{30}$	giga, billion	g, b, G, B	bytes per second	Bps
$10^{6} \approx 2^{20}$	mega	m, M	instructions per second	ips
$10^{3} \approx 2^{10}$	kilo	k, K	transactions per second	tps
$10^{0} \approx 2^{0}$				
10^{-3}	milli	m		
10^{-6}	micro	μ		
10^{-9}	nano	n		
10^{-12}	pico	p		
10^{-15}	femto	f		

Price-Performance Tradeoff for Memory

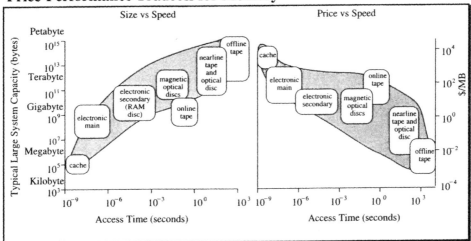

Typical Performance Figures of Commercial Systems

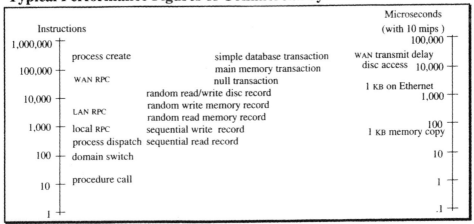

Terms and Definitions

The ACID Properties

Atomicity. A transaction's changes to the state are atomic: either all happen or none happen. These changes include database changes, messages, and actions on transducers.

Consistency. A transaction is a correct transformation of the state. The actions taken as a group do not violate any of the integrity constraints associated with the state. This requires that the transaction be a correct program.

Isolation. Even though transactions execute concurrently, it appears to each transaction, T, that others executed either before T or after T, but not both.

Durability. Once a transaction completes successfully (commits), its changes to the state survive failures.

Issue	Degree 0	Degree 1	Degree 2	Degree 3
Common Name	Chaos	Browse	Cursor stability	Isolated serializable repeatable reads
Protection Provided	Lets others run at higher isolation	0° and no lost updates	No lost updates No dirty reads	No lost updates No dirty reads Repeatable reads
Committed Data	Writes visible immediately	Writes visible at EOT	Same as 1°	Same as 1°
Dirty Data	You don't overwrite dirty data	0° and others do not over-write your dirty data	0°, 1°, and you don't read dirty data	0°,1°,2° and others don't dirty data you read
Lock Protocol	Set short exclusive locks on data you write	Set long exclusive locks on data you write	1° and set short share locks on data you read	1° and set long share locks on data you read
Transaction Structure	Well-formed WRT writes	Well-formed WRT writes and two-phase WRT writes	Well-formed and two-phase WRT writes	Well-formed and two-phase
Concurrency	Greatest: only set short write locks	Great: only wait for write locks	Medium: hold few read locks	Lowest: any data touched is locked to EOT
Overhead	Least: only set short write locks	Small: only set write locks	Medium: set both kinds of locks but need not store read locks	Medium: set and store both kinds of locks
Rollback	Undo cascades can't rollback	Undo incomplete transactions	Same as 1°	Same as 1°
System Recovery	Dangerous updates may be lost and violate 3°	Apply log in 1° order	Same as 1°	Same as 1° or can rerun in any <<< order
Dependencies	None	WRITE → WRITE	WRITE → WRITE WRITE → READ	WRITE → WRITE WRITE → READ READ→ WRITE

Components Involved in Distributed Transaction Processing

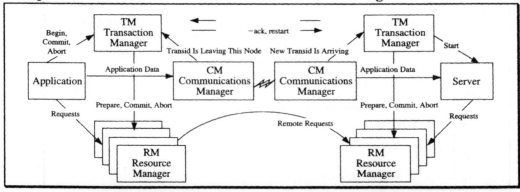

Printed and bound by CPI Group (UK) Ltd, Croydon, CR0 4YY

03/10/2024

01040339-0002